The Language of Liberty

The Political Speeches and Writings of
Abraham Lincoln

The Language of Liberty

The Political Speeches and Writings of Abraham Lincoln

EDITED WITH AN INTRODUCTION AND NOTES BY
JOSEPH R. FORNIERI

REVISED BICENTENNIAL EDITION

Since 1947
**REGNERY
PUBLISHING, INC.**
An Eagle Publishing Company • Washington, DC

ISBN: 978-1-59698-084-6

Published in the United States by
Regnery Publishing, Inc.
An Eagle Publishing Company
One Massachusetts Avenue, NW
Washington, DC 20001

Printed on acid-free paper

Manufactured in the United States of America

10 9 8 7 6 5 4 3 2 1

Books are available in quantity for promotional or premium use. Write to Director of Special Sales, Regnery Publishing, Inc., One Massachusetts Avenue, NW, Washington, DC 20001, for information on discounts and terms or call (202) 216-0600.

PREFACE TO THE
BICENTENNIAL EDITION

The publication of the revised edition of this book coincides with the occasion of Abraham Lincoln's bicentennial, 1809-2009. This bicentennial edition includes a revised, corrected, and expanded version of the 2003 edition with some new material.

This work was originally designed for my students. In teachings classes on Abraham Lincoln's political thought and leadership, I soon discovered that I could not presume that a majority of students had a working knowledge of American History and the Constitution, without which the speeches and writings of the Sixteenth President cannot be fully understood and appreciated. In order to remedy this gap, I have attempted to provide a broad overview of the historical, legal, and political context of Lincoln's thought and leadership, defining crucial terms, events and issues. I also wanted to equip students with a single volume of Lincoln's most important speeches and writings, in which those included would be published in their entirety, rather than in mere excerpts. Fortuitously, Series Editor Christopher B. Briggs's objectives for this leadership series corresponded exactly with the vision I intended for my students.

With these common pedagogical objectives in mind, I have chronologically divided Lincoln's speeches and writings based upon the major events in his life and the life of the nation into five chapters/sections. Each chapter includes a broad historical and political overview of the major events related to Lincoln's life and the life of the nation during that particular time. The final chapter/section of the volume, however, is thematic, offering a compilation of Lincoln's speeches and writings on the important subject of religion and politics.

Though the volume was designed originally for students, it will be useful to the Lincoln aficionado and scholar alike who now have access to a single volume collection of his great political speeches and writings, which are now published in their entirety, not merely excerpted. Moreover, my introductory essay on "Lincoln, The Natural Law and Prudence" should be of interest to students, general readers, and scholars alike.

Finally, it should be emphasized that the concise chapter overviews are in no way intended as a substitute to the more elegant and in-depth histories and biographies of the following Lincoln scholars to whom I am particularly indebted: Roy P. Basler, Gabor S. Boritt, Richard N. Current, Kelly Hanlon, David Herbert Donald, Don E. Fehrenbacher, Allen C. Guelzo, Lewis E. Lehrman, James M. McPherson, Mark E. Neely, Allan Nevins, Stephen B. Oates, and Benjamin P. Thomas. Any study of Abraham Lincoln should either include or refer to the magisterial works of these scholars. I also owe a great debt of gratitude to Hadley Arkes, whose Lincolnian logic is truly an inspiration.

In addition to the historians above, my own scholarship on the subject of Lincoln's political thought is indebted to the magisterial work of Harry V. Jaffa. I am also grateful to George Anastaplo for his scholarship on Lincoln and the Constitution. And I have found William Lee Miller's *Lincoln's Virtues: An Ethical Biography* to be an indispensable guide for understanding the character of our most admired President.

In sum, my own work has built upon the sturdy foundation laid by these scholars (See The Selected Bibliography). My hope is that this modest volume may contribute in some way to inspiring others to learn from our greatest president—Abraham Lincoln.

Joe Fornieri
Rochester New York,
April 2008.

To Pam

ACKNOWLEDGMENTS

I would like to express my gratitude to my wife Pam for her support; my parents Joseph P. and Beatrice A. Fornieri; My in-laws, Alice and Dick Hawkins, who embody so many of Lincoln's virtues.

Three cheers for Christopher B. Briggs whose friendship, tenacity, and vision was indispensable in bringing about the revised, bicentennial edition of this book.

Thanks to Bruce "Meister" Frohnen; Lee Cheek, Southern Gentleman, who knows that deep down in his heart that he really loves Lincoln; Dick Kieffer, whose advice and conversations over the years have been greatly appreciated; my friends and colleagues in the political science department at RIT including John Murley, Sean Sutton, Ivan Keneally, Lauren Hall.

Thanks to my students Adam Botzenhart and Angelo Valente for assisting me with the revisions and corrections.

I must also thank my Lincoln friends for their correspondence, counsel, advice and support throughout the years: Wendy Allen, Herman Belz, Joseph Garrera, Allen C. Guelzo, Phil Henderson, Harold Holzer, Father Matt Kawiak, Lew Lehrman, William Lee Miller, Lucas Morel, James Oakes, Richard Striner, David Walsh, and Frank J. Williams.

A special thanks to Sara V. Gabbard at the Lincoln Museum in Fort Wayne and Editor of Lincoln Lore for her extraordinary work throughout the years. She is a living testimony to the greatness of "the greatest generation."

Thanks to Ralph Lerner and Dennis J. Hutchinson for using the book in their Lincoln Seminar at the University of Chicago and for bringing its errors to my attention.

Last but not least, I word of thanks to Kenneth L. Deutsch. It has been said that, "You can take the New Yorker out of New York, but you can't take New York out of the New Yorker"—thank goodness!

CONTENTS

INTRODUCTION

LINCOLN, THE NATURAL LAW, AND PRUDENCE[*]

L INCOLN'S LEADERSHIP is of enduring significance because it reveals the important connection between law and morality. In his related struggle to preserve the Union and to end slavery, he sought to bring the regime into conformity with the principles of the Declaration, America's Decalogue, which promulgated the creed of its political faith. Those who would wish to learn about the theory of natural law and the virtue associated with its practice—prudence—would do well to ponder his example. It is the purpose of this essay to reveal how Lincoln prudently applied the moral precepts of the natural law to the circumstances of the Civil War era. More specifically, it will demonstrate how his leadership on the Emancipation Proclamation was exemplary in this regard. In recent times, the theory and practice of natural law so exemplified by the sixteenth president is in grave danger of being eclipsed by the increasing public acceptance of moral relativism or moral idealism as legitimate alternatives to resolve political conflicts. As will be seen, Lincoln relentlessly opposed both of these alternatives during the Civil War era, and revealed them as profoundly flawed interpretations of public life. His prudent statesmanship may thus serve as a guide for contemporary leaders who would seek to reinvigorate the moral foundations of the American regime, and to affirm its principles *vis á vis* the political circumstances and ethical challenges of the twenty-first century.

[*] Sections of this essay have appeared in: Joseph R. Fornieri, "Lincoln and the Emancipation Proclamation: A Model of Prudent Leadership" in *Tempered Strength: Studies in the Nature and Scope of Prudential Leadership* ed. Ethan Fishman (Lanham: Lexington Books, 2002), 125–149.

I. LINCOLN AND THE NATURAL LAW.

Lincoln's view of the relationship between law and morality was firmly rooted in the natural law tradition of western civilization derived from ancient Jewish, Neo-Platonic, and Roman sources, adapted by Christian thinkers; modified by modern political philosophers like John Locke; and embraced by the Founders of the American Republic.[1] This tradition presumed a trust in the ability of human reason to apprehend and discern principles of right conduct. The binding force and normative character of these principles were expressed in terms of a universal law; for like a law, their rational dictates commanded some moral obligation or duty concerning "how things ought to be." Thus, symbolically, the natural law represented a pre-existing moral order that was discovered rather than created by human beings, and it pointed to a transcendent ground or ultimate source of authority in the universe—namely, God, who was its author, promulgator, and judge. As a transcendent standard, the law constituted a rule and measure to judge the rectitude of human actions and institutions. Human laws, customs, and actions were judged in terms of their conformity with its rational dictates. The existence of an objective moral order that made claims upon human beings was taken for granted by the Founders; the difficulty was not in acknowledging the law, but in correctly applying its principles to particular and varying circumstances.

Unlike some modern conceptions of natural right that divorce duty (moral obligation) from right (equal entitlement), Lincoln saw duty and right as correlative. He believed that the gift of freedom necessarily implied a moral obligation or duty to exercise it responsibly in conformity with a transcendent standard. Freedom unbounded by duty was morally indistinguishable from license. Under such a conception, nothing in principle could prevent a majority of the people from freely choosing to enslave a minority. In fact, this is precisely how Lincoln's rival, Stephen A. Douglas, defined liberty—the freedom to do wrong. From the standpoint of duty, Lincoln maintained that the Declaration imposed a moral obligation upon the regime to resist the evil of slavery; however, from the standpoint of right, it entitled African-Americans to equal treatment by the regime. The moral duty on the part of leaders and the government to render equal justice to all human beings necessarily implied a right that each person was equally entitled to given his or her spiritual dignity created in the image of God. In this respect, Lincoln viewed duty and right as correlative; one implied the other.

From the time of the Founding to the Civil War era, the foregoing conception of natural law and right was taken for granted by leaders, judges, and the regime's cultural elite.[2] It was part of the nation's public philosophy.[3] Sir William Blackstone whose *Commentaries on the Laws of England* profoundly influenced generations of lawyers from the time of the Founding to the early twentieth century declared that "[T]he law of nature . . . dictated by God himself . . . is binding . . . in all countries and at all times; no human laws are of any validity if contrary to this; and such of them as are valid derive all force and all their authority, mediately or immediately, from this original."[4] Similarly, John Dickinson, patriot and chairman of the Committee for the Declaration of Independence, proclaimed during the Revolution that, "Our liberties do not come from charters; for these are only the declarations of preexisting rights. They do not depend on parchment or seals; but come from the King of Kings and the Lord of all the earth."[5] And John Adams affirmed the natural law when he stated, "Let it be known, that British liberties are not the grants of princes of parliaments, but original rights, conditions of original contracts. . . . Let them search for the foundations of British laws and government in the frame of human nature, in the constitution of the intellectual and moral world." Indeed, Founders like John Dickinson and John Adams admired the British constitutional tradition not simply because it was ancestral, but because it conformed to the dictates of an objective moral order found in nature and confirmed by revelation. While many of these rights were embodied concretely within the tradition of British constitutionalism, they were not merely the product of British convention or human artifice, but universal. For this reason, they were not subject to the whim of any human authority or institution, neither the King nor the Parliament.

The Declaration of Independence, the very foundation of the American experiment according to Lincoln, was predicated upon the foregoing view of natural law. It presumed the existence of a Creator God who established conditions of human flourishing. Indeed, there are four references to the divinity in the Declaration: God is represented as a lawgiver, ("the laws of nature and nature's God"), a creator ("all men are endowed by their Creator with certain unalienable rights"), a judge ("the Supreme Judge of the world"), and as a personal, Judeo-Christian deity who intervenes in Creation ("a firm reliance on the protection of Divine Providence"). The laws of God were apprehended by the Founders as self-evident truths, and subsequently promulgated as the inalienable rights to equality, life, liberty, and the pursuit of happiness. The binding force of these principles constituted a normative standard that served the regime as a guide, a moral compass, and boundary that circumscribed the actions of a just government.

In *A New Birth of Freedom*, Harry V. Jaffa concisely explains the conception of the natural law implicit to the Declaration:

...the perspective of the Declaration is in agreement with Thomas
Aquinas's conception of the natural law as the rational creature's participation in the eternal law, the law by which God governs the universe.
The Declaration also assumes the existence of an eternal law when it
speaks of an appeal to "the supreme judge of the world" and of "the protection of divine providence." The voice of right reason in the natural
law, therefore, is as much the voice of God as is divine revelation. Also,
since every member of the human species has the potentiality to participate in the natural law, in this decisive respect, all men are created
equal."[6]

Yet, despite the fact that the very moral foundations of the American
Republic are built upon the natural law, the concept has been reviled, repudiated, and tragically misunderstood in recent times. Those on both the left and
right wing of the political spectrum are equally suspicious of what they consider
to be an abstract, antiquated, and dangerous concept. Critics mistakenly associate the natural law with the puritanical imposition of morality upon others. Or
they dismiss it as a peculiarly sectarian (Roman Catholic) doctrine that violates
the separation of church and state. In any event, the invocation of the natural
law seems to carry a stigma in contemporary political discourse that gives pause
to today's leaders. It will be recalled that Democratic Senator Joseph Biden
attempted to discredit Justice Clarence Thomas during his confirmation hearing by alleging that the latter was a practitioner of the "natural law." And the
ostensibly conservative chief justice of the United States Supreme Court,
William Rehnquist, likewise eschewed the natural law in opposing the notion
of a living constitution and defending original intent:

> [t]he . . . difficulty with the . . . notion of the living Constitution is that
> it seems to ignore totally the nature of political value judgments in a
> democratic society. If such a society adopts a constitution and incorpo-
> rates in that constitution safeguards for individual liberty, these safeguards
> do indeed take on a generalized moral rightness or goodness. They
> assume a general social acceptance neither because of any intrinsic worth
> nor because of any unique origins in someone's idea of natural justice,
> but instead simply because they have been incorporated in a constitution
> by a people. Within the limits of our Constitution, the representatives of
> the people in the executive branches of the state and national govern-
> ments enact laws. The laws that emerge after a typical political struggle

in which various individual value judgments are debated likewise take on a form or moral goodness because they have been enacted into positive law. It is the fact of their enactment that gives them whatever moral claim they have upon us as a society, however, and not any independent virtue they may have in any particular citizen's own scale of values."[7]

Remarkably, Rehnquist seems to deny the intrinsic goodness or evil of political norms. He suggests that the "moral rightness or goodness" of "value judgments" is entirely relative to what people find socially acceptable at a given time and thus incorporate in their constitution and laws. Though he correctly warns against the dangers of a living constitution, Rehnquist's prescription of legal positivism—the idea that justice and moral right are completely relative to the commands and enactments of those in power—is entirely foreign to the political philosophy of the Founders who penned the Declaration.

The immense moral evil of slavery magnifies the erroneous practical reasoning of critics who reject the natural law. It should never be forgotten that at one time in America's history slavery assumed "a general social acceptance" and was thereby "incorporated" by southern people into their state and local constitutions. If consistently applied to the politics of the Civil War era, the complete separation of law and morality endorsed by today's cultural elite would have dictated the toleration of slavery. Indeed, far too many of today's liberals and conservatives alike embrace a defective philosophy of law that dangerously obscures the moral clarity so desperately needed to resist the new and subtle threats that technology poses to the integrity of human life and the preservation of human liberty.

Lincoln's appeal to the Declaration as a normative standard against slavery raises timeless questions about the relationship between law and morality. Can the appeal to moral absolutes be reconciled with the rule of law? How does Lincoln's invocation of equality differ from the utopian prescriptions of idealists like the radical abolitionists? Most importantly, if Lincoln's prudence involved a harmonization between law and morality, then how did he reconcile his moral obligation to the precepts of the Declaration with his legal obligation to the Constitution and the rule of law?

Though the tension between different spheres of moral, legal, and political obligation is an insoluble fact of human experience, the prudential balancing of these spheres has remained primarily a historical aspiration, not a reality. More often than not, leaders have either sought to divorce morality from politics or to coerce their idealistic visions through the instrumentality of the state at the expense of ordered liberty. The former solution to resolving the dynamic tension between law and morality is indicative of contemporary liberal democracy; the latter is characteristic of both secular and religious utopianism. Both visions of the public good are myopic and flawed. Although the invocation of moral authority is an inevitable part of public life, under American republicanism, the national enforcement of moral aspirations is legally constrained by the Constitution to ensure an ordered liberty that balances both freedom and authority. As Lincoln recognized, the public good of a nation involves the prudential balancing of moral right within the legal confines of the rule of law.

II. LINCOLN AND THE VIRTUE OF PRUDENCE.

What then is the virtue of prudence, and how does it relate to Lincoln's approach to law and morality? Prudence may be defined as the ability to judge well in practical matters; it is tantamount to right reason applied to the realm of moral and political action.[8] Prudent judgment involves the just application of means to ends. Aquinas states, "it belongs to prudence chiefly to direct something aright to an end; and this is not done aright unless both the end be good, and the means good and suitable."[9] In politics, this end represents the overarching common good affirmed by the regime.[10] However, the end of a particular regime may or may not accord with true justice as measured by the natural law. A nation may be dedicated to the apparent good of racial supremacy, or the selfish interest of a particular faction. In such a case, the prudent leader must seek to move the regime towards a truly just end as much as possible. In contradistinction to the ends, the means of prudent decision-making represent all just measures and policies adapted to reach the common good. In making decisions to benefit the common good, the prudent leader is bound to consider both universal ethical principles and the application or determination of these principles to a myriad of legal, social, and political contingencies.[11] Prudence thus involves the harmonization of universal moral precepts under the circumstances. St. Thomas Aquinas states: "But no man can conveniently apply one thing to another, unless he knows both the thing to be applied, and the thing to which it has to be applied. Now actions are in singular matters; and so it is necessary for the prudent man to know both the universal principles of reason, and the singulars about which actions are concerned."[12]

Prudence and natural law are logical corollaries; one implies the other. Those who act in accordance with the dictates of the natural law, or who make efficacious its general principles by applying them under the circumstances, act in a prudent manner. Prudence is the excellence associated with the human agent's virtuous practice of the natural law. Comparatively speaking, this virtue may be viewed as a mean between the two extremes or vices of (a) moral idealism, and (b) political pragmatism. Each vice involves a crucial defect or omission in right reasoning through precipitous or thoughtless practical judgment. Political idealism, for example, precipitously omits the consideration of particular circumstances in decision-making.[13] It involves "a negligence and blindness to the concrete realities" that surround political action.[14] The tenacious adherence to moral principle in its abstract purity blinds the idealist to the consequences of his actions and to the inherent limits of human nature and politics.

The policy of prohibition provides an instructive example of political idealism. Through its precipitous disregard of the extent to which the consumption of alcohol was an ingrained custom in American culture, the prohibition movement had the unintended consequence of stimulating the activities of organized crime in purveying bootleg liquor. The moral crusade to abolish the evils of alcohol actually backfired by undermining respect for the rule of law and by enhancing the public status of organized crime.

The vice or extreme of political pragmatism, on the other hand, misjudges moral principle in practical decision-making. Pragmatism implies an ethical relativism. It views moral standards as merely conventional and therefore relative to short-term interest, utility, or expediency. Its crucial defect or omission consists in an ethical myopia that is blind to the authoritativeness of moral claims in guiding public policy. Pragmatism thus resembles "[c]unning (*astutia*)...the most characteristic form of false prudence."[15] Those politicians who decide policies almost exclusively upon the basis of public opinion polls to further their own selfish interests without any consideration of whether or not the underlying principles governing such policies are intrinsically right or wrong provide a vivid contemporary example of political pragmatism. In short, the pragmatist believes that politics should be freed from absolute moral boundaries, and that the notions of "right and wrong" and "good and evil" are not inherently so, but relative to what people decide at a given moment.

The moral end of Lincoln's prudent leadership was to preserve an ordered liberty that secured the long-term freedom, safety, and happiness of the American people. Daniel Webster, Lincoln's Whig predecessor, tersely articulated this end for a generation of nationalist leaders, "liberty and Union, one and inseparable." For Lincoln, Clay, and Webster the inseparability of liberty and Union meant the perpetuation of a national Union dedicated to both the moral precepts of the Declaration and the legal framework of the Constitution. That is to say, freedom was best secured under the auspices of a national Union committed to civil and religious liberty found in the Declaration. These leaders were correctly convinced that the fate of the American experiment in Republican government depended upon the maintenance of a strong national Union committed to legitimate moral ends. For this reason, the Founders replaced the weaker Articles of Confederation with a "more perfect Union" established by the Constitution of 1787.

Lincoln interpreted the Declaration as the moral covenant of American republicanism. He regarded it as the foundation of the American experiment. He viewed the principles of Jefferson as the "definitions and axioms of free society."[16] And he confessed that, "All the political sentiments I entertain have been drawn. . . . from the Declaration of Independence."[17] Indeed, Lincoln interpreted the Declaration as a declaration of natural law and right.[18] It promulgated "universal principles of reason" that were to guide the regime. As an expression of the natural law, the Declaration provided a transcendent rule and measure— a normative standard, to judge the moral and political progress of the nation. The moral imperatives of the Declaration included both positive injunctions to extend freedom and negative prohibitions against its deprivation.[19] Among the principles of the Declaration, Lincoln assigned priority to the self-evident truth of equality, which he understood to be "the father of all moral principle" and the "central idea" of the American regime.[20]

In Lincoln's view, the moral precepts of the Declaration were confirmed by the complementary traditions of republicanism, reason, and revelation.[21] The teachings of these traditions coincided, validated, and confirmed one another in providing guidance for public life. The political thought of Sir William Blackstone whose *Commentaries on the Laws of England* profoundly influenced the legal mind of both the Founders and Lincoln envisioned a harmony between the laws of reason and revelation in jurisprudence: "Upon these two foundations, the law of nature and the law of revelation, depend all human laws; that is to say, no human law should be suffered to contradict these." James Wilson, a Founder at the Constitutional Convention and Supreme Court justice, characterized the compatibility between faith and reason in these terms: "How shall we, in particular cases, discover the will of God? We discover it by our conscience, our reason, and by the Holy Scriptures. The law of nature and the law of revelation are both divine; they flow, though in different channels, from the same adorable source. It is, indeed, preposterous to separate them from each other. The object of both is—to discover the will of God—and both are necessary for the accomplishment of that end."[22]

In a like manner, Lincoln maintained that the Declaration's assertion of equality coincided with the biblical precept of Genesis 1:27 which taught that all human beings possessed an equal rational and spiritual dignity created in the image of God *(imago Dei):* "nothing stamped with the Divine image and likeness was sent into the world to be trodden on, and degraded, and imbruted by its fellows."²³ According to Lincoln, the biblical precept of "The Golden Rule" in Matthew 7:12 likewise confirmed the republican principle of equal consent in the Declaration: "As I would not be a *slave* so I would not be a *master*. This expresses my idea of democracy. Whatever differs from this, to the extent of the difference, is no democracy."²⁴ Because no one himself would wish to be treated as a slave, no one was entitled to enslave another: "I never knew a man who wished to be himself a slave. Consider if you know any good thing, that no man desires for himself."²⁵

Perhaps the biblical precept most often cited by Lincoln to validate the republican principle of free labor in the Declaration was derived from Genesis 3:19 whereby God decreed that all human beings must labor as a consequence of their fallen condition:

> In the early days of the world, the Almighty said to the first of our race "In the sweat of thy face shalt thou eat bread" [Genesis 3:19]; and since then, if we except the *light* and the *air* of heaven, no good thing has been, or can be enjoyed by us, without having first cost labour. And, inasmuch [as] most good things are produced by labour, it follows that [all] such things of right belong to those whose labour has produced them. But it has so happened in all ages of the world, that *some* have laboured, and *others* have, without labour, enjoyed a large proportion of the fruits. This is wrong, and should not continue. To [secure] to each labourer the whole product of his labour or as nearly as possible, is a most worthy object of any good government.²⁶

Based on Lincoln's interpretation of Genesis 3:19, God had obliged the entire human race to labor as a condition of its existence. Such an exemption from laboring constituted a transgression of cosmic justice because it attempted to elevate one above the human condition at the expense of another. In Lincoln's mind, the God-given right to enjoy the fruits of one's own labor was thus confirmed by the Bible, the principle of equal consent in the Declaration, and the teaching of John Locke that each person has a right to property in himself.²⁷ The precepts of the Declaration were further complemented by what

Lincoln described as natural theology: "I think that if anything can be proved by natural theology, it is that slavery is morally wrong. God gave man a mouth to receive bread, hands to feed it, and his hand has a right to carry bread to his mouth without controversy."[28]

Although Lincoln believed that the moral precepts of the Bible could serve as a guide to public life, it is important to emphasize that he did not believe that its teachings could be applied literally to politics without prudential mediation. The Bible did not clearly point out what to do under particular circumstances. He knew full well that a literal interpretation of the Bible could be misinterpreted and exploited for political purposes, as it was to justify proslavery theology. In his *Second Inaugural Address*, he noted the supreme irony of both sides reading the same Bible and invoking the same God against each other.

Lincoln conveyed the limitations of a literal interpretation of the Bible to a group of abolitionist ministers who were convinced that the Good Book dictated the policy of immediate, uncompensated emancipation during the war:

> The subject presented in the memorial is one upon which I have thought much for weeks past, and I may even say for months. I am approached with the most opposite opinions and advice, and that by religious men, who are equally certain that they represent the Divine will. I am sure that either the one or the other class is mistaken in that belief, and perhaps in some respects both. I hope it will not be irreverent for me to say that if it is probable that God would reveal his will to others, on a point so connected with my duty, it might be supposed he would reveal it directly to me; for, unless I am more deceived in myself than I often am, it is my earnest desire to know the will of Providence in this matter. *And if I can learn what it is I will do it!* These are not, however, the days of miracles, and I suppose it will be granted that I am not to expect a direct revelation. I must study the plain physical facts of the case, ascertain what is possible and learn what appears to be wise and right. The subject is difficult, and good men do not agree.[29]

Lincoln's acknowledgment that "good men do not agree" on difficult moral questions reflected a humility that is diametrically opposed to the dogmatism of contemporary ideological thinking that demonizes one's political opponents. While humbly acknowledging the vast gulf between human pretence and divine intent, Lincoln nevertheless strove for greatness in his endeavor to serve both God and country. This rare combination of a Christian humility and pagan grandeur may be characterized as a biblical magnanimity.[30]

III. STEPHEN A. DOUGLAS'S POPULAR SOVEREIGNTY: THE ALTERNATIVE OF MORAL RELATIVISM.

The policy of popular sovereignty championed by Stephen A. Douglas represented a pragmatic alternative to resolving the slavery question before the outbreak of war. This policy granted territorial settlers the right to decide for themselves whether or not to have slavery. In Douglas's view, popular sovereignty was the most democratic way of resolving political conflict over slavery, and the one most consistent with the liberal virtues of self-determination, diversity, and local autonomy: "I hold to that great principle of self-government which asserts the right of every people to decide for themselves the nature and character of the domestic institutions and fundamental law under which they are to live." As long as the democratic process followed correct procedures, popular sovereignty was indifferent to its substantive moral outcome. Outside of the process itself, Douglas rejected the public relevance of a transcendent standard to judge policy.

It is instructive to consider the philosophical implications of popular sovereignty. The doctrine is predicated upon two related concepts: legal positivism and ethical relativism. Legal positivism identifies law and justice simply as the command of those in power. The legal positivist understands law to be univocal: justice is tantamount to the decrees of a duly constituted authority. Political institutions and public policies are thus self-legitimating. Because law is strictly identified with the will of those in power, the attempt to measure human enactments in terms of their conformity with an ultimate standard is meaningless. According to legal positivists, the appeal to an ultimate moral standard to judge the actions of the state illegitimately introduces a competing authority that necessarily undermines the concrete rule of law and established legal procedure in the name of utopian goals.

In an effort to diffuse sectional strife over slavery, Douglas suggested that moral and religious claims were neither absolute nor universal, but relative to the varying standards of each political community:

> I am now speaking of rights under the constitution, and not of moral or religious rights. I do not discuss the morals of the people of Missouri, but let them settle that matter for themselves. I hold that the people of

the slaveholding States are civilized men as well as ourselves, that they bear consciences as well as we, and that they are accountable to God and their posterity and not to us. It is for them to decide therefore the moral and religious right of the slavery question for themselves within their own limits."[31]

Rejecting a transcendent moral standard like so many contemporary theorists of jurisprudence, Douglas believed that the law should merely reflect "the community sense of what is expedient."[32]

Indeed, there is a striking resemblance between Douglas's nineteenth century legal positivism and John Rawls's contemporary theory of justice. Like Douglas, Rawls seeks to remove moral and religious absolutes from public life. In terms that bear comparison to Douglas, Rawls states:

> Thus, the aim of justice as fairness as a political conception is practical, and not metaphysical or epistemological. That is, it presents itself not as a conception of justice that is true, but one that can serve as a basis of informed and willing political agreement between citizens viewed as free and equal persons. . . . To secure this agreement we try, so far as we can, to avoid disputed philosophical, as well as disputed moral and religious, questions. . . . The hope is that, by this method of avoidance, as we might call it, existing differences between contending political views can at least be moderated, even if not entirely removed, so that social cooperation on the basis of mutual respect can be maintained.[33]

What both Douglas and Rawls fail to see is that the public recognition of each person as free and equal is itself predicated on an absolute moral standard that affirms the spiritual dignity of all human beings. By admitting that it is "good" and "fair" to treat all citizens equally and that each person ought to be treated on the "basis of mutual respect," Rawls presumes the very absolute values he seeks to reject. In fact, his theory of justice provides no fixed, external standard to choose freedom over slavery, tolerance over intolerance, and justice over injustice.

The Little Giant's legal positivism is revealed even more clearly in his defense of the Dred Scott Decision. Because he viewed the Supreme Court as the ultimate arbiter of the democratic process, he interpreted Lincoln's repudiation of the Dred Scott Decision as a prescription for anarchy:

The Dred Scott decision was pronounced by the highest tribunal on earth. From that decision there is no appeal this side of Heaven. Yet, Mr. Lincoln says he is going to reverse that decision. By what tribunal will he reverse it? Will he appeal to a mob? Does he intend to appeal to violence, to Lynch law? Will he stir up strife and rebellion in the land and over-throw the court by violence?...He who attempts to stir up odium and rebellion in the country against the constituted authorities, is stimulating the passions of men to resort to violence and to mobs instead of to the law. Hence, I tell you that I take the decisions of the Supreme Court as the law of the land, and I intend to obey them as such.[34]

Attempting to brand Lincoln as a radical abolitionist who would trample upon the rule of law in the name of abstract moral right, Douglas stated:

Mr. Lincoln, following the example and lead of all the little Aboli-tion orators, who go around and lecture in the basements of schools and churches, reads from the Declaration of Independence, that all men were created equal, and then asks how can you deprive a negro of that equal-ity which God and the Declaration of Independence awards to him. He and they maintain negro equality is guarantied by the laws of God, and that it is asserted in the Declaration of Independence.[35]

In addition to legal positivism, Douglas's version of popular sovereignty implied the related concept of ethical relativism. As seen, he asserted that domestic institutions were neither inherently good nor evil, but rather desirable or undesirable depending upon the varying interests of local communities. Jus-tice was relative to the preferences and tastes of each territory.

Like some modern communitarians and libertarians, Douglas maintained that the federal government should not "legislate morality" by preferring one set of "values" to another. Sociopolitical conflict could be resolved by treating moral and religious claims as matters of subjective taste to be chosen or rejected by the people through their territorial and state legislatures. In effect, Douglas viewed sectional disputes as a clash over different perspectives, each moral perspective being equal to all others, and relative to the will of the majority within a given community: "The great principle of this government is that each State has the right to do as it pleases on all these questions, and no other State, or power on earth has the right to interfere with us, or complain of us merely because our system differs from theirs."[36] Indeed, Douglas's ethical relativism even prevented him from distinguishing between slavery and other domestic institutions like agriculture. In his view, the decision of territorial settlers to choose or reject slavery was comparable to the decision to plant corn or stock cattle.

Moreover, Douglas exhorted national leaders to refrain from even raising vexing moral questions about public policies. Because such questions were insoluble, inflammatory, and divisive, leaders should entertain moral neutrality in judging policies. In his view, the liberal virtues of pluralism and diversity demanded not only the toleration of slavery, but also the cessation of all opposition to it. Thus, he characterized the abolitionists' moral condemnation of slavery as a fanatical expression of intolerance, one that undermined political compromise and exacerbated sectional strife. The only alternative to pluralism, toleration, and diversity was a coercive national uniformity—i.e. a puritanism that sought to coerce one way of life upon all others. According to Douglas, Lincoln's use of the House Divided metaphor, which emphasized the underlying need for a national moral consensus regarding the evil of slavery and its threat to the Union, was an expression of abolitionist intolerance and moral fanaticism:

> Mr. Lincoln likens that bond of the federal constitution joining free and slave States together to a house divided against itself, and says that it is contrary to the law of God and cannot stand. When did he learn, and by what authority does he proclaim, that this government is contrary to the law of God, and cannot stand?.... [O]ur government was formed on the principle of diversity in the local institutions and laws and not on that of uniformity.[37]

In response to Douglas's argument for an ethically neutral pluralism, Lincoln argued that the logic of popular sovereignty dictated the toleration of polygamy as well, a practice that was viewed by many nineteenth-century Victorians as even more odious than slavery. By associating slavery with polygamy, Lincoln attempted to show that the embrace of popular sovereignty necessarily led to the toleration of virtually any practice no matter how intuitively morally repugnant.

Douglas's version of popular sovereignty was unique in combining the seemingly incompatible principles of local autonomy with a national Union. Popular sovereignty fused the nationalist sentiment of manifest destiny with the self-determination. Though the Little Giant concurred with southern Democrats of his time that one of the principal aims of national authority was to secure local autonomy, he disagreed with them on the appropriate means to secure this end. Unlike his southern brethren, he believed that the goal of local autonomy and self-determination was assured most effectively under the auspices of the national Union that expanded ever westward to secure new territories for the country's teeming population. Douglas conveyed his political vision in these terms: "Hence, the great mission of the Democracy is to unite the fraternal feelings of the whole country, restore peace and quiet by teaching each State to mind its own business, and regulate its own domestic affairs, and all to unite carrying out the constitution as our fathers made it, and thus to preserve the Union and render it perpetual in all time to come."[38]

While Lincoln agreed with Douglas that the perpetuity of a national Union was the *sine qua non* of liberty, his understanding of the term differed radically from Douglas's view. For Lincoln, liberty did not mean the right to do wrong, but consisted in the responsible exercise of freedom in conformity with the standards of the natural law. The equal dignity of all human beings placed a moral imperative upon the regime to resist slavery. Paradoxically, the conception of liberty implicit to Douglas's moral relativism sanctioned the freedom of one people to enslave another. Because it perverted the meaning of liberty, Lincoln characterized popular sovereignty as a "false philosophy" and a "pseudo philosophy" that sought to replace the authentic political faith of the Founders with a contradictory doctrine that undermined the regime's first principles:

> The doctrine of self government is right—absolutely and eternally right—but [Douglas's version of popular sovereignty] has no just application, as here attempted. Or perhaps I should rather say that whether it has such just application depends upon whether a negro is *not* or *is* a man. If he is *not* a man, why in that case, he who *is* a man may, as a matter of self-government, do just as he pleases with him. But if the negro *is* a man, is it not to that extent, a total destruction of self-government, to say that he too shall not govern *himself*? When the white man governs himself that is self-government; but when he governs himself, and also governs *another* man, that is *more* than self-government—that is despotism. If the negro is a *man*, why then my ancient faith teaches me that "all men are created equal;" and that there can be no moral right in connection with one man's making a slave of another.[39]

Indeed, Lincoln's inclusive vision of the Union contrasted sharply with Douglas's racist vision of a Union dedicated to white supremacy emphatically proclaimed during their debates: "I believe this government was made on the

white basis. I believe it was made by white men, for the benefit of white men
and their posterity for ever, and I am in favor of confining citizenship to white
men, men of European birth and descent, instead of conferring it upon Negroes,
Indians and other inferior races."[40]

Does it follow that the public invocation of moral claims necessarily undermines the rule of law as Douglas contended? Though Douglas correctly discerned the theological grounding of his opponent's political thought, he
confounded Lincoln's natural law outlook with the moral idealism of the radical abolitionists in order to discredit both as extremist alternatives. He deroga-
torily referred to the Republicans as the Abolition party: "But the Abolition
party really think that under the Declaration of Independence the Negro is
equal to the white man, and that negro equality is an inalienable right conferred
by the Almighty, and hence, that all human laws are in violation of it are null
and void."

In sum, Douglas imposed a false dilemma: the invocation of moral principle
does not necessarily lead to the "violation" of the rule of law. Like many of
today's opponents of natural law, Douglas fallaciously equated the public appeal
to moral principle with the puritanical attempt to coerce belief through the
force of law and a divine imperative to overturn the established rule of law if it
does not enforce the most grandiose ideals. On the contrary, Lincoln maintained
that while the moral participates in the legal, the two are not strictly identical.
The application of principle must take into consideration the limits of human
nature and politics. As will be shown, Douglas's condemnation of moral idealism applied not to Lincoln, but to the radical abolitionists.

The noted transcendentalist writer and abolitionist Henry David Thoreau
advocated an idealistic vision of law and morality diametrically opposed to
Douglas's pragamatism: "It is not desirable to cultivate a respect for the law,
so much as for the right. The only obligation which I have a right to assume
is to do at any time what I think right.... Law never made men a whit more
just; and, by means of their respect for it, even the well-disposed are daily
made the agents of injustice."[41] Thoreau believed that the canker of slavery
had corrupted the entire nation beyond redemption: "I do not hesitate to say,
that those who call themselves Abolitionists should at once effectually withdraw their support, both in person and property, from the government of
Massachusetts, and not wait till they constitute a majority of one, before they
suffer the right to prevail through them. I think that it is enough if they have
God on their side, without waiting for that other one."[42] While reaching
opposite conclusions Thoreau and Douglas both agreed that the invocation of

moral principles in politics was necessarily revolutionary and subversive of the rule of law. Both conceived of a necessary antipathy between moral and legal obligation. However, while Douglas repudiated the public appeal to universal moral principles for pragmatic reasons, Thoreau upheld them for idealistic reasons. Indeed, Thoreau celebrated the very political idealism that Douglas condemned.

IV. THE RADICAL ABOLITIONISTS: THE ALTERNATIVE OF MORAL IDEALISM.

Radical abolitionism constituted the other extreme alternative, which was proffered by Northerners to resolve the slavery question before the war. The moral idealism of the radical abolitionists involved a dangerous fixation upon moral principles to the exclusion of practical circumstances. In demanding "immediate and uncompensated emancipation," they ignored the inherent limits of politics. Before the war, many of the radical abolitionists endorsed nonparticipation in the political process to maintain the moral purity of their principled stance against slavery. They disavowed any legal obligation to the Union and to the Constitution in view of its concessions to slavery. Their motto was, "No Union with slaveholders."

An early indication of Lincoln's prudence as a leader was revealed in his opposition to the moral idealism of the Liberty Party, an abolitionist third party, which cost Henry Clay the election of 1844. Lincoln campaigned for Whig candidate Clay, his "beau ideal of a statesman," in this election. He was discouraged when New York abolitionists bolted the Whig Party because they could not support Clay as a slaveholder, even though he was committed to the containment of the institution. Lincoln predicted that their uncompromising refusal to vote for Clay because he was a slaveholder would result in an even greater evil, the election of a proslavery candidate who would annex Texas and thereby aid and abet the spread of the institution throughout the Union. In a letter to Williamson Durley dated October 3, 1845, Lincoln chastised the Liberty Party for its flawed practical reasoning:

> What was their process of reasoning, I can only judge from what a single one of them told me. It was this: "We are not to do *evil* that *good* may come." This general, proposition is doubtless correct; but did it apply? If by your votes you could have prevented the *extention* (sic), &c. of slavery, would it not have been *good* and not *evil* so to have used your

votes, even though it involved the casting of them for a slaveholder? By the *fruit* the tree is to be known. An *evil* tree can not bring forth *good* fruit. If the fruit of electing Mr. Clay would have been to prevent the extension of slavery, could the act of electing him have been *evil*?[43]

As with the election in 1844, in the next election of 1848, Lincoln consistently opposed an antislavery third party that threatened to split the Whig Party, thereby resulting in a victory for the proslavery Democrats. Speaking in Worcester Massachusetts, he criticized the flawed practical reasoning of those who sought to leave the Whigs for the Free Soil Party:

> The "Free Soil".... [in] declaring that they would "do their duty and leave the consequences to God," merely gave an excuse for taking a course that they were not able to maintain by a fair and full argument. To make this declaration did not show what their duty was. If it did we should have no use for judgment, we might as well be made without intellect, and when divine or human law does not clearly point out what *is* our duty, we have no means of finding out what it is by using our most intelligent judgment of the consequences.

Though he consistently opposed human servitude, Lincoln rejected the political idealism of the more radical antislavery factions. Their actions would lead to consequences that hurt the cause of freedom—namely, the election of a proslavery Democrat. In both the election of 1844 and 1848, he emphasized that prudent decision making must weigh the consequences of each action. Moral principles are not applied in a theoretical vacuum apart from determinations of what is actually achievable. The fixation upon moral principles in their abstract purity may actually undermine what is politically possible under the circumstances leading to consequences that are entirely contrary to one's moral aspirations.

Before the war, Lincoln's prudential reconciliation of moral obligation to the Declaration and legal obligation to the Constitution may be understood as a mean between the disunionist extremes of the northern radical abolitionists and southern fire-eaters. Ironically, northern radical abolitionists and southern fire-eaters alike regarded the Constitution as a proslavery document. Consequently, both welcomed disunion as a means of establishing a more suitable form of government consonant with their own political ends. If the right to property in slave was expressly and distinctly affirmed by the Constitution as Justice Taney asserted in the Dred Scott decision, then it was unlawful to deny

Southerners the right to take their property in the territories. Surely this would constitute a most fundamental violation of their liberty. On the other hand, the alleged proslavery status of the Constitution led the abolitionists to forsake the rule of law. They conscientiously believed that a Union dedicated to the immoral end of slavery was not worth keeping.

However, was the constitution a proslavery document as both extremes contended? Did the Union really stand for slavery? As a lawyer himself—a seasoned veteran of forensic battles—Lincoln brought to bear the entire force of his incisive legal mind to provide a devastating critique of Dred Scott. Carefully analyzing each aspect of the decision in the light of logic, history, precedent, and the language of the Constitution itself, he demonstrated that Taney's legal reasoning was based upon an erroneous interpretation of the Declaration, the intentions of the Founders, and the Constitution. In Lincoln's words, it was based on "assumed historical facts which were not really true." It is no exaggeration to say that from the time of the decision in 1857 to his election as president in 1860, Lincoln devoted a considerable amount of time and energy vindicating the principles of the American regime from Taney's proslavery reinterpretation of the Constitution.

What then was the relationship between slavery and the Constitution? In sum, Lincoln viewed slavery as an anomaly within the American republic. It was condemned in principle by the Declaration, but tolerated in practice as a matter of political necessity where it already existed at the time of the founding. He clearly defined the anomalous status of slavery to the Constitution in his celebrated *Peoria Address* of October 16, 1854:

> I object... that there CAN be MORAL RIGHT in the enslaving of one man by another.... I object to it because the fathers of the republic eschewed, and rejected it. The argument of "Necessity" was the only argument they ever admitted in favor of slavery.... They found the institution existing among us, which they could not help; and they cast blame upon the British King for having permitted its introduction. Before the constitution, they prohibited its introduction in the north-western Territory—the only country we owned, then free from it. At the framing and adoption of the constitution they forbore to so much as mention the word "slave" or "slavery" in the whole instrument. In the provision for the recovery of fugitives, the slave is spoken of as a "PERSON HELD TO SERVICE OR LABOR." In... prohibiting the abolition of the African slave trade for twenty years, the trade is spoken of as "The

migration or importation of such persons as any of the States NOW
EXISTING, shall think proper to admit . . . Thus, the thing is hid away,
in the constitution, just as an afflicted man hides away a wen or a cancer,
which he dares not cut out at once, lest he bleed to death; with the
promise, nevertheless, that the cutting begin at the end of a given time.

The effort to abolish slavery in the southern states through federal power
would have aborted the Constitutional Convention, and, along with it, the
hopes, liberty, and security of the new republic. The rule of law thus obliged
Lincoln to tolerate slavery in the southern states as a matter of "necessity," limiting circumstances that seriously constrained the moral possibilities of the time.
Despite the necessary evil of slavery, the Constitution and the rule of law were
worth upholding because the regime was dedicated to the just ends of the Declaration, which morally obligated the regime to place the institution on a path
of ultimate extinction.

The legal toleration of slavery as a necessary evil, however, did not mean
that Lincoln espoused, like Stephen A. Douglas, a moral neutrality towards
the institution. On the contrary, the ends of the Declaration were nevertheless to be approximated through all appropriate means. In the case of the territories, Lincoln maintained that the coercive use of federal power to contain
the spread of slavery was a lawful and legitimate means authorized by the
Constitution. In the case of the states where slavery already existed, he
believed that persuasion and moral stewardship were the legitimate means.
This meant persuading the public mind that slavery was anathema to the
nation's republican institutions and, for the good of the entire nation, con-
stricting the institution and also encouraging the slave states to consent to its
gradual abolition. Under the Constitution, the lawful abolition of slavery in
the states required their consent. Some of the more moderate policies to this
end included plans for colonization, repatriation, and gradual, compensated
emancipation.

The moral campaign against cigarette smoking, and teen pregnancy for that
matter, demonstrates how persuasion may be used to contain the spread of an
evil. While the criminalization of cigarette smoking would be utopian and
imprudent, leaders at all levels of government have successfully provided public incentives and disincentives to discourage its use, especially among the youth.
Without being criminalized, the social and health risks of smoking demand that
is should be restricted and contained as much as possible through a public aware-
ness campaign. For this reason, public advertising in favor of cigarette smoking

has been severely restricted on television while advertising against it has been promoted.

At Peoria, Lincoln likened slavery to a cancer eating away at the body politic. In attempting to remedy the disease of slavery, the statesman was analogous to a doctor seeking to restore health to a patient. Like a surgeon, the statesman must proceed cautiously in treating the disease of slavery. The indiscriminate and reckless cutting of tissue could result in the death of the patient—that is, the body politic. Proverbially speaking, the cure may be worse than the disease. Indeed, Lincoln viewed the disunionism of the radical abolitionists as a cure worse than the disease of slavery. So long as the Constitution and the Union were bound to the moral principles of the Declaration, the rule of law was worth upholding. A Union dedicated to the principles of the regime would inevitably strive toward the containment of slavery and its eventual extinction through peaceful and gradual means.

Lincoln's adherence to the rule of law may be contrasted to the political idealism of radical abolitionist like Garrison who burnt a copy of the Constitution calling it a "covenant with death" and an "agreement with hell." He triumphantly proclaimed that, "if slaves have a right to their freedom, it ought to be given them, regardless of the consequences."[44] Similarly, Charles Sumner declared that, "The Antislavery Enterprise is right; and the right is always practicable."[45] The radical abolitionists' utopian expectations of politics led them to endorse disunion because the abstract principles of liberty and equality could not be applied immediately and perfectly to all human beings regardless of circumstance. Invoking divine justice, Garrison agitated for a revolutionary transfiguration of society that would usher in a new order purified from the corruption of human servitude:

> Let the American Union perish; let these allied States be torn with faction, or drenched in blood; let this republic realize the fate of Rome and Carthage, of Babylon and Tyre; still, those rights would remain undiminished in strength, unsullied in purity, unaffected in value, and sacred as their Divine Author. . . . Man is superior to all political compacts, all government arrangements, all religious institutions. As means to an end, these may sometimes be useful, though never indispensable; but that end must always be the freedom and happiness of man, INDIVIDUAL MAN. . . . [The Union] was conceived in sin, and brought forth in iniquity; and its career has been marked by unparalleled hypocrisy; by high-handed tyranny, by a bold defiance of the omniscience and omnipotence of God.[46]

Along with Garrison, Wendell Phillips was perhaps the most notable voice in the chorus for disunion:

> In my soul, I believe that the dissolution of the Union, sure to result speedily in the abolition of slavery, would be a lesser evil than the slow, faltering, diseased, gradual dying-out of slavery, constantly poisoning us with the festering remains of this corrupt political, social, and literary state. I believe a sudden conclusive, definite disunion, resulting in the abolition of slavery, in the disruption of the Northern mind from all connection with it, all vassalage to it, *immediately*, would be a better, healthier, and more wholesome cure, than to let the Republican Party exert this gradual influence through the power of the government for thirty or sixty years. . . . [47]

Garrison, Thoreau, and Phillips were joined by a host of other abolitionists like Gerrit Smith, a member of "the Secret Six" who financed John Brown's murderous raid on Harper's Ferry. Smith explained, "I insist that the Nation has a right and is therefore bound to abolish Slavery. But if it will not do so, then let there be Disunion & Abolition will follow."[48] John Jay similarly warned, "if we cannot have liberty & union in any new readjustment, I go for liberty without union."[49] And an abolitionist newspaper from Des Moines contended that, "the most effectual way to bring about the enfranchisement of every slave on this continent, is to dissolve this Union."[50] During the secession crisis, Frank Sanborn, another member of the "Secret Six," noted that, "the present condition of National affairs gives me much hope for the Slave. Whatever may be the issue—and I think it will be real disunion—Slavery will be greatly weakened."[51] Sanborn continued, "The Union is evidently on its last legs and Buchanan is laboring to tear it in pieces. Treason will not be treason much longer, but patriotism."[52]

V. LINCOLN'S PRUDENT BALANCING OF MORAL AND LEGAL OBLIGATION.

Contrary to the views of these radical abolitionists, Lincoln considered it unconstitutional, unethical, and self-defeating to dissolve the Union while legal remedies to slavery existed. In the long run, disunion (both northern and southern) would only augment the evil of slavery: freed from the moral bonds of the Union, an independent southern slave empire would ensure the indefinite perpetuation and spread of the institution throughout the continent and into the Caribbean basin. Thus, he explained: "Much as I hate slavery, I would consent to the extension of it rather than see the Union dissolved, just as I would consent to any *great* evil, to avoid a *greater* one."[53] The prudent counsel of this statement may be further appreciated in contrast to the moral idealism of William Lloyd Garrison who proclaimed, "To do evil, that good may come, is...absurd and criminal."[54] Unlike the extremists of his time, Lincoln acknowledged the limits of politics: "The true rule, in determining to embrace, or reject any thing, is not whether it have *any* evil in it; but whether it have more of evil, than of good. There are few things *wholly* evil, or *wholly* good. Almost every thing, especially of governmental policy, is an inseparable compound of the two; so that our best judgment of the preponderance between them is continually demanded."[55] Because few things in human life are absolutely good or absolutely evil, the statesman must prudently work to minimize evil and maximize good. The attempt to apply moral principles must always account for the various contingencies of politics. Despite slavery's inherent moral evil, before the war, Lincoln rejected the coercive use of national authority to bring about its extirpation in the states where it already existed. The use of such force was *ultra vires*—beyond the scope of federal power. To take this step would be to cross a constitutional Rubicon, marking the irrevocable step from the lawful use of executive power to the unbridled wielding of executive despotism.

In sum, Lincoln's moral stewardship (a) assimilated the merits, and (b) transcended the defects of the alternatives proposed by northern Democrats like Stephen A. Douglas, and abolitionists like Phillips and Garrison. While Lincoln shared Douglas's commitment to the rule of law, he transcended the defects of the Little Giant's moral relativism by acknowledging higher moral obligations in the determination of practical judgment. Conversely, while he shared the radical abolitionists' commitment to moral principle, he transcended the defect of their political idealism by upholding the rule of law and by considering the particular circumstances under which the application of principle was inevitably constrained. Counterpoised to either extreme, he harmonized moral principle with legal, political, and historical circumstances. His example is instructive to the contemporary moral relativist and moral absolutist alike.

Despite slavery's inherent evil, Lincoln acknowledged that the Founders of 1787 made concessions to it that as an elected official he was bound to uphold. Interpreting the affirmation of equality at the time of the Revolution as an aspiration to guide public life, he noted that the authors of the Declaration:

...did not mean to assert the obvious untruth, that all were then enjoying that equality, nor yet, that they were about to confer it immediately upon them. In fact they had no power to confer such a boon. They meant simply to declare the right, so that the enforcement of it might follow as fast as circumstances should permit. They meant to set up a standard maxim for free society, which should be familiar to all, and revered by all; constantly looked to, constantly labored for....[56]

Even though it was applied imperfectly due to the inherent limits of politics, the principle of equality nonetheless served as a normative guide to public life. Once prudent statesmen have acknowledged the initial preeminence of moral claims in guiding public life, they must subsequently address a set of derivative, but equally important questions—that is to say, they must address the specific legal and constitutional determinations of policy-making. The application of moral principle to practice is circumscribed by different jurisdictions of authority. As St. Thomas Aquinas explains, "the general principles of the natural law cannot be applied to all men in the same way on account of the great variety of human affairs: and hence arises the diversity of positive laws among various people."[57]

As seen, although he viewed human servitude as inherently evil in principle, Lincoln distinguished legally between slavery as a national, state, and territorial institution. These important legal distinctions mandated different courses of action in prudently determining the appropriate legal means for dealing with slavery depending upon where it existed. Although the national right to slavery was never expressly and distinctly affirmed in the Constitution by the Founders, the Federal division of powers prohibited the national government from interfering with the institution where it already existed in the states at the time of the Constitution. However, as noted, since Lincoln believed that the territories fell under national jurisdiction, he maintained that the federal government had both a compelling moral obligation and a corresponding legal authorization to restrict it in this area.

In his Fifth Debate with Douglas at Galesburg on October 7, 1858, Lincoln distinguished between state and territorial slavery claiming that while the former was outside of the jurisdiction of the federal government, the latter was within its scope:

I have never manifested any impatience with the necessities that spring from the actual presence of black people amongst us, and the actual existence of slavery amongst us where it does already exist; but I have insisted that, in legislating for new countries, where it does not exist, there is no just rule other than that of moral and abstract right! With reference to those new countries, those maxims as to the right of a people to "life, liberty and the pursuit of happiness," were the just rules to be constantly referred to.[58]

In sum, Lincoln endorsed the prudential council of his Whig predecessor: "Mr. Clay says *it is true as an abstract principle* that all men are created equal, but that we cannot practically apply it in all cases."[59] Prior to the exigencies of the Civil War and the passage of the Thirteenth, Fourteenth, and Fifteenth Amendments, the federal government was prohibited legally from abolishing slavery where it existed in the states. The attempt to do so would have constituted a gross usurpation of state and local authority by the national government, not to mention the almost certain possibility that public opinion would have supported the South in such an event, guaranteeing its independence and the indefinite perpetuity of slavery as well.

Although Lincoln agreed in principle with the radical abolitionists that slavery was evil in principle and that it ultimately should be abolished, he opposed their immoderate demands for disunion and immediate, uncompensated abolition. Prior to the exigencies of the Civil War and without an amendment, he regarded forcible emancipation of state slavery as imprudent, impractical, and illegal. He thus prudently opposed the disunionist extremes of both the radical abolitionists and southern fire-eaters:

> Stand with anybody that stands RIGHT. Stand with him while he is right and PART with him when he goes wrong. Stand WITH the abolitionist in restoring the Missouri Compromise; and stand AGAINST him when he attempts to repeal the fugitive slave law. In the latter case you stand with the Southern disunionist. What of that? You are still right. In both cases you are right. In both cases you oppose the dangerous extremes. In both you stand on middle ground and hold the ship level and steady. In both you are national and nothing less than national. This is good old whig ground.[60]

In sum, Lincoln's view of the inseparability of liberty and Union may be contrasted to the popular sovereign and radical abolitionist approach to law and morality. In effect, the abolitionists demanded "liberty without Union" while

Douglas demanded a "Union without liberty"—that is, without the universal promise of freedom for all human beings. The dissolution of the Union would have made any opposition to slavery a moot point. Freed from the moral bounds of the Union, the South would certainly have perpetuated and extended its "peculiar institution" indefinitely. In order to appreciate Lincoln's view of the inseparability of liberty and Union, one need only consider what "Liberty" would have meant in a Union that was dedicated to the ethically neutral principle of popular sovereignty or to the moral right to slavery.

VI. LINCOLN'S EMANCIPATION PROCLAMATION: A MODEL OF PRUDENT LEADERSHIP.

Before the transforming circumstances of the Civil War, Lincoln sought to contain the spread of slavery where he was legally authorized to do so in the territories, and to place it on a path of ultimate extinction. His moral stewardship involved guiding public in accordance with the overarching ends of the regime promulgated by the Declaration. The principles of the Declaration were to be actualized within the constraints of the rule of law. This meant upholding those legal concessions made to slavery at the time of the Constitution, which had become established precedent. However, the South's rebellion led to a new set of circumstances that made possible the prudent abolition of slavery as a war measure to preserve both the Union and the very principles for which it stood.

Traditionally, Lincoln has been lauded for performing one of the greatest acts in American history: the Emancipation Proclamation. Since the view of law and morality that informed Lincoln's decision-making has been so misunderstood, it is no surprise that his leadership on emancipation has been likewise derided by both the left and right wing of the political spectrum. Critics on the right contend that Lincoln was our most unconstitutional president; that the Emancipation Proclamation was illegal; and that his broad use of executive power during the war established a precedent for the imperial presidency. Critics on the left deride him as an unrepentant racist who was spurred on by the more principled radical abolitionists, who, in their view, are the true heroes of the Civil War era.

While it may be an exaggeration to claim that Lincoln was solely responsible for freeing the slaves, it is altogether false to deny that his role was less than instrumental in securing the twin goals of preserving the Union and extending equality to all human beings. The traditional view of Lincoln as "The Great

Emancipator" who freed the slaves is much closer to the truth than the deconstructionist view of him as an unprincipled, Machiavellian leader, who sought
his own personal glory at the expense of African-Americans. In response to contemporary critics, it should be noted that Lincoln was assailed from both
extremes of the political spectrum in his own time as well. His ability to navi-
gate the ship of state between the moral idealism of the radical abolitionists, who
demanded "Liberty first, Union afterwards;" and the pragmatism of the War
Democrats, who demanded, in effect, "a Union without Liberty," prudently
achieved the correlative aims of preserving the Union and ending slavery. His
prudence during the war in this regard may likewise be understood as a mean
between the political vices of pragmatism and moral idealism.[61]

According to Lincoln, the preservation of a Union dedicated to the rule of
law in the Constitution and the moral principles of the Declaration was the *sine
qua non* of attaining the loftier goal of extending the principle of equality to
African-Americans. Consequently, those legal concessions that he made to slavery during emancipation were prudent means adapted to the Union's preservation, an objective that implied the eventual end of slavery. Even when
exigencies legally justified emancipation as an executive action, Lincoln prudently cautioned that under the circumstances the act could nevertheless undermine Border State and War Democrat support for the war, thus precipitating a
Confederate victory. By failing to appreciate the extent to which the application of moral principle is constrained by the limits of politics, Lincoln's critics
inevitably fail to appreciate his prudent leadership. And this failure to recognize
Abraham Lincoln as a prudential statesman *par excellence* deprives students and
citizens alike of a moral compass and a valuable resource to evaluate the actions
of contemporary leaders.

As seen, the moral idealism of the radical abolitionists blinded them to the
limits of politics and the importance of maintaining the established rule of law.
Wendell Phillips derisively referred to the president elect as the "slave hound
from Illinois" for his concessions to slavery in order to preserve the Union and
arrogantly described him as an unwitting pawn of radical abolitionists:

> Not an Abolitionist, hardly an antislavery man, Mr. Lincoln consents
> to represent an antislavery idea. A pawn on the political chessboard, his
> value is in his position; with fair effort, we may soon change him for
> knight, bishop, or queen, and sweep the board. . . . The Republican party
> have undertaken a problem, the solution of which will force them to our
> position. . . . Not Mr. Seward's 'Union and Liberty,' which he stole and

poisoned from Webster's 'Liberty and Union.' No: their motto will soon be 'Liberty first,' 'Union afterwards.'[62]

Phillips' substitution of "Liberty First," "Union Afterwards" for "Liberty and Union, One and Inseparable" expresses rather concisely the moral idealism of the radical abolitionists. Unlike Lincoln, he was willing to risk the dissolution of the Union and the abandonment of the Constitution to achieve the abstract promise of equality. As a political idealist who completely disregarded the rule of law, which required that the consent of states within the Union be given to abolish slavery in their own borders, Phillips and the other radical abolitionists were unaware that their abstract commitment to principle may actually have subverted their moral aspirations. Phillips' political immoderation, so reminiscent of French Jacobinism, alienated southern moderates, undermined rational dialogue, and thereby hastened the Civil War. In fact, a member of the South Carolina state legislature quoted Phillips' speech "as one justification for his state's secession from the Union."[63]

From the start of the war and after secession, the radical wing of the Republican Party, constituted by former abolitionists like Garrison and Phillips, pressured Lincoln to decree immediate and unconditional emancipation throughout the entire Union, including the Border States—those states that remained loyal to the Union yet nevertheless had slaves.[64] Secession provided radicals with an opportune moment to implement their utopian agenda since the southern states no longer stood in the way of their moral aspirations.

Although Lincoln opposed slavery in principle, his fidelity to the Constitution and his oath of office prevented him from issuing emancipation without proper legal authorization and without broad public support. In a reply to Albert Hodges, editor of a Frankfurt, Kentucky newspaper who visited the White House to inform the president of "much dissatisfaction" in his state over the "enlistment of black soldiers," Lincoln distinguished his personal feelings from his political duty:

> I am naturally anti-slavery. If slavery is not wrong, nothing is wrong. I can not remember when I did not so think, and feel. And yet I have never understood that the Presidency conferred upon me an unrestricted right to act officially upon this judgment and feeling. It was in the oath I took that I would, to the best of my ability, preserve, protect, and defend the Constitution of the United States. I could not take the office without taking the oath. Nor was it my view that I might take an oath to get power, and break the oath in using the power.[65]

As incontrovertible proof that Lincoln's commitment to ending slavery was a sham, critics point to the facts that the Emancipation Proclamation did not apply to the Border States, that it was justified only as a war measure, and that it was not issued until after two years of war. To further confirm this view, they cite Lincoln's revocation of two prior emancipation edicts and his statement that his "paramount objective" in the war was to preserve the Union, not to abolish slavery. The deconstructionist view of the Emancipation Proclamation teaches that Lincoln was a cunning Machiavellian leader who treated blacks as nothing more than pawns on a political chessboard. If this view is indeed the case, Lincoln should no longer be praised as the "Great Emancipator," but ridiculed as the "Great Manipulator."

Yet, Lincoln's critics fail to take into account the concrete alternatives at the time. His position on emancipation should be viewed in its proper historical context as a prudential mean between the Radical Republicans who demanded immediate, uncompensated emancipation; and the War Democrats who not only opposed extending the principle of equality to African-Americans, but who were also most willing to reverse any strides made in the direction of black freedom. An immediate emancipation may have assuaged the North's feelings of self-righteousness in the short term; but, in the long term, it would have jeopardized the support of War Democrats and the Border States necessary to win the war. The loss of the war by the North and the dissolution of the Union would have rendered the discussion of black freedom moot. It would have resulted in the abandonment of African-Americans to a Confederacy dedicated to the principle of human inequality. On the other side of the political spectrum, a coalition of War Democrats, Border States, and conservative Republicans retarded steps toward black freedom by proposing a return to the *status quo antebellum* in regard to slavery. The pragmatic outlook of this coalition would have resulted in "a Union without Liberty"—that is, a Union dedicated exclusively to white freedom, and the retraction of all strides toward ending slavery. Lincoln's prudent leadership served the greater public good of both liberty and Union by avoiding the extreme alternatives proposed by the Radical Republicans and War Democrats from the Border States.

Lincoln's response to Horace Greeley is often adduced as incontrovertible proof that emancipation was merely an expedient devoid of any higher moral aspiration. In August of 1862, Horace Greeley, editor of the *New York Tribune,* wrote an editorial to the president entitled "The Prayer of Twenty Millions" criticizing Lincoln for his reluctance to emancipate: "We think you are unduly influenced by the councils, the representations, the menaces, of certain fossil politicians hailing from the Border States." Mindful that his response would be scrutinized in papers throughout the nation, Lincoln cautiously, but clearly stated the North's objective during the war:

> My paramount object in this struggle is to save the Union, and is not either to save or to destroy slavery. If I could save the Union without freeing any slave I would do it; and if I could save it by freeing all the slaves I would do it; and if I could save it by freeing some and leaving others alone I would also do that. What I do about slavery, and the colored race, I do because it helps to save the Union; and what I forebear, I forebear because I do not believe it would help to save the Union....I have here stated my purpose according to my view of official duty; and I intend no modification of my oft-expressed personal wish that all men everywhere could be free.[66]

Though Lincoln admitted that his "paramount object" was to save the Union, it did not follow that this end excluded the ultimate goal of extending the principle of equality to all human beings. Critics who cite the letter to Greeley in defense of the claim that the president was unprincipled in his efforts to preserve the Union neglect his many efforts towards compensated emancipation in the Border States, disregard his commitment to the Constitution and rule of law, and ignore his vision of an inclusive and moral Union dedicated to the principles of the Declaration.[67] They also truncate or omit the concluding sentence of the letter whereby Lincoln conveyed his "personal wish that all men everywhere could be free." Here Lincoln clearly distinguished between his personal aspirations for universal freedom and the constitutional limitations of his public duty, which constrained his ability to apply principle under the circumstances. In a word, Lincoln's critics on the left posit a false dichotomy between the twin goals of preserving the Union and ending slavery. They presume that the two objectives are mutually exclusive. On the contrary, Lincoln envisioned the objectives of preserving the Union and freeing the slaves as compatible. David Herbert Donald explains the relationship between these two:

> In Lincoln's mind there was no necessary disjunction between a war for the Union and a war to end slavery. Like most Republicans, he had long held the belief that if slavery could be contained it would inevitably die; a war that kept the slave states within the Union would, therefore, bring about the ultimate extinction of slavery. For this reason, saving the Union was his "paramount object." But readers aware that Lincoln

always chose his words carefully should have recognized that "paramount" meant "foremost" or "principal"—not "sole."[68]

As Donald explains, a careful reading of Lincoln's reply to Greeley would recognize that the word "paramount" does not mean "sole" or "only," but rather "foremost" or "principal." That is to say, Lincoln's language makes clear that although the preservation of the Union was a priority, it was not the only political objective. The preservation of the Union was merely the precondition to ending slavery and extending the principle of equality. Thus, in order to maintain the support of a broad coalition of Border States and War Democrats, Lincoln equivocated when he spoke of his paramount objective in the war. This equivocation was also apparent in his letter James Conkling on August 26, 1863, which was published subsequently throughout the nation. The letter to Conkling not only helps one to appreciate the various factions the president had to balance in maintaining a winning war coalition, but it also subtly reveals his view of the inseparable relationship between preserving the Union and the promise of equality: "You say you will not fight to free Negroes. Some of them seem willing to fight for you; but, no matter. Fight you, then exclusively to save the Union. I issued the proclamation on purpose to save the Union." Lincoln then justified his decision in the Emancipation to use black soldiers: "I thought that whatever Negroes can be got to do as soldiers, leaves just so much less for white soldiers to do, in saving the Union . . . But Negroes, like other people, act upon motives. Why should they do any thing for us, if we will do nothing for them? If they stake their lives for us, they must be promoted by the strongest motive— even the promise of freedom. And the promise being made, must be kept." And as Lawanda Cox has noted in her important work *Lincoln and Black Freedom*, the sixteenth president saw the use of black soldiers as a step toward achieving equality for blacks. Much like the end of his letter to Greeley, at the end of his letter to Conkling, Lincoln reminded his audience of his wider moral aspirations. He offered thanks to all, "For the great republic—for the principle it lives by, and keeps alive—for man's vast future. . . . " To be sure, Lincoln believed that equality was the great principle the Union lives by. Thus, preserving the Union meant preserving the principle of equality and the promise of freedom for all. Finally, Lincoln chastised the political pragmatism and cynicism of those whites seeking to deprive black people of their deserved freedom:

> Peace does not appear so distant as it did. I hope it will come soon, and come to stay; and so come as to be worth the keeping in all future time. It will then have been proved that, among free men, there can be

no successful appeal from the ballot to the bullet; and that they who take such appeal are sure to lose their case, and pay the cost. And then, there will be some black men who can remember that, with silent tongue, and clenched teeth, and steady eye, and well-poised bayonet, they have helped mankind on to this great consummation; while, I fear, there will be some white ones, unable to forget that, with malignant heart, and deceitful speech, they have strove to hinder it.[69]

Lincoln's reference to a peace "worth keeping in all future time" was a subtle reminder that a meaningful peace must honor the promise of freedom to African-Americans. A peace that returns blacks to slavery, as the War Democrats and McClellan desired, was not worth keeping in his view. The caustic tone of Lincoln's reference to "some white ones . . . with malignant heart, and deceitful speech" is uncharacteristic of the president's usual sobriety. This strong language conveyed his righteous indignation for those who sought to hinder America's mission as an exemplar of democracy and as a standard bearer of the principles of equality in the Declaration. Significantly, Lincoln referred generically to whites—that is to say, he did not distinguish between Confederates and northern Democrats, thereby implicating both in the denial of freedom to African-Americans.

The joint objectives of emancipation involved a short-term and long-term goal: The primary, short-term objective was to defeat the enemy and to restore the territorial integrity of the Union; the related, long-term objective was to extend the principle of equality to all human beings. However, the success of the latter depended upon the success of the first. The final version of the Emancipation Proclamation expressed Lincoln's dual intent. The Emancipation Proclamation was "sincerely believed to be an act of justice, warranted by the Constitution, upon military necessity. . . . "[70] Lincoln scrupulous attention to legal detail should not obscure the complementary moral intention of emancipation as an "act of justice." Indeed, the South recognized that Lincoln was a principled and implacable foe of slavery—that is why it seceded in the first place. It correctly understood that slavery was eventually doomed to extinction in a regime committed to the principles of the Declaration and to a leader who would contain the spread of the institution.

Textual evidence further confirms that Lincoln envisioned the inseparability of liberty and Union to imply the complementary goals of preserving the Union and ending slavery. At Peoria in 1854, he emphasized that the Union must be "worthy of saving."[71] As noted, according to Lincoln, the Union was only worthy of saving in view of the moral principles for which it stood! Thus, in a speech at Bloomington in 1856 Lincoln emphasized that "*the Union must be preserved in the purity of its principles*. . . ."[72] And, as seen above, his praise for "The Great Republic" was based upon "the principle it lives by"—that is to say, the Union's promise of civil and religious liberty to all. In Lincoln's view, the consistent application of the Declaration's principle of equality to blacks was linked to the success of the American mission in guaranteeing equality to all human beings: "In *giving* freedom to the *slave*, we *assure* freedom to the *free*—honorable alike in what we give, and what we preserve. We shall nobly save, or meanly lose, the last best, hope of earth."[73] While en route to his inauguration, Lincoln delivered a speech at Trenton, New Jersey, an important historical site of the Revolutionary War, in which he vowed to uphold the Founding Fathers' revolutionary legacy of freedom: "I am exceedingly anxious that this Union, the Constitution, and the liberties of the people shall be perpetuated in accordance with the original idea for which that struggle was made. . . ."[74] Of course, the original idea of the revolution was embodied in the Declaration. And after the Border State of Maryland had pledged to abolish slavery, Lincoln exclaimed: "Maryland is secure to Liberty and Union for all the future."[75] Because the Union was dedicated to legitimate moral ends, Lincoln warned the Border States that slavery would eventually become a casualty of the war: "If the war continue long, as it must, if the object be not sooner attained, the institution in your states will be extinguished by mere friction and abrasion—by the mere incident of the war." In a letter to August Belmont, he explained that "broken eggs cannot be mended" implying that the shell of slavery was doomed to inevitable destruction by the war.[76] Finally, the intention of the Gettysburg Address as a statement of America's creed and a poignant reminder of its moral aspirations demonstrates Lincoln's commitment to the principle of equality. In a *New Birth of Freedom*, Harry V. Jaffa explains the political intention behind the Gettysburg Address: Lincoln asked the American people to ratify the Emancipation Proclamation, which he had issued earlier the same year.[77] Lincoln's affirmation of equality as the central proposition of the nation and his subsequent reference to "a new birth of freedom" held out the possibility of a Union freed from its original sin of slavery. The myriad utterances above testify to the inseparable connection between preserving the Union and extending liberty in Lincoln's mind.

Even if the preservation of the Union implied the eventual promise of equal rights for all, the abstract resolution of a moral claim does not prescribe a detailed set of guidelines for the determination of public policy. The concrete application of a moral principle like equality must be weighed and balanced against the competing legal, political, social, and economic claims. Lincoln once confessed that "[t]he difficulty is not in stating the principle, but in practically applying it."[78] An appreciation of Lincoln's prudent decision-making on the Emancipation Proclamation thus requires a further discussion of the circumstances he confronted at the time. What contingencies and variables did Lincoln have to consider? First, Lincoln was unsure about his constitutional authority to emancipate the slaves. He had consistently and repeatedly pledged that he could not touch slavery where it existed in the states: from his earliest statements on slavery until his presidency. As much as he hated slavery, he had sworn an oath to uphold the Constitution and that meant upholding its concessions to slavery as well. As noted prior to the Thirteenth Amendment, the federal division of power prohibited interference with slavery where it already existed at the time of the Constitution. A House Resolution in 1790 explicitly prohibited Congress from emancipating the slaves in the southern states.[79] An emancipation proclamation in defiance of the Constitution would lack legitimacy and would confirm the suspicion of Southerners and northern moderates alike that the Republican Party was composed of fanatics who had no respect for established legal procedure and the rule of law. Given his constitutional reservations, Lincoln believed that Emancipation Proclamation could only be legally justified as a "War Measure" under the president's power in Article Two as "commander and chief" of the armed forces. Lincoln maintained that it was a necessary and reasonable means (a war measure) taken by the nation's chief executive to impair the South's ability to make war: the act would encourage slaves laboring for the Confederacy to flee and support the advancing Union armies. In fact, this did happen and the Union's war effort benefited greatly from it.

The legal status of the Emancipation Proclamation as a war measure also explains why it did not apply to the Border States, which remained loyal to the Union, and to those southern lands, which were now occupied by federal forces. In a letter to Salmon P. Chase dated September 2, 1863, Lincoln explained that the Emancipation Proclamation could only be justified as a war measure, and that to act beyond this grant of authority would blatantly violate the rule of law, inviting future despotism, encouraging resistance to the administration, and undermining needed political support to win the war:

> If I take the step [of abolishing slavery in those federal held areas of Virginia and Louisiana exempted from emancipation] must I not do so, without the argument of military necessity, and so, without any argu-

ment, except the one that I think the measure politically expedient, and morally right? Would I not thus give up all footing upon the constitution or law? Would I not thus be in the boundless field of absolutism? Could this pass unnoticed, or unresisted? Could it fail to be perceived that without any further stretch, I might do the same in Delaware, Maryland, Kentucky, Tennessee, and Missouri; and even change any law in any state? Would not many of our own friends shrink away appalled? Would it not lose us the elections, and with them, the very cause we seek to advance?[80]

To some, the fact that the Emancipation Proclamation reads like a lawyer's brief detracts from its significance; however, the language actually shows Lincoln's attention to legal detail, his respect for the rule of law, and his careful effort to balance both legal and moral obligation. Historian Richard Hofstadter once ridiculed the Emancipation Proclamation claiming that it had "all the moral grandeur of a bill of lading."[81] However, reaching an opposite conclusion based upon a greater appreciation of Lincoln's dual role as both commander in chief and attorney in chief,[82] George Anastaplo has correctly described the Emancipation Proclamation as "the lawyers art in its perfection."[83] For example, in crafting the language of the Emancipation, Lincoln was careful not to use the word "abolition" in the document in order to distinguish his lawful action from the unlawful measures of the radical abolitionists. And as a measure of its legal and moral propriety, the act also explicitly discouraged freed blacks from wanton violence against their captors: "And I hereby enjoin upon the people so declared to be free to abstain from all violence, unless in necessary self-defense..."

Even if it was constitutional (legally authorized), was emancipation politically expedient? How could the act be enforced in rebel territory? Lincoln's primary political consideration was to maintain a fragile war coalition composed of radical and moderate republicans who favored emancipation and War Democrats, conservative Republicans and the Border States who opposed emancipation. In particular, he had to maintain the political support of the Border States that remained faithful to the Union, despite the presence of slavery. The support of Border States like Kentucky, Maryland, and Missouri was crucial to the strategic success of the Union. Alienating them would upset the balance of power in favor of the South. Lincoln once said, "to lose Kentucky is to lose the whole game." He correctly discerned that it was both illegal and inexpedient to abolish slavery in the Border States without their consent. The needed support of War Democrats and the Border States to win the war constrained Lincoln's political possibilities. To maintain a winning coalition he prudently equivocated on what preserving the Union meant in his reply to Greeley and elsewhere to placate those who feared that the war would degenerate into an abolitionist crusade.

As a prudent commander in chief, Lincoln was forced to consider the effect of the emancipation on the Union Army's already low morale by late 1862. In order to defeat the South it was necessary to maintain unity in the northern army. Some Union officers were so hostile towards blacks that they returned fugitive slaves to the Confederacy during cease-fires. Soldiers in the field had already threatened to desert if the cause of the Union was identified with abolitionism. After General Fremont unilaterally proclaimed emancipation in Missouri, a company of federal soldiers threw down their arms and deserted, claiming that they enlisted to save the Union, not to "free the niggers." In fact, Lincoln had revoked two prior emancipations because he considered them to be illegal. Lincoln's commander for the Army of the Potomac, General George B. McClellan, a War Democrat, so vehemently opposed emancipation that he wrote a letter to his troops apologizing for Lincoln's actions in this regard.[84]

Lincoln also had to consider whether or not domestic opinion would support emancipation. Prudent leaders must consult public opinion and be responsible to it if democratic government is meaningful. Paradoxically, they must guide public opinion without moving too far ahead of it and be constrained by public opinion when it is recalcitrant. In Lincoln's words, "a universal opinion, whether good or bad, cannot safely be disregarded." What would be the social impact of emancipation? How realistic was the prospect of racial adjustment between whites and blacks? What would be done with the blacks once they were emancipated? How could they be assimilated into society, given their servile condition and the prevailing opinion amongst both Southerners and Northerners that they were an inferior race? Would the bitterness of slavery and resentment amongst blacks incite them to slaughter whites? And while many Northerners opposed slavery in the abstract, they nevertheless opposed the full social and political equality of blacks, and still viewed them as an inferior race. Many immigrants resented having to compete for jobs with newly freed African-Americans. An example of public hostility to black freedom in the North was seen in the New York City draft riots, which erupted the summer after Lincoln issued the Emancipation. A black orphanage was burnt, and blacks were lynched as a demonstration against instituting the draft to support a war for equal rights.

Lincoln had reservations about the credibility of an Emancipation Proclamation without a Union victory. Perceptions do count in politics. After winning

many of the initial battles of the Civil War, the South hoped for foreign intervention to recognize or assist their cause. Lincoln presented a first draft of the
Emancipation to his cabinet as early as July 22, 1862. Secretary of State William
Seward voiced reservations that without a Union military victory, the Emancipation would lack credibility in the nation and in the eyes of the world. Instead
of a sublime triumph of freedom, it would be viewed as an act of desperation, "the
last shriek on our retreat."[85] Lincoln and Seward both feared a British intervention that would force peace, thus guaranteeing the independence of the Confederacy. Lincoln thus delayed Emancipation until it could be crowned with a Union
victory to bolster its credibility at home and abroad. The battle of Antietam on
September 17 gave the Union the victory it needed. Although it was more or less
a stalemate in terms of casualties (about 20,000 total dead and wounded), Antietam was a symbolic victory because Lee was driven out of Maryland.

The preliminary Emancipation was signed on September 22, 1862, but did
not go into effect until January 1, 1863, a hundred days afterward. This interval
was yet another prudent means to prepare public opinion for the subsequent
transformation of freeing three million people. There were some notable differences between the preliminary and final draft of the Emancipation. The first
draft mentioned compensation to slaveholders for their freed slaves if the slaveholders rejoined the Union. The final draft made no mention of compensation.
Furthermore, the final draft authorized the use of black soldiers for the Union,
which was not mentioned in the first draft. Lincoln saw the enlistment of black
soldiers as both an expedient means to support the Union cause and an important step toward black freedom. By proving their manhood on the battlefield,
African-Americans would further dispose public opinion toward the goal of
equality. The withdrawal of an offer to compensate slaveholders who returned
to the Union and the authorization of black soldiers in the final version of the
Emancipation was further consistent with Lincoln's belief that the institution of
slavery would become a casualty of the war. To placate the fears of moderates
who feared a universal, servile insurrection, the final version of the Emancipation prudently included an admonition to the free slaves to "abstain from all violence, unless in necessary self-defense."

Ultimately, Lincoln decided that the advantages of emancipation outweighed
its disadvantages. After judging the various contingencies, he decided that the
act was salutary in both its principle and in its effects or consequences. The transforming circumstances of the Civil War made emancipation "an indispensable
necessity" at the time it furthered the joint ends of the Union's preservation and
slavery's demise. The prudent leader must take into consideration not only

intentions, but also the consequences of actions and ideas. Prudent leadership thus involves foresight; it anticipates unintended consequences. Indeed, Aquinas notes that the word prudence is derived from providence—that is, foresight. What then were some of the positive consequences to be anticipated by the Emancipation Proclamation? First, it would cripple the South's capacity to make war by encouraging slaves to escape from their southern masters and to support the approaching Union Army. It would have achieved an important moral aspiration of the Union by extending the Declaration's principle of equality to African-Americans in the South. It would have prevented diplomatic recognition of the Confederacy and intervention. Lincoln and Seward believed that emancipation would discourage the foreign intervention of Great Britain and other foreign nations, which would be forced to recognize the moral high ground of the Union's cause. And in addition to helping to preserve the territorial and legal integrity of the Union, it would give the North a very concrete moral cause to fight for.

The sober language of the Emancipation, its legal authorization as a war measure, its delay until a Union victory, its exemption of the Border States and other Union held areas show that it was a prudent act that considered a variety of contingencies.[86] Lincoln's principled commitment to equality and black freedom in the Emancipation is confirmed by his subsequent speech and deeds. Not only can one point to the various speeches and writings where Lincoln consistently opposed slavery, but also to his actions in this regard as well. It is worth considering just a few of these actions as a testimony to Lincoln's genuine opposition to slavery. The contention that Lincoln was a hypocrite because the Emancipation did not apply to the Border States is refuted by the many efforts of the president to abolish slavery legally in those states through his policy of compensated emancipation. In March 1862, Lincoln steered a joint resolution through Congress that offered financial aid to any Border State that would take measures toward gradual, compensated emancipation. He argued that a million dollars or less than half a day's cost of the war would buy all the slaves in Delaware at $400 a head. Because the Border States remained loyal to the Union, they had to consent to the abolition of slavery; compensated emancipation was thus a legal means to achieving an important moral principle. If Lincoln was less committed to black freedom, he would not have invited Border State men to the White House and appealed on numerous occasions to adopt his plan for compensated emancipation.[86] The Border States' refusal each time to accept the offer is an indication of the recalcitrance of public opinion in this part of the war coalition against extending equality to the African-American. Lincoln's commitment to the principle of equality is demonstrated further by his demand that the abolition of slavery be a necessary condition to any southern state's readmission to the Union during reconstruction. His commitment is demonstrated through his vigorous support of the Thirteenth Amendment that abolished slavery throughout the country—in the Border States as well. During the election of 1864, opponents of the act argued that, since it was a war measure, it could be revoked after the termination of hostilities. His commitment is demonstrated by his abolition of slavery in District of Columbia, an area that was under the jurisdiction of the federal government. His commitment is demonstrated by his approval of African-Americans in the army—a step toward black suffrage. Finally, Lincoln's commitment is demonstrated through his efforts toward black suffrage in Louisiana, the first reconstructed state that would serve as a model for subsequent states' readmission to the Union. Towards the end of the war, he recommended to Governor Hahn of Louisiana in a personal letter that some blacks be given the franchise. It is important to note that prior to the Fifteenth Amendment suffrage was left to the discretion of the states and placed beyond the authority of the national government to regulate. Lincoln's letter conveyed a personal moral aspiration to the governor: "I barely suggest for your private consideration, whether some of the colored people may not be let in—as for instance, the very intelligent, and especially those who have fought gallantly in our ranks. They would probably help, in some trying time to come, to keep the jewel of liberty within the family of freedom."[87] According to Lincoln, the Founder's legacy of liberty should be bequeathed unto the entire family of mankind.[88]

Lincoln's unwillingness to retract emancipation in order to gain popularity during the summer of 1864, the nadir of his election campaign, further demonstrates his principled leadership.[89] In 1864, the Democratic Party ran George B. McClellan, who sought to revoke the Emancipation Proclamation and who might have succeeded had he been elected. McClellan's letter of apology to the army after Lincoln issued the act has already been mentioned. In the early stages of the campaign, it looked as though Lincoln was sure to lose. Indeed, there was a great deal of pressure to renounce emancipation during the summer months of 1864. The Union was exhausted by war: one-half million deaths of American soldiers. The "existence and growth of a substantial peace movement" increasingly voiced opposition to Lincoln's war policies.[90] A miscegenation hoax perpetrated by the *New York World* newspaper attempted to stir up racism and to embarrass the Republican Party by claiming that emancipation was done to promote interbreeding among the races.

Lincoln was under great pressure to revoke the Emancipation Proclamation in order to gain the support of moderate Democrats and to build a wider political coalition. In his reply to a War Democrat, Charles D. Robinson, who expressed concerns about his emancipation policy, Lincoln stated: "I am sure you would not desire me to say, or to leave an inference, that I am ready, whenever convenient to join in re-enslaving those who shall have served us in consideration of our promise. As matter of morals, could such treachery by any possibility, escape the curses of Heaven, or of any good man."[91] And in December of 1864, Lincoln stated:

> I repeat the declaration made a year ago, that "while I remain in my present position I shall not attempt to retract or modify the emancipation proclamation, nor shall I return to slavery any person who is free by the terms of that proclamation, or by any of the Acts of Congress." If the people should, by whatever mode or means, make it an Executive duty to re-enslave such persons, another, and not I, must be their instrument to perform it.[92]

Lincoln's campaign for reelection sunk to a low point in the summer of 1864. In August, Henry J. Raymond, Chairman of the Republican National Committee, informed the president that his prospects for reelection were bleak, primarily on account of "the want of military success, and the impression in some minds, the fear and suspicion in others, that we are not to have peace in any event under this administration until Slavery is abandoned." Raymond's remarks testify that Lincoln's commitment to ending slavery and upholding the Emancipation were maintained at great risk to his personal political ambitions.[93] A less principled leader would have "triangulated" to stay in office. But instead, Lincoln was willing to accept defeat rather than abandon his core principles. On August 23, he circulated a blind memorandum to his cabinet asking them to sign the unseen document that conceded defeat in the election. Inside the sealed envelope, the memorandum stated:

> This morning, as for some days past, it seems exceedingly probable that this Administration will not be re-elected. Then it will be my duty to so co-operate with the President elect, as to save the Union between the election and the inauguration; as he will have secured his election on such ground that he cannot possibly save it afterwards.[94]

If Lincoln was the astute Machiavellian described by critics, he surely would have retracted the Emancipation in the name of expediency rather than suffer defeat in the name of principle. On the contrary, he was willing to accept defeat rather than return the freedmen to bondage Thus, despite great pressure and contrary to his own popularity and standing in the polls, Lincoln prudently adhered to his principles. Fortunately, Sherman's victory at the Battle of Atlanta in early September and the Democrat's suicidal endorsement of peace with the Confederacy all but ensured Lincoln's victory in 1864. There is no doubt that if McClellan had won the election of 1864, he would have attempted to reverse the many strides made toward black freedom.[95]

The words of Frederick Douglass at the dedication to the Freedman's monument in Washington, D.C. on April 14, 1876 commemorating Lincoln and the Emancipation provides a valuable insight on the sixteenth president's prudent leadership:

> His great mission was to accomplish two things: first, to save his country from dismemberment and ruin; and, second, to free his country from the great crime of slavery. To do one or the other, or both, he must have the earnest sympathy and the powerful cooperation of his loyal fellow-countrymen. Without this primary and essential condition to success his efforts must have been vain and utterly fruitless. Had he put the abolition of slavery before the salvation of the Union, he would inevitably driven from him a powerful class of the American people and rendered resistance to the rebellion impossible. Viewed from the genuine abolition ground, Mr. Lincoln seemed tardy, cold, dull, and indifferent; but measuring him by the sentiment of his country, a sentiment he was bound as a statesman to consult, he was swift, zealous, radical and determined.[96]

NOTES

1. Richard Horsley, "The Law of Nature in Philo And Cicero" *The Harvard Theological Review* vol. 71, Number ½, January-April 1978, 35–59.

2. Charles E. Rice, "Some Reasons For A Restoration of Natural Law Jurisprudence," Wake Forest Law Review, Volume 24, 1989, Number 3, 539–570.

3. Walter Lipmann, *The Public Philosophy* (Chicago: University of Chicago Press, 1978).

4. Blackstone cited in Rice, 540.

5. Michael Novak, *On Two Wings: Humble Faith and Common Sense at the American Founding* (San Francisco, Encounter Books, 2002), 95.

6. Harry V. Jaffa, *A New Birth of Freedom* (Lanham, Md.: Rowman and Littlefield, 2000), 509.

7. William H. Rehnquist, "The Notion of a Living Constitution" in *Views from the Bench: The Judiciary and Constitutional Politics*, ed. Mark W. Cannon and David M. O'Brien. Englewood Cliffs: Chatham House, 1985, 134–135; Also cited in Jaffa: 87.

8. St. Thomas Aquinas, *Summa Theologica: Volume Three: II-II* (Westminster, MD: Christian Classics, 1981), II-II, Q. 47–51, 1383-1406. (Hereafter cited as Aquinas, *S.T.)*

9. Aquinas, *S. T.*, II-II, Q. 49, Article 6, 1399.

10. Aquinas, *S. T.*, II-IIae, Q. 47, Article 10, p. 1389. Aquinas states, "Accordingly, since it belongs to prudence to rightly counsel, judge, and command concerning the means of obtaining a due end, it is evident that prudence regards not only the private good of the individual, but also the common good of the multitude."

11. Aquinas, *S. T.*, II-IIae, Q. 49, 2, 1396. Aquinas states, "The reasoning of prudence terminates, as in a conclusion, in the particular matter of action, to which, as stated above (Q. 47. AA. 3, 6), it applies the knowledge of some universal principle. Now a singular conclusion is argued from a universal and a singular proposition. Wherefore the reasoning of prudence must proceed from a twofold understanding. The one is cognizant of universals and this belongs to understanding which is an intellectual virtue, whereby we know naturally not only speculative principles, but also universal principles, such as One should do evil to no man, as shown above (Q. 47, A. 6). The other understanding, as stated in Ethic. Vi. 11, is cognizant of an extreme, i.e., of some primary singular and contingent practical matter, viz., the minor premises, which must needs be singular in the syllogism of prudence, as stated above (Q. 47, AA. 3, 6). Now this primary singular is some singular end, as stated in the same place. Wherefore the understanding which is a part of prudence is a right estimate of some particular end." Also see: Yves Simon, *A General Theory of Authority* (Notre Dame: Univ. of Notre Dame Press, 1980), 144.

12. Aquinas, *S. T.*, II, II, Q. 47, A. 2-3, 1384–1385.

13. Aquinas, *S. T.*, II, II, Q. 53-55, 1410–1420.

14. Josef Pieper, *The Four Cardinal Virtues* (Notre Dame: University of Notre Dame Press, 1966), 19.

15. Pieper, 19.

16. Abraham Lincoln, *The Collected Works of Abraham Lincoln*, ed. Roy P. Basler, 8 vols. (New Brunswick, N.J.: Rutgers University Press, 1953–1955), 3: 375. (Hereafter cited as *CWAL*).

17. *CWAL*, IV: 240.

18. Jaffa, 122–125, 509.

19. Joseph R. Fornieri, "Abraham Lincoln and the Declaration of Independence: The Meaning of Equality" in *Abraham Lincoln: Sources and Style of Leadership*, ed. Frank J. Williams, William D. Pederson, and Vincent J. Marsala (Westport, CT.: Greenwood Press, 1994), 45–69.

20. Harry V. Jaffa, *Equality and Liberty* (New York: Oxford University Press, 1965). Also See also: Harry V. Jaffa, *How to Think About the American Revolution* (Durham, N.C.: Carolina Academic Press, 1978).

21. I have explored how reason, revelation, and republicanism cooperate in Lincoln's political philosophy in much greater depth in my book: Joseph R. Fornieri, *Abraham Lincoln's Political Faith* (DeKalb: Northern Illinois University Press, 2003).

22. Novak, 37.

23. *CWAL*, II: 544–547.

24. *CWAL*, II: 532.

25. *CWAL*, VII: 260.

26. *CWAL*, I: 411-412.

27. Jaffa, *New Birth of Freedom*, 22–27.

28. *CWAL*, IV: 3. For Lincoln's appeal to natural theology against slavery, see the following: *CWAL*, II: 222; III: 462-463; 479-480; IV: 3, 9; X: 44-45.

29. *CWAL*, V: 419–420.

30. Fornieri, *Abraham Lincoln's Political Faith*, 106-108; Kenneth L. Deutsch, "Thomas Aquinas on Magnanimous and Prudent Statesmanship" in *Tempered Strength: Studies in the Nature and Scope of Prudential Leadership* ed. Ethan Fishman (Lanham: Lexington Books, 2002), 33–52.

31. *CWAL*, III: 274.

32. Rice, 540.

33. John Rawls, "Justice As Fairness: Political not Metaphysical," *Philosophy and Public Affairs* 14 (Summer 1985): 230–231.

34. *CWAL*, III: 267.

35. *CWAL*, III: 9-10.

36. *CWAL*, III: 217.

37. *CWAL*, III: 111–112.

38. *CWAL*, III: 116.

39. *CWAL*, II: 265–266.

40. *CWAL*, III: 9.

41. Carl Bode, ed., *The Portable Thoreau*, (New York, Penguin, 1977), 111.

42. Bode, 120–121.

43. *CWAL*, I: 347.

44. William Lloyd Garrison, *Selections From the Writings and Speeches of William Lloyd Garrison* (New York: Wallcut, 1852), 118.

45. David Herbert Donald, *Charles Sumner and the Coming of the Civil War* (Chicago: Univ. of Chicago Press, 1981), 228.

46. Garrison, 116–119.

47. Wendell Phillips, "The Argument for Disunion" in *On Civil Rights and Freedom*, ed. Louis Filler (New York: Hill and Wang, 1965), 133.

48. Cited in: James B. McPherson, *The Struggle for Equality: Abolitionists And The Negro In The Civil War And Reconstruction*, (Princeton: Princeton Univ Press, 1995), 37.

49. McPherson, 37.

50. McPherson, 36.

51. McPherson, 37.

52. Cited in: David M. Potter, *The Impending Crisis: 1848–1861.* ed. Don E. Fehrenbacher, (New York: Harper and Row, 1976), 366–367.

53. *CWAL*, II: 270.

54. Garrison, 117.

55. *CWAL*, I: 484.

56. *CWAL*, II: 406.

57. Aquinas, *S. T.*, I-II, Q. 95, A. 3.

58. *CWAL*, III: 222.

59. *CWAL*, III: 303-304.

60. *CWAL*, II: 273.

61. Ethan Fishman, "Under the Circumstances: Abraham Lincoln and Classical Prudence," in *Abraham Lincoln: Sources and Style of Leadership*, ed. Frank J. Williams, William D. Pederson, and Vincent J. Marsala (Westport, CT.: Greenwood Press, 1994), 4–7. See also: T. Harry Williams, "Abraham Lincoln: Principle and Pragmatism in Politics," *Mississippi Valley Historical Review* 40 (1953): 96–96.

62. McPherson, 27–28.

63. McPherson, 28.

64. See Harry T. Williams, *Lincoln and the Radicals* (Madison: University of Wisconsin Press, 1972).

65. *CWAL*: VII: 281–283.

66. *CWAL*, V: 388–389.

67. Rogan Kersh, *Dreams of a More Perfect Union* (Ithaca: Cornell University Press, 2001), 153–197.

68. David Herbert Donald, *Lincoln* (New York: Simon & Schuster, 1995), 368.

69. *CWAL*, VI: 406–410.

70. *CWAL*, VI: 30.

71. *CWAL*, II: 276.

72. *CWAL*, II: 340–341.

73. *CWAL*, V: 537.

74. *CWAL*, IV: 236.

75. *CWAL*, VIII: 148.

76. *CWAL*, V: 350.

77. Jaffa, *New Birth of Freedom*, 73–152.

78. *CWAL*, VII: 302.

79. Joseph Ellis, *Founding Brothers* (New York: Knopf, 2000), 81–119.

80. *CWAL*, VI: 428–429.

81. Richard Hofstadter, *The American Political Tradition* (New York: Vintage Books, 1961), 93.

82. For an important and cogent look at how Lincoln effectively combined the dual roles of attorney-in-chief and commander in chief based on his dual career in law and politics see: Frank J. Williams, *Judging Lincoln* (Urbana: Southern Illinois University Press, 2003).

83. For an outstanding textual analysis of the Emancipation Proclamation see: George Anastaplo: *A Constitutional Biography* (Lanham, Md.: Rowman and Littlefield, 1999), 199–227.

84. Benjamin Thomas, *Abraham Lincoln* (New York: Knopf, 1968), 345.

85. Thomas, 334.

86. For an outstanding and more extensive treatment of the Emancipation Proclamation, the reader is encouraged to study Allen C. Guelzo's *Lincoln's Emancipation Proclamation: The End of Slavery in America*, which was published in 2004, a year after the first edition of this volume.

87. *CWAL*, V: 144–146; 160–161; 317–319; 324; 527.

88. *CWAL*, VII: 243.

89. For a superb treatment of the Election of 1864 see: David E. Long, *The Jewel of Liberty: Abraham Lincoln's Reelection and the End of Slavery* (Mechanicsburg, Pa.: Stackpole, 1994).

90. David E. Long, "I Shall Not Recall A Word," in *Abraham Lincoln: Sources and Styles of Leadership*, ed. Frank J. Williams, William D. Pederson, and Vincent Marsala (Westport, Conn.: Greenwood Press, 1994), 89–108.

91. Long, "I Shall Not Recall A Word", 89–108.

92. *CWAL*, VII: 500.

93. *CWAL*, VIII: 152. Also see Anastaplo, 201.

94. Cited in Ronald C. White, Jr., *Lincoln's Greatest Speech: The Second Inaugural* (New York: Simon and Schuster, 2002), 46.

95. *CWAL*, VII: 514.

96. Long, *Jewel of Liberty*.

97. Frederick Douglass, *Selected Speeches and Writings*, ed. Philip S. Foner (Chicago: Lawrence Hill, 1999), 618–621.

SELECT BIBLIOGRAPHY

Anastaplo, George. "American Constitutionalism and The Virtue of Prudence: Philadelphia, Paris, Washington, Gettysburg." In *Abraham Lincoln The Gettysburg Address and American Constitutionalism*, ed. Leo Paul S. de Alvarez, 77–170. Irving, Texas: Univ. of Dallas Press, 1976.
_____. "Slavery and the Constitution: Explorations." *Texas Tech Law Review*, 20 (1989) : 677–786.
_____. *Abraham Lincoln: A Constitutional Biography*. Lanham: Rowman and Littlefield, 1999.
Barton, William E. *The Soul of Abraham Lincoln*. New York: George H. Doran Co., 1920.
Basler, Roy P., ed. *The Collected Works of Abraham Lincoln*. 8 vols. New Brunswick, N.J.: Rutgers Univ. Press, 1953.
Belz, Herman. *A new birth of freedom: The Republican Party and freedmen's rights, 1861 to 1866*. New York, Fordham University Press, 2000.
_____ *Abraham Lincoln, constitutionalism and equal rights during the Civil War Era*. New York: Fordham University Press, 1997
Bennett, Lerone Jr. "Was Abe Lincoln a White Supremacist?" in Ebony, 23, February 1968.
_____. *Forced Into Glory: Abraham Lincoln's White Dream*. Chicago: Johnson, 2000.
Boritt, Gabor. *Abraham Lincoln and the Economics of the American Dream*. Urbana and Chicago: University of Illinois Press, 1994.
_____ , ed. *The Historian's Lincoln: Pseudohistory, Psychohistory and History*. Urbana: Univ. of Illinois Press, 1988.
_____. The *Gettysburg Gospel: The Lincoln Speech that Nobody Knows*. New York: Simon and Schuster, 2006.
Bradford, M.E. *A Better Guide Than Reason: Studies in the American Revolution*. La Salle, Illinois: Sherwood Sugden, 1979.
_____. "The Lincoln Legacy: A Long View." *Modern Age*, 24 (1980), 355–63.
Burkhimer, Michael. *Lincoln's Christianity*. Yardley, PA: Westholme Publishing, 2007.
Burlingame, Michael. *The Inner World of Abraham Lincoln*. Chicago: University of Illinois Press, 1994.
Carnahan, Burrus M. *Act of Justice: Lincoln's Emancipation Proclamation and the Law of War*. Lexington: The University Press of Kentucky, 2007.
Carwardine, Richard J. *Lincoln: Profiles in Power*. London: Pearson Education, 2003.
Charnwood, Lord. *Abraham Lincoln*. New York: Pocket, 1917.
Corlett, William. "The Availability of Lincoln's Political Religion." In *Political Theory*, Vol. 10, 1982, 520–540.
Cox, LaWanda. *Lincoln and Black Freedom: A Study in Presidential Leadership*. Columbia, South Carolina: Univ. of South Carolina Press, 1994.

Current, Richard N. *The Lincoln Nobody Knows*. New York: Hill and Wang, 1984.

deAlvarez, Leo Paul S, ed. *Abraham Lincoln, The Gettysburg Address, and American Constitutionalism*. Irving, Texas: Univ. of Dallas Press, 1976.

Diggins, John P. *The Lost Soul of American Politics: Virtue, Self-Interest, and the Foundations of Liberalism*. Chicago: Univ. of Chicago Press, 1986.

DiLorenzo, Thomas J. *The Real Lincoln*. Roseville, CA: Forum-Prima Publishing, 2002.

Deutsch, Kenneth L. and Joseph R. Fornieri, eds. *Lincoln's American Dream: Clashing Political Perspectives*. Dulles, Virginia: Potomac, 2005.

Dirck, Brian, *Lincoln the Lawyer*. Urbana: University of Illinois Press, 2007.

_____. *Lincoln and Davis: Imagining America*. Lawrence: University Press of Kansas, 2001.

Donald, David Herbert. *Lincoln Reconsidered: Essays on the Civil War Era*. 2d ed. New York: Vintage, Knopf and Random House,1961.

_____. *Lincoln's Herndon*. New York: Knopf, 1948; reprint, New York: Da Capo,1989.

_____. *Lincoln*. New York: Simon & Schuster, 1995.

Douglass, Frederick. *Selected Speeches and Writings*. ed. Philip S. Foner. Chicago: Lawrence Hill Books, 1999.

Ericson, David F. *The Shaping Of American Liberalism: The Debates Over Ratification, Nullification And Slavery*. Chicago: Univ. Of Chicago Press, 1993.

Farber, Daniel. *Lincoln's Constitution*. Chicago: University of Chicago Press, 2003.

Fehrenbacher, Don E. *Prelude to Greatness: Lincoln in the 1850's*. Stanford: Stanford Univ. Press, 1962.

_____. *The Dred Scott Case: Its Significance in American Law and Politics*. New York: Oxford University Press, 1978.

_____. *Lincoln in Text and Context: Collected Essays*. Stanford: Stanford Univ. Press, 1987.

Fishman, Ethan. "Under the Circumstances: Abraham Lincoln and Classical Prudence." In *Abraham Lincoln: Sources and Styles of Leadership*. Westport Conn. Greenwood Press, 1994.

Forgie, George B. *Patricide in the House Divided*. New York: Norton, 1979.

Fornieri, Joseph R. *Abraham Lincoln's Political Faith*. DeKalb: Northern Illinois University Press, 2003.

Fornieri, Joseph R. and Sara Vaughn Gabbard, *Lincoln's America*. Carbondale: Southern Illinois University Press, 2008.

Genovese, Eugene D. The Slaveholders' Dilemma: Freedom and Progress in Southern Conservative Thought,1820-1860. Columbia, South Carolina: Univ. of South Carolina Press, 1992.

_____. *The Southern Tradition: The Achievement and Limitationsof an American Conservatism*. Cambridge Mass.: Harvard Univ. Press, 1994.

Greenstone, J. David. *The Lincoln Persuasion: Remaking American Liberalism*. Princeton: Princeton Univ. Press, 1993.

Guelzo, Allen C. *Abraham Lincoln: Redeemer President*. Grand Rapids: Eerdmans Publishing, 1999.

_____. *Lincoln's Emancipation Proclamation: The End of Slavery in America*. New York: Simon and Schuster, 2004.

_____. *Lincoln and Douglas: The Debates that Defined America*. New York: Simon and Schuster, 2008.

Harris, William C. *Lincoln's Rise to the Presidency*. Lawrence: University Press of Kansas, 2006.

Hein, David. "Lincoln's Theology and Political Ethics." *In Essays on Lincoln's Faith and Politics,* ed. Kenneth W. Thompson, 105-179. Lanham, Md.: Univ. Press of America, 1983.

Herndon, William H., and Jesse Weik. *Herndon's Life of Lincoln*. Cleveland: World, 1942; reprint, New York: Da Capo, 1983.

Oates, Stephen B. *With Malice Toward None: The Life Of Abraham Lincoln*. New York: Mentor-New American Library, 1978.

Paludan, Phillip Shaw. *The Presidency of Abraham Lincoln*. Lawrence: University Press of Kansas, 1994.

Peterson, Merril D. *Lincoln In American Memory*. New York: Oxford Univ. Press, 1994.

Pinsker, Matthew. *Lincoln's Sanctuary: Abraham Lincoln and the Soldiers' Home*. Oxford: Oxford University Press, 2004.

Potter, David M. *The Impending Crisis: 1848-1861*. Ed. by Don E. Fehrenbacher. New York: Harper & Row, 1976.

Randall, J. G. *Lincoln The President*. Vol. I, *Springfield to Gettysburg*. New York: Dodd, Mead, 1945.

_____. *Lincoln The President*. Vol. II, *Midstream*. New York: Dodd, Mead, 1952.

_____ , and Richard N. Current. *Lincoln The President*. Vol. III, *The   Last Full Measure*. New York: Dodd, Mead, 1955; reprint, Urbana: Univ. of Illinois Press, 1991.

Ross, Frederick A. *Slavery Ordained of God*. J.B. Lippincott,1857; reprint, Miami: Mnemosyne, 1969.

Sandburg, Carl. *Abraham Lincoln: The Prairie Years and the War Years, One Volume-Edition*. New York: Harcourt Brace Jovanovich, 1967.

Shenk, Joshua Wolf. *Lincoln's Melancholy: How Depression Challenged a President and Fueled His Greatness*. Boston: Houghton Mifflin, 2005.

Schneider, Thomas E. *Lincoln's Defense of Politics: The Public Man and His Opponents in the Crisis over Slavery*. Columbia: University of Missouri Press, 2006.

Simon, John Y, Harold Holzer and Dawn Vogel eds. *Lincoln Revisited*. New York: Fordham University Press, 2007.

Steers, Edward. *Blood on the Moon*. Lexington, University Press of Kentucky, 2001.

Steiner, Mark E. *An Honest Calling: The Law Practice of Abraham Lincoln*. DeKalb: Northern Illinois University Press, 2006.

Striner, Richard. *Father Abraham: Lincoln's Relentless Struggle To End Slavery*. New York: Oxford University Press, 2006.

Strozier, Charles B. *Lincoln's Quest for Union: Public and Private Meanings*. New York: Basic Books, 1982.

Thomas, Benjamin P. *Abraham Lincoln*. New York: Knopf, 1952.

Thurow, Glen E. *Abraham Lincoln And American Political Religion*. Albany: State Univ. of New York Press, 1976.

White, Ronald C. Jr. *Lincoln's Greatest Speech: The Second Inaugural*. New York: Simon & Schuster, 2002.

_____. *The Eloquent President*. New York: Random House, 2005.

Williams, Frank J, William D. Pederson and Vincent J. Marsala, eds. *Abraham Lincoln: Sources and Style of Leadership*. Westport,   Conn.: Greenwood Press, 1994.

_____. *Judging Lincoln*. Carbondale: Southern Illinois University Press, 2002.

Williams, Harry T. *Lincoln And The Radicals*. Madison: Univ. Of Wisconsin Press, 1972.

Wills, Garry. *Lincoln At Gettysburg: The Words That Remade America*.   New York: Simon & Schuster, 1992.

Wilson, Douglas L. *Honor's Voice: The Transformation of Abraham Lincoln*. New York: Knopf, 1998.

_____. *Lincoln's Sword: the Presidency and the Power of Words*. New York: Knopf, 2006.

Waugh, John C. *One Man Great Enough: Abraham Lincoln's Road to the Civil War*. Orlando: Harcourt Inc., 2007.

Winger, Stewart. *Lincoln Religion and Romantic Cultural Politics*. DeKalb: Northern Illinois University Press, 2002.

Wolf, William J. *The Religion of Abraham Lincoln*. New York: Seabury, 1963.

Holzer, Harold. *Lincoln At Cooper Union: The Speech That Made Abraham Lincoln President.* New York: Simon and Schuster, 2004.

Holzer, Harold and Sara Vaughn Gabbard. *Lincoln and Freedom: Slavery, Emancipation, and the Thirteenth Amendment.* Carbondale: Southern Illinois University Press, 2007.

Jaffa, Harry V. *Equality and Liberty: Theory And Practice In American Politics.* New York: Oxford Univ. Press, 1965.

_____. *The Conditions Of Freedom: Essays in Political Philosophy.* Baltimore: John Hopkins Univ. Press, 1975.

_____. *How To Think About the American Revolution: A Bicentennial Cerebration.* Durham: Carolina Academic Press, 1978.

_____. *Crisis of the House Divided: An Interpretation of the   Issues in the Lincoln-Douglas Debates.* Seattle: Univ. of Washington Press, Washington Paperbacks, 1973; reprint, Chicago: Univ. of Chicago Press, 1982.

_____. *A New Birth of Freedom.* Lanham, Rowman and Littlefield, 2000.

Kearns Goodwin, Doris. *Team of Rivals: The Political Genius of Abraham Lincoln.* New York: Simon and Schuster, 2005.

Kendall, Wilmoore, and George Carey. *The Basic Symbols of theAmerican Political Tradition.* Wash. D.C.: Catholic Univ. Press, 1995.

Lehrman, Lewis E. *Lincoln at Peoria: The Turning Point.* New York: Simon and Schuster, 2008.

Lerner, Ralph. "Lincoln's Revolution." Chap. in *Revolutions Revisited: Two Faces of the Politics of Enlightenment.* Chapel Hill: Univ. of North Carolina Press, 1994.

Long, David E. *The Jewel of Liberty: Abraham Lincoln's Re-election and the End of Slavery.* Mechan-icsburg, PA.: Stackpole, 1994.

McPherson, James M. *Battle Cry Of Freedom: The Civil War Era.* New York: Pallantine, 1988.

_____. *Abraham Lincoln And The Second American Revolution.* New York: Oxford Univ. Press, 1991.

_____. *The Struggle for Equality: Abolitionists And The Negro In The Civil War And Reconstruc-tion.* 2d ed. Princeton: Princeton Univ. Press, 1995.

Miller, William Lee. *Lincoln's Virtues: An Ethical Biography.* New York: Knopf, 2002.

_____. *President Lincoln: The Duty of a Statesman.* New York: Knopf, 2008.

Morel, Lucas E. *Lincoln's Sacred Effort.* Lanham: Lexington Books, 2000.

Murray, John Courtney. *We Hold These Truths: Catholic Reflections On The American Proposition.* Kansas City: Sheed and Ward, 1960.

Neely, Mark E., Jr. *The Fate of Liberty: Abraham Lincoln And Civil Liberties.* New York: Oxford, 1992.

_____. *The Last Best Hope Of Earth: Abraham Lincoln and the Promise of America.* Cambridge, Mass.: Harvard Univ. Press, 1993.

Noll, Mark A. "'Both…Pray to the Same God': The Singularity of Lincoln's Faith in the Era of the Civil War." *Journal of the Abraham Lincoln Association* 18 (Winter 1997): 1–26.

Nevins, Allan. *The Emergence of Lincoln.* Vol. I, *Douglas, Buchanan, and Party Chaos 1857-1859.* New York: Scribner's, 1950.

_____. *The Emergence of Lincoln.* Vol. II, *Prologue to Civil War, 1859-1861.* New York: Scribner's, 1950.

Niebuhr, Reinhold. "The Religion of Abraham Lincoln." In *Lincoln and the Gettysburg Address: Commemorative Papers,* ed. Allan Nevins, 72–87. Urbana: Univ. of Illinois Press, 1964.

Nicolay, John G., and John Hay. Abraham *Lincoln: A History.* 10 vols., New York: Century, 1890.

Oakes, James. *The Radical and the Republican: Frederick Douglass, Abraham Lincoln, and the Triumph of Antislavery Politics.* New York: Norton, 2007.

I.

"I Am Young and Unknown"

1832–1854

CHRONOLOGICALLY, the following compilation of speeches and writings span from Lincoln's first attempt at public office in 1832, to the Kansas-Nebraska Act of 1854, a turning point in his life and that of the nation's. Thematically, the section narrates the early development of Lincoln's political principles, his life in Springfield, his dual career in law and politics, his early opposition to slavery, his marriage to Mary Todd, and his single term in the United States House of Representatives, 1846-1848.

To appreciate the emergence of young Lincoln in public life, it is worth briefly mentioning some of the more notable events from his birth to his first successful run for office in 1834. Abraham Lincoln was born in a log cabin in Hardin County, Kentucky on February 12, 1809 to Thomas Lincoln and Nancy Hanks Lincoln. Due to his abhorrence of slavery, Thomas Lincoln joined a Baptist Church in Kentucky whose congregation was made up of people who had broken with their former churches in opposition to the institution. In 1816, the family moved to Indiana. When Lincoln was only nine years old, his mother, Nancy Hanks, died of the "milk sickness"—an illness caused from a poisonous weed digested by cows and passed through their milk. Shortly thereafter, Thomas Lincoln made a trip to Kentucky to find a suitable stepmother for his two children back in Indiana—Sarah and Abraham. In 1819, he married Sarah Bush Johnston who, contrary to the stereotype of the wicked stepmother, "bonded" with the young Lincoln and "took him under her maternal wing." Indeed, she helped fill an emotional void after the death of young Abraham's biological mother. Without her nurturing love, the emergent personality of the youthful Lincoln may have been stunted, permanently damaged, or even warped.

Although Lincoln's formal education amounted to no more than a year, he sought every opportunity to improve himself through learning. Much to the frustration of his father, who discouraged his son's educational endeavors, Lincoln persisted, reading all the books he could gather. The relationship between father and son was increasingly strained. It seemed that Thomas was unable to comprehend his son's intellectual aspirations and that the young Lincoln resented his father's provincialism in this regard. In a campaign autobiography from 1859, he described his upbringing in the back woods of Indiana in prosaic terms: "It was a wild region, with many bears and other wild animals still in the woods. There I grew up. There were some schools, so called; but no qualification was ever required of a teacher, beyond *"reading, writin, and cipherin,"* to the Rule of Three. If a straggler supposed to understand latin (sic), happened to sojourn in the neighborhood, he was looked upon as a wizard. There was absolutely nothing to excite ambition for education. Of course when I came of age I did not know much. Still somehow, I could read, write, and cipher to the Rule of Three; but that was all. I have not been to school since. The little advance I now have upon this store of education, I have picked up from time to time under the pressure of necessity. I was raised to farmwork, which I continued till I was twenty two."

In 1831, Lincoln moved to New Salem, Illinois. By his late teens, he was accustomed to hardship and death: a younger brother had died, his mother had died, and his sister Sarah had recently died in childbirth. It was around this time that Lincoln rode a flatboat down the Mississippi, carrying goods from Springfield, Illinois, to New Orleans, Louisiana. There he witnessed the abysmal sight of slaves shackled in irons. The bitter memory of this remained with him. Upon returning, he worked as a store clerk for Denton Offutt, the same merchant who sponsored his trip down the Mississippi.

In March of 1832, Lincoln made his first run for public office in the Illinois House of Representatives. A month later, after Offutt's business had collapsed, he enlisted in the Black Hawk War. To his great satisfaction, he was elected captain of his company. However, Lincoln did not see any action during the war. Deprecating his own experience, he would later poke fun at other politicians who exaggerated their exploits in the military, "I had a good many bloody struggles with the musquetoes (sic); and, although I never fainted from loss of blood, I can truly say I was very often hungry." Nonetheless, the Black Hawk War was significant in both revealing something about the young Lincoln's character, and in shaping his future destiny. First, the fact that Lincoln was elected captain by his men testified to his natural charisma as a leader. Second, when an Indian scout bearing a safe pass from American authorities wandered into their camp, Lincoln courageously kept his men from killing him as an alleged spy. Though his grandfather was slain by Indians in years gone-by, he did not allow himself to be dominated by a tribal hatred or revenge for an entire race of people. Third, during the war, Lincoln met John Stuart, who would become influential in helping him pursue a career as a lawyer. Indeed, after the war, Lincoln would join Stuart's legal practice.

Lincoln's participation in the Black Hawk War cost him the election, since he was unable to campaign during his absence. But though he lost the general election, Lincoln won 277 out of 300 votes in his town of New Salem, an indication of his popularity with those who knew him. Seeking new employment after the election, he became a co-owner of a general store with a partner whose alcohol problems led to bankruptcy. Because he was liable for all debts as a co-proprietor, Lincoln worked diligently for the next few years to pay off everything he owed. Later, he served as the postmaster of New Salem. In 1834, Lincoln ran a second time for public office and won as a Whig member of the Illinois House of Representatives. The Whig party to which Lincoln belonged was formed in opposition to the populist democracy of Andrew Jackson, which was seen as a threat to constitutional law and order. The Whigs were nationalists who favored a strong monetary system, a state bank, internal improvements, and Clay's American System, a nationalist vision that promoted economic integration, protective tariffs to support incipient American business, and independence for Latin America. In the state capital at Vandalia, Lincoln became known as one of the "Long Nine"—the nine delegates from Sangamo were called this on account of their unusual height. Lincoln and the "Long Nine" were instrumental in relocating the Illinois state capital from Vandalia to Springfield and in supporting an internal improvement policy for the state.

In 1839, Lincoln met Mary Todd, a vivacious, cultured, young belle from a well-established Kentucky family who came to Springfield to live with her sister and brother-in-law. Not a few of the major political figures of Illinois, Stephen A. Douglas for example, vied for Mary's affections. To her credit, Mary recognized Lincoln's potential for greatness early on. The two were opposite in many respects: socially, she moved in aristocratic circles; he was a self-made man of humble origin; she was vivacious, outgoing, and tempestuous; he was brooding, introspective, and cautious; she paid great attention to social conventions and graces; he was unpolished in appearance and mannerism. Despite these differences, however, both of them shared a common love for politics. The two were engaged in 1840. Shortly afterward, Lincoln inexplicably broke off the engagement and plunged into a severe depression, explaining to his friend Stuart, "I am now the most miserable man living." Fearing that he was suicidal, Lincoln's friends removed all sharp objects from his room. Eventually the couple reconciled. They were wed on November 4, 1842. Upon later reflection, Lincoln referred to the fact of his marriage as a "matter of profound wonder."

The young Lincoln's character was forged in the crucible of the frontier. Growing up in the backwoods of America, he acquired the virtues of self-reliance, rugged individualism, and a tireless work ethic. Within this context, politics and the law were the avenues for ambitious young men to advance in the race of life. Throughout much of his life, Lincoln would pursue a dual legal and political career. The tragedy and hardship he endured as a young man strengthened him for future trials. The physical prowess developed through intense, manual labor prepared him for the exhausting burden of the presidency.

Yet, although Lincoln was a product of the frontier, he also transcended many of its vices, limitations, and prejudices. Possessed of great strength of character, he refused to conform to the prevailing conventions around him. For example, he disliked both hunting and drinking—two of the most popular past-times of frontier youth. In fact, he was noted for his kindness to animals. He once felt guilty for being forced to shoot a turkey while he and his sister were virtually starving during a long, cold winter. And though he was extremely powerful and large, he was not a bully. He neither reveled in dueling nor drunken brawling— two other popular diversions of frontier youth. Indeed, as captain of a company during the Black Hawk War, he prevented a gang of ruffians from killing a captured Indian and making him their war trophy. Neither was Lincoln a ladies man. Instead, he confessed to being extremely shy and awkward around the fairer sex. And, unlike his father, he disdained manual labor. Looking back on his life, Lincoln was somewhat apprehensive about his rustic origins and lack of formal schooling. He himself never glamorized farm work and manual labor.

The young Lincoln's political views were also inconsistent with his frontier background and class origins. By all indications, he should have been a member of the populist Democratic Party whose president, Andrew Jackson, was born in a log cabin. The Democrats envisioned themselves as the defenders of the common man against the northeastern and southern aristocracies. Yet Lincoln joined the Whig Party, which was identified as the party of the middle-class and the aristocracy.

The young Lincoln's various pursuits as a manual laborer, a store clerk, surveyor, postmaster, soldier, and lawyer earned him a reputation as a person of integrity. These endeavors prepared him for a career in public life by exposing him to different walks of life. He seemed to have a gift in dealing and communicating with others. And his peers looked to him as a natural leader.

An understanding of Lincoln's speeches and writings during this time period also requires that they be placed in the historical context of the major national events from the Mexican War in 1846 to the Kansas-Nebraska Act of 1854. The acquisition of new territories from the Mexican War intensified sectional conflict over slavery. Lincoln and the Whig Party opposed the war as an act of American aggression perpetrated by an imperialist, Democratic administration bent on spreading human servitude throughout the continent. The acquisition of new lands from Mexico raised a number of important questions about slavery's relationship to the Union. Should the institution be allowed to spread into these new western regions? Did the Constitution authorize the national government to prohibit or restrict slavery in the territories? Or were the territories the common property of the states, merely held in trust by the national government? If they were held merely for the benefit of the states, as John C. Calhoun argued, then the national government was not only barred from interfering with territorial slavery, but it was also positively obliged to protect it.

During the Mexican War, David Wilmot, a Democrat from Pennsylvania, proposed an amendment to an appropriations bill, which sought to exclude involuntary servitude from all newly acquired territories. This antislavery proposal was known as the Wilmot Proviso, its principle—the prohibition of slavery in all new territories acquired by the United States—would constitute the core belief of the future Republican Party. Serving as the sole Whig representative from Illinois in the United States House of Representatives, Lincoln voted consistently in favor of the Wilmot Proviso in its various forms on numerous occasions. The proviso passed twice in the House, but it was defeated in the southern-controlled Senate each time.

The creation of the Free Soil Party, a new antislavery party, during the election of 1848 further polarized sectional conflict. The Free Soil Party nominated former president and New York Democrat Martin Van Buren as its presidential candidate. Its coalition consisted of antislavery Whigs (conscience Whigs), antislavery Democrats like Van Buren, and abolitionist members of the former Liberty Party, which had cost the Whigs the previous election.

During the election of 1844, Lincoln had campaigned for Henry Clay, the Whig candidate whom he admired as his "beau ideal of a statesman." While he opposed the extension of slavery, Clay was nevertheless a slaveholder. Much to Lincoln's dismay, during the 1844 election, a group of New York abolitionists bolted the Whig Party and formed the Liberty Party because they could not, in principle, support a slaveholder. These crucial votes cost Clay the presidency and ironically led to the victory of James K. Polk, a southern slaveholder and expansionist. Around the same time, the Methodist and Baptist churches split into northern and southern congregations based on their respective condemnation and defense of slavery in the eyes of God. It is an early indication of Lincoln's prudence that he viewed the policies of third party, antislavery factions as self-defeating. In his view, their political idealism and immoderation led to consequences that directly contradicted their moral aspirations: as with the Liberty Party in 1844, a vote for the Free Soil Party in 1848 would split the Whig vote resulting in the victory of southern, proslavery Democrats who were far more disposed toward the extension of slavery than Taylor and the Whigs. Like

Clay, Taylor was a slaveholder who seemed to oppose the national extension of slavery.

The Free Soil Party was dedicated to prohibiting slavery in the virgin territories and reserving it for free, white laborers who found it degrading to compete with slave labor. In general, the free soil movement was less concerned with the actual plight of African-Americans than with securing economic opportunity for white laborers. The party's motto was "free soil, free speech, free labor, and free men." Its demand for "free speech" was in opposition to southern gag laws that sought to suppress the inflammatory rhetoric of abolitionists as unconstitutional and dangerous to the security, rights, and way of life of the southern states. Southerners feared that the subversive doctrines of the abolitionists would incite a servile rebellion. The South was haunted by memories of Nat Turner's slave uprising in 1831, which resulted in the death of sixty whites and at least one hundred slaves.

The debate over slavery in those territories acquired from Mexico culminated with the Compromise of 1850—a measure that helped to avert a sectional upheaval in the short-term, but which failed to resolve the underlying problem of human servitude in the long-term. While Henry Clay began the initial version of the compromise, Stephen A. Douglas, champion of popular sovereignty and political nemesis of Lincoln in Illinois, finalized it and shepherded it through Congress. For the South, the Compromise included a stricter enforcement of the Constitution's fugitive slave provision, a guarantee for the protection of slavery in Washington, D.C., and a guarantee for the protection of the interstate slave trade. For the North, it included the abolition of the slave trade in Washington, D.C., the compensation of Texas with a sum of ten million dollars to relinquish its claim to the eastern portion of New Mexico, and the admission of California as a free state. Significantly, the new territories of Utah and New Mexico would be organized without explicit mention of slavery. Remarkably, the major issue that led to the Compromise of 1850 was left precariously unresolved by it. In a dress rehearsal of the ordeal that would occur ten years later, a group of Southerners met in Nashville in contemplation of secession if their rights as slaveholders were not secured by the Compromise. Northern abolitionists were equally determined to oppose the Compromise. In particular, they vilified its odious fugitive slave provision. This law permitted nearby citizens to be enlisted in the service of slave catchers, encouraged the capture and enslavement of free blacks, and paid federal judges twice the amount of money if they upheld a conviction under the law instead of acquitting the alleged fugitive. In response to the fugitive slave act, Harriet Beecher Stowe published *Uncle Tom's Cabin* in 1852, a novel that dramatized the plight of the slave and the evils of slavery, particularly its destruction of the family. The book mobilized northern public opinion against slavery to such an extent that, according to legend, when Lincoln met its author he remarked, "So this is the little lady who made this big war."

Historically, the Compromise of 1850 has been viewed as a high point in American oratory. And it marked the passing of one generation of leaders and the emergence of another. In particular, the debates over the Compromise between John C. Calhoun and Daniel Webster provided two rival interpretations of the Union that would define public opinion in the North and South for the next generation. The leadership of the great triumvirate of Clay, Calhoun, and Webster passed on to men like William Seward, Stephen A. Douglas, Samuel Chase, and Jefferson Davis. The Mexican Territories, the Wilmot Proviso, the rise of purely sectional antislavery third parties in the North, abolitionist agitation, the split in the Baptist and Methodist Churches over human servitude, the Compromise of 1850 and its strict fugitive slave provision—all of these developments quickened the process of sectional polarization over slavery that culminated with the South's secession in 1860.

TO THE PEOPLE OF SANGAMO COUNTY:
POLITICAL ANNOUNCEMENT
MARCH 9, 1832[1]

This handbill represents the earliest public statement of Lincoln's political principles. It was composed during his first attempt to run for political office as a candidate for the Illinois State Legislature. At the time, Lincoln was only twenty-three years old and was working as a store clerk in New Salem. The popularity he gained through this small-town job encouraged him to pursue a career in politics. It was common at this time for political aspirants to advertise their candidacy in handbills printed in local newspapers. Lincoln, who did not have the endorsement of a political party, published his platform in the local newspaper, the Sangamo Journal *and addressed it to the people of Sangamo County—the district in which he was running in. His participation in the Black Hawk War cost him the election since he was unable to campaign while away. Although he lost the election, Lincoln won 277 of the 300 votes cast in his home district of New Salem, a testimony to the popularity and esteem he enjoyed amongst the locals. Notable features of Lincoln's platform include internal improvements, a law to limit interest rates and an educational plan.*

1. Unless otherwise indicated, the selections comprised by this book are taken from *Abraham Lincoln: His Speeches and Writings,* ed. Roy P. Basler. Cleveland: The World Publishing Company, 1946.

He referred to education "as the most important subject which we as a people can be engaged in." Clearly, in his view, education was necessary for responsible citizenship in a democratic republic based on the people's participation and consent. Lincoln also included the reading of scripture as part of the character formation and education of American youth. Towards the end of the platform, he sounded an auto-biographical note by acknowledging his own ambition: "Everyman is said to have his peculiar ambition . . . I have no other so great as that of being truly esteemed of my fellow men." He concluded by reminding his audience of his political obscurity, which was a virtue compared to the being a "professional politician." And he reminded them of his common origins, "I am young and unknown to many of you. I was born and have remained in the most humble walks of life."

FELLOW CITIZENS:

Having become a candidate for the honorable office of one of your representatives in the next General Assembly of this state, in accordance with an established custom, and the principles of true republicanism, it becomes my duty to make known to you—the people whom I propose to represent—my sentiments with regard to local affairs.

Time and experience have verified to a demonstration, the public utility of internal improvements. That the poorest and most thinly populated countries would be greatly benefitted by the opening of good roads, and in the clearing of navigable streams within their limits, is what no person will deny. But yet it is folly to undertake works of this or any other kind, without first knowing that we are able to finish them—as half finished work generally proves to be labor lost. There cannot justly be any objection to having rail roads and canals, any more than to other good things, provided they cost nothing. The only objection is to paying for them; and the objection to paying arises from the want of ability to pay.

With respect to the County of Sangamo, some more easy means of communication than we now possess, for the purpose of facilitating the task of exporting the surplus products of its fertile soil, and importing necessary articles from abroad, are indispensably necessary. A meeting has been held of the citizens of Jacksonville, and the adjacent country, for the purpose of deliberating and enquiring into the expediency of constructing a railroad from some eligible point on the Illinois river, through the town of Jacksonville, in Morgan county, to the town of Springfield, in Sangamo county. This is, indeed, a very desirable object. No other improvement that reason will justify us in hoping for, can equal in utility the rail road. It is a never failing source of communication, between places of business remotely situated from each other. Upon the rail road the regular progress of commercial intercourse is not interrupted by either high or low water, or freezing weather, which are the principal difficulties that render our future hopes of water communication precarious and uncertain. Yet, however desirable an object the construction of a rail road through our country may be; however high our imaginations may be heated at thoughts of it—there is always a heart appalling shock accompanying the account of its cost, which forces us to shrink from our pleasing anticipations. The probable cost of this contemplated rail road is estimated at $290,000,—the bare statement of which, in my opinion, is sufficient to justify the belief, that the improvement of the Sangamo river is an object much better suited to our infant resources.

Respecting this view, I think I may say, without the fear of being contradicted, that its navigation may be rendered completely practicable, as high as the mouth of the South Fork, or probably higher, to vessels of from 25 to 30 tons burthen, for at least one half of all common years, and to vessels of much greater burthen a part of that time. From my peculiar circumstances, it is probable that for the last twelve months I have given as particular attention to the stage of the water in this river as any other person in the country. In the month of March, 1831, in company with others, I commenced the building of a flat boat on the Sangamo, and finished and took her out in the course of the spring. Since that time, I have been concerned in the mill at New Salem. These circumstances are sufficient evidence, that I have not been very inattentive to the stages of the water.—The time at which we crossed the mill dam, being in the last days of April the water was lower than it had been since the breaking of winter in February, or than it was for several weeks after. The principal difficulties we encountered in descending the river, were from the drifted timber, which obstructions all know is not difficult to be removed. Knowing almost precisely the height of water at that time, I believe I am safe in saying that it has as often been higher as lower since.

From this view of the subject, it appears that my calculations with regard to the navigation of the Sangamo cannot be unfounded in reason; but whatever may be its natural advantages, certain it is, that it never can be practically useful to any great extent, without being greatly improved by art. The drifted timber, as I have before mentioned, is the most formidable barrier to this object. Of all parts of this river, none will require so much labor in proportion, to make it navigable, as the last thirty or thirty-five miles; and going with the meanderings of the channel, when we are this distance above its mouth, we are only between twelve and eighteen miles above Beardstown, in something near a straight direction; and this route is upon such low ground as to retain water in many places during the season, and in all parts such as to draw two-thirds or three-fourths of the river water at all high stages.

This route is upon prairie land the whole distance;—so that it appears to me, by removing the turf, a sufficient width and damming up the old channel, the whole river in a short time would wash its way through, thereby curtailing the distance, and increasing the velocity of the current very considerably, while there would be no timber upon the banks to obstruct its navigation in future; and being nearly straight, the timber which might float in at the head, would be apt to go clear through. There are also many places above this where the river, in its zig zag course, forms such complete peninsulas, as to be easier cut through at the necks than to remove the obstructions from the bends—which, if done, would also lessen the distance.

What the cost of this work would be, I am unable to say. It is probable, however, it would not be greater than is common to streams of the same length. Finally, I believe the improvement of the Sangamo river, to be vastly important and highly desirable to the people of this county; and if elected, any measure in the legislature having this for its object, which may appear judicious, will meet my approbation, and shall receive my support.

It appears that the practice of loaning money at exorbitant rates of interest, has already been opened as a field for discussion; so I suppose I may enter upon it without claiming the honor, or risking the danger, which may await its first explorer. It seems as though we are never to have an end to this baneful and corroding system, acting almost as prejudicial to the general interests of the community as a direct tax of several thousand dollars annually laid on each county, for the benefit of a few individuals only, unless there be a law made setting a limit to the rates of usury. A law for this purpose, I am of opinion, may be made without materially injuring any class of people. In cases of extreme necessity there could always be means found to cheat the law, while in all other cases it would have its intended effect. I would not favor the passage of a law upon this subject, which might be very easily evaded. Let it be such that the labor and difficulty of evading it, could only be justified in cases of the greatest necessity.

Upon the subject of education, not presuming to dictate any plan or system respecting it, I can only say that I view it as the most important subject which we as a people can be engaged in. That every man may receive at least, a moderate education, and thereby be enabled to read the histories of his own and other countries, by which he may duly appreciate the value of our free institutions, appears to be an object of vital importance, even on this account alone, to say nothing of the advantages and satisfaction to be derived from all being able to read the scriptures and other works, both of a religious and moral nature, for themselves. For my part, I desire to see the time when education, and by its means, morality, sobriety, enterprise and industry, shall become much more general than at present, and should be gratified to have it in my power to contribute something to the advancement of any measure which might have a tendency to accelerate the happy period.

With regard to existing laws, some alterations are thought to be necessary. Many respectable men have suggested that our estray laws—the law respecting the issuing of executions, the road law, and some others, are deficient in their present form, and require alterations. But considering the great probability that the framers of those laws were wiser than myself, I should prefer [not?] meddling with them, unless they were first attacked by others, in which case I should feel it both a privilege and a duty to take that stand, which in my view, might tend most to the advancement of justice.

But, Fellow-Citizens, I shall conclude.—Considering the great degree of modesty which should always attend youth, it is probable I have already been more presuming than becomes me. However, upon the subjects of which I have treated, I have spoken as I thought. I may be wrong in regard to any or all of them; but holding it a sound maxim, that it is better to be only sometimes right, than at all times wrong, so soon as I discover my opinions to be erroneous, I shall be ready to renounce them.

Every man is said to have his peculiar ambition. Whether it be true or not, I can say for one that I have no other so great as that of being truly esteemed of my fellow men, by rendering myself worthy of their esteem. How far I shall succeed in gratifying this ambition, is yet to be developed. I am young and unknown to many of you. I was born and have ever remained in the most humble walks of life. I have no wealthy or popular relations to recommend me. My case is thrown exclusively upon the independent voters of this county, and if elected they will have conferred a favor upon me, for which I shall be unremitting in my labors to compensate. But if the good people in their wisdom shall see fit to keep me in the back ground, I have been too familiar with disappointments to be very much chagrined.

Your friend and fellow-citizen,

A. Lincoln

New Salem, March 9, 1832.

TO THE EDITOR OF THE SANGAMO JOURNAL
JUNE 13, 1836

In running for reelection in the Illinois legislature, Lincoln took the opportunity to explain his views on suffrage. The franchise had become a controversial issue given the increasing number of immigrants in Illinois at the time who were denied the right to vote until they became fully naturalized citizens. Seeking the immigrant vote, the Democrats sought to confer suffrage upon Irish immigrants regardless of whether or not they had been made naturalized citizens. On the contrary, Lincoln subscribed to the Whig position that the right of suffrage be tied to the responsibilities of citizenship.

To the Editor of the *Journal:*

In your paper of last Saturday, I see a communication over the signature of ``Many Voters,'' in which the candidates who are announced in the Journal, are called upon to ``show their hands.'' Agreed. Here's mine!

I go for all sharing the privileges of the government, who assist in bearing its burthens. Consequently I go for admitting all whites to the right of suffrage, who pay taxes or bear arms, (by no means excluding females.)

If elected, I shall consider the whole people of Sangamon my constituents, as well those that oppose, as those that support me.

While acting as their representative, I shall be governed by their will, on all subjects upon which I have the means of knowing what their will is; and upon all others, I shall do what my own judgment teaches me will best advance their interests. Whether elected or not, I go for distributing the proceeds of the sales of the public lands to the several states, to enable our state, in common with others, to dig canals and construct rail roads, without borrowing money and paying interest on it.

If alive on the first Monday in November, I shall vote for Hugh L. White for President.

Very respectfully, A. LINCOLN.

SPEECH IN THE ILLINOIS LEGISLATURE
January 11, 1837

Two principal Whig themes of the young Lincoln are found in this speech: support for a flexible monetary policy to stimulate internal improvements and defense of the rule of law against the populist democracy unleashed during the Age of Jackson. The speech occurred within the historical context of Andrew Jackson's war against the Second Bank of the United States. "King Andrew," as the Whigs referred to him, viewed the bank as a "monster," a hydra of corruption" and a parasitical institution devised by the privileged elite to protect their own economic interest against the common man. To kill the bank, Jackson withdrew federal funds and deposited them in state banks, called "pet banks." As a member of the Whigs, the opposition party to Jackson's Democratic Party, Lincoln supported both the Second Bank of the United States and internal improvements. After Jackson had killed the Bank of the United States, Lincoln supported the creation of an Illinois State Bank that would make capital available for needed internal improvements in his home state.

MR. CHAIRMAN:

Lest I should fall into the too common error, of being mistaken in regard to which side I design to be upon, I shall make it my first care to remove all doubt on that point, by declaring that I am opposed to the resolution under consideration, in toto. Before I proceed to the body of the subject, I will further remark, that it is not without a considerable degree of apprehension, that I venture to cross the track of the gentleman from Coles (Mr. Linder). Indeed, I do not believe I could muster a sufficiency of courage to come in contact with that gentleman, were it not for the fact, that he, some days since, most graciously condescended to assure us that he would never be found wasting ammunition on *small game*. On the same fortunate occasion, he further gave us to understand, that he regarded *himself* as being decidedly the *superior* of our common friend from Randolph (Mr. Shields); and feeling, as I really do, that I, to say the most of myself, am nothing more than the peer of our friend from Randolph, I shall regard the gentleman from Coles as decidedly my superior also, and consequently, in the course of what I shall have to say, whenever I shall have occasion to allude to that gentleman, I shall endeavor to adopt that kind of court language which I understand to be due to *decided superiority*. In one faculty, at least, there can be no dispute of the gentleman's superiority over me, and most other men; and that is, the faculty of entangling a subject, so that neither himself, or any other man, can find head or tail to it. Here he has introduced a resolution, embracing ninety-nine printed lines across common writing paper, and yet more than one half of his opening speech has been made upon subjects about which there is not one word said in his resolution.

Though his resolution embraces nothing in regard to the constitutionality of the Bank, much of what he has said has been with a view to make the impression that it was unconstitutional in its inception. Now, although I am satisfied that an ample field may be found within the pale of the resolution, at least for small game, yet as the gentleman has travelled out of it, I feel that I may, with all due humility, venture to follow him. The gentleman has discovered that some gentleman at Washington city has been upon the very eve of deciding our Bank unconstitutional, and that he would probably have completed his very authentic decision, had not some one of the Bank officers placed his hand upon his mouth, and begged him to withhold it. The fact that the individuals composing our Supreme Court have, in an official capacity, decided in favor of the constitutionality of the Bank, would, in my mind, seem a sufficient answer to this. It is a fact known to all, that the members of the Supreme Court, together with the Governor, form a Council of Revision, and that this Council approved this Bank Charter. I ask, then, if the extra-judicial decision—not quite, but only almost made, by the gentleman at Washington, before whom, by the way, the question of the constitutionality of our Bank never has, nor never can come— is to be taken as paramount to a decision officially made by that tribunal, by which and which alone, the constitutionality of the Bank can ever be settled? But, aside from this view of the subject, I would ask, if the committee which this resolution proposes to appoint, are to examine into the constitutionality of the Bank? Are they to be clothed with power to send for persons and papers, for this object? And after they have found the bank to be unconstitutional, and decided it so, how are they to enforce their decision? What will their decision amount to? They cannot compel the Bank to cease operations, or to change the course of its operations. What good, then, can their labors result in? Certainly none.

The gentleman asks, if we, without an examination, shall, by giving the State deposits to the Bank, and by taking the stock reserved for the State, legalize its former misconduct. Now I do not pretend to possess sufficient legal knowledge to decide, whether a legislative enactment, proposing to, and accepting from, the Bank, certain terms, would have the effect to legalize or wipe out its former errors, or not; but I can assure the gentleman, if such should be the effect, he has already got behind the settlement of accounts; for it is well known to all, that the Legislature, at its last session, passed a supplemental Bank charter, which the Bank has since accepted, and which, according to his doctrine, has legalized all the alleged violations of its original charter in the distribution of its stock.

I now proceed to the resolution. By examination it will be found that the first thirty-three lines, being precisely one third of the whole, relate exclusively to the distribution of the stock by the commissioners appointed by the State. Now, Sir, it is clear that no question can arise on this portion of the resolution, except a question between capitalists in regard to the ownership of stock. Some gentlemen have the stock in their hands, while others, who have more money than they know what to do with, want it; and this, and this alone, is the question, to settle which we are called on to squander thousands of the people's money. What interest, let me ask, have the people in the settlement of this question? What difference is it to them whether the stock is owned by Judge Smith, or Sam. Wiggins? If any gentleman be entitled to stock in the Bank, which he is kept out of possession of by others, let him assert his right in the Supreme Court, and let him or his antagonist, whichever may be found in the wrong, pay the costs of suit. It is an old maxim, and a very sound one, that he that dances should always pay the fiddler. Now, sir, in the present case, if any gentlemen, whose money is a burden to them, choose to lead off a dance, I am decidedly opposed to the people's money being used to pay the fiddler. No one can doubt that the examination proposed by this resolution must cost the State some ten or twelve thousand dollars; and all this to settle a question in which the people have no interest, and about which they care nothing. These capitalists generally act harmoniously and in concert, to fleece the people, and now, that they have got into a quarrel with themselves, we are called upon to appropriate the people's money to settle the quarrel.

I leave this part of the resolution, and proceed to the remainder. It will be found that no charge in the remaining part of the resolution, if true, amounts to the violation of the Bank charter, except one, which I will notice in due time. It might seem quite sufficient, to say no more upon any of these charges or insinuations, than enough to show they are not violations of the charter; yet, as they are ingeniously framed and handled, with a view to deceive and mislead, I will notice in their order, all the most prominent of them. The first of these, is in relation to a connexion between our Bank and several Banking institutions in other States. Admitting this connection to exist, I should like to see the gentleman from Coles, or any other gentleman, undertake to show that there is any harm in it.—What can there be in such a connexion, that the people of Illinois are willing to pay their money to get a peep into? By a reference to the tenth section of the Bank charter, any gentleman can see that the framers of the act contemplated the holding of stock in the institutions of other corporations. Why, then, is it, when neither law nor justice forbids it, that we are asked to spend our time and money, in inquiring into its truth?

The next charge, in the order of time, is, that some officer, director, clerk or servant of the Bank, has been required to take an oath of secrecy in relation to the affairs of said Bank. Now, I do not know whether this be true or false—neither do I believe any honest man cares. I know that the seven section of the charter expressly guarantees to the Bank the right of making, under certain restrictions, such by-laws as it may think fit; and I further know that the requiring an oath of secrecy would not transcend those restrictions. What, then, if the Bank has chosen to exercise this right? Who can it injure? Does not every merchant have his secret mark? and who is ever silly enough to complain of it? I presume if the Bank does require any such oath of secrecy, it is done through a motive of delicacy to those individuals who deal with it.—Why, sir, not many days since, one gentleman upon this floor, who, by the way, I have no doubt is now ready to join this hue and cry against the Bank, indulged in a philippic against one of the Bank officers, because, as he said, he had *divulged a secret*.

Immediately following this last charge, there are several insinuations in the resolution, which are too silly to require any sort of notice, were it not for the fact, that they conclude by saying, *"to the great injury of the people at large."* In answer to this I would say, that it is strange enough, that the people are suffering these "great injuries," and yet are not sensible of it! Singular indeed that the people should be writhing under oppression and injury, and yet not one among them to be found to raise the voice of complaint. If the Bank be inflicting injury upon the people, why is it, that not a single petition is presented to this body on the subject? If the Bank really be a grievance, why is it, that no one of the real people is found to ask redress of it? The truth is, no such oppression exists. If it did, our table would groan with memorials and petitions, and we would not be permitted to rest day or night, till we had put it down. The people know their rights; and they are never slow to assert and maintain them, when they are invaded. Let them call for an investigation, and I shall ever stand ready to respond to the call. But they have made no such call. I make the assertion boldly, and without fear of contradiction, that no man, who does not hold an office, or does not aspire to one, has ever found any fault of the Bank. It has doubled the prices of the products of their farms, and filled their pockets with a sound circulating medium, and they are all well pleased with its operations. No, Sir, it is the *politician* who is the first to sound the alarm, (which, by the way, is a false one.) It is he, who, by these unholy means, is endeavoring to blow up a storm that he may ride upon and direct. It is he, and he alone, that here proposes to spend thousands of the people's public treasure, for no other advantage to them, than to make valueless in their pockets the reward of their industry. Mr. Chairman, this work is exclusively the work of politicians; a set of men who have interests aside from the interests of the people, and who, to say the most of them, are, taken as a mass, at least one long step removed from honest men. I say this with the greater freedom, because, being a politician myself, none can regard it as personal.

Again, it is charged, or rather insinuated, that officers of the Bank have loaned money at usurious rates of interest. Suppose this to be true, are we to send a committee of this House to enquire into it? Suppose the committee should find it true can they redress the injured individuals? Assuredly not. If any individual had been injured in this way, is there not an ample remedy, to be found in the laws of the land? Does the gentleman from Coles know, that there is a statute standing in full force, making it highly penal, for an individual to loan money at a higher rate of interest than twelve per cent? If he does not he is too ignorant to be placed at the head of the committee which his resolution proposes; and if he does, his neglect to mention it, shows him to be too uncandid to merit the respect or confidence of any one.

But besides all this, if the Bank were struck from existence, could not the owners of the capital still loan it usuriously, as well as now? Whatever the Bank, or its officers, may have done, I know that usurious transactions were much more frequent and enormous before the commencement of its operations, than they have ever been since.

The next insinuation is, that the Bank has refused specie payments. This, if true, is a violation of the charter. But there is not the least probability of its truth; because, if such had been the fact, the individual to whom payment was refused, would have had an interest in making it public, by suing for the damages to which the charter entitles him. Yet no such thing has been done; and the strong presumption is, that the insinuation is false and groundless.

From this to the end of the resolution, there is nothing that merits attention—I therefore drop the particular examination of it.

By a general view of the resolution, it will be seen that a principal object of the committee is, to examine into, and ferret out, a mass of corruption, supposed to have been committed by the commissioners who apportioned the stock of the Bank. I believe it is universally understood and acknowledged, that all men will ever act correctly, unless they have a motive to do otherwise. If this be true, we can only suppose that the commissioners acted corruptly, by also supposing that they were bribed to do so. Taking this view of the subject, I would ask if the Bank is likely to find it more difficult to bribe the committee of seven, which we are about to appoint, than it may have found it to bribe the commissioners?

(Here Mr. Linder called to order. The Chair decided that Mr. Lincoln was not out of order. Mr. Linder appealed to the House;—but, before the question was put, withdrew his appeal, saying, he preferred to let the gentleman go on; he thought he would break his own neck. Mr. Lincoln proceeded:)—

Another *gracious condescension*. I acknowledge it with gratitude. I know I was not out of order; and I know every sensible man in the House knows it. I was not saying that the gentleman from Coles could be bribed, nor, on the other hand, will I say he could not. In that particular, I leave him where I found him. I was only endeavoring to show that there was at least as great a probability of *any* seven members that could be selected from this House, being bribed to act corruptly, as there was, that the twenty-four commissioners had been so bribed. By a reference to the ninth section of the Bank charter, it will be seen that those commissioners were John Tilson, Robert K. McLaughlin, Daniel Wann, A. G. S. Wight, John C. Riley, W. H. Davidson, Edward M. Wilson, Edward L. Pierson, Robert R. Green, Ezra Baker, Aquilla Wren, John Taylor, Samuel C. Christy, Edmund Roberts, Benjamin Godfrey, Thomas Mather, A. M. Jenkins, W. Linn, W. S. Gilman, Charles Prentice, Richard I. Hamilton, A. H. Buckner, W. F. Thornton, and Edmund D. Taylor.

These are twenty-four of the most respectable men in the State. Probably no twenty-four men could be selected in the State, with whom the people are better acquainted, or in whose honor and integrity, they would more readily place confidence. And I now repeat, that there is less probability that those men have been bribed and corrupted, than that *any* seven men, or rather any *six* men, that could be selected from the members of this House, might be so bribed and corrupted; even though they were headed and led on by "decided superiority" himself.

In all seriousness, I ask every reasonable man, if an issue be joined by these twenty-four commissioners, on the one part, and *any* other seven men, on the other part, and the whole depend upon the honor and integrity of the contending parties, to which party would the greatest degree of credit be due? Again: Another consideration is, that we have no right to make the examination. What I shall say upon this head I design exclusively for the law-loving and law-abiding part of the House. To those who claim omnipotence for the Legislature, and who in the plenitude of their assumed powers, are disposed to disregard the Constitution, law, good faith, moral right, and every thing else, I have not a word to say. But to the law-abiding part I say, examine the Bank charter, go examine the Constitution; go examine the acts that the General Assembly of this State has passed, and you will find just as much authority given in each and every of them, to compel the Bank to bring its coffers to this hall, and to pour their contents upon this floor, as to compel it to submit to this examination which this resolution proposes. Why, sir, the gentleman from Coles, the mover of this resolution, very lately denied on this floor, that the Legislature had any right to repeal, or otherwise meddle with its own acts, when those acts were made in the nature of contracts, and had been accepted and acted on by other parties. Now I ask, if this resolution does not propose, for this House alone, to do, what he, but the other day, denied the right of the whole Legislature to do? He must either abandon the position he then took, or he must now vote against his own resolution. It is no difference to me, and I presume but little to any one else, which he does.

I am by no means the special advocate of the Bank. I have long thought that it would be well for it to report its condition to the General Assembly, and that cases might occur, when it might be proper to make an examination of its affairs by a committee. Accordingly, during the last session, while a bill supplemental to the Bank charter, was pending before the House, I offered an amendment to the same, in these words: "The said corporation shall, at the next session of the General Assembly, and at each subsequent General Session, during the existence of its charter, report to the same the amount of debts due *from* said corporation; the amount of debts due *to* the same; the amount of specie in its vaults, and an account of all lands then owned by the same, and the amount for which such lands have been taken; and moreover, if said corporation shall at any time neglect or refuse to submit its books, papers, and all and everything necessary for a full and fair examination of its affairs, to any person or persons appointed by the General Assembly, for the purpose of making such examination, the said corporation shall forfeit its charter."

This amendment was negatived by a vote of 34 to 15. Eleven of the 34 who voted against it, are now members of this House; and though it would be out of order to call their names, I hope they will all recollect themselves, and not vote for this examination to be made without authority, inasmuch as they refused to reserve the authority when it was in their power to do so.

I have said that cases might occur, when an examination might be proper; but I do not believe any such case has now occurred; and if it has, I should still be opposed to making an examination without legal authority. I am opposed to encouraging that lawless and mobocratic spirit, whether in relation to the Bank or any thing else, which is already abroad in the land; and is spreading with rapid and fearful impetuosity, to the ultimate overthrow of every institution, or even moral principle, in which persons and property have hitherto found security.

But supposing we had the authority, I would ask what good can result from the examination? Can we declare the Bank unconstitutional, and compel it to cease operations? Can we compel it to desist from the abuses of its power, provided we find such abuses to exist? Can we repair the injuries which it may have done to individuals? Most certainly we can do none of these things. Why then shall we spend the public money in such employment? O, say the examiners, we can injure the credit of the Bank, if nothing else.—Please tell me, gentlemen, who will suffer most by that? You cannot injure, to any extent, the stockholders. They are men of wealth—of large capital; and consequently, beyond the power of fortune, or even the shafts of malice. But by injuring the credit of the Bank, you will depreciate the value of its paper in the hands of the honest and unsuspecting farmer and mechanic, and that is all you can do. But suppose you could effect your whole purpose; suppose you could wipe the Bank from existence, which is the grand *ultimatum* of the project, what would be the consequence? Why, sir, we should spend several thousand dollars of the public treasure in the operation, annihilate the currency of the State, render valueless in the hands of our people that reward of their former labors, and finally, be once more under the comfortable obligation of paying the Wiggins' loan, principal and interest.

PROTEST IN ILLINOIS LEGISLATURE ON SLAVERY[2]
MARCH 3, 1837

This protest constituted Lincoln's first explicit, public opposition to slavery. At the time, he was only twenty-eight years old serving in the Illinois General Assembly, a body composed of fifty-five representatives and twenty-six senators. The protest was in response to a southern "gag resolution" requesting the State of Illinois to censure abolitionist societies for their inflammatory rhetoric and to affirm that the Constitution protected slavery. Although slavery was prohibited in Illinois, the General Assembly approved the resolution as a gesture of solidarity with the South. Because public opinion in the state of Illinois was notoriously hostile to both abolitionists and free blacks, Lincoln had nothing to gain politically from his protest. Indeed, as one of only six in the assembly who voted against the censorious measure, Lincoln was both courageous and principled in his first public stance against slavery.

THE FOLLOWING PROTEST was presented to the House, which was read and ordered to be spread on the journals, to wit:

"Resolutions upon the subject of domestic slavery having passed undersigned hereby protest against the passage of the same.

They believe that the institution of slavery is founded on both injustice and bad policy; but that the promulgation of abolition doctrines tends rather to increase than to abate its evils.

They believe that the Congress of the United States has no power, under the constitution, to interfere with the institution of slavery in the different States.

2. Taken from Roy P. Basler, ed., Marion Dolores Pratt and Lloyd A. Dunlap, asst. eds., *The Collected Works of Abraham Lincoln,* 9 vols. (New Brunswick: Rutgers University Press, 1953–55): I, 74–75. Herein after cited: *CWAL.*

They believe that the Congress of the United States has the power, under the constitution, to abolish slavery in the District of Columbia; but that that power ought not to be exercised unless at the request of the people of said District.

The difference between these opinions and those contained in the said resolutions, is their reason for entering this protest."

DAN STONE,

A. LINCOLN,

Representatives from the county of Sangamon.

LETTER TO MISS MARY OWENS
MAY 7, 1837

Mary Owens was actually the second of three known romances in Lincoln's life. She stands between Lincoln's first love, Anne Rutledge, who died young, and his wife Mary Todd. Mary Owens was a Kentucky belle considerably more sophisticated than the coarse young Lincoln. Their courtship began shortly after Mary moved to New Salem to live with her sister. Although this letter captures something of the budding romance between the two, their infatuation soon fizzled out. Mary became frustrated with Lincoln's lack of refinement, in particular, his inattentiveness to the subtle courtesies required by well-bred females. On the other hand, Lincoln realized he was not physically attracted to Mary. In a subsequent letter to a friend, he would mockingly describe her as plump, toothless and "weather-beaten" in appearance. In this letter, Lincoln confessed his lack of church attendance due to his inability "to behave himself." Lincoln never became a formal member of a church, perhaps due to his aversion to the emotionalism and literalism of frontier religion.

SPRINGFIELD MAY 7, 1837

FRIEND MARY

I have commenced two letters to send you before this, both of which displeased me before I got half done, and so I tore them up. The first I thought was'nt serious enough, and the second was on the other extreme. I shall send this, turn out as it may.

This thing of living in Springfield is rather a dull business after all, at least it is so to me. I am quite as lonesome here as [I?] ever was anywhere in my life. I have been spoken to by but one woman since I've been here, and should not have been by her, if she could have avoided it. I've never been to church yet, nor probably shall not be soon. I stay away because I am conscious I should not know how to behave myself.

I am often thinking about what we said of your coming to live at Springfield. I am afraid you would not be satisfied. There is a great deal of flourishing about in carriages here, which it would be your doom to see without shareing [sic] in it. You would have to be poor without the means of hiding your poverty. Do you believe you could bear that patiently? Whatever woman may cast her lot with mine, should any ever do so, it is my intention to do all in my power to make her happy and contented; and there is nothing I can immagine [sic], that would make me more unhappy than to fail in the effort. I know I should be much happier with you than the way I am, provided I saw no signs of discontent in you. What you have said to me may have been in jest, or I may have misunderstood it. If so, then let it be forgotten; if otherwise, I much wish you would think seriously before you decide. For my part I have already decided. What I have said I will most positively abide by, provided you wish it. My opinion is that you had better not do it. You have not been accustomed to hardship, and it may be more severe than you now immagine [sic]. I know you are capable of thinking correctly on any subject, and if you deliberate maturely upon this, before you decide, then I am willing to abide your decision.

You must write me a good long letter after you get this. You have nothing else to do, and though it might not seem interesting to you, after you had written it, it would be a good deal of company to me in this "busy wilderness." Tell your sister I dont want to hear any more about selling out and moving. That gives me the hypo whenever I think of it.

Yours &c—

Lincoln

THE PERPETUATION OF OUR POLITICAL INSTITUTIONS: ADDRESS BEFORE THE YOUNG MEN'S LYCEUM OF SPRINGFIELD, ILLINOIS
JANUARY 27, 1838

The Lyceum Address is among the most controversial of Lincoln's speeches and writings. It has generated acrimonious debate amongst scholars who have interpreted it as the psychological or philosophical key that unlocks Lincoln's subsequent motivations and actions. The basic elements of the speech include Lincoln's diagnosis of mob rule sweeping the land and its threat to the nation's republican institutions, his call for a "political religion" that will remedy the dangers of populist democracy, and his warning against an ambitious, "towering genius" who will exploit sectional conflict for his own glory, "whether at the expense of emancipating slaves, or enslaving freemen." It has been argued that this statement was a self-referential warning by the young Lincoln of his own tower-ing ambition.

Psychohistorian scholars George Forgie and Dwight Anderson have claimed that Lin-coln "projected" himself into the role of the tyrannical figure he warned against in the speech. They maintain that his actions during the Civil War Era constituted a self-ful-filling prophecy: he exploited sectional conflict to aggrandize himself as the nation's polit-ical savior of the Union. From a somewhat different perspective, Straussian scholars like Harry V. Jaffa, George Anastaplo, Glen Thurow, et al. argue that a combined reading of Lincoln's Lyceum Address and Temperance Address of 1842 provides a systematic guide for understanding his "political religion." The distinction between Lincoln's exoteric (overt) teaching on religion and politics addressed to the general public and his esoteric (covert) teaching addressed to those with "superior minds and education" is crucial to the Straussian interpretation of his "political religion." In short, the Straussians maintain that publicly Lincoln invoked religious symbolism for its political utility; however, pri-vately, he questioned it between the lines to the careful reader as metaphysically false.

Southern conservative scholars M.E. Bradford and Willmoore Kendall insist that Lin-coln's reference to "political religion" and his biblical allusion to St. John's gospel at the end of the speech imply a messianic fusion of religion and politics. They revile Lincoln as an American Cromwell who saw politics not as the art of compromise, but as an armaged-don struggle between "the children of light and children of darkness." Failing to recognize Lincoln's prudence and to distinguish between the Sixteenth President and the radical abo-litionists whom he disagreed with in practice, they portray him as a secular messiah who waged a crusade against the South's "peculiar institution" with the millenarian expecta-tion of transfiguring the imperfections of political life into an egalitarian utopia.

While the Lyceum Address prefigures certain republican political themes in the mature Lincoln's political thought such as the important role of religion in maintaining the nation's republican institutions, it provides neither a systematic treatise of his political reli-gion nor the definitive statement of his political thought. Rather, its historical context, political intention, style and literary form suggest that it was primarily a rhetorical denun-ciation of mob rule. As both a lawyer committed to legal process and a member of the Whig party opposed to the plebiscitarian democracy unleashed during the Age of Jackson, Lin-coln upheld the rule of law against the growing tide of anarchy and lawlessness engulfing the nation. Indeed, the sub-text of the speech, The Perpetuation of our Political Institu-tions, conveys this intention. Implicit to Lincoln's narrative of "the effects of mob law" was the recent lynching of the renowned abolitionist Elijah P. Lovejoy in nearby Alton, Illinois. This event, fresh in the mind of his audience, provides the context for under-standing Lincoln's repudiation of mob rule and his call for the perpetuation of the nation's political institutions.

The design, argument and theme of the Lyceum Address also suggest that Lincoln modeled the speech after George Washington's celebrated Farewell Address, a work that Lincoln was eminently familiar with through his readings of Parson Weems's Farewell Address and David Ramsey's biographies of the Founder Father. These famous biographies provide an important textual link between the two addresses. Thematically, both speeches begin by surveying the strengths of the Union and then proceed to identify specific threats to it. Both speeches defend the rule of law, invoke religion and emphasize the need for public virtue (selfless devotion to the common good). Indeed, Washington's prescient warning of a sectional conflict and his admonition in the Farewell Address against "designing men" who would exploit sectional differences for personal glory and fame was reiterated by Lincoln in the Lyceum Address. The fact that Lincoln concluded his speech by praising Washington further confirms the parallels between the two addresses. Given their thematic continuities, the Farewell Address and Lyceum Address may be viewed as parallel texts of the American republican political tradition as envisioned by the nation's political founder and savior respectively.

Finally, the rhetorical, stylistic and cultural context of the Lyceum Address is crucial to understanding the young Lincoln's intention. The lyceums of the antebellum period in American history were public debate and speech societies; they provided a forum for aspiring young statesman to practice their oratorical skills by serving as institutions of civil discourse and debate. The florid writing style of the speech indicates that the young Lincoln, at age twenty-nine, seemed to be practicing his rhetoric. Indeed, Lincoln's speech was composed during the silver age of oratory dominated by giants like Everett, Parker, Calhoun and Webster. The age was also defined by a cult of filial piety in which George Washington was at the center. Especially in a land without a hereditary aristocracy, the founders of the republic replaced family ancestors as inspirational role models for politically ambitious youth.

AS A SUBJECT for the remarks of the evening, THE PERPETUATION OF OUR POLITICAL INSTITUTIONS, is selected.

In the great journal of things happening under the sun, we, the American People, find our account running, under date of the nineteenth century of the Christian era.—We find ourselves in the peaceful possession, of the fairest portion of the earth, as regards extent of territory, fertility of soil, and salubrity of climate. We find ourselves under the government of a system of political institutions, conducing more essentially to the ends of civil and religious liberty, than any of which the history of former times tell us. We, when mounting the stage of existence, found ourselves the legal inheritors of these fundamental blessings. We toiled not in the acquirement or establishment of them—they are a legacy bequeathed us, by a *once* hardy, brave, and patriotic, but *now* lamented and departed race of ancestors. Their's was the task (and nobly they performed it) to possess themselves, and through themselves, us, of this goodly land; and to uprear upon its hills and its valleys, a political edifice of liberty and equal rights; 'tis ours only, to transmit these, the former, unprofaned by the foot of an invader; the latter, undecayed by the lapse of time and untorn by usurpation, to the latest generation that fate shall permit the world to know. This task gratitude to our fathers, justice to ourselves, duty to posterity, and love for our species in general, all imperatively require us faithfully to perform.

How then shall we perform it?—At what point shall we expect the approach of danger? By what means shall we fortify against it?—Shall we expect some transatlantic military giant, to step the Ocean, and crush us at a blow? Never!—All the armies of Europe, Asia and Africa combined, with all the treasure of the earth (our own excepted) in their military chest; with a Buonaparte for a commander, could not by force, take a drink from the Ohio, or make a track on the Blue Ridge, in a trial of a thousand years.

At what point then is the approach of danger to be expected? I answer, if it ever reach us, it must spring up amongst us. It cannot come from abroad. If destruction be our lot, we must ourselves be its author and finisher. As a nation of freemen, we must live through all time, or die by suicide.

I hope I am over wary; but if I am not, there is, even now, something of ill-omen, amongst us. I mean the increasing disregard for law which pervades the country; the growing disposition to substitute the wild and furious passions, in lieu of the sober judgment of Courts; and the worse than savage mobs, for the executive ministers of justice. This disposition is awfully fearful in any community; and that it now exists in ours, though grating to our feelings to admit, it would be a violation of truth, and an insult to our intelligence, to deny. Accounts of outrages committed by mobs, form the every-day news of the times. They have pervaded the country, from New England to Louisiana;—they are neither peculiar to the eternal snows of the former, nor the burning suns of the latter;—they are not the creature of climate—neither are they confined to the slave-holding, or the non-slave-holding States. Alike, they spring up among the pleasure hunting masters of Southern slaves, and the order loving citizens of the land of steady habits.—Whatever, then, their cause may be, it is common to the whole country.

It would be tedious, as well as useless, to recount the horrors of all of them. Those happening in the State of Mississippi, and at St. Louis, are, perhaps, the most dangerous in example and revolting to humanity. In the Mississippi case, they first commenced by hanging the regular gamblers; a set of men, certainly not following for a livelihood, a very useful, or very honest occupation; but one which, so far from being forbidden by the laws, was actually licensed by an act of the Legislature, passed but a single year before. Next, negroes, suspected of conspiring to raise an insurrection, were caught up and hanged in all parts of the State: then, white men, supposed to be leagued with the negroes; and finally, strangers, from neighboring States, going thither on business, were, in many instances subjected to the same fate. Thus went on this process of hanging, from gamblers to negroes, from negroes to white citizens, and from these to strangers; till, dead men were seen literally dangling from the boughs of trees upon every road side; and in numbers almost sufficient, to rival the native Spanish moss of the country, as a drapery of the forest.

Turn, then, to that horror-striking scene at St. Louis. A single victim was only sacrificed there. His story is very short; and is, perhaps, the most highly tragic, of anything of its length, that has ever been witnessed in real life. A mulatto man, by the name of McIntosh, was seized in the street, dragged to the suburbs of the city, chained to a tree, and actually burned to death; and all within a single hour from the time he had been a freeman, attending to his own business, and at peace with the world.

Such are the effects of mob law; and such are the scenes, becoming more and more frequent in this land so lately famed for love of law and order; and the stories of which, have even now grown too familiar, to attract any thing more, than an idle remark.

But you are, perhaps, ready to ask, "What has this to do with the perpetuation of our political institutions?" I answer, it has much to do with it. Its direct consequences are, comparatively speaking, but a small evil; and much of its danger consists, in the proneness of our minds, to regard its direct, as its only consequences. Abstractly considered, the hanging of the gamblers at Vicksburg, was of but little consequence. They constitute a portion of population, that is worse than useless in any community; and their death, if no pernicious example be set by it, is never matter of reasonable regret with any one. If they were annually swept, from the stage of existence, by the plague or small pox, honest men would, perhaps, be much profited, by the operation.—Similar too, is the correct reasoning, in regard to the burning of the negro at St. Louis. He had forfeited his life, by the perpetration of an outrageous murder, upon one of the most worthy and respectable citizens of the city; and had he not died as he did, he must have died by the sentence of the law, in a very short time afterwards. As to him alone, it was as well the way it was, as it could otherwise have been.—

But the example in either case, was fearful.—When men take it in their heads to day, to hang gamblers, or burn murderers, they should recollect, that, in the confusion usually attending such transactions, they will be as likely to hang or burn some one who is neither a gambler nor a murderer as one who is; and that, acting upon the example they set, the mob of to-morrow, may, and probably will, hang or burn some of them by the very same mistake. And not only so; the innocent, those who have ever set their faces against violations of law in every shape, alike with the guilty, fall victims to the ravages of mob law; and thus it goes on, step by step, till all the walls erected for the defence of the persons and property of individuals, are trodden down, and disregarded. But all this even, is not the full extent of the evil.—By such examples, by instances of the perpetrators of such acts going unpunished, the lawless in spirit, are encouraged to become lawless in practice; and having been used to no restraint, but dread of punishment, they thus become, absolutely unrestrained.—Having ever regarded Government as their deadliest bane, they make a jubilee of the suspension of its operations; and pray for nothing so much, as its total annihilation. While, on the other hand, good men, men who love tranquility, who desire to abide by the laws, and enjoy their benefits, who would gladly spill their blood in the defence of their country; seeing their property destroyed; their families insulted, and their lives endangered; their persons injured; and seeing nothing in prospect that forebodes a change for the better; become tired of, and disgusted with, a Government that offers them no protection; and are not much averse to a change in which they imagine they have nothing to lose. Thus, then, by the operation of this mobocratic spirit, which all must admit, is now abroad in the land, the strongest bulwark of any Government, and particularly of those constituted like ours, may effectually be broken down and destroyed—I mean the *attachment* of the People. Whenever this effect shall be produced among us; whenever the vicious portion of population shall be permitted to gather in bands of hundreds and thousands, and burn churches, ravage and rob provision-stores, throw printing presses into rivers, shoot editors, and hang and burn obnoxious persons at pleasure, and with impunity; depend on it, this Government cannot last. By such things, the feelings of the best citizens will become more or less alienated from it; and thus it will be left without friends, or with too few, and those few too weak, to make their friendship effectual. At such a time and under such circumstances, men of sufficient talent and ambition will not be wanting to seize the opportunity, strike the blow, and overturn that fair fabric, which for the last half century, has been the fondest hope, of the lovers of freedom, throughout the world.

I know the American People are *much* attached to their Government;—I know they would suffer *much* for its sake;—I know they would endure evils long and patiently, before they would ever think of exchanging it for another. Yet, notwithstanding all this, if the laws be continually despised and disregarded, if their rights to be secure in their persons and property, are held by no better tenure than the caprice of a mob, the alienation of their affections from the Government is the natural consequence; and to that, sooner or later, it must come.

Here then, is one point at which danger may be expected.

The question recurs, "how shall we fortify against it?" The answer is simple. Let every American, every lover of liberty, every well wisher to his posterity, swear by the blood of the Revolution, never to violate in the least particular, the laws of the country; and never to tolerate their violation by others. As the patriots of seventy-six did to the support of the Declaration of Independence, so to the support of the Constitution and Laws, let every American pledge his life, his property, and his sacred honor;—let every man remember that to violate the law, is to trample on the blood of his father, and to tear the character of his own, and his children's liberty. Let reverence for the laws, be breathed by every American mother, to the lisping babe, that prattles on her laplet it be taught in schools, in seminaries, and in colleges; let it be written in Primers, spelling books, and in Almanacs;—let it be preached from the pulpit, proclaimed in legislative halls, and enforced in courts of justice. And, in short, let it become the *political religion* of the nation; and let the old and the young, the rich and the poor, the grave and the gay, of all sexes and tongues, and colors and conditions, sacrifice unceasingly upon its altars.

While ever a state of feeling, such as this, shall universally, or even, very generally prevail throughout the nation, vain will be every effort, and fruitless every attempt, to subvert our national freedom.

When I so pressingly urge a strict observance of all the laws, let me not be understood as saying there are no bad laws, nor that grievances may not arise, for the redress of which, no legal provisions have been made.—I mean to say no such thing. But I do mean to say, that, although bad laws, if they exist, should be repealed as soon as possible, still while they continue in force, for the sake of example, they should be religiously observed. So also in unprovided cases. If such arise, let proper legal provisions be made for them with the least possible delay; but, till then, let them, if not too intolerable, be borne with.

There is no grievance that is a fit object of redress by mob law. In any case that arises, as for instance, the promulgation of abolitionism, one of two positions is necessarily true; that is, the thing is right within itself, and therefore

deserves the protection of all law and all good citizens; or, it is wrong, and therefore proper to be prohibited by legal enactments; and in neither case, is the
interposition of mob law, either necessary, justifiable, or excusable.

But, it may be asked, why suppose danger to our political institutions? Have
we not preserved them for more than fifty years? And why may we not for fifty
times as long?

We hope there is *no sufficient* reason. We hope all dangers may be overcome;
but to conclude that no danger may ever arise, would itself be extremely dangerous. There are now, and will hereafter be, many causes, dangerous in their tendency, which have not existed heretofore; and which are not too insignificant to
merit attention. That our government should have been maintained in its original form from its establishment until now, is not much to be wondered at. It had
many props to support it through that period, which now are decayed, and crumbled away. Through that period, it was felt by all, to be an undecided experiment;
now, it is understood to be a successful one.—Then, all that sought celebrity and
fame, and distinction, expected to find them in the success of that experiment.
Their *all* was staked upon it:—their destiny was *inseparably* linked with it. Their
ambition aspired to display before an admiring world, a practical demonstration
of the truth of a proposition, which had hitherto been considered, at best no better, than problematical; namely, *the capability of a people to govern themselves.* If they
succeeded, they were to be immortalized; their names were to be transferred to
counties and cities, and rivers and mountains; and to be revered and sung, and
toasted through all time. If they failed, they were to be called knaves and fools,
and fanatics for a fleeting hour; then to sink and be forgotten. They succeeded.
The experiment is successful; and thousands have won their deathless names in
making it so. But the game is caught; and I believe it is true, that with the catching, end the pleasures of the chase. This field of glory is harvested, and the crop
is already appropriated. But new reapers will arise, and *they,* too, will seek a field.
It is to deny, what the history of the world tells us is true, to suppose that men of
ambition and talents will not continue to spring up amongst us. And, when they
do, they will as naturally seek the gratification of their ruling passion, as others
have so done before them. The question then, is, can that gratification be found
in supporting and maintaining an edifice that has been erected by others? Most
certainly it cannot. Many great and good men sufficiently qualified for any task
they should undertake, may ever be found, whose ambition would aspire to nothing beyond a seat in Congress, a gubernatorial or a presidential chair; *but such belong
not to the family of the lion, or the tribe of the eagle.* What! think you these places would
satisfy an Alexander, a Caesar, or a Napoleon?—Never! Towering genius disdains

a beaten path. It seeks regions hitherto unexplored.—It sees *no distinction* in adding story to story, upon the monuments of fame, erected to the memory of others. It *denies* that it is glory enough to serve under any chief. It *scorns* to tread in the footsteps of *any* predecessor, however illustrious. It thirsts and burns for distinction; and, if possible, it will have it, whether at the expense of emancipating slaves, or enslaving freemen. Is it unreasonable then to expect, that some man possessed of the loftiest genius, coupled with ambition sufficient to push it to its utmost stretch, will at some time, spring up among us? And when such a one does, it will require the people to be united with each other, attached to the government and laws, and generally intelligent, to successfully frustrate his designs.

Distinction will be his paramount object, and although he would as willingly, perhaps more so, acquire it by doing good as harm; yet, that opportunity being past, and nothing left to be done in the way of building up, he would set boldly to the task of pulling down.

Here then, is a probable case, highly dangerous, and such a one as could not have well existed heretofore.

Another reason which *once was;* but which, to the same extent, is *now no more,* has done much in maintaining our institutions thus far. I mean the powerful influence which the interesting scenes of the revolution had upon the *passions* of the people as distinguished from their judgment. By this influence, the jealousy, envy, and avarice, incident to our nature, and so common to a state of peace, prosperity, and conscious strength, were, for the time, in a great measure smothered and rendered inactive; while the deep-rooted principles of *hate,* and the powerful motive of *revenge,* instead of being turned against each other, were directed exclusively against the British nation. And thus, from the force of circumstances, the basest principles of our nature, were either made to lie dormant, or to become the active agents in the advancement of the noblest of cause— that of establishing and maintaining civil and religious liberty.

But this state of feeling *must fade, is fading, has faded,* with the circumstances that produced it.

I do not mean to say, that the scenes of the revolution *are now* or *ever will* be entirely forgotten; but that like every thing else, they must fade upon the memory of the world, and grow more and more dim by the lapse of time. In history, we hope, they will be read of, and recounted, so long as the bible shall be read;—but even granting that they will, their influence *cannot be* what it heretofore has been. Even then, they *cannot be* so universally known, nor so vividly felt, as they were by the generation just gone to rest. At the close of that struggle, nearly every adult male had been a participator in some of its scenes. The consequence was, that of those scenes, in the form of a husband, a father, a son or a brother, *a living history* was to be found in every family—a history bearing the indubitable testimonies of its own authenticity, in the limbs mangled, in the scars of wounds received, in the midst of the very scenes related—a history, too, that could be read and understood alike by all, the wise and the ignorant, the learned and the unlearned.—But *those* histories are gone. They *can* be read no more forever. They *were* a fortress of strength; but, what invading foeman could *never do,* the silent artillery of time *has done;* the leveling of its walls. They are gone.—They *were* a forest of giant oaks; but the all-resistless hurricane has swept over them, and left only, here and there, a lonely trunk, despoiled of its verdure, shorn of its foliage; unshading and unshaded, to murmur in a few more gentle breezes, and to combat with its mutilated limbs, a few more ruder storms, then to sink, and be no more.

They *were* the pillars of the temple of liberty; and now, that they have crumbled away, that temple must fall, unless we, their descendants, supply their places with other pillars, hewn from the solid quarry of sober reason. Passion has helped us; but can do so no more. It will in future be our enemy. Reason, cold, calculating, unimpassioned reason, must furnish all the materials for our future support and defence.—Let those materials be moulded into *general intelligence, sound morality,* and, in particular, *a reverence for the constitution and laws:* and, that we improved to the last; that we remained free to the last; that we revered his name to the last; that, during his long sleep, we permitted no hostile foot to pass over or desecrate his resting place; shall be that which to learn the last trump shall awaken our WASHINGTON.

Upon these let the proud fabric of freedom rest, as the rock of its basis; and as truly as has been said of the only greater institution, *"the gates of hell shall not prevail against it."*

LETTER TO MRS. O. H. BROWNING
APRIL 1, 1838

Mrs. Browning was the wife of Illinois State Senator Orville Browning, an acquaintance of Lincoln's in the Illinois State legislature. In this letter, Lincoln humorously describes how he was able to terminate his courtship with Mary Owens without loss of honor. It is unclear to what extent Lincoln's unflattering description of Mary Owens as a toothless, "weather-beaten," "old maid," and "a fair match for Falstaff" was exaggerated as part of an April Fool's joke. The letter is of interest because it reveals Lincoln's sense of humor, which was self-deprecating at times. He jested not only about Mary Owens's physical appearance, but also about his own vanity and presumption.

The letter concludes with a version of the familiar Grouch Marx quip: "I would never want to be part of any group that would have me as a member."

SPRINGFIELD, APRIL 1, 1838—

DEAR MADAM:

Without appologising [*sic*] for being egotistical, I shall make the history of so much of my own life, as has elapsed since I saw you, the subject of this letter. And by the way I now discover, that in order to give a full and inteligible [*sic*] account of the things I have done and suffered *since* I saw you, I shall necessarily have to relate some that happened *before*.

It was, then, in the autumn of 1836, that a married lady of my acquaintance, and who was a great friend of mine, being about to pay a visit to her father and other relatives residing in Kentucky, proposed to me, that on her return she would bring a sister of hers with her, upon condition that I would engage to become her brother-in-law with all convenient dispach [*sic*]. I, of course, accepted the proposal; for you know I could not have done otherwise, had I really been averse to it; but privately, between you and me, I was most confoundedly well pleased with the project. I had seen the said sister some three years before, thought her inteligent [*sic*] and agreeable, and saw no good objection to plodding life through hand in hand with her. Time passed on, the lady took her journey, and in due time returned, sister in company sure enough. This stomached me a little; for it appeared to me, that her coming so readily showed that she was a trifle too willing; but on reflection it occured [*sic*] to me, that she might have been prevailed on by her married sister to come, without any thing concerning me ever having been mentioned to her; and so I concluded that if no other objection presented itself, I would consent to waive this. All this occurred to me upon my *hearing* of her arrival in the neighborhood; for, be it remembered, I had not yet *seen* her, except about three years previous, as before mentioned.

In a few days we had an interview, and although I had seen her before, she did not look as my immagination [*sic*] had pictured her. I knew she was oversize, but she now appeared a fair match for Falstaff; I knew she was called an "old maid," and I felt no doubt of the truth of at least half of the appelation [*sic*]; but now, when I beheld her, I could not for my life avoid thinking of my mother; and this, not from withered features, for her skin was too full of fat to permit of its contracting in to wrinkles; but from her want of teeth, weatherbeaten appearance in general, and from a kind of notion that ran in my head, that *nothing* could have commenced at the size of infancy, and reached her present bulk in less than thirty-five or forty years; and, in short, I was not all pleased with her. But what could I do?—I had told her sister that I would take her for better or for worse; and I made a point of honor and conscience in all things, to stick to my word, especially if others had been induced to act on it, which in this case, I doubted not they had, for I was now fairly convinced, that no other man on earth would have her, and hence the conclusion that they were bent on holding me to my bargain. Well, thought I, I have said it, and, be consequences what they may, it shall not be my fault if I fail to do it. At once I determined to consider her my wife; and this done, all my powers of discovery were put to the rack, in search of perfections in her, which might be fairly set-off against her defects. I tried to immagine [sic] she was handsome, which, but for her unfortunate corpulency, was actually true. Exclusive of this, no woman that I have ever seen, has a finer face. I also tried to convince myself, that the mind was much more to be valued than the person; and in this, she was not inferior, as I could discover, to any with whom I had been acquainted.

Shortly after this, without attempting to come to any positive understanding with her, I set out for Vandalia, where and when you first saw me. During my stay there, I had letters from her, which did not change my opinion of either her intellect or intention; but on the contrary, confirmed it in both.

All this while, although I was fixed "firm as the surge repelling rock" in my resolution, I found I was continually repenting the rashness which had led me to make it. Through life I have been in no bondage, either real or imaginary, from the thraldom of which I so much desired to be free. After my return home, I saw nothing to change my opinion of her in any particular. She was the same and so was I. I now spent my time between planing [sic] how I might get along through life after my contemplated change of circumstances should have taken place; and how I might procrastinate the evil day for a time, which I really dreaded as much—perhaps more, than an irishman [sic] does the halter.

After all my suffering upon this deeply interesting subject, here I am, wholly unexpectedly, completely out of the "scrape"; and I now want to know, if you can guess how I got out of it. Out clear in every sense of the term; no violation of word, honor or conscience. I don't believe you can guess, and so I might as well tell you at once. As the lawyers say, it was done in the manner following, towit. After I had delayed the matter as long as I thought I could in honor do, which by the way had brought me round into the last fall, I concluded I might as well bring it to a consumation [sic] without further delay; and so I mustered my resolution, and made the proposal to her direct; but, shocking to relate, she answered, No. At first I supposed she did it through an affectation of modesty, which I thought but ill-became her, under the peculiar circumstances of her case; but on my renewal of the charge, I found she repeled [*sic*] it with greater firmness than before. I tried it again and again, but with the same success, or rather with the same want of success.

I finally was forced to give it up, at which I very unexpectedly found myself mortified almost beyond endurance. I was mortified, it seemed to me, in a hundred different ways. My vanity was deeply wounded by the reflections, that I had so long been too stupid to discover her intentions, and at the same time never doubting that I understood them perfectly; and also, that she whom I had taught myself to believe nobody else would have, had actually rejected me with all my fancied greatness; and to cap the whole, I then, for the first time, began to suspect that I was really a little in love with her. But let it all go. I'll try and out live it. Others have been made fools of by the girls; but this can never with truth be said of me. I most emphatically, in this instance, made a fool of myself. I have now come to the conclusion never again to think of marrying, and for this reason; I can never be satisfied with any one who would be block-head enough to have me.

When you receive this, write me a long yarn about something to amuse me. Give my respects to Mr. Browning.

Your sincere friend

A. Lincoln

Mrs. O. H. Browning—

THE SUBTREASURY: SPEECH AT A POLITICAL DISCUSSION IN THE HALL OF THE HOUSE OF REPRESENTATIVES AT SPRINGFIELD, ILLINOIS
DECEMBER [26], 1839

The Subtreasury or Independent Treasury was created as a fiscal expedient by Martin Van Buren after Jackson had killed the Second Bank of the United States by removing federal deposits and placing them in state "pet banks." The death of the Second Bank of the United States, the fiscal irresponsibility of the pet banks, and Jackson's economically disastrous decision to curb over-speculation by the specie circular, an act that required public land to be purchased only with hard money, helped to precipitate the Panic of 1837. While the creation of the Subtreasury restored federal deposits to the national vault, the government would use only hard money to pay for its expenditures. As a Whig who favored government promotion of a sound currency, Lincoln opposed the Subtreasury fearing that its hard money policy would discourage investment for internal improvements. Throughout his early career, Lincoln consistently supported the creation of a state bank of Illinois.

FELLOW-CITIZENS:

It is peculiarly embarrassing to me to attempt a continuance of the discussion, on this evening, which has been conducted in this Hall on several preceding ones. It is so, because on each of those evenings, there was a much fuller attendance than now, without any reason for its being so, except the greater *interest* the community feel in the *Speakers* who addressed them *then,* than they do in *him* who is to do so *now.* I am, indeed, apprehensive, that the few who have attended, have done so, more to spare me of mortification, than in the hope of being interested in any thing I may be able to say.—This circumstance casts a damp upon my spirits, which I am sure I shall be unable to overcome during the evening. But enough of preface.

The subject heretofore, and now to be discussed, is the Sub-Treasury scheme of the present Administration, as a means of collecting, safe-keeping, transferring, and disbursing the revenues of the Nation, as contrasted with a National Bank for the same purposes. Mr. Douglas has said that we (the Whigs) have not dared to meet them, (the Locos.) in argument on this question. I protest against this assertion. I say that we have again and again, during this discussion, urged facts and arguments against the Sub-Treasury, which they have neither dared to deny nor attempted to answer. But lest some may be led to believe that we really wish to avoid the question, I now propose, in my humble way, to urge those arguments again; at the same time, begging the audience to mark well the positions I shall take, and the proof I shall offer to sustain them, and that they will not again permit Mr. Douglas or his friends, to escape the force of them, by a round and groundless assertion, that we "dare not meet them argument."

Of the Sub-Treasury then, as contrasted with a National Bank, for the before enumerated purposes, I lay down the following propositions, to wit:

1st. It will injuriously affect the community by its operation on the circulating medium.

2d. It will be a more expensive fiscal agent.

3d. It will be a less secure depository for the public money.

To show the truth of the first proposition, let us take a short review our condition under the operation of a National Bank. It was the depository of the public revenues.—Between the collection of those revenues and the disbursements of them by the government, the Bank was permitted to, and did actually loan them out to individuals, and hence the large amount of money annually collected for revenue purposes, which by any other plan would have been idle, a great portion of time, was kept almost constantly in circulation. Any person who will reflect, that money is only valuable while in circulation,

will readily perceive, that any device which will keep the government revenues, in constant circulation, instead of being locked up in idleness, is no
inconsiderable advantage.

By the Sub-Treasury, the revenue is to be collected, and kept in iron boxes
until the government wants it for disbursement; thus robbing the people of the
use of it, while the government does not itself need it, and while the money is
performing no nobler office than that of rusting in iron boxes. The natural effect
of this change of policy, every one will see, is to reduce the quantity of money
in circulation.

But again, by the Sub-Treasury scheme the revenue is to be collected in
specie. I anticipate that this will be disputed. I expect to hear it said, that it is not
the policy of the Administration to collect the revenue in specie. If it shall, I
reply, that Mr. Van Buren, in his message recommended the Sub-Treasury,
expended nearly a column of that document in an attempt to persuade Congress
to provide for the collection of the revenue in specie exclusively; and he concluded with these words. "It may be safely assumed, that no motive of *convenience* to the *citizen,* requires the reception of Bank paper." In addition to this,
Mr. Silas Wright, Senator from New York, and the political, personal and confidential friend of Mr. Van Buren, drafted and introduced into the Senate the
first Sub-Treasury Bill, and that bill provided for ultimately collecting the revenue in specie. It is true, I know, that that clause was stricken from the bill, but
it was done by the votes of the Whigs, aided by a portion only of the Van Buren
Senators.—No Sub-Treasury bill has yet become a law, though two or three
have been considered by Congress, some with and some without the specie
clause; so that I admit there is room for quibbling upon the question of whether
the Administration favor the exclusive specie doctrine or not; but I take it, that
the fact that the President at first urged the specie doctrine, and that under his
recommendation the first bill introduced embraced it, warrants us in charging
it as the policy of the party until their head as publicly recants it, as he at first
espoused it.—I repeat then, that by the Sub-Treasury, the revenue is to be collected in *specie*. Now mark what the effect of this must be. By all estimates ever
made, there are but between 60 and 80 millions of specie in the United States.
The expenditures of the Government for the year 1838, the last for which we
have had the report, were 40 millions. Thus it is seen, that if the whole revenue
be collected in specie, it will take more than half of all the specie in the nation
to do it. By this means, more than half of all the specie belonging to the fifteen
million of souls, who compose the whole population of the country, is thrown
into the hands of the public office-holders, and other public creditors, compos-

ing in number perhaps not more than one quarter of a million; leaving the other fourteen millions and three quarters to get along as they best can, with less than one half of the specie of the country, and whatever rags, and shin-plasters they may be able to put, and keep, in circulation. By this means, every office-holder, and other public creditor may, and most likely will, set up shaver; and a most glorious harvest will the specie men have of it; each specie man, upon a fair division, having to his share, the fleecing of about 59 rag-men.*—In all candor, let

*On January 4, 1839, the Senate of the United States passed the following resolution, to wit:

> "*Resolved,* That the Secretary of the Treasury be directed to communicate to the Senate any information he may recently have received in respect to the mode of collecting, keeping, and disbursing public moneys in foreign countries."
>
> Under this resolution, the Secretary communicated to the Senate a letter, the following extract from which clearly shows that the collection of the revenue in *specie* will establish a sound currency for the office-holders, and a depreciated one for the people; and that the office-holders and other public creditors will turn shavers upon all the rest of the community. Here is the extract from the letter, being all of it that relates to the question:
>
> "Hague, October 12, 1838.
>
> "The financial system of Hamburg is, as far as is known, very simple, as may be supposed from so small a territory. The whole amount of Hamburg coined money is about four and a half millions of marks current, or one million two hundred and eighty-two thousand five hundred dollars; and, except under very extraordinary circumstances, *not more than one half that amount is in circulation,* and all duties, taxes, and excise must be paid in Hamburg currency. *The consequence is that it invariably commands a premium of one to three per centum.* Every year one senator and ten citizens are appointed to transact the whole of the financial concern, both as to receipt and disbursement of the funds, *which is always in cash,* and is every day deposited in the bank, to the credit of the chancery; and, on being paid out, the citizen to whose department the payment belongs must appear personally with the check or order, stating the amount and to whom to be paid. The person receiving very seldom keeps the money, *preferring to dispose of it to a money-changer at a premium,* and taking other coin at a discount, of which there is a great variety and a large amount constantly in circulation, and on which in his daily payment *he loses nothing;* and those who have payments to make to the government apply to the *money-changers again for Hamburg currency,* which keeps it in constant motion, and I believe it frequently occurs that the bags, which are sealed and labeled with the amount, are returned again to the bank without being opened.
>
> "With great respect, your obedient servant,
>
> "John Cuthbert."
>
> "To the Hon. Levi Woodbury,
>
> "Secretary of the Treasury,
>
> Washington, D.C."

This letter is found in Senate documents, p. 113 of the session of 1838–9 [Lincoln's note].

me ask, was such a system for benefiting the few at the expense of the many, ever before devised? And was the sacred name of Democracy, ever before made to endorse such an enormity against the rights of the people?

I have already said that the Sub-Treasury will reduce the quantity of money in circulation. This position is strengthened by the recollection that the revenue is to be collected in specie, so that the mere amount of revenue is not all that is withdrawn, but the amount of paper circulation that the 40 millions would serve to as a basis, is withdrawn; which would be in a sound state at least 100 millions.—When 100 millions, or more, of the circulation we now have, shall be withdrawn, who can contemplate, without terror, the distress, ruin, bankruptcy and beggary, that must follow?

The man who has purchased any article, say a horse, on credit, at 100 dollars, when there are 200 millions circulating in the country, if the quantity be reduced to 100 millions by the arrival of pay-day, will find the horse but sufficient to pay half the debt; and the other half must either be paid out of his other means, and thereby become a clear loss to him, or go unpaid, and thereby become a clear loss to his creditor. What I have here said of a single case of the purchase of a horse, will hold good in every case of a debt existing at the time a reduction in the quantity of money occurs, by whomsoever, and for whatsoever it may have been contracted. It may be said that what the debtor loses, the creditor gains by this operation—but on examination this will be found true only to a very limited extent. It is more generally true, that *all* lose by it.—The *creditor,* by losing more of his debts, than he gains by the increased value of those he collects; the *debtor* by either parting with more of his property to pay his debts, than he received in contracting them; or, by entirely breaking up in his business, and thereby being thrown upon the world in idleness.

The general distress thus created, will, to be sure, be *temporary;* because whatever change may occur in the quantity of money in any community, *time* will adjust the derangement produced; but while that adjustment is progressing, all suffer more or less, and very many lose everything that renders life desirable. Why then, shall we suffer a severe difficulty, even though it be *but temporary,* unless we receive some equivalent for it?

What I have been saying as to the effect produced by a reduction of the quantity of money, relates to the *whole* country. I now propose to show, that it would produce a *peculiar* and *permanent* hardship upon the citizens of those States and Territories in which the public lands lie. The Land Officers in those States and Territories, as all know, form the great gulf by which all, or nearly all the money in them, is swallowed up. When the quantity of money shall be reduced,

and consequently every thing under individual control brought down in proportion, the price of those lands, being fixed by law, will remain as now. Of
necessity it will follow, that the *produce* or *labor* that *now* raises money sufficient
to purchase 80 acres, will *then* raise but sufficient to purchase 40, or perhaps not
that much.—And this difficulty and hardship, will last as long, in some degree,
as any portion of these lands shall remain undisposed of. Knowing, as I well do,
the difficulty that poor people *now* encounter in procuring homes, I hesitate not
to say, that when the price of the public lands shall be doubled or trebled; or,
which is the same thing, produce and labor cut down to one half, or one third
of their present prices, it will be little less than impossible for them to procure
those homes at all.

In answer to what I have said as to the effect the Sub-Treasury would have
upon the currency, it is often urged that the money collected for revenue purposes will *not lie idle* in the vaults of the Treasury; and, farther, that a National
Bank produces greater derangement in the currency, by a system of contractions and expansions, than the Sub-Treasury would produce in any way. In
reply, I need only show, that experience proves the contrary of both these
propositions. It is an undisputed fact, that the late Bank of the United States paid
the government $75,000 annually, for the *privilege* of using the public money
between the times of its collection and disbursement. Can any man suppose,
that the Bank would have paid this sum, annually for twenty years, and then
offered to renew its obligations to do so, if in reality there was no *time* intervening between the collection and disbursement of the revenue, and consequently no privilege of *using* the money extended to it?

Again, as to the contractions and expansions of a National Bank, I need only
point to the period intervening between the time that the late Bank got into successful operation and that at which the Government commenced war upon it, to
show that during that period, no such contractions or expansions took place. If
before, or after that period, derangement occurred in the currency, it proves
nothing. The Bank could not be expected to regulate the currency, either *before*
it got into successful operation or *after* it was crippled and thrown into death convulsions, by the removal of the deposits from it, and other hostile measures of the
Government, against it. We do not pretend that a National Bank can establish
and maintain a sound and uniform state of currency in the country in *spite* of the
National Government; but we do say, that it has established and maintained such
a currency, and can do so again, by the *aid* of that Government; and we further
say, that no duty is more imperative on that Government, than the duty it owes
the people, of furnishing them a sound and uniform currency.

I now leave the proposition as to the effect of the Sub-Treasury upon the currency of the country, and pass to that relative to the additional *expense* which must be incurred by it over that incurred by a National Bank, as a fiscal agent of the Government. By the late National Bank, we had the public revenue received, safely kept, transferred and disbursed, not only without expense, but we actually received of the Bank $75,000 annually for its privileges, while rendering us those services. By the Sub-Treasury, according to the estimate of the Secretary of the Treasury, who is the warm advocate of the system and which estimate is the lowest made by any one, the same services are to cost $60,000. Mr. Rives, who, to say the least, is equally talented and honest, estimates that these services, under the Sub-Treasury system, cannot cost less than $600,000. For the sake of liberality, let us suppose that the estimates of the Secretary and Mr. Rives, are the two extremes, and that their mean is about the true estimate, and we shall then find, that when to that sum is added the $75,000 which the Bank paid us, the difference between the two systems, in favor of the Bank and against the Sub-Treasury, is $405,000 a year. This sum, though small when compared to the many millions annually expended by the General Government, is when viewed by itself, very large; and much too large, when viewed in any light, to be thrown away once a year for nothing. It is sufficient to pay the pensions of more than 4,000 Revolutionary Soldiers, or to purchase a 40 acre tract of Government land, for each one of more than 8,000 poor families.

To the argument against the Sub-Treasury, on the score of additional expense, its friends, so far as I know, attempt no answer. They choose, so far as I can learn, to treat the throwing away $405,000 once a year as a matter entirely too small to merit their democratic notice.

I now come to the proposition, that it would be less secure than a National Bank, as a depository of the public money. The experience of the past, I think, proves the truth of this. And here, inasmuch as I rely chiefly upon experience to establish it, let me ask, how is it that we know any thing—that any event will occur, that any combination of circumstances will produce a certain result—except by the analogies of past experience? What has once happened, will invariably happen again, when the same circumstances, which combined to produce it shall again combine in the same way. We all feel that we know that a blast of wind would extinguish the flame of the candle that stands by me. How do we know it? We have never seen this flame thus extinguished. We know it, because we have seen through all our lives, that a blast of wind extinguishes the flame of a candle whenever it is thrown fully upon it. Again, we all feel to *know* that we have to die.—How? We have never died yet. We know it, because we know, or at least think we know, that of all the beings, just like ourselves, who have been coming into the world for six thousand years, not one is now living who was here two hundred years ago.

I repeat, then, that we know nothing of what will happen in future, but by the analogy of experience, and that the fair analogy of past experience fully proves that the Sub-Treasury would be a less safe depository of the public money than a National Bank. Examine it.—By the Sub-Treasury scheme, the public money is to be kept, between the times of its collection and disbursement, by Treasurers of the Mint, Custom-house officers, Land officers, and some new officers to be appointed in the same way that those first enumerated are. Has a year passed, since the organization of the Government, that numerous defalcations have not occurred among this class of officers? Look at Swartwout with his $1,200,000, Price with his $75,000, Harris with his $109,000, Hawkins with his $100,000, Linn with his $55,000, together with some twenty-five hundred lesser lights. Place the public money again in these same hands, and will it not again go the same way? Most assuredly it will. But turn to the history of the National Bank in this country, and we shall there see, that those Banks performed the fiscal operations of the Government thro' a period of 40 years, received, safely kept, transferred, disbursed, an aggregate of nearly five hundred millions of dollars; and that, in all that time, and with all that money, not one dollar, nor one cent, did the Government lose by them. Place the public money again in a similar depository, and will it not again be safe?

But, conclusive as the experience of fifty years is, that individuals are unsafe depositories of the public money, and of forty years that National Banks are safe depositories, we are not left to rely solely upon that experience for the truth of those propositions.—If experience were silent upon the subject, conclusive reasons could be shown for the truth of them.

It is often urged that to say the public money will be more secure in a National Bank, than in the hands of individuals, as proposed in the Sub-Treasury, is to say, that Bank directors and Bank officers are more honest than sworn officers of the Government. Not so. We insist on no such thing. We say that public officers, selected with reference to their capacity and honesty, (which by the way, we deny is the practice in these days,) stand an equal chance, precisely, of being capable and honest, with Bank officers selected by the same rule.—We further say, that with however much care selections may be made, there will be some unfaithful and dishonest in both classes. The experience of the whole world, in all by-gone times, proves this true. The Saviour of the world chose twelve disciples, and even one of that small number, selected by super-human wisdom, turned out a traitor and a devil. And, it may not be improper here to add, that Judas carried the bag—was the Sub-Treasurer of the Saviour and his disciples.

We, then, do not say, nor need we say, to maintain our proposition, that Bank officers are more honest than Government officers, selected by the same rule. What we do say, is, that the *interest* of the Sub-Treasurer is *against his duty*—while the *interest* of the Bank is *on the side of its duty*.—Take instances—a Sub-Treasurer has in his hands one hundred thousand dollars of public money; his *duty* says,—"You ought to pay this money over"—but his *interest* says, "You ought to run away with this sum, and be a nabob the balance of your life." And who that knows any thing of human nature, doubts that, in many instances, interest will prevail over duty, and that the Sub-Treasurer will prefer opulent knavery in a foreign land, to honest poverty at home? But how different is it with a Bank. Besides the Government money deposited with it, it is doing business upon a large capital of its own. If it proves faithful to the Government, it continues its business, if unfaithful it forfeits its charter, breaks up its business, and thereby loses more than all it can make by seizing upon the Government funds in its possession. Its *interest,* therefore, is on the side of its duty—is to be faithful to the Government, and consequently, even the dishonest amongst its managers, have no temptation to be faithless to it. Even if robberies happen in the Bank, the losses are borne by the Bank, and the Government loses nothing. It is for this reason then, that we say a Bank is the more secure. It is because of that admirable feature in the Bank system, which places the *interest* and the *duty* of the depository both on one side; whereas that feature can never enter into the Sub-Treasury system. By the latter, the *interest* of the individuals keeping the public money, will wage an eternal war with their *duty,* and in very many instances must be victorious. In answer to the argument drawn from the fact that individual depositories of public money, have always proved unsafe, it is urged that, even if we had a National Bank, the money has to *pass through* the same individual hands, that it will under the Sub-Treasury. This is only partially true in fact, and wholly fallacious in argument.

It is only partially true, in fact, because by the Sub-Treasury bill, four Receivers-General are to be appointed by the President and Senate. These are new officers, and consequently, it cannot be true that the money, or any portion of it, has heretofore passed thro' their hands. These four new officers are to be located at New York, Boston, Charleston, and St. Louis, and consequently are to be depositories of all the money collected at or near those points; so that more than three-fourths of the public money will fall into the keeping of these four new officers, which did not exist as officers under the National Bank system. It is only partially true, then, that the money passes through the same hands, under a National Bank, as it would do under the Sub-Treasury.

It is true that under either system, individuals must be employed as Collectors of the Customs, Receivers at the Land Offices, &c. &c., but the difference is, that under the Bank system, the Receivers of all sorts, receive the money and pay it over to the Bank once a week when the collections are large, and once a month when they are small, whereas, by the Sub-Treasury system, individuals are not only to collect the money, but they are to *keep* it also, or pay it over to other individuals equally as unsafe as themselves, to be by them kept, until wanted for disbursement. It is during the time that it is thus lying idle in their hands, that opportunity is afforded, and temptation held out to them to embezzle and escape with it. By the Bank system, each Collector or Receiver, is to deposit in Bank all the money in his hands at the end of each month at most, and to send the Bank certificates of deposit, to the Secretary of the Treasury. Whenever that certificate of deposit fails to arrive at the proper time, the Secretary *knows* that the officer thus failing, is acting the knave; and if he is himself disposed to do his duty, he has him immediately removed from office, and thereby cuts him off from the possibility of embezzling but little more than the receipts of a single month. But by the Sub-Treasury System, the money is to lie month after month in the hands of individuals; larger amounts are to accumulate in the hands of the Receivers General, and some others, by perhaps ten to one, than ever accumulated in the hands of individuals before; yet during all this time, in relation to this great stake, the Secretary of the Treasury can comparatively know nothing. Reports, to be sure, he will have; but reports are often false, and always false when made by a knave to cloak his knavery. Long experience has shown, that nothing short of an actual demand of the money will expose an adroit peculator. Ask him for reports and he will give them to your heart's content, send agents to examine and count the money in his hands, and he will borrow of a friend, merely to be counted and then returned, a sufficient sum to make the sum square. Try what you will, it will all fail till you demand the money—then, and not till then, the truth will come.

The sum of the whole matter, I take to be this: Under the Bank system, while sums of money, by the law, were permitted to lie in the hands of individuals, *for very short periods only,* many and very large defalcations occurred by those individuals. Under the Sub-Treasury system, *much larger sums* are to lie in the hands of individuals *for much longer periods,* thereby multiplying *temptation* in proportion as the sums *are larger;* and multiplying *opportunity* in proportion as the periods *are longer* to, and for, those individuals to embezzle and escape with the public treasure; and therefore, just in the proportion, that the *temptation* and the *opportunity* are greater under the Sub-Treasury than the Bank system, will the peculations and defalcations be greater under the former than they have been under the latter. The truth of this, independent of actual experience, is but little less than self-evident. I, therefore, leave it.

But it is said, and truly too, that there is to be a *Penitentiary Department* to the Sub-Treasury. This, the advocates of the system will have it, will be a "king-cure-all." Before I go further, may I not ask if the Penitentiary Department, is not itself an admission that they expect the public money to be stolen? Why build a cage if they expect to catch no birds? But to the question how effectual the Penitentiary will be in preventing defalcations. How effectual have Penitentiaries heretofore been in preventing the crimes they were established to suppress? Has not confinement in them long been the legal penalty of larceny, forgery, robbery, and many other crimes, in almost all the States? And yet, are not those crimes committed weekly, daily, nay, and even hourly, in every one of those States? Again, the gallows has long been the penalty of murder, and yet we scarcely open a newspaper, that does not relate a new case of crime. If then, the Penitentiary has *heretofore* failed to prevent larceny, forgery, and robbery, and the gallows and halter have likewise failed to prevent murder, by what process of reasoning, I ask, is it that we are to conclude the Penitentiary will hereafter prevent the stealing of the public money? But our opponents seem to think they answer the charge, that the money will be stolen, fully, if they can show that they will bring the offenders to punishment. Not so. Will the punishment of the thief bring back the stolen money? No more so than the hanging of a murderer restores his victim to life. What is the object desired? Certainly not the greatest number of thieves we can catch, but that the money may not be stolen. If, then, any plan can be devised for depositing the public treasure where it will be never stolen, never embezzled, is not that the plan to be adopted? Turn, then, to a National Bank, and you have that plan, fully and completely successful, as tested by the experience of forty years.

I have now done with the three propositions that the Sub-Treasury would injuriously affect the currency, and would be more *expensive* and *less secure* as a depository of the public money than a National Bank. How far I have succeeded in establishing their truth is for others to judge.

Omitting, for want of time, what I had intended to say as to the effect of the Sub-Treasury, to bring the public money under the more immediate control of the President, than it has ever heretofore been, I now only ask the audience, when Mr. Calhoun shall answer me, *to hold him to the questions.* Permit him not to escape them. Require him *either* to show that the Sub-Treasury *would not* injuriously affect the *currency*, or that we should in some way receive an equiv-alent for that injurious effect. Require him *either* to show that the Sub-Treasury *would not be more expensive* as a fiscal agent, than a Bank, or that we should, in some way, be compensated for that additional expense. And particularly require him to show that the public money *would be as secure* in the Sub-Treasury as in a National Bank, or that the additional *insecurity* would be overbalanced by some good result of the proposed change.

No one of them, in my humble judgment, will he be able to do; and I ven-ture the prediction, and ask that it may be especially noted, *that he will not attempt to answer the proposition, that the Sub-Treasury would be more expensive than a National Bank, as a fiscal agent of the Government.*

As a sweeping objection to a National Bank, and consequently an argument in favor of the Sub-Treasury as a substitute for it, it often has been urged, and doubtless will be again, that such a bank is unconstitutional. We have often heretofore shown, and therefore, need not in detail, do so again, that a major-ity of the Revolutionary patriarchs, whoever acted officially upon the question, commencing with Gen. Washington, and embracing Gen. Jackson, the larger number of the signers of the Declaration, and of the framers of the Constitu-tion, who were in the Congress of 1791, have decided upon their oaths that such a Bank is constitutional. We have also shown that the votes of Congress have more often been in favor of, than against its constitutionality. In addition to all this, we have shown that the Supreme Court—that tribunal which the Constitution has itself established to decide Constitutional questions—has solemnly decided that such a Bank is constitutional. Protesting that these authorities ought to settle the question and ought to be conclusive, I will not urge them further now. I now propose to take a view of the question, which I have not known to be taken by any one before. It is that whatever objection ever has, or ever can be made to the constitutionality of a Bank, will apply with equal force in its whole length, breadth and proportions, to the Sub-Treasury. Our opponents say, there is no *express* authority in the Constitution to establish a *Bank* and therefore a Bank is unconstitutional; but we, with equal truth, may say, there is no *express* authority in the Constitution to establish a *Sub-Treasury,* and therefore a Sub-Treasury is unconstitutional. Who, then, has the advantage of this "*express authority*" argument? Does it not cut equally both ways? Does it not wound them as deeply and as deadly as it does us?

Our position is that both are constitutional. The Constitution enumerates expressly several powers which Congress may exercise, super-added to which is a general authority, "to make all laws necessary and proper," for carrying into effect "all the powers vested by the Constitution of the Government of the United States." One of the express powers given Congress is, "to lay and collect taxes; duties, imposts, and excises; to pay the debts, and provide for the common defence and general welfare of the United States."—Now, Congress is expressly authorized to make all laws necessary and proper for carrying this power into execution. To carry it into execution, it is indispensably necessary to collect, safely keep, transfer, and disburse a revenue. To do this, a Bank is "necessary and proper." But, say our opponents, to authorize the making of a Bank, the *necessity* must be so great, that the power just recited, would be nugatory without it; and that that *necessity* is expressly negatived by the fact, that they have got along *ten* whole years without such a *Bank*. Immediately we turn on them, and say, that that sort of *necessity* for a *Sub-Treasury* does not exist, because we have got along *forty* whole years without one. And this time, it may be observed, that we are not merely equal with them in the argument, but we beat them *forty* to *ten,* or which is the same thing, *four* to *one.* On examination, it will be found, that the absurd rule, which prescribes that before we can constitutionally adopt a National Bank as a fiscal agent, we must show an *indispensable necessity* for it, will exclude every sort of fiscal agent that the mind of man can conceive. A *Bank* is not *indispensable,* because we can take the *Sub-Treasury;* the *Sub-Treasury* is not *indispensable* because we can take the *Bank.*

The rule is too absurd to need further comment. Upon the phrase *"necessary and proper"* in the Constitution, it seems to me more reasonable to say that *some* fiscal agent is *indispensably necessary;* but, inasmuch as no *particular sort* of agent is thus *indispensable,* because some *other* sort might be adopted, we are left to choose that sort of agent, which may be most *"proper"* on grounds of expediency.

But it is said the Constitution gives no power to Congress to pass acts of incorporation. Indeed!—What is the passing an act of incorporation, but the *making of a law?* Is any one wise enough to tell? The Constitution expressly gives Congress power *"to pass all laws necessary and proper,"* &c. If, then, the passing of a Bank charter, be the *"making a law necessary and proper,"* is it not clearly within the constitutional power of Congress to do so?

I now leave the Bank and the Sub-Treasury to try to answer, in a brief way, some of the arguments which, on previous evenings here, have been urged by Messrs. Lamborn and Douglas. Mr. Lamborn admits, that *"errors,"* as he charitably calls them have occurred under the present and late administrations; but he insists that as great *"errors"* have occurred under all administrations. This, we respectfully deny. We admit that errors may have occurred under all administrations: but we insist that there is *no parallel* between them and those of the two last. If they can show that their errors are no greater in number and magnitude, than those of former times, we call off the dogs.

But they can do no such thing. To be brief, I will now attempt a contrast of the "errors" of the two latter, with those of former administrations, in relation to the public expenditures only. What I am now about to say, as to the expenditures, will be, in all cases exclusive of payments on the National debt. By an examination of authentic public documents, consisting of the regular series of annual reports, made by all the Secretaries of the Treasury from the establishment of the Government down to the close of the year 1838, the following contrasts will be presented.

1st. The last *ten* years under Gen. Jackson and Mr. Van Buren, cost more money than the first *twenty-seven* did, (including the heavy expenses of the late British war,) under Washington, Adams, Jefferson, and Madison.

2d. The last year of J. Q. Adams' Administration cost, in round numbers, *thirteen* millions, being about *one* dollar to each soul in the nation; the last (1838) of Mr. Van Buren's cost *forty* millions, being about *two dollars and fifty cents* to each soul; and being larger than the expenditures of Mr. Adams in the proportion of *five* to *two*.

3d. The highest annual expenditure during the late British war, being in 1814, and while he had in actual service rising 188,000 militia, together with the whole regular army, swelling the number to greatly over 200,000, and they to be clad, fed, and transported from point to point, with great rapidity and corresponding expense, and to be furnished with arms and ammunition, and they to be transported in like manner, and at like expense, was no more in round numbers than *thirty* millions; whereas the annual expenditure of 1838, under Mr. Van Buren, and while we were at peace with every government in the world, was *forty* millions; being over the highest year of the late and very expensive war, in the proportion of *four* to *three*.

4th. Gen. Washington administered the government *eight* years for *sixteen* millions; Mr. Van Buren administered it *one* year (1838) for *forty* millions; so that Mr. Van Buren expended *twice and a half* as much in *one* year, as Gen. Washington did in *eight,* and being in the proportion of *twenty* to *one*—or, in other words, had Gen. Washington administered the Government *twenty* years, at the same average expense that he did for *eight,* he would have carried us through the whole *twenty* for no more money than Mr. Van Buren has expended in getting us through the single *one* of 1838.

Other facts, equally astounding, might be presented from the same authentic document; but I deem the foregoing abundantly sufficient to establish the proposition, that there is no parallel between the *"errors"* of the present and late administrations, and those of former times, and that Mr. Van Buren is wholly out of the line of all precedents.

But, Mr. Douglas, seeing that the enormous expenditure of 1838, has no parallel in the olden times, comes in with a long list of excuses for it. This list of excuses, I will rapidly examine, and show, as I think, that the few of them which are true, prove nothing; and that the majority of them are wholly untrue in fact. He first says, that the expenditures of that year were made under the appropriations of Congress—*one branch of which was a Whig body.* It is true that those expenditures were made under the appropriations of Congress; but it is *untrue* that either branch of Congress was a *Whig* body. The Senate had fallen into the hands of the administration, more than a year before, as proven by the passage of the Expunging Resolution; and at the time those appropriations were made, there were too few Whigs in that body, to make a respectable struggle, in point of numbers, upon any question.—This is notorious to all. The House of Representatives that voted those appropriations, was the same that first assembled at the called session of September, 1838. Although it refused to pass the Sub-Treasury Bill, a majority of its members were elected as friends of the administration, and proved their adherence to it, by the election of a Van Buren Speaker, and two Van Buren clerks. It is clear then, that both branches of the Congress that passed those appropriations were in the hands of Mr. Van Buren's friends, so that the Whigs had no power to arrest them, as Mr. Douglas would insist. And is not the charge of extravagant expenditures, equally well sustained, if shown to have been made by a Van Buren Congress, as if shown to have been made in any other way? A Van Buren Congress passed the bills, and Mr. Van Buren himself approved them, and consequently the party are wholly responsible for them.

Mr. Douglas next says, that a portion of the expenditures of that year, was made for the purchase of Public Lands from the Indians. Now it happens that no such purchase was made during that year. It is true, that some money was paid that year in pursuance of Indian treaties; but no more, or rather not as much, as had been paid on the same account in each of several preceding years.

Next, he says, that the Florida was created many millions of this year's expenditures. This is true, and it is also true, that during that and every other year, that that war has existed, it has cost three or four times as much as it would have done under an honest and judicious administration of the Government. The large sums foolishly, not to say corruptly, thrown away in that war, constitute one of the just causes of complaint against the administration. Take a single instance. The agents of the Government in connexion with that war, needed a certain Steam boat; the owner proposed to sell it for ten thousand dollars; the agents refused to give that sum, but hired the boat at one hundred dollars per day, and kept it at hire till it amounted to ninety-two thousand dollars. This fact is not found in the public reports, but depends with me on the verbal statement of an officer of the navy, who said he knew it to be true.

That the administration ought to be credited for the *reasonable* expenses of the Florida war, we have never denied. Those *reasonable* charges, we say, could not exceed one or two millions a year. Deduct such a sum from the forty million expenditure of 1838, and the remainder will still be without a parallel as an annual expenditure.

Again, Mr. Douglas says, that the removal of the Indians to the country west of the Mississippi created much of the expenditure of 1838. I have examined the public documents in relation to this matter, and find that less was paid for the removal of Indians in that, than in some former years. The whole sum expended on that account in that year, did not much exceed one quarter of a million. For this small sum, altho' we do not think the administration entitled to credit, because large sums have been expended in the same way in former years, we consent it may take one and make the most of it.

Next, Mr. Douglas says, that five millions of the expenditures of 1838, consisted of the payment of the French indemnity money to its individual claimants. I have carefully examined the public documents, and thereby find this statement to be wholly untrue. Of the forty millions of dollars expended in 1838, I am enabled to say positively, that not one dollar consisted of payments on the French indemnities. So much for that excuse.

Next comes the Post Office.—He says that five millions were expended during that year to sustain that Department. By a like examination of public documents, I find this also, wholly untrue. Of the so often mentioned forty millions, not one dollar went to the Post Office. I am glad, however, that the Post Office has been referred to, because it warrants me in digressing a little, to enquire how it is, that that department of the Government has become a *charge* upon the Treasury, whereas under Mr. Adams and the Presidents before him, it not only, to use a homely phrase, cut its own fodder, but actually threw a surprlus into the Treasury.—Although nothing of the forty millions was paid on that account, in 1838; it is true that five millions are appropriated *to be so expended* in 1839; showing clearly that the department has become a *charge* upon the Treasury.—How has this happened?

I account for it in this way—the chief expense of the Post Office Department consists of the payments of Contractors for carrying the mails—contracts for carrying the mails, are, by law, let to the lowest bidders, after advertisement. This plan introduces competition, and insures the transportation of the mails at fair prices, so long as it is faithfully adhered to. It has ever been adhered to until Mr. Barry was made Post Master General. When he came into office, he formed the purpose of throwing the mail contracts into the hands of his friends to the exclusion of his opponents. To effect this, the plan of letting to the lowest bidder must be evaded, and it must be done in this way—The favorite bid less by perhaps three, or four hundred per cent, than the contract could be performed for, and consequently, shutting out all honest competition, became the contractor. The Post Master General would immediately add some slight additional duty to the contract, and under the pretence of extra allowance for extra services, run the contract to double, triple, and often quadruple what honest and fair bidders had proposed to take it at. In 1834 the finances of the department had become so deranged, that total concealment was no longer possible, and consequently a committee of the Senate were directed to make a thorough investigation of its affairs. Their report is found in the Senate Documents of 1833—'34—vol. 5, Doc. 422—which Documents may be seen at the Secretary's office, and I presume elsewhere in the State. The report shows numerous cases, of similar import, of one of which I give the substance—The contract for carrying the mail upon a certain route, had expired, and of course was to be let again. The old contractor offered to take it for $300 a year, the mail to be transported thereon three times a week, or for $600 transported daily. One James Reeside, bid $40 for three times a week; or $99 daily, and of course received the contract. On the examination of the committee, it was discovered that Reeside had received for the service on this route, which he had contracted to render for less than $100, the enormous sum of $1,999! This is but a single case.—Many similar ones, covering some ten or twenty pages of a large volume, are given in that report. The department was found to be insolvent to the amount of half a million; and to have been so grossly mismanaged, or rather so corruptly managed, in almost every particular, that the best friends of the Post Master General made no defence of his administration of it. They admitted that he was wholly unqualified for that office; but still he was retained in it by the President, until he resigned it voluntarily about a year afterwards. And when he resigned it what do you think became of him? Why, he sunk into obscurity and disgrace, to be sure, you will say. No such thing. Well, then, what did become of him? Why the President immediately expressed his high disapprobation of his almost unequalled incapability and corruption, by appointing him to a foreign mission, with a salary and outfit of $18,000 a year.—The party now attempt to throw *Barry* off and to avoid the responsibility of his sins.—Did not the President endorse those sins, when on the very heel of their commission, he appointed their author to the very highest and most honorable office in his gift, and which is but a single step behind the very *goal* of American political ambition?

I return to another of Mr. Douglas's excuses for the expenditures of 1838, at the same time announcing the pleasing intelligence, that this is the last one. He says that ten millions of that year's expenditures, was a contingent appropriation, to prosecute an anticipated war with Great Britain, on the Maine boundary question. Few words will settle this. First: that the ten millions appropriated was not *made* till 1839, and consequently could not have been expended in 1838, and, second; although it was appropriated, it has never been expended at all.—Those who heard Mr. Douglas, recollect that he indulged himself in a contemptuous expression of pity for me. "Now he's got me," thought I.—But when he went on to say that five millions of the expenditure of 1838, were payments of the French indemnities, *which I knew to be untrue;* that five millions had been for the Post Office, *which I knew to be untrue,* that ten millions had been for the Maine boundary war, *which I not only knew to be untrue but supremely ridiculous also;* and when I saw that he was stupid enough to hope, that I would permit such groundless and audacious assertions to go unexposed, I readily consented, that on the score of both veracity and sagacity, the audience should judge whether he or I were the more deserving of the world's contempt.

Mr. Lamborn insists that the difference between the Van Buren Party, and the Whigs is, that although the former sometimes err in *practice,* they are always correct in *principle*—whereas the latter are wrong in *principle*—and the better to impress this proposition, he uses a figurative expression in these words: *"The Democrats are vulnerable in the heel, but they are sound in the head and the heart."* The first branch of the figure, that is that the Democrats are vulnerable in the heel, I admit is not merely figuratively, but literally true. Who that looks but for a moment at their Swartwouts, their Prices, their Harringtons, and their hundreds of others, scampering away with the public money to Texas, to Europe, and to every spot of the earth where a villain may hope to find refuge from justice, can at all doubt that they are most distressingly affected in their *heels* with a species of *"running itch."* It seems that this malady of their heels, operates on these *sound-headed* and *honest-hearted* creatures, very much like the cork-leg, in the comic song, did on its owner, which, when he had once got started on it, the more he tried to stop it, the more it would run away. At the hazard of wearing this point thread bare, I will relate an anecdote, which seems too strikingly in point to be omitted. A witty Irish soldier, who was always boasting of his bravery, when no danger was near, but who invariably retreated without orders at the first charge of an engagement, being asked by his Captain why he did so, replied: "Captain, I have as brave a *heart* as Julius Caesar ever had; but somehow or other, whenever danger approaches, my *cowardly* legs will run away with it." So with Mr. Lamborn's party. They take the public money *into* their hand for the most laudable purpose, that *wise heads* and *honest hearts* can dictate; but before they can possibly get it *out* again, their rascally *"vulnerable heels"* will run away with them.

Seriously: this proposition of Mr. Lamborn is nothing more or less, than a request that his party may be tried by their *professions* instead of their *practices*. Perhaps no position that the party assumes is more liable to, or more deserving of exposure, than this very modest request; and nothing but the unwarrantable length to which I have already extended these remarks, forbids me now attempting to expose it. For the reason given, I pass it by.

I shall advert to but one more point.

Mr. Lamborn refers to the late elections in the States, and from their results, confidently predicts, that every State in the Union will vote for Mr. Van Buren at the next Presidential election. Address *that* argument to *cowards* and to *knaves;* with the *free* and the *brave* it will affect nothing. It *may* be true, if it *must,* let it. Many free countries have lost their liberty, and *ours may* lose hers; but if she shall, be it my proudest plume, not that I was the *last* to desert, but that I *never* deserted her.—I know that the great volcano at Washington, aroused and directed by the evil spirit that reigns there, is belching forth the lava of political corruption, in a current broad and deep, which is sweeping with frightful velocity over the whole length and breadth of the land, bidding fair to leave unscathed no green spot or living thing, while on its bosom are riding like demons on the waves of Hell, the imps of that evil spirit, and fiendishly taunting all those who dare resist its destroying course, with the hopelessness of their effort; and knowing this, I cannot deny that all may be swept away. Broken by it, I too, may be; bow to it, I never will. The *probability* that we may fall in the struggle *ought not* to deter us from the support of a cause we believe to be just; it *shall not* deter me. If ever I feel the soul within me elevate and expand to those dimensions not wholly unworthy of its Almighty Architect, it is when I contemplate the cause of my country, deserted by all the world beside, and I standing up boldly alone, and hurling defiance at her victorious oppressors. Here, without contemplating consequences, before High Heaven, and in the face of the world, I swear eternal fidelity to the just cause, as I deem it, of the land of my life, my liberty and my love.—And who, that thinks with me, will not fear-lessly adopt the oath that I take. Let none falter, who thinks he is right, and we may succeed. But, if after all, we shall fail, be it so.—We still shall have the proud consolation of saying to our consciences, and to the departed shade of our country's freedom, that the cause approved of our judgment, and adored of our hearts, in disaster, in chains, in torture, in death, we never faltered in defending.

LETTER TO MISS MARY SPEED
SEPTEMBER 27, 1841

Mary Speed was the half sister of Lincoln's best friend, Joshua Speed. In this letter, Lincoln described his trip through Kentucky where he witnessed slaves shackled together and torn apart from their families only to be sold to crueler masters in the Deep South. The scene prompted Lincoln to ponder "the effect of condition upon human happiness." His conclusion seems to reveal the melancholic part of his character.

BLOOMINGTON, ILLINOIS. SEPT. 27TH, 1841
MISS MARY SPEED
LOUISVILLE, KY.
MY FRIEND:

Having resolved to write to some of your mother's family, and not having the express permission of any one of them [to?] do so, I have had some little diffi-culty in determining on which to inflict the task of reading what I now feel must be a most dull and silly letter; but when I remembered that you and I were some-thing of cronies while I was at Farmington, and that while there, I was under the necessity of shutting you up in a room to prevent your committing an assault and battery upon me, I instantly decided that you should be the devoted one.

I assume that you have not heard from Joshua & myself since we left, because I think it doubtful whether he has written.

You remember there was some uneasiness about Joshua's health when we left. That little indisposition of his turned out to be nothing serious; and it was pretty nearly forgotten when we reached Springfield. We got on board the Steam Boat Lebanon, in the locks of the Canal about 12 o'clock M. of the day we left, and reached St. Louis the next Monday at 8 P. M. Nothing of interest happened during the passage, except the vexatious delays occasioned by the sand bars he thought interesting. By the way, a fine example was presented on board the boat for contemplating the effect of *condition* upon human happiness.

A gentleman had purchased twelve negroes in different parts of Kentucky, and was taking them to a farm in the South. They were chained six and six together. A small iron clevis was around the left wrist of each, and this fastened to the main chain by a shorter one at a convenient distance from the others; so that the negroes were strung together precisely like so many fish upon a trot-line. In this condition they were being separated forever from the scenes of their childhood, their friends, their fathers and mothers, and brothers and sisters, and many of them, from their wives and children, and going into perpetual slavery where the lash of the master is proverbially more ruthless and unrelenting than any other where; and yet amid all these distressing circumstances, as we would think them, they were the most cheerful and apparently happy creatures on board. One whose offence for which he had been sold was an over-fondness for his wife, played the fiddle almost continually; and the others danced, sung, cracked jokes, and played various games with cards from day to day. How true it is that "God tempers the wind to the shorn lamb," or in other words, that he renders the worst of human conditions tolerable, while he permits the best, to be nothing better than tolerable.

To return to the narative [sic]. When we reached Springfield, I staid [sic] but one day when I started on this tedious Circuit where I now am. Do you remember my going to the city, while I was in Kentucky, to have a tooth extracted, and making a failure of it? Well, that same old tooth got to paining me so much, that about a week since I had it torn out, bringing with it a bit of the jawbone; the consequence of which is that my mouth is now so sore that I can neither talk nor eat. I am litterally [sic] "subsisting on savoury remembrances"—that is, being unable to eat, I am living upon the remembrance of the delicious dishes of peaches and cream we used to have at your house.

When we left, Miss Fanny Henning was owing you a visit, as I understood. Has she paid it yet? If she has are you not convinced that she is one of the sweetest girls in the world? There is but one thing about her, so far as I could perceive, that I would have otherwise than as it is. That is something of a tendency to mellancholly [sic]. This, let it be observed, is a misfortune not a fault. Give her an assurance of my very highest regard when you see her.

Is little Siss Eliza Davis at your house yet? If she is kiss her "o'er and o'er again" for me.

Tell your mother that I have not got her "present" with me; but that I intend to read it regularly when I return home. I doubt not that it is really, as she says, the best cure for the "Blues" could one but take it according to the truth.

Give my respects to all your sisters (including "Aunt Emma") and brothers. Tell Mrs. Peay, of whose happy face I shall long retain a pleasant remembrance, that I have been trying to think of a name for her homestead, but as yet, can not satisfy myself with one. I shall be very happy to receive a line from you, soon after you receive this; and, in case you choose to favour me with one, address it to Charleston, Coles County, Ills as I shall be there about the time to receive it.

Your sincere friend
A. Lincoln.

LETTER TO JOSHUA F. SPEED
JANUARY 3, 1842

Joshua Speed was perhaps Lincoln's best friend in Springfield. The two became room-mates when Lincoln moved to the town in 1837. Lincoln's correspondence with Joshua Speed reveals a more intimate side of the young adult. In this letter, Lincoln applied his characteristically logical bent of mind to dispel his friend's prenuptial anxieties.

MY DEAR SPEED:

Feeling, as you know I do, the deepest solicitude for the success of the enterprise you are engaged in, I adopt this as the last method I can invent to aid you, in case (which God forbid) you shall need any aid. I do not place what I am going to say on paper, because I can say it any better in that way than I could by word of mouth; but because, were I to say it orrally [*sic*], before we part, most likely you would forget it at the very time when it might do you some good. As I think it reasonable that you will feel very badly some time between this and the final consummation of your purpose, it is intended that you shall read this just at such a time.

Why I say it is reasonable that you will feel very badly yet, is, because of *three special causes,* added to the *general one* which I shall mention.

The general cause is, that you are *naturally of a nervous temperament;* and this I say from what I have seen of you personally, and what you have told me concerning your mother at various times, and concerning your brother William at the time his wife died.

The first special cause is, *your exposure to bad weather* on your journey, which my experience clearly proves to be very severe on defective nerves. The second is, *the absence of all business and conversation of friends,* which might divert your mind, and give it occasional rest from the *intensity* of thought, which will sometimes wear the sweetest idea threadbare and turn it to the bitterness of death.

The third is, *the rapid and near approach of that crisis on which all your thoughts and feelings concentrate.*

If from all these causes you shall escape and go through triumphantly, without another "twinge of the soul" I shall be most happily, but most egregiously deceived.

If, on the contrary, you shall, as I expect you will at some time, be agonized and distressed, let me, who have some reason to speak with judgment on such a subject, beseech you, to ascribe it to the causes I have mentioned; and not to some false and ruinous suggestion of the Devil.

"But" you will say "do not your causes apply to every one engaged in a like undertaking?"

By no means. *The particular causes,* to a greater or less extent, perhaps do apply in all cases; but the *general one,*—nervous debility, which is the key and conductor of all the particular ones, and without which *they* would be utterly harmless, though it *does* pertain to you, *does not* pertain to one in a thousand. It is out of this, that the painful difference between you and the mass of the world springs.

I know what the painful point with you is, at all times when you are unhappy. It is an apprehension that you do not love her as you should. What nonsense!—How came you to court her? Was it because you thought she desired it, and that you had given her reason to expect it? If it was for that, why did not the same reason make you court Ann Todd, and at least twenty others of whom you can think, to whom it would apply with greater force than to *her?* Did you court her for her wealth? Why, you know she had none. But you say you reasoned yourself *into* it. What do you mean by that? Was it not, that you found yourself unable to *reason* yourself *out of it?* Did you not think, and partly form the purpose, of courting her the first time you ever saw or heard of her? What had reason to do with it, at that early stage? There was nothing *at that time* for reason to work upon. Whether she was moral, amiable, sensible, or even of good character, you did not, nor could then know; except, perhaps you might infer the last from the company you found her in. All you then did or could know of her, was her personal *appearance and deportment;* and these, if they impress at all, impress the *heart,* and not the head.

Say candidly, were not those heavenly *black eyes,* the whole basis of all your early *reasoning* on the subject?

After you and I had once been at her residence, did you not go and take me all the way to Lexington and back, for no other purpose but to get to see her again, on our return, in that seeming to take a trip for that express object?

What earthly consideration would you take to find her scouting and despising you, and giving herself up to another? But of this you have no apprehension; and therefore you can not bring it home to your feelings.

I shall be so anxious about you, that I want you to write every mail.

Your friend

Lincoln

LETTER TO JOSHUA F. SPEED
FEBRUARY 3, 1842

Seeking to encourage his friend to go through with his marriage, Lincoln pointed out that Speed's anxiety over the near death of his fiance was confirmation of true love. At the end of the letter, Lincoln reported that he had been clear of "hypo" or hypochondria, an allusion to one of his periodic bouts of melancholy.

SPRINGFIELD, ILLS. FEBY. 3—1842—

DEAR SPEED:

Your letter of the 25th. Jany. came to hand to-day. You well know that I do not feel my own sorrows much more keenly than I do yours, when I know of them; and yet I assure you I was not much hurt by what you wrote me of your excessively bad feeling at the time you wrote. Not that I am less capable of sympathising with you now than ever; not that I am less your friend than ever; but because I hope and believe, that your present anxiety and distress about *her* health and *her* life, must and will forever banish those horid [*sic*] doubts, which I know you sometimes felt, as to the truth of your affection for her. If they can be once and forever removed, (and I almost feel a presentiment that the Almighty has sent your present affliction expressly for that object) surely, nothing can come in their stead, to fill their immeasurable measure of misery. The death scenes of those we love, are surely painful enough; but these we are prepared to, and expect to see. They happen to all, and all know they must happen. Painful as they are, they are not an unlooked-for-sorrow. Should she, as you fear, be destined to an early grave, it is indeed a great consolation to know that she is so well prepared to meet it. Her religion, which you once disliked so much, I will venture you now prize most highly.

But I hope your melancholly [sic] bodings as to her early death, are not well founded. I even hope, that ere this reaches you, she will have returned with improved and still improving health; and that you will have met her, and forgotten the sorrows of the past, in the enjoyment of the present.

I would say more if I could, but it seems I have said enough. It really appears to me that you yourself ought to rejoice, and not sorrow, at this indubitable evidence of your undying affection for her. Why Speed, if you did not love her, although you might not wish her death, you would most calmly be resigned to it. Perhaps this point is no longer a question with you, and my pertinacious dwelling upon it, is a rude intrusion upon your feelings. If so, you must pardon me. You know the Hell I have suffered on that point, and how tender I am upon it. You know I do not mean wrong.

I have been quite clear of hypo since you left—even better than I was along in the fall.

I have seen Sarah but once. She seemed verry [sic] cheerful, and so, I said nothing to her about what we spoke of.

Old Uncle Billy Herndon is dead; and it is said this evening that Uncle Ben Ferguson will not live. This I believe is all the news, and enough at that unless it were better.

Write me immediately on the receipt of this.

Your friend as ever

Lincoln

TEMPERANCE ADDRESS DELIVERED BEFORE THE SPRINGFIELD WASHINGTON TEMPERANCE SOCIETY
FEBRUARY 22, 1842

The crusade for temperance was part of a broad social reform movement along with abolitionism, women's rights, and care for the mentally ill that swept the nation during the antebellum period. Lincoln's Temperance Speech reveals some of his insights on human nature as well as his political moderation. As with his opposition to slavery, Lincoln spoke against a moral evil while avoiding self-righteousness. A close look at the speech shows that he sought "to prick the conscience" of his audience by eliciting compassion for the addicts. Although he was not a member of the Temperance Society, Lincoln avoided alcohol claiming that it made him "flabby and undone." Straussian scholars have emphasized the philosophical implications of Lincoln's exaltation of the mind over the body at the end of the speech. They interpret the following passage not as a rhetorical flourish but as evidence of Lincoln's secular rationalism and his deterministic ontology: "Happy day, when all appetites controlled, all passions subdued, all matters subjected, mind, all conquering mind, shall live and move the monarch of the world. Glorious consummation! Hail fall of Fury! Reign of Reason, all hail!"

ALTHOUGH THE TEMPERANCE cause has been in progress for near twenty years, it is apparent to all, that it is, *just now,* being crowned with a degree of success, hitherto unparalleled.

The list of its friends is daily swelled by the additions of fifties, of hundreds, and of thousands. The cause itself seems suddenly transformed from a cold abstract theory, to a living, breathing, active, and powerful chieftain, going forth "conquering and to conquer." The citadels of his great adversary are daily being stormed and dismantled; his temples and his altars, where the rites of his idolatrous worship have long been performed, and where human sacrifices have long been wont to be made, are daily desecrated and deserted. The trump of the conqueror's fame is sounding from hill to hill, from sea to sea, and from land to land, and calling millions to his standard at a blast.

For this new and splendid success, we heartily rejoice. That that success is so much greater *now* than *heretofore,* is doubtless owing to rational causes; and if we would have it to continue, we shall do well to enquire what those causes are. The warfare heretofore waged against the demon of Intemperance, has, some how or other, been erroneous. Either the champions engaged, or the tactics they adopted, have not been the most proper. These champions for the most part, have been Preachers, Lawyers, and hired agents.—Between these and the mass of mankind, there is a want of *approachability,* if the term be admissible, partially at least, fatal to their success. They are supposed to have no sympathy of feeling or interest, with those very persons whom it is their object to convince and persuade.

And again, it is so easy and so common to ascribe motives to men of these classes, other than those they profess to act upon. The *preacher,* it is said, advocates temperance because he is a fanatic, and desires a union of the Church and State; the *lawyer,* from his pride and vanity of hearing himself speak; and the *hired agent,* for his salary. But when one, who has long been known as a victim of intemperance, bursts the fetters that have bound him, and appears before his neighbors "clothed, and in his right mind," a redeemed specimen of long lost humanity, and stands up with tears of joy trembling in eyes, to tell of the miseries *once* endured, *now* to be endured no more forever; of his once naked and starving children, now clad and fed comfortably; of a wife, long weighed down with woe, weeping, and a broken heart, now restored to health, happiness and renewed affection; and how easily it all is done, once it is resolved to be done; however simple his language, there is a logic, and an eloquence in it, that few, with human feelings, can resist. They cannot say that *he* desires a union of church and state, for he is not a church member; they can not say *he* is vain of hearing himself speak, for his whole demeanor shows, he would gladly avoid speaking at all; they cannot say *he* speaks for pay for he receives none, and asks for none. Nor can his sincerity in any way be doubted; or his sympathy for those he would persuade to imitate his example, be denied.

In my judgment, it is to the battles of this new class of champions that our late success is greatly, perhaps chiefly, owing.—But, had the old school champions themselves, been of the most wise selecting, was their *system* of tactics, the most judicious? It seems to me, it was not. Too much denunciation against dram sellers and dram drinkers was indulged in. This, I think, was both impolitic and unjust. It was *impolitic,* because, it is not much in the nature of man to be driven to any thing; still less to be driven about that which is exclusively his own business; and least of all, where such driving is to be submitted to, at the expense of pecuniary interest, or burning appetite. When the dram-seller and drinker, were incessantly told, not in the accents of entreaty and persuasion, diffidently addressed by erring man to an erring brother, but in the thundering tones of anathema and denunciation, with which the lordly Judge often groups together all the crimes of the felon's life, and thrusts them in his face just ere he passes sentence of death upon him, that *they* were the authors of all the vice and misery and crime in the land; that *they* were the manufacturers and material of all the thieves and robbers and murderers that infested the earth; that *their* houses were the workshops of the devil; and that *their persons* should be shunned by all the good and virtuous, as moral pestilences—I say, when they were told all this, and in this way, it is not wonderful that they were slow, *very slow,* to acknowledge the truth of such denunciations, and to join the ranks of their denouncers, in a hue and cry against themselves.

To have expected them to do otherwise than as they did—to have expected them not to meet denunciation with denunciation, crimination with crimination, and anathema with anathema, was to expect a reversal of human nature, which is God's decree, and never can be reversed. When the conduct of men is designed to be influenced, *persuasion,* kind, unassuming persuasion, should ever be adopted. It is an old and a true maxim "that a drop of honey catches more flies than a gallon of gall."—So with men. If you would win a man to your cause, *first* convince him that you are his sincere friend. Therein is a drop of honey that catches his heart, which, say what he will, is the great high road to his reason, and which, when once gained, you will find but little trouble in convincing his judgment of the justice of your cause, if indeed that cause really be a just one. On the contrary, assume to dictate to his judgment, or to command his action, or to mark him as one to be shunned and despised, and he will retreat within himself, close all the avenues to his head and his heart; and though your cause be naked truth itself, transformed to the heaviest lance, harder than steel, and sharper than steel can be made, and tho' you throw it with more than Herculean force and precision, you shall be no more able to pierce him, than to penetrate the hard shell of a tortoise with a rye straw.

Such is man, and so *must* he be understood by those who would lead him, even to his own best interest.

On this point, the Washingtonians greatly excel the temperance advocates of former times. Those whom *they* desire to convince and persuade, are their old friends and companions. They know they are not demons, nor even the worst of men. *They* know that generally, they are kind, generous, and charitable, even beyond the example of their more staid and sober neighbors. *They* are practical philanthropists; and *they* glow with a generous and brotherly zeal, that mere theorizers are incapable of feeling.—Benevolence and charity possess *their* hearts entirely; and out of the abundance of their hearts, their tongues give utterance. "Love through all their actions runs, and all their words are mild." In this spirit they speak and act, and in the same, they are heard and regarded. And when such is the temper of the advocate, and such of the audience, no good cause can be unsuccessful.

But I have said that denunciations against dram-sellers and dram-drinkers are *unjust,* as well as impolitic. Let us see.

I have not enquired at what period of time the use of intoxicating drinks commenced; nor is it important to know. It is sufficient that to all of us who now inhabit the world, the practice of drinking them, is just as old as the world itself,— that is, we have seen the one, just as long as we have seen the other. When all such of us, as have now reached the years of maturity, first opened our eyes upon the stage of existence, we found intoxicating liquor, recognized by every body, used by every body, and repudiated by nobody. It commonly entered into the first draught of the infant, and the last draught of the dying man. From the sideboard of the parson, down to the ragged pocket of the houseless loafer, it was constantly found. Physicians prescribed it in this, that, and the other disease. Government provided it for its soldiers and sailors; And to have a rolling or raising, a husking or hoe-down, any where without it was *positively insufferable.*

So too, it was every where a respectable article of manufacture and of merchandize. The making of it was regarded as an honorable livelihood; and he who could make most, was the most enterprising and respectable. Large and small manufactories of it were every where erected, in which all the earthly goods of their owners were invested. Wagons drew it from town to town—boats bore it from clime to clime, and the winds wafted it from nation to nation; and merchants bought and sold it, by wholesale and by retail, with precisely the same feelings, on the part of the seller, buyer, and by-stander as are felt at the selling and buying of flour, beef, bacon, or any other of the real necessaries of life. Universal public opinion not only tolerated, but recognized and adopted its use.

It is true, that even *then,* it was known and acknowledged, that many were greatly injured by it; but none seemed to think the injury arose from the *use* of a *bad thing,* but from the *abuse* of a *very good thing.*—The victims to it were pitied, and compassionated, just as now are, the heirs of consumptions, and other hereditary diseases. Their failing was treated as a *misfortune,* and not as a *crime,* or even as a *disgrace.*

If, then, what I have been saying be true, is it wonderful that *some* should think and act *now,* as *all* thought and acted *twenty years ago?* And is it *just* to assail, contemn, or despise them, for doing so? The universal *sense* of mankind, on any subject, is an argument, or at least an *influence,* not easily overcome. The success of the argument in favor of the existence of an overruling Providence, mainly depends upon that sense; and men ought not, in justice, to be denounced for yielding to it in any case, or for giving it up slowly, *especially,* where they are backed by interest, fixed habits, or burning appetites.

Another error, as it seems to me, into which the old reformers fell, was, the position that all habitual drunkards were utterly incorrigible, and therefore, must be turned adrift, and damned without remedy, in order that the grace of temperance might abound to the temperate *then,* and to all mankind some hundred years *thereafter.*—There is in this something so repugnant to humanity, so uncharitable, so cold-blooded and feelingless, that it never did, nor ever can enlist the enthusiasm of a popular cause. We could not love the man who taught it—we could not hear him with patience. The heart could not throw open its portals to it. The generous man could not adopt it. It could not mix with his blood. It looked so fiendishly selfish, so like throwing fathers and brothers overboard, to lighten the boat for our security—that the noble minded shrank from the manifest meanness of the thing.

And besides this, the benefits of a reformation to be effected by such a system, were too remote in point of time, to warmly engage many in its behalf.

Few can be induced to labor exclusively for posterity; and none will do it enthu-siastically. Posterity has done nothing for us; and theorise on it as we may, prac-tically we shall do very little for it, unless we are made to think, we are, at the same time, doing something for ourselves. What an ignorance of human nature does it exhibit, to ask or expect a whole community to rise up and labor for the *temporal* happiness of *others,* after *themselves* shall be consigned to the dust, a majority of which community take no pains whatever to secure their own eter-nal welfare, at no greater distant day? Great distance, in either time or space, has wonderful power to lull and render quiescent the human mind. Pleasures to be enjoyed, or pains to be endured, *after* we shall be dead and gone, are but little regarded, even in our *own* cases, and much less in the cases of others.

Still, in addition to this, there is something so ludicrous in *promises* of good, or *threats* of evil, a great way off, as to render the whole subject with which they are connected, easily turned into ridicule. "Better lay down that spade you're stealing, Paddy,—if you don't you'll pay for it at the day of judgment." "By the powers, if ye'll credit me so long, I'll take another, jist."

By the Washingtonians, this system of consigning the habitual drunkard to hopeless ruin, is repudiated. *They* adopt a more enlarged philanthropy. *They* go for present as well as future good. *They* labor for all *now* living, as well as all *here-after* to live.—*They* teach *hope* to all—*despair* to none. As applying to *their* cause, *they* deny the doctrine of unpardonable sin. As in Christianity it is taught, so in this *they* teach, that

> "While the lamp holds out to burn,
> The vilest sinner may return."

And, what is a matter of the most profound gratulation, they, by experiment upon experiment, and example upon example, prove the maxim to be no less true in the one case than in the other. On every hand we behold those, who but yesterday, were the chief of sinners, now the chief apostles of the cause. Drunken devils are cast out by ones, by sevens, and by legions; and their unfor-tunate victims, like the poor possessed, who was redeemed from his long and lonely wanderings in the tombs, are publishing to the ends of the earth how great things have been done for them.

To these *new champions,* and this *new* system of tactics, our late success is mainly owing; and to *them* we must chiefly look for the final consummation. The ball is now rolling gloriously on, and none are so able as *they* to increase its speed and its bulk—to add to its momentum, and its magnitude.—Even though unlearned in letters, for this task, none others are so well educated. To fit them for this work, they have been taught in the true school. *They* have been in *that* gulf, from which they would teach others the means of escape. *They* have passed that prison wall, which others have long declared impassable; and who that has not, shall dare to weigh opinions with *them,* as to the mode of passing?

But if it be true, as I have insisted, that those who have suffered by intemperance *personally,* and have reformed, are the most powerful and efficient instruments to push the reformation to ultimate success, it does not follow, that those who have not suffered, have no part left them to perform. Whether or not the world would be vastly benefitted by a total and final banishment from it of all intoxicating drinks, seems to me not *now* to be an open question. Three-fourths of mankind confess the affirmative with their *tongues,* and, I believe, all the rest acknowledge it in their *hearts.*

Ought *any,* then, to refuse their aid in doing what the good of the *whole* demands?—Shall he, who cannot do *much,* be for that reason, excused if he do *nothing*? "But," says one, "what good can I do by signing the pledge? I never drink even without signing." This question has already been asked and answered more than millions of times. Let it be answered once more. For the man to suddenly, or in any other way, to break off from the use of drams, who has indulged in them for a long course of years, and until his appetite for them has become ten or a hundred fold stronger, and more craving, than any natural appetite can be, requires a most powerful moral effort. In such an undertaking, he needs every moral support and influence, that can possibly be brought to his aid, and thrown around him. And not only so; but every moral prop, should be taken *from* whatever argument might rise in his mind to lure him to his backsliding. When he casts his eyes around him, he should be able to see, all that he respects, all that he admires, and all that [he?] loves, kindly and anxiously pointing him onward; and none beckoning him back, to his former miserable "wallowing in the mire."

But it is said by some, that men will *think* and *act* for themselves; that none will disuse spirits or anything else, merely because his neighbors do; and that *moral influence* is not that powerful engine contended for. Let us examine this. Let me ask the man who would maintain this position most stiffly, what compensation he will accept to go to church some Sunday and sit during the sermon with his wife's bonnet upon his head? Not a trifle, I'll venture. And why not? There would be nothing irreligious in it: nothing immoral, nothing uncomfortable.— Then why not? Is it not because there would be something egregiously unfashionable in it? Then it is the influence of *fashion;* and what is the influence of fashion, but the influence that *other* people's actions have on our actions, the strong inclination each of us feels to do as we see all our neighbors do? Nor is the influence of fashion confined to any particular thing or class of things. It is just as strong on one subject as another. Let us make it as unfashionable to withhold our names from the temperance pledge as for husbands to wear their wives' bonnets to church, and instances will be just as rare in the one case as the other.

"But," say some, "we are no drunkards; and we shall not acknowledge ourselves such by joining a reformed drunkards' society, whatever our influence might be." Surely no Christian will adhere to this objection.—If they believe, as they profess, that Omnipotence condescended to take on himself the form of sinful man, and as such, to die an ignominious death for their sakes, surely they will not refuse submission to the infinitely lesser condescension, for the temporal, and perhaps eternal salvation, of a large, erring, and unfortunate class of their own fellow creatures. Nor is the condescension very great.

In my judgment, such of us as have never fallen victims, have been spared more from the absence of appetite, than from any mental or moral superiority over those who have. Indeed, I believe, if we take habitual drunkards as a class, their heads and their hearts will bear an advantageous comparison with those of any other class. There seems ever to have been a proneness in the brilliant, and the warm-blooded, to fall into this vice—the demon of intemperance ever seems to have delighted in sucking the blood of genius and of generosity. What one of us but can call to mind some dear relative, more promising in youth than all his fellows, who has fallen a sacrifice to his rapacity? He ever seems to have gone forth, like the Egyptian angel of death, commissioned to slay if not the first, the fairest born of every family. Shall he now be arrested in his desolating career? In that arrest, all can give aid that will; and who shall be excused that *can* and will not? Far around as human breath has ever blown, he keeps our fathers, our brothers, our sons, and our friends prostrate in the chains of moral death. To all the living every where, we cry, "come sound the moral resurrection trump, that these may rise and stand up, an exceeding great army"—"Come from the four winds, O breath! and breathe upon these slain, that they may live."

If the relative grandeur of revolutions shall be estimated by the great amount of human misery they alleviate, and the small amount they inflict, then indeed, will this be the grandest the world shall ever have seen.—Of our political revolution of '76 we all are justly proud. It has given us a degree of political freedom, far exceeding that of any other of the nations of the earth. In it the world has found a solution of the long mooted problem, as to the capability of man to govern himself. In it was the germ which has vegetated, and still is to grow and expand into the universal liberty of mankind.

But with all these glorious results, past, present, and to come, it had its evils too.—It breathed forth famine, swam in blood and rode on fire; and long, long after, the orphan's cry, and the widow's wail, continued to break the sad silence that ensued. These were the price, the inevitable price, paid for the blessings it bought.

Turn now, to the temperance revolution. In *it* we shall find a stronger bondage broken; a viler slavery manumitted; a greater tyrant deposed. In *it,* more of want supplied, more disease healed, more sorrow assuaged. By *it* no orphans starving, no widows weeping. By *it,* none wounded in feeling, none injured in interest. Even the dram maker and dram seller, will have glided into other occupations *so* gradually, as never to have felt the shock of change; and will stand ready to join all others in the universal song of gladness.

And what a noble ally this, to the cause of political freedom. With such an aid, its march cannot fail to be on and on, till every son of earth shall drink in rich fruition, the sorrow quenching draughts of perfect liberty. Happy day, when, all appetites controlled, all passions subdued, all matters subjected, *mind,* all conquering *mind,* shall live and move the monarch of the world. Glorious consummation! Hail, fall of Fury! Reign of Reason, all hail!

And when the victory shall be complete—when there shall be neither a slave nor a drunkard on the earth—how proud the title of that *Land,* which may truly claim to be the birthplace and the cradle of both those revolutions, that shall have ended in that victory. How nobly distinguished that People, who shall have planted, and nurtured to maturity, both the political and moral freedom of their species.

This is the one hundred and tenth anniversary of the birthday of Washington.—We are met to celebrate this day. Washington is the mightiest name of earth—*long since* mightiest in the cause of civil liberty; *still* mightiest in moral reformation. On that name an eulogy is expected. It cannot be. To add brightness to the sun, or glory to the name of Washington, is alike impossible. Let none attempt it. In solemn awe pronounce the name, and in its naked deathless splendor, leave it shining on.

LETTER TO JOSHUA F. SPEED
JULY 4, 1842

Lincoln's letters to Joshua Speed on February 3 ("I Am Young and Unknown," above) and this one on July 4, 1842, manifest the core elements of his biblical faith. Though his faith deepened with maturity—especially after the death of his son, Willie,

and during the turbulent war years—Lincoln's articulation of this faith remained consis-
tent throughout his life. In this private correspondence, Lincoln assured his friend that life
is guided by a providential design. Things happen for a reason; life is not a series of uncon-
nected random events. Using biblical language existentially, Lincoln conveyed his per-
sonal experience of the divine at work in his own life. He believed that God had made
him "an instrument" in bringing Speed and his fiance, Fanny, together. The letter man-
ifests Lincoln's trust in the graciousness of divine being and his personal reliance upon
God's power. As a faithful servant, he bore witness to God's providence, quoting Exodus *14:13: "Stand still and see the salvation of the Lord," which communicated existen-*
tially his own experience of biblical faith. Despite the inscrutability of the Divine will,
Lincoln trusted that God would bring about some greater good out of his present suffering.

SPRINGFIELD, ILLS—JULY 4TH, 1842—
DEAR SPEED:

Yours of the 16th. June was received only a day or two since. It was not mailed at Louisville till the 25th. You speak of the great time that has elapsed since I wrote you. Let me explain that. Your letter reached here a day or two after I started on the circuit; I was gone five or six weeks, so that I got the letter only a few weeks before Butler started to your country. I thought it scarcely worth while to write you the news, which he could and would tell you more in detail. On his return, he told me you would write me soon; and so I waited for your letter. As to my having been displeased with your advice, surely you know better than that. I know you do; and therefore I will not labor to convince you. True, that subject is painful to me; but it is not your silence, or the silence of all the world that can make me forget it. I acknowledge the correctness of your advice too; but before I resolve to do the one thing or the other, I must regain my confidence in my own ability to keep my resolves when they are made. In that ability, you know, I once prided myself as the only, or at least the chief, gem of my character; that gem I lost—how, and where, you too well know. I have not yet regained it; and until I do, I can not trust myself in any matter of much importance. I believe now that had you understood my case at the time, as well as I understood yours afterwards, by the aid you would have given me, I should have sailed through clear; but that does not now afford me sufficient confidence, to begin that, or the like of that, again.

You make a kind acknowledgment of your obligations to me for your present happiness. I am pleased with that acknowledgment; but a thousand times more am I pleased to know, that you enjoy a degree of happiness, worthy of an acknowledgment. The truth is, I am not sure that there was any merit, with me, in the part I took in your difficulty; I was drawn to it as by fate; if I would, I could not have done less than I did. I always was superstitious; and as part of my superstition, I believe God made me one of the instruments of bringing your Fanny and you together, which union, I have no doubt He had fore-ordained. Whatever he designs, he will do for *me* yet. "Stand *still,* and see the salvation of the Lord" is my text just now. If, as you say, you have told Fanny *all,* I should have no objection to her seeing this letter, but for its reference to our friend here. Let her seeing it, depend upon whether she has ever known anything of my affair; and if she has not, do not let her.

I do not think I can come to Kentucky this season. I am so poor, and make so little headway in the world, that I drop back in a month of idleness, as much as I gain in a year's rowing. I should like to visit you again. I should like to see that "Sis" of yours, that was absent when I was there; tho I suppose she would run away again, if she were to hear I was coming.

About your collecting business. We have sued Branson; and will sue the others to the next court, unless they give deeds of trust as you require. Col Allen happened in the office since I commenced this letter, and promises to give a deed of trust. He says he had made the arrangement to pay you, and would have done it, but for the going down of the Shawnee money. We did not get the note in time to sue Hall at the last Tazewell court. Lockridge's property is levied on for you. John Irwin has done nothing with that Baker & Van Bergen matter. We will not fail to bring the suits for your use, where they are in the name of James Bell & Co. I have made you a suscriber to the Journal; and also sent the number containing the temperance speech. My respect and esteem to all your friends there; and, by your permission, my love to your Fanny.

Ever yours—

Lincoln

CORRESPONDENCE ABOUT THE LINCOLN-SHIELDS DUEL
SEPTEMBER 17, 1842

James Shields was an Illinois State auditor who infuriated Whigs by insisting that tax collectors must accept payment of notes at their actual value, less than half of their inflated value. Under the pseudonym of Rebecca, Lincoln, a devoted Whig, lampooned Shields in a series of articles called the "Lost Townships." The articles were published in the Sangamo Journal, *a Whig newspaper. Upon discovering its author, Shields promptly challenged Lincoln to a duel for "character assassination." In this instance, Lincoln's immoderate political humor almost led to disastrous consequences. However, he would learn from his mistakes. After the fiasco with Shields, he would tone down his personal attacks on political rivals. And he would never publish anonymously again. To protect the honor of his future wife, Mary Todd, Lincoln concealed the fact that the she had written one of the insulting articles.*

TREMONT, SEPT. 17TH, 1842.
A. LINCOLN, ESQ.

I regret that my absence on public business compelled me to postpone a matter of private consideration a little longer than I could have desired. It will only be necessary, however, to account for it by informing you that I have been to Quincy on business that would not admit of delay. I will now state briefly the reasons of my troubling you with this communication, the disagreeable nature of which I regret—as I had hoped to avoid any difficulty with any one in Springfield, while residing there, by endeavoring to conduct myself in such a way amongst both my political friends and opponents, as to escape the necessity of any. Whilst thus abstaining from giving provocation, I have become the object of slander, vituperation and personal abuse, which were I capable of submitting to, I would prove myself worthy of the whole of it.

In two or three of the last numbers of The Sangamo Journal, articles of the most personal nature and calculated to degrade me, have made their appearance. On enquiring I was informed by the editor of that paper, through the medium of my friend, Gen. Whiteside, that you are the author of those articles. This information satisfies me that I have become by some means or other, the object of your secret hostility. I will not take the trouble of enquiring into the reason of all this, but I will take the liberty of requiring a full, positive and absolute retraction of all offensive allusions used by you in these communications, in relation to my private character and standing as a man, as an apology for the insults conveyed in them.

This may prevent consequences which no one will regret more than myself.
Your ob't serv't,
Jas. Shields.

TREMONT, SEPT. 17, 1842.
JAS. SHIELDS, ESQ.

Your note of to-day was handed me by Gen. Whiteside. In that note you say you have been informed, through the medium of the editor of the Journal, that I am the author of certain articles in that paper which you deem personally abusive of you: and without stopping to inquire whether I really am the author, or to point out what is offensive in them, you demand an unqualified retraction of all that is offensive; and then proceed to hint at consequences.

Now, sir, there is in this so much assumption of facts, and so much of menace as to consequences, that I cannot submit to answer that note any farther than I have, and to add, that the consequence to which I suppose you allude, would be matter of as great regret to me as it possibly could to you.

Respectfully,

A. Lincoln.

TREMONT, SEPT. 17, 1842.

A. LINCOLN, ESQ.

In reply to my note of this date, you intimate that I assume facts and menace consequences, and that you cannot submit to answer it further. As now, sir, you desire it, I will be a little more particular. The editor of the Sangamo Journal gave me to understand that you are the author of an article which appeared I think in that paper of the 2d Sept. inst, headed the Lost Townships, and signed Rebecca or Becca. I would therefore take the liberty of asking whether you are the author of said article or any other over the same signature, which has appeared in any of the late numbers of that paper. If so, I repeat my request of an absolute retraction of all offensive allusion contained therein in relation to my private character and standing. If you are not the author of any of the articles, your denial will be sufficient. I will say further, it is not my intention to menace, but to do myself justice.

Your obd't serv't,

Jas. Shields.

MEMORANDUM OF INSTRUCTIONS TO E. H. MERRYMAN, LINCOLN'S SECOND
SEPTEMBER 19, 1842

In response to the lost township articles, Shields challenged Lincoln to a duel. Refusal would have branded Lincoln a coward and seriously undermined his reputation and honor on the frontier where the virtue of courage was paramount. Etiquette demanded that Lincoln prescribe the manner of combat to his second, Elias H. Merryman. Using his wits to avoid both dishonor and bloodshed, Lincoln proposed an absurd scenario in which the two would fight across a plank using cavalry broad swords. If followed, the terms of combat would have given Lincoln a clear advantage on account of his longer reach over his opponent. Fortunately, the duel never took place and the quarrel was resolved without inci-

dent. Apparently, Lincoln was quite ashamed of the entire episode, since he refused to
speak of it again.

IN CASE WHITESIDE SHALL SIGNIFY a wish to adjust this affair without further difficulty, let him know that if the present papers be withdrawn, and a note from Mr. Shields asking to know if I am the author of the articles of which he complains, and asking that I shall make him gentlemanly satisfaction, if I am the author, and this without menace, or dictation as to what that satisfaction shall be, a pledge is made that the following answer shall be given:

> "I did write the 'Lost Townships' letter which appeared in the Journal of the 2d inst., but had no participation in any form, in any other article alluding to you. I wrote that, wholly for political effect. I had no intention of injuring your personal or private character or standing as a man or a gentleman; and I did not then think, and do not now think that that article could produce or has produced that effect against you; and had I anticipated such an effect would have forborne to write it. And I will add that your conduct toward me, so far as I knew, had always been gentlemanly; and that I had no personal pique against you, and no cause for any."

If this should be done, I leave it with you to manage what shall and what shall not be published.

If nothing like this is done, the preliminaries of the fight are to be—

1st. WEAPONS —Cavalry broad swords of the largest size precisely equal in all respects—and such as now used by the cavalry company at Jacksonville.

2d. POSITION—A plank ten feet long, and from nine to twelve inches broad, to be firmly fixed on edge, on the ground, as the line between us, which neither is to pass his foot over upon forfeit of his life. Next a line drawn on the ground on either side of said plank and parallel with it, each at the distance of the whole length of the sword and three feet additional from the plank; and the passing of his own such line by either party during the fight, shall be deemed a surrender of the contest.

3d. TIME —On Thursday evening at 5 o'clock if you can get it so; but in no case to be at a greater distance of time than Friday evening, at 5 o'clock.

4th. PLACE—Within three miles of Alton, on the opposite side of the river, the particular spot to be agreed on by you.

Any preliminary details coming within the above rules, you are at liberty to make at your discretion, but you are in no case to swerve from these rules or to pass beyond their limits.

"MY CHILDHOOD HOME I SEE AGAIN" AND "THE BEAR HUNT" [1846]

These two poems were inspired when Lincoln briefly revisited his childhood home in Indiana. They convey a bleak but poignant reflection on the ephemeral character of life, the nostalgic longing for lost youth, the propensity for human cruelty, the tragedy of madness, and the omnipresence of death.

[I]
My childhood-home I see again,
And gladden with the view;
And still as mem'ries crowd my brain,
There's sadness in it too.

O memory! thou mid-way world
'Twixt Earth and Paradise,
Where things decayed, and loved ones lost
In dreamy shadows rise.

And freed from all that's gross or vile,
Seem hallowed, pure, and bright,
Like scenes in some enchanted isle,
All bathed in liquid light.

As distant mountains please the eye,
When twilight chases day—
As bugle-tones, that, passing by,
In distance die away—

As leaving some grand water-fall
We ling'ring, list it's roar,
So memory will hallow all
We've known, but know no more.

Now twenty years have passed away,
Since here I bid farewell
To woods, and fields, and scenes of play
And school-mates loved so well.

Where many were, how few remain
Of old familiar things!
But seeing these to mind again
The lost and absent brings.

The friends I left that parting day—
How changed, as time has sped!
Young childhood grown, strong manhood gray,
And half of all are dead.

I hear the lone survivors tell
How nought from death could save,
Till every sound appears a knell,
And every spot a grave.

I range the fields with pensive tread,
And pace the hollow rooms;
And feel (companions of the dead)
I'm living in the tombs.

[II]

A[nd] here's an object more of dread,
Than aught the grave contains—
A human-form, with reason fled,
While wretched life remains.

Poor Matthew! Once of genius bright,—
A fortune-favored child—
Now locked for aye, in mental night,
A haggard mad-man wild.

Poor Matthew! I have ne'er forgot
When first with maddened will,
Yourself you maimed, your father fought,
And mother strove to kill;

And terror spread, and neighbors ran,
Your dang'rous strength to bind;
And soon a howling crazy man,
Your limbs were fast confined.

How then you writhed and shrieked aloud,
Your bones and sinews bared;
And fiendish on the gaping crowd,
With burning eye-balls glared.

And begged, and swore, and wept, and prayed,
With maniac laughter joined—
How fearful are the signs displayed,
By pangs that kill the mind!

And when at length, the drear and long
Time soothed your fiercer woes—
How plaintively your mournful song,
Upon the still night rose.

I've heard it oft, as if I dreamed,
Far-distant, sweet, and lone;
The funeral dirge it ever seemed
Of reason dead and gone.

To drink its strains, I've stole away,
All silently and still,
Ere yet the rising god of day
Had streaked the Eastern hill.

Air held his breath; the trees all still
Seemed sorr'wing angels round.
Their swelling tears in dew-drops fell
Upon the list'ning ground.

But this is past, and naught remains
That raised you o'er the brute.
Your mad'ning shrieks, and soothing strains
Are like forever mute.

Now fare thee well: more thou the cause
Than subject now of woe.
All mental pangs, by time's kind laws,
Hast lost the power to know.

O death! thou awe-inspiring prince,
That keepst the world in fear;
Why dost thou tear more blest ones hence,
And leave him ling'ring here?—

And now away to seek some scene
Less painful than the last—
With less of horror mingled in
The present and the past.

The very spot where grew the bread
That formed my bones, I see.
How strange, old field, on thee to tread
And feel I'm part of thee!

"THE BEAR HUNT." [1846]
A wild-bear chace, didst never see?
Then hast thou lived in vain.
Thy richest bump of glorious glee,
Lies desert in thy brain.

When first my father settled here,
'Twas then the frontier line:
The panther's scream, filled night with fear
And bears preyed on the swine.

But wo for Bruin's short lived fun,
When rose the squealing cry;
Now man and horse, with dog and gun,
For vengeance, at him fly.

A sound of danger strikes his ear;
He gives the breeze a snuff;
Away he bounds, with little fear,
And seeks the tangled *rough*.

On press his foes, and reach the ground,
Where's left his half munched meal;
The dogs, in circles, scent around,
And find his fresh made trail.

With instant cry, away they dash,
And men as fast pursue;
O'er logs they leap, through water splash,
And shout the brisk halloo.

Now to elude the eager pack,
Bear shuns the open ground;
Though [sic] matted vines, he shapes his track
And runs it, round and round.

The tall fleet cur, with deep-mouthed voice,
Now speeds him, as the wind;
While half-grown pup, and short-legged fice,
Are yelping far behind.

And fresh recruits are dropping in
To join the merry *corps:*
With yelp and yell,—a mingled din—
The woods are in a roar.

And round, and round the chace now goes,
The world's alive with fun;
Nick Carter's horse, his rider throws,
And more, Hill drops his gun.

Now sorely pressed, bear glances back,
And lolls his tired tongue;
When is, to force him from his track,
An ambush on him sprung.

Across the glade he sweeps for flight,
And fully is in view.
The dogs, new-fired, by the sight,
Their cry, and speed, renew.

The foremost ones, now reach his rear,
He turns, they dash away;
And circling now, the wrathful bear,
They have him full at bay.

At top of speed, the horse-men come,
All screaming in a row.
"Whoop! Take him Tiger—Seize him Drum"—
Bang,—Bang—the rifles go.

And furious now, the dogs he tears.
And crushes in his ire—
Wheels right and left, and upward rears,
With eyes of burning fire.

But leaden death is at his heart,
Vain all the strength he plies—
And, spouting blood from every part,
He reels, and sinks, and dies.

And now a dinsome clamor rose,
'Bout who should have his skin;
Who first draws blood, each hunter knows,
This prize must always win.

But who did this, and how to trace
What's true from what's a lie,
Like lawyers, in a murder case
They stoutly *argufy*.

Aforesaid fice, of blustering mood,
Behind, and quite forgot,
Just now emerging from the wood,
Arrives upon the spot.

With grinning teeth, and up-turned hair—
Brim full of spunk and wrath,
He growls, and seizes on dead bear,
And shakes for life and death.

And swells as if his skin would tear,
And growls and shakes again;
And swears, as plain as dog can swear,
That he has won the skin.

Conceited whelp! we laugh at thee—
Nor mind, that not a few
Of pompous, two-legged dogs there be,
Conceited quite as you.

RESOLUTIONS IN THE UNITED STATES HOUSE OF REPRESENTATIVES
DECEMBER 22, 1847

Lincoln wrote these resolutions when he was serving his first and only term in the United States House of Representatives of the Thirtieth Congress. The fighting during the Mexican war had ended shortly before he arrived in Washington D.C. When he entered the House, the Whigs and Democrats were debating the question of whether or not the war was just. The Whigs, led by Lincoln's hero Henry Clay, claimed that the Democratic president, James K. Polk, had provoked the Mexican War by sending troops into Mexican territory. Lincoln agreed and joined his party in condemning American aggression. When a Democratic representative from Illinois proposed a resolution that vindicated Polk and blamed Mexico for initiating hostilities in order to gain congressional support for a greater indemnity, Lincoln countered with his "Spot Resolutions." Rejecting Polk's justification of the war as a purely defensive action, Lincoln alleged that hostilities were commenced on Mexican, not American, soil. He then challenged the president to identify the very spot where first blood was spilled. Lincoln's stance did not make him popular back home in Illinois. William Herndon, his law partner, worried that it would ruin Lincoln's political career.

WHEREAS the President of the United States, in his message of May 11, 1846, has declared that "the Mexican Government not only refused to receive him, [the envoy of the United States,] or listen to his propositions, but, after a long-continued series of menaces, has at last invaded *our territory* and shed the blood of our fellow-citizens on our *own soil:*"

And again, in his message of December 8, 1846, that "we had ample cause of war against Mexico long before the breaking out of hostilities; but even then we forbore to take redress into our own hands until Mexico herself became the aggressor, by invading *our soil* in hostile array, and shedding the blood of our citizens:"

And yet again, in his message of December 7, 1847, that "the Mexican Government refused even to hear the terms of adjustment which he [our minister of peace] was authorized to propose, and finally, under wholly unjustifiable pretexts, involved the two countries in war, by invading the territory of the State of Texas, striking the first blow, and shedding the blood of our citizens on *our own soil.*"

And whereas this House is desirous to obtain a full knowledge of all the facts which go to establish whether the particular spot on which the blood of our citizens was so shed was or was not at that time *our own soil:* Therefore,

Resolved By the House of Representatives, That the President of the United States be respectfully requested to inform this House—

1*st.* Whether the spot on which the blood of our citizens was shed, as in his messages declared, was or was not within the territory of Spain, at least after the treaty of 1819, until the Mexican revolution.

2*d.* Whether that spot is or is not within the territory which was wrested from Spain by the revolutionary Government of Mexico.

3*d.* Whether that spot is or is not within a settlement of people, which settlement has existed ever since long before the Texas revolution, and until its inhabitants fled before the approach of the United States army.

4*th.* Whether that settlement is or is not isolated from any and all other settlements by the Gulf and the Rio Grande on the south and west, and by wide uninhabited regions on the north and east.

5*th.* Whether the people of that settlement, or a majority of them, or any of them, have ever submitted themselves to the government or laws of Texas or of the United States, by consent or by compulsion, either by accepting office, or voting at elections, or paying tax, or serving on juries, or having process served upon them, or in any other way.

6*th.* Whether the people of that settlement did or did not flee from the approach of the United States army, leaving unprotected their homes and their growing crops, *before* the blood was shed, as in the messages stated; and whether the first blood, so shed, was or was not shed within the enclosure of one of the people who had thus fled from it.

7*th.* Whether our *citizens,* whose blood was shed, as in his message declared, were or were not, at that time, armed officers and soldiers, sent into that settlement by the military order of the President, through the Secretary of War.

8*th.* Whether the military force of the United States was or was not so sent into that settlement after General Taylor had more than once intimated to the

War Department that, in his opinion, no such movement was necessary to the defence or protection of Texas.

THE WAR WITH MEXICO: SPEECH IN THE UNITED STATES HOUSE OF REPRESENTATIVES
JANUARY 12, 1848

Admonishing Polk for his abuse of executive power, Lincoln invoked the example of George Washington, his inspirational model whom he praised in the Lyceum Address. Lincoln used the biblical story of Abel and Caine to convey didactically a teaching about moral guilt and political accountability. Although Polk may have escaped legal punishment, he was still accountable to God the Almighty, the ultimate moral authority. A day of reckoning was at hand. Polk's guilty conscience would not allow him to evade responsibility since "the blood of this war, like the blood of Abel, is crying to Heaven against him." Even a cursory reading of Lincoln's speeches and writings reveals that they were imbued profoundly with a biblical ethos and style.

MR. CHAIRMAN:

Some, if not all, the gentlemen on the other side of the House, who have addressed the committee within the last two days, have spoken rather complainingly, if I have rightly understood them, of the vote given a week or ten days ago, declaring that the war with Mexico was unnecessarily and unconstitutionally commenced by the President. I admit that such a vote should not be given in mere party wantonness, and that the one given is justly censurable, if it have no other or better foundation. I am one of those who joined in that vote; and I did so under my best impression of the *truth* of the case. How I got this impression, and how it may possibly be removed, I will now try to show. When the war began, it was my opinion that all those who, because of knowing too *little,* or because of knowing too *much,* could not conscientiously approve the conduct of the President, (in the beginning of it,) should, nevertheless, as good citizens and patriots, remain silent on that point, at least till the war should be ended. Some leading Democrats, including ex-President Van Buren, have taken this same view, as I understand them; and I adhered to it and acted upon it, until since I took my seat here; and I think I should still adhere to it, were it not that the President and his friends will not allow it to be so. Besides, the continual effort of the President to argue every silent vote given for supplies into an endorsement of the justice and wisdom of his conduct; besides that singularly candid paragraph in his late message, in which he tells us that Congress, with great unanimity, (only two in the Senate and fourteen in the House dissenting,) had declared that "by the act of the Republic of Mexico a state of war exists between that Government and the United States;" when the same journals that informed him of this, also informed him that, when that declaration stood disconnected from the question of supplies, sixty-seven in the House, and not fourteen, merely, voted against it; besides this open attempt to prove by telling the *truth,* what he could not prove by telling the *whole truth,* demanding of all who will not submit to be misrepresented, in justice to themselves, to speak out; besides all this, one of my colleagues, [MR. RICHARDSON,] at a very early day in the session, brought in a set of resolutions, expressly indorsing the original justice of the war on the part of the President. Upon these resolutions, when they shall be put on their passage, I shall be *compelled* to vote; so that I cannot be silent if I would. Seeing this, I went about preparing myself to give the vote understandingly, when it should come. I carefully examined the President's messages, to ascertain what he himself had said and proved upon the point. The result of this examination was to make the impression, that, taking for true all the President states as facts, he falls far short of proving his justification; and that the President would have gone further with his proof, if it had not been for the small matter that the *truth* would not permit him. Under the impression thus made, I gave the vote before mentioned. I propose now to give, concisely, the process of the examination I made, and how I reached the conclusion I did.

The President, in his first message of May, 1846, declares that the soil was *ours* on which hostilities were commenced by Mexico; and he repeats that declaration, almost in the same language, in each successive annual message—thus showing that he esteems that point a highly essential one. In the importance of that point, I entirely agree with the President. To my judgment, it is the *very point* upon which he should be justified or condemned. In his message of December, 1846, it seems to have occurred to him, as is certainly true, that title, ownership to soil or anything else, is not a simple fact, but is a conclusion following one or more simple facts; and that it was incumbent upon him to present the facts from which he concluded the soil was ours on which the first blood of the war was shed.

Accordingly, a little below the middle of page twelve, in the message last referred to, he enters upon that task; forming an issue and introducing testimony, extending the whole to a little below the middle of page fourteen. Now, I propose to try to show that the whole of this—issue and evidence—is, from beginning to end, the sheerest deception. The issue, as he presents it, is in these words: "But there are those who, conceding all this to be true, assume the ground that the true western boundary of Texas is the Nueces, instead of the

Rio Grande; and that, therefore, in marching our army to the east bank of the latter river, we passed the Texan line, and invaded the territory of Mexico." Now, this issue is made up of two affirmatives and no negative. The main deception of it is, that it assumes as true that *one* river or the *other* is necessarily the boundary, and cheats the superficial thinker entirely out of the idea that *possibly* the boundary is somewhere *between* the two, and not actually at either. A further deception is, that it will let in *evidence* which a true issue would exclude. A true issue made by the President would be about as follows: "I say the soil *was ours* on which the first blood was shed; there are those who say it was not."

I now proceed to examine the President's evidence, as applicable to such an issue. When that evidence is analyzed, it is all included in the following propositions:

1. That the Rio Grande was the western boundary of Louisiana, as we purchased it of France in 1803.
2. That the Republic of Texas always *claimed* the Rio Grande as her western boundary.
3. That, by various acts, she had claimed it *on paper*.
4. That Santa Anna, in his treaty with Texas, recognized the Rio Grande as her boundary.
5. That Texas *before,* and the United States *after* annexation, had *exercised* jurisdiction *beyond* the Nueces, *between* the two rivers.
6. That our Congress *understood* the boundary of Texas to extend beyond the Nueces.

Now for each of these in its turn:

His first item is, that the Rio Grande was the western boundary of Louisiana, as we purchased it of France in 1803; and, seeming to expect this to be disputed, he argues over the amount of nearly a page to prove it true; at the end of which, he lets us know that, by the treaty of 1819, we sold to Spain the whole country, from the Rio Grande eastward to the Sabine. Now, admitting, for the present, that the Rio Grande was the boundary of Louisiana, what, under heaven, had that to do with the *present* boundary between us and Mexico? How, Mr. Chairman, the line that once divided your land from mine can *still* be the boundary between us *after* I have sold my land to you, is, to me, beyond all comprehension. And how any man, with an honest purpose only of proving the truth, could ever have *thought* of introducing such a fact to prove such an issue, is equally incomprehensible. The outrage upon common *right,* of seizing as our own what we have once sold, merely because it *was* ours *before* we sold it, is only equalled by the outrage on common *sense* of any attempt to justify it.

The President's next piece of evidence is, that "the Republic of Texas always *claimed* this river (Rio Grande) as her western boundary." That is not true, in fact. Texas *has* claimed it, but she has not *always* claimed it. There is, at least, one distinguished exception. Her State constitution—the Republic's most solemn and well-considered act; that which may, without impropriety, be called her last will and testament, revoking all others—makes no such claim. But suppose she had always claimed it. Has not Mexico always claimed the contrary? So that there is but *claim* against *claim,* leaving nothing proved until we get back of the claims, and find which has the better *foundation*.

Though not in the order in which the President presents his evidence, I now consider that class of his statements, which are, in substance, nothing more than that Texas has, by various acts of her Convention and Congress, claimed the Rio Grande as her boundary—*on paper*. I mean here what he says about the fixing of the Rio Grande as her boundary, in her old constitution, (not her State constitution,) about forming congressional districts, counties, &c. Now, all of this is but naked *claim;* and what I have already said about claims is strictly applicable to this. If I should claim your land by word of mouth, that certainly would not make it mine; and if I were to claim it by a deed which I had made myself, and with which you had had nothing to do, the claim would be quite the same in substance, or rather in utter nothingness.

I next consider the President's statement that Santa Anna, in his *treaty* with Texas, recognized the Rio Grande as the western boundary of Texas. Besides the position so often taken that Santa Anna, while a prisoner of war—a captive—*could* not bind Mexico by a treaty, which I deem conclusive; besides this, I wish to say something in relation to this treaty,* so called by the President, with Santa Anna. If any man would like to be amused by a sight at that *little* thing, which the President calls by that *big* name, he can have it by turning to Niles's Register, volume 50, page 336. And if any one should suppose that Niles's Register is a curious repository of so mighty a document as a solemn treaty between nations, I can only say that I learned, to a tolerable degree of certainty, by inquiry at the State Department, that the President himself never saw it anywhere else. By the way, I believe I should not err if I were to declare, that during the first ten years of the existence of that document, it was never by anybody *called* a treaty; that it was never so called till the President, in his extremity, attempted, by so calling it, to wring something from it in justification of himself in connection with the Mexican war. It has none of the distinguishing features of a treaty. It does not call itself a treaty. Santa Anna does not therein assume to bind Mexico; he assumes only to act as the President, Commander-in-chief of the Mexican army and navy; stipulates that the then present hostilities should cease, and that he would not *himself* take up arms, nor *influence* the Mexican people to take up arms, against Texas, during the existence of the war of independence. He did not recognize the independence of Texas; he did not assume to put an end to the war, but clearly indicated his expectation of its continuance; he did not say one word about boundary, and most probably never thought of it. It *is* stipulated therein that the Mexican forces should evacuate the territory of Texas, *passing to the other side of the Rio Grande;* and in another article it is stipulated, that to prevent collisions between the armies, the Texan army should not approach nearer than within five leagues—of *what* is not said—but clearly, from the object stated, it is of the Rio Grande. Now, if this is a treaty recognizing the Rio Grande as the boundary of Texas, it contains the singular feature of stipulating that Texas shall not go within five leagues of *her own* boundary.

Next comes the evidence of Texas before annexation, and the United States afterwards, *exercising* jurisdiction *beyond* the Nueces, and *between* the two rivers. This actual *exercise* of jurisdiction is the very class or quality of evidence we want. It is excellent so far as it goes; but does it go far enough? He tells us it went *beyond* the Nueces, but he does not tell us it went *to* the Rio Grande. He tells us jurisdiction was exercised *between* the two rivers, but he does not tell us it was exercised over *all* the territory between them. Some simple-minded people think it *possible* to cross one river and go *beyond* it, without going *all the way* to the next; that jurisdiction may be exercised *between* two rivers without covering *all* the country between them. I know a man, not very unlike myself, who exercises jurisdiction over a piece of land between the Wabash and the Mississippi; and yet so far is this from being *all* there is between those rivers, that it is just one hundred and fifty-two feet long by fifty wide, and no part of it much within a hundred miles of either. He has a neighbor between him and the Mississippi— that is, just across the street, in that direction—whom, I am sure, he could neither *persuade* nor *force* to give up his habitation; but which, nevertheless, he could certainly annex, if it were to be done, by merely standing on his own side of the street and *claiming* it, or even sitting down and writing a *deed* for it.

But next, the President tells us, the Congress of the United States *understood* the State of Texas they admitted into the Union to extend *beyond* the Nueces. Well, I suppose they did—I certainly so understand it—but how *far* beyond? That Congress did *not* understand it to extend clear to the Rio Grande, is quite certain by the fact of their joint resolutions for admission expressly leaving all questions of boundary to future adjustment. And, it may be added, that Texas herself is proved to have had the same understanding of it that our Congress had, by the fact of the exact conformity of her new constitution to those resolutions.

I am now through the whole of the President's evidence; and it is a singular fact, that if any one should declare the President sent the army into the midst of a settlement of Mexican people, who had never submitted, by consent or by force to the authority of Texas or of the United States, and that *there,* and *thereby,* the first blood of the war was shed, there is not one word in all the President has said which would either admit or deny the declaration. In this strange omission chiefly consists the deception of the President's evidence—an omission which, it does seem to me, could scarcely have occurred but by design. My way of living leads me to be about the courts of justice; and there I have sometimes seen a good lawyer, struggling for his client's neck, in a desperate case, employing every artifice to work round, befog, and cover up with many words some position pressed upon him by the prosecution, which he *dared* not admit, and yet *could* not deny. Party bias may help to make it appear so; but, with all the allowance I can make for such bias, it still does appear to me that just such, and from just such necessity, is the President's struggles in this case.

Some time after my colleague [MR. RICHARDSON] introduced the resolutions I have mentioned, I introduced a preamble, resolution, and interrogatories, intended to draw the President out, if possible, on this hitherto untrodden ground. To show their relevancy, I propose to state my understanding of the true rule for ascertaining the boundary between Texas and Mexico. It is, that *wherever* Texas was *exercising* jurisdiction was hers; and *wherever Mexico* was exercising jurisdiction was hers; and that *whatever* separated the actual exercise of jurisdiction of the one from that of the other, was the true boundary between them. If, as is probably true, Texas was exercising jurisdiction along the western bank of the Nueces, and Mexico was exercising it along the eastern bank of the Rio Grande, then *neither* river was the boundary, but the uninhabited country between the two was. The extent of our territory in that region depended, not on any *treaty-fixed* boundary, (for no treaty had attempted it,) but on revolution. Any people anywhere, being inclined and having the power, have the *right* to rise up and shake off the existing government, and form a new one that suits them better. This is a most valuable, a most sacred right—a right which, we hope and believe, is to liberate the world. Nor is this right confined to cases in which the whole people of an existing government may choose to exercise it. Any portion of such people that *can may* revolutionize, and make their *own* of so much of the territory as they inhabit. More than this, a *majority* of any portion of such people may revolutionize, putting down a *minority,* intermingled with, or near about them, who may oppose their movements. Such minority was precisely the case of the Tories of our own Revolution. It is a quality of revolutions not to go by *old* lines, or *old* laws; but to break up both, and make new ones. As to the country now in question, we bought it of France in 1803, and sold it to Spain in 1819, according to the President's statement. After this, all Mexico, including Texas, revolutionized against Spain; and still later, Texas revolutionized against Mexico. In my view, just so far as she carried her revolution, by obtaining the *actual,* willing or unwilling, submission of the people, *so far* the country was hers, and no farther.

Now, sir, for the purpose of obtaining the very best evidence as to whether Texas had actually carried her revolution to the place where the hostilities of the present war commenced, let the President answer the interrogatories I proposed, as before mentioned, or some other similar ones. Let him answer fully, fairly, and candidly. Let him answer with *facts,* and not with arguments. Let him remember he sits where Washington sat; and, so remembering, let him answer as Washington would answer. As a nation *should* not, and the Almighty *will* not, be evaded, so let him attempt no evasion, no equivocation. And if, so answering, he can show that the soil was ours where the first blood of the war was shed—that it was not within an inhabited country, or, if within such, that the inhabitants had submitted themselves to the civil authority of Texas, or of the United States, and that the same is true of the site of Fort Brown—then I am with him for his justification. In that case, I shall be most happy to reverse the vote I gave the other day. I have a selfish motive for desiring that the President may do this; I expect to give some votes, in connection with the war, which, without his so doing, will be of doubtful propriety, in my own judgment, but which will be free from the doubt, if he does so. But if he *cannot* or *will not* do this—if, on any pretence, or no pretence, he shall refuse or omit it—then I shall be fully convinced, of what I more than suspect already, that he is deeply conscious of being in the wrong; that he feels the blood of this war, like the blood of Abel, is crying to Heaven against him; that he ordered General Taylor into the midst of a peaceful Mexican settlement, purposely to bring on a war; that originally having some strong motive—what I will not stop now to give my opinion concerning—to involve the two countries in a war, and trusting to escape scrutiny by fixing the public gaze upon the exceeding brightness of military glory—that attractive rainbow that rises in showers of blood—that serpent's eye that charms to destroy—he plunged into it, and has swept *on* and *on,* till, disappointed in his calculation of the ease with which Mexico might be subdued, he now finds himself he knows not where. How like the half-insane mumbling of a fever dream is the whole war part of the late message! At one time telling us that Mexico has nothing whatever that we can get but territory; at another, showing us how we can support the war by levying contributions on Mexico. At one time urging the national honor, the security of the future, the prevention of foreign interference, and even the good of Mexico herself, as among the objects of the war; at another, telling us that, "to reject indemnity, by refusing to accept a cession of territory, would be to abandon all our just demands, and to wage the war, bearing all its expenses, *without a purpose or definite object.*" So, then, the national honor, security of the future, and everything but territorial indemnity, may be considered the *no-purposes* and *indefinite* objects of the war! But, having it now settled that territorial indemnity is the only object, we are urged to seize, by legislation here, all that he was content to take a few months ago, and the whole province of Lower California to boot, and to still carry on the war—to take *all* we are fighting for, and *still* fight on. Again, the President is resolved, under all circumstances, to have full territorial indemnity for the expenses of the war; but he forgets to tell us how we are to get the *excess* after those expenses shall have surpassed the value of the *whole* of the Mexican territory. So, again, he insists that the separate national existence of Mexico shall be maintained; but he does not tell us *how* this can be done after we shall have taken *all* her territory. Lest the questions I here suggest be considered speculative merely, let me be indulged a moment in trying to show they are not.

The war has gone on some twenty months; for the expenses of which, together with an inconsiderable old score, the President now claims about one half of the Mexican territory, and that by far the better half, so far as concerns our ability to make anything out of it. *It* is comparatively uninhabited; so that we could establish land offices in it, and raise some money in that way. But the other half is already inhabited, as I understand it, tolerably densely for the nature of the country; and all its lands, or all that are valuable, already appropriated as private property. How, then, are we to make anything out of these lands with this encumbrance on them, or how remove the encumbrance? I suppose no one will say we should kill the people, or drive them out, or make slaves of them, or even confiscate their property? How, then, can we make much out of this part of the territory? If the prosecution of the war has, in expenses, already equaled the *better* half of the country, how long its future prosecution will be in equaling the less valuable half is not a *speculative,* but a *practical* question, pressing closely upon us; and yet it is a question which the President seems never to have thought of.

As to the mode of terminating the war and securing peace, the President is equally wandering and indefinite. First, it is to be done by a more vigorous prosecution of the war in the vital parts of the enemy's country; and, after apparently talking himself tired on this point, the President drops down into a half despairing tone, and tells us, that "with a people distracted and divided by contending factions, and a Government subject to constant changes, by successive revolutions, *the continued success of our arms may fail to obtain a satisfactory peace.*" Then he suggests the propriety of wheedling the Mexican people to desert the counsels of their own leaders, and, trusting in our protection, to set up a Government from which we can secure a satisfactory peace, telling us that *"this may become the only mode of obtaining such a peace."* But soon he falls into doubt of this too, and then drops back on to the already half-abandoned ground of "more vigorous prosecution." All this shows that the President is in no wise satisfied with his own positions. First, he takes up one, and, in attempting to argue us *into* it, he argues himself *out* of it; then seizes another, and goes through the same process; and then, confused at being able to think of nothing new, he snatches up the old one again, which he has some time before cast off. His mind, tasked beyond its power, is running hither and thither, like some tortured creature on a burning surface, finding no position on which it can settle down and be at ease.

Again, it is a singular omission in this message, that it nowhere intimates *when* the President expects the war to terminate. At its beginning, General Scott was, by this same President, driven into disfavor, if not disgrace, for intimating that peace could not be conquered in less than three or four months. But now, at the end of about twenty months, during which time our arms have given us the most splendid successes—every department, and every part, land and water, officers and privates, regulars and volunteers, doing all that men *could* do, and hundreds of things which it had ever before been thought men could *not* do; after all this, this same President gives us a long message without showing us that, *as to the end,* he has himself even an imaginary conception. As I have before said, he knows not where he is. He is a bewildered, confounded, and miserably-perplexed man. God grant he may be able to show there is not something about his conscience more painful than all his mental perplexity!

LETTER TO WILLIAM H. HERNDON
FEBRUARY 15, 1848

William Herndon was Lincoln's law partner and friend in Springfield. He would later publish important revisionist accounts of the Sixteenth President's early life. Seeing the popular backlash in Illinois against Lincoln's stance on the Mexican War, Herndon wrote to his partner in Washington advising him to tone down his attack on President Polk. Excoriating Lincoln as a coward and traitor, Democrats contemptuously referred to him as "Spotty Lincoln,"—a reference to his spot resolutions which challenged the president to identify the very spot where American blood was first spilled. Lincoln's reply to Herndon manifests the virtue of integrity that made him worthy of the name "honest Abe." He explained that despite popularity and expedience, he would not vote against his conscience. To have voted for a resolution that vindicated Polk would have constituted a "bald faced" lie.

WASHINGTON, FEB. 15, 1848
DEAR WILLIAM:

Your letter of the 29th. Jany. was receved [*sic*] last night. Being exclusively a constitutional argument, I wish to submit some reflections upon it in the same spirit of kindness that I know actuates you. Let me first state what I understand to be your position. It is, that if it shall become *necessary, to repel invasion,* the President may, without violation of the Constitution, cross the line, and *invade* the teritory [*sic*] of another country; and that whether such *necessity* exists in any given case, the President is to be the *sole* judge.

Before going further, consider well whether this is, or is not your position. If it is, it is a position that neither the President himself, nor any friend of his, so far as I know, has ever taken. Their only positions are first, that the soil was *ours* where hostilities commenced, and second, that whether it was rightfully *ours* or not, *Congress had annexed it,* and the President, for that reason was bound to defend it, both of which are as clearly proved to be false in fact, as you can prove that your house is not mine. That soil was not ours; and Congress did not annex or attempt to annex it. But to return to your position: Allow the President to invade a neighboring nation, whenever *he* shall deem it necessary to repel an invasion, and you allow him to do so, *whenever he may choose to say* he deems it necessary for such purpose—and you allow him to make war at pleasure. Study to see if you can fix *any limit* to his power in this respect, after you have given him so much as you propose. If, to-day, he should choose to say he thinks it necessary to invade Canada, to prevent the British from invading us, how could you stop him? You may say to him, "I see no probability of the British invading us" but he will say to you "be silent; I see it, if you dont."

The provision of the Constitution giving the war-making power to Congress, was dictated, as I understand it, by the following reasons. Kings had always been involving and impoverishing their people in wars, pretending generally, if not always, that the good of the people was the object. This, our convention understood to be the most oppressive of all Kingly oppressions; and they resolved to so frame the Constitution that *no one man* should hold the power of bringing this oppression upon us. But your view destroys the whole matter, and places our President where Kings have always stood. Write soon again.

Yours truly,

A Lincoln

SPEECH IN UNITED STATES HOUSE OF REPRESENTATIVES ON INTERNAL IMPROVEMENTS[3]
JUNE 20, 1848

Consonant with Whig party ideology and its philosophy of economic nationalism, Lincoln proposed an internal improvement program while serving in the House of Representatives. Such improvements were crucial to the general welfare of the newly developing West. The speech begins by stating critics' objections and then proceeds to answer them point-by-point. It provides an early manifestation of Lincoln's political prudence, one of the virtues that made him a great statesman. After weighing the pros and cons of the legislation, Lincoln explained that the "true rule in determining to embrace, or reject anything, is not whether it have any evil in it; but whether it have more of evil, than of good. There are few things wholly evil, or wholly good. Almost every thing, especially of government policy, is an inseparable compound of the two; so that our best judgment between the preponderance between them is continually demanded." This early recognition of the limits of politics and the necessity of compromise helps to dispel the illusion that Lincoln was a political idealist or utopian and it confirms the common sense view of him as a statesman par excellence who balanced principle with practice. Throughout his public life, Lincoln would consistently apply the prudential maxim stated above to his political judgments, especially when confronting the momentous challenges of slavery extension, disunion, emancipation, and reconstruction.

JUNE 20, 1848

IN COMMITTEE OF THE WHOLE ON THE STATE OF THE UNION, ON THE CIVIL AND DIPLOMATIC APPROPRIATION BILL—

MR. CHAIRMAN

I wish at all times in no way to practice any fraud upon the House or the committee, and I also desire to do nothing which may be very disagreeable to any of the members. I therefore state in advance that my object in taking the

3. *CWAL*, I, 480-90.

floor is to make a speech on the general subject of internal improvements; and if I am out of order in doing so, I give the chair the oppertunity of so deciding, and I will take my seat.

The Chair: I will not undertake to anticipate what the gentleman may say on the subject of internal improvements. He will, therefore, proceed in his remarks, and if any question of order shall be made, the chair will then decide it.

Mr. Lincoln: At an early day of this session the president sent us what may properly be called an internal improvement veto message. The late democratic convention which sat at Baltimore, and which nominated Gen: Cass for the presidency, adopted a set of resolutions, now called the democratic platform, among which is one in these words:

> "That the constitution does not confer upon the general government the power to commence, and carry on a general system of internal improvements."

Gen: Cass, in his letter accepting the nomination, holds this language:

> "I have carefully read the resolutions of the Democratic National convention, laying down the platform of our political faith, and I adhere to them as firmly, as I approve them cordially."

These things, taken together, show that the question of internal improvements is now more distinctly made—has become more intense—than at any former period. It can no longer be avoided. The veto message, and the Baltimore resolution, I understand to be, in substance, the same thing; the latter being the mere general statement, of which the former is the amplification—the bill of particulars. While I know there are many democrats, on this floor and elsewhere, who disapprove that message, I understand that all who shall vote for Gen: Cass, will thereafter be counted as having approved it—as having endorsed all it's doctrines. I suppose all, or nearly all the democrats will vote for him. Many of them will do so, not because they like his position on this question, but because they prefer him, being wrong in this, to another whom they consider farther wrong on other other [sic] questions. In this way, the internal improvement democrats are to be, by a sort of forced consent, carried over, and arrayed against themselves on this measure of policy. Gen: Cass, once elected, will not trouble himself to make a constitutional argument, or, perhaps, any argument at all, when he shall veto a river or harbor bill; he will consider it a sufficient answer to all democratic murmers, to point to Mr. Polk's message, and to the "democratic platform." This being the case, the question of improvements is verging to a final crisis; and the friends of the policy must now battle, and battle manfully, or surrender all. In this view, humble as I am, I wish to review, and contest as well as I may, the general positions of this veto message. When I say *general* positions, I mean to exclude from consideration so much as relates to the present embarrassed state of the Treasury in consequence of the Mexican war.

Those general positions are: That internal improvements ought not to be made by the general government—

1. Because they would overwhelm the Treasury.
2. Because, while their *burthens* would be general, their *benefits* would be *local* and *partial;* involving an obnoxious inequality—and
3. Because they would be unconstitutional.
4. Because the states may do enough by the levy and collection of tonnage duties—or if not
5. That the constitution may be amended.

"Do nothing at all, lest you do something wrong" is the sum of these positions—is the sum of this message. And this, with the exception of what is said about constitutionality, applying as forcibly to making improvements by state authority, as by the national authority. So that we must abandon the improvements of the country altogether, by any, and every authority, or we must resist, and repudiate the doctrines of this message. Let us attempt the latter.

The first position is, that a system of internal improvements would overwhelm the treasury.

That, in such a system there is a *tendency* to undue expansion, is not to be denied. Such tendency is founded in the nature of the subject. A member of congress will prefer voting for a bill which contains an appropriation for his district, to voting for one which does not; and when a bill shall be expanded till every district shall be provided for, that it will be too greatly expanded, is obvious. But is this any more true in congress, than in a state legislature? If a member of congress must have an appropriation for his district, so, a member of a legislature must have one for his county. And if one will overwhelm the national treasury, so the other will overwhelm the state treasury. Go where we will, the difficulty is the same. Allow it to drive us from the halls of congress, and it will, just as easily, drive us from the state legislatures.

Let us, then, grapple with it, and test it's strength. Let us, judging of the future by the past, ascertain whether there may not be, in the discretion of congress, a sufficient power to limit, and restrain this expansive tendency, within reasonable, and proper bounds. The president himself values the evidence of the past. He tells us that at a certain point of our history, more than two hundred millions of dollars had been, *applied for,* to make improvements; and this he does to prove that the treasury would be overwhelmed by such a system. Why did he not tell us how much was *granted?* Would not that have been better evidence? Let us turn to it, and see what it proves. In the message, the president tells us that "During the four succeeding years, embraced by the administration of president Adams, the power not only to appropriate money, but to apply it, under the direction and authority of the General Government, as well [as] to the construction of roads, as to the improvement of harbors and rivers, was fully asserted and exercised."

This, then, was the period of greatest enormity. These, if any, must have been the days of the two hundred millions. And how much do you suppose was really expended for improvements, during that four years? Two hundred millions? One hundred? Fifty? Ten? Five? No sir, less than two millions. As shown by authentic documents, the expenditures on improvements, during 1825 1826–1827 and 1828, amounted to $1-879-627-01. These four years were the period of Mr. Adams' administration, nearly, and substantially. This fact shows, that when the power to make improvements "was fully asserted and exercised" the congress *did* keep within reasonable limits; and what has been done, it seems to me, can be done again.

Now for the second position of the message, namely, that the burthens of improvements would be *general,* while their *benefits* would [be] *local* and *partial,* involving an obnoxious inequality. That there is some degree of truth in this position, I shall not deny. No commercial object of government patronage can be so exclusively *general,* as to not be of some peculiar *local* advantage; but, on the other hand, nothing is so *local,* as to not be of some general advantage. The Navy, as I understand it, was established, and is maintained at a great annual expense, partly to be ready for war when war shall come, but partly also, and perhaps chiefly, for the protection of our commerce on the high seas. This latter object is, for all I can see, in principle, the same as internal improvements. The driving a pirate from the track of commerce on the broad ocean, and the removing a snag from it's more narrow path in the Mississippi river, can not, I think, be distinguished in principle. Each is done to save life and property, and for nothing else.

The Navy, then, is the most general in it's benefits of all this class of objects; and yet even the Navy is of some peculiar advantage to Charleston, Baltimore,

Philadelphia, New-York and Boston, beyond what it is to the interior towns of Illinois. The next most general object I can think of would be improvements on the Mississippi river and it's tributaries. They touch thirteen of our states, Pennsylvania, Virginia, Kentucky, Tennessee, Mississippi, Louisiana, Arkansas, Missouri, Illinois, Indiana, Ohio, Wisconsin and Iowa. Now I suppose it will not be denied, that these thirteen states are a little more interested in improvements on that great river, than are the remaining seventeen. These instances of the Navy, and the Miss[iss]ippi river, show clearly that there is something of local advantage in the most general objects. But the converse is also true. Nothing is so *local* as to not be of some *general* benefit. Take, for instance, the Illinois and Michigan canal. Considered apart from it's effects, it is perfectly local. Every inch of it is within the state of Illinois. That canal was first opened for business last April. In a very few days we were all gratified to learn, among other things, that sugar had been carried from New-Orleans through this canal to Buffalo in New-York. This sugar took this route, doubtless because it was cheaper than the old route. Supposing the benefit of the reduction in the cost of carriage to be shared between seller and buyer, the result is, that the New Orleans merchant sold his sugar a little *dearer;* and the people of Buffalo sweetened their coffee a little *cheaper,* than before—a benefit resulting *from* the canal, not to Illinois where the canal *is,* but to Louisiana and New-York where it is *not.* In other transactions Illinois will, of course, have her share, and perhaps the larger share too, in the benefits of the canal; but the instance of the sugar clearly shows that the *benefits* of an improvement, are by no means confined to the particular locality of the improvement itself.

The just conclusion from all this is, that if the nation refuse to make improvements, of the more general kind, because their benefits may be somewhat local, a state may, for the same reason, refuse to make an improvement of a local kind, because it's benefits may be somewhat general. A state may well say to the nation "If you will do nothing for me, I will do nothing for you." Thus it is seen, that if this argument of "inequality" is sufficient any where,— it is sufficient every where; and puts an end to improvements altogether. I hope and believe, that if both the nation and the states would, in good faith, in their respective spheres, do what they could in the way of improvements, what of inequality might be produced in one place, might be compensated in another, and that the sum of the whole might not be very unequal.

But suppose, after all, there should be some degree of inequality. Inequality is certainly never to be embraced for it's own sake; but is every good thing to be discarded, which may be inseparably connected with some degree of it? If so, we must discard all government. This capitol is built at the public expense, for the public benefit[;] but does any one doubt that it is of some peculiar local advantage to the property holders, and business people of Washington? Shall we remove it for this reason? and if so, where shall we set it down, and be free from the difficulty? To make sure of our object, shall we locate it nowhere? and have congress hereafter to hold it's sessions, as the loafer lodged "in spots about"? I make no special allusion to the present president when I say there are few stronger cases in this in this [sic] world, of "burthen to the many, and benefit to the few"—of "inequality"—than the presidency itself is by some thought to be. An honest laborer digs coal at about seventy cents a day, while the president digs abstractions at about seventy dollars a day. The *coal* is clearly worth more than the *abstractions,* and yet what a monstrous inequality in the prices! Does the president, for this reason, propose to abolish the presidency? He *does* not, and he *ought* not. The true rule, in determining to embrace, or reject any thing, is not whether it have *any* evil in it; but whether it have more of evil, than of good. There are few things *wholly* evil, or *wholly* good. Almost everything, especially of governmental policy, is an inseparable compound of the two; so that our best judgment of the preponderance between them is continually demanded. On this principle the president, his friends, and the world generally, act on most subjects. Why not apply it, then, upon this question? Why, as to improvements, magnify the *evil,* and stoutly refuse to see any *good* in them?

Mr. Chairman, on the third position of the message, the constitutional question, I have not much to say. Being the man I am, and speaking when I do, I feel, that in any attempt at an original constitutional argument, I should not be, and ought not to be, listened to patiently. The ablest, and the best of men, have gone over the whole ground long ago. I shall attempt but little more than a brief notice of what some of them have said. In relation to Mr. Jeffersons views, I read from Mr. Polk's veto message—

President Jefferson, in his message to Congress in 1806, recommended an amendment of the constitution, with a view to apply an anticipated surplus in the Treasury "to the great purposes of the public education, roads, rivers, canals, and such other objects of public improvements as it may be thought proper to add to the constitutional enumeration of the federal powers;" and he adds: "I suppose an amendment to the constitution, by consent of the States, necessary, because the objects now recommended are not among those enumerated in the constitution, and to which it permits the public moneys to be applied." In 1825, he repeated, in his published letters, the opinion that no such power has been conferred upon Congress.

I introduce this, not to controvert, just now, the constitutional opinion, but to show that on the question of *expediency,* Mr. Jeffersons opinion was against the present president—that this opinion of Mr. Jefferson, in one branch at least, is, in the hands of Mr. Polk, like McFingal's gun:—"Bears wide, and kicks the owner over."

But to the constitutional question—In 1826, Chancellor Kent first published his Commentaries on American Law. He devoted a portion of one of the lectures to the question of the authority of congress to appropriate public moneyes for internal improvements. He mentions that the question had never been brought under judicial consideration, and proceeds to give a brief summary of the discussions it had undergone between the legislative, and executive branches of the government. He shows that the legislative branch had usually been *for,* and the executive against the power, till the period of Mr. J. Q. Adams' administration, at which point he considers the executive influence as withdrawn from opposition, and added to the support of the power. In 1844 the chancellor published a new edition of his commentaries, in which he adds some notes of what had transpired on the question since 1826. I have not time to read the original text, or the notes; but the whole may be found on page 267, and the two or three following pages of the first volume of the edition of 1844. As what Chancellor Kent seems to consider the sum of the whole, I read from one of the notes:

"Mr. Justice Story, in his commentaries on the constitution of the United States, vol. ii p 429–440, and again p 519–538 has stated at large the arguments for and and [sic] against the proposition, that congress have a constitutional authority to lay taxes, and to apply the power to regulate commerce as a means directly to encourage and protect domestic manufactures; and without giving any opinion of his own on the contested doctrine, he has left the reader to draw his own conclusions. I should think, however, from the arguments as stated, that every mind which has taken no part in the discussions, and felt no prejudice or teritorial bias on either side of the question, would deem the arguments in favor of the congressional power vastly superior." It will be seen, that in this extract the power to make improvements is not directly mentioned; but by examining the context, both of Kent and Story, it will be seen that the power mentioned in the extract, and the power to make improvements are regarded as identical. It is not to be denied that many great and good men have been *against* the power; but it is insisted that quite as many, as great and as good, have been *for* it; and it is shown that, on a full survey of the whole, Chancellor Kent was of opinion that the arguments of the latter were *vastly* superior. This is but the opinion of a man, but who was that man? He was one of the ablest and most learned lawyers of his age, or of any age. It is no disparagement to Mr. Polk, nor, indeed to any one who devotes much time to politics, to be placed far behind Chancellor Kent as a lawyer. His attitude was most favorable to correct conclusions. He wrote coolly, and in retirement. He was struggling to rear a durable [an enduring] monument of fame; and he well knew that *truth* and thoroughly sound reasoning were the only sure foundations. Can the party opinion of a party president, on a law question, as this purely is, be at all compared, or set in in opposition to that of such a man, in such an attitude, as Chancellor Kent?

This constitutional question will probably never be better settled than it is, until it shall pass under judicial consideration; but I do think no man, who is clear on the questions of expediency, needs feel his conscience much pricked upon this.

Mr. Chairman, the president seems to think that enough may be done, in the way of improvements, by means of tonnage duties, under state authority, with the consent of the General Government. Now I suppose this matter of tonnage duties is well enough in it's own sphere. I suppose it may be efficient, and perhaps, *sufficient,* to make slight improvements and repairs, in harbors already in use, and not much out of repair. But if I have any correct general idea of it, it must be wholly inefficient for any generally beneficent purposes of improvement. I know very little, or rather nothing at all, of the practical matter of levying and collecting tonnage duties; but I suppose one of it's principles must be, to lay a duty for the improvement of any particular harbor, *upon the tonnage coming into that harbor.* To do otherwise—to collect money in *one* harbor, to be expended on improvements in *another,* would be an extremely aggravated form of that inequality which the president so much deprecates. If I be right in this, how could we make any entirely new improvement by means of tonnage duties? How make a road, a canal, or clear a greatly obstructed river? The idea that we could, involves the same absurdity of the irish bull about the new boots—"I shall niver git em on" says Patrick "till I wear em a day or two, and strech em a little[.]" We shall never make a canal by tonnage duties, u[n]til it shall already have been made awhile, so the tonnage can get into it.

After all, the president, concludes that possibly there may be some great objects of improvements which can not be effected by tonnage duties, and which, therefore, may be expedient for the General Government to take in hand. Accordingly he suggests, in case any such be discovered, the propriety of amending the constitution. Amend it for what? If, like Mr. Jefferson, the president thought improvements *expedient,* but not constitutional, it would be natural enough for him to recommend such an amendment; but hear what he says in this very message:

> "In view of these portentous consequences, I can not but think that this course of legislation should be arrested, even were there nothing to forbid it in the fundamental laws of our union."

For what, then, would *he* have the constitution amended? With *him* it is a proposition to remove *one* impediment, merely to be met by *others,* which, in his opinion, can not be removed—to enable congress to do what, in his opinion they ought not to do, if they could!—(Here Mr. Meade, of Virginia, enquired if Mr. L. understood the president to be opposed, on grounds of expediency to any and every improvement; to which Mr. L. answered). In the very part of his message of which I am [now] speaking, I understand him as giving some vague expression in favor of some possible objects of improvements; but in doing so, I understand him to be directly in the teeth of his own arguments, in other parts of it. Neither the president, nor any one, can possibly specify an improvement, which shall not be clearly liable to one or another of the objections he has urged on the score of expediency. I have shown, and might show again, that no work—no object—can be so general, as to dispense it's benefits with precise equality; and this inequality, is chief among the "portentous consequences" for which he declares that improvements should be arrested. No sir, when the president intimates that something, in the way of improvements, may properly be done by the General Government, he is shrinking from the conclusions to which his own arguments would force him. He feels that the improvements of this broad and goodly land, are a mighty interest; and he is unwilling to confess to the people, or perhaps to himself, that he has built an argument which, when pressed to it's conclusions, entirely anihilates this interest.

I have already said that no one, who is satisfied of the expediency of making improvements, needs be much uneasy in his conscience about it's constitutionality. I wish now to submit a few remarks on the general proposition of amending the constitution. As a general rule, I think, we would [do] much better [to] let it alone. No slight occasion should tempt us to touch it. Better not take the first step, which may lead to a habit of altering it. Better, rather, habituate ourselves to think of it, as unalterable. It can scarcely be made better than it is. New provisions, would introduce new difficulties, and thus create, and increase appetite for still further change. No sir, let it stand as it is. New hands have never touched it. The men who made it, have done their work, and have passed away. Who shall improve, on what *they* did?

Mr. Chairman, for the purpose of reviewing this message in the least possible time, as well as for the sake of distinctness, I had analized it's arguments, as well as I could, and reduced them to the propositions I have stated. I have now examined them in detail. I wish to detain the committee only a little while longer with some general remarks upon the subject of improvements. That the subject is a difficult one, can not be denied. Still it is no more difficult in congress, than in the state legislatures, in the counties, or in the smallest municipal districts, which any where exist. All can recur to instances of this difficulty in the case of county-roads, bridges, and the like. One man is offended because a road passes over his land, and another is offended because it does *not* pass over his; one is dissatisfied because the bridge, for which he is taxed, crosses the river on a different road from that which leads from his house to town; another can not bear that the county should be got in debt for these same roads and bridges; while not a few struggle hard to have roads located over their lands, and then stoutly refuse to let them be opened until they are first paid the damages. Even between the different wards, and streets, of towns and cities, we find this same wrangling, and difficulty. Now these are no other than the very difficulties, against which and out of which, the president constructs his objections of "inequality" "speculation" and "crushing the treasury." There is but a single alternative about them; they are *sufficient,* or they are *not.* If sufficient, they are sufficient *out* of congress as well as *in* it, and there is the end. We must reject them, as insufficient, or lie down and do nothing, by any authority. Then, difficulty though there be, let us meet, and encounter [overcome] it.

> Attempt the end, and never stand to doubt;
> Nothing so hard, but search will find it out.

Determine that the thing can and shall be done, and then we shall find the way. The tendency to undue expansion is unquestionably the chief difficulty. How to do *something*, and still not do *too much*, is the desideratum. Let each contribute his mite in the way of suggestion. The late Silas Wright, in a letter to the Chicago convention, contributed his, which was worth something; and I now contribute mine, which may be worth nothing. At all events, it will mislead nobody, and, therefore will do no harm. I would not borrow money. I am against an overwhelming, crushing system. Suppose, that at each session, congress shall first determine *how much* money can, for that year, be spared for improvements; then apportion that sum to the most *important* objects. So far all is easy; but how shall we determine which *are* the most important? On this question comes the collision of interests. *I* shall be slow to acknowledge, that *your* harbor, or *your* river is more important than *mine*—and *vice versa*. To clear this difficulty, let us have that same statistical information, which the gentleman from Ohio (Mr. Vinton) suggested at the beginning of this session. In that information, we shall have a stern, unbending basis of *facts*—a basis, in nowise subject to whim, caprice, or local interest. The pre-limited amount of means, will save us from doing *too much,* and the statistics, will save us from doing, what we do, in *wrong places*. Adopt, and adhere to this course, and it seems to me, the difficulty is cleared.

One of the gentlemen from South Carolina (Mr. Rhett) very much deprecates these statistics. He particularly objects, as I understand him, to counting all the pigs and chickens in the land. I do not perceive much force in the objection. It is true that if every thing be enumerated, a portion of such statistics may not be very useful to this object. Such products of the country as are to be *consumed* where they are *produced* need no roads or rivers—no means of transportation, and have no very proper connection with this subject. The *surplus*—that which is produced in *one* place, to be consumed in *another;* the capacity of each locality for producing a *greater* surplus; the natural means of transportation, and their susceptability of improvement; the hindrances, delays, and losses of life and property during transportation, and the causes of each, would be among the most valuable statistics in this connection. From these, it would readily appear where a given amount of expenditure would do the most good. These statistics might be equally accessable, as they would be equally useful, to both the nation and the states. In this way, and by these means, let the nation take hold of the larger works, and the states the smaller ones; and thus, working in a meeting direction, discreetly, but steadily and firmly, what is made unequal in one place may be equalized in another, extravagance avoided, and the whole country put on that career of prosperity, which shall correspond with it's extent of teritory, its natural resources, and the intelligence and enterprize of its people.

LETTERS TO MARY TODD LINCOLN
April 16, 1848

Lincoln wrote the following letters to Mary in Springfield while he was in Washington D.C. They provide a rare glimpse of his domestic life. Perhaps mindful of his wife's volatility, he asked her, "Will you be a good girl in all things, if I consent? Then come along, and that as soon as possible." There are conflicting accounts of Lincoln's marriage, some positive, others extremely negative. Anticipations of Mary's anxiety and lack of stability are perhaps seen in the letter where Lincoln alludes to his wife's headaches. The carefree tone of these early letters would be shattered by future tragedy in the White House. Whatever one thinks of Mary Todd, she suffered greatly. And she deteriorated rapidly after surviving the death of her son William in February 1862 and the assassination of her husband three years later. Her son Robert eventually had her committed to an insane asylum.

WASHINGTON, APRIL 16—1848.

DEAR MARY:

In this troublesome world we are never quite satisfied. When you were here, I thought you hindered me some in attending to business; but now, having nothing but business—no variety—it has grown exceedingly tasteless to me. I hate to sit down and direct documents, and I hate to stay in this old room by myself. You know I told you in last Sunday's letter, I was going to make a little speech during the week; but the week has passed away without my getting a chance to do so; and now my interest in the subject has passed away too. Your second and third letters have been received since I wrote before. Dear Eddy thinks father is "gone tapila." Has any further discovery been made as to the breaking into your grand-mother's house? If I were she, I would not remain there alone. You mention that your Uncle John Parker is likely to be at Lexington. Dont forget to present him my very kindest regards.

I went yesterday to hunt the little plaid stockings as you wished; but found that McKnight has quit business and Allen had not a single pair of the description you give and only one plaid pair of any sort that I thought would fit "Eddy's dear little feet." I have a notion to make another trial to-morrow morning. If I could get them, I have an excellent chance of sending them. Mr. Warrich Tunstall, of St. Louis is here. He is to leave early this week and to go by Lexington. He says he knows you and will call to see you; and he voluntarily asked if I had not some package to send to you.

I wish you to enjoy yourself in every possible way, but is there no danger of wounding the feelings of your good father, by being so openly intimate with the Wickliffe family?

Mrs. Broome has not removed yet; but she thinks of doing so to-morrow. All the house—or rather, all with whom you were on decided good terms— send their love to you. The others say nothing.

Very soon after you went away I got what I think a very pretty set of shirt-bosom studs—modest little ones, jet set in gold, only costing 50 cents a piece or 1.50 for the whole.

Suppose you do not prefix the "Hon" to the address on your letters to me any more. I like the letters very much but I would rather they should not have that upon them. It is not necessary, as I suppose you have thought, to have them to come free.

And you are entirely free from headache? That is good—good considering it is the first spring you have been free from it since we were acquainted. I am afraid you will get so well, and fat, and young, as to be wanting to marry again. Tell Louisa I want her to watch you a little for me. Get weighed and write me how much you weigh.

I did not get rid of the impression of that foolish dream about dear Bobby till I got your letter written the same day. What did he and Eddy think of the little letters father sent them? Dont let the blessed fellows forget father.

A day or two ago Mr. Strong, here in Congress, said to me that Matilda would visit here within two or three weeks. Suppose you write her a letter, and enclose it in one of mine, and if she comes I will deliver it to her, and if she does not, I will send it to her.

Most affectionately
A. Lincoln

LETTER TO MARY TODD LINCOLN
JUNE 12, 1848

WASHINGTON, JUNE 12, 1848—
MY DEAR WIFE:

On my return from Philadelphia, yesterday, where, in my anxiety I had been led to attend the whig convention, I found your last letter. I was so tired and sleepy, having ridden all night, that I could not answer it till to-day; and how I have to do so in the H. R. The leading matter in your letter, is your wish to return to the side of the mountains. Will you be a *good girl* in all things, if I consent? Then come along, and that as *soon* as possible. Having got the idea in my head, I shall be impatient till I see you. You will not have money enough to bring you; but I presume your uncle will supply you, and I will refund him here. By the way you do not mention whether you have received the fifty dollars I sent you. I do not much fear but that you got it; because the want of it would have induced you [to?] say something in relation to it. If your uncle is already at Lexington, you might induce him to start on earlier than the first of July; he could stay in Kentucky longer on his return, and so make up for lost time. Since I began this letter, the H. R. has passed a resolution for adjourning on the 17th. July, which probably will pass the Senate. I hope this letter will not be disagreeable to you; which, together with the circumstances under which I write, I hope will excuse me from not writing a longer one. Come on just as soon as you can. I want to see you, and our dear—*dear* boys very much. Every body here wants to see our dear Bobby.

Affectionately

A Lincoln

LETTER TO MARY TODD LINCOLN
JULY 2, 1848

WASHINGTON, JULY 2, 1848

MY DEAR WIFE:

Your letter of last sunday came last night. On that day (sunday) I wrote the principal part of a letter to you, but did not finish it, or send it till tuesday, when I had provided a draft for $100 which I sent in it. It is now probable that on that day (tuesday) you started to Shelbyville; so that when the money reaches Lexington, you will not be there. Before leaving, did you make any provision about letters that might come to Lexington for you? Write me whether you got the draft, if you shall not have already done so, when this reaches you. Give my kindest regards to your uncle John, and all the family. Thinking of them reminds me that I saw your acquaintance, Newton, of Arkansas, at the Philadelphia Convention. We had but a single interview, and that was so brief, and in so great a multitude of strange faces, that I am quite sure I should not recognize him, if I were to meet him again. He was a sort of Trinity, three in one, having the right, in his own person, to cast the three votes of Arkansas. Two or three days ago I sent your uncle John, and a few of our other friends each a copy of the speech I mentioned in my last letter; but I did not send any to you, thinking you would be on the road here, before it would reach you. I send you one now. Last wednesday, P. H. Hood & Co, dunned me for a little bill of $5.38 cents, and Walter Harper & Co, another for $8.50 cents, for goods which they say you bought. I hesitated to pay them, because my recollection is that you told me when you went away, there was nothing left unpaid. Mention in your next letter whether they are right. Mrs. Richardson is still here; and what is more, has a baby—so Richardson says, and he ought to know. I believe Mary Hewett has left here and gone to Boston. I met her on the street about fifteen or twenty days ago, and she told me she was going soon. I have seen nothing of her since. The music in the Capitol grounds on saturdays, or, rather, the interest in it, is dwindling down to nothing. Yesterday evening the attendance was rather thin. Our two girls, whom you remember seeing first at Carusis, at the exhibition of the Ethiopian Serenaders, and whose peculiarities were the wearing of black fur bonnets, and never being seen in close company with other ladies, were at the music yesterday. One of them was attended by their brother, and the other had a member of Congress in tow. He went home with her; and if I were to guess, I would say, he went away a somewhat altered man—most likely in his pockets, and in some other particular. The fellow looked conscious of guilt, although I believe he was unconscious that every body around knew who it was that had caught him.

I have had no letter from home, since I wrote you before, except short business letters, which have no interest for you.

By the way, you do not intend to do without a girl, because the one you had has left you? Get another as soon as you can to take charge of the dear codgers. Father expected to see you all sooner; but let it pass; stay as long as you please, and come when you please. Kiss and love the dear rascals.

Affectionately

A. Lincoln

THE PRESIDENTIAL QUESTION: SPEECH IN THE UNITED STATES HOUSE OF REPRESENTATIVES
JULY 27, 1848

Despite their opposition to the Mexican War, the Whigs nominated a war hero for president, Zachary Taylor, a slaveholder from Louisiana who had never before voted in an election. Lincoln supported the nomination of Taylor because he practically recognized that his hero from the west, Henry Clay, who had already been defeated in three previous presidential contests, could not possibly win. Because he had worked so diligently for Taylor's campaign, Lincoln was disappointed when he was passed over for the patronage job of commissioner of the General Land Office at Washington. This coveted position, which was promised to the state of Illinois, was awarded to someone else. After the election of 1848, Lincoln retired from public life and resumed his law practice until 1854, the year of the Kansas-Nebraska Act. Toward the end of the speech, Lincoln exposed the absurdity of the Democrats attempting to portray Lewis Cass, their presidential candidate, as a hero of the Mexican War by comparing his own exploits during the Black Hawk

War: "I guess I surpassed him in charges upon the wild onions. If he saw any live, fighting indians (sic), it was more than I did; but I had good many bloody struggles with the musquetoes (sic); and, although I never fainted from the loss of blood, I can truly say I was often very hungry." To be sure, Lincoln was a master in using self-deprecating humor to disarm his political opponents.

THE MESSAGE OF THE PRESIDENT IN RELATION TO THE BOUNDARIES OF THE TERRITORIES CEDED BY MEXICO TO THE UNITED STATES, BEING UNDER CONSIDERATION

MR. SPEAKER:

Our Democratic friends seem to be in great distress because they think our candidate for the Presidency don't suit *us*. Most of them cannot find out that General Taylor has any principles at all; some, however, have discovered that he has *one,* but that that one is entirely wrong. This one principle is his position on the veto power. The gentleman from Tennessee [MR. STANTON,] who has just taken his seat, indeed, has said there is very little if any difference on this question between General Taylor and all the Presidents; and he seems to think it sufficient detraction from General Taylor's position on it, that it has nothing new in it. But all others, whom I have heard speak, assail it furiously. A new member from Kentucky, [MR. CLARK] of very considerable ability, was in particular concern about it. He thought it altogether novel and unprecedented for a President, or a Presidential candidate, to think of approving bills whose constitutionality may not be entirely clear to his own mind. He thinks the ark of our safety is gone, unless Presidents shall always veto such bills as, in their judgment, may be of *doubtful* constitutionality. However clear Congress may be of their authority to pass any particular act, the gentleman from Kentucky thinks the President must veto it if *he* has *doubts* about it. Now I have neither time nor inclination to argue with the gentleman on the veto power as an original question; but I wish to show that General Taylor, and not he, agrees with the earlier statesmen on this question. When the bill chartering the first Bank of the United States passed Congress, its constitutionality was questioned; Mr. Madison, then in the House of Representatives, as well as others, had opposed it on that ground. General Washington, as President, was called on to approve or reject it. He sought and obtained, on the constitutional question, the separate written opinion of Jefferson, Hamilton, and Edmund Randolph, they then being respectively Secretary of State, Secretary of the Treasury, and Attorney-General. Hamilton's opinion was for the power; while Randolph's and Jefferson's were both against it. Mr. Jefferson, after giving his opinion decidedly against the constitutionality of that bill, closes his letter with the paragraph which I now read:

> "It must be admitted, however, that unless the President's mind, on a view of everything which is urged for and against this bill, is tolerably clear that it is unauthorized by the Constitution; if the pro and the con hang so even as to balance his judgment, a just respect for the wisdom of the legislature would naturally decide the balance in favor of their opinion; it is chiefly for cases where they are clearly misled by error, ambition, or interest, that the Constitution has placed a check in the negative of the President.
> "Thomas Jefferson
> "February 15, 1791."

General Taylor's opinion, as expressed in his Allison letter, is as I now read:

> "The power given by the veto is a high conservative power; but, in my opinion, should never be exercised, except in cases of clear violation of the Constitution, or manifest haste and want of consideration by Congress."

It is here seen that, in Mr. Jefferson's opinion, if, on the constitutionality of any given bill, the President *doubts,* he is not to veto it, as the gentleman from Kentucky would have him do, but is to defer to Congress and approve it. And if we compare the opinions of Jefferson and Taylor, as expressed in these paragraphs, we shall find them more exactly alike than we can often find any two expressions having any literal difference. None but interested fault-finders, I think, can discover any substantial variation.

But gentlemen on the other side are unanimously agreed that General Taylor has no other principles. They are in utter darkness as to his opinions on any of the questions of policy which occupy the public attention. But is there any doubt as to what he will *do* on the prominent questions, if elected? Not the least. It is not possible to know what he will or would do in every imaginable case; because many questions have passed away, and others doubtless will arise which none of us have yet thought of; but on the prominent questions of currency, tariff, internal improvements, and Wilmot proviso, General Taylor's course is at least as well defined as is General Cass's. Why, in their eagerness to get at General Taylor, several Democratic members here have desired to know whether, in case of his election, a bankrupt law is to be established. Can they tell us General Cass's opinion on this question? [Some member answered, "He is against it."] Aye, how do you know he is? There is nothing about it in the platform, nor elsewhere, that I have seen. If the gentleman knows anything which I do not, he can show it. But to return: General Taylor, in his Allison letter, says:

"Upon the subject of the tariff, the currency, the improvement of our great highways, rivers, lakes, and harbors, the will of the people, as expressed through their Representatives in Congress, ought to be respected and carried out by the Executive."

Now, this is the whole matter—in substance, it is this: The people say to General Taylor, "If you are elected, shall we have a national bank?" He answers, "*Your* will, gentlemen, not *mine*." "What about the tariff?" "Say yourselves." "Shall our rivers and harbors be improved?" "Just as you please." "If you desire a bank, an alteration of the tariff, internal improvements, any or all, I will not hinder you; if you do not desire them, I will not attempt to force them on you." "Send up your members of Congress from the various districts, with opinions according to your own, and if they are for these measures, or any of them, I shall have nothing to oppose; if they are not for them, I shall not, by any appliances whatever, attempt to dragoon them into their adoption." Now, can there be any difficulty in understanding this? To you, Democrats, it may not seem like principle; but surely you cannot fail to perceive the position plainly enough. The distinction between it and the position of your candidate is broad and obvious, and I admit you have a clear right to show it is wrong, if you can; but you have no right to pretend you cannot see it at all. We see it, and to us it appears like principle, and the best sort of principle at that—the principle of allowing the people to do as they please with their own business. My friend from Indiana [MR. C. B. SMITH] has aptly asked, "Are you willing to trust the people?" Some of you answered, substantially, "We are willing to trust the people; but the President is as much the representative of the people as Congress." In a certain sense, and to a certain extent, he is the representative of the people. He is elected by them, as well as Congress is. But can he, in the nature of things, know the wants of the people as well as three hundred other men coming from all the various localities of the nation? If so, where is the propriety of having a Congress? That the Constitution gives the President a negative on legislation, all know; but that this negative should be so combined with platforms and other appliances as to enable him, and, in fact, almost compel him, to take the whole of legislation into his own hands, is what we object to—is what General Taylor objects to—and is what constitutes the broad distinction between you and us. To thus transfer legislation is clearly to take if from those who understand with minuteness the interest of the people, and give it to one who does not and cannot so well understand it. I understand your idea, that if a Presidential candidate avow his opinion upon a given question, or rather upon all questions, and the people, with full knowledge of this, elect him, they thereby distinctly approve all those opinions. This, though plausible, is a most pernicious deception. By means of it measures are adopted or rejected, contrary to the wishes of the whole of one party, and often nearly half of the other. The process is this: Three, four, or half a dozen questions are prominent at a given time; the party selects its candidate, and he takes his position on each of these questions. On all but one his positions have already been endorsed at former elections, and his party fully committed to them; but that one is new, and a large portion of them are against it. But what are they to do? The whole are strung together, and they must take all or reject all. They cannot take what they like and leave the rest. What they are already committed to, being the majority, they shut their eyes and gulp the whole. Next election, still another is introduced in the same way. If we run our eyes along the line of the past, we shall see that almost, if not quite, all the articles of the present Democratic creed have been at first forced upon the party in this very way. And just now, and just so, opposition to internal improvements is to be established if General Cass shall be elected. Almost half the Democrats here are for improvements, but they will vote for Cass, and if he succeeds, their votes will have aided in closing the doors against improvements. Now, this is a process which we think is wrong. We prefer a candidate who, like General Taylor, will allow the people to have their own way regardless of his private opinion; and I should think the internal-improvement Democrats at least, ought to prefer such a candidate. He would force nothing on them which they don't want, and he would allow them to have improvements, which their own candidate, if elected, will not.

Mr. Speaker, I have said General Taylor's position is as well defined as is that of General Cass. In saying this, I admit I do not certainly know what he would do on the Wilmot proviso. I am a northern man, or, rather, a western free State man, with a constituency I believe to be, and with personal feelings I know to be, against the extension of slavery. As such, and with what information I have, I hope, and *believe,* General Taylor, if elected, would not veto the proviso; but I do not *know* it. Yet, if I knew he would, I still would vote for him. I should do so, because, in my judgment, his election alone can defeat General Cass; and because, *should* slavery thereby go into the territory we now have, just so much will certainly happen by the election of Cass; and, in addition, a course of policy leading to new wars, new acquisitions of territory, and still further extensions of slavery. One of the two is to be President: which is preferable?

But there is as much doubt of Cass on improvements as there is of Taylor on the proviso. I have no doubt myself of General Cass on this question, but I know the Democrats differ among themselves as to his position. My internal-improvement colleague [MR. WENTWORTH] stated on this floor the other day, that he was satisfied Cass was for improvements, because he had voted all the bills that he [MR. W.] had. So far so good. But Mr. Polk vetoed some of these very bills; the Baltimore Convention passed a set of resolutions, among other things, approving these vetoes, and Cass declares, in his letter accepting the nomination, that he has carefully read these resolutions, and that he adheres to them as firmly as he approves them cordially. In other words, General Cass voted for the bills, and thinks the President did right to veto them; and his friends here are amiable enough to consider him as being on one side or the other, just as one or the other may correspond with their own respective inclinations. My colleague admits that the platform declares against the constitutionality of a general system of improvements, and that General Cass endorses the platform; but he still thinks General Cass is in favor of some sort of improvements. Well, what are they? As he is against *general* objects, those he *is for,* must be *particular* and *local.* Now, this is taking the subject precisely by the wrong end. *Particularity*—expending the money of the *whole* people for an object which will benefit only a *portion* of them, is the greatest real objection to improvements, and has been so held by General Jackson, Mr. Polk, and all others, I believe, till now. But now, behold, the objects most general, nearest free from this objection, are to be rejected, while those most liable to it are to be embraced. To return: I cannot help believing that General Cass, when he wrote his letter of acceptance, well understood he was to be claimed by the advocates of both sides of this question, and that he then closed the door against all further expressions of opinion, purposely to retain the benefits of that double position. His subsequent equivocation at Cleveland, to my mind, proves such to have been the case.

One word more, and I shall have done with this branch of the subject. You Democrats, and your candidate, in the main, are in favor of laying down, in advance, a platform—a set of party positions, as a unit; and then of enforcing the people, by every sort of appliance, to ratify them, however unpalatable some of them may be. We, and our candidate, are in favor of making Presidential elections and the legislation of the country distinct matters; so that the people can elect whom they please, and afterwards, legislate just *as* they please, without any hindrance, save only so much as may guard against infractions of the Constitution, undue haste, and want of consideration. The difference between us is clear as noon-day. That we are right we cannot doubt. We hold the true Republican position. In leaving the people's business in their hands, we cannot be wrong. We are willing, and even anxious, to go to the people on this issue.

But I suppose I cannot reasonably hope to convince you that we have any principles. The most I can expect is, to assure you that we think we have, and are quite contented with them. The other day, one of the gentlemen from Georgia [MR. IVERSON], an eloquent man, and a man of learning, so far as I can judge, not being learned myself, came down upon us astonishingly. He spoke in what the Baltimore American calls the "scathing and withering style." At the end of his second severe flash I was struck blind, and found myself feeling with my fingers for an assurance of my continued physical existence. A little of the bone was left, and I gradually revived. He eulogized Mr. Clay in high and beautiful terms, and then declared that we had deserted all our principles, and had turned Henry Clay out, like an old horse, to root. This is terribly severe. It cannot be answered by argument; at least, I cannot so answer it. I merely wish to ask the gentleman if the Whigs are the only party he can think of, who sometimes turn old horses out to root. Is not a certain Martin Van Buren an old horse, which your own party have turned out to root? and is he not rooting a little to your discomfort about now? But in not nominating Mr. Clay, we deserted our principles, you say. Ah! in what? Tell us, ye men of principles, what principle we violated? We say you did violate principle in discarding Van Buren, and we can tell you how. You violated the primary, the cardinal, the one great living principle of all Democratic representative government—the principle that the representative is bound to carry out the known will of his constituents. A large majority of the Baltimore Convention of 1844 were, by their constituents, instructed to procure Van Buren's nomination if they could. In violation, in utter, glaring contempt of this, you rejected him—rejected him, as the gentleman from New York, [MR. BIRDSALL], the other day expressly admitted, for *availability*—that same "general availability" which you charge upon us, and daily chew over here, as something exceedingly odious and unprincipled. But the gentleman from Georgia [MR. IVERSON,] gave us a second speech yesterday, all well considered and put down in writing, in which Van Buren was scathed and withered a "few" for his present position and movements. I cannot remember the gentleman's precise language, but I do remember he put Van Buren down, down, till he got him where he was finally to "stink" and "rot."

Mr. Speaker, it is no business or inclination of mine to defend Martin Van Buren. In the war of extermination now waging between him and his old admirers, I say, devil take the hindmost—and the foremost. But there is no mistaking the origin of the breach; and if the curse of "stinking" and "rotting" is to fall on the first and greatest violators of principle in the matter, I disinterestedly suggest, that the gentleman from Georgia and his present co-workers are bound to take it upon themselves.

But the gentleman from Georgia further says, we have deserted all our principles, and taken shelter under General Taylor's military coat tail; and he seems to think this is exceedingly degrading. Well, as his faith is, so be it unto him. But can he remember no other military coat tail under which a certain other party have been sheltering for near a quarter of a century? Has he no acquaintance with the ample military coat tail of General Jackson? Does he not know that his own party have run the last five Presidential races under that coat tail, and that they are now running the sixth under that same cover? Yes, sir, that coat tail was used, not only for General Jackson himself, but has been clung to with the grip of death by every Democratic candidate since. You have never ventured, and dare not now venture, from under it. Your campaign papers have constantly been "Old Hickories," with rude likenesses of the old General upon them; hickory poles and hickory brooms your never-ending emblems; Mr. Polk, himself, was "Young Hickory," "Little Hickory," or something so; and even now your campaign paper here is proclaiming that Cass and Butler are of the true "Hickory stripe." No, sir; you dare not give it up. Like a horde of hungry ticks, you have stuck to the tail of the Hermitage lion to the end of his life, and you are still sticking to it, and drawing a loathsome sustenance from it after he is dead. A fellow once advertised that he had made a discovery, by which he could make a new man out of an old one, and have enough of the stuff left to make a little yellow dog. Just such a discovery has General Jackson's popularity been to you. You not only twice made President of him out of it, but you have had enough of the stuff left to make Presidents of several comparatively small men since; and it is your chief reliance now to make still another.

Mr. Speaker, old horses and military coat tails, or tails of any sort, are not figures of speech such as I would be the first to introduce into discussions here; but as the gentleman from Georgia has thought fit to introduce them, he and you are welcome to all you have made, or can make, by them. If you have any more old horses, trot them out; any more tails, just cock them, and come at us.

I repeat, I would not introduce this mode of discussion here; but I wish gentlemen on the other side to understand, that the use of degrading figures is a game at which they may not find themselves able to take all the winnings. [We give it up.] Aye, you give it up, and well you may, but from a very different reason from that which you would have us understand. The point—the power to hurt—of all figures, consists in the *truthfulness* of their application; and understanding this, you may well give it up. They are weapons which hit you, but miss us.

But, in my hurry, I was very near closing on the subject of military tails, before I was done with it. There is one entire article of the sort I have not discussed yet; I mean the military tail you Democrats are now engaged in dovetailing on to the great Michigander. Yes, sir, all his biographers (and they are legion) have him in hand, tying him to a military tail, like so many mischievous boys tying a dog to a bladder of beans. True, the material they have is very limited; but they drive at it, might and main. He *in*vaded Canada without resistance, and he *out*vaded it without pursuit. As he did both under orders, I suppose there was, to him, neither credit nor discredit in them; but they are made to constitute a large part of the tail. He was not at Hull's surrender, but he was close by. He was volunteer aid to General Harrison on the day of the battle of the Thames; and, as you said in 1840, Harrison was picking whortleberries two miles off, while the battle was fought, I suppose it is a just conclusion, with you, to say Cass was aiding Harrison to pick whortleberries. This is about all, except the mooted question of the broken sword. Some authors say he broke it; some say he threw it away; and some others, who ought to know, say nothing about it. Perhaps it would be a fair historical compromise to say, if he did not break it, he did not do anything else with it.

By the way, Mr. Speaker, did you know I am a military hero? Yes, sir, in the days of the Black Hawk war, I fought, bled, and came away. Speaking of General Cass's career, reminds me of my own. I was not at Stillman's defeat, but I was about as near it as Cass was to Hull's surrender; and, like him, I saw the place very soon afterwards. It is quite certain I did not break my sword, for I had none to break; but I bent a musket pretty badly on one occasion. If Cass broke his sword, the idea is, he broke it in desperation; I bent the musket by accident. If General Cass went in advance of me in picking whortleberries, I guess I surpassed him in charges upon the wild onions. If he saw any live fighting Indians, it was more than I did, but I had a good many bloody struggles with the mosquitoes; and although I never fainted from loss of blood, I can truly say I was often very hungry.

Mr. Speaker, if I should ever conclude to doff whatever our Democratic friends may suppose there is of black-cockade Federalism about me, and, thereupon, they shall take me up as their candidate for the Presidency, I protest they shall not make fun of me, as they have of General Cass, by attempting to write me into a military hero.

While I have General Cass in hand, I wish to say a word about his political principles. As a specimen, I take the record of his progress on the Wilmot proviso. In the Washington Union, of March 2, 1847, there is a report of a speech of General Cass, made the day before in the Senate, on the Wilmot proviso, during the delivery of which Mr. Miller, of New Jersey, is reported to have interrupted him as follows, to wit:

> "MR. MILLER expressed his great surprise at the change in the sentiments of the Senator from Michigan, who had been regarded as the great champion of freedom in the northwest, of which he was a distinguished ornament. Last year the Senator from Michigan was understood to be decidedly in favor of the Wilmot proviso; and, as no reason had been stated for the change, he (Mr. M.) could not refrain from the expression of his extreme surprise."

To this General Cass is reported to have replied as follows, to wit:

> "Mr. Cass said, that the course of the Senator from New Jersey was most extraordinary. Last year he (Mr. C.) should have voted for the proposition had it come up. But circumstances had altogether changed. The honorable Senator then read several passages from the remarks as given above, which he had committed to writing, in order to refute such a charge as that of the Senator from New Jersey."

In the "remarks above committed to writing," is one numbered 4, as follows, to wit:

> "4th. Legislation would now be wholly inoperative, because no territory hereafter to be acquired can be governed without an act of Congress providing for its government. And such an act, on its passage, would open the whole subject, and leave the Congress, called on to pass it, free to exercise its own discretion, entirely uncontrolled by any declaration found in the statute book."

In Nile's Register, vol. 73, page 293, there is a letter of General Cass to A. O. P. Nicholson, of Nashville, Tennessee, dated December 24, 1847, from which the following are correct extracts:

"The Wilmot proviso has been before the country some time. It has been repeatedly discussed in Congress, and by the public press. I am strongly impressed with the opinion that a great change has been going on in the public mind upon this subject—in my own as well as others; and that doubts are resolving themselves into convictions, that the principle it involves should be kept out of the National Legislature, and left to the people of the Confederacy in their respective local Governments..."

"Briefly, then, I am opposed to the exercise of any jurisdiction by Congress over this matter; and I am in favor of leaving the people of any territory which may be hereafter acquired the right to regulate it themselves, under the general principles of the Constitution. Because,

"1. I do not see in the Constitution any grant of the requisite power to Congress; and I am not disposed to extend a doubtful precedent beyond its necessity—the establishment of territorial governments when needed—leaving to the inhabitants all the rights compatible with the relations they bear to the Confederation."

These extracts show that, in 1846, General Cass was for the proviso *at once;* that in March, 1847, he was still for it, *but not just then;* and that, in December, 1847, he was *against* it altogether. This is a true index to the whole man. When the question was raised in 1846, he was in a blustering hurry to take ground for it. He sought to be in advance, and to avoid the uninteresting position of a mere follower; but soon he began to see glimpses of the great Democratic ox-gad waving in his face, and to hear, indistinctly, a voice saying, "Back," "back, sir," "Back a little." He shakes his head; and bats his eyes, and blunders back to his position of March, 1847; but still the gad waves, and the voice grows more distinct, and sharper still—"Back, sir!" "Back, I say!" "Further back!" and back he goes to the position of December, 1847; at which the gad is still, and the voice soothingly says—"So!" "Stand at that."

Have no fears, gentlemen, of your candidate; he exactly suits you, and we congratulate you upon it. However much you may be distressed about *our* candidate, you have all cause to be contented and happy with your own. If elected, he may not maintain all, or even any, of his positions previously taken; but he will be sure to do whatever the party exigency, for the time being, may require;

and that is precisely what you want. He and Van Buren are the same "manner of men;" and, like Van Buren, he will never desert *you* till you first desert *him*.

Mr. Speaker, I adopt the suggestion of a friend, that General Cass is a general of splendidly successful *charges*—charges, to be sure, not upon the public enemy, but upon the public treasury.

He was Governor of Michigan Territory, and, *ex-officio,* superintendent of Indian affairs, from the 9th of October, 1813, till the 31st of July, 1831—a period of seventeen years, nine months, and twenty-two days. During this period, he received from the United States treasury, for personal services and personal expenses, the aggregate sum of $96,028—being an average sum of $14.79 per day for every day of the time. This large sum was reached by assuming that he was doing service and incurring expenses at several different *places,* and in several different *capacities* in the *same* place, all at the same *time.* By a correct analysis of his accounts during that period, the following propositions may be deduced:

First. He was paid in *three* different capacities during the *whole* of the time—that is to say:

1. As Governor's salary, at the rate, per year, of $2,000.
2. As estimated for office rent, clerk hire, fuel, &c., in superintendence of Indian affairs *in* Michigan, at the rate, per year, of $1,500.
3. As compensation and expenses, for various miscellaneous items of Indian service *out* of Michigan, an average, per year, of $625.

Second. During *part* of the time, that is, from the 9th of October, 1813, to the 29th of May, 1822, he was paid in *four* different capacities—that is to say:

The three as above, and in addition thereto the commutation of ten rations per day, amounting per year, to $730.

Third. During *another* part of the time, that is, from the beginning of 1822 to the 31st of July, 1831, he was also paid in *four* different capacities—that is to say:

The *first* three, as above, (the rations being dropped after the 29th of May, 1822,) and, in addition thereto, for superintending Indian agencies at Piqua, Ohio, Fort Wayne, Indiana, and Chicago, Illinois, at the rate, per year, of $1,500. It should be observed here, that the last item, commencing at the beginning of 1822, and the item of rations, ending on the 29th of May, 1822, lap on each other during so much of the time as lies between those two dates.

Fourth. Still another part of the time, that is, from the 31st of October, 1821, to the 29th of May, 1822, he was paid in *six* different capacities—that is to say:

The three first, as above; the item of rations, as above; and, in addition thereto, another item of ten rations per day while at Washington, settling his accounts; being at the rate, per year, of $730.

And, also, an allowance for expenses travelling to and from Washington, and while there, of $1,022; being at the rate, per year, of $1,793.

Fifth. And yet, during the little portion of time which lies between the 1st of January, 1822, and the 29th of May, 1822, he was paid in *seven* different capacities; that is to say:

The six last mentioned, and also at the rate of $1,500 per year for the Piqua, Fort Wayne, and Chicago service, as mentioned above.

These accounts have already been discussed some here; but when we are amongst them, as when we are in the Patent Office, we must peep about a good while before we can see all the curiosities. I shall not be tedious with them. As to the large item of $1,500 per year, amounting in the aggregate to $26,715, for office rent, clerk hire, fuel, &c., I barely wish to remark that, so far as I can discover in the public documents, there is no evidence, by word or inference, either from any disinterested witness, or of General Cass himself, that he ever rented or kept a separate office, ever hired or kept a clerk, or ever used any extra amount of fuel, &c., in consequence of his Indian services. Indeed, General Cass's entire silence in regard to these items in his two long letters, urging his claims upon the Government, is, to my mind, almost conclusive that no such items had any real existence.

But I have introduced General Cass's accounts here, chiefly to show the wonderful physical capacities of the man. They show that he not only did the labor of several men at the same *time,* but that he often did it at several *places* many hundred miles apart, *at the same time.* And at eating, too, his capacities are shown to be quite as wonderful. From October, 1821, to May, 1822, he ate ten rations a day in Michigan, ten rations a day here in Washington, and near five dollars' worth a day besides, partly on the road between the two places. And then there is an important discovery in his example—the art of being paid for what one eats, instead of having to pay for it. Hereafter, if any nice young man shall owe a bill which he cannot pay in any other way, he can just board it out. Mr. Speaker, we have all heard of the animal standing in doubt between two stacks of hay, and starving to death; the like of that would never happen to General Cass. Place the stacks a thousand miles apart, he would stand stock-still midway between them, and eat them both at once; and the green grass along the line would be apt to suffer some too, at the same time. By all means, make him President, gentlemen. He will feed you bounteously—if—if there is any left after he shall have helped himself.

But as General Taylor is, par excellence, the hero of the Mexican War; and, as you Democrats say we Whigs have always opposed the war, you think it must be very awkward and embarrassing for us to go for General Taylor. The declaration that we have always opposed the war is true or false, accordingly as one may understand the term "opposing the war." If to say "the war was unnecessarily and unconstitutionally commenced by the President," be opposing the war, then the Whigs have very generally opposed it. Whenever they have spoken at all, they have said this; and they have said it on what has appeared good reason to them. The marching an army into the midst of a peaceful Mexican settlement, frightening the inhabitants away, leaving their growing crops, and other property to destruction, to *you* may appear a perfectly amiable, peaceful, unprovoking procedure; but it does not appear so to *us*. So to call such an act, to us appears no other than a naked, impudent absurdity, and we speak of it accordingly. But if, when the war had begun, and had become the cause of the country, the giving of our money and our blood, in common with yours, was support of the war, then it is not true that we have always opposed the war. With few individual exceptions, you have constantly had our votes here for all the necessary supplies. And, more than this, you have had the services, the blood, and the lives of our political brethren in every trial, and on every field. The beardless boy, and the mature man—the humble and the distinguished, you have had them. Through suffering and death, by disease, and in battle, they have endured, and fought, and fell with you. Clay and Webster each gave a son, never to be returned. From the State of my own residence, besides other worthy but less known Whig names, we sent Marshall, Morrison, Baker, and Hardin; they all fought, and one fell, and in the fall of that one, we lost our best Whig man. Nor were the Whigs few in number, or laggard in the day of danger. In that fearful, bloody, breathless struggle at Buena Vista, where each man's hard task was to beat back five foes or die himself, of the five high officers who perished, four were Whigs.

In speaking of this, I mean no odious comparison between the lion-hearted Whigs and Democrats who fought there. On other occasions, and among the lower officers and privates on *that* occasion, I doubt not the proportion was different. I wish to do justice to all. I think of all those brave men as Americans, in whose proud fame, as an American, I too have a share. Many of them, Whigs and Democrats, are my constituents and personal friends; and I thank them—more than thank them—one and all, for the high imperishable honor they have conferred on our common State.

But the distinction between the cause of the *President* in beginning the war, and the cause of the *country* after it was begun, is a distinction which you cannot perceive. To *you,* the President, and the country, seem to be all one. You are interested to see no distinction between them; and I venture to suggest that *possibly* your interest blinds you a little. We see the distinction, as we think, clearly enough; and our friends who have fought in the war have no difficulty in seeing it also. What those who have fallen would say, were they alive and here, of course we can never know; but with those who have returned there is no difficulty. Colonel Haskell and Major Gaines, members here, both fought in the war; and one of them underwent extraordinary perils and hardships; still they, like all other Whigs here, vote on the record that the war was unnecessarily and unconstitutionally commenced by the President. And even General Taylor himself, the noblest Roman of them all, has declared that, as a citizen, and particularly as a soldier, it is sufficient for him to know that his country is at war with a foreign nation, to do all in his power to bring it to a speedy and honorable termination, by the most vigorous and energetic operations, without inquiring about its justice, or anything else connected with it.

Mr. Speaker, let our Democratic friends be comforted with the assurance, that we are content with our position, content with our company, and content with our candidate; and that, although they, in their generous sympathy, think we ought to be miserable, we really are not, and that they may dismiss the great anxiety they have on *our* account.

Mr. Speaker, I see I have but three minutes left, and this forces me to throw out one whole branch of my subject. A single word on still another. The Democrats are kind enough to frequently remind us that we have some dissensions in our ranks. Our good friend from Baltimore, immediately before me [MR. MC LANE,] expressed some doubt the other day as to which branch of our party General Taylor would ultimately fall into the hands of. That was a new idea to me. I knew we had dissenters, but I did not know they were trying to get our candidate away from us. I would like to say a word to our dissenters, but I have not the time. Some such *we* certainly have; have *you* none, gentlemen Democrats? Is it all union and harmony in *your* ranks? No bickerings? No divisions? If there be doubt as to which of our divisions will get our candidate, is there no doubt as to which of your candidates will get your party? I have heard some things from New York; and if they are true, we might well say of your party there, as a drunken fellow once said when he heard the reading of an indictment for hog-stealing. The clerk read on till he got to, and through the words "did steal, take, and carry away, ten boars, ten sows, ten shoats, and ten pigs," at which he exclaimed—"Well, by golly, that is the most equally divided gang of hogs I ever did hear of." If there is any gang of hogs more equally divided than the Democrats of New York are about this time, I have not heard of it.

REMARKS AND RESOLUTION INTRODUCED IN UNITED STATES HOUSE OF REPRESENTATIVES CONCERNING THE ABOLITION OF SLAVERY IN THE DISTRICT OF COLUMBIA
JANUARY 10, 1849

Lincoln proposed this compensated emancipation plan for the District of Columbia as a substitute for a resolution in the Thirtieth Congress, which had proposed that slavery be abolished there without the consent of its inhabitants. Attempting to steer a moderate course between northern and southern extremists, arguing that slavery could only be lawfully abolished with the consent of citizens who lived there, Lincoln's resolution asked for a referendum on the institution in the District of Columbia. Notably, this plan had a provision for the support and education of children born of slave mothers on or after January 1,1850, the date compensated emancipation would take effect. Lincoln considered proposing his resolution as a bill, but gave up in despair, "finding that I was abandoned by my former backers and having little personal influence, I dropped the matter knowing that it was useless to prosecute business at that time." Northern antislavery men objected to Lincoln's proposal because they opposed its fugitive slave provision and because they worried that any payment for liberating the slaves would tacitly legitimize the institution. Lincoln's proposal for compensated emancipation in D.C. in 1849 bears comparison to his subsequent compensated emancipation plans for the Border States while president.

JANUARY 10, 1849

Mr. Lincoln appealed to his colleague [Mr. Wentworth] to withdraw his motion, to enable him to read a proposition which he intended to submit, if the vote should be reconsidered.

Mr. Wentworth again withdrew his motion for that purpose.

Mr. Lincoln said, that by the courtesy of his colleague, he would say, that if the vote on the resolution was reconsidered, he should make an effort to introduce an amendment, which he should now read.

And Mr. Lincoln read as follows:

STRIKE OUT ALL before and after the word "Resolved" and insert the following, towit: That the Committee on the District of Columbia be instructed to report a bill in substance as follows, towit:

Section 1.   Be it enacted by the Senate and House of Representatives of the United States of America, in Congress assembled: That no person not now within the District of Columbia, nor now owned by any person or persons now resident within it, nor hereafter born within it, shall ever be held in slavery within said District.

Section 2.   That no person now within said District, or now owned by any person, or persons now resident within the same, or hereafter born within it, shall ever be held in slavery without the limits of said District: *Provided,* that officers of the government of the United States, being citizens of the slave-holding states, coming into said District on public business, and remaining only so long as may be reasonably necessary for that object, may be attended into, and out of, said District, and while there, by the necessary servants of themselves and their families, without their right to hold such servants in service, being thereby impaired.

Section 3.   That all children born of slave mothers within said District on, or after the first day of January in the year of our Lord one thousand, eight hundred and fifty shall be free; but shall be reasonably supported and educated, by the respective owners of their mothers or by their heirs or representatives, and shall owe reasonable service, as apprentices, to such owners, heirs, and representatives until they respectively arrive at the age of——years when they shall be entirely free; and the municipal authorities of Washington and Georgetown, within their respective jurisdictional limits, are hereby empowered and required to make all suitable and necessary provisions for enforcing obedience to this section, on the part of both masters and apprentices.

Section 4.   That all persons now within said District lawfully held as slaves, or now owned by any person or persons now resident within said District, shall remain such, at the will of their respective owners, their heirs and legal representatives: *Provided* that any such owners, or his legal representative, may at any time receive from the treasury of the United States the full value of his or her slave, of the class in this section mentioned, upon which such slave shall be forthwith and forever free: and provided further that the President of the United States, the Secretary of State, and the Secretary of the Treasury shall be a board for determining the value of such slaves as their owners may desire emancipation under this section; and whose duty it shall be to hold a session for the purpose, on the first Monday of each calendar month; to receive all applications; and, on satisfactory evidence in each case, that the person presented for valuation, is a slave, and of the class in this section mentioned, and is owned by the applicant, shall value such slave at his or her full cash value, and give to the applicant an order on the treasury for the amount; and also to such slave a certificate of freedom.

Section 5.   That the municipal authorities of Washington and George-town, within their respective jurisdictional limits, are hereby empowered and required to provide active and efficient means to arrest, and deliver up to their owners, all fugitive slaves escaping into said District.

Section 6.   That the election of officers within said District of Columbia, are hereby empowered and required to open polls at all the usual places of hold-ing elections, on the first Monday of April next, and receive the vote of every free white male citizen above the age of twentyone years, having resided within said District for the period of one year or more next preceding the time of such voting, for, or against this act; to proceed, in taking said votes, in all respects not herein specified, as at elections under the municipal laws; and, with as little delay as possible, to transmit correct statements of the votes so cast to the President of the United States. And it shall be the duty of the President to canvass said votes immediately, and, if a majority of them be found to be for this act, to forthwith issue his proclamation giving notice of the fact; and this act shall only be in full force and effect on, and after the day of such proclamation.

Section 7.   That involuntary servitude for the punishment of crime, whereof the party shall have been duly convicted shall in no wise be prohibited by this act.

Section 8.   That for all purposes of this act the jurisdictional limits of Washington are extended to all parts of the District of Columbia not now included within the present limits of Georgetown.

Mr. Lincoln the said, that he was authorized to say, that of about fifteen of the leading citizens of the District of Columbia to whom this proposition had been submitted, there was not one but who approved of the adoption of such a proposition. He did not wish to be misunderstood. He did not know whether or not they would vote for this bill on the first Monday of April; but he repeated, that out of fifteen persons to whom it had been submitted, he had authority to say that every one of them desired that some proposition like this should pass.

FRAGMENT: NOTES FOR A LAW LECTURE[4]
[JULY 1, 1850?]

Many of Lincoln's best qualities were honed through his practice of the law: prudence, precision, clarity, logic, persuasion, and a deep respect for the rule of law and legal proce-dure. Lincoln was a self-taught lawyer who established a successful legal practice by riding

4. *CWAL*, II, 81–2.

the Illinois circuit. This speech reveals his personal and professional integrity. While the legal profession is often maligned today, there are many honorable lawyers who strive to embody Lincoln's model. His admonition at the end of the lecture should be required reading for law students, and posted in law firms throughout the nation: "resolve to be honest at all events; and if in your own judgment you cannot be an honest lawyer, resolve to be honest without being a lawyer."

[JULY 1, 1850?]

I am not an accomplished lawyer. I find quite as much material for a lecture in those points wherein I have failed, as in those wherein I have been moderately successful. The leading rule for the lawyer, as for the man of every other calling, is diligence. Leave nothing for to-morrow which can be done to-day. Never let your correspondence fall behind. Whatever piece of business you have in hand, before stopping, do all the labor pertaining to it which can then be done. When you bring a common-law suit, if you have the facts for doing so, write the declaration at once. If a law point be involved, examine the books, and note the authority you rely on upon the declaration itself, where you are sure to find it when wanted. The same of defenses and pleas. In business not likely to be litigated,—ordinary collection cases, foreclosures, partitions, and the like,—make all examinations of titles, and note them, and even draft orders and decrees in advance. This course has a triple advantage; it avoids omissions and neglect, saves your labor when once done, performs the labor out of court when you have leisure, rather than in court when you have not. Extemporaneous speaking should be practised and cultivated. It is the lawyer's avenue to the public. However able and faithful he may be in other respects, people are slow to bring him business if he cannot make a speech. And yet there is not a more fatal error to young lawyers than relying too much on speech-making. If any one, upon his rare powers of speaking, shall claim an exemption from the drudgery of the law, his case is a failure in advance.

Discourage litigation. Persuade your neighbors to compromise whenever you can. Point out to them how the nominal winner is often a real loser—in fees, expenses, and waste of time. As a peacemaker the lawyer has a superior opportunity of being a good man. There will still be business enough.

Never stir up litigation. A worse man can scarcely be found than one who does this. Who can be more nearly a fiend than he who habitually overhauls the register of deeds in search of defects in titles, whereon to stir up strife, and put money in his pocket? A moral tone ought to be infused into the profession which should drive such men out of it.

The matter of fees is important, far beyond the mere question of bread and butter involved. Properly attended to, fuller justice is done to both lawyer and client. An exorbitant fee should never be claimed. As a general rule never take your whole fee in advance, nor any more than a small retainer. When fully paid beforehand, you are more than a common mortal if you can feel the same interest in the case, as if something was still in prospect for you, as well as for your client. And when you lack interest in the case the job will very likely lack skill and diligence in the performance. Settle the amount of fee and take a note in advance. Then you will feel that you are working for something, and you are sure to do your work faithfully and well. Never sell a fee note—at least not before the consideration service is performed. It leads to negligence and dishonesty—negligence by losing interest in the case, and dishonesty in refusing to refund when you have allowed the consideration to fail.

There is a vague popular belief that lawyers are necessarily dishonest. I say vague, because when we consider to what extent confidence and honors are reposed in and conferred upon lawyers by the people, it appears improbable that their impression of dishonesty is very distinct and vivid. Yet the impression is common, almost universal. Let no young man choosing the law for a calling for a moment yield to the popular belief—resolve to be honest at all events; and if in your own judgment you cannot be an honest lawyer, resolve to be honest without being a lawyer. Choose some other occupation, rather than one in the choosing of which you do in advance, consent to be a knave.

LETTER TO JOHN D. JOHNSTON[5]
JANUARY 12, 1851

John D. Johnston was Lincoln's step-brother, the son of Mary Bush Johnston who remarried Lincoln's father after the untimely death of his biological mother. Johnston asked Lincoln to return home and visit his dying father before he passed away. Lincoln's responded with this letter of consolation. Sadly, it betrays a strained relationship between father and son that was never reconciled. Lincoln did not attend his father's funeral.

SPRINGFIELD, JANY. 12, 1851—
DEAR BROTHER:

On the day before yesterday I received a letter from Harriett, written at Greenup. She says she has just returned from your house; and that Father is very low and will hardly recover. She also say[s you] have written me two letters;

5. *CWAL*, II, 96–97.

and that [although] you do not expect me to come now, you [wonder] that I do not write. I received both your [letters, and] although I have not answered them, it is no[t because] I have forgotten them, or been uninterested about them—but because it appeared to me I could write nothing which could do any good. You already know I desire that neither Father or Mother shall be in want of any comfort either in health or sickness while they live; and I feel sure you have not failed to use my name, if necessary, to procure a doctor, or any thing else for Father in his present sickness. My business is such that I could hardly leave home now, if it were not, as it is, that my own wife is sick-abed. (It is a case of baby sickness, and I suppose is not dangerous.) I sincerely hope Father may yet recover his health; but at all events tell him to remember to call upon, and confide in, our great, and good, and merciful Maker, who will not turn away from him in any extremity. He notes the fall of a sparrow, and numbers the hairs of our heads; and He will not forget the dying man who puts his trust in Him. Say to him that if we could meet now, it is doubtful whether it would not be more painful than pleasant; but that if it be his lot to go now, he will soon have a joyous [meeting] with many loved ones gone before; and where [the rest] of us, through the help of God, hope ere long [to join] them.

Write to me again when you receive this.

Affectionately

A. Lincoln

RESOLUTIONS IN BEHALF OF HUNGARIAN FREEDOM[6]
JANUARY 9, 1852

Shortly after Russia and Austria suppressed the Hungarian Revolution, Louis Kossuth fled to the United States in an effort to continue the struggle for Magyar independence. In response to Kossuth's freedom tour, the Illinois legislature was summoned to deliberate on whether or not the United States should intervene to aid the Hungarians in their struggle for democracy. Given the circumstances, Lincoln spoke at the meeting in favor of sympathy, but nonintervention. At the same time, he made it clear that American interventionism could be justified if a belligerent nation invaded the sovereignty of the free state. Thus, while Lincoln consistently affirmed the right of revolution for peoples struggling against despotism, this right did not obligate the United States as the standard bearer of self-government to intervene militarily when democracy was threatened abroad. America's mission could be affirmed through noninterventionist means such as extending moral support, sanctions against foes of democracy, and sympathy to struggling

6. *CWAL*, II, 115-116.

revolutionaries. As with his domestic policy, he believed that the principled commitment to democracy must be guided by the prudent determination of what is actually possible under the circumstances.

Whereas, in the opinion of this meeting, the arrival of Kossuth in our country, in connection with the recent events in Hungary, and with the appeal he is now making in behalf of his country, presents an occasion upon which we, the American people, cannot remain silent, without justifying an inference against our continued devotion to the principles of our free institutions, therefore,

Resolved,

1. That it is the right of any people, sufficiently numerous for national independence, to throw off, to revolutionize, their existing form of government, and to establish such other in its stead as they may choose.

2. That it is the duty of our government to neither foment, nor assist, such revolutions in other governments.

3. That, as we may not legally or warrantably interfere abroad, *to aid,* so no other government may interfere abroad, *to suppress* such revolutions; and that we should at once, announce to the world, our determinations to insist upon this *mutuality* of non-intervention, as a sacred principle of the international law.

4. That the late interference of Russia in the Hungarian struggle was, in our opinion, such illegal and unwarrantable interference.

5. That to have resisted Russia in that case, or to resist any power in a like case, would be no violation of our own cherished principles of non-intervention, but, on the contrary, would be ever meritorious, in us, or any independent nation.

6. That whether we will, in fact, interfere in such case, is purely a question of policy, to be decided when the exigency arrives.

7. That we recognize in Governor Kossuth of Hungary the most worthy and distinguished representative of the cause of civil and religious liberty on the continent of Europe. A cause for which he and his nation struggled until they were overwhelmed by the armed intervention of a foreign despot, in violation of the more sacred principles of the laws of nature and of nations—principles held dear by the friends of freedom everywhere, and more especially by the people of these United States.

8. That the sympathies of this country, and the benefits of its position, should be exerted in favor of the people of every nation struggling to be

free; and whilst we meet to do honor to Kossuth and Hungary, we should not fail to pour out the tribute of our praise and approbation to the patriotic efforts of the Irish, the Germans and the French, who have unsuccessfully fought to establish in their several governments the supremacy of the people.

9. That there is nothing in the past history of the British government, or in its present expressed policy, to encourage the belief that she will aid, in any manner, in the delivery of continental Europe from the yoke of despotism; and that her treatment of Ireland, of O'Brien, Mitchell, and other worthy patriots, forces the conclusion that she will join her efforts to the despots of Europe in suppressing every effort of the people to establish free governments, based upon the principles of true religious and civil liberty.

EULOGY ON HENRY CLAY DELIVERED IN THE STATE HOUSE AT SPRINGFIELD, ILLINOIS
JULY 6, 1852

Henry Clay was a leading statesman, economic nationalist and standard bearer of the Whig party during the antebellum period. Known as "the Great Compromiser," he helped preserve sectional peace on three important occasions: 1) the Missouri Compromise of 1820; 2) the Compromise of 1833 over the Nullification Crisis; and 3) The Compromise of 1850. Lincoln delivered this eulogy for Henry Clay at a public gathering in Springfield. If Washington was Lincoln's role model among the first generation of great American statesman, Clay was his model among the second generation. Clay's western roots, economic nationalism, devotion to the Union, principled opposition to the extension of slavery, and his colonization plan for dealing with the problem of slavery made a lasting impression on the young Lincoln. In particular, Clay's ability to reach compromise and to balance a variety of moral and legal claims resonated with Lincoln's prudential approach to politics.

ON THE FOURTH DAY OF JULY, 1776, the people of a few feeble and oppressed colonies of Great Britain, inhabiting a portion of the Atlantic coast of North America, publicly declared their national independence, and made their appeal to the justice of their cause, and to the God of battles, for the maintainance of that declaration. That people were few in numbers, and without resources, save only their own wise heads and stout hearts. Within the first year of that declared independence, and while its maintainance was yet problematical—while the bloody struggle between those resolute rebels, and their haughty would-be-masters, was still waging, of undistinguished parents, and in an obscure district of one of those colonies, Henry Clay was born. The infant nation, and the infant child began the race of life together. For three quarters of a century they have travelled hand in hand. They have been companions ever. The nation has passed its perils, and is free, prosperous, and powerful. The child has reached his manhood, his middle age, his old age, and is dead. In all that has concerned the nation the man ever sympathised; and now the nation mourns for the man.

The day after his death, one of the public Journals, opposed to him politically, held the following pathetic and beautiful language, which I adopt, partly because such high and exclusive eulogy, originating with a political friend, might offend good taste, but chiefly, because I could not, in any language of my own, so well express my thoughts—

"Alas! who can realize that Henry Clay is dead! Who can realize that never again that majestic form shall rise in the council-chambers of his country to beat back the storms of anarchy which may threaten, or pour the oil of peace upon the troubled billows as they rage and menace around? Who can realize, that the workings of that mighty mind have ceased—that the throbbings of that gallant heart are stilled—that the mighty sweep of that graceful arm will be felt no more, and the magic of that eloquent tongue, which spake as spake no other tongue besides, is hushed—hushed forever! Who can realize that freedom's champion—the champion of a civilized world, and of all tongues and kindreds and people, has indeed fallen! Alas, in those dark hours, which, as they come in the history of all nations, must come in ours—those hours of peril and dread which our land has experienced, and which she may be called to experience again—to whom now may her people look up for that counsel and advice, which only wisdom and experience and patriotism can give, and which only the undoubting confidence of a nation will receive? Perchance, in the whole circle of the great and gifted of our land, there remains but one on whose shoulders the mighty mantle of the departed statesman may fall—one, while we now write, is doubtless pouring his tears over the bier of his brother and his friend—brother, friend ever, yet in political sentiment, as far apart as party could make them. Ah, it is at times like these, that the petty distinctions of mere party disappear. We see only the great, the grand, the noble features of the departed statesman; and we do not even beg permission to bow at his feet and mingle our tears with those who have ever been his political adherents—we do [not?] beg this permission—we claim it as a right, though we feel it as a privilege. Henry Clay belonged to his country—to the world, mere party cannot claim men like him. His career has been national—his fame has filled the earth—his memory will endure to "the last syllable of recorded time."

"Henry Clay is dead!—He breathed his last on yesterday at twenty minutes after eleven, in his chamber at Washington. To those who followed his lead in public affairs, it more appropriately belongs to pronounce his eulogy, and pay specific honors to the memory of the illustrious dead—but all Americans may show the grief which his death inspires, for, his character and fame are national property. As on a question of liberty, he knew no North, no South, no East, no West, but only the Union, which held them all in its sacred circle, so now his countrymen will know no grief, that is not as wide-spread as the bounds of the confederacy. The career of Henry Clay was a public career. From his youth he has been devoted to the public service, at a period too, in the world's history justly regarded as a remarkable era in human affairs. He witnessed in the beginning the throes of the French Revolution. He saw the rise and fall of Napoleon. He was called upon to legislate for America, and direct her policy when all Europe was the battle-field of contending dynasties, and when the struggle for supremacy imperilled the rights of all neutral nations. His voice spoke war and peace in the contest with Great Britain.

"When Greece rose against the Turks and struck for liberty, his name was mingled with the battle-cry of freedom. When South America threw off the thraldom of Spain, his speeches were read at the head of her armies by Bolivar. His name has been, and will continue to be, hallowed in two hemispheres, for it is—

"One of the few the immortal names
That were not born to die,"

"To the ardent patriot and profound statesman, he added a quality possessed by few of the gifted on earth. His eloquence has not been surpassed. In the effective power to move the heart of man, Clay was without an equal, and the heaven born endowment, in the spirit of its origin, has been most conspicuously exhibited against intestine feud. On at least three important occasions, he has quelled our civil commotions, by a power and influence, which belonged to no other statesman of his age and times. And in our last internal discord, when this Union trembled to its center—in old age, he left the shades of private life and gave the death blow to fraternal strife, with the vigor of his earlier years in a series of Senatorial efforts, which in themselves would bring immortality, by challenging comparison with the efforts of any statesman in any age. He exorcised the demon which possessed the body politic, and gave peace to a distracted land. Alas! the achievement cost him his life! He sank day by day to the tomb—his pale, but noble brow, bound with a triple wreath, put there by a grateful country. May his ashes rest in peace, while his spirit goes to take its station among the great and good men who preceded him!"

While it is customary, and proper, upon occasions like the present, to give a brief sketch of the life of the deceased, in the case of Mr. Clay, it is less necessary than most others; for his biography has been written and re-written, and read and re-read, for the last twenty-five years; so that, with the exception of a few of the latest incidents of his life, all is as well known, as it can be. The short sketch which I give is, therefore, merely to maintain the connection of this discourse.

Henry Clay was born on the twelfth of April 1777, in Hanover County, Virginia. Of his father, who died in the fourth or fifth year of Henry's age, little seems to be known, except that he was a respectable man, and a preacher of the Baptist persuasion. Mr. Clay's education, to the end of life, was comparatively limited. I say *"to the end of life,"* because I have understood that, from time to time, he added something to his education during the greater part of his whole life. Mr. Clay's lack of a more perfect early education, however it may be regretted generally, teaches at least one profitable lesson: it teaches that in this country, one can scarcely be so poor, but that, if he *will,* he *can* acquire sufficient education to get through the world respectably. In his twenty-third year Mr. Clay was licensed to practise law, and emigrated to Lexington, Kentucky. Here he commenced and continued the practice till the year 1803, when he was first elected to the Kentucky legislature. By successive elections he was continued in the Legislature till the latter part of 1806, when he was elected to fill a vacancy, of a single session, in the United States Senate. In 1807 he was again elected to the Kentucky House of Representatives, and by that body, chosen its Speaker. In 1808 he was re-elected to the same body. In 1809 he was again chosen to fill a vacancy of two years in the United States Senate. In 1811 he was elected to the United States House of Representatives, and on the first day of taking his seat in that body, he was chosen its Speaker. In 1813 he was again elected Speaker. Early in 1814, being the period of our last British war, Mr. Clay was sent as commissioner, with others, to negotiate a treaty of peace, which treaty was concluded in the latter part of the same year. On his return from Europe he was again elected to the lower branch of Congress, and on taking his seat in December 1815, was called to his old post—the Speaker's chair, a position in which he was retained by successive elections, with one brief intermission, till the inauguration of John Q. Adams, in March, 1825. He was then appointed Secretary of State, and occupied that important station till the inauguration of Gen. Jackson in March 1829. After this he returned to Kentucky, resumed the practice of the law, and continued it till the autumn of 1831, when he was by the legislature of Kentucky, again placed in the United States Senate. By a re-election he continued in the Senate till he resigned his seat, and retired, in March 1848. In December 1849 he again took his seat in the Senate, which he again resigned only a few months before his death.

By the foregoing it is perceived that the period from the beginning of Mr. Clay's official life, in 1803, to the end of it in 1852, is but one year short of half a century; and that the sum of all the intervals in it, will not amount to ten years. But mere duration of time in office, constitutes the smallest part of Mr. Clay's history. Throughout that long period, he has constantly been the most loved, and most implicitly followed by friends, and the most dreaded by opponents, of all living American politicians. In all the great questions which have agitated the country, and particularly in those fearful crises, the Missouri question—the Nullification question, and the late slavery question, as connected with the newly acquired territory, involving and endangering the stability of the Union, his has been the leading and most conspicuous part. In 1824 he was first a candidate for the Presidency, and was defeated; and although he was successively defeated for the same office in 1832 and in 1844, there has never been a moment since 1824 till after 1848 when a very large portion of the American people did not cling to him with an enthusiastic hope and purpose of still elevating him to the Presidency. With other men, to be defeated, was to be forgotten; but to him, defeat was but a trifling incident, neither changing him, or the world's estimate of him. Even those of both political parties who have been preferred to him for the highest office, have run far briefer courses than he, and left him, still shining high in the heavens of the political world. Jackson, Van Buren, Harrison, Polk, and Taylor, all rose *after,* and set long before him. The spell—the long-enduring spell—with which the souls of men were bound to him, is a miracle. Who

can compass it? It is probably true he owed his pre-eminence to no one quality, but to a fortunate combination of several. He was surpassingly eloquent; but
many eloquent men fail utterly; and they are not, as a class, generally successful. His judgment was excellent; but many men of good judgment, live and die
unnoticed.—His will was indomitable; but this quality often secures to its owner
nothing better than a character for useless obstinacy. These then were Mr.
Clay's leading qualities. No one of them is very uncommon; but all together are
rarely combined in a single individual; and this is probably the reason why such
men as Henry Clay are so rare in the world.

Mr. Clay's eloquence did not consist, as many fine specimens of eloquence
do, of types and figures—of antithesis, and elegant arrangement of words and
sentences; but rather of that deeply earnest and impassioned tone, and manner,
which can proceed only from great sincerity, and thorough conviction, in the
speaker of the justice and importance of his cause. This it is, that truly touches
the chords of sympathy; and those who heard Mr. Clay never failed to be moved
by it, or ever afterwards, forgot the impression. All his efforts were made for
practical effect. He never spoke merely to be heard. He never delivered a Fourth
of July oration, or an eulogy on an occasion like this. As a politician or statesman, no one was so habitually careful to avoid all sectional ground. Whatever
he did, he did for the whole country. In the construction of his measures he
ever carefully surveyed every part of the field, and duly weighed every conflicting interest. Feeling as he did, and as the truth surely is, that the world's best
hope depended on the continued Union of these States, he was ever jealous of,
and watchful for, whatever might have the slightest tendency to separate them.

Mr. Clay's predominant sentiment, from first to last, was a deep devotion to
the cause of human liberty—a strong sympathy with the oppressed everywhere,
and an ardent wish for their elevation. With him, this was a primary and all controlling passion. Subsidiary to this was the conduct of his whole life. He loved
his country partly because it was his own country, but mostly because it was a
free country; and he burned with a zeal for its advancement, prosperity and
glory, because he saw in such, the advancement, prosperity, and glory, of
human liberty, human right and human nature. He desired the prosperity of his
countrymen partly because they were his countrymen, but chiefly to show to
the world that freemen could be prosperous.

That his views and measures were always the wisest, needs not to be affirmed;
nor should it be, on this occasion, where so many, thinking differently, join in
doing honor to his memory. A free people, in times of peace and quiet—when
pressed by no common danger—naturally divide into parties. At such times the

man who is of neither party, is not—cannot be, of any consequence. Mr. Clay, therefore, was of a party. Taking a prominent part, as he did, in all the great political questions of his country for the last half century, the wisdom of his course on many, is doubted and denied by a large portion of his countrymen; and of such it is not now proper to speak particularly.—But there are many others, about his course upon which, there is little or no disagreement amongst intelligent and patriotic Americans. Of these last are the war of 1812, the Missouri question, Nullification, and the now recent compromise measures. In 1812 Mr. Clay, though not unknown, was still a young man. Whether we should go to war with Great Britain, being the question of the day, a minority opposed the declaration of war by Congress, while the majority, though apparently inclining to war, had for years, wavered, and hesitated to act decisively. Meanwhile British aggressions multiplied, and grew more daring and aggravated. By Mr. Clay, more than any other man, the struggle was brought to a decision in Congress. The question, being now fully before congress, came up in a variety of ways, in rapid succession, on most of which occasions Mr. Clay spoke. Adding to all the logic, of which the subject was susceptible, that noble inspiration, which came to him as it came to no other, he aroused, and nerved, and inspired his friends, and confounded and bore down all opposition. Several of his speeches, on these occasions, were reported, and are still extant, but the best of these all never was. During its delivery the reporters forgot their vocations, dropped their pens, and sat enchanted from near the beginning to quite the close. The speech now lives only in the memory of a few old men; and the enthusiasm with which they cherish their recollection of it is absolutely astonishing. The precise language of this speech we shall never know; but we do know—we cannot help knowing—that, with deep pathos, it pleaded the cause of the injured sailor—that it invoked the genius of the revolution—that it apostrophized the names of Otis, of Henry and of Washington—that it appealed to the interest, the pride, the honor and the glory of the nation—that it shamed and taunted the timidity of friends—that it scorned, and scouted, and withered the temerity of domestic foes—that it bearded and defied the British Lion—and rising, and swelling, and maddening in its course, it sounded the onset, till the charge, the shock, the steady struggle, and the glorious victory, all passed in vivid review before the entranced hearers.

Important and exciting as was the war question, of 1812, it never so alarmed the sagacious statesmen of the country for the safety of the republic, as afterward did the Missouri question. This sprang from that unfortunate source of discord—negro slavery. When our Federal Constitution was adopted, we owned no territory beyond the limits or ownership of the States, except the territory North-West of the River Ohio, and east of the Mississippi.—What has since been formed into the States of Maine, Kentucky, and Tennessee, was, I believe, within the limits of or owned by Massachusetts, Virginia, and North Carolina. As to the North Western Territory, provision had been made, even before the adoption of the Constitution, that slavery should never go there. On the admission of the States into the Union carved from the territory we owned before the constitution, no question—or at most, no considerable question—arose about slavery—those which were within the limits of or owned by the old states, following respectively, the condition of the parent state, and those within the North West territory, following the previously made provision. But in 1803 we purchased Louisiana of the French; and it included with much more, what has since been formed into the State of Missouri. With regard to it, nothing had been done to forestall the question of slavery. When, therefore, in 1819, Missouri, having formed a State constitution, without excluding slavery, and with slavery already actually existing within its limits, knocked at the door of the Union for admission, almost the entire representation of the non-slaveholding states, objected. A fearful and angry struggle instantly followed. This alarmed thinking men, more than any previous question, because, unlike all the former, it divided the country by geographical lines. Other questions had their opposing partizans in all localities of the country and in almost every family; so that no division of the Union could follow such, without a separation of friends, to quite as great an extent, as that of opponents.—Not so with the Missouri question. On this a geographical line could be traced which, in the main, would separate opponents only. This was the danger. Mr. Jefferson, then in retirement, wrote:

"I had for a long time ceased to read newspapers, or to pay any attention to public affairs, confident they were in good hands, and content to be a passenger in our bark to the shore from which I am not distant. But this momentous question, like a fire bell in the night, awakened, and filled me with terror. I considered it at once as the knell of the Union. It is hushed, indeed, for the moment. But this is a reprieve only, not a final sentence. A geographical line, co-inciding with a marked principle, moral and political, once conceived and held up to the angry passions of men, will never be obliterated, and every irritation will mark it deeper and deeper. I can say with conscious truth, that there is not a man on earth who would sacrifice more than I would to relieve us from this heavy reproach, in any *practicable* way. The cession of that kind of property, for so it is misnamed, is a bagatelle which would not cost me a second thought, if, in that way, a general emancipation, and *expatriation* could be effected; and, gradually, and with due sacrifices I think it might be. But as it is, we have the wolf by the ears, and we can neither hold him, nor safely let him go. Justice is in one scale, and self-preservation in the other."

Mr. Clay was in congress, and, perceiving the danger, at once engaged his whole energies to avert it. It began, as I have said, in 1819; and it did not terminate till 1821. Missouri would not yield the point; and congress—that is, a majority in congress—by repeated votes, showed a determination to not admit the State unless it should yield. After several failures, and great labor on the part of Mr. Clay to so present the question that a majority could consent to the admission, it was by a vote, rejected, and as all seemed to think, finally. A sullen gloom hung over the nation. All felt that the rejection of Missouri, was equivalent to a dissolution of the Union, because those states which already had, what Missouri was rejected for refusing to relinquish, would go with Missouri. All deprecated and deplored this, but none saw how to avert it. For the judgment of members to be convinced of the necessity of yielding, was not the whole difficulty; each had a constituency to meet, and to answer to. Mr. Clay, though worn down, and exhausted, was appealed to by members, to renew his efforts at compromise.—He did so, and by some judicious modifications of his plan, coupled with laborious efforts with individual members, and his own over-mastering eloquence upon the floor, he finally secured the admission of the State. Brightly, and captivating as it had previously shown, it was now perceived that his great eloquence, was a mere embellishment, or at most, but a helping hand to his inventive genius, and his devotion to his country in the day of her extreme peril.

After the settlement of the Missouri question, although a portion of the American people have differed with Mr. Clay, and a majority even, appear generally to have been opposed to him on questions of ordinary administration, he seems constantly to have been regarded by all, as *the* man for a crisis. Accordingly, in the days of Nullification, and more recently in the re-appearance of the slavery question, connected with our territory newly acquired of Mexico, the task of devising a mode of adjustment, seems to have been cast upon Mr. Clay, by common consent—and his performance of the task, in each case, was little else than, a literal fulfilment of the public expectation.

Mr. Clay's efforts in behalf of the South Americans, and afterwards, in behalf of the Greeks, in the times of their respective struggles for civil liberty are among the finest on record, upon the noblest of all themes, and bear ample corroboration of what I have said was his ruling passion—a love of liberty and right, unselfishly, and for their own sakes.

Having been led to allude to domestic slavery so frequently already, I am unwilling to close without referring more particularly to Mr. Clay's views and conduct in regard to it. He ever was on principle and in feeling, opposed to slavery. The very earliest, and one of the latest public efforts of his life, separated by a period of more than fifty years;—were both made in favor of gradual emancipation of the slave in Kentucky. He did not perceive, that on a question of human right, the negroes were to be excepted from the human race. And yet Mr. Clay was the owner of slaves. Cast into life where slavery was already widely spread and deeply seated, he did not perceive, as I think no wise man has perceived, how it could be at *once* eradicated, without producing a greater evil, even to the cause of human liberty itself. His feeling and his judgment, therefore, ever led him to oppose both extremes of opinion on the subject. Those who would shiver into fragments the Union of these States; tear to tatters its now venerated constitution; and even burn the last copy of the Bible, rather than slavery should continue a single hour, together with all their more halting sympathisers, have received, and are receiving their just execration; and the name, and opinions, and influence of Mr. Clay, are fully, and, as I trust, effectually and enduringly, arrayed against them. But I would also, if I could, array his name, opinions, and influence against the opposite extreme—against a few, but an increasing number of men, who, for the sake of perpetuating slavery, are beginning to assail and to ridicule the white man's charter of freedom—the declaration that "all men are created free and equal." So far as I have learned, the first American, of any note, to do or attempt this, was the late John C. Calhoun; and if I mistake not, it soon after found its way into some of the messages of the Governors of South Carolina. We, however, look for and are not much shocked by, political eccentricities and heresies in South Carolina. But, only last year, I saw with astonishment, what purported to be a letter of a very distinguished and influential clergyman of Virginia, copied, with apparent approbation, into a St. Louis newspaper, containing the following, to me, very unsatisfactory language—

"I am fully aware that there is a text in some Bibles that is not in mine. Professional abolitionists have made more use of it, than of any passage in the Bible. It came, however, as I trace it, from Saint Voltaire, and was baptized by Thomas Jefferson, and since almost universally regarded as canonical authority, '*All men are born free and equal.*'

"This is a genuine coin in the political currency of our generation. I am sorry to say that I have never seen two men of whom it is true. But I must admit I never saw the Siamese Twins, and therefore will not dogmatically say that no man ever saw a proof of this sage aphorism."

This sounds strangely in republican America.—The like was not heard in the fresher days of the Republic. Let us contrast with it the language of that truly national man, whose life and death we now commemorate and lament. I quote from a speech of Mr. Clay delivered before the American Colonization Society in 1827:

"We are reproached with doing mischief by the agitation of this question. The society goes into no household to disturb its domestic tranquility; it addresses itself to no slaves to weaken their obligations of obedience. It seeks to affect no man's property. It neither has the power nor the will to affect the property of any one contrary to his consent.— The execution of its scheme would augment instead of diminishing the value of the property left behind. The society, composed of free men, concerns itself only with the free. Collateral consequences we are not responsible for. It is not this society which has produced the great moral revolution which the age exhibits. What would they, who thus reproach us, have done? If they would repress all tendencies towards liberty, and ultimate emancipation, they must do more than put down the benevolent efforts of this society. They must go back to the era of our liberty and independence, and muzzle the cannon which thunders its annual joyous return. They must renew the slave trade with all its train of atrocities. They must suppress the workings of British philanthropy, seeking to meliorate the condition of the unfortunate West Indian slave. They must arrest the career of South American deliverance from thraldom. They must blow out the moral lights around us, and extinguish that greatest torch of all which America presents to a benighted world— pointing the way to their rights, their liberties, and their happiness. And when they have achieved those purposes their work will be yet incomplete. They must penetrate the human soul, and eradicate the light of reason and the love of liberty. Then, and not till then, when universal darkness and despair prevail, can you perpetuate slavery, and repress all sympathy, and all humane, and benevolent efforts among free men, in behalf of the unhappy portion of our race doomed to bondage."

The American Colonization Society was organized in 1816. Mr. Clay, though not its projector, was one of its earliest members; and he died, as for the many preceding years he had been, its President.—It was one of the most cherished objects of his direct care and consideration; and the association of his name with it has probably been its very greatest collateral support. He considered it no demerit in the society, that it tended to relieve slave-holders from the troublesome presence of the free negroes; but this was far from being its whole merit in his estimation. In the same speech from which I have quoted he says:

"There is a moral fitness in the idea of returning to Africa her children, whose ancestors have been torn from her by the ruthless hand of fraud and violence. Transplanted in a foreign land, they will carry back to their native soil the rich fruits of religion, civilization, law and liberty. May it not be one of the great designs of the Ruler of the universe, (whose ways are often inscrutable by short-sighted mortals,) thus to transform an original crime, into a signal blessing to that most unfortunate portion of the globe?"

This suggestion of the possible ultimate redemption of the African race and African continent, was made twenty-five years ago. Every succeeding year has added strength to the hope of its realization.—May it indeed be realized! Pharaoh's country was cursed with plagues, and his hosts were drowned in the Red Sea for striving to retain a captive people who had already served them more than four hundred years. May like disasters never befall us! If as the friends of colonization hope, the present and coming generations of our countrymen shall by any means, succeed in freeing our land from the dangerous presence of slavery; and, at the same time, in restoring a captive people to their long-lost father-land, with bright prospects for the future; and this too, so gradually, that neither races nor individuals shall have suffered by the change, it will indeed be a glorious consummation. And if, to such a consummation, the efforts of Mr. Clay shall have contributed, it will be what he most ardently wished, and none of his labors will have been more valuable to his country and his kind.

But Henry Clay is dead. His long and eventful life is closed. Our country is prosperous and powerful; but could it have been quite all it has been, and is, and is to be, without Henry Clay? Such a man the times have demanded, and such, in the providence of God was given us. But he is gone. Let us strive to deserve, as far as mortals may, the continued care of Divine Providence, trusting that in future national emergencies, He will not fail to provide us the instruments of safety and security.

FRAGMENTS ON GOVERNMENT[7]
July 1, 1854

Contrary to those who claim that Lincoln endorsed a highly consolidated federal government at the expense of state and local authority, these fragments define a more limited role for the state during times of peace. They manifest an appreciation of the principle of subsidiarity: the recognition that there are different spheres of authority corresponding to the particular circumstances that each is best suited to govern. The exigencies of the Civil War, however, led to an inevitable increase in national power at the expense of state authority and, for better or worse, tilted the balance between the state and national authority in the direction of a more consolidated Union. It is noteworthy that Lincoln's reconstruction plan intended to give states greater authority and discretion in reconstituting their governments and in rejoining the Union than the alternatives proposed by the Radical Republicans.

[July 1, 1854?]

The legitimate object of government, is to do for a community of people, whatever they need to have done, but can not do, *at all,* or can not, *so well do,* for themselves—in their separate, and individual capacities.

In all that the people can individually do as well for themselves, government ought not to interfere.

The desirable things which the individuals of a people can not do, or can not well do, for themselves, fall into two classes: those which have relation to *wrongs,* and those which have not. Each of these branch off into an infinite variety of subdivisions.

The first—that in relation to wrongs—embraces all crimes, misdemesnors, and non-performance of contracts. The other embraces all which, in its nature, and without wrong, requires combined action, as public roads and highways, public schools, charities, pauperism, orphanage, estates of the deceased, and the machinery of government itself.

From this it appears that if all men were just, there still would be *some,* though not *so much,* need of government.

---

7. This fragment and the following one: CWAL, II, 220-22.

[JULY 1, 1854?]

Government is a combination of the people of a country to effect certain objects by joint effort. The best framed and best administered governments are necessarily expensive; while by errors in frame and maladministration most of them are more onerous than they need be, and some of them very oppressive. Why, then, should we have government? Why not each individual take to himself the whole fruit of his labor, without having any of it taxed away, in services, corn, or money? Why not take just so much land as he can cultivate with his own hands, without buying it of any one?

The legitimate object of government is "to do for the people what needs to be done, but which they can not, by individual effort, do at all, or do so well, for themselves." There are many such things—some of them exist independently of the injustice in the world. Making and maintaining roads, bridges, and the like; providing for the helpless young and afflicted; common schools; and disposing of deceased men's property, are instances.

But a far larger class of objects springs from the injustice of men. If one people will make war upon another, it is a necessity with that other to unite and coöperate for defense. Hence the military department. If some men will kill, or beat, or constrain others, or despoil them of property, by force, fraud, or noncompliance with contracts, it is a common object with peaceful and just men to prevent it. Hence the criminal and civil departments.

II.

"A House Divided"

1854–1858

T HIS SELECTION OF SPEECHES AND WRITINGS comprises events from the
time of the Kansas–Nebraska Act of 1854 to Lincoln's candidacy for the
United States Senate in 1858, just prior to the celebrated debates with
Douglas. They chronicle Lincoln's return to public life, the development of his
antislavery views, and the occurrence of a great political realignment—the dis-
ruption of the established political party system by the slavery issue and the shift-
ing of party loyalties culminating with the formation of the new Republican
Party. Events such as "Bleeding Kansas" in 1856 and the infamous Dred Scott
Decision of 1857 further polarized sectional conflict. The chronology ends with
Lincoln's nomination as the Republican candidate for the Illinois seat in the
United States Senate in 1858. It includes the opening salvos of his battle against
Democratic opponent Stephen A. Douglas.

The Kansas–Nebraska Act marked an important turning point in Lincoln's
life and the life of the nation. In response to it, Lincoln concentrated his political energies against slavery and its challenge to America's meaning and destiny.
The author of the Kansas–Nebraska Act was Stephen A. Douglas, a young
Democratic Senator from Illinois, co–author of the Compromise of 1850, and
then–Chairman of the United States Senate Committee on Territories. This
powerful committee was confronted with the combustible issue of slavery
extension, still smoldering from the Mexican Cession. Perhaps in hopes of
securing a transcontinental railroad route through the Midwest and of hasten-
ing westward expansion, Douglas sponsored a bill that would have rapidly
developed the as–yet–unorganized Northern territories of Kansas and Nebraska.
Significantly, slavery was prohibited in these territories by the Missouri Compromise since they fell north of the 36–30 line of demarcation. In order to gain
Southern support for his measure, Douglas agreed to an explicit repeal of the
Missouri Compromise. He then proposed that the question of human servitude
in the territories be resolved through the principle of popular sovereignty, the
right of territorial settlers to decide for themselves whether or not to have slavery. As a champion of manifest destiny, Douglas argued that popular sovereignty
was the most democratic and expedient way to resolve the slavery controversy,
which he believed distracted the nation from the more important task of nation-
building and westward expansion. He further contended that the principle of
self–determination in the Kansas–Nebraska Act was entirely consistent with the

precedent set by the Compromise of 1850 whose silence regarding slavery in the territories of Utah and New Mexico amounted to popular sovereignty in both principle and practice.

The Kansas–Nebraska Act stirred Lincoln to reenter politics after he had retired from office to focus on his law career. When considering the motives of Lincoln's leadership, this principled orientation should be kept in mind to balance recent scholarship that has made much of his personal ambition. Lincoln maintained that the Kansas–Nebraska Act profoundly jeopardized the founding ideals of the republic by placing slavery on a new basis. It extended the institution into the virgin territories and promoted the idea that it was a matter of moral indifference to the Union. In sum, the Kansas–Nebraska Act polarized sectional conflict, precipitated an incipient civil war in Kansas, caused a realignment resulting in the formation of the Republican Party, and led to the emergence of Lincoln in national politics.

In the winter of 1855, Lincoln threw his hat in the ring as a candidate for the Illinois seat in the United States Senate. As was customary before the Seventeenth Amendment mandated the direct election of senators, the Illinois State Legislature would choose a candidate to represent the state in Washington. In effect, the contest was a referendum on the Kansas–Nebraska Act. However, before the consolidation of the Republican Party, which would occur a year later, there was no firm antislavery coalition. Lincoln led the vote on the initial ballot, but lacked a majority needed to clinch the election. When a pro-Nebraska candidate threatened to win, Lincoln threw his support for Lyman Trumbell, an anti-Nebraska Democrat, thereby placing the greater good of the antislavery cause over his personal ambition. Trumbell was elected, but Lincoln would have another chance in the next senatorial contest against Stephen A. Douglas, which would be held in 1858.

In May of 1856, proslavery border ruffians from Missouri sacked Lawrence, Kansas, the free soil capital of the state, thereby sparking an incipient civil war in the state known as "Bleeding Kansas." In retaliation for the sack of Lawrence, the abolitionist John Brown raided a proslavery encampment at Pottawotomie Creek where he hacked to pieces five innocent men as their families watched in horror. Brown envisioned himself as a scourge commissioned by God to punish slaveholders. He literally subscribed to the motto that, "there can be no remission for sin without the spilling of blood." As violence often begets violence, Missouri border ruffians then retaliated for Pottawatomie and attacked a free soil settlement at Ossawatomie, killing one of Brown's sons.

The violence in Kansas reverberated throughout the halls of the United States Senate. Upon hearing of the sack of Lawrence, Charles Sumner, an abolitionist senator from Massachusetts, delivered an incendiary speech entitled *The Crime Against Kansas,* which included insulting remarks about Senator A. P. Butler of South Carolina. Two days later, Preston S. Brooks, Butler's nephew and a congressman also from South Carolina, entered the Senate chamber where Sumner was seated at his desk and pummeled him repeatedly over the head with a cane until he was knocked senseless. Apparently, the Southern code of honor demanded this form of chastisement, for dueling was a method of redress reserved only for equals. Because Southern gentlemen held Sumner in such contempt, the proper method of his chastisement called for a caning or a whipping rather than a duel.

In his Inaugural Address of March 4, 1857, President Buchanan alluded to a forthcoming decision that he hoped would resolve the slavery agitation convulsing the nation. Two days later, on March 6, 1857, Chief Justice Roger B. Taney, an appointment of Democratic President Andrew Jackson, handed down the infamous Dred Scott Decision. Scott was a Missouri slave who was taken by his master to the free state of Illinois and the free territory of Wisconsin wherein slavery was prohibited by the Compromise of 1820. After residing in free soil for about four years, Scott returned to the slave state of Missouri in 1838 and sued for his freedom, arguing that his residency upon free soil made him a free man. The Missouri Court ruled in Scott's favor; however, the case went on appeal to the Supreme Court. In effect, Taney's decision transformed the status of slavery from that of a narrowly circumscribed state institution to that of a broadly defined national institution.

There were three elements to Taney's decision: (1) his denial of Negro Citizenship and natural rights; (2) his denial of Federal Authority to restrict slavery in the Territories; and (3) his decree that "the right to property in a slave is distinctly and expressly affirmed in the Constitution." According to Taney, blacks were an inferior race having "no rights which the white man was bound to respect." After determining that the federal government lacked authority to regulate slavery in the territories, the Dred Scott Decision pronounced the Missouri Compromise null and void. In part, Taney's legal reasoning was based upon a substantive interpretation of the due process clause of the Fifth Amendment, meaning that the term "liberty" in the Fifth Amendment implied the national right of chattel slavery: "Thus the rights of property are united with the rights of person and placed on the same ground by the Fifth Amendment to the Constitution, which provides that no person shall be deprived of life, liberty, and property without due process of law. . . . [T]he right of property in a slave is distinctly and expressly affirmed in the Constitution. The right to traffic in it, like an ordinary article of merchandise and property, was guaranteed to the citizens of the United States. . . . " Since chattel slavery was upheld as a national right guaranteed by the Fifth Amendment, the federal government could no more restrict its spread than it could deny someone the right to transport "an ordinary article of merchandise" from one place to another. Any attempt to restrict slavery in the territories was therefore unconstitutional. Thus, Dred Scott subverted the core belief of the Republican Party. Proslavery forces felt vindicated by the opinion, which called into question the very existence of the Republican Party. Opposition to Dred Scott was interpreted as yet another instance of abolitionist fanaticism and the North's utter disregard for the rule of law, leaving secession as the South's only alternative to protect its right to slavery.

Ironically, the Dred Scott Decision also undermined Stephen Douglas's doctrine of popular sovereignty. By affirming chattel slavery as a national right, it deprived settlers of the freedom of choice to exclude slavery if they so wished. Settlers had no more right to exclude slave property from their territory than they did to deprive someone of transporting any other movable property or possessions from one place to another. Consequently, the Dred Scott Decision precipitated a split between Northern Douglas Democrats who favored popular sovereignty, and Southern Democrats who demanded a national slave code to protect and extend the institution, a demand which was perfectly consistent given Taney's logic.

Lincoln dissected Taney's legal reasoning in Dred Scott. He argued that the decision was based upon an erroneous interpretation of the Declaration, the intention of the Founders, and the text of the Constitution. He refused to accept the opinion as an authoritative precedent for settling national policy on slavery, since it was based on "assumed historical facts which were not really true." For example, in his speech at Springfield on July 26, 1857, Lincoln pointed out that African-Americans were considered citizens at the time of the Founding, and even voted in state ratifying conventions of the Constitution. Furthermore, he demonstrated that there was eighty years of historical precedent from the time of the Northwest Ordinance in 1787 onward validating the federal government's authority to restrict slavery in the territories, a grant of power that was based upon Article Four, Section Three in the Constitution: "The Congress shall have Power to dispose of and make all needful Rules and Regulations respecting the Territory or other Property belonging to the United States." Finally, contrary to Taney's assertion that "the right of property in a slave is distinctly and expressly affirmed in the Constitution," Lincoln explained that neither the word "slave" nor "slavery" was explicitly mentioned in the document, nor was the term slavery ever mentioned in any connection with property. Indeed, Lincoln had made this argument three years earlier in his Peoria address of October 16, 1854. In his view, the Founders' deliberate avoidance of the word slave or slavery in the Constitution conveyed a moral dubiousness about the institution.

In addition, Lincoln's critique of Dred Scott contemplated the sinister motives behind the decision and the pernicious consequences thereof. In his controversial House Divided speech of June 16, 1858, Lincoln repudiated the decision as part of an aggressive proslavery conspiracy that sought to nationalize the institution and to supplant the founding ideals of the nation, thereby replacing them with a new creed of human inequality. If chattel slavery was a national right guaranteed by the Constitution, then how could it be prevented from entering a free state as well? Indeed, the Taney Court had an opportunity to extend the precedent of chattel slavery to the free states in the impending case of *Lemmon v. the People of Virginia,* a companion case to Dred Scott in which a slaveholder sued for the right to bring his slaves into the free state of New York while en route to Texas.

It is no exaggeration to say that from the time of the Dred Scott in 1857 to his election as president in 1860, Lincoln devoted a considerable amount of time and energy vindicating the principles of the American regime from Taney's proslavery *re-interpretation* of the Constitution. In view of Lincoln's exhaustive, cogent, and detailed critique, it is therefore remarkable that today Taney's proslavery construction of the Constitution is still accepted in far too many circles as the correct interpretation of the Founders' intent on slavery.

FRAGMENTS: ON SLAVERY
[JULY 1, 1854?]

These two fragments on slavery seem to have been prepared by Lincoln for lectures. The date of April 1, 1854, was attributed by Lincoln's secretaries Nicolay and Hay and cannot be verified. While the exact wording of these fragments do not appear in any known speech by Lincoln, their overall logic and sentiments permeate his political thought and writing.

This fragment displays the incisive logic that distinguished Lincoln as a lawyer and statesman, testifying to his rare ability to express ideas clearly and forcefully in plain, simple language. Here, Lincoln cut to the principal justification for the South's "peculiar institution" forcing its apologists who defended it in the abstract to deduce consistently its abhorrent practical consequences. Those who justified slavery claimed that the possession of some quality to a greater degree—like intelligence—entitled them to a mastery over others. Lincoln noted that if applied consistently, the principle justifying servitude would pertain to anyone who was inferior or deficient in the possession of this quality, not merely to blacks, but to whites as well. Significantly, his argument made no mention of race thereby implying that differences between groups are only differences in degree based on incidental qualities like complexion or skin color. Affirming the unity of our common humanity, Lincoln maintained that differences among the same species do not amount to a difference in kind. As a result, such incidental differences did not constitute a legitimate basis for enslaving those who lacked them to the same degree.

IF A. CAN PROVE, however conclusively, that he may, of right, enslave B.— why may not B. snatch the same argument, and prove equally, that he may enslave A?—

You say A. is white, and B. is black. It is *color,* then; the lighter, having the right to enslave the darker? Take care. By this rule, you are to be slave to the first man you meet, with a fairer skin than your own.

You do not mean *color* exactly? You mean the whites are *intellectually* the superiors of the blacks; and, therefore have the right to enslave them? Take care again. By this rule, you are to be slave to the first man you meet, with an intellect superior to your own.

But, say you, it is a question of *interest;* and, if you can make it your *interest,* you have the right to enslave another. Very well. And if he can make it his interest, he has the right to enslave you.

*   *   *   *   *   *

This second fragment provides an enduring statement of the American dream.

[text missing] dent truth. Made so plain by our good Father in Heaven, that all *feel* and understand it, even down to brutes and creeping insects. The ant who has toiled and dragged a crumb to his nest, will furiously defend the fruit of his labor, against whatever robber assails him. So plain, that the most dumb and stupid slave that ever toiled for a master, does constantly *know* that he is wronged. So plain that no one, high or low, ever does mistake it, except in a plainly *selfish* way; for although volume upon volume is written to prove slavery a very good thing, we never hear of the man who wishes to take the good of it *by being a slave himself.*

Most governments have been based, practically, on the denial of the equal rights of men, as I have, in part, stated them; *ours* began by *affirming* those rights. *They* said, some men are too *ignorant,* and *vicious* to share in government. Possibly so, said we; and, by your system, you would always keep them ignorant, and vicious. We proposed to give *all* a chance; and we expected the weak to grow stronger, the ignorant, wiser; and all better, and happier together.

We made the experiment; and the fruit is before us. Look at it—think of it. Look at it in its aggregate grandeur, of extent of country, and numbers of population—of ship, and steamboat, and rail-

THE REPEAL OF THE MISSOURI COMPROMISE AND THE PROPRIETY OF ITS RESTORATION: SPEECH AT PEORIA, ILLINOIS, IN REPLY TO SENATOR DOUGLAS
OCTOBER 16, 1854

Lincoln's Peoria Address, which was partly based on a speech delivered at Springfield roughly a week earlier, is among his greatest. The speech was given as a reply to Douglas who toured Illinois in September of 1854 in defense of the Kansas-Nebraska Act. It marked the beginning of Lincoln's sustained moral critique of slavery, and his emphasis upon the Declaration as the regime's moral covenant. He saw the Declaration as an American Decalogue, which promulgated the first principles of the nation's republican creed, its "ancient faith." The design of Lincoln's argument at Peoria drew upon and integrated various constitutional, biblical, legal, and republican sources against slavery extension. In particular, he explained slavery's anomalous relationship to the Constitution, describing it as a cancer that was "hidden away" in the body politic with the promise and expectation that someday it would be "cut" out. Lincoln also professed his devotion to the Union, repudiating the disunionist extremes of the radical abolitionists and southern fire-eaters alike. The dissolution of the Union would be a greater evil, because it would put an end to the American experiment, and its promise of liberty to all human beings. As a moderate antislavery man, Lincoln distinguished legally between the existence of slavery, which was beyond the scope of federal power to regulate, and the extension of it in the territories, which fell under the jurisdiction of the federal government. Though he opposed human servitude in principle, Lincoln acknowledged the difficulty of ridding the nation of slavery where it already existed and in solving the difficult question of racial adjustment once blacks were freed. The early exchange between Lincoln and Douglas at Peoria may be viewed as a prelude to their great debates in 1858. Indeed, the design and argument of many of Lincoln's subsequent speeches against slavery can be found in his Peoria Address.

THE REPEAL OF THE MISSOURI COMPROMISE, and the propriety of its restoration, constitute the subject of what I am about to say.

As I desire to present my own connected view of this subject, my remarks will not be, specifically, an answer to Judge Douglas; yet, as I proceed, the main points he has presented will arise, and will receive such respectful attention as I may be able to give them.

I wish further to say, that I do not propose to question the patriotism, or to assail the motives of any man, or class of men; but rather to strictly confine myself to the naked merits of the question.

I also wish to be no less than National in all the positions I may take; and whenever I take ground which others have thought, or may think, narrow, sectional, and dangerous to the Union, I hope to give a reason, which will appear sufficient, at least to some, why I think differently.

And, as this subject is no other, than part and parcel of the larger general question of domestic slavery, I wish to MAKE and to KEEP the distinction between the EXISTING institution, and the EXTENSION of it, so broad, and so clear, that no honest man can misunderstand me, and no dishonest one, successfully misrepresent me.

In order to [get?] a clear understanding of what the Missouri Compromise is, a short history of the preceding kindred subjects will perhaps be proper. When we established our independence, we did not own, or claim, the country to which this compromise applies. Indeed, strictly speaking, the confederacy then owned no country at all; the States respectively owned the country within their limits; and some of them owned territory beyond their strict State limits. Virginia thus owned the North-Western territory—the country out of which the principal part of Ohio, all Indiana, all Illinois, all Michigan and all Wisconsin, have since been formed. She also owned (perhaps within her then limits) what has since been formed into the State of Kentucky. North Carolina thus owned what is now the State of Tennessee; and South Carolina and Georgia, in separate parts, owned what are now Mississippi and Alabama. Connecticut, I think, owned the little remaining part of Ohio—being the same where they now send Giddings to Congress, and beat all creation at making cheese. These territories, together with the States themselves, constituted all the country over which the confederacy then claimed any sort of jurisdiction. We were then living under the Articles of Confederation, which were superseded by the

Constitution several years afterwards. The question of ceding these territories to the general government was set on foot. Mr. Jefferson, the author of the Declaration of Independence, and otherwise a chief actor in the Revolution; then a delegate in Congress; afterwards twice President; who was, is, and perhaps will continue to be, the most distinguished politician of our history; a Virginian by birth and continued residence, and withal, a slave-holder; conceived the idea of taking that occasion, to prevent slavery ever going into the north-western territory. He prevailed on the Virginia legislature to adopt his views, and to cede the territory, making the prohibition of slavery therein, a condition of the deed. Congress accepted the cession, with the condition; and in the first Ordinance (which the acts of Congress were then called) for the government of the territory, provided that slavery should never be permitted therein. This is the famed ordinance of '87 so often spoken of. Thenceforward, for sixty-one years, and until in 1848, the last scrap of this territory came into the Union as the State of Wisconsin, all parties acted in quiet obedience to this ordinance. It is now what Jefferson foresaw and intended—the happy home of teeming millions of free, white, prosperous people, and no slave amongst them.

Thus, with the author of the declaration of Independence, the policy of prohibiting slavery in new territory originated. Thus, away back of the Constitution, in the pure, fresh, free breath of the revolution, the State of Virginia, and the National Congress put that policy in practice.—Thus, through sixty odd of the best years of the republic did that policy steadily work to its great and beneficent end. And thus, in those five states, and five millions of free, enterprising people, we have before us the rich fruits of this policy. But *now* new light breaks upon us.—Now Congress declares this ought never to have been; and the like of it, must never be again.—The sacred right of self-government is grossly violated by it! We even find some men, who drew their first breath, and every other breath of their lives, under this very restriction, now live in dread of absolute suffocation, if they should be restricted in the "sacred right" of taking slaves to Nebraska. That *perfect* liberty they sigh for—the liberty of making slaves of other people—Jefferson never thought of; their own father never thought of, they never thought of themselves, a year ago. How fortunate for them, they did not sooner become sensible of their great misery! Oh, how difficult it is to treat with respect such assaults upon all we have ever really held sacred!

But to return to history. In 1803 we purchased what was then called Louisiana, of France. It included the now States of Louisiana, Arkansas, Missouri, and Iowa; also the territory of Minnesota, and the present bone of contention, Kansas and Nebraska. Slavery already existed among the French at New Orleans;

and to some extent at St. Louis. In 1812 Louisiana came into the Union as a slave state, without controversy. In 1818 or '19, Missouri showed signs of a wish to come in with slavery. This was resisted by Northern members of Congress; and thus began the first great slavery agitation in the nation. This controversy lasted several months, and became very angry and exciting; the House of Representatives voting steadily for the prohibition of slavery in Missouri, and the Senate voting as steadily against it. Threats of breaking up the Union were freely made; and the ablest public men of the day became seriously alarmed. At length a compromise was made, in which, like all compromises, both sides yielded something. It was a law passed on the 6th day of March, 1820, providing that Missouri might come into the Union *with* slavery, but that in all the remaining part of the territory purchased of France, which lies north of 36 degrees and 30 minutes north latitude, slavery should never be permitted. This provision of law, *is the Missouri Compromise.* In excluding slavery north of the line, the same language is employed as in the ordinance of '87. It directly applied to Iowa, Minnesota, and to the present bone of contention, Kansas and Nebraska. Whether there should or should not, be slavery south of that line, nothing was said in the law; but Arkansas constituted the principal remaining part, south of the line; and it has since been admitted as a slave state, without serious controversy. More recently, Iowa, north of the line, came in as a free state without controversy. Still later, Minnesota, north of the line, had a territorial organization without controversy. Texas principally south of the line, and west of Arkansas; though originally within the purchase from France, had, in 1819, been traded off to Spain, in our treaty for the acquisition of Florida. It had thus become a part of Mexico. Mexico revolutionized and became independent of Spain. American citizens began settling rapidly, with their slaves, in the southern part of Texas. Soon they revolutionized against Mexico, and established an independent government of their own, adopting a constitution, with slavery, strongly resembling the constitutions of our slave states. By still another rapid move, Texas, claiming a boundary much further West, than when we parted with her in 1819, was brought back to the United States, and admitted into the Union as a slave state. There then was little or no settlement in the northern part of Texas, a considerable portion of which lay north of the Missouri line; and in the resolutions admitting her into the Union, the Missouri restriction was expressly extended westward across her territory. This was in 1845, only nine years ago.

Thus originated the Missouri Compromise; and thus has it been respected down to 1845.—And even four years later, in 1849, our distinguished Senator, in a public address, held the following language in relation to it:

"The Missouri Compromise had been in practical operation for about a quarter of a century, and had received the sanction and approbation of men of all parties in every section of the Union. It had allayed all sectional jealousies and irritations growing out of this vexed question, and harmonized and tranquilized the whole country. It has given to Henry Clay, as its prominent champion, the proud sobriquet of the "*Great Pacificator,*" and by that title and for that service, his political friends had repeatedly appealed to the people to rally under his standard, as a presidential candidate, as the man who had exhibited the patriotism and the power to suppress, an unholy and treasonable agitation, and preserve the Union. He was not aware that any man or any party from any section of the Union, had ever urged as an objection to Mr. Clay, that he was the great champion of the Missouri Compromise. On the contrary, the effort was made by the opponents of Mr. Clay, to prove that he was not entitled to the exclusive merit of that great patriotic measure, and that the honor was equally due to others as well as to him, for securing its adoption—that it had its origin in the hearts of all patriotic men, who desired to preserve and perpetuate the blessings of our glorious Union—an origin akin that of the Constitution of the United States, conceived in the same spirit of fraternal affection, and calculated to remove forever, the only danger, which seemed to threaten, at some distant day, to sever the social bond of union. All the evidences of public opinion at that day, seemed to indicate that this Compromise had been canonized in the hearts of the American people, as a sacred thing which no ruthless hand would ever be reckless enough to disturb."

I do not read this extract to involve Judge Douglas in an inconsistency—If he afterwards thought he had been wrong, it was right for him to change—I bring this forward merely to show the high estimate placed on the Missouri Compromise by all parties up to so late as the year 1849.

But, going back a little, in point of time, our war with Mexico broke out in 1846. When Congress was about adjourning that session, President Polk asked them to place two millions of dollars under his control, to be used by him in the recess, if found practicable and expedient, in negotiating a treaty of peace with Mexico, and acquiring some part of her territory.—A bill was duly got up, for the purpose, and was progressing swimmingly, in the House of Representatives, when a member by the name of David Wilmot, a democrat from Pennsylvania, moved as an amendment "Provided that in any territory thus acquired, there shall never be slavery."

This is the origin of the far-famed "Wilmot Proviso." It created a great flutter; but it stuck like wax, was voted into the bill, and the bill passed with it through the House. The Senate, however, adjourned without final action on it and so both appropriation and proviso were lost, for the time.—The war continued, and at the next session, the President renewed his request for the appropriation, enlarging the amount, I think, to three million. Again came the proviso; and defeated the measure.—Congress adjourned again, and the war went on. In Dec. 1847, the new congress assembled.—I was in the lower House that term.— The "Wilmot Proviso" or the principle of it, was constantly coming up in some shape or other, and I think I may venture to say I voted for it at least forty times; during the short term I was there. The Senate, however, held it in check, and it never became a law. In the spring of 1848 a treaty of peace was made with Mexico; by which we obtained that portion of her country which now constitutes the territories of New Mexico and Utah, and the now state of California. By this treaty the Wilmot Proviso was defeated, as so far as it was intended to be a condition of the acquisition of territory. Its friends, however, were still determined to find some way to restrain slavery from getting into the new country. This new acquisition lay directly west of our old purchase from France, and extended west to the Pacific Ocean—and was so situated that if the Missouri line should be extended straight west, the new country would be divided by such extended line, leaving some north and some south of it. On Judge Douglas' motion a bill, or provision of a bill, passed the Senate to so extend the Missouri line. The Proviso men in the House, including myself, voted it down, because by implication, it gave up the southern part to slavery, while we were bent on having it *all* free.

In the fall of 1848 the gold mines were discovered in California. This attracted people to it with unprecedented rapidity, so that on, or soon after, the meeting of the new congress in Dec., 1849, she already had a population of nearly a hundred thousand, had called a convention, formed a state constitution, excluding slavery, and was knocking for admission into the Union.—The Proviso men, of course, were for letting her in, but the Senate, always true to the other side, would not consent to her admission. And there California stood, kept *out* of the Union, because she would not let slavery *into* her borders. Under all the circumstances perhaps this was not wrong. There were other points of dispute, connected with the general question of slavery, which equally needed adjustment. The South clamored for a more efficient fugitive slave law. The North clamored for the abolition of a peculiar species of slave trade in the District of Columbia, in connection with which, in view from the windows of the capitol, a sort of negro-livery stable, where droves of negroes were collected, temporarily kept, and finally taken to Southern markets, precisely like droves of horses, had been openly maintained for fifty years. Utah and New Mexico needed territorial governments; and whether slavery should or should not be prohibited within them, was another question. The indefinite western boundary of Texas was to be settled. She was received a slave state; and consequently the farther west the slavery men could push her boundary, the more slave country they secured. And the farther east the slavery opponents could thrust the boundary back, the less slave ground was secured. Thus this was just as clearly a slavery question as any of the others.

These points all needed adjustment; and they were held up, perhaps wisely, to make them help to adjust one another. The Union, now, as in 1820, was thought to be in danger; and devotion to the Union rightfully inclined men to yield somewhat, in points where nothing else could have so inclined them. A compromise was finally effected. The South got their new fugitive-slave law; and the North got California, (the far best part of our acquisition from Mexico,) as a free State. The South got a provision that New Mexico and Utah, *when admitted as States,* may come in *with* or *without* slavery as they may then choose; and the North got the slave-trade abolished in the District of Columbia. The North got the western boundary of Texas, thence further back eastward than the South desired; but, in turn, they gave Texas ten millions of dollars, with which to pay her old debts. This is the compromise of 1850.

Preceding the presidential election of 1852, each of the great political parties, democrats and whigs, met in convention and adopted resolutions endorsing the compromise of '50, as a "finality," a final settlement, so far as these parties could make it so, of all slavery agitation. Previous to this, in 1851, the Illinois Legislature had indorsed it.

During this long period of time Nebraska had remained, substantially an uninhabited country, but now emigration to, and settlement within it began to take place. It is about one third as large as the present United States, and its importance so long overlooked, begins to come into view. The restriction of slavery by the Missouri Compromise directly applies to it; in fact, was first made, and has since been maintained, expressly for it. In 1853; a bill to give it a territorial government passed the House of Representatives, and, in the hands of Judge Douglas, failed of passing the Senate only for want of time. This bill contained no repeal of the Missouri Compromise. Indeed, when it was assailed because it did not contain such repeal, Judge Douglas defended it in its existing form. On January 4th, 1854, Judge Douglas introduces a new bill to give Nebraska territorial government. He accompanies this bill with a report, in which last, he expressly recommends that the Missouri Compromise shall neither be affirmed nor repealed.

Before long the bill is so modified as to make two territories instead of one; calling the southern one Kansas.

Also, about a month after the introduction of the bill, on the judge's own motion, it is so amended as to declare the Missouri Compromise inoperative and void; and, substantially, that the people who go and settle there may establish slavery, or exclude it, as they may see fit. In this shape the bill passed both branches of congress, and became a law.

This is the *repeal* of the Missouri Compromise. The foregoing history may not be precisely accurate in every particular; but I am sure it is sufficiently so, for all the uses I shall attempt to make of it, and in it, we have before us, the chief material enabling us to correctly judge whether the repeal of the Missouri Compromise is right or wrong.

I think, and shall try to show, that it is wrong; wrong in its direct effect, letting slavery into Kansas and Nebraska—and wrong in its prospective principle, allowing it to spread to every other part of the wide world, where men can be found inclined to take it.

This *declared* indifference, but, as I must think, covert *real zeal* for the spread of slavery, I can not but hate. I hate it because of the monstrous injustice of slavery itself. I hate it because it deprives our republican example of its just influence in the world—enables the enemies of free institutions, with plausibility, to taunt us as hypocrites—causes the real friends of freedom to doubt our sincerity, and especially because it forces so many really good men amongst ourselves into an open war with the very fundamental principles of civil liberty—criticizing the Declaration of Independence, and insisting that there is no right principle of action but *self-interest*.

Before proceeding, let me say that I think I have no prejudice against the Southern people. They are just what we would be in their situation. If slavery did not now exist amongst them, they would not introduce it. If it did now exist amongst us, we should not instantly give it up.—This I believe of the masses north and south.—Doubtless there are individuals on both sides, who would not hold slaves under any circumstances; and others who would gladly introduce slavery anew, if it were out of existence. We know that some southern men do free their slaves, go north, and become tip-top abolitionists; while some northern ones go south, and become most cruel slave-masters.

When southern people tell us they are no more responsible for the origin of slavery, than we; I acknowledge the fact. When it is said that the institution exists, and that it is very difficult to get rid of it, in any satisfactory way, I can understand and appreciate the saying. I surely will not blame them for not doing what I should not know how to do myself. If all earthly power were given me, I should not know what to do, as to the existing institution. My first impulse would be to free all the slaves, and send them to Liberia,—to their own native land. But a moment's reflection would convince me, that whatever of high hope, (as I think there is) there may be in this, in the long run, its sudden execution is impossible. If they were all landed there in a day, they would all perish in the next ten days; and there are not surplus shipping and surplus money enough in the world to carry them there in many times ten days. What then? Free them all, and keep them among us as underlings? Is it quite certain that this betters their condition? I think I would not hold one in slavery, at any rate; yet the point is not clear enough to me to denounce people upon. What next?—Free them, and make them politically and socially, our equals? My own feelings will not admit of this; and if mine would, we well know that those of the great mass of white people will not. Whether this feeling accords with justice and sound judgment, is not the sole question, if indeed, it is any part of it. A universal feeling, whether well or ill-founded, can not be safely disregarded. We can not, then, make them equals. It does seem to me that systems of gradual emancipation might be adopted; but for their tardiness in this, I will not undertake to judge our brethren of the south.

When they remind us of their constitutional rights, I acknowledge them, not grudgingly, but fully, and fairly; and I would give them any legislation for the reclaiming of their fugitives, which should not, in its stringency, be more likely to carry a free man into slavery, than our ordinary criminal laws are to hang an innocent one.

But all this, to my judgment, furnishes no more excuse for permitting slavery to go into our own free territory, than it would for reviving the African slave trade by law. The law which forbids the bringing of slaves *from* Africa; and that which has so long forbid the taking them *to* Nebraska, can hardly be distinguished on any moral principle; and the repeal of the former could find quite as plausible excuses as that of the latter.

The arguments by which the repeal of the Missouri Compromise is sought to be justified, are these:

First, that the Nebraska country needed a territorial government.

Second, that in various ways, the public had repudiated it, and demanded the repeal; and therefore should not now complain of it.

And lastly, that the repeal establishes a principle, which is intrinsically right.

I will attempt an answer to each of them in its turn.

First, then, if that country was in need of a territorial organization, could it not have had it as well without as with the repeal? Iowa and Minnesota, to both of which the Missouri restriction applied, had, without its repeal, each in succession, territorial organizations. And even, the year before, a bill for Nebraska itself, was within an ace of passing, without the repealing clause; and this in the hands of the same men who are now the champions of repeal. Why no necessity then for the repeal? But still later, when this very bill was first brought in, it contained no repeal. But, say they, because the public had demanded, or rather commanded the repeal, the repeal was to accompany the organization, whenever that should occur.

Now, I deny that the public ever demanded any such thing—ever repudiated the Missouri Compromise—ever commanded its repeal. I deny it, and call for the proof. It is not contended, I believe, that any such command has ever been given in express terms. It is only said that it was done *in principle*. The support of the Wilmot Proviso, is the first fact mentioned, to prove that the Missouri restriction was repudiated in *principle,* and the second is, the refusal to extend the Missouri line over the country acquired from Mexico. These are near enough alike to be treated together. The one was to exclude the chances of slavery from the *whole* new acquisition by the lump; and the other was to reject a division of it, by which one *half* was to be given up to those chances. Now whether this was a repudiation of the Missouri line, in *principle,* depends upon whether the Missouri law contained any *principle* requiring the line to be extended over the country acquired from Mexico. I contend it did not. I insist that it contained no general principle, but that it was, in every sense, specific. That its terms limit it to the country purchased from France, is undenied and undeniable. It could have no principle beyond the intention of those who made it. They did not intend to extend the line to country which they did not own. If they intended to extend it, in the event of acquiring additional territory, why did they not say so? It was just as easy to say, that "in all the country west of the Mississippi, which we now own, *or may hereafter acquire* there shall never be slavery," as to say what they did say; and they would have said it if they had meant it. An intention to extend the law is not only not mentioned in the law, but is not mentioned in any contemporaneous history. Both the law itself, and the history of the times are a blank as to any *principle* of extension; and by neither the known rules of construing statutes and contracts, nor by common sense, can any such *principle* be inferred.

Another fact showing the *specific* character of the Missouri law—showing that it intended no more than it expressed—showing that the line was not intended as a universal dividing line between free and slave territory, present and prospective—north of which slavery could never go—is the fact that by that very law, Missouri came in as a slave State, *north* of the line. If that law contained any prospective *principle,* the whole law must be looked to in order to ascertain what the *principle* was. And by this rule, the South could fairly contend that inasmuch as they got one slave state north of the line at the inception of the law, they have the right to have another given them *north* of it occasionally— now and then in the indefinite westward extension of the line. This demonstrates the absurdity of attempting to deduce a prospective *principle* from the Missouri Compromise line.

When we voted for the Wilmot Proviso, we were voting to keep slavery *out* of the whole Missouri [Mexican?] acquisition; and little did we think we were thereby voting, to let it *into* Nebraska, laying several hundred miles distant. When we voted against extending the Missouri line, little did we think we were voting to destroy the old line, then of near thirty years standing. To argue that we thus repudiated the Missouri Compromise is no less absurd than it would be to argue that because we have, so far, forborne to acquire Cuba, we have thereby, *in principle,* repudiated our former acquisitions, and determined to throw them out of the Union! No less absurd than it would be to say that because I may have refused to build an addition to my house, I thereby have decided to destroy the existing house! And if I catch you setting fire to my house, you will turn upon me and say I INSTRUCTED you to do it! The most conclusive argument, however, that, while voting for the Wilmot Proviso, and while voting against the EXTENSION of the Missouri line, we never thought of disturbing the original Missouri Compromise, is found in the fact that there was then, and still is, an unorganized tract of fine country, nearly as large as the State of Missouri, lying immediately west of Arkansas, and south of the Missouri Compromise line; and that we never attempted to prohibit slavery as to it. I wish particular attention to this. It adjoins the original Missouri Compromise line, by its northern boundary; and consequently is part of the country, into which, by implication, slavery was permitted to go, by that compromise. There it has lain open ever since, and there it still lies. And yet no effort has been made at any time to wrest it from the South. In all our struggles to prohibit slavery within our Mexican acquisitions, we never so much as lifted a finger to prohibit it, as to this tract. Is not this entirely conclusive that at all times, we have held the Missouri Compromise as a sacred thing; even when against ourselves, as well as when for us?

Senator Douglas sometimes says the Missouri line itself was, *in principle,* only an extension of the line of the ordinance of '87—that is to say, an extension of the Ohio River. I think this is weak enough on its face. I will remark, however, that, as a glance at the map will show, the Missouri line is a long way farther south than the Ohio; and that if our Senator, in proposing his extension, had stuck to the *principle* of jogging southward, perhaps it might not have been voted down so readily.

But next it is said that the compromises of '50 and the ratification of them by both political parties, in '52, established a *new principle,* which required the repeal of the Missouri Compromise. This again I deny. I deny it, and demand the proof. I have already stated fully what the compromises of '50 are. The particular part of those measures, for which the virtual repeal of the Missouri Compromise is sought to be inferred (for it is admitted they contain nothing about it, in express terms) is the provision in the Utah and New Mexico laws, which permits them when they seek admission into the Union as States, to come in with or without slavery as they shall then see fit. Now I insist this provision was made for Utah and New Mexico, and for no other place whatever. It had no more direct reference to Nebraska than it had to the territories of the moon. But, say they, it had reference to Nebraska, *in principle.* Let us see. The North consented to this provision, not because they considered it right in itself; but because they were compensated—paid for it.—They, at the same time, got California into the Union as a free State. This was far the best part of all they had struggled for by the Wilmot Proviso. They also got the area of slavery somewhat narrowed in the settlement of the boundary of Texas. Also, they got the slave trade abolished in the District of Columbia. For all these desirable objects the North could afford to yield something; and they did yield to the South the Utah and New Mexico provision. I do not mean that the whole North, or even a majority, yielded, when the law passed; but enough yielded, when added to the vote of the South, to carry the measure. Now can it be pretended that the *principle* of this arrangement requires us to permit the same provision to be applied to Nebraska, *without any equivalent at all?* Give us another free State; press the boundary of Texas still further back; give us another step toward the destruction of slavery in the District, and you present us a similar case. But ask us not to repeat, for nothing, what you paid for in the first instance. If you wish the thing again, pay again. That is the *principle* of the compromises of '50, if indeed they had any principles beyond their specific terms—it was the system of equivalents.

Again, if Congress, at that time, intended that all future territories should, when admitted as States, come in with or without slavery, at their own option, why did it not say so? With such an universal provision, all know the bills could not have passed. Did they, then—could they—establish a *principle* contrary to their own intention? Still further, if they intended to establish the principle that wherever Congress had control, it should be left to the people to do as they thought fit with slavery, why did they not authorize the people of the District of Columbia at their adoption to abolish slavery within these limits? I personally know that this has not been left undone, because it was unthought of. It was frequently spoken of by members of Congress and by citizens of Washington six years ago; and I heard no one express a doubt that a system of gradual emancipation, with compensation to owners, would meet the approbation of a large majority of the white people of the District. But without the action of Congress they could say nothing; and Congress said "no." In the measures of 1850, Congress had the subject of slavery in the District expressly on hand. If they were then establishing the *principle* of allowing the people to do as they please with slavery, why did they not apply the *principle* to that people?

Again, it is claimed that by the Resolutions of the Illinois Legislature, passed in 1851, the repeal of the Missouri Compromise was demanded. This I deny also. Whatever may be worked out by a criticism of the language of those resolutions, the people have never understood them as being any more than an endorsement of the compromises of 1850, and a release of our Senators from voting for the Wilmot Proviso. The whole people are living witnesses, that this only, was their view. Finally, it is asked "If we did not mean to apply the Utah and New Mexico provision, to all future territories, what did we mean, when we, in 1852, endorsed the compromise of '50?"

For myself, I can answer this question most easily. I meant not to ask a repeal, or modification of the fugitive slave law. I meant not to ask for the abolition of slavery in the District of Columbia. I meant not to resist the admission of Utah and New Mexico, even should they ask to come in as slave States. I meant nothing about additional territories, because, as I understood, we then had no territory whose character as to slavery was not already settled. As to Nebraska, I regarded its character as being fixed, by the Missouri Compromise, for thirty years—as unalterably fixed as that of my own home in Illinois. As to new acquisitions I said "sufficient unto the day is the evil thereof."—When we make new acquaintances [acquisitions?], we will, as heretofore, try to manage them somehow. That is my answer. That is what I meant and said; and I appeal to the people to say, each for himself, whether that was not also the universal meaning of the free States.

And now, in turn, let me ask a few questions. If by any, or all these matters, the repeal of the Missouri Compromise was commanded, why was not the command sooner obeyed? Why was the repeal omitted in the Nebraska bill of 1853?—Why was it omitted in the original bill of 1854? Why, in the accompanying report, was such a repeal characterized as a *departure* from the course pursued in 1850? and its continued omission recommended?

I am aware Judge Douglas now argues that the subsequent express repeal is no substantial alteration of the bill. This argument seems wonderful to me. It is as if one should argue that white and black are not different. He admits, however, that there is a literal change in the bill; and that he made the change in difference to other Senators, who would not support the bill without. This proves that those other Senators thought the change a substantial one; and that the Judge thought their opinions worth deferring to. His own opinions, therefore, seem not to rest on a very firm basis even in his own mind—and I suppose the world believes, and will continue to believe, that precisely on the substance of that change this whole agitation has arisen.

I conclude then, that the public never demanded the repeal of the Missouri Compromise.

I now come to consider whether the repeal, with its avowed principle, is intrinsically right. I insist that it is not. Take the particular case. A controversy had arisen between the advocates and opponents of slavery, in relation to its establishment within the country we had purchased of France. The southern, and then best part of the purchase, was already in as a slave State.—The controversy was settled by also letting Missouri in as a slave State; but with the agreement that within all the remaining part of the purchase, north of a certain line, there should never be slavery. As to what was to be done with the remaining part south of the line, nothing was said; but perhaps the fair implication was, that it should come in with slavery if it should so choose. The southern part, except a portion heretofore mentioned, afterwards did come in with slavery, as the State of Arkansas. All these many years since 1820, the Northern part had remained a wilderness. At length settlements began in it also. In due course, Iowa, came in as a free State, and Minnesota was given a territorial government, without removing the slavery restriction. Finally the sole remaining part, north of the line, Kansas and Nebraska, was to be organized; and it is proposed, and carried, to blot out the old dividing line of thirty-four years standing, and to open the whole of that country to the introduction of slavery. Now, this, to my mind, is manifestly unjust. After an angry and dangerous controversy, the parties made friends by dividing the bone of contention. The one party first appropriates her own share, beyond all power to be disturbed in the possession of it; and then seizes the share of the other party. It is as if two starving men had divided their only loaf; the one had hastily swallowed his half, and then grabbed the other half just as he was putting it to his mouth.

Let me here drop the main argument, to notice what I consider rather an inferior matter. It is argued that slavery will not go to Kansas and Nebraska, *in any event*. This is a *palliation*—a *lullaby*. I have some hope that it will not; but let us not be too confident. As to climate, a glance at the map shows that there are five slave States—Delaware, Maryland, Virginia, Kentucky, and Missouri—and also the District of Columbia, all north of the Missouri Compromise line. The census returns of 1850 show that, within these, there are 867,276 slaves—being more than one-fourth of all the slaves in the nation.

It is not climate, then, that will keep slavery out of these territories. Is there any thing in the peculiar nature of the country? Missouri adjoins these territories, by her entire western boundary, and slavery is already within every one of her western counties. I have even heard it said that there are more slaves, in proportion to whites, in the north western county of Missouri, than within any county of the State. Slavery pressed entirely up to the old western boundary of the State, and when, rather recently, a part of that boundary, at the north-west was moved out a little farther west, slavery followed on quite up to the new line. Now, when the restriction is removed, what is to prevent it from going still further? Climate will not.—No peculiarity of the country will—nothing in *nature* will. Will the disposition of the people prevent it? Those nearest the scene, are all in favor of the extension. The yankees, who are opposed to it, may be more numerous; but, in military phrase, the battle-field is too far from *their* base of operations.

But it is said, there now is *no* law in Nebraska on the subject of slavery; and that, in such case, taking a slave there, operates his freedom. That is good book-law; but is not the rule of actual practice. Wherever slavery is, it has been first introduced without law. The oldest laws we find concerning it, are not laws introducing it; but *regulating* it, as an already existing thing. A white man takes his slave to Nebraska now; who will inform the negro that he is free?—Who will take him before court to test the question of his freedom? In ignorance of his legal emancipation, he is kept chopping, splitting and plowing. Others are brought, and move on in the same track. At last, if ever the time for voting comes, on the question of slavery, the institution already in fact exists in the country, and cannot well be removed. The facts of its presence, and the difficulty of its removal, will carry the vote in its favor. Keep it out until a vote is taken, and a vote in favor of it, can not be got in any population of forty thousand, on earth, who have been drawn together by the ordinary motives of emigration and settlement. To get slaves into the country simultaneously with the whites, in the incipient stages of settlement, is the precise stake played for, and won in this Nebraska measure.

The question is asked us, "If slaves will go in, notwithstanding the general principle of law liberates them, why would they not equally go in against positive statute law?—go in, even if the Missouri restriction were maintained?" I answer, because it takes a much bolder man to venture in, with his property, in the latter case, than in the former—because the positive congressional enactment is known to, and respected by all, or nearly all; whereas the negative principle that *no* law is free law, is not much known except among lawyers. We have some experience of this practical difference. In spite of the Ordinance of '87, a few negroes were brought into Illinois, and held in a state of quasi slavery; not enough, however, to carry a vote of the people in favor of the institution when they came to form a constitution. But in the adjoining Missouri country, where there was no ordinance of '87—was no restriction—they were carried ten times, nay a hundred times, as fast, and actually made a slave State. This is fact—naked fact.

Another LULLABY argument is, that taking slaves to new countries does not increase their number, does not make any one slave who otherwise would be free. There is some truth in this, and I am glad of it, but it is not WHOLLY true. The African slave trade is not yet effectually suppressed; and if we make a reasonable deduction for the white people amongst us, who are foreigners, and the descendants of foreigners, arriving here since 1808, we shall find the increase of the black population out-running that of the white, to an extent unaccountable, except by supposing that some of them too, have been coming from Africa. If this be so, the opening of new countries to the institution, increases the demand for, and augments the price of slaves, and so does, in fact, make slaves of freemen by causing them to be brought from Africa, and sold into bondage.

But, however this may be, we know the opening of new countries to slavery, tends to the perpetuation of the institution, and so does KEEP men in slavery who otherwise would be free. This result we do not FEEL like favoring, and we are under no legal obligation to suppress our feelings in this respect.

Equal justice to the South, it is said, requires us to consent to the extending of slavery to new countries. That is to say, inasmuch as you do not object to my taking my hog to Nebraska, therefore I must not object to you taking your slave. Now, I admit this is perfectly logical, if there is no difference between hogs and negroes. But while you thus require me to deny the humanity of the negro, I wish to ask whether you of the south yourselves, have ever been willing to do as much? It is kindly provided that of all those who come into the world, only a small percentage are natural tyrants. That percentage is no larger in the slave States than in the free. The great majority, south as well as north, have human sympathies, of which they can no more divest themselves than they can of their sensibility to physical pain. These sympathies in the bosoms of the southern people, manifest in many ways, their sense of the wrong of slavery, and their consciousness that, after all, there is humanity in the negro. If they deny this, let me address them a few plain questions. In 1820 you joined the north, almost unanimously, in declaring the African slave trade piracy, and in annexing to it the punishment of death. Why did you do this? If you did not feel that it was wrong, why did you join in providing that men should be hung for it? The practice was no more than bringing wild negroes from Africa, to sell to such as would buy them. But you never thought of hanging men for catching and selling wild horses, wild buffaloes or wild bears.

Again, you have amongst you, a sneaking individual, of the class of native tyrants, known as the "SLAVE-DEALER." He watches your necessities, and crawls up to buy your slave, at a speculating price. If you cannot help it, you sell to him; but if you can help it, you drive him from your door. You despise him utterly. You do not recognize him as a friend, or even as an honest man. Your children must not play with his; they may rollick freely with the little negroes, but not with the "slave-dealer's" children. If you are obliged to deal with him, you try to get through the job without so much as touching him. It is common with you to join hands with the men you meet; but with the slave-dealer you avoid the ceremony—instinctively shrinking from the snaky contact. If he grows rich and retires from business, you still remember him, and still keep up the ban of non-intercourse upon him and his family. Now why is this? You do not so treat the man who deals in corn, cattle or tobacco.

And yet again, there are in the United States and territories, including the District of Columbia, 433,643 free blacks. At $500 per head they are worth over two hundred millions of dollars. How comes this vast amount of property to be running about without owners? We do not see free horses or free cattle running at large. How is this? All these free blacks are the descendants of slaves, or have been slaves themselves, and they would be slaves now, but for SOMETHING which has operated on their white owners, inducing them, at vast pecuniary sacrifices, to liberate them. What is that SOMETHING? Is there any mistaking it? In all these cases it is your sense of justice, and human sympathy, continually telling you, that the poor negro has some natural right to himself—that those who deny it, and make mere merchandise of him, deserve kickings, contempt and death.

And now, why will you ask us to deny the humanity of the slave? and estimate him only as the equal of the hog? Why ask us to do what you will not do yourselves? Why ask us to do for *nothing,* what two hundred million of dollars could not induce you to do?

But one great argument in the support of the repeal of the Missouri Compromise, is still to come. That argument is "the sacred right of self government." It seems our distinguished Senator has found great difficulty in getting his antagonists, even in the Senate, to meet him fairly on this argument. Some poet has said:

"Fools rush in where angels fear to tread."

At the hazzard [*sic*] of being thought one of the fools of this quotation, I meet that argument—I rush in, I take that bull by the horns.

I trust I understand, and truly estimate the right of self-government. My faith in the proposition that each man should do precisely as he pleases with all which is exclusively his own, lies at the foundation of the sense of justice there is in me. I extend the principles to communities of men, as well as to individuals. I so extend it, because it is politically wise, as well as naturally just; politically wise in saving us from broils about matters which do not concern us.—Here or at Washington, I would not trouble myself with the oyster laws of Virginia, or the cranberry laws of Indiana.

The doctrine of self-government is right—absolutely and eternally right—but it has no just application, as here attempted. Or perhaps I should rather say that whether it has such application depends upon whether a negro is *not* or *is* a man. If he is *not* a man, why in that case, he who *is* a man may, as a matter of self-government, do just as he pleases with him. But if the negro *is* a man, is it not to that extent a total destruction of self-government, to say that he too shall not govern *himself?* When the white man governs himself that is self-government; but when he governs himself, and also governs *another* man, that is *more* than self-government—that is despotism. If the negro is a *man,* why then my ancient faith teaches me that "all men are created equal;" and that there can be no moral right in connection with one man's making a slave of another.

Judge Douglas frequently, with bitter irony and sarcasm, paraphrases our argument by saying: "The white people of Nebraska are good enough to govern themselves, *but they are not good enough to govern a few miserable negroes!!*"

Well I doubt not that the people of Nebraska are, and will continue to be as good as the average of people elsewhere. I do not say the contrary. What I do say is, that no man is good enough to govern another man, *without that other's consent.* I say this is the leading principle—the sheet anchor of American republicanism. Our Declaration of Independence says:

"We hold these truths to be self evident: That all men are created equal; that they are endowed by their Creator with certain inalienable rights; that among these are life, liberty and the pursuit of happiness. That to secure these rights, governments are instituted among men, DERIVING THEIR JUST POWERS FROM THE CONSENT OF THE GOVERNED."

I have quoted so much at this time merely to show that according to our ancient faith, the just powers of governments are derived from the consent of the governed. Now the relation of masters and slaves is PROTANTO, a total violation of this principle. That master not only governs the slave without his consent; but he governs him by a set of rules altogether different from those which he prescribes for himself. Allow ALL the governed an equal voice in the government, and that, and that only, is self-government.

Let it not be said I am contending for the establishment of political and social equality between the whites and blacks. I have already said the contrary. I am not now combating the argument of NECESSITY, arising from the fact that the blacks are already amongst us; but I am combating what is set up as MORAL argument for allowing them to be taken where they have never yet been—arguing against the EXTENSION of a bad thing, which where it already exists we must of necessity, manage as we best can.

In support of his application of the doctrine of self-government, Senator Douglas has sought to bring to his aid the opinions and examples of our revolutionary fathers. I am glad he has done this. I love the sentiments of those old-time men; and shall be most happy to abide by their opinions. He shows us that when it was in contemplation for the colonies to break off from Great Britain, and set up a new government for themselves, several of the states instructed their delegates to go for the measure, PROVIDED EACH STATE SHOULD BE ALLOWED TO REGULATE ITS DOMESTIC CONCERNS IN ITS OWN WAY. I do not quote; but this in substance. This was right. I see nothing objectionable in it. I also think it probable that it had some reference to the existence of slavery amongst them. I will not deny that it had. But had it, in any reference, to the carrying of slavery into NEW COUNTRIES? That is the question; and we will let the fathers themselves answer it.

This same generation of men, and mostly the same individuals of the generation, who declared this principle—who declared independence—who fought the war of the revolution through—who afterwards made the constitution under which we still live—these same men passed the ordinance of '87, declaring that slavery should never go to the north-west territory. I have no doubt Judge Douglas thinks they were very inconsistent in this. It is a question of discrimination between them and him. But there is not an inch of ground left for his claiming that their opinions—their example—their authority—are on his side in this controversy.

Again, is not Nebraska, while a territory, a part of us? Do we not own the country? And if we surrender the control of it, do we not surrender the right of self-government? It is part of ourselves. If you say we shall not control it because it is ONLY part, the same is true of every other part; and when all the parts are gone, what has become of the whole? What is then left of us? What use for the General Government, when there is nothing left for it [to?] govern?

But you say this question should be left to the people of Nebraska, because they are more particularly interested. If this be the rule, you must leave it to each individual to say for himself whether he will have slaves. What better moral right have thirty-one citizens of Nebraska to say, that the thirty-second shall not hold slaves, than the people of the thirty-one States have to say that slavery shall not go into the thirty-second State at all?

But if it is a sacred right for the people of Nebraska to take and hold slaves there, it is equally their sacred right to buy them where they can buy them cheapest; and that undoubtedly will be on the coast of Africa; provided you will consent to not hang them for going there to buy them. You must remove this restriction too, from the sacred right of self-government. I am aware you say that taking slaves from the States to Nebraska, does not make slaves of freemen; but the African slave-trader can say just as much. He does not catch free negroes and bring them here. He finds them already slaves in the hands of their black captors, and he honestly buys them at the rate of about a red cotton handker-chief a head. This is very cheap, and it is a great abridgment of the sacred right of self-government to hang men for engaging in this profitable trade!

Another important objection to this application of the right of self-govern-ment, is that it enables the first FEW, to deprive the succeeding MANY, of a free exercise of the right of self-government. The first few may get slavery IN, and the subsequent many cannot easily get it OUT. How common is the remark now in the slave States—"If we were only clear of our slaves, how much better it would be for us." They are actually deprived of the privilege of governing themselves as they would, by the action of a very few, in the beginning. The same thing was true of the whole nation at the time our constitution was formed.

Whether slavery shall go into Nebraska, or other new territories, is not a matter of exclusive concern to the people who may go there. The whole nation is interested that the best use shall be made of these territories. We want them for the homes of free white people. This they cannot be, to any considerable extent, if slavery shall be planted within them. Slave States are places for poor white people to remove FROM; not to remove TO. New free States are the places for poor people to go to and better their condition. For this use, the nation needs these territories.

Still further; there are constitutional relations between the slave and free States, which are degrading to the latter. We are under legal obligations to catch and return their runaway slaves to them—a sort of dirty, disagreeable job which I believe, as a general rule, the slave-holders will not perform for one another. Then again, in the control of the government—the management of the partnership affairs—they have greatly the advantage of us. By the constitution, each State has two Senators, each has a number of Representatives, in proportion to the number of its people—and each has a number of presidential electors, equal to the whole number of its Senators and Representatives together. But in ascertaining the number of the people, for this purpose, five slaves are counted as being equal to three whites. The slaves do not vote; they are only counted and so used as to swell the influence of the white people's votes. The practical effect of this is more aptly shown by a comparison of the States of South Carolina and Maine. South Carolina has six representatives, and so has Maine; South Carolina has eight presidential electors, and so has Maine. This is precise equality so far; and, of course they are equal in Senators, each having two. Thus in the control of the government, the two States are equals precisely. But how are they in the number of their white people? Maine has 581,813—while South Carolina has 274,567. Maine has twice as many as South Carolina, and 32,679 over.—Thus each white man in South Carolina is more than the double of any man in Maine. This is all because South Carolina, besides her free people, has 384,984 slaves. The South Carolinian has precisely the same advantage over the white man in every other free State, as well as in Maine. He is more than the double of any one of us in this crowd. The same advantage, but not to the same extent, is held by all the citizens of the slave States, over those of the free; and it is an absolute truth, without an exception, that there is no voter in any slave State, but who has more legal power in the government, than any voter in any free State. There is no instance of exact equality; and the disadvantage is against us the whole chapter through. This principle, in the aggregate, gives the slave States in the present Congress, twenty additional representatives—being seven more than the whole majority by which they passed the Nebraska bill.

Now all this is manifestly unfair; yet I do not mention it to complain of it, in so far as it is already settled. It is in the constitution; and I do not, for that cause, or any other cause, propose to destroy, or alter, or disregard the constitution. I stand to it, fairly, fully, and firmly.

But when I am told I must leave it altogether to OTHER PEOPLE to say whether new partners are to be bred up and brought into the firm, on the same degrading terms against me, I respectfully demur. I insist, that whether I shall be a whole man, or only the half of one, in comparison with others, is a question in which I am somewhat concerned; and one which no other man can have a sacred right of deciding for me. If I am wrong in this—if it really be a sacred right of self-government, in the man who shall go to Nebraska, to decide whether he will be the EQUAL of me or the DOUBLE of me, then, after he shall have exercised that right, and thereby shall have reduced me to a still smaller fraction of a man than I already am, I should like for some gentleman, deeply skilled in the mysteries of sacred rights, to provide himself with a microscope, and peep about, and find out, if he can, what has become of my sacred rights!— They will surely be too small for detection with the naked eye.

Finally, I insist that if there is ANY THING which it is the duty of the WHOLE PEOPLE to never entrust to any hands but their own, that thing is the preservation and perpetuity, of their own liberties, and institutions. And if they shall think, as I do, that the extension of slavery endangers them, more than any, or all other causes, how recreant to themselves, if they submit the question, and with it, the fate of their country, to a mere handfull of men, bent only on temporary self-interest. If this question of slavery extension were an insignificant one—one having no power to do harm—it might be shuffled aside in this way. But being, as it is, the great Behemoth of danger, shall the strong gripe of the nation be loosened upon him, to entrust him to the hands of such feeble keepers?

I have done with this mighty argument, of self-government. Go, sacred thing! Go in peace.

But Nebraska is urged as a great Union-saving measure. Well, I too, go for saving the Union. Much as I hate slavery, I would consent to the extension of it rather than see the Union dissolved, just as I would consent to any GREAT evil, to avoid a GREATER one. But when I go to Union saving, I must believe, at east, that the means I employ have some adaptation to the end. To my mind, Nebraska has no such adaptation.

"It hath no relish of salvation in it."

It is an aggravation, rather, of the only one thing which ever endangers the Union. When it came upon us, all was peace and quiet. The nation was looking to the forming of new bonds of Union; and a long course of peace and prosperity seemed to lie before us. In the whole range of possibility, there scarcely appears to me to have been any thing, out of which the slavery agitation could have been revived, except the very project of repealing the Missouri Compromise.—Every inch of territory we owned, already had a definite settlement of the slavery question, and by which all parties were pledged to abide. Indeed, there was no uninhabited country on the continent, which we could acquire; if we except some extreme northern regions, which are wholly out of the question. In this state of case, the genius of Discord himself, could scarcely have invented a way of again setting us by the ears, but by turning back and destroying the peace measures of the past. The councils of that genius seem to have prevailed, the Missouri Compromise was repealed; and here we are, in the midst of a new slavery agitation, such, I think, as we have never seen before. Who is responsible for this? Is it those who resist the measure; or those who, causelessly, brought it forward, and pressed it through, having reason to know, and, in fact, knowing it must and would be so resisted? It could not but be expected by its author, that it would be looked upon as a measure for the extension of slavery, aggravated by a gross breach of faith. Argue as you will, and long as you will, this is the naked FRONT and ASPECT, of the measure. And in this aspect, it could not but produce agitation. Slavery is founded in the selfishness of man's nature—opposition to it, is [sic] his love of justice. These principles are an eternal antagonism; and when brought into collision so fiercely, as slavery extension brings them, shocks, and throes, and convulsions must ceaselessly follow. Repeal the Missouri compromise—repeal all compromises—repeal the declaration of independence—repeal all past history, you still can not repeal human nature. It still will be the abundance of man's heart, that slavery extension is wrong; and out of the abundance of his heart, his mouth will continue to speak.

The structure, too, of the Nebraska bill is very peculiar. The people are to decide the question of slavery for themselves; but WHEN they are to decide, or HOW they are to decide; or whether, when the question is once decided, it is to remain so, or is to be subject to an indefinite succession of new trials, the law does not say. Is it to be decided by the first dozen settlers who arrive there? or is it to await the arrival of a hundred? Is it to be decided by a vote of the people? or a vote of the legislature? or, indeed, by a vote of any sort? To these questions, the law gives no answer. There is a mystery about this; for when a member proposed to give the legislature express authority to exclude slavery, it was hooted down by the friends of the bill. This fact is worth remembering. Some Yankees, in the east, are sending emigrants to Nebraska to exclude slavery from it; and, so far as I can judge, they expect the question to be decided by voting, in some way or other. But the Missourians are awake too. They are within a stone's throw of the contested ground. They hold meetings, and pass resolutions, in which not the slightest allusion to voting is made. They resolve that slavery already exists in the territory; that more shall go there; that they, remaining in Missouri, will protect it; and that abolitionists shall be hung, or driven away. Through all this, bowie-knives and six-shooters are seen plainly enough; but never a glimpse of the ballot-box. And, really, what is to be the result of this? Each party WITHIN, having numerous and determined backers WITHOUT, is it not probable that the contest will come to blows, and bloodshed? Could there be a more apt invention to bring about collision and violence, on the slavery question, than this Nebraska project is? I do not charge, or believe, that such was intended by Congress; but if they had literally formed a ring, and placed champions within it to fight out the controversy, the fight could be no more likely to come off, than it is. And if this fight should begin, is it likely to take a very peaceful, Union-saving turn? Will not the first drop of blood so shed, be the real knell of the Union?

The Missouri Compromise ought to be restored. For the sake of the Union, it ought to be restored. We ought to elect a House of Representatives which will vote its restoration. If by any means, we omit to do this, what follows!— Slavery may or may not be established in Nebraska. But whether it be or not, we shall have repudiated—discarded from the councils of the Nation—the SPIRIT OF COMPROMISE; for who after this will ever trust in a national compromise? The spirit of mutual concession—that spirit which first gave us the constitution, and which has thrice saved the Union—we shall have strangled and cast from us forever. And what shall we have in lieu of it? The South flushed with triumph and tempted to excesses; the North, betrayed, as they believe, brooding on wrong and burning for revenge. One side will provoke; the other resent. The one will taunt, the other defy; one agrees [aggresses?], the other retaliates. Already a few in the North, defy all constitutional restraints, resist the execution of the fugitive slave law, and even menace the institution of slavery in the states where it exists.

Already a few in the South, claim the constitutional right to take and to hold slaves in the free states—demand the revival of the slave trade: and demand a treaty with Great Britain by which fugitive slaves may be reclaimed from

Canada. As yet they are but few on either side. It is a grave question for the lovers of the Union, whether the final destruction of the Missouri Compromise, and with it the spirit of all compromise will or will not embolden and embitter each of these, and fatally increase the numbers of both.

But restore the compromise, and what then? We thereby restore the national faith, the national confidence, the national feeling of brotherhood. We thereby reinstate the spirit of concession and compromise—that spirit which has never failed us in past perils, and which may be safely trusted for all the future. The south ought to join in doing this. The peace of the nation is as dear to them as to us. In memories of the past and hopes of the future, they share as largely as we. It would be on their part a great act—great in its spirit, and great in its effect. It would be worth to the nation a hundred years purchase of peace and prosperity. And what of sacrifice would they make? They only surrender to us, what they gave us for a consideration long, long ago; what they have not now, asked for, struggled or cared for; what has been thrust upon them, not less to their own astonishment than to ours.

But it is said we cannot restore it; that though we elect every member of the lower house, the Senate is still against us. It is quite true, that of the Senators who passed the Nebraska bill, a majority of the whole Senate will retain their seats in spite of the elections of this and the next year. But if at these elections, their several constituencies shall clearly express their will against Nebraska, will these Senators disregard their will? Will they neither obey, nor make room for those who will?

But even if we fail to technically restore the compromise, it is still a great point to carry a popular vote in favor of the restoration. The moral weight of such a vote can not be estimated too highly. The authors of Nebraska are not at all satisfied with the destruction of the compromise—an endorsement of this PRINCIPLE they proclaim to be the great object. With them, Nebraska alone is a small matter—to establish a principle, for FUTURE USE, is what they particularly desire.

That future use is to be the planting of slavery wherever in the wide world, local and unorganized opposition can not prevent it. Now if you wish to give them this endorsement—if you wish to establish this principle—do so. I shall regret it; but it is your right. On the contrary if you are opposed to the principle—intend to give it no such endorsement—let no wheedling, no sophistry, divert you from throwing a direct vote against it.

Some men, mostly whigs, who condemn the repeal of the Missouri Compromise, nevertheless hesitate to go for its restoration, lest they be thrown in company with the abolitionists. Will they allow me as an old whig to tell them good humoredly, that I think this is very silly? Stand with anybody that stands RIGHT. Stand with him while he is right and PART with him when he goes wrong. Stand WITH the abolitionist in restoring the Missouri Compromise; and stand AGAINST him when he attempts the repeal of the fugitive slave law. In the latter case you stand with the southern disunionist. What of that? you are still right. In both cases you are right. In both cases you expose the dangerous extremes. In both you stand on middle ground and hold the ship level and steady. In both you are national and nothing less than national. This is the good old whig ground. To desert such ground, because of any company, is to be less than a whig—less than a man—less than an American.

I particularly object to the NEW position which the avowed principle of this Nebraska law gives to slavery in the body politic. I object to it because it assumes that there can be MORAL RIGHT in the enslaving of one man by another. I object to it as a dangerous dalliance for a few people—a sad evidence that, feeling prosperity, we forget right—that liberty, as a principle, we have ceased to revere. I object to it because the fathers of the republic eschewed, and rejected it. The argument of "Necessity" was the only argument they ever admitted in favor of slavery; and so far, and so far only as it carried them, did they ever go. They found the institution existing among us, which they could not help; and they cast blame upon the British King for having permitted its introduction. BEFORE the constitution, they prohibited its introduction into the northwestern Territory—the only country we owned, then free from it. AT the framing and adoption of the constitution, they forbore to so much as mention the word "slave" or "slavery" in the whole instrument. In the provision for the recovery of fugitives, the slave is spoken of as a "PERSON HELD TO SERVICE OR LABOR." In that prohibiting the abolition of the African slave trade for twenty years, that trade is spoken of as "The migration of importation of such persons as any of the States NOW EXISTING, shall think proper to admit," &c. These are the only provisions alluding to slavery. Thus, the thing is hid away, in the constitution, just as an afflicted man hides away a wen or a cancer, which he dares not cut out at once, lest he bleed to death; with the promise, nevertheless, that the cutting may begin at the end of a given time.—Less than this our fathers COULD not do; and MORE they WOULD not do. Necessity drove them so far, and further, they would not go. But this is not all. The earlier Congress, under the constitution, took the same view of slavery. They hedged and hemmed it in to the narrowest limits of necessity.

In 1794, they prohibited an out-going slave trade—that is, the taking of slaves FROM the United States to sell.

In 1798, they prohibited the bringing of slaves from Africa INTO the Mississippi Territory, this territory then comprising what are now the States of Mississippi and Alabama. This was TEN YEARS before they had the authority to do the same thing as to the States existing at the adoption of the constitution.

In 1800 they prohibited AMERICAN CITIZENS from trading in slaves between foreign countries—as, for instance, from Africa to Brazil.

In 1803 they passed a law in aid of one or two State laws, in restraint of the internal slave trade.

In 1807, in apparent hot haste, they passed the law, nearly a year in advance, to take effect the first day of 1808—the very first day the constitution would permit—prohibiting the African slave trade by heavy pecuniary and corporal penalties.

In 1820, finding these provisions ineffectual, they declared the trade piracy, and annexed to it, the extreme penalty of death. While all this was passing in the general government, five or six of the original slave States had adopted systems of gradual emancipation; by which the institution was rapidly becoming extinct within these limits.

Thus we see, the plain unmistakable spirit of that age, towards slavery, was hostility to the PRINCIPLE, and toleration, ONLY BY NECESSITY.

But now it is to be transformed into a "sacred right." Nebraska brings it forth, places it on the high road to extension and perpetuity; and, with a pat on its back, says to it, "Go, and God speed you." Henceforth it is to be the chief jewel of the nation—the very figurehead of the ship of State. Little by little, but steadily as man's march to the grave, we have been giving up the OLD for the NEW faith. Near eighty years ago we began by declaring that all men are created equal; but now from that beginning we have run down to the other declaration, that for SOME men to enslave OTHERS is a "sacred right of self-government." These principles can not stand together. They are as opposite as God and mammon; and whoever holds to the one, must despise the other. When Pettit, in connection with his support of the Nebraska bill, called the Declaration of Independence "a self-evident lie," he only did what consistency and candor require all other Nebraska men to do. Of the forty odd Nebraska Senators who sat present and heard him, no one rebuked him. Nor am I apprized that any Nebraska newspaper, or any Nebraska orator, in the whole nation, has ever yet rebuked him. If this had been said among Marion's men, Southerners though they were, what would have become of the man who said it? If this had been said to the men who captured Andre, the man who said it, would probably have been hung sooner than Andre was. If it had been said in old Indepen-

dence Hall, seventy-eight years ago, the very door-keeper would have throt-
tled the man, and thrust him into the street.

Let no one be deceived. The spirit of seventy-six and the spirit of Nebraska,
are utter antagonisms; and the former is being rapidly displaced by the latter.

Fellow-countrymen—Americans south, as well as north, shall we make no
effort to arrest this? Already the liberal party throughout the world, express the
apprehension "that the one retrograde institution in America, is undermining
the principles of progress, and fatally violating the noblest political system the
world ever saw." This is not the taunt of enemies, but the warning of friends.
Is it quite safe to disregard it—to despise it? Is there no danger to liberty itself,
in discarding the earliest practice, and first precept of our ancient faith? In our
greedy chase to make profit of the negro, let us beware, lest we "cancel and tear
to pieces" even the white man's charter of freedom.

Our republican robe is soiled, and trailed in the dust. Let us re-purify it. Let
us turn and wash it white, in the spirit, if not the blood, of the Revolution. Let
us turn slavery from its claims of "moral right" back upon its existing legal rights,
and its arguments of "necessity."—Let us return it to the position our fathers
gave it; and there let it rest in peace. Let us re-adopt the Declaration of Independence, and with it, the practices, and policy, which harmonize with it. Let
north and south—let all Americans—let all lovers of liberty everywhere—join
in the great and good work. If we do this, we shall not only have saved the
Union; but we shall have so saved it, as to make, and to keep it, forever worthy
of the saving. We shall have so saved it, that the suceeding millions of free happy
people, the world over, shall rise up, and call us blessed, to the latest generations.

At Springfield, twelve days ago, where I had spoken substantially as I have
here, Judge Douglas replied to me—and as he is to reply to me here, I shall
attempt to anticipate him, by noticing some of the points he made there.

He commenced by stating I had assumed all the way through, that the principle of the Nebraska bill, would have the effect of extending slavery. He denied
that this was INTENDED, or that this EFFECT would follow.

I will not re-open the argument upon this point. That such WAS the intention, the world believed at the start, and will continue to believe. This was the
COUNTENANCE of the thing; and, both friends and enemies, instantly recognized
it as such. That countenance can not now be changed by argument. You can as
easily argue the color out of the negro's skin. Like the "bloody hand" you may
wash it, and wash it, the red witness of guilt still sticks, and stares horribly at you.

Next he says, congressional intervention never prevented slavery any where—
that it did not prevent it in the north west territory, now in Illinois—that in fact,

Illinois came into the Union as a slave State—that the principle of the Nebraska bill expelled it from Illinois, from several old States, from every where.

Now this is mere quibbling all the way through. If the ordinance of '87 did not keep slavery out of the north west territory, how happens it that the north west shore of the Ohio River is entirely free from it; while the south east shore, less than a mile distant, along nearly the whole length of the river, is entirely covered with it?

If that ordinance did not keep it out of Illinois, what was it that made the difference between Illinois and Missouri? They lie side by side, the Mississippi river only dividing them; while their early settlements were within the same latitude. Between 1810 and 1820 the number of slaves in Missouri INCREASED 7,211; while in Illinois, in the same ten years, they DECREASED 51.—This appears by the census returns. During nearly all of that ten years, both were territories—not States. During this time the ordinance forbid slavery to go into Illinois; and NOTHING forbid it to go into Missouri. It DID go into Missouri, and did NOT go into Illinois.—That is the fact. Can any one doubt as to the reason of it?

But, he says, Illinois came into the Union as a slave State. Silence, perhaps, would be the best answer to this flat contradiction of the known history of the country. What are the facts upon which this bold assertion is based? When we first acquired the country, as far back as 1787, there were some slaves within it, held by the French inhabitants at Kaskaskia. The territorial legislation, admitted a few negroes, from the slave States, as indentured servants. One year after the adoption of the first State constitution the whole number of them was—what do you think? just 117—while the aggregate free population was 55,094—about 470 to one. Upon this state of facts, the people framed their constitution prohibiting the further introduction of slavery, with a sort of guaranty to the owners of the few indentured servants, giving freedom to their children to be born thereafter, and making no mention whatever, of any supposed slave for life. Out of this small matter, the Judge manufactures his argument that Illinois came into the Union as a slave State. Let the facts be the answer to the argument.

The principles of the Nebraska bill, he says, expelled slavery from Illinois. The principle of that bill first planted it here—that is, it first came, because there was no law to prevent it—first came before we owned the country; and finding it here, and having the ordinance of '87 to prevent its increasing, our people struggled along, and finally got rid of it as best they could.

But the principle of the Nebraska bill abolished slavery in several of the old States.—Well, it is true that several of the old States, in the last quarter of the last century, did adopt systems of gradual emancipation, by which the institution has finally become extinct within their limits; but it MAY or MAY NOT be true that the principle of the Nebraska bill was the cause that led to the adoption of these measures. It is now more than fifty years, since the last of these States adopted its system of emancipation. If Nebraska Bill is the real author of these benevolent works, it is rather deplorable, that he has, for so long a time, ceased working altogether. Is there not some reason to suspect that it was the principle of the REVOLUTION, and not the principle of Nebraska Bill, that led to emancipation in these old States? Leave it to the people of these old emancipating States, and I am quite sure they will decide, that neither that, nor any other good thing, ever did, or ever will come of Nebraska Bill.

In the course of my main argument, Judge Douglas interrupted me to say, that the principle of the Nebraska bill was very old; that it originated when God made man and placed good and evil before him, allowing him to choose for himself, being responsible for the choice he should make. At the time I thought this was merely playful; and I answered it accordingly. But in his reply to me he renewed it, as a serious argument. In seriousness then, the facts of this proposition are not true as stated. God did not place good and evil before man, telling him to make his choice. On the contrary, he did tell him there was one tree, of the fruit of which, he should not eat, upon pain of certain death. I should searcely with so strong a prohibition against slavery in Nebraska.

But this argument strikes me as not a little remarkable in another particular—in its strong resemblance to the old argument for the 'Divine right of Kings.' By the latter, the King is to do just as he pleases with his white subjects, being responsible to God alone. By the former, the white man is to do just as he pleases with his black slaves, being responsible to God alone. The two things are precisely alike, and it is but natural that they should find similar arguments to sustain them.

I had argued, that the application of the principle of self-government, as contended for, would require the revival of the African slave trade—that no argument could be made in favor of a man's right to take slaves to Nebraska, which could not be equally well made in favor of his right to bring them from the coast of Africa.—The judge replied that the Constitution requires the suppression of the foreign slave-trade; but does not require the prohibition of slavery in the territories. That is a mistake, in point of fact. The Constitution does NOT require the action of Congress in either case; and it does AUTHORIZE it in both. And so, there is still no difference between the cases.

In regard to what I had said, the advantage the slave States have over the free, in the matter of representation, the Judge replied that we, in the free States, count five free negroes as five white people, while in the slave States, they count five slaves as three whites only; and that the advantage, at last, was on the side of the free States.

Now, in the slave States, they count free negroes just as we do; and it so happens that besides their slaves, they have as many free negroes as we have, and thirty-three thousand over.—Thus their free negroes more than balance ours; and their advantage over us, in consequence of their slaves, still remains as I stated it.

In reply to my argument, that the compromise measures of 1850, were a system of equivalents; and that the provisions of no one of them could fairly be carried to other subjects, without its corresponding equivalent being carried with it, the judge denied out-right, that these measures had any connection with, or dependence upon, each other. This is mere desperation. If they have no connection, why are they always spoken of in connection? Why has he so spoken of them, a thousand times? Why has he constantly called them a SERIES of measures? Why does everybody call them a compromise? Why was California kept out of the Union, six or seven months, if it was not because of its connection with the other measures? Webster's leading definition of the verb "to compromise" is "to adjust and settle a difference, by mutual agreement, with concessions of claims by the parties." This conveys precisely the popular understanding of the word "compromise." We knew, before the judge told us, that these measures passed separately, and in distinct bills; and that no two of them were passed by the votes of precisely the same members. But we also know, and so does he know, that no one of them could have passed both branches of Congress but for the understanding that the others were to pass also. Upon this understanding each got votes, which it could have got in no other way. It is this fact, which gives to the measures their true character; and it is the universal knowledge of this fact, that has given them the name of "compromise," so expressive of that true character.

I had asked "If in carrying the provisions of the Utah and New Mexico laws to Nebraska, you could clear away other objection, how can you leave Nebraska "perfectly free" to introduce slavery BEFORE she forms a constitution—during her territorial government?—while the Utah and New Mexico laws only authorize it WHEN they form constitutions, and are admitted into the Union?" To this Judge Douglas answered that the Utah and New Mexico laws, also authorized it BEFORE; and to prove this, he read from one of their laws, as follows: "That the legislative power of said territory shall extend to all rightful subjects of legislation consistent with the constitution of the United States and the provisions of this act."

Now it is perceived from the reading of this, that there is nothing express upon the subject; but that the authority is sought to be implied merely, for the general provision of "all rightful subjects of legislation." In reply to this, I insist, as a legal rule of construction, as well as the plain popular view of the matter, that the EXPRESS provision for Utah and New Mexico coming in with slavery if they choose, when they shall form constitutions, is an EXCLUSION of all implied authority on the same subject—that Congress, having the subject distinctly in their minds, when they made the express provision, they therein expressed their WHOLE meaning on that subject.

The judge rather insinuated that I had found it convenient to forget the Washington territorial law passed in 1853. This was a division of Oregon, organizing the northern part, as the territory of Washington. He asserted that, by this act, the ordinance of '87 theretofore existing in Oregon, was repealed; that nearly all the members of Congress voted for it, beginning in the H. R., with Charles Allen of Massachusetts, and ending with Richard Yates, of Illinois; and that he could not understand how those who now oppose the Nebraska bill, so voted then, unless it was because it was then too soon after both the great political parties had ratified the compromises of 1850, and the ratification therefore too fresh, to be then repudiated.

Now I had seen the Washington act before; and I have carefully examined it since; and I aver that there is no repeal of the ordinance of '87, or of any prohibition of slavery, in it. In express terms, there is absolutely nothing in the whole law upon the subject—in fact, nothing to lead a reader to THINK of the subject. To my judgment, it is equally free from every thing from which such repeal can be legally implied; but however this may be, are men now to be entrapped by a legal implication, extracted from covert language, introduced perhaps, for the very purpose of entrapping them? I sincerely wish every man could read this law quite through, carefully watching every sentence, and every line, for a repeal of the ordinance of '87 or any thing equivalent to it.

Another point on the Washington act. If it was intended to be modelled after the Utah and New Mexico acts, as Judge Douglas insists, why was it not inserted in it, as in them, that Washington was to come in with or without slavery as she may choose at the adoption of her constitution? It has no such provision in it; and I defy the ingenuity of man to give a reason for the omission, other than that it was not intended to follow the Utah and New Mexico laws in regard to the question of slavery.

The Washington act not only differs vitally from the Utah and New Mexico acts; but the Nebraska act differs vitally from both.—By the latter act the people are left "perfectly free" to regulate their own domestic concerns, &c.; but in all the former, all their laws are to be submitted to Congress, and if disapproved are to be null. The Washington act goes even further; it absolutely prohibits the territorial legislation, by very strong and guarded language, from establishing banks, or borrowing money on the faith of the territory. Is this the sacred right of self-government we hear vaunted so much? No sir, the Nebraska bill finds no model in the acts of '50 or the Washington act. It finds no model in any law from Adam till to-day. As Phillips says of Napoleon, the Nebraska act is grand, gloomy, and peculiar; wrapped in the solitude of its own originality; without a model, and without a shadow upon the earth.

In the course of his reply, Senator Douglas remarked, in substance, that he had always considered this government was made for the white people and not for the negroes. Why, in point of mere fact, I think so too. But in this remark of the Judge, there is a significance, which I think is the key to the great mistake (if there is any such mistake) which he has made in this Nebraska measure. It shows that the Judge has no very vivid impression that the negro is a human; and consequently has no idea that there can be any moral question in legislating about him. In his view, the question of whether a new country shall be slave or free, is a matter of as utter indifference, as it is whether his neighbor shall plant his farm with tobacco, or stock it with horned cattle. Now, whether this view is right or wrong, it is very certain that the great mass of mankind take a totally different view.—They consider slavery a great moral wrong; and their feeling against it, is not evanescent, but eternal. It lies at the very foundation of their sense of justice; and it cannot be trifled with.—It is a great and durable element of popular action, and I think, no statesman can safely disregard it.

Our Senator also objects that those who oppose him in this measure do not entirely agree with one another. He reminds me that in my firm adherence to the constitutional rights of the slave States, I differ widely from others who are co-operating with me in opposing the Nebraska bill; and he says it is not quite fair to oppose him in this variety of ways. He should remember that he took us by surprise—astounded us—by this measure. We were thunderstruck and stunned; and we reeled and fell in utter confusion. But we rose each fighting, grasping whatever he could first reach—a scythe—a pitchfork—a chopping axe,

or a butcher's cleaver. We struck in the direction of the sound, and we are
rapidly closing in upon him. He must not think to divert us from our purpose,
by showing us that our drill, our dress, and our weapons, are not entirely perfect and uniform. When the storm shall be past, he shall find us still Americans;
no less devoted to the continued Union and prosperity of the country than
heretofore.

Finally, the Judge invokes against me, the memory of Clay and of Webster.
They were great men, and men of great deeds. But where have I assailed them?
For what is it, that their life-long enemy, shall now make profit, by assuming
to defend them against me, their life-long friend? I go against the repeal of the
Missouri Compromise; did they ever go for it? They went for the compromise
of 1850; did I ever go against them? They were greatly devoted to the Union;
to the small measure of my ability, was I ever less so? Clay and Webster were
dead before this question arose; by what authority shall our Senator say they
would espouse his side of it, if alive? Mr. Clay was the leading spirit in making
the Missouri Compromise; is it very credible that if now alive, he would take
the lead in the breaking of it? The truth is that some support from whigs is now
a necessity with the Judge, and for this it is, that the names of Clay and Webster are now invoked. His old friends have deserted him in such numbers as to
leave too few to live by. He came to his own, and his own received him not,
and Lo! he turns unto the Gentiles.

A word now as to the Judge's desperate assumption that the compromises of
'50 had no connection with one another; that Illinois came into the Union as a
slave State, and some other similar ones. This is no other than a bold denial of
the history of the country. If we do not know that the compromises of '50 were
dependent on each other; if we do not know that Illinois came into the Union
as a free State—we do not know any thing. If we do not know these things, we
do not know that we ever had a revolutionary war, or such a chief as Washington. To deny these things is to deny our national axioms, or dogmas, at least;
and it puts an end to all argument. If a man will stand up and assert, and repeat,
and re-assert, that two and two do not make four, I know nothing in the power
of argument that can stop him. I think I can answer the Judge so long as he sticks
to the premises; but when he flies from them, I cannot work an argument into
the consistency of a maternal gag, and actually close his mouth with it. In such
a case I can only commend him to the seventy thousand answers just in from
Pennsylvania, Ohio and Indiana.

LETTER TO OWEN LOVEJOY
AUGUST 11, 1855

Owen Lovejoy was an abolitionist leader who became interested in joining forces with Lincoln against the Kansas-Nebraska Act. At this time, the Whig party was in decay, split along sectional lines between northern "Conscience Whigs" who opposed slavery, and southern "Cotton Whigs," who defended it. The incipient Republican Party was beginning to emerge as an anti-slavery party that could potentially gather together a broad coalition of northern Whigs, anti-Nebraska Democrats and abolitionists. Lincoln explored the possibility of fusing with this gathering coalition. However, as an experienced politician, he remained circumspect, avoiding a hasty and reckless decision that would threaten his own political career and the future of the anti-Nebraska movement. Though Lincoln shared many of Lovejoy's antislavery views, he was not an abolitionist. Furthermore, he did not want to provoke a direct confrontation with the Know-Nothings, a nativist party whose principles he abhorred, but whose support was potentially needed to strengthen the Anti-Nebraska coalition.

Nativism was a movement primarily of native-born Protestants who viewed the wave of nineteenth century immigration as a corrupting influence upon the purity of American government and culture. Secret societies like the Order of the Star Spangled Banner were formed to roll back the tide of immigration and to restrict the rights of foreigners, particularly Irish Catholics who had come to the United States in droves as a result of the Potato-Famine of the 1840's. When asked about their participation in the nativist movement, members of the party were sworn to secrecy and instructed to reply: "I know nothing." Hence, the nativist party was referred to as The Know Nothing Party.

True to his moral convictions, Lincoln was unwilling "to fuse" with a coalition that would have compromised its integrity by subordinating its core principles to the Know-Nothings: "I do not perceive how any one professing to be sensitive to the wrongs of negroes, can join in a league to degrade a class of white men." Lincoln thus hoped that the Know-Nothing Party, already in disarray, would disintegrate completely and that its scattered elements would be incorporated into an anti-slavery coalition based on sounder principles. This would force the disparate elements of the Know-Nothings to fuse on the terms of the new party rather than vice versa.

SPRINGFIELD, AUGUST 11—1855
HON: OWEN LOVEJOY:
MY DEAR SIR:

Yours of the 7th. was received the day before yesterday. Not even *you* are more anxious to prevent the extension of slavery than I; and yet the political atmosphere is such, just now, that I fear to do anything, lest I do wrong.

Knownothingism has not yet entirely tumbled to pieces—nay, it is even a little encouraged by the late elections in Tennessee, Kentucky & Alabama. Until we can get the elements of this organization, there is not sufficient materials to successfully combat the Nebraska democracy with. We can not get them so long as they cling to a hope of success under their own organization; and I fear an open push by us now, may offend them, and tend to prevent our ever getting them. About us here, they are mostly my old political and personal friends; and I have hoped their organization would die out without the painful necessity of my taking an open stand against them. Of their principles I think little better than I do of those of the slavery extentionists [sic]. Indeed I do not perceive how any one professing to be sensitive to the wrongs of the negroes, can join in a league to degrade a class of white men.

I have no objection to "fuse" with any body provided I can fuse on ground which I think is right; and I believe the opponents of slavery extension could now do this, if it were not for the K. N.ism. In many speeches last summer I advised those who did me the honor of a hearing to "stand with any body who stands right"—and I am still quite willing to follow my own advice. I lately saw, in the Quincy Whig, the report of a preamble and resolutions, made by Mr. Williams, as chairman of a Committee, to a public meeting and adopted by the meeting. I saw them but once, and have them not now at command; but so far as I can remember them, they occupy about the ground I should be willing to "fuse" upon.

As to my personal movements this summer, and fall, I am quite busy trying to pick up my lost crumbs of last year. I shall be here till September; then to the circuit till the 20th. then to Cincinnati, awhile, after a Patent right case; and back to the circuit to the end of November. I can be seen here any time this month; and at Bloomington at any time from the 10th. to the 17th. of September. As to an extra session of the Legislature, I should know no better how to bring that about, than to lift myself over a fence by the straps of my boots.

Yours truly
A. Lincoln—

LETTER TO GEORGE ROBERTSON
AUGUST 15, 1855

George Robertston, a Judge and Law Professor at Transylvania College in Kentucky, served as a legal counsel for Lincoln in the 1840s. While visiting Springfield in July 1855, he left Lincoln an inscribed volume of speeches called Scrap Book on Law and Politics, Men and Times. *Lincoln thanked Robertson and then expressed his apprehensions concerning the peaceful resolution of the slavery agitation. As seen in this letter, Lincoln often pointed out that the principle of divine right monarchy and proslavery theology were the same, and that both were antithetical to the nation's republican ideals. Like Frederick Douglass who revealed America's hypocrisy on the Fourth of July, Lincoln agreed that the embrace of slavery had made a mockery of the once glorious celebration. Anticipating his House Divided Speech, which would be delivered three years later, Lincoln ended his letter with a foreboding question, "Can we, as a nation, continue together permanently— forever—half slave, and half free?"*

SPRINGFIELD, ILLS. AUG: 15, 1855
HON: GEO. ROBERTSON
LEXINGTON, KY.
MY DEAR SIR:

The volume you left for me has been received. I am really grateful for the honor of your kind remembrance, as well as for the book. The partial reading I have already given it, has afforded me much of both pleasure and instruction. It was new to me that the exact question which led to the Missouri Compromise, has arisen before it arose in regard to Missouri; and that you had taken so prominent a part in it. Your short, but able and patriotic speech upon that occasion, has not been improved upon since, by those holding the same views; and, with all the lights you then had, the views you took appear to me as very reasonable.

You are not a friend to slavery in the abstract. In that speech you spoke of *"the peaceful extinction of slavery"* and used other expressions indicating your belief that the thing was, at some time, to have an end Since then we have had thirty six years of experience; and this experience has demonstrated, I think, that there is no peaceful extinction of slavery in prospect for us. The signal failure of Henry Clay, and other good and great men, in 1849, to effect anything in favor of gradual emancipation in Kentucky, together with a thousand other signs, extinguishes that hope utterly. On the question of liberty, as a principle, we are not what we have been.

When we were the political slaves of King George, and wanted to be free, we called the maxim that "all men are created equal" a self evident truth; but now when we have grown fat, and have lost all dread of being slaves ourselves, we have become so greedy to be *masters* that we call the same maxim "a self-evident lie" The fourth of July has not quite dwindled away; it is still a great day—*for burning fire-crackers!!!*

That spirit which desired the peaceful extinction of slavery, has itself become extinct, with the *occasion,* and the *men* of the Revolution. Under the impulse of that occasion, nearly half the states adopted systems of emancipation at once; and it is a significant fact, that not a single state has done the like since. So far as peaceful, voluntary emancipation is concerned, the condition of the negro slave in America, scarcely less terrible to the contemplation of a free mind, is now so fixed, and hopeless of change for the better, as that of the lost souls of the finally impenitent. The Autocrat of all the Russias will resign his crown, and proclaim his subjects free republicans, sooner than will our American masters voluntarily give up their slaves.

Our political problem now is "Can we, as a nation, continue together *permanently—forever—*half slave, and half free?" The problem is too mighty for me. May God, in his mercy, superintend the solution.

Your much obliged friend,

and humble servant

A. Lincoln—

LETTER TO JOSHUA F. SPEED
AUGUST 24, 1855

In this letter to Joshua Speed, his friend from Springfield, Lincoln replied to critics who argued that the containment of slavery necessarily implied violation of the rule of law and disunion. Lincoln pricked his friends' conscience by reminding him of their trip to St. Louis where they witnessed the appalling sight of slaves shackled together like fish on a stringer. Apparently, the memory of this ghastly sight haunted Lincoln. Testifying to his consistent opposition to slavery, he further explained that during the one term he served as a congressman in the United States House of Representatives, he voted for the Wilmot Proviso more than forty times. He then repudiated the nativist ideals of the Know Nothing Party as equally subversive to the principles of the American regime and its credibility in the eyes of the world. Indeed, it was utter hypocrisy for a nation founded on equality to affirm the moral right to slavery. In their affirmation of a superior race or group, proponents of slavery and Nativism alike would turn the regime away from its progressive aspirations towards the backwards path of Old-World despotism.

SPRINGFIELD, AUG: 24, 1855

DEAR SPEED:

You know what a poor correspondent I am. Ever since I received your very agreeable letter of the 22nd. of May I have been intending to write you in answer to it. You suggest that in political action now, you and I would differ. I suppose we would; not quite as much, however, as you may think. You know I dislike slavery; and you fully admit the abstract wrong of it. So far there is no cause of difference. But you say that sooner than yield your legal right to the slave—especially at the bidding of those who are not themselves interested, you would see the Union dissolved. I am not aware that *any one* is bidding you to yield that right; very certainly *I* am not. I leave that matter entirely to yourself. I also acknowledge *your* rights and *my* obligations, under the constitution, in regard to your slaves. I confess I hate to see the poor creatures hunted down, and caught, and carried back to their stripes, and unrewarded toils; but I bite my lip and keep quiet. In 1841 you and I had together a tedious low-water trip, on a Steam Boat from Louisville to St. Louis. You may remember, as I well do, that from Louisville to the mouth of the Ohio, there were, on board, ten or a dozen slaves, shackled together with irons. That sight was a continued torment to me; and I see something like it every time I touch the Ohio, or any other slave-border. It is hardly fair for you to assume, that I have no interest in a thing which has, and continually exercises, the power of making me miserable. You ought rather to appreciate how much the great body of the Northern people do crucify their feelings, in order to maintain their loyalty to the Constitution and the Union.

I do oppose the extension of slavery, because my judgment and feelings so prompt me; and I am under no obligation to the contrary. If for this you and I must differ, differ we must. You say if you were President, you would send an army and hang the leaders of the Missouri outrages upon the Kansas elections; still, if Kansas fairly votes herself a slave state, she must be admitted, or the Union must be dissolved. But how if she votes herself a slave State *unfairly*—that is, by the very means for which you say you would hang men? Must she still be admitted, or the Union be dissolved? That will be the phase of the question when it first becomes a practical one. In your assumption that there may be a *fair* decision of the slavery question in Kansas, I plainly see you and I would differ about the Nebraska-law. I look upon that enactment not as a *law,* but as *violence* from the beginning. It was conceived in violence, passed in violence, is maintained in violence, and is being executed in violence. I say it was *conceived* in violence, because the destruction of the Missouri Compromise, under the circumstances, was nothing less than violence. It was *passed* in violence, because it could not have passed at all but for the votes of many members in violence of the known will of their constituents. It is *maintained* in violence because the elections since, clearly demand it's repeal, and this demand is openly disregarded. *You* say men ought to be hung for the way they are executing that law; and *I* say the way it is being executed is quite as good as any of its antecedents. It is being executed in the precise way which was intended from the first; else why does no Nebraska man express astonishment or condemnation? Poor Reeder is the only public man who has been silly enough to believe that any thing like fairness was ever intended; and he has been bravely undeceived.

That Kansas will form a Slave Constitution, and, with it, will ask to be admitted into the Union, I take to be an already settled question; and so settled by the very means you so pointedly condemn. By every principle of law, ever held by any court, North or South, every negro taken to Kansas is free; yet, in utter disregard of this—in the spirit of violence merely—that beautiful Legislature gravely passes a law to hang men who shall venture to inform a negro of his legal rights. This is the substance, and real object of the law. If, like Haman, they should hang upon the gallows of their own building, I shall not be among the mourners for their fate.

In my humble sphere, I shall advocate the restoration of the Missouri Compromise, so long as Kansas remains a territory; and when, by all these foul means, it seeks to come into the Union as a Slave-state, I shall oppose it. I am very loth, in any case, to withhold my assent to the enjoyment of property *acquired,* or *located,* in good faith; but I do not admit that *good faith,* in taking a negro to Kansas, to be held in slavery, is a *possibility* with any man. Any man who has sense enough to be the controller of his own property, has too much sense to misunderstand the outrageous character of this whole Nebraska business. But I digress. In my opposition to the admission of Kansas I shall have some company; but we may be beaten. If we are, I shall not, on that account, attempt to dissolve the Union. On the contrary, if we succeed, there will be enough of us to take care of the Union. I think it probable, however, we shall be beaten. Standing as a unit among yourselves, you can, directly, and indirectly, bribe enough of our men to carry the day—as you could on an open proposition to establish monarchy. Get hold of some man in the North, whose position and ability in such, that he can make the support of your measure— whatever it may be—*a democratic party necessity,* and the thing is done. *Appropos* [sic] of this, let me tell you an anecdote. Douglas introduced the Nebraska bill in January. In February afterwards, there was a call session of the Illinois Legislature. Of the one hundred members composing the two branches of that body, about seventy were democrats. These latter held a caucus, in which the Nebraska bill was talked of, if not formally discussed. It was thereby discovered that just three, and no more, were in favor of the measure. In a day or two Dougla's [sic] orders came on to have resolutions passed approving the bill;

and they were passed by large majorities!!! The truth of this is vouched for by a bolting democratic member. The masses too, democratic as well as whig, were even, nearer unanamous [sic] against it; but as soon as the party necessity of supporting it, became apparent, the way the democracy began to see the *wisdom* and *justice* of it, was perfectly astonishing.

You say if Kansas fairly votes herself a free state, as a Christian you will rather rejoice at it. All decent slaveholders *talk* that way; and I do not doubt their candor. But they never *vote* that way. Although in a private letter, or conversation, you will express your preference that Kansas shall be free, you would vote for no man for Congress who would say the same thing publicly. No such man could be elected from any district in a slave-state. You think Stringfellow & Co ought to be hung; and yet, at the next presidential election you will vote for the exact type and representative of Stringfellow. The slave-breeders and slave-traders, are a small, odious and detested class, among you; and yet in politics, they dictate the course of all of you, and are as completely your masters, as you are the master of your own negroes. You inquire where I now stand. That is a disputed point—I think I am a whig; but others say there are no whigs, and that I am an abolitionist. When I was at Washington I voted for the Wilmot Proviso as good as forty times, and I never heard of any one attempting to unwhig me for that. I now do no more than oppose the *extension* of slavery.

I am not a Know-Nothing. That is certain. How could I be? How can any one who abhors the oppression of negroes, be in favor of degrading classes of white people? Our progress in degeneracy appears to me to be pretty rapid. As a nation, we began by declaring that *"all men are created equal."* We now practically read it "all men are created equal, *except negroes"* When the Know-Nothings get control, it will read "all men are created equal, except negroes, *and foreigners, and Catholics."* When it comes to this I should prefer emigrating to some country where they make no pretence of loving liberty—to Russia, for instance, where despotism can be taken pure, and without the base alloy of hypocracy [sic].

Mary will probably pass a day to two in Louisville in October. My kindest regards to Mrs. Speed. On the leading subject of this letter, I have more of her sympathy than I have of yours. And yet let me say I am

Your friend forever

A. Lincoln.

---

1. *CWAL,* II, 482.

SPEECH AT BLOOMINGTON, ILLINOIS[1]
MAY 29, 1856

Lincoln's speech at Bloomington coincided with the formation of the Illinois Republican Party and his role as its standard-bearer. In February 1856, he took an important step in assuming leadership of the anti-Nebraska movement in Illinois. He met in Decatur, Illinois, with a group of journalists to coordinate a unified opposition against the Kansas-Nebraska Act. Three months later, an anti-Nebraska Illinois State convention was announced for Bloomington, Illinois, on May 29, 1856. The convention was an effort by the newly formed Republican Party to organize the state for the coming presidential election of 1856. Lincoln was elected as one of 270 delegates. Some of Lincoln's Whig colleagues thought that his decision to attend the Convention would prove disastrous to his political career since radical abolitionists were known to be part of the Republican Party coalition. Lincoln, however, had already made up his mind. His decision to attend the convention represented a final commitment to fuse with the Republican Party.

Lincoln helped frame both the Decatur Declaration and the Bloomington Platform, moderate antislavery documents that eschewed abolitionist positions by acknowledging legal obligations to slaveholders. In addition, Lincoln was honored by being chosen as the final speaker at the Bloomington meeting, a testimony to his crucial leadership of the antislavery movement. Unfortunately, only fragments remain of Lincoln's speech. However, the fragment that was recorded provides a crucial insight concerning Lincoln's moral view of the Union. His dictum that "the Union must be preserved in the purity of its principles" is an important corollary to Webster's "Liberty and Union, now and forever, one and inseparable." Contrary to those who have claimed that Lincoln's effort to preserve the Union was indifferent to black freedom, he emphasized quite early in his career that preserving the Union meant preserving the moral principles for which the Union stood for, including the promise of equality in the Declaration.

Apparently, Lincoln's speech at Bloomington captivated his audience and left the crowd spellbound. Herndon claimed that it was "full of fire and energy and force, it was logic; it was pathos; it was enthusiasm; it was justice, equity, truth, and right set ablaze by the divine fires of a soul maddened by the wrong; it was hard, heavy, knotty, gnarly, backed with wrath."

MAY 29, 1856

Abraham Lincoln, of Sangamon, came upon the platform amid deafening applause. He enumerated the pressing reasons of the present movement. He was here ready to fuse with anyone who would unite with him to oppose slave power; spoke of the bugbear disunion which was so vaguely threatened. It was to be remembered that the *Union must be preserved in the purity of its principles as well as in the integrity of its territorial parts.* It must be "Liberty and Union, now and forever, one and inseparable." The sentiment in favor of white slavery now prevailed in all the slave state papers, except those of Kentucky, Tennessee and Missouri and Maryland. Such was the progress of the National Democracy. Douglas once claimed against him that Democracy favored more than his principles, the individual rights of man. Was it not strange that he must stand there now to defend those rights against their former eulogist? The Black Democracy were endeavoring to cite Henry Clay to reconcile old Whigs to their doctrine, and repaid them with the very cheap compliment of National Whigs.

SECTIONALISM
[OCTOBER 1?], 1856

The following fragment was written in the context of Lincoln's support for John C. Fremont and William L. Dayton, the respective presidential and vice-presidential candidates of the Republican Party in the election of 1856. The Republican campaign slogan was: "Free soil, free speech, and Fremont." It included a condemnation of slavery as a "great moral, social and political evil," called for the containment of slavery in the national territories, the repeal of the Kansas-Nebraska Act, the repeal of the Fugitive Slave Act, and the abolition of slavery in the District of Columbia. Many principled opponents of slavery were hesitant in supporting the incipient Republican Party since it was perceived as a purely sectional party that would endanger the bonds of Union. Republicans were derisively called "Black Republicans" because of their antislavery views. Attempting to vindicate his new party, Lincoln responded to the objections of critics who opposed it as a purely sectional party by defining the naked, moral issue.

SECTIONALISM

IT IS CONSTANTLY objected to Fremont & Dayton, that they are supported by a *sectional* party, who, by their *sectionalism,* endanger the National Union. This objection, more than all other, causes men, really opposed to slavery extension, to hesitate. Practically, it is the most difficult objection we have to meet.

For this reason, I now propose to examine it, a little more carefully than I have heretofore done, or seen it done by others.

First, then, what is the question between the parties, respectively represented by Buchanan and Fremomont [*sic*]?

Simply this: *"Shall slavery be allowed to extend into U. S. terrtories [sic], now legally free?"* Buchanan says it *shall;* and Fremont says it shall *not.*

That is the *naked* issue, and the *whole* of it. Lay the respective platforms side by side; and the difference between them, will be found to amount to precisely that.

True, each party charges upon the other, *designs* much beyond what is involved in the issue, as stated; but as these charges can not be fully proved either way, it is probably better to reject them on both sides, and stick to the naked issue, as it is clearly made up on the record.

And now, to restate the question *"Shall slavery be allowed to extend into U. S. terrtories [sic], now legally free?* I beg to know *how one* side of that question is more sectional than the other? Of course I expect to effect nothing with the man who makes this charge of sectionalism, without caring whether it is just or not. But of the *candid, fair,* man who has been puzzled with this charge, I do ask how is *one* side of this question, more *sectional,* than the other? I beg of him to consider well, and answer calmly.

If one side be as sectional as the other, nothing is gained, as to sectionalism, by changing sides; so that each must choose sides of the question on some other ground. As I should think, according, as the one side or the other, shall appear nearest right. If he shall really think slavery *ought* to be extended, let him go to Buchanan; if he think it ought *not* let [him?] go to Fremont.

But, Fremont and Dayton, are both residents of the free-states; and this fact has been vaunted, in high places, as excessive *sectionalism.*

While interested individuals become *indignant* and *excited,* against this manifestation of *sectionalism,* I am very happy to know, that the Constitution remains calm—keeps cool—upon the subject. It does say that President and Vice President shall be resident of different states; but it does not say one must live in a *slave,* and the other in a *free* state.

It has been a *custom* to take one from a slave, and the other from a free state; but the custom has not, at all been uniform. In 1828 Gen. Jackson and Mr. Calhoun, both from slave states, were placed on the same ticket; and Mr. Adams and Dr. Rush both from the free-states, were pitted against them. Gen. Jackson and Mr. Calhoun were elected; and qualified and served under the election; yet the whole thing never suggested the idea of sectionalism.

In 1841, the president, Gen. Harrison, died, by which Mr. Tyler, the Vice-President & a slave state man, became president. Mr. Mangum, another slave-state man, was placed in the Vice Presidential chair, served out the term, and no fuss about it—no sectionalism thought of.

In 1853 the present president came into office. He is a freestate man. Mr. King, the new Vice President elect, was a slave state man; but he died without entering on the duties of his office. At first, his vacancy was filled by Atchison, another slave-state man; but he soon resigned, and the place was supplied by Bright, a free-state man. So that right now, and for the year and a half last past, our president and vice-president are both actually free-state men.

But, it is said, the friends of Fremont, avow the purpose of electing him exclusively by free-state votes, and that this is unendurable sectionalism.

This statement of fact, is not exactly true. With the friends of Fremont, it is an *expected necessity,* but it is not an *"avowed purpose,"* to elect him, if at all, principally, by free state votes; but it is, with equal intensity, true that Buchanan's friends expect to elect him, if at all, chiefly by slave-state votes.

Here, agan [*sic*], the sectionalism, is just as much on one side as the other.

The thing which gives most color to the charge of Sectionalism, made against those who oppose the spread of slavery into free terrtory [*sic*], is the fact that *they* can get no votes in the slave-states, while their opponents get all, or nearly so, in the slave-states, and also, a large number in the free States. To state it in another way, the Extensionists, can get votes all over the Nation, while the Restrictionists can get them only in the free states.

This being the fact, *why* is it so? It is not because one *side* of the question dividing them, is more sectional than the *other;* nor because of any difference in the mental or moral structure of the people North and South. It is because, in that question, the people of the South have an immediate palpable and immenesly [*sic*] great pecuniary interest; while, with the people of the North, it is merely an abstract question of moral right, with only *slight,* and *remote* pecuniary interest added.

The slaves of the South, at a moderate estimate, are worth a thousand millions of dollars. Let it be permanently settled that this property may extend to new teritory [*sic*], without restraint, and it greatly *enhances,* perhaps quite *doubles,* its value at once. This immense, palpable pecuniary interest, on the question of extending slavery, unites the Southern people, as one man. But it can not be demonstrated that the *North* will gain a dollar by restricting it.

Moral principle is all, or nearly all, that unites us of the North. Pity 'tis, it is so, but this is a looser bond than pecuniary interest. Right here is the plain cause of *their perfect* union and *our want of it.* And see how *it* works. If a Southern man aspires to be president, they choke him down instantly, in order that the glittering prize of the presidency, may be held up, on Southern terms, to the greedy eyes of Northern ambition. With this they tempt us, and break in upon us.

The democratic party, in 1844, elected a Southern president. Since then, they have neither had a Southern candidate for *election,* or *nomination.* Their conventions of 1848–1852 and 1856, have been struggles exclusively among

Northern men, each vieing [*sic*] to outbid the other for the Southern vote—the South standing calmly by to finally cry going, going, gone, to the highest bidder; and, at the same time, to make its power more distinctly seen, and thereby to secure a still higher bid at the next succeeding struggle.

"Actions speak louder than words" is the maxim; and, if true, the South now distinctly says to the North "Give us the *measures,* and you take the *men.*"

The total withdrawal of Southern aspirants, for the presidency, multiplies the number of Northern ones. These last, in competing with each other, commit themselves to the utmost verge that, through their own greediness, they have the least hope their Northern supporters will bear. Having got committed, in a race of competition, necessity drives them into union to sustain themselves. Each, at first secures all he can, on personal attachments to him, and through *hopes* resting on him personally. Next, they unite with one another, and with the perfectly banded South, to make the offensive position they have got into, "a party measure." This done, large additional members are secured. When the repeal of the Missouri Compromise was first proposed, at the North there was litterally [*sic*] *"nobody"* in favor of it. In February 1854 our Legislature met in call, or extra, session. From them Douglas sought an indorsement of his then pending measure of Repeal. In our Legislature were about 70 democrats to 30 whigs. The former held a caucus, in which it was resolved to give Douglas the desired indorsement. Some of the members of that caucus bolted—would not stand it—and they now divulge the secrets. They say that the caucus fairly confessed that the Repeal was wrong; and they placed their determination to indorse it, solely on the ground that it was *necessary* to sustain Douglas. Here we have the direct evidence of how the Nebraska-bill obtained its strength in Illinois. It was given, not in a sense of right, but in the teeth of a sense of wrong, to *sustain Douglas.* So Illinois was divided. So New England, for Pierce; Michigan for Cass, Pensylvania [*sic*] for Buchan [*sic*], and all for the Democratic party.

And when, by such means, they have got a large portion of the Northern people into a position contrary to their own honest impulses, and sense of right; they have the impudence to turn upon those who do stand firm, and call them *sectional.*

Were it not too serious a matter, this cool impudence would be laughable, to say the least.

Recurring to the question *"Shall slavery be allowed to extend into U.S. terrtory* [sic] *now legal* [sic] *free?*

This *is* a sectional question—that is to say, it is a question, in its nature calculated to divide the American people geographically. Who is to *blame* for that?

Who can help it? Either side *can* help it; but how? Simply by yielding to the other side. There is no other way. In the whole range of possibility, there is no other way. Then, which side shall yield? To this again, there can be but one answer— the side which is in the *wrong*. True, we differ, as to which side *is* wrong; and we boldly say, let all who really think slavery ought to spread into free terrtory [*sic*], openly go over against us. There is where they rightfully belong.

But why should any go, who really think slavery ought not to spread? Do they really think the *right* ought to yield to the wrong? Are they afraid to stand by the *right?* Do they fear that the constitution is too weak to sustain them in the right? Do they really think that by right surrendering to wrong, the hopes of our Constitution, our Union, and our liberties, can possibly be bettered?

SPEECH AT A REPUBLICAN BANQUET, CHICAGO, ILLINOIS
[DECEMBER 10, 1856]

The short speech below is significant in revealing Lincoln's debt to his Whig prede-
cessor Daniel Webster on the inseparability of liberty and Union. Lincoln and the Whigs
believed that liberty was best safeguarded under the auspices of a national Union dedi-
cated to the principles of the Declaration and the rule of law in the Constitution. In this
same speech, Lincoln identifies equality as "the central idea" of the American Republic
and warns of the effort to replace this fundamental principle of the nation's creed with a
new, substitute creed of inequality.

... THE PRESIDENT THEN READ the first regular toast: "1st THE UNION— The North will maintain it—the South will not depart therefrom."

Hon. Abram Lincoln of Springfield, amid most deafening cheers, arose to reply to this toast. He said he could most heartily indorse the sentiment expressed in the toast. During the whole canvass we had been assailed as the enemies of the Union, and he often had occasion to repudiate the sentiments attributed to us. He said that the Republican party was the friend of the Union. [Cheers.] It was the friend of the Union now; and if it had been entirely suc-cessful, it would have been the friend of the Union more than ever, [Loud and long continued cheers]. He maintained that the Liberty for which we con-tended could best be obtained by a firm, a steady adherence to the Union. As Webster said, "Not Union without liberty, nor liberty without Union; but Union and liberty, now and forever, one and inseparable." [Loud Cheers.] The speaker said we had selected and elected a Republican State ticket. We have done what we supposed to be our duty. It is now the duty of those elected to give us a good Republican Administration. In regard to the Governor-elect, Col. Bissell,—[Loud and long-continued cheers and waving of handker-chiefs]—he referred to the opposite party saying that "he couldn't take the oath." Well, they said "he couldn't be elected," and as they were mistaken once, he thought they were not unlikely to be mistaken again. "*They* wouldn't take such an oath!" Oh, no! [Laughter.] "They would cut off their right arm first." He would like to know one of them who would not part with his right arm to have the privilege of taking the oath. Their conduct reminded him of the darky who, when a bear had put its head into the hole and shut out the daylight, cried out, "What was darkening de hole?" "Ah," cried the other darky, who was on to the tail of the animal, "if de tail breaks you'll find out." [Laughter and cheers.] Those darkies at Springfield see something darkening the hole, but wait till the tail breaks on the 1st of January, and they will see. [Cheers.] The speaker referred to the anecdote of the boy who was talking to another as to whether Gen. Jackson could ever get to Heaven. Said the boy "He'd get there if he had a mind to." [Cheers and laughter.] So was it with Col. Bissell,—he'd do what-ever he had a mind to. [Cheers.]

We have another annual Presidential Message. Like a rejected lover, mak-ing merry at the wedding of his rival, the President felicitates hugely over the late Presidential election. He considers the result a signal triumph of good prin-ciples and good men, and a very pointed rebuke of bad ones. He says the peo-ple did it. He forgets that the "people," as he complacently calls only those who voted for Buchanan, are in a minority of the whole people, by about four hun-dred thousand voters—one full tenth of all the voters. Remembering this, he might perceive that the "Rebuke" may not be quite as durable as he seems to think—that the majority may not choose to remain permanently rebuked by that minority.

The President thinks the great body of us Fremonters, being ardently attached to liberty, in the abstract, were duped by a few wicked and designing men. There is a slight difference of opinion on this. We think *he*, being ardently attached to the hope of a second term, *in the concrete*, was duped by men who had liberty every way. He is in the cat's paw. By much dragging of chestnuts from the fire for others to eat, his claws are burnt off to the gristle, and he is thrown aside as unfit for further use. As the fool said to King Lear, when his daughters had turned him out of doors, "He's a shelled pea's cod."

So far as the President charges us "with a desire to change the domestic insti-tutions of existing States;" and of "doing every thing in our power to deprive the Constitution and the laws of moral authority," for the whole party, on *belief*, and for myself, on *knowledge* I pronounce the charge an unmixed, and unmitigated falsehood.

Our government rests in public opinion. Whoever can change public opinion, can change the government, practically just so much. Public opinion, or [on?] any subject, always has a *"central idea,"* from which all its minor thoughts radiate. That "central idea" in our political public opinion, at the beginning was, and until recently has continued to be, "the equality of men." And although it was always submitted patiently to whatever of inequality there seemed to be as matter of actual necessity, its constant working has been a steady progress towards the practical equality of all men. The late Presidential election was a struggle, by one party, to discard that central idea, and to substitute for it the opposite idea that slavery is right, in the abstract, the workings of which, as a central idea, may be the perpetuity of human slavery, and its extension to all countries and colors. Less than a year ago, the Richmond *Enquirer*, an avowed advocate of slavery, regardless of color, in order to favor his views, invented the phrase, "State equality," and now the President, in his Message, adopts the *Enquirer's* catch-phrase, telling us the people "have asserted the constitutional equality of each and all of the States of the Union as States." The President flatters himself that the new central idea is completely inaugurated; and so, indeed, it is, so far as the mere fact of a Presidential election can inaugurate it. To us it is left to know that the majority of the people have not yet declared for it, and to hope that they never will.

All of us who did not vote for Mr. Buchanan, taken together, are a majority of four hundred thousand. But, in the late contest we were divided between Fremont and Fillmore. Can we not come together, for the future. Let every one who really believes, and is resolved, that free society is not, *and shall not be*, a failure, and who can conscientiously declare that in the past contest he has done only what he thought best—let every such one have charity to believe that every other one can say as much. Thus let bygones be bygones. Let past differences, as nothing be; and with steady eye on the real issue, let us reinaugurate the good old "central ideas" of the Republic. We *can* do it. The human heart *is* with us—God is with us. We shall again be able not to declare, that "all States as States, are equal," nor yet that "all citizens as citizens are equal," but to renew the broader, better declaration, including both these and much more, that "all *men* are created equal."

FIRST LECTURE ON DISCOVERIES AND INVENTIONS
[APRIL 6, 1858]

Lincoln first made this speech in Bloomington at the Young Men's Association on April 6, 1858. He delivered a second, revised lecture in February of 1859, which is also included below. These lectures displays Lincoln's scientific and speculative cast of mind. Drawing extensively from the Bible, he traces the progress of human discovery and invention through time to provide a theological defense of free labor and self-improvement.

ALL CREATION IS A MINE, and every man, a miner.

The whole earth, and all *within* it, *upon* it, and *round about* it, including *himself*, in his physical, moral, and intellectual nature, and his susceptabilities, are the infinitely various "leads" from which, man, from the first, was to dig out his destiny.

In the beginning, the mine was unopened, and the miner stood *naked*, and *knowledgeless*, upon it.

Fishes, birds, beasts, and creeping things, are not miners, but *feeders* and *lodgers*, merely. Beavers build houses; but they build them in nowise differently, or better now, than they did, five thousand years ago. Ants, and honey-bees, provide food for winter; but just in the *same way* they did, when Solomon refered the sluggard to them as patterns of prudence.

Man is not the only animal who labors; but he is the only one who *improves* his workmanship. This improvement, he effects by *Discoveries*, and *Inventions*. His first important discovery was the fact that he was naked; and his first invention was the fig-leaf-apron. This simple article—the apron—made of leaves, seems to have been the origin of *clothing*—the one thing for which nearly Page 438 half of the toil and care of the human race has ever since been expended. The most important improvement ever made in connection with clothing, was the invention of *spinning* and *weaving*. The spinning jenny, and power-loom, invented in modern times, though great *improvements*, do not, *as inventions*, rank with the ancient arts of spinning and weaving. Spinning and weaving brought into the department of clothing such abundance and variety of material. Wool, the hair of several species of animals, hemp, flax, cotten, silk, and perhaps other articles, were all suited to it, affording garments not only adapted to wet and dry, heat and cold, but also susceptable of high degrees of ornamental finish. Exactly *when*, or *where*, spinning and weaving originated is not known. At the first interview of the Almighty with Adam and Eve, after the fall, He made ``coats of skins, and clothed them" Gen: 3-21.

The Bible makes no other alusion to clothing, *before* the flood. Soon *after* the deluge Noah's two sons covered him with a *garment*; but of what *material* the garment was made is not mentioned. Gen. 9-23.

Abraham mentions "*thread*" in such connection as to indicate that spinning and weaving were in use in his day—Gen. 14.23—and soon after, reference to the art is frequently made. "*Linen breeches*, ['] are mentioned,—Exod. 28.42—and it is said "all the women that were wise hearted, did *spin* with their hands" (35-25) and, "all the women whose hearts stirred them up in wisdom, *spun* goat's hair" (35-26). The work of the "*weaver*" is mentioned—(35-35). In the book of Job, a very old book, date not exactly known, the "*weavers shuttle*" is mentioned.

The above mention of "*thread*" by Abraham is the oldest recorded alusion to spinning and weaving; and *it* was made about two thousand years after the creation of man, and now, near four thousand years ago. Profane authors think these arts originated in Egypt; and this is not contradicted, or made improbable, by any thing in the Bible; for the alusion of Abraham, mentioned, was not made until after he had sojourned in Egypt.

The discovery of the properties of *iron*, and the making of *iron tools*, must have been among the earliest of important discoveries and inventions. We can scarcely conceive the possibility of making much of anything else, without the use of iron tools. Indeed, an iron *hammer* must have been very much needed to make the *first* iron hammer with. A *stone* probably served as a substitute. How could the "*gopher wood*" for the Ark, have been gotten out without an axe? It seems to me an axe, or a miracle, was indispensable. Corresponding with the prime necessity for iron, we find at least Page 439 one very early notice of it. Tubal-cain was ``an instructer of every artificer in *brass* and *iron*[']—Gen: 4-22. Tubal-cain was the seventh in decent from Adam; and his birth was about one thousand years before the flood. *After* the flood, frequent mention is made of *iron*, and *instruments* made of iron. Thus "instrument of iron" at Num: 35-16; "bed-stead of iron" at Deut. 3-11—"the iron furnace [']" at 4-20—and "iron tool" at 27-5. At 19-5—very distinct mention of "the ax to cut down the tree" is made; and also at 8-9, the promised land is described as "a land whose stones are iron, and out of whose hills thou mayest dig brass." From the somewhat frequent mention of brass in connection with iron, it is not improbable that brass—perhaps what we now call copper—was used by the ancients for some of the same purposes as iron.

Transportation—the removal of person, and goods—from place to plac—would be an early *object*, if not a *necessity*, with man. By his natural powers of locomotion, and without much assistance from Discovery and invention, he could move himself about with considerable facility; and even, could carry small burthens with him. But very soon he would wish to lessen the labor, while he might, at the same time, extend, and expedite the business. For this object, wheel-carriages, and water-crafts—wagons and boats—are the most important inventions. The use of the wheel & axle, has been so long known, that it is difficult, without reflection, to estimate it at it's true value.

The oldest recorded allusion to the wheel and axle is the mention of a "chariot" Gen: 41-43. This was in Egypt, upon the occasion of Joseph being made Governor by Pharaoh. It was about twentyfive hundred years after the creation of Adam. That the chariot then mentioned was a wheel-carriage drawn by animals, is sufficiently evidenced by the mention of chariot-*wheels*, at Exod. 14-25, and the mention of chariots in connection with *horses*, in the same chapter, verses 9 & 23. So much, at present, for land-transportation.

Now, as to transportation by *water*, I have concluded, without sufficient authority perhaps, to use the term "boat" as a general name for all water-craft. The boat is indispensable to navigation. It is not probable that the philosophical principle upon which the use of the boat primarily depends—towit, the *principle*, that any thing will float, which can not sink without displacing more than it's own *weight* of water—was known, or even thought of, before the first boats were made. The sight of a crow standing on a piece of drift-wood floating down the swolen current of a creek or river, might well enough suggest the specific idea to a savage, that he could himself get upon a log, or on two logs tied together, and somehow work his way to the opposite shore of the same stream. Such a suggestion, so taken, would be the birth of navigation; and such, not improbably, it really was. The leading idea was thus caught; and whatever came afterwards, were but improvements upon, and auxiliaries to, it.

As man is a land animal, it might be expected he would learn to travel by land somewhat earlier than he would by water. Still the crossing of streams, somewhat too deep for wading, would be an early necessity with him. If we pass by the Ark, which may be regarded as belonging rather to the *miracalous*, than to *human* invention the first notice we have of water-craft, is the mention of "ships" by Jacob—Gen: 49-13. It is not till we reach the book of Isaiah that we meet with the mention of "oars" and "sails."

As mans *food*—his first necessity—was to be derived from the vegitation of the earth, it was natural that his first care should be directed to the assistance of that vegitation. And accordingly we find that, even before the fall, the man was put into the garden of Eden ``to dress it, and to keep it." And when afterwards, in consequence of the first transgression, *labor* was imposed on the race, as a *penalty*—a *curse*—we find the first born man—the first heir of the curse—was "a tiller of the ground." This was the beginning of agriculture; and although, both in point of time, and of importance, it stands at the head of all branches of human industry, it has derived less direct advantage from Discovery and Invention, than almost any other. The plow, of very early origin; and reaping, and threshing, machines, of modern invention are, at this day, the principle improvements in agriculture. And even the oldest of these, the plow, could not have been conceived of, until a precedent conception had been caught, and put into practice—I mean the conception, or idea, of substituting other forces in nature, for man's own muscular power. These other forces, as now used, are principally, the *strength* of animals, and the *power* of the wind, of running streams, and of steam.

Climbing upon the back of an animal, and making it carry us, might not, occur very readily. I think the back of the camel would never have suggested it. It was, however, a matter of vast importance.

The earliest instance of it mentioned, is when "Abraham rose up early in the morning, and saddled his ass,['] Gen. 22-3 preparatory to sacraficing Isaac as a burnt-offering; but the allusion to the *saddle* indicates that riding had been in use some time; for it is quite probable they rode bare-backed awhile, at least, before they invented saddles.

The *idea*, being once conceived, of riding *one* species of animals, would soon be extended to others. Accordingly we find that when the servant of Abraham went in search of a wife for Isaac, he took ten *camels* with him; and, on his return trip, "Rebekah arose, and her damsels, and they rode upon the camels, and followed the man" Gen 24-61[.]

The *horse*, too, as a riding animal, is mentioned early. The Redsea being safely passed, Moses and the children of Israel sang to the Lord "the *horse*, and his *rider* hath he thrown into the sea." Exo. 15-1.

Seeing that animals could bear *man* upon their backs, it would soon occur that they could also bear other burthens. Accordingly we find that Joseph's bretheren, on their first visit to Egypt, "laded their asses with the corn, and departed thence" Gen. 42-26.

Also it would occur that animals could be made to *draw* burthens *after* them, as well as to bear them upon their backs; and hence plows and chariots came into use early enough to be often mentioned in the books of Moses—Deut. 22-10. Gen. 41-43. Gen. 46-29. Exo. 14-25[.]

Of all the forces of nature, I should think the *wind* contains the largest amount of *motive power*—that is, power to move things. Take any given space of the earth's surface—for instance, Illinois—and all the power exerted by all the men, and beasts, and running-water, and steam, over and upon it, shall not equal the one hundredth part of what is exerted by the blowing of the wind over and upon the same space. And yet it has not, so far in the world's history, become proportionably *valuable* as a motive power. It is applied extensively, and advantageously, to sail-vessels in navigation. Add to this a few wind-mills, and pumps, and you have about all. That, as yet, no very successful mode of *controlling*, and *directing* the wind, has been discovered; and that, naturally, it moves by fits and starts—now so gently as to scarcely stir a leaf, and now so roughly as to level a forest—doubtless have been the insurmountable difficulties. As yet, the wind is an *untamed*, Page 442 and *unharnessed* force; and quite possibly one of the greatest discoveries hereafter to be made, will be the taming, and harnessing of the wind. That the difficulties of controlling this power are very great is quite evident by the fact that they have already been perceived, and struggled with more than three thousand years; for that power was applied to sail-vessels, at least as early as the time of the prophet Isaiah.

In speaking of *running streams*, as a motive power, I mean it's application to mills and other machinery by means of the "*water wheel*"—a thing now well known, and extensively used; but, of which, no mention is made in the bible, though it is thought to have been in use among the romans—(Am. Ency. tit— Mill) [.] The language of the Saviour "Two women shall be grinding at the mill &c" indicates that, even in the populous city of Jerusalem, at that day, mills were operated by hand—having, as yet had no other than human power applied to them.

The advantageous use of *Steam-power* is, unquestionably, a modern discovery.

And yet, as much as two thousand years ago the power of steam was not only observed, but an ingenius toy was actually made and put in motion by it, at Alexandria in Egypt.

What appears strange is, that neither the inventor of the toy, nor any one else, for so long a time afterwards, should perceive that steam would move *useful* machinery as well as a toy.

SECOND LECTURE ON DISCOVERIES AND INVENTIONS
[FEBRUARY 11, 1859]

WE HAVE ALL HEARD OF YOUNG AMERICA. He is the most *current* youth of the age. Some think him conceited, and arrogant; but has he not reason to entertain a rather extensive opinion of himself? Is he not the inventor and owner of the *present*, and sole hope of the *future*? Men, and things, everywhere, are ministering unto him. Look at his apparel, and you shall see cotten fabrics from Manchester and Lowell; flax-linen from Ireland; wool-cloth from [Spain;] silk from France; furs from the Arctic regions, with a buffalo-robe from the Rocky Mountains, as a general out-sider. At his table, besides plain bread and meat made at home, are sugar from Louisiana; coffee and fruits from the tropics; salt from Turk's Island; fish from New-foundland; tea from China, and spices from the Indies. The whale of the Pacific furnishes his candle-light; he has a diamond-ring from Brazil; a gold-watch from California, and a spanish cigar from Havanna. He not only has a present supply of all these, and much more; but thousands of hands are engaged in producing fresh supplies, and other thousands, in bringing them to him. The iron horse is panting, and impatient, to carry him everywhere, in no time; and the lightening stands ready harnessed to take and bring his tidings in a trifle less than no time. He owns a large part of the world, by right of possessing it; and all the rest by right of *wanting* it, and *intending* to have it. As Plato had for the immortality of the soul, so Young America has "a pleasing hope—a fond desire—a longing after" teritory. He has a great passion—a perfect rage—for the "*new*"; particularly new men for office, and the new earth mentioned in the revelations, in which, being no more sea, there must be about three times as much land as in the present. He is a great friend of humanity; and his desire for land is not selfish, but merely an impulse to extend the area of freedom. He is very anxious to fight for the liberation of enslaved nations and colonies, provided, always, they *have* land, and have *not* any liking for his interference. As to those who have no land, and would be glad of help from any quarter, he considers *they* can afford to wait a few hundred years longer. In knowledge he is particularly rich. He knows all that can possibly be known; inclines to believe in spiritual rappings, and is the unquestioned inventor of "*Manifest Destiny*." His horror is for all that is old, particularly "Old Fogy"; and if there be any thing old which he can endure, it is only old whiskey and old tobacco.

If the said Young America really is, as he claims to be, the owner of all present, it must be admitted that he has considerable advantage of Old Fogy. Take, for instance, the first of all fogies, father Adam. There he stood, a very perfect physical man, as poets and painters inform us; but he must have been very ignorant, and simple in his habits. He had had no sufficient time to learn much by observation; and he had no near neighbors to teach him anything. No part of his breakfast had been brought from the other side of the world; and it is quite probable, he had no conception of the world having any other side. In all of these things, it is very plain, he was no equal of Young America; the most that can be said is, that *according to his chance* he may have been quite as much of a man as his very self-complaisant descendant. Little as was what he knew, let the Youngster discard all he has learned from others, and then show, if he can, any advantage on his side. In the way of *land*, and *live stock*, Adam was quite in the ascendant. He had dominion over all the earth, and all the living things upon, and round about it. The land has been sadly divided out since; but never fret, Young America will *re-annex* it.

The great difference between Young America and Old Fogy, is the result of *Discoveries*, *Inventions*, and *Improvements*. These, in turn, are the result of *observation*, *reflection* and *experiment*. For instance, it is quite certain that ever since water has been boiled in covered vessels, men have seen the lids of the vessels rise and fall a little, with a sort of fluttering motion, by force of the steam; but so long as this was not specially observed, and reflected and experimented upon, it came to nothing. At length however, after many thousand years, some man observes this long-known effect of hot water lifting a pot-lid, and begins a train of reflection upon it. He says "Why, to be sure, the force that lifts the pot-lid, will lift any thing else, which is no heavier than the pot-lid." "And, as man has much hard lifting to do, can not this hot-water power be made to help him?" He has become a little excited on the subject, and he fancies he hears a voice answering "Try me" He does try it; and the *observation, reflection*, and *trial* gives to the world the control of that tremendous, and now well known agent, called steam-power. This is not the actual history in detail, but the general principle.

But was this first inventor of the application of steam, wiser or more ingenious than those who had gone before him? Not at all. Had he not learned much of them, he never would have succeeded—probably, never would have thought of making the attempt. To be fruitful in invention, it is indispensable to have a *habit* of observation and reflection; and this *habit*, our steam friend acquired, no doubt, from those who, to him, were old fogies. But for the difference in *habit* of observation, why did yankees, almost instantly, discover gold in California, which had been trodden upon, and over-looked by indians and Mexican greasers, for centuries? Gold-mines are not the only mines overlooked in the same way. There are more mines above the Earth's surface than below it. All nature—the whole world, material, moral, and intellectual,—is a mine; and, in Adam's day, it was a wholly unexplored mine. Now, it was the destined work of Adam's race to develope, by discoveries, inventions, and improvements, the hidden treasures of this mine. But Adam had nothing to turn his attention to the work. If he should do anything in the way of invention, he had first to invent the art of invention—the *instance* at least, if not the *habit* of observation and reflection. As might be expected he seems not to have been a very observing man at first; for it appears he went about naked a considerable length of time, before he even noticed that obvious fact. But when he did observe it, the observation was not lost upon him; for it immediately led to the first of all inventions, of which we have any direct account—*the fig-leaf apron.*

The inclination to exchange thoughts with one another is probably an original impulse of our nature. If I be in pain I wish to let you know it, and to ask your sympathy and assistance; and my pleasurable emotions also, I wish to communicate to, and share with you. But to carry on such communication, some *instrumentality* is indispensable. Accordingly speech—articulate sounds rattled off from the tongue—was used by our first parents, and even by Adam, before the creation of Eve. He gave names to the animals while she was still a bone in his side; and he broke out quite volubly when she first stood before him, the best present of his maker. From this it would appear that speech was not an invention of man, but rather the direct gift of his Creator. But whether Divine gift, or invention, it is still plain that if a mode of communication had been left to invention, *speech* must have been the first, from the superior adaptation to the end, of the organs of speech, over every other means within the whole range of nature. Of the organs of speech the tongue is the principal; and if we shall test it, we shall find the capacities of the tongue, in the utterance of articulate sounds, absolutely wonderful. You can count from one to one hundred, quite distinctly in about forty seconds. In doing this two hundred and eighty three distinct sounds or syllables are uttered, being seven to each second; and yet there shall be enough difference between every two, to be easily recognized by the ear of the hearer. What other *signs* to represent *things* could possibly be produced so rapidly? or, even, if ready made, could be *arranged* so rapidly to express the sense? *Motions* with the hands, are no adequate substitute. *Marks* for the recognition of the eye—*writing*—although a wonderful auxiliary for speech, is no worthy substitute for it. In addition to the more slow and laborious process of getting up a communication in writing, the materials—pen, ink, and paper—are not always at hand. But one always has his tongue with him, and the breath of his life is the ever-ready material with which it works. Speech, then, by enabling different individuals to interchange thoughts, and thereby to combine their powers of observation and reflection, greatly facilitates useful discoveries and inventions. What one observes, and would himself infer nothing from, he tells to another, and that other at once sees a valuable hint in it. A result is thus reached which neither *alone* would have arrived at.

And this reminds me of what I passed unnoticed before, that the very first invention was a joint operation, Eve having shared with Adam in the getting up of the apron. And, indeed, judging from the fact that sewing has come down to our times as "woman's work" it is very probable she took the leading part; he, perhaps, doing no more than to stand by and thread the needle. That proceeding may be reckoned as the mother of all "Sewing societies"; and the first and most perfect "world's fair" all inventions and all inventors then in the world, being on the spot.

But speech alone, valuable as it ever has been, and is, has not advanced the condition of the world much. This is abundantly evident when we look at the degraded condition of all those tribes of human creatures who have no considerable additional means of communicating thoughts. *Writing*—the art of communicating thoughts to the mind, through the eye—is the great invention of the world. Great in the astonishing range of analysis and combination which necessarily underlies the most crude and general conception of it—great, very great in enabling us to converse with the dead, the absent, and the unborn, at all distances of time and of space; and great, not only in its direct benefits, but greatest help, to all other inventions. Suppose the art, with all conception of it, were this day lost to the world, how long, think you, would it be, before even Young America could get up the letter A. with any adequate notion of using it to advantage? The precise period at which writing was invented, is not known; but it certainly was as early as the time of Moses; from which we may safely infer that it's inventors were very old fogies.

Webster, at the time of writing his Dictionary, speaks of the English Language as then consisting of seventy or eighty thousand words. If so, the language in which the five books of Moses were written must, at that time, now thirtythree or four hundred years ago, have consisted of at least one quarter as many, or, twenty thousand. When we remember that words are *sounds* merely, we shall conclude that the idea of representing those sounds by *marks*, so that whoever should at any time after see the marks, would understand what sounds they meant, was a bold and ingenius conception, not likely to occur to one man of a million, in the run of a thousand years. And, when it did occur, a distinct mark for each word, giving twenty thousand different marks first to be learned, and afterwards remembered, would follow as the second thought, and would present such a difficulty as would lead to the conclusion that the whole thing was impracticable. But the *necessity* still would exist; and we may readily suppose that the idea was conceived, and lost, and reproduced, and dropped, and taken up again and again, until at last, the thought of dividing sounds into parts, and making a mark, not to represent a whole sound, but only a part of one, and then of

combining these marks, not very many in number, upon the principles of per-
mutation, so as to represent any and all of the whole twenty thousand words,
and even any additional number was somehow conceived and pushed into practice. This was the invention of *phoenetic* writing, as distinguished from the
clumsy picture writing of some of the nations. That it was difficult of conception and execution, is apparant, as well by the foregoing reflections, as by the
fact that so many tribes of men have come down from Adam's time to ours
without ever having possessed it. It's utility may be conceived, by the reflection
that, to *it* we owe everything which distinguishes us from savages. Take it from
us, and the Bible, all history, all science, all government, all commerce, and
nearly all social intercourse go with it.

The great activity of the tongue, in articulating sounds, has already been
mentioned; and it may be of some passing interest to notice the wonderful powers of the *eye*, in conveying ideas to the mind from writing. Take the same
example of the numbers from *one* to *one hundred*, written down, and you can
run your eye over the list, and be assured that every number is in it, in about
one half the time it would require to pronounce the words with the voice; and
not only so, but you can, in the same short time, determine whether every word
is spelled correctly, by which it is evident that every separate letter, amounting
to eight hundred and sixty four, has been recognized, and reported to the mind,
within the incredibly short space of twenty seconds, or one third of a minute.

I have already intimated my opinion that in the world's history, certain
inventions and discoveries occurred, of peculiar value, on account of their great
efficiency in facilitating all other inventions and discoveries. Of these were the
arts of writing and of printing—the discovery of America, and the introduction
of Patent-laws. The date of the first, as already stated, is unknown; but it certainly was as much as fifteen hundred years before the Christian era; the second—printing—came in 1436, or nearly three thousand years after the first. The
others followed more rapidly—the discovery of America in 1492, and the first
patent laws in 1624. Though not apposite to my present purpose, it is but justice to the fruitfulness of that period, to mention two other important events—
the Lutheran Reformation in 1517, and, still earlier, the invention of negroes,
or, of the present mode of using them, in 1434. But, to return to the consideration of printing, it is plain that it is but the *other* half—and in real utility, the
better half—of writing; and that both together are but the assistants of speech in
the communication of thoughts between man and man. When man was possessed of speech alone, the chances of invention, discovery, and improvement,
were very limited; but by the introduction of each of these, they were greatly

multiplied. When writing was invented, any important observation, likely to lead to a discovery, had at least a chance of being written down, and consequently, a better chance of never being forgotten; and of being seen, and reflected upon, by a much greater number of persons; and thereby the chances of a valuable hint being caught, proportionably augmented. By this means the observation of a single individual might lead to an important invention, years, and even centuries after he was dead. In one word, by means of writing, the seeds of invention were more permanently preserved, and more widely sown. And yet, for the three thousand years during which printing remained undiscovered after writing was in use, it was only a small portion of the people who could write, or read writing; and consequently the field of invention, though much extended, still continued very limited. At length printing came. It gave ten thousand copies of any written matter, quite as cheaply as ten were given before; and consequently a thousand minds were brought into the field where there was but one before. This was a great *gain*; and history shows a great *change* corresponding to it, in point of time. I will venture to consider *it*, the true termination of that period called "the dark ages." Discoveries, inventions, and improvements followed rapidly, and have been increasing their rapidity ever since. The effects could not come, all at once. It required time to bring them out; and they are still coming. The *capacity* to read, could not be multiplied as fast as the *means* of reading. Spelling-books just began to go into the hands of the children; but the teachers were not very numerous, or very competent; so that it is safe to infer they did not advance so speedily as they do now-a-days. It is very probable—almost certain—that the great mass of men, at that time, were utterly unconscious, that their *conditions*, or their *minds* were capable of improvement. They not only looked upon the educated few as superior beings; but they supposed themselves to be naturally incapable of rising to equality. To immancipate the mind from this false and under estimate of itself, is the great task which printing came into the world to perform. It is difficult for us, *now* and *here*, to conceive how strong this slavery of the mind was; and how long it did, of necessity, take, to break it's shackles, and to get a habit of freedom of thought, established. It is, in this connection, a curious fact that a new country is most favorable—almost necessary—to the immancipation of thought, and the consequent advancement of civilization and the arts. The human family originated as is thought, somewhere in Asia, and have worked their way princip[al]ly Westward. Just now, in civilization, and the arts, the people of Asia are entirely behind those of Europe; those of the East of Europe behind those of the West of it; while we, here in America, *think* we discover, and invent, and improve, faster than any of them. *They* may think this is arrogance; but they can not deny that Russia has called on us to show her how to build steam-boats and rail-roads—while in the older parts of Asia, they scarcely know that such things as S.Bs & RR.s. exist. In anciently inhabited countries, the dust of ages—a real downright old-fogyism—seems to settle upon, and smother the intellects and energies of man. It is in this view that I have mentioned the discovery of America as an event greatly favoring and facilitating useful discoveries and inventions.

Next came the Patent laws. These began in England in 1624; and, in this country, with the adoption of our constitution. Before then [these?], any man might instantly use what another had invented; so that the inventor had no special advantage from his own invention. The patent system changed this; secured to the inventor, for a limited time, the exclusive use of his invention; and thereby added the fuel of *interest* to the *fire* of genius, in the discovery and production of new and useful things.

THE DRED SCOTT DECISION:
SPEECH AT SPRINGFIELD, ILLINOIS.
JUNE 26, 1857

Partly in response to an earlier speech by Stephen A. Doulgas, Lincoln's remarks at Springfield represented his first public reply to Dred-Scott v. Sanford, *which was decided in March the same year. In this particular instance, Lincoln focused on Taney's denial of Negro citizenship and his assertion that blacks had "no rights which the white man was bound to respect." Contrary to Taney, Lincoln claimed that the same Founders had included African Americans in the Declaration, which the Founders, according to Lincoln, regarded as a standard maxim for free society to be approximated as much as possible.*

In order to avoid the charge of radical abolitionism, Lincoln distinguished his opposition to the decision from resistance to the rule of law. Denying the Supreme Court the final say on the question, he pledged to abide by the particular decision regarding whether or not Scott was entitled to his freedom; however, he would not accept the general ruling of Dred Scott as an authoritative precedent binding upon future slavery policies. The Springfield Speech is of enduring significance because it provides guidelines for dealing with the abuse of judicial power. Lincoln clearly rejected the doctrine of judicial supremacy. Echoing Andrew Jackson, he declared that each public official has taken an oath to support the Constitution "as he understands it."

FELLOW-CITIZENS:——

I am here to-night, partly by the invitation of some of you, and partly by my own inclination. Two weeks ago Judge Douglas spoke here on the several subjects of Kansas, the Dred Scott decision, and Utah. I listened to the speech at the time, and have read the report of it since. It was intended to controvert opinions which I think just, and to assail (politically, not personally,) those men who, in common with me, entertain those opinions. For this reason I wished then, and still wish, to make some answer to it, which I now take the opportunity of doing.

I begin with Utah. If it prove to be true, as is probable, that the people of Utah are in open rebellion to the United States, then Judge Douglas is in favor of repealing their territorial organization, and attaching them to the adjoining States for judicial purposes. I say, too, if they are in rebellion, they ought to be somehow coerced to obedience; and I am not now prepared to admit or deny that the Judge's mode of coercing them is not as good as any. The Republicans can fall in with it without taking back anything they have ever said. To be sure, it would be a considerable backing down by Judge Douglas from his much-vaunted doctrine of self-government for the territories; but this is only additional proof of what was very plain from the beginning, that that doctrine was a mere deceitful pretense for the benefit of slavery. Those who could not see that much in the Nebraska act itself, which forced Governors, and Secretaries, and Judges on the people of the territories, without their choice or consent, could not be made to see, though one should rise from the dead to testify.

But in all this, it is very plain the Judge evades the only question the Republicans have ever pressed upon the Democracy in regard to Utah. That question the Judge well knows to be this: "If the people of Utah shall peacefully form a State Constitution tolerating polygamy, will the Democracy admit them into the Union?" There is nothing in the United States Constitution or law against polygamy; and why is it not a part of the Judge's "sacred right of self-government" for that people to have it, or rather to *keep* it, if they choose? These questions, so far as I know, the Judge never answers. It might involve the Democracy to answer them either way, and they go unanswered.

As to Kansas. The substance of the Judge's speech on Kansas is an effort to put the free State men in the wrong for not voting at the election of delegates to the Constitutional Convention. He says: *"There is every reason to hope and believe that the law will be fairly interpreted and impartially executed, so as to insure to every bona fide inhabitant the free and quiet exercise of the elective franchise."*

It appears extraordinary that Judge Douglas should make such a statement. He knows that, by the law, no one can vote who has not been registered; and he knows that the free State men place their refusal to vote on the ground that but few of them have been registered. It is *possible* this is not true, but Judge Douglas knows it is asserted to be true in letters, newspapers, and public speeches, and borne by every mail, and blown by every breeze to the eyes and ears of the world. He knows it is boldly declared that the people of many whole counties, and many whole neighborhoods in others, are left unregistered; yet, he does not venture to contradict the declaration, nor to point out how they *can* vote without being registered; but he just slips along, not seeming to know there is any such question of fact, and complacently declares: "There is every reason to hope and believe that the law will be fairly and impartially executed, so as to insure to every *bona fide* inhabitant the free and quiet exercise of the elective franchise."

I readily agree that if all had a chance to vote, they ought to have voted. If, on the contrary, as they allege, and Judge Douglas ventures not to particularly contradict, few only of the free State men had a chance to vote, they were perfectly right in staying from the polls in a body.

By the way since the Judge spoke, the Kansas election has come off. The Judge expressed his confidence that all the Democrats in Kansas would do their duty—including "free state Democrats" of course. The returns received here as yet are very incomplete; but so far as they go, they indicate that only about one sixth of the registered voters, have really voted; and this too, when not more, perhaps, than one half of the rightful voters have been registered, thus showing the thing to have been altogether the most exquisite farce ever enacted. I am watching with considerable interest, to ascertain what figure "the free-state Democrats" cut in the concern. Of course they voted—all democrats do their duty—and of course they did not vote for slave-state candidates. We soon shall know how many delegates *they* elected, how many candidates they had, pledged for a free state; and how many votes were cast for them.

Allow me to barely whisper my suspicion that there were no such things in Kansas as "free state Democrats"—that they were altogether mythical, good only to figure in newspapers and speeches in the free states. If there should prove to be one real living free state Democrat in Kansas, I suggest that it might be well to catch him, and stuff and preserve his skin, as an interesting specimen of that soon-to-be-extinct variety of the genus, Democrat.

And now as to the Dred Scott decision. That decision declares two propositions—first, that a negro cannot sue in the U.S. Courts; and secondly, that Congress cannot prohibit slavery in the Territories. It was made by a divided court—dividing differently on the different points. Judge Douglas does not discuss the merits of the decision; and, in that respect, I shall follow his example, believing I could no more improve on McLean and Curtis, than he could on Taney.

He denounces all who question the correctness of that decision, as offering violent resistance to it. But who resists it? Who has, in spite of the decision, declared Dred Scott free, and resisted the authority of his master over him?

Judicial decisions have two uses—first, to absolutely determine the case decided; and secondly, to indicate to the public how other similar cases will be decided when they arise. For the latter use, they are called "precedents" and "authorities."

We believe, as much as Judge Douglas, (perhaps more) in obedience to, and respect for, the judicial department of government. We think its decisions on Constitutional questions, when fully settled, should control, not only the particular cases decided, but the general policy of the country, subject to be disturbed only by amendments of the Constitution as provided in that instrument itself. More than this would be revolution. But we think the Dred Scott decision is erroneous. We know the court that made it, has often overruled its own decisions, and we shall do what we can to have it to over rule this. We offer no *resistance* to it.

Judicial decisions are of greater or less authority as precedents, according to circumstances. That this should be so, accords both with common sense, and the customary understanding of the legal profession.

If this important decision had been made by the unanimous concurrence of the judges, and without any apparent partisan bias, and in accordance with legal public expectation, and with the steady practice of the departments throughout our history, and had been in no part, based on assumed historical facts which are not really true; or, if wanting in some of these, it had been before the court more than once, and had there been affirmed and re-affirmed through a course of years, it then might be, perhaps would be, factious, nay, even revolutionary, not to acquiesce in it as a precedent.

But when, as it is true we find it wanting in all these claims to the public confidence, it is not resistance, it is not factious, it is not even disrespectful, to treat it as not having yet quite established a settled doctrine for the country. But Judge Douglas considers this view awful. Hear him:

> "The courts are the tribunals prescribed by the Constitution and created by the authority of the people to determine, expound and enforce

the law. Hence, whoever resists the final decision of the highest judicial tribunal, aims a deadly blow to our whole Republican system of government—a blow, which if successful would place all our rights and liberties at the mercy of passion, anarchy and violence. I repeat, therefore, that if resistance to the decisions of the Supreme Court of the United States, in a matter like the points decided in the Dred Scott case, clearly within their jurisdiction as defined by the Constitution, shall be forced upon the country as a political issue, it will become a distinct and naked issue between the friends and enemies of the Constitution—the friends and the enemies of the supremacy of the laws."

Why, this same Supreme court once decided a national bank to be constitutional; but Gen. Jackson, as President of the United States, disregarded the decision, and voted a bill for a re-charter, partly on constitutional ground, declaring that each public functionary must support the Constitution, *"as he understands it."* But hear the General's own words. Here they are, taken from his veto message:

"It is maintained by the advocates of the bank, that its constitutionality, in all its features, ought to be considered as settled by precedent, and by the decision of the Supreme Court. To this conclusion I cannot assent. Mere precedent is a dangerous source of authority, and should not be regarded as deciding questions of constitutional power, except where the acquiescence of the people and the States can be considered as well settled. So far from this being the case on this subject, an argument against the bank might be based on precedent. One Congress in 1791, decided in favor of a bank; another in 1811, decided against it. Once Congress in 1815 decided against a bank; another in 1816 decided in its favor. Prior to the present Congress, therefore, the precedents drawn from that source were equal. If we resort to the States, the expressions of legislative, judicial and executive opinions against the bank have been probably to those in its favor as four to one. There is nothing in precedent, therefore, which if its authority were admitted, ought to weigh in favor of the act before me."

I drop the quotations merely to remark that all there ever was, in the way of precedent up to the Dred Scott decision, on the points therein decided, had been against that decision. But hear Gen. Jackson further—

"If the opinion of the Supreme Court covered the whole ground of this act, it ought not to control the co-ordinate authorities of this Government. The Congress, the executive and the court must each for itself be guided by its own opinion of the Constitution. Each public officer, who takes an oath to support the Constitution, swears that he will support it as he understands it, and not as it is understood by others."

Again and again have I heard Judge Douglas denounce that bank decision, and applaud Gen. Jackson for disregarding it. It would be interesting for him to look over his recent speech, and see how exactly his fierce philippics against us for resisting Supreme Court decisions, fall upon his own head. It will call to his mind a long and fierce political war in this country, upon an issue which, in his own language, and, of course, in his own changeless estimation, was "a distinct and naked issue between the friends and the enemies of the Constitution," and in which war he fought in the ranks of the enemies of the Constitution.

I have said, in substance, that the Dred Scott decision was, in part, based on assumed historical facts which were not really true; and I ought not to leave the subject without giving some reasons for saying this; I therefore give an instance or two, which I think fully sustain me. Chief Justice Taney, in delivering the opinion of the majority of the Court, insists at great length that negroes were no part of the people who made, or for whom was made, the Declaration of Independence, or the Constitution of the United States.

On the contrary, Judge Curtis, in his dissenting opinion, shows that in five of the then thirteen States, to wit, New Hampshire, Massachusetts, New York, New Jersey and North Carolina, free negroes were voters, and, in proportion to their numbers, had the same part in making the Constitution that the white people had. He shows this with so much particularity as to leave no doubt of its truth; and, as a sort of conclusion on that point, holds the following language:

"The Constitution was ordained and established by the people of the United States, through the action, in each State, of those persons who were qualified by its laws to act thereon in behalf of themselves and all other citizens of the State. In some of the States, as we have seen, colored persons were among those qualified by law to act on the subject. These colored persons were not only included in the body of 'the people of the United States,' by whom the Constitution was ordained and established; but in at least five of the States they had

2. *CWAL,* II, 482.

the power to act, and, doubtless, did act, by their suffrages, upon the question of its adoption."

Again, Chief Justice Taney says: "It is difficult, at this day, to realize the state of public opinion in relation to that unfortunate race, which prevailed in the civilized and enlightened portions of the world at the time of the Declaration of Independence, and when the Constitution of the United States was framed and adopted." And again, after quoting from the Declaration, he says: "The general words above quoted would seem to include the whole human family, and if they were used in a similar instrument at this day, would be so understood."

In these the Chief Justice does not directly assert, but plainly assumes, as a fact, that the public estimate of the black man is more favorable *now* than it was in the days of the Revolution. This assumption is a mistake. In some trifling particulars, the condition of that race has been ameliorated; but, as a whole, in this country, the change between then and now is decidedly the other way; and their ultimate destiny has never appeared so hopeless as in the last three or four years. In two of the five States—New Jersey and North Carolina—that then gave the free negro the right of voting, the right has since been taken away; and in a third—New York—it has been greatly abridged; while it has not been extended, so far as I know, to a single additional State, though the number of the States has more than doubled. In those days, as I understand, masters could, at their own pleasure, emancipate their slaves; but since then, such legal restraints have been made upon emancipation, as to amount almost to prohibition. In those days, Legislatures held the unquestioned power to abolish slavery in their respective States, but now it is becoming quite fashionable for State Constitutions to withhold that power from the Legislatures. In those days, by common consent, the spread of the black man's bondage to new countries was prohibited; but now, Congress decides that it *will* not continue the prohibition, and the Supreme Court decides that it *could* not if it would. In those days, our Declaration of Independence was held sacred by all, and thought to include all; but now, to aid in making the bondage of the negro universal and eternal, it is assailed, and sneered at, and construed, and hawked at, and torn, till, if its framers could rise from their graves, they could not at all recognize it. All the powers of earth seem rapidly combining against him. Mammon is after him; ambition follows, and philosophy follows, and the Theology of the day is fast joining the cry. They have him in his prison house; they have searched his person, and left no prying instrument with him. One after another they have closed the heavy iron doors upon him, and now they have him, as it were, bolted in with a lock of a hundred keys, which can never be unlocked without the concurrence of every key; the keys in the hands of a hundred different men, and they scattered to a hundred different and distant places; and they stand musing as to what invention, in all the dominions of mind and matter, can be produced to make the impossibility of his escape more complete than it is.

It is grossly incorrect to say or assume, that the public estimate of the negro is more favorable now than it was at the origin of the government.

Three years and a half ago, Judge Douglas brought forward his famous Nebraska bill. The country was at once in a blaze. He scorned all opposition, and carried it through Congress. Since then he has seen himself superseded in a Presidential nomination, by one indorsing the general doctrine of his measure, but at the same time standing clear of the odium of its untimely agitation, and its gross breach of national faith; and he has seen that successful rival Constitutionally elected, not by the strength of friends, but by the division of adversaries, being in a popular minority of nearly four hundred thousand votes. He has seen his chief aids in his own State, Shields and Richardson, politically speaking, successively tried, convicted, and executed, for an offense not their own, but his. And now he sees his own case, standing next on the docket for trial.

There is a natural disgust in the minds of nearly all white people, to the idea of an indiscriminate amalgamation of the white and black races; and Judge Douglas evidently is basing his chief hope upon the chances of his being able to appropriate the benefit of this disgust to himself. If he can, by much drumming and repeating, fasten the odium of that idea upon his adversaries, he thinks he can struggle through the storm. He therefore clings to this hope, as a drowning man to the last plank. He makes an occasion for lugging it in from the opposition to the Dred Scott decision. He finds the Republicans insisting that the Declaration of Independence includes ALL men, black as well as white; and forthwith he boldly denies that it includes negroes at all, and proceeds to argue gravely that all who contend it does, do so only because they want to vote, and eat, and sleep, and marry with negroes! He will have it that they cannot be consistent else. Now I protest against that counterfeit logic which concludes that, because I do not want a black woman for a *slave* I must necessarily want her for a *wife*. I need not have her for either, I can just leave her alone. In some respects she certainly is not my equal; but in her natural right to eat the bread she earns with her own hands without asking leave of any one else, she is my equal, and the equal of all others.

Chief Justice Taney, in his opinion in the Dred Scott case, admits that the language of the Declaration is broad enough to include the whole human family, but he and Judge Douglas argue that the authors of that instrument did not intend to include negroes, by the fact that they did not at once, actually place them on an equality with the whites. Now this grave argument comes to just nothing at all, by the other fact, that they did not at once, *or ever afterwards,* actually place all white people on an equality with one another. And this is the staple argument of both the Chief Justice and the Senator, for doing this obvious violence to the plain, unmistakable language of the Declaration. I think the authors of that notable instrument intended to include *all* men, but they did not intend to declare all men equal *in all respects.* They did not mean to say all were equal in color, size, intellect, moral developments, or social capacity. They defined with tolerable distinctness, in what respects they did consider all men created equal—equal in "certain inalienable rights, among which are life, liberty, and the pursuit of happiness." This they said, and this they meant. They did not mean to assert the obvious untruth, that all were then actually enjoying that equality, nor yet, that they were about to confer it immediately upon them. In fact they had no power to confer such a boon. They meant simply to declare the *right,* so that the *enforcement* of it might follow as fast as circumstances should permit. They meant to set up a standard maxim for free society, which could be familiar to all, and revered by all; constantly looked to, constantly labored for, and even though never perfectly attained, constantly approximated, and thereby constantly spreading and deepening its influence, and augmenting the happiness and value of life to all people of all colors everywhere. The assertion that "all men are created equal" was of no practical use in effecting our separation from Great Britain; and it was placed in the Declaration, not for that, but for future use. Its authors meant it to be, thank God, it is now proving itself, a stumbling block to those who in after times might seek to turn a free people back into the hateful paths of despotism. They knew the proneness of prosperity to breed tyrants, and they meant when such should re-appear in this fair land and commence their vocation they should find left for them at least one hard nut to crack.

I have now briefly expressed my view of the *meaning* and *objects* of that part of the Declaration of Independence which declares that "all men are created equal."

Now let us hear Judge Douglas' view of the same subject, as I find it in the printed report of his late speech. Here it is:

"No man can vindicate the character, motives and conduct of the signers of the Declaration of Independence, except upon the hypothesis that they referred to the white race alone, and not to the African, when they declared all men to have been created equal—that they were speaking of British subjects on this continent being equal to British subjects born and residing in Great Britain—that they were entitled to the same inalienable rights, and among them were enumerated life, liberty and the pursuit of happiness. The Declaration was adopted for the purpose of justifying the colonists in the eyes of the civilized world in withdrawing their allegiance from the British crown, and dissolving their connection with the mother country."

My good friends, read that carefully over some leisure hour, and ponder well upon it—see what a mere wreck—mangled ruin—it makes of our once glorious Declaration.

"They were speaking of British subjects on this continent being equal to British subjects born and residing in Great Britain!" Why, according to this, not only negroes but white people outside of Great Britain and America are not spoken of in that instrument. The English, Irish and Scotch, along with white Americans, were included to be sure, but the French, Germans and other white people of the world are all gone to pot along with the Judge's inferior races.

I had thought the Declaration promised something better than the condition of British subjects; but no, it only meant that we should be *equal* to them in their own oppressed and *unequal* condition. According to that, it gave no promise that having kicked off the King and Lords of Great Britain, we should not at once be saddled with a King and Lords of our own.

I had thought the Declaration contemplated the progressive improvement in the condition of all men everywhere; but no, it merely "was adopted for the purpose of justifying the colonists in the eyes of the civilized world in withdrawing their allegiance from the British crown, and dissolving their connection with the mother country." Why, that object having been effected some eighty years ago, the Declaration is of no practical use now—mere rubbish—old wadding left to rot on the battle-field after the victory is won.

I understand you are preparing to celebrate the "Fourth," tomorrow week. What for? The doings of that day had no reference to the present; and quite half of you are not even descendants of those who were referred to at that day. But I suppose you will celebrate; and will even go so far as to read the Declaration. Suppose after you read it once in the old fashioned way, you read it once more with Judge Douglas' version. It will then run thus: "We hold these truths to be self-evident that all British subjects who were on this continent eighty-one years ago, were created equal to all British subjects born and *then* residing in Great Britain."

And now I appeal to all—to Democrats as well as others,—are you really willing that the Declaration shall be thus frittered away?—thus left no more at most, than an interesting memorial of the dead past? thus shorn of its vitality, and practical value; and left without the *germ* or even the *suggestion* of the individual rights of man in it?

But Judge Douglas is especially horrified at the thought of the mixing of blood by the white and black races: agreed for once—a thousand times agreed. There are white men enough to marry all the white women, and black men enough to marry all the black women; and so let them be married. On this point we fully agree with the Judge; and when he shall show that his policy is better adapted to prevent amalgamation than ours we shall drop ours, and adopt his. Let us see. In 1850 there were in the United States 405,751 mulattoes. Very few of these are the offspring of whites and *free* blacks; nearly all have sprung from black *slaves* and white masters. A separation of the races is the only perfect preventive of amalgamation; but as an immediate separation is impossible the next best thing is to *keep* them apart *where* they are not already together. If white and black people never get together in Kansas, they will never mix blood in Kansas. That is at least one self-evident truth. A few free colored persons may get into the free States, in any event; but their number is too insignificant to amount to much in the way of mixing blood. In 1850 there were in the free States, 56,649 mulattoes; but for the most part they were not born there—they came from the slave States, ready made up. In the same year the slave States had 348,874 mulattoes, all of home production. The proportion of free mulattoes to free blacks— the only colored classes in the free states—is much greater in the slave than in the free states. It is worthy of note too, that among the free states those which make the colored man the nearest to equal the white, have proportionably the fewest mulattoes, the least of amalgamation. In New Hampshire, the State which goes farthest toward equality between the races, there are just 184 mulattoes, while there are in Virginia—how many do you think?—79,775, being 23,126 more than in all the free States together.

These statistics show that slavery is the greatest source of amalgamation; and next to it, not the elevation, but the degradation of the free blacks. Yet Judge Douglas dreads the slightest restraints on the spread of slavery, and the slightest human recognition of the negro, as tending horribly to amalgamation.

The very Dred Scott case affords a strong test as to which party most favors amalgamation, the Republicans or the dear Union-saving Democracy. Dred Scott, his wife and two daughters were all involved in the suit. We desired the court to have held that they were citizens so far at least as to entitle them to a hearing as to whether they were free or not; and then, also, that they were in fact and in law really free. Could we have had our way, the chances of these black girls ever mixing their blood with that of white people, would have been diminished at least to the extent that it could not have been without their consent. But Judge Douglas is delighted to have them decided to be slaves, and not human enough to have a hearing, even if they were free, and thus left subject to the forced concubinage of their masters, and liable to become the mothers of mulattoes in spite of themselves—the very state of case that produces nine tenths of all the mulattoes—all the mixing of blood in the nation.

Of course, I state this case as an illustration only, not meaning to say or intimate that the master of Dred Scott and his family, or any more than a per centage of masters generally, are inclined to exercise this particular power which they hold over their female slaves.

I have said that the separation of the races is the only perfect preventive of amalgamation. I have no right to say all the members of the Republican party are in favor of this, nor to say that as a party they are in favor of it. There is nothing in their platform directly on the subject. But I can say a very large proportion of its members are for it, and that the chief plank in their platform—opposition to the spread of slavery—is most favorable to that separation.

Such separation, if ever effected at all, must be effected by colonization; and no political party, as such, is now doing anything directly for colonization. Party operations at present only favor or retard colonization incidentally. The enterprise is a difficult one; but "where there is a will there is a way," and what colonization needs most is a hearty will. Will springs from the two elements of moral sense and self-interest. Let us be brought to believe it is morally right, and at the same time, favorable to, or, at least, not against, our interest, to transfer the African to his native clime, and we shall find a way to do it, however great the task may be. The children of Israel, to such numbers as to include four hundred thousand fighting men, went out of Egyptian bondage in a body.

How differently the respective courses of the Democratic and Republican parties incidentally bear on the question of forming a will—a public sentiment—for colonization, is easy to see. The Republicans inculcate, with whatever of ability they can, that the negro is a man, that his bondage is cruelly wrong, and that the field of his oppression ought not to be enlarged. The Democrats deny his manhood; deny, or dwarf to insignificance, the wrong of his bondage; so far as possible, crush all sympathy for him, and cultivate and excite hatred and disgust against him; compliment themselves as Union-savers for doing so; and call the indefinite outspreading of his bondage "a sacred right of self-government."

The plainest print cannot be read through a gold eagle; and it will be ever hard to find many men who will send a slave to Liberia, and pay his passage, while they can send him to a new country Kansas, for instance, and sell him for fifteen hundred dollars, and the rise.

A HOUSE DIVIDED: SPEECH DELIVERED AT SPRINGFIELD, ILLINOIS, AT THE CLOSE OF THE REPUBLICAN STATE CONVENTION
JUNE 16, 1858

The House Divided Speech was Lincoln's acceptance speech after the Illinois State Convention in Springfield nominated him as the Republican candidate for the United States Senate. It was also one of his most controversial. During the Lincoln-Douglas debates, Douglas repudiated the House Divided speech as an abolitionist manifesto that proclaimed the forcible abolition of slavery in the states and territories alike.

However, the political motive of Lincoln's House Divided Speech was not to proclaim universal abolition, but to prevent Republicans from defecting to Stephen Douglas's camp after the latter had repudiated the pro-slavery Kansas Lecompton Constitution. This would have guaranteed that Kansas entered the Union as a slave state. The Democratic Party split over Lecompton Constitution: the Buchanan administration favored it, but Douglas opposed it on procedural grounds, not because he believed slavery to be wrong in principle, but because it was enacted through fraudulent means. The break over Lecompton led some prominent northeastern Republicans to consider Douglas as a viable anti-slavery leader. In effect, the House Divided Speech sought to destroy Douglas's moral credibility as standard-bearer of the antislavery cause. The House Divided metaphor from Matthew 12:25 accentuated the underlying importance of a moral consensus to the public mind. Such a consensus, in Lincoln's view, was a necessary condition of resolving subsequent political conflict. The speech sought to prevent Illinois Republicans from compromising their core principles—the moral repudiation of slavery and the legal right to restrict it in the territories—through an "unholy alliance" with Douglas who was utterly indifferent to its evil and spread.

Lincoln's allegation of a conspiracy to nationalize slavery was another controversial element of the House Divided Speech. His references to "Stephen, Franklin, Roger and James" provide the first names of the four alleged Democratic conspirators: Stephen A. Douglas (author of the Kansas-Nebraska Act); Franklin Pierce (President at the time of the Kansas Nebraska Act in 1854); Roger B. Taney (author of the Dred Scott decision, and James Buchanan (President at the time of the Dred Scott decision).

Friends had warned Lincoln that the speech was inflammatory. Its rhetoric would come back to haunt him. During the secession crisis, the South seized upon his observation that "this government cannot endure permanently half slave and half free" as a declaration of sectional war. Indeed, South Carolina quoted the speech in its Declaration of Causes for Secession.

IF WE COULD FIRST know *where* we are, and *whither* we are tending, we could better judge *what* to do, and *how* to do it.

We are now far into the *fifth* year, since a policy was initiated, with the *avowed* object, and *confident* promise, of putting an end to slavery agitation.

Under the operation of that policy, that agitation has not only, *not ceased,* but has *constantly augmented.*

In my opinion, it *will* not cease, until a *crisis* shall have been reached, and passed—

"A house divided against itself cannot stand."

I believe this government cannot endure, permanently half *slave* and half *free.*

I do not expect the Union to be *dissolved*—I do not expect the house to *fall*—but I *do* expect it will cease to be divided.

It will become *all* one thing, or *all* the other.

Either the *opponents* of slavery, will arrest the further spread of it, and place it where the public mind shall rest in the belief that it is in course of ultimate extinction; or its *advocates* will push it forward, till it shall become alike lawful in *all* the States, *old* as well as *new*—North as well as *South.*

Have we no *tendency* to the latter condition?

Let any one who doubts, carefully contemplate that now almost complete legal combination—piece of *machinery* so to speak—compounded of the Nebraska doctrine, and the Dred Scott decision. Let him consider not only *what work* the machinery is adapted to do, and *how well* adapted; but also, let him study the history of its construction, and trace, if he can, or rather *fail,* if he can, to trace the evidences of design, and concert of action, among its chief bosses, from the beginning.

The new year of 1854 found slavery excluded from more than half the States by State Constitutions, and from most of the national territory by congressional prohibition.

Four days later, commenced the struggle, which ended in repealing that congressional prohibition.

This opened all the national territory to slavery; and was the first point gained.

But, so far, *Congress* only, had acted; and an *indorsement* by the people, *real* or *apparent,* was indispensable, to *save* the point already gained, and give chance for more.

This necessity had not been overlooked; but had been provided for, as well as might be, in the notable argument of "squater sovereignty," otherwise called *"sacred right of self government,"* which latter phrase, though expressive of the only rightful basis of any government, was so perverted in this attempted use of it as to amount to just this: That if any *one* man, choose to enslave *another,* no *third* man shall be allowed to object.

That argument was incorporated into the Nebraska bill itself, in the language which follows: *"It being the true intent and meaning of this act not to legislate slavery into any Territory or State, nor to exclude it therefrom; but to leave the people thereof perfectly free to form and regulate their domestic institutions in their own way, subject only to the Constitution of the United States."*

Then opened the roar of loose declamation in favor of "Squatter Sovereignty," and "Sacred right of self government."

"But," said opposition members, "let us be more *specific*—let us *amend* the bill so as to expressly declare that the people of the Territory *may* exclude slavery." "Not we," said the friends of the measure; and down they voted the amendment.

While the Nebraska bill was passing through congress, a *law case,* involving the question of a negro's freedom, by reason of his owner having voluntarily taken him first into a free State and then a territory covered by the congressional prohibition, and held him as a slave for a long time in each, was passing through the U. S. Circuit Court for the District of Missouri; and both Nebraska bill and law suit were brought to a decision in the same month of May, 1854. The negro's name was "Dred Scott," which name now designates the decision finally made in the case.

Before the *then* next Presidential election, the law case came *to,* and was argued *in* the Supreme Court of the United States; but the *decision* of it was deferred until *after* the election. Still, *before* the election, Senator Trumbull, on the floor of the Senate, requests the leading advocate of the Nebraska bill to state *his opinion* whether the people of a territory can constitutionally exclude slavery from their limits; and the latter answers, "That is a question for the Supreme Court."

The election came. Mr. Buchanan was elected, and the *indorsement,* such as it was, secured. That was the *second* point gained. The indorsement, however, fell short of a clear popular majority by nearly four hundred thousand votes, and so, perhaps, was not over-whelmingly reliable and satisfactory.

The *outgoing* President, in his last annual message, as impressively as possible *echoed back* upon the people the *weight* and *authority* of the indorsement.

The Supreme Court met again; *did not* announce their decision, but ordered a re-argument.

The Presidential inauguration came, and still no decision of the court; but the *incoming* President, in his inaugural address, fervently exhorted the people to abide by the forthcoming decision, *whatever it might be.*

Then, in a few days, came the decision.

The reputed author of the Nebraska bill finds an early occasion to make a speech at this capitol indorsing the Dred Scott Decision, and vehemently denouncing all opposition to it.

The new President, too, seizes the early occasion of the Silliman letter to indorse and strongly *construe* that decision, and to express his *astonishment* that any different view had ever been entertained.

At length a squabble springs up between the President and the author of the Nebraska bill, on the *mere* question of *fact,* whether the Lecompton constitution was or was not, in any just sense, made by the people of Kansas; and in that quarrel the latter declares that all he wants is a fair vote for the people, and that he *cares* not whether slavery be voted *down* or voted *up.* I do not understand his declaration that he cares not whether slavery be voted down or voted up, to be intended by him other than as an *apt definition* of the *policy* he would impress upon the public mind—the *principle* for which he declares he has suffered much, and is ready to suffer to the end.

And well may he cling to that principle. If he has any parental feeling, well may he cling to it. That principle, is the only shred left of his original Nebraska doctrine. Under the Dred Scott decision, "squatter sovereignty" squatted out of existence, tumbled down like temporary scaffolding—like the mold at the foundry served through one blast and fell back into loose sand—helped to carry an election, and then was kicked to the winds. His late *joint* struggle with the Republicans, against the Lecompton Constitution, involves nothing of the original Nebraska doctrine. That struggle was made on a point, the right of a people to make their own constitution, upon which he and the Republicans have never differed.

The several points of the Dred Scott decision, in connection with Senator Douglas' "care not" policy, constitute the piece of machinery, in its *present* state of advancement.

The *working* points of that machinery are:

First, that no negro slave, imported as such from Africa, and no descendant of such slave can ever be a *citizen* of any State, in the sense of that term as used in the Constitution of the United States.

This point is made in order to deprive the negro, in every possible event, of the benefit of that provision of the United States Constitution, which declares that—

> "the citizens of each State shall be entitled to all privileges and immunities of citizens in the several States."

Secondly, that "subject to the Constitution of the United States," neither *Congress* nor a *Territorial Legislature* can exclude slavery from any United States Territory.

This point is made in order that individual men may *fill up* the territories with slaves, without danger of losing them as property, and thus enhance the chances of *permanency* to the institution through all the future.

Thirdly, that whether the holding a negro in actual slavery in a free State, makes him free, as against the holder, the United States courts will not decide, but will leave to be decided by the courts of any slave State the negro may be forced into by the master.

This point is made, not to be pressed *immediately;* but, if acquiesced in for a while, and apparently *indorsed* by the people at an election, *then* to sustain the logical conclusion that what Dred Scott's master might lawfully do with Dred Scott, in the free State of Illinois, every other master may lawfully do with any other *one* or one *thousand* slaves, in Illinois, or in any other free State.

Auxiliary to all this, and working hand in hand with it, the Nebraska doctrine, or what is left of it, is to *educate* and *mould* public opinion, at least *Northern* public opinion, to not *care* whether slavery is voted *down* or voted *up*.

This shows exactly where we now *are;* and *partially* also, whither we are tending.

It will throw additional light on the latter, to go back, and run the mind over the string of historical facts already stated. Several things will *now* appear less *dark* and *mysterious* than they did *when* they were transpiring. The people were to be left "perfectly free" "subject only to the Constitution." What the *Constitution* had to do with it, outsiders could not *then* see. Plainly enough *now*, it was an exactly fitted *nitch* for the Dred Scott decision to afterward come in, and declare that *perfect freedom* of the people, to be just no freedom at all.

228 THE LANGUAGE OF LIBERTY

Why was the amendment, expressly declaring the right of the people to exclude slavery, voted down? Plainly enough *now,* the adoption of it, would have spoiled the nitch for the Dred Scott decision.

Why was the court decision held up? Why, even a Senator's individual opinion withheld, till *after* the Presidential election? Plainly enough *now,* the speaking out *then* would have damaged the *"perfectly free"* argument upon which the election was to be carried.

Why the *outgoing* President's felicitation on the indorsement? Why the delay of a reargument? Why the incoming President's *advance* exhortation in favor of the decision?

These things *look* like the cautious *patting* and *petting* of a spirited horse, preparatory to mounting him, when it is dreaded that he may give the rider a fall.

And why the hasty after indorsements of the decision by the President and others?

We cannot absolutely *know* that all these exact adaptations are the result of preconcert. But when we see a lot of framed timbers, different portions of which we know have been gotten out at different times and places and by different workmen—Stephen, Franklin, Roger, and James, for instance—and we see these timbers joined together, and see they exactly make the frame of a house or a mill, all the tenons and mortises exactly fitting, and all the lengths and proportions of the different pieces exactly adapted to their respective places, and not a piece too many or too few—not omitting even scaffolding—or, if a single piece be lacking, we see the place in the frame exactly fitted and prepared to yet bring such piece in—in *such* a case, we find it impossible not to *believe* that Stephen and Franklin and Roger and James all understood one another from the beginning, and all worked upon a common *plan* or *draft* drawn up before the first lick was struck.

It should not be overlooked that, by the Nebraska bill, the people of a *State* as well as *Territory,* were to be left *"perfectly free"* *"subject only to the Constitution."*

Why mention a *State?* They were legislating for *territories,* and not *for* or *about* States. Certainly the people of a *State are* and *ought to be* subject to the Constitution of the United States; but why is mention of this *lugged* into this merely *territorial* law? Why are the people of a *territory* and the people of a *state* therein *lumped* together, and their relation to the Constitution therein treated as being *precisely* the same?

While the opinion of the Court, by Chief Justice Taney, in the Dred Scott case, and the separate opinions of all the concurring Judges, expressly declare that the Constitution of the United States neither permits Congress nor a territorial legislature to exclude slavery from any United States territory, they all *omit* to declare whether or not the same Constitution permits a state, or the people of a State, to exclude it.

Possibly, this is a mere *omission;* but who can be *quite* sure, if McLean or Curtis had sought to get into the opinion a declaration of unlimited power in the people of a state to exclude slavery from their limits, just as Chase and Mace sought to get such declaration, in behalf of the people of a territory, into the Nebraska bill—I ask, who can be quite *sure* that it would not have been voted down, in the one case, as it had been in the other?

The nearest approach to the point of declaring the power of a State over slavery, is made by Judge Nelson. He approaches it more than once, using the precise idea, and *almost* the language too, of the Nebraska act. On one occasion his exact language is, "except in cases where the power is restrained by the Constitution of the United States, the law of the State is supreme over the subject of slavery within its jurisdiction."

In what *cases* the power of the *states* is so restrained by the U. S. Constitution is left an *open* question, precisly [*sic*] as the same question, as to the restraint on the power of the *territories* was left open in the Nebraska act. Put *that* and *that* together, and we have another nice little nitch, which we may, ere long, see filled with another Supreme Court decision, declaring that the Constitution of the United States does not permit a state to exclude slavery from its limits.

And this may especially be expected if the doctrine of "care not whether slavery be voted *down* or voted *up,*" shall gain upon the public mind sufficiently to give promise that such a decision can be maintained when made.

Such a decision is all that slavery now lacks of being alike lawful in all the States.

Welcome or unwelcome, such decision *is* probably coming, and will soon be upon us, unless the power of the present political dynasty shall be met and overthrown. We shall *lie down* pleasantly dreaming that the people of *Missouri* are on the verge of making their State *free;* and we shall *awake* to the *reality,* instead, that the *Supreme* Court has made *Illinois* a *slave* State.

To meet and overthrow the power of that dynasty, is the work now before all those who would prevent that consummation.

That is *what* we have to do.

But *how* can we best do it?

There are those who denounce us *openly* to their *own* friends, and yet whisper *us softly,* that *Senator Douglas* is the *aptest* instrument there is, with which to effect that object. *They* do *not* tell us, nor has *he* told us, that he *wishes* any such object to be effected. They wish us to *infer* all, from the facts, that he now has a little quarrel with the present head of the dynasty; and that he has regularly voted with us, on a single point, upon which, he and we, have never differed.

They remind us that *he* is a *great* man, and that the largest of *us* are very small ones. Let this be granted. But "a *living dog* is better than a *dead lion*." Judge Douglas, if not a *dead* lion *for this work,* is at least a *caged* and *toothless* one. How can he oppose the advances of slavery? He don't *care* nothing about it. His avowed *mission is impressing* the "public heart" to *care* nothing about it.

A leading Douglas Democratic newspaper thinks Douglas' superior talent will be needed to resist the revival of the African slave trade.

Does Douglas believe an effort to revive that trade is approaching? He has not said so. Does he *really* think so? But if it is, how can he resist it? For years he has labored to prove it a *sacred right* of white men to take negro slaves into the new territories. Can he possibly show that it is *less* a sacred right to *buy* them where they can be bought cheapest? And, unquestionably they can be bought *cheaper* in *Africa* than in *Virginia*.

He has done all in his power to reduce the whole question of slavery to one of a mere *right of property;* and as such, how can *he* oppose the foreign slave trade—how can he refuse that trade in that "property" shall be "perfectly free"— unless he does it as a *protection* to the home production? And as the home *producers* will probably not *ask* the protection, he will be wholly without a ground of opposition.

Senator Douglas holds, we know, that a man may rightfully be *wiser to-day* than he was *yesterday*—that he may rightfully *change* when he finds himself wrong.

But, can we for that reason, run ahead, and *infer* that he *will* make any particular change, of which he, himself, has given no intimation? Can we *safely* base *our* action upon any such *vague* inference?

Now, as ever, I wish to not misrepresent Judge Douglas' *position,* question his *motives,* or do aught that can be personally offensive to him.

Whenever, *if ever,* he and we can come together on *principle* so that *our great cause* may have assistance from *his great ability,* I hope to have interposed no adventitious obstacle.

But clearly, he is not *now* with us—he does not *pretend* to be—he does not *promise* to *ever* be.

Our cause, then, must be intrusted to, and conducted by its own undoubted friends—those whose hands are free, whose hearts are in the work—who *do care* for the result.

Two years ago the Republicans of the nation mustered over thirteen hundred thousand strong.

We did this under the single impulse of resistance to a common danger, with every external circumstance against us.

Of *strange, discordant,* and even, *hostile* elements, we gathered from the four winds, and *formed* and fought the battle through, under the constant hot fire of a disciplined, proud, and pampered enemy.

Did we brave all *then* to *falter* now?—now—when that same enemy is *wavering,* dissevered, and belligerent?

The result is not doubtful. We shall not fail—if we stand firm, we shall not fail.

Wise counsels may *accelerate* or *mistakes delay* it, but sooner or later the victory is *sure* to come.

FRAGMENT ON THE STRUGGLE AGAINST SLAVERY[2]
JULY 1858

Lincoln's eldest son, Robert Todd, reported that this fragment was a portion of a speech prepared by his father for the Lincoln-Douglas Debates. The fragment is valuable in revealing Lincoln's complex motives in pursuing politics. While admitting that he "never professed an indifference to the honors of official station," he also professed that he was motivated by "a higher aim than mere office." Much has been made of Lincoln's ambition. However, is the drive for honor necessarily a vice? Ambition often serves as spur to greatness when it is bounded by moral standards and directed toward some legitimate moral end. On the other hand, ambition becomes dangerous when divorced from an external moral standard thereby becoming an end in itself, as was the case with Napoleon and Alexander. In assessing Lincoln's character, one must determine whether or not his ambition was of the former or latter type.

[C. JULY, 1858]

I have never professed an indifference to the honors of official station; and were I to do so now, I should only make myself ridiculous. Yet I have never failed—do not now fail—to remember that in the republican cause there is a higher aim than that of mere office. I have not allowed myself to forget that the abolition of the Slave-trade by Great Brittain, was agitated a hundred years before it was a final success; that the measure had it's open fire-eating opponents; it's stealthy "dont care" opponents; it's dollar and cent opponents; it's inferior race opponents; its negro equality opponents; and its religion and good order opponents; that all these opponents got offices, and their adversaries got none. But I have also remembered that though they blazed, like tallow-candles for a century, at last they flickered in the socket, died out, stank in the dark for a brief season, and were remembered no more, even by the smell. Schoolboys know that Wilbe[r]force, and Granville Sharpe [*sic*], helped that cause forward; but who can now name a single man who labored to retard it? Remembering these things I can not but regard it as possible that the higher object of this contest may not be completely attained within the term of my natural life. But I can not doubt either that it will come in due time. Even in this view, I am proud, in my passing speck of time, to contribute an humble mite to that glorious consummation, which my own poor eyes may not last to see.

SPEECH IN REPLY TO DOUGLAS AT CHICAGO, ILLINOIS
JULY 10, 1858

Lincoln's reply to Douglas at Chicago may be viewed as a prelude to the Lincoln-Douglas Debates that would take place a month later. Douglas fired an opening salvo in Chicago on July 9 where he repudiated Lincoln for his House Divided Speech, claiming that the demand for moral consensus undermined the pluralism and diversity of established by the American republic. Lincoln was present when Douglas gave his speech and offered a reply the next day. Attempting to vindicate himself from the charge of inciting a sectional war, he reaffirmed equality as the central idea of the American republic.

In his speech at Chicago, Lincoln identified equality as the "father of all moral principle," thereby characterizing it as a principle of justice. He maintained that the Declaration constituted the basis of a political creed that bound together the disparate elements of the American republic into a corpus mysticum. *The common moral aspiration of liberty and equality were the vital links of the regime providing unity and fellowship amidst pluralism. Shared fidelity to the principles of the Declaration transformed the many into one, hence the nation's motto of* e pluribus unum—*out of many, one. Much like his Peoria Address four years earlier, Lincoln would reiterate the argument and design of the Chicago speech throughout his debates with Douglas.*

MY FELLOW-CITIZENS:—

On yesterday evening, upon the occasion of the reception given to Senator Douglas, I was furnished with a seat very convenient for hearing him, and was otherwise very courteously treated by him and by his friends, and for which I thank him and them. During the course of his remarks my name was mentioned in such a way, as I suppose renders it at least not improper that I should make some sort of reply to him. I shall not attempt to follow him in the precise order in which he addressed the assembled multitude upon that occasion, though I shall perhaps do so in the main.

There was one question to which he asked the attention of the crowd, which I deem of somewhat less importance—at least of propriety for me to dwell upon—than the others, which he brought in near the close of his speech, and which I think it would not be entirely proper for me to omit attending to, and yet if I were not to give some attention to it now, I should probably forget it altogether. While I am upon this subject, allow me to say that I do not intend to indulge in that inconvenient mode sometimes adopted in public speaking, of reading from documents; but I shall depart from that rule so far as to read a little scrap from his speech, which notices this first topic of which I shall speak—that is, provided I can find it in the paper:

"I have made up my mind to appeal to the people against the combination that has been made against me:—the Republican leaders having formed an alliance, an unholy and unnatural alliance, with a portion of unscrupulous federal office-holders. I intend to fight that allied army wherever I meet them. I know they deny the alliance, but yet these men who are trying to divide the Democratic party for the purpose of electing a Republican Senator in my place, are just as much the agents and tools of the supporters of Mr. Lincoln. Hence, I shall deal with this allied army just as the Russians dealt with the Allies at Sebastopol—that is, the Russians did not stop to inquire, when they fired a broadside, whether it hit an Englishman, a Frenchman, or a Turk. Nor will I stop to inquire, nor shall I hesitate, whether my blows shall hit these Republican leaders or their allies who are holding the federal offices and yet acting in concert with them."

Well, now, gentlemen, is not that very alarming? Just to think of it! right at the outset of his canvass, I, a poor, kind, amiable, intelligent gentlemen, I am to be slain in this way. Why, my friend, the Judge, is not only, as it turns out, not a dead lion; nor even a living one—he is the rugged Russian Bear!

But if they will have it—for he says that we deny it—that there is any such alliance, as he says there is—and I don't propose hanging very much upon this question of veracity—but if he will have it that there is such an alliance—that the Administration men and we are allied, and we stand in the attitude of English, French, and Turk, and he occupying the position of the Russian, in that case, I beg that he will indulge us while we barely suggest to him, that these allies took Sebastopol.

Gentlemen, only a few more words as to this alliance. For my part, I have to say, that whether there be such an alliance, depends, so far as I know, upon what may be a right definition of the term *alliance*. If for the Republican party to see the other great party to which they are opposed divided among themselves, and not try to stop the division and rather be glad of it—if that is an alliance I confess I am in; but if it is meant to be said that the Republicans had formed an alliance going beyond that, by which there is contribution of money or sacrifice of principle on the one side or the other, so far as the Republican party is concerned, if there be any such thing, I protest that I neither know of it, nor do I believe it. I will however say—as I think this branch of the argument is lugged in—I would, before I leave it, state, for the benefit of those concerned, that one of those same Buchanan men did once tell me of an argument that he made for his opposition to Judge Douglas. He said that a friend of our Senator Douglas has been talking to him, and had among other things said to him: "Why, you don't want to beat Douglas?" "Yes" said he, "I do want to beat him, and I will tell you why. I believe his original Nebraska Bill was right in the abstract, but it was wrong in the time that it was brought forward. It was wrong in the application to a Territory in regard to which the question had been settled; it was brought forward at a time when nobody asked him; it was tendered to the South when the South had not asked for it, but when they could not well refuse it; and for this same reason he forced that question upon our party: it has sunk our best men all over the nation, everywhere; and now when our President, struggling with the difficulties of this man's getting up, has reached the very hardest point to turn in the case, he deserts him, and I *am* for putting him where he will trouble us no more."

Now, gentlemen, that is not my argument—that is not my argument at all. I have only been stating to you an argument of a Buchanan man. You will judge if there is any force in it. Popular Sovereignty! everlasting Popular Sovereignty! Let us for a moment inquire into this vast matter of Popular Sovereignty. What is Popular Sovereignty? We recollect that at an early period in the history of this struggle there was another name for this same thing—*Squatter Sovereignty*. It was not exactly Popular Sovereignty, but Squatter Sovereignty. What do those terms mean? What do they mean when used now? And vast credit is taken by our friend, the Judge, in regard to his support of it, when he declares the last years of his life have been, and all the future years of his life shall be, devoted to this matter of Popular Sovereignty. What is it? Why, it is the sovereignty of the people. What was Squatter Sovereignty? I suppose if it had any significance at all, it was the right of the people to govern themselves, to be sovereign over their own affairs, while they were squatted down in a country not their own, while they had squatted on a territory that did not belong to them, in the sense that a State belongs to the people who inhabit it,—when it belonged to the nation—such right to govern themselves was called "Squatter Sovereignty."

Now, I wish you to mark. What has become of that Squatter Sovereignty? What has become of it? Can you get anybody to tell you now that the people of a Territory have any authority to govern themselves, in regard to this mooted question of slavery, before they form a State Constitution? No such thing at all, although there is a general running fire, and although there has been a hurrah made in every speech on that side, assuming that that policy had given the people of a Territory the right to govern themselves upon this question: yet the point is dodged. To-day it has been decided—no more than a year ago it was decided by the Supreme Court of the United States, and is insisted upon to-day, that the people of a Territory have no right to exclude slavery from a Territory, that if any one man chooses to take slaves into a Territory, all the rest of the people have no right to keep them out. This being so, and this decision being made one of the points that the Judge approved, and one in the approval of which he says he means to keep me down—*put* me down I should not say, for I have never been up. He says he is in favor of it, and sticks to it, and expects to win his battle on that decision, which says that there is no such thing as Squatter Sovereignty, but that any one man may take slaves into a Territory, and all the other men of the Territory may be opposed to it, and yet by reason of the constitution they cannot prohibit it. When that is so, how much is left of this vast matter of Squatter Sovereignty, I should like to know?

When we get back, we get to the point of the right of the people to make a constitution. Kansas was settled, for example, in 1854. It was a Territory yet, without having formed a constitution, in a very regular way, for three years. All this time negro slavery could be taken in by any few individuals, and by that decision of the Supreme Court, which the Judge approves, all the rest of the people cannot keep it out; but when they come to make a constitution, they may say they will not have slavery. But it is there; they are obliged to tolerate it in some way, and all experience shows that it will be so—for they will not take the negro slaves and absolutely deprive the owners of them. All experience shows this to be so. All that space of time that runs from the beginning of the settlement of the Territory until there is a sufficiency of people to make a State Constitution—all that portion of time Popular Sovereignty is given up. The seal is absolutely put down upon it by the Court decision, and Judge Douglas puts his on the top of that; yet he is appealing to the people to give him vast credit for his devotion to Popular Sovereignty.

Again, when we get to the question of the right of the people to form a State Constitution as they please, to form it with slavery or without slavery—if that is anything new, I confess I don't know it. Has there ever been a time when any one said that anybody other than the people of a Territory itself should form their constitution? What is new in it, that Judge Douglas should have fought several years of his life, and pledge himself to fight all the remaining years of his life for? Can Judge Douglas find anybody on earth that said that anybody else should form a constitution for a people? (A voice, "Yes.") Well, I should like you to name him; I should like to know who he was. (Same voice, "John Calhoun.")

Mr. Lincoln—No, Sir, I never heard of even John Calhoun saying such a thing. He insisted on the same principle as Judge Douglas; but his mode of applying it in fact, was wrong. It is enough for my purpose to ask this crowd, when ever a Republican said anything against it? They never said anything against it, but they have constantly spoken for it; and whosoever will undertake to examine the platform, and the speeches of responsible men of the party, and of irresponsible men, too, if you please, will be unable to find one word from anybody in the Republican ranks, opposed to that Popular Sovereignty which Judge Douglas thinks that he has invented. I suppose that Judge Douglas will claim, in a little while, that he is the inventor of the idea that the people should govern themselves; that nobody ever thought of such a thing until he brought it forward. We do remember that in that old Declaration of Independence, it is said that "We hold these truths to be self-evident, that all men are created equal; that they are endowed by their Creator with certain inalienable rights; that among these are life, liberty, and the pursuit of happiness; that to secure these rights, governments are instituted among men, deriving their just powers from the consent of the governed." There is the origin of Popular Sovereignty. Who, then, shall come in at this day and claim that he invented it?

The Lecompton Constitution connects itself with this question, for it is in this matter of the Lecompton Constitution that our friend Judge Douglas claims such vast credit. I agree that in opposing the Lecompton Constitution, so far as I can perceive, he was right. I do not deny that at all; and gentlemen, you will readily see why I could not deny it, even if I wanted to. But I do not wish to; for all the Republicans in the nation opposed it, and they would have opposed it just as much without Judge Douglas' aid, as with it. They had all taken ground against it long before he did. Why, the reason that he urges against that Constitution, I urged against him a year before. I have the printed speech in my hand. The argument that he makes, why that Constitution should not be adopted, that the people were not fairly represented nor allowed to vote, I pointed out in a speech a year ago, which I hold in my hand now, that no fair chance was to be given the people. ("Read it, Read it.") I shall not waste your time by trying to read it. ("Read it, Read it.") Gentlemen, reading from speeches is a very tedious business, particularly for an old man that has to put on spectacles, and the more so if the man be so tall that he has to bend over to the light.

A little more, now, as to this matter of popular sovereignty and the Lecompton Constitution. The Lecompton Constitution, as the Judge tells us, was defeated. The defeat of it was a good thing or it was not. He thinks the defeat of it was a good thing and so do I, and we agree in that. Who defeated it?

A voice—"Judge Douglas."

Mr. Lincoln—Yes, he furnished himself, and if you suppose he controlled the other Democrats that went with him, he furnished *three* votes; while the Republicans furnished *twenty*.

That is what he did to defeat it. In the House of Representatives he and his friends furnished some twenty votes, and the Republicans furnished *ninety odd*. Now who was it that did the work?

A voice—"Douglas."

Mr. Lincoln—Why yes, Douglas did it! To be sure he did.

Let us, however, put that proposition another way. The Republicans could not have done it without Judge Douglas. Could he have done it without them? Which could have come the nearest to doing it without the other?

A voice—"Who killed the bill?"

Another voice—"Douglas."

Mr. Lincoln—Ground was taken against it by the Republicans long before Douglas did it. The proportion of opposition to that measure is about five to one.

A voice—"Why don't they come out on it?"

Mr. Lincoln—You don't know what you are talking about, my friend. I am quite willing to answer any gentleman in the crowd who asks an *intelligent* question.

Now, who in all this country has ever found any of our friends of Judge Douglas' way of thinking, and who have acted upon this main question, that has ever thought of uttering a word in behalf of Judge Trumbull? (A voice— "We have.") I defy you to show a printed resolution passed in a Democratic meeting—I take it upon myself to defy any man to show a printed resolution of a Democratic meeting, large or small, in favor of Judge Trumbull, or any of the five to one Republicans who beat that bill. Everything must be for the Democrats! They did everything, and the five to one that really did the thing, they snub over, and they do not seem to remember that they have an existence upon the face of the earth.

Gentlemen: I fear that I shall become tedious. I leave this branch of the subject to take hold of another. I take up that part of Judge Douglas' speech in which he respectfully attended to me.

Judge Douglas makes two points upon my recent speech at Springfield. He says they are to be the issues of this campaign. The first one of these points he bases upon the language in a speech which I delivered at Springfield, which I believe I can quote correctly from memory. I said there that "we are now far into the fifth year since a policy was instituted for the avowed object and with the confident promise of putting an end to slavery agitation; under the operation of that policy, that agitation had [not?] only not ceased, but has constantly augmented. I believe it will not cease until a crisis shall have been reached and passed. A house divided against itself cannot stand. I believe this government cannot endure permanently half slave and half free. I do not expect the Union to be dissolved,"—I am quoting from my speech—"I do not expect the house to fall, but I do expect it will cease to be divided. It will become all one thing or all the other. Either the opponents of slavery will arrest the spread of it, and place it where the public mind shall rest in the belief that it is in the course of ultimate extinction, or its advocates will push it forward until it shall become alike lawful in all the States North as well as South."

What is the paragraph? In this paragraph which I have quoted in your hearing, and to which I ask the attention of all, Judge Douglas thinks he discovers great political heresy. I want your attention particularly to what he has inferred from it. He says I am in favor of making all the States of this Union uniform in all their internal regulations; that in all their domestic concerns I am in favor of making them entirely uniform. He draws this inference from the language I have quoted to you. He says that I am in favor of making war by the North upon the South for the extinction of slavery; that I am also in favor of inviting, as he expresses it, the South to a war upon the North for the purpose of nationalizing slavery. Now, it is singular enough, if you will carefully read that passage over, that I did not say that I was in favor of anything in it. I only said what I expected would take place. I made a prediction only—it may have been a foolish one perhaps. I did not even say that I desired that slavery should be put in course of ultimate extinction. I do say so now, however, so there need be no longer any difficulty about that. It may be written down in the next speech.

Gentlemen, Judge Douglas informed you that this speech of mine was probably carefully prepared. I admit that it was. I am not master of language; I have not a fine education; I am not capable of entering into a disquisition upon dialectics, as I believe you call it; but I do not believe the language I employed bears any such construction as Judge Douglas put upon it. But I don't care about a quibble in regard to words. I know what I meant, and I will not leave this crowd in doubt, if I can explain it to them, what I really meant in the use of that paragraph.

I am not, in the first place, unaware that this Government has endured eighty-two years, half slave and half free. I know that. I am tolerably well acquainted with the history of the country, and I know that it has endured eighty-two years, half slave and half free. I *believe*—and that is what I meant to allude to there—I *believe* it has endured because, during all that time, until the introduction of the Nebraska Bill, the public mind did rest, all the time, in the belief that slavery was in course of ultimate extinction. That was what gave us the rest that we had through that period of eighty-two years;—at least, so I believe. I have always hated slavery, I think, as much as any Abolitionist. I have been an Old Line Whig. I have always hated it, but I have always been quiet about it until this new era of the introduction of the Nebraska Bill began. I always believed that everybody was against it, and that it was in course of ultimate extinction. (Pointing to Mr. Browning, who stood near by,) Browning thought so; the great mass of the nation have rested in the belief that slavery was in course of ultimate extinction. They had reason so to believe.

The adoption of the Constitution and its attendant history led the people to believe so; and that such was the belief of the framers of the Constitution itself. Why did those old men, about the time of the adoption of the Constitution, decree that slavery should not go into the new Territory, where it had not already gone? Why declare that within twenty years the African Slave Trade, by which slaves are supplied, might be cut off by Congress? Why were all these acts? I might enumerate more of such acts—but enough. What were they but a clear indication that the framers of the Constitution intended and expected the ultimate extinction of that institution? And now when I say, as I say in this speech, that Judge Douglas has quoted from, when I say that I think the opponents of slavery will resist the farther spread of it, and place it where the public mind shall rest with the belief that it is in course of ultimate extinction, I only mean to say, that they will place it where the founders of this government originally placed it.

I have said a hundred times, and I have now no inclination to take it back, that I believe there is no right, and ought to be no inclination, in the people of the free States to enter into the slave States, and interfere with the question of slavery at all. I have said that always. Judge Douglas has heard me say it—if not quite a hundred times, at least as good as a hundred times; and when it is said that I am in favor of interfering with slavery where it exists, I know it is unwarranted by anything I have ever *intended,* and, as I believe, by anything I have ever *said.* If, by any means, I have ever used language which could fairly be so construed, (as, however, I believe I never have,) I now correct it.

So much, then, for the inference that Judge Douglas draws, that I am in favor of setting the sections at war with one another. I know that I never meant any such thing, and I believe that no fair mind can infer any such thing from anything I have ever said.

Now, in relation to his inference that I am in favor of a general consolidation of all the local institutions of the various States. I will attend to that for a little while, and try to inquire if I can how on earth it could be that any man could draw such an inference from anything I said. I have said, very many times, in Judge Douglas' hearing, that no man believed more than I in the principle of self-government; that it lies at the bottom of all my ideas of just government from beginning to end. I have denied that his use of that term applies properly. But for the thing itself I deny that any man has ever gone ahead of me in his devotion to the principle, whatever he may have done in efficiency in advocating it. I think that I have said it in your hearing—that I believe each individual is naturally entitled to do as he pleases with himself and the fruit of his labor, so far as it in no wise interferes with any other man's rights, that each community, as a State, has a right to do exactly as it pleases with all the concerns within that State that interfere with the rights of no other State, and that the general government, upon principle, has no right to interfere with any thing other than that general class of things that does concern the whole. I have said that at all times. I have said, as illustrations, that I do not believe in the right of Illinois to interfere with the cranberry laws of Indiana, the oyster laws of Virginia, or the Liquor Laws of Maine. I have said these things over and over again and I repeat them here as my sentiments.

How is it, then, that Judge Douglas infers, because I hope to see slavery put where the public mind shall rest in the belief that it is in the course of ultimate extinction, that I am in favor of Illinois going over and interfering with the cranberry laws of Indiana? What can authorize him to draw any such inference? I suppose there might be one thing that at least enabled *him* to draw such an inference that would not be true with me or with many others—that is, because he looks upon all this matter of slavery as an exceedingly little thing—this matter of keeping one sixth of the population of the whole nation in a state of oppression and tyranny unequalled in the world. He looks upon it as being an exceedingly little thing—only equal to the question of the cranberry laws of Indiana—as something having no moral question in it—as something on a par with the question of whether a man shall pasture his land with cattle, or plant it with tobacco—so little and so small a thing, that he concludes if I could desire that anything should be done to bring about the ultimate extinction of that little thing, I must be in favor of bringing about an amalgamation of all the other little things in the Union. Now, it so happens—and there, I presume, is the foundation of this mistake—that the Judge thinks thus; and it so happens that there is a vast portion of the American people that do *not* look upon that matter as being this very little thing. They look upon it as a vast moral evil; they can prove it is such by the writings of those who gave us the blessings of liberty which we enjoy, and that they so looked upon it and not as an evil merely confining itself to the States where it is situated; and while we agree that, by the Constitution we assented to, in the States where it exists we have no right to interfere with it because it is in the Constitution and we are by both duty and inclination to stick by that Constitution in all its letter and spirit from beginning to end.

So much then as to my disposition—my wish—to have all the State legislatures blotted out, and to have one general consolidated government, and a uniformity of domestic regulations in all the States, by which I suppose it is meant if we raise corn here, we must make sugar-cane grow here too, and we must make those things grow North, grow in the South. All this I suppose the Judge understands I am in favor of doing. Now, so much for all this nonsense—for I must call it so. The Judge can have no issue with me on a question of establishing uniformity in the domestic regulations of the States.

A little now on the other point—the Dred Scott Decision. Another one of the issues he says that is to be made with me, is upon his devotion to the Dred Scott Decision, and my opposition to it.

I have expressed heretofore, and I now repeat, my opposition to the Dred Scott Decision, but I should be allowed to state the nature of that opposition, and I ask your indulgence while I do so. What is fairly implied by the term Judge Douglas has used, "resistance to the Decision?" I do not resist it. If I wanted to take Dred Scott from his master, I would be interfering with property, and that terrible difficulty that Judge Douglas speaks of, of interfering with property, would arise. But I am doing no such thing as that, but all that I am doing is refusing to obey it as a political rule. If I were in Congress, and a vote should come up on a question whether slavery should be prohibited in a new Territory, in spite of that Dred Scott Decision, I would vote that it should.

That is what I would do. Judge Douglas said last night, that before the Decision he might advance his opinion, and it might be contrary to the decision when it was made; but *after* it was made he would abide by it until it was reversed. Just so! We let this property abide by the decision, but we will try to reverse that decision. We will try to put it where Judge Douglas would not object, for he says he will obey it until it is reversed. Somebody has to reverse that decision, since it is made, and we mean to reverse it, and we mean to do it peaceably.

What are the uses of decisions of courts? They have two uses. As rules of property they have to uses. First—they decide upon the question before the court. They decide in this case that Dred Scott is a slave. Nobody resists that. Not only that, but they say to everybody else, that persons standing just as Dred Scott stands, are as he is. That is, they say that when a question comes up upon another person it will be so decided again, unless the court decides another way, unless the court overrules its decision. Well, we mean to do what we can to have the court decide the other way. That is one thing we mean to try to do.

The sacredness that Judge Douglas throws around this decision, is a degree of sacredness that has never been before thrown around any other decision. I have never heard of such a thing. Why, decisions apparently contrary to that decision, or that good lawyers thought were contrary to that decision, have been made by that very court before. It is the first of its kind; it is an *astonisher* in legal history. It is a new wonder of the world. It is based upon falsehood in the main as to the facts—allegations of facts upon which it stands are not facts at all in many instances, and no decision made on any question—the first instance of a decision made under so many unfavorable circumstances—thus placed has ever been held by the profession as law, and it has always needed confirmation before the lawyers regarded it as a settled law. But Judge Douglas will have it that all hands must take this extraordinary decision, made under these extraordinary circumstances, and give their vote in Congress in accordance with it, yield to it and obey it in every possible sense. Circumstances alter cases. Do not gentlemen here remember the case of that same Supreme Court, some twenty-five or thirty years ago, deciding that a National Bank was constitutional? I ask, if somebody does not remember that a National Bank was declared to be constitutional? Such is the truth, whether it be remembered or not. The Bank charter ran out, and a re-charter was granted by Congress. That re-charter was laid before Gen. Jackson. It was urged upon him, when he denied the constitutionality of the bank, that the Supreme Court had decided that it was constitutional; and Gen. Jackson then said that the Supreme Court had no right to lay down a rule to govern a co-ordinate branch of the government, the members of which had sworn to support the Constitution—that each member had sworn to support that Constitution as he understood it. I will venture here to say, that I have heard Judge Douglas say that he approved of Gen. Jackson for that act. What has now become of all his tirade about "resistance to the Supreme Court?"

My fellow-citizens, getting back a little, for I pass from these points, when Judge Douglas makes his threat of annihilation upon the "alliance," he is cautious to say that that warfare of his is to fall upon the leaders of the Republican party. Almost every word he utters and every distinction he makes, has its significance. He means for the Republicans that do not count themselves as leaders, to be his friends; he makes no fuss over them; it is the leaders that he is making war upon. He wants it understood that the mass of the Republican party are really his friends. It is only the leaders that are doing something, that are intolerant, and that require extermination at his hands. As this is clearly and unquestionably the light in which he presents that matter, I want to ask your attention, addressing myself to the Republicans here, that I may ask you some questions, as to where you, as the Republican party, would be placed if you sustained Judge Douglas in his present position by a re-election? I do not claim, gentlemen, to be unselfish; I do not pretend that I would not like to go to the United States Senate, I make no such hypocritical pretense, but I do say to you that in this mighty issue, it is nothing to you—nothing to the mass of the people of the nation, whether or not Judge Douglas or myself shall ever be heard of after this night; it may be a trifle to either of us, but in connection with this mighty question, upon which hang the destinies of the nation, perhaps, it is absolutely nothing; but where will you be placed if you re-endorse Judge Douglas? Don't you know how apt he is—how exceedingly anxious he is at all times to seize upon anything and everything to persuade you that something *he* has done *you* did yourselves? Why, he tried to persuade you last night that our Illinois Legislature instructed him to introduce the Nebraska Bill. There was nobody in that Legislature ever thought of such a thing; and when he first introduced the bill, he never thought of it; but still he fights furiously for the proposition, and that he did it because there was a standing instruction to our Senators to be always introducing Nebraska bills. He tells you he is for the Cincinnati Platform, he tells you he is for the Dred Scott Decision. He tells you, not in his speech last night, but substantially in a former speech, that he cares not if slavery is voted up or down—he tells you the struggle on Lecompton is passed—it may come up again or not and if it does he stands where he stood when in spite of him and his opposition you built up the Republican party. If you endorse him, you tell him you do not care whether slavery be voted up or down, and he will close, or try to close your mouths with his declaration, repeated by the day, the week, the month, and the year. Is that what you mean? (Cries of "no;" one voice "yes.") Yes, I have no doubt you who have always been for him, if you mean that. No doubt of that, soberly I have said, and I repeat it. I think, in the position in which Judge Douglas stood in opposing the Lecompton Constitution he was right; he does not know that it will return, but if it does we may know where to find him, and if it does not we may know where to look for him, and that is on the Cincinnati Platform. Now I could ask the Republican party, after all the hard names that Judge Douglas has called them by—all his repeated charges of their inclination to marry with and hug negroes, all his declarations of Black Republicanism—by the way, we are improving, the black has got rubbed off—but with all that, if he be endorsed by Republican votes, where do you stand? Plainly, you stand ready saddled, bridled and harnessed and waiting to be driven over into the slavery extension camp of the nation,—just ready to be driven over, tied together in a lot—to be driven over, every man with a rope around his neck, that halter being held by Judge Douglas. That is the question. If Republican men have been in earnest in what they have done, I think they had better not do it, but I think that the Republican party is made up of those who, as far as they can peaceably, will oppose the extension of slavery, and who will hope for its ultimate extinction—who will believe, if it ceases to spread, that it is in course of ultimate extinction. If they believe it is wrong in grasping up the new lands of the continent, and keeping them from the settlement of free white laborers, who want the land to bring up their families upon; if they are in earnest, although they may make a mistake, they will grow restless, and the time will come when they will come back again and reorganize, if not by the same name, at least upon the same principles as their party now has. It is better, then, to save the work while it is begun. You have done the labor; maintain it—keep it. If men choose to serve you, go with them; but as you have made up your organization upon principle, stand by it; for, as surely as God reigns over you, and has inspired your mind, and given you a sense of propriety, and continues to give you hope, so surely will you still cling to these ideas, and you will at last come back again after your wanderings, merely to do your work over again.

We were often—more than once, at least—in the course of Judge Douglas' speech last night, reminded that this government was made for white men— that he believed it was made for white men! Well, that is putting it in a shape in which no one wants to deny it; but the Judge then goes into his passion for drawing inferences that are not warranted. I protest, now and forever, against that counterfeit logic which presumes that because I did not want a negro woman for a slave, I do necessarily want her for a wife. My understanding is that I need not have her for either, but, as God made us separate, we can leave one another alone, and do one another much good thereby. There are white men enough to marry all the white women, and enough black men to marry all the black women, and in God's name let them be so married. The Judge regales us with the terrible enormities that take place by the mixture of races; that the inferior race bears the superior down. Why, Judge, if we will not let them get together in the Territories, they won't mix there.

A voice—"Three cheers for Lincoln." (The cheers were given with a hearty good-will.)

Mr. Lincoln—I should say at least that that is a self-evident truth.

Now, it happens that we meet together once every year, sometimes about the 4th of July for some reason or other. These 4th of July gatherings, I suppose, have their uses. If you will indulge me, I will state what I suppose to be some of them.

We are now a mighty nation, we are thirty—or about thirty millions of people, and we own and inhabit about one-fifteenth part of the dry land of the whole earth. We run our memory back over the pages of history for about eighty-two years, and we discover that we were then a very small people in point of numbers, vastly inferior to what we are now, with a vastly less extent of country,—with vastly less of everything we deem desirable among men,—we look upon the change as exceedingly advantageous to us and to our posterity,—and we fix upon something that happened away back, as in some way or other being connected with this rise of prosperity. We find a race of men living in that day whom we claim as our fathers and grandfathers; they were iron men; they fought for the principle that they were contending for; and we understand that by what they then did it has followed that the degree of prosperity that we now enjoy has come to us. We hold this annual celebration to remind ourselves of all the good done in this process of time, of how it was done and who did it, and how we are historically connected with it; and we go from these meetings in better humor with ourselves—we feel more attached the one to the other, and more firmly bound to the country we inhabit. In every way we are better men in the age, and race, and country in which we live, for these celebrations. But after we have done all this we have not yet reached the whole. There is something else connected with it. We have besides these men—

descended by blood from our ancestors—among us perhaps half our people who are not descendants at all of these men, they are men who have come from Europe—German, Irish, French and Scandinavian—men that have come from Europe themselves, or whose ancestors have come hither and settled here, finding themselves our equals in all things. If they look back through this history to trace their connection with those days by blood, they find they have none, they cannot carry themselves back into that glorious epoch and make themselves feel that they are part of us, but when they look through that old Declaration of Independence, they find that those old men say that "We hold these truths to be self-evident, that all men are created equal," and then they feel that that moral sentiment taught in that day evidences their relation to those men, that it is the father of all moral principle in them, and that they have a right to claim it as though they were blood of the blood, and flesh of the flesh, of the men who wrote that Declaration, and so they are. That is the electric cord in that Declaration that links the hearts of patriotic and liberty-loving men together, that will link those patriotic hearts as long as the love of freedom exists in the minds of men throughout the world.

Now, sirs, for the purpose of squaring things with this idea of "don't care if slavery is voted up or voted down," for sustaining the Dred Scott Decision, for holding that the Declaration of Independence did not mean anything at all, we have Judge Douglas giving his exposition of what the Declaration of Independence means, and we have him saying that the people of America were equal to the people of England. According to his construction, you Germans are not connected with it. Now, I ask you in all soberness, if all these things, if indulged in, if ratified, if confirmed and endorsed, if taught to our children and repeated to them, do not tend to rub out the sentiment of liberty in the country, and to transform this government into a government of some other form. These arguments that are made, that the inferior race are to be treated with as much allowance as they are capable of enjoying; that as much is to be done for them as their condition will allow. What are these arguments? They are the arguments that kings have made for enslaving the people in all ages of the world. You will find that all the arguments in favor of kingcraft were of this class; they always bestrode the necks of the people, not that they wanted to do it, but because the people were better off for being ridden. That is their argument, and this argument of the Judge is the same old serpent that says, you work, and I eat, you toil, and I will enjoy the fruits of it. Turn it whatever way you will—whether it come from the mouth of a King, an excuse for enslaving the people of his country, or from the mouth of men of one race as a reason for enslaving the men of another race, it is all the same old serpent, and I hold if that course of argumentation that is made for the purpose of convincing the public mind that we should not care about this, should be granted, it does not stop with the negro. I should like to know if taking this old Declaration of Independence, which declares that all men are equal upon principle, and making exceptions to it, where will it stop? If one man says it does not mean a negro, why may not another say it does not mean some other man? If that Declaration is not the truth, let us get the Statute book in which we find it and tear it out! Who is so bold as to do it! If it is not true let us tear it out! (cries of "no, no,") let us stick to it then (cheers). Let us stand firmly by it then (applause).

It may be argued that there are certain conditions that make necessities and impose them upon us, and to the extent that a necessity is imposed upon a man, he must submit to it. I think that was the condition in which we found ourselves when we established this government. We have slavery among us, we could not get our Constitution unless we permitted them to remain in slavery, we could not secure the good we did secure if we grasped for more, and having by necessity submitted to that much, it does not destroy the principle that is the charter of our liberties. Let that charter stand as our standard.

My friend has said to me that I am a poor hand to quote Scripture. I will try it again, however. It is said in one of the admonitions of the Lord, "As your Father in heaven is perfect, be ye also perfect." The Saviour, I suppose, did not expect that any human creature could be perfect as the Father in Heaven; but He said, "As your Father in Heaven is perfect, be ye also perfect." He set that up as a standard, and he who did most towards reaching that standard, attained the highest degree of moral perfection. So I say in relation to the principle that all men are created equal, let it be as nearly reached as we can. If we cannot give freedom to every creature, let us do nothing that will impose slavery upon any other creature. Let us then turn this government back into the channel in which the framers of the Constitution originally placed it. Let us stand firmly by each other. If we do not do so, we are turning in the contrary direction, that our friend Judge Douglas proposes—not intentionally—as working in the traces that tend to make this one universal Slave Nation. He is one that runs in that direction, and as such I resist him.

My friends, I have detained you about as long as I desired to do, and I have only to say, let us discard all this quibbling about this man and the other man—this race and that race and the other race being inferior, and therefore they must be placed in an inferior position—discarding our standard that we have left us.

Let us discard all these things, and unite as one people throughout this land, until we shall once more stand up declaring that all men are created equal.

My friends, I could not, without launching off upon some new topic, which would detain you too long, continue to-night. I thank you for this most extensive audience that you have furnished me to-night. I leave you, hoping that the lamp of liberty will burn in your bosoms until there shall no longer be a doubt that all men are created free and equal.

SPEECH IN REPLY TO DOUGLAS AT SPRINGFIELD, ILLINOIS
JULY 17, 1858

As was the case a week before at Chicago, Lincoln stalked Douglas at Springfield, replying to him afterward. At this time, Douglas was a prominent national figure while Lincoln was still a local figure in Illinois. Lincoln's strategy of following Douglas was an attempt to gain greater public visibility for his campaign. Shortly after the Springfield Speech, Lincoln challenged Douglas to a series of formal debates.

Lincoln's appeal to his political predecessors is noteworthy in the Springfield Speech. Attempting to establish republican continuity between himself, the Founders and the Second Generation of Whig Nationalists, he invoked the authority of Thomas Jefferson, Andrew Jackson, Daniel Webster, and Henry Clay against Douglas and the tendency towards the nationalization of slavery. In a nation devoid of a hereditary aristocracy, aspiring politicians turned to the actions and deeds of the natural aristocracy of statesman and political leaders as standards to measure their own virtue. The tradition of political filial piety and ancestral reverence was taken seriously in mid–nineteenth century America.

FELLOW CITIZENS:

Another election, which is deemed an important one, is approaching, and, as I suppose, the Republican party will without much difficulty elect their State ticket. But in regard to the Legislature, we, the Republicans, labor under some disadvantages. In the first place, we have a Legislature to elect upon an apportionment of the representation made several years ago, when the proportion of the population was far greater in the south (as compared with the north) than it now is; and in as much as our opponents hold almost entire sway in the south, and we a correspondingly large majority in the north, the fact that we are now to be represented as we were years ago, when the population was different, is to us a very great disadvantage. We had, in the year 1855, according to law, a census or an enumeration of the inhabitants, taken for the purpose of a new apportionment of representation. We know what a fair apportionment of representation upon that census would give us. We know that it could not, if fairly made, fail to give the Republican party from six to ten more members of the Legislature than they can probably get as the law now stands. It so happened at the last session of the Legislature, that our opponents, holding the control of both branches of the Legislature, steadily refused to give us such an apportionment as we were rightfully entitled to have upon the census then taken. The Legislature steadily refused to give us such an apportionment as we were rightfully entitled to have upon the census taken of the population of the State. The Legislature would pass no bill upon that subject, except such as was at least as unfair to us as the old one, and in which, in some instances, two men in the Democratic regions were allowed to go as far toward sending a member to the Legislature as three were in the Republican regions. Comparison was made at the time as to representative and senatorial districts, which completely demonstrated that such was the fact. Such a bill was passed, and tendered to the Republican Governor for his signature; but principally for the reasons I have stated, he withheld his approval, and the bill fell without becoming a law.

Another disadvantage under which we labor, is, that there are one or two Democratic Senators who will be members of the next legislature, and will vote for the election of Senator, who are holding over in districts in which we could, on all reasonable calculation, elect men of our own, if we only had the chance of an election. When we consider that there are but twenty-five Senators in the Senate, taking two from the side where they rightfully belong, and adding them to the other, is to us a disadvantage not to be lightly regarded. Still, so it is. We have this to contend with. Perhaps there is no ground of complaint on our part. In attending to the many things involved in the last general election for President, Governor, Auditor, Treasurer, Superintendent of Public Instruction, Members of Congress, of the Legislature, county officers and so on, we allowed these things to happen by want of sufficient attention, and we have no cause to complain of our adversaries, so far as this matter is concerned. But we have some cause to complain of the refusal to give us a fair apportionment.

There is still another disadvantage under which we labor, and to which I will ask your attention. It arises out of the relative positions of the two persons who stand before the State as candidates for the Senate. Senator Douglas is of world wide renown. All the anxious politicians of his party, or who have been of his party, for years past, have been looking upon him, as certainly, at no very distant day to be the President of the United States. They have seen in his round, jolly, fruitful face, postoffices, land offices, marshalships and cabinet appoint-

ments, chargeships and foreign missions, bursting and sprouting out in wonderful exuberance, ready to be laid hold of by their greedy hands. And as they
have been gazing upon this attractive picture so long they cannot, in the little
distraction that has taken place in the party, bring themselves to quite give up
the charming hope; but with greedier anxiety they rush about him, sustain him,
and give him marches, triumphal entries, and receptions beyond what even in
the days of his highest prosperity they could have brought about in his favor.
On the contrary, no body has ever expected me to be President. In my poor,
lean, lank face nobody has ever seen that any cabbages were sprouting out.
These are disadvantages all taken together that the Republicans labor under. *We*
have to fight this battle upon principle, and upon principle alone. I am, in a certain sense made the standard bearer in behalf of the Republicans. I was made so,
merely because there had to be some one so placed—I being, in no wise preferable to any other one of the twenty—fifty—perhaps a hundred we have in the
Republican ranks. Then I say I wish it to be distinctly understood, and borne
in mind, that we have to fight this battle without many—perhaps without any—
of the external aids, which are brought to bear against us. So I hope those with
whom I am surrounded have principle enough to nerve themselves for the task
and leave nothing undone that can be fairly done, to bring about the right result.

After Senator Douglas left Washington, as his movements were made
known by the public prints, he tarried a considerable time in the city of New
York; and it was heralded that, like another Napoleon, he was lying by, and
framing the plan of his campaign. It was telegraphed to Washington City, and
published in the *Union,* that he was framing this plan for the purpose of going
to Illinois to pounce upon and annihilate the treasonable and disunion speech
which Lincoln had made here on the 16th of June. Now, I do suppose that the
Judge really spent some time in New York maturing the plan of the campaign,
as his friends heralded for him. I have been able, by noting his movements since
his arrival in Illinois, to discover evidences confirmatory of that allegation. I
think I have been able to see what are the material points of that plan. I will, for
a little while, ask your attention to some of them. What I shall point out, though
not showing the whole plan, are, nevertheless, the main points, as I suppose.

They are not very numerous. The first is popular sovereignty. The second
and third are attacks upon my speech made on the 16th of June. Out of these
three points—drawing within the range of popular sovereignty the question of
the Lecompton Constitution—he makes his principal assault. Upon these his
successive speeches are substantially one and the same. On this matter of popular sovereignty I wish to be a little careful. Auxiliary to these main points, to

be sure, are their thunderings of cannon, their marching and music, their fiz-
zle-gigs and fireworks; but I will not waste time with them. They are but the
little trappings of the campaign.

Coming to the substance—the first point—"popular sovereignty." It is to
be labeled upon the cars in which he travels; put upon the hacks he rides in;
to be flaunted upon the arches he passes under, and the banners which wave
over him. It is to be dished up in as many varieties as a French cook can produce soups from potatoes. Now, as this is so great a staple of the plan of the
campaign, it is worth while to examine it carefully; and if we examine only a
very little, and do not allow ourselves to be misled, we shall be able to see that
the whole thing is the most arrant Quixotism that was ever enacted before a
community. What is this matter of popular sovereignty? The first thing, in
order to understand it, is to get a good definition of what it is, and after that to
see how it is applied.

I suppose almost every one knows, that in this controversy, whatever has
been said, has had reference to the question of negro slavery. We have not been
in a controversy about the right of the people to govern themselves in the *ordinary* matters of domestic concern in the States and Territories. Mr. Buchanan
in one of his late messages (I think when he sent up the Lecompton Constitution), urged that the main points to which the public attention had been
directed, was not in regard to the great variety of small domestic matters, but
was directed to the question of negro slavery; and he asserted, that if the people had had a fair chance to vote on that question, there was no reasonable
ground of objection in regard to minor questions. Now, while I think that the
people had *not* had given, or offered them, a fair chance upon that slavery question; still, if there had been a fair submission to a vote upon that main question,
the President's proposition would have been true to the uttermost. Hence,
when hereafter, I speak of popular sovereignty, I wish to be understood as
applying what I say to the question of slavery only, and not to other minor
domestic matters of a territory or a State.

Does Judge Douglas, when he says that several of the past years of his life
have been devoted to the question of "popular sovereignty," and that all the
remainder of his life shall be devoted to it, does he mean to say that he has been
devoting his life to securing to the people of the Territories the right to exclude
slavery from the Territories? If he means so to say, he means to deceive; because
he, and every one knows that the decision of the Supreme Court, which he
approves and makes special ground of attack upon me for disapproving, forbids
the people of a Territory to exclude slavery. This covers the whole ground,

from the settlement of a Territory till it reaches the degree of maturity entitling it to form a State Constitution. So far as all that ground is concerned, the Judge is not sustaining popular sovereignty, but absolutely opposing it. He sustains the decision which declares that the popular will of the Territories has no constitutional power to exclude slavery during their territorial existence. This being so, the period of time from the first settlement of a Territory, till it reaches the point of forming a State Constitution, is not the thing that the Judge has fought for, or is fighting for, but on the contrary, he has fought for, and is fighting for, the thing that annihilates and crushes out that same popular sovereignty.

Well, so much being disposed of, what is left? Why, he is contending for the right of the people, when they come to make a State Constitution, to make it for themselves, and precisely as best suits themselves. I say again, that is Quixotic. I defy contradiction when I declare that the Judge can find no one to oppose him on that proposition. I repeat, there is no body opposing that proposition on *principle*. Let me not be misunderstood. I know that, with reference to the Lecompton Constitution, I may be misunderstood; but when you understand me correctly, my proposition will be true and accurate. No body is opposing or has opposed the right of the people, when they form a constitution, to form it for themselves. Mr. Buchanan and his friends have not done it; they, too, as well as the Republicans and the anti-Lecompton Democrats, have not done it; but, on the contrary, they together have insisted on the right of the people to form a constitution for themselves. The difference between the Buchanan men on the one hand, and the Douglas men and the Republicans on the other, has not been on a question of principle, but on a question of *fact*.

The dispute was upon the question of fact, whether the Lecompton Constitution had been fairly formed by the people or not. Mr. Buchanan and his friends have not contended for the contrary principle any more than the Douglas men or the Republicans. They have insisted that whatever of small irregularities existed in getting up the Lecompton Constitution, were such as happen in the settlement of all new Territories. The question was, was it a fair emanation of the people? It was a question of fact and not of principle. As to the principle, all were agreed. Judge Douglas voted with the Republicans upon that matter of fact.

He and they, by their voices and votes, denied that it was a fair emanation of the people. The Administration affirmed that it was. With respect to the evidence bearing upon that question of fact, I readily agree that Judge Douglas and the Republicans had the right on their side, and that the Administration was wrong. But I state again that as a matter of principle, there is no dispute upon the right of the people in a Territory merging into a State to form a Constitution for themselves without outside interference from any quarter. This being so, what is Judge Douglas going to spend his life for?—Is he going to spend his life in maintaining a principle that no body on earth opposes?—Does he expect to stand up in majestic dignity, and go through his *apotheosis* and become a God, in the maintaining of a principle which, neither a man nor a mouse in all God's creation is opposing? Now something in regard to the Lecompton Constitution more specifically; for I pass from this other question of popular sovereignty as the most arrant humbug that has ever been attempted on an intelligent community.

As to the Lecompton Constitution I have already said that on the question of fact as to whether it was a fair emanation of the people or not, Judge Douglas with the Republicans and some Americans had greatly the argument against the Administration; and while I repeat this, I wish to know what there is in the opposition of Judge Douglas to the Lecompton Constitution that entitles him to be considered the only opponent to it—as being *par excellence* the very *quintessence* of that opposition. I agree to the rightfulness of his opposition. He in the Senate and his class of men there formed the number *three* and no more. In the House of Representatives his class of men—the anti-Lecompton Democrats—formed a number of about twenty. It took one hundred and twenty to defeat the measure against one hundred and twelve. Of the votes of that one hundred and twenty, Judge Douglas' friends furnished twenty, to add to which there were six Americans and ninety-four Republicans. I do not say that I am precisely accurate in their numbers, but I am sufficiently so for any use I am making of it.

Why is it that twenty shall be entitled to all the credit of doing that work, and the hundred none of it? Why, if, as Judge Douglas says, the honor is to be divided and due credit is to be given to other parties, why, is just so much given as is consonant with the wishes, the interests and advancement of the twenty? My understanding is, when a common job is done, or a common enterprize prosecuted, that if I put in five dollars to your one, I have a right to take out five dollars to your one. But he does not so understand it. He declares the dividend of credit for defeating Lecompton upon a basis which seems unprecedented and incomprehensible.

Let us see. Lecompton, in the run was defeated. It afterwards took a sort of cooked up shape, and was passed in the English bill. It is said by the Judge, that the defeat was a good and proper thing. If it was a good thing, why is he entitled to more credit than others, for the performance of that good act, unless there was something in the antecedents of the Republicans that might induce every one to expect that they would join in that good work, and at the same time, something leading them to doubt that he would? Does he place his superior claim to credit, on the ground that he performed a good, which was never expected of him? He says I have a proneness for quoting scripture. If I should do so now, it occurs, that perhaps he places himself somewhat upon the ground of the parable of the lost sheep which went astray upon the mountains, and when the owner of the hundred sheep found the one that was lost, and threw it upon his shoulders, and came home rejoicing, it was said that there was more rejoicing over the one sheep that was lost and had been found, than over the ninety and nine in the fold. The moral is applied by the Saviour in this parable, thus—"Verily, I say unto you, there is more rejoicing in Heaven, over one sinner that repenteth, than over ninety and nine just persons that need no repentance." And now, if the Judge claims the benefit of this parable, *let him repent.* Let him not come up here and say: "I am the only just person; and you are the ninety-nine sinners!" *Repentance,* before *forgiveness* is a provision of the Christian system, and on that condition alone will the Republicans grant his forgiveness.

How will he prove that we have ever occupied a different position in regard to this Lecompton Constitution or any principle in it? He says he did not make his opposition on the ground as to whether it was a free or slave constitution, and he would have you understand that the Republicans made their opposition, because it ultimately became a slave constitution. To make proof in favor of himself on this point, he reminds us that he opposed Lecompton before the vote was taken declaring whether the State was to be free or slave. But he forgets to say that our Republican Senator, Trumbull, made a speech against Lecompton, even before he did.

Why did he oppose it? Partly, as he declares, because the members of the Convention who framed it were not fairly elected by the people; that the people were not allowed to vote unless they had been registered; and that the people of whole counties, in some instances, were not registered. For these reasons he declares the constitution was not an emanation, in any true sense, from the people. He also has an additional objection as to the mode of submitting the constitution back to the people. But bearing on the question of whether the delegates were fairly elected, a speech of his, made something more than twelve months ago, from this stand, becomes important. It was made a little while before the election of the delegates who made Lecompton. In that speech he declared there was every reason to hope and believe the election would be fair; and if any one failed to vote, it would be his own culpable fault.

I, a few days after, made a sort of answer to that speech. In that answer, I made, substantially, the very argument with which he combatted his Lecompton adversaries in the Senate last winter. I pointed to the facts that the people could not vote without being registered, and that the time for registering had gone by. I commented on it as wonderful that Judge Douglas could be ignorant of these facts, which every one else in the nation so well knew.

I now pass from popular sovereignty and Lecompton. I may have occasion to refer to one or both.

When he was preparing his plan of campaign, Napoleon like, in New York, as appears by two speeches I have heard him deliver since his arrival in Illinois, he gave special attention to a speech of mine, delivered here on the 16th of June last. He says that he carefully read that speech. He told us that at Chicago a week ago last night, and he repeated it at Bloomington last night. Doubtless, he repeated it again to-day, though I did not hear him. In the two first places—Chicago and Bloomington—I heard him; to-day I did not. He said he had carefully examined that speech; *when,* he did not say; but there is no reasonable doubt it was when he was in New York preparing his plan of campaign. I am glad he did read it carefully. He says it was evidently prepared with great care. I freely admit it was prepared with care. I claim not to be more free from errors than others—perhaps scarcely so much; but I was very careful not to put anything in that speech as a matter of fact, or make any inferences which did not appear to me to be true, and fully warrantable. If I had made any mistake, I was willing to be corrected; if I had drawn any inference in regard to Judge Douglas, or any one else, which was not warranted, I was fully prepared to modify it as soon as discovered. I planted myself upon the truth, and the truth only, so far as I knew it, or could be brought to know it.

Having made that speech, with the most kindly feelings towards Judge Douglas, as manifested therein, I was gratified that the care and caution used in that speech, left it so that he, most of all others interested in discovering error, has not been able to point out one thing against him which he could say was wrong. He seizes upon the doctrines he supposes to be included in that speech, and declares that upon them will turn the issues of this campaign. He then quotes, or attempts to quote, from my speech. I will not say that he willfully misquotes, but he does fail to quote accurately. His attempt at quoting is from a passage which I believe I can quote accurately from memory. I shall make the quotation now, with some comments upon it, as I have already said, in order that the Judge shall be left entirely without excuse for misrepresenting me. I do so now, as I hope, for the last time. I do this in great caution, in order that if he repeats his misrepresentation, it shall be plain to all that he does so willfully. If, after all, he still persists, I shall be compelled to reconstruct the course I have marked out for myself, and draw upon such humble resources as I have, for a new course, better suited to the real exigencies of the case. I set out in this campaign, with the intention of conducting it strictly as a gentleman, in substance at least, if not in the outside polish. The latter I shall never be, but that which constitutes the inside of a gentleman I hope I understand, and am not less inclined to practice than others. [Cheers.] It was my purpose and expectations that this canvass would be conducted upon principle, and with fairness on both sides; and it shall not be my fault, if this purpose and expectation shall be given up.

He charges, in substance, that I invite a war of sections; that I propose all the local institutions of the different States shall become consolidated and uniform. What is there in the language of that speech which expresses such purpose, or bears such construction? I have again and again said that I would not enter into any of the States to disturb the institution of slavery. Judge Douglas said, at Bloomington, that I used language most able and ingenious for concealing what I really meant; and that while I had protested against entering into the slave States, I nevertheless did mean to go on the banks of the Ohio and throw missiles into Kentucky, to disturb them in their domestic institutions.

I said in that speech, and I meant no more, that the institution of slavery ought to be placed in the very attitude where the framers of this government placed it, and left it. I do not understand that the framers of our Constitution left the people of the free States in the attitude of firing bombs or shells into the slave States. I was not using that passage for the purpose for which he infers I did use it. I said, "We are now far advanced into the fifth year since a policy was created for the avowed object and with the confident promise of putting an end to slavery agitation. Under the operation of that policy that agitation has not only not ceased, but has constantly augmented. In my opinion it will not cease till a crisis shall have been reached and passed. `A house divided against itself cannot stand.' I believe that this government cannot endure permanently half slave and half free. It will become all one thing or all the other. Either the opponents of slavery will arrest the further spread of it, and place it where the public mind shall rest in the belief that it is in the course of ultimate extinction, or its advocates will push it forward till it shall become alike lawful in all the States, old as well as new, North as well as South."

Now you all see, from that quotation, I did not express my *wish* on any thing. In that passage I indicated no wish or purpose of my own; I simply expressed my *expectation*. Can not the Judge perceive a distinction between a *purpose* and an *expectation?* I have often expressed an expectation to die, but I have never expressed a *wish* to die. I said at Chicago, and now repeat, that I am quite aware this government has endured, half slave and half free, for eighty two years. I understand that little bit of history. I expressed the opinion I did, because I perceived—or thought I perceived—a new set of causes introduced. I did say, at Chicago, in my speech then, that I do wish to see the spread of slavery arrested, and to see it placed where the public mind shall rest in the belief that it is in the course of ultimate extinction. I said that because I supposed, when the public mind shall rest in that belief, we shall have peace on the slavery question. I have believed—and now believe—the public mind did rest in that belief up to the introduction of the Nebraska bill.

Although I have ever been opposed to slavery, so far I rested in the hope and belief that it was in the course of ultimate extinction. For that reason, it had been a minor question with me. I might have been mistaken; but I had believed, and now believe, that the whole public mind, that is, the mind of the great majority, had rested in that belief up to the repeal of the Missouri Compromise. But, upon that event, I became convinced, that either I had been resting in a delusion, or the institution was being placed on a new basis; a basis for making it perpetual, national, and universal. Subsequent events have greatly confirmed me in that belief. I believe that bill to be the beginning of a conspiracy for that purpose. So believing, I have since then, considered that question a paramount one. So believing, I have thought the public mind will never rest till the power of Congress to restrict the spread of it, shall again be acknowledged and exercised on the one hand; or on the other, all resistance be entirely crushed out. I have expressed that opinion, and I entertain it to-night. It is denied that there is any tendency to the nationalization of slavery in these States.

Mr. Brooks of South Carolina, in one of his speeches, when they were presenting him with canes, silver plate, gold pitchers and the like, for assaulting Senator Sumner, distinctly affirmed his opinion that when this Constitution was formed, it was the belief of no man that slavery would last to the present day.

He said what I think, that the framers of our Constitution placed the institution of slavery where the public mind rested in the hope that it was in course of ultimate extinction. But he went on to say that the men of the present age, by their experience, have become wiser than the framers of the Constitution; and the inventor of the cotton-gin had made the perpetuity of slavery a necessity in this country.

As another piece of evidence tending to the same point, quite recently in Virginia, a man—the owner of slaves—made a will providing that after his death certain of his slaves should have their freedom, if they should so choose, and go to Liberia, rather than remain in slavery. They chose to be liberated. But the persons to whom they would descend as property, claimed them as slaves. A suit was instituted, which finally came to the Supreme Court of Virginia, and was therein decided against the slaves, upon the ground that a negro cannot make a choice—that they had no legal power to choose—could not perform the condition upon which their freedom depended.

I do not mention this with any purpose of criticizing, but to connect it with the arguments as affording additional evidence of the change of sentiment upon this question, of slavery in the direction of making it perpetual and national. I argue now as I did before, that there is such a tendency, and I am backed, not merely, by the facts, but by the open confession in the slave States.

And now as to the Judge's inference, that because I wish to see slavery placed in the course of ultimate extinction—placed where our fathers originally placed it—I wish to annihilate the State Legislatures—to force the cotton to grow upon the tops of the Green Mountains—to freeze ice in Florida—to cut timber on the broad Illinois prairies—that I am in favor of all these ridiculous and impossible things.

It seems to me it is a complete answer to all this, to ask if, when Congress did have the fashion of restricting slavery from free territory, when courts did have the fashion of deciding that taking a slave into a free country made him free, I say it is a sufficient answer, to ask, if any of this ridiculous nonsense about consolidation, and uniformity, did actually follow. Who heard of any such thing, because of the ordinance of '87? because of the Missouri Restriction? because of the numerous court decisions of that character?

Now as to the Dred Scott decision: for upon that he makes his last point upon me. He boldly takes ground in favor of that decision.

This is one half the onslaught, and one third of the entire plan of the campaign. I am opposed to that decision in a certain sense, but not in the sense which he puts on it. I say that in so far as it decided in favor of Dred Scott's master, and against Dred Scott and his family, I do not propose to disturb or resist the decision.

I never have proposed to do any such thing. I think, that in respect for judicial authority, my humble history would not suffer in a comparison with that of Judge Douglas. He would have the citizen conform his vote, to that decision; the member of Congress, his; the President his use of the veto power. He would make it a rule of political action, for the people and all the departments of the government. I would not. By resisting it as a political rule, I disturb no right of property, create no disorder, excite no mobs.

When he spoke at Chicago, on Friday evening of last week, he made this same point upon me. On Saturday evening I replied and reminded him of a Supreme Court decision which he opposed for at least several years. Last night at Bloomington he took some notice of that reply; but entirely forgot to remember that part of it.

He renews his onslaughts upon me, forgetting to remember that I have turned the tables against himself on that very point. I renew the effort to draw his attention to it. I wish to stand erect before the country, as well as before Judge Douglas, on this question of judicial authority, and therefore I add something to the authority in favor of my own position. I wish to show that I am sustained by authority, in addition to that heretofore presented. I do not expect to convince the Judge. It is part of the plan of his campaign, and he will cling to it with a desperate grip. Even, turn it upon him—turn the sharp point against him, and gaff him through—he will still cling to it till he can invent some new dodge to take the place of it.

In public speaking it is tedious reading from documents; but I must beg to indulge the practice to a limited extent. I shall read from a letter written by Mr. Jefferson in 1820, and now to be found in the seventh volume of his correspondence, at page 177. It seems he had been presented by a gentleman of the name of Jarvis with a book, or essay, or periodical, called the "Republican," and he was writing in acknowledgment of the present, and noting some of its contents. After expressing the hope that the work will produce a favorable effect upon the minds of the young, he proceeds to say:

"That it will have this tendency may be expected, and for that reason I feel an urgency to note what I deem an error in it, the more requiring notice as your opinion is strengthened by that of many others. You seem, in pages 84 and 148, to consider the judges as the ultimate arbiters of all constitutional questions—a very dangerous doctrine indeed, and one which would place us under the despotism of an oligarchy. Our judges are as honest as other men, and not more so. They have, with others, the same passions for party, for power, and the privilege for their corps. Their maxim is, `boni judicis est ampliare jurisdictionem;' and their power the more dangerous as they are in office for life, and not responsible, as the other functionaries are, to the elective control. The Constitution has

erected no such single tribunal, knowing that to whatever hands confided, with the corruptions of time and party, its members would become
despots. It has more wisely made all the departments co-equal and co-
sovereign within themselves."

Thus we see the power claimed for the Supreme Court by Judge Douglas,
Mr. Jefferson holds, would reduce us to the despotism of an oligarchy.

Now, I have said no more than this—in fact, never quite so much as this—
at least, I am sustained by Mr. Jefferson.

Let us go a little further. You remember we once had a national bank. Some
man owed the bank a debt, he was sued and sought to avoid payment, on the
ground that the bank was unconstitutional. The case went to the Supreme
Court, and then it was decided that the bank was constitutional. The whole
Democratic party revolted against that decision. General Jackson himself
asserted that he, as President, would not be bound to hold a national bank to be
constitutional, even though the court had decided it to be so. He fell in precisely with the view of Mr. Jefferson, and acted upon it under his official oath,
in vetoing a charter for a national bank. The declaration that Congress does not
possess this constitutional power to charter a bank, has gone into the Democratic platforms, at their national conventions, and was brought forward and reaffirmed in their last convention at Cincinnati. They have contended for that
declaration, in the very teeth of the Supreme Court, for more than a quarter of
a century. In fact, they have reduced the decision to an absolute nullity. That
decision, I repeat, is repudiated in the Cincinnati platform; and still, as if to show
that effrontery can go no farther, Judge Douglas vaunts in the very speeches in
which he denounces me for opposing the Dred Scott decision, that he stands
on the Cincinnati platform.

Now, I wish to know what the Judge can charge upon me, with respect to
decisions of the Supreme Court which does not lie in all its length, breadth, and
proportions at his own door. The plain truth is simply this: Judge Douglas is *for*
Supreme Court decisions when he likes them, and against them when he does
not like them. He is for the Dred Scott decision because it tends to nationalize
slavery—because it is part of the original combination for that object. It so happens singularly enough, that I never stood opposed to a decision of the Supreme
Court till this. On the contrary, I have no recollection that he was ever particularly in favor of one till this. He never was in favor of any, nor I opposed to
any, till the present one, which helps to nationalize slavery.

Free men of Sangamon, free men of Illinois—free men everywhere—judge ye between him and me, upon this issue.

He says this Dred Scott case is a very small matter at most—that it has no practical effect; that at best, or rather, I suppose, at worst, it is but an abstraction. I submit that the proposition that the thing which determines whether a man is free or a slave, is rather *concrete* than *abstract*. I think you would conclude that it was, if your liberty depended upon it, and so would Judge Douglas if his liberty depended upon it. But suppose it was on the question of slavery over the new Territories that he considers it as being merely an abstract matter, and one of no practical importance. How has the planting of slavery in new countries always been effected? It has now been decided that slavery cannot be kept out of our new Territories by any legal means. In what do our new Territories now differ in this respect, from the old Colonies when slavery was first planted within them? It was planted, as Mr. Clay once declared, and as history proves true, by industrious men in spite of the wishes of the people; the mother government refusing to prohibit it, and withholding from the people of the Colonies the authority to prohibit it for themselves. Mr. Clay says this was one of the great and just causes of complaint, against Great Britain by the Colonies, and the best apology we can now make for having the institution amongst us. In that precise condition, our Nebraska politicians have at last succeeded in placing our own new Territories: the government will not prohibit slavery within them, nor allow the people to prohibit it.—

I defy any man to find any difference between the policy which originally planted slavery in these Colonies and that policy which now prevails in our new Territories. If it does not go into them, it is only because no individual wishes it to go. The Judge indulged himself, doubtless, to-day, with the question as to what I am going to do with or about the Dred Scott decision. Well, Judge, will you please tell me what you did about the Bank decision? Will you not graciously allow us to do with the Dred Scott decision precisely as you did with the Bank decision? You succeeded in breaking down the moral effect of that decision; did you find it necessary to amend the Constitution? or to set up a court of negroes in order to do it?

There is one other point. Judge Douglas has a very affectionate leaning towards the Americans and old Whigs. Last evening, in a sort of weeping tone, he described to us a death-bed scene. He had been called to the side of Mr. Clay, in his last moments, in order that the genius of "popular sovereignty" might duly descend from the dying man and settle upon him, this loving and most worthy successor. He could do no less than promise that he would devote the remainder of his life to "popular sovereignty;" and then the great statesman departed in peace. By this part of the "plan of the campaign," the Judge has evidently promised himself, that tears shall be drawn down the cheeks of all old Whigs, as large as half-grown apples.

Mr. Webster, too, was mentioned; but it did not quite come to a death-bed scene, as to him. It would be amusing, if it were not disgusting, to see how quick these compromise-breakers administer on the political effects of their dead adversaries, trumping up claims never before heard of, and dividing the assets among themselves. If I should be found dead to-morrow morning, nothing but my insignificance could prevent a speech being made on my authority, before the end of next week. It so happens that in that "popular sovereignty" with which Mr. Clay was identified, the Missouri Compromise was expressly reserved; and it was a little singular if Mr. Clay cast his mantle upon Judge Douglas on purpose to have that compromise repealed.

Again, the Judge did not keep faith with Mr. Clay when he first brought in his Nebraska bill. He left the Missouri Compromise unrepealed, and in his report accompanying the bill, he told the world he did it on purpose. The manes of Mr. Clay must have been in great agony, till thirty days later, when "popular sovereignty" stood forth in all its glory.

One more thing. Last night Judge Douglas tormented himself with horrors about my disposition to make negroes perfectly equal with white men in social and political relations. He did not stop to show that I have said any such things, or that they legitimately follow from anything I have said, but he rushes on with his assertions. I adhere to the Declaration of Independence. If Judge Douglas and his friends are not willing to stand by it, let them come up and amend it. Let them make it read that all men are created equal, except negroes. Let us have it decided, whether the Declaration of Independence, in this blessed year of 1858, shall be thus amended. In his construction of the Declaration last year, he said it only meant that Americans in America, were equal to Englishmen in England. Then, when I pointed out to him that by that rule, he excludes the Germans, the Irish, the Portuguese, and all the other people who have come amongst us since the Revolution, he reconstructs his construction. In his last speech he tells us it meant Europeans.

I press him a little further, and ask if it meant to include the Russians in Asia? or does he mean to exclude that vast population from the principles of our Declaration of Independence? I expect ere long, he will introduce another amendment to his definition. He is not at all particular. He is satisfied with anything which does not endanger the nationalizing of negro slavery. It may draw white men down, but it must not lift negroes up. Who shall say, "I am the superior, and you are the inferior?"

My declarations upon this subject of negro slavery may be misrepresented, but cannot be misunderstood. I have said I do not understand the Declaration to mean that all men were created equal in all respects. They are not our equal in color; but I suppose that it does mean to declare that all men are equal in some respects; they are equal in their right to "life, liberty and the pursuit of happiness." Certainly the negro is not our equal in color—perhaps not in many other respects; still, in the right to put into his mouth the bread that his own hands have earned, he is the equal of every other man, white or black. In pointing out that more has been given you, you can not be justified in taking away the little which has been given him. All I ask for the negro is that if you do not like him, let him alone. If God gave him but little, that little let him enjoy.

When our government was established, we had the institution of slavery among us. We were in a certain sense compelled to tolerate its existence. It was a sort of necessity. We had gone through our struggle and secured our own independence. The framers of the Constitution found the institution of slavery amongst their other institutions at the time. They found that by an effort to eradicate it, they might lose much of what they had already gained. They were obliged to bow to the necessity. They gave power to Congress to abolish the slave trade at the end of twenty years. They also prohibited it in the Territories where it did not exist. They did what they could and yielded to necessity for the rest. I also yield to all which follows from that necessity. What I would most desire would be the separation of the white and black races.

One more point in this Springfield speech which Judge Douglas says he has read so carefully. I had expressed my belief in the existence of a conspiracy to perpetuate and nationalize slavery. I did not profess to know it, nor do I now. I showed the part Judge Douglas had played in the string of facts, constituting to my mind, the proof of that conspiracy. I showed the parts played by others.

I charged that the people had been deceived into carrying the last Presidential election, by the impression that the people of the Territories might exclude slavery if they chose, when it was known in advance by the conspirators, that the court was to decide that neither Congress nor the people could so exclude slavery. These charges are more distinctly made than anything else in the speech.

Judge Douglas has carefully read and re-read that speech. He has not, so far as I know, contradicted those charges. In the two speeches which I heard, he certainly did not. On his own tacit admission I renew that charge. I charge him with having been a party to that conspiracy and to that deception for the sole purpose of nationalizing slavery.

FRAGMENT: ON SLAVERY
[AUGUST 1, 1858?]

Lincoln's terse, yet profound definition of democracy was an expression of the golden rule in Matthew 7:12: *"So always treat others as you would like them to treat you; that is the Law and the Prophets." Lincoln's political philosophy combined the biblical teaching of the golden rule with the republican teaching of consent. Democracy implied a rudimentary sense of justice and fairness to others. It was possible only to the extent that citizens recognized each other's equal dignity as human beings and therefore renounced any claims to mastery over others. Based upon a biblical view of human nature that recognized both the dignity of man created in the image of God (Genesis 1:27) and the depravity of his fallen nature, Lincoln consistently maintained no human being was good enough to govern another without that other's consent.*

As I WOULD NOT BE a *slave*, so I would not be a *master*. This expresses my idea of democracy. Whatever differs from this, to the extent of the difference, is not democracy.

   A. Lincoln—

III.

The Lincoln-Douglas Debates

1858

A FTER REPLYING TO DOUGLAS at Chicago, Bloomington, and Springfield in the summer of 1858, Lincoln challenged the "Little Giant" to
a series of formal debates, vying for the Illinois seat in the United States
Senate. In 1855, Lincoln had run for the other U.S. Senate seat from Illinois,
but had lost. Douglas, who did not have as much to gain from the challenge as
an incumbent, was obliged to accept Lincoln's challenge, lest he appear cowardly. Shortly after Douglas agreed to the debates, he confessed, "I shall have
my hands full . . . he [Lincoln] is as honest as he is shrewd; and if I beat him, my
victory will be hardly won." With the exception of the two districts where they
had already spoken, Lincoln and Douglas agreed to debate within a town from
each of the seven remaining congressional districts of Illinois. There would be
a total of seven formal debates in the corresponding towns of Ottawa on August
21, Freeport on August 27, Jonesboro (or Egypt as it was called) on September
15, Charleston on September 18, Galesburg on October 7, Quincy on October
13, and Alton on October 15. The northern districts tended to be Republican,
the southern districts Democratic. The format of the debates included an opening speech, an hour-and-a-half rebuttal, concluding with a half-hour rejoinder.
The candidates alternated opening speeches; Douglas, as incumbent, began the
first and last debate. Each candidate brought along his own reporter to transcribe
the speeches accurately. Although the official debates occurred in the respective towns for which they are named, the candidates stumped tirelessly and
spoke informally on numerous other occasions in nearby towns every day for
two months.

As a New York newspaper reported, the Great Debates set the Illinois prairie
on fire. To be sure, the campaign also provided a popular form of entertainment
for Westerners. It was a festival of the democratic spirit, a carnival for the common man complete with pomp, parade, and spectacle. Douglas rode on a train
with a mounted canon that sounded his arrival from town to town. Bands trum-
peted, guns thundered, taverns overflowed, streets flooded, and barbecues smol-
dered as crowds thronged to hear the speakers. The physical contrast between
the candidates must have been striking. At five feet Douglas was short, compact
and burly; at six-foot-four, Lincoln was long, lean, and lanky. Douglas had a
booming baritone voice, which was often melodious but became coarse and
gruff by the end of the debates. Lincoln, contrary to most stereotypes of him,

had a high-pitched, shrill tenor voice, which projected long distances, but would crack when he became impassioned. Vocal projection was certainly an asset in an era in which candidates without amplification addressed huge outdoor gatherings. At Ottawa, for example, there was an estimated ten thousand people in attendance; at Freeport, an estimated fifteen thousand. During the debates, Douglas was said to have worn a "wrathful frown," defiantly shaking his hands, stamping his feet, and clenching his fists. The lanky Lincoln, with his great height and long frame, would bend his knees, crouch down, and then burst upward, gesticulating to emphasize a point.

The Lincoln-Douglas Debates provided two Union-saving alternatives to resolving the slavery crisis. Both candidates attempted to gather a broad coalition by rejecting the extreme disunionist views of the northern abolitionists and southern fire-eaters. The debates focused almost entirely on slavery, testifying to the fact that it was indeed the *causa sine qua non (cause without which)* of the Civil War. In considering the dominance of the slavery issue in 1858, it is instructive to consider what the candidates did not discuss. During the debates little to no mention was made of the tariff, foreign policy, immigration, and the bank, hitherto traditional issues of contention between the two parties. Indeed, one cannot read the historical documents of the Civil War era without acknowledging the centrality of slavery as an "apple of discord" as Lincoln referred to it.

The debates constituted a struggle to form public opinion, which began to crystallize into two irreconcilable camps, consisting of those who were committed to the containment and eventual extinction of slavery and those who were committed to its extension and indefinite perpetuation. Although Douglas won the senatorial election, he lost in the court of national public opinion. As will be discussed, during the debates, Lincoln trapped Douglas in a dilemma that further alienated him from the southern wing of the Democratic Party leading to an eventual split at the convention during the election of 1860.

Most profoundly, however, the Lincoln-Douglas Debates are of enduring significance in providing two rival interpretations of American political order. They raised fundamental questions about the meaning and destiny of democracy in general, and the American experiment more specifically. Indeed, Douglas and Lincoln defined two radically opposed versions of the Union, which vied against each other for public authoritativeness. The Union, liberty, and the American dream represented something different for each candidate. Both sides invoked the Founders, the Constitution, and the Declaration in support of their views, but reached different conclusions about each.

In Lincoln's view, republican government was ruled and measured by a pre-existing moral standard. The will of the majority was not necessarily just, but bound to and limited by the moral imperatives of the Declaration of Independence. These imperatives or laws derived from an ultimate authority, the "laws of nature and nature's God," and constituted part of an external moral order that was rationally discernible. Because rights came from the hand of the Creator, they were not relative to human convention. Such rationally discernible laws and rights provided a normative standard to guide public life by commanding what must be done and prohibiting what must be forbidden. Lincoln envisioned an inclusive Union, which promised equality to African-Americans. Because the principles of the Declaration applied universally to all human beings, African-Americans were included in its equality clause. At the very least, equality promised them the right to enjoy the fruits of their own labor.

Douglas, on the other hand, envisioned a Union unbounded by moral absolutes. He saw an expanding American empire that would be based upon white supremacy. Douglas, argued, that the Founders never intended for African-Americans and other "inferior races" to be included in the Declaration: "I believe this government was made on the white basis. I believe it was made by white men, for the benefit of white men and their posterity for ever, and I am in favor of confining citizenship to white men, men of European birth and descent, instead of conferring it upon negroes, Indians and other inferior races."

Douglas attributed the agitation over slavery to people like Lincoln and the abolitionists who injected their moral and religious views into the public realm. His solution for resolving the vexing problem of slavery, and placing the country back on track with the more important task of nation-building, was popular sovereignty: the federal government should entertain moral neutrality regarding slavery, leaving territorial settlers the freedom of choice to decide the issue for themselves. Contrary to Lincoln's view of law and morality, Douglas's policy of popular sovereignty was based upon ethical relativism—the belief that nothing is inherently good or evil, but relative to the tastes, preferences, and will of the people at a given time. In addition, popular sovereignty constituted a nineteenth-century version of legal positivism—the belief that justice is relative to the command of those in power. Douglas maintained that the decision of territorial settlers to choose or reject slavery was morally indistinguishable from their decision to plant corn or tobacco. As long as the process was fair, its moral outcomes were necessarily just, no matter how repugnant they seemed.

In effect, Douglas's vision of democracy placed no moral boundaries on the will of the majority, which was absolute so long as the proper legal procedures

were followed. He regarded the appeal to any moral and religious standard outside of the legal process itself as illegitimate and meaningless. In fact, such appeals
were anarchic. To question the outcome of the democratic process in the name
of some higher moral standard, as Lincoln did by invoking the Declaration, was
subversive of political order. In response, Lincoln argued that people did not
have a right to do wrong. True liberty, as distinguished from license, was
defined by moral boundaries.

Lincoln characterized slavery as the very antithesis of republican government.
It undermined America's moral credibility in the eyes of the world and corrupted
its habits. Popular sovereignty, or squatter sovereignty, as he derisively referred
to it, subverted the very moral foundations of the regime by teaching the public
to "care nothing" about such a pernicious evil. The Founders framed the Declaration of Independence as a moral compass and a stumbling block to those who
would try and steer the nation toward the paths of despotism. The principles of
the American regime, according to Lincoln, did not entitle people to enslave others; on the contrary, they mandated slavery's ultimate extinction. Paradoxically,
Douglas's conception of liberty meant the freedom to enslave others. As Lincoln
reminded him, Douglas's popular sovereignty amounted to tyranny of the white
majority over the black minority. Moreover, popular sovereignty's moral indifference to the vast evil of slavery debauched public opinion and prepared the
nation for the indefinite perpetuation and nationalization of the institution: "In
this and like communities, public sentiment is everything. With public sentiment,
nothing can fail; without it nothing can succeed. Consequently he who molds
public sentiment goes deeper than he who enacts statutes or pronounces decisions. He makes statutes and decisions possible or impossible to be executed."
According to Lincoln, public policy and opinion were reciprocal. Public opinion was debauched through the corrupt teaching that people should not really
care about slavery. In turn, this led to corrupt public policies that entrenched the
institution. Throughout his struggle against slavery, Lincoln emphasized that the
American public mind had to reach a moral consensus regarding the inherent
moral evil of slavery before the issue could be firmly resolved. His task as a statesman was to guide public opinion toward this end.

Douglas defended popular sovereignty as an expression of American pluralism and diversity. Why couldn't the house remain divided, asked Douglas? The
division between slave and free states was part of America's diversity, not a
source of discord, as Lincoln claimed. In Douglas's view, democracy should tolerate a diversity of values, none of which are good or evil per se; but entirely
relative to the subjective tastes and preferences of the people. Lincoln's moral

crusade against slavery turned the strength of diversity into a weakness. Unlike the Founders who prized freedom of choice and pluralism, Lincoln sought to impose a strangulating uniformity upon those who did not accept his moral vision. The best way to resolve political conflict over different values was to grant the territories the right of self-determination, local autonomy to choose for themselves what was expedient and just. One wonders if Douglas's vision of American freedom has prevailed? Today, Douglas's moral relativism has reappeared in the guise of individual autonomy rather than local autonomy.

The debates also focused upon the legal and constitutional issue of whether or not the federal government had the authority to restrict slavery in the territories. Douglas claimed that the Kansas-Nebraska Act of 1854, the Compromise of 1850, and the Dred Scott Decision of 1857 all provided precedents against the federal restriction of slavery in the territories, and in support of popular sovereignty. Slavery, according to Douglas, was a local issue, which should be left to the states and territories. On the contrary, Lincoln responded that slavery was not merely a local issue, but a national issue. Consequently, it could not be left to a small territorial minority to determine its outcome. Slavery affected the entire character and destiny of the republic. Furthermore, Lincoln maintained that the federal government did indeed have legal authority to restrict the spread of the institution. He pointed to Article IV, section 4 of the Constitution. The Northwest Ordinance of 1787; the prohibition of the foreign slave trade after 1808; and the Missouri Compromise of 1820 as compelling precedents justifying federal restriction of the institution.

Douglas's strategy during the debates was to discredit Lincoln as a radical abolitionist fanatic who undermined the rule of law and incited sectional war. To support this claim Douglas repudiated Lincoln's House Divided Speech, challenged his opposition to Dred Scott, characterized the Republican Party as a purely sectional party, and stigmatized him for invoking moral and religious absolutes. Thus, Douglas accused "Lincoln [of] following the example and lead of all the little Abolition orators, who go around and lecture in basements of schools and churches, reads from the Declaration of Independence, that all men were created equal, and then asks how can you deprive a negro of that equality which God and the Declaration of Independence awards to him. He and they maintain that negro equality is guarantied by the laws of God. . . . "

Lincoln's strategy was to push the conspiracy charge against Douglas and to drive a wedge between the Little Giant and the Buchanan administration. One cannot appreciate fully Lincoln's intention without understanding the historical context of Douglas's split with Buchanan over Lecompton and the English

Bill. As noted, Douglas opposed the proslavery Lecompton Constitution on pragmatic grounds because the voting process was fraudulent, not because he objected to slavery in principle. Free soil advocates who constituted the majority of the population in Kansas refused to vote. Eager to resolve the conflict in Kansas, President Buchanan supported Lecompton and then offered a face-saving expedient known as the English Bill, which waived the normal population number required for a territory's admission to the Union and offered immediate admission for Kansas, whose population fell far below. Douglas rejected both the English Bill and the Lecompton Constitution.

In view of the Dred Scott Decision, which undermined the principle of popular sovereignty by affirming the right of slaveholders to take their property in the territories, Lincoln attempted to drive a wedge between Douglas and Buchanan southern Democrats. During the second debate at Freeport, Lincoln asked Douglas a "fatal question" that presented a dilemma to the Little Giant: "Can the people of a United States Territory, in any lawful way, against the wish of any citizen of the United States, exclude slavery from its limits prior to the formation of a State Constitution." By agreeing that a territory could exclude slavery, Douglas would have consistently affirmed popular sovereignty, but he would have contradicted the Dred Scott Decision (something he had repudiated Lincoln for), thereby alienating southern Democrats in Illinois. On the other hand, by denying the people's right to exclude slavery, Douglas would have contradicted popular sovereignty, the very principle he purported to champion throughout his public life.

Douglas responded to these questions with what would be known as his "Freeport Doctrine," an attempt to reconcile popular sovereignty with the Dred Scott Decision. The Freeport Doctrine suggested that although the people of a territory could not exclude slavery *de jure* (by right), they could do so, *de facto*, through "unfriendly legislation," which prevented it from taking root. The people of a territory could simply decline to pass laws that would protect and foster slavery. In the absence of such protective laws, argued Douglas, slavery would never become permanently established. Thus, Douglas explained: "It matters not what way the Supreme Court may hereafter decide as to the abstract question whether slavery may or may not go into a territory under the constitution, the people have the lawful means to introduce or exclude it as they please, for the reason that slavery cannot exist a day or an hour anywhere, unless it is supported by local police regulations. Those police regulations can only be established by the local legislature, and if the people are opposed to slavery they will elect representatives to that body who will by unfriendly legislation effectually prevent the introduction of it into their midst."

Douglas also played the "race card" during the debates. He attempted to paint Lincoln as a radical abolitionist referring to him as a "Black Republican" and pandering to the public's racism and Negrophobia. It was within this context that Lincoln made his most controversial remarks about race. During the debate at Charleston, Lincoln replied:

> I am not, nor ever have been in favor of bringing about in any way the social and political equality of the white and black races,—-that I am not nor ever have been in favor of making voters or jurors of negroes, nor of qualifying them to hold office, nor to intermarry with white people; and I will say in addition to this that there is a physical difference between the white and black races which I believe will for ever forbid the two races living together on terms of social and political equality. And inasmuch as they cannot so live, while they do remain together there must be the position of superior and inferior, and I as much as any other man am in favor of having the superior position assigned to the white race. I say upon this occasion I do not perceive that because the white man is to have the superior position the negro should be denied everything. I do not understand that because I do not want a negro woman for a slave I must necessarily want her for a wife. My understanding is that I can just let her alone. I am now in my fiftieth year, and I certainly never have had a black woman for either a slave or a wife. So it seems to me quite possible for us to get along without making either slaves or wives of negroes.

Deconstructionist scholars cite the passage as incontrovertible proof that Lincoln was an unrepentant racist, unscrupulously driven by his own ambition, completely insensitive to the plight of African-Americans. However, a careful reading of Lincoln's speeches and writings reveals an incongruity between the tone and content of this single statement and the abundance of statements he made attacking slavery as inhuman, cruel, immoral, and unjust institution. What accounts for the discrepancy? Was Lincoln a closet racist and white supremacist?

The testimony of Frederick Douglas is helpful in determining the mature Lincoln's view of the African race. Douglas commended Lincoln for "his entire freedom from popular prejudice against the colored race." He even described

Lincoln as "the first great man that I talked with in the United States freely who in no single instance reminded me of the difference between himself and myself, of the difference of color." Testifying to the respect and courtesy Lincoln accorded him, Douglas stated: "Perhaps you would like to know how I, a negro, was received at the White House by the President of the United States. Why, Precisely as one gentleman would be received by another."

What then accounted for Lincoln's discordant statement on race during the debates? True, Lincoln did not believe in 1858 that blacks should receive full social and political equality. In the context of 1858 Illinois politics, no public official standing for a senatorial election could make such a claim without committing political suicide. However, he did believe that slavery was wrong and that the principles of the Declaration applied to African-Americans. The aspiration to apply fairly and consistently these principles was the crux of the argument between himself and Douglas. Lincoln's reply implicitly distinguishes between political rights like suffrage and citizenship and natural rights guaranteed by the Declaration of Independence. Before the Fourteenth Amendment, these political rights were left to the discretion of states. According to Lincoln the states could therefore deny them to African-Americans contingent upon the circumstances of racial adjustment. However, the natural rights of the Declaration were universal and not relative in principle to the discretion of the states. At the very least, the national government could not deny African-Americans their natural, God-given right to enjoy the fruits of their own labor in those areas that it had legal jurisdiction over. Douglas had pressed Lincoln on the issue to undermine his support in the southern districts of Illinois. Douglas was guilty of a non sequitur in arguing that because Lincoln opposed slavery, he necessarily favored full social and political equality for blacks. Lincoln's reply at Charleston must be seen in this context.

As notable scholars like Lawanda Cox, David Herbert Donald, and Harry V. Jaffa have pointed out, Lincoln's remarks at Charleston should be viewed as a political expedient that accommodates the political limits of his audience. Demographically, the Charleston audience was predominately made up of voters who were of southern origin. Donald states: "This was a politically expedient thing to say in a state where the majority of the inhabitants were of Southern origin; perhaps it was a necessary thing to say in a state where only ten years earlier 70 percent of the voters had favored a constitutional amendment to exclude all blacks from Illinois." Lincoln's accommodation to the prejudices of the audience does not mention that they accord with justice. Indeed, Lincoln's statements are equivocal. His use of the subjunctive in the unexpurgated version like

"I suppose," "inasmuch" seriously qualify his statements. They cannot be taken either categorically or unequivocally.

The vote was held on November 2, 1858. Neither Lincoln's nor Douglas's name appeared on the ballot. As was predicted, the northern counties of Illinois voted primarily Republican, whereas the southern counties went Democratic. Although Lincoln won the popular vote, he lost the election. Before the Seventeenth Amendment, senatorial races were determined by the state legislatures. The popular vote was held merely to get an indication of the people's will; it was by no means binding. Because the Republicans failed to gain a majority of seats in the Illinois legislature where the contest would actually be decided, Lincoln lost the election.

However, the debates propelled Lincoln into the national spotlight making him a serious candidate for the Republican Party in the upcoming presidential election of 1860. Douglas won the senatorial seat, but alienated the southern wing of the Democratic Party. Ironically, it was this split in the Democratic Party that cost Douglas the election when he competed against Lincoln once again in the race for the presidency only two years later in 1860.

FIRST JOINT DEBATE, AT OTTAWA[1]
AUGUST 21, 1858.

MR. DOUGLAS'S OPENING SPEECH.

LADIES AND GENTLEMEN: I appear before you to-day for the purpose of discussing the leading political topics which now agitate the public mind. By an arrangement between Mr. Lincoln and myself, we are present here to-day for the purpose of having a joint discussion, as the representatives of the two great political parties of the State and Union, upon the principles in issue between those parties; and this vast concourse of people shows the deep feeling which pervades the public mind in regard to the questions dividing us.

Prior to 1854 this country was divided into two great political parties, known as the Whig and Democratic parties. Both were national and patriotic, advocating principles that were universal in their application. An old line Whig could proclaim his principles in Louisiana and Massachusetts alike. Whig principles had no boundary sectional line—they were not limited by the Ohio river, nor by the Potomac, nor by the line of the free and slave States, but applied and were proclaimed wherever the Constitution ruled or the American flag waved

1. The source for these famous debates is *Political Debates between Hon. Abraham Lincoln and Hon. Stephen A. Douglas.* Columbus, Ohio: Follet, Foster and Company, 1860.

over the American soil. So it was, and so it is with the great Democratic party, which, from the days of Jefferson until this period, has proven itself to be the historic party of this nation. While the Whig and Democratic parties differed in regard to a bank, the tariff, distribution, the specie circular and the sub-treasury, they agreed on the great slavery question which now agitates the Union. I say that the Whig party and the Democratic party agreed on this slavery question, while they differed on those matters of expediency to which I have referred. The Whig party and the Democratic party jointly adopted the Compromise measures of 1850 as the basis of a proper and just solution of this slavery question in all its forms. Clay was the great leader, with Webster on his right and Cass on his left, and sustained by the patriots in the Whig and Democratic ranks, who had devised and enacted the Compromise measures of 1850.

In 1851, the Whig party and the Democratic party united in Illinois in adopting resolutions indorsing and approving the principles of the Compromise measures of 1850, as the proper adjustment of that question. In 1852, when the Whig party assembled in Convention at Baltimore for the purpose of nominating a candidate for the Presidency, the first thing it did was to declare the Compromise measures of 1850, in substance and in principle, a suitable adjustment of that question. [Here the speaker was interrupted by loud and long-continued applause.] My friends, silence will be more acceptable to me in the discussion of these questions than applause. I desire to address myself to your judgment, your understanding, and your consciences, and not to your passions or your enthusiasm. When the Democratic Convention assembled in Baltimore in the same year, for the purpose of nominating a Democratic candidate for the Presidency, it also adopted the Compromise measures of 1850 as the basis of Democratic action. Thus you see that up to 1853-'54, the Whig party and the Democratic party both stood on the same platform with regard to the slavery question. That platform was the right of the people of each State and each Territory to decide their local and domestic institutions for themselves, subject only to the Federal Constitution.

During the session of Congress of 1853-'54, I introduced into the Senate of the United States a bill to organize the Territories of Kansas and Nebraska on that principle which had been adopted in the Compromise measures of 1850, approved by the Whig party and the Democratic party in Illinois in 1851, and indorsed by the Whig party and the Democratic party in National Convention in 1852. In order that there might be no misunderstanding in relation to the principle involved in the Kansas and Nebraska bill, I put forth the true intent and meaning of the act in these words: "It is the true intent and meaning of this act not to legislate slavery into any State or Territory, or to exclude it therefrom, but to leave the people thereof perfectly free to form and regulate their domestic institutions in their own way, subject only to the Federal Constitution." Thus, you see, that up to 1854, when the Kansas and Nebraska bill was brought into Congress for the purpose of carrying out the principles which both parties had up to that time indorsed and approved, there had been no division in this country in regard to that principle except the opposition of the Abolitionists. In the House of Representatives of the Illinois Legislature, upon a resolution asserting that principle, every Whig and every Democrat in the House voted in the affirmative, and only four men voted against it, and those four were old line Abolitionists.

In 1854, Mr. Abraham Lincoln and Mr. Trumbull entered into an arrangement, one with the other, and each with his respective friends, to dissolve the old Whig party on the one hand, and to dissolve the old Democratic party on the other, and to connect the members of both into an Abolition party, under the name and disguise of a Republican party. The terms of that arrangement between Mr. Lincoln and Mr. Trumbull have been published to the world by Mr. Lincoln's special friend, James H. Matheny, Esq., and they were, that Lincoln should have Shields's place in the United States Senate, which was then about to become vacant, and that Trumbull should have my seat when my term expired. Lincoln went to work to Abolitionize the old Whig party all over the State, pretending that he was then as good a Whig as ever; and Trumbull went to work in his part of the State preaching Abolitionism in its milder and lighter form, and trying to Abolitionize the Democratic party, and bring old Democrats handcuffed and bound hand and foot into the Abolition camp. In pursuance of the arrangement, the parties met at Springfield in October, 1854, and proclaimed their new platform. Lincoln was to bring into the Abolition camp the old line Whigs, and transfer them over to Giddings, Chase, Fred. Douglass, and Parson Lovejoy, who were ready to receive them and christen them in their new faith. They laid down on that occasion a platform for their new Republican party, which was to be thus constructed. I have the resolutions of their State Convention ever held, which was the first mass State Convention ever held in Illinois by the Black Republican party, and I now hold them in my hands and will read a part of them, and cause the others to be printed. Here are the most important and material resolutions of this Abolition platform:

1. *Resolved,* That we believe this truth to be self-evident, that when parties become subversive of the ends for which they are established, or incapable of restoring the Government to the true principles of the Constitution, it

is the right and duty of the people to dissolve the political bands by which they may have been connected therewith, and to organize new parties upon such principles and with such views as the circumstances and exigencies of the nation may demand.

2. *Resolved,* That the times imperatively demand the reorganization of parties, and, repudiating all previous party attachments, names and predilections, we unite ourselves together in defense of the liberty and Constitution of the country, and will hereafter cooperate as the Republican party, pledged to the accomplishment of the following purposes: To bring the administration of the Government back to the control of first principles; to restore Nebraska and Kansas to the position of free Territories; that, as the Constitution of the United States vests in the States, and not in Congress, the power to legislate for the extradition of fugitives from labor, to repeal and entirely abrogate the Fugitive Slave law; to restrict slavery to those Status in which it exists; to prohibit the admission of any more slave States into the Union; to abolish slavery in the District of Columbia; to exclude slavery from all the Territories over which the General Government has exclusive jurisdiction; and to resist the acquirements of any more Territories unless the practice of slavery therein forever shall have been prohibited.

3. *Resolved,* That in furtherance of these principles we will use such Constitutional and lawful means as shall seem best adapted to their accomplishment, and that we will support no man for office, under the General or State Government, who is not positively and fully committed to the support of these principles, and whose personal character and conduct is not a guaranty that he is reliable, and who shall not have abjured old party allegiance and ties.

Now, gentlemen, your Black Republicans have cheered every one of those propositions, and yet I venture to say that you cannot get Mr. Lincoln to come out and say that he is now in favor of each one of them. That these propositions, one and all, constitute the platform of the Black Republican party of this day, I have no doubt; and when you were not aware for what purpose I was reading them, your Black Republicans cheered them as good Black Republican doctrines. My object in reading these resolutions, was to put the question to Abraham Lincoln this day, whether he now stands and will stand by each article in that creed, and carry it out. I desire to know whether Mr. Lincoln to-day stands as he did in 1854, in favor of the unconditional repeal of the Fugitive Slave law. I desire him to answer whether he stands pledged to-day, as he did in 1854, against the admission of any more slave States into the Union, even if the people want them. I want to know whether he stands pledged against the admission of a new State into the Union with such a Constitution as the people of that State may see fit to make. I want to know whether he stands to-day pledged to the abolition of slavery in the District of Columbia. I desire him to answer whether he stands pledged to the prohibition of the slave trade between the different States. I desire to know whether he stands pledged to prohibit slavery in all the Territories of the United States, North as well as South of the Missouri Compromise line. I desire him to answer whether he is opposed to the acquisition of any more territory unless slavery is prohibited therein. I want his answer to these questions. Your affirmative cheers in favor of this Abolition platform is not satisfactory. I ask Abraham Lincoln to answer these questions, in order that, when I trot him down to lower Egypt, I may put the same questions to him. My principles are the same everywhere. I can proclaim them alike in the North, the South, the East, and the West. My principles will apply wherever the Constitution prevails and the American flag waves. I desire to know whether Mr. Lincoln's principles will bear transplanting from Ottawa to Jonesboro? I put these questions to him to-day distinctly, and ask an answer. I have a right to an answer, for I quote from the platform of the Republican party, made by himself and others at the time that party was formed, and the bargain made by Lincoln to dissolve and kill the old Whig party, and transfer its members, bound hand and foot, to the Abolition party, under the direction of Giddings and Fred Douglass. In the remarks I have made on this platform, and the position of Mr. Lincoln upon it, I mean nothing personally disrespectful or unkind to that gentleman. I have known him for nearly twenty-five years. There were many points of sympathy between us when we first got acquainted. We were both comparatively boys, and both struggling with poverty in a strange land. I was a school-teacher in the town of Winchester, and he a flourishing grocery-keeper in the town of Salem. He was more successful in his occupation than I was in mine, and hence more fortunate in this world's goods. Lincoln is one of those peculiar men who perform with admirable skill everything which they undertake. I made as good a school-teacher as I could, and when a cabinet maker I made a good bedstead and tables, although my old boss said I succeeded better with bureaus and secretaries than with anything else; but I believe that Lincoln was always more successful in business than I, for his business enabled him to get into the Legislature. I met him there, however, and had a sympathy with him, because of the up-hill struggle we both had in life. He was then just as good at telling an anecdote as now. He could beat any of the boys wrestling, or running a foot-race, in pitching quoits or tossing a copper; could ruin more liquor than all the boys of the town together, and the dignity and impartiality with which he presided at a horserace or fist-fight, excited the admiration and won the praise of everybody that was present and participated. I sympathised with him, because he was struggling with difficulties, and so was I. Mr. Lincoln served with me in the Legislature in 1836, when we both retired, and he subsided, or became submerged, and he was lost sight of as a public man for some years. In 1846, when Wilmot introduced his celebrated proviso, and the Abolition tornado swept over the country, Lincoln again turned up as a member of Congress from the Sangamon district. I was then in the Senate of the United States, and was glad to welcome my old friend and companion. Whilst in Congress, he distinguished himself by his opposition to the Mexican war, taking the side of the common enemy against his own country; and when he returned home he found that the indignation of the people followed him everywhere, and he was again submerged or obliged to retire into private life, forgotten by his former friends. He came up again in 1854, just in time to make this Abolition or Black Republican platform, in company with Giddings, Love-joy, Chase and Fred Douglass, for the Republican party to stand upon. Trum-bull, too, was one of our own cotemporaries. He was born and raised in old Connecticut, was bred a Federalist, but removing to Georgia, turned Nullifier, when nullification was popular, and as soon as he disposed of his clocks and wound up his business, migrated to Illinois, turned politician and lawyer here, and made his appearance in 1841, as a member of the Legislature. He became noted as the author of the scheme to repudiate a large portion of the State debt of Illinois, which, if successful, would have brought infamy and disgrace upon the fair escuteheon of our glorious State. The odium attached to that measure consigned him to oblivion for a time. I helped to do it. I walked into a public meeting in the hall of the House of Representatives, and replied to his repudi-ating speeches, and resolutions were carried over his head denouncing repudi-ation, and asserting the moral and legal obligation of Illinois to pay every dollar of the debt she owed and every bond that bore her seal. Trumbull's malignity has followed me since I thus defeated his infamous scheme.

These two men having formed this combination to abolitionize the old Whig party and the old Democratic party, and put themselves into the Senate of the United States, in pursuance of their bargain, are now carrying out that arrangement. Matheny states that Trumbull broke faith; that the bargain was that Lincoln should be the Senator in Shields's place, and Trumbull was to wait for mine; and the story goes, that Trumbull cheated Lincoln, having control of four or five abolitionized Democrats who were holding over in the Senate; he would not let them vote for Lincoln, and which obliged the rest of the Abolitionists to support him in order to secure an Abolition Senator. There are a number of authorities for the truth of this besides Matheny, and I suppose that even Mr. Lincoln will not deny it.

Mr. Lincoln demands that he shall have the place intended for Trumbull, as Trumball cheated him and got his, and Trumbull is stumping the State traducing me for the purpose of securing the position for Lincoln, in order to quiet him. It was in consequence of this arrangement that the Republican Convention was empaneled to instruct for Lincoln and nobody else, and it was on this account that they passed resolutions that he was their first, their last, and their only choice. Archy Williams was nowhere, Browning was nobody, Wentworth was not to be considered; they had no man in the Republican party for the place except Lincoln, for the reason that he demanded that they should carry out the arrangement.

Having formed this new party for the benefit of deserters from Whiggery, and deserters from Democracy, and having laid down the Abolition platform which I have read, Lincoln now takes his stand and proclaims his Abolition doctrines. Let me read a part of them. In his speech at Springfield to the Convention, which nominated him for the Senate, he said:

> "In my opinion it will not cease until a crisis shall have been reached and passed. 'A house divided against itself cannot stand.' I believe this government *cannot endure permanently half Slave and half Free.* I do not expect the Union to be dissolved—I do not expect the house to fall—*but I do expect it will cease to be divided.* It will become all one thing, or all the other. Either the opponents of slavery *will arrest the further spread of it,* and place it where the public mind shall rest in the belief *that it is in the course of ultimate extinction:* or its advocates *will push it forward till it shall become alike lawful in all the States*—old as well as new, North as well as South."

["Good," "good," and cheers.]

I am delighted to hear you Black Republicans say "good." I have no doubt that doctrine expresses your sentiments, and I will prove to you now, if you will listen to me, that it is revolutionary and destructive of the existence of this Government. Mr. Lincoln, in the extract from which I have read, says that this Government cannot endure permanently in the same condition in which it was made by its framers—divided into free and slave States. He says that it has existed for about seventy years thus divided, and yet he tells you that it cannot endure permanently on the same principles and in the same relative condition in which our fathers made it. Why can it not exist divided into free and slave States? Washington, Jefferson, Franklin, Madison, Hamilton, Jay, and the great men of that day, made this Government divided into free States and slave States, and left each State perfectly free to do as it pleased on the subject of slavery. Why can it not exist on the same principles on which our fathers made it? They knew when they framed the Constitution that in a country as wide and broad as this, with such a variety of climate, production and interest, the people necessarily required different laws and institutions in different localities. They knew that the laws and regulations which would suit the granite hills of New Hampshire would be unsuited to the rice plantations of South Carolina, and they, therefore, provided that each State should retain its own Legislature and its own sovereignty, with the full and complete power to do as it pleased within its own limits, in all that was local and not national. One of the reserved rights of the States, was the right to regulate the relations between Master and Servant, on the slavery question. At the time the Constitution was framed, there were thirteen States in the Union, twelve of which were slaveholding States and one a free State. Suppose this doctrine of uniformity preached by Mr. Lincoln, that the States should all be free or all be slave had prevailed, and what would have been the result? Of course, the twelve slaveholding States would have overruled the one free State, and slavery would have been fastened by a Constitutional provision on every inch of the American Republic, instead of being left as our fathers wisely left it, to each State to decide for itself. Here I assert that uniformity in the local laws and institutions of the different States is neither possible or desirable. If uniformity had been adopted when the Government was established, it must inevitably have been the uniformity of slavery everywhere, or else the uniformity of negro citizenship and negro equality everywhere.

We are told by Lincoln that he is utterly opposed to the Dred Scott decision, and will not submit to it, for the reason that he says it deprives the negro of the rights and privileges of citizenship. That is the first and main reason which he assigns for his warfare on the Supreme Court of the United States and its decision. I ask you, are you in favor of conferring upon the negro the rights and privileges of citizenship? Do you desire to strike out of our State Constitution that clause which keeps slaves and free negroes out of the State, and allow the free negroes to flow in, and cover your prairies with black settlements? Do you desire to turn this beautiful State into a free negro colony, in order that when Missouri abolishes slavery she can send one hundred thousand emancipated slaves into Illinois, to become citizens and voters, on an equality with your-selves? If you desire negro citizenship, if you desire to allow them to come into the State and settle with the white man, if you desire them to vote on an equal-ity with yourselves, and-to make them eligible to office, to serve on juries, and to adjudge your rights, then support. Mr. Lincoln and the Black Republican party, who are in favor of the citizenship of the negro. For one, I am opposed to negro citizenship in any and every form. I believe this Government was made on the white basis. I believe it was made by white men, for the benefit of white men and their posterity for ever, and I am in favor of confining citizenship to white men, men of European birth and descent, instead of conferring it upon negroes, Indians, and other inferior races.

Mr. Lincoln, following the example and lead of all the little Abolition ora-tors, who go around and lecture in the basements of schools and churches, reads from the Declaration of Independence, that all men were created equal, and then asks, how can you deprive a negro of that equality which God and the Declara-tion of Independence awards to him? He and they maintain that negro equality is guarantied by the laws of God, and that it is asserted in the Declaration of Inde-pendence. If they think so, of course they have a right to say so, and so vote. I do not question Mr. Lincoln's conscientious belief that the negro was made his equal, and hence is his brother; but for my own part, I do not regard the negro as my equal, and positively deny that he is my brother or any kin to me what-ever. Lincoln has evidently learned by heart Parson Lovejoy's catechism. He can repeat it as well as Farnsworth, and be is worthy of a medal from Father Gid-dings and Fred Douglass for his Abolitionism. He holds that the negro was born his equal and yours, and that he was endowed with equality by the Almighty, and that no human law can deprive him of these rights which were guarantied to him by the Supreme ruler of the Universe. Now, I do not believe that the Almighty ever intended the negro to be the equal of the white man. If he did, he has been a long time demonstrating the fact. For thousands of years the negro has been a race upon the earth, and during all that time, in all latitudes and cli-mates, wherever he has wandered or been taken, he has been inferior to the race which he has there met. He belongs to an inferior race, and must always occupy an inferior position. I do not hold that because the negro is our inferior that therefore he ought to be a slave. By no means can such a conclusion be drawn from what I have said. On the contrary, I hold that humanity and Christianity both require that the negro shall have and enjoy every right, every privilege, and every immunity consistent with the safety of the society in which he lives. On that point, I presume, there can be no diversity of opinion. You and I are bound to extend to our inferior and dependent beings every right, every privilege, every facility and immunity consistent with the public good. The question then arises, what rights and privileges are consistent with the public good? This is a question which each State and each Territory must decide for itself—Illinois has decided it for herself. We have provided that the negro shall not be a slave, and we have also provided that he shall not be a citizen, but protect him in his civil rights, in his life, his person and his property, only depriving him of all political rights whatsoever, and refusing to put him on an equality with the white man. That policy of Illinois is satisfactory to the Democratic party and to me, and if it were to the Republicans, there would then be no question upon the subject; but the Republicans say that he ought to be made a citizen, and when he becomes a citizen he becomes your equal, with all your rights and privileges. They assert the Dred Scott decision to be monstrous because it denies that the negro is or can be a citizen under the Constitution. Now, I hold that Illinois had a right to abolish and prohibit slavery as she did, and I hold that Kentucky has the same right to continue and protect slavery that Illinois had to abolish it. I hold that New York had as much right to abolish slavery as Virginia has to continue it, and that each and every State of this Union is a sovereign power, with the right to do as it pleases upon this question of slavery, and upon all its domestic institutions. Slavery is not the only question which comes up in this controversy. There is a far more important one to you, and that is, what shall be done with the free negro? We have settled the slavery question as far as we are concerned; we have prohibited it in Illinois forever, and in doing so, I think we have done wisely, and there is no man in the State who would be more strenuous in his opposition to the introduction of slavery than I would; but when we settled it for ourselves, we exhausted all our power over that subject. We have done our whole duty, and can do no more. We must leave each and every other State to decide for itself the same question. In relation to the policy to be pursued toward the free negroes, we have said that they shall not vote; whilst Maine, on the other hand, has said that they shall vote. Maine is a sovereign State, and has the power to regulate the qualifications of voters within her limits. I would never consent to confer the right of voting and of citizenship upon a negro, but still I am not going to quarrel with Maine for differing from me in opinion. Let Maine take care of her own negroes and fix the qualifications of her own voters to suit herself, without interfering with Illinois, and Illinois will not interfere with Maine. So with the State of New York. She allows the negro to vote provided he owns two hundred and fifty dollars' worth of property, but not otherwise. While I would not make any distinction whatever between a negro who held property and one who did not, yet if the sovereign State of New York chooses to make that distinction it is her business and not mine, and I will not quarrel with her for it. She can do as she pleases on this question if she minds her own business, and we will do the same thing. Now, my friends, if we will only act conscientiously and rigidly upon this great principle of popular sovereignty, which guaranties to each State and Territory the right to do as it pleases on all things, local and domestic, instead of Congress interfering, we will continue at peace one with another. Why should Illinois be at war with Missouri, or Kentucky with Ohio, or Virginia with New York, merely because their institutions differ? Our fathers intended that our institutions should differ. They knew that the North and the South, having different climates, productions and interests, required different institutions. This doctrine of Mr. Lincoln, of uniformity among the institutions of the different States, is a new doctrine, never dreamed of by Washington, Madison, or the framers of this Government. Mr. Lincoln and the Republican party set themselves up as wiser than these men who made this Government, which has flourished for seventy years under the principle of popular sovereignty, recognizing the right of each State to do as it pleased. Under that principle, we have grown from a nation of three or four millions to a nation of about thirty millions of people; we have crossed the Allegheny mountains and filled up the whole North-west, turning the prairie into a garden, and building up churches and schools, thus spreading civilization and Christianity where before there was nothing but savage barbarism. Under that principle we have become, from a feeble nation, the most powerful on the face of the earth, and if we only adhere to that principle, we can go forward increasing in territory, in power, in strength and in glory until the Republic of America shall be the North Star that shall guide the friends of freedom throughout the civilized world. And why can we not adhere to the great principle of self-government, upon which our institutions were originally based? I believe that this new doctrine preached by Mr. Lincoln and his party will dissolve the Union if it succeeds. They are trying to array all the Northern States in one body against the South, to excite a sectional war between the free States and the slave States, in order that the one or the other may be driven to the wall.

I am told that my time is out. Mr. Lincoln will now address you for an hour and a half, and I will then occupy an half hour in replying to him.

MR. LINCOLN'S REPLY.

MY FELLOW-CITIZENS: When a man hears himself somewhat misrepresented, it provokes him—at least, I find it so with myself; but when misrepresentation

becomes very gross and palpable, it is more apt to amuse him. The first thing I
see fit to notice, is the fact that Judge Douglas alleges, after running through the
history of the old Democratic and the old Whig parties, that Judge Trumbull and
myself made an arrangement in 1854, by which I was to have the place of Gen.
Shields in the United States Senate, and Judge Trumbull was to have the place
of Judge Douglas. Now, all I have to say upon that subject is, that I think no
man—not even Judge Douglas—can prove it, *because it is not true*. I have no
doubt he is *"conscientious"* in saying it. As to those resolutions that he took such
a length of time to read, as being the platform of the Republican party in 1854,
I say I never had anything to do with them, and I think Trumbull never had.
Judge Douglas cannot show that either of us ever did have anything to do with
them. I believe *this* is true about those resolutions: There was a call for a Convention to form a Republican party at Springfield, and I think that my friend,
Mr. Lovejoy, who is here upon this stand, had a hand in it. I think this is true,
and I think if he will remember accurately, he will be able to recollect that he
tried to get me into it, and I would not go in. I believe it is also true that I went
away from Springfield when the Convention was in session, to attend court in
Tazewell county. It is true they did place my name, though without authority,
upon the committee, and afterward wrote me to attend the meeting of the committee, but I refused to do so, and I never had anything to do with that organization. This is the plain truth about all that matter of the resolutions.

Now, about this story that Judge Douglas tells of Trumbull bargaining to sell
out the old Democratic party, and Lincoln agreeing to sell out the old Whig
party, I have the means of *knowing* about that; Judge Douglas cannot have; and
I know there is no substance to it whatever. Yet I have no doubt he is *"conscientious"* about it. I know that after Mr. Lovejoy got into the Legislature that winter, he complained of me that I had told all the old Whigs of his district that the
old Whig party was good enough for them, and some of them voted against him
because I told them so. Now, I have no means of totally disproving such charges
as this which the Judge makes. A man cannot prove a negative, but he has a right
to claim that when a man makes an affirmative charge, he must offer some proof
to show the truth of what he says. I certainly cannot introduce testimony to show
the negative about things, but I have a right to claim that if a man says he *knows*
a thing, then he must show *how* he knows it. I always have a right to claim this,
and it is not satisfactory to me that he may be "conscientious" on the subject.

Now, gentlemen, I hate to waste my time on such things, but in regard to that
general Abolition tilt that Judge Douglas makes, when he says that I was engaged
at that time in selling out and abolitionizing the old Whig party—I hope you will

permit me to read a part of a printed speech that I made then at Peoria, which will show altogether a different view of the position I took in that contest of 1854.

Voice—"Put on your specs."

Mr. Lincoln—Yes, sir, I am obliged to do so. I am no longer a young man.

"This is the *repeal* of the Missouri Compromise.* The foregoing history may not be precisely accurate in every particular; but I am sure it is sufficiently so for all the uses I shall attempt to make of it, and in it we have before us, the chief materials enabling us to correctly judge whether the repeal of the Missouri Compromise is right or wrong.

"I think, and shall try to show, that it is wrong; wrong in its direct effect, letting slavery into Kansas and Nebraska—and wrong in its prospective principle, allowing it to spread to every other part of the wide world, where men can be found inclined to take it.

"This *declared* indifference, but, as I must think, covert *real* zeal for the spread of slavery, I cannot but hate. I hate it because of the monstrous injustice of slavery itself. I hate it because it deprives our republican example of its just influence in the world—enables the enemies of free institutions, with plausibility, to taunt us as hypocrites—causes the real friends of freedom to doubt our sincerity, and especially because it forces so many really good men amongst ourselves into an open war with the very fundamental principles of civil liberty—criticising the Declaration of Independence, and insisting that there is no right principle of action but *self-interest*.

"Before proceeding, let me say I think I have no prejudice against the Southern people. They are just what we would be in their situation. If slavery did not now exist among them, they would not introduce it. If it did now exist amongst us, we should not instantly give it up. This I believe of the masses North and South. Doubtless there are individuals on both sides, who would not hold slaves under any circumstances; and others who would gladly introduce slavery anew, if it were out of existence. We know that some Southern men do free their slaves, go North, and become tip-top Abolitionists; while some Northern ones go South, and become most cruel slave-masters.

"When Southern people tell us they are no more responsible for the origin of slavery than we, I acknowledge the fact. When it is said that the

---

*This extract from Mr. Lincoln's Peoria speech of 1854, was read by him in the Ottawa debate, but was not reported fully or accurately in either the *Times* or *Press* and *Tribune*. It is inserted now as necessary to a complete report of the debate [this footnote in the original].

institution exists, and that it is very difficult to get rid of it, in any satisfactory way, I can understand and appreciate the saying. I surely will not
blame them for not doing what I should not know how to do myself. If
all earthly power were given me, I should not know what to do, as to
the existing institution. My first impulse would be to free all the slaves,
and send them to Liberia—to their own native land. But a moment's
reflection would convince me, that whatever of high hope (as I think
there is) there may be in this, in the long run, its sudden execution is
impossible. If they were all landed there in a day, they would all perish
in the next ten days; and there are not surplus shipping and surplus
money enough in the world to carry them there in many times ten days.
What then? Free them all, and keep them among us as underlings? Is it
quite that this betters their condition? I think I would not hold one in
slavery at any rate; yet the point is not clear enough to me to denounce
people upon. What next? Free them, and make them politically and
socially our equals? My own feelings will not admit of this; and if mine
would, we well know that those of the great mass of white people will
not. Whether this feeling accords with justice and sound judgment, is not
the sole question, if, indeed, it is any part of it. A universal feeling,
whether well or ill-founded, cannot be safely disregarded. We cannot,
then, make them equals. It does seem to me that systems of gradual
emancipation might be adopted; but for their tardiness in this, I will not
undertake to judge our brethren of the South.

"When they remind us of their constitutional rights, I acknowledge
them, not grudgingly, but fully and fairly; and I would give them any
legislation for the reclaiming of their fugitives, which should not, in its
stringency, be more likely to carry a free man into slavery, than our ordinary criminal laws are to hang an innocent one.

"But all this, to my judgment, furnishes no more excuse for permitting slavery to go into our own free territory, than it would for reviving the African slave-trade by law. The law which forbids the bringing
of slaves *from* Africa, and that which has so long forbid the taking of
them *to* Nebraska, can hardly be distinguished on any moral principle;
and the repeal of the former could find quite as plausible excuses as that
of the latter."

I have reason to know that Judge Douglas *knows* that I said this. I think he
has the answer here to one of the questions he put to me. I do not mean to allow

him to catechise me unless he pays back for it in kind. I will not answer questions one after another, unless he reciprocates; but as he has made this inquiry, and I have answered it before, he has got it without my getting anything in return. He has got my answer on the Fugitive Slave law.

Now, gentlemen, I don't want to read at any greater length, but this is the true complexion of all I have ever said in regard to the institution of slavery and the black race. This is the whole of it, and anything that argues me into his idea of perfect social and political equality with the negro, is but a specious and fantastic arrangement of words, by which a man can prove a horse-chestnut to be a chestnut horse. I will say here, while upon this subject, that I have no purpose, directly or indirectly, to interfere with the institution of slavery in the States where it exists. I believe I have no lawful right to do so, and I have no inclination to do so. I have no purpose to introduce political and social equality between the white and the black races. There is a physical difference between the two, which, in my judgment, will probably forever forbid their living together upon the footing of perfect equality, and inasmuch as it becomes a necessity that there must be a difference, I, as well as Judge Douglas, am in favor of the race to which I belong having the superior position. I have never said anything to the contrary, but I hold that, notwithstanding all this, there is no reason in the world why the negro is not entitled to all the natural rights enumerated in the Declaration of Independence, the right to life, liberty, and the pursuit of happiness. I hold that he is as much entitled to these as the white man. I agree with Judge Douglas he is not my equal in many respects—certainly not in color, perhaps not in moral or intellectual endowment. But in the right to eat the bread, without the leave of anybody else, which his own hand earns, *he is my equal and the equal of Judge Douglas, and the equal of every living man.*

Now I pass on to consider one or two more of these little follies. The Judge is wofully at fault about his early friend Lincoln being a "grocery-keeper." I don't know as it would be a great sin, if I had been; but he is mistaken. Lincoln never kept a grocery anywhere in the world. It is true that Lincoln did work the latter part of one winter in a little still-house, up at the head of a hollow. And so I think my friend, the Judge, is equally at fault which he charges me at the time when I was in Congress of having opposed our soldiers who were fighting in the Mexican war. The Judge did not make his charge very distinctly, but I can tell you what he can prove, by referring to the record. You remember I was an old Whig, and whenever the Democratic party tried to get me to vote that the war had been righteously begun by the President, I would not do it. But whenever they asked for any money, or land-warrants, or anything to pay the soldiers there, during all that time, I gave the same vote that Judge Douglas did. You can think as you please as to whether that was consistent. Such is the truth; and the Judge has the right to make all he can out of it. But when he, by a general charge, conveys the idea that I withheld supplies from the soldiers who were fighting in the Mexican war, or did anything else to hinder the soldiers, he is, to say the least, grossly and altogether mistaken, as a consultation of the records will prove to him.

As I have not used up so much of my time as I had supposed, I will dwell a little longer upon one or two of these minor topics upon which the Judge has spoken. He has read from my speech in Springfield, in which I say that "a house divided against itself cannot stand." Does the Judge say it *can* stand? I don't know whether he does or not. The Judge does not seem to be attending to me just now, but I would like to know if it is his opinion that a house divided against itself *can stand*. If he does, then there is a question of veracity, not between him and me, but between the Judge and an authority of a somewhat higher character.

Now, my friends, I ask your attention to this matter for the purpose of saying something seriously. I know that the Judge may readily enough agree with me that the maxim which was put forth by the Saviour is true, but he may allege that I misapply it; and the Judge has a right to urge that, in my application, I do misapply it, and then I have a right to show that I do *not* misapply it. When he undertakes to say that because I think this nation, so far as the question of slavery is concerned, will all become one thing or all the other, I am in favor of bringing about a dead uniformity in the various States, in all their institutions, he argues erroneously. The great variety of the local institutions in the States, springing from differences in the soil, differences in the face of the country, and in the climate, are bonds of Union. They do not make "a house divided against itself," but they make a house united. If they produce in one section of the country what is called for by the wants of another section, and this other section can supply the wants of the first, they are not matters of discord but bonds of union, true bonds of union. But can this question of slavery be considered as among *these* varieties in the institutions of the country? I leave it to you to say whether, in the history of our Government, this institution of slavery has not always failed to be a bond of union, and, on the contrary, been an apple of discord, and an element of division in the house. I ask you to consider whether, so long as the moral constitution of men's minds shall continue to be the same, after this generation and assemblage shall sink into the grave, and another race shall arise, with the same moral and intellectual development we have—whether, if that institution is standing in the same irritating position in which it now is, it will not continue an element of division? If so, then I have a right to say that, in regard to this question, the Union is a house divided against itself; and when the Judge reminds me that I have often said to him that the institution of slavery has existed for eighty years in some States, and yet it does not exist in some others, I agree to the fact, and I account for it by looking at the position in which our fathers originally placed it—restricting it from the new Territories where it had not gone, and legislating to cut off its source by the abrogation of the slave-trade, thus putting the seal of legislation *against its spread.* The public mind *did* rest in the belief that it was in the course of ultimate extinction. But lately, I think—and in this I charge nothing on the Judge's motives—lately, I think, that he, and those acting with him, have placed that institution on a new basis, which looks to the *perpetuity and nationalization of slavery.* And while it is placed upon this new basis, I say, and I have said, that I believe we shall not have peace upon the question until the opponents of slavery arrest the further spread of it, and place it where the public mind shall rest in the belief that it is in the course of ultimate extinction; or, on the other hand, that its advocates will push it forward until it shall become alike lawful in all the States, old as well as new, North as well as South. Now, I believe if we could arrest the spread, and place it where Washington, and Jefferson, and Madison placed it, it *would be* in the course of ultimate extinction, and the public mind *would,* as for eighty years past, believe that it was in the course of ultimate extinction. The crisis would be past and the institution might be let alone for a hundred years, if it should live so long, in the States where it exists, yet it would be going out of existence in the way best for both the black and the white races.

A Voice—"Then do you repudiate Popular Sovereignty?"

Mr. Lincoln—Well, then, let us talk about Popular Sovereignty! What is Popular Sovereignty? Is it the right of the people to have slavery or not have it, as they see fit, in the Territories? I will state—and I have an able man to watch me—my understanding is that Popular Sovereignty, as now applied to the question of slavery, does allow the people of a Territory to have slavery if they want to, but does not allow them *not* to have it if they *do not* want it. I do not mean that if this vast concourse of people were in a Territory of the United States, any one of them would be obliged to have a slave if he did not want one; but I do say that, as I understand the Dred Scott decision, if any one man wants slaves, all the rest have no way of keeping that one man from holding them.

When I made my speech at Springfield, of which the Judge complains, and from which he quotes, I really was not thinking of the things which he ascribes to me at all. I had no thought in the world that I was doing anything to bring about a war between the free and slave States. I had no thought in the world that I was doing anything to bring about a political and social equality of the black and white races. It never occurred to me that I was doing anything or favoring anything to reduce to a dead uniformity all the local institutions of the various States. But I must say, in all fairness to him, if he thinks I am doing something which leads to these bad results, it is none the better that I did not mean it. It is just as fatal to the country, if I have any influence in producing it, whether I intend it or not. But can it be true, that placing this institution upon the original basis—the basis upon which our fathers placed it—can have any tendency to set the Northern and the Southern States at war with one another, or that it can have any tendency to make the people of Vermont raise sugarcane, because they raise it in Louisiana, or that it can compel the people of Illinois to cut pine logs on the Grand Prairie, where they will not grow, because they cut pine logs in Maine, where they do grow? The Judge says this is a new principle started in regard to this question. Does the Judge claim that he is working on the plan of the founders of Government? I think he says in some of his speeches—indeed, I have one here now—that he saw evidence of a policy to allow slavery to be south of a certain line, while north of it it should be excluded, and he saw an indisposition on the part of the country to stand upon that policy, and therefore he set about studying the subject upon *original principles,* and upon *original principles* he got up the Nebraska bill! I am fighting it upon these "original principles"—fighting it in the Jeffersonian, Washingtonian, and Madisonian fashion.

Now, my friends, I wish you to attend for a little while to one or two other things in that Springfield speech. My main object was to show, so far as my humble ability was capable of showing to the people of this country, what I believed was the truth—that there was a *tendency,* if not a conspiracy among those who have engineered this slavery question for the last four or five years, to make slavery perpetual and universal in this nation. Having made that speech principally for that object, after arranging the evidences that I thought tended to prove my proposition, I concluded with this bit of comment:

"We cannot absolutely know that these exact adaptations are the result of preconcert, but when we see a lot of framed timbers, different portions of which we know have been gotten out at different times and places, and by different workmen—Stephen, Franklin, Roger and James, for instance—and when we see these timbers joined together, and see they exactly make the frame of a house or a mill, all the tenons and mortices exactly fitting, and all the lengths and proportions of the different pieces exactly adapted to their respective places, and not a piece too many or too few—not omitting even the scaffolding—or if a single piece be lacking, we see the place in the frame exactly fitted and prepared yet to bring such piece in—in such a case we feel it impossible not to believe that Stephen and Franklin, and Roger and James, all understood one another from the beginning, and all worked upon a common plan or draft drawn before the first blow was struck."

When my friend, Judge Douglas, came to Chicago, on the 9th of July, this speech having been delivered on the 16th of June, he made an harangue there, in which he took hold of this speech of mine, showing that he had carefully read it; and while he paid no attention to *this* matter at all, but complimented me as being a "kind, amiable and intelligent gentleman," notwithstanding I had said this, he goes on and eliminates, or draws out, from my speech this tendency of mine to set the States at or with one another, to make all the institutions uniform, and set the niggers and white people to marrying together. Then, as the Judge had complimented me with these pleasant titles (I must confess to my weakness), I was a little "taken," for it me from a great man. I was not very much accustomed to fluttery, and it came a sweeter to me. I was rather like the Hoosier, with the gingerbread, when he said he reckoned he loved it better than any other man, and got less of it. As the Judge had so flattered me, I could not make up my mind that he meant to deal unfairly with me; so I went to work to show him that he misunderstood the whole scope of my speech, and that I really never intended to set the people at war with one another. As an illustration, the next time I met him, which was at Springfield, I used this expression, that I claimed no right under the Constitution, nor had I any delination to enter into the slave States and interfere with the institutions of slavery. He says upon that: Lincoln will not enter into the slave States, but will go to the banks of the Ohio, on this side, and shoot over! He runs on, step by step, in the horse-chestnut style of argument, until in the Springfield speech he says, "Unless he shall be successful in firing his batteries, until he shall have extinguished slavery in all the States, the Union shall be dissolved." Now I don't think that was exactly the way to treat "a kind, amiable, intelligent gentleman." I know if I had asked the Judge to show when or where it was I had said that, if I didn't succeed in firing into the slave States until slavery should be extinguished, the Union should be dissolved, he could not have shown it. I understand what he would do. He would say, "I don't mean to quote from you, but this was the *result* of what you say." But I have the right to ask, and I do ask now, Did you not put it in such a form that an ordinary reader or listener would take it as an expression *from me?*

In a speech at Springfield, on the night of the 17th; I thought I might as well attend to my own business a little, and I recalled his attention as well as I could to this charge of conspiracy to nationalize slavery. I called his attention to the fact that he had acknowledged, in my hearing twice, that he had carefully read the speech, and, in the language of the lawyers, as he had twice read the speech, and still had put in no plea or answer, I took a default on him. I insisted that I had a right then to renew that charge of conspiracy. Ten days afterward I met the Judge at Clinton—that is to say, I was on the ground, but not in the discussion—and heard him make a speech. Then he comes in with his plea to this charge, for the first time, and his plea when put in, as well as I can recollect it, amounted to this: that he never had any talk with Judge Taney or the President of the United States with regard to the Dred Scott decision before it was made. I (Lincoln) ought to know that the man who makes a charge without knowing it to be true, falsifies as much as he who knowingly tells a falsehood; and lastly, that he would pronounce the whole thing a falsehood; but he would make no personal application of the charge of falsehood, not because of any regard for the "kind, amiable, intelligent gentleman," but because of his own personal self-respect! I have understood since then (but [turning to Judge Douglas] will not hold the Judge to it if he is not willing) that he has broken through the "self-respect," and has got to saying the thing *out.* The Judge nods to me that it is so. It is fortunate for me that I can keep as good-humored as I do, when the Judge acknowledges that he has been trying to make a question of veracity with me. I know the Judge is a great man, while I am only a small man, but *I feel that I have got him.* I demur to that plea. I waive all objections that it was not filed till after default was taken, and demur to it upon the merits. What if Judge Douglas never did talk with Chief Justice Taney and the President, before the Dred Scott decision was made, does it follow that he could not have had as perfect an understanding without talking as with it? I am not disposed to stand upon my legal advantage. I am disposed to take his denial as being like an answer in chancery, that he neither had any knowledge, information or belief in the existence of such a conspiracy. I am disposed to take his answer as being as broad as though he had put it in these words. And now, I ask, even if he had done so, have not I a right to *prove it on him,* and to offer the evidence of more than two witnesses, by whom to prove it; and if the evidence proves the existence of the conspiracy, does his broad answer denying all knowledge, information, or belief, disturb the fact? It can only show that he was *used* by conspirators, and was not a *leader* of them.

Now, in regard to his reminding me of the moral rule that persons who tell what they do not know to be true, falsify as much as those who knowingly tell falsehoods. I remember the rule, and it must be borne in mind that in what I have read to you, I do not say that I *know* such a conspiracy to exist. To that I reply, *I believe it*. If the Judge says that I do *not* believe it, then *he* says what *he* does not know, and falls within his own rule, that he who asserts a thing which he does not know to be true, falsifies as much as he who knowingly tells a falsehood. I want to call your attention to a little discussion on that branch of the case, and the evidence which brought my mind to the conclusion which I expressed as my *belief*. If, in arraying that evidence, I had stated anything which was false or erroneous, it needed but that Judge Douglas should point it out, and I would have taken it back with all the kindness in the world. I do not deal in that way. If I have brought forward anything not a fact, if he will point it out, it will not even ruffle me to take it back. But if he will not point out anything erroneous in the evidence, is it not rather for him to show, by a comparison of the evidence, that I have *reasoned* falsely, than to call the "kind, amiable, intelligent gentleman" a liar? If I have reasoned to a false conclusion, it is the vocation of an able debater to show by argument that I have wandered to an erroneous conclusion. I want to ask your attention to a portion of the Nebraska bill, which Judge Douglas has quoted: "It being the true intent and meaning of this act, not to legislate slavery into any Territory or State, nor to exclude it therefrom, but to leave the people thereof perfectly free to form and regulate their domestic institutions in their own way, subject only to the Constitution of the United States." Thereupon Judge Douglas and others began to argue in favor of "Popular Sovereignty"—the right of the people to have slaves if they wanted them, and to exclude slavery if they did not want them. "But," said, in substance, a Senator from Ohio (Mr. Chase, I believe), "we more than suspect that you do not mean to allow the people to exclude slavery if they wish to, and if you do mean it, accept an amendment which I propose expressly authorizing the people to exclude slavery." I believe I have the amendment here before me, which was offered, and under which the people of the Territory, through their proper representatives, might, if they saw fit, prohibit the existence of slavery therein. And now I state it as a *fact,* to be taken back if there is any mistake about it, that Judge Douglas and those acting with him *voted that amendment down.* I now think that those men who voted it down, had a *real reason* for doing so. They know what that reason was. It looks to us, since we have seen the Dred

Scott decision pronounced, holding that, "under the Constitution," the people cannot exclude slavery—I say it looks to outsiders, poor, simple, "amiable, intelligent gentlemen," as though the niche was left as a place to put that Dred Scott decision in—a niche which would have been spoiled by adopting the amendment. And now, I say again, if *this* was not the reason, it will avail the Judge much more to calmly and good-humoredly point out to these people what that *other* reason was for voting the amendment down, than, swelling himself up, to vociferate that he may be provoked to call somebody a liar.

Again: there is in that same quotation from the Nebraska bill this clause— "It being the true intent and meaning of this bill not to legislate slavery into any Territory or *State*." I have always been puzzled to know what business the word "State" had in that connection. Judge Douglas knows. *He put it there.* He knows what he put it there for. We outsiders cannot say what he put it there for. The law they were passing was not about States, and was not making provisions for States. What was it placed there for? After seeing the Dred Scott decision, which holds that the people cannot exclude slavery from a *Territory,* if another Dred Scott decision shall come, holding that they cannot exclude it from a *State,* we shall discover that when the word was originally put there, it was in view of something which was to come in due time, we shall see that it was the *other half* of something. I now say again, if there is any different reason for putting it there, Judge Douglas, in a good humored way, without calling anybody a liar, *can tell what the reason was.*

When the Judge spoke at Clinton, he came very near making a charge of falsehood against me. He used, as I found it printed in a newspaper, which, I remember, was very nearly like the real speech, the following language:

> "I did not answer the charge [of conspiracy] before, for the reason that I did not suppose there was a man in America with a heart so corrupt as to believe such a charge could be true. I have too much respect for Mr. Lincoln to suppose he is serious in making the charge."

I confess this is rather a curious view, that out of respect for me he should consider I was making what I deemed rather a grave charge in fun. I confess it strikes me rather strangely. But I let it pass. As the Judge did not for a moment believe that there was a man in America whose heart was so "corrupt" as to make such a charge, and as he places me among the "men in America" who have hearts base enough to make such a charge, I hope he will excuse me if I hunt out another charge very like this; and if it should turn out that in hunting

I should find that other, and it should turn out to be Judge Douglas himself who made it, I hope he will reconsider this question of the deep corruption of heart he has thought fit to ascribe to me. In Judge Douglas's speech of March 22d, 1858, which I hold in my hand, he says:

"In this connection there is another topic to which I desire to allude. I seldom refer to the course of newspapers, or notice the articles which they publish in regard to myself; but the course of the Washington *Union* has been so extraordinary, for the last two or three months, that I think it well enough to make some allusion to it. It has read me out of the Democratic party every other day, at least for two or three months, and keeps reading me out, and, as if it had not succeeded, still continues to read me out, using such terms as "traitor," "renegade," "deserter," and other kind and polite epithets of that nature. Sir, I have no vindication to make of my Democracy against the Washington *Union,* or any other newspapers. I am willing to allow my history and action for the last twenty years to speak for themselves as to my political principles, and my fidelity to political obligations. The Washington *Union* has a personal grievance. When its editor was nominated for public printer I declined to vote for him, and stated that at some time I might give my reasons for doing so. Since I declined to give that vote, this scurrilous abuse, these vindictive and constant attacks have been repeated almost daily on me. Will my friend from Michigan read the article to which I allude?"

This is a part of the speech. You must excuse me from reading the entire article of the Washington *Union,* as Mr. Stuart read it for Mr. Douglas. The Judge goes on and sums up, as I think, correctly:

"Mr. President, you here find several distinct propositions advanced boldly by the Washington *Union* editorially, and apparently *authoritatively,* and any man who questions any of them is denounced as an Abolitionist, a Freesoiler, a fanatic. The propositions are, first, that the primary object of all government at its original institution is the protection of person and property; second, that the Constitution of the United States declares that the citizens of each State shall be entitled to all the privileges and immunities of citizens in the several States; and that, therefore, thirdly, all State laws, whether organic or otherwise, which prohibit the citizens of one State from settling in another with their slave property, and especially declaring it forfeited, are direct violations of the original intention of the Government and Constitution of the United States; and, fourth, that the emancipation of the slaves of the Northern States was a gross outrage on the rights of property, inasmuch as it was involuntarily done on the part of the owner."

"Remember that this article was published in the *Union* on the 17th of November, and on the 18th appeared the first article giving the adhesion of the *Union* to the Lecompton Constitution. It was in these words:

"'KANSAS AND HER CONSTITUTION.—The vexed question is settled. The problem is solved. The dead point of danger is passed. All serious trouble to Kansas affairs is over and gone'—

"And a column, nearly, of the same sort. Then, when you come to look into the Lecompton Constitution, you find the same doctrine incorporated in it which was put forth editorially in the *Union*. What is it?

"'ARTICLE 7, *Section* 1. The right of property is before and higher than any Constitutional sanction; and the right of the owner of a slave to such slave and its increase is the same and as inviolable as the right of the owner of any property whatever.'

"Then in the schedule is a provision that the Constitution may be amended after 1864 by a two-thirds vote.

"'But no alteration shall be made to affect the right of property in the ownership of slaves.'

"It will be seen by these clauses in the Lecompton Constitution, that they are identical in spirit with the *authoritative* article in the Washington *Union* of the day previous to its indorsement of this Constitution."

I pass over some portions of the speech, and I hope that any one who feels interested in this matter will read the entire section of the speech, and see whether I do the Judge injustice. He proceeds:

"When I saw that article in the *Union* of the 17th of November, followed by the glorification of the Lecompton Constitution on the 18th of November, and this clause in the Constitution asserting the doctrine that a State has no right to prohibit slavery within its limits, I saw that there was a *fatal blow* being struck at the sovereignty of the States of this Union."

I stop the quotation there, again requesting that it may all be read. I have read all of the portion I desire to comment upon. What is this charge that the

Judge thinks I must have a very corrupt heart to make? It was a purpose on the part of certain high functionaries to make it impossible for the people of one State to prohibit the people of any other State from entering it with their "property," so called, and making it a slave State. In other words, it was a charge implying a design to make the institution of slavery national. And now I ask your attention to what Judge Douglas has himself done here. I know he made that part of the speech as a reason why he had refused to vote for a certain man for public printer, but when we get at it, the charge itself is the very one I made against him, that he thinks I am so corrupt for uttering. Now, whom does he make that charge against? Does he make it against that newspaper editor merely? No; he says it is identical in spirit with the Lecompton Constitution, and so the framers of that Constitution are brought in with the editor of the newspaper in that "fatal blow being struck." He did not call it a "conspiracy." In his language it is a "fatal blow being struck." And if the words carry the meaning better when changed from a "conspiracy" into a "fatal blow being struck," I will change *my* expression and call it "fatal blow being struck." We see the charge made not merely against the editor of the *Union,* but all the framers of the Lecompton Constitution; and not only so, but the article was an *authoritative* article. By whose authority? Is there any question but he means it was by the authority of the President and his Cabinet—the Administration?

Is there any sort of question but he means to make that charge? Then there are the editors of the *Union,* the framers of the Lecompton Constitution, the President of the United States and his Cabinet, and all the supporters of the Lecompton Constitution, in Congress and out of Congress, who are all involved in this "fatal blow being struck." I commend to Judge Douglas's consideration the question of *how corrupt a man's heart must be to make such a charge!*

Now, my friends, I have but one branch of the subject, in the little time I have left, to which to call your attention, and as I shall come to a close at the end of that branch, it is probable that I shall not occupy quite all the time alloted to me. Although on these questions I would like to talk twice as long as I have, I could not enter upon another head and discuss it properly without running over my time. I ask the attention of the people here assembled and elsewhere, to the course that Judge Douglas is pursuing every day as bearing upon this question of making slavery national. Not going back to the records, but taking the speeches he makes, the speeches he made yesterday and day before, and makes constantly all over the country—I ask your attention to them. In the first place, what is necessary to make the Institution national? Not war. There is no danger that the people of Kentucky will shoulder their muskets, and, with a young nigger stuck on every bayonet, march into Illinois and force them upon us. There is no danger of our going over there and making war upon them. Then what is necessary for the nationalization of slavery? It is simply the next Dred Scott decision. It is merely for the Supreme Court to decide that no *State* under the Constitution can exclude it, just as they have already decided that under the Constitution neither Congress nor the Territorial Legislature can do it. When that is decided and acquiesced in, the whole thing is done. This being true, and this being the way, as I think, that slavery is to be made national, let us consider what Judge Douglas is doing every day to that end. In the first place, let us see what influence he is exerting on public sentiment. In this and like communities, public sentiment is everything. With public sentiment, nothing can fail; without it nothing can succeed. Consequently he who moulds public sentiment, goes deeper than he who enacts statutes or pronounces decisions. He makes statutes and decisions possible or impossible to be executed. This must be borne in mind, as also the additional fact that Judge Douglas is a man of vast influence, so great that it is enough for many men to profess to believe anything, when they once find out that Judge Douglas professes to believe it. Consider also the attitude he occupies at the head of a large party—a party which he claims has a majority of all the voters in the country. This man sticks to a decision which forbids the people of a Territory from excluding slavery, and he does so not because he says it is right in itself—he does not give any opinion on that—but because it has been *decided by the court,* and being decided by the court, he is, and you are bound to take it in your political action as *law*—not that he judges at all of its merits, but because a decision of the court is to him a "*Thus saith the Lord.*" He places it on that ground alone, and you will bear in mind that, thus committing himself unreservedly to this decision, *commits him to the next one* just as firmly as to this. He did not commit himself on account of the merit or demerit of the decision, but it is a *Thus saith the Lord*. The next decision, as much as this, will be a *Thus saith the Lord*. There is nothing that can divert or turn him away from this decision. It is nothing that I point out to him that his great prototype, Gen. Jackson, did not believe in the binding force of decisions. It is nothing to him that Jefferson did not so believe. I have said that I have often heard him approve of Jackson's course in disregarding the decision of the Supreme Court pronouncing a National Bank constitutional. He says, I did not hear him say so. He denies the accuracy of my recollection. I say he ought to know better than I, but I will make no question about this thing, though it still seems to me that I heard him say it twenty times. I will tell him though, that he now claims to stand on the Cincinnati platform, which affirms that Congress *cannot* charter a National Bank, in the teeth of that old standing decision that Congress can charter a bank. And I remind him of another piece of history on the question of respect for judicial decisions, and it is a piece of Illinois history, belonging to a time when the large party to which Judge Douglas belonged, were displeased with a decision of the Supreme Court of Illinois, because they had decided that a Governor could not remove a Secretary of State. You will find the whole story in Ford's History of Illinois, and I know that Judge Douglas will not deny that he was then in favor of overslaughing that decision by the mode of adding five new Judges, so as to vote down the four old ones. Not only so, but it ended in *the Judge's sitting down on that very bench as one of the five new Judges to break down the four old ones.* It was in this way precisely that he got his title of Judge. Now, when the Judge tells me that men appointed conditionally to sit as members of a court, will have to be catechised beforehand upon some subject, I say, "You know, Judge; you have tried it." When he says a court of this kind will lose the confidence of all men, will be prostituted and disgraced by such a proceeding, I say, "You know best, Judge; you have been through the mill." But I cannot shake Judge Douglas's teeth loose from the Dred Scott decision. Like some obstinate animal (I mean no disrespect), that will hang on when he has once got his teeth fixed; you may cut off a leg, or you may tear away an arm, still he will not relax his hold. And so I may point out to the Judge, and say that he is bespattered all over, from the beginning of his political life to the present time, with attacks upon judicial decisions—I may cut off limb after limb of his public record, and strive to wrench him from a single dictum of the court—yet I cannot divert him from it. He hangs, to the last, to the Dred Scott decision. These things show there is a purpose *strong as death and eternity* for which he adheres to this decision, and for which he will adhere to *all other decisions* of the same court.

A Hibernian—"Give us something besides Drid Scott."

Mr. Lincoln—Yes; no doubt you want to hear something that don't hurt. Now, having spoken of the Dred Scott decision, one more word and I am done. Henry Clay, my beau ideal of a statesman, the man for whom I fought all my humble life—Henry Clay once said of a class of men who would repress all tendencies to liberty and ultimate emancipation, that they must, if they would do this, go back to the era of our Independence, and muzzle the cannon which thunders its annual joyous return; they must blow out the moral lights around us; they must penetrate the human soul, and eradicate there the love of liberty; and then, and not till then, could they perpetuate slavery in this country! To my thinking, Judge Douglas is, by his example and vast influence, doing that very thing in this community, when he says that the negro has nothing in the Declaration of Independence. Henry Clay plainly understood the contrary. Judge Douglas is going back to the era of our Revolution, and to the extent of his ability, muzzling the cannon which thunders its annual joyous return. When he invites any people, willing to have slavery, to establish it, he is blowing out the moral lights around us. When he says he "cares not whether slavery is voted down or voted up"—that it is a sacred right of self-government—he is, in my judgment, penetrating the human soul and eradicating the light of reason and the love of liberty in this American people. And now I will only say that when, by all these means and appliances, Judge Douglas shall succeed in bringing public sentiment to an exact accordance with his own views—when these vast assemblages shall echo back all these sentiments—when they shall come to repeat his views and to avow his principles, and to say all that he says on these mighty questions—then it needs only the formality of the second Dred Scott decision, which he indorses in advance, to make slavery alike lawful in all the States—old as well as new, North as well as South.

My friends, that ends the chapter. The Judge can take his half hour.

MR. DOUGLAS'S REJOINDER.

FELLOW-CITIZENS: I will now occupy the half hour allotted to me in replying to Mr. Lincoln. The first point to which I will call your attention is, as to what I said about the organization of the Republican party in 1854, and the platform that was formed on the fifth of October, of that year, and I will then put the question to Mr. Lincoln, whether or not, he approves of each article in that platform, and ask for a specific answer. I did not charge him with being a member of the committee which reported that platform. I charged that that platform was the platform of the Republican party adopted by them. The fact that it was the platform of the Republican party is not denied, but Mr. Lincoln now says, that although his name was on the committee which reported it, that he does not think he was there, but thinks he was in Tazewell, holding court. Now, I want to remind Mr. Lincoln that he was a Springfield when that Convention was held and those resolutions adopted.

The point I am going to remind Mr. Lincoln of is this: that after I had made my speech in 1854, during the fair, he gave me notice that he was going to reply to me the next day. I was sick at the time, but I staid over in Springfield to hear his reply and to reply to him. On that day this very Convention, the resolutions adopted by which I have read, was to meet in the Senate chamber. He spoke in the hall of the House; and when he got through his speech—my recollection is distinct, and I shall never forget it—Mr. Codding walked in as I took the stand to reply, and gave notice that the Republican State Convention would meet instantly in the Senate chamber, and called upon the Republicans to retire there and go into this very Convention, instead of remaining and listening to me.

In the first place, Mr. Lincoln was selected by the very men who made the Republican organization, on that day, to reply to me. He spoke for them and for that party, and he was the leader of the party; and on the very day he made his speech in reply to me, preaching up this same doctrine of negro equality, under the Declaration of Independence, this Republican party met in Convention. Another evidence that he was acting in concert with them is to be found in the fact that that Convention waited an hour after its time of meeting to hear Lincoln's speech, and Codding one of their leading men, marched in the moment Lincoln got through, and gave notice that they did not want to hear me, and would proceed with the business of the Convention. Still another fact. I have here a newspaper printed at Springfield. Mr. Lincoln's own town, in October, 1854, a few days afterward, publishing these resolutions, charging Mr. Lincoln with entertaining these sentiments, and trying to prove that they were also the sentiments of Mr. Yates, then candidate for Congress. This has been published on Mr. Lincoln over and over again, and never before has he denied it.

But, my friends, this denial of his that he did not act on the committee, is a miserable quibble to avoid the main issue, which is, that this Republican platform declares in favor of the unconditional repeal of the Fugitive Slave law. Has Lincoln answered whether he indorsed that or not? I called his attention to it when I first addressed you, and asked him for an answer, and I then predicted that he would not answer. How does he answer? Why, that he was not on the committee that wrote the resolutions. I then repeated the next proposition contained in the resolutions, which was to restrict slavery in those States in which it exists, and asked him whether he indorsed it. Does he answer yes, or no? He says in reply, "I was not on the committee at the time; I was up in Tazewell." The next question I put to him was, whether he was in favor of prohibiting the admission of any more slave States into the Union. I put the question to him distinctly, whether, if the people of the Territory, when they had sufficient population to make a State, should form their Constitution recognizing slavery, he would vote for or against its admission. He is a candidate for the United States Senate, and it is possible, if he should be elected, that he would have to vote directly on that question. I asked him to answer me and you, whether he would vote to admit a State into the Union, with slavery or without it, as its own people might choose. He did not answer that question. He dodges that question also, under the cover that he was not on the Committee at the time, that he was not present when the platform was made. I want to know if he should happen to be in the Senate when a State applied for admission, with a Constitution acceptable to her own people, he would vote to admit that State, if slavery was one of its institutions. He avoids the answer.

It is true he gives the Abolitionists to understand by a hint that he would not vote to admit such a State. And why? He goes on to say that the man who would talk about giving each State the right to have slavery, or not, as it pleased, was akin to the man who would muzzle the guns which thundered forth the annual joyous return of the day of our independence. He says that that kind of talk is casting a blight on the glory of this country. What is the meaning of that? That he is not in favor of each State to have the right of doing as it pleases on the slavery question: I will put the question to him again and again, and I intend to force it out of him.

Then again, this platform which was made at Springfield by his own party, when he was its acknowledged head, provides that Republicans will insist on the abolition of slavery in the District of Columbia, and I asked Lincoln specifically whether he agreed with them in that? ["Did you get an answer?"] He is afraid to answer it. He knows I will trot him down to Egypt. I intend to make him answer there, or I will show the people of Illinois that he does not intend to answer these questions. The Convention to which I have been alluding goes a little further, and pledges itself to exclude slavery from all the Territories over which the General Government has exclusive jurisdiction north of 36 deg. 30 min., as well as South. Now I want to know whether he approves that provision. I want him to answer, and when he does, I want to know his opinion on another point, which is, whether he will redeem the pledge of this platform and resist the acquirement of any more territory unless slavery therein shall be forever prohibited. I want him to answer this last question. Each of the questions I have put to him are practical questions—questions based upon the fundamental principles of the Black Republican party, and I want to know whether he is the first, last, and only choice of a party with whom he does not agree in principle. He does not deny but that that principle was unanimously adopted by the Republican party; he does not deny that the whole Republican party is pledged to it; he does not deny that a man who is not faithful to it is faithless to the Republican party; and now I want to know whether that party is unanimously in favor of a man who does not adopt that creed and agree with them in their principles: I want to know whether the man who does not agree with them, and who is afraid to avow his differences, and who dodges the issue, is the first, last, and only choice of the Republican party.

A voice—"How about the conspiracy?"

Mr. Douglas—Never mind, I will come to that soon enough. But the platform which I have read to you, not only lays down these principles, but it adds:

Resolved, That in furtherance of these principles we will use such constitutional and lawful means as shall seem best adapted to their accomplishment, and that we will support no man for office, under the General or State Government, who is not positively and fully committed to the support of these principles, and whose personal character and conduct is not a guaranty that he is reliable, and who shall not have abjured old party allegiance and ties.

The Black Republican party stands pledged that they will never support Lincoln until he has pledged himself to that platform, but he cannot devise his answer; he has not made up his mind whether he will or not. He talked about everything else he could think of to occupy his hour and a half, and when he could not think of anything more to say, without an excuse for refusing to answer these questions, he sat down long before his time was out.

In relation to Mr. Lincoln's charge of conspiracy against me, I have a word to say. In his speech to-day he quotes a playful part of his speech at Springfield, about Stephen, and James, and Franklin, and Roger, and says that I did not take exception to it. I did not answer it, and he repeats it again. I did not take exception to this figure of his. He has a right to be as playful as he pleases in throwing his arguments together, and I will not object; but I did take objection to his second Springfield speech, in which he stated that he intended his first speech as a charge of corruption or conspiracy against the Supreme Court of the United States, President Pierce, President Buchanan, and myself. That gave the offensive character to the charge. He then said that when he made it he did not know whether it was true or not, but inasmuch as Judge Douglas had not denied it, although he had replied to the other parts of his speech three times, he repeated it as a charge of conspiracy against me, thus charging me with moral turpitude. When he put it in that form, I did say, that inasmuch as he repeated the charge simply because I had not denied it, I would deprive him of the opportunity of ever repeating it again, by declaring that it was in all its bearings, an infamous lie. He says he will repeat it until I answer his fully and nonsense, about Stephen, and Franklin, and Roger, and Bob, and James.

He studied that out—prepared that one sentence with the greatest care, committed it to memory, and put it in his first Springfield speech, and now he carries that speech around and reads that sentence to show how pretty it is. His vanity is wounded because I will not go into that beautiful figure of his about the building of a house. All I have to say is, that I am not green enough to let him make a large which he acknowledges he does not know to be true, and then take up any time in answering it, when I know it to be false and nobody else knows it to be true.

I have not brought a charge of moral turpitude against him. When he, or any other man, brings one against me, instead of disproving it, I will say that it is a lie, and let him prove it if he can.

I have lived twenty-five years in Illinois. I have served you with all the fidelity and ability which I possess, and Mr. Lincoln is at liberty to attack my public action, my votes, and my conduct; but when he dares to attack my moral integrity, by a charge of conspiracy between myself, Chief Justice Taney and the Supreme Court, and two Presidents of the United States, I will repel it.

Mr. Lincoln has not character enough for integrity and truth, merely on his own *ipse dixit,* to arraign President Buchanan, President Pierce, and nine Judges of the Supreme Court, not one of whom would be complimented by being put on an equality with him. There is an unpardonable presumption in a man putting himself up before thousands of people, and pretending that his *ipse dixit,* without proof, without fact and without truth, is enough to bring down and destroy the purest and best of living men.

Fellow-citizens, my time is fast expiring; I must pass on. Mr. Lincoln wants to know why I voted against Mr. Chase's amendment to the Nebraska bill. I will tell him. In the first place, the bill already conferred all the power which Congress had, by giving the people the whole power over the subject. Chase offered a provise that they might abolish slavery, which by implication would convey the idea that they could prohibit by not introducing that institution. Gen. Cass asked him to modify his amendment, so as to provide that the people might either prohibit or introduce slavery, and thus make it fair and equal. Chase refused to so modify his proviso, and then Gen. Cass and all the rest of us, voted it down. Those facts appear on the journals and debates of Congress, where Mr. Lincoln found the charge and if he had told the whole truth, there would have been no necessity for me to occupy your time in explaining the matter.

Mr. Lincoln wants to know why the word "State," as well as "Territory," was put into the Nebraska bill? I will tell him. It was put there to meet just such false arguments as he has been adducing. That first, not only the people of the Territories should do as they pleased, but that when they come to be admitted as States, they should come into the Union with or without slavery, as the people determined. I meant to knock in the head this Abolition doctrine of Mr. Lincoln's, that there shall be no more slave States, even if the people want them. And it does not do for him to say, or for any other Black Republican to say, that there is nobody in favor of the doctrine of no more slave States, and that nobody wants to interfere with the right of the people to do as they please. What was the origin of the Missouri difficulty and the Missouri Compromise? The people of Missouri formed a Constitution as a slave State, and asked admission into the Union, but the Freesoil party of the North being in a majority, refused to admit her because she had slavery as one of her institutions. Hence this first slavery agitation arose upon a State and not upon a Territory, and yet Mr. Lincoln does not know why the word State was placed in the Kansas-Nebraska bill. The whole Abolition agitation arose on that doctrine of prohibiting a State from coming in with Slavery or not, as it pleased, and that same doctrine is here in this Republican platform of 1854; it has never been repealed; and every Black Republican stands pledged by that platform, never to vote for any man who is not in favor of it. Yet Mr. Lincoln does not know that there is a man in the world who is in favor of preventing a State from coming in as it pleases, notwithstanding. The Springfield platform says that they, the Republican party, will not allow a State to come in under such circumstances. He is an ignorant man.

Now you see that upon these very points I am as far from bringing Mr. Lincoln up to the line as I ever was before. He does not want to avow his principles. I do want to avow mine, as clear as sunlight in mid-day. Democracy is founded upon the eternal principle of right. The plainer these principles are avowed before the people, the stronger will be the support which they will receive. I only wish I had the power to make them so clear that they would shine in the heavens for every man, woman, and child to read. The first of those principles that I would proclaim would be in opposition to Mr. Lincoln's doctrine of uniformity between the different States, and I would declare instead the sovereign right of each State to decide the slavery question as well as all other domestic questions for themselves, without interference from any other State or power whatsoever.

When that principle is recognized, you will have peace and harmony and fraternal feeling between all the States of this Union; until you do recognize that doctrine, there will be sectional warfare agitating and distracting the country. What does Mr. Lincoln propose? He says that the Union cannot exist divided into free and slave States. If it cannot endure thus divided, then he must strive to make them all free or all slave, which will inevitably bring about a dissolution of the Union.

Gentlemen, I am told that my time is out, and I am obliged to stop.

SECOND JOINT DEBATE, AT FREEPORT
AUGUST 27, 1858

MR. LINCOLN'S OPENING SPEECH.

LADIES AND GENTLEMEN: On Saturday last, Judge Douglas and myself first met in public discussion. He spoke one hour, I an hour and a half, and he replied for half an hour. The order is now reversed. I am to speak an hour, he an hour and a half, and then I am to reply for half an hour. I propose to devote myself during the first hour to the scope of what was brought within the range of his half-hour speech at Ottawa. Of course there was brought within the scope in that half-hour's speech something of his own opening speech. In the course of that opening argument Judge Douglas proposed to me seven distinct interrogatories. In my speech of an hour and a half, I attended to some other parts of his speech, and incidentally, as I thought, answered one of the interrogatories then. I then distinctly intimated to him that I would answer the rest of his interrogatories on condition only that he should agree to answer as many for me. He made no intinuation at the time of the proposition, nor did he in his reply allude at all to that suggestion of mine. I do him no injustice in saying that he occupied at least half of his reply in dealing with me as though I had *refused* to answer his interrogatories. I now propose that I will answer any of the interrogatories, upon condition that he will answer questions from me not exceeding the same number. I give him an opportunity to respond. The Judge remains silent. I now say that I will answer his interrogatories, whether he answers mine or not; and that after I have done so, I shall propound mine to him.

I have supposed myself, since the organization of the Republican party at Bloomington, in May, 1856, bound as a party man by the platforms of the party, then and since. If in any interrogatories which I shall answer I go beyond the scope of what is within these platforms, it will be perceived that no one is responsible but myself.

Having said thus much, I will take up the Judge's interrogatories as I find them printed in the Chicago *Times,* and answer them *seriatim.* In order that there may be no mistake about it, I have copied the interrogatories in writing, and also my answers to them. The first one of these interrogatories is in these words:

Question 1. "I desire to know whether Lincoln to-day stands, as he did in 1854, in favor of the unconditional repeal of the Fugitive Slave law?"

Answer. I do not now, nor ever did, stand in favor of the unconditional repeal of the Fugitive Slave law.

Q. 2. "I desire him to answer whether he stands pledged to-day, as he did in 1854, against the admission of any more slave States into the Union, even if the people want them?"

A. I do not now, or ever did, stand pledged against the admission of any more slave States into the Union.

Q. 3. "I want to know whether he stands pledged against the admission of a new State into the Union with such a Constitution as the people of that State may see fit to make?"

A. I do not stand pledged against the admission of a new State into the Union, with such a Constitution as the people of that State may see fit to make.

Q. 4. "I want to know whether he stands to-day pledged to the abolition of slavery in the District of Columbia?"

A. I do not stand to-day pledged to the abolition of slavery in the District of Columbia.

Q. 5. "I desire him to answer whether he stands pledged to the prohibition of the slave-trade between the different States?"

A. I do not stand pledged to the prohibition of the slave-trade between the different States.

Q. 6. "I desire to know whether he stands pledged to prohibit slavery in all the Territories of the United States, North as well as South of the Missouri Compromise line?"

A. I am impliedly, if not expressly, pledged to a belief in the *right* and *duty* of Congress to prohibit slavery in all the United States Territories.

Q. 7. "I desire him to answer whether he is opposed to the acquisition of any new territory unless slavery is first prohibited therein?"

A. I am not generally opposed to honest acquisition of territory; and, in any given case, I would or would not oppose such acquisition, accordingly as I might think such acquisition would or would not aggravate the slavery question among ourselves.

Now, my friends, it will be perceived upon an examination of these questions and answers, that so far I have only answered that I was not *pledged* to this, that or the other. The Judge has not framed his interrogatories to ask me anything more than this, and I have answered in strict accordance with the interrogatories, and have answered truly that I am not *pledged* at all upon any of the points to which I have answered. But I am not disposed to hang upon the exact form of his interrogatory. I am rather disposed to take up at least some of these questions, and state what I really think upon them.

As to the first one, in regard to the Fugitive Slave law, I have never hesitated to say, and I do not now hesitate to say, that I think, under the Constitution of the United States, the people of the Southern States are entitled to a Congressional Fugitive Slave law. Having said that, I have had nothing to say in regard to the existing Fugitive Slave law, further than that I think it should have been framed so as to be free from some of the objections that pertain to it, without lessening its efficiency. And inasmuch as we are not now in an agitation in regard to an alteration or modification of that law, I would not be the man to introduce it as a new subject of agitation upon the general question of slavery.

In regard to the other question, of whether I am pledged to the admission of any more slave States into the Union, I state to you very frankly that I would be exceedingly sorry ever to be put in a position of having to pass upon that question. I should be exceedingly glad to know that there would never be another slave State admitted into the Union; but I must add, that if slavery shall be kept out of the Territories during the territorial existence of any one given Territory, and then the people shall, having a fair chance and a clear field, when they come to adopt the Constitution, do such an extraordinary thing as to adopt a slave Constitution, uninfluenced by the actual presence of the institution among them, I see no alternative, if we own the country, but to admit them into the Union.

The third interrogatory is answered by the answer to the second, it being, as I conceive, the same as the second.

The fourth one is in regard to the abolition of slavery in the District of Columbia. In relation to that, I have my mind very distinctly made up. I should be exceedingly glad to see slavery abolished in the District of Columbia. I believe that Congress possesses the constitutional power to abolish it. Yet as a member of Congress, I should not with my present views, be in favor of *endeavoring* to abolish slavery in the District of Columbia, unless it would be upon these conditions: *First,* that the abolition should be gradual. *Second,* that it should be on a vote of the majority of qualified voters in the District; and *third,* that compensation should be made to unwilling owners. With these three conditions, I confess I would be exceedingly glad to see Congress abolish slavery in the District of Columbia, and, in the language of Henry Clay, "sweep from our Capital that foul blot upon our nation."

In regard to the fifth interrogatory, I must say here, that as to the question of the abolition of the slave-trade between the different States, I can truly answer, as I have, that I am *pledged* to nothing about it. It is a subject to which I have not given that mature consideration that would make me feel authorized to state a position so as to hold myself entirely bound by it. In other words, that question has never been prominently enough before me to induce me to investigate whether we really have the constitutional power to do it. I could investigate it if I had sufficient time, to bring myself to a conclusion upon that subject; but I have not done so, and I say so frankly to you here, and to Judge Douglas. I must say, however, that if I should be of opinion that Congress does possess the constitutional power to abolish the slave-trade among the different States, I should still not be in favor of the exercise of that power unless upon some conservative principle as I conceive it, akin to what I have said in relation to the abolition of slavery in the District of Columbia.

My answer as to whether I desire that slavery should be prohibited in all the Territories of the United States, is full and explicit within itself, and cannot be made clearer by any comments of mine. So I suppose in regard to the question whether I am opposed to the acquisition of any more territory unless slavery is first prohibited therein, my answer is such that I could add nothing by way of illustration, or making myself better understood, than the answer which I have placed in writing.

Now in all this, the Judge has me, and he has me on the record. I suppose he had flattered himself that I was really entertaining one set of opinions for one place and another set for another place—that I was afraid to say at one place what I uttered at another. What I am saying here I suppose I say to a vast audience as strongly tending to Abolitionism as any audience in the State of Illinois, and I believe I am saying that which, if it would be offensive to any persons and render them enemies to myself, would be offensive to persons in this audience.

I now proceed to propound to the Judge the interrogatories, so far as I have framed them. I will bring forward a new installment when I get them ready. I will bring these forward now, only reaching to number four.

The first one is:

Question 1.   If the people of Kansas shall, by means entirely unobjectionable in all other respects, adopt a State Constitution, and ask admission into the Union under it, *before* they have the requisite number of inhabitants according to the English bill—some ninety-three thousand—will you vote to admit them?

Q. 2.Can the people of a United States Territory, in any lawful way, against the wish of any citizen of the United States, exclude slavery from its limits prior to the formation of a State Constitution?

Q. 3.If the Supreme Court of the United States shall decide that States cannot exclude slavery from their limits, are you in favor of acquiescing in, adopting and following such decision as a rule of political action?

Q. 4.Are you in favor of acquiring additional territory, in disregard of how such acquisition may affect the nation on the slavery question?

As introductory to these interrogatories which Judge Douglas propounded to me at Ottawa, he read a set of resolutions which he said Judge Trumbull and myself had participated in adopting, in the first Republican State Convention, held at Springfield, in October, 1854. He insisted that I and Judge Trumbull, and perhaps the entire Republican party, were responsible for the doctrines contained in the set of resolutions which he read, and I understand that it was from that set of resolutions that he deduced the interrogatories which he propounded to me, using these resolutions as a sort of authority for propounding those questions to me. Now I say here to-day that I do not answer his interrogatories because of their springing at all from that set of resolutions which he read. I answered them because Judge Douglas thought fit to ask them. I do not now, nor never did, recognize any responsibility upon myself in that set of resolutions. When I replied to him on that occasion, I assured him that I never had anything to do with them. I repeat here to-day, that I never in any possible form had anything to do with that set of resolutions. It turns out, I believe, that those resolutions were never passed in any Convention held in Springfield. It turns out that they were never passed at any Convention or any public meeting that I had any part in. I believe it turns out in addition to all this, that there was not, in the fall of 1854, any Convention holding a session in Springfield, calling itself a Republican State Convention; yet it is true there was a Convention, or assemblage of men calling themselves a Convention, at Springfield, that did pass some resolutions. But so little did I really know of the proceedings of that Convention, or what set of resolutions they had passed, though having a general knowledge that there had been such an assemblage of men there, that when Judge Douglas read the resolutions, I really did not know but they had been the resolutions passed then and there. I did not question that they were the resolutions adopted. For I could not bring myself to suppose that Judge Douglas could say what he did upon this subject without *knowing* that it was true. I contented myself, on that occasion, with denying, as I truly could, all connection with them, not denying or affirming whether they were passed at Springfield. Now it turns out that he had got hold of some resolutions passed at some Convention or public meeting in Kane county I wish to say here, that I don't conceive that in any fair and just mind this discovery relieves me at all. I had just as much to do with the Convention in Kane county as that at Springfield. I am just as much responsible for the resolutions at Kane county as those at Springfield, the amount of the responsibility being exactly nothing in either case; no more than there would be in regard to a set of resolutions passed in the moon.

I allude to this extraordinary matter in this canvass for some further purpose than anything yet advanced. Judge Douglas did not make his statement upon that occasion as matters that he believed to be true, but he stated them roundly as *being true,* in such form as to pledge his veracity for their truth. When the whole matter turns out as it does, and when we consider who Judge Douglas is—that he is a distinguished Senator of the United States—that he has served nearly twelve years as such—that his character is not at all limited as an ordinary Senator of the United States, but that his name has become of world-wide renown—it is *most extraordinary* that he should so far forget all the suggestions of justice to an adversary, or of prudence to himself, as to venture upon the assertion of that which the slightest investigation would have shown him to be wholly false. I can only account for his having done so upon the supposition that that evil genius which has attended him through his life, giving to him an apparent astonishing prosperity, such as to lead very many good men to doubt there being any advantage in virtue over vice—I say I can only account for it on the supposition that the evil genius has at last made up its mind to forsake him.

And I may add that another extraordinary feature of the Judge's conduct in this canvass—made more extraordinary by this incident—is, that he is in the habit, in almost all the speeches he makes, of charging falsehood upon his adversaries, myself and others. I now ask whether he is able to find in any thing that Judge Trumbull, for instance, has said, or in any thing that I have said, a justification at all compared with what we have, in this instance, for that sort of vulgarity.

I have been in the habit of charging as a matter of belief on my part, that, in the introduction of the Nebraska bill into Congress, there was a conspiracy to make slavery perpetual and national. I have arranged from time to time the evidence which establishes and proves the truth of this charge. I recurred to this charge at Ottawa. I shall not now have time to dwell upon it at very great length; but, inasmuch as Judge Douglas in his reply of half an hour, made some points upon me in relation to it, I propose noticing a few of them.

The Judge insists that, in the first speech I made, in which I very distinctly made that charge, he thought for a good while I was in fun!—that I was playful—that I was not sincere about it—and that he only grew angry and somewhat excited when he found that I insisted upon it as a matter of earnestness. He says he characterized it as a falsehood as far as I implicated his *moral character* in that transaction. Well, I did not know, till he presented that view, that I had implicated his moral character. He is very much in the habit, when he argues me up into a position I never thought of occupying, of very cosily saying he has no doubt Lincoln is "conscientious" in saying so. He should remember that I did not know but what *he* was ALTOGETHER "CONSCIENTOUS" in that matter. I can conceive it possible for men to conspire to do a good thing, and I really find nothing in Judge Douglas's course or arguments that is contrary to or inconsistent with his belief of a conspiracy to nationalize and spread slavery as being a good and blessed thing, and so I hope he will understand that I do not at all question but that in all this matter he is entirely "conscientious."

But to draw your attention to one of the points I made in this case, beginning at the beginning. When the Nebraska bill was introduced, or a short time afterward, by an amendment, I believe, it was provided that it must be considered "the true intent and meaning of this act not to legislate slavery into any State or Territory, or to exclude it therefrom, but to leave the people thereof perfectly free to form and regulate their own domestic institutions in their own way, subject only to the Constitution of the United States." I have called his attention to the fact that when he and some others began arguing that they were giving an increased degree of liberty to the people in the Territories over and above what they formerly had on the question of slavery, a question was raised whether the law was enacted to give such unconditional liberty to the people, and to test the sincerity of this mode of argument, Mr. Chase, of Ohio, introduced an amendment, in which he made the law—if the amendment were adopted—expressly declare that the people of the Territory should have the power to exclude slavery if they saw fit. I have asked attention also to the fact that Judge Douglas and those who acted with him, voted that amendment down, notwithstanding it expressed exactly the thing they said was the true intent and meaning of the law. I have called attention to the fact that in subsequent times, a decision of the Supreme Court has been made, in which it has been declared that a Territorial Legislature has no constitutional right to exclude slavery. And I have argued and said that for men who did intend that the people of the Territory should have the right to exclude slavery absolutely and unconditionally, the voting down of Chase's amendment is wholly inexplica-

ble. It is a puzzle—a riddle. But I have said that with men who did look forward to such a decision, or who had it in contemplation, that such a decision
of the Supreme Court would or might be made, the voting down of that
amendment would be perfectly rational and intelligible. It would keep Congress from coming in collision with the decision when it was made. Any body
can conceive that if there was an intention or expectation that such a decision
was to follow, it would not be a very desirable party attitude to get into for the
Supreme Court—all or nearly all its members belonging to the same party—to
decide one way, when the party in Congress had decided the other way. Hence
it would be very rational for men expecting such a decision, to keep the niche
is that law clear for it. After pointing this out, I tell Judge Douglas that it looks
to me as though here was the reason why Chase's amendment was voted down.
I tell him that as he did it, and knows why he did it, if it was done for a reason
different from this, *he knows what that reason was, and can tell us what it was.* I tell
him, also, it will be vastly more satisfactory to the country for him to give some
other plausible, intelligible reason *why* it was voted down than to stand upon
his dignity and call people liars. Well, on Saturday he did make his answer, and
what do you think it was? He says if I had only taken upon myself to tell the
whole truth about that amendment of Chase's, no explanation would have been
necessary on his part—or words to that effect. Now, I say here, that I am quite
unconscious of having suppressed any thing material to the case, and I am very
frank to admit if there is any sound reason other than that which appeared to
me material, it is quite fair for him to present it. What reason does he propose?
That when Chase came forward with his amendment expressly authorizing the
people to exclude slavery from the limits of every Territory, Gen. Cass proposed to Chase, if he (Chase) would add to his amendment that the people
should have the power to *introduce* or exclude, they would let it go. This is substantially all of his reply. And because Chase would not do that, they voted his
amendment down. Well, it turns out, I believe, upon examination, that General Cass took some part in the little running debate upon that amendment, and
then ran *away and did not vote on it at all.* Is not that the fact? So confident, as I
think, was General Cass that there was a snake somewhere about, he chose to
run away from the whole thing. This is an inference I draw from the fact that,
though he took part in the debate, his name does not appear in the ayes and
noes. But does Judge Douglas's reply amount to a satisfactory answer? [Cries of
"yes," "yes," and "no," "no."] There is some little difference of opinion here.
But I ask attention to a few more views bearing on the question of whether it
amounts to a satisfactory answer. The men who were determined that that

amendment should not get into the bill and spoil the place where the Dred Scott decision was to come in, sought an excuse to get rid of it somewhere. One of these ways—one of these excuses—was to ask Chase to add to his proposed amendment a provision that the people might *introduce* slavery if they wanted to. They very well knew Chase would do no such thing—that Mr. Chase was one of the men differing from them on the broad principle of his insisting that freedom was *better* than slavery—a man who would not consent to enact a law, penned with his own hand, by which he was made to recognize slavery on the one hand and liberty on the other as *precisely equal;* and when they insisted on his doing this, they very well knew they insisted on that which he would not for a moment think of doing, and that they were only bluffing him. I believe (I have not, since he made his answer, had a chance to examine the journals or *Congressional Globe,* and therefore speak from memory)—I believe the state of the bill at that time, according to parliamentary rules, was such that no member could propose an additional amendment to Chase's amendment. I rather think this is the truth—the Judge shakes his head. Very well. I would like to know, then *if they wanted Chase's amendment fixed over, somebody else could not have offered to do it?* If they wanted it amended, why did they not offer the amendment? Why did they stand there taunting and quibbling at Chase? Why did they not *put it in themselves?* But to put it on the other ground; suppose that there was such an amendment offered, and Chase's was an amendment to an amendment; until one is disposed of by parliamentary law, you cannot pile another on. Then all these gentlemen had to do was to vote Chase's on, and then in the amended form in which the whole stood, add their own amendment to it if they wanted to put it in that shape. This was all they were obliged to do, and the eyes and nose show that there were thirty-six who voted it down, against ten who voted in favor of it. The thirty-six held entire sway and control. They could in some form or other have put that bill in the exact shape they wanted. If there was a rule preventing their amending it at the time, they could pass that, and then Chase's amendment being merged, put it in the shape they wanted. They did not choose to do so, but they went into a quibble with Chase to get him to add what they knew he would not add, and because he would not, they stand upon that flimsy pretext for voting down what they argued was the meaning and intent of their own bill. They left room thereby for this Dred Scott decision, which goes very far to make slavery national throughout the United States.

I pass one or two points I have because my time will very soon expire, but I must be allowed to say that Judge Douglas recurs again, as he did upon one or two other occasions, to the enormity of Lincoln—an insignificant individual like

Lincoln—upon his *ipse dixit* charging a conspiracy upon a large number of members of Congress, the Supreme Court and two Presidents, to nationalize slavery. I want to say that, in the first place, I have made no charge of this sort upon my *ipse dixit*. I have only arrayed the evidence tending to prove it, and presented it to the understanding of others, saying what I think it proves, but giving you the means of judging whether it proves it or not. This is precisely what I have done. I have not placed it upon my *ipse dixil* at all. On this occasion, I wish to recall his attention to a piece of evidence which I brought forward at Ottawa on Saturday, showing that he had made substantially the *same charge* against substantially the *same persons,* excluding his dear self from the category. I ask him to give some attention to the evidence which I brought forward, that he himself had discovered a "fatal blow being struck" against the right of the people to exclude slavery from their limits, which fatal blow he assumed as in evidence in an article in the Washington *Union,* published "by authority." I ask by whose authority? He discovers a similar or identical provision in the Lecompton Constitution. Made by whom? The framers of that Constitution. Advocated by whom? By all the members of the party in the nation, who advocated the introduction of Kansas into the Union under the Lecompton Constitution.

I have asked his attention to the evidence that he arrayed to prove that such a fatal blow was being struck, and to the facts which he brought forward in support of that charge—being identical with the one which he thinks so villainous in me. He pointed it not at a newspaper editor merely, but at the President and his Cabinet and the members of Congress advocating the Lecompton Constitution and those framing that instrument. I must again be permitted to remind him, that although my *ipse dixit* may not be as great as his, yet it somewhat reduces the force of his calling my attention to the *enormity* of my making a like charge against him.

Go on, Judge Douglas.

MR. DOUGLAS'S REPLY.

LADIES AND GENTLEMEN: The silence with which you have listened to Mr. Lincoln during his hour is creditable to this vast audience, composed of men of various political parties. Nothing is more honorable to any large mass of people assembled for the purpose of a fair discussion, than that kind and respectful attention that is yielded not only to your political friends, but to those who are opposed to you in politics.

I am glad that at last I have brought Mr. Lincoln to the conclusion that he had better define his position on certain political questions to which I called his attention at Ottawa. He there showed no disposition, no inclination, to answer them. I did not present idle questions for him to answer merely for my gratification. I laid the foundation for those interrogatories by showing that they constituted the platform of the party whose nominee he is for the Senate. I did not presume that I had the right to catechise him as I saw proper, unless I showed that his party, or a majority of it, stood upon the platform and were in favor of the propositions upon which my questions were based. I desired simply to know, inasmuch as he had been nominated as the first, last, and only choice of his party, whether he concurred in the platform which that party had adopted for its government. In a few moments I will proceed to review the answers which he has given to these interrogatories; but in order to relieve his anxiety I will first respond to these which he has presented to me. Mark you, he has not presented interrogatories which have ever received the sanction of the party with which I am acting, and hence he has no other foundation for them than his own curiosity.

First, he desires to know if the people of Kansas shall form a Constitution by means entirely proper and unobjectionable and ask admission into the Union as a State, before they have the requisite population for a member of Congress, whether I will vote for that admission. Well, now, I regret exceedingly that he did not answer that interrogatory himself before he put it to me, in order that we might understand, and not be left to infer, on which side he is. Mr. Trumbull, during the last session of Congress, voted from the beginning to the end against the admission of Oregon, although a free State, because she had not the requisite population for a member of Congress. Mr. Trumbull would not consent, under any circumstances, to let a State, free or slave, come into the Union until it had the requisite population. As Mr. Trumbull is in the field, fighting for Mr. Lincoln, I would like to have Mr. Lincoln answer his own question and tell me whether he is fighting Trumbull on that issue or not. But I will answer his question. In reference to Kansas, it is my opinion, that as she has population enough to constitute a slave State, she has people enough for a free State. I will not make Kansas an exceptional case to the other States of the Union. I hold it to be a sound rule of universal application to require a Territory to contain the requisite population for a member of Congress, before it is admitted as a State into the Union. I made that proposition in the Senate in 1856, and I renewed it during the last session, in a bill providing that no Territory of the United States should form a Constitution and apply for admission until it had the requisite population. On another occasion I proposed that neither Kansas, or any other Territory, should be admitted until it had the requisite population. Congress did not adopt any of my propositions containing this general rule, but did make an exception of Kansas. I will stand by that exception. Either Kansas must come in as a free State, with whatever population she may have, or the rule must be applied to all the other Territories alike. I therefore answer at once, that it having been decided that Kansas has people enough for a slave State, I hold that she has enough for a free State. I hope Mr. Lincoln is satisfied with my answer; and now I would like to get his answer to his own interrogatory—whether or not he will vote to admit Kansas before she has the requisite population. I want to know whether he will vote to admit Oregon before that Territory has the requisite population. Mr. Trumbull will not, and the same reason that commits Mr. Trumbull against the admission of Oregon, commits him against Kansas, even if she should apply for admission as a free State. If there is any sincerity, any truth, in the argument of Mr. Trumbull in the Senate, against the admission of Oregon because she had not 93,420 people, although her population was larger than that of Kansas, he stands pledged against the admission of both Oregon and Kansas until they have 93,420 inhabitants. I would like Mr. Lincoln to answer this question. I would like him to take his own medicine. If he differs with Mr. Trumbull, let him answer his argument against the admission of Oregon, instead of poking questions at me.

The next question propounded to me by Mr. Lincoln is, can the people of a Territory in any lawful way, against the wishes of any citizen of the United States, exclude slavery from their limits prior to the formation of a State Constitution? I answer emphatically, as Mr. Lincoln has heard me answer a hundred times from every stump in Illinois, that in my opinion the people of a Territory can, by lawful means, exclude slavery from their limits prior to the formation of a State Constitution. Mr. Lincoln knew that I had answered that question over and over again. He heard me argue the Nebraska bill on that principle all over the State in 1854, in 1855, and in 1856, and he has no excuse for pretending to be in doubt as to my position on that question. It matters not what way the Supreme Court may hereafter decide us to the abstract question whether slavery may or may not go into a Territory under the Constitution, the people have the lawful means to introduce it or exclude it as they please, for the reason that slavery cannot exist a day or an hour anywhere, unless it is supported by local police regulations. Those police regulations can only be established by the local legislature, and if the people are opposed to slavery they will elect representatives to that body who will by unfriendly legislation effectually prevent the introduction of it into their midst. If, on the contrary, they are for it, their legislation will favor its extension. Hence, no matter what the decision of the

Supreme Court may be on that abstract question, still the right of the people to make a slave Territory or a free Territory is perfect and complete under the Nebraska bill. I hope Mr. Lincoln deems my answer satisfactory on that point.

In this connection, I will notice the charge which he has introduced in relation to Mr. Chase's amendment. I thought that I had chased that amendment out of Mr. Lincoln's brain at Ottawa; but it seems that still haunts his imagination, and he is not yet satisfied. I had supposed that he would be ashamed to press that question further. He is a lawyer, and has been a member of Congress, and has occupied his time and amused you by telling you about parliamentary proceedings. He ought to have known better than to try to palm off his miserable impositions upon this intelligent audience. The Nebraska bill provided that the legislative power, and authority of the said Territory, should extend to all rightful subjects of legislation consistent with the organic act and the Constitution of the United States. It did not make any exception as to slavery, but gave all the power that it was possible for Congress to give, without violating the Constitution to the Territorial Legislature, with no exception or limitation on the subject of slavery at all. The language of that bill which I have quoted, gave the full power and the full authority over the subject of slavery, affirmatively and negatively, to introduce it or exclude it, so far as the Constitution of the United States would permit. What more could Mr. Chase give by his amendment? Nothing. He offered his amendment for the identical purpose for which Mr. Lincoln is using it, to enable demagogues in the country to try and deceive the people.

His amendment was to this effect. It provided that the Legislature should have the power to exclude slavery: and General Cass suggested, "why not give the power to introduce as well as exclude?" The answer was, they have the power already in the bill to do both. Chase was afraid his amendment would be adopted if he put the alternative proposition and so make it fair both ways, but would not yield. He offered it for the purpose of having it rejected. He offered it, as he has himself avowed over and over again, simply to make capital out of it for the stump. He expected that it would be capital for small politicians in the country, and that they would make an effort to deceive the people with it, and he was not mistaken, for Lincoln is carrying out the plan admirably. Lincoln knows that the Nebraska bill, without Chase's amendment, gave all the power which the Constitution would permit. Could Congress confer any more? Could Congress go beyond the Constitution of the country? We gave all a full grant, with no exception in regard to slavery one way or the other. We left that question as we left all others, to be decided by the people for themselves, just as they pleased. I will not occupy my time on this question. I have argued it before all over Illinois. I have argued it in this beautiful city of Freeport; I have argued it in the North, the South, the East, and the West, avowing the same sentiments and the same principles. I have not been afraid to avow my sentiments up here for fear I would be trotted down into Egypt.

The third question which Mr. Lincoln presented is, if the Supreme Court of the United States shall decide that a State of this Union cannot exclude slavery from its own limits, will I submit to it? I am amazed that Lincoln should ask such a question. ["A school-boy knows better."] Yes, a school-boy does know better. Mr. Lincoln's object is to cast an imputation upon the Supreme Court. He knows that there never was but one man in America, claiming any degree of intelligence or decency, who ever for a moment pretended such a thing. It is true that the Washington *Union,* in an article published on the 17th of last December, did put forth that doctrine, and I denounced the article on the floor of the Senate, in a speech which Mr. Lincoln now pretends was against the President. The *Union* had claimed that slavery had a right to go into the free States, and that any provision in the Constitution or laws of the free States to the contrary were null and void. I denounced it in the Senate, as I said before, and I was the first man who did. Lincoln's friends, Trumbull, and Seward, and Hale, and Wilson, and the whole Black Republican side of the Senate, were silent. They left it to me to denounce it. And what was the reply made to me on that occasion? Mr. Toombs, of Georgia, got up and undertook to lecture me on the ground that I ought not to have deemed the article worthy of notice, and ought not to have replied to it; that there was not one man, woman or child of the Potomac, in any slave State, who did not repudiate any such pretension. Mr. Lincoln knows that that reply was made on the spot, and yet now he asks this question. He might as well ask me, suppose Mr. Lincoln should steal a horse, would I sanction it; and it would be as genteel in me to ask him, in the event he stole a horse, what ought to be done with him. He casts an imputation upon the Supreme Court of the United States, by supposing that they would violate the Constitution of the United States. I tell him that such a thing is not possible. It would be an act of moral treason that no man on the bench could ever descend to. Mr. Lincoln himself would never in his partisan feelings so far forget what was right as to be guilty of such an act.

The fourth question of Mr. Lincoln is, are you in favor of acquiring additional territory, in disregard as to how such acquisition may affect the Union on the slavery questions? This question is very ingeniously and cunningly put.

The Black Republican creed lays it down expressly, that under no circumstances shall we acquire any more territory unless slavery is first prohibited in the country. I ask Mr. Lincoln whether he is in favor of that proposition. Are you [addressing Mr. Lincoln] opposed to the acquisition of any more territory, under any circumstances, unless slavery is prohibited in it? That he does not like to answer. When I ask him whether he stands up to that article in the platform of his party, he turns, Yankee-fashion, and without answering it, asks me whether I am in favor of acquiring territory without regard to how it may affect the Union on the slavery question. I answer that whenever it becomes necessary, in our growth and progress, to acquire more territory, that I am in favor of it, without reference to the question of slavery, and when we have acquired it, I will leave the people free to do as they please, either to make it slave or free territory, as they prefer. It is idle to tell me on you that we have territory enough. Our fathers supposed that we had enough when our territory extended to the Mississippi river, but a few years' growth and expansion satisfied them that we needed more, and the Louisiana territory, from the West branch of the Mississippi to the British possessions, was acquired. Then we acquired Oregon, then California and New Mexico. We have enough now for the present, but this is a young and a growing nation. It swarms as often as a hive of bees, and as new swarms are turned out each year, there must be hives in which they can gather and make their honey. In less than fifteen years, if the same progress that has distinguished this country for the last fifteen years continues, every foot of vacant land between this and the Pacific ocean, owned by the United States, will be occupied. Will you not continue to increase at the end of fifteen years as well as now? I tell you, increase, and multiply, and expand, is the law of this nation's existence. You cannot limit this great Republic by mere boundary lines, saying, "thus far shalt thou go, and no further." Any one of you gentlemen might as well say to a son twelve years old that he is big enough, and must not grow any larger, and in order to prevent his growth put a hoop around him to keep him to his present size. What would be the result? Either the hoop must burst and be rent asunder, or the child must die. So it would be with this great nation. With our natural increase, growing with a rapidity unknown in any other part of the globe, with the tide of emigration that is fleeing from despotism in the old world to seek refuge in our own, there is a constant torrent pouring into this country that requires more land, more territory upon which to settle, and just as fast as our interests and our destiny require additional territory in the North, in the South, or on the Islands of the ocean, I am for it, and when we acquire it, will leave the people, according to the Nebraska bill, free to do as they please on the subject of slavery and every other question.

I trust now that Mr. Lincoln will deem himself answered on his four points. He racked his brain so much in devising these four questions that he exhausted himself, and had not strength enough to invent the others. As soon as he is able to hold a council with his advisers, Lovejoy, Farnsworth, and Fred Douglas, he will frame and propound others. ["Good, good."] You Black Republicans who say good, I have no doubt think that they are all good men. I have reason to recollect that some people in this country think that Fred Douglass is a very good man. The last time I came here to make a speech, while talking from the stand to you, people of Freeport, as I am doing to-day, I saw a carriage, and a magnificent one it was, drive up and take a position on the outside of the crowd; a beautiful young lady was sitting on the box-seat, whilst Fred Douglass and her mother reclined inside, and the owner of the carriage acted as driver. I saw this in your own town. ["What of it?"] All I have to say of it is this, that if you, Black Republicans, think that the negro ought to be on a social equality with your wives and daughters, and ride in a carriage with your wife, whilst you drive the team, you have perfect right to do so. I am told that one of Fred Douglass's kinsmen, another rich black negro, is now traveling in this part of the State making speeches for his friend Lincoln as the champion of black men. ["What have you to say against it?"] All I have to say on that subject is, that those of you who believe that the negro is your equal and ought to be on an equality with you socially, politically, and legally, have a right to entertain those opinions, and of course will vote for Mr. Lincoln.

I have a word to say on Mr. Lincoln's answer to the interrogatories contained in my speech at Ottawa, and which he has pretended to reply to here to-day. Mr. Lincoln makes a great parade of the fact that I quoted a platform as having been adopted by the Black Republican party at Springfield in 1854, which, it turns out, was adopted at another place. Mr. Lincoln loses sight of the thing itself in his ecstacies over the mistake I made in stating the place where it was done. He thinks that that platform was not adopted on the right "spot."

When I put the direct questions to Mr. Lincoln to ascertain whether he now stands pledged to that creed—to the unconditional repeal of the Fugitive Slave law, a refusal to admit any more slave States into the Union even if the people want them, a determination to apply the Wilmot Proviso, not only to all the territory we now have, but all that we may hereafter acquire, he refused to answer, and his followers say, in excuse, that the resolutions upon which I based my interrogatories were not adopted at the *"right spot."* Lincoln and his political friends are great on *"spots."* In Congress, as a representative of this State, he declared the Mexican war to be unjust and infamous, and would not support it, or acknowledge his own country to be right in the contest, because he said that American blood was not shed on American soil in the *"right spot."* And now he cannot answer the questions I put to him at Ottawa because the resolutions I read were not adopted at the *"right spot."* It may be possible that I was led into an error as to the *spot* on which the resolutions I then read were proclaimed, but I was not, and am not in error as to the fact of their forming the basis of the creed of the Republican party when that party was first organized. I will state to you the evidence I had, and upon which relied for my statement that the resolutions in question were adopted at Springfield on the 5th of October, 1854. Although I was aware that such resolutions had been passed in this district, and nearly all the northern Congressional Districts and County Conventions, I had not noticed whether or not they had been adopted by my State Convention. In 1856, a debate arose in Congress between Major Thomas L. Harris, of the Springfield District, and Mr. Norton, of the Joliet District, on political matters connected with our State, in the course of which, Major Harris quoted those resolutions as having been passed by the first Republican State Convention that ever assembled in Illinois. I knew that Major Harris was remarkable for his accuracy, that he was a very conscientious and sincere man, and I also noticed that Norton did not question the accuracy of this statement. I therefore took it for granted that it was so, and the other day when I concluded to use the resolutions at Ottawa, I wrote to Charles H. Lanphier, editor of the *State Register,* at Springfield, calling his attention to them, telling him that I had been informed that Major Harris was lying sick at Springfield, and desiring him to call upon him and ascertain all the facts concerning the resolutions, the time and the place where they were adopted. In reply, Mr. Lanphier sent me two copies of his paper, which I have here. The first is a copy of the *State Register,* published at Springfield, Mr. Lincoln's own town, on the 16th of October, 1854, only eleven days after the adjournment of the Convention, from which I desire to read the following:

> "During the late discussions in this city, Lincoln made a speech, to which Judge Douglas replied. In Lincoln's speech he took the broad ground that, according to the Declaration of Independence, the whites and blacks are equal. From this he drew the conclusion, which he several times repeated, that the white man had no right to pass laws for the government of the black man without the nigger's consent. This speech of Lincoln's was heard and applauded by all the Abolitionists assembled in Springfield. So soon as Mr. Lincoln was done speaking, Mr. Codding arose and

requested all the delegates to the Black Republican Convention to with-draw into the Senate chamber. They did so, and after long deliberation, they laid down the following Abolition platform as the platform on which they stood. We call the particular attention of all our readers to it."

Then follows the identical platform, word for word, which I read at Ottawa. Now, that was published in Mr. Lincoln's own town, eleven days after the Convention was held, and it has remained on record up to this day never contradicted.

When I quoted the resolutions at Ottawa and questioned Mr. Lincoln in relation to them, he said that his name was on the committee that reported them, but he did not serve, nor did he think he served, because he was, or thought he was, in Tazewell county at the time the Convention was in session. He did not deny that the resolutions were passed by the Springfield Convention. He did not know better, and evidently thought that they were, but afterward his friends declared that they had discovered that they varied in some respects from the resolutions passed by that Convention. I have shown you that I had good evidence for believing that the resolutions had been passed at Springfield. Mr. Lincoln ought to have known better; but not a word is said about his ignorance on the subject, whilst I, notwithstanding the circumstances, am accused of forgery.

Now, I will show you that if I have made a mistake as to the place where these resolutions were adopted—and when I get down to Springfield I will investigate the matter and see whether or not I have—that the principles they enunciate were adopted as the Black Republican platform ["white, white"], in the various countries and Congressional Districts throughout the north end of the State in 1854. This platform was adopted in nearly every county that gave a Black Republican majority for the Legislature in that year, and here is a man [pointing to Mr. Denio, who sat on the stand near Deacon Bross] who knows as well as any living man that it was the creed of the Black Republican party at that time. I would be willing to call Denio as a witness, or any other honest man belonging to that party. I will now read the resolutions adopted at the Rockford Convention on the 90th of August, 1854, which nominated Washburne for Congress. You elected him on the following platform:

> Resolved, That the continued and increasing aggressions of slavery in our country are destructive of the best rights of a free people, and that such aggressions cannot be successfully resisted without the united political action of all good men.

Resolved, That the citizens of the United States hold in their hands peaceful, constitutional and efficient remedy against the encroachments of the slave power, the ballot-box, and, if that remedy is boldly and wisely applied, the principles of liberty and eternal justice will be established.

Resolved, That we accept this issue forced upon us by the slave power, and, in defense of freedom, will co-operate and he known as Republicans, pledged to the accomplishment of the following purposes:

To bring the Administration of the Government back to the control of first principles; to restore Kansas and Nebraska to the position of free Territories; to repeal and entirely abrogate the Fugitive Slave law; to restrict slavery to those States in which it exists; to prohibit the admission of any more slave States into the Union; to exclude slavery from all the Territories over which the General Government has exclusive jurisdiction, and to resist the acquisition of any more Territories unless the introduction of slavery therein forever shall have been prohibited.

Resolved, That in furtherance of these principles we will use such constitutional and lawful means as shall seem best adapted to their accomplishment, and that we will support no man for office under the General or State Government who is not positively committed to the support of theme principles, and whose personal character and conduct is not a guaranty that he is reliable and shall abjure all party allegiance and ties.

Resolved, That we cordially invite persons of all former political parties whatever in favor of the object expressed in the above resolutions to units with us in carrying them into effect.

Well, you think that is a very good platform, do you not? If you do, if you approve it now, and think it is all right, you will not join with those men who say that I libel you by calling these your principles, will you? Now, Mr. Lincoln complains; Mr. Lincoln charges that I did you and him injustices by saying that this was the platform of your party. I am told that Washburne made a speech in Galena last night, in which he abused me awfully for bringing to light this platform, on which he was elected to Congress. He thought that you had forgotten it, as he and Mr. Lincoln desires to. He did not deny but that you had adopted it, and that he had subscribed to and was pledged by it, but he did not think it was fair to call it up and remind the people that it was their platform.

But I am glad to find that you are more honest in your abolitionism than your leaders, by avowing that it is your platform, and right in your opinion.

In the adoption of that platform, you not only declared that you would resist the admission of any more slave States, and work for the repeal of the Fugitive Slave law, but you pledged yourselves not to vote for any man for State or Federal offices who was not committed to these principles. You were thus committed. Similar resolutions to those were adopted in your country Convention here, and now with your admissions that they are your platform and embody your sentiments now as they did then, what do you think of Mr. Lincoln, your candidate for the U.S. Senate, who is attempting to dodge the responsibility of this platform, because it was not adopted in the right spot. I thought that it was adopted in Springfield, but it turns out it was not, that it was adopted at Rockford, and in the various counties which comprise this Congressional District. When I get into the next district, I will show that the same platform was adopted there, and so on through the State, until I nail the responsibility of it upon the back of the Black Republican party throughout the State.

A voice—"Couldn't you modify and call it brown?"

Mr. Douglas—Not a bit. I thought that you were becoming a little brown when your members in Congress voted for the Crittenden-Montgomery bill, but since you have backed out from that position and gone back to Abolitionism, you are black and not brown.

Gentlemen, I have shown you what your platform was in 1854. You still adhere to it. The same platform was adopted by nearly all the counties where the Black Republican party had a majority in 1854. I wish now to call your attention to the action of your representatives in the Legislature when they assembled together at Springfield. In the first place, you must remember that this was the organization of a new party. It is so declared in the resolutions themselves, which say that you are going to dissolve all old party ties and call the new party Republican. The old Whig party was to have its throat cut from ear to ear, and the Democratic party was to be annihilated and blotted out of existence, whilst in lieu of these parties the Black Republican party was to be organized on this Abolition platform. You know who the chief leaders were in breaking up and destroying these two great parties. Lincoln on the one hand and Trumbull on the other, being disappointed politicians, and having retired or been driven to obscurity by an outraged constituency because of their political sins, formed a scheme to abolitionize the two parties and lead the old line Whigs and old line Democrats captive, bound hand and foot, into the Abolition camp. Giddings, Chase, Fred Douglass and Lovejoy were here to christen them whenever they were brought in. Lincoln went to work to dissolve the old line Whig party. Clay was dead, and although the sod was not yet green on his grave, this man undertook to bring into disrepute those great Compromise measures of 1850, with which Clay and Webster were identified. Up to 1854 the old Whig party and the Democratic party had stood on a common platform so far as this slavery question was concerned. You Whigs and we Democrats differed about the bank, the tariff, distribution, the specie circular and the sub-treasury, but we agreed on this slavery question and the true mode of preserving the peace and harmony of the Union. The Compromise measures of 1850 were introduced by Clay, were defended by Webster, and supported by Cass, and were approved by Fillmore, and sanctioned by the National men of both parties. They constituted a common plank upon which both Whigs and Democrats stood. In 1852 the Whig party, in its last National Convention at Baltimore, indorsed and approved these measures of Clay, and so did the National Convention of the Democratic party held that same year. Thus the old line Whigs and the old line Democrats stood pledged to the great principle of self-government, which guaranties to the people of each Territory the right to decide the slavery question for themselves. In 1854, after the death of Clay and Webster, Mr. Lincoln, on the part of the Whigs, undertook to Abolition-ize the Whig party, by dissolving it, transferring the members into the Aboli-tion camp and making them train under Giddings, Fred Douglass, Lovejoy, Chase, Farnsworth, and other Abolition leaders. Trumbull undertook to dis-solve the Democratic party by taking old Democrats into the Abolition camp. Mr. Lincoln was aided in his efforts by many leading Whigs throughout the State. Your member of Congress, Mr. Washburne, being one of the most active. Trumbull was aided by many renegades from the Democratic party, among whom were John Wentworth, Tom Turner, and others, with whom you are familiar.

[Mr. Turner, who was one of the moderators, here interposed and said that he had drawn the resolutions which Senator Douglas had read.]

Mr. Douglas—Yes, and Turner says that he drew these resolutions. ["Hurra for Turner," "Hurra for Douglas."] That is right, give Turner cheers for draw-ing the resolutions if you approve them. If he drew those resolutions he will not deny that they are the creed of the Black Republican party.

Mr. Turner—"They are our creed exactly."

Mr. Douglas—And yet Lincoln denies that he stands on them. Mr. Turner says that the creed of the Black Republican party is the admission of no more slave States, and yet Mr. Lincoln declares that he would not like to be placed in a position where he would have to vote for them. All I have to say to friend Lincoln is, that I do not think there is much danger of his being placed in such a position. As Mr. Lincoln would be very sorry to be placed in such an embarrassing position as to be obliged to vote on the admission of any more slave States, I propose, out of mere kindness, to relieve him from any such necessity.

When the bargain between Lincoln and Trumbull was completed for Abolitionizing the Whig and Democratic parties, they "spread" over the State, Lincoln still pretending to be an old line Whig, in order to "rope in" the Whigs, and Trumbull pretending to be as good a Democrat as he ever was, in order to coax the Democrats over into the Abolition ranks. They played the part that "decoy ducks" play down on the Potomac river. In that part of the country they make artificial ducks and put them on the water in places where the wild ducks are to be found, for the purpose of decoying them. Well, Lincoln and Trumbull played the part of these "decoy ducks" and deceived enough old line Whigs and old line Democrats to elect a Black Republican Legislature. When that Legislature met, the first thing it did was to elect as Speaker of the House, the very man who is now boasting that he wrote the Abolition platform on which Lincoln will not stand. I want to know of Mr. Turner whether or not, when he was elected, he was a good embodiment of Republican principles?

Mr. Turner—"I hope I was then and am now."

Mr. Douglas—He swears that he hopes he was then and is now. He wrote that Black Republican platform, and is satisfied with it now. I admire and acknowledge Turner's honesty. Every man of you know that what he says about these resolutions being the platform of the Black Republican party is true, and you also know that each one of these men who are shuffling and trying to deny it are only trying to cheat the people out of their votes for the purpose of deceiving them still more after the election. I propose to trace this thing a little further, in order that you can see what additional evidence there is to fasten thin revolutionary platform upon the Black Republican party. When the Legislature assembled, there was an United States Senator to elect in the place of Gen. Shields, and before they proceeded to ballot, Lovejoy insisted on laying down certain principles by which to govern the party. It has been published to the world and satisfactorily proven that there was, at the time the alliance was made between Trumbull and Lincoln to Abolitionize the two parties, an agreement that Lincoln should take Shields's place in the United States Senate, and Trumbull should have mine so soon as they could conveniently get rid of me. When Lincoln was beaten for Shields's place, in a manner I will refer to in a few minutes, he felt very sore and restive; his friends grumbled, and some of them came out and charged that the most infamous treachery had been practiced against him; that the bargain was that Lincoln was to have had Shields's place, and Trumbull was

to have waited for mine, but that Trumbull having the control of a few Abolitionized Democrats, he prevented them from voting for Lincoln, thus keeping
him within a few votes of an election until he succeeded in forcing the party to
drop him and elect Trumbull. Well, Trumbull having cheated Lincoln, his
friends made a fuss, and in order to keep them and Lincoln quiet, the party were
obliged to come forward, in advance, at the last State election, and make a pledge
that they would go for Lincoln and nobody else. Lincoln could not be silenced
in any other way.

Now, there are a great many Black Republicans of you who do not know
this thing was done. ["White, white," and great clamor.] I wish to remind you
that while Mr. Lincoln was speaking there was not a Democrat vulgar and
blackguard enough to interrupt him. But I know that the shoe is pinching you.
I am clinching Lincoln now, and you are scared to death for the result. I have
seen this thing before. I have seen men make appointments for joint discussions,
and the moment their man has been heard, try to interrupt and prevent a fair
hearing of the other side. I have seen your mobs before, and defy your wrath.
[Tremendous applause.] My friends, do not cheer, for I need my whole time.
The object of the opposition is to occupy my attention in order to prevent me
from giving the whole evidence and nailing this double dealing on the Black
Republican party. As I have before said, Lovejoy demanded a declaration of
principles on the part of the Black Republicans of the Legislature before going
into an election for United States Senator. He offered the following preamble
and resolutions which I hold in my hand:

> WHEREAS. Human slavery is a violation of the principles of natural
> and revealed rights; and whereas, the fathers of the Revolution, fully
> imbued with the spirit of these principles, declared freedom to be the
> inalienable birthright of all men; and whereas, the preamble to the Con-
> stitution of the United States avers that that instrument was ordained to
> establish justice, and secure the blessings of liberty to ourselves and our
> posterity; and whereas, in furtherance of the above principles, slavery was
> forever prohibited in the old North-west Territory, and more recently
> in all that Territory lying west and north of the State of Missouri, by the
> act of the Federal Government; and whereas, the repeal of the prohibi-
> tion last referred to, was contrary to the wishes of the people of Illinois,
> a violation of an implied compact, long deemed sacred by the citizens of
> the United States, and a wide departure from the uniform action of the
> General Government in relation to the extension of slavery; therefore,

Resolved by the House of Representatives, the Senate concurring therein, That our Senators in Congress be instructed, and our Representatives requested to introduce, if not otherwise introduced, and to vote for a bill to restore such prohibition to the aforesaid Territories, and also to extend a similar prohibition to all territory which now belongs to the United States, or which may hereafter come under their jurisdiction.

Resolved, That our Senators in Congress be instructed, and our Representatives requested, to vote against the admission of any State into the Union, the Constitution of which does not prohibit slavery, whether the territory out of which such State may have been formed shall have been acquired by conquest, treaty, purchase, or from original territory of the United States.

Resolved, That our Senators in Congress be instructed, and our Representatives requested, to introduce and vote for a bill to repeal an act entitled "an act respecting fugitives from justice and persons escaping from the service of their masters; and, failing in that, for such a modification of it as shall secure the right of *habeaus corpus* and trial by jury before the regularly-constituted authorities of the State, to all persons claimed as owing service or labor.

Those resolutions were introduced by Mr. Lovejoy immediately preceding the election of Senator. They declared first, that the Wilmot Proviso must be applied to all territory north of 36 deg. 30 min. Secondly, that it must be applied to all territory south of 36 deg. 30 min. Thirdly, that it must be applied to all territory hereafter to be acquired by the United States. The next resolution declares that no more slave States shall be admitted into this Union under any circumstances whatever, no matter whether they are formed out of territory now owned by us or that we may hereafter acquire, by treaty, by Congress, or in any manner whatever. The next resolution demands the unconditional repeal of the Fugitive Slave law, although its unconditional repeal would leave no provision for carrying out that clause of the Constitution of the United States which guaranties the surrender of fugitives. If they could not get an unconditional repeal, they demanded that that law should be so modified as to make it as nearly useless as possible. Now, I want to show you who voted for these resolutions. When the vote was taken on the first resolution it was decided in the affirmative—yeas 41, nays 32. You will find that this is a strict party vote, between the Democrats on the one hand and the Black Republicans on the other. [Cries of "White, white," and clamor.] I know your name, and always call things by their right name. The point I wish to call your attention to, is this: that these resolutions were adopted on the 7th day of February, and that on the 8th they went into an election for a United States Senator, and that day every man who voted for these resolutions, with but two exceptions, voted for Lincoln for the United States Senate. ["Give us their names."] I will read the names over to you if you want them, but I believe your object is to occupy my time.

On the next resolution the vote stood—yeas 33, nays 40, and on the third resolution—yeas 35, nays 47. I wish to impress it upon you, that every man who voted for those resolutions, with but two exceptions, voted on the next day for Lincoln for U.S. Senator. Bear in mind that the members who thus voted for Lincoln were elected to the Legislature pledged to vote for no man for office under the State or Federal Government who was not committed to this Black Republican platform. They were all so pledged. Mr. Turner, who stands by me, and who then represented you, and who says that he wrote those resolutions, voted for Lincoln, when he was pledged not to do so unless Lincoln was in favor of those resolutions. I now ask Mr. Turner [turning to Mr. Turner], did you violate your pledge in voting for Mr. Lincoln, or did he commit himself to your platform before you cast your vote for him?

I could go through the whole list of names here and show you that all the Black Republicans in the Legislature, who voted for Mr. Lincoln, had voted on the day previous for these resolutions. For instance, here are the names of Sargent and Little of Jo Daviess and Carroll, Thomas J. Turner of Stephenson, Lawrence of Boone and McHenry, Swan of Lake, Pinckney of Ogle county, and Lyman of Winnebago. Thus you see every member from your Congressional District voted for Mr. Lincoln, and they were pledged not to vote for him unless he was committed to the doctrine of no more slave States, the prohibition of slavery in the Territories, and the repeal of the Fugitive Slave law. Mr. Lincoln tells you to-day that he is not pledged to any such doctrine. Either Mr. Lincoln was then committed to those propositions, or Mr. Turner violated his pledges to you when he voted for him. Either Lincoln was pledged to each one of those propositions, or else every Black Republican Representative from this Congressional District violated his pledge of honor to his constituents by voting for him. I ask you which horn of the dilemma will you take? Will you hold Lincoln up to the platform of his party, or will you accuse every Representative you had in the Legislature of violating his pledge of honor to his constituents? There is no escape for you. Either Mr. Lincoln was committed to those propositions, or your members violated their faith. Take either horn of the dilemma you choose. There is no dodging the question; I want Lincoln's answer. He says he was not pledged to repeal the Fugitive Slave law, that he does not quite like to do it; he will not introduce a law to repeal it, but thinks there ought to be some law; he does not tell what it ought to be; upon the whole, he is altogether undecided, and don't know what to think or do. That is the substance of his answer upon the repeal of the Fugitive Slave law. I put the question to him distinctly, whether he indorsed that part of the Black Republican platform which calls for the entire abrogation and repeal of the Fugitive Slave law. He answers no! that he does not indorse that, but he does not tell what be is for, or what he will vote for. His answer is, in fact, no answer at all. Why cannot he speak out and say what he is for and what he will do?

In regard to there being no more slave States, he is not pledged to that. He would not like, he says, to be put in a position where he would have to vote one way or another upon that question. I pray you, do not put him in a position that would embarass him so much. Gentlemen, if he goes to the Senate, he may be put in that position, and then which way will he vote?

[A Voice—"How will you vote?"]

Mr. Douglas—I will vote for the admission of just such a State as by the form of their Constitution the people show they want; if they want slavery, they shall have it; if they prohibit slavery it shall be prohibited. They can form their institutions to please themselves, subject only to the Constitution; and I for one stand ready to receive them into the Union. Why cannot your Black Republican candidates talk out as plain as that when they are questioned?

I do not want to cheat any man out of his vote. No man is deceived in regard to my principles if I have the power to express myself in terms explicit enough to convey my ideas.

Mr. Lincoln made a speech when he was nominated for the United States Senate which covers all these Abolition platforms. He there lays down a proposition so broad in its abolitionism as to cover the whole ground.

"In my opinion it [the slavery agitation] will not cease until a crisis shall have been reached and passed. 'A house divided against itself cannot stand.' I believe this Government cannot endure permanently half slave and half free. I do not expect the house to fall—but I do expect it will cease to be divided. It will become all one thing or all the other. Either the opponents of Slavery will arrest the further spread of it, and place it where the public mind shall rest in the belief that is in the course of ultimate extinction, or its advocates will push it forward till it shall become alike lawful in all the States—old as well as new. North as well as South."

There you find that Mr. Lincoln lays down the doctrine that this Union cannot endure divided as our fathers made it, with free and slave States. He says they must all become one thing, or all the other; that they must all be free or all slave, or else the Union cannot continue to exist. It being his opinion that to admit any more slave States, to continue to divide the Union into free and slave States, will dissolve it. I want to know of Mr. Lincoln whether he will vote for the admission of another slave State.

He tells you the Union cannot exist unless the States are all free or all slave; he tells you that he is opposed to making them all slave, and hence he is for making them all free, in order that the Union may exist; and yet he will not say that he will not vote against another slave State, knowing that the Unions must be dissolved if he votes for it. I ask you if that is fair dealing? The true intent and inevitable conclusion to be drawn from his first Springfield speech is, that he is opposed to the admission of any more slave States under any circumstance. If he is so opposed, why not say so? If be believes this Union cannot endure divided into free and slave States, that they must all become free in order to save the Union, he is bound as an honest man, to vote against any more slave States. If he believes it he is bound to do it. Show me that it is my duty in order to save the Union to do a particular act, and I will do it if the Constitution does not prohibit it. I am not for the dissolution of the Union under any circumstances. I will pursue no course of conduct that will give just cause for the dissolution of the Union. The hope of the friends of freedom throughout the world rests upon the perpetuity of this Union. The down-trodden and oppressed people who are suffering under European despotism all look with hope and anxiety to the American. Union as the only resting place and permanent home of freedom and self-government.

Mr. Lincoln says that he believes that this Union cannot continue to endure with slave States in it, and yet he will not tell you distinctly whether he will vote for or against the admission of any more slave States, but says he would not like to be put to the test. I do not think he will be put to the test. I do not think that the people of Illinois desire a man to represent them who would not like to be put to the test on the performances of a high constitutional duty. I will retire in shame from the Senate of the United States when I am not willing to be put to the test in the performance of my duty. I have been put to severe tests. I have stood by my principles in fair weather and in foul, in the sunshine and in the rain. I have defended the great principles of self-government here among you when Northern sentiment ran in a torrent against me, and I have defended that same great principle when Southern sentiment came down like an avalanche upon me. I was not afraid of any test they put to me. I knew I was right—I knew my principles were sound—I knew that the people would see in the end that I had done right, and I knew that the God of Heaven would smile upon me if I was faithful in the performance of my duty.

Mr. Lincoln makes a charge of corruption against the Supreme Court of the United States, and two Presidents of the United States, and attempts to bolster it up by saying that I did the same against the Washington *Union.* Suppose I did make that charge of corruption against the Washington *Union,* when it was true, does that justify him in making a false charge against me and others? That is the question I would put. He says that at the time the Nebraska bill was introduced, and before it was passed, there was a conspiracy between the Judges of the Supreme Court, President Pierce, President Buchanan and myself by that bill, and the decision of the court to break down the barrier and establish slavery all over the Union. Does he not know that that charge is historically false as against President Buchanan? He knows that Mr. Buchanan was at that time in England, representing this country with distinguished ability at the Court of St. James, that he was there for a long time before, and did not return for a year or more after. He knows that to be true, and that fact proves his charge to be false as against Mr. Buchanan. Then again, I wish to call his attention to the fact that at the time the Nebraska bill was passed, the Dred Scott case was not before the Supreme Court at all; it was not upon the docket of the Supreme Court; it had not been brought there, and the Judges in all probability knew nothing of it. Thus the history of the country proves the charge to be false as against them. As to President Pierce, his high character as a man of integrity and honor is enough to vindicate him from such a charge; and as to myself, I pronounce the charge an infamous lie, whenever and wherever made, and by whomsoever made. I am willing that Mr. Lincoln should go and rake up every public act of mine, every measure I have introduced, report I have made, speech delivered, and criticise them, but when he charges upon me a corrupt conspiracy for the purpose of perverting the institutions of the country, I brand it as it deserves. I say the history of the country proves it to be false, and that it could not have been possible at the time. But now he tries to protect himself in this charge, because I made a charge against the Washington *Union.* My speech in the Senate against the Washington *Union* was made because it advocated a revolutionary doctrine, by declaring that the free States had not the right to prohibit slavery within their own limits. Because I made that charge against the Washington *Union,* Mr. Lincoln says it was a charge against Mr. Buchanan. Suppose it was; is Mr. Lincoln the peculiar defender of Mr. Buchanan? Is he so interested in the Federal Administration, and so bound to it, that he must jump to the rescue and defend it from every attack that I may make against it? I understand the whole thing. The Washington *Union,* under that most corrupt of all men, Cornelius Wendell, is advocating Mr. Lincoln's claim to the Senate. Wendell was the printer of the last Black Republican House of Representatives; he was a candidate before the present Democratic House, but was ignominiously kicked out, and then he took the money which he had made out of the public printing by means of the Black Republicans, bought the Washington *Union,* and is now publishing it in the name of the Democratic party, and advocating Mr. Lincoln's election to the Senate. Mr. Lincoln therefore considers an attack upon Wendell and his corrupt gang as a personal attack upon him. This only proves what I have charged, that there is an alliance between Lincoln and his supporters, and the Federal office-holders of this State, and Presidential aspirants out of it, to break me down at home.

Mr. Lincoln feels bound to come in to the rescue of the Washington *Union.* In that speech which I delivered in answer to the Washington *Union,* I made it distinctly against the *Union,* and against the *Union* alone. I did not choose to go beyond that. If I have occasion to attack the President's conduct, I will do it in language that will not be misunderstood. When I differed with the President, I spoke out so that you all heard me. That question passed away; it resulted in the triumph of my principle by allowing the people to do as they please, and there is an end of the controversy. Whenever the great principle of self-government—the right of the people to make their own Constitution, and come into the Union with slavery or without it, as they see proper, shall again arise, you will find me standing firm in defense of that principle, and fighting whoever fights it. If Mr. Buchanan stands as I doubt not he will, by the recommendation contained in his Message, that hereafter all State Constitutions ought to be submitted to the people before the admission of the State into the Union, he will find me standing by him firmly, shoulder to shoulder, in carrying it out. I know Mr. Lincoln's object; he wants to divide the Democratic party, in order that he may defeat me and get to the Senate.

Mr. Douglas's time here expired, and he stopped on the moment.

MR. LINCOLN'S REJOINDER.

MY FRIENDS: It will readily occur to you that I cannot, in half an hour, notice all the things that so able a man as Judge Douglas can say in an hour and a half; and I hope, therefore, if there be any thing that he has said upon which you would like to hear something from me, but which I omit to comment upon, you will bear in mind that it would be expecting an impossibility for me to go over his whole ground. I can but take up some of the points that he has dwelt upon, and employ my half-hour specially on them.

The first thing I have to say to you is a word in regard to Judge Douglas's declaration about the "vulgarity and blackguardian" in the audience—that no such thing, as he says, was shown by any Democrat while I was speaking. Now, I only wish, by way of reply on this subject, to say that while *I* was speaking, *I* used no "vulgarity or blackguardism" toward any Democrat.

Now, my friends, I come to all this long portion of the Judge's speech—perhaps half of it—which he has devoted to the various resolutions and platforms that have been adopted in the different counties in the different Congressional Districts, and in the Illinois Legislature—which he supposes are at variance with the positions I have assumed before you to-day. It is true that many of these resolutions are at variance with the positions I have here assumed. All I have to ask is that we talk reasonably and rationally about it. I happen to know, the Judge's opinion to the contrary notswithstanding, that I have never tried to conceal my opinions, nor tried to deceive any one in reference to them. He may go and examine all the members who voted for me for United States Senator in 1855, after the election of 1854. They were pledged to certain things here at home, and were determined to have pledges from me, and if he will find any of these persons who will tell him any thing inconsistent with what I say now, I will resign, or rather retire from the race, and give him no more trouble. The plain truth is this: At the introduction of the Nebraska policy, we believed there was a new era being introduced in the history of the Republic, which tended to the spread and perpetuation of slavery. But in our opposition to that measure we did not agree with one another in every thing. The people in the north end of the State were for stronger measures of opposition than we of the central and Southern portions of the State, but we were all opposed to the Nebraska doctrine. We had that one feeling and that one sentiment in common. You at the north end met in your Conventions and passed your resolutions. We in the middle of the State and further south did not hold such Conventions and pass the same resolutions, although we had in general a common view and a common sentiment. So that these meetings which the Judge has alluded to, and the resolutions he has read from, were local, and did not spread over the whole State. We at last met together in 1856, from all parts of the State, and we agreed upon a common platform. You, who held more extreme notions, either yielded those notions, or if not wholly yielding them, agreed to yield them practically, for the sake of embodying the opposition to the measures which the opposite party were pushing forward at that time. We met you then, and if there was any thing yielded, it was for practical purposes. We agreed then upon a platform for the party throughout the entire State of Illinois, and now we are all bound as a party, *to that platform*. And I say here to you, if any one expects of me—in the case of my election—that I will do any thing not signified by our Republican platform and my answers here to-day, I tell you very frankly that person will be deceived. I do not ask for the vote of any one who supposes that I have secret purposes or pledges that I dare not speak out. Cannot the Judge be satisfied? If he fears, in the unfortunate case of my election, that my going to Washington will enable me to advocate sentiments contrary to those which I expressed when you voted for and elected me, I assure him that his fears are wholly needless and groundless. Is the Judge really afraid of any such thing? I'll tell you what he is afraid of. *He is afraid we'll all pull together.* This is what alarms him more than any thing else. For my part, I do hope that all of us, entertaining a common sentiment in opposition to what appears to us a design to nationalize and perpetuate slavery, will waive minor differences on questions which either belong to the dead past or the distant future, and all pull together in this struggle. What are your sentiments? If it be true, that on the ground which I occupy—ground which I occupy as frankly and boldly as Judge Douglas does his—my views, though partly coinciding with yours, are not as perfectly in accordance with your feelings as his are, I do say to you in all candor, go for him and not for me. I hope to deal in all things, fairly with Judge Douglas, and with the people of the State, in this contest. And if I should never be elected to any office, I trust I may go down with no stain of falsehood upon my reputation—notwithstanding the hard opinions Judge Douglas chooses to entertain of me.

The Judge has again addressed himself to the abolition tendencies of a speech of mine, made at Springfield in June last. I have so often tried to answer what he is always saying on that melacholy theme, that I almost turn with disgust from the discussion—from the repetition of an answer to it. I trust that nearly all of this intelligent audience have rend that speech. If you have, I may venture to leave it to you to inspect it closely, and see whether it contains any of those "bugaboos" which frighten Judge Douglas.

The Judge complains that I did not fully answer his questions. If I have the sense to comprehend and answer those questions, I have done so fairly. If it can be pointed out to me how I can more fully and fairly answer him, I aver I have not the sense to see how it is to be done. He says I do not declare I would in any event vote for the admission of a slave State into the Union. If I have been fairly reported he will see that I did give an explicit answer to his interrogatories, I did not merely say that I would dislike to be put to the test; but I said clearly, if I were put to the test, and a Territory from which slavery had been excluded should present herself with a State Constitution sanctioning slavery— a most extraordinary thing and wholly unlikely to happen—I did not see how I could avoid voting for her admission. But he refuses to understand that I said so, and he wants this audience to understand that I did not say so. Yet it will be so reported in the printed speech that he cannot help seeing it.

He says if I should vote for the admission of a slave State I would be voting for a dissolution of the Union, because I hold that the Union cannot permanently exist half slave and half free. I repeat that I do not believe this Government *can* endure permanently half slave and half free, yet I do not admit, nor does it at all follow, that the admission of a single slave State will permanently fix the character and establish this as a universal slave nation. The Judge is very happy indeed at working up these quibbles. Before leaving the subject of answering questions I aver as my confident belief, when you come to see our speeches in print, that you will find every question which he has asked me more fairly and boldly and fully answered than he has answered those which I put to him. Is not that so? The two speeches may be placed side by side; and I will venture to leave it to impartial judges whether his questions have not been more directly and circumstantially answered than mine.

Judge Douglas says he made a charge upon the editor of the Washington *Union, alone,* of entertaining a purpose to rob the States of their power to exclude slavery from their limits. I undertake to say, and I make the direct issue, that he did *not* make his charge against the editor of the *Union* alone. I will undertake to prove by the record here, that he made that charge against more and higher dignitaries than the editor of the Washington *Union.* I am quite aware that he was shirking and dodging around the form in which he put it, but I can make it manifest that he leveled his "fatal blow" against more persons than this Washington editor. Will he dodge it now by alleging that I am trying to defend Mr. Buchanan against the charge? Not at all. Am I not making the same charge myself? I am trying to show that you, Judge Douglas, are a witness on my side. I am not defending Buchanan, and I will tell Judge Douglas that in my opinion, when he made that charge, he had an eye farther north than he was to-day. He was then fighting against people who called *him* a Black Republican and an Abolitionist. It is mixed all through his speech, and it is tolerably manifest that his eye was a great deal farther north than it is to-day. The Judge says that though he made this charge, Toombs got up and declared there was not a man in the United States, except the editor of the *Union,* who was in favor of the doctrines put forth in that article. And thereupon, I understand that the

Judge withdrew the charge. Although he had taken extracts from the newspaper, and then from the Lecompton Constitution, to show the existence of a conspiracy to bring about a "fatal blow," by which the States were to be deprived of the right of excluding slavery, it all went to pot as soon as Toombs got up and told him it was not true. It reminds me of the story that John Phoenix, the California railroad surveyor, tells. He says they started out from the Plaza to the Mission of Dolores. They had two ways of determining distances. One was by a chain and pins taken over the ground. The other was by a "go-it-ometer"—an invention of his own—a three-legged instrument, with which he computed a series of triangles between the points. At night he turned to the chain-man to ascertain what distance they had come, and found that by some mistake he had merely dragged the chain over the ground without keeping any record. By the "go-it-ometer" he found he had made ten miles. Being skeptical about this, he asked a drayman who was passing how far it was to the plaza. The drayman replied it was just half a mile, and the surveyor put it down in his book—just as Judge Douglas says, after he had made his calculations and computations, he took Toomba's statement. I have no doubt that after Judge Douglas had made his charge, he was as easily satisfied about its truth as the surveyor was of the drayman's statement of the distance to the plaza. Yet it is a fact that the man who put forth all that matter which Douglas deemed a "fatal alow" at State eovereignty, was elected by the Democrats as public printer.

Now, gentlemen, you may take Judge Douglas's speech of March 22d, 1858, beginning about the middle of page 21, and reading to the bottom of page 24, and you will find the evidence on which I say that he did not make his charge against the editor of the *Union* alone. I cannot stop to read it, but I will give it to the reporters. Judge Douglas said:

> "Mr. President, you here find several distinct propositions advanced boldly by the Washington *Union* editorially and apparently *authoritatively*, and every man who questions any of them is denounced as an Abolitionist, a Freesoiler, a fanatic. The propositions are, first, that the primary object of all government at its original institution is the protection of persons and property; second, that the Constitution of the United States declares that the citizens of each State shall be entitled to all the privileges and immunities of citizens in the several States; and that, therefore, thirdly, all State laws, whether organic or otherwise, which prohibit the citizens of one State from settling in another with their slave property, and especially declaring it forfeited, are direct violations of the original

intention of the Government and Constitution of the United States; and fourth, that the emancipation of the slaves of the Northern States was a gross outrage on the rights of property, inasmuch as it was involuntarily done on the part of the owner."

"Remember that this article was published in the *Union* on the 17th of November, and on the 18th appeared the first article giving the adhesion of the *Union* to the Lecompton Constitution. It was in these words:

"'KANSAS AND HER CONSTITUTION.—The vexed question is settled. The problem is solved. The dead point of danger is passed. All serious trouble to Kansas affairs is over and gone'—

"And a column, nearly, of the same sort. Then, when you come to look into the Lecompton Constitution, you find the same doctrine incorporated in it which was put forth editorially in the *Union*. What is it?

"'ARTICLE 7, *Section* 1. The right of property is before and higher than any constitutional sanction; and the right of the owner of a slave to such slave and its increase is the same and as invariable as the right of the owner of any property whatever.'

"Then in the schedule is a provision that the Constitution may be amended after 1864 by a two-thirds vote.

"'But no alteration shall be made to affect the right of property in the ownership of slaves.'

"It will be seen by these clauses in the Lecompton Constitution that they are identical in spirit with this *authoritative* article in the Washington *Union* of the day previous to its indorsement of this Constitution.

"When I saw that article in the *Union* of the 17th of November, followed by the glorification of the Lecompton Constitution on the 18th of November, and this clause in the Constitution asserting the doctrine that a State has no right to prohibit slavery within its limits, I saw that there was a *fatal blow* being struck at the sovereignty of the States of this Union."

Here he says, "Mr. President, you here find several distinct propositions advanced boldly, and apparently *authoritatively*." By whose authority, Judge Douglas? Again, he says in another place, "It will be seen by these clauses in the Lecompton Constitution, that they are identical in spirit with this *authoritative* article." *By whose authority?* Who do you mean to say authorized the publication of these articles? He knows that the Washington *Union* is considered the organ of the Administration. *I* demand of Judge Douglas *by whose authority* he meant to say those articles were published, if not by the authority of the President of the United States and his Cabinet? I defy him to show whom he referred to, if not to these high functionaries in the Federal Government. More than this, he says the articles in that paper and the provisions of the Lecompton Constitution are "identical," and being identical, he argues that the authors are co-operating and conspiring together. He does not use the word "conspiring," but what other construction can you put upon it? He winds up with this:

"When I saw that article in the *Union* of the 17th of November, followed by the glorification of the Lecompton Constitution on the 18th of November, and this clause in the Constitution asserting the doctrine that a State has no right to prohibit slavery within its limits, I saw that there was a *fatal blow* being struck at the sovereignty of the States of this Union."

I ask him if all this fuss was made over the editor of this newspaper. It would be a terribly "*fatal* blow" indeed which a single man could strike, when no President, no Cabinet officer, no member of Congress, was giving strength and efficiency to the moment. Out of respect to Judge Douglas's good sense I must believe be didn't manufacture his idea of the "fatal" character of that blow out of such a miserable scapegrace as he represents that editor to be. But the Judge's eye is farther south now. Then, it was very peculiarly and decidedly north. His hope rested on the idea of visiting the great "Black Republican" party, and making it the tail of his new kite. He knows he was then expecting from day to day to turn Republican and place himself at the head of our organization. He has found that these despised "Black Republicans" estimate him by a standard which he has taught them none too well. Hence he is crawling back into his old camp, and you will find him eventually installed in full fellowship among those whom he was then battling, and with whom he now pretends to be at such fearful variance. [Loud applause and cries of "go on, go on."] I cannot, gentlemen, my time has expired.

THIRD JOINT DEBATE, AT JONESBORO
SEPTEMBER 15, 1858

MR. DOUGLAS'S SPEECH.

LADIES AND GENTLEMEN: I appear before you to-day in pursuance of a previous notice, and have made arrangements with Mr. Lincoln to divide time, and discuss with him the leading political topics that now agitate the country.

Prior to 1854 this country was divided into two great political parties known as Whig and Democratic. These parties differed from each other on certain questions which were then deemed to be important to the best interests of the Republic. Whig and Democrats differed about a bank, the tariff, distribution, the specie circular and the sub-treasury. On those issues we went before the country and discussed the principles, objects and measures of the two great parties. Each of the parties could proclaim its principles in Louisiana as well as in Massachusetts, in Kentucky as well as in Illinois. Since that period, a great revolution has taken place in the formation of parties, by which they now seem to be divided by a geographical line, a large party in the North being arrayed under the Abolition or Republican banner, in hostility to the Southern States, Southern people, and Southern institutions. It becomes important for us to inquire how this transformation of parties has occurred, made from those of national principles to geographical factions. You remember that in 1850—this country was agitated from its center to its circumference about this slavery question—it became necessary for the leaders of the great Whig party and the leaders of the great Democratic party to postpone, for the time being, their particular disputes, and unite first to save the Union before they should quarrel as to the mode in which it was to be governed. During the Congress of 1849–'50, Henry Clay was the leader of the Union men, supported by Cass and Webster, and the leaders of the Democracy and the leaders of the Whigs, in opposition to Northern Abolitionists or Southern Disunionists. That great contest of 1850 resulted in the establishment of the Compromise Measures of that year, which measures rested on the great principle that the people of each State and each Territory of this Union ought to be permitted to regulate their own domestic institutions in their own way, subject to no other limitation than that which the Federal Constitution imposes.

I now wish to ask you whether that principle was right or wrong which guarantied to every State and every community the right to form and regulate their domestic institutions to suit themselves. These measures were adopted, as I have previously said, by the joint action of the Union Whigs and Union Democrats in opposition to Northern Abolitionists and Southern Disunionists. In 1858, when the Whig party assembled at Baltimore, in National Convention for the last time, they adopted the principle of the Compromise Measures of 1850 as their rule of party action in the future. One month thereafter the Democrats assembled at the same place to nominate a candidate for the Presidency, and declared the same great principle as the rule of action by which the Democracy would be governed. The Presidential election of 1852 was fought on that basis. It is true that the Whigs claimed special merit for the adoption of those measures, because they asserted that their great Clay originated them, their

344 THE LANGUAGE OF LIBERTY

god-like Webster defended them and their Fillmore signed the bill making them the law of the land; but on the other hand, the Democrats claimed special credit for the Democracy, upon the ground that we gave twice as many votes in both Houses of Congress for the passage of these measures as the Whig party.

Thus you see that in the Presidential election of 1852, the Whigs were pledged by their platform and their candidate to the principle of the Compromise Measures of 1850, and the Democracy were likewise pledged by our principles, our platform, and our candidate to the same line of policy, to preserve peace and quiet between the different sections of this Union. Since that period the Whig party has been transformed into a sectional party, under the name of the Republican party, whilst the Democratic party continues the same national party it was at that day. All sectional men, all men of Abolition sentiments and principles, no matter whether they were old Abolitionists or had been Whigs or Democrats, rally under the sectional Republican banner, and consequently all national men, all Union-loving men, whether Whigs, Democrats, or by whatever name they have been known, ought to rally under the stars and stripes in defense of the Constitution as our fathers made it, and of the Union as it has existed under the Constitution.

How has this departure from the faith of the Democracy and the faith of the Whig party been accomplished? In 1854, certain restless, ambitious, and disappointed politicians throughout the land took advantage of the temporary excitement created by the Nebraska bill to try and dissolve the old Whig party and the old Democratic party, to abolitionize their members, and lead them, bound band and foot, captives into the Abolition camp. In the State of New York a Convention was held by some of these men and a platform adopted, every plank of which was as black as night, each one relating to the negro, and not one referring to the interests of the white man. That example was followed throughout the Northern States, the effect being made to combine all the free States in hostile array against the slave States. The men who thus thought that they could build up a great sectional party, and through its organization control the political destinies of this country, based all their hopes on the single fact that the North was the stronger division of the nation, and hence, if the North could be combined against the South, a sure victory awaited their efforts. I am doing no more than justice to the truth of history when I say that in this State Abraham Lincoln, on behalf of the Whigs, and Lyman Trumbull, on behalf of the Democrats, were the leaders who undertook to perform this grand scheme of abolitionizing the two parties to which they belonged. They had a private arrangement as to what should be the political destiny of each of the contracting parties before they went into the operation. The arrangement was that Mr. Lincoln was to take the old line Whigs with him, claiming that he was still as good a Whig as ever, over to the Abolitionists, and Mr. Trumbull was to run for Congress in the Belleville District, and, claiming to be a good Democrat, coax the old Democrats into the Abolition camp, and when, by the joint efforts of the abolitionized Whigs, the abolitionized Democrats, and the old line Abolition and Freesoil party of this State, they should secure a majority in the Legislature. Lincoln was then to be made United States Senator in Shields's place, Trumbull remaining in Congress until I should be accommodating enough to die or resign, and give him a chance to follow Lincoln. That was a very nice little bargain so far as Lincoln and Trumbull were concerned, if it had been carried out in good faith, and friend Lincoln had attained to Senatorial dignity according to the contract. They went into the contest in every part of the State, calling upon all disappointed politicians to join in the crusade against the Democracy, and appealed to the prevailing sentiments and prejudices in all the northern counties of the State. In three Congressional Districts in the north end of the State they adopted, as the platform of this new party thus formed by Lincoln and Trumbull in the connection with the Abolitionists, all of those principles which aimed at a warfare on the part of the North against the South. They declared in that platform that the Wilmot Proviso was to be applied to all the Territories of the United States, North as well as South of 36 deg. 30 min., and not only to all the territory we then had, but all that we might hereafter acquire; that hereafter no more slave States should be admitted into this Union, even if the people of such State desired slavery; that the Fugitive Slave law should be absolutely and unconditionally repealed; that slavery should be abolished in the District of Columbia; that the slave-trade should be abolished between the different States, and, in fact, every article in their creed related to this slavery question, and pointed to a Northern geographical party in hostility to the Southern States of this Union. Such were their principles in Northern Illinois. A little further South they became bleached and grew paler just in proportion as public sentiment moderated and changed in this direction. They were Republicans or Abolitionists in the North, anti-Nebraska men down about Springfield, and in this neighborhood they contented themselves with talking about the inexpediency of the repeal of the Missouri Compromise. In the extreme northern counties they brought out men to canvass the State whose complexion suited their political creed, and hence Fred Douglass, the negro, was to be found there, following Gen. Cass, and attempting to speak on behalf of Lincoln, Trumbull and Abolitionism, against that illustrious Senator. Why, they brought Fred Douglass to Freeport, when I was addressing a meeting there, in a carriage driven by the white owner, the negro sitting inside with the white lady and her daughter. When I got through canvassing the northern counties that year, and progressed as far south as Springfield, I was met and opposed in discussion by Lincoln, Lovejoy, Trumbull, and Sidney Breese, who were on one side. Father Giddings, the high-priest of Abolitionism, had just been there, and Chase came about the time I left. ["Why didn't you shoot him?"] I did take a running shot at them, but as I was single-handed against the white, black and mixed drove, I had to use a shot-gun and fire into the crowd instead of taking them off singly with a ride. Trumbull had for his lieutenants, in aiding him to abolitionize the Democracy, such men as John Wentworth, of Chicago, Gov. Reynolds, of Belleville, Sidney Breese, of Carlisle, and John Dougherty, of Union, each of whom modified his opinions to suit the locality he was in. Dougherty, for instance, would not go much further than to talk about the inexpediency of the Nebraska bill, whilst his allies at Chicago, advocated negro citizenship and negro equality, putting the white man and the negro on the same basis under the law. Now these men, four years ago, were engaged in a conspiracy to break down the Democracy; to-day they are again acting together for the same purpose! They do not hoist the same flag; they do not own the same principles, or profess the same faith; but conceal their union for the sake of policy. In the northern counties, you find that all the Conventions are called in the name of the Black Republican party; at Springfield, they dare not call a Republican Convention, but invite all the enemies of the Democracy to unite, and when they get down into Egypt, Trumbull issues notices calling upon the "*Free Democracy*" to assemble and hear him speak. I have one of the handbills calling a Trumbull meeting at Waterloo the other day, which I received there, which is in the following language:

A meeting of the Free Democracy will take place in Waterloo, on Monday, Sept. 13th inst., whereat Hon. Lyman Trumbull, Hon. John Baker and others, will address the people upon the different political topics of the day. Members of all parties are cordially invited to be present, and hear and determine for themselves.

THE MONROE FREE DEMOCRACY.

What is that name of "Free Democrats" put forth for unless to deceive the people, and make them believe that Trumbull and his followers are not the same party as that which raises the black flag of Abolitionism in the northern part of this State, and makes war upon the Democratic party throughout the State.

When I put that question to them at Waterloo on Saturday last, one of them rose and stated that they had changed their name for political effect in order to get votes. There was a candid admission. Their object in changing their party organization and principles in different localities was avowed to be an attempt to cheat and deceive some portion of the people until after the election. Why cannot a political party that is conscious of the rectitude of its purposes and the soundness of its principles declare them every where alike? I would disdain to hold any political principles that I could not avow in the same terms in Kentucky that I declared in Illinois, in Charleston as well as in Chicago, in New Orleans as well as in New York. So long as we live under a Constitution common to all the States, our political faith ought to be as broad, as liberal, and just as that Constitution itself, and should be proclaimed alike in every portion of the Union. But it is apparent that our opponents find it necessary, for partisan effect, to change their colors in different counties in order to catch the popular breeze, and hope with these discordant materials combined together to secure a majority in the Legislature for the purpose of putting down the Democratic party. This combination did succeed in 1854 so far as to elect a majority of their confederates to the Legislature, and the first important act which they performed was to elect a Senator in the place of the eminent and gallant Senator Shields. His term expired in the United States Senate at that time, and he had to be crushed by the Abolition coalition for the simple reason that he would not join in their conspiracy to wage war against one-half of the Union. That was the only objection to General Shields. He had served the people of the State with ability in the Legislature, he had served you with fidelity and ability as Auditor, he had performed his duties to the satisfaction of the whole country at the head of the Land Department at Washington, he had covered the State and the Union with immortal glory on the bloody fields of Mexico in defense of the honor of our flag, and yet he had to be stricken down by this unholy combination. And for what cause? Merely because he would not join a combination of one-half of the States to make war upon the other half, after having poured out his heart's blood for all the States in the Union. Trumbull was put in his place by Abolitionism. How did Trumbull get there? Before the Abolitionists would consent to go into an election for United States Senator they required all the members of this new combination to show their hands upon this question of Abolitionism. Lovejoy, one of their high-priests, brought in resolutions defining the Abolition creed, and required them to commit themselves on it by their votes—yea or nay. In that creed, as laid down by Lovejoy, they declared first, that the Wilmot Proviso must be put on all the Territories of the United States, North as well as

South of 36 deg. 30 min., and that no more territory should ever be acquired unless slavery was at first prohibited therein; second, that no more States should ever be received into the Union unless slavery was first prohibited, by Constitutional provision, in such States; third, that the Fugitive Slave law must be immediately repealed, or, failing in that, then such amendments were to be made to it as would render it useless and inefficient for the objects for which it was passed, etc. The next day after these resolutions were offered they were voted upon, part of them carried, and the others defeated, the same men who voted for them, with only two exceptions, voting soon after for Abraham Lincoln as their candidate for the United States Senate. He came within one or two votes of being elected, but he could not quite get the number required, for the simple reason that his friend Trumbull, who was a party to the bargain by which Lincoln was to take Shield's place, controlled a few abolitionized Democrats in the Legislature, and would not allow them all to vote for him, thus wronging Lincoln by permitting him on each ballot to be almost elected, but not quite, until he forced them to drop Lincoln and elect him (Trumbull), in order to unite the party. Thus you find, that although the Legislature was carried that year by the bargain between Trumbull, Lincoln, and the Abolitionists, and the union of these discordant elements in one harmonious party; yet Trumbull violated his pledge, and played a Yankee trick on Lincoln when they came to divide the spoils. Perhaps you would like a little evidence on this point. If you would, I will call Col. James H. Matheny, of Springfield, to the stand, Mr. Lincoln's especial confidential friend for the last twenty years, and see what he will say upon the subject of this bargain. Matheny is now the Black Republican or Abolition candidate for Congress in the Springfield District against the gallant Col. Harris, and is making speeches all over that part of the State against me and in favor of Lincoln, in concert with Trumbull. He ought to be a good witness, and I will read an extract from a speech which he made in 1856, when he was mad because his friend Lincoln had been cheated. It is one of numerous speeches of the same tenor that were made about that time, exposing this bargain between Lincoln, Trumbull and the Abolitionists. Matheny then said:

"The Whigs, Abolitionists, Know Nothings and renegade Democrats made a solemn compact for the purpose of carrying this State against the Democracy, on this plan: 1st. That they would all combine and elect Mr. Trumbull to Congress, and thereby carry his district for the Legislature, in order to throw all the strength that could be obtained into that body against the Democrats. 2d. That when the Legislature should meet, the officers of that body, such as speaker, clerks, door-keepers, etc., would be given to the Abolitionists; and 3d. That the Whigs were to have the United States Senator. That, accordingly, in good faith, Trumbull was elected to Congress, and his district carried for the Legislature, and, when it convened, the Abolitionists got all the officers of that body, and thus far the "bond" was fairly executed. The Whigs, on their part, demanded the election of Abraham Lincoln to the United States Senate, that the bond might be fulfilled, the other parties to the contract having already secured to themselves all that was called for. But, in the most perfidious manner, they refused to elect Mr. Lincoln; and the mean, lowlived, sneaking Trumbull succeeded, by pledging all that was required by any party, in thrusting Lincoln aside and foisting himself, an excrescence from the rotten bowels of the Democracy, into the United States Senate; and thus it has ever been, that an *honest* man makes a bad bargain when he conspires or contracts with rogues."

Matheny thought that his friend Lincoln made a bad bargain when he conspired and contracted with such rogues as Trumbull and his Abolition associates in that campaign. Lincoln was shoved off the track, and he and his friends all at once began to mope; became sour and mad, and disposed to tell, but dare not; and thus they stood for a long time, until the Abolitionists coaxed and flattered him back by their assurances that he should certainly be a Senator in Douglas's place. In that way the Abolitionists have been enabled to hold Lincoln to the alliance up to this time, and now they have brought him into a fight against me, and he is to see if he is again to be cheated by them. Lincoln this time, though, required more of them than a promise, and holds their bond, if not security, that Lovejoy shall not cheat him as Trumbull did.

When the Republican Convention assembled at Springfield, in June last, for the purpose of nominating State officers only, the Abolitionists could not get Lincoln and his friends into it until they would pledge themselves that Lincoln should be their candidate for the Senate; and you will find, in proof of this, that that Convention passed a resolution unanimously declaring that Abraham Lincoln was the "first, last and only choice" of the Republicans for United States Senator. He was not willing to have it understood that he was merely their first choice, or their last choice, but their *only* choice. The Black Republican party had nobody else. Browning was nowhere; Gov. Bissell was of no account; Archie Williams was not to be taken into consideration; John Wentworth was not worth mentioning; John M. Palmer was degraded; and their party presented the extraordinary spectacle of having but one—the first, the last, and only choice for the Senate. Suppose that Lincoln should die, what a horrible condition the Republican party would be in! They would have nobody left. They have no other choice, and it was necessary for them to put themselves before the world in this ludicrous, ridiculous attitude of having no other choice in order to quiet Lincoln's suspicions, and assure him that he was not to be cheated by Lovejoy, and the trickery by which Trumbull outgeneraled him. Well, gentlemen, I think they will have a nice time of it before they get through. I do not intend to give them any chance to cheat Lincoln at all this time. I intend to relieve him of all anxiety upon that subject, and spare them the mortification of more exposures of contracts violated, and the pledged honor of rogues forfeited.

But I wish to invite your attention to the chief points at issue between Mr. Lincoln and myself in this discussion. Mr. Lincoln knowing that he was to be the candidate of his party on account of the arrangement of which I have already spoken, knowing that he was to receive the nomination of the Convention for the United States Senate, had his speech, accepting that nomination, all written and committed to memory, ready to be delivered the moment the nominations was announced. Accordingly when it was made, he was in readiness, and delivered his speech, a portion of which I will read, in order that I may state his political principles fairly, by repeating them in his own language:

"We are now far into the fifth year since a policy was instituted for the avowed object, and with the confident promise of putting an end to slavery agitation; under the operation of that policy, that agitation has not only not ceased, but has constantly augmented. I believe it will not cease until a crisis shall have been reached and passed. 'A house divided against itself cannot stand.' I believe this Government cannot endure permanently half slave and half free. I do not expect the Union to be dissolved. I do not expect the house to fall, but I do expect it will cease to be divided. It will become all one thing or all the other. Either the opponents of slavery will arrest the spread of it, and place it where the public mind shall rest in the belief that it is in the course of ultimate extinction, or its advocates will push it forward until it shall become alike lawful in all the States, North as well as South."

There you have Mr. Lincoln's first and main proposition, upon which he bases his claims, stated in his own language. He tells you that this Republic cannot endure permanently divided into slave and free States, as our fathers made it. He says that they must all become free or all become slave, that they must all be one thing or all be the other, or this Government cannot last. Why can it not last, if we will execute the Government in the same spirit and upon the same principles upon which it is founded? Lincoln, by his proposition, says to the South, "If you desire to maintain your institutions as they are now, you must not be satisfied with minding your own business, but you must invade Illinois and all the other Northern States, establish slavery in them, and make it universal;" and in the same language he says to the North, "You must not be content with regulating your own affairs, and minding your own business, but if you desire to maintain your freedom, you must invade the Southern States, abolish slavery there and every where, in order to have the States all one thing or all the other." I say that this is the inevitable and irresistible result of Mr. Lincoln's argument, inviting a warfare between the North and the South, to be carried on with ruthless vengeance, until the one section or the other shall be driven to the wall, and become the victim of the rapacity of the other. What good would follow such a system of warfare? Suppose the North should succeed in conquering the South, how much would she be the gainer? or suppose the South should conquer the North, could the Union be preserved in that way? Is this sectional warfare to be waged between Northern States and Southern States until they all shall become uniform in their local and domestic institutions merely because Mr. Lincoln says that a house divided against itself cannot stand, and pretends that this scriptural quotation, this language of our Lord and Master, is applicable to the American Union and the American Constitution? Washington and his compeers, in the Convention that framed the Constitution, made this Government divided into free and slave States. It was composed then of thirteen sovereign and independent States, each having sovereign authority over its local and domestic institutions, and all bound together by the Federal Constitution. Mr. Lincoln likens that bond of the Federal Constitution, joining free and slave States together, to a house divided against itself, and says that it is contrary to the law of God and cannot stand. When did he learn, and by what authority does he proclaim, that this Government is contrary to the law of God and cannot stand? It has stood thus divided into free and slave States from its organization up to this day. During that period we have increased from four millions to thirty millions of people; we have extended our territory from the Mississippi to the Pacific ocean; we have acquired the Florida and Texas, and other territory sufficient to double our geographical extent; we have increased in population, in wealth, and in power beyond any example on earth; we have risen from a weak and feeble power to become the terror and admiration of the civilized world; and all this has been done under a Constitution which Mr. Lincoln, in substance, says is in violation of the law of God, and under a Union divided into free and slave States, which Mr. Lincoln thinks, because of such division, cannot stand. Surely, Mr. Lincoln is a wiser man than those who framed the Government. Washington did not believe, nor did his compatriots, that the local laws and domestic institutions that were well adapted to the Green Mountains of Vermont were suited to the rice plantations of South Carolina; they did not believe at that day that in a Republic so broad and expanded as this, containing such a variety of climate, soil, and interest, that uniformity in the local laws and domestic institutions was either desirable or possible. They believed then as our experience has proved to us now, that each locality, having different interests, a different climate and different surroundings, required different local laws, local policy and local institutions, adapted to the wants of that locality. Thus our Government was formed on the principle of diversity in the local institutions and laws, and not on that of uniformity.

As my time flies, I can only glance at these points and not present them as fully as I would wish, because I desire to bring all the points in controversy between the two parties before you in order to have Mr. Lincoln's reply. He makes war on the decision of the Supreme Court, in the case known as the Dred Scott case. I wish to say to you, fellow-citizens, that I have no war to make on that decision, or any other ever rendered by the Supreme Court. I am content to take that decision as it stands delivered by the highest judicial tribunal on earth, a tribunal established by the Constitution of the United States for that purpose, and hence that decision becomes the law of the land, binding on you, on me, and on every other good citizen, whether we like it or not. Hence I do not choose to go into an argument to prove, before this audience, whether or not Chief Justice Taney understood the law better than Abraham Lincoln.

Mr. Lincoln objects to that decision, first and mainly because it deprives the negro of the rights of citizenship. I am as much opposed to his reason for that objection as I am to the objection itself. I hold that a negro is not and never ought to be a citizen of the United States. I hold that this Government was made on the white basis, by white men, for the benefit of white men and their posterity forever, and should be administered by white men and none others. I do not believe that the Almighty made the negro capable of self-government. I am aware that all the Abolitionist lecturers that you find traveling about through the country, are in the habit of reading the Declaration of Independence to prove that all men were created equal and endowed by their Creator with certain inalienable rights, among which are life, liberty, and the pursuit of happiness. Mr. Lincoln is very much in the habit of following in the track of Love-joy in this particular, by reading that part of the Declaration of Independence to prove that the negro was endowed by the Almighty with the inalienable right of equality with white men. Now, I say to you, my fellow-citizens, that in my opinion, the signers of the Declaration had no reference to the negro whatever, when they declared all men to be created equal. They desired to express by that phrase white men, men of European birth and European descent, and had no reference either to the negro, the savage Indians, the Fejee, the Malay, or any other inferior and degraded race, when they spoke of the equality of men. One great evidence that such was their understanding, is to be found in the fact that at that time every one of the thirteen colonies was a slaveholding colony, every signer of the Declaration represented a slaveholding constituency, and we knew that no one of them emancipated his slaves, much less offered citizenship to them when they signed the Declaration; and yet, if they intended to declare that the negro was the equal of the white man, and entitled by divine right to an equality with him, they were bound, as honest men, that day and hour to have put their negroes on an equality with themselves. Instead of doing so, with uplifted eyes to heaven they implored the divine blessing upon them, during the seven years' bloody war they had to fight to maintain that Declaration, never dreaming that they were violating divine law by still holding the negroes in bondage and depriving them of equality.

My friends, I am in favor of preserving this Government as our fathers made it. It does not follow by any means that because a negro is not your equal or mine, that hence he must necessarily be a slave. On the contrary, it does follow that we ought so extend to the negro every right, every privilege, every immunity which he is capable of enjoying, consistent with the good of society. When you ask me what these rights are, what their nature and extent is, I tell you that that is a question which each State of this Union must decide for itself. Illinois has already decided the question. We have decided that the negro must not be a slave within our limits, but we have also decided that the negro shall not be a citizen within our limits; that he shall not vote, hold office, or exercise any political rights. I maintain that Illinois, as a sovereign State, has a right thus to fix her policy with reference to the relation between the white man and the negro; but while we had that right to decide the question for ourselves, we must recognize the same right in Kentucky and in every other State to make the same decision, or a different one. Having decided our own policy with reference to the black race, we must leave Kentucky and Missouri and every other State perfectly free to make just such a decision as they see proper on that question.

Kentucky has decided that question for herself. She has said that within her limits a negro shall not exercise any political rights, and she has also said that a portion of the negroes under the laws of that State shall be slaves. She had as much right to adopt that as her policy as we had to adopt the contrary for our policy. New York has decided that in that State a negro may vote if he has $250 worth of property, and if he owns that much he may vote upon an equality with the white man. I, for one, am utterly opposed to negro suffrage any where and under any circumstances yet, inasmuch as the Supreme Court have decided in the celebrated Dred Scott case that a State has a right to confer the privilege of voting upon free negroes, I am not going to make war upon New York because she has adopted a policy repugnant to my feelings. But New York must mind her own business, and keep her negro suffrage to herself, and not attempt to force it upon us.

In the State of Maine they have decided that a negro may vote and hold office on an equality with a white man. I had occasion to say to the Senators from Maine, in a discussion last session, that if they thought that the white people within the limits of their State were no better than negroes, I would not quarrel with them for it, but they must not say that my white constituents of Illinois were no better than negroes, or we would be sure to quarrel.

The Dred Scott decision covers the whole question, and declares that each State has the right to settle this question of suffrage for itself, and all questions as to the relations between the white man and the negro. Judge Taney expressly lays down the doctrine. I receive it as law, and I say that while those States are adopting regulations on that subject disgusting and abhorrent, according to my views, I will not make war on them if they will mind their own business and let us alone.

I now come back to the question, why cannot this Union exist forever divided into free and slave States, as our fathers made it? It can thus exist if each State will carry out the principles upon which our institutions were founded, to wit: the right of each State to do as it pleases, without meddling with its neighbors. Just act upon that great principle, and this Union will not only live forever, but it will extend and expand until it covers the whole continent, and makes this confederacy one grand, ocean-bound Republic. We must bear in mind that we are yet a young nation, growing with a rapidity unequaled in the history of the world, that our national increase is great, and that the emigration from the old world is increasing, requiring us to expand and acquire new territory from time to time, in order to give our people land to live upon. If we live upon the principle of State rights and State sovereignty, each State regulating its own affairs and minding its own business, we can go on and extend indefinitely, just as fast and as far as we need the territory. The time may come, indeed has now come, when our interests would be advanced by the requisition of the Island of Cuba. When we get Cuba we must take it as we find it, leaving the people to decide the question of slavery for themselves, without interference on the part of the Federal Government, or of any State of this Union. So, when it becomes necessary to acquire any portion of Mexico or Canada, or of this continent or the adjoining islands, we must take them as we find them, leaving the people free to do as they please—to have slavery or not, as they choose. I never have inquired and never will inquire whether a new State, applying for admission, has slavery or not for one of her institutions. If the Constitution that is presented be the act and deed of the people, and embodies their will, and they have the requisite population, I will admit them with slavery or without it, just as that people shall determine. My objection to the Lecompton Constitution did not consist in the fact that it made Kansas a slave State. I would have been as much opposed to its admission under such a Constitution as a free State as I was opposed to its admission under it as a slave State. I hold that that was a question which that people had a right to decide for themselves, and that no power on earth ought to have interfered with that decision. In my opinion, the Lecompton Constitution was not the act and deed of the people of Kansas, and did not embody their will, and the recent election in that Territory, at which it was voted down by nearly ten to one, shows conclusively that I was right in saying, when the Constitution was presented, that it was not the act and deed of the people, and did not embody their will.

If we wish to preserve our institutions in their purity, and transmit them unimpaired to our latest posterity, we must preserve with religious good faith that great principle of self-government which guaranties to each and every State, old and new, the right to make just such Constitutions as they desire, and come into the Union with their own Constitution, and not one palmed upon them. Whenever you sanction the doctrine that Congress may crowd a Constitution down the throats of an unwilling people, against their consent, you will subvert the great fundamental principle upon which all our free institutions rest. In the future I have no fear that the attempt will ever be made. President Buchanan declared in his annual message, that hereafter the rule adopted in the Minnesota case, requiring a Constitution to be submitted to the people, should be followed in all future cases, and if he stands by that recommendation there will be no division in the Democratic party on that principle in the future. Hence, the great mission of the Democracy is to unite the fraternal feeling of the whole country, restore peace and quiet, by teaching each State to mind its own business, and regulate its own domestic affairs, and all to unite in carrying out the Constitution as our fathers made it, and thus to preserve the Union and render it perpetual in all time to come. Why should we not act as our fathers who made the Government? There was no sectional strife in Washington's army. They were all brethren of a common confederacy; they fought under a common flag that they might bestow upon their posterity a common destiny, and to this end they poured out their blood in common streams, and shared, in some instances, a common grave.

MR. LINCOLN'S REPLY.

LADIES AND GENTLEMEN: There is very much in the principles that Judge Douglas has here enunciated that I most cordially approve, and over which I shall have no controversy with him. In so far as he has insisted that all the States have the right to do exactly as they please about all their domestic relations, including that of slavery, I agree entirely with him. He places me wrong in spite of all I can tell him, though I repeat it again and again, insisting that I have no difference with him upon this subject. I have made a great many speeches, some of which have been printed, and it will be utterly impossible for him to find any thing that I have ever put in print contrary to what I now say upon this subject. I hold myself under constitutional obligations to allow the people in all the States, without interference, direct or indirect, to do exactly as they please, and I deny that I have any inclination to interfere with them, even if there were no such constitutional obligation. I can only say again that I am placed improperly—altogether improperly, in spite of all I can say—when it is insisted that I entertain any other view or purposes in regard to that matter.

While I am upon this subject, I will make some answers briefly to certain propositions that Judge Douglas has put. He says, "Why can't this Union endure permanently, half slave and half free?" I have said that I supposed it could not, and I will try, before this new audience, to give briefly some of the reasons for entertaining that opinion. Another form of his question is, "Why can't we let it stand as our fathers placed it?" That is the exact difficulty between us. I say, that Judge Douglas and his friends have changed them from the position in which our fathers originally placed it. I say, in the way our fathers originally left the slavery question, the institution was in the course of ultimate extinction, and the public mind rested in the belief that it *was* in the course of ultimate extinction. I say when this Government was first established, it was the policy of its founders to prohibit the spread of slavery into the new Territories of the United States, where it had not existed. But Judge Douglas and his friends have broken up that policy, and placed it upon a new basis by which it is to become national and perpetual. All I have asked or desired any where is that it should be placed back again upon the basis that the fathers of our Government originally placed it upon. I have no doubt that it *would* become extinct, for all time to come, if we but readopted the policy of the fathers by restricting it to the limits it has already covered—restricting it from the new Territories.

I do not wish to dwell at great length on this branch of the subject at this time, but allow me to repeat one thing that I have stated before. Brooks, the man who assaulted Senator Summer on the floor of the Senate, and who was complimented with dinners, and silver pitchers, and gold-headed canes, and a good many other things for that feat, in one of his speeches declared that when this Government was originally established, nobody expected that the institution of slavery would last until this day. That was but the opinion of one man, but it was such an opinion as we can never get from Judge Douglas or anybody in favor of slavery in the North at all. You *can* sometimes get it from a Southern man. He said at the same time that the framers of our Government did not have the knowledge that experience has taught us—that experience and the invention of the cotton-gin have taught us that the perpetuation of slavery is a necessity. He insisted, therefore, upon its being changed from the basis upon which the fathers of the Government left it to the basis of its perpetuation and nationalization.

I insist that this is the difference between Judge Douglas and myself—that Judge Douglas is helping that change along. I insist upon this Government being placed where our fathers originally placed it.

I remember Judge Douglas once said that he saw the evidences on the statute books of Congress, of a policy in the origin of Government to divide slavery and freedom by a geographical line—that he saw an indisposition to maintain that policy, and therefore he set about studying up a way to settle the institution on the right basis—the basis which he thought it ought to have been placed upon at first; and in that speech he confesses that he seeks to place it, not upon the basis that the fathers placed it upon, but upon one gotten up on "original principles." When he asks me why we cannot get along with it in the attitude where our fathers placed it, he had better clear up the evidences that he has himself changed it from that basis; that he has himself been chiefly instrumental in changing the policy of the fathers. Any one who will read his speech of the 22d of last March, will see that he there makes an open confession, showing that he set about fixing the institution upon an altogether different set of principles. I think I have fully answered him when he asks me why we cannot let it alone upon the basis where our fathers left it, by showing that he has himself changed the whole policy of the Government in that regard.

Now, fellow-citizens, in regard to this matter about a contract that was made between Judge Trumbull and myself, and all that long portion of Judge Douglas's speech on this subject—I wish simply to say what I have said to him before, that he cannot know whether it is true or not, and I *do know* that there is not a word of truth in it. And I have told him so before. I don't want any harsh language indulged in, but I do not know how to deal with this persistent insisting on a story that I know to be utterly without truth. It used to be a fashion amongst men that when a charge was made, some sort of proof was brought forward to establish it, and if no proof was found to exist, the charge was dropped. I don't know how to meet this kind of an argument. I don't want to have a fight with Judge Douglas, and I have no way of making an argument up into the consistency of a corn-cob and stopping his mouth with it. All I can do is, good-humoredly to say that, from the beginning to the end of all that story about a bargain between Judge Trumbull and myself, *there is not a word of truth in it.* I can only ask him to show some sort of evidence of the truth of his story. He brings forward here and reads from what he contends is a speech by James H. Matheny, charging such a bargain between Trumbull and myself. My own opinion is that Matheny did do some such immoral thing as to tell a story that he knew nothing about. I believe he did. I contradicted it instantly, and it has been contradicted by Judge Trumbull, while nobody has produced any proof, because there is none. Now, whether the speech which the Judge brings forward here is really the one Matheny made I do not know, and I hope the Judge will pardon me for doubting the genuineness of this document, since his production of those Springfield resolutions at Ottawa. I do not wish to dwell at any great length upon this matter. I can say nothing when a long story like this is told, except it is not true, and demand that he who insists upon it shall produce some proof. That is all any man can do, and I leave it in that way, for I know of no other way of dealing with it.

The Judge has gone over a long account of the old Whig and Democratic parties, and it connects itself with this charge against Trumbull and myself. He says that they agreed upon a compromise in regard to the slavery question in 1850; that in a National Democratic Convention resolutions were passed to abide by that compromises as a finality upon the slavery question. He also says that the Whig party in National Convention agreed to abide by and regard as a finality the Compromise of 1850. I understand the Judge to be altogether right about that; I understand that part of the history of the country as stated by him to be correct. I recollect that I, as a member of that party, acquiesced in that compromise. I recollect in the Presidential election which followed, when we had General Scott up for the Presidency, Judge Douglas was around berating us Whigs as Abolitionists, precisely as he does to-day—not a bit of difference. I have often heard him. We could do nothing when the old Whig party was alive that was not Abolitionism, but it has got an extremely good name since it has passed away.

When that Compromise was made it did not repeal the old Missouri Compromise. It left a region of United States territory half as large as the present territory of the United States, north of the line of 36 degrees 30 minutes, in which slavery was prohibited by act of Congress. This compromise did not repeal that one. It did not affect or propose to repeal it. But at last it became Judge Douglas's duly, as he thought (and I find no fault with him), as Chairman of the Committee on Territories, to bring in a bill for the organization of a Territorial Government—first of one, then of two Territories north of that line. When he did so it ended in his inserting a provision substantially repealing the Missouri Compromise. That was because the Compromise of 1850 *had not* repealed it. And now I ask why he could not have let that compromise alone? We were quiet from the agitation of the slavery question. We were making no fuss about it. All had acquiesced in the Compromise measures of 1850. We never had been seriously disturbed by any abolition agitation before that period. When he came to form governments for the Territories north of the line of 36 degrees 30 minutes, why could he not have let that matter stand as it was standing? Was it necessary to the organization of a Territory? Not at all. Iowa lay north of the line and had been organized as a Territory and come into the Union as a State without disturbing that Compromise. There was no sort of necessity for destroying it to organize these Territories. But, gentlemen, it would take up all my time to meet all the little quibbling arguments of Judge Douglas to show that the Missouri Compromise was repealed by the Compromise of 1850. My own opinion is, that a careful investigation of all the arguments to sustain the position that that Compromise was virtually repealed by the Compromise of 1850, would show that they are the merest fallacies. I have the Report that Judge Douglas first brought into Congress at the time of the introduction of the Nebraska bill, which in its original form *did not* repeal the Missouri Compromise, and he there expressly stated that he had forborne to do so *because it had not been done by the Compromise of 1850.* I close this part of the discussion on my part by asking him the question again, "Why, when we had peace under the Missouri Compromise, could you not have let it alone?"

In complaining of what I said in my speech at Springfield, in which he says I accepted my nomination for the Senatorship (where, by the way, he is at fault, for if be will examine it, he will find no acceptance in it), he again quotes that portion in which I said that "a house divided against itself cannot stand." Let me say a word in regard to that matter.

He tries to persuade us that there must be a variety in the different institutions of the States of the Union; that that variety necessarily proceeds from the variety of soil, climate, of the face of the country, and the difference in the natural feature of the States. I agree to all that. Have these very matters ever produced any difficulty amongst us? Not at all. Have we ever had any quarrel over the fact that they have laws in Louisiana designed to regulate the commerce that springs from the production of sugar? Or because we have a different class relative to the production of flour in this State? Have they produced any differences? Not at all. They are the very cements of this Union. They don't make the house a house divided against itself. They are the props that hold up the house and sustain the Union.

But has it been so with this element of slavery? Have we not always had quarrels and difficulties over it? And when will we cease to have quarrels over it? Like causes produce like effects. It is worth while to observe that we have generally had comparative peace upon the slavery question, and that there has been no cause for alarm until it was excited by the effort to spread it into new territory. Whenever it has been limited to its present bounds, and there has been no effort to spread it, there has been peace. All the trouble and convulsion has proceeded from efforts to spread it over more territory. It was thus at the date of the Missouri Compromise. It was so again with the annexation of Texas; so with the territory acquired by the Mexican war, and it is so now. Whenever there has been an effort to spread it there has been agitation and resistance. Now, I appeal to this audience (very few of whom are my political friends), as national men, whether we have reason to expect that the agitation in regard to this subject will cease while the causes that tend to reproduce agitation are actively at work? Will not the same cause that produced agitation in 1820, when the Missouri Compromise was formed—that which produced the agitation upon the annexation of Texas, and at other times—work out the same results always? Do you think that the nature of man will be changed—that the same causes that produced agitation at one time will not have the same effect at another?

This has been the result so far as my observation of the slavery question and my reading in history extends. What right have we then to hope that the trouble will cease—that the agitation will come to an end—until it shall either be placed back where it originally stood, and where the fathers originally placed it, or, on the other hand, until it shall entirely master all opposition? This is the view I entertain, and this is the reason why I entertained it, as Judge Douglas has read from my Springfield speech.

Now, my friends, there is one other thing that I feel myself under some sort of obligation to mention. Judge Douglas has here to-day—in a very rambling way, I was about saying—spoken of the platforms for which he seeks to hold me responsible. He says, "Why can't you come out and make an open avowal of principles in all places alike?" and he reads from an advertisement that he says was used to notify the people of a speech to be made by Judge Trumbull at Waterloo. In commenting on it he desires to know whether we cannot speak frankly and manfully as he and his friends do! How, I ask, do his friends speak out their own sentiments? A Convention of his party in this State met on the 21st of April, at Springfield, and passed a set of resolutions which they proclaim to the country as their platform. This does constitute their platform, and it is because Judge Douglas claims it is his platform—that these are his principles and purposes—that he has a right to declare he speaks his sentiments "frankly and manfully." On the 9th of June, Col. John Dougherty, Gov. Reynolds and others, calling themselves National Democrats, met in Springfield and adopted a set of resolutions which are as easily understood, as plain and as definite in stating to the country and to the world what they believed in and would stand upon, as Judge Douglas's platform. Now, what is the reason, that Judge Douglas is not willing that Col. Dougherty and Gov. Reynolds should stand upon their own written and printed platform as well as he upon his? Why must he look farther than their platform when he claims himself to stand by his platform?

Again, in reference to our platform: On the 16th of June the Republicans had their Convention and published their platform, which is as clear and distinct as Judge Douglas's. In it they spoke their principles as plainly and as definitely to the world. What is the reason that Judge Douglas is not willing I should stand upon that platform? Why must he go around hunting for some one who is supporting me, or has supported me at some time in his life, and who has said something at some time contrary to that platform? Does the Judge regard that rule as a good one? If it turn out that the rule is a good one for me—that I am responsible for any and every opinion that any man has expressed who is my friend—then it is a good rule for him. I ask, is it not as good a rule for him as it is for me? In my opinion, it is not a good rule for either of us. Do you think differently, Judge?

Mr. Douglas—"I do not."

Mr. Lincoln—Judge Douglas says he does not think differently. I am glad of it. Then can he tell me why he is looking up resolutions of five or six years ago, and insisting that they were my platform, notwithstanding my protest that they are not, and never were my platform, and my pointing out the platform of the State Convention which he delights to say nominated me for the Senate? I cannot see what he means by parading these resolutions, if it is not to hold me responsible for them in some way. If he says to me here, that he does not hold the rule to be good, one way or the other, I do not comprehend how he could answer me more fully if he answered me at greater length. I will therefore put in as my answer to the resolutions that he has hunted up against me, what I, as a lawyer, would call a good plea to a bad declaration. I understand that it is a maxim of law, that a poor plea may be a good plea to a bad declaration. I think that the opinions the Judge brings from those who support me, yet differ from me, is a bad declaration against me; but if I can bring the same things against him, I am putting in a good plea to that kind of declaration, and now I propose to try it.

At Freeport Judge Douglas occupied a large part of his time in producing resolutions and documents of various sorts, as I understood, to make me somehow responsible for them; and I propose now doing a little of the same sort of thing for him. In 1850 a very clever gentleman by the name of Thompson Campbell, a personal friend of Judge Douglas and myself, a political friend of Judge Douglas and opponent of mine, was a candidate for Congress in the Galena District. He was interrogated as to his views on this same slavery question. I have here before me the interrogatories and Campbell's answers to them. I will read them:

INTERROGATORIES.

1st. Will you, if elected, vote for and cordially support a bill prohibiting slavery in the Territories of the United States?

2d. Will you vote for and support a bill abolishing slavery in the District of Columbia?

3d. Will you oppose the admission of any slave States which may be formed out of Texas or the Territories?

4th. Will you vote for and advocate the repeal of the Fugitive Slave law passed at the recent session of Congress?

5th. Will you advocate and vote for the election of a Speaker of the House of Representatives who shall be willing to organize the committee of that House so as to give the free States their just influence in the business of legislation?

6th. What are your views, not only as to the constitutional right of Congress to prohibit the slave-trade between the States, but also as to the expediency of exercising that right immediately?

CAMPBELL'S REPLY.

To the first and second interrogatories, I answer unequivocally in the affirmative.

To the third interrogatory I reply, that I am opposed to the admission of any more slave States into the Union, that may be formed out of Texan or any other Territory.

To the fourth and fifth interrogatories I unhesitatingly answer in the affirmative.

To the sixth interrogatory I reply, that so long as the slave States continue to treat slaves as articles of commerce, the Constitution confers power on Congress to pass laws regulating that peculiar COMMERCE, and that the protection of Human Rights imperatively demands the interposition of every constitutional means to prevent this most inhuman and iniquitous traffic.

T. CAMPBELL

I want to say here that Thompson Campbell was elected to Congress on that platform, as the Democratic candidate in the Galena District, against Martin P. Sweet.

Judge Douglas—"Give me the date of the letter."

Mr. Lincoln—The time Campbell ran was in 1850. I have not the exact date here. It was some time in 1850 that these interrogatories were put and the answer given. Campbell was elected to Congress, and served out his term. I think a second election came up before he served out his term and he was not re-elected. Whether defeated or not nominated, I do not know. [Mr. Campbell was nominated for re-election by the Democratic party, by acclamation.] At the end of his term his very good friend, Judge Douglas, got him a high office from President Pierce, and sent him off to California. Is not that the fact? Just at the end of his term in Congress it appears that our mutual friend Judge Douglas got our mutual friend Campbell a good office, and sent him to California upon it. And not only so, but on the 27th of last month, when Judge Douglas and myself spoke at Freeport in joint discussion, there was his same friend Campbell, come all the way from California, to help the Judge beat me; and there was poor Martin P. Sweet standing on the platform, trying to help poor me to be elected. That is true of one of Judge Douglas's friends.

So again, in that same race of 1850, there was a Congressional Convention assembled at Joliet, and it nominated R. S. Molony for Congress, and unanimously adopted the following resolution:

> Resolved, That we are uncompromisingly opposed to the extension of slavery; and while we would not make much opposition a ground of interference with the interests of the States where it exists, yet we moderately but firmly insist that it is the duty of Congress to oppose its extension into Territory now free, by all means compatible with the obligations of the Constitution, and with good faith to our sister States; that these principles were recognized by the Ordinance of 1787, which received the sanotion of Thomas Jefferson, who is acknowledged by all to be the great oracle and expounder of our faith.

Subsequently the same interrogatories were propounded to Dr. Molony which had been addressed to Campbell, as above, with the exception of the 6th, respecting the inter-State slave-trade, to which Dr. Molony, the Democratic nominee for Congress, replied as follows:

> I received the written interrogatories this day, and as you will see by the La Salle *Democrat* and Ottawa *Free Trader,* I look at Peru on the 5th and at Ottawa on the 7th, the affirmative side of interrogatories 1st and 2d, and in relation to the admission of any more slave States from free Territory, my position taken at these meetings, as correctly reported in said papers, was *emphatically* and *distinctly* opposed to it. In relation to the admission of any more slave States from Texas, whether I shall go against it or not will depend upon the opinion that I may hereafter form of the true meaning and nature of the resolutions of annexation. If, by said resolutions, the honor and good faith of the nation is pledged to admit more slave States from Texas when she (Texas) may supply for the admission of such State, then I should, if in Congress, vote for their admission. But if not so PLEDGED and bound by sacred contract, then a bill for the admission of more slave States from Texas would never receive my vote.
>
> To your fourth interrogatory I answer *most decidedly* in the affirmative, and for reasons set forth in my reported remarks at Ottawa last Monday.

To your fifth interrogatory I also reply in the affirmative *most cordially*, and that I will use my utmost exertions to secure the nomination and election of a man who will accomplish the objects of said interrogatories. I most cordially approve of the resolutions adopted at the union meeting held at Princeton on the 27th September ult.

Yours, etc.,

H. S. MOLONY.

All I have to say in regard to Dr. Molony is, that he was the regularly nominated Democratic candidate for Congress in his district—was elected at that time, at the end of his term was appointed to a land-office at Danville. (I never heard any thing of Judge Douglas's instrumentality in this.) He held this office a considerable time, and when we were at Freeport the other day, there were handbills scattered about notifying the public that after our debate was over, R. S. Molony would make a Democratic speech in favor of Judge Douglas. That is all I know of my own personal knowledge. It is added here to this resolution, and truly I believe, that—

"Among those who participated in the Joliet Convention, and who supported its nominee, with his platform as laid down in the resolution of the Convention and in his reply as above given, we call at random the following names, all of which are recognized at this day as leading Democrats:"

"Cook County—E. B. Williams, Charles McDonell, Arno Voss, Thomas Hoyne, Isaac Cook."

I reckon we ought to except Cook.

"F. C. Sherman."

"Will—Joel A. Matteson, S. W. Bowen."

"Kane—B. F. Hall, G. W. Renwick, A. M. Herrington, Elijah Wilcox."

"McHenry—W. M. Jackson, Enos W. Smith, Neil Donnelly."

"La Salle—John Hise, William Reddick."

William Reddick! another one of Judge Douglas's friends that stood on the stand with him at Ottawa, at the time the Judge says my knees trembled so that I had to be carried away. The names are all here:

"DuPage—Nathan Allen."

"DeKalb—Z. B. Mayo."

Here is another set of resolutions which I think are apposite to the matter in hand.

On the 28th of February of the same year, a Democratic District Convention was held at Naperville, to nominate a candidate for Circuit Judge. Among the delegates were Bowen and Kelly, of Will; Captain Naper, H. H. Cody, Nathan Allen, of Du Page; W. M. Jackson, J. M. Strode, P. W. Platt and Enos W. Smith, of McHenry; J. Horsman and others, of Winnebago. Col. Strode presided over the Convention. The following resolutions were unanimously adopted—the first on motion of P. W. Platt, the second on motion of William M. Jackson:

Resolved, That this Convention is in favor of the Wilmot Proviso, both in *Principle* and *Practice,* and that we know of no good reason why any *person* should oppose the largest latitude in *Free Soil, Free Territory* and *Free Speech.*

Resolved, That in the opinion of this Convention, the time has arrived when *all men should be free,* whites as well as others.

Judge Douglas—"What is the date of those resolutions?"

Mr. Lincoln—I understand it was in 1850, but I do not *know* it. I do not state a thing and say I know it, when I do not. But I have the highest belief that this is so. I know of no way to arrive at the conclusion that there is an error in it. I mean to put a case no stronger than the truth will allow. But what I was going to comment upon is an extract from a newspaper in DeKalb county, and it strikes me as being rather singular, I confess, under the circumstances. There is a Judge Mayo in that county, who is a candidate for the Legislature, for the purpose, if he, secures his election, of helping to re-elect Judge Douglas. He is the editor of a newspaper [DeKalb County *Sentinel*], and in that paper I find the extract I am going to read. It is part of an editorial article in which he was electioneering as fiercely as he could for Judge Douglas and against me. It was a curious thing, I think, to be in such a paper. I will agree to that, and the Judge may make the most of it:

"Our education has been such, that we have ever been rather *in favor of the equality of the blacks; that is, that they should enjoy all the privileges of the whites where they reside.* We are aware that this is not a very popular doctrine. We have had many a confab with some who are now strong `Republicans,' we taking the broad ground of equality and they the opposite ground.

"We were brought up in a State where blacks were voters, and we do not know of any inconvenience resulting from it, though perhaps it would not work as well where the blacks are more numerous. We have no doubt of the right of the whites to guard against such an evil, if it is one. Our opinion is that it would be best for all concerned to have the colored population in a State by themselves [in this I agree with him]; but if within the jurisdiction of the United States, *we say by all means they should have the right to have their Senators and Representatives in Congress, and to vote for President.* With us `worth makes the man, and want of it the fellow.' We have seen many a `nigger' that we thought more of than some white men."

That is one of Judge Douglas's friends. Now I do not want to leave myself in an attitude where I can be misrepresented, so I will say I do not think the Judge is responsible for this article; but he is quite as responsible for it as I would be if one of my friends had said it. I think that is fair enough.

I have here also a set of resolutions passed by a Democratic State Convention in Judge Douglas's own good old State of Vermont, that I think ought to be good for him too:

Resolved, That liberty is a right inherent and inalienable is man, and that herein *all men are equal.*

Resolved, That we claim no authority in the Federal Government to abolish slavery in the several States, but we do claim for it Constitutional power perpetually to prohibit the introduction of slavery into territory now free, and abolish it wherever, under the jurisdiction of Congress, it exists.

Resolved, That this power ought immediately to be exercised in prohibiting the introduction and existence of slavery in New Mexico and California, in abolishing slavery and the slave-trade in the District of Columbia, on the high seas, and wherever else, under the Constitution, it can be reached.

Resolved, That no more slave States should be admitted into the Federal Union.

Resolved, That the Government ought to return to its ancient policy, not to extend, nationalize or encourage, but to limit, localize and discourage slavery.

At Freeport I answered several interrogatories that had been propounded to me by Judge Douglas at the Ottawa meeting. The Judge has yet not seen it

to find any fault with the position that I took in regard to those seven interrogatories, which were certainly broad enough, in all conscience, to cover the
entire ground. In my answers, which have been printed, and all have had the
opportunity of seeing, I take the ground that those who elect me must expect
that I will do nothing which will not be in accordance with those answers. I
have some right to assert that Judge Douglas has no fault to find with them.
But he chooses to still try to thrust me upon different ground without paying
any attention to my answers, the obtaining of which from me cost him so
much trouble and concern. At the same time, I propounded four interrogatories to him, claiming it as a right that he should answer as many interrogatories for me as I did for him, and I would reserve myself for a future installment
when I got them ready. The Judge in answering me upon that occasion, put
in what I suppose he intends as answers to all four of my interrogatories. The
first one of these interrogatories I have before me, and it is in these words:

"Question 1. If the people of Kansas shall, by means entirely unobjectionable in all other respects, adopt a State Constitution, and ask
admission into the Union under it, *before* they have the requisite number
of inhabitants according to the English bill—some ninety-three thousand—will you vote to admit them?"

As I read the Judge's answer in the newspaper, and as I remember it as pronounced at the time, he does not give any answer which is equivalent to yes or
no—I will or I wont. He answers at very considerable length, rather quarreling
with me for asking the question, and insisting that Judge Trumbull had done
something that I ought to say something about; and finally getting out such
statements as induce me to infer that he means to be understood he will, in that
supposed case, vote for the admission of Kansas. I only bring this forward now
for the purpose of saying that if he chooses to put a different construction upon
his answer he may do it. But if he does not, I shall from this time forward assume
that he will vote for the admission of Kansas in disregard of the English bill. He
has the right to remove any misunderstanding I may have. I only mention it
now that I may hereafter assume this to be the true construction of his answer,
if he does not now choose to correct me.

The second interrogatory that I propounded to him, was this:

"Question 2. Can the people of a United States Territory, in any lawful way, against the wish of any citizen of the United States, exclude slavery from its limits prior to the formation of a State Constitution?"

To this Judge Douglas answered that they can lawfully exclude slavery from the Territory prior to the formation of a Constitution. He goes on to tell us how it can be done. As I understand him, he holds that it can be done by the Territorial Legislature refusing to make any enactments for the protection of slavery in the Territory, and especially by adopting unfriendly legislation to it. For the sake of clearness I state it again; that they can exclude slavery from the Territory, 1st, by withholding what he assumes to be an indispensable assistance to it in the way of legislation; and, 2d, by unfriendly legislation. If I rightly understand him, I wish to ask your attention for a while to his position.

In the first place, the Supreme Court of the United States has decided that any Congressional prohibition of slavery in the Territories is unconstitutional— that they have reached this proposition as a conclusion from their former proposition, that the Constitution of the United States expressly recognizes property in slaves, and from that other Constitutional provision, that no person shall be deprived of property without due process of law. Hence they reach the conclusion that as the Constitution of the United States expressly recognizes property in slaves, and prohibits any person from being deprived of property without due process of law, to pass an act of Congress by which a man who owned a slave on one side of a line would be deprived of him if he took him on the other side, is depriving him of that property without due process of law. That I understand to be the decision of the Supreme Court. I understand also that Judge Douglas adheres most firmly to that decision; and the difficulty is, how is it possible for any power to exclude slavery from the Territory unless in violation of that decision? That is the difficulty.

In the Senate of the United States, in 1850, Judge Trumball, in a speech, substantially, if not directly, put the same interrogatory to Judge Douglas, as to whether the people of a Territory had the lawful power to exclude slavery prior to the formation of a Constitution? Judge Douglas then answered at considerable length, and his answer will be found in the *Congressional Globe,* under date of June 9th, 1856. The Judge said that whether the people could exclude slavery prior to the formation of a Constitution or not *was a question to be decided by the Supreme Court.* He put that proposition, as will be seen by the *Congressional Globe,* in a variety of forms, all running to the same thing in substance—that it was a question for the Supreme Court. I maintain that when he says, after the Supreme Court have decided the question, that the people may yet exclude slavery by any means whatever, he does virtually say, that it is *not* a question for the Supreme Court. He shifts his ground. I appeal to you whether he did not say it was a question for the Supreme Court? Has not the Supreme Court decided that question? When he now says the people *may* exclude slavery, does he not make it a question for the people? Does he not virtually shift his ground and say that it is *not* a question for the court, but for the people? This is a very simple proposition—a very plain and naked one. It seems to me that there is no difficulty in deciding it. In a variety of ways he said that it was a question for the Supreme Court. He did not stop then to tell us that whatever the Supreme Court decides, the people can by withholding necessary "police regulations" keep slavery out. He did not make any such answer. I submit to you now, whether the new state of the case has not induced the Judge to sheer away from his original ground. Would not this be the impression of every fair-minded man?

I hold that the proposition that slavery cannot enter a new country without police regulations is historically false. It is not true at all. I hold that the history of this country shows that the institution of slavery was originally planted upon this continent *without* these "police regulations" which the Judge now thinks necessary for the actual establishment of it. Not only so, but is there not another fact—how came this Dred Scott decision to be made? It was made upon the case of a negro being taken and actually held in slavery in Minnesota Territory, claiming his freedom because the act of Congress prohibited his being so held there. *Will the Judge pretend that Dred Scott was not held there without police regulations?* There is at least one matter of record as to his having been held in slavery in the Territory, not only without police regulations, but in the teeth of Congressional legislation supposed to be valid at the time. This shows that there is vigor enough in slavery to plant itself in a new country even against unfriendly legislation. It takes not only law but the *enforcement* of law to keep it out. That is the history of this country upon the subject.

I wish to ask one other question. It being understood that the Constitution of the United States guaranties property in slaves in the Territories, if there is any infringement of the right of that property, would not the United States Courts, organized for the government of the Territory, apply such remedy as might be necessary in that case? It is a maxim held by the courts, that there is no wrong without its remedy; and the courts have a remedy for whatever is acknowledged and treated as a wrong.

Again: I will ask you, my friends, if you were elected members of the Legislature, what would be the first thing you would have to do before entering upon your duties? *Swear to support the Constitution of the United States.* Suppose you believe, as Judge Douglas does, that the Constitution of the United States guaranties to your neighbor the right to hold slaves in that Territory—that they are his property—how can you clear your oaths unless you give him such legislation as is necessary to enable him to enjoy that property? What do you understand by supporting the Constitution of a State, or of the United States? Is it not to give each Constitutional helps to the rights established by that Constitution as may be practically needed? Can you, if you swear to support the Constitution, and believe that the Constitution establishes a right, clear your oath, without giving it support? Do you support the Constitution if, knowing or believing there is a right established under it which needs specific legislation, you withhold that legislation? Do you not violate and disregard your oath? I can conceive of nothing plainer in the world. There can be nothing in the words "support the Constitution," if you may run counter to it by refusing support to any right established under the Constitution. And what I say here will hold with still more force against the Judge's doctrine of "unfriendly legislation." How could you, having sworn to support the Constitution and believing it guarantied the right to hold slaves in the Territories, assist in legislation *intended to defeat that right?* That would be violating your own view of the Constitution. Not only so, but if you were to do so, how long would it take the courts to hold your votes unconstitutional and void? Not a moment.

Lastly I would ask—is not Congress, itself, under obligation to give legislative support to any right that is established under the United States Constitution? I repeat the question—is not Congress, itself, bound to give legislative support to any right that is established in the United States Constitution? A member of Congress swears to support the Constitution of the United States, and if he sees a right established by that Constitution which needs specific legislative protection, can he clear his oath without giving that protection? Let me ask you why many of us who are opposed to slavery upon principle, give our acquiescence to a Fugitive Slave law? Why do we hold ourselves under obligations to pass such a law, and abide by it when it is passed? Because the Constitution makes provision that the owners of slaves shall have the right to reclaim them. It gives the right to reclaim slaves, and that right is, as Judge Douglas says, a barren right, unless there is legislation that will enforce it.

The mere declaration, "No person held to service or labor in one State under the laws thereof, escaping into another, shall in consequence of any law or regulation therein be discharged from such service or labor, but shall be delivered up on claim of the party to whom such service or labor may be due," is powerless without specific legislation to enforce it. Now, on what ground would a member of Congress who is supposed to slavery in the abstract, vote for a Fugitive law, as I would deem it my duty to do? Because there is a Constitutional right which needs legislation to enforce it. And although it is distasteful to me, I have sworn to support the Constitution, and having so sworn,

I cannot conceive that I do support it if I withhold from that right any necessary legislation to make it practical. And if that is true in regard to a Fugitive Slave law, is the right to have fugitive slaves reclaimed any better fixed in the Constitution than the right to hold slaves in the Territories? For this decision is a just exposition of the Constitution, as Judge Douglas thinks. Is the one right any better than the other? Is there any man who, while a member of Congress, would give support to the one any more than the other? If I wished to refuse to give legislative support to slave property in the Territories, if a member of Congress, I could not do it, holding the view that the Constitution establishes that right. If I did it at all, it would be because I deny that this decision properly construes the Constitution. But if I acknowledge, with Judge Douglas, that this decision properly construes the Constitution, I cannot conceive that I would be less than a perjured man if I should refuse in Congress to give such protection to that property as in its nature it needed.

At the end of what I have said here I propose to give the Judge my fifth interrogatory, which he may take and answer at his leisure. My fifth interrogatory is this:

If the slaveholding citizens of a United States Territory should need and demand Congressional legislation for the protection of their slave property in such Territory, would you, as a member of Congress, vote for or against such legislation?

Judge Douglas—"Will you repeat that? I want to answer that question."

Mr. Lincoln—If the slaveholding citizens of a United States Territory should need and demand Congressional legislation for the protection of their slave property in such Territory, would you, as a member of Congress, vote for or against such legislation?

I am aware that in some of the speeches Judge Douglas has made, he has spoken as if he did not know or think that the Supreme Court had decided that a Territorial Legislature cannot exclude slavery. Precisely what the Judge would say upon the subject—whether he would say definitely that he does not understand they have so decided, or whether he would say he does understand that the court have so decided, I do not know; but I know that in his speech at Springfield he spoke of it as a thing they had not decided yet; and in his answer to me at Freeport, he spoke of it so far again, as I can comprehend it, as a thing that had not yet been decided. Now I hold that if the Judge does entertain that view, I think that he is not mistaken in so far as it can be said that the court has not decided any thing save the mere question of jurisdiction. I know the legal arguments that can be made—that after a court has decided that it cannot take jurisdiction in a case, it then has decided all that is before it, and that is the end of it. A plausible argument can be made in favor of that proposition, but I know that Judge Douglas has said in one of his speeches that the court went forward, *like honest men as they were,* and decided all the points in the case. If any points are really extra-judicially decided because not necessarily before them, then this one as to the power of the Territorial Legislature to exclude slavery is one of them, as also the one that the Missouri Compromise was null and void. They are both extra-judicial, or neither is, according as the court held that they had no jurisdiction in the case between the parties, because of want of capacity of one party to maintain a suit in that court. I want, if I have sufficient time, to show that the court did *pass its opinion,* but that is the only thing actually done in the case. If they did not decide, they showed what they were ready to decide whenever the matter was before them. What is that opinion? After having argued that Congress had no power to pass a law excluding slavery from a United States Territory, they then used language to this effect: That inasmuch as Congress itself could not exercise such a power, it followed as a matter of course that it could not authorize a Territorial Government to exercise it, for the Territorial Legislature can do no more than Congress could do. Thus it expressed its opinion emphatically against the power of a Territorial Legislature to exclude slavery, leaving us in just as little doubt on that point as upon any other point they really decided.

Now, my fellow-citizens, I will detain you only a little while longer. My time is nearly out. I find a report of a speech made by Judge Douglas at Joliet, since we last met at Freeport—published, I believe, in the *Missouri Republican*—on the 9th of this month, in which Judge Douglas says:

"You know at Ottawa, I read this platform, and asked him if he concurred in each and all of the principles set forth in it. He would not answer these questions. At last I said frankly, I wish you to answer them, because when I get them up here where the color of your principles are a little darker than in Egypt, I intend to trot you down to Jonesboro. The very notice that I was going to take him down to Egypt made him tremble in the knees so that he had to be carried from the platform. He laid up seven days, and in the meantime held a consultation with his political physicians; they had Lovejoy and Farnsworth and all the leaders of the Abolition party, they consulted it all over, and at last Lincoln came to the conclusion that he would answer, so he came up to Freeport last Friday."

Now that statement altogether furnishes a subject for philosophical con-templation. I have been treating it in that way, and I have really come to the conclusion that I can explain it in no other way than by believing the Judge is crazy. If he was in his right mind, I cannot conceive how he would have risked disgusting the four or five thousand of his own friends who stood there, and knew, as to my having been carried from the platform, that there was not a word of truth in it.

Judge Douglas—"Didn't they carry you off?"

Mr. Lincoln—There; that question illustrates the character of this man Dou-glas, exactly. He smiles now and says, "Didn't they carry you off?" But he said then, *"he had to be carried off;"* and he said it to convince the country that he had so completely broken me down by his speech that I had to be carried away. Now he seeks to dodge it, and asks, "Didn't they carry you off?" Yes, they did. *"But, Judge Douglas, why didn't you tell the truth?"* I would like to know why you didn't tell the truth about it. And then again, "He laid up seven days." He puts this in print for the people of the country to read as a serious document. I think if he had been in his sober senses he would not have risked that barefacedness in the presence of thousands of his own friends, who knew that I made speeches within six of the seven days at Henry, Marshall county; Augusta, Hancock county, and Macomb, McDonough county, including all the necessary travel to meet him again at Freeport at the end of the six days. Now, I say, there is no charitable way to look at that statement, except to conclude that he is actually crazy. There is another thing in that statement that alarmed me very greatly as he states it, that he was going to "trot me down to Egypt." Thereby he would have you to infer that I would not come to Egypt unless he forced me—that I could not be got here, unless he, giant-like, had hauled me down here. That statement he makes, too, in the teeth of the knowledge that I had made the stip-ulation to come down here, *and that he himself had been very reluctant to enter into the stipulation.* More than all this, Judge Douglas, when he made that statement, must have been crazy, and wholly out of his sober senses, or else he would have known that when he got me down here—that promise—that windy promise—of his powers to annihilate me, wouldn't amount to anything. Now, how little do I look like being carried away trembling? Let the Judge go on, and after he is done with his half hour, I want you all, if I can't go home myself, to let me stay and rot here; and if anything happens to the Judge, if I cannot carry him to the hotel and put him to bed, let me stay here and rot. I say, then, there is some-thing *extraordinary* in this statement. I ask you if you know any other living man who would make such a statement? I will ask my friend Casey, over there, if he would do such a thing? Would he send that out and have his men take it as the truth? Did the Judge talk of trotting me down to Egypt to scare me to death? Why, I know this people better than he does. I was raised just a little east of here. I am a part of this people. But the Judge was raised further north, and perhaps be has some horrid idea of what this people might be induced to do. But really I have talked about this matter perhaps longer than I ought, for it is no great thing, and yet the smallest are often the most difficult things to deal with. The Judge has set about seriously trying to make the impression that when we meet at different places I am literally in his clutches—that I am a poor, helpless, decrepit mouse, and that I can do nothing at all. This is one of the ways he has taken to create that impression. I don't know any other way to meet it, except this. I don't want to quarrel with him—to call him a liar—but when I come square up to him I don't know what else to call him, if I must tell the truth out. I want to be at peace, and reserve all my fighting powers for necessary occasions. My time, now, is very nearly out, and I give up the trifle that is left to the Judge, to let him set my knees trembling again, if he can.

MR. DOUGLAS'S REJOINDER.

MY FRIENDS, while I am very grateful to you for the enthusiasm which you show for me, I will say in all candor, that your quietness will be much more agreeable than your applause, inasmuch as you deprive me of some part of my time whenever you cheer.

I will commence where Mr. Lincoln left off, and make a remark upon this serious complaint of his about my speech at Joliet. I did say there in a playful manner that when I put these questions to Mr. Lincoln at Ottawa he failed to answer, and that he trembled and had to be carried off the stand, and required seven days to get up his reply. That he did not walk off from that stand he will not deny. That when the crowd went away from the stand with me, a few persons carried him home on their shoulders and laid him down, he will admit. I wish to say to you that whenever I degrade my friends and myself by allowing them to carry me on their backs along through the public streets, when I am able to walk, I am willing to be deemed crazy. I did not say whether I beat him or he beat me in the argument. It is true I put these questions to him, and I put them not as mere idle questions, but showed that I based them upon the creed of the Black Republican party as declared by their Conventions in that portion of the State which he depends upon to elect him, and desired to know whether he indorsed that creed. He would not answer. When I reminded him that I intended bringing him into Egypt and renewing my questions if he refused to answer, he then consulted and did get up his answers one week after,—answers which I may refer to in a few minutes and show you how equivocal they are. My object was to make him avow whether or not he stood by the platform of his party; the resolutions I then read, and upon which I based my questions, had been adopted by his party in the Galena Congressional District, and the Chicago and Bloomington Congressional Districts, composing a large majority of the counties in this State that give Republican or Abolition majorities. Mr. Lincoln cannot and will not deny that the doctrines laid down in these resolutions were in substance put forth in Lovejoy's resolutions, which were voted for by a majority of his party, some of them, if not all, receiving the support of every man of his party. Hence, I laid a foundation for my questions to him before I asked him whether that was or was not the platform of his party. He says that he answered my questions. One of them was whether he would vote to admit any more slave States into the Union. The creed of the Republican party as set forth in the resolutions of their various Conventions was, that they would under no circumstances vote to admit another slave State. It was put forth in the Love-joy resolutions in the Legislature; it was put forth and passed in a majority of all the counties of this State which give Abolition or Republican majorities, or elect members to the Legislature of that school of politics. I had a right to know whether he would vote for or against the admission of another slave State in the event the people wanted it. He first answered that he was not pledged on the subject, and then said, "In regard to the other question, of whether I am pledged to the admission of any more slave States into the Union, I state to you very frankly that I would be exceedingly sorry ever to be put in the position of having to pass on that question. I should be exceedingly glad to know that there would never be another slave State admitted into the Union; but I must add that if slavery shall be kept out of the Territories during the territorial existence of any one given Territory, and then the people, having a fair chance and clean field when they come to adopt a Constitution, do such an extraordinary thing as adopt a slave Constitution, uninfluenced by the actual presence of the institution among them, I see no alternative, if we own the country, but to admit them into the Union."

Now analyze that answer. In the first place he says he would be exceedingly sorry to be put in a position where he would have to vote on the question of the admission of a slave State. Why is he a candidate for the Senate if he would be sorry to be put in that position? I trust the people of Illinois will not put him in a position which he would be so sorry to occupy. The next position he takes is that he would be glad to know that there would never be another slave State, yet, in certain contingencies, he might have to vote for one. What is that contingency? "If Congress keeps slavery out by law while it is a Territory, and then the people should have a fair chance and should adopt slavery, uninfluenced by the presence of the institution," he supposed he would have to admit the State. Suppose Congress should not keep slavery out during their territorial existence, then how would he vote when the people applied for admission into the Union with a slave Constitution? That he does not answer, and that is the condition of every Territory we have now got. Slavery is not kept out of Kansas by act of Congress, and when I put the question to Mr. Lincoln, whether he will vote for the admission with or without slavery, as her people may desire, he will not answer, and you have not got an answer from him. In Nebraska slavery is not prohibited by act of Congress, but the people are allowed, under the Nebraska bill, to do as they please on the subject; and when I ask him whether he will vote to admit Nebraska with a slave Constitution if her people desire it, he will not answer. So with New Mexico, Washington Territory, Arizona, and the four new States to be admitted from Texas. You cannot get an answer from him to these questions. His answer only applies to a given case, to a condition—things which he knows does not exist in any one Territory in the Union. He tries to give you to understand that he would allow the people to do as they please, and yet he dodges the question as to every Territory in the Union. I now ask why cannot Mr. Lincoln answer to each of these Territories? He has not done it, and he will not do it. The Abolitionists up North understand that this answer is made with a view of not committing himself on any one Territory now in existence. It is so understood there, and you cannot expect an answer from him on a case that applies to any one Territory, or applies to the new States which by compact we are pledged to admit out of Texas, when they have the requisite population and desire admission. I submit to you whether he has made a frank answer, so that you can tell how he would vote in any one of these cases. "He would be sorry to be put in the position." Why would he be sorry to be put in this position if his duty required him to give the vote? If the people of a Territory ought to be permitted to come into the Union as a State, with slavery or without it, as they pleased, why not give the vote admitting them cheerfully? If in his opinion they might not to come in with slavery, even if they wanted to, why not say that he would cheerfully vote against their admission? His intimation is that conscience would not let him vote "No," and he would be sorry to do that which his conscience would compel him to do as an honest man.

In regard to the contract or bargain between Trumbull, the Abolitionists and him, which he denies, I wish to say that the charge can be proved by notorious historical facts. Trumbull, Lovejoy, Giddings, Fred Douglass, Hale, and Banks, were traveling the State at that time making speeches on the same side and in the same cause with him. He contents himself with the simple denial that no such thing occurred. Does he deny that he, and Trumbull, and Breese, and Giddings, and Chase, and Fred Douglass, and Lovejoy, and all those Abolitionists and deserters from the Democratic party, did make speeches all over this State in the same common cause? Does he deny that Jim Matheny was then, and is now, his confidential friend, and does he deny that Matheny made the charge of the bargain and fraud in his own language, as I have read it from his printed speech. Matheny spoke of his own personal knowledge of that bargain existing between Lincoln, Trumbull, and the Abolitionists. He still remains Lincoln's confidential friend, and is now a candidate for Congress, and is canvassing the Springfield District for Lincoln. I assert that I can prove the charge to be true in detail if I can ever get it where I can summon and compel the attendance of witnesses. I have the statement of another man to the same effect as that made by Matheny, which I am not permitted to use yet, but Jim Matheny is a good witness on that point, and the history of the country is conclusive upon it. That Lincoln up to that time had been a Whig, and then undertook to Abolitionize the Whigs and bring them into the Abolition camp, is beyond denial; that Trumbull up to that time had been a Democrat, and deserted, and undertook to Abolitionize the Democracy, and take them into the Abolition camp, is beyond denial; that they are both now active, leading, distinguished members of this Abolition Republican party, in full communion, is a fact that cannot be questioned or denied.

But Lincoln is not willing to be responsible for the creed of his party. He complains because I hold him responsible, and in order to avoid the issue, he attempts to show that individuals in the Democratic party, many years ago, expressed Abolition sentiments. It is true that Tom Campbell, when a candidate for Congress in 1850, published the letter which Lincoln read. When I asked Lincoln for the date of that letter he could not give it. The date of the letter has been suppressed by other speakers who have used it, though I take it for granted that Lincoln did not know the date. If he will take the trouble to examine, he will find that the letter was published only two days before the election, and was never seen until after it, except in one county. Tom Campbell would have been beat to death by the Democratic party if that letter had been made public in his district. As to Molony, it is true he uttered sentiments of the kind referred to by Mr. Lincoln, and the best Democrats would not vote for him for that reason. I returned from Washington after the passage of the Compromise

Measures in 1850, and when I found Molony running under John Wentworth's tutelage, and on his platform, I denounced him, and declared that he was no Democrat. In my speech at Chicago, just before the election that year, I went before the infuriated people of that city and vindicated the Compromise Measures of 1850. Remember the city council had passed resolutions nullifying acts of Congress and instructing the police to withhold their assistance from the execution of the laws, and as I was the only man in the city of Chicago who was responsible for the passage of the Compromise Measures, I went before the crowd, justified each and every one of those measures, and let it be said to the eternal honor of the people of Chicago, that when they were convinced by my exposition of those measures that they were right and they had done wrong in opposing them, they repealed their nullifying resolutions and declared that they would acquiesce in and support the laws of the land. These facts are well known, and Mr. Lincoln can only get up individual instances, dating back to 1849–'50, which are contradicted by the whole tenor of the Democratic creed.

But Mr. Lincoln does not want to be held responsible for the Black Republican doctrine of no more slave States. Farnsworth is the candidate of his party to-day in the Chicago District, and he made a speech in the last Congress in which he called upon God to palsy his right arm if he ever voted for the admission of another slave State, whether the people wanted it or not. Lovejoy is making speeches all over the State for Lincoln now, and taking ground against any more slave States. Washburne, the Black Republican candidate for Congress in the Galena District, is making speeches in favor of this same Abolition platform declaring no more slave States. Why are men running for Congress in the northern districts, and taking that Abolition platform for their guide, when Mr. Lincoln does not want to be held to it down here in Egypt and in the center of the State, and objects to it so as to get votes here. Let me tell Mr. Lincoln that his party in the northern part of the State hold to that Abolition platform, and that if they do not in the South and in the center they present the extraordinary spectacle of a "house divided against itself," and hence "cannot stand." I now bring down upon him the vengeance of his own scriptural quotation, and give it a more appropriate application than he did, when I say to him that his party, Abolition in one end of the State and opposed to it in the other, is a house divided against itself, and cannot stand, and ought not to stand, for it attempts to cheat the American people out of their votes by disguising its sentiments.

Mr. Lincoln attempts to cover up and get over his Abolitionism by telling you that he was raised a little east of you, beyond the Wabash in Indiana, and he thinks that makes a mighty sound and good man of him on all these questions.

I do not know that the place where a man is born or raised has much to do with his political principles. The worst Abolitionist I have ever known in Illinois have been men who have sold their slaves in Alabama and Kentucky, and have come here and turned Abolitionists whilst spending the money got for the negroes they sold, and I do not know that an Abolitionist from Indiana or Kentucky ought to have any more credit because he was born and raised among slaveholders. I do not know that a native of Kentucky is more excusable because raised among slaves, his father and mother having owned slaves, he comes to Illinois, turns Abolitionist, and slanders the graves of his father and mother, and breathes curses upon the institutions under which he was born, and his father and mother bred. True, I was not born out west here. I was born away down in Yankee land, I was born in a valley in Vermont, with the high mountains around me. I love the old green mountains and valleys of Vermont, where I was born, and where I played in my childhood. I went up to visit them some seven or eight years ago, for the first time for twenty odd years. When I got there they treated me very kindly. They invited me to the commencement of their college, placed me on the seats with their distinguished guests, and conferred upon me the degree of LL. D. in Latin (doctor of laws), the same as they did old Hickory, at Cambridge, many years ago, and I give you my word and honor I understood just as much of the Latin as he did. When they got through conferring the honorary degree, they called upon me for a speech, and I got up with my heart full and swelling with gratitude for their kindness, and I said to them, "My friends, Vermont is the most glorious spot on the face of this globe for a man to be born in, *provided* he emigrates when he is very young."

I emigrated when I was very young. I came out here when I was a boy, and I found my mind liberalized, and my opinions enlarged when I got on these broad prairies, with only the Heavens to bound my vision, instead of having them circumscribed by the little narrow ridges that surrounded the valley where I was born. But, I discard all things of the land where a man was born. I wish to be judged by my principles, by those great public measures and Constitutional principles upon which the peace, the happiness and the perpetuity of this Republic now rest.

Mr. Lincoln has framed another question, propounded it to me, and desired my answer. As I have said before, I did not put a question to him that I did not first lay a foundation for by showing that it was a part of the platform of the party whose votes he is now seeking, adopted in a majority of the counties where he now hopes to get a majority, and supported by the candidates of his party now running in those counties. But I will answer his question. It is as follows: "If the slaveholding citizens of a United States Territory should need and demand Congressional legislation for the protection of their slave property in such Territory, would you, as a member of Congress, vote for or against such legislation?" I answer him that it is a fundamental article in the Democratic creed that there should be non-interference and non-intervention by Congress with slavery in the States or Territories. Mr. Lincoln could have found an answer to his question in the Cincinnati platform, if he had desired it. The Democratic party have always stood by that great principle of non-interference and non-intervention by Congress with slavery in the States and Territories alike, and I stand on that platform now.

Now I desire to call your attention to the fact that Lincoln did not define his own position in his own question. How does he stand on that question? He put the question to me at Freeport whether or not I would vote to admit Kansas into the Union before she had 93,420 inhabitants. I answered him at once that it having been decided that Kansas had now population enough for a slave State, she had population enough for a free State.

I answered the question unequivocally, and then I asked him whether he would vote for or against the admission of Kansas before she had 93,420 inhabitants, and he would not answer me. To-day he has called attention to the fact that, in his opinion, my answer on that question was not quite plain enough, and yet he has not answered it himself. He now puts a question in relation to Congressional interference in the Territories to me. I answer him direct, and yet he has not answered the question himself. I ask you whether a man has any right, in common decency, to put questions in these public discussions, to his opponent, which he will not answer himself, when they are pressed home to him. I have asked him three times, whether he would vote to admit Kansas whenever the people applied with a Constitution of their own making and their own adoption, under circumstances that were fair, just and unexceptionable, but I cannot get an answer from him. Nor will he answer the question which he put to me, and which I have just answered in relation to Congressional interference in the Territories, by making a slave code there.

It is true that he goes on to answer the question by arguing that under the decision of the Supreme Court it is the duty of a man to vote for a slave code in the Territories. He says that it is his duty, under the decision that the court has made, and if he believes in that decision he would be a perjured man if he did not give the vote. I want to know whether he is not bound to a decision which is contrary to his opinions just as much as to one in accordance with his opinions. If the decision of the Supreme Court, the tribunal created by the

Constitution to decide the question, is final and binding, is he not bound by it just as strongly as if he was for it instead of against it originally? Is every man in this land allowed to resist decisions he does not like, and only support those that meet his approval? What are important courts worth unless their decisions are binding on all good citizens? It is the fundamental principles of the judiciary that its decisions are final. It is created for that purpose, so that when you cannot agree among yourselves on a disputed point you appeal to the judicial tribunal which steps in and decides for you, and that decision is then binding on every good citizen. It is the law of the land just as much with Mr. Lincoln against it as for it. And yet he says that if that decision is binding he is a perjured man if he does not vote for a slave code in the different Territories of this Union. Well, if you [turning to Mr. Lincoln] are not going to resist the decision, if you obey it, and do not intend to array mob law against the constituted authorities, then, according to your own statement, you will be a perjured man if you do not vote to establish slavery in these Territories. My doctrine is, that even taking Mr. Lincoln's view that the decision recognizes the right of a man to carry his slaves into the Territories of the United States, if he pleases, yet after he gets there he needs affirmative law to make that right of any value. The same doctrine not only applies to slave property, but all other kinds of property. Chief Justice Taney places it upon the ground that slave property is on an equal footing with other property. Suppose one of your merchants should move to Kansas and open a liquor store; he has a right to take groceries and liquors there, but the mode of selling them, and the circumstances under which they shall be sold, and all the remedies must be prescribed by local legislation, and if that is unfriendly it will drive him out just as effectually as if there was a Constitutional provision against the sale of liquor. So the absence of local legislation to encourage and support slave property in a Territory excludes it practically just as effectually as if there was a positive Constitutional provision against it. Hence, I assert that under the Dred Scott decision you cannot maintain slavery a day in a Territory where there is an unwilling people and unfriendly legislation. If the people are opposed to it, our right is a barren, worthless, useless right, and if they are for it, they will support and encourage it. We come right back, therefore, to the practical question, if the people of a Territory want slavery they will have it, and if they do not want it you cannot force it on them. And this is the practical question, the great principle, upon which our institutions rest. I am willing to take the decision of the Supreme Court as it was pronounced by that august tribunal without stopping to inquire whether I would have decided that way or not. I have had many a decision made against me on questions of law which I did not like, but I was bound by them just as much as if I had had a hand in making them, and approved them. Did you ever see a lawyer or a client lose his case that he approved the decision of the court? They always think the decision unjust when it is given against them. In a Government of laws like ours we must sustain the Constitution as our fathers made it, and maintain the rights of the States as they are guarantied under the Constitution, and then we will have peace and harmony between the different States and sections of this glorious Union.

FOURTH JOINT DEBATE, AT CHARLESTON
SEPTEMBER 18, 1858

MR. LINCOLN'S SPEECH.

LADIES AND GENTLEMEN: It will be very difficult for an audience so large as this to hear distinctly what a speaker says, and consequently it is important that as profound silence be preserved as possible.

While I was at the hotel to-day, an elderly gentleman called upon me to know whether I was really in favor of producing a perfect equality between the negroes and white people. While I had not proposed to myself on this occasion to say much on that subject, yet as the question was asked me I thought I would occupy perhaps five minutes in saying something in regard to it. I will say then that I am not, nor ever have been, in favor of bringing about in any way the social and political equality of the white and black races—that I am not nor ever have been in favor of making voters or jurors of negroes, nor of qualifying them to hold office, nor to intermarry with white people; and I will say in addition to this that there is a physical difference between the white and black races which I believe will forever forbid the two races living together on terms of social and political equality. And inasmuch as they cannot so live, while they do remain together there must be the position of superior and inferior, and I as much as any other man am in favor of having the superior position assigned to the white race. I say upon this occasion I do not perceive that because the white man is to have the superior position the negro should be denied every thing. I do not understand that because I do not want a negro woman for a slave I must necessarily want her for a wife. My understanding is that I can just let her alone. I am now in my fiftieth year, and I certainly never have had a black woman for either a slave or a wife. So it seems to me quite possible for us to get along without making either slaves or wives of negroes. I will add to this that I have never seen, to my knowledge, a man, woman or child who was in favor of producing a perfect equality, social and political, between negroes and white men. I recollect of but one distinguished instance that I ever heard of so frequently as to be entirely satisfied of its correctness—and that is the case of Judge Douglas's old friend Col. Richard M. Johnson. I will also add to the remarks I have made (for I are not going to enter at large upon this subject), that I have never had the least apprehension that I or my friends would marry negroes if there was no law to keep them from it; but as Judge Douglas and his friends seem to be in great apprehension that they might, if there were no law to keep them from it, I give him the most solemn pledge that I will to the very last stand by the law of this State, which forbids the marrying of white people with negroes. I will add one further word, which is this: that I do not understand that there is any place where an alteration of the social and political relations of the negro and the white man can be made except in the State Legislature—not in the Congress of the United States—and as I do not really apprehend the approach of any such thing myself, and as Judge Douglas seems to be in constant horror that some such danger is rapidly approaching, I propose as the best means to prevent it that the Judge be kept at home and placed in the State Legislature to fight the measure. I do not propose dwelling longer at this time on this subject.

When Judge Trumbull, our other Senator in Congress, returned to Illinois in the month of August, he made a speech at Chicago, in which he made what may be called *a charge* against Judge Douglas, which I understand proved to be very offensive to him. The Judge was at that time out upon one of his speaking tours through the country, and when the news of it reached him, as I am informed, he denounced Judge Trumbull in rather harsh terms for having said what he did in regard to that matter. I was traveling at that time, and speaking at the same places with Judge Douglas on subsequent days, and when I heard of what Judge Trumbull had said of Douglas, and what Douglas had said back again, I felt that I was in a position where I could not remain entirely silent in regard to the matter. Consequently, upon two or three occasions I alluded to it, and alluded to it in no otherwise than to say that in regard to the charge brought by Trumbull against Douglas, I *personally* knew nothing, and sought to say nothing about it—that I did personally know Judge Trumbull—that I believed him to be a man of veracity—that I believed him to be a man of capacity sufficient to know very well whether an assertion he was making, as a conclusion drawn from a set of facts, was true or false; and as a conclusion of my own from that, I stated it as my belief, if Trumbull should ever be called upon, he would prove every thing he had said. I said this upon two or three occasions. Upon a subsequent occasion, Judge Trumbull spoke again before an audience at Alton, and upon that occasion not only repeated his charge against Douglas, but arrayed the evidence he relied upon to substantiate it. This speech was published at length; and subsequently at Jacksonville Judge Douglas alluded to the matter. In the course of his speech, and near the close of it, he stated in regard to myself what I will now read: "Judge Douglas proceeded to remark that he should not hereafter occupy his time in refuting such charges made by Trumbull, but that Lincoln having indorsed the character of Trumbull for veracity, he should hold him (Lincoln) responsible for the slanders." I have done simply what I have told you, to subject me to this invitation to notice the charge. I now wish to say that it had not originally been my purpose to discuss that matter at all. But inasmuch as it seems to be the wish of Judge Douglas to hold me responsible for it, then for once in my life I will play General Jackson, and to the just extent I take the responsibility.

I wish to say at the beginning that I will hand to the reporters that portion of Judge Trumbull's Alton speech which was devoted to this matter, and also that portion of Judge Douglas's speech made at Jacksonville in answer to it. I shall thereby furnish the readers of this debate with the complete discussion between Trumbull and Douglas. I cannot now read them, for the reason that it would take half of my first hour to do so. I can only make some comments upon them. Trumbull's charge is in the following words: "Now, the charge is, that there was a plot entered into to have a Constitution formed for Kansas, and put in force, without giving the people an opportunity to vote upon it, and that Mr. Douglas was in the plot." I will state, without quoting further, for all will have an opportunity of reading it hereafter, that Judge Trumbull brings forward what he regards as sufficient evidence to substantiate this charge.*

It will be perceived Judge Trumbull shows that Senator Bigler, upon the floor of the Senate, had declared there had been a conference among the Senators, in which conference it was determined to have an Enabling Act passed for the people of Kansas to form a Constitution under, and in this conference it was agreed among them that it was best not to have a provision for submitting the Constitution to a vote of the people after it should be formed. He then brings forward to show, and showing, as he deemed, that Judge Douglas reported the bill back to the Senate with that clause stricken out. He then shows that there was a new clause inserted into the bill, which would in its nature *prevent* a reference of the Constitution back for a vote of the people—if, indeed, upon a mere silence in the law, it could be assumed that they had the right to vote upon it. These are the general statements that he has made.

I propose to examine the points in Judge Douglas's speech, in which he attempts to answer that speech of Judge Trumbull's. When you come to

---

* See Trumbull's speech at the close of this debate [this footnote in the original].

examine Judge Douglas's speech, you will find that the first point he makes is: "Suppose it were true that there was such a change in the bill, and that I struck it out—is that a proof of a plot to force a Constitution upon them against their will?" His striking out such a provision, if there was such a one in the bill, he argues, does not establish the proof that it was stricken out for the purpose of robbing the people of that right. I would say, in the first place, that that would be a *most manifest* reason for it. It is true, as Judge Douglas states, that many Territorial bills have passed without having such a provision in them. I believe it is true, though I am not certain, that in some instances, Constitutions framed under such bills have been submitted to a vote of the people, with the law silent upon the subject, but it does not appear that they once had their Enabling Acts framed with an express provision *for* submitting the Constitution to be framed to a vote of the people, and then that they were stricken out when Congress did not mean to alter the effect of the law. That there have been bills which never had the provision in, I do not question; but when was that provision taken out of one that it was in? More especially does this evidence tend to prove the proposition that Trumbull advanced, when we remember that the provision was stricken out of the bill almost simultaneously with the time that Bigler says there was a conference among certain Senators, and in which it was agreed that a bill should be passed leaving that out. Judge Douglas, in answering Trumbull, omits to attend to the testimony of Bigler, that there was a meeting in which it was agreed they should so frame the bill that there should be no submission of the Constitution to a vote of the people. The Judge does not notice this part of it. If you take this as one piece of evidence, and then ascertain that simultaneously Judge Douglas struck out a provision that did require it to be submitted, and put the two together, I think it will make a pretty fair show of proof that Judge Douglas did, as Trumbull says, enter into a plot to put in force a Constitution for Kansas without giving the people any opportunity of voting upon it.

But I must hurry on. The next proposition that Judge Douglas puts is this: "But upon examination it turns out that the Toombs bill never did contain a clause requiring the Constitution to be submitted." This is a mere question of fact, and can be determined by evidence. I only want to ask this question—why did not Judge Douglas say that these words were not stricken out of the Toombs bill, or this bill from which it is alleged the provision was stricken out—a bill which goes by the name of Toombs, because he originally brought it forward? I ask why, if the Judge wanted to make a direct issue with Trumbull, did he not take the exact proposition Trumbull made in his speech, and say it was not stricken out? Trumbull has given the exact words that he says were in the Toombs bill, and he alleges that when the bill came back, they were stricken out. Judge Douglas does not say that the words which Trumbull says were stricken out, were not so stricken out, but he says there was no provision in the Toombs bill to submit the Constitution to a vote of the people. We see at once that he is merely making an issue upon the meaning of the words. He has not undertaken to say that Trumbull tells a lie about these words being stricken out; but he is really, when pushed up to it, only taking an issue upon the meaning of the words. Now, then, if there be any issue upon the meaning of the words, or if there be upon the question of fact as to whether these words were stricken out, I have before me what I suppose to be a genuine copy of the Toombs bill, in which it can be shown that the words Trumbull says were in it, were, in fact, originally there. If there be any dispute upon the fact, I have got the documents here to show they were there. If there be any controversy upon the sense of the words—whether these words which were stricken out really constituted a provision for submitting the matter to a vote of the people, as that is a matter of argument, I think I may as well use Trumbull's own argument. He says that the proposition is in these words:

> "That the following propositions be and the same are hereby offered to the said Convention of the people of Kansas when formed, for their free acceptance or rejection; which, if accepted by the Convention *and ratified by the people at the election for the adoption of the Constitution,* shall be obligatory upon the United States and the said State of Kansas."

Now, Trumbull alleges that these last words were stricken out of the bill when it came back, and he says this was a provision for submitting the Constitution to a vote of the people, and his argument is this: "Would it have been possible to ratify the land propositions at the election for the adoption of the Constitution, unless such an election was to be held?" That is Trumbull's argument. Now Judge Douglas does not meet the charge at all, but he stands up and says there was no such proposition in that bill for submitting the Constitution to be framed to a vote of the people. Trumbull admits that the language is not a direct provision for submitting it, but it is a provision necessarily implied from another provision. He asks you how it is possible to ratify the land proposition at the election for the adoption of the Constitution, if there was no election to be held for the adoption of the Constitution. And he goes on to show that it is not any less a law because the provision is put in that indirect shape than it would be if it was put directly. But I presume I have said enough to draw attention to this point, and I pass it by also.

Another one of the points that Judge Douglas makes upon Trumbull, and at very great length, is, that Trumbull, while the bill was pending, said in a speech in the Senate that he supposed the Constitution to be made would have to be submitted to the people. He asks, if Trumbull thought so then, what ground is there for any body thinking otherwise now? Fellow-citizens, this much may be said in reply: That bill had been in the hands of a party to which Trumbull did not belong. It had been in the hands of the committee at the head of which Judge Douglas stood. Trumbull perhaps had a printed copy of the original Toombs bill. I have not the evidence on that point, except a sort of inference I draw from the general course of business there. What alterations, or what provisions in the way of altering, were going on in committee, Trumbull had no means of knowing, until the altered bill was reported back. Soon afterward, when it was reported back, there was a discussion over it, and perhaps Trumbull in reading it hastily in the altered form did not perceive all the bearings of the alterations. He was hastily borne into the debate, and it does not follow that because there was something in it Trumbull did not perceive, that something did not exist. More than this, is it true that what Trumbull did can have any effect on what Douglas did? Suppose Trumbull had been in the plot with these other men, would that let Douglas out of it? Would it exonerate Douglas that Trumbull didn't then perceive he was in the plot? He also asks the question: Why didn't Trumbull propose to amend the bill if he thought it needed any amendment? Why, I believe that every thing Judge Trumbull had proposed, particularly in connection with this question of Kansas and Nebraska, since he had been on the floor of the Senate, had been promptly voted down by Judge Douglas and his friends. He had no promise that an amendment offered by him to any thing on this subject would receive the slightest consideration. Judge Trumbull did bring to the notice of the Senate at that time to the fact that there was no provision for submitting the Constitution about to be made for the people of Kansas, to a vote of the people. I believe I may venture to say that Judge Douglas made some reply to this speech of Judge Trumbull's, *but he never noticed that part of it at all.* And so the thing passed by. I think, then, the fact that Judge Trumbull offered no amendment, does not throw much blame upon him; and if it did, it does not reach the question of fact *as to what Judge Douglas was doing.* I repeat, that if Trumbull had himself been in the plot, it would not at all relieve the others who were in it from blame. If I should be indicted for murder, and upon the trial it should be discovered that I had been implicated in that murder, but that the prosecuting witness was guilty too, that would not at all touch the question of my crime. It would be no relief to my neck that they discovered this other man who charged the crime upon me to be guilty too.

Another one of the points Judge Douglas makes upon Judge Trumbull is, that when he spoke in Chicago he made his charge to rest upon the fact that the bill had the provision in it for submitting the Constitution to a vote of the people, when it went into his (Judge Douglas's) hands, that it was missing when he reported it to the Senate, and that in a public speech he had subsequently said the alteration in the bill was made while it was in committee, and that they were made in consultation between him (Judge Douglas) and Toombs. And Judge Douglas goes on to comment upon the fact of Trumbull's adducing in his Alton speech the proposition that the bill not only came back with that proposition stricken out, but with another clause and another provision in it, saying that "until the complete execution of this act there shall be no election in said Territory,"— which Trumbull argued was not only taking the provision for submitting to a vote of the people out of the bill, but was adding an affirmative one, in that it prevented the people from exercising the right under a bill that was merely silent on the question. Now in regard to what he says, that Trumbull shifts the issue—that he shifts his ground—and I believe he uses the term, that "it being proven false, he has changed ground"—I call upon all of you, when you come to examine that portion of Trumbull's speech (for it will make a part of mine), to examine whether Trumbull has shifted his ground or not. I say he did not shift his ground, but that he brought forward his original charge and the evidence to sustain it yet more fully, but precisely as he originally made it. Then, in addition thereto, he brought in a new piece of evidence. He shifted no ground. He brought no no new piece of evidence inconsistent with his former testimony, but he brought a new piece, tending, as he thought, and as I think, to prove his proposition. To illustrate: A man brings an accusation against another, and on trial the man making the charge introduces A and B to prove the accusation. At a second trial he introduces the same witnesses, who tell the same story as before, and a third witness, who tells the same thing and in addition, gives further testimony corroborative of the charge. So with Trumbull. There was no shifting of ground, nor inconsistency of testimony between the new piece of evidence and what he originally introduced.

But Judge Douglas says that he himself moved to strike out that last provision of the bill, and that on his motion it was stricken out and a substitute inserted. That I presume is the truth. I presume it is true that that last proposition was stricken out by Judge Douglas. Trumbull has not said it was not. Trumbull has himself said that it was so stricken out. He says: "I am speaking of the bill as Judge Douglas reported it back. It was amended somewhat in the Senate before it passed, but I am speaking of it as he brought it back." Now when Judge Douglas parades the fact that the provision was stricken out of the bill when it came back, he asserts nothing contrary to what Trumbull alleges. Trumbull has only said that he originally put it in—not that he did not strike it out. Trumbull says it was not in the bill when it went to the committee. When it came back it was in, and Judge Douglas said the alterations were made by him in consultation with Toombs. Trumbull alleges therefore, as his conclusion, that Judge Douglas put it in. Then if Douglas wants to contradict Trumbull and call him a liar, let him say he did not put it in, and not that he didn't take it out again. It is said that a bear is sometimes hard enough pushed to drop a cub, and so I presume it was in this case. I presume the truth is that Douglas put it in and afterward took it out. That I take it is the truth about it. Judge Trumbull says one thing; Douglas says another thing, and the two don't contradict one another at all. The question is, what did he put it in for? In the first place what did he take the other provision out of the bill for?—the provision which Trumbull argued was necessary for submitting the Constitution to a vote of the people? What did he take that out for? and having taken it out, what did he put this in for? I say that in the run of things, it is not unlikely forces conspire to render it vastly expedient for Judge Douglas to take that latter clause out again. The question that Trumbull has made is that Judge Douglas put it in, and he don't meet Trumbull at all unless he denies that.

In the clause of Judge Douglas's speech upon this subject he uses this language toward Judge Trumbull. He says: "He forges his evidence from beginning to end, and by falsifying the record he endeavors to bolster up his false charge." Well, that is a pretty serious statement. Trumbull forges his evidence from beginning to end. Now upon my own authority I say that it is not true. What is a forgery? Consider the evidence that Trumbull has brought forward. When you come to read the speech, as you will be able to, examine whether the evidence is a forgery from beginning to end. He had the bill or document in his hand like that [holding up a paper]. He says that is a copy of the Toombs bill—the amendment offered by Toombs. He says that is a copy of the bill as it was introduced and went into Judge Douglas's hands. Now, does Judge Douglas say that is a forgery? That is one thing Trumbull brought forward. Judge Douglas says he forged it from beginning to end! That is the "beginning" we will say. Does Douglas say that is a forgery? Let him say it to-day and we will have a subsequent examination upon this subject. Trumbull then holds up another document like this and says, that is an exact copy of the bill as it came back in the amended form out of Judge Douglas's hands. Does Judge Douglas say that is a forgery? Does he say it in his general sweeping charge? Does he say so now? If he does not, then take this Toombs bill and the bill in the amended form, and it only needs to compare them to see that the provision is in the one and not in the other; it leaves the inference inevitable that it was taken out.

But while I am dealing with this question, let us see what Trumbull's other evidence is. One other piece of evidence I will read. Trumbull says there are in this original Toombs bill these words: "That the following propositions be, and the same are hereby offered to the said Convention of the people of Kansas, when formed, for their free acceptance or rejection; which, if accepted by the Convention and ratified by the people at the election for the adoption of the Constitution, shall be obligatory upon the United States and the said State of Kansas." Now, if it is said that this is a forgery, we will open the paper here and see whether it is or not. Again, Trumbull says, as he goes along, that Mr. Bigler made the following statement in his place in the Senate, December 9, 1857:

"I was present when that subject was discussed by Senators before the bill was introduced, and the question was raised and discussed, whether the Constitution, when formed, should be submitted to a vote of the people. It was held by those most intelligent on the subject, that in view of all the difficulties surrounding that Territory, the danger of any experiment at that time of a popular vote, it would be better there should be no such provision in the Toombs bill; and it was my understanding, in all the intercourse I had, that the Convention would make a Constitution, and send it here without submitting it to the popular vote."

Then Trumbull follows on: "In speaking of this meeting again on the 21st December, 1857 [*Congressional Globe,* same vol., page 113], Senator Bigler said:

"'Nothing was further from my mind than to allude to any social or confidential interview. The meeting was not of that character. Indeed, it was semi-official and called to promote the public good. My recollection was clear that I left the conference under the impression that it had been deemed best to adopt measures to admit Kansas as a State through the agency of one popular election, and that for delegates to this Convention. This impression was stronger because I thought the spirit of the bill infringed upon the doctrine of non-intervention, to which I had great aversion; but with the hope of accomplishing a great good, and as no movement had been made in that direction in the Territory, I waived this objection, and concluded to support the measure. I have a few items of testimony as to the correctness of these impressions, and with their submission I shall be content. I have before me the bill reported by the Senator from Illinois on the 7th of March, 1856, providing for the admission of Kansas as a State, the third section of which reads as follows:

"'That the following propositions be, and the same are hereby offered to the said Convention of the people of Kansas, when formed, for their free acceptance or rejection; which, if accepted by the Convention and ratified by the people at the election for the adoption of the Constitution, shall be obligatory upon the United States and the said State of Kansas.'

"'The bill read in his place by the Senator from Georgia, on the 25th of June, and referred to the Committee on Territories, contained the same section word for word. Both these bills were under consideration at the conference referred to; but, sir, when the Senator from Illinois reported the Toombs bill to the Senate with amendments, the next morning it did not contain that portion of the third section which indicated to the Convention that the Constitution should be approved by the people. The words, `and ratified by the people at the election for the adoption of the Constitution,' had been stricken out.'"

Now these things Trumbull says were stated by Bigler upon the floor of the Senate on certain days, and that they are recorded in the *Congressional Globe* on certain pages. Does Judge Douglas say this is a forgery? Does he say there is no such thing in the *Congressional Globe?* What does he mean when he says Judge Trumbull forges his evidence from beginning to end? So again he says in another place, that Judge Douglas, in his speech December 9, 1857 [*Congressional Globe,* part 1, page 15], stated:

"That during the last session of Congress, I [Mr. Douglas] reported a bill from the Committee on Territories, to authorize the people of Kansas to assemble and form a Constitution for themselves. Subsequently the Senator from Georgia [Mr. Toombs] brought forward a substitute for my bill, which, *after having been modified by him and myself in consultation,* was passed by the Senate."

Now Trumbull says this is a quotation from a speech of Douglas, and is recorded in the *Congressional Globe.* Is *it* a forgery? Is it there or not? It may not be there, but I want the Judge to take these pieces of evidence, and distinctly say they are forgeries if he dare do it.

A voice—"He will."

Mr. Lincoln—Well, sir, you had better not commit him. He gives other quotations—another from Judge Douglas. He says:

> "I will ask the Senator to show me an intimation, from any one member of the Senate, in the whole debate on the Toombs bill, and in the Union, from any quarter, that the Constitution was not to be submitted to the people. I will venture to say that on all sides of the chamber it was so understood at the time. If the opponents of the bill had understood it was not, they would have made the point on it; and if they had made it, we should certainly have yielded to it, and put in the clause. That is a discovery made since the President found out that it was not safe to take it for granted that that would be done, which ought in fairness to have been done."

Judge Trumbull says Douglas made that speech, and it is recorded. Does Judge Douglas say it is a forgery, and was not true? Trumbull says somewhere, and I propose to skip it, but it will be found by any one who will read this debate, that he did distinctly bring it to the notice of those who were engineering the bill, that it lacked that provision, and then he goes on to give another quotation from Judge Douglas, where Judge Trumbull uses this language:

> "Judge Douglas, however, on the same day and in the same debate, probably recollecting or being reminded of the fact that I had objected to the Toombs bill when pending that it did not provide for a submission of the Constitution to the people, made another statement, which is to be found in the same volume of the *Globe,* page 22, in which he says:
>
> "'That the bill was silent on this subject was true, and my attention was called to that about the time it was passed; and I took the fair construction to be, that powers not delegated were reserved, and that of course the Constitution would be submitted to the people.'
>
> "Whether this statement is consistent with the statement just before made, that had the point been made it would have been yielded to, or that it was a new discovery, you will determine."

So I say. I do not know whether Judge Douglas will dispute this, and yet maintain his position that Trumbull's evidence "was forged from beginning to end." I will remark that I have not got these *Congressional Globes* with me. They are large books and difficult to carry about, and if Judge Douglas shall say that on these points where Trumbull has quoted from them, there are no such passages there, I shall not be able to prove they are there upon this occasion, but I will have another chance. Whenever he points out the forgery and says, "I declare that this particular thing which Trumbull has uttered is not to be found where he says it is," then my attention will be drawn to that, and I will arm myself for the contest—stating now that I have not the slightest doubt on earth that I will find every quotation just where Trumbull says it is. Then the question is, how can Douglas call that a forgery? How can he make out that it is a forgery? What is a forgery? It is the bringing forward something in writing or in print purporting to be of certain effect when it is altogether untrue. If you come forward with my note for one hundred dollars when I have never given such a note, there is a forgery. If you come forward with a letter purporting to be written by me which I never wrote, there is another forgery. If you produce anything in writing or in print saying it is so and so, the document not being genuine, a forgery has been committed. How do you make this a forgery when every piece of the evidence is genuine? If Judge Douglas does say these documents and quotations are false and forged, he has a full right to do so, but until he does it specifically we don't know how to get at him. If he does say they are false and forged, I will then look further into it, and I presume I can procure the certificates of the proper officers that they are genuine copies. I have no doubt each of these extracts will be found exactly where Trumbull says it is. Then I leave it to you if Judge Douglas, in making his sweeping charge that Judge Trumbull's evidence is forged from beginning to end, at all meets the case—if that is the way to get at the facts. I repeat again, if he will point out which one is a forgery, I will carefully examine it, and if it proves that any one of them is really a forgery it will not be me who will hold to it any longer. I have always wanted to deal with every one I meet candidly and honestly. If I have made any assertion not warranted by facts, and it is pointed out to me, I will withdraw it cheerfully. But I do not choose to see Judge Trumbull calumniated, and the evidence he has brought forward branded in general terms, "a forgery from beginning to end." This is not the legal way of meeting a charge, and I submit to all intelligent persons, both friends of Judge Douglas and of myself, whether it is.

The point upon Judge Douglas is this. The bill that went into his hands had the provision in it for a submission of the Constitution to the people; and I say its language amounts to an express provision for a submission, and that he took the provision out. He says it was known that the bill was silent in this particular; *but I say, Judge Douglas, it was not silent when you got it.* It was vocal with the declaration when you got it, for a submission of the Constitution to the people. And now, my direct question to Judge Douglas is, to answer why, if he deemed the bill silent on this point, he found it necessary to strike out those particular harmless words. If he had found the bill silent and without this provision, he might say what he does now. If he supposes it was implied that the Constitution would be submitted to a vote of the people, how could these two lines so encumber the statute as to make it necessary to strike them out? How could he infer that a submission was still implied, after its express provision had been stricken from the bill? I find the bill vocal with the provision, while he silenced it. He took it out, and although he took out the other provision preventing a submission to a vote of the people, I ask, *why did you first put it in?* I ask him whether he took the original provision out, which Trumbull alleges was in the bill? If he admits that he did take it, *I ask him what he did for it?* It looks to us as if he had altered the bill. If it looks differently to him—if he has a different reason for his action from the one we assign him—he can tell it. I insist upon knowing why he made the bill silent upon that point when it was vocal before he put his hands upon it.

I was told, before my last paragraph, that my time was within three minutes of being out. I presume it is expired now. I therefore close.

Mr. Douglas's Reply.

LADIES AND GENTLEMEN: I had supposed that we assembled here to-day for the purpose of a joint discussion between Mr. Lincoln and myself, upon the political questions that now agitate the whole country. The rule of such discussions is, that the opening speaker shall touch upon all the points he intends to discuss, in order that his opponent, in reply, shall have the opportunity of answering them. Let me ask you what questions of public policy, relating to the welfare of this State or the Union, has Mr. Lincoln discussed before you? Mr. Lincoln simply contented himself at the outset by saying, that he was not in favor of social and political equality between the white man and the negro, and did not desire the law so changed as to make the latter voters or eligible to office. I am glad that I have at last succeeded in getting an answer out of him upon this question of negro citizenship and eligibility to office, for I have been trying to bring him to the point on it ever since this canvass commenced.

I will now call your attention to the question which Mr. Lincoln has occupied his entire time in discussing. He spent his whole hour in retailing a charge made by Senator Trumbull against me. The circumstances out of which that charge was manufactured, occurred prior to the last Presidential election, over two years ago. If the charge was true, why did not Trumbull make it in 1856, when I was discussing the questions of that day all over this State with Lincoln and him, and when it was pertinent to the then issue? He was then as silent as the grave on the subject. If that charge was true, the time to have brought it forward was the canvass of 1856, the year when the Toombs bill passed the Senate. When the facts were fresh in the public mind, when the Kansas question was the paramount question of the day, and when such a charge would have had a material bearing on the election, why did he and Lincoln remain silent then, knowing that such a charge could be made and proven if true? Were they not false to you and false to the country in going through that entire campaign, concealing their knowledge of this enormous conspiracy which, Mr. Trumbull says, he then knew and would not tell? Mr. Lincoln intimates, in his speech, a good reason why Mr. Trumbull would not tell, for, he says, that it might be true, as I proved that it was at Jacksonville, that Trumbull was also in the plot, yet that the fact of Trumbull's being in the plot would not in any way relieve me. He illustrates this argument by supposing himself on trial for murder, and says that it would be no extenuating circumstance if, on his trial, another man was found to be a party to his crime. Well, if Trumbull was in the plot, and concealed it in order to escape the odium which would have fallen upon himself, I ask you whether you can believe him now when he turns State's evidence, and avows his own infamy in order to implicate me. I am amazed that Mr. Lincoln should now come forward and indorse that charge, occupying his whole hour in reading Mr. Trumbull's speech in support of it. Why, I ask, does not Mr. Lincoln make a speech of his own instead of taking up his time reading Trumbull's speech at Alton? I supposed that Mr. Lincoln was capable of making a public speech on his own account, or I should not have accepted the banter from him for a joint discussion. ["How about the charges?"] Do not trouble yourselves, I am going to make my speech in my own way, and I trust, as the Democrats listened patiently and respectfully to Mr. Lincoln, that his friends will not interrupt me when I am answering him. When Mr. Trumbull returned from the East, the first thing he did when he landed at Chicago was to make a speech wholly devoted to assaults upon my public character and public action.

Up to that time I had never alluded to his course in Congress, or to him directly or indirectly, and hence his assaults upon me were entirely without provocation and without excuse. Since then he has been traveling from one end of the State to the other repeating his vile charge. I propose now to read it in his own language:

> "Now, fellow-citizens, I make the distinct charge, that there was a pre-concerted arrangement and plot entered into by the very men who now claim credit for opposing a Constitution formed and put in force without giving the people any opportunity to pass upon it. This, my friends, is a serious charge, but I charge it to-night that the very men who traverse the country under banners proclaiming popular sovereignty, by design concocted a bill on purpose to force a Constitution upon that people."

In answer to some one in the crowd, who asked him a question, Trumbull said:

> "And you want to satisfy yourself that he was in the plot to force a Constitution upon that people? I will satisfy you. I will cram the truth down any honest man's throat until he cannot deny it. And to the man who does deny it, I will cram the lie down his throat till he shall cry enough.
>
> "It is preposterous—it is the most damnable effrontery that man ever put on, to conceal a scheme to defraud and cheat the people out of their rights and then claim credit for it."

That is the polite language Senator Trumbull applied to me, his colleague, when I was two hundred miles off. Why did he not speak out as boldly in the Senate of the United States, and cram the lie down my throat when I denied the charge, first made by Bigler, and made him take it back? You all recollect how Bigler assaulted me when I was engaged in a hand-to-hand fight, resisting a scheme to force a Constitution on the people of Kansas against their will. He then attacked me with this charge; but I proved its utter falsity; nailed the slander to the counter, and made him take the back track. There is not an honest man in America who read that debate who will pretend that the charge is true. Trumbull was then present in the Senate, face to face with me, and why did he not then rise and repeat the charge, and say he would cram the lie down my throat? I tell you that Trumbull then knew it was a lie. He knew that Toombs denied that there ever was a clause in the bill he brought forward, calling for and requiring a submission of the Kansas Constitution to the people. I will tell you what the facts of the case were. I introduced a bill to authorize the people of Kansas to form a Constitution, and come into the Union as a State whenever they should have the requisite population for a member of Congress, and Mr. Toombs proposed a substitute, authorizing the people of Kansas, with their then population of only 25,000, to form a Constitution, and come in at once. The question at issue was, whether we would admit Kansas with a population of 25,000, or, make her wait until she had the ratio entitling her to a representative in Congress, which was 93,420. That was the point of dispute in the Committee of Territories, to which both my bill and Mr. Toombs's substitute had been referred. I was overruled by a majority of the committee, my proposition rejected, and Mr. Toombs's proposition to admit Kansas then, with her population of 25,000, adopted. Accordingly, a bill to carry out his idea of immediate admission was reported as a substitute for mine—the only points at issue being, as I have already said, the question of population, and the adoption of safeguards against frauds at the election. Trumbull knew this—the whole Senate knew it—and hence he was silent at that time. He waited until I became engaged in this canvass, and finding that I was showing up Lincoln's Abolitionism and negro equality doctrines, that I was driving Lincoln to the wall, and white men would not support his rank Abolitionism, he came back from the East and trumped up a system of charges against me, hoping that I would be compelled to occupy my entire time in defending myself, so that I would not be able to show up the enormity of the principles of the Abolitionists. Now the only reason, and the true reason, why Mr. Lincoln has occupied the whole of his first hour in this issue between Trumbull and myself, is, to conceal from this vast audience the real questions which divide the two great parties.

I am not going to allow them to waste much of my time with these personal matters. I have lived in this State twenty-five years, most of that time have been in public life, and my record is open to you all. If that record is not enough to vindicate me from these petty, malicious assaults, I despise ever to be elected to office by slandering my opponents and traducing other men. Mr. Lincoln asks you to elect him to the United States Senate to-day solely because he and Trumbull can slander me. Has he given any other reason? Has he avowed what he was desirous to do in Congress on any one question? He desires to ride into office, not upon his own merits, not upon the merits and soundness of his principles, but upon his success in fastening a stale old slander upon me.

I wish you to bear in mind that up to the time of the introduction of the Toombs bill, and after its introduction, there had never been an act of Congress for the admission of a new State which contained a clause requiring its Constitution to be submitted to the people. The general rule made the law silent on the subject, taking it for granted that the people would demand and compel a popular vote on the ratification of their Constitution. Such was the general rule under Washington, Jefferson, Madison, Jackson and Polk, under the Whig Presidents and the Democratic Presidents from the beginning of the Government down, and nobody dreamed that an effort would ever be made to abuse the power thus confided to the people of a Territory. For this reason our attention was not called to the fact of whether there was or was not a clause in the Toombs bill compelling submission, but it was taken for granted that the Constitution would be submitted to the people whether the law compelled it or not.

Now, I will read from the report by me as Chairman of the Committee on Territories at the time I reported back the Toombs substitute to the Senate. It contained several things which I had voted against in committee, but had been overruled by a majority of the members, and it was my duty as chairman of the committee to report the bill back as it was agreed upon by them. The main point upon which I had been overruled was the question of population. In my report accompanying the Toombs bill, I said:

> "In the opinion of your Committee, whenever a Constitution shall be formed in any Territory, preparatory to its admission into the Union as a State, justice, the genius of our institutions, the whole theory of our republican system, imperatively demand that the voice of the people shall be fairly expressed, and their will embodied in that fundamental law, without fraud, or violence, or intimidation, or any other improper or unlawful influence, and subject to no other restrictions than those imposed by the Constitution of the United States."

There you find that we took it for granted that the Constitution was to be submitted to the people, whether the bill was silent on the subject or not. Suppose I had reported it so, following the example of Washington, Adams, Jefferson, Madison Monroe, Adams, Jackson, Van Buren, Harrison, Tyler, Polk, Taylor, Fillmore, and Pierce, would that fact have been evidence of a conspiracy to force a Constitution upon the people of Kansas against their will? If the charge which Mr. Lincoln makes be true against me, it is true against Zachary

Taylor, Millard Fillmore, and every Whig President, as well as every Democratic President, and against Henry Clay, who, in the Senate or House, for forty years advocated bills similar to the one I reported, no one of them containing a clause compelling the submission of the Constitution to the people. Are Mr. Lincoln and Mr. Trumbull prepared to charge upon all those eminent men from the beginning of the Government down to the present day, that the absence of a provision compelling submission, in the various bills passed by them, authorizing the people of Territories to form State Constitutions, is evidence of a corrupt design on their part to force a Constitution upon an unwilling people?

I ask you to reflect on these things, for I tell you that there is a conspiracy to carry this election for the Black Republicans by slander, and not by fair means. Mr. Lincoln's speech this day is conclusive evidence of the fact. He has devoted his entire time to an issue between Mr. Trumbull and myself, and has not uttered a word about the politics of the day. Are you going to elect Mr. Trumbull's colleague upon an issue between Mr. Trumbull and me? I thought I was running against Abraham Lincoln, that he claimed to be my opponent, had challenged me to a discussion of the public questions of the day with him, and was discussing these questions with me; but it turns out that his only hope is to ride into office on Trumbull's back, who will carry him by falsehood.

Permit me to pursue this subject a little further. An examination of the record proves that Trumbull's charge—that the Toombs bill originally contained a clause requiring the Constitution to be submitted to the people—*is false.* The printed copy of the bill which Mr. Lincoln held up before you, and which he pretends contains such a clause, merely contains a clause requiring a submission of the land grant, and *there is no clause in it requiring a submission of the Constitution.* Mr. Lincoln cannot find such a clause in it. My report shows that we took it for granted that the people would require a submission of the Constitution, and secure it for themselves. There never was a clause in the Toombs bill requiring the Constitution to be submitted; Trumbull knew it at the time, and his speech made on the night of its passage discloses the fact that he knew it was silent or the subject; Lincoln pretends, and tells you that Trumbull has not changed his evidence in support of his charge since he made his speech in Chicago. Let us see. The Chicago *Times* took up Trumbull's Chicago speech, compared it with the official records of Congress, and proved that speech to be false in its charge that the original Toombs bill required a submission of the Constitution to the people. Trumbull then saw that he was caught—and his falsehood exposed—and he went to Alton, and, under the very walls of the penitentiary, made a new speech, in which he predicated his assault upon me in the allegation that I had caused to be voted into the Toombs bill a clause which prohibited the Convention from submitting the Constitution to the people, and quoted what he pretended was the clause. Now, has not Mr. Trumbull entirely changed the evidence on which he bases his charge? The clause which he quoted in his Alton speech (which he has published and circulated broadcast over the State) as having been put into the Toombs bill by me, is in the following words:

> "And until the complete execution of this act, no other election shall be held in said Territory."

Trumbull says that the object of that amendment was to prevent the Convention from submitting the Constitution to a vote of the people.

Now, I will show you that when Trumbull made that statement at Alton he knew it to be untrue. I read from Trumbull's speech in the Senate on the Toombs bill on the night of its passage. He then said:

> "There is nothing said in this bill, so far as I have discovered, about submitting the Constitution, which is to be formed, to the people for their sanction or rejection. Perhaps the Convention will have the right to submit it, if it should think proper, but it is certainly not compelled to do so according to the provisions of the bill."

Thus you see that Trumbull, when the bill was on its passage in the Senate, said that it was silent on the subject of submission, and that there was nothing in the bill one way or the other on it. In his Alton speech he says there was a clause in the bill preventing its submission to the people, and that I had it voted in as an amendment. Thus I convict him of falsehood and slander by quoting from him on the passage of the Toombs bill in the Senate of the United States, his own speech, made on the night of July 2, 1856, and reported in the *Congressional Globe* for the first session of the thirty-fourth Congress, vol. 33. What will you think of a man who makes a false charge and falsifies the records to prove it? I will now show you that the clause which Trumbull says was put in the bill on my motion, was never put in at all by me, but was stricken out on my motion and another substituted in its place. I call your attention to the same volume of the *Congressional Globe* to which I have already referred, page 795, where you will find the following report of the proceedings of the Senate:

"Mr. Douglas—I have an amendment to offer from the Committee on Territories. On page 8, section 11, strike out the words 'until the complete execution of this act, no other election shall be held in said Territory,' and insert the amendment which I hold in my hand."

You see from this that I moved to strike out the very words that Trumbull says I put in. The Committee on Territories overruled me in Committee and put the clause in, but as soon as I got the bill back into the Senate, I moved to strike it out and put another clause in its place. On the same page you will find that my amendment was agreed to *unanimously*. I then offered another amendment, recognizing the right of the people of Kansas, under the Toombs bill, to order just such elections as they saw proper. You can find it on page 796 of the same volume. I will read it:

"Mr. Douglas—I have another amendment to offer from the Committee, to follow the amendment which has been adopted. The bill reads now: 'And until the complete execution of this act, no other election shall be held in said Territory.' It has been suggested that it should be modified in this way: 'And to avoid conflict is the complete execution of this act, all other elections in said Territory are hereby postponed until such time as said Convention shall appoint,' so that they can appoint the day in the event that there should be a failure to come into the Union."

The amendment was *unanimously* agreed to—clearly and distinctly recognizing the right of the Convention to order just as many elections as they saw proper in the execution of the act. Trumbull concealed in his Alton speech the fact that the clause he quoted had been stricken out in my motion, and the other fact that this other clause was put in the hill on my motion, and made the false charge that I incorporated into the bill a clause preventing submission, in the face of the fact, that, on my motion, the bill was so amended before it passed as to recognize in express words the right and duty of submission.

On this record that I have produced before you, I repeat my charge that Trumbull did falsify the public records of the country, in order to make his charge against me, and I tell Mr. Abraham Lincoln that if he will examine these records, he will then know that what I state is true. Mr. Lincoln has this day indorsed Mr. Trumbull's veracity after he had my word for it that that veracity was proved to be violated and forfeited by the public records. It will not do for Mr. Lincoln in parading his calumnies against me, to put Mr. Trumbull between him and the odium and responsibility which justly attaches to such calumnies. I tell him that I am as ready to prosecute the indorser as the maker of a forged note. I regret the necessity of occupying my time with these petty personal matters. It is unbecoming the dignity of a canvass for an office of the character for which we are candidates. When I commenced the canvass at Chicago, I spoke of Mr. Lincoln in terms of kindness as an old friend—I said that he was a good citizen, of unblemished character, against whom I had nothing to say. I repeated these complimentary remarks about him in my successive speeches, until he became the indorser for these and other slanders against me. If there is any thing personally disagreeable, uncourteous or disreputable in these personalities, the sole responsibility rests on Mr. Lincoln, Mr. Trumbull and their backers.

I will show you another charge made by Mr. Lincoln against me, as an offset to his determination of willingness to take back any thing that is incorrect, and to correct any false statement he may have made. He has several times charged that the Supreme Court, President Pierce, President Buchanan, and myself, at the time I introduced the Nebraska bill in January, 1854, at Washington, entered into a conspiracy to establish slavery all over this country. I branded this charge as a falsehood, and then he repeated it, asked me to analyze its truth and answer it. I told him, "Mr. Lincoln, I know what you are after—you want to occupy my time in personal matters, to prevent me from showing up the revolutionary principles which the Abolition party—whose candidate you are—have proclaimed to the world." But he asked me to analyze his proof, and I did so. I called his attention to the fact that at the time the Nebraska bill was introduced, there was no such case as the Dred Scott case pending in the Supreme Court, nor was it brought there for years afterward, and hence that it was impossible there could have been any such conspiracy between the Judges of the Supreme Court and the other parties involved. I proved by the record that the charge was false, and what did he answer? Did he take it back like an honest man and say that he had been mistaken? No; he repeated the charge, and said, that although there was no such case pending that year, there was an understanding between the Democratic owners of Dred Scott and the Judges of the Supreme Court and other parties involved, that the case should be brought up. I then demanded to know who these Democratic owners of Dred Scott were. He could not or would not tell; he did not know. In truth, there were no Democratic owners of Dred Scott on the face of the land. Dred Scott was owned at that time by the Rev. Dr. Chaffee, an Abolition member of Congress from Springfield, Massachusetts, and his wife; and Mr. Lincoln ought to have known that Dred Scott was so owned, for the reason that as soon as the decision was announced by the court, Dr. Chaffee and his wife executed a deed eman-cipating him, and put that deed on record. It was a matter of public record, therefore, that at the time the case was taken to the Supreme Court, Dred Scott was owned by an Abolition member of Congress, a friend of Lincoln's, and a leading man of his party, while the defense was conducted by Abolition lawyers—and thus the Abolitionists managed both sides of the case. I have exposed these facts to Mr. Lincoln, and yet he will not withdraw his charge of conspiracy. I now submit to you whether you can place any confidence in a man who continues to make a charge when its utter falsity is proven by the pub-lic records. I will state another fact to show how utterly reckless and unscrupu-lous this charge against the Supreme Court, President Pierce, President Buchanan and myself is. Lincoln says that President Buchanan was in the con-spiracy at Washington in the winter of 1854, when the Nebraska bill was intro-duced. The history of this country shows that James Buchanan was at that time representing this country at the Court of St. James, Great Britain, with distin-guished ability and usefulness, that he had not been in the United States for nearly a year previous, and that he did not return until about three years after. Yet Mr. Lincoln keeps repeating this charge of conspiracy against Mr. Buchanan when the public records prove it to be untrue. Having proved it to be false as far as the Supreme Court and President Buchanan are concerned, I drop it, leav-ing the public to say whether I, by myself, without their concurrence, could have gone into a conspiracy with them. My friends, you see that the object clearly is to conduct the canvass on personal matters, and hunt me down with charges that are proven to be false by the public records of the country. I am willing to throw open my whole public and private life to the inspection of any man, or all men who desire to investigate it. Having resided among you twenty-five years, during nearly the whole of which time a public man, exposed to more assaults, perhaps more abuse than any man living of my age, or who ever did live, and having survived it all and still commanded your confidence, I am willing to trust to your knowledge of me and my public conduct without mak-ing any more defense against these assaults.

Fellow-citizens, I came here for the purpose of discussing the leading polit-ical topics which now agitate the country. I have no charges to make against Mr. Lincoln, none against Mr. Trumbull, and none against any man who is a candidate, except in repelling their assaults upon me. If Mr. Lincoln is a man of bad character, I leave you to find it out; if his votes in the past are not satisfac-tory, I leave others to ascertain the fact; if his course on the Mexican war was not in accordance with your notions of patriotism and fidelity to our own country as against a public enemy, I leave you to ascertain the fact. I have no assaults to make upon him, except to trace his course on the questions that now divide the country and engross so much of the people's attention.

You know that prior to 1854 this country was divided into two great political parties, one the Whig, the other the Democratic. I, as a Democrat for twenty years prior to that time, had been in public discussions in this State as an advocate of Democratic principles, and I can appeal with confidence to every old line Whig within the hearing of my voice to bear testimony that during all that period I fought you Whigs like a man on every question that separated the two parties. I had the highest respect for Henry Clay as a gallant party leader, as an eminent statesman, and as one of the bright ornaments of this country; but I conscientiously believed that the Democratic party was right on the questions which separated the Democrats from the Whigs. The man does not live who can say that I ever personally assailed Henry Clay or Daniel Webster, or any one of the leaders of that great party, whilst I combated with all my energy the measures they advocated. What did we differ about in those days? Did Whigs and Democrats differ about this slavery question? On the contrary, did we not, in 1850, unite to a man in favor of that system of Compromise measures which Mr. Clay introduced, Webster defended, Case supported, and Fillmore approved and made the law of the land by his signature. While we agreed on those Compromise measures, we differed about a bank, the tariff, distribution, the specie circular, the sub-treasury, and other questions of that description. Now, let me ask you, which one of those questions on which Whigs and Democrats then differed now remains to divide the two great parties? Every one of those questions which divided Whigs and Democrats has passed away, the country has outgrown them, they have passed into history. Hence it is immaterial whether you were right or I was right on the bank, the sub-treasury, and other questions, because they no longer continue living issues. What, then, has taken the place of those questions about which we once differed? The slavery question has now become the leading and controlling issue; that question on which you and I agreed, on which the Whigs and Democrats united, has now become the leading issue between the National Democracy on the one side, and the Republican or Abolition party on the other.

Just recollect for a moment the memorable contest of 1850, when this country was agitated from its center to its circumference by the slavery agitation. All eyes in this nation were then turned to the three great lights that survived the days of the Revolution. They looked to Clay, then in retirement at Ashland, and to Webster and Cass in the United States Senate. Clay had retired to

Ashland, having, as he supposed, performed his mission on earth, and was preparing himself for a better sphere of existence in another world. In that retirement he heard the discordant, harsh and grating sounds of sectional strife and disunion, and he aroused and came forth and resumed his seat in the Senate, that great theater of his great deeds. From the moment that Clay arrived among as he became the leader of all the Union men, whether Whigs or Democrats. For nine months we each assembled, each day, in the council-chamber, Clay in the chair, with Cass upon his right hand and Webster upon his left, and the Democrats and Whigs gathered around, forgetting differences, and only animated by one common, patriotic sentiment to devise means and measures by which we could defeat the mad and revolutionary scheme of the Northern Abolitionist and Southern disunionists. We did devise those means. Clay brought them forward, Cass advocated them, the Union Democrats and Union Whigs voted for them, Fillmore signed them, and they gave peace and quiet to the country. Those Compromise measures of 1850 were founded upon the great fundamental principle that the people of each State and each Territory ought to be left free to form and regulate their own domestic institutions in their own way, subject only to the Federal Constitution. I will ask every old line Democrat and every old line Whig within the hearing of my voice, if I have not truly stated the issues as they then presented themselves to the country. You recollect that the Abolitionists raised a howl of indignation, and cried for vengeance and the destruction of Democrats and Whigs both, who supported those Compromise measures of 1850. When I returned home to Chicago, I found the citizens inflamed and infuriated against the authors of those great measures. Being the only man in that city who was held responsible for affirmative votes on all those measures, I came forward and addressed the assembled inhabitants, defended each and every one of Clay's Compromise measures as they passed the Senate and the House, and were approved by President Fillmore. Previous to that time, the city council had passed resolutions nullifying the act of Congress, and instructing the police to withhold all assistance from its execution; but the people of Chicago listened to my defense, and like candid, frank, conscientious men, when they became convinced that they had done an injustice to Clay, Webster, Cass, and all of us who had supported those measures, they repealed their nullifying resolutions and declared that the laws should be executed and the supremacy of the Constitution maintained. Let it always be recorded in history to the immortal honor of the people of Chicago, that they returned to their duty when they found that they were wrong, and did justice to those whom they had blamed and abused unjustly. When the Legislature of this State assembled that year, they proceeded to pass resolutions approving the Compromise measures of 1850. When the Whig party assembled in 1852 at Baltimore in National Convention for the last time, to nominate Scott for the Presidency, they adopted as a part of their platform the Compromise measures of 1850 as the cardinal plank upon which every Whig would stand and by which he would regulate his future conduct. When the Democratic party assembled at the same place one month after, to nominate General Pierce, we adopted the same platform so far as those Compromise measures were concerned, agreeing that we would stand by those glorious measures as a cardinal article in the Democratic faith. Thus you see that in 1852 all the old Whigs and all the old Democrats stood on a common plank so far as this slavery question was concerned, differing on other questions.

Now, let me ask, how is it that since that time so many of you Whigs have wandered from the true path marked out by Clay and carried out broad and wide by the great Webster? How is it that so many old line Democrats have abandoned the old faith of their party, and joined with Abolitionism and Freesoilism to overturn the platform of the old Democrats, and the platform of the old Whigs? You cannot deny that since 1854 there has been a great revolution on this one question. How has it been brought about? I answer, that no sonner was the sod grown green over he grave of the immortal Clay, no sooner was the rose planted on the tomb of the god-like Webster, than many of the leaders of the Whig party, such as Seward, of New York, and his followers, led off and attempted to abolitionize the Whig party, and transfer all your old Whigs, bound head and foot, into the Abolition camp. Seizing hold of the temporary excitement produced in this country by the introduction of the Nebraska bill, the disappointed politicians in the Democratic party united with the disappointed politicians in the Whig party, and endeavored to form a new party composed of all the Abolitionists, of abolitionized Democrats and abolitionized Whigs, banded together in an Abolition platform.

And who led that crusade against National principles in this State? I answer, Abraham Lincoln on behalf of the Whigs, and Lyman Trumbull on behalf of the Democrats, formed a scheme by which they would abolitionize the two great parties in this State on condition that Lincoln should be sent to the United States Senate in place of General Shields, and that Trumbull should go to Congress from the Belleville District, until I would be accommodating enough either to die or resign for his benefit, and then he was to go to the Senate in my place. You all remember that during the year 1854, these two worthy gentlemen, Mr. Lincoln and Mr. Trumbull, one an old line Whig and the other an old line Democrat, were hunting in partnership to elect a Legislature against the

Democratic party. I canvassed the State that year from the time I returned home until the election came off, and spoke in every county that I could reach during that period. In the northern part of the State I found Lincoln's ally, in the person of FRED DOUGLASS, THE NEGRO, preaching Abolition doctrines, while Lincoln was discussing the same principles down here, and Trumbull, a little farther down, was advocating the election of members to the Legislature who would act in concert with Lincoln's and Fred Douglass's friends. I witnessed an effort made at Chicago by Lincoln's then associates, and now supporters, to put Fred Douglass, the negro, on the stand at a Democratic meeting, to reply to the illustrious General Cass, when he was addressing the people there. They had the same negro hunting me down, and they now have a negro traversing the northern counties of the State, and speaking in behalf of Lincoln. Lincoln knows that when we were at Freeport in joint discussion, there was a distinguished colored friend of his there then who was on the stump for him, and who made a speech there the night before we spoke, and another the night after, a short distance from Freeport, in favor of Lincoln, and in order to show how much interest the colored brethren felt in the success of their brother Abe, I have with me here, and would read it if it would not occupy too much of my time, a speech made by Fred Douglass in Poughkeepsie, N. Y., a short time since, to a large Convention, in which he conjures all the friends of negro equality and negro citizenship to rally as one man around Abraham Lincoln, the perfect embodiment of their principles, and by all means to defeat Stephen A. Douglas. Thus you find that this Republican party in the northern part of the State had colored gentlemen for their advocates in 1854, in company with Lincoln and Trumbull, as they have now. When, in October, 1854, I went down to Springfield to attend the State Fair, I found the leaders of this party all assembled together under the title of an anti-Nebraska meeting. It was Black Republicans up north, and anti-Nebraska at Springfield. I found Lovejoy, a high-priest of Abolitionism, and Lincoln, one of the leaders who was towing the old line Whigs into the Abolition camp, and Trumbull, Sidney Breese, and Governor Reynolds, all making speeches against the Democratic party and myself, at the same place and in the same cause. The same men who are now fighting the Democratic party and the regular Democratic nominees in this State, were fighting us then. They did not then acknowledge that they had become Abolitionists, and many of them deny it now. Breese, Dougherty and Reynolds were then fighting the Democracy under the title of anti-Nebraska men, and now they are fighting the Democracy under the pretense that they are *simon pure* Democrats, saying that they are authorized to have every office-holder in Illinois beheaded who prefers

the election of Douglas to that of Lincoln, or the success of the Democratic
ticket in preference to the Abolition ticket for members of Congress, State officers, members of the Legislature, or any office in the State. They canvassed the
State against us in 1854, as they are doing now, owning different names and different principles in different localities, but having a common object in view, viz:
The defeat of all men holding national principles in opposition to this sectional
Abolition party. They carried the Legislature in 1854, and when it assembled in
Springfield they proceeded to elect a United States Senator, all voting for Lincoln with one or two exceptions, which exceptions prevented them from quite
electing him. And why should they not elect him? Had not Trumbull agreed
that Lincoln should have Shields's place? Had not the Abolitionists agreed to it?
Was it not the solemn compact, the condition on which Lincoln agreed to abolitionize the old Whigs that he should be Senator? Still, Trumbull having control of a few abolitionized Democrats, would not allow them all to vote for
Lincoln on any one ballot, and thus kept him for some time within one or two
votes of an election, until he worried out Lincoln's friends, and compelled them
to drop him and elect Trumbull in violation of the bargain. I desire to read you
a piece of testimony in confirmation of the notoriously public facts which I have
stated to you. Col. James H. Matheny, of Springfield, is, and for twenty years
has been, the confidential personal and political friend and manager of Mr. Lincoln. Matheny is this very day the candidate of the Republican or Abolition
party for Congress against the gallant Major Thos. L. Harris, in the Springfield
District, and is making speeches for Lincoln and against me. I will read you the
testimony of Matheny about this bargain between Lincoln and Trumbull when
they undertook to abolitionize Whigs and Democrats only four years ago.
Matheny being mad at Trumbull for having played a Yankee trick on Lincoln,
exposed the bargain in a public speech two years ago, and I will read the published report of that speech, the correctness of which Mr. Lincoln will not deny:

> "The Whigs, Abolitionists, Know Nothings, and renegade Democ-
> rats, made a solemn compact for the purpose of carrying this State against
> the Democracy on this plan: 1st. That they would all combine and elect
> Mr. Trumbull to Congress, and thereby carry his district for the Legisla-
> ture, in order to throw all the strength that could be obtained into that
> body against the Democrats. 2d. That when the Legisture should meet,
> the officers of that body, such as speaker, clerks, door-keepers, etc., would
> be given to the Abolitionists; and 3d. That the Whigs were to have the
> United States Senator. That, accordingly, in good faith Trumbull was

elected to Congress, and his district carried for the Legislature, and when it convened the Abolitionists got all the officers of that body, and thus far the 'bond' was fairly executed. The Whigs, on their part, demanded the election of Abraham Lincoln to the United States Senate, that the bond might be fulfilled, the other parties to the contract having already secured to themselves all that was called for. But, in the most perfidious manner, they refused to elect Mr. Lincoln; and the mean, low-lived, sneaking Trumbull succeeded by pleading all that was required by any party, in thrusting Lincoln aside and foisting himself, an excrescence from the rotten bowels of the Democracy, into the United States Senate; and thus it has ever been, that an *honest* man makes a bad bargain when he conspires or contracts with rogues."

Lincoln's confidential friend, Matheny, thought that Lincoln made a bad bargain when he conspired with such rogues as Trumbull and the Abolitionists. I would like to know whether Lincoln had as high opinion of Trumbull's veracity when the latter agreed to support him for the Senate, and then cheated him as he does now, when Trumbull comes forward and makes charges against me. You could not then prove Trumbull an honest man either by Lincoln, by Matheny, or by any of Lincoln's friends. They charged every where that Trumbull had cheated them out of the bargain, and Lincoln found sure enough that it was a *bad bargain* to contract and conspire with rogues.

And now I will explain to you what has been a mystery all over the State and Union, the reason why Lincoln was nominated for the United States Senate by the Black Republican Convention. You know it has never been usual for any party, or any Convention, to nominate a candidate for United States Senator. Probably this was the first time that such a thing was ever done. The Black Republican Convention had not been called for that purpose, but to nominate a State ticket, and every man was surprised and many disgusted when Lincoln was nominated. Archie Williams thought he was entitled to it, Browning knew that he deserved it, Wentworth was certain that he would get it, Peck had hopes, Judd felt sure that he was the man, and Palmer had claims and had made arrangements to secure it; but to their utter amazement, Lincoln was nominated by the Convention, and not only that, but he received the nomination unanimously, by a resolution declaring that Abraham Lincoln was "the first, last, and only choice" of the Republican party. How did this occur? Why, because they could not get Lincoln's friends to make another bargain with "rogues," unless the whole party would come up as one man and pledge their honor that they would stand by Lincoln first, last and all the time, and that he should not be cheated by Lovejoy this time, as he was by Trumbull before. Thus, by passing this resolution, the Abolitionists are all for him, Lovejoy and Farnsworth are canvassing for him, Giddings is ready to come here in his behalf, and the negro speakers are already on the stump for him, and he is sure not to be cheated this time. He would not go into the arrangement until he got their bond for it, and Trumbull is compelled now to take the stump, get up false charges against me, and travel all over the State to try and elect Lincoln, in order to keep Lincoln's friends quiet about the bargain in which Trumbull cheated them four years ago. You see, now, why it is that Lincoln and Trumbull are so mighty fond of each other. They have entered into a conspiracy to break me down by these assaults on my public character, in order to draw my attention from a fair exposure of the mode in which they attempted to abolitionize the old Whig and the old Democratic parties and lead them captive into the Abolition camp. Do you not all remember that Lincoln went around here four years ago making speeches to you, and telling that you should all go for the Abolition ticket, and swearing that he was as good a Whig as he ever was; and that Trumbull went all over the State making pledges to the old Democrats, and trying to coax them into the Abolition camp, swearing by his Maker, with the uplifted hand, that he was still a Democrat, always intended to be, and that never would he desert the Democratic party. He got your votes to elect an Abolition Legislature, which passed Abolition resolutions, attempted to pass Abolition laws, and sustained Abolitionists for office, State and National. Now, the same game is attempted to be played over again. Then Lincoln and Trumbull made captives of the old Whigs and old Democrats and carried them into the Abolition camp, where Father Giddings, the high-priest of Abolitionism, received and christened them in the dark cause just as fast as they were brought in. Giddings found the converts so numerous that he had to have assistance, and be sent for John P. Hale, N. P. Banks, Chase, and other Abolitionists, and they came on, and with Lovejoy and Fred Douglass, the negro, helped to baptize these new converts as Lincoln, Trumbull, Breese, Reynolds, and Dougherty could capture them and bring them within the Abolition clutch. Gentlemen, they are now around making the same kind of speeches. Trumbull was down in Monroe county the other day assailing me, and making a speech in favor of Lincoln, and I will show you under what notice his meeting was called. You see these people are Black Republicans or Abolitionists up north, while at Springfield today, they dare not call their Convention "Republican," but are obliged to say "a Convention of all men opposed to the Democratic party," and in Monroe county and lower Egypt Trumbull advertises their meetings as follows:

A meeting of the Free Democracy will take place at Waterloo, on Monday, September 12th, inst., whereat Hon. Lyman Trumbull, Hon. John Baker, and others, will address the people upon the different political topics of the day. Members of all parties are cordially invited to be present, and hear and determine for themselves.

September 9, 1858.

THE FREE DEMOCRACY.

Did you ever before hear of this new party called the "Free Democracy?"

What object have these Black Republicans in changing their name in every county? They have one name in the north, another in the center, and another in the South. When I used to practice law before my distinguished judicial friend, whom I recognize in the crowd before me, if a man was charged with horse-stealing and the proof showed that he went by one name in Stephenson county, another in Sangamon, a third in Monroe, and a fourth in Randolph, we thought that the fact of his changing his name so often to avoid detection, was pretty strong evidence of his guilt. I would like to know why it is that this great Freesoil Abolition party is not willing to avow the same name in all parts of the State? If this party believes that its course is just, why does it not avow the same principles in the North, and in the South, in the East and in the West, wherever the American flag waves over American soil?

A voice—"The party does not call itself Black Republican in the North."

Mr. Douglas—Sir if you, will get a copy of the paper published at Waukegan, fifty miles from Chicago, which advocates the election of Mr. Lincoln, and has his name flying at its mast-head, you will find that it declares that "this paper is devoted to the cause" of *Black Republicanism.* I had a copy of it and intended to bring it down here into Egypt to let you see what name the party rallied under up in the northern part of the State, and to convince you that their principles are as different in the two sections of the State as is their name. I am sorry that I have mislaid it and have not got it here. Their principles in the north are jet-black, in the center they are in color a decent mulatto, and in lower Egypt they are almost white. Why, I admired many of the white sentiments contained in Lincoln's speech at Jonesboro, and could not help but contrast them with the speeches of the same distinguished orator made in the northern part of the State. Down here he denies that the Black Republican party is opposed to the admission of any more slave States, under any circumstances, and says that they are willing to allow the people of each State, when it wants to come into the Union, to do just as it pleases on the question of slavery. In the North, you find Lovejoy, their candidate for Congress in the Bloomington District, Farmsworth, their candidate in the Chicago District, and Washburne, their candidate in the Galena District, all declaring that never will they consent, under any circumstances, to admit another slave State, even if the people want it. Thus, while they avow one set of principles up there, they avow another and entirely different set down here. And here let me recall to Mr. Lincoln the scriptural quotation which he has applied to the Federal Government, that a house divided against itself cannot stand, and ask him how does he expect this Abolition party to stand when in one-half of the State it advocates a set of principles which it has repudiated in the other half?

I am told that I have but eight minutes more. I would like to talk to you an hour and a half longer, but I will make the best use I can of the remaining eight minutes. Mr. Lincoln said in his first remarks that he was not in favor of the social and political equality of the negro with the white man. Every where up north he has declared that he was not in favor of the social and political equality of the negro, but he would not say whether or not he was opposed to negroes voting and negro citizenship. I want to know whether he is for or against negro citizenship? He declared his utter opposition to the Dred Scott decision, and advanced as a reason that the court had decided that it was not possible for a negro to be a citizen under the Constitution of the United States. If he is opposed to the Dred Scott decision for that reason, he must be in favor of confering the right and privilege of citizenship upon the negro! I have been trying to get an answer from him on that point, but have never yet obtained one, and I will show you why. In every speech he made in the north he quoted the Declaration of Independence to prove that all men were created equal, and insisted that the phrase "all men," included the negro as well as the white man, and that the equality rested upon Divine law. Here is what he said on that point:

"I should like to know if, taking this old Declaration of Independence, which declares that all men are equal upon principle, and making exceptions to it, where will it stop? If one man says it does not mean a negro, why may not another say it does not mean some other man? If that declaration is not the truth, let us get the statute book in which we find it and bear it out."

Lincoln maintains there that the Declaration of Independence asserts that the negro is equal to the white man, and that under Divine law, and if he believes so it was rational for him to advocate negro citizenship, which, when allowed, puts the negro on an equality under the law. I say to you in all frankness, gentlemen, that in my opinion a negro is not a citizen, cannot be, and ought not to be, under the Constitution of the United States. I will not even qualify my opinion to meet the declaration of one of the Judges of the Supreme Court in the Dred Scott case, "that a negro descended from African parents, who was imported into this country as a slave is not a citizen, and cannot be." I say that this Government was established on the white basis. It was made by white men, for the benefit of white men and their posterity forever, and never should be administered by any except white men. I declare that a negro ought not to be a citizen, whether his parents were imported into this country as slaves or not, or whether or not he was born here. It does not depend upon the place a negro's parents were born, or whether they were slaves or not, but upon the fact that he is a negro, belonging to a race incapable of self-government, and for that reason ought not to be on an equality with white men.

My friends, I am sorry that I have not time to pursue this argument further, as I might have done but for the fact that Mr. Lincoln compelled me to occupy a portion of my time in repelling those gross slanders and falsehoods that Trumbull has invented against me and put in circulation. In conclusion, let me ask you why should this Government be divided by a geographical line—arraying all men North in one great hostile party against all men South? Mr. Lincoln tells you, in his speech at Springfield, "that a house divided against itself cannot stand; that this Government, divided into free and slave States, cannot endure permanently; that they must either be all free or all slave; all one thing or all the other." Why cannot this Government endure divided into free and slave States, as our fathers made it? When this Government was established by Washington, Jefferson, Madison, Jay, Hamilton, Franklin, and the other sages and patriots of that day, it was composed of free States and slave States, bound together by one common Constitution. We have existed and prospered from that day to this thus divided, and have increased with a rapidity never before equaled in wealth, the extension of territory, and all the elements of power and greatness, until we have become the first nation on the face of the globe. Why can we not thus continue to prosper? We can if we will live up to and execute the Government upon those principles upon which our fathers established it. During the whole period of our existence Divine Providence has smiled upon us, and showered upon our nation richer and more abundant blessings than have ever been conferred upon any other.

MR. LINCOLN'S REJOINDER.

FELLOW-CITIZENS: It follows as a matter of course that a half-hour answer to a speech of an hour and a half can be but a very hurried one. I shall only be able to touch upon a few of the points suggested by Judge Douglas, and give them a brief attention, while I shall have to totally omit others for the want of time.

Judge Douglas has said to you that he has not been able to get from me an answer to the question whether I am in favor of negro citizenship. So far as I know, the Judge never asked me the question before. He shall have no occasion to ever ask it again, for I tell him very frankly that I am not in favor of negro citizenship. This furnishes me an occasion for saying a few words upon the subject. I mentioned in a certain speech of mine which has been printed, that the Supreme Court had decided that a negro could not possibly be made a citizen, and without saying what was my ground of complaint in regard to that, or whether I had any ground of complaint, Judge Douglas has from that thing manufactured nearly every thing that he ever says about my disposition to produce an equality between the negroes and the white people. If any one will read my speech, he will find I mentioned that as one of the points decided in the course of the Supreme Court opinions, but I did not state what objection I had to it. But Judge Douglas tells the people what my objection was when I did not tell them myself. Now my opinion is that the different States have the power to make a negro a citizen under the Constitution of the United States if they choose. The Dred Scott decision decides that they have not that power. If the State of Illinois had that power I should be opposed to the exercise of it. That is all I have to say about it.

Judge Douglas has told me that he heard my speeches north and my speeches south—that he had heard me at Ottawa and at Freeport in the north, and recently at Jonesboro in the south, and there was a very different cast of sentiment in the speeches made at the different points. I will not charge upon Judge Douglas that he willfully misrepresents me, but I call upon every fair-minded man to take these speeches and read them, *and I dare him to point out any difference between my speeches north and south.* While I am here perhaps I ought to say a word, if I have the time, in regard to the latter portion of the Judge's speech, which was a sort of declamation in reference to my having said I entertained the belief that this Government would not endure, half slave and half free. I have said so, and I did not say it without what seemed to me to be good reasons. It perhaps would require more time than I have now to set forth these reasons in detail; but let me ask you a few questions. Have we ever had any peace on this slavery question? When are we to have peace upon it if it is kept in the position it now occupies? How are we ever to have peace upon it? That is an important question. To be sure, if we will all stop and allow Judge Douglas and his friends to march on in their present career until they plant the institution all over the nation, here and wherever else our flag waves, and we acquiesce in it, there will be peace. But let me ask Judge Douglas how he is going to get the people to do that? They have been wrangling over this question for at least forty years. This was the cause of the agitation resulting in the Missouri Compromise—this produced the troubles at the annexation of Texas, in the acquisition of the territory acquired in the Mexican war. Again, this was the trouble which was quieted by the Compromise of 1850, when it was settled "*forever,*" as both the great political parties declared in their National Conventions. That "forever" turned out to be just four years, *when Judge Douglas himself reopened it.* When is it likely to come to an end? He introduced the Nebraska bill in 1854 to put *another end* to the slavery agitation. He promised that it would finish it all up immediately, and he has never made a speech since until he got into a quarrel with the President about the Lecompton Constitution, in which he has not declared that we are *just at the end* of the slavery agitation. But in one speech, I think last winter, he did say that he didn't quite see when the end of the slavery agitation would come. Now he tells us again that it is all over, and the people of Kansas have voted down the Lecompton Constitution. How is it over? That was only one of the attempts at putting an end to the slavery agitation—one of these "final settlements." Is Kansas in the Union? Has she formed a Constitution that she is likely to come in under? Is not the slavery agitation still an open question in that Territory? Has the voting down of that Constitution put an end to all the trouble? Is that more likely to settle it than every one of these previous attempts to settle the slavery agitation? Now, at this day in the history of the world we can no more foretell where the end of this slavery agitation will be than we can see the end of the world itself. The Nebraska-Kansas bill was introduced four years and a half ago, and if the agitation is ever to come to an end, we may say we are four years and a half nearer the end. So, too, we can say we are four years and a half nearer the end of the world; and we can just as clearly see the end of the world as we can see the end of this agitation. The Kansas settlement did not conclude it. If Kansas should sink to-day, and leave a great vacant space in the earth's surface, this vexed question would still be among us. I say, then, there is no way of putting an end to the slavery agitation amongst us but to put it back upon the basis where our fathers placed it, no way but to keep it out of our new Territories—to restrict it forever to the old States where it now exists. Then the public mind *will* rest in the belief that it is in the course of ultimate extinction. That is one way of putting an end to the slavery agitation.

The other way is for us to surrender and let Judge Douglas and his friends have their way and plant slavery over all the States—cease speaking of it as in any way a wrong—regard slavery as one of the common matters of property, and speak of negroes as we do of our horses and cattle. But while it drives on in its state of progress as it is now driving, and as it has driven for the last five years, I have ventured the opinion, and I say to-day, that we will have no end to the slavery agitation until it takes one turn or the other. I do not mean that when it takes a turn toward ultimate extinction it will be in a day, nor in a year, nor in two years. I do not suppose that in the most peaceful way ultimate extinction would occur in less than a hundred years at least; but that it will occur in the best way for both races, in God's own good time, I have no doubt. But, my friends, I have used up more of my time than I intended on this point.

Now, in regard to this matter about Trumbull and myself having made a bargain to sell out the entire Whig and Democratic parties in 1854—Judge Douglas brings forward no evidence to sustain his charge, except the speech Matheny is said to have made in 1856, in which he told a cock-and-bull story of that sort, upon the same moral principles that Judge Douglas tells it here to-day. This is the simple truth. I do not care greatly for the story, but this is the truth of it, and I have twice told Judge Douglas to his face, that from beginning to end there is not one word of truth in it. I have called upon him for the proof, and he does not at all meet me as Trumbull met him upon that of which we were just talking, by producing the record. He didn't bring the record, because there was no record for him to bring. When he asks if I am ready to indorse Trumbull's veracity after he has broken a bargain with me, I reply that if Trumbull *had* broken a bargain with me, I would not be likely to indorse his veracity; but I am ready to indorse his veracity because *neither in that thing, nor in any other, in all the years that I have known Lyman Trumbull, have I known him to fail of his word or tell a falsehood, large or small.* It is for that reason that I indorse Lyman Trumbull.

Mr. James Brown (*Douglas Post Master*)—"What does Ford's history any about him?"

Mr. Lincoln—Some gentleman asks me what Ford's History says about him. My own recollection is, that Ford speaks of Trumbull in very disrespectful terms in several portions of his book, *and that he talks a great deal worse of Judge Douglas.* I refer you, sir, to the history for examination.

Judge Douglas complains, at considerable length, about a disposition on the part of Trumbull and myself to attack him personally. I want to attend to that suggestion a moment. I don't want to be unjustly accused of dealing illiberally or unfairly with an adversary, either in court, or in a political canvass, or any where else. I would despise myself if I supposed myself ready to deal less liberally with an adversary than I was willing to be treated myself. Judge Douglas, in a general way, without putting it in a direct shape, revives the old charge against me in reference to the Mexican war. He does not take the responsibility of putting it in a very definite form, but makes a general reference to it. That charge is more than ten years old. He complains of Trumbull and myself, because he says we bring charges against him one or two years old. He knows, too, that in regard to the Mexican war story, the more respectable papers of his own party throughout the State have been compelled to take it back and acknowledge that it was a lie.

Here Mr. Lincoln turned to the crowd on the platform, and selecting Hon. Orlando B. Ficklin, led him forward and said:

I do not mean to do any thing with Mr. Ficklin, except to present his face and tell you that *he personally knows it to be a lie!* He was a member of Congress at the only time I was in Congress, and he [Ficklin] knows that whenever there was an attempt to procure a vote of mine which would indorse the origin and justice of the war, I refused to give such indorsement, and voted against it; but I never voted against the supplies for the army, and he knows, as well as Judge Douglas, that whenever a dollar was asked by way of compensation or other-wise, for the benefit of the soldiers, *I gave all the votes that Ficklin or Douglas did, and perhaps more.*

Mr. Ficklin—My friends, I wish to say this in reference to the matter. Mr. Lincoln and myself are just as good personal friends as Judge Douglas and myself. In reference to this Mexican war, my recollection is that when Ashmun's resolution [amendment] was offered by Mr. Ashmun of Massachusetts, in which he declared that the Mexican war was unnecessarily and unconstitutionally commenced by the President—my recollection is that Mr. Lincoln voted for that resolution.

Mr. Lincoln—That is the truth. Now you all remember that was a resolution censuring the President for the manner in which the war was *begun.* You know they have charged that I voted against the supplies, by which I starved the soldiers who were out fighting the battles of their country. I say that Ficklin knows it is false. When that charge was brought forward by the Chicago *Times,* the Springfield *Register* [Douglas organ] reminded the *Times* that the charge really applied to John Henry; and I do know that John Henry is *now mak-ing speeches and fiercely battling for Judge Douglas.* If the Judge now says that he offers this as a sort of set-off to what I said to-day in reference to Trumbull's charge, then I remind him that he made this charge before I said a word about Trumbull's. He brought this forward at Ottawa, the first time we met face to face; and in the opening speech that Judge Douglas made, he attacked me in regard to a matter ten years old. Isn't he a pretty man to be whining about people making charges against him only *two* years old!

The Judge thinks it is altogether wrong that I should have dwelt upon this charge of Trumbull's at all. I gave the apology for doing so in my opening speech. Perhaps it didn't fix your attention. I said that when Judge Douglas was speaking at places where I spoke on the succeeding day, he used very harsh language about this charge. Two or three times afterward I said I had confidence in Judge Trumbull's veracity and intelligence; and my own opinion was, from what I knew of the character of Judge Trumbull, that he would vindicate his position, and prove whatever he had stated to be true. This I repeated two or three times; and then I dropped it, without saying any thing more on the subject for weeks—perhaps a month. I passed it by without noticing it at all till I found at Jacksonville, Judge Douglas, in the plenitude of his power, is not willing to answer Trumbull and let me alone; but he comes out there and uses this language: "He should not hereafter occupy his time in refuting such charges made by Trumbull, but that Lincoln, having indorsed the character of Trumbull for veracity, he should hold him [Lincoln] responsible for the slanders." What was Lincoln to do? Did he not do right, when he had the fit opportunity of meeting Judge Douglas here, to tell him he was ready for the responsibility? I ask a candid audience whether in doing thus Judge Douglas was not the assailant rather than I? Here I meet him face to face and say I am ready to take the responsibility so far as it rests on me.

Having done so, I ask the attention of this audience to the question whether I have succeeded in sustaining the charge, and whether Judge Douglas has at all succeeded in rebutting it? You all heard me call upon him to say *which of these pieces of evidence was a forgery?* Does he say that what I present here as a copy of the original Toombs bill is a forgery? Does he say that what I present as a copy of the bill reported by himself is a forgery? Or what is presented as a transcript from the *Globe,* of the quotations from Bigler's speech, is a forgery? Does he say the quotations from his own speech are forgeries? Does he say this transcript from Trumbull's speech is a forgery? ["He didn't deny one of them."] *I would then like to know how it comes about, that when each piece of a story is true, the whole story turns out false?* I take it these people have some sense; they see plainly that Judge Douglas is playing cuttle-fish, a small species of fish that has no mode of defending itself when pursued except by throwing out a black fluid, which makes the water so dark the enemy cannot see it, and thus it escapes. Ain't the Judge playing the cuttle-fish?

Now I would ask very special attention to the consideration of Judge Douglas's speech at Jacksonville; and when you shall read his speech of to-day, I ask you to watch closely and see which of these pieces of testimony, every one of which he says is a forgery, he has shown to be such. *Not one of them has he shown to be a forgery.* Then I ask the original question, if each of the pieces of testimony is true, *how is it possible that the whole is a falsehood?*

In regard to Trumbull's charge that he [Douglas] inserted a provision into the bill to prevent the Constitution being submitted to the people, what was his answer? He comes here and reads from the *Congressional Globe* to show that on his motion that provision was struck out of the bill. Why, Trumbull has not said it was not stricken out, but Trumbull says he [Douglas] put it in, and it is no answer to the charge to say he afterward took it out. Both are perhaps true. It was in regard to that thing precisely that I told him he had dropped the cub. Trumbull shows you that by his introducing the bill it was his cub. It is no answer to that assertion to call Trumbull a liar merely because he did not specially say that Douglas struck it out. Suppose that were the case, does it answer Trumbull? I assert that you [pointing to an individual] are here to-day, and you undertake to prove me a liar by showing that you were in Mattoon yesterday. I say that you took your hat off your head, and you prove me a liar by putting it on your head. That is the whole force of Douglas's argument.

Now, I want to come back to my original question. Trumbull says that Judge Douglas had a bill with a provision in it for submitting a Constitution to be made to a vote of the people of Kansas. Does Judge Douglas deny that fact? Does he deny that the provision which Trumbull reads was put in that bill? Then Trumbull says he struck it out. Does he dare to deny that? He does not, and I have the right to repeat the question—*why Judge Douglas took it out?* Bigler has said there was a combination of certain Senators, among whom he did not include Judge Douglas, by which it was agreed that the Kansas bill should have a clause in it not to have the Constitution formed under it submitted to a vote of the people. He did not say that Douglas was among them, but we prove by another source that about the same time Douglas comes into the Senate *with that provision stricken out of the bill.* Although Bigler cannot say they were all working in concert, yet it looks very much as if the thing was agreed upon and done with a mutual understanding after the conference; and while we do not know that it was absolutely so, yet it looks so probable that we have a right to call upon the man who knows the true reason why it was done, *to tell what the true reason was.* When he will not tell what the true reason was, he stands in the attitude of an accused thief who has stolen goods in his possession, and when called to account, refuses to tell where he got them. Not only is this the evidence, but when he comes in with the bill having the provision stricken out, he tells us in a speech, not then, but since, that these alterations and modifications in the bill *had been made by* HIM, *in consultation with Toombs, the originator of the bill.* He tells us the same to-day. He says there were certain modifications made in the bill in Committee that he did not vote for. I ask you to remember while certain amendments were made which he disapproved of, but which a majority of the Committee voted in, he has himself told us that in this particular *the alterations and modifications were made by him upon consultation with Toombs.* We have his own word that these alterations were made *by him* and not by the Committee. Now, I ask what is the reason Judge Douglas is so chary about coming to the exact question? What is the reason he will not tell you any thing about HOW it was made, BY WHOM it was made, or that he remembers it being made at all? Why does he stand playing upon the meaning of words, and quibbling around the edges of the evidence? If he can explain all this, but leaves it unexplained, I have a right to infer that Judge Douglas understood it was the purpose of his party, in engineering that bill through, to make a Constitution, and have Kansas come into the Union with that Constitution, *without its being submitted to a vote of the people.* If he will explain his action on this question, by giving a *better reason* for the facts that happened, than he has done, it will be satisfactory. But until he does that—until he gives a better or more plausible reason than he has offered against the evidence in the case—*I suggest to him it will not avail him at all that he swells himself up, takes on dignity, and calls people liars.* Why, sir, there is not a word in Trumbull's speech that depends on Trumbull's veracity at all. He has only arrayed the evidence and told you what follows as a matter of reasoning. There is not a statement in the whole speech that depends on Trumbull's word. If you have ever studied geometry, you remember that by a course of reasoning, Euclid proves that all the angles in a triangle are equal to two right angles. Euclid has shown you how to work it out. Now, if you undertake to disprove that proposition, and to show that it is erroneous, would you prove it to be false by calling Euclid a liar? They tell me that my time is out, and therefore I close.

EXTRACT FROM MR. TRUMBULL'S SPEECH MADE AT ALTON,
REFERRED TO BY MR. LINCOLN IN HIS OPENING AT CHARLESTON.

I come now to another extract from a speech of Mr. Douglas, made at Beardstown, and reported in the *Missouri Republican*. This extract has reference to a statement made by me at Chicago, wherein I charged that an agreement had been entered into by the very persons now claiming credit for opposing a

Constitution not submitted to the people, to have a Constitution formed and put in force without giving the people of Kansas an opportunity to pass upon it. Without meeting this charge, which I substantiated by a reference to the record, my colleague is reported to have said:

"For when this charge was once made in a much milder form, in the Senate of the United States, I did brand it as a lie in the presence of Mr. Trumbull, and Mr. Trumbull sat and heard it thus branded, without daring to say it was true. I tell you he knew it to be false when he uttered it at Chicago; and yet he says he is going to cram the lie down his throat until he should cry enough. The miserable craven-hearted wretch! he would rather have both ears cut off than to use that language in my presence, where I could call him to account. I see the object is to draw me into a personal controversy, with the hope thereby of concealing from the public the enormity of the principles to which they are committed. I shall not allow much of my time in this canvass to be occupied by these personal assaults—I have none to make on Mr. Lincoln; I have none to make on Mr. Trumbull; I have none to make on any other political opponent. If I cannot stand on my own public record, on my own private and public character as history will record it, I will not attempt to rise by traducing the character of other men. I will not make a blackguard of myself by imitating the course they have pursued against me. I have no charges to make against them."

This is a singular statement taken altogether. After indulging in language which would disgrace a loafer in the filthiest purlieus of a fish-market, he winds up by saying that he will not make a blackguard of himself, that he has no charges to make against me. So I suppose he considers, that to say of another that he knew a thing to be false when he uttered it, that he was a "miserable craven-hearted wretch," does not amount to a personal assault, and does not make a man a blackguard. A discriminating public will judge of that for themselves; but as he says he has "no charges to make on Mr. Trumbull," I suppose politeness requires I should believe him. At the risk of again offending this mighty man of war, and losing something more than my ears, I shall have the audacity to again read the record upon him and prove and pin upon him, so that he cannot escape it, the truth of every word I uttered at Chicago. You, fellow-citizens, are the judges to determine whether I do this. My colleague says he is willing to stand on his public record. By that he shall be tried, and if he had been able to discriminate between the exposure of a public act by the record, and a personal attack upon the individual, he would have discovered that there was nothing personal in my Chicago remarks, unless the condemnation of himself by his own public record is personal, and then you must judge who is most to blame for the torture his public record inflicts upon him, he for making, or I for reading it after it was made. As an individual I care very little about Judge Douglas one way or the other. It is his public acts with which I have to do, and if they condemn, disgrace and consign him to oblivion, he has only himself, not me to blame.

Now, the charge is that there was a plot entered into to have a Constitution formed for Kansas, and put in force, without giving the people an opportunity to pass upon it, and that Mr. Douglas was in the plot. This is as susceptible of proof by the record as is the fact that the State of Minnesota was admitted into the Union at the last session of Congress.

On the 25th of June, 1856, a bill was pending in the United States Senate to authorize the people of Kansas to form a Constitution and come into the Union. On that day Mr. Toombs offered an amendment which he intended to propose to the bill which was ordered to be printed, and, with the original bill and other amendments, recommended to the Committee on Territories, of which Mr. Douglas was Chairman. This amendment of Mr. Toombs, printed by order of the Senate, and a copy of which I have here present, provided for the appointment of commissioners who were to take a census of Kansas, divide the Territory into election districts, and superintend the election of delegates to form a Constitution, and contains a clanse in the 18th section which I will read to you, requiring the Constitution which should be formed to be submitted to the people for adoption. It reads as follows:

> "That the following propositions be and the same are hereby offered to the said Convention of the people of Kansas, when formed, for their free acceptance or rejection, which, if accepted by the Convention, and ratified by the people at the election for the adoption of the Constitution, shall be obligatory on the United States, and upon the said State of Kansas," etc.

It has been contended by some of the newspaper press, that this section did not require the Constitution which should be formed to be submitted to the people for approval, and that it was only the land propositions which were to be submitted. You will observe the language is that the propositions are to be

"ratified by the people at the election for the adoption of the Constitution."
Would it have been possible to ratify the land propositions "at the election for
the adoption of the Constitution," unless such an election was to be held?

When one thing is required by a contract or law to be done, the doing of
which is made dependent upon and cannot be performed without the doing of
some other thing, is not that other thing just as much required by the contract
or law as the first? It matters not in what part of the act, nor in what phraseology the intention of the Legislature is expressed, so you can clearly ascertain
what it is; and whenever that intention is ascertained from an examination of
the language used, such intention is part of and a requirement of the law. Can
any candid, fair-minded man, read the section I have quoted, and say that the
intention to have the Constitution which should be formed submitted to the
people for their adoption, is not clearly expressed? In my judgment there can
be no controversy among honest men upon a proposition so plain as this. Mr.
Douglas has never pretended to deny, so far as I am aware, that the Toombs
amendment, as originally introduced, did require a submission of the Constitution to the people. This amendment of Mr. Toombs was referred to the committee of which Mr. Douglas was Chairman, and reported back by him on the
30th of June, with the words, "And ratified by the people at the election for the
adoption of the Constitution" stricken out. I have here a copy of the bill as
reported back by Mr. Douglas to substantiate the statement I make. Various
other alterations were also made in the bill to which I shall presently have occasion to call attention. There was no other clause in the original Toombs bill
requiring a submission of the Constitution to the people than the one I have
read, and there was no clause whatever, after that was struck out, in the bill, as
reported back by Judge Douglas, requiring a submission. I will now introduce
a witness whose testimony cannot be impeached, he acknowledging himself to
have been one of the conspirators and privy to the fact about which he testifies.

Senator Bigler alluding to the Toombs bill, as it was called, and which, after
sundry amendments, passed the Senate, and to the propriety of submitting the
Constitution which should be formed to a vote of the people, made the following statement in his place in the Senate, December 9th, 1857. I read from
part 1, *Congressional Globe* of last session, paragraph 21:

> "I was present when that subject was discussed by Senators, before
> the bill was introduced, and the question was raised and discussed
> whether the Constitution, when formed, should be submitted to a vote
> of the people. It was held by the most intelligent on the subject, that in

view of all the difficulties surrounding that Territory, the danger of any experiment at that time of a popular vote, it would be better that there should be no such provision in the Toombs bill; and it is my understanding, in all the intercourse I had, that that Convention would make a Constitution and send it here without submitting it to the popular vote."

In speaking of this meeting again on the 21st December, 1857 (*Congressional Globe,* same vol., page 113), Senator Bigler said:

"Nothing was farther from my mind than to allude to any social or confidential interview. The meeting was not of that character. Indeed, it was semi-official, and called to promote the public good. My recollection was clear that I left the conference, under the impression that it had been deemed best to adopt measures to admit Kansas as a State through the agency of one popular election, and that for delegates to the Convention. This impression was the stronger, because I thought the spirit of the bill infringed upon the doctrine of non-intervention, to which I had great aversion; but with the hope of accomplishing great good, and as no movement had been made in that direction in the Territory, I waived this objection, and concluded to support the measure. I have a few items of testimony as to the correctness of these impressions, and with their submission I shall be content. I have before me the bill reported by the Senator from Illinois, on the 7th of March, 1856, providing for the admission of Kansas as a State, the third section of which reads as follows:

"'That the following propositions be, and the same are hereby offered to the said Convention of the people of Kansas, when formed, for their free acceptance or rejection; which, if accepted by the Convention and ratified by the people at the election for the adoption of the Constitution, shall be obligatory upon the United States, and upon the said State of Kansas.'

"The bill read in place by the Senator from Georgia, on the 25th of June, and referred to the Committee on Territories, contained the same section, word for word. Both these bills were under consideration at the conference referred to, but, sir, when the Senator from Illinois reported the Toombs bill to the Senate, with amendments, the next morning, it did not contain that portion of the third section which indicated to the Convention that the Constitution should be approved by the people.

The words 'and ratified by the people at the election for the adoption of the Constitution' had been stricken out."

I am not now seeking to prove that Douglas was in the plot to force a Constitution upon Kansas without allowing the people to vote directly upon it. I shall attend to that branch of the subject by and by. My object now is to prove the existence of the plot, what the design was, and I ask if I have not already done so. Here are the facts:

The introduction of a bill on the 7th of March, 1856, providing for the calling of a Convention in Kansas, to form a State Constitution, and providing that the Constitution should be submitted to the people for adoption; an amendment to this bill, proposed by Mr. Toombs, containing the same requirement; a reference of these various bills to the Committee on Territories; a consultation of Senators to determine whether it was advisable to have the Constitution submitted for ratification; the determination that it was not advisable; and a report of the bill back to the Senate next morning, with the clause providing for the submission stricken out. Could evidence be more complete to establish the first part of the charge I have made of a plot having been entered into by somebody, to have a Constitution adopted without submitting it to the people?

Now, for the other part of the charge, that Judge Douglas was in this plot, whether knowingly or ignorantly, is not material to my purpose. The charge is that he was an instrument co-operating in the project to have a Constitution formed and put into operation, without affording the people an opportunity to pass upon it. The first evidence to sustain the charge is the fact that he reported back the Toombs amendment with the clause providing for the submission stricken out. This, in connection with his speech in the Senate on the 9th of December, 1857 (*Congressional Globe,* part 1, page 14), wherein he stated:

> "That during the last Congress, I [Mr. Douglas] reported a bill from the Committee on Territories, to authorize the people of Kansas to assemble and form a Constitution for themselves. Subsequently the Senator from Georgia (Mr. Toombs) brought forward a substitute for my bill, which, after having been modified by him and myself in consultation, was passed by the Senate."

This of itself ought to be sufficient to show that my colleague was an instrument in the plot to have a Constitution put in force without submitting it to the people, and to forever close his mouth from attempting to deny. No man can reconcile his acts and former declarations with his present denial, and the only charitable conclusion would be that he was being used by others without knowing it. Whether he is entitled to the benefit of even this excuse, you must judge on a candid hearing of the facts I shall present. When the charge was first made in the United States Senate, by Mr. Bigler, that my colleague had voted for an Enabling Act which put a Government in operation without submitting the Constitution to the people, my colleague (*Congressional Globe,* last session, part 1, page 24) stated:

"I will ask the Senator to show me an intimation from any one member of the Senate; in the whole debate on the Toombs bill, and in the Union from any quarter, that the Constitution was not to be submitted to the people. I will venture to say that on all sides of the chamber it was so understood at the time. If the opponents of the bill had understood it was not, they would have made the point on it; and if they had made it we should certainly have yielded to it, and put in the clause. That is a discovery made since the President found out that it was not safe to take it for granted that that would be done which ought in fairness to have been done."

I knew at the time this statement was made, that I had urged the very objection to the Toombs bill two years before, that it did not provide for the submission of the Constitution. You will find my remarks, made on the 2d of July, 1856, in the appendix to the *Congressional Globe* of that year, page 179, urging this very objection. Do you ask why I did not expose him at the time? I will tell you—Mr. Douglas was then doing good service against the Lecompton iniquity. The Republicans were then engaged in a hand-to-hand fight with the National Democracy, to prevent the bringing of Kansas into the Union as a slave State against the wishes of its inhabitants, and of course I was unwilling to turn our guns from the common enemy to strike down an ally. Judge Douglas, however, on the same day, and in the same debate, probably recollecting, or being reminded of the fact, that I had objected to the Toombs bill when pending, that it did not provide for the submission of the Constitution to the people, made another statement which is to be found in the same volume of the *Congressional Globe,* page 22, in which he says:

"That the bill was silent on the subject is true, and my attention was called to that about the time it was passed; and I took the fair construction to be, that powers not delegated were reserved, and that of course the Constitution would be submitted to the people. Whether this statement is consistent with the statement just before made, that had the point been made it would have been yielded to, or that it was a new discovery, you will determine; for if the public records do not convict and condemn him, he may go uncondemned, so far as I am concerned. I make no use hero of the testimony of Senator Bigler to show that Judge Douglas must have been privy to the consultation held at his house, when it was determined not to submit the Constitution to the people, because Judge Douglas denies it, and I wish to use his own acts and declarations, which are abundantly sufficient for my purpose.

I come to a piece of testimony which disposes of all these various pretenses which have been set up for striking out of the original Toombs proposition, the clause requiring a submission of the Constitution to the people, and shows that it was not done either by accident, by inadvertence, or because it was believed that the bill, being silent on the subject, the Constitution would necessarily be submitted to the people for approval. What will you think, after listening to the facts already presented, to show that there was a design with those who concoeted the Toombs bill as amended, not to submit the Constitution to the people, if I now bring before you the amended bill as Judge Douglas reported it back, and show the clause of the original bill requiring submission, was not only struck out, but that other clauses were inserted in the bill putting it absolutely out of the power of the Convention to submit the Constitution to the people for approval, had they desired to do so? If I can produce such evidence as that, will you not all agree that it clinches and establishes forever all I charged at Chicago, and more too?

I propose now to furnish that evidence. It will be remembered that Mr. Toombs's bill provided for holding an election for delegates to form a Constitution under the supervision of commissioners to be appointed by the President, and in the bill as reported back by Judge Douglas, these words, *not to be found in the original bill,* are inserted at the close of the 11th section, viz:

> "And until the complete execution of this act no other election shall be held in said Territory."

This clause put it out of the power of the Convention to refer to the people for adoption; it absolutely prohibited the holding of any other election than that for the election of delegates, till that act was completely executed, which would not have been until Kansas was admitted as a State, or at all events till her Constitution was fully prepared and ready for submission to Congress for admission. Other amendments reported by Judge Douglas to the original Toombs bill, clearly show that the intention was to enable Kansas to become a State without any further action than simply a resolution of admission. The amendment reported by Mr. Douglas, that "until the next Congressional apportionment, the said State shall have one representative," clearly shows this, no such provision being contained in the original Toombs bill. For what other earthly purpose could the clause to prevent any other election in Kansas, except that of delegates, till it was admitted as a State, have been inserted except to prevent a submission of the Constitution, when formed, to the people?

The Toombs bill did not pass in the exact shape in which Judge Douglas reported it. Several amendments were made to it in the Senate. I am now dealing with the action of Judge Douglas as connected with that bill, and speak of the bill as he recommended it. The facts I have stated in regard to this matter appear upon the records, which I have here present to show to any man who wishes to look at them. They establish beyond the power of controversey, all the charges I have made, and show that Judge Douglas was made use of as an instrument by others, or else knowingly was a party to the scheme to have a Government put in force over the people of Kansas, without giving them an opportunity to pass upon it. That others high in position in the so-called Democratic party were parties to such a scheme is confessed by Gov. Bigler; and the only reason why the scheme was not carried, and Kansas long ago forced into the Union as a slave State, is the fact, that the Republicans were sufficiently strong in the House of Representatives to defeat the measure.

EXTRACT FROM MR. DOUGLAS'S SPEECH MADE AT JACKSONVILLE,
AND REFERRED TO BY MR. LINCOLN IN HIS OPENING AT CHARLESTON.

I have been reminded by a friend behind me that there is another topic upon which there has been a desire expressed that I should speak. I am told that Mr. Lyman Trumbull, who has the good fortune to hold a seat in the United States Senate, in violation of the bargain between him and Lincoln, was here the other day and occupied his time in making certain charges against me, involving, if they be true, moral turpitude. I am also informed that the charges he made here were substantially the same as those made by him in the city of Chicago, which were printed in the newspapers of that city. I now propose to answer those charges and to annihilate every pretext that an honest man has ever had for repeating them.

In order that I may meet these charges fairly, I will read them, as made by Mr. Trumbull, in his Chicago speech, in his own language. He says:

> "Now, fellow-citizens. I make the distinct charge that there was a preconcerted arrangement and plot entered into by the very men who now claim credit for opposing a Constitution not submitted to the people, to have a Constitution formed and put in force without giving the people an opportunity to pass upon it. This, my friends, is a serious charge, but I charge it to-night, that the very men who traverse the country under banners, proclaiming popular sovereignty, by design, concocted a bill on purpose to force a Constitution upon that people."

Again, speaking to some one in the crowd, he says:

> "And you want to satisfy yourself that he was in the plot to force a Constitution upon that people? I will satisfy you. I will cram the truth down any honest man's throat, until he cannot deny it, and to the man who does deny it, I will cram the lie down his throat till he shall cry enough! It is preposterous—it is the most damnable effrontery that man ever put on to conceal a scheme to defraud and cheat the people out of their rights, and then claim credit for it."

That is polite and decent language for a Senator of the United States. Remember that that language was used without any provocation whatever from me. I had not alluded to him in any manner in any speech that I had made, hence without provocation. As soon as he sets his foot within the State, he makes the direct charge that I was a party to a plot to force a Constitution upon the people of Kansas against their will, and knowing that it would be denied, he talks about cramming the lie down the throat of any man who shall deny it, until he cries enough.

Why did he take it for granted that it would be denied, unless he knew it to be false? Why did he deem it necessary to make a threat in advance that he would "cram the lie" down the throat of any man that should deny it? I have no doubt that the entire Abolition party consider it very polite for Mr. Trumbull to go round uttering calumnies of that kind, bullying and talking of cramming lies down men's throats; but if I deny any of his lies by calling him a liar, they are shocked at the indecency of the language; hence, to-day, instead of calling him a liar I intend to prove that he is one.

I wish in the first place to refer to the evidence adduced by Trumbull, at Chicago, to sustain his charge. He there declared that Mr. Toombs, of Georgia, introduced a bill into Congress authorizing the people of Kansas to form a Constitution and come into the Union, that when introduced it contained a clause requiring the Constitution to be submitted to the people, and that I struck out the words of that clause.

Suppose it were true that there was such a clause in the bill, and that I struck it out, is that proof of a plot to force a Constitution upon a people against their will? Bear in mind, that from the days of George Washington to the Administration of Franklin Pierce, there had never been passed by Congress a bill requiring the submission of a Constitution to the people. If Trumbull's charge, that I struck out that clause, were true, it would only prove that I had reported the bill in the exact shape of every bill of like character that passed under Washington, Jefferson, Madison, Monroe, Jackson, or any other President, to the time of the then present Administration. I ask you, would that be evidence of a design to force a Constitution on a people against their will? If it were so, it would be evidence against Washington, Jefferson, Madison, Jackson, Van Buren, and every other President.

But upon examination, it turns out that the Toombs bill never did contain a clause requiring the Constitution to be submitted. Hence no such clause was ever stricken out by me or any body else. It is true, however, that the Toombs bill and its authors all took it for granted that the Constitution would be submitted. There had never been, in the history of this Government, any attempt made to force a Constitution upon an unwilling people, and nobody dreamed that any such attempt would be made, or deemed it necessary to provide for such a contingency. If such a clause was necessary in Mr. Trumbull's opinion, why did he not offer an amendment to that effect?

In order to give more pertinency to that question, I will read an extract from Trumbull's speech in the Senate, on the Toombs bill, made on the 2d of July, 1856. He said:

"We are asked to amend this bill, and make it perfect, and a liberal spirit seems to be manifested on the part of some Senators to have a fair bill. It is difficult, I admit, to frame a bill that will give satisfaction to all, but to approach it, or come near it, I think two things must be done."

The first, then, he goes on to say, was the application of the Wilmot Proviso to the Territories, and the second the repeal of all the laws passed by the

Territorial Legislature. He did not then say that it was necessary to put in a clause requiring the submission of the Constitution. Why, if he thought such a provision necessary, did he not introduce it? He says in his speech that he was invited to offer amendments. Why did he not do so? He cannot pretend that he had no chance to do this, for he did offer some amendments, but none requiring submission.

I now proceed to show that Mr. Trumbull knew at the time that the bill was silent as to the subject of submission, and also that he, and every body else, took it for granted that the Constitution would be submitted. Now for the evidence. In his second speech he says: "The bill in many of its features meets my approbation." So he did not think it so very bad.

Further on he, says:

"In regard to the measure introduced by the Senator from Georgia [Mr. Toombs], and recommended by the Committee, I regard it, in many respects, as a most excellent bill; but we must look at it in the light of surrounding circumstances. In the condition of things now existing in the country, I do not consider it as a safe measure, nor one which will give peace, and I will give my reasons. First, it affords no immediate relief. It provides for taking a census of the voters in the Territory, for an election in November, and the assembling of a Convention in December, to form, if it thinks proper, a Constitution for Kansas, preparatory to its admission into the Union as a State. It is not until December that the Convention is to meet. It would take some time to form a Constitution. *I suppose that Constitution would have to be ratified by the people before it becomes valid.*"

He there expressly declared that he supposed, under the bill, the Constitution would have to be submitted to the people before it became valid. He went on to say:

"No provision is made in this bill for such a ratification. This is objectionable to my mind. I do not think the people should be bound by a Constitution, without passing upon it directly, themselves."

Why did he not offer an amendment providing for such a submission, if he thought it necessary? Notwithstanding the absence of such a clause, he took it for granted that the Constitution would have to be ratified by the people, under the bill.

In another part of the same speech, he says:

"There is nothing said in this bill, so far as I have discovered, about submitting the Constitution which is to be framed, to the people, for their sanction or rejection. Perhaps the Convention would have the right to submit it, if it should think proper; but it is certainly not compelled to do so, according to the provisions of the bill. If it is to be submitted to the people, it will take time, and it will not be until some time next year that this new Constitution, affirmed and ratified by the people, would be submitted here to Congress for its acceptance, and what is to be the condition of that people in the meantime?"

You see that his argument then was that the Toombs bill would not get Kansas into the Union quick enough and was objectionable on that account. He had no fears about this submission, or why did he not introduce an amendment to meet the case?

A voice—"Why didn't you? You were Chairman of the Committee."

Mr. Douglas—I will answer that question for you.

In the first place, such provision had ever before been put in any similar act passed by Congress. I did not suppose that there was an honest man who would pretend that the omission of such a clause furnished evidence of a conspiracy or attempt to impose on the people. It could not be expected that such of us as did not think that omission was evidence of such a scheme, would offer such an amendment; but if Trumbull then believed what he now says, why did he not offer the amendment, and try to prevent it, when he was, as he says, invited to do so?

In this connection I will tell you what the main point of discussion was: There was a bill pending to admit Kansas whenever she should have a population of 93,420, that being the ratio required for a member of Congress. Under that bill Kansas could not have become a State for some years, because she could not have had the requisite population. Mr. Toombs took it into his head to bring in a bill to admit Kansas then, with only twenty-five or thirty thousand people, and the question was whether we would allow Kansas to come in under this bill, or keep her out under mine until she had 93,420 people. The Committee considered that question, and overruled me by deciding in favor of the immediate admission of Kansas, and I reported accordingly. I hold in my hand a copy of the Report which I made at that time. I will read from it.

> "The point upon which your Committee have entertained the most serious and grave doubts in regard to the propriety of indorsing the proposition, relates to the fact that, in the absence of any census of the inhabitants, there is reason to apprehend that the Territory does not contain sufficient population to entitle them to demand admission under the treaty with France, if we take the ratio of representation for a member of Congress as the rule."

Thus you see that in the written report accompanying the bill, I said that the great difficulty with the Committee was the question of population. In the same report I happened to refer to the question of submission. Now, listen to what I said about that:

> "In the opinion of your Committee, whenever a Constitution shall be formed in any Territory, preparatory to its admission into the Union as a State, justice, the genius of our institutions, the whole theory of our republican system, imperatively demands that the voice of the people shall be fairly expressed, and their will embodied in that fundamental law without fraud or violence, or intimidation, or any other improper or unlawful influence, and subject to no other restrictions than those imposed by the Constitution of the United States."

I read this from the Report I made at the time, on the Toombs bill. I will read yet another passage from the same Report; after setting out the features of the Toombs bill, I contrast it with the proposition of Senator Seward, saying:

> "The revised proposition of the Senator from Georgia refers all matters in dispute to the decision of the present population, with guaranties of fairness and safeguards against frauds and violence, to which no reasonable man can find just grounds of exception, while the Senator from New York, if his proposition is designed to recognize and impart vitality to the Topeka Constitution, proposes to disfranchise not only all the emigrants who have arrived in the Territory this year, but all the law-abiding men who refused to join in the act of open rebellion against the constituted authorities of the

Territory last year by making the unauthorized and unlawful action of a political party the fundamental law of the whole people."

Then, again, I repeat that under that bill the question is to be referred to the present population to decide for or against coming into the Union under the Constitution they may adopt.

Mr. Trumbull, when at Chicago, rested his charge upon the allegation that the clause requiring submission was originally in the bill, and was stricken out by me. When that falsehood was exposed by a publication of the record, he went to Alton and made another speech, repeating the charge and referring to other and different evidence to sustain it. He saw that he was caught in his first falsehood, so he changed the issue, and instead of resting upon the allegation of striking out, he made it rest upon the declaration that I had introduced a clause into the bill prohibiting the people from voting upon the Constitution. I am told that he made the same charge here that he made at Alton, that I had actually introduced and incorporated into the bill, a clause which prohibited the people from voting upon their Constitution. I hold his Alton speech in my hand, and will read the amendment, which he alleges that I offered. It is in these words:

> "And until the complete executions of this act no other election shall be held in said Territory."

Trumbull says the object of that amendment was to prevent the Convention from submitting the Constitution to a vote of the people. I will read what he said at Alton on that subject:

> "This clause put it out of the power of the Convention, had it been so disposed, to submit the Constitution to the people for adoption; for it absolutely prohibited the holding of any other election, than that for the election of delegates, till that act was completely executed, which would not have been till Kansas was admitted as a State, or, at all events, till her Constitution was fully prepared and ready for submission to Congress for admission."

Now, do you suppose that Mr. Trumbull supposed that that clause prohibited the Convention from submitting the Constitution to the people, when, in his speech in the Senate, be declared that the Convention had a right to submit it? In his Alton speech, as will be seen by the extract which I have read, he

declared that the clause put it out of the power of the Convention to submit
the Constitution, and in his speech in the Senate he said:

> "There is *nothing said in this bill,* so far as I have discovered, about sub-
> mitting the Constitution which is to be formed, to the people, for their
> sanction or rejection. Perhaps the Convention could have the right to
> submit it, if it should think proper, but it is certainly not compelled to
> do so according to the provisions of the bill."

Thus you see that, in Congress, he declared the bill to be silent on the subject, and a few days since, at Alton, he made a speech, and said that there was a
provision in the bill prohibiting submission.

I have two answers to make to that. In the first place, the amendment which
he quotes as depriving the people of an opportunity to vote upon the Constitution, *was stricken out on my motion*—absolutely stricken out and not voted on
at all! In the second place, in lieu of it, a provision was voted in authorizing the
Convention to order an election whenever it pleased. I will read. After Trumbull had made his speech in the Senate, declaring that the Constitution would
probably be submitted to the people, although the bill was silent upon that subject, I made a few remarks, and offered two amendments, which you may find
in the Appendix to the *Congressional Globe,* volume thirty-three, first session of
the thirty-fourth Congress, page 795.

I quote:

> "Mr. Douglas—I have an amendment to offer from the Committee
> on Territories. On page 8, section 11, *strike out the words* 'until the com-
> plete execution of this act no other election shall be held in said Terri-
> tory,' and insert the amendment which I hold in my hand."

The amendment was as follows:

> "That all persons who shall possess the other qualifications prescribed
> for voters under this act, and who shall have been *bona fide* inhabitants of
> said Territory since its organization, and who shall have absented them-
> selves therefrom in consequence of the disturbances therein, and who
> shall return before the first day of October next, and become *bona fide*
> inhabitants of the Territory, with the intent of making it their permanent
> home, and shall present satisfactory evidence of these facts to the Board

of Commissioners, shall be entitled to vote at said election, and shall have their names placed on said corrected list of voters for that purpose."

That amendment was adopted unanimously. After its adoption, the record shows the following:

"Mr. Douglas—I have another amendment to offer from the Committee, to follow the amendment which has been adopted. The bill reads now, 'and until the complete execution of this act, no other election shall be held in said Territory.' It has been suggested that it should be modified in this way, 'and to avoid all conflict in the complete execution of this act, all other elections in said Territory are hereby postponed until such time as said Convention shall appoint,' so that they can appoint the day in the event that there should be a failure to come into the Union."

This amendment was also agreed to without dissent.

Thus you see that the amendment quoted by Trumbull, at Alton, as evidence against me, instead of being put into the bill by me, was stricken out on my motion, and never became a part thereof at all. You also see that the substituted clause expressly authorized the Convention to appoint such day of election as it should deem proper.

Mr. Trumbull when he made that speech knew these facts. He forged his evidence from beginning to end, and by falsifying the record he endeavors to bolster up his false charge. I ask you what you think of Trumbull thus going around the country, falsifying and garbling the public records. I ask you whether you will sustain a man who will descend to the infamy of such conduct.

Mr. Douglas proceeded to remark that he should not hereafter occupy his time in refuting such charges made by Trumbull, but that Lincoln having indorsed the character of Trumbull for veracity, he should hold him [Lincoln] responsible for the slanders.

FIFTH JOINT DEBATE, AT GALESBURG
OCTOBER 7, 1858

MR. DOUGLAS'S SPEECH.

LADIES AND GENTLEMEN: Four years ago I appeared before the people of Knox county for the purpose of defending my political action upon the Compromise measures of 1850 and the passage of the Kansas-Nebraska bill. Those of

you before me, who were present then, will remember that I vindicated myself
for supporting those two measures by the fact that they rested upon the great fundamental principle that the people of each State and each Territory of this Union
have the right, and ought to be permitted to exercise the right, of regulating their
own domestic concerns in their own way, subject to no other limitation or
restriction than that which the Constitution of the United States imposes upon
them. I then called upon the people of Illinois to decide whether that principle
of self-government was right or wrong. If it was and is right, then the Compromise measures of 1850 were right, and, consequently, the Kansas and Nebraska
bill, based upon the same principle, must necessarily have been right.

The Kansas and Nebraska bill declared, in so many words, that it was the true
intent and meaning of the act not to legislate slavery into any State or Territory,
nor to exclude it therefrom, but to leave the people thereof perfectly free to form
and regulate their domestic institutions in their own way, subject only to the
Constitution of the United States. For the last four years I have devoted all my
energies, in private and public, to commend that principle to the American people. Whatever else may be said in condemnation or support of my political
course, I apprehend that no honest man will doubt the fidelity with which, under
all circumstances, I have stood by it.

During the last year a question arose in the Congress of the United States
whether or not that principle would be violated by the admission of Kansas into
the Union under the Lecompton Constitution. In my opinion, the attempt to
force Kansas in under that Constitution, was a gross violation of the principle
enunciated in the Compromise measures of 1850, and Kansas and Nebraska bill
of 1854, and therefore I led off in the fight against the Lecompton Constitution,
and conducted it until the effort to carry that Constitution through Congress
was abandoned. And I can appeal to all men, friends and foes, Democrats and
Republicans, Northern men and Southern men, that during the whole of that
fight I carried the banner of Popular Sovereignty aloft, and never allowed it to
trail in the dust, or lowered my flag until victory perched upon our arms. When
the Lecompton Constitution was defeated, the question arose in the minds of
those who had advocated it what they should next resort to in order to carry
out their views. They devised a measure known as the English bill, and granted
a general amnesty and political pardon to all men who had fought against the
Lecompton Constitution, provided they would support that bill. I for one did
not choose to accept the pardon, or to avail myself of the amnesty granted on
that condition. The fact that the supporters of Lecompton were willing to for-
give all differences of opinion at that time in the event those who opposed it

favored the English bill, was an admission they did not think that opposition to Lecompton impaired a man's standing in the Democratic party. Now the question arises, what was that English bill which certain men are now attempting to make a test of political orthodoxy in this country. It provided, in substance, that the Lecompton Constitution should be sent back to the people of Kansas for their adoption or rejection, at an election which was held in August last, and in case they refused admission under it, that Kansas should be kept out of the Union until she had 93,420 inhabitants. I was in favor of sending the Constitution back in order to enable the people to say whether or not it was their act and deed, and embodied their will; but the other proposition, that if they refused to come into the Union under it, they should be kept out until they had double or treble the population they then had, I never would sanction by my vote. The reason why I could not sanction it is to be found in the fact that by the English bill, if the people of Kansas had only agreed to become a slave-holding State under the Lecompton Constitution, they could have done so with 35,000 people, but if they insisted on being a free State, as they had a right to do, then they were to be punished by being kept out of the Union until they had nearly three times that population. I then said in my place in the Senate, as I now say to you, that whenever Kansas has population enough for a slave State she has population enough for a free State. I have never yet given a vote, and I never intend to record one, making an odious and unjust distinction between the different States of this Union. I hold it to be a fundamental principle in our republican form of government that all the States of this Union, old and new, free and slave, stand on an exact equality. Equality among the different States is a cardinal principle on which all our institutions rest. Wherever, therefore, you make a discrimination, saying to a slave State that it shall be admitted with 35,000 inhabitants, and to a free State that it shall not be admitted until it has 93,000 or 100,000 inhabitants, you are throwing the whole weight of the Federal Government into the scale in favor of one class of States against the other. Nor would I on the other hand any sooner sanction the doctrine that a free State could be admitted into the Union with 35,000 people, while a slave State was kept out until it had 93,000. I have always declared in the Senate my willingness, and I am willing now to adopt the rule, that no Territory shall ever become a State, until it has the requisite population for a member of Congress, according to the then existing ratio. But while I have always been, and am now willing to adopt that general rule, I was not willing and would not consent to make an exception of Kansas, as a punishment for her obstinacy, in demanding the right to do as she pleased in the formation of her Constitution. It is proper that

I should remark here, that my opposition to the Lecompton Constitution did not rest upon the peculiar position taken by Kansas on the subject of slavery. I held then, and hold now, that if the people of Kansas want a slave State, it is their right to make one and be received into the Union under it; if, on the contrary, they want a free State, it is their right to have it, and no man should ever oppose their admission because they ask it under the one or the other. I hold to that great principle of self-government which asserts the right of every people to decide for themselves the nature and character of the domestic institutions and fundamental law under which they are to live.

The effort has been and is now being made in this State by certain postmasters and other Federal office-holders, to make a test of faith on the support of the English bill. These men are now making speeches all over the State against me and in favor of Lincoln, either directly or indirectly, because I would not sanction a discrimination between slave and free States by voting for the English bill. But while that bill is made a test in Illinois for the purpose of breaking up the Democratic organization in this State, how is it in the other States? Go to Indiana, and there you find English himself, the author of the English bill, who is a candidate for re-election to Congress, has been forced by public opinion to abandon his own darling project, and to give a promise that he will vote for the admission of Kansas at once, whenever she forms a Constitution in pursuance of law, and ratifies it by a majority vote of her people. Not only is this the case with English himself, but I am informed that every Democratic candidate for Congress in Indiana takes the same ground. Pass to Ohio, and there you find that Groesbeck, and Pendleton, and Cox, and all the other anti-Lecompton men who stood shoulder to shoulder with me against the Lecompton Constitution, but voted for the English bill, now repudiate it and take the same ground that I do on that question. So it is with the Joneses and others of Pennsylvania, and so it is with every other Lecompton Democrat in the free States. They now abandon even the English bill, and come back to the true platform which I proclaimed at the time in the Senate, and upon which the Democracy of Illinois now stand. And yet, notwithstanding the fact, that every Lecompton and anti-Lecompton Democrat in the free States has abandoned the English bill, you are told that it is to be made a test upon me, while the power and patronage of the Government are all exerted to elect men to Congress in the other States who occupy the same position with reference to it that I do. It seems that my political offense consists in the fact that I first did not vote for the English bill, and thus pledge myself to keep Kansas out of the Union until she has a population of 93,420, and then return home, violate that pledge, repudiate the bill, and take the opposite ground. If I had done this, perhaps the Administration would now be advocating my re-election, as it is that of the others who have pursued this course. I did not choose to give that pledge, for the reason that I did not intend to carry out that principle. I never will consent, for the sake of conciliating the frowns of power, to pledge myself to do that which I do not intend to perform. I now submit the question to you as my constituency, whether I was not right, first, in resisting the adoption of the Lecompton Constitution; and secondly, in resisting the English bill. I repeat, that I opposed the Lecompton Constitution because it was not the act and deed of the people of Kansas, and did not embody their will. I denied the right of any power on earth, under our system of Government, to force a Constitution on an unwilling people. There was a time when some men could pretend to believe that the Lecompton Constitution embodied the will of the people of Kansas, but that time has passed. The question was referred to the people of Kansas under the English bill last August, and then, at a fair election, they rejected the Lecompton Constitution by a vote of from eight to ten against it to one in its favor. Since it has been voted down by so overwhelming a majority, no man can pretend that it was the act and deed of that people. I submit the question to you whether or not, if it had not been for me, that Constitution would have been crammed down the throats of the people of Kansas against their consent. While at least ninety-nine out of every hundred people here present, agree that I was right in defeating that project, yet my enemies use the fact that I did defeat it by doing right, to break me down and put another man in the United States in my place. The very men who acknowledge that I was right in defeating Lecompton, now form an alliance with Federal office-holders, professed Lecompton men, to defeat me, because I did right. My political opponent, Mr. Lincoln, has no hope on earth, and has never dreamed that he had a chance of success, were it not for the aid that he is receiving from Federal office-holders, who are using their influence and the patronage of the Government against me in revenge for my having defeated the Lecompton Constitution. What do you Republicans think of a political organization that will try to make an unholy and unnatural combination with its professed foes to beat a man merely because he has done right? You know such is the fact with regard to your own party. You know that the ax of decapitation is suspended over every man in office in Illinois, and the terror of proscription is threatened every Democrat by the present Administration, unless he supports the Republican ticket in preference to my Democratic associates and myself. I could find an instance in the postmaster of the city of Galesburgh, and in every other postmaster in this vicinity, all of whom have been stricken down simply because they discharged the duties of their offices honestly, and supported the regular Democratic ticket in this State in the right. The Republican party is availing itself of every unworthy means in the present contest to carry the election, because its leaders know that if they let this chance slip they will never have another, and their hopes of making this a Republican State will be blasted forever.

Now, let me ask you whether the country has any interest in sustaining this organization, known as the Republican party. That party is unlike all other political organizations in this country. All other parties have been national in their character—have avowed their principles alike in the slave and free States, in Kentucky as well as Illinois, in Louisiana as well as in Massachusetts. Such was the case with the old Whig party, and such was and is the case with the Democratic party. Whigs and Democrats could proclaim their principles boldly and fearlessly in the North and in the South, in the East and in the West, wherever the Constitution ruled and the American flag waved over American soil.

But now you have a sectional organization, a party which appeals to the Northern section of the Union against the Southern, a party which appeals to Northern passion, Northern pride, Northern ambition, and Northern prejudices, against Southern people, the Southern States, and Southern institutions. The leaders of that party hope that they will be able to unite the Northern States in one great sectional party, and inasmuch as the North is the strongest section, that they will thus be enabled to out vote, conquer, govern, and control the South. Hence you find that they now make speeches advocating principles and measures which cannot be defended in any slaveholding State of this Union. Is there a Republican residing in Galesburgh who can travel into Kentucky and carry his principles with him across the Ohio? What Republican from Massachusetts can visit the Old Dominion without leaving his principles behind him when he crosses Mason and Dixon's line? Permit me to say to you in perfect good humor, but in all sincerity, that no political creed is sound which cannot be proclaimed fearlessly in every State of this Union where the Federal Constitution is not the supreme law of the land. Not only is this Republican party unable to proclaim its principles alike in the North and in the South, in the free States and in the slave States, but it cannot even proclaim them in the same forms and give them the same strength and meaning in all parts of the same State. My friend Lincoln finds it extremely difficult to manage a debate in the center part of the State, where there is a mixture of men from the North and the South. In the extreme Northern part of Illinois he can proclaim as bold and radical Abolitionism as ever Giddings, Lovejoy, or Garrison enunciated, but when he gets down a little further South he claims that he is an old line Whig, a disciple of Henry Clay, and declares that he still adheres to the old line Whig creed, and has nothing whatever to do with Abolitionism, or negro equality, or negro citizenship. I once before hinted this of Mr. Lincoln in a public speech, and at Charleston he defied me to show that there was any difference between his speeches in the North and in the South, and that they were not in strict harmony. I will now call your attention to two of them, and you can then say whether you would be apt to believe that the same man ever uttered both. In a speech in reply to me at Chicago in July last, Mr. Lincoln, in speaking of the equality of the negro with the white man, used the following language:

> "I should like to know, if taking this old Declaration of Independence, which declares that all men are equal upon principle, and making exceptions to it, where will it stop? If one man says it does not mean a negro, why may not another man say it does not mean another man? If the Declaration is not the truth, let us get the statute book in which we find it and tear it out. Who is so bold as to do it? If it is not true, let us tear it out."

You find that Mr. Lincoln there proposed that if the doctrine of the Declaration of Independence, declaring all men to be born equal, did not include the negro and put him on an equality with the white man, that we should take the statute book and tear it out. He there took the ground that the negro race is included in the Declaration of Independence as the equal of the white race, and that there could be no such thing as a distinction in the races, making one superior and the other inferior. I read now from the same speech:

> "My friends [he says], I have detained you about as long as I desire to do, and I have only to say let us discard all this quibbling about this man and the other man—this race and that race and the other race being inferior, and therefore they must be placed in an inferior position, discarding our standard that we have left us. Let us discard all these things, and unite as one people throughout this land, until we shall once more stand up declaring that all men are created equal."

["That's right," etc.]

Yes, I have no doubt that you think it is right, but the Lincoln men down in Coles, Tazewell and Sangamon counties *do not* think it is right. In the conclusion of the same speech, talking to the Chicago Abolitionists, he said: "I leave

you, hoping that the lamp of liberty will burn in your bosoms until there shall
no longer be a doubt that all men are created free and equal." ["Good, good."]
Well, you say good to that, and you are going to vote for Lincoln because he
holds that doctrine. I will not blame you for supporting him on that ground,
but I will show you in immediate contrast with that doctrine, what Mr. Lincoln said down in Egypt in order to get votes in that locality where they do not
hold to such a doctrine. In a joint discussion between Mr. Lincoln and myself,
at Charleston, I think, on the 18th of last month, Mr. Lincoln, referring to this
subject, used the following language:

> "I will say then, that I am not nor never have been in favor of bring-
> ing about in any way the social and political equality of the white and
> black races; that I am not nor never have been in favor of making voters
> of the free negroes, or jurors, or qualifying them to hold office, or hav-
> ing them to marry with white people. I will say in addition, that there is
> a physical difference between the white and black races, which, I sup-
> pose, will forever forbid the two races living together upon terms of
> social and political equality, and inasmuch as they cannot so live, that
> while they do remain together, there must be the position of superior
> and inferior, that I as much as any other man am in favor of the superior
> position being assigned to the white man."

["Good for Lincoln."]

Fellow-citizens, here you find men hurraing for Lincoln and saying that he
did right, when in one part of the State he stood up for negro equality, and in
another part for political effect, discarded the doctrine and declared that there
always must be a superior and inferior race. Abolitionists up north are expected
and required to vote for Lincoln because he goes for the equality of the races,
holding that by the Declaration of Independence the white man and the negro
were created equal, and endowed by the Divine law with that equality, and
down south he tells the old Whigs, the Kentuckians, Virginians, and Tennes-
seans, that there is a physical difference in the races, making one superior and
the other inferior, and that he is in favor of maintaining the superiority of the
white race over the negro. Now, how can you reconcile those two positions of
Mr. Lincoln? He is to be voted for in the south as a pro-slavery man, and he is
to be voted for in the north as an Abolitionist. Up here he thinks it is all nonsense to talk about a difference between the races, and says that we must "discard all quibbling about this race and that race and the other race being inferior,

and therefore they must be placed in an inferior position." Down south he makes this "quibble" about this race and that race and the other race being inferior as the creed of his party, and declares that the negro can never be elevated to the position of the white man. You find that his political meetings are called by different names in different counties in the State. Here they are called Republican meetings, but in old Tazewell, where Lincoln made a speech last Tuesday, he did not address a *Republican* meeting, but "a grand rally of the *Lincoln men*." There are very few Republicans there, because Tazewell county is filled with old Virginians and Kentuckians, all of whom are Whigs or Democrats, and if Mr. Lincoln had called an Abolition or Republican meeting there, he would not get many votes. Go down into Egypt and you find that he and his party are operating under an alias there, which his friend Trumbull has given them, in order that they may cheat the people. When I was down in Monroe county a few weeks ago addressing the people, I saw handbills posted announcing that Mr. Trumbull was going to speak in behalf of Lincoln, and what do you think the name of his party was there? Why the "*Free Democracy*." Mr. Trumbull and Mr. Jehu Baker were announced to address the Free Democracy of Monroe county, and the bill was signed "Many Free Democrats." The reason that Lincoln and his party adopted the name of "Free Democracy" down there was because Monroe county has always been an old-fashioned Democratic county, and hence it was necessary to make the people believe that they were Democrats, sympathized with them, and were fighting for Lincoln as Democrats. Come up to Springfield, where Lincoln now lives and always has lived, and you find that the Convention of his party which assembled to nominate candidates for Legislature, who are expected to vote for him if elected, dare not adopt the name of Republican, but assembled under the title of "all opposed to the Democracy." Thus you find that Mr. Lincoln's creed cannot travel through even one half of the counties of this State, but that it changes its hues and becomes lighter and lighter, as it travels from the extreme north, until it is nearly white, when it reaches the extreme south end of the State. I ask you, my friends, why cannot Republicans avow their principles alike every where? I would despise myself if I thought that I was procuring your votes by concealing my opinions, and by avowing one set of principles in one part of the State, and a different set in another part. If I do not truly and honorably represent your feelings and principles, then I ought not to be your Senator; and I will never conceal my opinions, or modify or change them a hair's brendth in order to get votes. I tell you that this Chicago doctrine of Lincoln's—declaring that the negro and the white man are made equal by the Declaration of Independence and by Divine Providence—is a monstrous heresy. The signers of the Declaration of Independence never dreamed of the negro when they were writing that document. They referred to white men, to men of European birth and European descent, when they declared the equality of all men. I see a gentleman there in the crowd shaking his head. Let me remind him that when Thomas Jefferson wrote that document, he was the owner, and so continued until his death, of a large number of slaves. Did he intend to say in that Declaration, that his negro slaves, which he held and treated as property, were created his equals by Divine law, and that he was violating the law of God every day of his life by holding them as slaves? It must be borne in mind that when that Declaration was put forth, every one of the thirteen Colonies were slave-holding Colonies, and every man who signed that instrument represented a slave-holding constituency. Recollect, also, that no one of them emancipated his slaves, much less put them on an equality with himself, after he signed the Declaration. On the contrary, they all continued to hold their negroes as slaves during the revolutionary war. Now, do you believe—are you willing to have it said—that every man who signed the Declaration of Independence declared the negro his equal, and then was hypocrite enough to continue to hold him as a slave, in violation of what he believed to be the Divine law? And yet when you say that the Declaration of Independence includes the negro, you charge the signers of it with hypocrisy.

I say to you, frankly, that in my opinion, this Government was made by our father on the white basis. It was made by white men for the benefit of white men and their posterity forever, and was intended to be administered by white men in all time to come. But while I hold that under our Constitution and political system the negro is not a citizen, cannot be a citizen, and ought not to be a citizen, it does not follow by any means that he should be a slave. On the contrary it does follow that the negro, as an inferior race, ought to possess every right, every privilege, every immunity which he can safely exercise consistent with the safety of the society in which he lives. Humanity requires, and Christianity commands, that you shall extend to every inferior being, and every dependent being, all the privileges, immunities and advantages which can be granted to them consistent with the safety of society. If you ask me the nature and extent of these privileges, I answer that that is a question which the people of each State must decide for themselves. Illinois has decided that question for herself. We have said that in this State the negro shall not be a slave, nor shall he be a citizen. Kentucky holds a different doctrine. New York holds one different from either, and Maine one different from all. Virginia, in her policy on this question, differs in many respects from the others, and so on, until there is hardly two States whose policy is exactly alike in regard to the relation of the white man and the negro. Nor can you reconcile them and make them alike. Each State must do as it pleases. Illinois had as much right to adopt the policy which we have on that subject as Kentucky had to adopt a different policy. The great principle of this Government is, that each State has the right to do as it pleases on all these questions, and no other State, or power on earth has the right to interfere with us, or complain of us merely because our system differs from theirs. In the Compromise Measures of 1850, Mr. Clay declared that this great principle ought to exist in the Territories as well as in the States, and I reasserted his doctrine in the Kansas and Nebraska bill in 1854.

But Mr. Lincoln cannot be made to understand, and those who are determined to vote for him, no matter whether he is a pro-slavery man in the south and a negro equality advocate in the north, cannot be made to understand how it is that in a Territory the people can do as they please on the slavery question under the Dred Scott decision. Let us see whether I cannot explain it to the satisfaction of all impartial men. Chief Justice Taney has said in his opinion in the Dred Scott case, that a negro slave being property, stands on an equal footing with other property, and that the owner may carry them into United States territory the same as he does other property. Suppose any two of you, neighbors, should conclude to go to Kansas, one carrying $100,000 worth of negro slaves and the other $100,000 worth of mixed merchandise, including quantities of liquors. You both agree that under that decision you may carry your property to Kansas, but when you get it there, the merchant who is possessed of the liquors is met by the Maine liquor law, which prohibits the sale or use of his property, and the owner of the slaves is met by equally unfriendly legislation, which makes his property worthless after he gets it there. What is the right to carry your property into the Territory worth to either, when unfriendly legislation in the Territory renders it worthless after you get it there? The slaveholder when he gets his slaves there finds that there is no local law to protect him in holding them, no slave code, no police regulation maintaining and supporting him in his right, and he discovers at once that the absence of such friendly legislation excludes his property from the Territory, just as irresistibly as if there was a positive Constitutional prohibition excluding it. Thus you find it is with any kind of property in a Territory, it depends for its protection on the local and municipal law. If the people of a Territory want slavery, they make friendly legislation to introduce it, but if they do not want it, they withhold all protection from it, and then it cannot exist there. Such was the view taken on the subject by different Southern men when the Nebraska bill passed. See the speech

of Mr. Orr, of South Carolina, the present Speaker of the House of Representatives of Congress, made at that time, and there you will find this whole
doctrine argued out at full length. Read the speeches of other Southern Con-
gressmen, Senators and Representatives, made in 1854, and you will find that
they took the same view of the subject as Mr. Orr—that slavery could never be
forced on a people who did not want it. I hold that in this country there is no
power on the face of the globe that can force any institution on an unwilling
people. The great fundamental principle of our Government is that the people
of each State and each Territory shall be left perfectly free to decide for themselves what shall be the nature and character of their institutions. When this
Government was made, it was based on that principle. At the time of its formation there were twelve slaveholding States and one free State in this Union.
Suppose this doctrine of Mr. Lincoln and the Republicans, of uniformity of laws
of all the States on the subject of slavery, had prevailed; suppose Mr. Lincoln
himself had been a member of the Convention which framed the Constitution,
and that he had risen in that august body, and addressing the father of his country, had said as he did at Springfield:

> "A house divided against itself cannot stand. I believe this Government
> cannot endure permanently half slave and half free. I do not expect the
> Union to be dissolved—I do not expect the house to fall, but I do expect
> it will cease to be divided. It will become all one thing or all the other."

What do you think would have been the result? Suppose he had made that
Convention believe that doctrine and they had acted upon it, what do you think
would have been the result? Do you believe that the one free State would have
outvoted the twelve slaveholding States, and thus abolish slavery? On the contrary, would not the twelve slaveholding States have outvoted the one free State,
and under his doctrine have fastened slavery by an irrevocable Constitutional
provision upon every inch of the American Republic? Thus you see that the
doctrine he now advocates, if proclaimed at the beginning of the Government,
would have established slavery every where throughout the American continent, and are you willing, now that we have the majority section, to exercise a
power which we never would have submitted to when we were in the minority? If the Southern States had attempted to control our institutions, and make
the States all slave when they had the power, I ask would you have submitted
to it? If you would not, are you willing now, that we have become the strongest
under that great principle of self-government that allows each State to do as it

pleases, to attempt to control the Southern institutions? Then, my friends, I say to you that there is but one path of peace in this Republic, and that is to administer this Government as our fathers made it, divided into free and slave States, allowing each State to decide for itself whether it wants slavery or not. If Illinois will settle the slavery question for herself, and mind her own business and let her neighbors alone, we will be at peace with Kentucky, and every other Southern State. If every other State in the Union will do the same there will be peace between the North and the South, and in the whole Union.

MR. LINCOLN'S REPLY.

MY FELLOW-CITIZENS: A very large portion of the speech which Judge Douglas has addressed to you has previously been delivered and put in print. I do not mean that for a hit upon the Judge at all. If I had not been interrupted. I was going to say that such an answer as I was able to make to a very large portion of it, had already been more than once made and published. There has been an opportunity afforded to the public to see our respective views upon the topics discussed in a large portion of the speech which he has just delivered. I make these remarks for the purpose of excusing myself for not passing over the entire ground that the Judge has traversed. I however desire to take up some of the points that he has attended to, and ask your attention to them, and I shall follow him backwards upon some notes which I have taken, reversing the order by beginning where he concluded.

The Judge has alluded to the Declaration of Independence, and insisted that negroes are not included in that Declaration; and that it is a slander upon the framers of that instrument, to suppose that negroes were meant therein; and he asks you: Is it possible to believe that Mr. Jefferson, who penned the immortal paper, could have supposed himself applying the language of that instrument to the negro race, and yet held a portion of that race in slavery? Would be not at once have freed them? I only have to remark upon this part of the Judge's speech (and that, too, very briefly, for I shall not detain myself, or you, upon that point for any great length of time), that I believe the entire records of the world; from the date of the Declaration of Independence up to within three years ago, may be searched in vain for one single affirmation, from one single man, that the negro was not included in the Declaration of Independence; I think I may defy Judge Douglas to show that he ever said so, that Washington ever said so, that any President ever said so, that any member of Congress ever said so, or that any living man upon the whole earth ever said so, until the necessities of the present policy of the Democratic party, in regard to slavery, had to invent that affirmation. And I will remind Judge Douglas and this audience, that while Mr. Jefferson was the owner of slaves, as undoubtedly he was, in speaking upon this very subject, he used the strong language that "he trembled for his country when he remembered that God was just;" and I will offer the highest premium in my power to Judge Douglas if he will show that he, in all his life, ever uttered a sentiment at all akin to that of Jefferson.

The next thing to which I will ask your attention is the Judge's comments upon the fact, as he assumes it to be, that we cannot call our public meetings as Republican meetings; and he instances Tazewell county as one of the places where the friends of Lincoln have called a public meeting and have not dared to name it a Republican meeting. He instances Monroe county as another where Judge Trumbull and Jehu Baker addressed the persons whom the Judge assumes to be the friends of Lincoln, calling them the "Free Democracy." I have the honor to inform Judge Douglas that he spoke in that very county of Tazewell last Saturday, and I was there on Tuesday last, and when he spoke there he spoke under a call not venturing to use the word "Democrat." [Turning to Judge Douglas.] What think you of this?

So again, there is another thing to which I would ask the Judge's attention upon this subject. In the contest of 1856 his party delighted to call themselves together as the "National Democracy," but now, if there should be a notice put up any where for a meeting of the "National Democracy," Judge Douglas and his friends would not come. They would not suppose themselves invited. They would understand that it was a call for those hateful postmasters whom he talks about.

Now a few words in regard to these extracts from speeches of mine, which Judge Douglas has read to you, and which he supposes are in very great contrast to each other. Those speeches have been before the public for a considerable time, and if they have any inconsistency in them, if there is any conflict in them, the public have been able to detect it. When the Judge says, in speaking on this subject, that I make speeches of one sort for the people of the northen end of the State, and of a different sort for the southern people, he assumes that I do not understand that my speeches will be put in print and read north and south. I knew all the while that the speech that I made at Chicago, and the one I made at Jonesboro and the one at Charleston, would all be put in print and all the reading and intelligent men in the community would see them and know all about my opinions. And I have not supposed, and do not now suppose, that there is any conflict whatever between them. But the Judge will have it that if we do not confess that there is a sort of inequality between the white and black races, which justifies us in making them slaves, we must, then, insist that there is a degree of equality that requires us to make them our wives. Now, I have all the while taken a broad distinction in regard to that matter; and that is all there is in these different speeches which he arrays here, and the entire reading of either of the speeches will show that that distinction was made. Perhaps by taking two parts of the same speech, he could have got up as much of a conflict as the one he has found. I have all the while maintained, that in so far as it should be insisted that there was an equality between the white and black races that should produce a perfect social and political equality, it was an impossibility. This you have seen in my printed speeches, and with it I have said, that in their right to "life, liberty and the pursuit of happiness," as proclaimed in that old Declaration, the inferior races are our equals. And these declarations I have constantly made in reference to the abstract moral question, to contemplate and consider when we are legislating about any new country which is not already cursed with the actual presence of the evil—slavery. I have never manifested any impatience with the necessities that spring from the actual presence of black people amongst us, and the actual existence of slavery amongst us where it does already exist; but I have insisted that, in legislating for new countries, where it does not exist, there is no just rule other than that of moral and abstract right! With reference to those new countries, those maxims as to the right of a people to "life, liberty and the pursuit of happiness," were the just rules to be constantly referred to. There is no misunderstanding this, except by men interested to misunderstand it. I take it that I have to address an intelligent and reading community, who will peruse what I say, weigh it, and then judge whether I advance improper or unsound views, or whether I advance hypocritical, and deceptive, and contrary views in different portions of the country. I believe myself to be guilty of no such thing as the latter, though, of course, I cannot claim that I am entirely free from all error in the opinions I advance.

The Judge has also detained us awhile in regard to the distinction between his party and our party. His he assumes to be a national party—ours a sectional one. He does this in asking the question whether this country has any interest in the maintenance of the Republican party? He assumes that our party is altogether sectional—that the party to which he adheres is national; and the argument is, that no party can be a rightful party—can be based upon rightful principles—unless it can announce its principles every where. I presume that Judge Douglas could not go into Russia and announce the doctrine of our national Democracy; he could not denounce the doctrine of kings and emperors and monarchies in Russia; and it may be true of this country, that in some places we may not be able to proclaim a doctrine as clearly true as the truth of Democracy, because there is a section so directly opposed to it that they will not tolerate us in doing so. Is it the true test of the soundness of a doctrine, that in some places people won't let you proclaim it? Is that the way to test the truth of any doctrine? Why, I understood that at one time the people of Chicago would not let Judge Douglas preach a certain favorite doctrine of his. I commend to his consideration the question, whether he takes that as a test of the unsoundness of what he wanted to preach.

There is another thing to which I wish to ask attention for a little while on this occasion. What has always been the evidence brought forward to prove that the Republican party is a sectional party? The main one was that in the Southern portion of the Union the people did not let the Republicans proclaim their doctrines amongst them. That has been the main evidence brought forward—that they had no supporters, or substantially none, in the slave States. The South have not taken hold of our principles as we announce them; nor does Judge Douglas now grapple with those principles. We have a Republican State Platform, laid down in Springfield in June last, stating our position all the way through the questions before the country. We are now far advanced in this canvass. Judge Douglas and I have made perhaps forty speeches apiece, and we have now for the fifth time met face to face in debate, and up to this day I have not found either Judge Douglas or any friend of his taking hold of the Republican platform or laying his finger upon anything in it that is wrong. I ask you all to recollect that. Judge Douglas turns away from the platform of principles to the fact that he can find people somewhere who will not allow us to announce those principles. If he had great confidence that our principles were wrong, he would take hold of them and demonstrate them to be wrong. But he does not do so. The only evidence he has of their being wrong is in the fact that there are people who won't allow us to preach them. I ask again is that the way to test the soundness of a doctrine?

I ask his attention also to the fact that by the rule of nationality he is himself fast becoming sectional. I ask his attention to the fact that his speeches would not go as current now south of the Ohio river as they have formerly gone there. I ask his attention to the fact that he felicitates himself to-day that all the Democrats of the free States are agreeing with him, while he omits to tell us that the Democrats of any slave State agree with him. If he has not thought of this, I commend to his consideration the evidence in his own declaration, on this day, of his becoming sectional too. I see it rapidly approaching. Whatever may be the result of this ephemeral contest between Judge Douglas and myself, I see the day rapidly approaching when his pill of sectionalism, which he has been thrusting down the throats of Republicans for years past, will be crowded down his own throat.

Now in regard to what Judge Douglas said (in the beginning of his speech) about the Compromise of 1850, containing the principle of the Nebraska bill, although I have often presented my views upon that subject, yet as I have not done so in this canvass, I will, if you please, detain you a little with them. I have always maintained, so far as I was able, that there was nothing of the principle of the Nebraska bill in the Compromise of 1850 at all—nothing whatever. Where can you find the principle of the Nebraska bill in that Compromise? If any where, in the two pieces of the Compromise organizing the Territories of New Mexico and Utah. It was expressly provided in these two acts, that, when they came to be admitted into the Union, they should be admitted with or without slavery, as they should choose, by their own Constitutions. Nothing was said in either of those acts as to what was to be done in relation to slavery during the territorial existence of those Territories, while Henry Clay constantly made the declaration (Judge Douglas recognizing him as a leader) that, in his opinion, the old Mexican laws would control that question during the territorial existence, and that these old Mexican laws excluded slavery. How can that be used as a principle for declaring that during the territorial existence as well as at the time of framing the Constitution, the people, if you please, might have slaves if they wanted them? I am not discussing the question whether it is right or wrong; but how are the New Mexican and Utah laws patterns for the Nebraska bill? I maintain that the organization of Utah and New Mexico *did not* establish a general principle at all. It had no feature of establishing a general principle. The acts to which I have referred were a part of a general system of Compromises. They did not lay down what was proposed as a regular policy for the Territories; only an agreement in this particular case to do in that way, because other things were done that were to be a compensation for it. They were allowed to come in in that shape, because in another way it was paid for—considering that as a part of that system of measures called the Compromise of 1850, which finally included half a dozen acts. It included the admission of California as a free State, which was kept out of the Union for half a year because it had formed a free Constitution. It included the settlement of the boundary of Texas, which had been undefined before, which was in itself a slavery question: for, if you pushed the line farther west, you made Texas larger, and made more slave Territory; while, if you drew the line toward the east, you narrowed the boundary and diminished the domain of slavery, and by so much increased free

Territory. It included the abolition of the slave-trade in the District of Columbia. It included the passage of a new Fugitive Slave law. All these things were put together, and though passed in separate acts, were nevertheless in legislation (as the speeches at the time will show), made to depend upon each other. Each got votes, with the understanding that the other measures were to pass, and by this system of Compromise, in that series of measures, those two bills—the New Mexico and Utah bills—were passed; and I say for that reason they could not be taken as models, framed upon their own intrinsic principle, for all future Territories. And I have the evidence of this in the fact that Judge Douglas, a year afterward, or more than a year afterward, perhaps, when he first introduced bills for the purpose of framing new Territories, did not attempt to follow these bills of New Mexico and Utah; and even when he introduced this Nebraska bill, I think you will discover that he did not exactly follow them. But I do not wish to dwell at great length upon this branch of the discussion. My own opinion is, that a thorough investigation will show most plainly that the New Mexico and Utah bills were part of a system of Compromise, and not designed as patterns for future territorial legislation; and that this Nebraska bill did not follow them as a pattern at all.

The Judge tells, in proceeding, that he is opposed to making any odious distinctions between free and slave States. I am altogether unaware that the Republicans are in favor of making any odious distinctions between the free and slave States. But there still is a difference, I think, between Judge Douglas and the Republicans in this. I suppose that the real difference between Judge Douglas and his friends, and the Republicans on the contrary, is, that the Judge is not in favor of making any difference between slavery and liberty—that he is in favor of eradicating, of pressing out of view, the questions of preference in this country for free or slave institutions; and consequently every sentiment he utters discards the idea that there is any wrong in slavery. Every thing that emanates from him or his coadjutors in their course of policy, carefully excludes the thought that there is any thing wrong in slavery. All their arguments, if you will consider them, will be seen to exclude the thought that there is any thing whatever wrong in slavery. If you will take the Judge's speeches, and select the short and pointed sentences expressed by him—as his declaration that he "don't care whether slavery is voted up or down"—you will see at once that this is perfectly logical, if you do not admit that slavery is wrong. If you do admit that it is wrong, Judge Douglas cannot logically say he don't care whether a wrong is voted up or voted down. Judge Douglas declares that if any community want slavery they have a right to have it. He can say that logically, if he says that there is no wrong in slavery; but if you admit that there is a wrong in it, he cannot logically say that any body has a right to do wrong. He insists that, upon the score of equality, the owners of slaves and owners of property—of horses and every other sort of property—should be alike and hold them alike in a new Territory. That is perfectly logical, if the two species of property are alike and are equally founded in right. But if you admit that one of them is wrong, you cannot institute any equality between right and wrong. And from this difference of sentiment—the belief on the part of one that the institution is wrong, and a policy springing from that belief which looks to the arrest of the enlargement of that wrong; and this other sentiment, that it is no wrong, and a policy sprung from that sentiment which will tolerate no idea of prerenting that wrong from growing larger, and looks to there never being an end of it through all the existence of things,—arises the real difference between Judge Douglas and his friends on the one hand, and the Republicans on the other. Now, I confess myself as belonging to that class in the country who contemplate slavery as a moral, social and political evil, having due regard for its actual existence amongst us and the difficulties of getting rid of it in any satisfactory way, and to all the Constitutional obligations which have been thrown about it; but, nevertheless, desire a policy that looks to the prevention of it as a wrong, and looks hopefully to the time when as a wrong it may come to an end.

Judge Douglas has again, for, I believe, the fifth time, if not the seventh, in my presence, reiterated his charge of a conspiracy or combination between the National Democrats and Republicans. What evidence Judge Douglas has upon this subject I know not, inasmuch as he never favors us with any. I have said upon a former occasion, and I do not choose to suppress it now, that I have no objection to the division in the Judge's party. He got it up himself. It was all his and their work. He had, I think, a great deal more to do with the steps that led to the Lecompton Constitution than Mr. Buchanan had; though at last, when they reached it, they quarreled over it, and their friends divided upon it. I am very free to confess to Judge Douglas that I have no objection to the division; but I defy the Judge to show any evidence that I have in any way promoted that division, unless he insists on being a witness himself in merely saying so. I can give all fair friends of Judge Douglas here to understand exactly the view that Republicans take in regard to that division. Don't you remember how two years ago the opponents of the Democratic party were divided between Fremont and Fillmore? I guess you do. Any Democrat who remembers that division, will remember also that he was at the time very glad of it, and then he will be able to see all there is between the National Democrats and the Republicans. What we now think of the two divisions of Democrats, you then thought of the Fremont and Fillmore divisions. That is all there is of it.

But, if the Judge continues to put forward the declaration that there is an unholy and unnatural alliance between the Republican and the National Democrats, I now want to enter my protest against receiving him as an entirely competent witness upon that subject. I want to call to the Judge's attention an attack he made upon me in the first one of these debates, at Ottawa, on the 21st of August. In order to fix extreme Abolitionism upon me, Judge Douglas read a set of resolutions which he declared had been passed by a Republican State Convention, in October, 1854, at Springfield, Illinois, and he declared I had taken part in that Convention. It turned out that although a few men calling themselves an anti-Nebraska State Convention had sat at Springfield about that time, yet neither did I take any part in it, nor did it pass the resolutions or any such resolutions as Judge Douglas read. So apparent had it become that the resolutions which he read had not been passed at Springfield at all, nor by a State Convention in which I had taken part, that seven days afterward, at Freeport, Judge Douglas declared that he had been misled by Charles H. Lanphier, editor of the *State Register,* and Thomas L. Harris, member of Congress in that District, and he promised in that speech that when he went to Springfield he would investigate the matter. Since then Judge Douglas has been to Springfield, and I presume has made the investigation; but a month has passed since he has been there, and so far as I know, he has made no report of the result of his investigation. I have waited as I think sufficient time for the report of that investigation, and I have some curiosity to see and hear it. A fraud—an absolute forgery was committed, and the perpetration of it was traced to the three—Lanphier, Harris and Douglas. Whether it can be narrowed in any way so as to exonerate any one of them, is what Judge Douglas's report would probably show.

It is true that the set of resolutions read by Judge Douglas were published in the Illinois *State Register* on the 16th of October, 1854, as being the resolutions of an anti-Nebraska Convention, which had sat in that same month of October, at Springfield. But it is also true that the publication in the *Register* was a forgery then, and the question is still behind, which of the three, if not all of them, committed that forgery? The idea that it was done by mistake, is absurd. The article in the Illinois *State Register* contains part of the real proceedings of that Springfield Convention, showing that the writer of the article had the real proceedings before him, and purposely threw out the genuine resolutions passed by the Convention, and fraudulently substituted the others. Lanphier then, as now, was the editor of the *Register,* so that there seems to be but little room for his escape. But then it is to be borne in mind that Lanphier had less interest in the object of that forgery than either of the other two. The main object of that forgery at that time was to beat Yates and elect Harris to Congress, and that object was known to be exceedingly dear to Judge Douglas at that time. Harris and Douglas were both in Springfield when the Convention was in session, and although they both left before the fraud appeared in the *Register,* subsequent events show that they have both had their eyes fixed upon that Convention.

The fraud having been apparently successful upon the occasion, both Harris and Douglas have more than once since then been attempting to put it to new uses. As the fisherman's wife, whose drowned husband was brought home with his body full of eels, said when she was asked, "What was to be done with him?" *"Take the eels out and set him again;"* so Harris and Douglas have shown a disposition to take the eels out of that stale fraud by which they gained Harris's election, and set the fraud again more than once. On the 9th of July, 1856, Douglas attempted a repetition of it upon Trumbull on the floor of the Senate of the United States, as will appear from the appendix of the *Congressional Globe* of that date.

On the 9th of August, Harris attempted it again upon Norton in the House of Representatives, as will appear by the same documents—the appendix to the *Congressional Globe* of that date. On the 21st of August last, all three—Lanphier, Douglas and Harris—reattempted it upon me at Ottawa. It has been clung to and played out again and again as an exceedingly high trump by this blessed trio. And now that it has been discovered publicly to be a fraud, we find that Judge Douglas manifests no surprise at it at all. He makes no complaint of Lanphier, who must have known it to be a fraud from the beginning. He, Lanphier and Harris, are just as cozy now, and just as active in the concoction of new schemes as they were before the general discovery of this fraud. Now all this is very natural if they are all alike guilty in that fraud, and it is very unnatural if any one of them is innocent. Lanphier perhaps insists that the rule of honor among thieves does not quite require him to take all upon himself, and consequently my friend Judge Douglas finds it difficult to make a satisfactory report upon his investigation. But meanwhile the three are agreed that each is *"a most honorable man."*

Judge Douglas requires an indorsement of his truth and honor by a re-election to the United States Senate, and he makes and reports against me and against Judge Trumbull, day after day, charges which we know to be utterly untrue, without for a moment seeming to think that this one unexplained fraud, which he promised to investigate, will be the least drawback to his claim to belief. Harris ditto. He asks a re-election to the lower House of Congress without seeming to remember at all that he is involved in this dishonorable fraud! The Illinois *State Register,* edited by Lanphier, then, as now, the central organ of both Harris and Douglas, continues to din the public ear with this assertion without seeming to suspect that these assertions are at all lacking in title to belief.

After all, the question still recurs upon us, how did that fraud originally get into the *State Register?* Lanphier then, as now, was the editor of that paper. Lanphier knows. Lanphier cannot be ignorant of how and by whom it was originally concocted. Can he be induced to tell, or if he has told, can Judge Douglas be induced to tell how it originally was concocted? It may be true that Lanphier insists that the two men for whose benefit it was originally devised, shall at least bear their share of it! How that is, I do not know, and while it remains unexplained, I hope to be pardoned if I insist that the mere fact of Judge Douglas making charges against Trumbull and myself is not quite sufficient evidence to establish them!

While we were at Freeport, in one of these joint discussions, I answered certain interrogatories which Judge Douglas had propounded to me, and there in turn propounded some to him, which he in a sort of way answered. The third one of these interrogatories I have with me and wish now to make some comments upon it. It was in these words: "If the Supreme Court of the United States shall decide that the States cannot exclude slavery from their limits, are you in favor of acquiescing in, adhering to and following such decision, as a rule of political action?"

To this interrogatory Judge Douglas made no answer in any just sense of the word. He contented himself with sneering at the thought that it was possible for the Supreme Court ever to make such a decision. He sneered at me for propounding the interrogatory. I had not propounded it without some reflection, and I wish now to address to this audience some remarks upon it.

In the second clause of the sixth article, I believe it is, of the Constitution of the United States, we find the following language: "This Constitution and the laws of the United States which shall be made in pursuance thereof; and all treaties made, or which shall be made under the authority of the United States, shall be the supreme law of the land; and the judges in every State shall be bound thereby, any thing in the Constitution or laws of any State to the contrary notwithstanding."

The essence of the Dred Scott case is compressed into the sentence which I will now read: "Now, as we have already said in an earlier part of this opinion, upon a different point, the right of property in a slave is distinctly and expressly affirmed in the Constitution." I repeat it, "*The right of property in a slave is dis-*

tinctly and expressly affirmed in the Constitution!" What is it to be "*affirmed*" in the Constitution? Made firm in the Constitution—so made that it cannot be separated from the Constitution without breaking the Constitution—durable as the Constitution, and part of the Constitution. Now, remembering the provision of the Constitution which I have read, affirming that that instrument is the supreme law of the land; that the Judges of every State shall be bound by it, any law or Constitution of any State to the contrary notwithstanding; that the right of property in a slave is affirmed in that Constitution, is made, formed into, and cannot be separated from it without breaking it; durable as the instrument; part of the instrument;—what follows as a short and even syllogistic argument from it? I think it follows, and I submit to the consideration of men capable of arguing, whether as I state it, in syllogistic form, the argument has any fault in it?

Nothing in the Constitution or laws of any State can destroy a right distinctly and expressly affirmed in the Constitution of the United States.

The right of property in a slave is distinctly and expressly affirmed in the Constitution of the United States.

Therefore, nothing in the Constitution or laws of any State can destroy the right of property in a slave.

I believe that no fault can be pointed out in that argument; assuming the truth of the premises, the conclusion, so far as I have capacity at all to understand it, follows inevitably. There is a fault in it as I think, but the fault is not in the reasoning; but the falsehood in fact is a fault of the premises. I believe that the right of property in a slave *is not* distinctly and expressly affirmed in the Constitution, and Judge Douglas thinks it *is*. I believe that the Supreme Court and the advocates of that decision may search in vain for the place in the Constitution where the right of a slave is distinctly and expressly affirmed. I say, therefore, that I think one of the premises is not true in fact. But it is true with Judge Douglas. It is true with the Supreme Court who pronounced it. They are estopped from denying it, and being estopped from denying it, the conclusion follows that the Constitution of the United States being the supreme law, no constitution or law can interfere with it. It being affirmed in the decision that the right of property in a slave is distinctly and expressly affirmed in the Constitution, the conclusion inevitably follows that no State law or constitution can destroy that right. I then say to Judge Douglas and to all others, that I think it will take a better answer than a sneer to show that those who have said that the right of property in a slave is distinctly and expressly affirmed in the Constitution, are not prepared to show that no constitution or law can destroy that right. I say I believe it will take a far better argument than a mere sneer to show to the minds of intelligent men that whoever has so said, is not prepared, whenever public sentiment is so far advanced as to justify it, to say the other. This is but an opinion, and the opinion of one very humble man; but it is my opinion that the Dred Scott decision, as it is, never would have been made in its present form if the party that made it had not been sustained previously by the elections. My own opinion is, that the new Dred Scott decision, deciding against the right of the people of the States to exclude slavery, will never be made, if that party is not sustained by the elections. I believe, further, that it is just as sure to be made as to-morrow is to come, if that party shall be sustained. I have said, upon a former occasion, and I repeat it now, that the course of argument that Judge Douglas makes use of upon this subject (I charge not his motives in this), is preparing the public mind for that new Dred Scott decision. I have asked him again to point out to me the reasons for his first adherence to the Dred Scott decision as it is. I have turned his attention to the fact that General Jackson differed with him in regard to the political obligation of a Supreme Court decision. I have asked his attention to the fact that Jefferson differed with him in regard to the political obligation of a Supreme Court decision. Jefferson said, that "Judges are as honest as other men, and not more so." And he said, substantially, that "whenever a free people should give up in absolute submission to any department of government, retaining for themselves no appeal from it, their liberties were gone." I have asked his attention to the fact that the Cincinnati platform, upon which he says he stands, disregards a time-honored decision of the Supreme Court, in denying the power of Congress to establish a National Bank. I have asked his attention to the fact that he himself was one of the most active instruments at one time in breaking down the Supreme Court of the State of Illinois, because it had made a decision distasteful to him—a struggle ending in the remarkable circumstance of his sitting down as one of the new Judges who were to overslaugh that decision—getting his title of Judge in that very way.

So far in this controversy I can get no answer at all from Judge Douglas upon these subjects. Not one can I get from him, except that he swells himself up and says, "All of us who stand by the decision of the Supreme Court are the friends of the Constitution; all you fellows that dare question it in any way, are the enemies of the Constitution." Now, in this very devoted adherence to this decision, in opposition to all the great political leaders whom he has recognized as leaders—in opposition to his former self and history, there is something very marked. And the manner in which he adheres to it—not as being right upon the merits, as he conceives (because he did not discuss that at all), but as being absolutely obligatory upon every one simply because of the source from whence it comes—as that which no man can gainsay, whatever it may be—this is another marked feature of his adherence to that decision. It marks it in this respect, that it commits him to the next decision, whenever it comes, as being as obligatory as this one, since he does not investigate it, and won't inquire whether this opinion is right or wrong. So he takes the next one without inquiring whether *it* is right or wrong. He teaches men this doctrine, and in so doing prepares the public mind to take the next decision when it comes, without any inquiry. In this I think I argue fairly (without questioning motives at all), that Judge Douglas is most ingeniously and powerfully preparing the public mind to take that decision when it comes; and not only so, but he is doing it in various other ways. In these general maxims about liberty—in his assertions that he "don't care whether slavery is voted up or voted down;" that "whoever wants slavery has a right to have it;" that "upon principles of equality it should be allowed to go every where;" that "there is no inconsistency between free and slave institutions." In this he is also preparing (whether purposely or not) the way for making the institution of slavery national! I repeat again, for I wish no misunderstanding, that I do not charge that he means it so; but I call upon your minds to inquire, if you were going to get the best instrument you could, and then set it to work in the most ingenious way, to prepare the public mind for this movement, operating in the free States, where there is now an abhorrence of the institution of slavery, could you find an instrument so capable of doing it as Judge Douglas? or one employed in so apt a way to do it?

I have said once before, and I will repeat it now, that Mr. Clay, when he was once answering an objection to the Colonization Society, that it had a tendency to the ultimate emancipation of the slaves, said that "those who would repress all tendencies to liberty and ultimate emancipation must do more than put down the benevolent efforts of the Colonization Society—they must go back to the era of our liberty and independence, and muzzle the cannon that thunders its annual joyous return—they must blot out the moral lights around us—they must penetrate the human soul, and eradicate the light of reason and the love of liberty!" And I do think—I repeat, though I said it on a former occasion—that Judge Douglas, and whoever like him teaches that the negro has no share, humble though it may be, in the Declaration of Independence, is going back to the era of our liberty and independence, and, so far as in him lies, muzzling the cannon that thunders its annual joyous return; that he is blowing out the moral lights around us, when he contends that whoever wants slaves has a right to hold them; that he is penetrating, so far as lies in his power, the human soul, and eradicating the light of reason and the love of liberty, when he is in every possible way preparing the public mind, by his vast influence, for making the institution of slavery perpetual and national.

There is, my friends, only one other point to which I will call your attention for the remaining time that I have left me, and perhaps I shall not occupy the entire time that I have, as that one point may not take me clear through it.

Among the interrogatories that Judge Douglas propounded to me at Freeport, there was one in about this language: "Are you opposed to the acquisition of any further territory to the United States, unless slavery shall first be prohibited therein?" I answered as I thought, in this way, that I am not generally opposed to the acquisition of additional territory, and that I would support a proposition for the acquisition of additional territory, according as my supporting it was or was not calculated to aggravate this slavery question amongst us. I then proposed to Judge Douglas another interrogatory, which was correlative to that: "Are you in favor of acquiring additional territory in disregard of how it may affect us upon the slavery question?" Judge Douglas answered, that is, in his own way he answered it. I believe that, although he took a good many words to answer it, it was a little more fully answered than any other. The substance of his answer was, that this country would continue to expand—that it would need additional territory—that it was as absurd to suppose that we could continue upon our present territory, enlarging in population as we are, as it would be to hoop a boy twelve years of age, and expect him to grow to man's size without bursting the hoops. I believe it was something like that. Consequently he was in favor of the acquisition of further territory, as fast as we might need it, in disregard of how it might affect the slavery question. I do not say this as giving his exact language, but he said so substantially, and he would leave the question of slavery where the territory was acquired, to be settled by the people of the acquired territory. ["That's the doctrine."] May be it is; let us consider that for a while. This will probably, in the run of things, become one of the concrete manifestations of this slavery question. If Judge Douglas's policy upon this question succeeds and gets fairly settled down, until all opposition is crushed out, the next thing will be a grab for the territory of poor Mexico, an invasion of the rich lands of South America, then the adjoining islands will follow, each one of which promises additional slave fields. And this question is to be left to the people of those countries for settlement. When we shall get Mexico, I don't know whether the Judge will be in favor of the Mexican people that we get with it settling that question for themselves and all others; because we know the Judge has a great horror for mongrels, and I understand that the people of Mexico are most decidedly a race of mongrels. I understand that there is not more than one person there out of eight who is pure white, and I suppose from the Judge's previous declaration that when we get Mexico or any considerable portion of it, that he will be in favor of these mongrels settling the question, which would bring him somewhat into collision with his horror of an inferior race.

It is to be remembered, though, that this power of acquiring additional territory is a power confided to the President and Senate of the United States. It is a power not under the control of the representatives of the people any further than they, the President and the Senate, can be considered the representatives of the people. Let me illustrate that by a case we have in our history. When we acquired the territory from Mexico in the Mexican war, the House of Representatives, composed of the immediate representatives of the people, all the time insisted that the territory thus to be acquired should be brought in upon condition that slavery should be forever prohibited therein, upon the terms and in the language that slavery had been prohibited from coming into this country. That was insisted upon constantly, and never failed to call forth an assurance that any territory thus acquired should have that prohibition in it, so far as the House of Representatives was concerned. But at last the President and Senate acquired the territory without asking the House of Representatives any thing about it, and took it without that prohibition. They have the power of acquiring territory without the immediate representatives of the people being called upon to say any thing about it, and thus furnishing a very apt and powerful means of bringing new territory into the Union, and when it is once brought into the country, involving us anew in this slavery agitation. It is, therefore, as I think, a very important question for the consideration of the American people, whether the policy of bringing in additional territory, without considering at all how it will operate upon the safety of the Union in reference to this one great disturbing element in our national politics, shall be adopted as the policy of the country. You will bear in mind that it is to be acquired, according to the Judge's view, as fast as it is needed, and the indefinite part of this proposition is that we have only Judge Douglas and his class of men to decide how fast it is needed. We have no clear and certain way of determining or demonstrating how fast territory is needed by the necessities of the country. Whoever wants to go out fillibustering, then, thinks that more territory is needed. Whoever wants wider slave fields, feels sure that some additional territory is needed as slave territory. Then it is as easy to show the necessity of additional slave territory as it is to assert any thing that is incapable of absolute demonstration. Whatever motive a man or a set of men may have for making annexation of property or territory, it is very easy to assert, but much less easy to disprove, that it is necessary for the wants of the country.

And now it only remains for me to say that I think it is a very grave question for the people of this Union to consider whether, in view of the fact that this slavery question has been the only one that has ever endangered our Republican institutions—the only one that has ever threatened or menaced a dissolution of the Union—that has ever disturbed us in such a way as to make us fear for the perpetuity of our liberty—in view of these facts, I think it is an exceedingly interesting and important question for, this people to consider, whether we shall engage in the policy of acquiring additional territory, discarding altogether from our consideration, while obtaining new territory, the question how it may affect us in regard to this the only endangering element to our liberties and national greatness. The Judge's view has been expressed. I, in my answer to his question, have expressed mine. I think it will become an important and practical question. Our views are before the public. I am willing and anxious that they should consider them fully—that they should turn it about and consider the importance of the question, and arrive at a just conclusion as to whether it is or is not wise in the people of this Union, in the acquisition of new territory, to consider whether it will add to the disturbance that is existing amongst us—whether it will add to the one only danger that has ever threatened the perpetuity of the Union or our own liberties. I think it is extremely important that they shall decide, and rightly decide, that question before entering upon that policy.

And now, my friends, having said the little I wish to say upon this head, whether I have occupied the whole of the remnant of my time or not, I believe I could not enter upon any new topics so as to treat it fully without transcending my time, which I would not for a moment think of doing. I give way to Judge Douglas.

MR. DOUGLAS'S REJOINDER.

GENTLEMEN: The highest compliment you can pay me during the brief half hour that I have to conclude is by observing a strict silence. I desire to be heard rather than to be applauded.

The first criticism that Mr. Lincoln makes on my speech was that it was in substance what I have said every where else in the State where I have addressed the people. I wish I could say the same of his speech. Why, the reason I complain of him is because he makes one speech north and another south. Because he has one set of sentiments for the Abolition counties and another set for the counties opposed to Abolitionism. My point of complaint against him is that I cannot induce him to hold up the same standard, to carry the same flag in all parts of the State. He does not pretend, and no other man will, that I have one set of principles for Galesburgh and another for Charleston. He does not pretend that I hold to one doctrine in Chicago and an opposite one in Jonesboro. I have proved that he has a different set of principles for each of these localities. All I asked of him was that he should deliver the speech that he has made here to-day in Coles county instead of in old Knox. It would have settled the question between us in that doubtful county. Here I understand him to reaffirm the doctrine of negro equality, and to assert that by the Declaration of Independence the negro is declared equal to the white man. He tells you to-day that the negro was included in the Declaration of Independence when it asserted that all men were created equal. ["We believe it."] Very well.

Mr. Lincoln asserts to-day as he did at Chicago, that the negro was included in that clause of the Declaration of Independence which says that all men were created equal and endowed by the Creator with certain inalienable rights, among which are life, liberty, and the pursuit of happiness. If the negro was made his equal and mine, if that equality was established by Divine law, and was the negro's inalienable right, how came he to say at Charleston to the Kentuckians residing in that section of our State, that the negro was physically inferior to the white man, belonged to an inferior race, and he was for keeping him always in that inferior condition. I wish you to bear these things in mind. At Charleston he said that the negro belonged to an inferior race, and that he was for keeping him in that inferior condition. There he gave the people to understand that there was no moral question involved, because the inferiority being established, it was only a question of degree and not a question of right; here, to day, instead of making it a question of degree, he makes it a moral question, says that it is a great crime to hold the negro in that inferior condition. ["He's right."] Is he right now or was he right in Charleston? ["Both."] He is right then, sir, in your estimation, not because he is consistent, but because he can trim his principles any way in any section, so as to secure votes. All I desire of him is that he will declare the same principles in the south that he does in the north.

But did you notice how he answered my position that a man should hold the same doctrines throughout the length and breadth of this Republic? He said, "Would Judge Douglas go to Russia and proclaim the same principles he does here?" I would remind him that Russia is not under the American Constitution. If Russia was a part of the American Republic, under our Federal Constitution, and I was sworn to support the Constitution, I would maintain the same doctrine in Russia that I do in Illinois. The slaveholding States are governed by the same Federal Constitution as ourselves, and hence a man's principles, in order to be in harmony with the Constitution, must be the same in the south as they are in the north, the same in the free States as they are in the slave States. Whenever a man advocates one set of principles in one section, and another set in another section, his opinions are in violation of the spirit of the Constitution which he has sworn to support. When Mr. Lincoln went to Congress in 1847, and laying his hand upon the Holy Evangelists, made a solemn vow in the presence of high Heaven that he would be faithful to the Constitution—what did he mean? the Constitution as he expounds it in Galesburgh, or the Constitution as he expounds it in Charleston.

Mr. Lincoln has devoted considerable time to the circumstance that at Ottawa I read a series of resolutions as having been adopted at Springfield, in this State, on the 4th or 5th of October, 1854, which happened not to have been adopted there. He has used hard names; has dared to talk about fraud, about forgery, and has insinuated that there was a conspiracy between Mr. Lanphier, Mr. Harris, and myself to perpetrate a forgery. Now, bear in mind that he does not deny that these resolutions were adopted in a majority of all the Republican counties of this State in that year; he does not deny that they were declared to be the platform of this Republican party in the first Congressional District, in the second, in the third, and in many counties of the fourth, and that they thus became the platform of his party in a majority of the counties upon which he now relies for support; he does not deny the truthfulness of the resolutions, but takes exception to the *spot* on which they were adopted. He takes to himself great merit because he thinks they were not adopted on the right spot for me to use them against him, just as he was very severe in Congress upon the Government of his country when he thought that he had discovered that the Mexican war was not begun in the right *spot,* and was therefore unjust. He tries very hard to make out that there is something very extraordinary in the place where the thing was done, and not in the thing itself. I never believed before that Abraham Lincoln would be guilty of what he has done this day in regard to those resolutions. In the first place, the moment it was intimated to me that they had been adopted at Aurora and Rockford instead of Springfield, I did not wait for him to call my attention to the fact, but led off and explained in my first meeting after the Ottawa debate, what the mistake was, and how it had been made. I supposed that for an honest man, conscious of his own rectitude, that explanation would be sufficient. I did not wait for him, after the mistake was made, to call my attention to it, but frankly explained it at once as an honest man would. I also gave the authority on which I had stated that these resolutions were adopted by the Springfield Republican Convention. That I had seen them quoted by Major Harris in a debate in Congress, as having been adopted by the first Republican State Convention in Illinois, and that I had written to him and asked him for the authority as to the time and place of their adoption; that Major Harris being extremely ill, Charles H. Lanphier had written to me for him, that they were adopted at Springfield, on the 5th of October, 1854, and had sent me a copy of the Springfield paper containing them. I read them from the newspaper just as Mr. Lincoln reads the proceedings of meetings held years ago from the newspapers. After giving that explanation, I did not think there was an honest man in the State of Illinois who doubted that I had been led into the error, if it was such, innocently, in the way I detailed; and I will now say that I do not now believe that there is an honest man on the face of the globe who will not regard with abhorrence and disgust Mr. Lincoln's insinuations of my complicity in that forgery, if it was a forgery. Does Mr. Lincoln wish to push these things to the point of personal difficulties here? I commenced this contest by treating him courteously and kindly; I always spoke of him in words of respect, and in return he has sought, and is now seeking, to divert public attention from the enormity of his revolutionary principles by impeaching men's sincerity and integrity, and inviting personal quarrels.

I desired to conduct this contest with him like a gentleman, but I spurn the insinuation of complicity and fraud made upon the simple circumstance of an editor of a newspaper having made a mistake as to the place where a thing was done, but not as to the thing itself. These resolutions were the platform of this Republican party of Mr. Lincoln's of that year. They were adopted in a majority of the Republican counties in the State; and when I asked him at Ottawa whether they formed the platform upon which he stood, he did not answer, and I could not get an answer out of him. He then thought, as I thought, that those resolutions were adopted at the Springfield Convention, but excused himself by saying that he was not there when they were adopted, but had gone to Tazewell court in order to avoid being present at the Convention. He saw them published as having been adopted at Springfield, and so did I, and he knew that if there was a mistake in regard to them, that I had nothing under heaven to do with it. Besides, you find that in all these northern countries where the Republican candidates are running pledged to him, that the Conventions which nominated them adopted that identical platform. One cardinal point in that platform which he shrinks from is this—that there shall be no more slave States admitted into the Union, even if the people went them. Lovejoy stands pledged against the admission of any more slave States. ["Right, so do we."] So do you, you say. Farnsworth stands pledged against the admission of any more slave States. Washburne stands pledged the same way. The candidate for the Legislature who is running on Lincoln's ticket in Henderson and Warren, stands committed by his vote in the Legislature to the same thing, and I am informed, but do not know of the fact, that your candidate here is also so pledged. ["Hurra for him, good."] Now, you Republicans all hurra for him, and for the doctrine of "no more slave States," and yet Lincoln tells you that his conscience will not permit him to sanction that doctrine. And complains because the resolutions I read at Ottawa made him, as a member of the party, responsible for sanctioning the doctrine of no more slave States. You are one way, you confess, and he is or pretends to be the other, and yet you are both governed by *principle* in supporting one another. If it be true, as I have shown it is, that the whole Republican party in the northern part of the State stands committed to the doctrine of no more slave States, and that this same doctrine is repudiated by the Republicans in the other part of the State, I wonder whether Mr. Lincoln and his party do not present the case which he cited from the Scriptures, of a house divided against itself which cannot stand! I desire to know what are Mr. Lincoln's principles and the principles of his party? I hold, and the party with which I am identified hold, that the people of each State, old and new, have the right to decide the slavery question for themselves, and when I used the remark that I did not care whether slavery was voted up or down, I used it in the connection that I was for allowing Kansas to do just as she pleased on the slavery question. I said that I did not care whether they voted slavery up or down, because they had the right to do as they pleased on the question, and therefore my action would not be controlled by any such consideration. Why cannot Abraham Lincoln, and the party with which he acts, speak out their principles so that they may be understood? Why do they claim to be one thing in one part of the State and another in the other part? Whenever I allude to the Abolition doctrines, which he considers a slander to be charged with being in favor of, you all indorse them, and hurra for them, not knowing that your candidate is ashamed to acknowledge them.

I have a few words to say upon the Dred Scott decision, which has troubled the brain of Mr. Lincoln so much. He insists that that decision would carry slavery into the free States, notwithstanding that the decision says directly the opposite; and goes into a long argument to make you believe that I am in favor of, and would sanction the doctrine that would allow slaves to be brought here and held as slaves contrary to our Constitution and laws. Mr. Lincoln knew better when he asserted this; he knew that one newspaper, and so far as is within my knowledge but one, ever asserted that doctrine, and that I was the first man in either House of Congress that read that article in debate, and denounced it on the floor of the Senate as revolutionary. When the Washington *Union,* on the 17th of last November, published an article to that effect, I branded it at once, and denounced it, and hence the *Union* has been pursuing me ever since. Mr. Toombs, of Georgia, replied to me, and said that there was not a man in any of the slave States south of the Potomac river that held any such doctrine. Mr. Lincoln knows that there is not a member of the Supreme Court who holds that doctrine; he knows that every one of them, us shown by their opinions, holds the reverse. Why this attempt, then, to bring the Supreme Court into disrepute among the people? It looks as if there was an effort being made to destroy public confidence in the highest judicial tribunal on earth. Suppose he succeeds in destroying public confidence in the court, so that the people will not respect its decisions, but will feel at liberty to disregard them, and resist the laws of the land, what will he have gained? He will have changed the Government from one of laws into that of a mob, in which the strong arm of violence will be substituted for the decisions of the courts of justice. He complains because I did not go into an argument reviewing Chief Justice Taney's opinion, and the other opinions of the different judges, to determine whether their reasoning is right or wrong on the questions of law. What use would that be? He wants to take an appeal from the Supreme Court to this meeting to determine whether the questions of law were decided properly. He is going to appeal from the Supreme Court of the United States to every town meeting in the hope that he can excite a prejudice against that court, and on the wave of that prejudice ride into the Senate of the United States, when he could not get there on his own principles, or his own merits. Suppose he should succeed in getting into the Senate of the United States, what then will he have to do with the decision of the Supreme Court in the Dred Scott case? Can he reverse that decision when he gets there? Can he act upon it? Has the Senate any right to reverse it or revise it? He will not pretend that it has. Then why drag the matter into this contest, unless for the purpose of making a false issue, by which he can direct public attention from the real issue.

He has cited General Jackson in justification of the war he is making on the decision of the court. Mr. Lincoln misunderstands the history of the country, if he believes there is any parallel in the two cases. It is true that the Supreme Court once decided that if a Bank of the United States was a necessary fiscal agent of the Government, it was Constitutional, and if not, that it was unconstitutional, and also, that whether or not it was necessary for that purpose, was a political question for Congress and not a judicial one for the courts to determine. Hence the court would not determine the bank unconstitutional. Jackson respected the decision, obeyed the law, executed it and carried it into effect during its existence; but after the charter of the bank expired and a proposition was made to create a new bank, General Jackson said, "it is unnecessary and improper, and, therefore, I am against it on Constitutional grounds as well as those of expediency." Is Congress bound to pass every act that is Constitutional? Why, there are a thousand things that are Constitutional, but yet are inexpedient and unnecessary, and you surely would not vote for them merely because you had the right to? And because General Jackson would not do a thing which he had a right to do, but did not deem expedient or proper, Mr. Lincoln is going to justify himself in doing that which he has no right to do. I ask him, whether he is not bound to respect and obey the decisions of the Supreme Court as well as me? The Constitution has created that court to decide all Constitutional questions in the last resort, and when such decisions have been made, they become the law of the land, and you, and he, and myself, and every other good citizen are bound by them. Yet, he argues that I am bound by their decisions and he is not. He says that their decisions are binding on Democrats, but not on Republicans. Are not Republicans bound by the laws of the land as well as Democrats? And when the court has fixed the construction of the Constitution on the validity of a given law, is not their decision binding upon Republicans as well as upon Democrats? Is it possible that you Republicans have the right to raise your mobs and oppose the laws of the land and the constituted authorities, and yet hold us democrats bound to obey them? My time is within half a minute of expiring, and all I have to say is, that I stand by the laws of the land. I stand by the Constitution as our fathers made it, by the laws as they are enacted, and by the decisions of the court upon all points within their jurisdiction as they are pronounced by the highest tribunal on earth; and any man who resists these must resort to mob law and violence to overturn the government of laws.

SIXTH JOINT DEBATE, AT QUINCY
OCTOBER 13, 1858

MR. LINCOLN'S SPEECH.

LADIES AND GENTLEMEN: I have had no immediate conference with Judge Douglas, but I will venture to say that he and I will perfectly agree that your entire silence, both when I speak and when he speaks will be most agreeable to us.

In the month of May, 1856, the elements in the State of Illinois, which have since been consolidated into the Republican party, assembled together in a State Convention at Bloomington. They adopted at that time, what, in political language, is called a platform. In June of the same year, the elements of the Republican party in the nation assembled together in a National Convention at Philadelphia. They adopted what is called the National Platform. In June, 1858— the present year—the Republicans of Illinois reassembled at Springfield, in State Convention, and adopted again their platform, as I suppose, not differing in any essential particular from either of the former ones, but perhaps adding something in relation to the new developments of political progress in the country.

The Convention that assembled in June last did me the honor, if it be one, and I esteem it such, to nominate me as their candidate for the United States Senate. I have supposed that, in entering upon this canvass, I stood generally upon these platforms. We are now met together on the 13th of October of the same year, only four months from the adoption of the last platform, and I am unaware that in this canvass, from the beginning until to-day, any one of our adversaries has taken hold of our platforms, or laid his finger upon any thing that he calls wrong in them.

In the very first one of these joint discussions between Senator Douglas and myself, Senator Douglas, without alluding at all to these platforms, or any one of them, of which I have spoken, attempted to hold me responsible for a set of resolutions passed long before the meeting of either one of these Conventions of which I have spoken. And as a ground for holding me responsible for these resolutions, he assumed that they had been passed at a State Convention of the Republican party, and that I took part in that Convention. It was discovered afterward that this was erroneous, that the resolutions which he endeavored to hold me responsible for, had not been passed by any State Convention any where—had not been passed at Springfield, where he supposed they had, or assumed that they had, and that they had been passed in no Convention in which I had taken part. The Judge, nevertheless, was not willing to give up the point that he was endeavoring to make upon me, and he therefore thought to still hold me to the point that he was endeavoring to make, by showing that the resolutions that he read, had been passed at a local Convention in the northern part of the State, although it was not a local Convention that embraced my residence at all, nor one that reached, as I suppose, nearer than one hundred and fifty or two hundred miles of where I was when it met, nor one in which I took any part at all. He also introduced other resolutions, passed at other meetings, and by combining the whole, although they were all antecedent to the two State Conventions, and the one National Convention I have mentioned, still he insisted and now insists, as I understand, that I am in some way responsible for them.

At Jonesboro, on our third meeting, I insisted to the Judge that I was in no way rightfully held responsible for the proceedings of this local meeting or Convention in which I had taken no part, and in which I was in no way embraced; but I insisted to him that if he thought I was responsible for every man or every set of men every where, who happen to be my friends, the rule ought to work both ways, and he ought to be responsible for the acts and resolutions of all men or sets of men who were or are now his supporters and friends, and gave him a pretty long string of resolutions, passed by men who are now his friends, and announcing doctrines for which he does not desire to be held responsible.

This still does not satisfy Judge Douglas. He still adheres to his proposition, that I am responsible for what some of my friends in different parts of the State have done; but that he is not responsible for what his have done. At least, so I understand him. But in addition to that, the Judge, at our meeting in Galesburgh, last week, undertakes to establish that I am guilty of a species of double-dealing with the public—that I make speeches of a certain sort in the north, among the Abolitionists, which I would not make in the south, and that I make speeches of a certain sort in the south which I would not make in the north. I apprehend, in the course I have marked out for myself, that I shall not have to dwell at very great length upon this subject.

As this was done in the Judge's opening speech at Galesburgh, I had an opportunity, as I had the middle speech then, of saying something in answer to it. He brought forward a quotation or two from a speech of mine, delivered at Chicago, and then to contrast with it, he brought forward an extract from a speech of mine at Charleston, in which he insisted that I was greatly inconsistent, and insisted that his conclusion followed that I was playing a double part, and speaking in one region one way, and in another region another way. I have not time now to dwell on this as long as I would like, and wish only now to requote that portion of my speech at Charleston, which the Judge quoted, and then make some comments upon it. This he quotes from me as being delivered at Charleston, and I believe correctly: "I will say, then, that I am not, nor ever have been, in favor of bringing about in any way the social and political equality of the white and black races—that I am not nor ever have been in favor of making voters or jurors of negroes, nor of qualifying them to hold office, nor to intermarry with white people; and I will say in addition to this that there is a physical difference between the white and black races which will ever forbid the two races living together on terms of social and political equality. And inasmuch as they cannot so live, while they do remain together, there must be the position of superior and inferior. I am as much as any other man in favor of having the superior position assigned to the white race." This, I believe, is the entire quotation from the Charleston speech, as Judge Douglas made it. His comments are as follows:

> "Yes, here you find men who hurra for Lincoln, and say he is right when he discards all distinction between races, or when he declares that he discards the doctrine that there is such a thing as a superior and inferior race; and Abolitionists are required and expected to vote for Mr. Lincoln because he goes for the equality of races, holding that in the Declaration of Independence the white man and negro were declared equal, and endowed by divine law with equality. And down south with the old line Whigs, with the Kentuckians, the Virginians, and the Tennesseeans, he tells you that there is a physical difference between the races, making the one superior, the other inferior, and he is in favor of maintaining the superiority the white race over the negro."

Those are the Judge's comments. Now I wish to show you, that a month, or, only lacking three days of a month, before I made the speech at Charleston, which the Judge quotes from, he had himself heard me say substantially the same thing. It was in our first meeting, at Ottawa—and I will say a word about where it was, and the atmosphere it was in, after awhile—but at our first meeting, at Ottawa, I read an extract from an old speech of mine, made nearly four years ago, not merely to show my sentiments, but to show that my sentiments were long entertained and openly expressed; in which extract I expressly declared that my own feelings would not admit a social and political equality between the white and black races, and that even if my own feelings would admit of it, I still knew that the public sentiment of the country would not, and that such a thing was an utter impossibility, or substantially that. That extract from my old speech, the reporters, by some sort of accident, passed over, and it was not reported. I lay no blame upon any body. I suppose they thought that I would hand it over to them, and dropped reporting while I was reading it, but afterward went away without getting it from me. At the end of that quotation from my old speech, which I read at Ottawa, I made the comments which were reported at that time, and which I will now read, and ask you to notice how very nearly they are the same as Judge Douglas says were delivered by me, down in Egypt. After reading I added these words: "Now, gentlemen, I don't want to read at any great length, but this is the true complexion of all I have ever said in regard to the institution of slavery or the black race, and this is the whole of it; any thing that argues me into his idea of perfect social and political equality with the negro, is but a specious and fantastical arrangement of words by which a man can prove a horse-chestnut to be a chestnut horse. I will say here, while upon this subject, that I have no purpose, directly or indirectly, to interfere with the institution in the States where it exists. I believe I have no right to do so. I have no inclination to do so. I have no purpose to introduce political and social equality between the white and black races. There is a physical difference between the two, which, in my judgment, will probably forever forbid their living together on the footing of perfect equality, and inasmuch as it becomes a necessity that there must be a difference, I, as well as Judge Douglas, am in favor of the race to which I belong having the superior position. I have never said any thing to the contrary, but I hold that, notwithstanding all this, there is no reason in the world why the negro is not entitled to all the rights enumerated in the Declaration of Independence—the right of life, liberty, and the pursuit of happiness. I hold that he is as much entitled to these as the white man. I agree with Judge Douglas that he is not my equal in many respects, certainly not in color—perhaps not in intellectual and moral endowments; but in the right to eat the bread without the leave of any body else which his own hand earns, he is my equal and the equal of Judge Douglas, and the equal of every other man."

I have chiefly introduced this for the purpose of meeting the Judge's charge that the quotation he took from my Charleston speech was what I would say down south among the Kentuckians, the Virginians, etc., but would not say in the regions in which was supposed to be more of the Abolition element. I now make this comment: That speech from which I have now read the quotation, and which is there given correctly, perhaps too much so for good taste, was made away up north in the Abolition District of this State *par excellence*—in the Lovejoy District—in the personal presence of Lovejoy, for he was on the stand with as when I made it. It had been made and put in print in that region only three days less than a month before the speech made at Charleston, the like of which Judge Douglas thinks I would not make where there was any Abolition element. I only refer to this matter to say that I am altogether unconscious of having attempted any double-dealing any where—that upon one occasion I may say one thing and leave other things unsaid, and *vice versa;* but that I have said any thing on one occasion that is inconsistent with what I have said elsewhere, I deny—at least I deny it so far as the intention is concerned. I find that I have devoted to this topic a larger portion of my time than I had intended. I wished to show, but I will pass it upon this occasion, that in the sentiment I have occasionally advanced upon the Declaration of Independence, I am entirely borne out by the sentiments advanced by our old Whig leader, Henry Clay, and I have the book here to show it from; but because I have already occupied more time than I intended to do on that topic, I pass over it.

At Galesburgh, I tried to show that by the Dred Scott decision, pushed to its legitimate consequences, slavery would be established in all the States as well as in the Territories. I did this because, upon a former occasion, I had asked Judge Douglas whether, if the Supreme Court should make a decision declaring that the States had not the power to exclude slavery from their limits, he would adopt and follow that decision as a rule of political action; and because he had not directly answered that question, but had merely contented himself with sneering at it, I again introduced it, and tried to show that the conclusion that I stated followed inevitably and logically from the proposition already decided by the court. Judge Douglas had the privilege of replying to me at Galesburgh, and again he gave me no direct answer as to whether he would or would not sustain such a decision if made. I give him this third chance to say yes or no. He is not obliged to do either—probably he will not do either—but I give him the third chance. I tried to show then that this result—this conclusion inevitably followed from the point already decided by the court. The Judge, in his reply, again sneers at the thought of the court making any such decision, and in the course of his remarks upon this subject, uses the language which I will now read. Speaking of me the Judge says:

> "He goes on and insists that the Dred Scott decision would carry slavery into the free States, notwithstanding the decision itself says the contrary." And he adds: "Mr. Lincoln knows that there is no member of the Supreme Court that holds that doctrine. He knows that every one of them in their opinions held the reverse."

I especially introduce this subject again for the purpose of saying that I have the Dred Scott decision here, and I will thank Judge Douglas to lay his finger upon the place in the entire opinions of the court where any one of them "says the contrary." It is very hard to affirm a negative with entire confidence. I say, however, that I have examined that decision with a good deal of care, as a lawyer examines a decision, and so far as I have been able to do so, the court has no where in its opinions said that the States have the power to exclude slavery, nor have they used other language substantially that. I also say, so far as I can find, not one of the concurring Judges has said that the States can exclude slavery, nor said any thing that was substantially that. The nearest approach that any one of them has made to it, so far as I can flud, was by Judge Nelson, and the approach he made to it was exactly, in substance, the Nebraska Bill—that the States had the exclusive power over the question of slavery, so far as they are not limited by the Constitution of the United States. I asked the question therefore, if the non-concurring Judges, McLean or Curtis, had asked to get an express declaration that the States could absolutely exclude slavery from their limits, what reason have we to believe that it would not have been voted down by the majority of the Judges, just as Chase's amendment was voted down by Judge Douglas and his compeers when it was offered to the Nebraska Bill.

Also at Galesburgh, I said something in regard to those Springfield resolutions that Judge Douglas had attempted to use upon me at Ottawa, and commented at some length upon the fact that they were, as presented, not genuine. Judge Douglas in his reply to me seemed to be somewhat exasperated. He said he would never have believed that Abraham Lincoln, as he kindly called me, would have attempted such a thing as I had attempted upon that occasion; and among other expressions which he used toward me, was that I dared to say forgery—that I had *dared* to say forgery [turning to Judge Douglas]. Yes, Judge, I did dare to say forgery. But in this political canvass, the Judge ought to remember that I was not the first who *dared* to say forgery. At Jacksonville Judge Douglas made a speech in answer to something said by Judge Trumbull, and at the close of what he said upon that subject, he *dared* to say that Trumbull had forged his evidence. He said, too, that he should not concern himself with Trumbull any more, but thereafter he should hold Lincoln responsible for the slanders upon him. When I met him at Charleston after that, although I think that I should not have noticed the subject if he had not said he would hold me responsible for it, I spread out before him the statements of the evidence that Judge Trumbull had used, and I asked Judge Douglas, piece by piece, to put his finger upon one piece of all that evidence that he would say was a forgery! When I went through with each and every piece, Judge Douglas did not *dare* then to say that any piece of it was a forgery. So it seems that there are some things that Judge Douglas dares to do, and some that he dares not to do.

A voice—"It's the same thing with you."

Mr. Lincoln—Yes, sir, it's the same thing with me. I do dare to say forgery when it's true, and don't dare to say forgery when it's false. Now, I will say here to this audience and to Judge Douglas, I have not dared to say he committed a forgery, and I never shall until I know it; but I did dare to say—just to suggest to the Judge—that a forgery had been committed, which by his own showing had been traced to him and two of his friends. I dared to suggest to him that he had expressly promised in one of his public speeches to investigate that matter, and I dared to suggest to him that there was an implied promise that when he investigated it he would make known the result. I dared to suggest to the Judge that he could not expect to be quite clear of suspicion of that fraud, for since the time that promise was made he had been with those friends, and had not kept his promise in regard to the investigation and the report upon it. I am not a very daring man, but I dared that much, Judge, and I am not much scared about it yet. When the Judge says he wouldn't have believed of Abraham Lincoln that he would have made such an attempt as that, he reminds me of the fact that he entered upon this canvass with the purpose to treat me courteously; that touched me somewhat. It sets me to thinking. I was aware, when it was first agreed that Judge Douglas and I were to have these seven joint discussions, that they were the successive acts of a drama—perhaps I should say, to be enacted not merely in the face of audiences like this, but in the face of the nation, and to some extent, by my relation to him, and not from any thing in myself, in the face of the world; and I am anxious that they should be conducted with dignity and in the good temper which would be befitting the vast audience before which it was conducted. But when Judge Douglas got home from Washington and made his first speech in Chicago, the evening afterward I made some sort of a reply to it. His second speech was made at Bloomington, in which he commented upon my speech at Chicago, and said that I had used language ingeniously contrived to conceal my intentions, or words to that effect. Now, I understand that this is an imputation upon my veracity and my candor. I do not know what the Judge understood by it but in our first discussion at Ottawa, he led off by charging a bargain, somewhat corrupt in its character, upon Trumbull and myself—that we had entered into a bargain, one of the terms of which was that Trumbull was to abolitionize the old Democratic party, and I (Lincoln) was to abolitionize the old Whig party—I pretending to be as good an old line Whig as ever. Judge Douglas may not understand that he implicated my truthfulness and my honor, when he said I was doing one thing and pretending another; and I misunderstood him if he thought he was treating me in a dignified way, as a man of honor and truth, as he now claims he was disposed to treat me. Even after that time, at Galesburg, when he brings forward an extract from a speech made at Chicago, and an extract from a speech made at Charleston, to prove that I was trying to play a double part—that I was trying to cheat the public, and get votes upon one set of principles at one place and upon another set of principles at another place—I do not understand but what he impeaches my

honor, my veracity and my candor, and because *he* does this, I do not understand that I am bound, if I see a truthful ground for it, to keep my hands off of
him. As soon as I learned that Judge Douglas was disposed to treat me in this
way, I signified in one of my speeches that I should be driven to draw upon
whatever of humble resources I might have—to adopt a new course with him.
I was not entirely sure that I should be able to hold my own with him, but I at
least had the purpose made to do as well as I could upon him; and now I say
that I will not be the first to cry "hold." I think it originated with the Judge,
and when he quits, I probably will. But I shall not ask any favors at all. He asks
me, or he asks the audience, if I wish to push this matter to the point of personal difficulty. I tell him, no. He did not make a mistake, in one of his early
speeches, when he called me an "amiable" man, though perhaps he did when
he called me an "intelligent" man. It really hurts me very much to suppose that
I have wronged any body on earth. I again tell him, no! I very much prefer,
when this canvass shall be over, however it may result, that we at least part without any bitter recollections of personal difficulties.

The Judge, in his concluding speech at Galesburg, says that I was pushing
this matter to a personal difficulty, to avoid the responsibility for the enormity
of my principles. I say to the Judge and this audience now, that I will again state
our principles as well as I hastily can in all their enormity, and if the Judge hereafter chooses to confine himself to a war upon these principles, he will probably not find me departing from the same course.

We have in this nation this element of domestic slavery. It is a matter of
absolute certainty that it is a disturbing element. It is the opinion of all the great
men who have expressed an opinion upon it, that it is a dangerous element. We
keep up a controversy in regard to it. That controversy necessarily springs from
difference of opinion, and if we can learn exactly—can reduce to the lowest elements—what that difference of opinion is, we perhaps shall be better prepared
for discussing the different systems of policy that we would propose in regard
to that disturbing element. I suggest that the difference of opinion, reduced to
its lowest terms, is no other than the difference between the men who think
slavery a wrong and those who do not think it wrong. The Republican party
think it wrong—we think it is a moral, a social and a political wrong. We think
it as a wrong not confining itself merely to the persons or the States where it
exists, but that it is a wrong in its tendency, to say the least, that extends itself
to the existence of the whole nation. Because we think it wrong, we propose a
course of policy that shall deal with it as a wrong. We deal with it as with any
other wrong, in so far as we can prevent its growing any larger, and so deal with

it that in the run of time there may be some promise of an end to it. We have a due regard to the actual presence of it amongst us and the difficulties of getting rid of it in any satisfactory way, and all the Constitutional obligations thrown about it. I suppose that in reference both to its actual existence in the nation, and to our Constitutional obligations, we have no right at all to disturb it in the States where it exists, and we profess that we have no more inclination to disturb it than we have the right to do it. We go further than that; we don't propose to disturb it where, in one instance, we think the Constitution would permit us. We think the Constitution would permit us to disturb it in the District of Columbia. Still we do not propose to do that, unless it should be in terms which I don't suppose the nation is very likely soon to agree to—the terms of making the emancipation gradual and compensating the unwilling owners. Where we suppose we have the Constitutional right, we restrain ourselves in reference to the actual existence of the institution and the difficulties thrown about it. We also oppose it as an evil so far as it seeks to spread itself. We insist on the policy that shall restrict it to its present limits. We don't suppose that in doing this we violate any thing due to the actual presence of the institution, or any thing due to the Constitutional guaranties thrown around it.

We oppose the Dred Scott decision in a certain way, upon which I ought perhaps to address you a few words. We do not propose that when Dred Scott has been decided to be a slave by the court, we, as a mob, will decide him to be free. We do not propose that, when any other one, or one thousand, shall be decided by that court to be slaves, we will in any violent way disturb the rights of property thus settled but we nevertheless do oppose that decision as a political rule, which shall be binding on the voter to vote for nobody who thinks it wrong, which shall be binding on the members of Congress or the President to favor no measure that does not actually concur with the principles of that decision. We do not propose to be bound by it as a political rule in that way, because we think it lays the foundation not merely of enlarging and spreading out what we consider an evil, but it lays the foundation for spreading that evil into the States themselves. We propose so resisting it as to have it reversed if we can, and a new judicial rule established upon this subject.

I will add this, that if there be any man who does not believe that slavery is wrong in the three aspects which I have mentioned, or in any one of them, that man is misplaced, and ought to leave us. While, on the other hand, if there be any man in the Republican party who is impatient over the necessity springing from its actual presence, and is impatient of the Constitutional guaranties thrown around it, and would act in disregard of these, he too is misplaced, standing with us. He will find his place somewhere else; for we have a due regard, so far as we are capable of understanding them, for all these things. This, gentlemen, as well as I can give it, is a plain statement of our principles in all their enormity.

I will say now that there is a sentiment in the country contrary to me—a sentiment which holds that slavery is not wrong, and therefore it goes for the policy that does not propose dealing with it as a wrong. That policy is the Democratic policy, and that sentiment is the Democratic sentiment. If there be a doubt in the mind of any one of this vast audience that this is really the central idea of the Democratic party, in relation to this subject, I ask him to bear with me while I state a few things tending, as I think, to prove that proposition. In the first place, the leading man—I think I may do my friend Judge Douglas the honor of calling him such—advocating the present Democratic policy, never himself says it is wrong. He has the high distinction, so far as I know, of never having said slavery is either right or wrong. Almost every body else says one or the other, but the Judge never does. If there be a man in the Democratic party who thinks it is wrong, and yet clings to that party, I suggest to him in the first place that his leader don't talk as he does, for he never says that it is wrong. In the second place, I suggest to him that if he will examine the policy proposed to be carried forward, he will find that he carefully excludes the idea that there is any thing wrong in it. If you will examine the arguments that are made on it, you will find that every one carefully excludes the idea that there is any thing wrong in slavery. Perhaps that Democrat who says he is as much opposed to slavery as I am, will tell me that I am wrong about this. I wish him to examine his own course in regard to this matter a moment, and then see if his opinion will not be changed a little. You say it is wrong; but don't you constantly object to any body else saying so? Do you not constantly argue that this is not the right place to oppose it? You say it must not be opposed in the free States, because slavery is not here; it must not be opposed in the slave States, because it is there; it must not be opposed in politics, because that will make a fuss; it must not be opposed in the pulpit, because it is not religion. Then where is the place to oppose it? There is no suitable place to oppose it. There is no plan in the country to oppose this evil overspreading the continent, which you say yourself is coming. Frank Blair and Gratz Brown tried to get up a system of gradual emancipation in Missouri, had an election in August and got beat, and you, Mr. Democrat, threw up your hat, and hallooed "hurra for Democracy." So I say again, that in regard to the arguments that are made, when Judge Douglas says he "don't care whether slavery is voted up or voted down," whether he

means that as an individual expression of sentiment, or only as a sort of statement of his views on national policy, it is alike true to say that he can thus argue
logically if he don't see any thing wrong in it; but he cannot say so logically if
he admits that slavery is wrong. He cannot say that he would as soon see a wrong
voted up as voted down. When Judge Douglas says that whoever or whatever
community wants slaves, they have a right to have them, he is perfectly logical
if there is nothing wrong in the institution; but if you admit that it is wrong, he
cannot logically say that any body has a right to do wrong. When he says that
slave property and horse and hog property are, alike, to be allowed to go into
the Territories, upon the principles of equality, he is reasoning truly, if there is
no difference between them as property; but if the one is property, held rightfully, and the other is wrong, then there is no equality between the right and
wrong; so that, turn it in any way you can, in all the arguments sustaining the
Democratic policy, and in that policy itself, there is a careful, studied exclusion
of the idea that there is any thing wrong in slavery. Let us understand this. I am
not, just here, trying to prove that we are right and they are wrong. I have been
stating where we and they stand, and trying to show what is the real difference
between us; and I now say that whenever we can get the question distinctly
stated—can get all these men who believe that slavery is in some of these respects
wrong, to stand and act with us in treating it as a wrong—then, and not till then,
I think we will in some way come to an end of this slavery agitation.

MR. DOUGLAS'S REPLY.

LADIES AND GENTLEMEN: Permit me to say that unless silence is observed it
will be impossible for me to be heard by this immense crowd, and my friends
can confer no higher favor upon me than by omitting all expressions of applause
or approbation. I desire to be heard rather than to be applauded. I wish to
address myself to your reason, your judgment, your sense of justice, and not to
your passions.

I regret that Mr. Lincoln should have deemed it proper for him to again
indulge in gross personalities and base insinuations in regard to the Springfield
resolutions. It has imposed upon me the necessity of using some portion of my
time for the purpose of calling your attention to the facts of the case, and it will
then be for you to say what you think of a man who can predicate such a charge
upon the circumstances as he has in this. I had seen the platform adopted by a
Republican Congressional Convention held in Aurora, the Second Congressional District, in September, 1854, published as purporting to be the platform
of the Republican party. That platform declared that the Republican party was

pledged never to admit another slave State into the Union, and also that it pledged to prohibit slavery in all the Territories of the United States, not only all that we then had, but all that we should thereafter acquire, and to repeal unconditionally the Fugitive Slave law, abolish slavery in the District of Columbia, and prohibit the slave-trade between the different States. These and other articles against slavery were contained in this platform, and unanimously adopted by the Republican Congressional Convention in that District. I had also seen that the Republican Congressional Conventions at Rockford, in the First District, and at Bloomington, in the Third, had adopted the same platform that year, nearly word for word, and had declared it to be the platform of the Republican party. I had noticed that Major Thomas L. Harris, a member of Congress from the Springfield District, had referred to that platform in a speech in Congress as having been adopted by the first Republican State Convention which assembled in Illinois. When I had occasion to use the fact in this canvass, I wrote to Major Harris to know on what day that Convention was held, and to ask him to send me its proceedings. He being sick, Charles H. Lanphier answered my letter by sending me the published proceedings of the Convention held at Springfield on the 5th of October, 1854, as they appeared in the report of the *State Register*. I read those resolutions from that newspaper the same as any of you would refer back and quote any fact from the files of a newspaper which had published it. Mr. Lincoln pretends that after I had so quoted those resolutions he discovered that they had never been adopted at Springfield. He does not deny their adoption by the Republican party at Aurora, at Bloomington, and at Rockford, and by nearly all the Republican County Conventions in Northern Illinois where his party is in a majority, but merely because they were not adopted on the "*spot*" on which I said they were, he chooses to quibble about the place rather than meet and discuss the merits of the resolutions themselves. I stated when I quoted them that I did so from the *State Register*. I gave my authority. Lincoln believed at the time, as he has since admitted, that they had been adopted at Springfield, as published. Does he believe now, that I did not tell the truth when I quoted those resolutions? He knows, in his heart, that I quoted them in good faith, believing, at the time, that they had been adopted at Springfield. I would consider myself an infamous wretch, if, under such circumstances, I could charge any man with being a party to a trick or a fraud. And I will tell him, too, that it will not do to charge a forgery on Charles H. Lanphier or Thomas L. Harris. No man on earth, who knows them, and knows Lincoln, would take his oath against their word. There are not two men in the State of Illinois who have higher characters for truth, for integrity, for moral character, and for elevation of tone, as gentlemen, than Mr. Lanphier and Mr. Harris. Any man who attempts to make such charges as Mr. Lincoln has indulged in against them, only proclaims himself a slanderer.

I will now show you that I stated with entire fairness, as soon as it was made known to me, that there was a mistake about the spot where the resolutions had been adopted, although their truthfulness, as a declaration of the principles of the Republican party, had not and could not be questioned. I did not wait for Lincoln to point out the mistake; but the moment I discovered it, I made a speech, and published it to the world, correcting the error. I corrected it myself, as a gentleman, and an honest man, and as I always feel proud to do when I have made a mistake. I wish Mr. Lincoln could show that he has acted with equal fairness, and truthfulness, when I have convinced him that he has been mistaken. I will give you an illustration to show you how he acts in a similar case: In a speech at Springfield, he charged Chief Justice Taney, and his associates, President Pierce, President Buchanan, and myself, with having entered into a conspiracy at the time the Nebraska bill was introduced, by which the Dred Scott decision was to be made by the Supreme Court, in order to carry slavery every where under the Constitution. I called his attention to the fact, that at the time alluded to, to wit: the introduction of the Nebraska bill, it was not possible that such a conspiracy could have been entered into, for the reason that the Dred Scott case had never been taken before the Supreme Court, and was not taken before it for a year after; and I asked him to take back that charge. Did he do it? I showed him that it was impossible that the charge could be true; I proved it by the record, and I then called upon him to retract his false charge. What was his answer? Instead of coming out like an honest man and doing so, he reiterated the charge, and said that if the case had not gone up to the Supreme Court from the courts of Missouri at the time he charged that the Judges of the Supreme Court entered into the conspiracy, yet, that there was an understanding with the Democratic owners of Dred Scott that they would take it up. I have since asked him who the Democratic owners of Dred Scott were, but he could not tell, and why? Because there were no such Democratic owners in existence. Dred Scott at the time was owned by the Rev. Dr. Chaffee, an Abolition member of Congress, of Springfield, Massachusetts, in right of his wife. He was owned by one of Lincoln's friends, and not by Democrats at all; his case was conducted in court by Abolition lawyers, so that both the prosecution and the defense were in the hands of the Abolition political friends of Mr. Lincoln. Notwithstanding I thus proved by the record that his charge against the Supreme Court was false, instead of taking it back, he resorted to another false charge to sustain the infamy of it. He also charged President Buchanan with having been a party to the conspiracy. I directed his attention to the fact that the charge could not possibly be true, for the reason that at the time specified, Mr. Buchanan was not in America, but was three thousand miles off, representing the United States at the Court of St. James, and had been there for a year previous, and did not return until three years afterward. Yet, I never could get Mr. Lincoln to take back his false charge, although I have called upon him over and over again. He refuses to do it, and either remains silent, or resorts to other tricks to try and palm his slander off on the country. Therein you will find the difference between Mr. Lincoln and myself. When I make a mistake, as an honest man, I correct it without being asked to do so, but when he makes a false charge he sticks to it, and never corrects it. One word more in regard to these resolutions: I quoted them at Ottawa merely to ask Mr. Lincoln whether he stood on that platform. That was the purpose for which I quoted them. I did not think that I had a right to put idle questions to him, and I first laid a foundation for my questions by showing that the principles which I wished him either to affirm or deny had been adopted by some portion of his friends, at least as their creed. Hence I read the resolutions, and put the questions to him, and he then refused to answer them. Subsequently, one week afterward, he did answer a part of them, but the others he has not answered up to this day.

Now, let me call your attention for a moment to the answers which Mr. Lincoln made at Freeport to the questions which I propounded him at Ottawa, based upon the platform adopted by a majority of the Abolition counties of the State, which now as then supported him. In answer to my question whether he indorsed the Black Republican principle of "no more slave States," he answered that he was not pledged against the admission of any more slave States, but that he would be very sorry if he should ever be placed in a position where he would have to vote on the question; that he would rejoice to know that no more slave States would be admitted into the Union; "but," he added, "if slavery shall be kept out of the Territories during the territorial existence of any one given Territory, and then the people shall, having a fair chance and a clear field when they come to adopt the Constitution, do such an extraordinary thing as to adopt a slave Constitution, uninfluenced by the actual presence of the institution among them, I see no alternative, if we own the country, but to admit them into the Union." The point I wish him to answer is this: Suppose Congress should not prohibit slavery in the Territory, and it applied for admission with a Constitution recognizing slavery, then how would he vote?

His answer at Freeport does not apply to any territory in America. I ask you [turning to Lincoln], will you vote to admit Kansas into the Union, with just such a Constitution as her people want, with slavery or without, as they shall determine? He will not answer. I have put that question to him time and time again, and have not been able to get an answer out of him. I ask you again, Lincoln, will you vote to admit New Mexico when she has the requisite population with such a Constitution as her people adopt, either recognizing slavery or not, as they shall determine? He will not answer. I put the same question to him in reference to Oregon and the new States to be carved out of Texas, in pursuance of the contract between Texas and the United States, and he will not answer. He will not answer these questions in reference to any territory now in existence; but says, that if Congress should prohibit slavery in a Territory, and when its people asked for admission as a State, they should adopt slavery as one of their institutions, that he supposes he would have to let it come in. I submit to you whether that answer of his to my question does not justify me in saying that he has a fertile genius in devising language to conceal his thoughts. I ask you whether there is an intelligent man in America who does not believe, that that answer was made for the purpose of concealing what he intended to do. He wished to make the old line Whigs believe that he would stand by the Compromise measures of 1850, which declared that the States might come into the Union with slavery, or without, as they pleased, while Lovejoy and his Abolition allies up North, explained to the Abolitionists, that in taking this ground he preached good Abolition doctrine, because his proviso would not apply to any territory in America, and therefore there was no chance of his being governed by it. It would have been quite easy for him to have said, that he would let the people of a State do just as they pleased, if he desired to convey such an idea. Why did he not do it? He would not answer my question directly, because up north, the Abolition creed declares that there shall be no more slave States, while down south, in Adams county, in Coles, and in Sangamon, he and his friends are afraid to advance that doctrine. Therefore, he gives an evasive and equivocal answer, to be construed one way in the south and another way in the north, which, when analyzed, it is apparent is not an answer at all with reference to any territory now in existence.

Mr. Lincoln complains that, in my speech the other day at Galesburgh, I read an extract from a speech delivered by him at Chicago, and then another from his speech at Charleston, and compared them, thus showing the people that he had one set of principles in one part of the State and another in the other part. And how does he answer that charge? Why, he quotes from his Charleston speech as I quoted from it, and then quotes another extract from a speech which he made at another place, which he says is the same as the extract from his speech at Charleston; but he does not quote the extract from his Chicago speech, upon which I convicted him of double-dealing. I quoted from his Chicago speech to prove that he held one set of principles up north among the Abolitionists, and from his Charleston speech to prove that he held another set down at Charleston and in southern Illinois. In his answer to this charge, he ignores entirely his Chicago speech, and merely argues that he said the same thing which he said at Charleston at another place. If he did, it follows that he has twice, instead of once, held one creed in one part of the State and a different creed in another part. Up at Chicago, in the opening of the campaign, he reviewed my reception speech, and undertook to answer my argument attacking his favorite doctrine of negro equality. I had shown that it was a falsification of the Declaration of Independence to pretend that that instrument applied to and included negroes in the clause declaring that all men were created equal. What was Lincoln's reply? I will read from his Chicago speech and the one which he did not quote, and dare not quote, in this part of the State. He said:

> "I should like to know, if taking this old Declaration of Independence, which declares that all men are equal upon principle, and making exceptions to it, where will it stop? If one man says it does not mean a negro, why may not another man say it does not mean another man? If that declaration is not the truth, let us get this statute book in which we find it and tear it out."

There you find that Mr. Lincoln told the Abolitionists of Chicago that if the Declaration of Independence did not declare that the negro was created by the Almighty the equal of the white man, that you ought to take that instrument and tear out the clause which says that all men were created equal. But let me call your attention to another part of the same speech. You know that in his Charleston speech, an extract from which he has read, he declared that the negro belongs to an inferior race; is physically inferior to the white man, and should always be kept in an inferior position. I will now read to you what he said at Chicago on that point. In concluding his speech at that place, he remarked:

> "My friends, I have detained you about as long as I desire to do, and I have only to say let us discard all this quibbling about this man and the

other man—this race and that race, and the other race being inferior, and therefore they must be placed in an inferior position, discarding our standard that we have left us. Let us discard all these things, and unite as one people throughout this land until we shall once more stand up declaring that all men are created equal."

Thus you see, that when addressing the Chicago Abolitionists he declared that all distinctions of race must be discarded and blotted out, because the negro stood on an equal footing with the white man; that if one man said the Declaration of Independence did not mean a negro when it declared all men created equal, that another man would say that it did not mean another man; and hence we ought to discard all difference between the negro race and all other races, and declare them all created equal. Did old Giddings, when he came down among you four years ago, preach more radical Abolitionism than this? Did Lovejoy, or Lloyd Garrison, or Wendell Phillips, or Fred Douglass, ever take higher Abolition grounds than that? Lincoln told you that I had charged him with getting up these personal attacks to conceal the enormity of his principles, and then commenced talking about something else, omitting to quote this part of his Chicago speech which contained the enormity of his principles to which I alluded. He knew that I alluded to his negro-equality doctrines when I spoke of the enormity of his principles, yet he did not find it convenient to answer on that point. Having shown you what he said in his Chicago speech in reference to negroes being created equal to white men, and about discarding all distinctions between the two races, I will again read to you what he said at Charleston:

"I will say then, that I am not nor ever have been in favor of bringing about in any way, the social and political equality of the white and black races; that I am not nor ever have been in favor of making voters of the the free negroes, or jurors, or qualifying them to hold office, or having them to marry with white people. I will say in addition, that there is a physical difference between the white and black races, which, I suppose, will forever forbid the two races living together upon terms of social and political equality, and inasmuch as they cannot so live, that while they do remain together, there must be the position of superior and inferior, that I as much as any other man am in favor of the superior position being assigned to the white man."

A voice—"That's the doctrine."

Mr. Douglas—Yes, sir, that is good doctrine, but Mr. Lincoln is afraid to advocate it in the latitude of Chicago, where he hopes to get his votes. It is good doctrine in the anti-Abolition counties for him, and his Chicago speech is good doctrine in the Abolition counties. I assert, on the authority of these two speeches of Mr. Lincoln, that he holds one set of principles in the Abolition counties, and a different and contradictory set in the other counties. I do not question that he said at Ottawa what he quoted, but that only convicts him further, by proving that he has twice contradicted himself instead of once. Let me ask him why he cannot avow his principles the same in the North as in the South—the same in every county, if he has a conviction that they are just? But I forgot—he would not be a Republican, if his principles would apply alike to every part of the country. The party to which he belongs is bounded and limited by geographical lines. With their principles they cannot even cross the Mississippi river on your ferry-boats. They cannot cross over the Ohio into Kentucky. Lincoln himself cannot visit the land of his fathers, the scenes of his childhood, the graves of his ancestors, and carry his Abolition principles, as he declared them at Chicago, with him.

This Republican organization appeals to the North against the South; it appeals to northern passion, northern prejudice, and northern ambition, against southern people, southern States, and southern institutions, and its only hope of success is by that appeal. Mr. Lincoln goes on to justify himself in making a war upon slavery, upon the ground that Frank Blair and Gratz Brown did not succeed in their warfare upon the institutions in Missouri. Frank Blair was elected to Congress in 1856, from the State of Missouri, as a Buchanan Democrat, and he turned Freemonter after the people elected him, thus belonging to one party before his election, and another afterward. What right then had he to expect, after having thus cheated his constituency, that they would support him at another election? Mr. Lincoln thinks that it is his duty to preach a crusade in the free States against slavery, because it is a crime, as he believes, and ought to be extinguished; and because the people of the slave States will never abolish it. How is he going to abolish it? Down in the southern part of the State he takes the ground openly that he will not interfere with slavery where it exists, and says that he is not now and never was in favor of interfering with slavery where it exists in the States. Well, if he is not in favor of that, how does he expect to bring slavery in a course of ultimate extinction? How can he extinguish it in Kentucky, in Virginia, in all the slave States by his policy, if he will not pursue a policy which will interfere with it in the States where it exists? In his speech at Springfield before the Abolition or Republican Convention, he declared his hostility to any more slave States in this language:

"Under the operation of that policy the agitation has not only not ceased, but has constantly augmented. In my opinion it will not cease until a crisis shall have been reached and passed. 'A house divided against itself cannot stand.' I believe this Government cannot endure permanently half slave and half free. I do not expect the Union to be dissolved—I do not expect the house to fall—but I do expect it will cease to be divided. It will become all one thing or all the other. Either the opponents of slavery will arrest the further spread of it, and place it where the public mind shall rest in the belief that it is in the course of ultimate extinction; or, its advocates will push it forward until it shall become alike lawful in all the States—old as well as new, north as well as south."

Mr. Lincoln there told his Abolition friends that this Government could not endure permanently, divided into free and slave States as our fathers made it, and that it must become all free or all slave, otherwise, that the Government could not exist. How then does Lincoln propose to save the Union, unless by compelling all the States to become free, so that the house shall not be divided against itself? He intends making them all free; he will preserve the Union in that way, and yet, he is not going to interfere with slavery any where it now exists. How is he going to bring it about? Why, he will agitate, he will induce the North to agitate until the South shall be worried out, and forced to abolish slavery. Let us examine the policy by which that is to be done. He first tells you that he would prohibit slavery every where in the Territories. He would thus confine slavery within its present limits. When he thus gets it confined, and surrounded, so that it cannot spread, the natural laws of increase will go on until the negroes will be so plenty that they cannot live on the soil. He will hem them in until starvation seizes them, and by starving them to death, he will put slavery in the course of ultimate extinction. If he is not going to interfere with slavery in the States, but intends to interfere and prohibit it in the Territories, and thus smother slavery out, it naturally follows, that he can extinguish it only by extinguishing the negro race, for his policy would drive them to starvation. This is the humane and Christian remedy that he proposes for the great crime of slavery.

He tells you that I will not argue the question whether slavery is right or wrong. I tell you why I will not do it. I hold that under the Constitution of the United States, each State of this Union has a right to do as it pleases on the subject of slavery. In Illinois we have exercised that sovereign right by prohibiting slavery within our own limits. I approve of that line of policy. We have performed our whole duty in Illinois. We have gone as far as we have a right to go under the Constitution of our common country. It is none of our business whether slavery exists in Missouri or not. Missouri is a sovereign State of this Union, and has the same right to decide the slavery question for herself that Illinois has to decide it for herself. Hence I do not choose to occupy the time allotted to me in discussing a question that we have no right to act upon. I thought that you desired to hear us upon those questions coming within our Constitutional power or action. Lincoln will not discuss these. What one question has he discussed that comes within the power or calls for the action or interference of an United States Senator? He is going to discuss the rightfulness of slavery when Congress cannot act upon it either way. He wishes to discuss the merits of the Dred Scott decision when, under the Constitution, a Senator has no right to interfere with the decision of judicial tribunals. He wants your exclusive attention to two questions that he has no power to act upon; to two questions that he could not vote upon if he was in Congress, to two questions that are not practical, in order to conceal your attention from other questions which he might be required to vote upon should he ever become a member of Congress. He tells you that he does not like the Dred Scott decision. Suppose he does not, how is he going to help himself? He says that he will reverse it. How will he reverse it? I know of but one mode of reversing judicial decisions, and that is by appealing from the inferior to the superior court. But I have never yet learned how or where an appeal could be taken from the Supreme Court of the United States! The Dred Scott decision was pronounced by the highest tribunal on earth. From that decision there is no appeal this side of Heaven. Yet, Mr. Lincoln says he is going to reverse that decision. By what tribunal will he reverse it? Will he appeal to a mob? Does he intend to appeal to violence, to Lynch law? Will he stir up strife and rebellion in the land and overthrow the court by violence? He does not deign to tell you how he will reverse the Dred Scott decision, but keeps appealing each day from the Supreme Court of the United States to political meetings in the country. He wants me to argue with you the merits of each point of that decision before this political meeting. I say to you, with all due respect, that I choose to abide by the decisions of the Supreme Court as they are pronounced. It is not for me to inquire after a decision is made whether I like it in all the points or not. When I used to practice law with Lincoln, I never knew him to be beat in a case that he did not get mad at the judge and talk about appealing; and when I got beat I generally thought the court was wrong, but I never dreamed of going out of the court-house and making a stump speech to the people against the judge, merely because I had found out that I did not know the law as well as he did. If the decision did not suit me, I appealed until I got to the Supreme Court, and then if that court, the highest tribunal in the world, decided against me, I was satisfied, because it is the duty of every law-abiding man to obey the constitutions, the laws, and the constituted authorities. He who attempts to stir up odium and rebellion in the country against the constituted authorities, is stimulating the passions of men to resort to violence and to mobs instead of to the law. Hence, I tell you that I take the decisions of the Supreme Court as the law of the land, and I intend to obey them as such.

But Mr. Lincoln says that I will not answer his question as to what I would do in the event of the court making so ridiculous a decision as he imagines they would by deciding that the free State of Illinois could not prohibit slavery within her own limits. I told him at Freeport why I would not answer such a question. I told him that there was not a man possessing any brains in America, lawyer or not, who ever dreamed that such a thing could be done. I told him then, as I do now, that by all the principles set forth in the Dred Scott decision, it is impossible. I told him then, as I do now, that it is an insult to men's understanding, and a gross calumny on the court, to presume in advance that it was going to degrade itself so low as to make a decision known to be in direct violation of the Constitution.

A voice—"The same thing was said about the Dred Scott decision before it passed."

Mr. Douglas—Perhaps you think that the court did the same thing in reference to the Dred Scott decision: I have heard a man talk that way before. The principles contained in the Dred Scott decision had been affirmed previously in various other decisions. What court or judge ever held that a negro was a citizen? The State courts had decided that question over and over again, and the Dred Scott decision on that point only affirmed what every court in the land knew to be the law.

But, I will not be drawn off into an argument upon the merits of the Dred Scott decision. It is enough for me to know that the Constitution of the United States created the Supreme Court for the purpose of deciding all disputed questions touching the true construction of that instrument, and when such decisions are pronounced, they are the law of the land, binding on every good citizen. Mr. Lincoln has a very convenient mode of arguing upon the subject. He holds that because he is a Republican that he is not bound by the decisions of the court, but that I being a Democrat am so bound. It may be that Republicans do not hold themselves bound by the laws of the land and the Constitution of the country as expounded by the courts; it may be an article in the Republican creed that men who do not like a decision, have a right to rebel against it; but when Mr. Lincoln preaches that doctrine, I think he will find some honest Republican—some law-abiding men in that party—who will repudiate such a monstrous doctrine. The decision in the Dred Scott case is binding on every American citizen alike; and yet Mr. Lincoln argues that the Republicans are not bound by it, because they are opposed to it, whilst Democrats are bound by it, because we will not resist it. A Democrat cannot resist the constituted authorities of this country. A Democrat is a law-abiding man, a Democrat stands by the Constitution and the laws, and relies upon liberty as protected by law, and not upon mob or political violence.

I have never yet been able to make Mr. Lincoln understand, or can I make any man who is determined to support him, right or wrong, understand how it is that under the Dred Scott decision the people of a Territory, as well as a State, can have slavery or not, just as they please. I believe that I can explain that proposition to all Constitution-loving, law-abiding men in a way that they cannot fail to understand it. Chief Justice Taney, in his opinion in the Dred Scott case, said that slaves being property, the owner of them has a right to take them into a Territory the same as he would any other property; in other words, that slave property, so far as the right to enter a Territory is concerned, stands on the same footing with other property. Suppose we grant that proposition. Then any man has a right to go to Kansas and take his property with him, but when he gets there he must rely upon the local law to protect his property, whatever it may be. In order to illustrate this, imagine that three of you conclude to go to Kansas. One takes $10,000 worth of slaves, another $10,000 worth of liquors, and the third $10,000 worth of dry goods. When the man who owns the dry goods arrives out there and commences selling them, he finds that he is stopped and prohibited from selling until he gets a license, which will destroy all the profits he can make on his goods to pay for. When the man with the liquors gets there and tries to sell he finds a Maine liquor law in force which prevents him. Now, of what use is his right to go there with his property unless he is protected in the enjoyment of that right after he gets there? The man who goes there with his slaves finds that there is no law to protect him when he arrives there. He has no remedy if his slaves run away to another country: there is no slave code or police regulations; and the absence of them excludes his slaves from the Territory just as effectually and as positively as a Constitutional prohibition could.

Such was the understanding when the Kansas and Nebraska bill was pending in Congress. Read the speech of Speaker Orr, of South Carolina, in the House of Representatives, in 1856, on the Kansas question, and you will find that he takes the ground that while the owner of a slave has a right to go into a Territory, and carry his slaves with him, that he cannot hold them one day or hour unless there is a slave code to protect him. He tells you that slavery would not exist a day in South Carolina, or any other State, unless there was a friendly people and friendly legislation. Read the speeches of that giant in intellect, Alexander H. Stephens, of Georgia, and you will find them to the same effect. Read the speeches of Sam Smith, of Tennessee, and of all Southern men, and you will find that they all understood this doctrine then as we understand it now. Mr. Lincoln cannot be made to understand it, however. Down at Jonesboro, he went on to argue that if it be the law that a man has a right to take his slaves into territory of the United States under the Constitution, that then a member of Congress was perjured if he did not vote for a slave code. I ask him whether the decision of the Supreme Court is not binding upon him as well as on me? If so, and he holds that he would be perjured if he did not vote for a slave code under it, I ask him whether, if elected to Congress, he will so vote? I have a right to his answer, and I will tell you why. He put that question to me down in Egypt, and did it with an air of triumph. This was about the form of it: "In the event of a slaveholding citizen of one of the Territories should need and demand a slave code to protect his slaves, will you vote for it?" I answered him that a fundamental article in the Democratic creed, as put forth in the Nebraska bill and the Cincinnati platform, was non-intervention by Congress with slavery in the States and Territories, and hence, that I would not vote in Congress for any code of laws, either for or against slavery in any Territory. I will leave the people perfectly free to decide that question for themselves.

Mr. Lincoln and the Washington *Union* both think this a monstrous bad doctrine. Neither Mr. Lincoln nor the Washington *Union* like my Freeport speech on that subject. The *Union,* in a late number, has been reading me out of the Democratic party because I hold that the people of a Territory, like those of a State, have the right to have slavery or not, as they please. It has devoted three and a half columns to prove certain propositions, one of which I will read. It says:

"We propose to show that Judge Douglas's action in 1850 and 1854 was taken with especial reference to the announcement of doctrine and programme which was made at Freeport. The declaration at Freeport was, that 'in his opinion the people can, by lawful means, exclude slavery from a Territory before it comes in as a State;' and he declared that his competitor had 'heard him argue the Nebraska bill on that principle all over Illinois in 1854, 1855 and 1856, and had no excuse to pretend to have any doubt upon that subject.'"

The Washington *Union* there charges me with the monstrous crime of now proclaiming on the stump, the same doctrine that I carried out in 1850, by supporting Clay's Compromise measures. The *Union* also charges that I am now proclaiming the same doctrine that I did in 1854 in support of the Kansas and Nebraska bill. It is shocked that I should now stand where I stood in 1850, when I was supported by Clay, Webster, Cass, and the great men of that day, and where I stood in 1854, and in 1856, when Mr. Buchanan was elected President. It goes on to prove and succeeds in proving, from my speeches in Congress on Clay's Compromise measures, that I held the same doctrines at that time that I do now, and then proves that by the Kansas and Nebraska bill I advanced the same doctrine that I now advance. It remarks:

"So much for the course taken by Judge Douglas on the Compromises of 1850. The record shows, beyond the possibility of cavil or dispute, that he expressly intended in those bills to give the Territorial Legislatures power to exclude slavery. How stands his record in the memorable session of 1854, with reference to the Kansas–Nebraska bill itself? We shall not overhaul the votes that were given on that notable measure. Our space will not afford it. We have his own words, however, delivered in his speech closing the great debate on that bill on the night of March 3, 1854, to show that *he meant* to do in 1854 precisely what *he had meant* to do in 1858. The Kansas-Nebraska bill being upon its passage, he said:"

It then quotes my remarks upon the passage of the bill as follows:

"The principle which we propose to carry into effect by this bill is this: That Congress shall neither legislate slavery into any Territory or State nor out of the same; but the people shall be left free to regulate their domestic concerns in their own way, subject only to the Constitution of the United States. In order to carry this principle into practical operation, it becomes necessary to remove whatever legal obstacles might be found in the way of its free exercise. It is only for the purpose of carrying out this great fundamental principle of self-government that the bill renders the eighth section of the Missouri act inoperative and void.

"Now, let me ask, will those Senators who have arraigned me, or any one of them, have the assurance to rise in his place and declare that this great principle was never thought of or advocated as applicable to territorial bills, in 1850; that, from that session until the present, nobody ever thought of incorporating this principle in all new territorial organizations, etc., etc. I will begin with the Compromises of 1850. Any Senator who will take the trouble to examine our journals will find that on the 25th of March of that year I reported from the Committee on Territories two bills, including the following measures: the admission of California, a territorial government for Utah, a territorial government for New Mexico, and the adjustment of the Texas boundary. These bills proposed to leave the people of Utah and New Mexico free to decide the slavery question for themselves, *in the precise language of the Nebraska bill* now under discussion. A few weeks afterward the committee of thirteen took those bills and put a wafer between them and reported them back to the Senate as one bill, with some slight amendments. *One of these amendments was, that the Territorial Legislatures should not legislate upon the subject of African slavery. I objected to this provision,* upon the ground that it subverted the great principle of self-government, *upon which the bill had been originally framed by the Territorial Committee.* On the first trial the Senate refused to strike it out, but subsequently did so, upon full debate, in order to establish that principle as the rule of action in territorial organizations."

The *Union* comments thus upon my speech on that occesion.

"Thus it is seen that, in framing the Nebraska-Kansas bill, Judge Douglas framed it in the terms and upon the model of those of Utah and New Mexico, and that in the debate he took pains expressly to revive the recollection of the voting which had taken place upon amendments affecting the powers of the Territorial Legislatures over the subject of slavery in the bills of 1850, in order to give the same meaning, force, and effect to the Nebraska-Kansas bill on this subject as had been given to those of Utah and New Mexico."

The *Union* proves the following propositions: First, that I sustained Clay's Compromise measures on the ground that they established the principle of self-government in the Territories. Secondly, that I brought in the Kansas and Nebraska bill founded upon the same principles as Clay's Compromise measures of 1850; and thirdly, that my Freeport speech is in exact accordance with those principles. And what do you think is the imputation that the *Union* casts upon me for all this? It says that my Freeport speech is not Democratic, and that I was not a Democrat in 1854 or in 1850! Now is not that funny? Think that the author of the Kansas and Nebraska bill was not a Democrat when he introduced it. The *Union* says I was not a sound Democrat in 1850, nor in 1854, nor in 1856, nor am I in 1858, because I have always taken and now occupy the ground that the people of a Territory, like those of a State, have the right to decide for themselves whether slavery shall or shall not exist in a Territory. I wish to cite for the benefit of the Washington *Union* and the followers of that sheet, one authority on that point, and I hope the authority will be deemed satisfactory to that class of politicians. I will read from Mr. Buchanan's letter accepting the nomination of the Democratic Convention, for the Presidency. You know that Mr. Buchanan, after he was nominated, declared to the Keystone Club, in a public speech, that he was no longer James Buchanan, but the embodiment of the Democratic platform. In his letter to the committee which informed him of his nomination accepting it, he defined the meaning of the Kansas and Nebraska bill and the Cincinnati platform in these words:

> "The recent legislation of Congress respecting domestic slavery, derived as it has been from the original and pure fountain of legitimate political power, the will of the majority, promises ere long to allay the dangerous excitement. This legislation is founded upon principles as ancient as free government itself, and in accordance with them has simply declared that the people of a Territory, like those of a State, shall decide for themselves whether slavery shall or shall not exist within their limits."

Thus you see that James Buchanan accepted the nomination at Cincinnati, on the conditions that the people of a Territory, like those of a State, should be left to decide for themselves whether slavery should or should not exist within their limits. I sustained James Buchanan for the Presidency on that platform as adopted at Cincinnati, and expounded by himself. He was elected President on that platform, and now we are told by the Washington *Union* that no man is a true Democrat who stands on the platform on which Mr. Buchanan was nominated, and which he has explained and expounded himself. We are told that a man is not a Democrat who stands by Clay, Webster, and Cass, and the Compromise measures of 1850, and the Kansas and Nebraska bill of 1854. Whether a man be a Democrat or not on that platform, I intend to stand there as long as I have life. I intend to cling firmly to that great principle which declares that the right of each State and each Territory to settle the question of slavery, and every other domestic question, for themselves. I hold that if they want a slave State, they have a right under the Constitution of the United States to make it so, and if they want a free State, it is their right to have it. But the *Union,* in advocating the claims of Lincoln over me to the Senate, lays down two unpardonable heresies which it says I advocate. The first, is the right of the people of a Territory, the same as a State, to decide for themselves the question whether slavery shall exist within their limits, in the language of Mr. Buchanan; and the second is, that a Constitution shall be submitted to the people of a Territory for its adoption or rejection before their admission as a State under it. It so happens that Mr. Buchanan is pledged to both these heresies, for supporting which the Washington *Union* has read me out of the Democratic church. In his annual message he said he trusted that the example of the Minnesota case would be followed in all future cases, requiring a submission of the Constitution; and in his letter of acceptance, he said that the people of a Territory, the same as a State, had the right to decide for themselves whether slavery should exist within their limits. Thus you find that this little corrupt gang who control the *Union,* and wish to elect Lincoln in preference to me—because, as they say, of these two heresies which I support—denounce President Buchanan when they denounce me, if he stands now by the principles upon which he was elected. Will they pretend that he does not now stand by the principles on which he was elected? Do they hold that he has abandoned the Kansas-Nebraska bill, the Cincinnati platform, and his own letter accepting his nomination, all of which declare the right of the people of a Territory, the same as a State, to decide the slavery question for themselves? I will not believe that he has betrayed or intends to betray the platform which elected him; but if he does, I will not follow him. I will stand by that great principle, no matter who may desert it. I intend to stand by it for the purpose of preserving peace between the North and the South, the free and the slave States. If each State will only agree to mind its own business, and let its neighbors alone, there will be peace forever between us. We in Illinois tried slavery when a Territory, and found it was not good for us in this climate, and with our surroundings, and hence we abolished it. We then adopted a free State Constitution, as we had a right to do. In this State we have declared that a negro shall not be a citizen, and we have also declared that he shall not be a slave. We had a right to adopt that policy. Missouri has just as good a right to adopt the other policy. I am now speaking of rights under the Constitution, and not of moral or religious rights. I do not discuss the morals of the people of Missouri, but let them settle that matter for themselves. I hold that the people of the slave-holding States are civilized men as well as ourselves; that they bear consciences as well as we, and that they are accountable to God and their posterity, and not to us. It is for them to decide, therefore, the moral and religious right of the slavery question for themselves within their own limits. I assert that they had as much right under the Constitution to adopt the system of policy which they have as we had to adopt ours. So it is with every other State in this Union. Let each State stand firmly by that great Constitutional right, let each State mind its own business and let its neighbors alone, and there will be no trouble on this question. If we will stand by that principle, then Mr. Lincoln will find that this Republic can exist forever divided into free and slave States, as our fathers made it and the people of each State have decided. Stand by that great principle, and we can go on as we have done, increasing in wealth, in population, in power, and in all the elements of greatness, until we shall be the admiration and and terror of the world. We can go on and enlarge as our population increase, require more room, until we make this continent one ocean-bound republic. Under that principle the United States can perform that great mission, that destiny, which Providence has marked out for us. Under that principle we can receive with entire safety that stream of intelligence which is constantly flowing from the Old World to the New, filling up our prairies, clearing our wildernesses and building cities, towns, railroads and other internal improvements, and thus make this the asylum of the oppressed of the whole earth. We have this great mission to perform, and it can only be performed by adhering faithfully to that principle of self-government on which our institutions were all established. I repeat that the principle is the right of each State, each Territory, to decide this slavery question for itself, to have slavery or not, as it chooses, and it does not become Mr. Lincoln, or anybody else, to tell the people of Kentucky that they have no consciences, that they are living in a state of iniquity, and that they are cherishing an institution to their bosoms in violation of the law of God. Better for him to adopt the doctrine of "judge not lest ye shall be judged." Let him perform his own duty at home, and he will have a better fate in the future. I think there are objects of charity enough in the free States to excite the sympathies and open the pockets of all the benevolence we have amongst us, without going abroad in search of negroes, of whose condition we know nothing. We have enough objects of charity at home, and it is our duty to take care of our own poor, and our own suffering, before we go abroad to intermeddle with other people's business.

My friends, I am told that my time is within two minutes of expiring. I have omitted many topics that I would liked to have discussed before you at length. There were many points touched by Mr. Lincoln that I have not been able to take up for the want of time. I have hurried over each subject that I have discussed as rapidly as possible, so as to omit but few, but one hour and a half is not time sufficient for a man to discuss at length one half of the great questions which are now dividing the public mind.

In conclusion, I desire to return to you my grateful acknowledgments for the kindness and the courtesy with which you have listened to me. It is something remarkable that in an audience as vast as this, composed of men of opposite politics and views, with their passions highly excited, there should be so much courtesy, kindness and respect exhibited not only toward one another, but toward the speakers, and I feel that it is due to you that I should thus express my gratitude for the kindness with which you have treated me.

MR. LINCOLN'S REJOINDER.

MY FRIENDS: Since Judge Douglas has said to you in his conclusion that he had not time in an hour and a half to answer all I had said in an hour, it follows of course that I will not be able to answer in half an hour all that he said in an hour and a half.

I wish to return to Judge Douglas my profound thanks for his public annunciation here to-day; to be put on record, that his system of policy in regard to the institution of slavery *contemplates that it shall last forever*. We are getting a little nearer the true issue of this controversy, and I am profoundly grateful for this one sentence. Judge Douglas asks you, "Why cannot the institution of slavery, or rather, why cannot the nation, part slave and part free, continue as our fathers made it *forever*?" In the first place, I insist that our fathers *did not* make this nation half slave and half free, or part slave and part free. I insist that they found the institution of slavery existing here. They did not make it so, but they left it so because they knew of no way to get rid of it at that time. When Judge Douglas undertakes to say that, as a matter of choice, the fathers of the Government made this nation part slave and part free, *he assumes what is historically a falsehood.* More than that: when the fathers of the Government cut off the source of slavery by the abolition of the slave-trade, and adopted a system of restricting it from the new Territories where it had not existed, I maintain that they placed it where they understood, and all sensible men understood, it was in the course of ultimate extinction; and when Judge Douglas asks me why it cannot continue as our fathers made it, I ask him why he and his friends could not let it remain as our fathers made it?

It is precisely all I ask of him in relation to the institution of slavery, that it shall be placed upon the basis that our fathers placed it upon. Mr. Brooks, of South Carolina, once said, and truly said, that when this Government was established, no one expected the institution of slavery to last until this day; and that the men who formed this Government were wiser and better than the men of these days; but the men of these days had experience which the fathers had not, and that experience had taught them the invention of the cotton-gin, and this had made the perpetuation of the institution of slavery a necessity in this country. Judge Douglas could not let it stand upon the basis which our fathers placed it, but removed it, and *put it upon the cotton-gin basis*. It is a question, therefore, for him and his friends to answer—why they could not let it remain where the fathers of the Government originally placed it.

I hope nobody has understood me as trying to sustain the doctrine that we have a right to quarrel with Kentucky, or Virginia, or any of the slave States, about the institution of slavery—thus giving the Judge an opportunity to make himself eloquent and valiant against us in fighting for their rights. I expressly declared in my opening speech, that I had neither the inclination to exercise, nor the belief in the existence of the right to interfere with the States of Kentucky or Virginia in doing as they pleased with slavery or any other existing institution. Then what becomes of all his eloquence in behalf of the rights of States, which are assailed by no living man?

But I have to hurry on, for I have but a half hour. The Judge has informed me, or informed this audience, that the Washington *Union* is laboring for my election to the United States Senate. This is news to me—not very ungrateful news either. [Turning to Mr. W. H. Carlin, who was on the stand]—I hope that Carlin will be elected to the State Senate and will vote for me. [Mr. Carlin shook his head.] Carlin don't fall in, I perceive, and I suppose he will not do much for me, but I am glad of all the support I can get any where, if I can get it without practicing any deception to obtain it. In respect to this large portion of Judge Douglas's speech, in which he tries to show that in the controversy between himself and the Administration party, he is in the right, I do not feel myself at all competent or inclined to answer him. I say to him, "Give it to them—give it to them just all you can"—and, on the other hand, I say to Carlin, and Jake Davis, and to this man Wogley up here in Hancock, "Give it to Douglas—just pour it into him."

Now, in regard to this matter of the Dred Scott decision, I wish to say a word or two. After all, the Judge will not say whether, if a decision is made, holding that the people of the *States* cannot exclude slavery, he will support it or not. He obstinately refuses to say what he will do in that case. The Judges of the Supreme Court as obstinately refused to say what they would do on this subject. Before this I reminded him that at Galesburgh he said the Judges had expressly declared the contrary, and you remember that in my opening speech I told him I had the book containing that decision here, and I would thank him to lay his finger on the place where any such thing was said. He has occupied his hour and a half, and he has not ventured to try to sustain his assertion. *He never will.* But he is desirous of knowing how we are going to reverse the Dred Scott decision. Judge Douglas ought to know how. Did not he and his political friends find a way to reverse the decision of that same court in favor the Constitutionality of the National Bank? Didn't they find a way to do it so effectually that they have reversed it as completely as any decision ever was reversed, so far as its practical operation is concerned? And let me ask you, didn't Judge Douglas find a way to reverse the decision of our Supreme Court, when it decided that Carlin's father—old Governor Carlin—had not the Constitutional power to remove a Secretary of State? Did he not appeal to the "MOBS," as he calls them? Did he not make speeches in the lobby to show how villainous that decision was, and how it ought to be overthrown? Did he not succeed, too, in getting an act passed by the Legislature to have it overthrown? And didn't he himself sit down on that bench as one of the five added judges, who were to overslaugh the four old ones—getting his name of "Judge" in that way and no other? If there is a villainy in using disrespect or making opposition to Supreme Court decisions, I commend it to Judge Douglas's earnest consideration. I know of no man in the State of Illinois who ought to know so well about *how much* villainy it takes to oppose a decision of the Supreme Court as our honorable friend, Stephen A. Douglas.

Judge Douglas also makes the declaration that I say the Democrats are bound by the Dred Scott decision, while the Republicans are not. In the sense in which he argues, I never said it; but I will tell you what I have said and what I do not hesitate to repeat to-day. I have said that, as the Democrats believe that decision to be correct, and that the extension of slavery is affirmed in the National Constitution, they are bound to support it as such; and I will tell you here that General Jackson once said each man was bound to support the Constitution "as he understood it." Now, Judge Douglas understands the Constitution according to the Dred Scott decision, and he is bound to support it as he understands it. I understand it another way, and therefore I am bound to support it in the way in which I understand it. And as Judge Douglas believes that decision to be correct, I will remake that argument if I have time to do so. Let me talk to some gentleman down there among you who looks me in the face. We will say you are a member of the Territorial Legislature, and like Judge Douglas, you believe that the right to take and hold slaves there is a Constitutional right. The first thing you do, is to *swear you will support the Constitution* and all rights guarantied therein; that you will whenever your neighbor needs your legislation to support his Constitutional rights, not withhold that legislation. If you withhold that necessary legislation for the support of the Constitution and Constitutional rights, do you not commit perjury? I ask every sensible man, if that is not so? That is undoubtedly just so, say what you please. Now, that is precisely what Judge Douglas says; that this is a Constitutional right. Does the Judge mean to say that the Territorial Legislature in legislating may, by withholding necessary laws, or by passing unfriendly laws, *nullify that Constitutional right?* Does he mean to say that? Does he mean to ignore the proposition so long and well established in law, that what you cannot do directly, you cannot do indirectly? Does he mean that? The truth about the matter is this: Judge Douglas has sung pæans to his "Popular Sovereignty" doctrine until his Supreme Court, co-operating with him, has *squatted* his Squatter Sovereignty out. But he will keep up this species of humbuggery about Squatter Sovereignty. He has at last invented this sort of *do-nothing Sovereignty*—that the people may exclude slavery by a sort of "Sovereignty" that is exercised by doing nothing at all. Is not that running his Popular Sovereignty down awfully? Has it not got down as thin as the homeopathic soup that was made by boiling the shadow of a pigeon that had starved to death? But at last, when it is brought to the test of close reasoning, there is not even that thin decoction of it left. It is a presumption impossible in the domain of thought. It is precisely no other than the putting of that most unphilosophical proposition, that two bodies can occupy the same space at the same time. The Dred Scott decision covers the whole ground, and while it occupies it, there is no room even for the shadow of a starved pigeon to occupy the same ground.

Judge Douglas, in reply to what I have said about having upon a previous occasion made the speech at Ottawa as the one he took an extract from, at Charleston, says it only shows that I practiced the deception twice. Now, my friends, are any of you obtuse enough to swallow that? Judge Douglas had said I had made a speech at Charleston that I would not make up north, and I turned around and answered him by showing I *had* made that same speech up north—

had made it at Ottawa—made it in his hearing—made it in *the* Abolition District—in Lovejoy's District—in the personal presence of Lovejoy himself—in the same atmosphere exactly in which I had made my Chicago speech, of which he complains so much.

Now, in relation to my not having said any thing about the quotation from the Chicago speech: He thinks that is a terrible subject for me to handle. Why, gentlemen, I can show you that the substance of the Chicago speech I delivered two years ago in "Egypt," as he calls it. It was down at Springfield. That speech is here in this book, and I could turn to it and read it to you but for the lack of time. I have not now the time to read it. ["Read it, read it."] No, gentlemen, I am obliged to use discretion in disposing most advantageously of my brief time. The Judge has taken great exception to my adopting the heretical statement in the Declaration of Independence, that "all men are created equal," and he has a great deal to say about negro equality. I want to say that in sometimes alluding to the Declaration of Independence, I have only uttered the sentiments that Henry Clay used to hold. Allow me to occupy your time a moment with what he said. Mr. Clay was at one time called upon in Indiana, and in a way that I suppose was very insulting, to liberate his slaves, and he made a written reply to that application, and one portion of it is in these words:

> "What is the *foundation* of this appeal to me in Indiana, to liberate the slaves under my care in Kentucky? It is a general declaration in the act announcing to the world the independence of the thirteen American colonies, that '*men are created equal.*' Now, as an abstract principle, *there is no doubt of the truth of that declaration,* and it is desirable in the *original construction* of society, and in organized societies, to keep it in view as a great fundamental principle."

When I sometimes, in relation to the organization of new societies in new countries, where the soil is clean and clear, insisted that we should keep that principle in view, Judge Douglas will have it that I want a negro wife. He never can be brought to understand that there is any middle ground on this subject. I have lived until my fiftieth year, and have never had a negro woman either for a slave or a wife, and I think I can live fifty centuries, for that matter, without having had one for either. I maintain that you may take Judge Douglas's quotations from my Chicago speech, and from my Charleston speech, and the Galesburgh speech,—in his speech of to-day, and compare them over, and I am willing to trust them with you upon his proposition that they show rascality or double-dealing. I deny that they do.

The Judge does not seem at all disposed to have peace, but I find he is disposed to have a personal warfare with me. He says that my oath would not be taken against the bare word of Charles H. Lanphier or Thomas L. Harris. Well, that is altogether a matter of opinion. It is certainly not for me to vaunt my word against oaths of these gentlemen, but I will tell Judge Douglas again the facts upon which I "*dared*" to say they proved a forgery. I pointed out at Galesburgh that the publication of these resolutions in the Illinois *State Register* could not have been the result of accident, as the proceedings of that meeting bore unmistakable evidence of being done by a man who *knew* it was a forgery; that it was a publication partly taken from the real proceedings of the Convention, and partly from the proceedings of a Convention at another place; which showed that he had the real proceedings before him, and taking one part of the resolutions, he threw out another part and substituted false and fraudulent ones in their stead. I pointed that out to him, and also that his friend Lanphier, who was editor of the *Register* at that time and now is, must have known how it was done. Now whether *he* did it or got some friend to do it for him, I could not tell, but he certainly knew all about it. I pointed out to Judge Douglas that in his Freeport speech he had promised to *investigate* that matter. Does he now say he did not make that promise? I have a right to ask *why he did not keep it?* I call upon him to tell here to-day why he did not keep that promise? That fraud has been traced up so that it lies between him, Harris and Lanphier. There is little room for escape for Lanphier. Lanphier is doing the Judge good service, and Douglas desires his word to be taken for the truth. He desires Lanphier to be taken as authority in what he states in his newspaper. He desires Harris to be taken as a man of vast credibility, and when this thing lies among them, they will not press it to show where the guilt really belongs. Now, as he has said that he would investigate it, and implied that he would tell us the result of his investigation, I demand of him to tell why he did not investigate it, if he did not; and if he did, *why he won't tell the result.* I call upon him for that.

This is the third time that Judge Douglas has assumed that he learned about these resolutions by Harris's attempting to use them against Norton on the floor of Congress. I tell Judge Douglas the public records of the country show that *he* himself attempted it upon Trumbull a month before Harris tried them on Norton—that Harris had the opportunity of *learning it from him,* rather than he from Harris. I now ask his attention to that part of the record on the case. My friends, I am not disposed to detain you longer in regard to that matter.

I am told that I still have five minutes left. There is another matter I wish to call attention to. He says, when he discovered there was a mistake in that case, he came forward magnanimously, without my calling his attention to it, and explained it. I will tell you how he became so magnanimous. When the newspapers of our side had discovered and published it, and put it beyond his power to deny it, then he came forward and made a virtue of necessity by acknowledging it. Now he argues that all the point there was in those resolutions, although never passed at Springfield, is retained by their being passed at other localities. Is that true? He said I had a hand in passing them, in his opening speech—that I was in the Convention and helped to pass them. Do the resolutions touch me at all? It strikes me there is some difference between holding a man responsible for an act which he *has not* done, and holding him responsible for an act that he *has* done. You will judge whether there is any difference in the "*spots.*" And he has taken credit for great magnanimity in coming forward and acknowledging what is proved on him beyond even the capacity of Judge Douglas to deny, and he has more capacity in that way than any other living man.

Then he wants to know why I won't withdraw the charge in regard to a conspiracy to make slavery national, as he has withdrawn the one he made. May it please his worship, I will withdraw it *when it is proven false on the us that was proven false on him.* I will add a little more than that. I will withdraw it whenever a reasonable man shall be brought to believe that the charge is not true. I have asked Judge Douglas's attention to certain matters of fact tending to prove the charge of a conspiracy to nationalize slavery, and he says he convinces me that this is all untrue because Buchanan was not in the country at that time, and because the Dred Scott case had not then got into the Supreme Court; and he says that I say the *Democratic* owners of Dred Scott got up the case. I never did say that. I defy Judge Douglas to show that I ever said so, *for I never uttered it.* [One of Mr. Douglas's reporters gesticulated affirmatively at Mr. Lincoln.] I don't care if your hireling does say I did, I tell you myself that *I never said the "Democratic" owners of Dred Scott got up the case.* I have never pretended to know whether Dred Scott's owners were Democrats or Abolitionists, or Freesoilers or Border Ruffians. I have said that there is evidence about the case tending to show that it was a made up case, for the purpose of getting that decision. I have said that that evidence was very strong in the fact that when Dred Scott was declared to be a slave, the owner of him made him free, showing that he had had the case tried and the question settled for such use as could be made of that decision; he cared nothing about the property thus declared to be his by that decision. But my time is out and I can say no more.

SEVENTH JOINT DEBATE, AT ALTON
OCTOBER 15, 1858

MR. DOUGLAS'S SPEECH.

LADIES AND GENTLEMEN: It is now nearly four months since the canvass between Mr. Lincoln and myself commenced. On the 16th of June the Republican Convention assembled at Springfield and nominated Mr. Lincoln as their candidate for the United States Senate, and he, on that occasion, delivered a speech in which he laid down what he understood to be the Republican creed and the platform on which he proposed to stand during the contest. The principal points in that speech of Mr. Lincoln's were: First, that this Government could not endure permanently divided into free and slave States, as our fathers made it; that they must all become free or all become slave; all become one thing or all become the other, otherwise this Union could not continue to exist. I give you his opinions almost in the identical language he used. His second proposition was a crusade against the Supreme Court of the United States because of the Dred Scott decision; urging as an especial reason for his opposition to that decision that it deprived the negroes of the rights and benefits of that clause in the Constitution of the United States which guaranties to the citizens of each State all the rights, privileges, and immunities of the citizens of the several States. On the 10th of July I returned home, and delivered a speech to the people of Chicago, in which I announced it to be my purpose to appeal to the people of Illinois to sustain the course I had pursued in Congress. In that speech I joined issue with Mr. Lincoln on the points which he had presented. Thus there was an issue clear and distinct made up between us on these two propositions laid down in the speech of Mr. Lincoln at Springfield, and controverted by me in my reply to him at Chicago. On the next day, the 11th of July, Mr. Lincoln replied to me at Chicago, explaining at some length, and reaffirming the positions which he had taken in his Springfield speech. In that Chicago speech he even went further than he had before, and uttered sentiments in regard to the negro being on an equality with the white man. He adopted in support of this position the argument which Lovejoy and Codding, and other Abolition lecturers had made familiar in the northern and central portions of the State, to wit: that the Declaration of Independence having declared all men free and equal, by Divine law, also that negro equality was an inalienable right, of which they could not be deprived. He insisted, in that speech, that the Declaration of Independence included the negro in the clause, asserting that all men were created equal, and went so far as to say that if one man was allowed to take the position, that it did not include the negro, others might take the position that it did not include other men. He said that all these distinctions between this man and that man, this race and the other race, must be discarded, and we must all stand by the Declaration of Independence, declaring that all men were created equal.

The issue thus being made up between Mr. Lincoln and myself on three points, we went before the people of the State. During the following seven weeks, between the Chicago speeches and our first meeting at Ottawa, he and I addressed large assemblages of the people in many of the central counties. In my speeches I confined myself closely to those three positions which he had taken, controverting his proposition that this Union could not exist as our fathers made it, divided into free and slave States, controverting his proposition of a crusade against the Supreme Court because of the Dred Scott decision, and controverting his proposition that the Declaration of Independence included and meant the negroes as well as the white men, when it declared all men to be created equal. I supposed at that time that these propositions constituted a distinct issue between us, and that the opposite positions we had taken upon them we would be willing to be held to in every part of the State, I never intended to waver one hair's brendth from that issue either in the north or the south, or wherever I should address the people of Illinois. I hold that when the time arrives that I cannot proclaim my political creed in the same terms not only in the northern but the southern part of Illinois, not only in the Northern but the Southern States, and wherever the American flag waves over American soil, that then there must be something wrong in that creed. So long as we live under a common Constitution, so long as we live in a confederacy of sovereign and equal States, joined together as one for certain purposes, that any political creed is radically wrong which cannot be proclaimed in every State, and every section of that Union, alike. I took up Mr. Lincoln's three propositions in my several speeches, analyzed them, and pointed out what I believed to be the radical errors contained in them. First, in regard to his doctrine that this Government was in violation of the law of God, which says that a house divided against itself cannot stand, I repudiated it as a slander upon the immortal framers of our Constitution. I then said, I have often repeated, and now again assert, that in my opinion our Government can endure forever, divided into free and slave States as our fathers made it,—each State having the right to prohibit, abolish or sustain slavery, just as it pleases. This Government was made upon the great basis of the sovereignty of the States, the right of each State to regulate its own domestic institutions to suit itself, and that right was conferred with the understanding and expectation that inasmuch as each locality had separate interests, each locality must have different and distinct local and domestic institutions, corresponding to its wants and interests. Our fathers knew when they made the Government, that the laws and institutions which were well adapted to the green mountains of Vermont, were unsuited to the rice plantations of South Carolina. They knew then, as well as we know now, that the laws and institutions which would be well adapted to the beautiful prairies of Illinois would not be suited to the mining regions of California. They knew that in a Republic as broad as this, having such a variety of soil, climate and interest, there must necessarily be a corresponding variety of local laws—the policy and institutions of each State adapted to its condition and wants. For this reason this Union was established on the right of each State to do as it pleased on the question of slavery, and every other question; and the various States were not allowed to complain of, much less interfere with the policy, of their neighbors.

Suppose the doctrine advocated by Mr. Lincoln and the Abolitionists of this day had prevailed when the Constitution was made, what would have been the result? Imagine for a moment that Mr. Lincoln had been a member of the Convention that framed the Constitution of the United States, and that when its members were about to sign that wonderful document, he had arisen in that Convention as he did at Springfield this summer, and addressing himself to the President, had said, "A house divided against itself cannot stand; this Government, divided into free and slave States, cannot endure, they must all be free or all be slave, they must all be one thing or all the other, otherwise, it is a violation of the law of God, and cannot continue to exist;"—suppose Mr. Lincoln had convinced that body of sages that that doctrine was sound, what would have been the result? Remember that the Union was then composed of thirteen States, twelve of which were slaveholding and one free. Do you think that the one free State would have outvoted the twelve slaveholding States, and thus have secured the abolition of slavery? On the other hand, would not the twelve slaveholding States have outvoted the one free State, and thus have fastened slavery, by a Constitutional provision, on every foot of the American Republic forever? You see that if this Abolition doctrine of Mr. Lincoln had prevailed when the Government was made, it would have established slavery as a permanent institution, in all the States, whether they wanted it or not, and the question for us to determine in Illinois now as one of the free States is, whether or not we are willing, having become the majority section, to enforce a doctrine on the minority, which we would have resisted with our heart's blood had it been attempted on us when we were in a minority. How has the South lost her power as the majority section in this Union, and how have the free States gained it, except under the operation of that principle which declares the right of the people of each State and each Territory to form and regulate their domestic institutions in their own way. It was under that principle that slavery was abolished in New Hampshire, Rhode Island, Connecticut, New York, New Jersey, and Pennsylvania; it was under that principle that one half of the slaveholding States became free; it was under that principle that the number of free States increased until from being one out of twelve States, we have grown to be the majority of States of the whole Union, with the power to control the House of Representatives and Senate, and the power, consequently, to elect a President by Northern votes without the aid of a Southern State. Having obtained this power under the operation of that great principle, are you now prepared to abandon the principle and declare that merely because we have the power you will wage a war against the Southern States and their institutions until you force them to abolish slavery every where.

After having pressed these arguments home on Mr. Lincoln for seven weeks, publishing a number of my speeches, we met at Ottawa in joint discussion, and he then began to crawfish a little, and let himself down. I there propounded certain questions to him. Amongst others, I asked him whether he would vote for the admission of any more slave States in the event the people wanted them. He would not answer. I then told him that if he did not answer the question there I would renew it at Freeport, and would then trot him down into Egypt and again put it to him. Well, at Freeport, knowing that the next joint discussion took place in Egypt, and being in dread of it, he did answer my question in regard to no more slave States in a mode which he hoped would be satisfactory to me, and accomplish the object he had in view. I will show you what his answer was. After saying that he was not pledged to the Republican doctrine of "no more slave States," he declared:

> "I state to you freely, frankly, that I should be exceedingly sorry to ever be put in the position of having to pass upon that question. I should be exceedingly glad to know that there never would be another slave State admitted into this Union."

Here permit me to remark, that I do not think the people will ever force him into a position against his will. He went on to say:

"But I must add in regard to this, that if slavery shall be kept out of the Territory during the territorial existence of any one given Territory, and then the people should, having a fair chance and a clear field when they come to adopt a Constitution, if they should do the extraordinary thing of adopting a slave Constitution, uninfluenced by the actual presence of the institution among them, I see no alternative, if we own the country, but we must admit it into the Union."

That answer Mr. Lincoln supposed would satisfy the old line Whigs, composed of Kentuckians and Virginians, down in the southern part of the State. Now, what does it amount to? I desired to know whether he would vote to allow Kansas to come into the Union with slavery or not, as her people desired. He would not answer; but in a roundabout way said that if slavery should be kept out of a Territory during the whole of its territorial existence, and then the people, when they adopted a State Constitution, asked admission as a slave State, he supposed he would have to let the State come in. The case I put to him was an entirely different one. I desired to know whether he would vote to admit a State if Congress had not prohibited slavery in it during its territorial existence, as Congress never pretended to do under Clay's Compromise measures of 1850. He would not answer, and I have not yet been able to get an answer from him. I have asked him whether he would vote to admit Nebraska if her people asked to come in as a State with a Constitution recognizing slavery, and he refused to answer. I have put the question to him with reference to New Mexico, and he has not uttered a word in answer. I have enumerated the Territories, one after another, putting the same question to him with reference to each, and he has not said, and will not say, whether, if elected to Congress, he will vote to admit any Territory now in existence with such a Constitution as her people may adopt. He invents a case which does not exist, and cannot exist under this Government, and answers it; but he will not answer the question I put to him in connection with any of the Territories now in existence. The contract we entered into with Texas when she entered the Union obliges us to allow four States to be formed out of the old State, and admitted with or without slavery as the respective inhabitants of each may determine. I have asked Mr. Lincoln three times in our joint discussions whether he would vote to redeem that pledge, and he has never yet answered. He is as silent as the grave on the subject. He would rather answer as to a state of the case which will never arise than commit himself by telling what he would do in a case which would come up for his action soon after his election to Congress. Why can he not say whether he is willing to allow the people of each State to have slavery or not as they please, and to come into the Union when they have the requisite population as a slave or a free State as they decide? I have no trouble in answering the question. I have said every where, and now repeat it to you, that if the people of Kansas want a slave State they have a right, under the Constitution of the United States, to form such a State, and I will let them come into the Union with slavery or without, as they determine. If the people of any other Territory desire slavery, let them have it. If they do not want it, let them prohibit it. It is their business, not mine. It is none of our business in Illinois whether Kansas is a free State or a slave State. It is none of your business in Missouri whether Kansas shall adopt slavery or reject it. It is the business of her people and none of yours. The people of Kansas have as much right to decide that question for themselves as you have in Missouri to decide it for yourselves, or we in Illinois to decide it for ourselves.

And here I may repeat what I have said in every speech I have made in Illinois, that I fought the Lecompton Constitution to its death, not because of the slavery clause in it, but because it was not the act and deed of the people of Kansas. I said then in Congress, and I say now, that if the people of Kansas want a slave State, they have a right to have it. If they wanted the Lecompton Constitution, they had a right to have it. I was opposed to that Constitution because I did not believe that it was the act and deed of the people, but on the contrary, the act of a small, pitiful minority acting in the name of the majority. When at last it was determined to send that Constitution back to the people, and accordingly, in August last, the question of admission under it was submitted to a popular vote, the citizens rejected it by nearly ten to one, thus showing conclusively, that I was right when I said that the Lecompton Constitution was not the act and deed of the people of Kansas, and did not embody their will.

I hold that there is no power on earth, under our system of Government, which has the right to force a Constitution upon an unwilling people. Suppose that there had been a majority of ten to one in favor of slavery in Kansas, and suppose there had been an Abolition President, and an Abolition Administration, and by some means the Abolitionists succeeded in forcing an Abolition Constitution on those slave-holding people, would the people of the South have submitted to that act for one instant? Well, if you of the South would not have submitted to it a day, how can you, as fair, honorable and honest men, insist on putting a slave Constitution on a people who desire a free State? Your safety and ours depend upon both of as acting in good faith, and living up to that great principle which asserts the right of every people to form and regulate their domestic institutions to suit themselves, subject only to the Constitution of the United States.

Most of the men who denounced my course on the Lecompton question, objected to it not because I was not right, but because they thought it expedient at that time, for the sake of keeping the party together, to do wrong. I never knew the Democratic party to violate any one of its principles out of policy or expediency, that it did not pay the debt with sorrow. There is no safety or success for our party unless we always do right, and trust the consequences to God and the people. I chose not to depart from principle for the sake of expediency in the Lecompton question, and I never intend to do it on that or any other question.

But I am told that I would have been all right if I had only voted for the English bill after Lecompton was killed. You know a general pardon was granted to all political offenders on the Lecompton question, provided they would only vote for the English bill. I did not accept the benefits of that pardon, for the reason that I had been right in the course I had pursued, and hence did not require any forgiveness. Let us see how the result has been worked out. English brought in his bill referring the Lecompton Constitution back to the people, with the provision that if it was rejected Kansas should be kept out of the Union until she had the full ratio of population required for a member of Congress, thus in effect declaring that if the people of Kansas would only consent to come into the Union under the Lecompton Constitution, and have a slave State when they did not want it, they should be admitted with a population of 35,000, but that if they were so obstinate as to insist upon having just such a Constitution as they thought best, and to desire admission as a free State, then they should be kept out until they had 93,420 inhabitants. I then said, and I now repeat to you, that whenever Kansas has people enough for a slave State she has people enough for a free State. I was and am willing to adopt the rule that no State shall ever come into the Union until she has the full ratio of population for a member of Congress, provided that rule is made uniform. I made that proposition in the Senate last winter, but a majority of the Senators would not agree to it; and I then said to them if you will not adopt the general rule I will not consent to make an exception of Kansas.

I hold that it is a violation of the fundamental principles of this Government to throw the weight of federal power into the scale, either in favor of the free or the slave States. Equality among all the States of this Union is a fundamental principle in our political system. We have no more right to throw the weight of the Federal Government into the scale in favor of the slaveholding than the free States, and last of all should our friends in the South consent for a moment that Congress should withhold its powers either way when they know that there is a majority against them in both Houses of Congress.

Fellow-citizens, how have the supporters of the English bill stood up to their pledges not to admit Kansas until she obtained a population of 93,420 in the event she rejected the Lecompton Constitution? How? The newspapers inform us that English himself, whilst conducting his canvass for re-election, and in order to secure it, pledged himself to his constituents that if returned he would disregard his own bill and vote to admit Kansas into the Union with such population as she might have when she made application. We are informed that every Democratic candidate for Congress in all the States where elections have recently been held, was pledged against the English bill, with perhaps one or two exceptions. Now, if I had only done as these anti-Lecompton men who voted for the English bill in Congress, pledging themselves to refuse to admit Kansas if she refused to become a slave State until she had a population of 93,420, and then returned to their people, forfeited their pledge, and made a new pledge to admit Kansas at any time she applied, without regard to population, I would have had no trouble. You saw the whole power and patronage of the Federal Government wielded in Indiana, Ohio, and Pennsylvania to re-elect anti-Lecompton men to Congress who voted against Lecompton, then voted for the English bill, and then denounced the English bill, and pledged themselves to their people to disregard it. My sin consists in not having given a pledge, and then in not having afterward forfeited it. For that reason, in this State, every postmaster, every route agent, every collector of the ports, and every federal office-holder, forfeits his head the moment he expresses a preference for the Democratic candidates against Lincoln and his Abolition associates. A Democratic Administration which we helped to bring into power, deems it consistent with its fidelity to principle and its regard to duty, to wield its power in this State in behalf of the Republican Abolition candidates in every county and every Congressional District against the Democratic party. All I have to say in reference to the matter is, that if that Administration have not regard enough for principle, if they are not sufficiently attached to the creed of the Democratic party to bury forever their personal hostilities in order to succeed in carrying out our glorious principles, I have. I have no personal difficulty with Mr. Buchanan or his cabinet. He chose to make certain recommendations to Congress, as he had a right to do, on the Lecompton question. I could not vote in favor of them. I had as much right to judge for myself how I should vote as he had how he should recommend. He undertook to say to me, if you do not vote as I tell you, I will take off the heads of your friends. I replied to him, "You did not elect me, I represent Illinois and I am accountable to Illinois, as my constituency, and to God, but not to the President or to any other power on earth."

And now this warfare is made on me because I would not surrender my connections of duty, because I would not abandon my constituency, and receive the orders of the executive authorities how I should vote in the Senate of the United States. I hold that an attempt to control the Senate on the part of the Executive is subversive of the principles of our Constitution. The Executive department is independent of the Senate, and the Senate is independent of the President. In matters of legislation the President has a veto on the action of the Senate, and in appointments and treaties the Senate has a veto on the President. He has no more right to tell me how I shall vote on his appointments than I have to tell him whether he shall veto or approve a bill that the Senate has passed. Whenever you recognize the right of the Executive to say to a Senator, "Do this, or I will take off the heads of your friends," you convert this Government from a republic into a despotism. Whenever you recognize the right of a President to say to a member of Congress, "Vote as I tell you, or I will bring a power to bear against you at home which will crush you," you destroy the independence of the representative, and convert him into a tool of Executive power. I resisted this invasion of the constitutional rights of a Senator, and I intend to resist it as long as I have a voice to speak, or a vote to give. Yet, Mr. Buchanan cannot provoke me to abandon one iota of Democratic principles out of revenge or hostility to his course. I stand by the platform of the Democratic party, and by its organization, and support its nominees. If there are any who choose to bolt, the fact only shows that they are not as good Democrats as I am.

My friends, there never was a time when it was as important for the Democratic party, for all national men, to rally and stand together as it is to-day. We find all sectional men giving up past differences and continuing the one question of slavery, and when we find sectional men thus uniting, we should unite to resist them and their treasonable designs. Such was the case in 1850, when Clay left the quiet and peace of his home, and again entered upon public life to quell agitation and restore peace to a distracted Union. Then we Democrats, with Cass at our head, welcomed Henry Clay, whom the whole nation regarded as having been preserved by God for the times. He became our leader in that great fight, and we rallied around him the same as the Whigs rallied around old Hickory in 1832, to put down nullification. Thus you see that whilst Whigs and Democrats fought fearlessly in old times about banks, the tariff, distribution, the specie circular, and the sub-treasury, all united as a band of brothers when the peace, harmony, or integrity of the Union was imperiled. It was so in 1850, when Abolitionism had even so far divided this country, North and South, as to endanger the peace of the Union; Whigs and Democrats united in establishing the Compromise measures of that year, and restoring tranquillity and good feeling. These measures passed on the joint action of the two parties. They rested on the great principle that the people of each State and each Territory should be left perfectly free to form and regulate their domestic institutions to suit themselves. You Whigs and we Democrats justified them in that principle. In 1854, when it became necessary to organize the Territories of Kansas and Nebraska, I brought forward the bill on the same principle. In the Kansas-Nebraska bill you find it declared to be the true intent and meaning of the act not to legislate slavery into any State or Territory, nor to exclude it therefrom, but to leave the people thereof perfectly free to form and regulate their domestic institutions in their own way. I stand on that same platform in 1858 that I did in 1850, 1854, and 1856. The Washington *Union* pretending to be the organ of the Administration, in the number of the 5th of this month, devotes three columns and a half to establish these propositions: First, that Douglas, in his Freeport speech, held the same doctrine that he did in his Nebraska bill in 1854; second, that in 1854 Douglas justified the Nebraska bill upon the ground that it was based upon the same principle as Clay's Compromise measures of 1856. The *Union* thus proved that Douglas was the same in 1858 that he was in 1856, 1854, and 1850, and consequently argued that he was never a Democrat. Is it not funny that I was never a Democrat? There is no pretense that I have changed a hair's breadth. The *Union* proves by my speeches that I explained the Compromise measures of 1850 just as I do now, and that I explained the Kansas and Nebraska bill in 1854 just as I did in my Freeport speech, and yet says that I am not a Democrat, and cannot be trusted, because I have not changed during the whole of that time. It has occured to me that in 1854 the author of the Kansas and Nebraska bill was considered a pretty good Democrat. It has occurred to me that in 1856, when I was exerting every nerve and every energy for James Buchanan, standing on the same platform then that I do now, that I was a pretty good Democrat. They now tell me that I am not a Democrat, because I assert that the people of a Territory, as well as those of a State, have the right to decide for themselves whether slavery can or cannot exist in such Territory. Let me read what James Buchanan said on that point when he accepted the Democratic nomination for the Presidency in 1856. In his letter of acceptance, he used the following language:

"The recent legislation of Congress respecting domestic slavery, derived as it has been from the original and pure fountain of legitmate political power, the will of the majority, promises ere long to allay the dangerous excitement. This legislation is founded upon principles as ancient as free government itself, and in accordance with them has simply declared that the people of a Territory, like those of a State, shall decide for themselves whether slavery shall or shall not exist within their limits."

Dr. Hope will there find my answer to the question he propounded to me before I commenced speaking. Of course no man will consider it an answer, who is outside of the Democratic organization, bolts Democratic nominations, and indirectly aids to put Abolitionists into power over Democrats. But whether Dr. Hope considers it an answer or not, every fair-minded man will see that James Buchanan has answered the question, and has asserted that the people of a Territory, like those of a State, shall decide for themselves whether slavery shall or shall not exist within their limits. I answer specifically if you want a further answer, and say that while under the decision of the Supreme Court, as recorded in the opinion of Chief Justice Taney, slaves are property like all other property, and can be carried into any Territory of the United States the same as any other description of property, yet when you get them there they are subject to the local law of the Territory just like all other property. You will find in a recent speech delivered by that able and eloquent statesman, Hon. Jefferson Davis, at Bangor, Maine, that he took the same view of this subject that I did in my Freeport speech. He there said:

"If the inhabitants of any Territory should refuse to enact such laws and police regulations as would give security to their property or to his, it would be rendered more or less valueless in proportion to the difficulties of holding it without such protection. In the case of property in the labor of man, or what is usually called slave property, the insecurity would be so great that the owner could not ordinarily retain it. Therefore, though the right would remain, the remedy being withheld, it would follow that the owner would be practically debarred, by the circumstances of the case, from taking slave property into a Territory where the sense of the inhabitants was opposed to its introduction. So much for the oft-repeated fallacy of forcing slavery upon any community."

You will also find that the distinguished Speaker of the present House of Representatives, Hon. Jas. L. Orr, construed the Kansas and Nebraska bill in this same way in 1856, and also that great intellect of the South, Alex. H. Stephens, put the same construction upon it in Congress that I did in my Freeport speech. The whole South are rallying to the support of the doctrine that if the people of a Territory want slavery they have a right to have it, and if they do not want it that no power on earth can force it upon them. I hold that there is no principle on earth more sacred to all the friends of freedom than that which says that no institution, no law, no constitution, should be forced on an unwilling people contrary to their wishes; and I assert that the Kansas and Nebraska bill contains that principle. It is the great principle contained in that bill. It is the principle on which James Buchanan was made President. Without that principle he never would have been made President of the United States. I will never violate or abandon that doctrine if I have to stand alone. I have resisted the blandishments and threats of power on the one side, and seduction on the other, and have stood immovably for that principle, fighting for it when assailed by Northern mobs, or threatened by Southern hostility. I have defended it against the North and the South, and I will defend it against who-ever assails it, and I will follow it wherever its logical conclusions lead me. I say to you that there is but one hope, one safety for this country, and that is to stand immovably by that principle which declares the right of each State and each Territory to decide these questions for themselves. This Government was founded on that principle, and must be administered in the same sense in which it was founded.

But the Abolition party really think that under the Declaration of Independence the negro is equal to the white man, and that negro equality is an inalienable right conferred by the Almighty, and hence that all human laws in violation of it are null and void. With such men it is no use for me to argue. I hold that the signers of the Declaration of Independence had no reference to negroes at all when they declared all men to be created equal. They did not mean negro, nor the savage Indians, nor the Fejee Islanders, nor any other barbarous race. They were speaking of white men. They alluded to men of European birth and European descent—to white men, and to none others, when they declared that doctrine. I hold that this Government was established on the white basis. It was established by white men for the benefit of white men and their posterity for-ever, and should be administered by white men, and none others. But it does not follow, by any means, that merely because the negro is not a citizen, and merely because he is not our equal, that, therefore, he should be a slave. On the contrary, it does follow that we ought to extend to the negro race, and to all other dependent races all the rights, all the privileges, and all the immunities which they can exercise consistently with the safety of society. Humanity requires that we should give them all these privileges; Christianity commands that we should extend those privileges to them. The question then arises what are those privileges, and what is the nature and extent of them. My answer is that that is a question which each State must answer for itself. We in Illinois have decided it for ourselves. We tried slavery, kept it up for twelve years, and finding that it was not profitable, we abolished it for that reason, and became a free State. We adopted in its stead the policy that a negro in this State shall not be a slave and shall not be a citizen. We have a right to adopt that policy. For my part I think it is a wise and sound policy for us. You in Missouri must judge for yourselves whether it is a wise policy for you. If you choose to follow our example, very good; if you reject it, still well, it is your business, not ours. So with Kentucky. Let Kentucky adopt a policy to suit herself. If we do not like it we will keep away from it, and if she does not like ours let her stay at home, mind her own business and let us alone. If the people of all the States will act on that great principle, and each State mind its own business, attend to its own affairs, take care of its own negroes and not meddle with its neighbors, then there will be peace between the North and the South, the East and the West, throughout the whole Union. Why can we not thus have peace? Why should we thus allow a sectional party to agitate this country, to array the North against the South, and convert us into enemies instead of friends, merely that a few ambitious men may ride into power on a sectional hobby? How long is it since these ambitious Northern men wished for a sectional organization? Did any one of them dream of a sectional party as long as the North was the weaker section and the South the stronger? Then all were opposed to sectional parties; but the moment the North obtained the majority in the House and Senate by the admission of California, and could elect a President without the aid of Southern votes, that moment ambitious Northern men formed a scheme to excite the North against the South, and make the people be governed in their votes by geographical lines, thinking that the North, being the stronger section, would outvote the South, and consequently they, the leaders, would ride into office on a sectional hobby. I am told that my hour is out. It was very short.

MR. LINCOLN'S REPLY.

LADIES AND GENTLEMEN: I have been somewhat, in my own mind, complimented by a large portion of Judge Douglas's speech—I mean that portion which he devotes to the controversy between himself and the present Administration. This is the seventh time Judge Douglas and myself have met in these joint discussions, and he has been gradually improving in regard to his war with the Administration. At Quincy, day before yesterday, he was a little more severe upon the Administration than I had heard him upon any occasion, and I took pains to compliment him for it. I then told him to "Give it to them with all the power he had;" and as some of them were present, I told them I would be very much obliged if they would *give it to him* in about the same way. I take it he has now vastly improved upon the attack he made then upon the Administration. I flatter myself he has really taken my advice on this subject. All I can say now is to re-commend to him and to them what I then commended—to prosecute the war against one another in the most vigorous manner. I say to them again— "Go it, husband!—Go it, bear!"

There is one other thing I will mention before I leave this branch of the discussion—although I do not consider it much of my business, any way. I refer to that part of the Judge's remarks where he undertakes to involve Mr. Buchanan in an inconsistency. He reads something from Mr. Buchanan, from which he undertakes to involve him in an inconsistency; and he gets something of a cheer for having done so. I would only remind the Judge that while he is very valiantly fighting for the Nebraska bill and the repeal of the Missouri Compromise, it has been but a little while since he was the *valiant advocate of* the Missouri Compromise. I want to know if Buchanan has not as much right to be inconsistent as Douglas has? Has Douglas the *exclusive right,* in this country, of being *on all sides of all questions?* Is nobody allowed that high privilege but himself? Is he to have an entire *monopoly* on that subject?

So far as Judge Douglas addressed his speech to me, or so far as it was about me, it is my business to pay some attention to it. I have heard the Judge state two or three times what he has stated to-day—that in a speech which I made at Springfield, Illinois, I had in a very especial manner complained that the Supreme Court in the Dred Scott case had decided that a negro could never be a citizen of the United States. I have omitted by some accident heretofore to analyze this statement, and it is required of me to notice it now. In point of fact it is *untrue.* I never have complained *especially* of the Dred Scott decision because it held that a negro could not be a citizen, and the Judge is always wrong when he says I ever did so complain of it. I have the speech here, and I will thank him or any of his friends to show where I said that a negro should be a citizen, and complained especially of the Dred Scott decision because it declared he could not be one. I have done no such thing, and Judge Douglas so persistently insisting that I have done so, has strongly impressed me with the belief of a predetermination on his part to misrepresent me. He could not get his foundation for insisting that I was in favor of this negro equality any where else as well he could by assuming that untrue proposition. Let me tell this audience what is true in regard to that matter; and the means by which they may correct me if I do not tell them truly is by a recurrence to the speech itself I spoke of the Dred Scott decision in my Springfield speech, and I was then endeavoring to prove that the Dred Scott decision was a portion of a system or scheme to make slavery national in this country. I pointed out what things had been decided by the court. I mentioned as a fact that they had decided that a negro could not be a citizen—that they had done so, as I supposed, to deprive the negro, under all circumstances, of the remotest possibility of ever becoming a citizen and claiming the rights of a citizen of the United States under a certain clause of the Constitution. I stated that, without making any complaint of it at all. I then went on and stated the other points decided in the case, namely: that the bringing of a negro into the State of Illinois and holding him in slavery for two years here was a matter in regard to which they would not decide whether it would make him free or not; that they decided the further point that taking him into a United States Territory where slavery was prohibited by act of Congress, did not make him free, because that act of Congress, as they held, was unconstitutional. I mentioned these three things as making up the points decided in that case. I mentioned them in a lump taken in connection with the introduction of the Nebraska bill, and the amendment of Chase, offered at the time, declaratory of the right of the people of the Territories to *exclude slavery,* which was voted down by the friends of the bill. I mentioned all these things together, as evidence tending to prove a combination and conspiracy to make the institution of slavery national. In that connection and in that way I mentioned the decision on the point that a negro could not be a citizen, and in no other connection.

Out of this, Judge Douglas builds up his beautiful fabrication—of my purpose to introduce a perfect, social, and political equality between the white and black races. His assertion that I made an "especial objection" (that is his exact language) to the decision on this account, is untrue in point of fact.

Now, while I am upon this subject, and as Henry Clay has been alluded to, I desire to place myself, in connection with Mr. Clay, as nearly right before this people as may be. I am quite aware what the Judge's object is here by all these allusions. He knows that we are before an audience, having strong sympathies southward by relationship, place of birth, and so on. He desires to place me in an extremely Abolition attitude. He read upon a former occasion, and alludes without reading today, to a portion of a speech which I delivered in Chicago. In his quotations from that speech, as he has made them upon former occasions, the extracts were taken in such a way as, I suppose, brings them within the definition of what is called *garbling*—taking portions of a speech which, when taken by themselves, do not present the entire sense of the speaker as expressed at the time. I propose, therefore, out of that same speech, to show how one portion of it which he skipped over (taking an extract before and an extract after) will give a different idea, and the true idea I intended to convey. It will take me some little time to read it, but I believe I will occupy the time that way.

You have heard him frequently allude to my controversy with him in regard to the Declaration of Independence. I confess that I have had a struggle with Judge Douglas on that matter, and I will try briefly to place myself right in regard to it on this occasion. I said—and it is between the extracts Judge Douglas has taken from this speech, and put in his published speeches:

> "It may be argued that there are certain conditions that make necessities and impose them upon us, and to the extent that a necessity is imposed upon a man he must submit to it. I think that was the condition in which we found ourselves when we established this Government. We had slaves among us, we could not get our Constitution unless we permitted them to remain in slavery, we could not secure the good we did secure if we grasped for more; and having by necessity submitted to that much, it does not destroy the principle that is the charter of our liberties. Let the charter remain as our standard."

Now I have upon all occasions declared as strongly as Judge Douglas against the disposition to interfere with the existing institution of slavery. You hear me read it from the same speech from which he takes garbled extracts for the purpose of proving upon me a disposition to interfere with the institution of slavery, and establish a perfect social and political equality between negroes and white people.

Allow me while upon this subject briefly to present one other extract from a speech of mine, more than a year ago, at Springfield, in discussing this very same question, soon after Judge Douglas took his ground that negroes were not included in the Declaration of Independence:

> "I think the authors of that notable instrument intended to include *all* men, but they did not mean to declare all men equal *in all respects.*

They did not mean to say all men were equal in color, size, intellect, moral development or social capacity. They defined with tolerable distinctness in what they did consider all men created equal—equal in certain inalienable rights, among which are life, liberty, and the pursuit of happiness. This they said, and this they meant. They did not mean to assert the obvious untruth, that all were then actually enjoying that equality, or yet that they were about to confer it immediately upon them. In fact they had no power to confer such a boon. They meant simply to declare the *right,* so that the *enforcement* of it might follow as fast as circumstances should permit.

"They meant to set up a standard maxim for free society which should be familiar to all: constantly looked to, constantly labored for, and even, though never perfectly attained, constantly approximated, and thereby constantly spreading and deepening its influence and augmenting the happiness and value of life to all people, of all colors, every where."

There again are the sentiments I have expressed in regard to the Declaration of Independence upon a former occasion—sentiments which have been put in print and read wherever any body cared to know what so humble an individual as myself chose to say in regard to it.

At Galesburgh the other day, I said in answer to Judge Douglas, that three years ago there never had been a man, so far as I knew or believed, in the whole world, who had said that the Declaration of Independence did not include negroes in the term "all men." I reassert it to-day. I assert that Judge Douglas and all his friends may search the whole records of the country, and it will be a matter of great astonishment to me if they shall be able to find that one human being three years ago had ever uttered the astounding sentiment that the term "all men" in the Declaration did not include the negro. Do not let me be misunderstood. I know that more than three years ago there were men who, finding this assertion constantly in the way of their schemes to bring about the ascendancy and perpetuation of slavery, *denied the truth of it.* I know that Mr. Calhoun and all the politicians of his school denied the truth of the Declaration. I know that it ran along in the mouth of some Southern men for a period of years, ending at last in that shameful though rather forcible declaration of Petit of Indiana, upon the floor of the United States Senate, that the Declaration of Independence was in that respect "a self-evident lie," rather than a self-evident truth. But I say, with a perfect knowledge of all this hawking at the Declaration without directly attacking it, that three years ago there never had lived a man who had ventured to assail it in the sneaking way of pretending to believe it and then asserting it did not include the negro. I believe the first man who ever said it was Chief Justice Taney in the Dred Scott case, and the next to him was our friend, Stephen A. Douglas. And now it has become the catch-word of the entire party. I would like to call upon his friends every where to consider how they have come in so short a time to view this matter in a way so entirely different from their former belief? to ask whether they are not being borne along by an irresistible current—whither, they know not?

In answer to my proposition at Galesburgh last week, I see that some man in Chicago has got up a letter addressed to the Chicago *Times,* to show, as he professes, that somebody *had* said so before; and he signs himself "An Old Line Whig," if I remember correctly. In the first place I would say he *was not* an old line Whig. I am somewhat acquainted with old line Whigs. I was with the old line Whigs from the origin to the end of that party; I became pretty well acquainted with them, and I know they always had some sense, whatever else you could ascribe to them. I know there never was one who had not more sense than to try to show by the evidence he produces that some man had, prior to the time I named, said that negroes were not included in the term "all men" in the Declaration of Independence. What is the evidence he produces? I will bring forward *his* evidence and let you see what *he* offers by way of showing that somebody more than three years ago had said negroes were not included in the Declaration. He brings forward part of a speech from Henry Clay—*the* part of *the* speech of Henry Clay which I used to bring forward to prove precisely the contrary. I guess we are surrounded to some extent to-day by the old friends of Mr. Clay, and they will be glad to hear any thing from that authority. While he was in Indiana a man presented a petition to liberate his negroes, and he (Mr. Clay) made a speech in answer to it, which I suppose he carefully wrote out himself and caused to be published. I have before me an extract from that speech which constitutes the evidence this pretended "Old Line Whig" at Chicago brought forward to show that Mr. Clay didn't suppose the negro was included in the Declaration of Independence. Hear what Mr. Clay said:

"And what is the foundation of this appeal to me in Indiana, to liberate the slaves under my care in Kentucky? It is a general declaration in the act announcing to the world the independence of the thirteen American colonies, that all men are created equal. Now, as an abstract principle, *there is no doubt of the truth of that declaration;* and it is desirable, *in the original construction of society, and in organized societies,* to keep it in view as a great fundamental principle. But, then, I apprehend that in no society that ever did exist, or ever shall be formed, was or can the equality asserted among the members of the human race, be practically enforced and carried out. There are portions, large portions, women, minors, insane, culprits, transient sojourners, that will always probably remain subject to the government of another portion of the community.

"That declaration, whatever may be the extent of its import, was made by the delegations of the thirteen States. In most of them slavery existed, and had long existed, and was established by law. It was introduced and forced upon the colonies by the paramount law of England. Do you believe, that in making that declaration the States that concurred in it intended that it should be tortured into a virtual emancipation of all the slaves within their respective limits? Would Virginia and other Southern States have ever united in a declaration which was to be interpreted into an abolition of slavery among them? Did any one of the thirteen colonies entertain such a design or expectation? To impute such a secret and unavowed purpose, would be to charge a political fraud upon the noblest band of patriots that ever assembled in council—a fraud upon the Confederacy of the Revolution—a fraud upon the union of those States whose Constitution not only recognized the lawfulness of slavery, but permitted the importation of slaves from Africa until the year 1808."

This is the entire quotation brought forward to prove that somebody previous to three years ago had said the negro was not included in the term "all men" in the Declaration. How does it do so? In what way has it a tendency to prove that? Mr. Clay says *it is true as an abstract principle* that all men are created equal, but that we cannot practically apply it in all cases. He illustrates this by bringing forward the cases of females, minors, and insane persons, with whom it cannot be enforced; out he says it is true as an abstract principle in the organization of society as well as in organized society, and it should be kept in view as a fundamental principle. Let me read a few words more before I add some comments of my own. Mr. Clay says a little further on:

"I desire no concealment of my opinions in regard to the institution of slavery. I look upon it as a great evil, and deeply lament that we have derived it from the parental Government, and from our ancestors. But here they are, and the question is, how can they be best dealt with? If a state of nature existed, and we were about to lay the foundations of society, *no man would be more strongly opposed than I should be, to incorporating the institution of slavery among its elements."*

Now, here in this same book—in this same speech—in this same extract brought forward to prove that Mr. Clay held that the negro was not included in the Declaration of Independence—no such statement on his part, but the declaration *that it is a great fundamental truth,* which should be constantly kept in view in the organization of society and in societies already organized. But if I say a word about it—if I attempt, as Mr. Clay said all good men ought to do, to keep it in view—if, in this "organized society," I ask to have the public eye turned upon it—if I ask, in relation to the organization of new Territories, that the public eye should be turned upon it—forthwith I am villified as you hear me to-day. What have I done, that I have not the license of Henry Clay's illustrious example here in doing? Have I done aught that I have not his authority for, while maintaining that in organizing new Territories and societies, this fundamental principle should be regarded, and in organized society holding it up to the public view and recognizing what *he* recognized as the great principle of free government?

And when this new principle—this new proposition that no human being ever thought of three years ago—is brought forward, *I combat it* as having an evil tendency, if not an evil design. I combat it as having a tendency to dehumanize the negro—to take away from him the right of ever striving to be a man. I combat it as being one of the thousand things constantly done in these days to prepare the public mind to make property, and nothing but property, of the *negro in all the States of this Union.*

But there is a point that I wish, before leaving this part of the discussion, to ask attention to. I have read and I repeat the words of Henry Clay:

> "I desire no concealment of my opinions in regard to the institution of slavery. I look upon it as a great evil, and deeply lament that we have derived it from the parental Government, and from our ancestors. I wish every slave in the United States was in the country of his ancestors. But here they are; the question is how they can best be dealt with? If a state of nature existed, and we were about to lay the foundations of society, no man would be more strongly opposed than I should be, to incorporate the institution of slavery among its elements."

The principle upon which I have insisted in this canvass, is in relation to laying the foundations of new societies. I have never sought to apply these principles to the old States for the purpose of abolishing slavery in those States. It is nothing but a miserable perversion of what I *have* said, to assume that I have declared Missouri, or any other slave State, shall emancipate her slaves. I have proposed no such thing. But when Mr. Clay says that in laying the foundation of societies in our Territories where it does not exist, he would be opposed to the introduction of slavery as an element, I insist that we have *his warrant*—his license for insisting upon the exclusion of that element which he declared in such strong and emphatic language *was most hateful to him.*

Judge Douglas has again referred to a Springfield speech in which I said "a house divided against itself cannot stand." The Judge has so often made the entire quotation from that speech that I can make it from memory. I used this language:

> "We are now far into the fifth year, since a policy was initiated with the avowed object and confident promise of putting an end to the slavery agitation. Under the operation of this policy, that agitation has not only not ceased, but has constantly augmented. In my opinion it will not cease until a crisis shall have been reached and passed. 'A house divided against itself cannot stand.' I believe this Government cannot endure permanently half slave and half free. I do not expect the house to fall—but I do expect it will cease to be divided. It will become all one thing, or all the other. Either the opponents of slavery will arrest the further spread of it, and place it where the public mind shall rest in the belief that it is in the course of ultimate extinction, or its advocates will push it forward till it shall become alike lawful in all the States—old as well as new, North as well as South."

That extract and the sentiments expressed in it, have been extremely offensive to Judge Douglas. He has warred upon them as Satan wars upon the Bible. His perversions upon it are endless. Here now are my views upon it in brief.

I said we were now far into the fifth year, since a policy was initiated with the avowed object and confident promise of putting an end to the slavery agitation. Is it not so? When that Nebraska bill was brought forward four years ago last January, was it not for the "avowed object" of putting an end to the slavery agitation? We were to have no more agitation in Congress it was all to be banished to the Territories. By the way, I will remark here that, as Judge Dou-

glas is very fond of complimenting Mr. Crittenden in these days, Mr. Crittenden has said there was a falsehood in that whole business, for there was *no slavery agitation at that time to allay*. We were for a little while *quiet* on the
troublesome thing, and that very allaying plaster of Judge Douglas's stirred it up
again. But was it not understood or intimated with the "confident promise" of
putting an end to the slavery agitation? Surely it was. In every speech you heard
Judge Douglas make, until he got into this "imbroglio," as they call it, with the
Administration about the Lecompton Constitution, every speech on that
Nebraska bill was full of his felicitations that we were *just at the end* of the slavery agitation. The last tip of the last joint of the old serpent's tail was just drawing out of view. But has it proved so? I have asserted that under that policy that
agitation "has not only not ceased, but has constantly augmented." When was
there ever a greater agitation in Congress than last winter? When was it as great
in the country as to-day?

There was a collateral object in the introduction of that Nebraska policy
which was to clothe the people of the Territories with a superior degree of self-
government, beyond what they had ever had before. The first object and the
main one of conferring upon the people a higher degree of "self-government,"
is a question of fact to be determined by you in answer to a single question.
Have you ever heard or known of a people any where on earth who had as little to do, as, in the first instance of its use, the people of Kansas had with this
same right of "self-government?" In its main policy and in its collateral object,
it has been nothing but a living, creeping lie from the time of its introduction till to-day.

I have intimated that I thought the agitation would not cease until a crisis
should have been reached and passed. I have stated in what way I thought it
would be reached and passed. I have said that it might go one way or the other.
We might, by arresting the further spread of it, and placing it where the fathers
originally placed it, put it where the public mind should rest in the belief that
it was in the course of ultimate extinction. Thus the agitation may cease. It may
be pushed forward until it shall become alike lawful in all the States, old as well
as new, North as well as South. I have said, and I repeat, my wish is that the
further spread of it may be arrested, and that it may be placed where the public mind shall rest in the belief that it is in the course of ultimate extinction. I
have expressed that as my wish. I entertain the opinion upon evidence sufficient to my mind, that the fathers of this Government placed that institution
where the public mind *did* rest in the belief that it was in the course of ultimate
extinction. Let me ask why they made provision that the source of slavery—
the African slave-trade—should be cut off at the end of twenty years? Why did

they make provision that in all the new territory we owned at that time, slavery should be forever inhibited? Why stop its spread in one direction and cut off its source in another, if they did not look to its being placed in the course of ultimate extinction?

Again; the institution of slavery is only mentioned in the Constitution of the United States two or three times, and in neither of these cases does the word "slavery" or "negro race" occur; but covert language is used each time, and for a purpose full of significance. What is the language in regard to the prohibition of the African slave-trade? It runs in about this way: "The migration or importation of such persons as any of the States now existing shall think proper to admit, shall not be prohibited by the Congress prior to the year one thousand eight hundred and eight."

The next allusion in the Constitution to the question of slavery and the black race, is on the subject of the basis of representation, and there the language used is, "Representatives and direct taxes shall be apportioned among the several States which may be included within this Union, according to their respective numbers, which shall be determined by adding to the whole number of free persons, including those bound to service for a term of years, and excluding Indians not taxed—three-fifths of all other persons."

It says "persons," not slaves, not negroes; but this "three-fifths" can be applied to no other class among us than the negroes.

Lastly, in the provision for the reclamation of fugitive slaves, it is said: "No person held to service or labor in one State, under the laws thereof, escaping into another, shall in consequence of any law or regulation therein, be discharged from such service or labor, but shall be delivered up, on claim of the party to whom such service or labor may be due." There again there is no mention of the word "negro" or of slavery. In all three of these places, being the only allusions to slavery in the instrument, covert language is used. Language is used not suggesting that slavery existed or that the black race were among us. And I understand the cotemporaneous history of those times to be that covert language was used with a purpose, and that purpose was that in our Constitution, which it was hoped and is still hoped will endure forever—when it should be read by intelligent and patriotic men, after the institution of slavery had passed from among us—there should be nothing on the face of the great charter of liberty suggesting that such a thing as negro slavery had ever existed among us. This is part of the evidence that the fathers of the Government expected and intended the institution of slavery to come to an end. They expected and intended that it should be in the course of ultimate extinction.

And when I say that I desire to see the further spread of it arrested, I only say I desire to see that done which the fathers have first done. When I say I desire to see it placed where the public mind will rest in the belief that it is in the course of ultimate extinction, I only say I desire to see it placed where they placed it. It is not true that our fathers, as Judge Douglas assumes, made this Government part slave and part free. Understand the sense in which he puts it. He assumes that slavery is a rightful thing within itself—was introduced by the framers of the Constitution. The exact truth is, that they found the institution existing among us, and they left it as they found it. But in making the Government they left this institution with many clear marks of disapprobation upon it. They found slavery among them, and they left it among them because of the difficulty—the absolute impossibility of its immediate removal. And when Judge Douglas asks me why we cannot let it remain part slave and part free, as the fathers of the Government made it, he asks a question based upon an assumption which is itself a falsehood; and I turn upon him and ask him the question, when the policy that the fathers of the Government had adopted in relation to this element among us was the best policy in the world—the only wise policy—the only policy that we can ever safely continue upon—that will ever give us peace, unless this dangerous element masters us all and becomes a national institution—*I turn upon him and ask him why he could not leave it alone.* I turn and ask him why he was driven to the necessity of introducing a *new policy* in regard to it. He has himself said he introduced a new policy. He said so in his speech on the 22d of March of the present year, 1858. I ask him why he could not let it remain where our fathers placed it. I ask, too, of Judge Douglas and his friends why we shall not again place this institution upon the basis on which the fathers left it. I ask you, when he infers that I am in favor of setting the free and slave States at war, when the institution was placed in that attitude by those who made the Constitution, *did they make any war?* If we had no war out of it, when thus placed, wherein is the ground of belief that we shall have war out of it, if we return to that policy? Have we had any peace upon this matter springing from any other basis? I maintain that we have not. I have proposed nothing more than a return to the policy of the fathers.

I confess, when I propose a certain measure of policy, it is not enough for me that I do not intend any thing evil in the result, but it is incumbent on me to show that it has not a *tendency* to that result. I have met Judge Douglas in that point of view. I have not only made the declaration that I do not *mean* to produce a conflict between the States, but I have tried to show by fair reasoning, and I think I have shown to the minds of fair men, that I propose nothing but what has a most peaceful tendency. The quotation that I happened to make in that Springfield speech, that "a house divided against itself cannot stand," and which has proved so offensive to the Judge, was part and parcel of the same thing. He tries to show that variety in the domestic institutions of the different States is necessary and indispensable. I do not dispute it. I have no controversy with Judge Douglas about that. I shall very readily agree with him that it would be foolish for us to insist upon having a cranberry law here, in Illinois, where we have no cranberries, because they have a cranberry law in Indiana, where they have cranberries. I should insist that it would be exceedingly wrong in us to deny to Virginia the right to enact oyster laws, where they have oysters, because we want no such laws here. I understand, I hope, quite as well as Judge Douglas or any body else, that the variety in the soil and climate and face of the country, and consequent variety in the industrial pursuits and productions of a country, require systems of law conforming to this variety in the natural features of the country. I understand quite as well as Judge Douglas, that if we here raise a barrel of flour more than we want, and the Louisianians raise a barrel of sugar more than they want, it is of mutual advantage to exchange. That produces commerce, brings us together, and makes us better friends. We like one another the more for it. And I understand as well as Judge Douglas, or any body else, that these mutual accommodations are the cements which bind together the different parts of this Union—that instead of being a thing to "divide the house"—figuratively expressing the Union—they tend to sustain it; they are the props of the bouse tending always to hold it up.

But when I have admitted all this, I ask if there is any parallel between these things and this institution of slavery? I do not see that there is any parallel at all between them. Consider it. When have we had any difficulty or quarrel amongst ourselves about the cranberry laws of Indiana, or the oyster laws of Virginia, or the pine lumber laws of Maine, or the fact that Louisiana produces sugar, and Illinois flour? When have we had any quarrels over these things? When have we had perfect peace in regard to this thing which I say is an element of discord in this Union? We have sometimes had peace, but when was it? It was when the institution of slavery remained quiet where it was. We have had difficulty and turmoil whenever it has made a struggle to spread itself where it was not. I ask, then, if experience does not speak in thunder-tones, telling us that the policy which has given peace to the country heretofore, being returned to, gives the greatest promise of peace again. You may say, and Judge Douglas has intimated the same thing, that all this difficulty in regard to the institution of slavery is the mere agitation of office-seekers and ambitious northern politicians. He thinks we want to get "his place," I suppose. I agree that there are office-seekers amongst us. The Bible says somewhere that we are desperately selfish. I think we would have discovered that fact without the Bible. I do not claim that I am any less so than the average of men, but I do claim that I am not more selfish than Judge Douglas.

But is it true that all the difficulty and agitation we have in regard to this institution of slavery springs from office-seeking—from the mere ambition of politicians? Is that the truth? How many times have we had danger from this question? Go back to the day of the Missouri Compromise. Go back to the Nullification question, at the bottom of which lay this same slavery question. Go back to the time of the Annexation of Texas. Go back to the troubles that led to the Compromise of 1850. You will find that every time, with the single exception of the Nullification question, they sprung from an endeavor to spread this institution. There never was a party in the history of this country, and there probably never will be, of sufficient strength to disturb the general peace of the country. Parties themselves may be divided and quarrel on minor questions, yet it extends not beyond the parties themselves. But does *not* this question make a disturbance outside of political circles? Does it not enter into the churches and rend them asunder? What divided the great Methodist Church into two parts, North and South? What has raised this constant disturbance in every Presbyterian General Assembly that meets? What disturbed the Unitarian Church in this very city two years ago? What has jarred and shaken the great American Tract Society recently, not yet splitting it, but sure to divide it in the end? Is it not this same mighty, deep-seated power that somehow operates on the minds of men, exciting and stirring them up in every avenue of society—in politics, in religion, in literature, in morals, in all the manifold relations of life? Is this the work of politicians? Is that irresistible power which for fifty years has shaken the Government and agitated the people to be stilled and subdued by pretending that it is an exceedingly simple thing, and we ought not to talk about it? If you will get every body else to stop talking about it, I assure you I will quit before they have half done so. But where is the philosophy or statesmanship which assumes that you can quiet that disturbing element in our society which has disturbed us for more than half a century, which has been the only serious danger that has threatened our institutions—I say, where is the philosophy or the statesmanship based on the assumption that we are to quit talking about it, and that the public mind is all at once to cease being agitated by it? Yet this is the policy here in the north that Douglas is advocating—that we are to care nothing about it! I ask you if it is not a false philosophy? Is it not a false statesmanship that undertakes to build up a system of policy upon the basis of caring nothing about *the very thing that every body does care the most about?*—a thing which all experience has shown we care a very great deal about?

The Judge alludes very often in the course of his remarks to the exclusive right which the States have to decide the whole thing for themselves. I agree with him very readily that the different States have that right. He is but fighting a man of straw when he assumes that I am contending against the right of the States to do as they please about it. Our controversy with him is in regard to the new Territories. We agree that when the States come in as States they have the right and the power to do as they please. We have no power as citizens of the free States or in our federal capacity as members of the Federal Union through the General Government, to disturb slavery in the States where it exists. We profess constantly that we have no more inclination than belief in the power of the Government to disturb it; yet we are driven constantly to defend ourselves from the assumption that we are warring upon the rights of the *States*. What I insist upon is, that the new Territories shall be kept free from it while in the Territorial condition. Judge Douglas assumes that we have no interest in them—that we have no right whatever to interfere. I think we have some interest. I think that as white men we have. Do we not wish for an outlet for our surplus population, if I may so express myself? Do we not feel an interest in getting to that outlet with such institutions as we would like to have prevail there? If *you* go to the Territory opposed to slavery and another man comes upon the same ground with his slave, upon the assumption that the things are equal, it turns out that he has the equal right all his way and you have no part of it your way. If he goes in and makes it a slave Territory, and by consequence a slave State, is it not time that those who desire to have it a free State were an equal ground. Let me suggest it in a different way. How many Democrats are there about here ["A thousand"] who have left slave States and come into the free State of Illinois to get rid of the institution of slavery? [Another voice—"A thousand and one."] I reckon there are a thousand and one. I will ask you, if the policy you are now advocating had prevailed when this country was in a Territorial condition, where would you have gone to get rid of it? Where would you have found your free State or Territory to go to? And when hereafter, for any cause, the people in this place shall desire to find new homes, if they wish to be rid of the institution, where will they find the place to go to?

Now irrespective of the moral aspect of this question as to whether there is a right or wrong in enslaving a negro, I am still in favor of our new Territories being in such a condition that white men may find a home—may find some spot where they can better their condition—where they can settle upon new soil and better their condition in life. I am in favor of this not merely (I must say it here as I have elsewhere) for our own people who are born amongst us, but as an outlet for *free white people every where,* the world over—in which Hans and Baptiste and Patrick, and all other men from all the world, may find new homes and better their conditions in life.

I have stated upon former occasions, and I may as well state again, what I understand to be the real issue in this controversy between Judge Douglas and myself. On the point of my wanting to make war between the free and the slave States, there has been no issue between us. So, too, when he assumes that I am in favor of introducing a perfect social and political equality between the white and black races. These are false issues, upon which Judge Douglas has tried to force the controversy. There is no foundation in truth for the charge that I maintain either of these propositions. The real issue in this controversy—the one pressing upon every mind—is the sentiment on the part of one class that looks upon the institution of slavery *as a wrong,* and of another class that *does not* look upon it as a wrong. The sentiment that contemplates the institution of slavery in this country as a wrong is the sentiment of the Republican party. It is the sentiment around which all their actions—all their arguments circle—from which all their propositions radiate. They look upon it as being a moral, social and political wrong; and while they contemplate it as such, they nevertheless have due regard for its actual existence among us, and the difficulties of getting rid of it in any satisfactory way and to all the constitutional obligations thrown about it. Yet having a due regard for these, they desire a policy in regard to it that looks to its not creating any more danger. They insist that it should as far as may be, *be treated* as a wrong, and one of the methods of treating it as a wrong is to *make provision that it shall grow no larger.* They also desire a policy that looks to a peaceful end of slavery at sometime, as being wrong. These are the views they entertain in regard to it as I understand them; and all their sentiments—all their arguments and propositions are brought within this range. I have said and I repeat it here, that if there be a man amongst us who does not think that the institution of slavery is wrong in any one of the aspects of which I have spoken, he is misplaced and ought not to be with us. And if there be a man amongst us who is so impatient of it as a wrong as to disregard its actual presence among us and the difficulty of getting rid of it suddenly in a satisfactory way, and to dis-regard the constitutional obligations thrown about it, that man is misplaced if he is on our platform. We disclaim sympathy with him in practical action. He is not placed properly with us.

On this subject of treating it as a wrong, and limiting its spread, let me say a word. Has any thing ever threatened the existence of this Union save and except this very institution of slavery? What is it that we hold most dear amongst us? Our own liberty and prosperity. What has ever threatened our liberty and prosperity save and except this institution of slavery? If this is true, how do you propose to improve the condition of things by enlarging slavery—by spreading it out and making it bigger? You may have a wen or cancer upon your person and not be able to cut it out lest you bleed to death; but surely it is no way to cure it, to engraft it and spread it over your whole body. That is no proper way of treating what you regard a wrong. You see this peaceful way of dealing with it as a wrong—restricting the spread of it, and not allowing it to go into new countries where it has not already existed. That is the peaceful way, the old-fashioned way, the way in which the fathers themselves set us the example.

On the other hand, I have said there is a sentiment which treats it as *not* being wrong. That is the Democratic sentiment of this day. I do not mean to say that every man who stands within that range positively asserts that it is right. That class will include all who positively assert that it is right, and all who like Judge Douglas treat it as indifferent and do not say it is either right or wrong. These two classes of men fall within the general class of those who do not look upon it as wrong. And if there be among you any body who supposes that he, as a Democrat, can consider himself "as much opposed to slavery as anybody," I would like reason with him. You never treat it as a wrong. What other thing that you consider as a wrong, do you deal with as you deal with that? Perhaps you *say* it wrong, *but your leader never does, and you quarrel with anybody who says it is wrong.* Although you pretend to say so yourself you can find no fit place to deal with it as a wrong. You must not say any thing about it in the free States, *because it is not here.* You must not say any thing about it in the slave States, *because it is there.* You must not say any thing about it in the pulpit, because that is religion and his nothing to do with it. You must not say any thing about it in politics, *because they will disturb the security of "my place."* There is no place to talk about it as being wrong, although you say yourself it *is* a wrong. But finally you will screw yourself up to the belief that if the people of the slave States should adopt a system of gradual emancipation on the slavery question, you would be in favor of it. You would be in favor of it. You say that is getting it in the right place, and you would be glad to see it succeed. But you are deceiving yourself. You all know that Frank Blair and Gratz Brown, down there in St. Louis, undertook to introduce a system in Missouri. They fought as valiantly as they could for the system of usual emancipation which you pretend you would be glad to see succeed. Now I bring you to the test. After a hard fight they were beaten, and when the news came over here you threw up your hats and *hurraed for Democracy*. More than that, take all the argument made in favor of the system you have proposed, and it carefully excludes the idea that there is any thing wrong in the institution of slavery. The arguments to sustain that policy carefully excluded it. Even here to-day you heard Judge Douglas quarrel with me because I uttered a wish that it might sometime come to an end. Although Henry Clay could say he wished every slave in the United States was in the country of his ancestors, I am denounced by those pretending to respect Henry Clay for uttering a wish that it might sometime, in some peaceful way, come to an end. The Democratic policy in regard to that institution will not tolerate the merest breath, the slightest hint, of the least degree of wrong about it. Try it by some of Judge Douglas's arguments. He says he "don't care whether it is voted up or voted down" in the Territories. I do not care myself in dealing with that expression, whether it is intended to be expressive of his individual sentiments on the subject, or only of the national policy he desires to have established. It is alike valuable for my purpose. Any man can say that who does not see any thing wrong in slavery, but no man can logically say it who does see a wrong in it; because no man can logically say he don't care whether a wrong is voted up or voted down. He may say he don't care whether an indifferent thing is voted up or down, but he must logically have a choice between a right thing and a wrong thing. He contends that whatever community wants slaves has a right to have them. So they have if it is not a wrong. But if it is a wrong, he cannot say people have a right to do wrong. He says that upon the score of equality, slaves should be allowed to go in a new Territory, like other property. This is strictly logical if there is no difference between it and other property. If it and other property are equal, his argument is entirely logical. But if you insist that one is wrong and the other right, there is no use to institute a comparison between right and wrong. You may turn over every thing in the Democratic policy from beginning to end, whether in the shape it takes on the statute book, in the shape it takes in the Dred Scott decision, in the shape it takes in conversation, or the shape it takes in short maxim-like arguments—it every where carefully excludes the idea that there is any thing wrong in it.

That is the real issue. That is the issue that will continue in this country when these poor tongues of Judge Douglas and myself shall be silent. It is the eternal struggle between these two principles—right and wrong—throughout the world. They are the two principles that have stood face to face from the beginning of time; and will ever continue to struggle. The one is the common right of humanity and the other the divine right of kings. It is the same principle in whatever shape it develops itself. It is the same spirit that says, "You work and toil and earn bread, and I'll eat it." No matter in what shape it comes, whether from the mouth of a king who seeks to bestride the people of his own nation and live by the fruit of their labor, or from one race of men as an apology for enslaving another race, it is the same tyrannical principle. I was glad to express my gratitude at Quincy, and I re-express it here to Judge Douglas—*that he looks to no end of the institution of slavery.* That will help the people to see where the struggle really is. It will hereafter place with us all men who really do wish the wrong may have an end. And whenever we can get rid of the fog which obscures the real question—when we can get Judge Douglas and his friends to avow a policy looking to its perpetuation—we can get out from among that class of men and bring them to the side of those who treat it as a wrong. Then there will soon be an end of it, and that end will be its "ultimate extinction." Whenever the issue can be distinctly made, and all extraneous matter thrown out so that men can fairly see the real difference between the parties, this controversy will soon be settled, and it will be done peaceably too. There will be no war, no violence. It will be placed again where the wisest and best men of the world placed it. Brooks of South Carolina once declared that when this Constitution was framed, its framers did not look to the institution existing until this day. When he said this, I think he stated a fact that is fully borne out by the history of the times. But he also said they were better and wiser men than the men of these days; yet the men of these days had experience which they had not, and by the invention of the cotton-gin it became a necessity in this country that slavery should be perpetual. I now say that, willingly or unwillingly, purposely or without purpose, Judge Douglas has been the most prominent instrument in changing the position of the institution of slavery which the fathers of the Government expected to come to an end ere this—*and putting it upon Brooks's cotton-gin basis*—placing it where he openly confesses he has no desire there shall ever be an end of it.

I understand I have ten minutes yet. I will employ it in saying something about this argument Judge Douglas uses, while he sustains the Dred Scott decision, that the people of the Territories can still somehow exclude slavery. The first thing I ask attention to is the fact that Judge Douglas constantly said, before the decision, that whether they could or not, *was a question for the Supreme Court.* But after the court has made the decision he virtually says it is *not* a question for the Supreme Court, but for the people. And how is it he tells us they can exclude it? He says it needs "police regulations," and that admits of "unfriendly legislation." Although it is a right established by the Constitution of the United States to take a slave into a Territory of the United States and hold him as property, yet unless the Territorial Legislature will give friendly legislation, and, more especially, if they adopt unfriendly legislation, they can practically exclude him. Now, without meeting this proposition as a matter of fact, I pass to consider the real Constitutional obligation. Let me take the gentleman who looks me in the face before me, and let us suppose that he is a member of the Territorial Legislature. The first thing he will do will be to swear that he will support the Constitution of the United States. His neighbor by his side in the Territory has slaves and needs Territorial legislation to enable him to enjoy that Constitutional right. Can he withhold the legislation which his neighbor needs for the enjoyment of a right which is fixed in his favor in the Constitution of the United States which he has sworn to support? Can he withhold it without violating his oath? And more especially, can he pass unfriendly legislation to violate his oath? Why, this is a *monstrous* sort of talk about the Constitution of the United States! *There has never been as outlandish or lawless a doctrine from the mouth of any respectable man on earth.* I do not believe it is a Constitutional right to hold slaves in a Territory of the United States. I believe the decision was improperly made and I go for reversing it. Judge Douglas is furious against those who go for reversing a decision. But he is for legislating it out of all force while the law itself stands. I repeat that there has never been so monstrous a doctrine uttered from the mouth of a respectable man.

I suppose most of us (I know it of myself) believe that the people of the Southern States are entitled to a Congressional Fugitive Slave law—that is a right fixed in the Constitution. But it cannot be made available to them without Congressional legislation. In the Judge's language, it is a "barren right" which needs legislation before it can become efficient and valuable to the persons to whom it is guarantied. And as the right is Constitutional I agree that the legislation shall be granted to it—and that not that we like the institution of slavery. We profess to have no taste for running and catching niggers—at least I profess no taste for that job at all. Why then do I yield support to a Fugitive Slave law? Because I do not understand that the Constitution, which guaranties that right, can be supported without it. And if I believed that the right to hold a slave in a Territory was equally fixed in the Constitution with the right to reclaim fugitives, I should be bound to give it the legislation necessary to support it. I say that no man can deny his obligation to give the necessary legislation to support slavery in a Territory, who believes it is a Constitutional right to have it there. No man can, who does not give the Abolitionists an argument to deny the obligation enjoined by the Constitution to enact a Fugitive Slave law. Try it now. It is the strongest Abolition argument ever made. I say if that Dred Scott decision is correct, then the right to hold slaves in a Territory is equally a Constitutional right with the right of a slaveholder to have his runaway returned. No one can show the distinction between them. The one is express, so that we cannot deny it. The other is construed to be in the Constitution, so that he who believes the decision to be correct believes in the right. And the man who argues that by unfriendly legislation, in spite of that Constitutional right, slavery may be driven from the Territories, cannot avoid furnishing an argument by which Abolitionists may deny the obligation to return fugitives, and claim the power to pass laws unfriendly to the right of the slaveholder to reclaim his fugitive. I do not know how such an argument may strike a popular assembly like this, but I defy any body to go before a body of men whose minds are educated to estimating evidence and reasoning, and show that there is an iota of difference between the Constitutional right to reclaim a fugitive, and the Constitutional right to hold a slave, in a Territory, provided this Dred Scott decision is correct. I defy any man to make an argument that will justify unfriendly legislation to deprive a slaveholder of his right to hold his slave in a Territory, that will not equally, in all its length, breadth and thickness, furnish an argument for nullifying the Fugitive Slave law. Why, there is not such an Abolitionist in the nation as Douglas, after all.

MR. DOUGLAS'S REJOINDER.

MR. LINCOLN has concluded his remarks by saying that there is not such an Abolitionist as I am in all America. If he could make the Abolitionists of Illinois believe that, he would not have much show for the Senate. Let him make the Abolitionists believe the truth of that statement and his political back is broken.

His first criticism upon me is the expression of his hope that the war of the Administration will be prosecuted against me and the Democratic party of this State with vigor. He wants that war prosecuted with vigor; I have no doubt of it. His hopes of success, and the hopes of his party depend solely upon it. They have no chance of destroying the Democracy of this State except by the aid of federal patronage. He has all the federal office-holders here as his allies, running separate tickets against the Democracy to divide the party, although the leaders all intend to vote directly the Abolition ticket, and only leave the greenhorns to vote this separate ticket who refuse to go into the Abolition camp. There is something really refreshing in the thought that Mr. Lincoln is in favor of prosecuting one war vigorously. It is the first war I ever knew him to be in favor of prosecuting. It is the first war that I ever knew him to believe to be just or Constitutional. When the Mexican war was being waged, and the American army was surrounded by the enemy in Mexico, he thought that war was unconstitutional, unnecessary, and unjust. He thought it was not commenced on the right *spot.*

When I made an incidental allusion of that kind in the joint discussion over at Charleston some weeks ago, Lincoln, in replying, said that I, Douglas, had charged him with voting against supplies for the Mexican war, and then he reared up, full length, and swore that he never voted against the supplies—that it was a slander—and caught hold of Ficklin, who sat on the stand, and said, "Here, Ficklin, tell the people that it is a lie." Well, Ficklin, who had served in Congress with him, stood up and told them all that he recollected about it. It was that when George Ashmun, of Massachusetts, brought forward a resolution declaring the war unconstitutional, unnecessary, and unjust, that Lincoln had voted for it. "Yes," said Lincoln, "I did." Thus he confessed that he voted that the war was wrong, that our country was in the wrong, and consequently that the Mexicans were in the right; but charged that I had slandered him by saying that he voted against the supplies. I never charged him with voting against the supplies in my life, because I knew that he was not in Congress when they were voted. The war was commenced on the 13th day of May, 1846, and on that day we appropriated in Congress ten millions of dollars and fifty thousand men to prosecute it. During the same session we voted more men and more money, and at the next session we voted more men and more money, so that by the time Mr. Lincoln entered Congress we had enough men and enough money to carry on the war, and had no occasion to vote for any more. When he got into the House, being opposed to the war, and not being able to stop the supplies, because they had all gone forward, all he could do was to follow the lead of Corwin, and prove that the war was not begun on the right spot, and that it was unconstitutional, unnecessary, and wrong. Remember, too, that this he did after the war had been begun. It is one thing to be opposed to the declaration of a war, another and very different thing to take sides with the enemy against your own country after the war has been commenced. Our army was in Mexico at the time, many battles had been fought; our citizens, who were defending the honor of their country's flag, were surrounded by the daggers, the guns and the poison of the enemy. Then it was that Corwin made his speech in which he declared that the American soldiers ought to be welcomed by the Mexicans with bloody hands and hospitable graves; then it was that Ashmun and Lincoln voted in the House of Representatives that the war was unconstitutional and unjust; and Ashmun's resolution, Corwin's speech, and Lincoln's vote, were sent to Mexico and read at the head of the Mexican army, to prove to them that there was a Mexican party in the Congress of the United States who were doing all in their power to aid them. That a man who takes sides with the common enemy against his own country in time of war should rejoice in a war being made on me now, is very natural. And in my opinion, no other kind of a man would rejoice in it.

Mr. Lincoln has told you a great deal to-day about his being an old line Clay Whig. Bear in mind that there are a great many old Clay Whigs down in this region. It is more agreeable, therefore, for him to talk about the old Clay Whig party than it is for him to talk Abolitionism. We did not hear much about the old Clay Whig party up in the Abolition districts. How much of an old line Henry Clay Whig was he? Have you read General Singleton's speech at Jacksonville? You know that Gen. Singleton was, for twenty-five years, the confidential friend of Henry Clay in Illinois, and he testified that in 1847, when the Constitutional Convention of this State was in session, the Whig members were invited to a Whig caucus at the house of Mr. Lincoln's brother-in-law, where Mr. Lincoln proposed to throw Henry Clay overboard and take up Gen. Taylor in his place, giving, as his reason, that if the Whigs did not take up Gen. Taylor the Democrats would. Singleton testifies that Lincoln, in that speech, urged, as another reason for throwing Henry Clay overboard, that the Whigs had fought long enough for principle and ought to begin to fight for success. Singleton also testifies that Lincoln's speech did have the effect of cutting Clay's throat, and that he (Singleton) and others withdrew from the caucus in indignation. He further states that when they got to Philadelphia to attend the National Convention of the Whig party, that Lincoln was there, the bitter and deadly enemy of Clay, and that he tried to keep him (Singleton) out of the Convention because he insisted on voting for Clay, and Lincoln was determined to have Taylor. Singleton says that Lincoln rejoiced with very great joy when he found the mangled remains of the murdered Whig statesman lying cold before him. Now, Mr. Lincoln tells you that he is an old line Clay Whig! Gen. Singleton testifies to the facts I have narrated, in a public speech which has been printed and circulated broadcast over the State for weeks, yet not a lisp have we heard from Mr. Lincoln on the subject, except that he is an old Clay Whig.

What part of Henry Clay's policy did Lincoln ever advocate? He was in Congress in 1848–9, when the Wilmot proviso warfare disturbed the peace and harmony of the country, until it shook the foundation of the Republic from its center to its circumference. It was that agitation that brought Clay forth from his retirement at Ashland again to occupy his seat in the Senate of the United States, to see if he could not, by his great wisdom and experience, and the renown of his name, do something to restore peace and quiet to a disturbed country. Who got up that sectional strife that Clay had to be called upon to quell? I have heard Lincoln boast that he voted forty-two times for the Wilmot proviso, and that he would have voted as many times more if he could. Lincoln is the man, in connection with Seward, Cliase, Giddings, and other Abolitionists, who got up that strife that I helped Clay to put down. Henry Clay came back to the Senate in 1849, and saw that he must do something to restore peace to the country. The Union Whigs and the Union Democrats welcomed him the moment he arrived, as the man for the occasion. We believed that be, of all men on earth, had been preserved by Divine Providence to guide us out of our difficulties, and we Democrats rallied under Clay then, as you Whigs in nullification time rallied under the banner of old Jackson, forgetting party when the country was in danger, in order that we might have a country first, and parties afterward.

And this reminds me that Mr. Lincoln told you that the slavery question was the only thing that ever disturbed the peace and harmony of the Union. Did not nullification once raise its head and disturb the peace of this Union in 1832? Was that the slavery question, Mr. Lincoln? Did not disunion raise its monster head during the last war with Great Britain? Was that the slavery question, Mr. Lincoln? The peace of this country has been disturbed three times, once during the war with Great Britain, once on the tariff question, and once on the slavery question. His argument, therefore, that slavery is the only question that has ever created dissension in the Union falls to the ground. It is true that agitators are enabled now to use this slavery question for the purpose of sectional strife. He admits that in regard to all things else, the principle that I advocate, making each State and Territory free to decide for itself, ought to prevail. He instances the cranberry laws, and the oyster laws, and he might have gone through the whole list with the same effect. I say that all these laws are local and domestic, and that local and domestic concerns should be left to each State and each Territory to manage for itself. If agitators would acquiesce in that principle, there never would be any danger to the peace and harmony of the Union.

Mr. Lincoln tries to avoid the main issue by attacking the truth of my proposition, that our fathers made this Government divided into free and slave States, recognizing the right of each to decide all its local questions for itself. Did they not thus make it? It is true that they did not establish slavery in any of the States, or abolish it in any of them; but finding thirteen States, twelve of which were slave and one free, they agreed to form a government uniting them together, as they stood divided into free and slave States, and to guaranty forever to each State the right to do as it pleased on the slavery question. Having thus made the government, and conferred this right upon each State forever, I assert that this Government can exist as they made it, divided into free and slave States, if any one State chooses to retain slavery. He says that he looks forward to a time when slavery shall be abolished every where. I look forward to a time when each State shall be allowed to do as it pleases. If it chooses to keep slavery forever, it is not my business, but its own; if it chooses to abolish slavery, it is its own business— not mine. I care more for the great principle of self-government, the right of the people to rule, than I do for all the negroes in Christendom. I would not endanger the perpetuity of this Union, I would not blot out the great inalienable rights of the white men for all the negroes that ever existed. Hence, I say, let us maintain this Government on the principles that our fathers made it, recognizing the right of each State to keep slavery as long as its people determine, or to abolish it when they please. But Mr. Lincoln says that when our fathers made this Government they did not look forward to the state of things now existing, and therefore he thinks the doctrine was wrong; and he quotes Brooks, of South Carolina, to prove that our fathers then thought that probably slavery would be abolished by each State acting for itself before this time. Suppose they did; suppose they did not foresee what has occurred,—does that change the principles of our Government? They did not probably foresee the telegraph that transmits intelligence by lightning, nor did they foresee the railroads that now form the bonds of union between the different States, or the thousand mechanical inventions that have elevated mankind. But do these things change the principles of the Government? Our fathers, I say, made this Government on the principles of the right of each State to do as it pleases in its own domestic affairs, subject to the Constitution, and allowed the people of each to apply to every new change of circumstances such remedy as they may see fit to improve their condition. This right they have for all time to come.

Mr. Lincoln went on to tell you that he does not at all desire to interfere with slavery in the States where it exists, nor does his party. I expected him to say that down here. Let me ask him then how he expects to put slavery in the course of ultimate extinction every where, if he does not intend to interfere with it in the States where it exists? He says that he will prohibit it in all Territories, and the inference is, then, that unless they make free States out of them he will keep them out of the Union; for, mark you, he did not say whether or not he would vote to admit Kansas with slavery or not, as her people might apply (he forgot that as usual, etc.); he did not say whether or not he was in favor of bringing the Territories now in existence into the Union on the principle of Clay's Compromise measures on the slavery question. I told you that he would not. His idea is that he will prohibit slavery in all the Territories and thus force them all to become free States, surrounding the slave States with a cordon of free States and hemming them in, keeping the slaves confined to their present limits whilst they go on multiplying until the soil on which they live will no longer feed them, and he will thus be able to put slavery in a course of ultimate extinction by starvation. He will extinguish slavery in the Southern States as the French general exterminated the Algerines when he smoked them out. He is going to extinguish slavery by surrounding the slave States, hemming in the slaves and starving them out of existence, as you smoke a fox out of his hole. He intends to do that in the name of humanity and Christianity, in order that we may get rid of the terrible crime and sin entailed upon our fathers of holding slaves. Mr. Lincoln makes out that line of policy, and appeals to the moral sense of justice and to the Christian feeling of the community to sustain him. He says that any man who holds to the contrary doctrine is in the position of the king who claimed to govern by Divine right. Let us examine for a moment and see what principle it was that overthrew the Divine right of George the Third to govern us. Did not these colonies rebel because the British parliament had no right to pass laws concerning our property and domestic and private institutions without our consent? We demanded that the British Government should not pass such laws unless they gave us representation in the body passing them,—and this the British government insisting on doing,—we went to war, on the principle that the Home Government should not control and govern distant colonies without giving them a representation. Now, Mr. Lincoln proposes to govern the Territories without giving them a representation, and calls on Congress to pass laws controlling their property and domestic concerns without their consent and against their will. Thus, he asserts for his party the identical principle asserted by George III. and the Tories of the Revolution.

I ask you to look into these things, and then tell me whether the Democracy or the Abolitionists are right. I hold that the people of a Territory, like those of a State (I use the language of Mr. Buchanan in his letter of acceptance), have the right to decide for themselves whether slavery shall or shall not exist within their limits. The point upon which Chief Justice Taney expresses his opinion is simply this, that slaves being property, stand on an equal footing with other property, and consequently that the owner has the same right to carry that property into a Territory that he has any other, subject to the same conditions. Suppose that one of your merchants was to take fifty or one hundred thousand dollars' worth of liquors to Kansas. He has a right to go there under that decision, but when he gets there he finds the Maine liquor law in force, and what can he do with his properly after he gets it there? He cannot sell it, he cannot use it, it is subject to the local law, and that law is against him, and the best thing he can do with it is to bring it back into Missouri or Illinois and sell it. If you take negroes to Kansas, as Col. Jeff. Davis said in his Bangor speech, from which I have quoted to-day; you must take them there subject to the local law. If the people want the institution of slavery they will protect and encourage it; but if they do not want it they will withhold that protection, and the absence of local legislation protecting slavery excludes it as completely as a positive prohibition. You slaveholders of Missouri might as well understand what you know practically, that you cannot carry slavery where the people do not want it. All you have a right to ask is that the people shall do as they please; if they want slavery let them have it; if they do not want it, allow them to refuse to encourage it.

My friends, if, as I have said before, we will only live up to this great fundamental principle, there will be peace between the North and the South. Mr. Lincoln admits that under the Constitution on all domestic questions, except slavery, we ought not to interfere with the people of each State. What right have we to interfere with slavery any more than we have to interfere with any other question? He says that this slavery question is now the bone of contention. Why? Simply because agitators have combined in all the free States to make war upon it. Suppose the agitators in the States should combine in one-half of the Union to make war upon the railroad system of the other half? They would thus be driven to the same sectional strife. Suppose one section makes war upon any other peculiar institution of the opposite section, and the same strife is produced. The only remedy and safety is that we shall stand by the Constitution as our fathers made it, obey the laws as they are passed, while they stand the proper test and sustain the decisions of the Supreme Court and the constituted authorities.

IV.

"I Would Save the Union"

1859–1863

THE LINCOLN-DOUGLAS DEBATES catapulted Lincoln into national prominence. As a result of his newly found fame, Lincoln was invited by the Republican establishment to address audiences on the East Coast. Indeed, one of his greatest speeches to date was delivered in New York at the Cooper Institute on February 27, 1860, where he provided a cogent interpretation of the Founders' intentions to restrict slavery and to stigmatize it as a necessary evil. Given the enthusiastic response of eastern audiences to his speeches, it became increasingly clear that Lincoln would become a candidate for the Republican Party in the election of 1860, vying against antislavery luminaries like William Seward from New York and Salmon P. Chase from Ohio. Lincoln's lack of national prominence prior to the debates was actually a political asset: the absence of a recent congressional voting record on slavery prevented his being cast as either a radical or a conservative. Yet another advantage in gaining the Republican nomination was Lincoln's western origins. This made him appear less objectionable, and more moderate than either a southern or northern candidate. It also allowed the Republican Party to compete with the Democratic Douglas for western votes. Finally, since the Republican National Convention was to be held in Illinois, Lincoln would have the "home field advantage." When the time came, local Lincoln men packed the convention and rallied behind their favorite son.

In the fall of 1859, sectional tensions reached a watershed. On October 16, 1859, John Brown and twenty-two of his followers raided a federal arsenal at Harper's Ferry, Virginia in an effort to incite a servile revolt throughout the South. Brown's crusade was supported by a group of abolitionist ministers and philanthropists known as the "Secret Six," a cabal that included such prominent figures as Gerritt Smith and Theodore Parker. Apparently, these men believed that the slaves were ripe for rebellion; that only a small spark was needed to touch off a general conflagration, thereby incinerating the South's "peculiar institution." However, the misguided and ill-conceived attempt was suppressed. Brown was captured and two of his sons were killed during the fighting. Ironically, future heroes of the Confederacy, Lieutenant-Colonel Robert E. Lee and Lieutenant J.E.B Stuart of the U.S. Cavalry, helped to put down the rebellion. In a highly dramatic and publicized trial, Brown was found guilty of treason and hanged by the State of Virginia on Decemer 2, 1859. His execution transfigured

him into a martyr. Abolitionists like Ralph Waldo Emerson exalted him as a
Christ figure, proclaiming that: "The new saint will make the gallows as glorious as the cross." The canonization of John Brown by northern abolitionists
enraged the South and confirmed its worst fears of Yankee fanaticism. How
could the rights of southern people ever be secure in a Union with radicals who
attempted to incite a bloody and remorseless servile insurrection that would claim
the lives of innocent women and children? The virulent passions unleashed by
John Brown's raid only further aroused political immoderation on each side of
the Mason-Dixon line.

Events continued to portend an impending crisis a year later in the fall of
1860, when the Democratic Party split along sectional lines over the issue of a
federal slave code. Charleston, South Carolina, a volatile hot bed of states rights,
secessionism, and nullification, was chosen as the site of the Democratic National
Convention for 1860. While the Little Giant was the frontrunner for the Democratic nomination, his stance on popular sovereignty, his opposition to Lecompton, and his Freeport Doctrine alienated him from the southern wing of the
party. The issue of slavery had become so polarized that Douglas's position of
ethical neutrality had become unacceptable to proslavery southerners who
demanded positive protection for slavery, a demand that followed from the logic
of the Dred Scott Decision. At the convention, Douglas reiterated his commitment to popular sovereignty and his policy of congressional noninterference
with slavery. Southern Democrats girded for battle by putting forth the
"Alabama Platform," which proposed a national slave code backed by positive,
federal protection for slavery. The South's support for the vigorous exercise of
federal power to extend, affirm, and protect the "peculiar institution" of slavery
was inconsistent with its usual mantra of states rights. This inconsistency testifies
to the centrality of slavery as the cause of the Civil War. Indeed, for southern
radicals, the abstract principle of states rights was clearly subordinate to the concrete interest of promoting and protecting slavery. Led by William Yancey of
Alabama, southern fire-eaters conspired to walk out of the convention if they
did not gain explicit recognition of their "peculiar institution" as a moral and
legal right. Yancey excoriated Douglas and northern Democrats for failing to
affirm slavery as a positive good: "If you had taken the position directly that slavery was right, and therefore ought to be . . . you could have triumphed, and antislavery would now be dead in your midst." Yancey argued that through his
failure to affirm unequivocally the moral right to slavery and the legal right of
the national government to protect and extend it through a slave code, Douglas
had lent credence to the antislavery movement. When the proslavery plank was

voted down, irate Southerners stormed out of the convention: The entire delegations from Mississippi, Louisiana, South Carolina, Texas, and Florida were soon joined by others from Arkansas, Missouri, Georgia, Virginia, and Delaware. Meanwhile, Douglas and the northern Democrats reconvened in Baltimore where the Little Giant was finally nominated. The Southern wing of the party gathered first in Richmond but subsequently moved to Baltimore, where they adopted a national slave code and nominated John C. Breckinridge of Kentucky as their candidate. Thus, the Democratic Party, the only national party that was held together by a tenuous coalition of both sections, had now been polarized along sectional lines as well. The actions and agenda of Yancey, Rhett, and other fire-eaters who precipitated the split in the Democratic Party further confirm Lincoln's view that the underlying issue dividing North and South was over the inherent right or wrong of slavery and its meaning to the Union. This intra-party split, however, clearly bode well for Lincoln's success in the election of 1860.

The Illinois State Republican Convention, which was held in Decatur on May 9–10, nominated Lincoln as the Republican candidate of 1860. Judge David Davis, who rode the circuit with Lincoln, served as an astute campaign manager. Six days later on May 16–18, the Republican National Convention was held in Chicago. An enormous Wigwam designed to hold 10,000 people was constructed for the occasion. Lincoln did not attend the convention, but remained in Springfield where he eagerly monitored events. During a climactic moment in the Wigwam, two men produced a set of fence rails that Lincoln had allegedly split in 1830, proclaiming him as the "Rail Candidate." Henceforth he would be known as the "Rail Splitter." Indeed, much of the democratic myth that surrounds Lincoln as a self-made man of log cabin origins can be traced to the image-making efforts of his campaign managers during this time. William Seward of New York was the frontrunner in the race for the nomination. Although Seward was actually a moderate on the slavery question, he had used incendiary language in his antislavery speeches appealing to "higher law" and warning of "an irrepressible conflict" that branded him as a radical. Seward was victorious on the first ballot, but did not gain the necessary majority of delegates needed to clinch the nomination. Lincoln won the nomination on the third ballot after the Ohio and Pennsylvania delegations threw their support to him.

The Republican platform included a program of economic nationalism: a moderate protective tariff, a homestead act, a Pacific railroad, and "a daily Overland Mail." To gain the German vote, it opposed restrictions on immigration. And to assuage southern fears, it guaranteed "the right of each State to order and control its own domestic institutions according to its own judgments exclusively." With the impression of John Brown's Raid fresh in the public mind, the Republicans denounced, "lawless invasion by armed force of the soil of any State or Territory, no matter under what pretext, as among the gravest of crimes." On the issue of slavery, the Republicans invoked the Declaration's promise of equality, reaffirmed the national government's legal authority to restrict the institution in the territories, and supported the admission of Kansas as a free state. The platform denounced popular sovereignty and the proposal to reopen the African slave trade.

Fearing that the rights of states to spread and protect slavery would be insecure under a "Black Republican" administration, voices from the lower South threatened to secede if Lincoln was elected. In an effort to prevent this from happening, a group of former Whigs formed the Constitutional Union Party, nominating John Bell and Edward Everett as their respective presidential and vice presidential candidates. Deliberately avoiding a firm moral stance against slavery, this party attempted to provide an acceptable alternative to the disunionist extremism of northern radical abolitionists and southern fire-eaters alike. Aided by the split in the Democratic Party, on November 6, Lincoln was elected as president of the United States with less than 40 percent of the popular vote. The results of the election were as follows: Lincoln, Republican 1,866,452 popular votes, 180 electoral votes; Douglas, northern Democrat, 1,376,957 popular, 12 electoral; Breckinridge, southern Democrat, 849,781 popular, 72 electoral; Bell, Constitutional Union, 588,879 popular, 39 electoral. Upon hearing of Republican victories in the states of Pennsylvania and Indiana, which all but ensured Lincoln's election, Stephen A. Douglas remarked, "Mr. Lincoln is the next President. . . . We must try to save the Union. I will go South." He then set off on a tour to dissuade the south from secession. This was perhaps Douglas's finest hour; he died shortly afterward.

In defiance of Lincoln's election, South Carolina seceded from the Union on December 20, 1860. President Buchanan impotently demurred, claiming that although he believed secession was unconstitutional, he had no legal authority to coerce a state back into the Union. Buchanan thus watched as the Union was dismembered, avoiding the weight of responsibility and bequeathing the crisis to the next administration. In a "last-ditch effort" to avert bloodshed, a Senate committee of thirteen led by John Crittenden and a House committee of thirty-three were assembled to resolve the crisis. They proposed to appease the South through a compromise measure known as the Crittenden Compromise, which proposed an extension of the Missouri Compromise line to the Pacific: territories south of 36-30 would be open to slavery; those north of the line would be closed to it. Though he remained silent publicly, Lincoln privately made it clear to the Republican Party faithful that he opposed any measure that would subvert the core belief of the party: the moral and legal right to restrict slavery in the territories. The Republicans, argued Lincoln, had carried the election fairly on the basis of these principles; to retreat from them would signify a betrayal to the entire antislavery movement. Such appeasement would only encourage further extortion. Thus, Lincoln was willing to risk war rather than compromise on the core principles of the antislavery movement and the Republican Party.

Perhaps one of Lincoln's greatest miscalculations as president was to underestimate the resolve of the South in seceding from the Union, and to overestimate the strength of southern unionism. Initially, Lincoln suspected that the South was once again bluffing to gain concessions for slavery. Events proved him wrong. Throughout the late fall of 1860 and the winter of 1861, Confederates seized federal property, forts, and arsenals. The only remaining forts under federal possession in the South were Fort Moultrie in South Carolina and Fort Pickens in Pensacola, Florida. On December 26, 1860, Major John Anderson, commander of Fort Moultrie in South Carolina and a Kentucky Unionist who refused to surrender to the rebel forces, moved his garrison to the more easily defended Fort Sumter, which was located on a sandbar in the middle of Charleston Harbor. By Febuary 1, 1861, Mississippi, Florida, Alabama, Georgia, Louisiana, and Texas had joined South Carolina in seceding from the Union—seven states in all. On February 4, in Montgomery, Alabama, the states of the lower South joined together in establishing a new government, the Confederate States of America. Jefferson Davis, senator from Mississippi, was sworn in as president of the new Confederacy. Thus, before Lincoln was inaugurated on March 4, 1861, seven states had seceded from the Union and formed a new government of their own. In addition, federal forts, property, and arsenals were confiscated throughout the South by rebel forces. On March 21, 1861, Alexander Stephens, Vice President of the newly formed Confederate States of America, proclaimed the new moral foundations of the Confederacy in his infamous "Corner Stone" speech:

> Our new government is founded upon exactly the opposite idea [to the principle of equality in the Declaration]; its foundations are laid, its corner stone rests upon the great truth that the negro is not equal to the white man. That slavery—subordination to the superior race, is his natural and normal condition. This, our new Government, is the first, in the history of the world, based upon this great physical and moral truth.

Lincoln began and ended his presidency under the ominous cloud of assassination. After winning the election in November, he embarked on a twelve-day trip from Springfield to the Capitol in mid-February. To his humiliation, Lincoln had to enter Washington in disguise, during the night, in view of revelations of a plot to assassinate him in Baltimore en route to the Capitol. Rumors circulated that he was disguised in a Scottish plaid cap and kilt. The press lampooned him mercilessly as an awkward baboon and a silly, uncouth, coward.

In his First Inaugural Address of March 4, 1861, Lincoln provided a point-by-point refutation of secession, claiming that the Union was perpetual and older than the Constitution, and that it had evolved into a national entity by the time of the Constitution. Denying both a constitutional and moral right to secession, Lincoln characterized it as "the essence of anarchy" claiming that a "majority, held in restraint by constitutional checks, and limitations, and always changing easily, with deliberate changes of popular opinions and sentiments, is the only true sovereign of a free people. Whoever rejects it, does of necessity, fly to anarchy or to despotism. Unanimity is impossible; the rule of a minority as a permanent arrangement, is wholly inadmissible; so that, rejecting the majority principle, anarchy or despotism in some form, is all that is left." At the beginning of his speech, Lincoln noted that the principles of the Republican platform were perfectly lawful and that the party had fairly carried an election on the basis of such principles. The administration had not perpetrated any unlawful act against the South, and it certainly had not committed a "long train of abuses" that would justify a moral right to revolution. Reassuring the South that he would not touch slavery where it already existed, Lincoln stated that, "I have no purpose directly, or indirectly, to interfere with the institution of slavery in the States where it exists. I believe I have no lawful right to do so, and I have no inclination to do so."

However, unlike Buchanan who watched the dismemberment of the Union without raising a finger, Lincoln clearly stated that his duty as chief executive obligated him to preserve the territorial integrity of the regime, "I therefore consider that, in view of the Constitution and the laws, the Union is unbroken; and, to the extent of my ability, I shall take care, as the Constitution itself expressly enjoins upon me, that the laws of the Union be faithfully executed in all States." Thus, he would "hold, occupy, and possess the property, and places belonging to the government," an allusion to Fort Sumter. Lincoln's careful use of the words "hold, occupy, and possess" intended to demonstrate resolution to the South without provocation. He concluded his First Inaugural with a poetic appeal to fraternity and patriotism, "I am loth to close. We are not enemies, but friends. We must not be enemies. Though passion may have strained, it must not break our bonds of affection. The mystic chords of memory, stretching from every battle-field, and patriot grave, to every living heart and hearthstone, all over this broad land, will yet swell the chorus of the Union, when again touched, as surely they will be, by the better angels of our nature."

On April 12 Fort Sumter was bombarded. Events then moved rapidly towards war. On April 15 Lincoln called on the states to supply 75,000 men for three months' service. In response to his call for troops, Virginia passed a secession ordinance on April 17, which was ultimately approved on May 22, 1861. Troubles mounted. On April 19 a Massachusetts infantry headed to protect Washington was mobbed in Baltimore by Confederate sympathizers. In response to this, a delegation from Baltimore was sent to Washington requesting that no more federal troops pass through the city en route to the Capitol. Ever perilous, Confederate troops were just across the Potomac River in Alexandria, Virginia. Lincoln agonized, fearing that the enemy would soon take Washington. To his relief, federal troops finally arrived to defend the city on April 25.

During the controversial "Eighty Days" from April 15 to July 4, Lincoln suspended the writ of habeas corpus, declared a blockade of southern ports, raised troops, and approved federal spending without congressional authorization. Though Congress was adjourned during this interval, he could have summoned a special session. Instead, Lincoln delayed the call until July 4, thereby giving himself a free hand in responding to the rebellion without congressional interference. And when Chief Justice Taney ruled against the suspension of the writ of habeas corpus, Lincoln simply ignored his decision.

It is quite likely that Lincoln delayed calling a special session of Congress to ensure the orderly and safe convocation of the new government. It would have seriously undermined the domestic and foreign credibility of the new administration if Confederate obstruction and subversion blocked Congress from meeting in Washington, D.C. It should be emphasized that the states adjacent to the capital, Maryland and Virginia, were tottering on the verge of rebellion. The latter may have been prevented from seceding through the palpable threat of a federal bombardment of its cities. The thwarting of the new Congress's ability to assemble and its vulnerability to a preemptive strike would have represented a *fait accompli* to many, thereby demoralizing the Union cause. Lincoln was clearly mindful of this when he explained: "it cannot be believed that the framers of the instrument intended, that in every case, the danger should run its course, until Congress could be called together; the very assembling of which might be prevented, as was intended in this case, by the rebellion."

Lincoln's extraordinary actions in suppressing the rebellion in its early stages illustrate the dynamic tension in a constitutional democracy between balancing liberty and security in times of crisis. Lincoln would justify his use of executive power in his celebrated message to Congress in a Special Session on July 4, 1861. The symbolic date of the speech appealed to the nation's patriotism in defense of its first principles enshrined in the Declaration. Defending his suspension of the writ of habeas corpus, Lincoln asked, "are all the laws, *but one*, to go unexecuted, lest that one be violated?" He then explained that even if the Constitution strictly forbid his action, under the circumstances he still would have been justified, given his duty to preserve the government. However, since the Constitution provides for the suspension of the writ in cases of rebellion (article 1, sec. 10), no law was violated. Did Lincoln bend the Constitution without breaking it? Or did he establish a constitutional dictatorship as some scholars have claimed?

Populations on the eve of conflict were as follows: For the North: 20,000,000; for the South: 6,000,000 whites and 3,500,000 slaves. The battles of the Civil War were divided into a western theatre around the Mississippi and an eastern theatre around the Chesapeake Peninsula. The Union strategy in the beginning of the war was to seize the southern capital of Richmond, split the Confederacy by controlling the Mississippi, and implement an "anaconda strategy," strangling the South through a blockade. Southern strategy was to gain diplomatic recognition and aid from a European ally, France or Britain, to seize Washington, D.C. and to shatter federal morale through an invasion of the North, thereby guaranteeing a peace that would recognize the Confederacy's independence. It is estimated that in total over 600,000 Americans died during the Civil War, more than all the combined wars fought by the United States, including World War I, World War II, Korea, and Vietnam!

The chronology of speeches in this section ends with Lincoln's preliminary draft of the Emancipation Proclamation on September 22, 1862, and his final draft, which took effect on January 1, 1863. From the beginning of the war, Lincoln was under pressure from radicals to free the slaves. Abolitionists saw an opportunity to extirpate the institution once and for all. Throughout the conflict slaves fled their masters seeking the protection of the Union armies. What should be done with these fugitives? One Union commander actually called for a ceasefire in order to return fugitive slaves back to the Confederate Army, claiming that he would not wage war against southern "property." In 1862, Union soldiers from Ohio wrote to their congressman telling him that they would not fight a war that led to a mass migration of blacks northward. These actions testify to northern racism, which was particularly vehement among Democrats, who opposed any efforts to free the slaves or to ameliorate their condition. To prevent further return of fugitive slaves, Congress passed a Confiscation Act on August 6, 1861. This authorized Union armies to confiscate as contraband any persons or property used by the enemy to make war on the government. The Confiscation Act was a first legal step towards emancipation. Radicals in Lincoln's own time and progressives today have criticized Lincoln for prudently delaying emancipation until public opinion could have supported it. Carefully measuring the consequences of his actions, Lincoln believed that to emancipate the slaves in defiance of the law and against public opinion could have seriously undermined the Union's war efforts, thereby granting the South victory and putting an end to the aspiration of liberty and equality for all human beings. He consistently maintained that the cause of liberty and equality was most secure under the auspices of a national Union, which was the *sine qua non* of achieving the loftier goal of black freedom. In order to defeat the Confederacy, Lincoln needed to maintain a broad war coalition, which consisted of the Border States of Kentucky, Missouri, Maryland and Delaware. Complicating matters for the president was the fact that these states had slaves, but remained loyal to the Union. In addition, Lincoln also needed the support of War Democrats who were willing to fight to preserve the Union, but much less willing to fight for blacks. He had revoked two unauthorized emancipations by his generals. After one of these, a company of Union soldiers threw down its arms complaining that they enlisted to save the Union, not to "free the niggers." Lincoln also delayed the Emancipation Proclamation until it could be crowned with a Union victory. Without such a victory the government's actions would lack public credibility, appearing to be the final, reckless act of a desperate administration. Although he had composed a draft of the Emancipation as early as July, he waited until events were ripe. The symbolic Union victory came at the Battle of Antietam on September 17, 1862 where Lee was driven out of Maryland. Five days later, Lincoln issued a preliminary Emancipation on September 22, 1862. He justified the Emancipation as a war measure under his authority as commander in chief of the armed forces. The final version of the Emancipation also provided for the enlistment of black soldiers. By encouraging slaves to flee from their captors and to join the Union army, the Emancipation served as dual purpose in crippling the South's ability to make war and strengthening the Union's ability to wage it. Because the Emancipation was legally justified as a war measure against an enemy combatant, it did not apply to those jurisdictions loyal to the Union—namely, the Border States, which had slaves. Thus, to prevent the Emancipation from being retracted by subsequent administrations and to ensure that slavery would be abolished everywhere throughout the Union, Lincoln endorsed the Thirteenth Amendment. And he shrewdly steered it through congressional approval in 1865.

Lincoln has been denigrated by some as a political pragmatist for placing the Union's preservation above the immediate goal of emancipation. In support of this view, critics cite Lincoln's letter to Greeley in which he claimed that his "paramount object" was to save the Union, not to free the slaves. However, as I demonstrate in the introduction to this volume, his commitment to equality was not compromised in his reply to Greely, if one recognizes that the twin goals of preserving the Union and ending slavery were inseparably linked in his mind. Preserving the Union, for Lincoln, always meant preserving the principles for which the Union stood. Because the Union was dedicated to the principle of equality, its preservation meant that slavery would ultimately be abolished. Indeed, this was standard Republican Party ideology. Lincoln clearly articulated his vision of a Union dedicated to just moral ends as early as 1854. In a speech at Bloomington, he noted that, "the Union must be preserved in the purity of its principles." The same year, at Peoria, he emphasized that "the Union must be worthy of saving!" However, the Union was only worthy of saving in light of those principles for which it stood. And while en route to his first inauguration, he noted at Trenton, New Jersey, that his goal as president elect was to preserve "the original idea" for which the nation was founded—that is, the ideas of liberty and equality affirmed by the Declaration.

Indeed, the South recognized that Lincoln was a principled and implacable foe of slavery—that is why it seceded in the first place. The South correctly understood that slavery was eventually doomed to extinction in a regime committed to the principles of the Declaration and by a leader committed to the containment of and eventual extinction of its peculiar institution.

LETTER TO J. W. FELL, ENCLOSING AUTOBIOGRAPHY
DECEMBER 20, 1859

Lincoln's brief autobiography to Jesse Fell was part of his movement toward candidacy for the Republican Party in the upcoming presidential election of 1860. Publicly, Lincoln feigned indifference to seeking the presidential office, while behind the scenes, he privately worked to secure the nomination. In December of 1859, he submitted this autobiography to Jesse Fell, an Illinois politician, who published it in a Pennsylvania newspaper to enhance Lincoln's reputation in the East. This particular autobiography became a primary source for other newspapers throughout the nation. However, it was extremely short and sparse. Without much embellishment or detail, Lincoln described his rustic origins, his

selection as a captain in the Black Hawk war, his dual legal and political career in Spring-
field, and his devotion to Whig principles. He ascribed his return to public life as an urgent
response to the proslavery threat of the Kansas-Nebraska Act. Perhaps due to his humor-
ous, self-deprecating nature, he concluded the biography with an unflattering physical
description of himself, playfully commenting, "no other marks or brands recollected."

SPRINGFIELD, DEC. 20, 1859
J. W. FELL, ESQ
MY DEAR SIR:

Herewith is a little sketch, as you requested. There is not much of it, for the reason, I suppose, that there is not much of me. If anything be made out of it, I wish it to be modest, and not to go beyond the materials. If it were thought necessary to incorporate any thing from any of my speeches, I suppose there would be no objection. Of course it must not appear to have been written by myself.

Yours very truly

A. Lincoln

I WAS BORN FEB. 12, 1809, in Hardin County, Kentucky. My parents were both born in Virginia, of undistinguished families—second families, perhaps I should say. My mother, who died in my tenth year, was of a family of the name of Hanks, some of whom now reside in Adams, and others in Macon Counties, Illinois. My paternal grandfather, Abraham Lincoln, emigrated from Rocking-ham County, Virginia, to Kentucky, about 1781 or 2, where, a year or two later, he was killed by indians, not in battle, but by stealth, when he was laboring to open a farm in the forest. His ancestors, who were Quakers, went to Virginia from Berks County, Pennsylvania. An effort to identify them with the New-England family of the same name ended in nothing more definite, than a similarity of Christian names in both families, such as Enoch, Levi, Mordecai, Solomon, Abraham, and the like.

My father, at the death of his father, was but six years of age; and he grew up, litterally [sic] without education. He removed from Kentucky to what is now Spencer County, Indiana, in my eighth year. We reached our new home about the time the State came into the Union. It was a wild region, with many bears and other wild animals, still in the woods. There I grew up. There were some schools, so called; but no qualification was ever required of a teacher beyond "readin, writin, and cipherin" to the Rule of Three. If a straggler supposed to understand latin happened to sojourn in the neighborhood, he was looked upon as a wizzard [sic]. There was absolutely nothing to excite ambition for education. Of course when I came of age I did not know much. Still some-how, I could read, write, and cipher to the Rule of Three; but that was all. I have not been to school since. The little advance I now have upon this store of education, I have picked up from time to time under the pressure of necessity.

I was raised to farm work, which I continued till I was twenty-two. At twenty one I came to Illinois, and passed the first year in Macon County. Then I got to New-Salem (at that time in Sangamon, now in Menard County, where I remained a year as a sort of Clerk in a store. Then came the Black-Hawk war; and I was elected a Captain of Volunteers—a success which gave me more pleasure than any I have had since. I went the campaign, was elated, ran for the Legislature the same year (1832) and was beaten—the only time I ever have been beaten by the people. The next, and three succeeding biennial elections, I was elected to the Legislature. I was not a candidate afterwards. During this Legislative period I had studied law, and removed to Springfield to practise it. In 1846 I was once elected to the lower House of Congress. Was not a candidate for re-election. From 1849 to 1854, both inclusive, practiced law more assiduously than ever before. Always a whig in politics, and generally on the whig electoral tickets, making active can-vasses—I was losing interest in politics, when the repeal of the Missouri Com-promise aroused me again. What I have done since then is pretty well known.

If any personal description of me is thought desirable, it may be said, I am, in height, six feet, four inches, nearly; lean in flesh, weighing on an average one hundred and eighty pounds; dark complexion, with coarse black hair, and grey eyes—no other marks or brands recollected.

Yours very truly
A. Lincoln.
Hon J W. Fell.

ADDRESS AT COOPER INSTITUTE, NEW YORK
FEBRUARY 27, 1860

After gaining national recognition through the debates with Douglas, Lincoln was invited by Henry Ward Beecher, the abolitionist preacher, to speak at Plymouth Church in Brooklyn. The venue was then changed to Cooper Union in Manhattan. Recognized as a tour de force, Lincoln's well-crafted speech won over the eastern establishment and catapulted him towards candidacy for the Republican Party. Indeed, the historian Harold Holzer claims that the Cooper Union Address made Lincoln President. It was crafted in response to Stephen A. Douglas's "Dividing Line" speech—the definitive case for pop-ular sovereignty published by Harper's New Monthly Magazine *in September of*

1859. With the assistance of the renowned historian George Bancroft, Douglas attempted to show that popular sovereignty reflected the Founders' views on slavery. "Our fathers," Douglas claimed, "understood this question just as well, and even better than we do now." Taking Douglas at his word, Lincoln seized upon this phrase and made it the rhetorical backbone of his speech. To prove his case that the Founders' actually supported the federal restriction of slavery in the territories, Lincoln exhaustively researched historical documents relating to the question. After identifying the thirty-nine signers of the Constitution as "our fathers," an allusion to the Lord's Prayer, he then cross examined their voting record on the federal government's right to restrict slavery in the territories. He showed that of the thirty-nine fathers who signed the Constitution, twenty-three left a clear voting record on slavery extension. Of these, twenty-one voted in favor of restriction. And of the sixteen who left no clear voting record, fifteen had expressed antislavery convictions. Lincoln's tally of the Founders' intent thus results in a thirty-six to three vote in favor of restricting slavery! Lincoln's characterization of the Republican Party as a conservative party and his condemnation of John Brown's raid were efforts to distinguish himself as an antislavery moderate from the disunionist extremism of the radical abolitionists.

MR. PRESIDENT AND FELLOW CITIZENS OF NEW YORK:—

The facts with which I shall deal this evening are mainly old and familiar; nor is there anything new in the general use I shall make of them. If there shall be any novelty, it will be in the mode of presenting the facts, and the inferences and observations following that presentation.

In his speech last autumn, at Columbus, Ohio, as reported in "The New-York Times," Senator Douglas said:

> "Our fathers, when they framed the Government under which we live, understood this question just as well, and even better, than we do now."

I fully indorse this, and I adopt it as a text for this discourse. I so adopt it because it furnishes a precise and an agreed starting point for a discussion between Republicans and that wing of the Democracy headed by Senator Douglas. It simply leaves the inquiry: *"What was the understanding those fathers had of the question mentioned?"*

What is the frame of government under which we live?

The answer must be: "The Constitution of the United States." That Constitution consists of the original, framed in 1787, (and under which the present government first went into operation,) and twelve subsequently framed amendments, the first ten of which were framed in 1789.

Who were our fathers that framed the Constitution? I suppose the "thirty-nine" who signed the original instrument may be fairly called our fathers who framed that part of the present Government. It is almost exactly true to say they framed it, and it is altogether true to say they fairly represented the opinion and sentiment of the whole nation at that time. Their names, being familiar to nearly all, and accessible to quite all, need not now be repeated.

I take these "thirty-nine," for the present, as being "our fathers who framed the Government under which we live."

What is the question which, according to the text, those fathers understood "just as well, and even better than we do now?"

It is this: Does the proper division of local from federal authority, or anything in the Constitution, forbid our *Federal Government* to control as to slavery in *our Federal Territories?*

Upon this, Senator Douglas holds the affirmative, and Republicans the negative. This affirmation and denial form an issue; and this issue—this question—is precisely what the text declares our fathers understood "better than we."

Let us now inquire whether the "thirty-nine," or any of them, ever acted upon this question; and if they did, how they acted upon it—how they expressed that better understanding?

In 1784, three years before the Constitution—the United States then owning the Northwestern Territory, and no other, the Congress of the Confederation had before them the question of prohibiting slavery in that Territory; and four of the "thirty-nine" who afterward framed the Constitution, were in that Congress, and voted on that question. Of these, Roger Sherman, Thomas Mifflin, and Hugh Williamson voted for the prohibition, thus showing that, in their understanding, no line dividing local from federal authority, nor anything else, properly forbade the Federal Government to control as to slavery in federal territory. The other of the four—James M'Henry—voted against the prohibition, showing that, for some cause, he thought it improper to vote for it.

In 1787, still before the Constitution, but while the Convention was in session framing it, and while the Northwestern Territory still was the only territory owned by the United States, the same question of prohibiting slavery in the territory again came before the Congress of the Confederation; and two more of the "thirty-nine" who afterward signed the Constitution, were in that Congress, and voted on the question. They were William Blount and William Few; and they both voted for the prohibition—thus showing that, in their understanding, no line dividing local from federal authority, nor anything else, properly forbids the Federal Government to control as to slavery in Federal territory. This time the prohibition became a law, being part of what is now well known as the Ordinance of '87.

The question of federal control of slavery in the territories, seems not to have been directly before the Convention which framed the original Constitution; and hence it is not recorded that the "thirty-nine," or any of them, while engaged on that instrument, expressed any opinion on that precise question.

In 1789, by the first Congress which sat under the Constitution, an act was passed to enforce the Ordinance of '87, including the prohibition of slavery in the Northwestern Territory. The bill for this act was reported by one of the "thirty-nine," Thomas Fitzsimmons, then a member of the House of Representatives from Pennsylvania. It went through all its stages without a word of opposition, and finally passed both branches without yeas and nays, which is equivalent to an unanimous passage. In this Congress there were sixteen of the thirty-nine fathers who framed the original Constitution. They were John Langdon, Nicholas Gilman, Wm. S. Johnson, Roger Sherman, Robert Morris, Thos. Fitzsimmons, William Few, Abraham Baldwin, Rufus King, William Paterson, George Clymer, Richard Bassett, George Read, Pierce Butler, Daniel Carroll, James Madison.

This shows that, in their understanding, no line dividing local from federal authority, nor anything in the Constitution, properly forbade Congress to prohibit slavery in the federal territory; else both their fidelity to correct principle, and their oath to support the Constitution, would have constrained them to oppose the prohibition.

Again, George Washington, another of the "thirty-nine," was then President of the United States, and, as such approved and signed the bill; thus completing its validity as a law, and thus showing that, in his understanding, no line dividing local from federal authority, nor anything in the Constitution, forbade the Federal Government, to control as to slavery in federal territory.

No great while after the adoption of the original Constitution, North Carolina ceded to the Federal Government the country now constituting the State of Tennessee; and a few years later Georgia ceded that which now constitutes the States of Mississippi and Alabama. In both deeds of cession it was made a condition by the ceding States that the Federal Government should not prohibit slavery in the ceded country. Besides this, slavery was then actually in the ceded country. Under these circumstances, Congress, on taking charge of these countries, did not absolutely prohibit slavery within them. But they did interfere with it—take control of it—even there, to a certain extent. In 1798, Congress organized the Territory of Mississippi. In the act of organization, they prohibited the bringing of slaves into the Territory, from any place without the United States, by fine, and giving freedom to slaves so brought. This act passed both branches of Congress without yeas and nays. In that Congress were three of the "thirty-nine" who framed the original Constitution. They were John Langdon, George Read and Abraham Baldwin. They all, probably, voted for it. Certainly they would have placed their opposition to it upon record, if, in their understanding, any line dividing local from federal authority, or anything in the Constitution, properly forbade the Federal Government to control as to slavery in federal territory.

In 1803, the Federal Government purchased the Louisiana country. Our former territorial acquisitions came from certain of our own States; but this Louisiana country was acquired from a foreign nation. In 1804, Congress gave a territorial organization to that part of it which now constitutes the State of Louisiana. New Orleans, lying within that part, was an old and comparatively large city. There were other considerable towns and settlements, and slavery was extensively and thoroughly intermingled with the people. Congress did not, in the Territorial Act, prohibit slavery; but they did interfere with it—take control of it—in a more marked and extensive way than they did in the case of Mississippi. The substance of the provision therein made, in relation to slaves, was:

First. That no slave should be imported into the territory from foreign parts.

Second. That no slave should be carried into it who had been imported into the United States since the first day of May, 1798.

Third. That no slave should be carried into it, except by the owner, and for his own use as a settler; the penalty in all the cases being a fine upon the violator of the law, and freedom to the slave.

This act also was passed without yeas and nays. In the Congress which passed it, there were two of the "thirty-nine." They were Abraham Baldwin and Jonathan Dayton. As stated in the case of Mississippi, it is probable they both voted for it. They would not have allowed it to pass without recording their opposition to it, if, in their understanding, it violated either the line properly dividing local from federal authority, or any provision of the Constitution.

In 1819–20, came and passed the Missouri question. Many votes were taken, by yeas and nays, in both branches of Congress, upon the various phases of the general question. Two of the "thirty-nine"—Rufus King and Charles Pinckney—were members of that Congress. Mr. King steadily voted for slavery prohibition and against all compromises, while Mr. Pinckney as steadily voted against slavery prohibition and against all compromises. By this, Mr. King showed that, in his understanding, no line dividing local from federal authority, nor anything in the Constitution, was violated by Congress prohibiting slavery in federal territory; while Mr. Pinckney, by his votes, showed that, in his understanding, there was some sufficient reason for opposing such prohibition in that case.

The cases I have mentioned are the only acts of the "thirty-nine," or of any of them, upon the direct issue, which I have been able to discover.

To enumerate the persons who thus acted, as being four in 1784, two in 1787, seventeen in 1789, three in 1798, two in 1804, and two in 1819–20—there would be thirty of them. But this would be counting John Langdon, Roger Sherman, William Few, Rufus King, and George Read each twice, and Abraham Baldwin, three times. The true number of those of the "thirty-nine" whom I have shown to have acted upon the question, which, by the text, they understood better than we, is twenty-three, leaving sixteen not shown to have acted upon it in any way.

Here, then, we have twenty-three out of our thirty-nine fathers "who framed the government under which we live," who have, upon their official responsibility and their corporal oaths, acted upon the very question which the text affirms they "understood just as well, and even better than we do now;" and twenty-one of them—a clear majority of the whole "thirty-nine"—so acting upon it as to make them guilty of gross political impropriety and wilful perjury, if, in their understanding, any proper division between local and federal authority, or anything in the Constitution they had made themselves, and sworn to support, forbade the Federal Government to control as to slavery in the federal territories. Thus the twenty-one acted; and, as actions speak louder than words, so actions, under such responsibility, speak still louder.

Two of the twenty-three voted against Congressional prohibition of slavery in the federal territories, in the instances in which they acted upon the question. But for what reasons they so voted is not known. They may have done so because they thought a proper division of local from federal authority, or some provision or principle of the Constitution, stood in the way; or they may, without any such question, have voted against the prohibition, on what appeared to them to be sufficient grounds of expediency. No one who has sworn to support the Constitution can conscientiously vote for what he understands to be an unconstitutional measure, however expedient he may think it; but one may and ought to vote against a measure which he deems constitutional, if, at the same time, he deems it inexpedient. It, therefore, would be unsafe to set down even the two who voted against the prohibition, as having done so because, in their understanding, any proper division of local from federal authority, or anything in the Constitution, forbade the Federal Government to control as to slavery in federal territory.

The remaining sixteen of the "thirty-nine," so far as I have discovered, have left no record of their understanding upon the direct question of federal control of slavery in the federal territories. But there is much reason to believe that their understanding upon that question would not have appeared different from that of their twenty-three compeers, had it been manifested at all.

For the purpose of adhering rigidly to the text, I have purposely omitted whatever understanding may have been manifested by any person, however distinguished, other than the thirty-nine fathers who framed the original Constitution; and, for the same reason, I have also omitted whatever understanding may have been manifested by any of the "thirty-nine" even, on any other phase of the general question of slavery. If we should look into their acts and declarations on those other phases, as the foreign slave trade, and the morality and policy of slavery generally, it would appear to us that on the direct question of federal control of slavery in federal territories, the sixteen, if they had acted at all, would probably have acted just as the twenty-three did. Among that sixteen were several of the most noted antislavery men of those times—as Dr. Franklin, Alexander Hamilton and Gouverneur Morris—while there was not one now known to have been otherwise, unless it may be John Rutledge, of South Carolina.

The sum of the whole is, that of our thirty-nine fathers who framed the original Constitution, twenty-one—a clear majority of the whole—certainly understood that no proper division of local from federal authority, nor any part of the Constitution, forbade the Federal Government to control slavery in the federal territories; while all the rest probably had the same understanding. Such, unquestionably, was the understanding of our fathers who framed the original Constitution; and the text affirms that they understood the question "better than we."

But, so far, I have been considering the understanding of the question manifested by the framers of the original Constitution. In and by the original instrument, a mode was provided for amending it; and, as I have already stated, the present frame of "the Government under which we live" consists of that original, and twelve amendatory articles framed and adopted since. Those who now insist that federal control of slavery in federal territories violates the Constitution, point us to the provisions which they suppose it thus violates; and, as I understand, that all fix upon provisions in these amendatory articles, and not in the original instrument. The Supreme Court, in the Dred Scott case, plant themselves upon the fifth amendment, which provides that no person shall be deprived of "life, liberty or property without due process of law;" while Senator Douglas and his peculiar adherents plant themselves upon the tenth amendment, providing that "the powers not delegated to the United States by the Constitution" "are reserved to the States respectively, or to the people."

Now, it so happens that these amendments were framed by the first Congress which sat under the Constitution—the identical Congress which passed the act already mentioned, enforcing the prohibition of slavery in the Northwestern Territory. Not only was it the same Congress, but they were the identical, same individual men who, at the same session, and at the same time within the session, had under consideration, and in progress toward maturity, these Constitutional amendments, and this act prohibiting slavery in all the territory the nation then owned. The Constitutional amendments were introduced before, and passed after the act enforcing the Ordinance of '87; so that, during the whole pendency of the act to enforce the Ordinance, the Constitutional amendments were also pending.

The seventy-six members of that Congress, including sixteen of the framers of the original Constitution, as before stated, were pre-eminently our fathers who framed that part of "the Government under which we live," which is now claimed as forbidding the Federal Government to control slavery in the federal territories.

Is it not a little presumptuous in any one at this day to affirm that the two things which that Congress deliberately framed, and carried to maturity at the same time, are absolutely inconsistent with each other? And does not such affirmation become impudently absurd when coupled with the other affirmation from the same mounth, that those who did the two things, alleged to be inconsistent, understood whether they really were inconsistent better than we—better than he who affirms that they are inconsistent?

It is surely safe to assume that the thirty-nine framers of the original Constitution, and the seventy-six members of the Congress which framed the amendments thereto, taken together, do certainly include those who may be fairly called "our fathers who framed the Government under which we live." And so assuming, I defy any man to show that any one of them ever, in his whole life, declared that, in his understanding, any proper division of local from federal authority, or any part of the Constitution, forbade the Federal Government to control as to slavery in the federal territories. I go a step further. I defy any one to show that any living man in the whole world ever did, prior to the beginning of the present century, (and I might almost say prior to the beginning of the last half of the present century,) declare that, in his understanding, any proper division of local from federal authority, or any part of the Constitution, forbade the

Federal Government to control as to slavery in the federal territories. To those who now so declare, I give, not only "our fathers who framed the Government under which we live," but with them all other living men within the century in which it was framed, among whom to search, and they shall not be able to find the evidence of a single man agreeing with them.

Now, and here, let me guard a little against being misunderstood. I do not mean to say we are bound to follow implicitly in whatever our fathers did. To do so, would be to discard all the lights of current experience—to reject all progress—all improvement. What I do say is, that if we would supplant the opinions and policy of our fathers in any case, we should do so upon evidence so conclusive, and argument so clear, that even their great authority, fairly considered and weighed, cannot stand; and most surely not in a case whereof we ourselves declare they understood the question better than we.

If any man at this day sincerely believes that a proper division of local from federal authority, or any part of the Constitution, forbids the Federal Government to control as to slavery in the federal territories, he is right to say so, and to enforce his position by all truthful evidence and fair argument which he can. But he has no right to mislead others, who have less access to history, and less leisure to study it, into the false belief that "our fathers who framed the Government under which we live" were of the same opinion—thus substituting falsehood and deception for truthful evidence and fair argument. If any man at this day sincerely believes "our fathers who framed the Government under which we live," used and applied principles, in other cases, which ought to have led them to understand that a proper division of local from federal authority or some part of the Constitution, forbids the Federal Government to control as to slavery in the federal territories, he is right to say so. But he should, at the same time, brave the responsibility of declaring that, in his opinion, he understands their principles better than they did themselves; and especially should he not shirk that responsibility by asserting that they "understood the question just as well, and even better, than we do now."

But enough! *Let all who believe that "our fathers, who framed the Government under which we live, understood this question just as well, and even better, than we do now," speak as they spoke, and act as they acted upon it. This is all Republicans ask— all Republicans desire—in relation to slavery. As those fathers marked it, so let it be again marked, as an evil not to be extended, but to be tolerated and protected only because of and so far as its actual presence among us makes that toleration and protection a necessity. Let all the guaranties those fathers gave it, be, not grudgingly, but fully and fairly, maintained.* For this Republicans contend, and with this, so far as I know or believe, they will be content.

And now, if they would listen—as I suppose they will not—I would address a few words to the Southern people.

I would say to them:—You consider yourselves a reasonable and a just people; and I consider that in the general qualities of reason and justice you are not inferior to any other people. Still, when you speak of us Republicans, you do so only to denounce us as reptiles, or, at the best, as no better than outlaws. You will grant a hearing to pirates or murderers, but nothing like it to "Black Republicans." In all your contentions with one another, each of you deems an unconditional condemnation of "Black Republicanism" as the first thing to be attended to. Indeed, such condemnation of us seems to be an indispensable prerequisite—license, so to speak—among you to be admitted or permitted to speak at all. Now, can you, or not, be prevailed upon to pause and to consider whether this is quite just to us, or even to yourselves? Bring forward your charges and specifications, and then be patient long enough to hear us deny or justify.

You say we are sectional. We deny it. That makes an issue; and the burden of proof is upon you. You produce your proof; and what is it? Why, that our party has no existence in your section—gets no votes in your section. The fact is substantially true; but does it prove the issue? If it does, then in case we should, without change of principle, begin to get votes in your section, we should thereby cease to be sectional. You cannot escape this conclusion; and yet, are you willing to abide by it? If you are, you will probably soon find that we have ceased to be sectional, for we shall get votes in your section this very year. You will then begin to discover, as the truth plainly is, that your proof does not touch the issue. The fact that we get no votes in your section, is a fact of your making, and not of ours. And if there be fault in that fact, that fault is primarily yours, and remains until you show that we repel you by some wrong principle or practice. If we do repel you by any wrong principle or practice, the fault is ours; but this brings you to where you ought to have started—to a discussion of the right or wrong of our principle. If our principle, put in practice, would wrong your section for the benefit of ours, or for any other object, then our principle, and we with it, are sectional, and are justly opposed and denounced as such. Meet us, then, on the question of whether our principle, put in practice, would wrong your section; and so meet it as if it were possible that something may be said on our side. Do you accept the challenge? No! Then you really believe that the principle which "our fathers who framed the Government under which we live" thought so clearly right as to adopt it, and indorse it again and again, upon their official oaths, is in fact so clearly wrong as to demand your condemnation without a moment's consideration.

Some of you delight to flaunt in our faces the warning against sectional parties given by Washington in his Farewell Address. Less than eight years before Washington gave that warning, he had, as President of the United States, approved and signed an act of Congress, enforcing the prohibition of slavery in the Northwestern Territory, which act embodied the policy of the Government upon that subject up to and at the very moment he penned that warning; and about one year after he penned it, he wrote LaFayette that he considered that prohibition a wise measure, expressing in the same connection his hope that we should at some time have a confederacy of free States.

Bearing this in mind, and seeing that sectionalism has since arisen upon this same subject, is that warning a weapon in your hands against us, or in our hands against you? Could Washington himself speak, would he cast the blame of that sectionalism upon us, who sustain his policy, or upon you who repudiate it? We respect that warning of Washington, and we commend it to you, together with his example pointing to the right application of it.

But you say you are conservative—eminently conservative—while we are revolutionary, destructive, or something of the sort. What is conservatism? Is it not adherence to the old and tried, against the new and untried? We stick to, contend for, the identical old policy on the point in controversy which was adopted by "our fathers who framed the Government under which we live;" while you with one accord reject, and scout, and spit upon that old policy, and insist upon substituting something new. True, you disagree among yourselves as to what that substitute shall be. You are divided on new propositions and plans, but you are unanimous in rejecting and denouncing the old policy of the fathers. Some of you are for reviving the foreign slave trade; some for a Congressional Slave-Code for the Territories; some for Congress forbidding the Territories to prohibit Slavery within their limits; some for maintaining Slavery in the Territories through the judiciary; some for the "gur-reat pur-rinciple" that "if one man would enslave another, no third man should object," fantastically called "Popular Sovereignty;" but never a man among you is in favor of federal prohibition of slavery in federal territories, according to the practice of "our fathers who framed the Government under which we live." Not one of all your various plans can show a precedent or an advocate in the century within which our Government originated. Consider, then, whether your claim of conservatism for yourselves, and your charge of destructiveness against us, are based on the most clear and stable foundations.

Again, you say we have made the slavery question more prominent than it formerly was. We deny it. We admit that it is more prominent, but we deny that we made it so. It was not we, but you, who discarded the old policy of the fathers. We resisted, and still resist, your innovation; and thence comes the greater prominence of the question. Would you have that question reduced to its former proportions? Go back to that old policy. What has been will be again, under the same conditions. If you would have the peace of the old times, read-opt the precepts and policy of the old times.

You charge that we stir up insurrections among your slaves. We deny it; and what is your proof? Harper's Ferry! John Brown!! John Brown was no Republican; and you have failed to implicate a single Republican in his Harper's Ferry enterprise. If any member of our party is guilty in that matter, you know it or you do not know it. If you do know it, you are inexcusable for not designating the man and proving the fact. If you do not know it, you are inexcusable for asserting it, and especially for persisting in the assertion after you have tried and failed to make the proof. You need not be told that persisting in a charge which one does not know to be true, is simply malicious slander.

Some of you admit that no Republican designedly aided or encouraged the Harper's Ferry affair, but still insist that our doctrines and declarations necessarily lead to such results. We do not believe it. We know we hold to no doctrine, and make no declaration, which were not held to and made by "our fathers who framed the Government under which we live." You never dealt fairly by us in relation to this affair. When it occurred, some important State elections were near at hand, and you were in evident glee with the belief that, by charging the blame upon us, you could get an advantage of us in those elections. The elections came, and your expectations were not quite fulfilled. Every Republican man knew that, as to himself at least, your charge was a slander, and he was not much inclined by it to cast his vote in your favor. Republican doctrines and declarations are accompanied with a continual protest against any interference whatever with your slaves, or with you about your slaves. Surely, this does not encourage them to revolt. True, we do, in common with "our fathers, who framed the Government under which we live," declare our belief that slavery is wrong; but the slaves do not hear us declare even this. For anything we say or do, the slaves would scarcely know there is a Republican party. I believe they would not, in fact, generally know it but for your misrepresentations of us, in their hearing. In your political contests among yourselves, each faction charges the other with sympathy with Black Republicanism; and then, to give point to the charge, defines Black Republicanism to simply be insurrection, blood and thunder among the slaves.

Slave insurrections are no more common now than they were before the Republican party was organized. What induced the Southampton insurrection, twenty-eight years ago, in which, at least three times as many lives were lost as at Harper's Ferry? You can scarcely stretch your very elastic fancy to the conclusion that Southampton was "got up by Black Republicanism." In the present state of things in the United States, I do not think a general, or even a very extensive slave insurrection is possible. The indispensable concert of action cannot be attained. The slaves have no means of rapid communication; nor can incendiary freemen, black or white, supply it. The explosive materials are everywhere in parcels; but there neither are, nor can be supplied, the indispensable connecting trains.

Much is said by Southern people about the affection of slaves for their masters and mistresses; and a part of it, at least, is true. A plot for an uprising could scarcely be devised and communicated to twenty individuals before some one of them, to save the life of a favorite master or mistress, would divulge it. This is the rule; and the slave revolution in Hayti was not an exception to it, but a case occurring under peculiar circumstances. The gunpowder plot of British history, though not connected with slaves, was more in point. In that case, only about twenty were admitted to the secret; and yet one of them, in his anxiety to save a friend, betrayed the plot to that friend, and, by consequence, averted the calamity. Occasional poisonings from the kitchen, and open or stealthy assassinations in the field, and local revolts extending to a score or so, will continue to occur as the natural results of slavery; but no general insurrection of slaves, as I think, can happen in this country for a long time. Whoever much fears, or much hopes for such an event, will be alike disappointed.

In the language of Mr. Jefferson, uttered many years ago, "It is still in our power to direct the process of emancipation, and deportation, peaceably, and in such slow degrees, as that the evil will wear off insensibly; and their places be, *pari passu,* filled up by free white laborers. If, on the contrary, it is left to force itself on, human nature must shudder at the prospect held up."

Mr. Jefferson did not mean to say, nor do I, that the power of emancipation is in the Federal Government. He spoke of Virginia; and, as to the power of emancipation, I speak of the slave-holding States only. The Federal Government, however, as we insist, has the power of restraining the extension of the institution—the power to insure that a slave insurrection shall never occur on any American soil which is now free from slavery.

John Brown's effort was peculiar. It was not a slave insurrection. It was an attempt by white men to get up a revolt among slaves, in which the slaves

refused to participate. In fact, it was so absurd that the slaves, with all their ignorance, saw plainly enough it could not succeed. That affair, in its philosophy,
corresponds with the many attempts, related in history, at the assassination of
kings and emperors. An enthusiast broods over the oppression of a people till
he fancies himself commissioned by Heaven to liberate them. He ventures the
attempt, which ends in little else than his own execution. Orsini's attempt on
Louis Napoleon, and John Brown's attempt at Harper's Ferry were, in their philosophy, precisely the same. The eagerness to cast blame on old England in the
one case, and on New England in the other, does not disprove the sameness of
the two things.

And how much would it avail you, if you could, by the use of John Brown,
Helper's Book, and the like, break up the Republican organization? Human
action can be modified to some extent, but human nature cannot be changed.
There is a judgment and a feeling against slavery in this nation, which cast at least
a million and a half of votes. You cannot destroy that judgment and feeling—that
sentiment—by breaking up the political organization which rallies around it. You
can scarcely scatter and disperse an army which has been formed into order in the
face of your heaviest fire; but if you could, how much would you gain by forcing the sentiment which created it out of the peaceful channel of the ballot-box,
into some other channel? What would that other channel probably be? Would
the number of John Browns be lessened or enlarged by the operation?

But you will break up the Union rather than submit to a denial of your Constitutional rights.

That has a somewhat reckless sound; but it would be palliated, if not fully
justified, were we proposing, by the mere force of numbers, to deprive you of
some right, plainly written down in the Constitution. But we are proposing no
such thing.

When you make these declarations, you have a specific and well-understood
allusion to an assumed Constitutional right of yours, to take slaves into the federal territories, and to hold them there as property. But no such right is specifically written in the Constitution. That instrument is literally silent about any
such right. We, on the contrary, deny that such a right has any existence in the
Constitution, even by implication.

Your purpose, then, plainly stated, is that you will destroy the Government,
unless you be allowed to construe and enforce the Constitution as you please,
on all points in dispute between you and us. You will rule or ruin in all events.

This, plainly stated, is your language. Perhaps you will say the Supreme
Court has decided the disputed Constitutional question in your favor. Not quite

so. But waiving the lawyer's distinction between dictum and decision, the Court have decided the question for you in a sort of way. The Court have substantially said, it is your Constitutional right to take slaves into the federal territories, and to hold them there as property. When I say the decision was made in a sort of way, I mean it was made in a divided Court, by a bare majority of the Judges, and they not quite agreeing with one another in the reasons for making it; that it is so made as that its avowed supporters disagree with one another about its meaning, and that it was mainly based upon a mistaken statement of fact—the statement in the opinion that "the right of property in a slave is distinctly and expressly affirmed in the Constitution."

An inspection of the Constitution will show that the right of property in a slave is not "*distinctly* and *expressly* affirmed" in it. Bear in mind, the Judges do not pledge their judicial opinion that such right is *impliedly* affirmed in the Constitution; but they pledge their veracity that it is "*distinctly* and *expressly*" affirmed there—"distinctly," that is, not mingled with anything else—"expressly," that is, in words meaning just that, without the aid of any inference, and susceptible of no other meaning.

If they had only pledged their judicial opinion that such right is affirmed in the instrument by implication, it would be open to others to show that neither the word "slave" nor "slavery" is to be found in the Constitution, nor the word "property" even, in any connection with language alluding to the things slave, or slavery; and that wherever in that instrument the slave is alluded to, he is called a "person;"—and wherever his master's legal right in relation to him is alluded to, it is spoken of as "service or labor which may be due,"—as a debt payable in service or labor. Also, it would be open to show, by contemporaneous history, that this mode of alluding to slaves and slavery, instead of speaking of them, was employed on purpose to exclude from the Constitution the idea that there could be property in man.

To show all this, is easy and certain.

When this obvious mistake of the Judges shall be brought to their notice, is it not reasonable to expect that they will withdraw the mistaken statement, and reconsider the conclusion based upon it?

And then it is to be remembered that "our fathers, who framed the Government under which we live"—the men who made the Constitution—decided this same Constitutional question in our favor, long ago—decided it without division among themselves, when making the decision; without division among themselves about the meaning of it after it was made, and, so far as any evidence is left, without basing it upon any mistaken statement of facts.

Under all these circumstances, do you really feel yourselves justified to break up this Government unless such a court decision as yours is, shall be at once submitted to as a conclusive and final rule of political action? But you will not abide the election of a Republican president! In that supposed event, you say, you will destroy the Union; and then, you say, the great crime of having destroyed it will be upon us! That is cool. A highwayman holds a pistol to my ear, and mutters through his teeth, "Stand and deliver, or I shall kill you, and then you will be a murderer!"

To be sure, what the robber demanded of me—my money—was my own; and I had a clear right to keep it; but it was no more my own than my vote is my own; and the threat of death to me, to extort my money, and the threat of destruction to the Union, to extort my vote, can scarcely be distinguished in principle.

A few words now to Republicans. *It is exceedingly desirable that all parts of this great Confederacy shall be at peace, and in harmony, one with another. Let us Republicans do our part to have it so. Even though much provoked, let us do nothing through passion and ill temper. Even though the southern people will not so much as listen to us, let us calmly consider their demands, and yield to them if, in our deliberate view of our duty, we possibly can.* Judging by all they say and do, and by the subject and nature of their controversy with us, let us determine, if we can, what will satisfy them.

Will they be satisfied if the Territories be unconditionally surrendered to them? We know they will not. In all their present complaints against us, the Territories are scarcely mentioned. Invasions and insurrections are the rage now. Will it satisfy them, if, in the future, we have nothing to do with invasions and insurrections? We know it will not. We so know, because we know we never had anything to do with invasions and insurrections; and yet this total abstaining does not exempt us from the charge and the denunciation.

The question recurs, what will satisfy them? Simply this: We must not only let them alone, but we must somehow, convince them that we do let them alone. This, we know by experience, is no easy task. We have been so trying to convince them from the very beginning of our organization, but with no success. In all our platforms and speeches we have constantly protested our purpose to let them alone; but this has had no tendency to convince them. Alike unavailing to convince them, is the fact that they have never detected a man of us in any attempt to disturb them.

These natural, and apparently adequate means all failing, what will convince them? This, and this only: cease to call slavery *wrong,* and join them in calling it *right*. And this must be done thoroughly—done in *acts* as well as in *words*. Silence will not be tolerated—we must place ourselves avowedly with them. Senator Douglas's new sedition law must be enacted and enforced, suppressing all declarations that slavery is wrong, whether made in politics, in presses, in pulpits, or in private. We must arrest and return their fugitive slaves with greedy pleasure. We must pull down our Free State constitutions. The whole atmosphere must be disinfected from all taint of opposition to slavery, before they will cease to believe that all their troubles proceed from us.

I am quite aware they do not state their case precisely in this way. Most of them would probably say to us, "Let us alone, do nothing to us, and say what you please about slavery." But we do let them alone—have never disturbed them—so that, after all, it is what we say, which dissatisfies them. They will continue to accuse us of doing, until we cease saying.

I am also aware they have not, as yet, in terms, demanded the overthrow of our Free-State Constitutions. Yet those Constitutions declare the wrong of slavery, with more solemn emphasis, than do all other sayings against it; and when all these other sayings shall have been silenced, the overthrow of these Constitutions will be demanded, and nothing be left to resist the demand. It is nothing to the contrary, that they do not demand the whole of this just now. Demanding what they do, and for the reason they do, they can voluntarily stop nowhere short of this consummation. Holding, as they do, that slavery is morally right, and socially elevating, they cannot cease to demand a full national recognition of it, as a legal right, and a social blessing.

Nor can we justifiably withhold this, on any ground save our conviction that slavery is wrong. If slavery is right, all words, acts, laws, and constitutions against it, are themselves wrong, and should be silenced, and swept away. If it is right, we cannot justly object to its nationality—its universality; if it is wrong, they cannot justly insist upon its extension—its enlargement. All they ask, we could readily grant, if we thought slavery right; all we ask, they could as readily grant, if they thought it wrong. Their thinking it right, and our thinking it wrong, is the precise fact upon which depends the whole controversy. Thinking it right, as they do, they are not to blame for desiring its full recognition, as being right; but, thinking it wrong, as we do, can we yield to them? Can we cast our votes with their view, and against our own? In view of our moral, social, and political responsibilities, can we do this?

Wrong as we think slavery is, we can yet afford to let it alone where it is, because that much is due to the necessity arising from its actual presence in the nation; but can we, while our votes will prevent it, allow it to spread into the

National Territories, and to overrun us here in these Free States? If our sense of duty forbids this, then let us stand by our duty, fearlessly and effectively. Let us be diverted by none of those sophistical contrivances wherewith we are so industriously plied and belabored—contrivances such as groping for some middle ground between the right and the wrong, vain as the search for a man who should be neither a living man nor a dead man—such as a policy of "don't care" on a question about which all true men do care—such as Union appeals beseeching true Union men to yield to Disunionists, reversing the divine rule, and calling, not the sinners, but the righteous to repentance—such as invocations to Washington, imploring men to unsay what Washington said, and undo what Washington did.

Neither let us be slandered from our duty by false accusations against us, nor frightened from it by menaces of destruction to the Government nor of dungeons to ourselves. LET US HAVE FAITH THAT RIGHT MAKES MIGHT, AND IN THAT FAITH, LET US, TO THE END, DARE TO DO OUR DUTY AS WE UNDERSTAND IT.

FRAGMENT: THE CONSTITUTION, THE DECLARATION, AND THE UNION
[1860?]

The apple of gold and picture of silver are biblical metaphors taken from Proverbs 25:11. Lincoln used this metaphor didactically to convey the complementary relationship between the Declaration and Constitution as cornerstones of the Union. The exact date of this fragment is unknown, perhaps sometime around the First Inaugural. The only clue to dating the fragment comes from Alexander Stephens who cited the same passage from the Bible in a letter he wrote to Lincoln on December 30, 1860. Stephens was a former Whig and congressional colleague of Lincoln who would later become Vice-President of the Confederate States. The fragment may have constituted a reply to Stephens, who initially gained Lincoln's respect. Stephens had supported the Union in a speech to the Georgia legislature. However, after he was elected as vice president of the Confederacy, Stephens proclaimed the Union's epitaph in his Inaugural Speech when he referred to slavery as the "corner stone" of the Confederacy (see editor's introduction to this section). Lincoln's fragment is of great significance to understanding his conception of the Union as bound by a moral obligation to the Declaration and a corresponding legal obligation to the Constitution. The metaphor expressed the complementary relationship between these two cornerstones of the American Union. The Declaration provided the spirit, which animated the Constitution. The Constitution, in turn, provided the legal framework whereby the aims of the Declaration could be realized prudently. According to Lincoln, the Constitution should be read in view of the moral aspirations of the Declaration: "The picture was made for the apple—not the apple for the picture." Clearly, for Lincoln, liberty and equality were best perpetuated under the auspices of a national Union dedicated to the principles of the Declaration.

ALL THIS IS NOT THE RESULT OF ACCIDENT. It has a philosophical cause. Without the *Constitution* and the *Union*, we could not have attained the result; but even these, are not the primary cause of our great prosperity. There is something back of these, entwining itself more closely about the human heart. That something, is the principle of "Liberty to all"—the principle that clears the *path* for all—gives *hope* to all—and, by consequence, *enterprize,* and *industry* to all.

The *expression* of that principle, in our Declaration of Independence, was most happy, and fortunate. *Without* this, as well as *with* it, we could have declared our independence of Great Brittain [*sic*]; but *without* it, we could not, I think, have secured our free government, and consequent prosperity. No oppressed people will *fight,* and *endure,* as our fathers did, without the promise of something better, than a mere change of masters.

The assertion of that *principle,* at *that time,* was *the* word, *"fitly spoken"* which has proved an "apple of gold" to us. The *Union,* and the *Constitution,* are the *picture* of *silver,* subsequently framed around it. The picture was made, not to *conceal,* or *destroy* the apple; but to *adorn,* and *preserve* it. The *picture* was made *for* the apple—*not* the apple for the picture.

So let us act, that neither *picture,* or *apple,* shall ever be blurred, or broken.

That we may so act, we must study, and understand the points of danger.

LETTER TO GEORGE ASHMUN
MAY 23, 1860

George Ashmun was the President of the Republican National Convention, which had nominated Lincoln in Chicago. Years earlier as the sole Whig congressman from Illinois, Lincoln had supported Ashmun's proposed resolution condemning Polk for his aggression during the Mexican War. Though Lincoln endorsed the Republican Party platform, he did not elaborate on specific policies or issues. Since he was already leading the election, and since he had made his position on slavery amply clear, Lincoln believed that nothing would be gained by emphasizing his stance on the divisive issue. To do so would only further alarm the south and potentially alienate northern moderates. Indeed, during the election and immediately after, Lincoln was extremely reticent in reiterating his anti-

slavery views, not because he had shifted principles, but because he was convinced that he had stated his position clearly and that any further elaboration would be misconstrued.

SPRINGFIELD. ILLS. MAY 23, 1860
HON: GEORGE ASHMUN:
PRESIDENT OF THE REPUBLICAN NATIONAL CONVENTION.
SIR:

I accept the nomination tendered me by the convention over which you presided, and of which I am formally apprised in the letter of yourself and others, acting as a committee of the convention, for that purpose.

The declaration of principles and sentiments, which accompanies your letter, meets my approval; and it shall be my care not to violate or disregard it, in any part.

Imploring the assistance of Divine Providence, and with due regard to the views and feelings of all who were represented in the Convention; to the rights of all the states, and territories, and people of the nation; to the inviolability of the Constitution, and the perpetual union, harmony, and prosperity of all, I am most happy to co-operate for the practical success of the principles declared by the Convention.

Your obliged friend, and fellow citizen
A. Lincoln

ADDRESS TO THE NEW JERSEY SENATE AT TRENTON, NEW JERSEY[1]

FEBRUARY 21, 1861

While making the twelve-day journey from Springfield to Washington, D.C., Lincoln delivered speeches at numerous points in-between. His Address to the New Jersey Senate at Trenton was made en route to the White House. In this brief but important speech, Lincoln noted the historical significance of Trenton, claiming that the glorious deeds of George Washington had inspired him as a child. Establishing continuity between himself and the Founders, he made it clear to the audience that he was dedicated to perpetuating the "original idea" for which the nation fought for during its independence— that is, the idea of liberty and equality in the Declaration. Finally, invoking Divine Providence, Lincoln characterized himself as a "humble instrument in the hands of the Almighty." He ironically referred to the American people as God's "almost chosen

1. *CWAL,* IV, 235-236.

people." This designation of Americans as God's "almost chosen people" introduced an ambiguity and qualification that recognized both the nation's blessings and its obligations.

FEBRUARY 21, 1861

Mr. President and Gentlemen of the Senate of the State of New-Jersey: I am very grateful to you for the honorable reception of which I have been the object. I cannot but remember the place that New-Jersey holds in our early history. In the early Revolutionary struggle, few of the States among the old Thirteen had more of the battle-fields of the country within their limits than old New-Jersey. May I be pardoned if, upon this occasion, I mention that away back in my childhood, the earliest days of my being able to read, I got hold of a small book, such a one as few of the younger members have ever seen, "Weem's Life of Washington." I remember all the accounts there given of the battle fields and struggles for the liberties of the country, and none fixed themselves upon my imagination so deeply as the struggle here at Trenton, New-Jersey. The crossing of the river; the contest with the Hessians; the great hardships endured at that time, all fixed themselves on my memory more than any single revolutionary event; and you all know, for you have all been boys, how these early impressions last longer than any others. I recollect thinking then, boy even though I was, that there must have been something more than common that those men struggled for. I am exceedingly anxious that that thing which they struggled for; that something even more than National Independence; that something that held out a great promise to all the people of the world to all time to come; I am exceedingly anxious that this Union, the Constitution, and the liberties of the people shall be perpetuated in accordance with the original idea for which that struggle was made, and I shall be most happy indeed if I shall be an humble instrument in the hands of the Almighty, and of this, his almost chosen people, for perpetuating the object of that great struggle. You give me this reception, as I understand, without distinction of party. I learn that this body is composed of a majority of gentlemen who, in the exercise of their best judgment in the choice of a Chief Magistrate, did not think I was the man. I understand, nevertheless, that they came forward here to greet me as the constitutional President of the United States—as citizens of the United States, to meet the man who, for the time being, is the representative man of the nation, united by a purpose to perpetuate the Union and liberties of the people. As such, I accept this reception more gratefully than I could do did I believe it was tendered to me as an individual.

ADDRESS IN INDEPENDENCE HALL, PHILADELPHIA, PENNSYLVANIA
FEBRUARY 22, 1861

Delivered the day after his speech at Trenton, Lincoln's Speech in Independence Hall is likewise notable in revealing the centrality of the Declaration as the inspirational source of his leadership. Lincoln's confession that he would rather be assassinated on the spot rather than surrender the principles of the regime was a defiant response to rumors of a plot to kill him as he passed through Baltimore en route *to Washington. The remark is chilling given that he was assassinated four years later.*

MR. CUYLER:

I am filled with deep emotion at finding myself standing here, in this place, where were collected together the wisdom, the patriotism, the devotion to principle, from which sprang the institutions under which we live. You have kindly suggested to me that in my hands is the task of restoring peace to the present distracted condition of the country. I can say in return, Sir, that all the political sentiments I entertain have been drawn, so far as I have been able to draw them, from the sentiments which originated and were given to the world from this hall. I have never had a feeling politically that did not spring from the sentiments embodied in the Declaration of Independence. I have often pondered over the dangers which were incurred by the men who assembled here, and framed and adopted that Declaration of Independence. I have pondered over the toils that were endured by the officers and soldiers of the army who achieved that Independence. I have often inquired of myself what great principle or idea it was that kept this Confederacy so long together. It was not the mere matter of the separation of the Colonies from the motherland; but that sentiment in the Declaration of Independence which gave liberty, not alone to the people of this country, but, I hope, to the world, for all future time. It was that which gave promise that in due time the weight would be lifted from the shoulders of all men. This is a sentiment embodied in the Declaration of Independence. Now, my friends, can this country be saved upon that basis? If it can, I will consider myself one of the happiest men in the world, if I can help to save it. If it cannot be saved upon that principle, it will be truly awful. But if this country cannot be saved without giving up that principle, I was about to say I would rather be assassinated on this spot than surrender it. Now, in my view of the present aspect of affairs, there need be no bloodshed or war. There is no necessity for it. I am not in favor of such a course, and I may say, in advance, that there will be no bloodshed unless it be forced upon the Government, and then it will be compelled to act in self-defense.

My friends, this is wholly an unexpected speech, and I did not expect to be called upon to say a word when I came here. I supposed it was merely to do something toward raising the flag. I may, therefore, have said something indiscreet. (Cries of "No, no") I have said nothing but what I am willing to live by and, if it be the pleasure of Almighty God, die by.

FIRST INAUGURAL ADDRESS
MARCH 4, 1861

The First Inaugural Address was delivered ten days after Lincoln's arrival in Washington. The lower South had already seceded, a new Confederate constitution had been framed in Montgomery, and rebels had seized federal forts, arsenals, and property throughout the South. Fort Pickens in Pensacola Florida and Fort Sumter in Charleston Bay were the only forts in the South still under federal control. Under these dire circumstances, Lincoln had to choose his words carefully; the upper South and Border States would be scrutinizing his response to events. Virginia and North Carolina had not yet seceded. If both Virginia and Maryland seceded, the capital would be surrounded by the Confederacy. Lincoln affirmed his constitutional duty to preserve the Union, to see "that the laws of the Union are faithfully executed in all the states." In the First Inaugural, Lincoln offered a point-by-point refutation of secession, claiming that it could not be justified, on either constitutional or moral grounds, as a God-given right to revolution. Although he made clear that the Union was perpetual and had to be preserved, he attempted to reassure the South: "I have no purpose, directly or indirectly, to interfere with the institution of slavery in the states where it exists, I believe I have no lawful right to do so, and I have no inclination to do so." Lincoln's use of the words "hold, occupy and possess . . . all . . . property and places belonging to the government, and to collect the duties on import" was noteworthy in the context of South Carolina's efforts to seize the federal Fort Sumter. In his original draft, Lincoln used the word "reclaim;" however, he replaced it with the less provocative, "hold, occupy and possess." They day after the inauguration, he received word from Major Anderson that Fort Sumter had only six weeks of provisions to hold out. Seward proposed a war with Great Britain in order to redirect national animosity toward a foreign enemy. Rejecting this proposal, Lincoln sent a message to Governor Pickens of South Carolina that he would re-provision the fort with food and supplies and that no attempt would be made to supply it with "men, arms or ammunition," provided South Carolina did not resist the attempt. Refusing any attempt to re-provision federal troops,

South Carolina commenced the bombardment of Fort Sumter. Thus, Lincoln baited the pugnacious South into firing the first shot of the war. If war was inevitable, it was important that the South be the aggressors so that the nation could rally behind the Federal Union. After reading Lincoln's first draft of the inaugural address, Seward, whom Lincoln had nominated as secretary of state, advised a more conciliatory tone. He urged Lincoln to delete any words or phrases that would be construed as provocative and to conclude the address with a gesture of fraternity. Although Seward wrote the initial concluding paragraph, Lincoln substantially revised it to reflect his own style and thought.

FELLOW-CITIZENS OF THE UNITED STATES:

In compliance with a custom as old as the government itself, I appear before you to address you briefly, and to take, in your presence, the oath prescribed by the Constitution of the United States, to be taken by the President "before he enters on the execution of his office."

I do not consider it necessary at present for me to discuss those matters of administration about which there is no special anxiety or excitement.

Apprehension seems to exist among the people of the Southern States, that by the accession of a Republican Administration, their property, and their peace, and personal security, are to be endangered. There has never been any reasonable cause for such apprehension. Indeed, the most ample evidence to the contrary has all the while existed, and been open to their inspection. It is found in nearly all the published speeches of him who now addresses you. I do but quote from one of those speeches when I declare that "I have no purpose, directly or indirectly, to interfere with the institution of slavery in the States where it exists. I believe I have no lawful right to do so, and I have no inclination to do so." Those who nominated and elected me did so with full knowledge that I had made this, and many similar declarations, and had never recanted them. And more than this, they placed in the platform, for my acceptance, and as a law to themselves, and to me, the clear and emphatic resolution which I now read:

> "*Resolved,* That the maintenance inviolate of the rights of the States, and especially the right of each State to order and control its own domestic institutions according to its own judgment exclusively, is essential to that balance of power on which the perfection and endurance of our political fabric depend; and we denounce the lawless invasion by armed force of the soil of any State or Territory, no matter under what pretext, as among the gravest of crimes."

I now reiterate these sentiments: and in doing so, I only press upon the public attention the most conclusive evidence of which the case is susceptible, that the property, peace and security of no section are to be in any wise endangered by the now incoming Administration. I add too, that all the protection which, consistently with the Constitution and the laws, can be given, will be cheerfully given to all the States when lawfully demanded, for whatever cause—as cheerfully to one section as to another.

There is much controversy about the delivering up of fugitives from service or labor. The clause I now read is as plainly written in the Constitution as any other of its provisions:

> "No person held to service or labor in one State, under the laws thereof, escaping into another, shall, in consequence of any law or regulation therein, be discharged from such service or labor, but shall be delivered up on claim of the party to whom such service or labor may be due."

It is scarcely questioned that this provision was intended by those who made it, for the reclaiming of what we call fugitive slaves; and the intention of the law-giver is the law. All members of Congress swear their support to the whole Constitution—to this provision as much as to any other. To the proposition, then, that slaves whose cases come within the terms of this clause, "shall be delivered up," their oaths are unanimous. Now, if they would make the effort in good temper, could they not, with nearly equal unanimity, frame and pass a law, by means of which to keep good that unanimous oath?

There is some difference of opinion whether this clause should be enforced by national or by state authority; but surely that difference is not a very material one. If the slave is to be surrendered, it can be of but little consequence to him, or to others, by which authority it is done. And should any one, in any case, be content that his oath shall go unkept, on a merely unsubstantial controversy as to *how* it shall be kept?

Again, in any law upon this subject, ought not all the safeguards of liberty known in civilized and humane jurisprudence to be introduced, so that a free man be not, in any case, surrendered as a slave? And might it not be well, at the same time to provide by law for the enforcement of that clause in the Constitution which guarantees that "the citizens of each State shall be entitled to all privileges and immunities of citizens in the several States"?

I take the official oath to-day, with no mental reservations, and with no purpose to construe the Constitution or laws, by any hypercritical rules. And while

I do not choose now to specify particular acts of Congress as proper to be enforced, I do suggest that it will be much safer for all, both in official and private stations, to conform to, and abide by, all those acts which stand unrepealed, than to violate any of them, trusting to find impunity in having them held to be unconstitutional.

It is seventy-two years since the first inauguration of a President under our national Constitution. During that period fifteen different and greatly distinguished citizens, have, in succession, administered the executive branch of the government. They have conducted it through many perils; and, generally, with great success. Yet, with all this scope for [of] precedent, I now enter upon the same task for the brief constitutional term of four years, under great and peculiar difficulty. A disruption of the Federal Union, heretofore only menaced, is now formidably attempted.

I hold, that in contemplation of universal law, and of the Constitution, the Union of these States is perpetual. Perpetuity is implied, if not expressed, in the fundamental law of all national governments. It is safe to assert that no government proper, ever had a provision in its organic law for its own termination. Continue to execute all the express provisions of our national Constitution, and the Union will endure forever—it being impossible to destroy it, except by some action not provided for in the instrument itself.

Again, if the United States be not a government proper, but an association of States in the nature of contract merely, can it, as a contract, be peaceably unmade, by less than all the parties who made it? One party to a contract may violate it—break it, so to speak; but does it not require all to lawfully rescind it?

Descending from these general principles, we find the proposition that, in legal contemplation, the Union is perpetual, confirmed by the history of the Union itself. The Union is much older than the Constitution. It was formed in fact, by the Articles of Association in 1774. It was matured and continued by the Declaration of Independence in 1776. It was further matured and the faith of all the then thirteen States expressly plighted and engaged that it should be perpetual, by the Articles of Confederation in 1778. And finally, in 1787, one of the declared objects for ordaining and establishing the Constitution, was *"to form a more perfect Union."*

But if [the] destruction of the Union, by one, or by a part only, of the States, be lawfully possible, the Union is *less* perfect than before the Constitution, having lost the vital element of perpetuity.

It follows from these views that no State, upon its own mere motion, can lawfully get out of the Union,—that *resolves* and *ordinances* to that effect are legally void, and that acts of violence, within any State or States, against the authority of the United States, are insurrectionary or revolutionary, according to circumstances.

I therefore consider that in view of the Constitution and the laws, the Union is unbroken; and to the extent of my ability I shall take care, as the Constitution itself expressly enjoins upon me, that the laws of the Union be faithfully executed in all the States. Doing this I deem to be only a simple duty on my part; and I shall perform it, so far as practicable, unless my rightful masters, the American people, shall withhold the requisite means, or, in some authoritative manner, direct the contrary. I trust this will not be regarded as a menace, but only as the declared purpose of the Union that it will constitutionally defend and maintain itself.

In doing this there needs to be no bloodshed or violence; and there shall be none, unless it be forced upon the national authority. The power confided to me will be used to hold, occupy, and possess the property and places belonging to the government, and to collect the duties and imposts; but beyond what may be necessary for these objects, there will be no invasion—no using of force against or among the people anywhere. Where hostility to the United States, in any interior locality, shall be so great and so universal, as to prevent competent resident citizens from holding the Federal offices, there will be no attempt to force obnoxious strangers among the people for that object. While the strict legal right may exist in the government to enforce the exercise of these offices, the attempt to do so would be so irritating, and so nearly impracticable with all, that I deem it better to forego, for the time, the uses of such offices.

The mails, unless repelled, will continue to be furnished in all parts of the Union. So far as possible, the people everywhere shall have that sense of perfect security which is most favorable to calm thought and reflection. The course here indicated will be followed, unless current events and experience shall show a modification or change to be proper; and in every case and exigency my best discretion will be exercised according to circumstances actually existing, and with a view and a hope of a peaceful solution of the national troubles, and the restoration of fraternal sympathies and affections.

That there are persons in one section or another who seek to destroy the Union at all events, and are glad of any pretext to do it, I will neither affirm or deny; but if there be such, I need address no word to them. To those, however, who really love the Union, may I not speak?

Before entering upon so grave a matter as the destruction of our national fabric, with all its benefits, its memories and its hopes, would it not be wise to ascertain precisely why we do it? Will you hazard so desperate a step, while there is any possibility that any portion of the ills you fly from have no real existence? Will you, while the certain ills you fly to, are greater than all the real ones you fly from? Will you risk the commission of so fearful a mistake?

All profess to be content in the Union, if all constitutional rights can be maintained. Is it true, then, that any right, plainly written in the Constitution, has been denied? I think not. Happily the human mind is so constituted, that no party can reach to the audacity of doing this. Think, if you can, of a single instance in which a plainly written provision of the Constitution has ever been denied. If, by the mere force of numbers, a majority should deprive a minority of any clearly written constitutional right, it might, in a moral point of view, justify revolution—certainly would, if such a right were a vital one. But such is not our case. All the vital rights of minorities, and of individuals, are so plainly assured to them, by affirmations and negations, guarantees and prohibitions, in the Constitution, that controversies never arise concerning them. But no organic law can ever be framed with a provision specifically applicable to every question which may occur in practical administration. No foresight can anticipate, nor any document of reasonable length contain express provisions for all possible questions. Shall fugitives from labor be surrendered by national or by State authority? The Constitution does not expressly say. *May* Congress prohibit slavery in the territories? The Constitution does not expressly say. *Must* Congress protect slavery in the territories? The Constitution does not expressly say.

From questions of this class spring all our constitutional controversies, and we divide upon them into majorities and minorities. If the minority will not acquiesce, the majority must, or the government must cease. There is no other alternative; for continuing the government, is acquiescence on one side or the other. If a minority, in such case, will secede rather than acquiesce, they make a precedent which, in turn, will divide and ruin them; for a minority of their own will secede from them whenever a majority refuses to be controlled by such minority. For instance, why may not any portion of a new confederacy, a year or two hence, arbitrarily secede again, precisely as portions of the present Union now claim to secede from it? All who cherish disunion sentiments, are now being educated to the exact temper of doing this.

Is there such perfect identity of interests among the States to compose a new Union, as to produce harmony only, and prevent renewed secession?

Plainly, the central idea of secession, is the essence of anarchy. A majority, held in restraint by constitutional checks and limitations, and always changing easily with deliberate changes of popular opinions and sentiments is the only true sovereign of a free people. Whoever rejects it, does, of necessity, fly to anarchy or to despotism. Unanimity is impossible; the rule of a minority, as a permanent arrangement, is wholly inadmissible; so that, rejecting the majority principle, anarchy or despotism in some form is all that is left.

I do not forget the position assumed by some, that constitutional questions are to be decided by the Supreme Court; nor do I deny that such decisions must be binding in any case, upon the parties to a suit, as to the object of that suit, while they are also entitled to very high respect and consideration in all parallel cases by all other departments of the government. And while it is obviously possible that such decision may be erroneous in any given case, still the evil effect following it, being limited to that particular case, with the chance that it may be over-ruled, and never become a precedent for other cases, can better be borne than could the evils of a different practice. At the same time, the candid citizen must confess that if the policy of the government upon vital questions, affecting the whole people, is to be irrevocably fixed by decisions of the Supreme Court, the instant they are made, in ordinary litigation between parties, in personal actions, the people will have ceased to be their own rulers, having to that extent practically resigned their government into the hands of that eminent tribunal. Nor is there in this view any assault upon the court or the judges. It is a duty from which they may not shrink, to decide cases properly brought before them; and it is no fault of theirs if others seek to turn their decisions to political purposes.

One section of our country believes slavery is *right,* and ought to be extended, while the other believes it is *wrong,* and ought not to be extended. This is the only substantial dispute. The fugitive slave clause of the Constitution, and the law for the suppression of the foreign slave trade, are each as well enforced, perhaps, as any law can ever be in a community where the moral sense of the people imperfectly supports the law itself. The great body of the people abide by the dry legal obligation in both cases, and a few break over in each. This, I think, cannot be perfectly cured; and it would be worse in both cases *after* the separation of the sections, than before. The foreign slave trade, now imperfectly suppressed, would be ultimately revived without restriction, in one section; while fugitive slaves, now only partially surrendered, would not be surrendered at all, by the other.

Physically speaking, we cannot separate. We cannot remove our respective sections from each other, nor build an impassable wall between them. A husband and wife may be divorced, and go out of the presence, and beyond the reach of each other; but the different parts of our country cannot do this. They cannot but remain face to face; and intercourse, either amicable or hostile, must continue between them. Is it possible, then, to make that intercourse more advantageous or more satisfactory, *after* separation than *before?* Can aliens make treaties easier than friends can make laws? Can treaties be more faithfully enforced between aliens than laws can among friends? Suppose you go to war, you cannot fight always; and when, after much loss on both sides, and no gain on either, you cease fighting, the identical old questions, as to terms of intercourse, are again upon you.

This country, with its institutions, belongs to the people who inhabit it. Whenever they shall grow weary of the existing government, they can exercise their *constitutional* right of amending it, or their *revolutionary* right to dismember or overthrow it. I cannot be ignorant of the fact that many worthy and patriotic citizens are desirous of having the national Constitution amended. While I make no recommendation of amendments, I fully recognize the rightful authority of the people over the whole subject to be exercised in either of the modes prescribed in the instrument itself; and I should under existing circumstances favor rather than oppose a fair opportunity being afforded the people to act upon it.

I will venture to add that to me the Convention mode seems preferable, in that it allows amendments to originate with the people themselves, instead of only permitting them to take or reject propositions, originated by others, not especially chosen for the purpose, and which might not be precisely such as they would wish to either accept or refuse. I understand a proposed amendment to the Constitution, which amendment, however, I have not seen, has passed Congress, to the effect that the federal government shall never interfere with the domestic institutions of the States, including that of persons held to service. To avoid misconstruction of what I have said, I depart from my purpose not to speak of particular amendments, so far as to say that holding such a provision to now be implied constitutional law, I have no objection to its being made express and irrevocable.

The Chief Magistrate derives all his authority from the people, and they have conferred none upon him to fix terms for the separation of the States. The people themselves can do this also if they choose; but the executive, as such, has nothing to do with it. His duty is to administer the present government, as it came to his hands, and to transmit it, unimpaired by him, to his successor.

Why should there not be a patient confidence in the ultimate justice of the people? Is there any better or equal hope, in the world? In our present differences, is either party without faith of being in the right? If the Almighty Ruler of nations, with his eternal truth and justice, be on your side of the North or on yours of the South, that truth, and that justice, will surely prevail, by the judgment of this great tribunal, the American people.

By the frame of the government under which we live, this same people have wisely given their public servants but little power for mischief; and have, with equal wisdom, provided for the return of that little to their own hands at very short intervals.

While the people retain their virtue and vigilance, no administration, by any extreme of wickedness or folly, can very seriously injure the government in the short space of four years.

My countrymen, one and all, think calmly and *well*, upon this whole subject. Nothing valuable can be lost by taking time. If there be an object to *hurry* any of you, in hot haste, to a step which you would never take *deliberately*, that object will be frustrated by taking time; but no good object can be frustrated by it. Such of you as are now dissatisfied, still have the old Constitution unimpaired, and, on the sensitive point, the laws of your own framing under it; while the new administration will have no immediate power, if it would, to change either. If it were admitted that you who are dissatisfied, hold the right side in the dispute, there still is no single good reason for precipitate action. Intelligence, patriotism, Christianity, and a firm reliance on Him, who has never yet forsaken this favored land, are still competent to adjust, in the best way, all our present difficulty.

In *your* hands, my dissatisfied fellow countrymen, and not in *mine,* is the momentous issue of civil war. The government will not assail *you.* You can have no conflict, without being yourselves the aggressors. *You* have no oath registered in Heaven to destroy the government, while *I* shall have the most solemn one to "preserve, protect and defend" it.

I am loth to close. We are not enemies, but friends. We must not be enemies. Though passion may have strained, it must not break our bonds of affection. The mystic chords of memory, stretching from every battle-field, and patriot grave, to every living heart and hearth-stone, all over this broad land, will yet swell the chorus of the Union, when again touched, as surely they will be, by the better angels of our nature.

MESSAGE TO CONGRESS IN SPECIAL SESSION
JULY 4, 1861

Because Congress was adjourned at the time of the secession crisis, Lincoln was obliged to convene a special session, which he scheduled for the historic date of July 4, 1861. Lin-

coln delayed calling a special session not only to give himself a "free-hand" in dealing with the crisis, but also to ensure the safe convocation of Congress, whose assemblage might have been thwarted by the surrounding rebel states and insurgents. The Fourth of July also represented a symbolic date to rally the Union in defense of its liberty. During the controversial eighty days—the interval between Lincoln's first call for troops on April 15 and his calling of a special session of Congress on July 4—Lincoln the president implemented a series of emergency measures without congressional approval. These included the call for troops, the raising of money, the suspension of the writ of habeas corpus, and the deployment of a blockade against the South. In this speech before a joint session of Congress, Lincoln attempted to provide a justification for his extraordinary actions as chief executive. Attempting to rouse the nation, he defined the struggle to preserve the Union in wider terms. Indeed, he characterized the struggle as test of democracy's viability as a form of government. Because America was the last bastion of self-government in a globe dominated by despotism, the fate of the Union was linked to the fate of democracy throughout the world. Lincoln's Fourth of July Speech also reiterated a critique of secession, reminding the South that, "ballots are the rightful, and peaceful, successors of bullets; and that when ballots have fairly, and constitutionally decided, there can be no successful appeal, back to bullets. . . . " Emphasizing the important role that the southern cultural elite played in disposing their people towards resisting their government, Lincoln claimed that the "movers" of rebellion had "commenced an insidious debauching of the public mind." Cutting through their sophistry, Lincoln scornfully characterized their arguments in behalf of states rights and secession as "sugar coated" rebellion.

FELLOW-CITIZENS OF THE SENATE AND HOUSE OF REPRESENTATIVES:

Having been convened on an extraordinary occasion, as authorized by the Constitution, your attention is not called to any ordinary subject of legislation.

At the beginning of the present presidential term, four months ago, the functions of the Federal Government were found to be generally suspended within the several States of South Carolina, Georgia, Alabama, Mississippi, Louisiana, and Florida, excepting only those of the Post Office Department.

Within these States all the forts, arsenals, dockyards, custom-houses, and the like, including the movable and stationary property in and about them, had been seized, and were held in open hostility to this Government, excepting only Forts Pickens, Taylor, and Jefferson, on and near the Florida coast, and Fort Sumter, in Charleston harbor, South Carolina. The forts thus seized had been put in improved condition, new ones had been built, and armed forces had been organized and were organizing, all avowedly with the same hostile purpose.

The forts remaining in the possession of the Federal Government in and near these States were either besieged or menaced by warlike preparations, and especially Fort Sumter was nearly surrounded by well-protected hostile batteries, with guns equal in quality to the best of its own, and outnumbering the latter as perhaps ten to one. A disproportionate share of the Federal muskets and rifles had somehow found their way into these States, and had been seized to be used against the Government. Accumulations of the public revenue, lying within them, had been seized for the same object. The Navy was scattered in distant seas, leaving but a very small part of it within the immediate reach of the Government. Officers of the Federal Army and Navy had resigned in great numbers; and of those resigning, a large proportion had taken up arms against the Government. Simultaneously, and in connection with all this, the purpose to sever the Federal Union was openly avowed. In accordance with this purpose, an ordinance had been adopted in each of these States, declaring the States, respectively, to be separated from the National Union. A formula for instituting a combined government of these States had been promulgated; and this illegal organization in the character of confederate States, was already invoking recognition, aid, and intervention, from foreign Powers.

Finding this condition of things, and believing it to be an imperative duty upon the incoming Executive to prevent, if possible, the consummation of such attempt to destroy the Federal Union, a choice of means to that end became indispensable. This choice was made, and was declared in the inaugural address. The policy chosen looked to the exhaustion of all peaceful measures, before a resort to any stronger ones. It sought only to hold the public places and property not already wrested from the Government, and to collect the revenue, relying for the rest on time, discussion, and the ballot-box. It promised a continuance of the mails, at Government expense, to the very people who were resisting the Government; and it gave repeated pledges against any disturbance to any of the people, or any of their rights. Of all that which a President might constitutionally and justifiably do in such a case, everything was forborne, without which it was believed possible to keep the government on foot.

On the 5th of March, (the present incumbent's first full day in office,) a letter of Major Anderson, commanding at Fort Sumter, written on the 28th of February, and received at the War Department on the 4th of March, was, by that Department, placed in his hands. This letter expressed the professional opinion of the writer, that reinforcements could not be thrown into that fort within the time for his relief, rendered necessary by the limited supply of provisions, and with a view of holding possession of the same, with a force of less than twenty thousand good and well disciplined men. This opinion was concurred in by all the officers of his command, and their *memoranda* on the subject were made inclosures of Major Anderson's letter. The whole was immediately laid before Lieutenant General Scott, who at once concurred with Major Anderson in opinion. On reflection, however, he took full time, consulting with other officers, both of the Army and the Navy, and, at the end of four days, came reluctantly, but decidedly, to the same conclusion as before. He also stated at the same time that no such sufficient force was then at the control of the Government, or could be raised and brought to the ground within the time when the provisions in the fort would be exhausted. In a purely military point of view, this reduced the duty of the Administration in the case, to the mere matter of getting the garrison safely out of the fort.

It was believed, however, that to so abandon that position, under the circumstances, would be utterly ruinous; that the *necessity* under which it was to be done would not be fully understood; that by many it would be construed as a part of a *voluntary* policy; that at home it would discourage the friends of the Union, embolden its adversaries, and go far to insure to the latter a recognition abroad; that, in fact, it would be our national destruction consummated. This could not be allowed. Starvation was not yet upon the garrison; and ere it would be reached *Fort Pickens* might be reinforced. This last would be a clear indication of *policy,* and would better enable the country to accept the evacuation of Fort Sumter as a military *necessity.* An order was at once directed to be sent for the landing of the troops from the steamship Brooklyn into Fort Pickens. This order could not go by land, but must take the longer and slower route by sea. The first return news from the order was received just one week before the fall of Fort Sumter. The news itself was that the officer commanding the Sabine, to which vessel the troops had been transferred from the Brooklyn, acting upon some *quasi* armistice of the late Administration, (and of the existence of which the present Administration, up to the time the order was dispatched, had only too vague and uncertain rumors to fix attention,) had refused to land the troops. To now reinforce Fort Pickens before a crisis would be reached at Fort Sumter was impossible—rendered so by the near exhaustion of provisions in the latter-named fort. In precaution against such a conjuncture, the Government had a few days before commenced preparing an expedition, as well adapted as might be, to relieve Fort Sumter, which expedition was intended to be ultimately used or not, according to circumstances. The strongest anticipated case for using it was now presented; and it was resolved to send it forward. As had been intended in this contingency, it was also resolved to notify the Governor of South Carolina that he might expect an attempt would be made to provision the fort; and that, if the attempt should not be resisted, there would be no effort to throw in men, arms, or ammunition, without further notice, or in case of an attack upon the fort. This notice was accordingly given; whereupon the fort was attacked and bombarded to its fall, without even awaiting the arrival of the provisioning expedition.

It is thus seen that the assault upon and reduction of Fort Sumter was in no sense a matter of self defense on the part of the assailants. They well knew that the garrison in the fort could by no possibility commit aggression upon them. They knew—they were expressly notified—that the giving of bread to the few brave and hungry men of the garrison was all which would on that occasion be attempted, unless themselves, by resisting so much, should provoke more. They knew that this Government desired to keep the garrison in the fort, not to assail them, but merely to maintain visible possession, and thus to preserve the Union from actual and immediate dissolution—trusting, as hereinbefore stated, to time, discussion, and the ballot-box, for final adjustment; and they assailed and reduced the fort for precisely the reverse object—to drive out the visible authority of the Federal Union, and thus force it to immediate dissolution. That this was their object, the Executive well understood; and having said to them in the inaugural address, "You can have no conflict without being yourselves the aggressors," he took pains not only to keep this declaration good, but also to keep the case so free from the power of ingenious sophistry that the world should not be able to misunderstand it. By the affair at Fort Sumter, with its surrounding circumstances, that point was reached. Then and thereby the assailants of the Government began the conflict of arms, without a gun in sight or in expectancy to return their fire, save only the few in the fort, sent to that harbor years before for their own protection, and still ready to give that protection in whatever was lawful. In this act, discarding all else, they have forced upon the country the distinct issue, "immediate dissolution or blood."

And this issue embraces more than the fate of these United States. It presents to the whole family of man the question, whether a constitutional republic, or democracy—a Government of the people by the same people—can or cannot maintain its territorial integrity against its own domestic foes. It presents the question, whether discontented individuals, too few in numbers to control administration, according to organic law, in any case, can always, upon the pretenses made in this case, or on any other pretenses, or arbitrarily, without any pretense, break up their Government, and thus practically put an end to free government upon the earth. It forces us to ask: "Is there, in all republics, this inherent and fatal weakness?" "Must a Government, of necessity, be too *strong* for the liberties of its own people, or too *weak* to maintain its own existence?"

So viewing the issue, no choice was left but to call out the war power of the Government; and so to resist force employed for its destruction, by force for its preservation.

The call was made, and the response of the country was most gratifying, surpassing in unanimity and spirit the most sanguine expectation. Yet none of the States commonly called slave States, except Delaware, gave a regiment through regular State organization. A few regiments have been organized within some others of those States by individual enterprise, and received into the Government service. Of course, the seceded States, so called, (and to which Texas had been joined about the time of the inauguration,) gave no troops to the cause of the Union. The border States, so called, were not uniform in their action, some of them being almost *for* the Union, while in others—as Virginia, North Carolina, Tennessee, and Arkansas—the Union sentiment was nearly repressed and silenced. The course taken in Virginia was the most remarkable—perhaps the most important. A convention, elected by the people of that State to consider this very question of disrupting the Federal Union, was in session at the capital of Virginia when Fort Sumter fell. To this body the people had chosen a large majority of *professed* Union men. Almost immediately after the fall of Sumter, many members of that majority went over to the original disunion minority, and, with them, adopted an ordinance for withdrawing the State from the Union. Whether this change was wrought by their great approval of the assault upon Sumter, or their great resentment at the Government's resistance to that assault, is not definitely known. Although they submitted the ordinance, for ratification, to a vote of the people, to be taken on a day then somewhat more than a month distant, the convention and the Legislature, (which was also in session at the same time and place,) with leading men of the State, not members of either, immediately commenced acting as if the State were already out of the Union. They pushed military preparations vigorously forward all over the State. They seized the United States armory at Harper's Ferry, and the navy-yard at Gosport, near Norfolk. They received—perhaps invited—into their State large bodies of troops, with their warlike appointments, from the so-called seceded States. They formally entered into a treaty of temporary alliance and cooperation with the so-called "Confederate States," and sent members to their congress at Montgomery; and, finally, they permitted the insurrectionary government to be transferred to their capital at Richmond.

The people of Virginia have thus allowed this giant insurrection to make its nest within her borders; and this Government has no choice left but to deal with it *where* it finds it. And it has the less regret, as the loyal citizens have in due form claimed its protection. Those loyal citizens this Government is bound to recognize and protect as being Virginia.

In the border States, so called—in fact, the Middle States—there are those who favor a policy which they call "armed neutrality;" that is, an arming of those States to prevent the Union forces passing one way, or the disunion the other, over their soil. This would be disunion completed. Figuratively speaking, it would be the building of an impassable wall along the line of separation—and yet not quite an impassable one; for, under the guise of neutrality, it would tie the hands of the Union men, and freely pass supplies from among them to the insurrectionists, which it could not do as an open enemy. At a stroke it would take all the trouble off the hands of secession, except only what proceeds from the external blockade. It would do for the disunionists that which of all things they most desire—feed them well and give them disunion without a struggle of their own. It recognizes no fidelity to the Constitution, no obligation to maintain the Union; and while very many who have favored it are doubtless loyal citizens, it is, nevertheless, treason in effect.

Recurring to the action of the Government, it may be stated that at first a call was made for seventy-five thousand militia; and rapidly following this a proclamation was issued for closing the ports of the insurrectionary districts by proceedings in the nature of a blockade. So far all was believed to be strictly legal. At this point the insurrectionists announced their purpose to enter upon the practice of privateering.

Other calls were made for volunteers to serve for three years, unless sooner discharged, and also for large additions to the regular Army and Navy. These measures, whether strictly legal or not, were ventured upon under what appeared to be a popular demand and a public necessity; trusting then as now that Congress would readily ratify them. It is believed that nothing has been done beyond the constitutional competency of Congress.

Soon after the first call for militia, it was considered a duty to authorize the commanding general in proper cases, according to his discretion, to suspend the privilege of the writ of *habeas corpus,* or, in other words, to arrest and detain, without resort to the ordinary processes and forms of law, such individuals as he might deem dangerous to the public safety. This authority has purposely been exercised but very sparingly. Nevertheless, the legality and propriety of what has been done under it are questioned, and the attention of the country has been called to the proposition that one who is sworn to "take care that the laws be faithfully executed" should not himself violate them. Of course some consideration was given to the questions of power and propriety before this matter was acted upon. The whole of the laws which were required to be faithfully executed were being resisted, and failing of execution in nearly one third of the States. Must they be allowed to finally fail of execution, even had it been perfectly clear that by the use of the means necessary to their execution some single law, made in such extreme tenderness of the citizen's liberty, that practically it relieves more of the guilty than of the innocent, should to a very limited extent be violated? To state the question more directly: are all the laws *but one* to go unexecuted, and the Government itself go to pieces, lest that one be violated? Even in such a case, would not the official oath be broken if the government should be overthrown, when it was believed that disregarding the single law would tend to preserve it? But it was not believed that this question was presented. It was not believed that any law was violated. The provision of the Constitution that "the privilege of the writ of *habeas corpus* shall not be suspended unless when, in cases of rebellion or invasion, the public safety may require it," is equivalent to a provision—is a provision—that such privilege may be suspended when, in case of rebellion or invasion, the public safety *does* require it. It was decided that we have a case of rebellion, and that the public safety does require the qualified suspension of the privilege of the writ which was authorized to be made. Now, it is insisted that Congress, and not the Executive, is vested with this power. But the Constitution itself is silent as to which or who is to exercise the power; and as the provision was plainly made for a dangerous emergency, it cannot be believed the framers of the instrument intended that in every case the danger should run its course until Congress could be called together; the very assembling of which might be prevented, as was intended in this case, by the rebellion.

No more extended argument is now offered, as an opinion, at some length, will probably be presented by the Attorney General. Whether there shall be any legislation upon the subject, and if any, what, is submitted entirely to the better judgment of Congress.

The forbearance of this Government had been so extraordinary, and so long continued, as to lead some foreign nations to shape their action as if they supposed the early destruction of our national Union was probable. While this, on discovery, gave the Executive some concern, he is now happy to say that the sovereignty and rights of the United States are now everywhere practically respected by foreign Powers; and a general sympathy with the country is manifested throughout the world.

The reports of the Secretaries of the Treasury, War, and the Navy, will give the information in detail deemed necessary and convenient for your deliberation and action; while the Executive and all the Departments will stand ready to supply omissions, or to communicate new facts considered important for you to know.

It is now recommended that you give the legal means for making this contest a short and a decisive one; that you place at the control of the Government, for the work, at least four hundred thousand men, and $400,000,000. That number of men is about one tenth of those of proper ages within the regions where, apparently, *all* are willing to engage; and the sum is less than a twenty-third part of the money value owned by the men who seem ready to devote the whole. A debt of $600,000,000 *now,* is a less sum per head than was the debt of our Revolution when we came out of that struggle; and the money value in the country now bears even a greater proportion to what it was *then,* than does the population. Surely each man has as strong a motive *now* to *preserve* our liberties, as each had *then* to *establish* them.

A right result, at this time, will be worth more to the world than ten times the men and ten times the money. The evidence reaching us from the country leaves no doubt that the material for the work is abundant, and that it needs only the hand of legislation to give it legal sanction, and the hand of the executive to give it practical shape and efficiency. One of the greatest perplexities of the Government is to avoid receiving troops faster than it can provide for them. In a word, the people will save their Government if the Government itself will do its part only indifferently well.

It might seem, at first thought, to be of little difference whether the present movement at the South be called "secession" or "rebellion." The movers, however, well understand the difference. At the beginning they knew they could never raise their treason to any respectable magnitude by any name which implies *violation* of law. They knew their people possessed as much of moral sense, as much of devotion to law and order, and as much pride in, and reverence for, the history and Government of their common country, as any other civilized and patriotic people. They knew they could make no advancement directly in the teeth of these strong and noble sentiments. Accordingly they commenced by an insidious debauching of the public mind. They invented an ingenious sophism, which, if conceded, was followed by perfectly logical steps, through all the incidents, to the complete destruction of the Union. The sophism itself is, that any State of the Union may, *consistently* with the national Constitution, and therefore *lawfully* and *peacefully,* withdraw from the Union without the consent of the Union or of any other State. The little disguise that the supposed right is to be exercised only for just cause, themselves to be the sole judge of its justice, is too thin to merit any notice.

With rebellion thus sugar-coated they have been drugging the public mind of their section for more than thirty years, and until at length they have brought many good men to a willingness to take up arms against the Government the day *after* some assemblage of men have enacted the farcical pretense of taking their State out of the Union, who could have been brought to no such thing the day *before*.

This sophism derives much, perhaps the whole, of its currency from the assumption that there is some omnipotent and sacred supremacy pertaining to a *State*—to each State of our Federal Union. Our States have neither more nor less power than that reserved to them in the Union by the Constitution—no one of them ever having been a State *out* of the Union. The original ones passed into the Union even *before* they cast off their British colonial dependence; and the new ones each came into the Union directly from a condition of dependence, excepting Texas. And even Texas, in its temporary independence, was never designated a State. The new ones only took the designation of States on coming into the Union, while that name was first adopted for the old ones in and by the Declaration of Independence. Therein the "United Colonies" were declared to be "free and independent States;" but, even then, the object plainly was not to declare their independence of *one another,* or of the *Union,* but directly the contrary, as their mutual pledge, and their mutual action, before, at the time, and afterwards, abundantly show. The express plighting of faith by each and all of the original thirteen in the Articles of Confederation, two years later, that the Union shall be perpetual, is most conclusive. Having never been States, either in substance or in name, *outside* of the Union, whence this magical omnipotence of "State rights," asserting a claim of power to lawfully destroy the Union itself? Much is said about the "sovereignty" of the States; but the word, even, is not in the national Constitution; nor, as is believed, in any of the State constitutions. What is "sovereignty," in the political sense of the term? Would it be far wrong to define it "a political community, without a political superior"? Tested by this, no one of our States, except Texas, ever was a sovereignty. And even Texas gave up the character on coming into the Union; by which act she acknowledged the Constitution of the United States and the laws and treaties of the United States made in pursuance of the Constitution to be, for her, the supreme law of the land. The States have their *status* in the Union, and they have no other legal *status*. If they break from this, they can only do so

against law and by revolution. The Union, and not themselves separately, procured their independence and their liberty. By conquest, or purchase, the
Union gave each of them whatever of independence and liberty it has. The
Union is older than any of the States, and, in fact, it created them as States. Originally some dependent colonies made the Union, and, in turn, the Union threw
off their old dependence for them, and made them States, such as they are. Not
one of them ever had a State constitution independent of the Union. Of course,
it is not forgotten that all the new States framed their constitutions before they
entered the Union; nevertheless, dependent upon, and preparatory to, coming
into the Union.

Unquestionably the States have the powers and rights reserved to them in
and by the national Constitution; but among these, surely, are not included all
conceivable powers, however mischievous or destructive; but, at most, such
only as were known in the world, at the time, as governmental powers; and certainly a power to destroy the Government itself had never been known as a governmental—as a merely administrative power. This relative matter of national
power and State rights, as a principle, is no other than the principle of *generality*
and *locality*. Whatever concerns the whole should be confided to the whole—
to the General Government; while whatever concerns *only* the State should be
left exclusively to the State. This is all there is of original principle about it.
Whether the National Constitution in defining boundaries between the two has
applied the principle with exact accuracy, is not to be questioned. We are all
bound by that defining, without question.

What is now combated, is the position that secession is *consistent* with the
Constitution—is *lawful* and *peaceful*. It is not contended that there is any express
law for it; and nothing should ever be implied as law which leads to unjust or
absurd consequences. The nation purchased with money the countries out of
which several of these States were formed: is it just that they shall go off without leave and without refunding? The nation paid very large sums (in the aggregate, I believe, nearly a hundred millions) to relieve Florida of the aboriginal
tribes: is it just that she shall now be off without consent, or without making
any return? The nation is now in debt for money applied to the benefit of these
so-called seceding States in common with the rest: is it just either that creditors
shall go unpaid, or the remaining States pay the whole? A part of the present
national debt was contracted to pay the old debts of Texas: is it just that she shall
leave and pay no part of this herself?

Again: if one State may secede, so may another; and when all shall have
seceded, none is left to pay the debts. Is this quite just to creditors? Did we notify

them of this sage view of ours when we borrowed their money? If we now recognize this doctrine by allowing the seceders to go in peace, it is difficult to see what we can do if others choose to go, or to extort terms upon which they will promise to remain.

The seceders insist that our Constitution admits of secession. They have assumed to make a national constitution of their own, in which, of necessity, they have either *discarded* or *retained* the right of secession, as they insist it exists in ours. If they have discarded it, they thereby admit that, on principle, it ought not to be in ours. If they have retained it, by their own construction of ours they show that, to be consistent, they must secede from one another whenever they shall find it the easiest way of settling their debts, or effecting any other selfish or unjust object. The principle itself is one of disintegration, and upon which no Government can possibly endure.

If all the States, save one, should assert the power to *drive* that one out of the Union, it is presumed the whole class of seceder politicians would at once deny the power, and denounce the act as the greatest outrage upon State rights. But suppose that precisely the same act, instead of being called "driving the one out," should be called "the seceding of the others from that one:" it would be exactly what the seceders claim to do; unless, indeed, they make the point that the one, because it is a minority, may rightfully do what the others, because they are a majority, may not rightfully do. These politicians are subtile and profound on the rights of minorities. They are not partial to that power which made the Constitution, and speaks from the preamble, calling itself "We, the People."

It may well be questioned whether there is, to-day, a majority of the legally-qualified voters of any State, except perhaps South Carolina, in favor of disunion. There is much reason to believe that the Union men are the majority in many, if not in every other one, of the so-called seceded States. The contrary has not been demonstrated in any one of them. It is ventured to affirm this even of Virginia and Tennessee; for the result of an election held in military camps, where the bayonets are all on one side of the question voted upon, can scarcely be considered as demonstrating popular sentiment. At such an election, all that large class who are at once *for* the Union, and *against* coercion, would be coerced to vote against the Union.

It may be affirmed, without extravagance, that the free institutions we enjoy have developed the powers and improved the condition of our whole people, beyond any example in the world. Of this we now have a striking and an impressive illustration. So large an army as the government has now on foot was never before known without a soldier in it but who had taken his place there of his own free choice. But more than this: there are many single regiments whose members, one and another, possess full practical knowledge of all the arts, sciences, professions, and whatever else, whether useful or elegant, is known in the world; and there is scarcely one from which there could not be selected a President, a Cabinet, a Congress, and perhaps a court, abundantly competent to administer the Government itself! Nor do I say this is not true also in the army of our late friends, now adversaries, in this contest; but if it is, so much better the reason why the Government which has conferred such benefits on both them and us should not be broken up. Whoever, in any section, proposes to abandon such a Government, would do well to consider, in deference to what principle it is that he does it; what better he is likely to get in its stead; whether the substitute will give, or be intended to give, so much of good to the people? There are some foreshadowings on this subject. Our adversaries have adopted some declarations of independence, in which, unlike the good old one, penned by Jefferson, they omit the words "all men are created equal." Why? They have adopted a temporary national constitution, in the preamble of which, unlike our good old one, signed by Washington, they omit "We, the People," and substitute "We, the deputies of the sovereign and independent States." Why? Why this deliberate pressing out of view the rights of men and the authority of the people?

This is essentially a people's contest. On the side of the Union, it is a struggle for maintaining in the world that form and substance of government whose leading object is to elevate the condition of men; to lift artificial weights from all shoulders; to clear the paths of laudable pursuit for all; to afford all an unfettered start and a fair chance in the race of life. Yielding to partial and temporary departures, from necessity, this is the leading object of the Government for whose existence we contend.

I am most happy to believe that the plain people understand and appreciate this. It is worthy of note, that while in this the Government's hour of trial, large numbers of those in the Army and Navy who have been favored with the offices have resigned and proved false to the hand which had pampered them, not one common soldier or common sailor is known to have deserted his flag.

Great honor is due to those officers who remained true, despite the example of their treacherous associates; but the greatest honor, and most important fact of all, is the unanimous firmness of the common soldiers and common sailors. To the last man, so far as known, they have successfully resisted the traitorous efforts of those whose commands, but an hour before, they obeyed as absolute law. This is the patriotic instinct of plain people. They understand, without an argument, that destroying the Government which was made by Washington means no good to them.

Our popular government has often been called an experiment. Two points in it our people have already settled—the successful *establishing* and the successful *administering* of it. One still remains—its successful *maintenance* against a formidable internal attempt to overthrow it. It is now for them to demonstrate to the world that those who can fairly carry an election can also suppress a rebellion; that ballots are the rightful and peaceful successors of bullets; and that when ballots have fairly and constitutionally decided, there can be no successful appeal back to bullets; that there can be no successful appeal except to ballots themselves, at succeeding elections. Such will be a great lesson of peace; teaching men that what they cannot take by an election, neither can they take by a war; teaching all the folly of being the beginners of a war.

Lest there be some uneasiness in the minds of candid men as to what is to be the course of the Government towards the southern States *after* the rebellion shall have been suppressed, the Executive deems it proper to say, it will be his purpose then, as ever, to be guided by the Constitution and the laws; and that he probably will have no different understanding of the powers and duties of the Federal Government relatively [relative?] to the rights of the States and the people, under the Constitution than that expressed in the inaugural address.

He desires to preserve the Government, that it may be administered for all, as it was administered by the men who made it. Loyal citizens everywhere have the right to claim this of their Government, and the Government has no right to withhold or neglect it. It is not perceived that, in giving it, there is any coercion, any conquest, or any subjugation, in any just sense of those terms.

The Constitution provides, and all the States have accepted the provision, that "the United States shall guaranty to every State in this Union a republican form of Government." But if a State may lawfully go out of the Union, having done so, it may also discard the republican form of Government; so that to prevent its going out is an indispensable *means* to the *end* of maintaining the guarantee mentioned; and when an end is lawful and obligatory, the indispensable means to it are also lawful and obligatory.

It was with the deepest regret that the Executive found the duty of employing the war power in defense of the Government forced upon him. He could but perform this duty, or surrender the existence of the Government. No compromise by public servants could in this case be a cure; not that compromises are not often proper, but that no popular Government can long survive a marked precedent that those who carry an election can only save the Government from immediate destruction by giving up the main point upon which the people gave the election. The people themselves, and not their servants, can safely reverse their own deliberate decisions.

As a private citizen, the Executive could not have consented that these institutions shall perish; much less could he, in betrayal of so vast and so sacred a trust as these free people have confided to him. He felt that he had no moral right to shrink, or even to count the chances of his own life, in what might follow. In full view of his great responsibility, he has, so far, done what he has deemed his duty. You will now, according to your own judgment, perform yours. He sincerely hopes that your views and your action may so accord with his as to assure all faithful citizens who have been disturbed in their rights of a certain and speedy restoration to them, under the Constitution and the laws.

And having thus chosen our course, without guile and with pure purpose, let us renew our trust in God, and go forward without fear and with manly hearts.

Abraham Lincoln.

July 4, 1861.

LETTER TO O. H. BROWNING
SEPTEMBER 22, 1861

From the beginning of the war, Lincoln was under pressure from radicals to emancipate the slaves. Abolitionists saw the conflict as an opportunity to extirpate the institution once and for all. While Lincoln was committed to extending the principle of equality, he also had consistently maintained that he had no legal authority to touch slavery where it already existed in the states. Even if the circumstance of the war made emancipation possible, in order to preserve the Union, Lincoln was obliged to consider the effect that it would have on public opinion, especially in the Border States—those states strategically located between the North and South like Missouri, Kentucky, and Maryland that remained loyal to the Union despite having slaves. As guerilla warfare raged in the Border State of Missouri, the commander of the Union forces in the western theatre, John C. Fremont, declared martial law, confiscated rebel property, and unilaterally freed the slaves. After hearing of Fremont's edict of emancipation, a company of soldiers threw down their weapons and disbanded, claiming that they had enlisted to save the Union, not to "free the niggers." Fremont's reckless actions flagrantly contradicted Lincoln's pledge in the First Inaugural, violated the due process provisions of the Confiscation Act, and threatened to undermine the fragile coalition of Border States and War Democrats necessary to win the war (see editor's introduction above). Lincoln ordered Fremont to change the decree to comply with the terms of the Confiscation Act. In his letter to Orville Browning, an old friend and anti-slavery political ally, Lincoln defended his revocation of Fremont's emancipation, describing it as a "dictatorship," a purely political act that was unlawful. Lincoln suggested that the legality of emancipation could only be sustained through an amendment or as a matter of military necessity.

PRIVATE & CONFIDENTIAL.
EXECUTIVE MANSION
WASHINGTON SEPT 22D 1861.
HON. O. H. BROWNING
MY DEAR SIR

Yours of the 17th is just received; and coming from you, I confess it astonishes me. That you should object to my adhering to a law, which you had assisted in making, and presenting to me, less than a month before, is odd enough. But this is a very small part. Genl. Fremont's proclamation, as to confiscation of property, and the liberation of slaves, is *purely political,* and not within the range of *military* law, or necessity. If a commanding General finds a necessity to seize the farm of a private owner, for a pasture, and encampment, or a fortification, he has the right to do so, and to so hold it, as long as the necessity lasts; and this is within military law, because within military necessity. But to say the farm shall no longer belong to the owner, or his heirs forever; and this as well when the farm is not needed for military purposes as when it is, is purely political, without the savor of military law about it. And the same is true of slaves. If the General needs them, he can seize them, and use them; but when the need is past, it is not for him to fix their permanent future condition. That must be settled according to laws made by law-makers, and not by military proclamations. The proclamation in the point in question, is simply "dictatorship." It assumes that the general may do *anything* he pleases—confiscate the lands and free the slaves of *loyal* people, as well as of disloyal ones. And going the whole figure I have no doubt would be more popular with some thoughtless people, than that which has been done! But I cannot assume this reckless position, nor allow others to assume it on my responsibility. You speak of it as being the only means of *saving* the government. On the contrary it is itself the surrender of the government. Can it be pretended that it is any longer the Government of the U. S.—any government of Constitution and laws,—wherein a General, or a President, may make permanent rules of property by proclamation?

I do not say Congress might not with propriety pass a law, on the point, just such as General Fremont proclaimed. I do not say I might not, as a member of Congress, vote for it. What I object to is, that I as President, shall expressly or impliedly seize and exercise the permanent legislative functions of the government.

So much as to principle. Now as to policy. No doubt the thing was popular in some quarters, and would have been more so if it had been a general declaration of emancipation. The Kentucky Legislature would not budge till that proclamation was modified; and Gen. Anderson telegraphed me that on the news of Gen. Fremont having actually issued deeds of manumission, a whole company of our Volunteers threw down their arms and disbanded. I was so assured, as to think it probable, that the very arms we had furnished Kentucky would be turned against us. I think to lose Kentucky is nearly the same as to lose the whole game. Kentucky gone, we can not hold Missouri, nor, as I think, Maryland. These all against us, and the job on our hands is too large for us. We would as well consent to separation at once, including the surrender of this capitol. On the contrary, if you will give up your restlessness for new positions, and back me manfully on the grounds upon which you and other kind friends gave me the election, and have approved in my public documents, we shall go through triumphantly.

You must not understand I took my course on the proclamation *because* of Kentucky. I took the same ground in a private letter to General Fremont before I heard from Kentucky.

You think I am inconsistent because I did not also forbid Gen. Fremont to shoot men under the proclamation. I understand that part to be within military law; but I also think, and so privately wrote Gen. Fremont, that it is impolitic in this, that our adversaries have the power, and will certainly exercise it, to shoot as many of our men as we shoot of theirs. I did not say this in the public letter, because it is a subject I prefer not to discuss in the hearing of our enemies.

There has been no thought of removing Gen. Fremont on any ground connected with his proclamation; and if there has been any wish for his removal on any ground, our mutual friend Sam Glover can probably tell you what it was. I hope no real necessity for it exists on any ground.

Suppose you write to Hurlbut and get him to resign.

Your friend as ever

A. Lincoln

ANNUAL MESSAGE TO CONGRESS
DECEMBER 3, 1861

In his message to Congress, Lincoln reviewed his policies during the war and defended the legality of the Confiscation Act, "An act to confiscate property used for insurrectionary

purposes," which passed on August 6, 1861. The Confiscation Act was an important step
towards emancipation. The Confederates were using slave labor to dig trenches, build for-
tifications, provide food, and to make weapons. Lincoln argued that Southerners had for-
feited any federal protection of slavery if they took arms up against the Union. The speech
proposed a colonization plan for the freed blacks. Following in the footsteps of his hero,
Henry Clay, Lincoln was an early proponent of colonization and repatriation for blacks
as a means to resolve the difficult question of racial adjustment. During the war, Lincoln
explored the idea of colonizing blacks in Central America. An actual colonization attempt
was tried on an island nearby Haiti, which ended in disaster; many of the colonists died
of exposure and starvation. To avert further tragedy, the administration sent an expedi-
tion back to the island to retrieve the survivors. Colonization was never again attempted.
As Frederick Douglass reminded Lincoln, most African-Americans wanted to remain in
the United States! Because he did not want the war to be perceived as a revolutionary abo-
litionist crusade, Lincoln emphasized that preserving the Union was "the primary object"
of the struggle, leaving all questions that were not of vital military importance to the more
deliberate action of the legislature. Lincoln concluded his speech with an elegant discussion
of America as the land of opportunity, once again emphasizing the worldwide significance
of the struggle.

FELLOW-CITIZENS OF THE SENATE AND HOUSE OF REPRESENTATIVES:

In the midst of unprecedented political troubles, we have cause of great gratitude to God for unusual good health, and most abundant harvests.

You will not be surprised to learn that, in the peculiar exigencies of the
times, our intercourse with foreign nations has been attended with profound
solicitude, chiefly turning upon our own domestic affairs.

A disloyal portion of the American people have, during the whole year, been
engaged in an attempt to divide and destroy the Union. A nation which endures
factious domestic division, is exposed to disrespect abroad; and one party, if not
both, is sure, sooner or later, to invoke foreign intervention.

Nations, thus tempted to interfere, are not always able to resist the counsels
of seeming expediency, and ungenerous ambition, although measures adopted
under such influences seldom fail to be unfortunate and injurious to those
adopting them.

The disloyal citizens of the United States who have offered the ruin of our
country, in return for the aid and comfort which they have invoked abroad,
have received less patronage and encouragement than they probably expected.
If it were just to suppose, as the insurgents have seemed to assume, that foreign
nations, in this case, discarding all moral, social, and treaty obligations, would

act solely, and selfishly, for the most speedy restoration of commerce, includ-ing, especially, the acquisition of cotton, those nations appear, as yet, not to have seen their way to their object more directly, or clearly, through the destruction, than through the preservation, of the Union. If we could dare to believe that foreign nations are actuated by no higher principle than this, I am quite sure a sound argument could be made to show them that they can reach their aim more readily, and easily, by aiding to crush this rebellion, than by giving encour-agement to it.

The principal lever relied on by the insurgents for exciting foreign nations to hostility against us, as already intimated, is the embarrassment of commerce. Those nations, however, not improbably, saw from the first, that it was the Union which made as well our foreign, as our domestic, commerce. They can scarcely have failed to perceive that the effort for disunion produces the exist-ing difficulty; and that one strong nation promises more durable peace, and a more extensive, valuable and reliable commerce, than can the same nation bro-ken into hostile fragments.

It is not my purpose to review our discussions with foreign states; because whatever might be their wishes, or dispositions, the integrity of our country, and the stability of our government, mainly depend, not upon them, but on the loyalty, virtue, patriotism, and intelligence of the American people. The corre-spondence itself, with the usual reservations, is herewith submitted.

I venture to hope it will appear that we have practised prudence, and liber-ality towards foreign powers, averting causes of irritation; and, with firmness, maintaining our own rights and honor.

Since, however, it is apparent that here, as in every other state, foreign dan-gers necessarily attend domestic difficulties, I recommend that adequate and ample measures be adopted for maintaining the public defences on every side. While, under this general recommendation, provision for defending our sea-coast line readily occurs to the mind, I also, in the same connexion, ask the attention of Congress to our great lakes and rivers. It is believed that some for-tifications and depots of arms and munitions, with harbor and navigation improvements, all at well selected points upon these, would be of great impor-tance to the national defence and preservation. I ask attention to the views of the Secretary of War, expressed in his report, upon the same general subject.

I deem it of importance that the loyal regions of East Tennessee and west-ern North Carolina should be connected with Kentucky, and other faithful parts of the Union, by railroad. I therefore recommend, as a military measure, that Congress provide for the construction of such road, as speedily as possible. Kentucky, no doubt, will co-operate, and, through her legislature, make the most judicious selection of a line. The northern terminus must connect with some existing railroad; and whether the route shall be from Lexington, or Nicholasville, to the Cumberland Gap; or from Lebanon to the Tennessee line, in the direction of Knoxville; or on some still different line, can easily be determined. Kentucky and the general government co-operating, the work can be completed in a very short time; and when done, it will be not only of vast present usefulness, but also a valuable permanent improvement, worth its cost in all the future.

Some treaties, designed chiefly for the interests of commerce, and having no grave political importance, have been negotiated, and will be submitted to the Senate for their consideration.

Although we have failed to induce some of the commercial powers to adopt a desirable melioration of the rigor of maritime war, we have removed all obstructions from the way of this humane reform, except such as are merely of temporary and accidental occurrence.

I invite your attention to the correspondence between her Britannic Majesty's minister accredited to this government, and the Secretary of State, relative to the detention of the British ship Perthshire in June last, by the United States steamer Massachusetts, for a supposed breach of the blockade. As this detention was occasioned by an obvious misapprehension of the facts, and as justice requires that we should commit no belligerent act not founded in strict right, as sanctioned by public law, I recommend that an appropriation be made to satisfy the reasonable demand of the owners of the vessel for her detention.

I repeat the recommendation of my predecessor, in his annual message to Congress in December last, in regard to the disposition of the surplus which will probably remain after satisfying the claims of American citizens against China, pursuant to the awards of the commissioners under the act of the 3rd of March, 1859. If, however, it should not be deemed advisable to carry that recommendation into effect, I would suggest that authority be given for investing the principal, over the proceeds of the surplus referred to, in good securities, with a view to the satisfaction of such other just claims of our citizens against China as are not unlikely to arise hereafter in the course of our extensive trade with that Empire.

By the act of the 5th of August last, Congress authorized the President to instruct the commanders of suitable vessels to defend themselves against, and to capture pirates. This authority has been exercised in a single instance only. For the more effectual protection of our extensive and valuable commerce, in the eastern seas especially, it seems to me that it would also be advisable to authorize the commanders of sailing vessels to re-capture any prizes which pirates might make of United States vessels and their cargoes, and the consular courts, now established by law in eastern countries, to adjudicate the cases, in the event that this should not be objected to by the local authorities.

If any good reason exists why we should persevere longer in withholding our recognition of the independence and sovereignty of Hayti and Liberia, I am unable to discern it. Unwilling, however, to inaugurate a novel policy in regard to them without the approbation of Congress, I submit for your consideration the expediency of an appropriation for maintaining a chargé d'affaires near each of those new states. It does not admit of doubt that important commercial advantages might be secured by favorable commercial treaties with them.

The operations of the treasury during the period which has elapsed since your adjournment have been conducted with signal success. The patriotism of the people has placed at the disposal of the government the large means demanded by the public exigencies. Much of the national loan has been taken by citizens of the industrial classes, whose confidence in their country's faith, and zeal for their country's deliverance from present peril, have induced them to contribute to the support of the government the whole of their limited acquisitions. This fact imposes peculiar obligations to economy in disbursement and energy in action.

The revenue from all sources, including loans, for the financial year ending on the 30th June, 1861, was eighty six million, eight hundred and thirty five thousand, nine hundred dollars, and twenty seven cents, ($86,835,900.27,) and the expenditures for the same period, including payments on account of the public debt, were eighty four million, five hundred and seventy eight thousand, eight hundred and thirty four dollars and forty seven cents, ($84,578,834.47;) leaving a balance in the treasury, on the 1st July, of two million, two hundred and fifty seven thousand, sixty five dollars and eighty cents, ($2,257,065.80). For the first quarter of the financial year, ending on the 30th September, 1861, the receipts from all sources, including the balance of first of July, were $102,532,509.27, and the expenses $98,239,733.09; leaving a balance on the 1st October, 1861, of $4,292,776.18.

Estimates for the remaining three quarters of the year, and for the financial year 1863, together with his views of ways and means for meeting the demands contemplated by them, will be submitted to Congress by the Secretary of the Treasury. It is gratifying to know that the expenditures made necessary by the rebellion are not beyond the resources of the loyal people, and to believe that the same patriotism which has thus far sustained the government will continue to sustain it till peace and union shall again bless the land.

I respectfully refer to the report of the Secretary of War for information respecting the numerical strength of the Army, and for recommendations having in view an increase of its efficiency and the well-being of the various branches of the service intrusted to his care. It is gratifying to know that the patriotism of the people has proved equal to the occasion, and that the number of troops tendered greatly exceeds the force which Congress authorized me to call into the field.

I refer with pleasure to those portions of his report which make allusion to the creditable degree of discipline already attained by our troops, and to the excellent sanitary condition of the entire army.

The recommendation of the secretary for an organization of the militia upon a uniform basis, is a subject of vital importance to the future safety of the country, and is commended to the serious attention of Congress.

The large addition to the regular Army, in connection with the defection that has so considerably diminished the number of its officers, gives peculiar importance to his recommendation for increasing the corps of cadets to the greatest capacity of the Military Academy.

By mere omission, I presume, Congress has failed to provide chaplains for hospitals occupied by volunteers. This subject was brought to my notice, and I was induced to draw up the form of a letter, one copy of which, properly addressed, has been delivered to each of the persons, and at the dates respectively named and stated, in a schedule, containing also the form of the letter, marked A, and herewith transmitted.

These gentlemen, I understand, entered upon the duties designated, at the times respectively stated in the schedule, and have labored faithfully therein ever since. I therefore recommend that they be compensated at the same rate as chaplains in the army. I further suggest that general provision be made for chaplains to serve at hospitals, as well as with regiments.

The report of the Secretary of the Navy presents in detail the operations of that branch of the service, the activity and energy which have characterized its administration, and the results of measures to increase its efficiency and power. Such have been the additions, by construction and purchase, that it may almost be said a navy has been created and brought into service since our difficulties commenced.

Besides blockading our extensive coast, squadrons larger than ever before assembled under our flag have been put afloat and performed deeds which have increased our naval renown.

I would invite special attention to the recommendation of the Secretary for a more perfect organization of the Navy by introducing additional grades in the service.

The present organization is defective and unsatisfactory, and the suggestions submitted by the Department will, it is believed, if adopted, obviate the difficulties alluded to, promote harmony, and increase the efficiency of the Navy.

There are three vacancies on the bench of the Supreme Court—two by the decease of Justices Daniel and McLean, and one by the resignation of Justice Campbell. I have so far forborne making nominations to fill these vacancies for reasons which I will now state. Two of the outgoing judges resided within the States now overrun by revolt; so that if successors were appointed in the same localities, they could not now serve upon their circuits; and many of the most competent men there probably would not take the personal hazard of accepting to serve, even here, upon the supreme bench. I have been unwilling to throw all the appointments northward, thus disabling myself from doing justice to the South on the return of peace; although I may remark that to transfer to the North one which has heretofore been in the South, would not, with reference to territory and population, be unjust.

During the long and brilliant judicial career of Judge McLean his circuit grew into an empire—altogether too large for any one judge to give the courts therein more than a nominal attendance—rising in population from one million four hundred and seventy thousand and eighteen in 1830, to six million one hundred and fifty-one thousand four hundred and five in 1860.

Besides this, the country generally has outgrown our present judicial system. If uniformity was at all intended, the system requires that all the States shall be accommodated with circuit courts, attended by supreme judges, while, in fact, Wisconsin, Minnesota, Iowa, Kansas, Florida, Texas, California, and Oregon, have never had any such courts. Nor can this well be remedied without a change of the system; because the adding of judges to the Supreme Court, enough for the accommodation of all parts of the country, with circuit courts, would create a court altogether too numerous for a judicial body of any sort. And the evil, if it be one, will increase as new States come into the Union. Circuit courts are useful, or they are not useful. If useful, no State should be denied them; if not useful, no State should have them. Let them be provided for all, or abolished as to all.

Three modifications occur to me, either of which, I think, would be an improvement upon our present system. Let the Supreme Court be of convenient number in every event. Then, first, let the whole country be divided into circuits of convenient size, the supreme judges to serve in a number of them corresponding to their own number, and independent circuit judges be provided for all the rest. Or, secondly, let the supreme judges be relieved from circuit duties, and circuit judges provided for all the circuits. Or, thirdly, dispense with circuit courts altogether, leaving the judicial functions wholly to the district courts and an independent Supreme Court.

I respectfully recommend to the consideration of Congress the present condition of the Statute laws, with the hope that Congress will be able to find an easy remedy for many of the inconveniences and evils which constantly embarrass those engaged in the practical administration of them. Since the organization of the government, Congress has enacted some five thousand acts and joint resolutions, which fill more than six thousand closely printed pages, and are scattered through many volumes. Many of these acts have been drawn in haste and without sufficient caution, so that their provisions are often obscure in themselves, or in conflict with each other, or at least so doubtful as to render it very difficult for even the best informed persons to ascertain precisely what the statute law really is.

It seems to me very important that the statute laws should be made as plain and intelligible as possible, and be reduced to as small a compass as may consist with the fullness and precision of the will of the legislature and the perspicuity of its language. This, well done, would, I think, greatly facilitate the labors of those whose duty it is to assist in the administration of the laws, and would be a lasting benefit to the people, by placing before them, in a more accessible and intelligible form, the laws which so deeply concern their interests and their duties.

I am informed by some whose opinions I respect, that all the acts of Congress now in force, and of a permanent and general nature, might be revised and rewritten, so as to be embraced in one volume (or at most, two volumes) of ordinary and convenient size. And I respectfully recommend to Congress to consider of the subject, and, if my suggestion be approved, to devise such plan as to their wisdom shall seem most proper for the attainment of the end proposed.

One of the unavoidable consequences of the present insurrection is the entire suppression, in many places, of all the ordinary means of administering civil justice by the officers and in the forms of existing law. This is the case, in whole or in part, in all the insurgent States; and as our armies advance upon and take possession of parts of those States, the principal evil becomes more apparent. There are no courts nor officers to whom the citizens of other States may apply for the enforcement of their lawful claims against citizens of the insurgent States; and there is a vast amount of debt constituting such claims. Some have estimated it as high as two hundred million dollars, due, in large part, from insurgents, in open rebellion, to loyal citizens who are, even now, making great sacrifices in the discharge of their patriotic duty to support the government.

Under these circumstances, I have been urgently solicited to establish, by military power, courts to administer summary justice in such cases. I have thus far declined to do it, not because I had any doubt that the end proposed—the collection of the debts—was just and right in itself, but because I have been unwilling to go beyond the pressure of necessity in the unusual exercise of power. But the powers of Congress I suppose are equal to the anomalous occasion, and therefore I refer the whole matter to Congress, with the hope that a plan may be devised for the administration of justice in all such parts of the insurgent States and Territories as may be under the control of this government, whether by a voluntary return to allegiance and order or by the power of our arms. This, however, not to be a permanent institution, but a temporary substitute, and to cease as soon as the ordinary courts can be reestablished in peace.

It is important that some more convenient means should be provided, if possible, for the adjustment of claims against the government, especially in view of their increased number by reason of the war. It is as much the duty of government to render prompt justice against itself, in favor of citizens, as it is to administer the same, between private individuals. The investigation and adjudication of claims, in their nature belong to the judicial department; besides, it is apparent that the attention of Congress will be more than usually engaged, for some time to come, with great national questions. It was intended, by the organization of the Court of Claims mainly to remove this branch of business from the Halls of Congress; but while the court has proved to be an effective and valuable means of investigation, it in great degree fails to effect the object of its creation, for want of power to make its judgments final.

Fully aware of the delicacy, not to say the danger, of the subject, I commend to your careful consideration whether this power of making judgments final may not properly be given to the court, reserving the right of appeal on questions of law to the Supreme Court, with such other provisions as experience may have shown to be necessary.

I ask attention to the report of the Postmaster General, the following being a summary statement of the condition of the department:

The revenue from all sources during the fiscal year ending June 30, 1861, including the annual permanent appropriation of seven hundred thousand dollars ($700,000) for the transportation of "free mail matter," was nine million, forty nine thousand, two hundred and ninety six dollars and forty cents ($9,049,296.40,) being about two per cent. less than the revenue for 1860.

The expenditures were thirteen million, six hundred and six thousand, seven hundred and fifty nine dollars and eleven cents ($13,606,759.11) showing a decrease of more than eight per cent. as compared with those of the previous year, and leaving an excess of expenditure over the revenue for the last fiscal year of four million, five hundred and fifty seven thousand, four hundred and sixty two dollars and seventy one cents ($4,557,462.71).

The gross revenue for the year ending June 30, 1863, is estimated at an increase of four per cent. on that of 1861, making eight million, six hundred and eighty three thousand dollars ($8,683,000) to which should be added the earnings of the department in carrying free matter, viz: seven hundred thousand dollars ($700,000,) making nine million, three hundred and eighty three thousand dollars ($9,383,000).

The total expenditures for 1863 are estimated at $12,528,000, leaving an estimated deficiency of $3,145,000, to be supplied from the treasury, in addition to the permanent appropriation.

The present insurrection shows, I think, that the extension of this District across the Potomac river, at the time of establishing the capital here, was eminently wise, and consequently that the relinquishment of that portion of it which lies within the State of Virginia was unwise and dangerous. I submit for your consideration the expediency of regaining that part of the District, and the restoration of the original boundaries thereof, through negotiations with the State of Virginia.

The report of the Secretary of the Interior, with the accompanying documents, exhibits the condition of the several branches of the public business pertaining to that department. The depressing influences of the insurrection have been especially felt in the operations of the Patent and General Land Offices. The cash receipts from the sales of public lands during the past year have exceeded the expenses of our land system only about $200,000. The sales have been entirely suspended in the southern States, while the interruptions to the business of the country, and the diversion of large numbers of men from labor to military service, have obstructed settlements in the new States and Territories of the northwest.

The receipts of the Patent Office have declined in nine months about $100,000, rendering a large reduction of the force employed necessary to make it self sustaining.

The demands upon the Pension Office will be largely increased by the insurrection. Numerous applications for pensions, based upon the casualties of the existing war, have already been made. There is reason to believe that many who are now upon the pension rolls and in receipt of the bounty of the government, are in the ranks of the insurgent army, or giving them aid and comfort. The Secretary of the Interior has directed a suspension of the payment of the pensions of such persons upon proof of their disloyalty. I recommend that Congress authorize that officer to cause the names of such persons to be stricken from the pension rolls.

The relations of the government with the Indian tribes have been greatly disturbed by the insurrection, especially in the southern superintendency and in that of New Mexico. The Indian country south of Kansas is in the possession of insurgents from Texas and Arkansas. The agents of the United States appointed since the 4th of March for this superintendency have been unable to reach their posts, while the most of those who were in office before that time have espoused the insurrectionary cause, and assume to exercise the powers of agents by virtue of commissions from the insurrectionists. It has been stated in the public press that a portion of those Indians have been organized as a military force, and are attached to the army of the insurgents. Although the government has no official information upon this subject, letters have been written to the Commissioner of Indian Affairs by several prominent chiefs, giving assurance of their loyalty to the United States, and expressing a wish for the presence of federal troops to protect them. It is believed that upon the repossession of the country by the federal forces the Indians will readily cease all hostile demonstrations, and resume their former relations to the government.

Agriculture, confessedly the largest interest of the nation, has, not a department, nor a bureau, but a clerkship only, assigned to it in the government. While it is fortunate that this great interest is so independent in its nature as to not have demanded and extorted more from the government, I respectfully ask Congress to consider whether something more cannot be given voluntarily with general advantage.

Annual reports exhibiting the condition of our agriculture, commerce, and manufacturers would present a fund of information of great practical value to the country. While I make no suggestion as to details, I venture the opinion that an agricultural and statistical bureau might profitably be organized.

The execution of the laws for the suppression of the African slave trade, has been confided to the Department of the Interior. It is a subject of gratulation that the efforts which have been made for the suppression of this inhuman traffic, have been recently attended with unusual success. Five vessels being fitted out for the slave trade have been seized and condemned. Two mates of vessels engaged in the trade, and one person in equipping a vessel as a slaver, have been convicted and subjected to the penalty of fine and imprisonment, and one captain, taken with a cargo of Africans on board his vessel, has been convicted of the highest grade of offence under our laws, the punishment of which is death.

The Territories of Colorado, Dakotah [sic] and Nevada, created by the last Congress, have been organized, and civil administration has been inaugurated therein under auspices especially gratifying, when it is considered that the leaven of treason was found existing in some of these new countries when the federal officers arrived there.

The abundant natural resources of these Territories, with the security and protection afforded by organized government, will doubtless invite to them a large immigration when peace shall restore the business of the country to its accustomed channels. I submit the resolutions of the legislature of Colorado, which evidence the patriotic spirit of the people of the Territory. So far the authority of the United States has been upheld in all the Territories, as it is hoped it will be in the future. I commend their interests and defence to the enlightened and generous care of Congress.

I recommend to the favorable consideration of Congress the interests of the District of Columbia. The insurrection has been the cause of much suffering and sacrifice to its inhabitants, and as they have no representative in Congress, that body should not overlook their just claims upon the government.

At your late session a joint resolution was adopted authorizing the President to take measures for facilitating a proper representation of the industrial interests of the United States at the exhibition of the industry of all nations to be holden at London in the year 1862. I regret to say I have been unable to give personal attention to this subject,—a subject at once so interesting in itself, and so extensively and intimately connected with the material prosperity of the world. Through the Secretaries of State and of the Interior a plan, or system, has been devised, and partly matured, and which will be laid before you.

Under and by virtue of the act of Congress entitled "An act to confiscate property used for insurrectionary purposes," approved August 6, 1861, the legal claims of certain persons to the labor and service of certain other persons have become forfeited; and numbers of the latter, thus liberated, are already dependent on the United States, and must be provided for in some way. Besides this, it is not impossible that some of the States will pass similar enactments for their own benefit respectively, and by operation of which persons of the same class will be thrown upon them for disposal. In such case I recommend that Congress provide for accepting such persons from such States, according to some mode of valuation, in lieu, *pro tanto,* of direct taxes, or upon some other plan to be agreed on with such States respectively; that such persons, on such acceptance by the general government, be at once deemed free; and that, in any event, steps be taken for colonizing both classes, (or the one first mentioned, if the other shall not be brought into existence,) at some place, or places, in a climate congenial to them. It might be well to consider, too, whether the free colored people already in the United States could not, so far as individuals may desire, be included in such colonization.

To carry out the plan of colonization may involve the acquiring of territory, and also the appropriation of money beyond that to be expended in the territorial acquisition. Having practiced the acquisition of territory for nearly sixty years, the question of constitutional power to do so is no longer an open one with us. The power was questioned at first by Mr. Jefferson, who, however, in the purchase of Louisiana, yielded his scruples on the plea of great expediency. If it be said that the only legitimate object of acquiring territory is to furnish homes for white men, this measure effects that object; for the emigration of colored men leaves additional room for white men remaining or coming here. Mr. Jefferson, however, placed the importance of procuring Louisiana more on political and commercial grounds than on providing room for population.

On this whole proposition, including the appropriation of money with the acquisition of territory, does not the expediency amount to absolute necessity—that, without which the government itself cannot be perpetuated? The war continues. In considering the policy to be adopted for suppressing the insurrection, I have been anxious and careful that the inevitable conflict for this purpose shall not degenerate into a violent and remorseless revolutionary struggle. I have, therefore, in every case, thought it proper to keep the integrity of the Union prominent as the primary object of the contest on our part, leaving all questions which are not of vital military importance to the more deliberate action of the legislature.

In the exercise of my best discretion I have adhered to the blockade of the ports held by the insurgents, instead of putting in force, by proclamation, the law of Congress enacted at the late session, for closing those ports. So, also, obeying the dictates of prudence, as well as the obligations of law, instead of transcending, I have adhered to the act of Congress to confiscate property used for insurrectionary purposes. If a new law upon the same subject shall be proposed, its propriety will be duly considered.

The Union must be preserved, and hence, all indispensable means must be employed. We should not be in haste to determine that radical and extreme measures, which may reach the loyal as well as the disloyal, are indispensable.

The inaugural address at the beginning of the Administration, and the message to Congress at the late special session, were both mainly devoted to the domestic controversy out of which the insurrection and consequent war have sprung. Nothing now occurs to add or subtract, to or from, the principles or general purposes stated and expressed in those documents.

The last ray of hope for preserving the Union peaceably, expired at the assault upon Fort Sumter; and a general review of what has occurred since may not be unprofitable. What was painfully uncertain then, is much better defined and more distinct now; and the progress of events is plainly in the right direction. The insurgents confidently claimed a strong support from north of Mason and Dixon's line; and the friends of the Union were not free from apprehension on the point. This, however, was soon settled definitely and on the right side. South of the line, noble little Delaware led off right from the first. Maryland was made to *seem* against the Union. Our soldiers were assaulted, bridges were burned, and railroads torn up, within her limits; and we were many days, at one time, without the ability to bring a single regiment over her soil to the capital. Now, her bridges and railroads are repaired and open to the government; she already gives seven regiments to the cause of the Union and none to the enemy; and her people, at a regular election, have sustained the Union, by a larger majority, and a larger aggregate vote than they ever before gave to any candidate, or any question. Kentucky, too, for some time in doubt, is now decidedly, and, I think, unchangeably, ranged on the side of the Union. Missouri is comparatively quiet; and I believe cannot again be overrun by the insurrectionists. These three States of Maryland, Kentucky, and Missouri, neither of which would promise a single soldier at first, have now an aggregate of not less than forty thousand in the field, for the Union; while, of their citizens, certainly not more than a third of that number, and they of doubtful whereabouts, and doubtful existence, are in arms against it. After a somewhat bloody struggle of months, winter closes on the Union people of western Virginia, leaving them masters of their own country.

An insurgent force of about fifteen hundred, for months dominating the narrow peninsular region, constituting the counties of Accomac and Northampton, and known as eastern shore of Virginia, together with some contiguous parts of Maryland, have laid down their arms; and the people there have renewed their allegiance to, and accepted the protection of, the old flag. This leaves no armed insurrectionist north of the Potomac, or east of the Chesapeake.

Also we have obtained a footing at each of the isolated points, on the southern coast, of Hatteras, Port Royal, Tybee Island, near Savannah, and Ship Island;

and we likewise have some general accounts of popular movements, in behalf of the Union, in North Carolina and Tennessee.

These things demonstrate that the cause of the Union is advancing steadily and certainly southward.

Since your last adjournment, Lieutenant General Scott has retired from the head of the army. During his long life, the nation has not been unmindful of his merit; yet, on calling to mind how faithfully, ably and brilliantly he has served the country, from a time far back in our history, when few of the now living had been born, and thenceforward continually, I cannot but think we are still his debtors. I submit, therefore, for your consideration, what further mark of recognition is due to him, and to ourselves, as a grateful people.

With the retirement of General Scott came the executive duty of appointing, in his stead, a general-in-chief of the army. It is a fortunate circumstance that neither in council nor country was there, so far as I know, any difference of opinion as to the proper person to be selected. The retiring chief repeatedly expressed his judgment in favor of General McClellan for the position; and in this the nation seemed to give a unanimous concurrence. The designation of General McClellan is therefore in considerable degree, the selection of the Country as well as of the Executive; and hence there is better reason to hope there will be given him, the confidence, and cordial support thus, by fair implication, promised, and without which, he cannot, with so full efficiency, serve the country.

It has been said that one bad general is better than two good ones; and the saying is true, if taken to mean no more than that an army is better directed by a single mind, though inferior, than by two superior ones, at variance, and cross-purposes with each other.

And the same is true, in all joint operations wherein those engaged, *can* have none but a common end in view, and *can* differ only as to the choice of means. In a storm at sea, no one on board *can* wish the ship to sink; and yet, not unfrequently, all go down together, because too many will direct, and no single mind can be allowed to control.

It continues to develop that the insurrection is largely, if not exclusively, a war upon the first principle of popular government—the rights of the people. Conclusive evidence of this is found in the most grave and maturely considered public documents, as well as in the general tone of the insurgents. In those documents we find the abridgement of the existing right of suffrage and the denial to the people of all right to participate in the selection of public officers, except the legislative boldly advocated, with labored arguments to prove that large control of the people in government, is the source of all political evil.

Monarchy itself is sometimes hinted at as a possible refuge from the power of the people.

In my present position, I could scarcely be justified were I to omit raising a warning voice against this approach of returning despotism.

It is not needed, not fitting here, that a general argument should be made in favor of popular institutions; but there is one point, with its connexions, not so hackneyed as most others, to which I ask a brief attention. It is the effort to place *capital* on an equal footing with, if not above *labor,* in the structure of government. It is assumed that labor is available only in connexion with capital; that nobody labors unless somebody else, owning capital, somehow by the use of it, induces him to labor. This assumed, it is next considered whether it is best that capital shall *hire* laborers, and thus induce them to work by their own consent, or *buy* them, and drive them to it without their consent. Having proceeded so far, it is naturally concluded that all laborers are either *hired* laborers, or what we call slaves. And further it is assumed that whoever is once a hired laborer, is fixed in that condition for life.

Now, there is no such relation between capital and labor as assumed; nor is there any such thing as a free man being fixed for life in the condition of a hired laborer. Both these assumptions are false, and all inferences from them are groundless. Labor is prior to, and independent of, capital. Capital is only the fruit of labor, and could never have existed if labor had not first existed. Labor is the superior of capital, and deserves much the higher consideration. Capital has its rights, which are as worthy of protection as any other rights. Nor is it denied that there is, and probably always will be, a relation between labor and capital, producing mutual benefits. The error is in assuming that the whole labor of community exists within that relation. A few men own capital, and that few avoid labor themselves, and, with their capital, hire or buy another few to labor for them. A large majority belong to neither class—neither work for others, nor have others working for them. In most of the southern states, a majority of the whole people of all colors are neither slaves nor masters; while in the northern a large majority are neither hirers nor hired. Men with their families—wives, sons, and daughters—work for themselves, on their farms, in their houses, and in their shops, taking the whole product to themselves, and asking no favors of capital on the one hand, nor of hired laborers or slaves on the other. It is not forgotten that a considerable number of persons mingle their own labor with capital—that is, they labor with their own hands, and also buy or hire others to labor for them; but this is only a mixed, and not a distinct class. No principle stated is disturbed by the existence of this mixed class.

Again: as has already been said, there is not, of necessity, any such thing as the free hired laborer being fixed to that condition for life. Many independent men everywhere in these States, a few years back in their lives, were hired laborers. The prudent, penniless beginner in the world, labors for wages awhile, saves a surplus with which to buy tools or land for himself; then labors on his own account another while, and at length hires another new beginner to help him. This is the just, and generous, and prosperous system, which opens the way to all—gives hope to all, and consequent energy, and progress, and improvement of condition to all. No men living are more worthy to be trusted than those who toil up from poverty—none less inclined to take, or touch, aught which they have not honestly earned. Let them beware of surrendering a political power which they already possess, and which, if surrendered, will surely be used to close the door of advancement against such as they, and to fix new disabilities and burdens upon them, till all of liberty shall be lost.

From the first taking of our national census to the last are seventy years; and we find our population at the end of the period eight times as great as it was at the beginning. The increase of those other things which men deem desirable has been even greater. We thus have at one view, what the popular principle applied to government, through the machinery of the States and the Union, has produced in a given time; and also what, if firmly maintained, it promises for the future. There are already among us those, who, if the Union be preserved, will live to see it contain two hundred and fifty millions. The struggle *of* to-day, is not altogether for to-day—it is for a vast future also. With a reliance on Providence, all the more firm and earnest, let us proceed in the great task which events have devolved upon us.

Abraham Lincoln

December 3, 1861

MESSAGE TO CONGRESS[2]
MARCH 6, 1862

Lincoln's Message to Congress on March 6 constituted the first of four appeals to achieve a gradual, compensated emancipation in the loyal Border States where the institution remained. Unfortunately, these persistent efforts toward black freedom have been neglected or forgotten by contemporary scholars who denigrate the Emancipation Proclamation of 1863 because it was justified as a military necessity and did not apply to the Border States. Lin-

2. *CWAL,* V, 144-46

coln's commitment to compensated emancipation shows that he attempted to achieve his
moral aspiration of equality and black freedom within legal boundaries. Under Lincoln's
plan, the federal government would provide aid to any state that would emancipate its
slaves. Although the plan was proposed by the national government under the auspices of
Lincoln's prudent leadership, its approval was left to the discretion and consent of the states
since the national government still lacked the authority to abolish slavery in those areas that
remained loyal to the Union.

MARCH 6, 1862

Fellow-citizens of the Senate, and House of Representatives, I recommend the adoption of a Joint Resolution by your honorable bodies which shall be substantially as follows:

"Resolved that the United States ought to co-operate with any state which may adopt gradual abolishment of slavery, giving to such state pecuniary aid, to be used by such state in it's discretion, to compensate for the inconveniences public and private, produced by such change of system."

If the proposition contained in the resolution does not meet the approval of Congress and the country, there is the end; but if it does command such approval, I deem it of importance that the states and people immediately interested, should be at once distinctly notified of the fact, so that they may begin to consider whether to accept or reject it. The federal government would find it's highest interest in such a measure, as one of the most efficient means of self-preservation. The leaders of the existing insurrection entertain the hope that this government will ultimately be forced to acknowledge the independence of some part of the disaffected region, and that all the slave states North of such part will then say "the Union, for which we have struggled, being already gone, we now choose to go with the Southern section." To deprive them of this hope, substantially ends the rebellion; and the initiation of emancipation completely deprives them of it, as to all the states initiating it. The point is not that *all* the states tolerating slavery would very soon, if at all, initiate emancipation; but that, while the offer is equally made to all, the more Northern shall, by such initiation, make it certain to the more Southern, that in no event, will the former ever join the latter, in their proposed confederacy. I say "initiation" because, in my judgment, gradual, and not sudden emancipation, is better for all. In the mere financial, or pecuniary view, any member of Congress, with the census-tables and Treasury-reports before him, can readily see for himself how very soon the current expenditures of this war would purchase, at fair valuation, all the slaves in any named State. Such a proposition, on the part of the general government, sets up no claim of a right, by federal authority, to interfere with slavery within state limits, referring, as it does, the absolute control of the subject, in each case, to the state and it's people, immediately interested. It is proposed as a matter of perfectly free choice with them.

In the annual message last December, I thought fit to say "The Union must be preserved; and hence all indispensable means must be employed." I said this, not hastily, but deliberately. War has been made, and continues to be, an indispensable means to this end. A practical re-acknowledgement of the national authority would render the war unnecessary, and it would at once cease. If, however, resistance continues, the war must also continue; and it is impossible to foresee all the incidents, which may attend and all the ruin which may follow it. Such as may seem indispensable, or may obviously promise great efficiency towards ending the struggle, must and will come.

The proposition now made, though an offer only, I hope it may be esteemed no offence to ask whether the pecuniary consideration tendered would not be of more value to the States and private persons concerned, than are the institution, and property in it, in the present aspect of affairs.

While it is true that the adoption of the proposed resolution would be merely initiatory, and not within itself a practical measure, it is recommended in the hope that it would soon lead to important practical results. In full view of my great responsibility to my God, and to my country, I earnestly beg the attention of Congress and the people to the subject.

ABRAHAM LINCOLN
March 6. 1862.

LETTER TO JAMES A. MCDOUGAL[3]
MARCH 14, 1862

Senator James A. McDougall was a War Democrat from California who opposed Lincoln's plan for gradual and compensated emancipation. In response to his critics, Lincoln demonstrated that compensated emancipation was in their pecuniary interest. Less than one half-day's cost of the war would pay for all the slaves in Delaware at four hundred dollars per head. Despite Lincoln's efforts, McDougal continued his opposition by questioning the constitutionality of the measure in a speech before the Senate on March 22.

3. *CWAL,* V, 160.

HON. JAMES A. MCDOUGAL
EXECUTIVE MANSION
U.S. SENATE
WASHINGTON, MARCH 14, 1862

My dear Sir: As to the expensiveness of the plan of gradual emancipation with compensation, proposed in the late Message, please allow me one or two brief suggestions.

Less than one half-day's cost of this war would pay for all the slaves in Delaware at four hundred dollars per head:

Thus, all the slaves in Delaware,

by the Census of 1860, are	1798
	400
Cost of the slaves	$719,200.
One day's cost of the war	$2,000,000.

Again, less than eighty seven days cost of this war would, at the same price, pay for all in Delaware, Maryland, District of Columbia, Kentucky, and Missouri.

Thus, slaves in Delaware	1798
" " Maryland	87,188
" " Dis. of Col.	3,181
" " Kentucky	225,490
" " Missouri	*114,965*
	432,622
	400
Cost of the slaves	$173,048,800
Eighty-seven days' cost of the war	$174,000,000.

Do you doubt that taking the initiatory steps on the part of those states and this District, would shorten the war more than eighty-seven days, and thus be an actual saving of expense?

A word as to the *time* and *manner* of incurring the expence. Suppose, for instance, a State devises and adopts a system by which the institution absolutely ceases therein by a named day—say January 1st, 1882. Then, let the sum to be paid to such state by the United States, be ascertained by taking from the Census of 1860, the number of slaves within the state, and multiplying that number by four hundred—the United States to pay such sum to the state in twenty equal annual instalments, in six per cent. bonds of the United States.

The sum thus given, as to *time* and *manner,* I think would not be half as oner-ous, as would be an equal sum, raised *now,* for the indefinite prossecution of the war; but of this you can judge as well as I.

I inclose a Census-table for your convenience. Yours very truly

A. LINCOLN

LETTER TO THE SENATE AND HOUSE OF REPRESENTATIVES
APRIL 16, 1862

In the absence of the southern states, the remaining northern members of Congress enacted a law providing for gradual and compensated emancipation in the District of Columbia. The same act also provided for the voluntary colonization of the freedmen to Haiti and Liberia. Lincoln voiced his approval of the twin goals of compensated emancipation and colonization. The law would finally remove the foul blight of slavery from the nation's capital. The legality of the act was based on Congress's jurisdiction over the District of Columbia.

FELLOW CITIZENS OF THE SENATE, AND HOUSE OF REPRESENTATIVES.

The Act entitled "An Act for the release of certain persons held to service, or labor in the District of Columbia" has this day been approved, and signed.

I have never doubted the constitutional authority of Congress to abolish slavery in this District; and I have ever desired to see the national capital freed from the institution in some satisfactory way. Hence there has never been; in my mind, any question upon the subject, except the one of expediency, aris-ing in view of all the circumstances. If there be matters within and above this act, which might have taken a course or shape, more satisfactory to my judg-ment, I do-not attempt to specify them. I am gratified that the two principles of compensation, and colonization, are both recognized, and practically applied in the act.

In the matter of compensation, it is provided that claims may be presented within ninety days from the passage of the act "but not thereafter"; and there is no saving for minors, femes-covert, insane, or absent persons. I presume this is an omission by mere over-sight, and I recommend that it be supplied by an amendatory or supplemental act.

Abraham Lincoln

April 16, 1862.

PROCLAMATION REVOKING GENERAL HUNTER'S ORDER OF MILITARY EMANCIPATION OF MAY 9, 1862[4]

On May 9, 1862, General Hunter, commander of Union forces in the southern the-atre, decreed the emancipation of slaves in Georgia, South Carolina, and Florida. As with Fremont's emancipation, Lincoln revoked Hunter's as unconstitutional. However, to show that he favored the possibility of legal abolition, Lincoln made a second appeal to the Border States in favor of compensated emancipation at the end of his Proclamation.

MAY 19, 1862
BY THE PRESIDENT OF THE UNITED STATES OF AMERICA.
A PROCLAMATION.

Whereas there appears in the public prints, what purports to be a proclama-tion, of Major General Hunter, in the words and figures following, towit:

> *Headquarters Department of the South,*
> Hilton Head, S.C., May 9, 1862.
> General Orders No. 11.—The three States of Georgia, Florida and South Carolina, comprising the military department of the south, hav-ing deliberately declared themselves no longer under the protection of the United States of America, and having taken up arms against the said United States, it becomes a military necessity to declare them under mar-tial law. This was accordingly done on the 25th day of April, 1862. Slav-ery and martial law in a free country are altogether incompatible; the persons in these three States—Georgia, Florida and South Carolina—heretofore held as slaves, are therefore declared forever free.
> DAVID HUNTER, (Official) Major General Commanding.
> ED. W. SMITH, Acting Assistant Adjutant General.

And whereas the same is producing some excitement, and misunderstand-ing: therefore

I, Abraham Lincoln, president of the United States, proclaim and declare, that the government of the United States, had no knowledge, information, or belief, of an intention on the part of General Hunter to issue such a proclama-tion; nor has it yet, any authentic information that the document is genuine. And further that neither General Hunter, nor any other commander, or person, has been authorized by the Government of the United States, to make proclamations declaring the slaves of any State free; and that the supposed proclamation, now in question, whether genuine or false, is altogether void, so far as respects such declaration.

I further make known that whether it be competent for me, as Commander-in-Chief of the Army and Navy, to declare the Slaves of any state or states, free, and whether at any time, in any case, it shall have become a necessity indispensable to the maintainance of the government, to exercise such supposed power, are questions which, under my responsibility, I reserve to myself, and which I can not feel justified in leaving to the decision of commanders in the field. These are totally different questions from those of police regulations in armies and camps.

On the sixth day of March last, by a special message, I recommended to Congress the adoption of a joint resolution to be substantially as follows:

Resolved, That the United States ought to co-operate with any State which may adopt a gradual abolishment of slavery, giving to such State pecuniary aid, to be used by such State in its discretion to compensate for the inconveniences, public and private, produced by such change of system.

The resolution, in the language above quoted, was adopted by large majorities in both branches of Congress, and now stands an authentic, definite, and solemn proposal of the nation to the States and people most immediately interested in the subject matter. To the people of those states I now earnestly appeal. I do not argue. I beseech you to make the arguments for yourselves. You can not if you would, be blind to the signs of the times. I beg of you a calm and enlarged consideration of them, ranging, if it may be, far above personal and partizan politics. This proposal makes common cause for a common object, casting no reproaches upon any. It acts not the pharisee. The change it contemplates would come gently as the dews of heaven, not rending or wrecking anything. Will you not embrace it? So much good has not been done, by one effort, in all past time, as, in the providence of God, it is now your high previlege to do. May the vast future not have to lament that you have neglected it.

In witness whereof, I have hereunto set my hand, and caused the seal of the United States to be affixed.

Done at the City of Washington this nineteenth day of [L.S.] May, in the year of our Lord one thousand eight hundred and sixty-two, and of the Independence of the United States the eighty-sixth.

ABRAHAM LINCOLN.

By the President:

WILLIAM H. SEWARD, Secretary of State.

APPEAL TO BORDER STATE REPRESENTATIVES TO FAVOR COMPENSATED EMANCIPATION[5]
JULY 12, 1862

This constituted Lincoln's third appeal to the Border States for compensated emancipation. For Lincoln, the twin goals of preserving the Union and ending slavery were related in the long-term. Lincoln warned that the Border States' failure to accept the proposal would be a missed opportunity to gain some compensation since it was only a matter of time before the institution of slavery would be a casualty of war. The proposal for compensated emancipation was passed in both houses of Congress, but was rejected by the state legislatures.

JULY 12, 1862

Gentlemen. After the adjournment of Congress, now very near, I shall have no opportunity of seeing you for several months. Believing that you of the border-states hold more power for good than any other equal number of members, I feel it a duty which I can not justifiably waive, to make this appeal to you. I intend no reproach or complaint when I assure you that in my opinion, if you all had voted for the resolution in the gradual emancipation message of last March, the war would now be substantially ended. And the plan therein proposed is yet one of the most potent, and swift means of ending it. Let the states which are in rebellion see, definitely and certainly, that, in no event, will the states you represent ever join their proposed Confederacy, and they can not, much longer maintain the contest. But you can not divest them of their hope to ultimately have you with them so long as you show a determination to perpetuate the institution within your own states. Beat them at elections, as you have overwhelmingly done, and, nothing daunted, they still claim you as their own. You and I know what the lever of their power is. Break that lever before their faces, and they can shake you no more forever.

Most of you have treated me with kindness and consideration; and I trust you will not now think I improperly touch what is exclusively your own, when, for the sake of the whole country I ask "Can you, for your states, do better than to take the course I urge? ["] Discarding *punctillio,* and maxims adapted to more manageable times, and looking only to the unprecedentedly stern facts of our case, can you do better in any possible event? You prefer that the constitutional relation of the states to the nation shall be practically restored, without disturbance of the institution; and if this were done, my whole duty, in this respect, under the constitution, and my oath of office,

5. *CWAL,* V, 317–319.

would be performed. But it is not done, and we are trying to accomplish it by war. The incidents of the war can not be avoided. If the war continue long, as it must, if the object be not sooner attained, the institution in your states will be extinguished by mere friction and abrasion—by the mere incidents of the war. It will be gone, and you will have nothing valuable in lieu of it. Much of it's value is gone already. How much better for you, and for your people, to take the step which, at once, shortens the war, and secures substantial compensation for that which is sure to be wholly lost in any other event. How much better to thus save the money which else we sink forever in the war. How much better to do it while we can, lest the war ere long render us pecuniarily unable to do it. How much better for you, as seller, and the nation as buyer, to sell out, and buy out, that without which the war could never have been, than to sink both the thing to be sold, and the price of it, in cutting one another's throats.

I do not speak of emancipation *at once,* but of a *decision* at once to emancipate *gradually.* Room in South America for colonization, can be obtained cheaply, and in abundance; and when numbers shall be large enough to be company and encouragement for one another, the freed people will not be so reluctant to go.

I am pressed with a difficulty not yet mentioned—one which threatens division among those who, united are none too strong. An instance of it is known to you. Gen. Hunter is an honest man. He was, and I hope, still is, my friend. I valued him none the less for his agreeing with me in the general wish that all men everywhere, could be free. He proclaimed all men free within certain states, and I repudiated the proclamation. He expected more good, and less harm from the measure, than I could believe would follow. Yet in repudiating it, I gave dissatisfaction, if not offence, to many whose support the country can not afford to lose. And this is not the end of it. The pressure, in this direction, is still upon me, and is increasing. By conceding what I now ask, you can relieve me, and much more, can relieve the country, in this important point. Upon these considerations I have again begged your attention to the message of March last. Before leaving the Capital, consider and discuss it among yourselves. You are patriots and statesmen; and, as such, I pray you, consider this proposition; and, at the least, commend it to the consideration of your states and people. As you would perpetuate popular government for the best people in the world, I beseech you that you do in no wise omit this. Our common country is in great peril, demanding the loftiest views, and boldest action to bring it speedy relief. Once relieved, it's form of government is saved to the world; it's beloved history, and cherished memories, are vindicated; and it's happy future fully assured, and rendered inconceivably grand. To you, more than to any others, the previlege is given, to assure that happiness, and swell that grandeur, and to link your own names therewith forever.

LETTER TO AUGUST BELMONT[6]
JULY 31, 1862

August Belmont was a New York businessman. He had provided Thurlow Weed, former editor of an Albany newspaper and leader of New York conservative Republicans, with a letter from a Louisianan who criticized Lincoln for vacillating on slavery. Apparently, the author of the letter anticipated a restoration of slavery to the status quo ante-bellum *once the Union was restored. Lincoln replied that, "Broken eggs cannot be mended." The war had progressed to such an extent that the institution of slavery would be crushed under its weight. The rebels could not secede from the Union and expect that slavery, the very cause of the war, would remain unscathed. Lincoln's response testified to his sincere belief that a Union victory would represent the eventual triumph of freedom over slavery.*

JULY 31, 1862.

Dear Sir: You send to Mr. W[eed] an extract from a letter written at New Orleans the 9th instant, which is shown to me. You do not give the writer's name; but plainly he is a man of ability, and probably of some note. He says: "The time has arrived when Mr. Lincoln must take a decisive course. Trying to please everybody, he will satisfy nobody. A vacillating policy in matters of importance is the very worst. Now is the time, if ever, for honest men who love their country to rally to its support. Why will not the North say officially that it wishes for the restoration of the Union as it was?"

And so, it seems, this is the point on which the writer thinks I have no policy. Why will he not read and understand what I have said?

The substance of the very declaration he desires is in the inaugural, in each of the two regular messages to Congress, and in many, if not all, the minor documents issued by the Executive since the inauguration.

Broken eggs cannot be mended; but Louisiana has nothing to do now but to take her place in the Union as it was, barring the already broken eggs. The sooner she does so, the smaller will be the amount of that which will be past mending. This government cannot much longer play a game in which it stakes all, and its enemies stake nothing. Those enemies must understand that they cannot experiment for ten years trying to destroy the government, and if they fail still come back into the Union unhurt. If they expect in any contingency to ever have the Union as it was, I join with the writer in saying, "Now is the time."

How much better it would have been for the writer to have gone at this, under the protection of the army at New Orleans, than to have sat down in a closet writing complaining letters northward!

Yours truly,   A. LINCOLN.

LETTER TO HORACE GREELEY
AUGUST 22, 1862

Horace Greeley was the notable and influential editor of the New York Tribune. *On August 20, 1862, he published an editorial entitled "The Prayer of Twenty Millions," which criticized the president for his reluctance to emancipate. The editorial stated: "We think you are strangely and disastrously remiss . . . with regard to the emancipating provisions or the new Confiscation Act. . . . We think you are unduly influenced by the counsels . . . of certain fossil politicians hailing from the Border Slave States. . . . We complain that the Union cause has suffered . . . from mistaken deference to Rebel Slavery." Despite the claim that emancipation was the prayer of twenty millions—the entire population of the North—northern public opinion was unwilling to support a war that turned into an abolitionist crusade. In the letter to Belmont above, Lincoln responded to conservative critics of black freedom who wanted to return to the status quo antebellum and who even anticipated a restoration of slavery. However, in this letter to Greeley, Lincoln responded to radical critics who favored immediate and unconditional emancipation. Some have criticized Lincoln's reply to Greeley claiming that it proves the president was indifferent to the plight of the slave and that his effort to preserve the Union was an unprincipled exercise in* realpolitik. *However, a careful reading of Lincoln's reply to Greeley would recognize that his use of the word "paramount" does not mean "exclusive" or "sole" objective, but rather the primary or foremost objective. For Lincoln the preservation of the Union was the priority because it was the necessary condition or means of achieving all loftier goals. Thus, the dispute between Lincoln and the abolitionists was not between ending slavery, but between what means were best conducive to the long-term goal. Contrary to the radicals, Lincoln prudently recognized that the preservation of the Union must take precedence to guarantee the long-term end of slavery, even if it meant delaying emancipation in the short-term. The Union's preservation was the indispensable means, the* sine qua non, *to ending slavery. The dissolution of the Union and the triumph of the Confederacy would render the slavery question moot. And significantly, Lincoln's critics often omit the crucial last sentence in his response to Greeley in which he states, "This does not change my personal wish that all men can enjoy freedom everywhere." To be sure, this last sentence affirmed an important moral aspiration that must be considered in a balanced assessment of Lincoln's leadership. The moral aspiration remained, but it had to be applied lawfully under the circumstances. Indeed, the letter to Greeley was the first time a president had even suggested that he would abolish slavery.*

EXECUTIVE MANSION,
WASHINGTON, AUGUST 22, 1862
HON. HORACE GREELEY:
DEAR SIR.

I have just read yours of the 19th. addressed to myself through the New-York Tribune. If there be in it any statements, or assumptions of fact, which I may know to be erroneous, I do not, now and here, controvert them. If there be in it any inferences which I may believe to be falsely drawn, I do not now and here, argue against them. If there be perceptable [*sic*] in it an impatient and dictatorial tone, I waive it in deference to an old friend, whose heart I have always supposed to be right.

As to the policy I "seem to be pursuing" as you say, I have not meant to leave any one in doubt.

I would save the Union. I would save it the shortest way under the Constitution. The sooner the national authority can be restored; the nearer the Union will be "the Union as it was." If there be those who would not save the Union, unless they could at the same time *save* slavery, I do not agree with them. If there be those who would not save the Union unless they could at the same time *destroy* slavery, I do not agree with them. My paramount object in this struggle *is* to save the Union, and is *not* either to save or to destroy slavery. If I could save the Union without freeing *any* slave I would do it, and if I could save it by freeing *all* the slaves, I would do it; and if I could save it by freeing some and leaving others alone I would also do that. What I do about slavery, and the colored race, I do because I believe it helps to save the Union; and what I forbear, I forbear because I do *not* believe it would help to save the Union. I shall do *less* whenever I shall believe what I am doing hurts the cause, and I shall do *more* whenever I shall believe doing more will help the cause. I shall try to correct errors when shown to be errors; and I shall adopt new views so fast as they shall appear to be true views.

I have here stated my purpose according to my view of *official* duty; and I intend no modification of my oft-expressed *personal* wish that all men everywhere could be free.

Yours,

A. Lincoln.

LETTER TO GENERAL G. B. MCCLELLAN
OCTOBER 13, 1862

At thirty-five years old, George B. McClellan was general in chief of the Union army. "Little Napoleon," as he was called, was second in his class at West Point and considered to be a prodigy by some. Although he was a great tactician and administrator, McClellan lacked daring needed to strike a decisive blow against the Confederate army. Politically, he was a War Democrat who became openly critical of the Republican administration. He vehemently opposed emancipation and even wrote a letter to his troops apologizing for the president's actions in this regard. McClellan would run against Lincoln in the election of 1864 on a platform that sought to end the war and to retract the Emancipation Proclamation.

EXECUTIVE MANSION,

WASHINGTON, D.C., OCTOBER 13, 1862.

MAJOR-GENERAL MCCLELLAN.

MY DEAR SIR:

You remember my speaking to you of what I called your over-cautiousness. Are you not over-cautious when you assume that you cannot do what the enemy is constantly doing? Should you not claim to be at least his equal in prowess, and act upon the claim? As I understand, you telegraphed General Halleck that you cannot subsist your army at Winchester unless the railroad from Harper's Ferry to that point be put in working order. But the enemy does now subsist his army at Winchester, at a distance nearly twice as great from railroad transportation as you would have to do without the railroad last named. He now wagons from Culpeper Court House, which is just about twice as far as you would have to do from Harper's Ferry. He is certainly not more than half as well provided with wagons as you are. I certainly should be pleased for you to have the advantage of the railroad from Harper's Ferry to Winchester, but it wastes all the remainder of autumn to give it to you, and in fact ignores the question of time, which cannot and must not be ignored. Again, one of the standard maxims of war, as you know, is to "operate upon the enemy's communications as much as possible without exposing your own." You seem to act as if this applies against you, but cannot apply in your favor. Change positions with the enemy, and think you not he would break your communication with Richmond within the next twenty-four hours? You dread his going into Pennsylvania; but if he does so in full force, he gives up his communications to you absolutely, and you have nothing to do but to follow and ruin him. If he does so with less than full force, fall upon and beat what is left behind all the easier. Exclusive of the water-line, you are now nearer Richmond than the enemy is by the route that you can and he must take. Why can you not reach there before him, unless you admit that he is more than your equal on a march? His route is the arc of a circle, while yours is the chord. The roads are as good on yours as on his. You know I desired, but did not order, you to cross the Potomac below, instead of above, the Shenandoah and Blue Ridge. My idea was that this would at once menace the enemy's communications, which I would seize if he would permit.

If he should move northward, I would follow him closely, holding his communications. If he should prevent our seizing his communications and move toward Richmond, I would press closely to him, fight him if a favorable opportunity should present, and at least try to beat him to Richmond on the inside track. I say "try"; if we never try, we shall never succeed. If he makes a stand at Winchester, moving neither north nor south, I would fight him there, on the idea that if we cannot beat him when he bears the wastage of coming to us, we never can when we bear the wastage of going to him. This proposition is a simple truth, and is too important to be lost sight of for a moment. In coming to us he tenders us an advantage which we should not waive. We should not so operate as to merely drive him away. As we must beat him somewhere or fail finally, we can do it, if at all, easier near to us than far away. If we cannot beat the enemy where he now is, we never can, he again being within the intrenchments of Richmond.

Recurring to the idea of going to Richmond on the inside track, the facility of supplying from the side away from the enemy is remarkable, as it were, by the different spokes of a wheel extending from the hub toward the rim, and this whether you move directly by the chord or on the inside arc, hugging the Blue Ridge more closely. The chord-line, as you see, carries you by Aldie, Hay Market, and Fredericksburg; and you see how turnpikes, railroads, and finally the Potomac, by Aquia Creek, meet you at all points from Washington; the same, only the lines lengthened a little, if you press closer to the Blue Ridge part of the way.

The gaps through the Blue Ridge I understand to be about the following distances from Harper's Ferry, to wit: Vestal's 5 miles; Gregory's, 13; Snicker's, 18; Ashby's, 28; Manassas, 38; Chester, 45; and Thornton's, 53. I should think it preferable to take the route nearest the enemy, disabling him to make an important move without your knowledge, and compelling him to keep his forces together for dread of you. The gaps would enable you to attack if you should wish. For a great part of the way you would be practically between the enemy and both Washington and Richmond, enabling us to spare you the greatest number of troops from here. When at length running for Richmond ahead of him enables him to move this way, if he does so, turn and attack him in rear. But I think he should be engaged long before such point is reached. It is all easy if our troops march as well as the enemy, and it is unmanly to say they cannot do it. This letter is in no sense an order.

Yours truly,

A. Lincoln.

TELEGRAM TO GENERAL G. B. MCCLELLAN
OCTOBER 24, 1862

Something of Lincoln's humor can be seen in this telegram regarding McClellan's delay in attacking the enemy.

WASHINGTON CITY, D. C. OCT. 24, 1862

MAJR. GENL. MCCLELLAN

I have just read your despatch about sore tongued and fatigued horses.

Will you pardon me for asking what the horses of your army have done since the battle of Antietam that fatigues anything?

A. Lincoln

ANNUAL MESSAGE TO CONGRESS
DECEMBER 1, 1862

Lincoln's Annual Message to Congress on the State of the Union barely mentioned the momentous act of the Emancipation Proclamation. The message constituted Lincoln's fourth appeal for gradual compensated emancipation. While Lincoln favored colonization, he did not oppose the decision of the freedmen to remain in the United States. Colonization would be voluntary. In this speech, Lincoln also replied to critics who feared that freed blacks would compete with white labor. The speech contains Lincoln's memorable

references to the war as a "Fiery Trial" and the American people as the "Last best hope
on earth." It also includes his poetic statement that, "The dogmas of the quiet past are
inadequate to the stormy present" and that in "giving freedom to the slave, we assure free-
dom to the free. . . ."

FELLOW-CITIZENS OF THE SENATE AND HOUSE OF REPRESENTATIVES:

Since your last annual assembling another year of health and bountiful harvests has passed. And while it has not pleased the Almighty to bless us with a
return of peace, we can but press on, guided by the best light He gives us, trusting that in His own good time, and wise way, all will yet be well.

The correspondence touching foreign affairs which has taken place during
the last year is herewith submitted, in virtual compliance with a request to that
effect, made by the House of Representatives near the close of the last session
of Congress.

If the condition of our relations with other nations is less gratifying than it
has usually been at former periods, it is certainly more satisfactory than a nation
so unhappily distracted as we are might reasonably have apprehended. In the
month of June last there were some grounds to expect that the maritime Powers which, at the beginning of our domestic difficulties, so unwisely and unnecessarily, as we think, recognized the insurgents as a belligerent, would soon
recede from that position, which has proved only less injurious to themselves
than to our own country. But the temporary reverses which afterwards befell
the national arms, and which were exaggerated by our own disloyal citizens
abroad have hitherto delayed that act of simple justice.

The civil war, which has so radically changed for the moment, the occupations and habits of the American people, has necessarily disturbed the social condition, and affected very deeply the prosperity of the nations with which we have
carried on a commerce that has been steadily increasing throughout a period of
half a century. It has, at the same time, excited political ambitions and apprehensions which have produced a profound agitation throughout the civilized
world. In this unusual agitation we have forborne from taking part in any controversy between foreign states, and between parties or factions in such states.
We have attempted no propagandism, and acknowledged no revolution. But we
have left to every nation the exclusive conduct and management of its own
affairs. Our struggle has been, of course, contemplated by foreign nations with
reference less to its own merits, than to its supposed, and often exaggerated effects
and consequences resulting to those nations themselves. Nevertheless, complaint
on the part of this government, even if it were just, would certainly be unwise.

The treaty with Great Britain for the suppression of the slave trade has been put into operation with a good prospect of complete success. It is an occasion of special pleasure to acknowledge that the execution of it, on the part of her Majesty's government has been marked with a jealous respect for the authority of the United States, and the rights of their moral and loyal citizens.

The convention with Hanover for the abolition of the stade dues has been carried into full effect, under the act of Congress for that purpose.

A blockade of three thousand miles of sea-coast could not be established, and vigorously enforced, in a season of great commercial activity like the present, without committing occasional mistakes, and inflicting unintentional injuries upon foreign nations and their subjects.

A civil war occurring in a country where foreigners reside and carry on trade under treaty stipulations, is necessarily fruitful of complaints of the violation of neutral rights. All such collisions tend to excite misapprehensions, and possibly to produce mutual reclamations between nations which have a common interest in preserving peace and friendship. In clear cases of these kinds I have, so far as possible, heard and redressed complaints which have been presented by friendly powers. There is still, however, a large and an augmenting number of doubtful cases upon which the government is unable to agree with the governments whose protection is demanded by the claimants. There are, moreover, many cases in which the United States, or their citizens, suffer wrongs from the naval or military authorities of foreign nations, which the governments of those states are not at once prepared to redress. I have proposed to some of the foreign states, thus interested, mutual conventions to examine and adjust such complaints. This proposition has been made especially to Great Britain, to France, to Spain, and to Prussia. In each case it has been kindly received, but has not yet been formally adopted.

I deem it my duty to recommend an appropriation in behalf of the owners of the Norwegian bark Admiral P. Tordenskiold, which vessel was, in May, 1861, prevented by the commander of the blockading force off Charleston from leaving that port with cargo, notwithstanding a similar privilege had, shortly before, been granted to an English vessel. I have directed the Secretary of State to cause the papers in the case to be communicated to the proper committees.

Applications have been made to me by many free Americans of African descent to favor their emigration, with a view to such colonization as was contemplated in recent acts of Congress. Other parties, at home and abroad—some from interested motives, others upon patriotic considerations, and still others influenced by philanthropic sentiments—have suggested similar measures; while, on the other hand, several of the Spanish-American republics have protested against the sending of such colonies to their respective territories. Under these circumstances, I have declined to move any such colony to any state, without first obtaining the consent of its government, with an agreement on its part to receive and protect such emigrants in all the rights of freemen; and I have, at the same time, offered to the several states situated within the tropics, or having colonies there, to negotiate with them, subject to the advice and consent of the Senate, to favor the voluntary emigration of persons of that class to their respective territories, upon conditions which shall be equal, just, and humane. Liberia and Hayti are, as yet, the only countries to which colonists of African descent from here, could go with certainty of being received and adopted as citizens; and I regret to say such persons, contemplating colonization do not seem so willing to migrate to those countries as to some others, nor so willing as I think their interest demands. I believe, however, opinion among them, in this respect, is improving; and that, ere long, there will be an augmented, and considerable migration to both these countries, from the United States.

The new commercial treaty between the United States and the Sultan of Turkey has been carried into execution.

A commercial and consular treaty has been negotiated, subject to the Senate's consent, with Liberia; and a similar negotiation is now pending with the republic of Hayti. A considerable improvement of our national commerce is expected to result from these measures.

Our relations with Great Britain, France, Spain, Portugal, Russia, Prussia, Denmark, Sweden, Austria, the Netherlands, Italy, Rome, and the other European states, remain undisturbed. Very favorable relations also continue to be maintained with Turkey, Morocco, China and Japan.

During the last year there has not only been no change of our previous relations with the independent states of our own continent, but, more friendly sentiments than have heretofore existed, are believed to be entertained by these neighbors, whose safety and progress, are so intimately connected with our own. This statement especially applies to Mexico, Nicaragua, Costa Rica, Honduras, Peru, and Chile.

The commission under the convention with the republic of New Granada closed its session, without having audited and passed upon, all the claims which were submitted to it. A proposition is pending to revive the convention, that it may be able to do more complete justice. The joint commission between the United States and the republic of Costa Rica has completed its labors and submitted its report.

I have favored the project for connecting the United States with Europe by an Atlantic telegraph, and a similar project to extend the telegraph from San Francisco, to connect by a Pacific telegraph with the line which is being extended across the Russian empire.

The Territories of the United States, with unimportant exceptions, have remained undisturbed by the civil war, and they are exhibiting such evidence of prosperity as justifies an expectation that some of them will soon be in a condition to be organized as States, and be constitutionally admitted into the federal Union.

The immense mineral resources of some of those Territories ought to be developed as rapidly as possible. Every step in that direction would have a tendency to improve the revenues of the government, and diminish the burdens of the people. It is worthy of your serious consideration whether some extraordinary measures to promote that end cannot be adopted. The means which suggests itself as most likely to be effective, is a scientific exploration of the mineral regions in those Territories, with a view to the publication of its results at home and in foreign countries—results which cannot fail to be auspicious.

The condition of the finances will claim your most diligent consideration. The vast expenditures incident to the military and naval operations required for the suppression of the rebellion, have hitherto been met with a promptitude, and certainty, unusual in similar circumstances, and the public credit has been fully maintained. The continuance of the war, however, and the increased disbursements made necessary by the augmented forces now in the field, demand your best reflections as to the best modes of providing the necessary revenue, without injury to business and with the least possible burdens upon labor.

The suspension of specie payments by the banks, soon after the commencement of your last session, made large issues of United States notes unavoidable. In no other way could the payment of the troops, and the satisfaction of other just demands, be so economically, or so well provided for. The judicious legislation of Congress, securing the receivability of these notes for loans and internal duties, and making them a legal tender for other debts, has made them an universal currency; and has satisfied, partially, at least, and for the time, the long felt want of an uniform circulating medium, saving thereby to the people, immense sums in discounts and exchanges.

A return to specie payments, however, at the earliest period compatible with due regard to all interests concerned, should ever be kept in view. Fluctuations in the value of currency are always injurious, and to reduce these fluctuations to the lowest possible point will always be a leading purpose in wise legislation. Convertibility, prompt and certain convertibility into coin, is generally acknowledged to be the best and surest safeguard against them; and it is extremely doubtful whether a circulation of United States notes, payable in coin, and sufficiently large for the wants of the people, can be permanently, usefully and safely maintained.

Is there, then, any other mode in which the necessary provision for the public wants can be made, and the great advantages of a safe and uniform currency secured?

I know of none which promises so certain results, and is, at the same time, so unobjectionable, as the organization of banking associations, under a general act of Congress, well guarded in its provisions. To such associations the government might furnish circulating notes, on the security of United States bonds deposited in the treasury. These notes, prepared under the supervision of proper officers, being uniform in appearance and security, and convertible always into coin, would at once protect labor against the evils of a vicious currency, and facilitate commerce by cheap and safe exchanges.

A moderate reservation from the interest on the bonds would compensate the United States for the preparation and distribution of the notes and a general supervision of the system, and would lighten the burden of that part of the public debt employed as securities. The public credit, moreover, would be greatly improved, and the negotiation of new loans greatly facilitated by the steady market demand for government bonds which the adoption of the proposed system would create.

It is an additional recommendation of the measure, of considerable weight, in my judgment, that it would reconcile, as far as possible, all existing interests, by the opportunity offered to existing institutions to reorganize under the act, substituting only the secured uniform national circulation for the local and various circulation, secured and unsecured, now issued by them.

The receipts into the treasury from all sources, including loans and balance from the preceding year, for the fiscal year ending on the 30th June, 1862, were $583,885,247.06, of which sum $49,056,397.62 were derived from customs; $1,795,331.73 from the direct tax; from public lands, $152,203.77; from miscellaneous sources, $931,787.64; from loans in all forms, $529,692,460.50. The remainder, $2,257,065.80, was the balance from last year.

The disbursements during the same period were for congressional, executive, and judicial purposes, $5,939,009.29; for foreign intercourse, $1,339,710.35; for miscellaneous expenses, including the mints, loans, post office deficiencies, collection of revenue, and other like charges, $14,129,771.50; for expenses under the Interior Department, $3,102,985.52; under the War Department, $394,368,407.36; under the Navy Department, $42,674,569.69; for interest on public debt, $13,190,324.45; and for payment of public debt, including reimbursement of temporary loan, and redemptions, $96,096,922.09; making an aggregate of $570,841,700.25, and leaving a balance in the treasury on the first day of July, 1862, of $13,043,546.81.

It should be observed that the sum of $96,096,922.09, expended for reimbursements and redemption of public debt, being included also in the loans made, may be properly deducted, both from receipts and expenditures, leaving the actual receipts for the year $487,788,324.97; and the expenditures, $474,744,778.16.

Other information on the subject of the finances will be found in the report of the Secretary of the Treasury, to whose statements and views I invite your most candid and considerate attention.

The reports of the Secretaries of War, and of the Navy, are herewith transmitted. These reports, though lengthy, are scarcely more than brief abstracts of the very numerous and extensive transactions and operations conducted through those departments. Nor could I give a summary of them here, upon any principle, which would admit of its being much shorter than the reports themselves. I therefore content myself with laying the reports before you, and asking your attention to them.

It gives me pleasure to report a decided improvement in the financial condition of the Post Office Department, as compared with several preceding years. The receipts for the fiscal year 1861 amounted to $8,349,296.40, which embraced the revenue from all the States of the Union for three quarters of that year. Notwithstanding the cessation of revenue from the so-called seceded States during the last fiscal year, the increase of the correspondence of the loyal States has been sufficient to produce a revenue during the same year of $8,299,820.90, being only $50,000 less than was derived from all the States of the Union during the previous year. The expenditures show a still more favorable result. The amount expended in 1861 was $13,606,759.11. For the last year the amount has been reduced to $11,125,364.13, showing a decrease of about $2,481,000 in the expenditures as compared with the preceding year and about $3,750,000 as compared with the fiscal year 1860. The deficiency in the department for the previous year was $4,551,966.98. For the last fiscal year it was reduced to $2,112,814.57. These favorable results are in part owing to the cessation of mail service in the insurrectionary States, and in part to a careful review of all expenditures in that department in the interest of economy. The efficiency of the postal service, it is believed, has also been much improved. The Postmaster General has also opened a correspondence, through the Department of State, with foreign governments, proposing a convention of postal representatives for the purpose of simplifying the rates of foreign postage, and to expedite the foreign mails. This proposition, equally important to our adopted citizens, and to the commercial interests of this country, has been favorably entertained, and agreed to, by all the governments from whom replies have been received.

I ask the attention of Congress to the suggestions of the Postmaster General in his report respecting the further legislation required, in his opinion, for the benefit of the postal service.

The Secretary of the Interior reports as follows in regard to the public lands:

"The public lands have ceased to be a source of revenue. From the 1st July, 1861, to the 30th September, 1862, the entire cash receipts from the sale of lands were $137,476.26—a sum much less than the expenses of our land system during the same period. The homestead law, which will take effect on the 1st of January next, offers such inducements to settlers, that sales for cash cannot be expected, to an extent sufficient to meet the expenses of the General Land Office, and the cost of surveying and bringing the land into market."

The discrepancy between the sum here stated as arising from the sales of the public lands, and the sum derived from the same source as reported from the Treasury Department, arises, as I understand, from the fact that the periods of time, though apparently, were not really, coincident at the beginning point— the Treasury report including a considerable sum now, which had previously been reported from the Interior—sufficiently large to greatly overreach the sum derived from the three months now reported upon by the Interior, and not by the Treasury.

The Indian tribes upon our frontiers have, during the past year, manifested a spirit of insubordination, and, at several points, have engaged in open hostilities against the white settlements in their vicinity. The tribes occupying the Indian country south of Kansas, renounced their allegiance to the United States, and entered into treaties with the insurgents. Those who remained loyal to the United States were driven from the country. The chief of the Cherokees has visited this city for the purpose of restoring the former relations of the tribe with the United States. He alleges that they were constrained, by superior force, to enter into treaties with the insurgents, and that the United States neglected to furnish the protection which their treaty stipulations required.

In the month of August last the Sioux Indians, in Minnesota, attacked the settlements in their vicinity with extreme ferocity, killing, indiscriminately, men, women, and children. This attack was wholly unexpected, and, therefore, no means of defence had been provided. It is estimated that not less than eight hundred persons were killed by the Indians, and a large amount of property was destroyed. How this outbreak was induced is not definitely known, and suspicions, which may be unjust, need not to be stated. Information was received by the Indian bureau, from different sources, about the time hostilities were commenced, that a simultaneous attack was to be made upon the white settlements by all the tribes between the Mississippi River and the Rocky mountains. The State of Minnesota has suffered great injury from this Indian war. A large portion of her territory has been depopulated, and a severe loss has been sustained by the destruction of property. The people of that State manifest much anxiety for the removal of the tribes beyond the limits of the State as a guarantee against future hostilities. The Commissioner of Indian Affairs will furnish full details. I submit for your especial consideration whether our Indian system shall not be remodelled. Many wise and good men have impressed me with the belief that this can be profitably done.

I submit a statement of the proceedings of commissioners, which shows the progress that has been made in the enterprise of constructing the Pacific railroad. And this suggests the earliest completion of this road, and also the favorable action of Congress upon the projects now pending before them for enlarging the capacities of the great canals in New York and Illinois, as being of vital and rapidly increasing importance to the whole nation, and especially to the vast interior region hereinafter to be noticed at some greater length. I propose having prepared and laid before you at an early day some interesting and valuable statistical information upon this subject. The military and commercial importance of enlarging the Illinois and Michigan canal, and improving the Illinois River, is presented in the report of Colonel Webster to the Secretary of War, and now transmitted to Congress. I respectfully ask attention to it.

To carry out the provisions of the act of Congress of the 15th of May last, I have caused the Department of Agriculture of the United States to be organized.

The commissioner informs me that within the period of a few months this department has established an extensive system of correspondence and exchanges, both at home and abroad, which promises to effect highly beneficial results in the development of a correct knowledge of recent improvements in agriculture, in the introduction of new products, and in the collection of the agricultural statistics of the different States.

Also, that it will soon be prepared to distribute largely seeds, cereals, plants and cuttings, and has already published, and liberally diffused, much valuable information in anticipation of a more elaborate report, which will in due time be furnished, embracing some valuable tests in chemical science now in progress in the laboratory.

The creation of this department was for the more immediate benefit of a large class of our most valuable citizens; and I trust that the liberal basis upon which it has been organized will not only meet your approbation, but that it will realize, at no distant day, all the fondest anticipations of its most sanguine friends, and become the fruitful source of advantage to all our people.

On the twenty-second day of September last a proclamation was issued by the Executive, a copy of which is herewith submitted.

In accordance with the purpose expressed in the second paragraph of that paper, I now respectfully recall your attention to what may be called "compensated emancipation."

A nation may be said to consist of its territory, its people, and its laws. The territory is the only part which is of certain durability. "One generation passeth away, and another generation cometh, but the earth abideth forever." It is of the first importance to duly consider, and estimate, this ever-enduring part. That portion of the earth's surface which is owned and inhabited by the people of the United States, is well adapted to be the home of one national family; and it is not well adapted for two, or more. Its vast extent, and its variety of climate and productions, are of advantage, in this age, for one people, whatever they might have been in former ages. Steam, telegraphs, and intelligence, have brought these, to be an advantageous combination for one united people.

In the inaugural address I briefly pointed out the total inadequacy of disunion, as a remedy for the differences between the people of the two sections. I did so in language which I cannot improve, and which, therefore, I beg to repeat:

> "One section of our country believes slavery is *right,* and ought to be extended, while the other believes it is *wrong,* and ought not to be extended. This is the only substantial dispute. The fugitive slave clause of the Constitution, and the law for the suppression of the foreign slave trade, are each as well enforced, perhaps, as any law can ever be in a community where the moral sense of the people imperfectly supports the law itself. The great body of the people abide by the dry legal obligation in both cases, and a few break over in each. This, I think, cannot be perfectly cured; and it would be worse in both cases *after* the separation of the sections, than before. The foreign slave trade, now imperfectly suppressed, would be ultimately revived without restriction in one section; while fugitive slaves, now only partially surrendered, would not be surrendered at all by the other.

"Physically speaking, we cannot separate. We cannot remove our respective sections from each other, nor build an impassable wall between them. A husband and wife may be divorced, and go out of the presence, and beyond the reach of each other; but the different parts of our country cannot do this. They cannot but remain face to face; and intercourse, either amicable or hostile, must continue between them. Is it possible, then, to make that intercourse more advantageous, or more satisfactory, *after* separation than *before*? Can aliens make treaties, easier than friends can make laws? Can treaties be more faithfully enforced between aliens, than laws can among friends? Suppose you go to war, you cannot fight always; and when, after much loss on both sides, and no gain on either, you cease fighting, the identical old questions, as to terms of intercourse, are again upon you."

There is no line, straight or crooked, suitable for a national boundary, upon which to divide. Trace through, from east to west, upon the line between the free and slave country, and we shall find a little more than one-third of its length are rivers, easy to be crossed, and populated, or soon to be populated, thickly upon both sides; while nearly all its remaining length are merely surveyor's lines, over which people may walk back and forth without any consciousness of their presence. No part of this line can be made any more difficult to pass, by writing it down on paper, or parchment, as a national boundary. The fact of separation, if it comes, gives up, on the part of the seceding section, the fugitive slave clause, along with all other constitutional obligations upon the section seceded from, while I should expect no treaty stipulation would be ever made to take its place.

But there is another difficulty. The great interior region, bounded east by the Alleghanies, north by the British dominions, west by the Rocky Mountains, and south by the line along which the culture of corn and cotton meets, and which includes part of Virginia, part of Tennessee, all of Kentucky, Ohio, Indiana, Michigan, Wisconsin, Illinois, Missouri, Kansas, Iowa, Minnesota, and the Territories of Dakota, Nebraska, and part of Colorado, already has above ten millions of people, and will have fifty millions within fifty years, if not prevented by any political folly or mistake. It contains more than one third of the country owned by the United States—certainly more than one million of square miles. Once half as populous as Massachusetts already is, it would have more than seventy-five millions of people. A glance at the map shows that, territorially speaking, it is the great body of the republic. The other parts are but marginal borders to it, the magnificent region sloping west from the Rocky Mountains to the Pacific, being the deepest and also the richest in undeveloped resources. In the production of provisions, grains, grasses, and all which proceed from them, this great interior region is naturally one of the most important in the world. Ascertain from the statistics the small proportion of the region which has, as yet, been brought into cultivation, and also the large and rapidly increasing amount of its products, and we shall be overwhelmed with the magnitude of the prospect presented. And yet this region has no sea-coast, touches no ocean anywhere. As part of one nation, its people now find, and may forever find, their way to Europe by New York, to South America and Africa by New Orleans, and to Asia by San Francisco. But separate our common country into two nations, as designed by the present rebellion, and every man of this great interior region is thereby cut off from some one or more of these outlets, not, perhaps, by a physical barrier, but by embarrassing and onerous trade regulations.

And this is true, *wherever* a dividing, or boundary line, may be fixed. Place it between the now free and slave country, or place it south of Kentucky, or north of Ohio, and still the truth remains, that none south of it, can trade to any port or place north of it, and none north of it, can trade to any port or place south of it, except upon terms dictated by a government foreign to them. These outlets, east, west, and south, are indispensable to the well-being of the people inhabiting, and to inhabit, this vast interior region. *Which* of the three may be the best, is no proper question. All, are better than either, and all, of right, belong to that people, and to their successors forever. True to themselves, they will not ask *where* a line of separation shall be, but will vow, rather, that there shall be no such line. Nor are the marginal regions less interested in these communications to, and through them, to the great outside world. They, too, and each of them, must have access to this Egypt of the West, without paying toll at the crossing of any national boundary.

Our national strife springs not from our permanent part; not from the land we inhabit; not from our national homestead. There is no possible severing of this, but would multiply, and not mitigate, evils among us. In all its adaptations and aptitudes, it demands union, and abhors separation. In fact, it would, ere long, force reunion, however much of blood and treasure the separation might have cost.

Our strife pertains to ourselves—to the passing generations of men; and it can, without convulsion, be hushed forever with the passing of one generation.

In this view, I recommend the adoption of the following resolution and articles amendatory to the Constitution of the United States:

"*Resolved by the Senate and House of Representatives of the United States of America in Congress assembled,* (two-thirds of both Houses concurring,) That the following articles be proposed to the legislatures (or conventions) of the several States as amendments to the Constitution of the United States, all or any of which articles when ratified by three fourths of the said legislatures (or conventions) to be valid as part or parts of the said Constitution, viz:

"Article —.

"Every State, wherein slavery now exists, which shall abolish the same therein, at any time, or times, before the first day of January, in the year of our Lord one thousand and nine hundred, shall receive compensation from the United States, as follows, to wit:

"The President of the United States shall deliver to every such State, bonds of the United States, bearing interest at the rate of __ percent, per annum, to an amount equal to the aggregate sum of ____ for each slave shown to have been therein, by the eighth census of the United States, said bonds to be delivered to such State by instalments, or in one parcel, at the completion of the abolishment, accordingly as the same shall have been gradual, or at one time, within such State; and interest shall begin to run upon any such bond, only from the proper time of its delivery as aforesaid. Any State having received bonds as aforesaid, and afterwards reintroducing or tolerating slavery therein, shall refund to the United States the bonds so received, or the value thereof, and all interest paid thereon.

"Article —.

"All slaves who shall have enjoyed actual freedom by the chances of the war, at any time before the end of the rebellion, shall be forever free; but all owners of such, who shall not have been disloyal, shall be compensated for them, at the same rates as is provided for States adopting abolishment of slavery, but in such way, that no slave shall be twice accounted for.

"Article —.

"Congress may appropriate money, and otherwise provide, for colonizing free colored persons, with their own consent, at any place or places without the United States."

I beg indulgence to discuss these proposed articles at some length. Without slavery the rebellion could never have existed; without slavery it could not continue.

Among the friends of the Union there is great diversity of sentiment, and of policy, in regard to slavery, and the African race amongst us. Some would perpetuate slavery; some would abolish it suddenly, and without compensation; some would abolish it gradually, and with compensation; some would remove the freed people from us, and some would retain them with us; and there are yet other minor diversities. Because of these diversities, we waste much strength in struggles among ourselves. By mutual concession we should harmonize, and act together. This would be compromise; but it would be compromise among the friends, and not with the enemies of the Union. These articles are intended to embody a plan of such mutual concessions. If the plan shall be adopted, it is assumed that emancipation will follow, at least, in several of the States.

As to the first article, the main points are: first, the emancipation; secondly, the length of time for consummating it—thirty-seven years; and thirdly, the compensation.

The emancipation will be unsatisfactory to the advocates of perpetual slavery; but the length of time should greatly mitigate their dissatisfaction. The time spares both races from the evils of sudden derangement—in fact, from the necessity of any derangement—while most of those whose habitual course of thought will be disturbed by the measure will have passed away before its consummation. They will never see it. Another class will hail the prospect of emancipation, but will deprecate the length of time. They will feel that it gives too little to the now living slaves. But it really gives them much. It saves them from the vagrant destitution which must largely attend immediate emancipation in localities where their numbers are very great; and it gives the inspiring assurance that their posterity shall be free forever. The plan leaves to each State, choosing to act under it, to abolish slavery now, or at the end of the century, or at any intermediate time, or by degrees, extending over the whole or any part of the period; and it obliges no two States to proceed alike. It also provides for compensation, and generally the mode of making it. This, it would seem, must further mitigate the dissatisfaction of those who favor perpetual slavery, and especially of those who are to receive the compensation. Doubtless some of those who are to pay, and not to receive will object. Yet the measure is both just and economical. In a certain sense the liberation of slaves is the destruction of property—property acquired by descent, or by purchase, the same as any other property. It is no less true for having been often said, that the people of the South are not more responsible for the original introduction of this property, than are the people of the North; and when it is remembered how unhesitatingly we all use cotton and sugar, and share the profits of dealing in them, it may not be quite safe to say, that the South has been more responsible than the North for its continuance. If then, for a common object, this property is to be sacrificed is it not just that it be done at a common charge?

And if, with less money, or money more easily paid, we can preserve the benefits of the Union by this means, than we can by the war alone, is it not also economical to do it? Let us consider it then. Let us ascertain the sum we have expended in the war since compensated emancipation was proposed last March, and consider whether, if that measure had been promptly accepted, by even some of the slave States, the same sum would not have done more to close the war, than has been otherwise done. If so the measure would save money, and in that view, would be a prudent and economical measure. Certainly it is not so easy to pay *something* as it is to pay *nothing;* but it is easier to pay a *large* sum than it is to pay a *larger* one. And it is easier to pay any sum *when* we are able, than it is to pay it *before* we are able. The war requires large sums, and requires them at once. The aggregate sum necessary for compensated emancipation, of course, would be large. But it would require no ready cash; nor the bonds even, any faster than the emancipation progresses. This might not, and probably would not, close before the end of the thirty-seven years. At that time we shall probably have a hundred millions of people to share the burden, instead of thirty-one millions, as now. And not only so, but the increase of our population may be expected to continue for a long time after that period, as rapidly as before; because our territory will not have become full. I do not state this inconsiderately. At the same ratio of increase which we have maintained, on an average, from our first national census, in 1790, until that of 1860, we should, in 1900, have a population of 103,208,415. And why may we not continue that ratio far beyond that period? Our abundant room—our broad national homestead—is our ample resource. Were our territory as limited as are the British Isles, very certainly our population could not expand as stated. Instead of receiving the foreign born, as now, we should be compelled to send part of the native born away. But such is not our condition. We have two millions nine hundred and sixty-three thousand square miles. Europe has three millions and eight hundred thousand, with a population averaging seventy-three and one-third persons to the square mile. Why may not our country, at some time, average as many? Is it less fertile? Has it more waste surface, by mountains, rivers, lakes, deserts, or other causes? Is it inferior to Europe in any natural advantage? If, then, we are, at some time, to be as populous as Europe, how soon? As to when this *may* be, we can judge by the past and the present; as to when it *will* be, if ever, depends much on whether we maintain the Union. Several of our States are already above the

average of Europe—seventy three and a third to the square mile. Massachusetts
has 157; Rhode Island, 133; Connecticut, 99; New York and New Jersey, each,
80; Also two other great States, Pennsylvania and Ohio, are not far below, the
former having 63, and the latter 59. The States already above the European average, except New York, have increased in as rapid a ratio, since passing that point,
as ever before; while no one of them is equal to some other parts of our country in natural capacity for sustaining a dense population.

Taking the nation in the aggregate, and we find its population and ratio of
increase, for the several decennial periods, to be as follows:—

1790	3,929,827						
1800	5,305,937	35.02	per cent. ratio of increase.				
1810	7,239,814	36.45	"	"	"	"	"
1820	9,638,131	33.13	"	"	"	"	"
1830	12,866,020	33.49	"	"	"	"	"
1840	17,069,453	32.67	"	"	"	"	"
1850	23,191,876	35.87	"	"	"	"	"
1860	31,443,790	35.58	"	"	"	"	"

This shows an average decennial increase of 34.60 per cent. in population
through the seventy years from our first, to our last census yet taken. It is seen
that the ratio of increase, at no one of these seven periods, is either two per cent.
below, or two per cent. above, the average; thus showing how inflexible, and,
consequently, how reliable, the law of increase, in our case, is. Assuming that it
will continue, gives the following results:—

1870	42,323,341
1880	56,967,216
1890	76,677,872
1900	103,208,415
1910	138,918,526
1920	186,984,335
1930	251,680,914

These figures show that our country *may* be as populous as Europe now is,
at some point between 1920 and 1930—say about 1925—our territory, at seventy-three and a third persons to the square mile, being of capacity to contain
217,186,000.

And we *will* reach this, too, if we do not ourselves relinquish the chance, by
the folly and evils of disunion, or by long, and exhausting war springing from

the only great element of national discord among us. While it cannot be foreseen exactly how much one huge example of secession, breeding lesser ones indefinitely, would retard population, civilization, and prosperity, no one can doubt that the extent of it would be very great and injurious.

The proposed emancipation would shorten the war, perpetuate peace, insure this increase of population, and proportionately the wealth of the country. With these, we should pay all the emancipation would cost, together with our other debt, easier than we should pay our other debt, without it. If we had allowed our old national debt to run at six per cent. per annum, simple interest, from the end of our revolutionary struggle until today, without paying anything on either principal or interest, each man of us would owe less upon that debt now, than each owed upon it then; and this because our increase of men, through the whole period, has been greater than six per cent.; has run faster than the interest upon the debt. Thus, time alone relieves a debtor nation, so long as its population increases faster than unpaid interest accumulates on its debt.

This fact would be no excuse for delaying payment of what is justly due; but it shows the great importance of time in this connexion—the great advantage of a policy by which we shall not have to pay until we number a hundred millions, what, by a different policy, we would have to pay now, when we number but thirty one millions. In a word, it shows that a dollar will be much harder to pay for the war, than will be a dollar for emancipation on the proposed plan. And then the latter will cost no blood, no precious life. It will be a saving of both.

As to the second article, I think it would be impracticable to return to bondage the class of persons therein contemplated. Some of them, doubtless, in the property sense, belong to loyal owners; and hence, provision is made in this article for compensating such.

The third article relates to the future of the freed people. It does not oblige, but merely authorizes, Congress to aid in colonizing such as may consent. This ought not to be regarded as objectionable, on the one hand, or on the other, in so much as it comes to nothing, unless by the mutual consent of the people to be deported, and the American voters, through their representatives in Congress.

I cannot make it better known than it already is, that I strongly favor colonization. And yet I wish to say there is an objection urged against free colored persons remaining in the country, which is largely imaginary, if not sometimes malicious.

It is insisted that their presence would injure, and displace white labor and white laborers. If there ever could be a proper time for mere catch arguments, that time surely is not now. In times like the present, men should utter nothing for which they would not willingly be responsible through time and in eternity. Is it true, then, that colored people can displace any more white labor, by being free, than by remaining slaves? If they stay in their old places, they jostle no white laborers; if they leave their old places, they leave them open to white laborers. Logically, there is neither more nor less of it. Emancipation, even without deportation, would probably enhance the wages of white labor, and, very surely, would not reduce them. Thus, the customary amount of labor would still have to be performed; the freed people would surely not do more than their old proportion of it, and very probably, for a time, would do less, leaving an increased part to white laborers, bringing their labor into greater demand, and, consequently, enhancing the wages of it. With deportation, even to a limited extent, enhanced wages to white labor is mathematically certain. Labor is like any other commodity in the market—increase the demand for it, and you increase the price of it. Reduce the supply of black labor, by colonizing the black laborer out of the country, and, by precisely so much, you increase the demand for, and wages of, white labor.

But it is dreaded that the freed people will swarm forth, and cover the whole land? Are they not already in the land? Will liberation make them any more numerous? Equally distributed among the whites of the whole country, and there would be but one colored to seven whites. Could the one, in any way, greatly disturb the seven? There are many communities now, having more than one free colored person, to seven whites; and this, without any apparent consciousness of evil from it. The District of Columbia, and the States of Maryland and Delaware, are all in this condition. The district has more than one free colored to six whites; and yet, in its frequent petitions to Congress, I believe it has never presented the presence of free colored persons as one of its grievances. But why should emancipation south, send the freed people north? People, of any color, seldom run, unless there be something to run from. *Heretofore* colored people, to some extent, have fled north from bondage; and *now,* perhaps, from both bondage and destitution. But if gradual emancipation and deportation be adopted, they will have neither to flee from. Their old masters will give them wages at least until new laborers can be procured; and the freed men, in turn, will gladly give their labor for the wages, till new homes can be found for them, in congenial climes, and with people of their own blood and race. This proposition can be trusted on the mutual interests involved. And, in any event, cannot the north decide for itself, whether to receive them?

Again, as practice proves more than theory, in any case, has there been any irruption of colored people northward, because of the abolishment of slavery in this District last spring?

What I have said of the proportion of free colored persons to the whites, in the District, is from the census of 1860, having no reference to persons called contrabands, nor to those made free by the act of Congress abolishing slavery here.

The plan consisting of these articles is recommended, not but that a restoration of the national authority would be accepted without its adoption.

Nor will the war, nor proceedings under the proclamation of September 22, 1862, be stayed because of the *recommendation* of this plan. Its timely *adoption,* I doubt not, would bring restoration and thereby stay both.

And, notwithstanding this plan, the recommendation that Congress provide by law for compensating any State which may adopt emancipation, before this plan shall have been acted upon, is hereby earnestly renewed. Such would be only an advance part of the plan, and the same arguments apply to both.

This plan is recommended as a means, not in exclusion of, but additional to, all others for restoring and preserving the national authority throughout the Union. The subject is presented exclusively in its economical aspect. The plan would, I am confident, secure peace more speedily, and maintain it more permanently, than can be done by force alone; while all it would cost, considering amounts, and manner of payment, and times of payment, would be easier paid than will be the additional cost of the war, if we rely solely upon force. It is much—very much—that it would cost no blood at all.

The plan is proposed as permanent constitutional law. It cannot become such without the concurrence of, first, two thirds of Congress, and, afterwards, three-fourths of the States. The requisite three-fourths of the States will necessarily include seven of the Slave States. Their concurrence, if obtained, will give assurance of their severally adopting emancipation, at no very distant day, upon the new constitutional terms. This assurance would end the struggle now, and save the Union forever.

I do not forget the gravity which should characterize a paper addressed to the Congress of the nation by the Chief Magistrate of the nation. Nor do I forget that some of you are my seniors, nor that many of you have more experience than I, in the conduct of public affairs. Yet I trust that in view of the great responsibility resting upon me, you will perceive no want of respect yourselves, in any undue earnestness I may seem to display.

Is it doubted, then, that the plan I propose, if adopted, would shorten the war, and thus lessen its expenditure of money and of blood? Is it doubted that it would restore the national authority and national prosperity, and perpetuate both indefinitely? Is it doubted that we here—Congress and Executive—can secure its adoption? Will not the good people respond to a united, and earnest appeal from us? Can we, can they, by any other means, so certainly, or so speedily, assure these vital objects? We can succeed only by concert. It is not "can *any* of us *imagine* better?" but, "can we *all* do better?" Object whatsoever is possible, still the question recurs, "can we do better?" The dogmas of the quiet past, are inadequate to the stormy present. The occasion is piled high with difficulty, and we must rise—with the occasion. As our case is new, so we must think anew, and act anew. We must disenthrall ourselves, and then we shall save our country.

Fellow-citizens, *we* cannot escape history. We of this Congress and this administration, will be remembered in spite of ourselves. No personal significance, or insignificance, can spare one or another of us. The fiery trial through which we pass, will light us down, in honor or dishonor, to the latest generation. We *say* we are for the Union. The world will not forget that we say this. We know how to save the Union. The world knows we do know how to save it. We—even *we here*—hold the power, and bear the responsibility. In *giving* freedom to the *slave,* we *assure* freedom to the *free*—honorable alike in what we give, and what we preserve. We shall nobly save, or meanly lose, the last best hope of earth. Other means may succeed; this could not fail. The way is plain, peaceful, generous, just—a way which, if followed, the world will forever applaud, and God must forever bless.

Abraham Lincoln.

December 1, 1862.

PRELIMINARY EMANCIPATION PROCLAMATION
SEPTEMBER 22, 1862
AND FINAL EMANCIPATION PROCLAMATION
JANUARY 1, 1863

Lincoln presented a first draft of the Emancipation Proclamation to his cabinet on July 22, 1862. Secretary of State William Seward voiced reservations that without a Union military victory, emancipation would lack credibility in the nation and in the eyes of the world. Instead of a sublime triumph of freedom, it would be viewed as an act of desperation, "the last shriek on our retreat." Lincoln and Seward feared a British intervention that would force peace, thereby guaranteeing the independence of the Confederacy. The battle of Antietam on September 17 provided the Union with its needed victory. Although the battle was more or less a stalemate in terms of casualties (about 20,000 total dead and wounded), it was a symbolic victory because Lee was driven out of Maryland. The Preliminary Emancipation Proclamation was signed on September

22, 1862, giving the South one hundred days to cease the rebellion before the final Emancipation Proclamation would go into effect on January 1, 1863. The legal and constitutional was based on the president's power as commander and chief. It was justified as a necessary war measure necessary to cripple the South's ability to fight by encouraging fugitives to flee the rebels and to join the Union cause. Since the act was justified as a military measure, it did not apply to slaves in the Border States and parts of Louisiana that remained in the Union. In sum, the act freed 3.5 million people and gave the Union a clear moral objective to fight for. The Union had taken the moral high ground, making it disgraceful in the eyes of world public opinion for any nation to aid the Confederacy and slavery. In contrast to the preliminary draft, the final emancipation authorized the use of black soldiers, an important step in moving public opinion toward black freedom and suffrage. Lincoln recognized that the willingness of black soldiers to make the supreme sacrifice on the battlefield would help dispose public opinion to support black freedom. Despite the First Draft's claim that the slaves in rebel territory were "forever free," some argued that the act could be revoked once the military necessity had ended. General McClellan and other War Democrats sought its retraction. These concerns along with the vestiges of slavery in the Border States led to the passage of the Thirteenth Amendment that freed the slaves in the Border States as well. And it guaranteed that the Emancipation would not be revoked. The congressional elections of 1862 demonstrated public dissatisfaction with the war and the Emancipation Proclamation. Democrats swept the Republicans in New York, Pennsylvania, Ohio, Indiana, and Illinois, states that voted for Lincoln in 1860. Overall, Democrats increased their representation in Congress from forty-four to seventy-five. Clearly, Lincoln did not have a public mandate in support of emancipation. In order to sustain it, he would have to dispose further public opinion towards black freedom. His address at Gettysburg provided such an opportunity. There, he would claim that the Emancipation Proclamation had given the nation a "new birth of freedom."

SEPTEMBER 22, 1862

BY THE PRESIDENT OF THE UNITED STATES OF AMERICA

A PROCLAMATION.

I, Abraham Lincoln, President of the United States of America, and Commander-in-chief of the Army and Navy thereof, do hereby proclaim and declare that hereafter, as heretofore, the war will be prossecuted for the object of practically restoring the constitutional relation between the United States, and each of the states, and the people thereof, in which states that relation is, or may be suspended, or disturbed.

That it is my purpose, upon the next meeting of Congress to again recommend the adoption of a practical measure tendering pecuniary aid to the free acceptance or rejection of all slave-states, so called, the people whereof may not then be in rebellion against the United States, and which states, may then have voluntarily adopted, or thereafter may voluntarily adopt, immediate, or gradual abolishment of slavery within their respective limits; and that the effort to colonize persons of African descent, with their consent, upon this continent, or elsewhere, with the previously obtained consent of the Governments existing there, will be continued.

That on the first day of January in the year of our Lord, one thousand eight hundred and sixty-three, all persons held as slaves within any state, or designated part of a state, the people whereof shall then be in rebellion against the United States shall be then, thenceforward, and forever free; and the executive government of the United States, including the military and naval authority thereof, will recognize and maintain the freedom of such persons, and will do no act or acts to repress such persons, or any of them, in any efforts they may make for their actual freedom.

That the executive will, on the first day of January aforesaid, by proclamation, designate the States, and parts of states, if any, in which the people thereof respectively, shall then be in rebellion against the United States; and the fact that any state, or the people thereof shall, on that day be, in good faith represented in the Congress of the United States, by members chosen thereto, at elections wherein a majority of the qualified voters of such state shall have participated, shall, in the absence of strong countervailing testimony, be deemed conclusive evidence that such state and the people thereof, are not then in rebellion against the United States.

That attention is hereby called to an act of Congress entitled "An act to make an additional Article of War" approved March 13, 1862, and which act is in the words and figure following:

Be it enacted by the Senate and House of Representatives of the United States of America in Congress assembled, That hereafter the following shall be promulgated as an additional article of war for the government of the army of the United States, and shall be obeyed and observed as such:

Article——. All officers or persons in the military or naval service of the United States are prohibited from employing any of the forces under their respective commands for the purpose of returning fugitives from service or labor, who may have escaped from any persons to whom such service or labor is claimed to be due, and any officer who shall be found guilty by a court-martial of violating this article shall be dismissed from the service.

SEC. 2. *And be it further enacted,* That this act shall take effect from and after its passage.

Also to the ninth and tenth sections of an act entitled "An Act to suppress Insurrection, to punish Treason and Rebellion, to seize and confiscate property of rebels, and for other purposes," approved July 17, 1862, and which sections are in the words and figures following:

SEC. 9. *And be it further enacted,* That all slaves of persons who shall hereafter be engaged in rebellion against the government of the United States, or who shall in any way give aid or comfort thereto, escaping from such persons and taking refuge within the lines of the army; and all slaves captured from such persons or deserted by them and coming under the control of the government of the United States; and all slaves of such persons found *on* (or) being within any place occupied by rebel forces and afterwards occupied by the forces of the United States, shall be deemed captives of war, and shall be forever free of their servitude and not again held as slaves.

SEC. 10. *And be it further enacted,* That no slave escaping into any State, Territory, or the District of Columbia, from any other State, shall be delivered up, or in any way impeded or hindered of his liberty, except for crime, or some offence against the laws, unless the person claiming said fugitive shall first make oath that the person to whom the labor or service of such fugitive is alleged to be due is his lawful owner, and has not borne arms against the United States in the present rebellion, nor in any way given aid and comfort thereto; and no person engaged in the military or naval service of the United States shall, under any pretence whatever, assume to decide on the validity of the claim of any person to the service or labor of any other person, or surrender up any such person to the claimant, on pain of being dismissed from the service.

And I do hereby enjoin upon and order all persons engaged in the military and naval service of the United States to observe, obey, and enforce, within their respective spheres of service, the act, and sections above recited.

And the executive will in due time recommend that all citizens of the United States who shall have remained loyal thereto throughout the rebellion, shall (upon the restoration of the constitutional relation between the United States, and their respective states, and people, if that relation shall have been suspended or disturbed) be compensated for all losses by acts of the United States, including the loss of slaves.

In witness whereof, I have hereunto set my hand, and caused the seal of the United States to be affixed.

L.S.   Done at the City of Washington, this twenty second day of September, in the year of our Lord, one thousand eight hundred and sixty two, and of the Independence of the United States, the eighty seventh.

By the President:

ABRAHAM LINCOLN

WILLIAM H. SEWARD, Secretary of State.

A PROCLAMATION

Whereas, on the twenty-second day of September, in the year of our Lord one thousand eight hundred and sixty two a proclamation was issued by the President of the United States, containing, among other things, the following, to wit:

"That on the first day of January, in the year of our Lord one thousand eight hundred and sixty-three, all persons held as slaves within any state, or designated part of a state, the people whereof shall then be in rebellion against the United States, shall be then, thenceforward and forever free; and the Executive Government of the United States, including the military and naval authority thereof, will recognize and maintain the freedom of such persons, and will do no act or acts to repress such persons, or any of them, in any efforts they may make for their actual freedom.

"That the executive will, on the first day of January aforesaid, by proclamation, designate the states and parts of states, if any, in which the people thereof, respectively, shall then be in rebellion against the United States, and the fact that any state, or the people thereof, shall on that day be in good faith represented in the Congress of the United States by members chosen thereto, at elections wherein a majority of the qualified voters of such state shall have participated, shall, in the absence of strong countervailing testimony, be deemed conclusive evidence that such state, and the people thereof, are not then in rebellion against the United States."

Now, therefore I, Abraham Lincoln President of the United States, by virtue of the power in me vested as Commander-in-Chief, of the Army and Navy of the United States in time of actual armed rebellion against authority and government of the United States, and as a fit and necessary war measure for suppressing said rebellion, do on this first day of January, in the year of our Lord one thousand eight hundred and sixty three, and in accordance with my purpose so to do publicly proclaimed for the full period of one hundred days, from the day first above mentioned, order and designate as the States and parts of States wherein the people thereof respectively, are this day in rebellion against the United States, the following, to wit

Arkansas, Texas, Louisiana, (except the Parishes of St. Bernard, Plaquemine, Jefferson, St. Johns, St. Charles, St. James, Ascension, Assumption, Terrebonne, Lafourche, St. Mary, St. Martin, and Orleans, including the City of New-Orleans) Mississippi, Alabama, Florida, Georgia, South-Carolina, North-Carolina, and Virginia, (except the forty-eight counties designated as West Virginia and also the counties of Berkeley, Accomac, Northampton, Elizabeth City, York, Princess-Ann, and Norfolk, including the cities of Norfolk & Portsmouth; and which excepted parts are for the present left precisely as if this proclamation were not issued.

And by virtue of the power and for the purpose aforesaid I do order and declare that all persons held as slaves within said designated States, and parts of States are and henceforward shall be free; and that the Executive government of the United States, including the military and naval authorities thereof, will recognize and maintain the freedom of said persons.

And I hereby enjoin upon the people so declared to be free to abstain from all violence, unless in necessary self-defense; and I recommend to them that in all cases when allowed, they labor faithfully for reasonable wages.

And I further declare and make known, that such persons of suitable condition, will be received into the armed service of the United States to garrison forts, positions, stations and other places, and to man vessels of all sorts in said service.

And upon this act sincerely believed to be an act of justice, warranted by the Constitution upon military necessity, I invoke the considerate judgment of mankind, and the gracious favor of Almighty God.

In witness whereof, I have hereunto set my hand and caused the seal of the United States to be affixed

[L. S.] Done at the city of Washington, this first day of January, in the year of our Lord one thousand eight hundred and sixty three, and of the Independence of the United States of America the eighty-seventh.

By the President: Abraham Lincoln
William H. Seward,
Secretary of State

V.

"The Last Full Measure"

1863–1865

FOUR RELATED ISSUES FIGURE prominently in Lincoln's speeches and writings from January 1863 to his tragic assassination on April 14, 1865: (1) defeating the Confederacy; (2) restoring the southern states to the Union; (3) winning the crucial election of 1864; and (4) ending slavery to secure a "new birth of freedom." Indeed, the Union's destiny hinged upon each of these defining and momentous challenges.

Though the Confederacy was far from vanquished, the summer of 1863 proved to be a turning point in the war, due to the Union's simultaneous victories at Gettysburg on July 3, and Vicksburg on July 4. At Gettysburg, Pennsylvania, federal forces led by George G. Meade defeated Robert E. Lee after a three-day battle in which the North suffered 23,000 casualties and the South 28,000. The "high tide of the Confederacy" was reached with Pickett's Charge: 14,000 Confederates surged forward across an open field in a frontal assault against the federal lines. After thirty minutes, less than half of them returned. Lee's second invasion of the North sought to demoralize the federal cause forcing the Lincoln Administration to sue for peace. Instead, it resulted in a costly defeat with staggering casualties the rebel army could not sustain in the long-term, forcing Lee to retreat back across the Potomac. In the western theatre, Ulysses S. Grant, who had distinguished himself in Lincoln's eyes as a tenacious and resolute fighter, captured the strategic southern port of Vicksburg, Mississippi after a prolonged siege, thereby splitting the Confederacy in half. Thus, July 4, 1863 brought glad tidings to the Union from both the eastern and western theatres of war. Independence Day was truly a cause for celebration in the North.

In view of the countless lives given on both sides at Gettysburg, it was decided to make the site of the battlefield a national cemetery, as an everlasting monument to the brave soldiers who gave the "last full measure" there. The renowned orator Edward Everett was invited to commemorate the opening of the cemetery on November 19, 1863. Lincoln received "second billing" and was invited, almost as an afterthought, to make a "few brief remarks." But while there, he provided an enduring statement of America's democratic identity and mission, distilling the essence of its political creed. Holding out the promise of a "new birth of freedom," which symbolized a Union redeemed from the

original sin of slavery, he asked the nation to confirm the Emancipation Proclamation issued in January of the same year.

Though sustaining great casualties, the relentless advance of federal armies
and their occupation of southern lands raised questions about how the seceded
states would be readmitted to the Union, and on what terms? Would they reenter with or without slavery? Could they reestablish slavery once they reentered?
This debate over reconstruction widened the political chasm between Lincoln
and a group of Radical Republicans that his secretary John Hay referred to as
"the Jacobins." After a series of federal military defeats earlier in the war, in January of 1862, the Radical Republicans in Congress formed a Committee on the
Conduct of the War whose ostensible purpose was to investigate reasons for the
Union's lack of success in battle. In actuality, the committee was a vehicle to
advance the radical political agenda of unconditional emancipation. Its proceedings took on an aura of McCarthyism. Democratic officers including
McClellan were accused of harboring southern sympathies. Blinded by narrow
partisanship, the radicals failed to see that a broad coalition including northern
Democrats was needed to prosecute the war to a successful conclusion.

In 1864, Lincoln and the Radicals debated over who had the authority to
preside over reconstruction, the Congress or the president? Would the terms
for the South's readmission be lenient or punitive? Lincoln's lenient terms proceeded from his interpretation of the technical legal status of the Confederate
states during the rebellion. Because he maintained that the Confederate states
had no legal authority to secede, that secession was, in fact, a domestic rebellion; he believed that they technically remained in the Union, thereby preserving their territorial integrity and retaining many of their rights from the *status
quo antebellum*. The exception was slavery, the abolition of which Lincoln
demanded as a condition of peace and the South's readmission to the Union.
Since the Civil War was a domestic rebellion, Lincoln also contended that the
task of reconstruction fell under his authority as commander in chief and chief
executive. He sought to readmit the seceded states as soon as possible, proposing a full pardon to all rebels who would swear an oath to the Union — with
the exception of its "ring leaders." Lincoln's "Ten Percent Reconstruction
Plan" allowed a seceded state to reenter the Union if 10 percent of its prewar
population swore an oath of loyalty to the Union and abolished slavery. However, this plan did not mandate that the southern states grant full civil and political equality to the freedmen. Although the national government had an
important stewardship role in guaranteeing black freedom and in providing
basic ladders of opportunity for African-Americans such as the Freedman's

Bureau, Lincoln maintained that, without an amendment, the federal division of powers under the Constitution left specific measures of racial adjustment to the discretion of the states. In sum, Lincoln's differences with the Radicals stemmed not so much from the goals of extending equality to all human beings, but the proper constitutional, social, and political means to achieve this end.

Contrary to Lincoln, the Radicals contended that Congress, not the president, should preside over Reconstruction. Their alternative Reconstruction proposal was known as the Wade-Davis Bill. This more punitive measure was based on the view that the Confederate states had committed political suicide during the war thereby forfeiting all of their rights. According to the Radicals, the Confederate states assumed the legal status of conquered provinces in a foreign war. In contrast to Lincoln's 10 percent plan, the Wade-Davis Bill required that a majority of citizens in each southern state swear an "iron clad oath" of "past purity and future loyalty" to gain readmission to the Union. It required them to swear that they had never participated in, aided, or abetted the rebellion. Since the stringency of this oath would have excluded most southern whites from participating in a Reconstruction government, Congress and the Freedmen, backed by the coercive force of federal generals, would control the southern state governments for at least a generation. Without an amendment, Lincoln believed this to be an unauthorized intrusion of federal power. He pocket vetoed the Wade-Davis Bill, arousing the fury of the Radical Republicans who schemed to dump him as their candidate in the election of 1864. His plea for "malice toward none and charity for all" in the Second Inaugural Address should be seen in the context of northern vindictiveness toward the South. Lincoln's assassination was indeed calamitous for the South. After his death, the Radicals impeached his successor, President Johnson, guaranteeing their virtual control over reconstruction. They imposed a military reconstruction plan that divided the South into five military districts presided over by a federal general. Though many of these measures were justified given the South's blatant defiance of federal law and its continued oppression of newly freed African-Americans, Lincoln's death deprived the nation of a prudent leader who might have been successful in dealing with the volatile issue of racial adjustment by drawing the southern states through both diplomatic and coercive means into a national moral consensus. In addition to the threat of force, it is likely that Lincoln would have found more subtle ways to make it in the South's interest to recognize black freedom. Avoiding the self-righteousness of the Radicals, he most likely would have reminded Northerners of their responsibility to help bear the burden of reconstruction rather than humiliating the South and exploiting its vulnerability. Intimations of this outlook and approach can be seen in his second inaugural address. Indeed, throughout his mature public life, Lincoln consistently manifested the virtue of prudence by politically navigating between the Skylla and Kharybdis of overzealous idealism and unprincipled pragmatism, both of which imperiled the long-term public good of the nation.

In the late summer of 1864 Lincoln's chances for election seemed futile. Ulysses S. Grant, who was promoted to the rank of lieutenant general, was transferred to the eastern theatre, where he suffered horrendous casualties in pursuit of Lee at the Battle of the Wilderness (May 5-6, 1864) and Cold Harbor (June 1-3). After twenty minutes of fighting at Cold Harbor, there were 7,000 federal casualties. Grant's critics branded him a "butcher" who callously hurled bodies into an enemy meat grinder. The advance of the Union Army seemed to be stalled; it seemed unable to break the neck of the Confederacy. How much longer would the war last, and at what cost? The North was becoming weary and exhausted of war. Political disintegration matched military failure. Copperheads, named by Union loyalists after a venomous snake, were Northern peace Democrats who vehemently criticized the administration, opposed the war, and encouraged resistance to the draft, in some cases even covertly aiding the rebellion. Lincoln referred to this subversive Copperhead threat in the North as "the enemy in the rear." In mid-July of 1863, draft riots erupted in New York City. Demonstrating their contempt for the Emancipation Proclamation, an angry mob, primarily made up of Irish immigrants who resented the idea of having to compete with free blacks for work, lynched African-Americans and burned down a black orphanage.

Lincoln's fragile war coalition was breaking apart as well: on the right wing, War Democrats and conservative Republicans criticized him for the Emancipation; on the Left wing, Radical Republicans and abolitionists like Wendell Phillips condemned him for his leniency toward the South. Threatening to undermine the fragile Republican coalition, Salmon P. Chase, Lincoln's secretary of treasury, conspired with Radicals to steal the Republican nomination from his chief. Prior to the Republican National Convention in June, a splinter group of Radicals Republicans calling themselves the "Radical Democracy" voiced opposition to Lincoln's policies, held their own convention in Cleveland, and nominated John Fremont as their presidential candidate. Chase's bid ultimately proved unsuccessful. Other critics claimed that Lincoln's second term in office would inevitably lead to an abuse of power. Since Andrew Jackson, no president had been reelected for a second term. Despite efforts to thwart him, Lincoln was renominated unanimously at the Republican National Convention in June. Most notably, the Republican platform linked the triumph of the Union's cause with the end of slavery: "Resolved. That, as slavery was the cause and now constitutes the strength of this rebellion, and as it must be, always and everywhere hostile to the principles of republican government, justice and the national safety demand its utter and complete extirpation from the soil of the republic." The platform called for the prosecution of the war with the "utmost vigor," defended the Emancipation as a "deathblow" against the "gigantic evil" of slavery, and called for an amendment that would "terminate and forever prohibit" slavery's existence in the United States. This would ultimately be achieved in 1865 by the Thirteenth Amendment.

The Democrats nominated George B. McClellan, former Union general, as their candidate. Testifying to the antiwar sentiment among Democrats, Clement Vallandigham, the notorious Copperhead representative from Ohio, wrote the party's platform. Vallandigham had become a martyr after he had been imprisoned and exiled for resisting Lincoln's suspension of the writ of habeas corpus. This controversial action haunted the Lincoln Administration, raising questions about the abuse of executive power. The Democratic platform called for an "immediate cessation of hostilities," a convention of states to secure peace, a condemnation of Lincoln's abridgement of civil liberties, and a repudiation of his use of executive authority to issue the Emancipation. Exhausted by war, many in the North were willing to accept a peace at any price: either recognizing the independence of the Confederacy or restoring the Union with slavery. In effect, the result would have been the same: the regime would have forfeited its promise of equality to African-Americans and to itself.

Lincoln stressed the importance of the election of 1864 as a "trial" testing the viability of the nation's Republican institutions in a time of crisis. He emphasized that the nation must demonstrate the integrity of its democratic process even in the midst of a Civil War. The election was also "a necessity" in guaranteeing the end of slavery. Significantly, Lincoln vigorously supported the Republican Party's endorsement of a Thirteenth Amendment permanently abolishing slavery throughout the entire Union. Despite the Emancipation Proclamation, this amendment was needed in order to abolish slavery in the Border States and to prevent its potential reestablishment by the southern states after the war. The success of the Democratic Party in the election of 1864 would have negated the many strides made toward black freedom during the war. The Democrats called for a peace that would have restored the Union with slavery intact, while Lincoln demanded an end to the institution as a condition of peace. And he refused to retract the Emancipation in the midst of great political pressure from conservative Republicans and War Democrats, even if it meant his defeat in the election.

Destiny would carry Lincoln forward to a consummation securing his election in 1864. On September 4, the North received word that General William Tecumseh Sherman had captured Atlanta. This fortuitous military success reinvigorated northern will and virtually ensured Lincoln's reelection. The election results were as follows: Lincoln won 55 percent of the popular vote, 221 electoral; McClellan, 45 percent of the popular vote. A dramatic reversal in events had occurred. McClellan had won only three states: New Jersey, Delaware, and Kentucky.

Lincoln's shrewd political maneuvering was crucial in securing passage of the Thirteenth Amendment through the Thirty-Eighth Congress on January 31, 1865. Availing himself to logrolling and arm-twisting, he shepherded the amendment through the House of Representatives, where it passed by two votes over the required two-thirds majority, 119-56. Historians have speculated about Lincoln's role in using patronage to influence eight Democrats who were mysteriously absent during the voting.

On March, 4, 1865, Lincoln delivered his celebrated Second Inaugural Address—the culmination of his civil theology and an expression of his living faith. With this profound speech, Lincoln pondered the ultimate significance of the war and affirmed the righteousness of a living God who would bring good out of the national suffering. Eschewing the self-righteousness and tribalism of those who vindictively sought to punish the South, he pointed to the North's culpability in events, referring to the root cause of the conflict in general terms as "American slavery" rather than blaming the war exclusively upon the South. Lincoln appealed to the "higher angels" of his audience to accept a magnanimous, just, and lasting peace: "With malice toward none; with charity for all; with firmness in the right, as God gives us to see the right, let us strive on to finish the work we are in; to bind up the nation's wounds; to care for him who shall have borne the battle, and for his widow, and his orphan—to do all which may achieve and cherish a just, and a lasting peace, among ourselves, and with all nations." In an important symbolic gesture after the speech, the president deliberately sought out Frederick Douglass, who, as a black, was prohibited from entering the congressional galleries. After inviting Douglass to a reception after the event, Lincoln personally solicited his view of the speech. This was the first time an African-American had been invited to a presidential social function.

The end came shortly afterward. On April 9, 1865, Palm Sunday, Lee surrendered to Grant at Appomattox. Lincoln was assassinated on April 14th, Good

Friday. The martyr of liberty had sacrificed "the last full measure" to ensure his nation "a new birth of freedom."

TO THE WORKINGMEN OF MANCHESTER, ENGLAND[1]
JANUARY 19, 1863

British public opinion was divided over the Civil War. In general, the aristocracy was sympathetic to the South, the working class to the North. On both sides of the Atlantic, the Civil War was viewed as a cultural struggle, a continuation of the English Civil War between the ancestors of the Puritan parliamentarians who settled in the North and the Cavalier royalists who settled in the South. In a touching gesture of support for the president and the Union cause, workers from Manchester England wrote to Lincoln saying: "As citizens of Manchester . . . we beg to express our fraternal sentiments. . . . We honor your free States, as a singular happy abode for the working millions. . . . One thing alone has, in the past, lessened our sympathy with your country and our confidence in it; we mean the ascendancy of politicians who not merely maintained negro slavery, but desired to extend and root it more firmly. Since we have discerned, however, that the victory of the free north, in the war which has so sorely distressed us as well as afflicted you, will strike off the fetters of the slave, you have attracted our warm and earnest sympathy. We joyfully honor you, as the President, and the Congress with you, for the many decisive steps towards practically exemplifying your belief in the words of your great founders, 'All men are created equal.' "

Since the federal blockade of southern ports harmed England's manufacturing centers by depriving them of cotton, Lincoln praised the workers sacrifice as an example of "sublime Christian heroism."

EXECUTIVE MANSION, WASHINGTON,
TO THE WORKINGMEN OF MANCHESTER: JANUARY 19, 1863.

I have the honor to acknowledge the receipt of the address and resolutions which you sent to me on the eve of the new year.

When I came, on the fourth day of March, 1861, through a free and constitutional election, to preside in the government of the United States, the country was found at the verge of civil war. Whatever might have been the cause, or whosoever the fault, one duty paramount to all others was before me, namely, to maintain and preserve at once the Constitution and the integrity of the federal republic. A conscientious purpose to perform this duty is a key to all the measures of administration which have been, and to all which will hereafter be pursued. Under our form of government, and my official oath, I could not depart from this purpose if I would. It is not always in the power of governments to enlarge or restrict the scope of moral results which follow the policies that they may deem it necessary for the public safety, from time to time, to adopt.

I have understood well that the duty of self-preservation rests solely with the American people. But I have at the same time been aware that favor or disfavor of foreign nations might have a material influence in enlarging and prolonging the struggle with disloyal men in which the country is engaged. A fair examination of history has seemed to authorize a belief that the past action and influences of the United States were generally regarded as having been beneficent towards mankind. I have therefore reckoned upon the forbearance of nations. Circumstances, to some of which you kindly allude, induced me especially to expect that if justice and good faith should be practiced by the United States, they would encounter no hostile influence on the part of Great Britain. It is now a pleasant duty to acknowledge the demonstration you have given of your desire that a spirit of peace and amity towards this country may prevail in the councils of your Queen, who is respected and esteemed in your own country only more than she is by the kindred nation which has its home on this side of the Atlantic.

I know and deeply deplore the sufferings which the workingmen at Manchester and in all Europe are called to endure in this crisis. It has been often and studiously represented that the attempt to overthrow this government, which was built upon the foundation of human rights, and to substitute for it one which should rest exclusively on the basis of human slavery, was likely to obtain the favor of Europe. Through the actions of our disloyal citizens the workingmen of Europe have been subjected to a severe trial, for the purpose of forcing their sanction to that attempt. Under these circumstances, I cannot but regard your decisive utterance upon the question as an instance of sublime Christian heroism which has not been surpassed in any age or in any country. It is, indeed, an energetic and reinspiring assurance of the inherent power of truth and of the ultimate and universal triumph of justice, humanity, and freedom. I do not doubt that the sentiments you have expressed will be sustained by your great nation, and, on the other hand, I have no hesitation in assuring you that they will excite admiration, esteem, and the most reciprocal feelings of friendship among the American people. I hail this interchange of sentiment, therefore, as an augury that, whatever else may happen, whatever misfortune may befall your country or my own, the peace and friendship which now exist between the two nations will be, as it shall be my desire to make them, perpetual.

ABRAHAM LINCOLN
LETTER TO GENERAL JOSEPH HOOKER
JANUARY 26, 1863

After appointing General "Fighting Joe" Hooker as the head of the Army of the Potomac, Lincoln provided him with some advice. Until he discovered Ulysses S. Grant, Lincoln's efforts to find a competent and tenacious general to lead the Union army proved frustrating. Reputedly, Hooker had made derogatory remarks that subverted General Burnside's authority. As a leader, Lincoln possessed the rare ability of offering constructive criticism to his subordinates without alienating them. Indeed, Hooker would later remark that he considered Lincoln's firm but friendly admonition as a kind of "fatherly advice."

EXECUTIVE MANSION,
WASHINGTON, JANUARY 26, 1863.
MAJOR-GENERAL HOOKER:
GENERAL.

I have placed you at the head of the Army of the Potomac. Of course I have done this upon what appear to me to be sufficient reasons. And yet I think it best for you to know that there are some things in regard to which, I am not quite satisfied with you. I believe you to be a brave and skilful soldier, which, of course, I like. I also believe you do not mix politics with your profession, in which you are right. You have confidence in yourself, which is a valuable, if not an indispensable quality. You are ambitious, which, within reasonable bounds, does good rather than harm. But I think that during Gen. Burnside's command of the Army, you have taken counsel of your ambition, and thwarted him as much as you could, in which you did a great wrong to the country, and to a most meritorious and honorable brother officer. I have heard, in such a way as to believe it, of your recently saying that both the Army and the Government needed a Dictator. Of course it was not *for* this, but in spite of it, that I have given you the command. Only those generals who gain successes, can set up dictators. What I now ask of you is military success, and I will risk the dictatorship. The government will support you to the utmost of it's ability, which is neither more nor less than it has done and will do for all commanders. I much fear that the spirit which you have aided to infuse into the Army, of criticizing their Commander, and withholding confidence from him, will now turn upon you. I shall assist you as far as I can, to put it down. Neither you, nor Napoleon, if he were alive again, could get any good out of an army, while such a spirit prevails in it.

And now, beware of rashness. Beware of rashness, but with energy, and sleepless vigilance, go forward, and give us victories.

Yours very truly

A. Lincoln.

LETTER TO MARY TODD LINCOLN
June 9, 1863

Lincoln sent this telegram to his wife Mary Todd about a nightmare premonition he had concerning his youngest son Tad. Apparently, Lincoln feared Tad would harm himself with his unloaded toy pistol. Perhaps Lincoln was especially sensitive at this time since his middle son Willie had tragically died in February of 1862. It is well documented that Lincoln had premonitions of his own death before his assassination.

Mrs. Lincoln
Executive Mansion,
Philadelphia, Pa.
Washington, June 9, 1863

Think you better put "Tad's" pistol away. I had an ugly dream about him.

A. LINCOLN.

LETTER TO ERASTUS CORNING AND OTHERS
June 12, 1863

Erastus Corning was President of the New York Central Railroad, and the leader of a Democratic delegation from Albany New York, that protested Lincoln's abridgement of civil liberties during the war, in particular, his suspension of the writ of habeas corpus. Opposition to Lincoln surged when General Burnside arrested Clement Vallandigham, who was a notable Ohio Democratic representative and Copperhead—a southern sympathizer who condemned the administration's war policies and urged opposition to the draft. In 1863, Lincoln suspended the writ of habeas corpus throughout the Union to check the subversive activities of Copperheads. Lincoln referred to these subversives as the "enemy in the rear." Democratic leaders like Erastus Corning argued that Lincoln had abridged civil liberties as a political weapon to silence Democratic dissent. Lincoln did not order the specific arrest of Vallandigham, but was forced to back general Burnside once the

decision was made. Burnside's repression transformed Vallandigham into a political mar-
tyr. In his response to Corning and the Albany Democrats, Lincoln provided his justifi-
cation for suspending the writ of habeas corpus. Frank Williams, the Chief Justice of the
Rhode Island Supreme Court and President of the Lincoln Forum, in his book Judging
Lincoln, *has described Lincoln as "bending the Constitution without breaking it."*
Williams correctly explains that in attempting to balance the nation's liberties and secu-
rity in times of crisis, Lincoln acted in the dual role of commander in chief and attorney
general in chief, a role he was uniquely suited for given his dual practice of law and poli-
tics in Springfield. While the Constitution does provide for the suspension of the writ of
habeas corpus in cases of rebellion, it does not specify who has the authority to suspend
the writ. Lincoln argued that the authority to suspend the writ of habeas corpus as a mil-
itary necessity logically fell to the commander in chief of the armed forces. Subsequently,
Congress approved his action. Lincoln's extraordinary use of executive power during the
war is still hotly debated amongst scholars today.

EXECUTIVE MANSION,
WASHINGTON, JUNE 12, 1863.
HON. ERASTUS CORNING AND OTHERS.
GENTLEMEN:

Your letter of May 19, inclosing the resolutions of a public meeting held at
Albany, New York, on the 16th of the same month, was received several days ago.

The resolutions, as I understand them, are resolvable into two propositions—
first, the expression of a purpose to sustain the cause of the Union, to secure
peace through victory, and to support the administration in every constitutional
and lawful measure to suppress the rebellion; and, secondly, a declaration of
censure upon the administration for supposed unconstitutional action, such as
the making of military arrests. And from the two propositions a third is deduced,
which is that the gentlemen composing the meeting are resolved on doing their
part to maintain our common government and country, despite the folly or
wickedness, as they may conceive, of any administration. This position is eminently patriotic, and as such I thank the meeting, and congratulate the nation
for it. My own purpose is the same; so that the meeting and myself have a common object, and can have no difference, except in the choice of means or measures for effecting that object.

And here I ought to close this paper, and would close it, if there were no
apprehension that more injurious consequences than any merely personal to
myself might follow the censures systematically cast upon me for doing what, in
my view of duty, I could not forbear. The resolutions promise to support me in

every constitutional and lawful measure to suppress the rebellion; and I have not knowingly employed, nor shall knowingly employ, any other. But the meeting, by their resolutions, assert and argue that certain military arrests, and proceedings following them, for which I am ultimately responsible, are unconstitutional. I think they are not. The resolutions quote from the Constitution the definition of treason, and also the limiting safeguards and guarantees therein provided for the citizen on trials for treason, and on his being held to answer for capital or otherwise infamous crimes, and in criminal prosecutions his right to a speedy and public trial by an impartial jury. They proceed to resolve "that these safeguards of the rights of the citizen against the pretensions of arbitrary power were intended more especially for his protection in times of civil commotion." And, apparently to demonstrate the proposition, the resolutions proceed: "They were secured substantially to the English people after years of protracted civil war, and were adopted into our Constitution at the close of the revolution." Would not the demonstration have been better if it could have been truly said that these safeguards had been adopted and applied during the civil wars and during our revolution, instead of after the one and at the close of the other? I, too, am devotedly for them after civil war, and before civil war, and at all times, "except when, in cases of rebellion or invasion, the public safety may require" their suspension. The resolutions proceed to tell us that these safeguards "have stood the test of seventy-six years of trial under our republican system, under circumstances which show that while they constitute the foundation of all free government, they are the elements of the enduring stability of the republic." No one denies that they have so stood the test up to the beginning of the present rebellion, if we except a certain occurrence at New Orleans hereafter to be mentioned; nor does any one question that they will stand the same test much longer after the rebellion closes. But these provisions of the Constitution have no application to the case we have in hand, because the arrests complained of were not made for treason—that is, not for the treason defined in the Constitution, and upon the conviction of which the punishment is death—nor yet were they made to hold persons to answer for any capital or otherwise infamous crimes; nor were the proceedings following, in any constitutional or legal sense, "criminal prosecutions." The arrests were made on totally different grounds, and the proceedings following accorded with the grounds of the arrests. Let us consider the real case with which we are dealing, and apply to it the parts of the Constitution plainly made for such cases.

Prior to my installation here it had been inculcated that any State had a lawful right to secede from the national Union, and that it would be expedient to exercise the right whenever the devotees of the doctrine should fail to elect a president to their own liking. I was elected contrary to their liking; and, accordingly, so far as it was legally possible, they had taken seven States out of the Union, had seized many of the United States forts, and had fired upon the United States flag, all before I was inaugurated, and, of course, before I had done any official act whatever. The rebellion thus begun soon ran into the present civil war; and, in certain respects, it began on very unequal terms between the parties. The insurgents had been preparing for it more than thirty years, while the government had taken no steps to resist them. The former had carefully considered all the means which could be turned to their account. It undoubtedly was a well-pondered reliance with them that in their own unrestricted effort to destroy Union, Constitution and law, all together, the government would, in great degree, be restrained by the same Constitution and law from arresting their progress. Their sympathizers pervaded all departments of the government and nearly all communities of the people. From this material, under cover of "liberty of speech," "liberty of the press," and "*habeas corpus,*" they hoped to keep on foot amongst us a most efficient corps of spies, informers, suppliers, and aiders and abettors of their cause in a thousand ways. They knew that in times such as they were inaugurating, by the Constitution itself the "*habeas corpus*" might be suspended; but they also knew they had friends who would make a question as to who was to suspend it; meanwhile their spies and others might remain at large to help on their cause. Or if, as has happened, the Executive should suspend the writ without ruinous waste of time, instances of arresting innocent persons might occur, as are always likely to occur in such cases; and then a clamor could be raised in regard to this, which might be at least of some service to the insurgent cause. It needed no very keen perception to discover this part of the enemy's programme, so soon as by open hostilities their machinery was fairly put in motion. Yet, thoroughly imbued with a reverence for the guaranteed rights of individuals, I was slow to adopt the strong measures which by degrees I have been forced to regard as being within the exceptions of the Constitution, and as indispensable to the public safety. Nothing is better known to history than that courts of justice are utterly incompetent to such cases. Civil courts are organized chiefly for trials of individuals, or, at most, a few individuals acting in concert—and this in quiet times, and on charges of crimes well defined in the law. Even in times of peace bands of horse-thieves and robbers frequently grow too numerous and powerful for the ordinary courts of justice. But what comparison, in numbers, have such bands ever borne to the insurgent sympathizers even in many of the loyal States? Again, a jury too frequently has at least one member more ready to hang the panel than to hang the traitor. And yet again, he who dissuades one man from volunteering, or induces one soldier to desert, weakens the Union cause as much as he who kills a Union soldier in battle. Yet this dissuasion or inducement may be so conducted as to be no defined crime of which any civil court would take cognizance.

Ours is a case of rebellion—so called by the resolutions before me—in fact, a clear, flagrant, and gigantic case of rebellion; and the provision of the Constitution that "the privilege of the writ of *habeas corpus* shall not be suspended unless when, in cases of rebellion or invasion, the public safety may require it," is the provision which specially applies to our present case. This provision plainly attests the understanding of those who made the Constitution that ordinary courts of justice are inadequate to "cases of rebellion"—attests their purpose that, in such cases, men may be held in custody whom the courts, acting on ordinary rules, would discharge. *Habeas corpus* does not discharge men who are proved to be guilty of defined crime; and its suspension is allowed by the Constitution on purpose that men may be arrested and held who cannot be proved to be guilty of defined crime, "when, in cases of rebellion or invasion, the public safety may require it."

This is precisely our present case—a case of rebellion wherein the public safety does require the suspension. Indeed, arrests by process of courts and arrests in cases of rebellion do not proceed altogether upon the same basis. The former is directed at the small percentage of ordinary and continuous perpetration of crime, while the latter is directed at sudden and extensive uprisings against the government, which, at most, will succeed or fail in no great length of time. In the latter case arrests are made not so much for what has been done, as for what probably would be done. The latter is more for the preventive and less for the vindictive than the former. In such cases the purposes of men are much more easily understood than in cases of ordinary crime. The man who stands by and says nothing when the peril of his government is discussed, cannot be misunderstood. If not hindered, he is sure to help the enemy; much more if he talks ambiguously—talks for his country with "buts," and "ifs" and "ands." Of how little value the constitutional provision I have quoted will be rendered if arrests shall never be made until defined crimes shall have been committed, may be illustrated by a few notable examples: General John C. Breckinridge, General Robert E. Lee, General Joseph E. Johnston, General John B. Magruder, General William B. Preston, General Simon B. Buckner, and Commodore Franklin Buchanan, now occupying the very highest places in the rebel war service, were all within the power of the government since the rebellion began, and were nearly as well known to be traitors then as now. Unquestionably if we had seized and held them, the insurgent cause would be much weaker. But no one of them had then committed any crime defined in the law. Every one of them, if arrested, would have been discharged on *habeas corpus* were the writ allowed to operate. In view of these and similar cases, I think the time not unlikely to come when I shall be blamed for having made too few arrests rather than too many.

By the third resolution the meeting indicate their opinion that military arrests may be constitutional in localities where rebellion actually exists, but that such arrests are unconstitutional in localities where rebellion or insurrection does not actually exist. They insist that such arrests shall not be made "outside of the lines of necessary military occupation and the scenes of insurrection." Inasmuch, however, as the Constitution itself makes no such distinction, I am unable to believe that there is any such constitutional distinction. I concede that the class of arrests complained of can be constitutional only when, in cases of rebellion or invasion, the public safety may require them; and I insist that in such cases they are constitutional wherever the public safety does require them, as well in places to which they may prevent the rebellion extending, as in those where it may be already prevailing; as well where they may restrain mischievous interference with the raising and supplying of armies to suppress the rebellion, as where the rebellion may actually be; as well where they may restrain the enticing men out of the army, as where they would prevent mutiny in the army; equally constitutional at all places where they will conduce to the public safety, as against the dangers of rebellion or invasion. Take the particular case mentioned by the meeting. It is asserted in substance, that Mr. Vallandigham was, by a military commander, seized and tried "for no other reason than words addressed to a public meeting in criticism of the course of the administration, and in condemnation of the military orders of the general." Now, if there be no mistake about this, if this assertion is the truth and the whole truth, if there was no other reason for the arrest, then I concede that the arrest was wrong. But the arrest, as I understand, was made for a very different reason. Mr. Vallandigham avows his hostility to the war on the part of the Union; and his arrest was made because he was laboring, with some effect, to prevent the raising of troops, to encourage desertions from the army, and to leave the rebellion without an adequate military force to suppress it. He was not arrested because he was damaging the political prospects of the administration or the personal interests of the commanding general, but because he was damaging the army, upon the existence and vigor of which the life of the nation depends. He was warring upon the military, and this gave the military constitutional jurisdiction to lay hands upon him. If Mr. Vallandigham was not damaging the military power of the country, then his arrest was made on mistake of fact, which I would be glad to correct on reasonably satisfactory evidence.

I understand the meeting whose resolutions I am considering to be in favor of suppressing the rebellion by military force—by armies. Long experience has shown that armies cannot be maintained unless desertion shall be punished by the severe penalty of death. The case requires, and the law and the Constitution sanction, this punishment. Must I shoot a simple-minded soldier boy who deserts, while I must not touch a hair of a wily agitator who induces him to desert? This is none the less injurious when effected by getting a father, or brother, or friend into a public meeting, and there working upon his feelings till he is persuaded to write the soldier boy that he is fighting in a bad cause, for a wicked administration of a contemptible government, too weak to arrest and punish him if he shall desert. I think that, in such a case, to silence the agitator and save the boy is not only constitutional, but withal a great mercy.

If I be wrong on this question of constitutional power, my error lies in believing that certain proceedings are constitutional when, in cases of rebellion or invasion, the public safety requires them, which would not be constitutional when, in absence of rebellion or invasion, the public safety does not require them: in other words, that the Constitution is not in its application in all respects the same in cases of rebellion or invasion involving the public safety, as it is in times of profound peace and public security. The Constitution itself makes the distinction, and I can no more be persuaded that the government can constitutionally take no strong measures in time of rebellion, because it can be shown that the same could not be lawfully taken in time of peace, than I can be persuaded that a particular drug is not good medicine for a sick man because it can be shown to not be good food for a well one. Nor am I able to appreciate the danger apprehended by the meeting, that the American people will by means of military arrests during the rebellion lose the right of public discussion, the liberty of speech and the press, the law of evidence, trial by jury, and *habeas corpus* throughout the indefinite peaceful future which I trust lies before them, any more than I am able to believe that a man could contract so strong an appetite for emetics during temporary illness as to persist in feeding upon them during the remainder of his healthful life.

In giving the resolutions that earnest consideration which you request of me, I cannot overlook the fact that the meeting speak as "Democrats." Nor can I, with full respect for their known intelligence, and the fairly presumed deliberation with which they prepared their resolutions, be permitted to suppose that this occurred by accident, or in any way other than that they preferred to designate themselves "Democrats" rather than "American citizens." In this time of national peril I would have preferred to meet you upon a level one step higher than any party platform, because I am sure that from such more elevated position we could do better battle for the country we all love than we possibly can from those lower ones where, from the force of habit, the prejudices of the past, and selfish hopes of the future, we are sure to expend much of our ingenuity and strength in finding fault with and aiming blows at each other. But since you have denied me this, I will yet be thankful for the country's sake that not all Democrats have done so. He on whose discretionary judgment Mr. Vallandigham was arrested and tried is a Democrat, having no old party affinity with me, and the judge who rejected the constitutional view expressed in these resolutions, by refusing to discharge Mr. Vallandigham on *habeas corpus,* is a Democrat of better days than these, having received his judicial mantle at the hands of President Jackson. And still more, of all those Democrats who are nobly exposing their lives and shedding their blood on the battle-field, I have learned that many approve the course taken with Mr. Vallandigham, while I have not heard of a single one condemning it. I cannot assert that there are none such. And the name of President Jackson recalls an instance of pertinent history. After the battle of New Orleans, and while the fact that the treaty of peace had been concluded was well known in the city, but before official knowledge of it had arrived, General Jackson still maintained martial or military law. Now that it could be said the war was over, the clamor against martial law, which had existed from the first, grew more furious. Among other things, a Mr. Louaillier published a denunciatory newspaper article. General Jackson arrested him. A lawyer by the name of Morel procured the United States Judge Hall to order a writ of *habeas corpus* to release Mr. Louaillier. General Jackson arrested both the lawyer and the judge. A Mr. Hollander ventured to say of some part of the matter that "it was a dirty trick." General Jackson arrested him. When the officer undertook to serve the writ of *habeas corpus,* General Jackson took it from him, and sent him away with a copy. Holding the judge in custody a few days, the general sent him beyond the limits of his encampment, and set him at liberty with an order to remain till the ratification of peace should be regularly announced, or until the British should have left the southern coast. A day or two more elapsed, the ratification of the treaty of peace was regularly announced, and the judge and others were fully liberated. A few days more, and the judge called General Jackson into court and fined him $1000 for having arrested him and the others named. The general paid the fine, and then the matter rested for nearly thirty years, when Congress refunded principal and interest. The late Senator Douglas, then in the House of Representatives, took a leading part in the debates in which the constitutional question was much discussed. I am not prepared to say whom the journals would show to have voted for the measure.

It may be remarked—first, that we had the same Constitution then as now; secondly, that we then had a case of invasion, and now we have a case of rebellion; and, thirdly, that the permanent right of the people to public discussion, the liberty of speech and of the press, the trial by jury, the law of evidence, and the *habeas corpus,* suffered no detriment whatever by that conduct of General Jackson, or its subsequent approval by the American Congress.

And yet, let me say that, in my own discretion, I do not know whether I would have ordered the arrest of Mr. Vallandigham. While I cannot shift the responsibility from myself, I hold that, as a general rule, the commander in the field is the better judge of the necessity in any particular case. Of course I must practise a general directory and revisory power in the matter.

One of the resolutions expresses the opinion of the meeting that arbitrary arrests will have the effect to divide and distract those who should be united in suppressing the rebellion, and I am specifically called on to discharge Mr. Vallandigham. I regard this as, at least, a fair appeal to me on the expediency of exercising a constitutional power which I think exists. In response to such appeal I have to say, it gave me pain when I learned that Mr. Vallandigham had been arrested (that is, I was pained that there should have seemed to be a necessity for arresting him), and that it will afford me great pleasure to discharge him so soon as I can by any means believe the public safety will not suffer by it.

I further say that, as the war progresses, it appears to me, opinion and action, which were in great confusion at first, take shape and fall into more regular channels, so that the necessity for strong dealing with them gradually decreases. I have every reason to desire that it should cease altogether, and far from the least is my regard for the opinions and wishes of those who, like the meeting at Albany, declare their purpose to sustain the government in every constitutional and lawful measure to suppress the rebellion. Still, I must continue to do so much as may seem to be required by the public safety.

A. Lincoln.

LETTER TO GENERAL N. P. BANKS
AUGUST 5, 1863

General Nathaniel Banks was the current commander of Federal forces in Louisiana, which had occupied New Orleans since April, 1862. Since the Emancipation Proclamation was a war measure against rebel states, it did not apply to parts of Louisiana that remained

within the Union. And as yet, there was no amendment that prohibited slavery in the
Border States and in those areas exempted from the Emancipation Proclamation. This
raised an ominous question: upon reentering the Union, could the people of the reconstructed
Louisiana government reestablish slavery in their new Constitution? To do so would set
back the cause of freedom and constitute a grave humiliation to the administration. To avoid
this, Lincoln encouraged Banks to hold elections for a new free state government in Louisi-
ana. Subsequently, the free government would either frame a new constitution abolishing
slavery or revise the antebellum constitution to accord with this end. In his letter to Banks,
Lincoln conveyed his vision for reconstruction. He hoped that the people of Louisiana would
recognize the Emancipation Proclamation, adopt a gradual policy of racial adjustment, and
provide for the education of young blacks.

EXECUTIVE MANSION,
WASHINGTON, AUGUST 5, 1863.
MY DEAR GENERAL BANKS

Being a poor correspondent is the only apology I offer for not having sooner
tendered my thanks for your very successful, and very valuable military operations this year. The final stroke in opening the Mississippi never should, and I
think never will, be forgotten.

Recent events in Mexico, I think, render early action in Texas more important than ever. I expect, however, the General-in-Chief, will address you more
fully upon this subject.

Governor Boutwell read me to-day that part of your letter to him, which
relates to Louisiana affairs. While I very well know what I would be glad for
Louisiana to do, it is quite a different thing for me to assume direction of the
matter. I would be glad for her to make a new constitution recognizing the
emancipation proclamation, and adopting emancipation in those parts of the
state to which the proclamation does not apply. And while she is at it, I think
it would not be objectionable for her to adopt some practical system by which
the two races could gradually live themselves out of their old relation to each
other, and both come out better prepared for the new. Education for young
blacks should be included in the plan. After all, the power, or element, of "contract" may be sufficient for this probationary period; and, by it's simplicity, and
flexibility, may be the better.

As an anti-slavery man I have a motive to desire emancipation, which proslavery men do not have; but even they have strong enough reason to thus place
themselves again under the shield of the Union, and to thus perpetually hedge
against the recurrence of the scenes through which we are now passing.

Gov. Shepley has informed me that Mr. Durant is now taking a registry, with a view to the election of a Constitutional Convention in Louisiana. This, to me, appears proper. If such convention were to ask my views, I could present little else than what I now say to you. I think the thing should be pushed forward, so that if possible, it's mature work may reach here by the meeting of Congress.

For my own part I think I shall not, in any event, retract the emancipation proclamation; nor, as executive, ever return to slavery any person who is free by the terms of that proclamation, or by any of the acts of Congress.

If Louisiana shall send members to Congress, then admission to seats will depend, as you know, upon the respective Houses, and not upon the President.

If these views can be of any advantage in giving shape, and impetus, to action there, I shall be glad for you to use them prudently for that object. Of course you will confer with intelligent and trusty citizens of the State, among whom I would suggest Messrs. Flanders, Hahn, and Durant; and to each of whom I now think I may send copies of this letter. Still it is perhaps better to not make the letter generally public.

Yours very truly

A. Lincoln

LETTER TO JAMES C. CONKLING
AUGUST 26, 1863

James C. Conkling held a rally for the reelection of the president in Springfield Illinois, Lincoln's hometown. The rally attempted to gain the votes of loyal Democrats to support Lincoln as the National Union candidate. Although Lincoln could not attend personally, he wrote Conkling this letter, which was read to the congregation and published subsequently in major newspapers throughout the country. In it, Lincoln carefully defended the administration's policies, including the Emancipation Proclamation.

EXECUTIVE MANSION,
WASHINGTON, AUGUST 26, 1863.
HON. JAMES C. CONKLING
MY DEAR SIR.

Your letter inviting me to attend a mass-meeting of unconditional Union-men, to be held at the Capitol of Illinois, on the 3d day of September, has been received.

It would be very agreeable to me, to thus meet my old friends, at my own home; but I can not, just now, be absent from here, so long as a visit there, would require.

The meeting is to be of all those who maintain unconditional devotion to the Union; and I am sure my old political friends will thank me for tendering, as I do, the nation's gratitude to those other noble men, whom no partizan malice, or partizan hope, can make false to the nation's life.

There are those who are dissatisfied with me. To such I would say: You desire peace; and you blame me that we do not have it. But how can we attain it? There are but three conceivable ways. First, to suppress the rebellion by force of arms. This I am trying to do. Are you for it? If you are, so far we are agreed. If you are not for it, a second way is to give up the Union. I am against this. Are you for it? If you are, you should say so plainly. If you are not for *force,* nor yet for *dissolution,* there only remains some imaginable *compromise.* I do not believe any compromise, embracing the maintenance of the Union, is now possible. All I learn, leads to a directly opposite belief. The strength of the rebellion, is its military—its army. That army dominates all the country, and all the people, within its range. Any offer of terms made by any man or men within that range, in opposition to that army, is simply nothing for the present; because such man or men, have no power whatever to enforce their side of a compromise, if one were made with them. To illustrate. Suppose refugees from the South, and peace men of the North, get together in convention, and frame and proclaim a compromise embracing a restoration of the Union; in what way can that compromise be used to keep Lee's army out of Pennsylvania? Meade's army can keep Lee's army out of Pennsylvania; and, I think, can ultimately drive it out of existence. But no paper compromise, to which the controllers of Lee's army are not agreed, can at all affect that army. In an effort at such compromise we should waste time, which the enemy would improve to our disadvantage; and that would be all. A compromise, to be effective, must be made either with those who control the rebel army, or with the people first liberated from the domination of that army, by the success of our own army. Now allow me to assure you, that no word or intimation, from that rebel army, or from any of the men controlling it, in relation to any peace compromise, has ever come to my knowledge or belief. All charges and insinuations to the contrary, are deceptive and groundless. And I promise you, that if any such proposition shall hereafter come, it shall not be rejected, and kept a secret from you. I freely acknowledge myself the servant of the people, according to the bond of service—the United States Constitution; and that, as such, I am responsible to them.

But to be plain, you are dissatisfied with me about the negro. Quite likely there is a difference of opinion between you and myself upon that subject. I certainly wish that all men could be free, while I suppose you do not. Yet I have neither adopted, nor proposed any measure, which is not consistent with even your view, provided you are for the Union. I suggested compensated emancipation; to which you replied you wished not to be taxed to buy negroes. But I had not asked you to be taxed to buy negroes, except in such way, as to save you from greater taxation to save the Union exclusively by other means.

You dislike the emancipation proclamation; and, perhaps, would have it retracted. You say it is unconstitutional—I think differently. I think the constitution invests its Commander-in-chief, with the law of war, in time of war. The most that can be said, if so much, is, that slaves are property. Is there—has there ever been—any question that by the law of war, property, both of enemies and friends, may be taken when needed? And is it not needed whenever taking it, helps us, or hurts the enemy? Armies, the world over, destroy enemie's property when they can not use it; and even destroy their own to keep it from the enemy. Civilized belligerents do all in their power to help themselves, or hurt the enemy, except a few things regarded as barbarous or cruel. Among the exceptions are the massacre of vanquished foes, and noncombatants, male and female.

But the proclamation, as law, either is valid, or is not valid. If it is not valid, it needs no retraction. If it is valid, it can not be retracted, any more than the dead can be brought to life. Some of you profess to think its retraction would operate favorably for the Union. Why better *after* the retraction, than *before* the issue? There was more than a year and a half of trial to suppress the rebellion before the proclamation issued, the last one hundred days of which passed under an explicit notice that it was coming, unless averted by those in revolt, returning to their allegiance. The war has certainly progressed as favorably for us, since the issue of the proclamation as before. I know, as fully as one can know the opinions of others, that some of the commanders of our armies in the field who have given us our most important successes believe the emancipation policy and the use of the colored troops constitute the heaviest blow yet dealt to the Rebellion, and that at least one of these important successes could not have been achieved when it was but for the aid of black soldiers. Among the commanders holding these views are some who have never had any affinity with what is called abolitionism or with the Republican party policies but who held them purely as military opinions. I submit these opinions as being entitled to some weight against the objections often urged that emancipation and arming the blacks are unwise as military measures and were not adopted as such in good faith.

You say you will not fight to free negroes. Some of them seem willing to fight for you; but, no matter. Fight you, then, exclusively to save the Union. I issued the proclamation on purpose to aid you in saving the Union. Whenever you shall have conquered all resistance to the Union, if I shall urge you to continue fighting, it will be an apt time, then, for you to declare you will not fight to free negroes.

I thought that in your struggle for the Union, to whatever extent the negroes should cease helping the enemy, to that extent it weakened the enemy in his resistance to you. Do you think differently? I thought that whatever negroes can be got to do as soldiers, leaves just so much less for white soldiers to do, in saving the Union. Does it appear otherwise to you? But negroes, like other people, act upon motives. Why should they do any thing for us, if we will do nothing for them? If they stake their lives for us, they must be prompted by the strongest motive—even the promise of freedom. And the promise being made, must be kept.

The signs look better. The Father of Waters again goes unvexed to the sea. Thanks to the great Northwest for it. Nor yet wholly to them. Three hundred miles up, they met New England, Empire, Key-stone, and Jersey, hewing their way right and left. The Sunny South too, in more colors than one, also lent a hand. On the spot, their part of the history was jotted down in black and white. The job was a great national one; and let none be banned who bore an honorable part in it. And while those who have cleared the great river may well be proud, even that is not all. It is hard to say that anything has been more bravely, and well done, than at Antietam, Murfreesboro, Gettysburg, and on many fields of lesser note. Nor must Uncle Sam's web-feet be forgotten. At all the watery margins they have been present. Not only on the deep sea, the broad bay, and the rapid river, but also up the narrow muddy bayou, and wherever the ground was a little damp, they have been, and made their tracks. Thanks to all. For the great republic—for the principle it lives by, and keeps alive—for man's vast future—thanks to all.

Peace does not appear so distant as it did. I hope it will come soon, and come to stay; and so come as to be worth the keeping in all future time. It will then have been proved that, among free men, there can be no successful appeal from the ballot to the bullet; and that they who take such appeal are sure to lose their case, and pay the cost. And then, there will be some black men who can remember that, with silent tongue, and clenched teeth, and steady eye, and well-poised bayonet, they have helped mankind on to this great consummation; while, I fear, there will be some white ones, unable to forget that, with malignant heart, and deceitful speech, they strove to hinder it.

Still, let us not be over-sanguine of a speedy final triumph. Let us be quite sober. Let us diligently apply the means, never doubting that a just God, in his own good time, will give us the rightful result.

Yours very truly

A. Lincoln.

ADDRESS DELIVERED AT THE DEDICATION OF THE CEMETERY AT GETTYSBURG
NOVEMBER 19, 1863

In November, Lincoln was invited to make "a few appropriate remarks" at the dedication of a national cemetery created on the site of the battle of Gettysburg, which was fought in July 1863. The feature speaker, however, was not Lincoln, whose presence was required to dignify the occasion, but the notable orator, Edward Everett. Everett's speech lasted about two hours while Lincoln's speech lasted about three minutes. Lincoln's 272 words at Gettysburg poetically distilled the essence of the American creed. The "Four score and seven years" of the speech—the term score was used by the King James Bible to designate a period of twenty years—placed the nation's birth at 1776, the year of the Declaration thereby emphasizing that equality was the "central idea" of the American experiment. A biblical cadence, ethos, and style pervaded the speech. The religious metaphors of death, redemption, and re-birth symbolically conveyed the nation's sacrificial suffering for its political faith in the Declaration. The blood of the nation's soldiers symbolically redeemed the nation from the original sin of slavery, leading to "a new birth of freedom," a Union freed from the stain of human servitude. Significantly, when speaking of the dead, Lincoln made no distinction between the South and the North, implicitly recognizing the courage and sacrifice of both sides. The memorable expression "of the people, by the people, for the people" continues to resonate throughout the world as one of the most terse definitions of democracy.

FOUR SCORE AND SEVEN YEARS AGO our fathers brought forth on this continent, a new nation, conceived in Liberty, and dedicated to the proposition that all men are created equal.

Now we are engaged in a great civil war, testing whether that nation, or any nation so conceived and so dedicated, can long endure. We are met on a great battle-field of that war. We have come to dedicate a portion of that field, as a final resting place for those who here gave their lives that that nation might live. It is altogether fitting and proper that we should do this.

But, in a larger sense, we can not dedicate—we can not consecrate—we can not hallow—this ground. The brave men, living and dead, who struggled here, have consecrated it, far above our poor power to add or detract. The world will little note, nor long remember what we say here, but it can never forget what they did here. It is for us the living, rather, to be dedicated here to the unfinished work which they who fought here have thus far so nobly advanced. It is rather for us to be here dedicated to the great task remaining before us—that from these honored dead we take increased devotion to that cause for which they gave the last full measure of devotion—that we here highly resolve that these dead shall not have died in vain—that this nation, under God, shall have a new birth of freedom—and that government of the people, by the people, for the people, shall not perish from the earth.

Abraham Lincoln.

November 19, 1863.

PROCLAMATION OF AMNESTY AND RECONSTRUCTION
DECEMBER 8, 1863

Lincoln's Proclamation of December 8 explained his Ten Percent Plan for Reconstruction. Lincoln offered a pardon to all members of the Confederacy who would swear an oath of loyalty to the Union and who would recognize the Emancipation. Lincoln's plan maintained that if one tenth of a seceded states' population swore an oath of loyalty, it would be re-admitted to the Union. Radical critics believed that his policy was far too lenient toward the South and even undemocratic since only a ten percent vote was needed to form a reconstructed government.

BY THE PRESIDENT OF THE UNITED STATES OF AMERICA:
A PROCLAMATION.

Whereas, in and by the Constitution of the United States, it is provided that the President "shall have power to grant reprieves and pardons for offences against the United States, except in cases of impeachment;" and

Whereas a rebellion now exists whereby the loyal State governments of several States have for a long time been subverted, and many persons have committed and are now guilty of treason against the United States; and

Whereas, with reference to said rebellion and treason, laws have been enacted by Congress, declaring forfeitures and confiscation of property and liberation of slaves, all upon terms and conditions therein stated, and also declaring that the President was thereby authorized at any time thereafter, by proclamation, to extend to persons who may have participated in the existing rebellion, in any State or part thereof, pardon and amnesty, with such exceptions and at such times and on such conditions as he may deem expedient for the public welfare; and

Whereas the congressional declaration for limited and conditional pardon accords with well-established judicial exposition of the pardoning power; and

Whereas, with reference to said rebellion, the President of the United States has issued several proclamations, with provisions in regard to the liberation of slaves; and

Whereas it is now desired by some persons heretofore engaged in said rebellion to resume their allegiance to the United States, and to reinaugurate loyal State governments within and for their respective States; therefore,

I, Abraham Lincoln, President of the United States, do proclaim, declare, and make known to all persons who have, directly or by implication, participated in the existing rebellion, except as hereinafter excepted, that a full pardon is hereby granted to them and each of them, with restoration of all rights of property, except as to slaves, and in property cases where rights of third parties shall have intervened, and upon the condition that every such person shall take and subscribe an oath, and thenceforward keep and maintain said oath inviolate; and which oath shall be registered for permanent preservation, and shall be of the tenor and effect following, to wit:

"I, _____, do solemnly swear, in presence of Almighty God, that I will henceforth faithfully support, protect and defend the Constitution of the United States, and the union of the States thereunder; and that I will, in like manner, abide by and faithfully support all acts of Congress passed during the existing rebellion with reference to slaves, so long and so far as not repealed, modified or held void by Congress, or by decision of the Supreme Court; and that I will, in like manner, abide by and faithfully support all proclamations of the President made during the existing rebellion having reference to slaves, so long and so far as not modified or declared void by decision of the Supreme Court. So help me God."

The persons excepted from the benefits of the foregoing provisions are all who are, or shall have been, civil or diplomatic officers or agents of the so-called confederate government; all who have left judicial stations under the United States to aid the rebellion; all who are, or shall have been, military or naval officers of said so-called confederate government above the rank of colonel in the army, or of lieutenant in the navy; all who left seats in the United States Congress to aid the rebellion; all who resigned commissions in the army or navy of the United States, and afterwards aided the rebellion; and all who have engaged in any way in treating colored persons or white persons, in charge of such, otherwise than lawfully as prisoners of war, and which persons may have been found in the United States service, as soldiers, seamen, or in any other capacity.

And I do further proclaim, declare, and make known that whenever, in any of the States of Arkansas, Texas, Louisiana, Mississippi, Tennessee, Alabama, Georgia, Florida, South Carolina, and North Carolina, a number of persons, not less than one-tenth in number of the votes cast in such State at the Presidential election of the year of our Lord one thousand eight hundred and sixty, each having taken the oath aforesaid and not having since violated it, and being a qualified voter by the election law of the State existing immediately before the so-called act of secession, and excluding all others, shall re-establish a State government which shall be republican, and in no wise contravening said oath, such shall be recognized as the true government of the State, and the State shall receive thereunder the benefits of the constitutional provision which declares that "The United States shall guaranty to every State in this union a republican form of government, and shall protect each of them against invasion; and, on application of the legislature, or the executive, (when the legislature cannot be convened,) against domestic violence."

And I do further proclaim, declare, and make known that any provision which may be adopted by such State government in relation to the freed people of such State, which shall recognize and declare their permanent freedom, provide for their education, and which may yet be consistent, as a temporary arrangement, with their present condition as a laboring, landless, and homeless class, will not be objected to by the national Executive. And it is suggested as not improper, that, in constructing a loyal State government in any State, the name of the State, the boundary, the subdivisions, the constitution, and the general code of laws, as before the rebellion, be maintained, subject only to the modifications made necessary by the conditions hereinbefore stated, and such others, if any, not contravening said conditions, and which may be deemed expedient by those framing the new State government.

To avoid misunderstanding, it may be proper to say that this proclamation, so far as it relates to State governments, has no reference to States wherein loyal State governments have all the while been maintained. And for the same reason, it may be proper to further say that whether members sent to Congress from any

State shall be admitted to seats, constitutionally rests exclusively with the respective Houses, and not to any extent with the Executive. And still further, that this proclamation is intended to present the people of the States wherein the national authority has been suspended, and loyal State governments have been subverted, a mode in and by which the national authority and loyal State governments may be re-established within said States, or in any of them; and, while the mode presented is the best the Executive can suggest, with his present impressions, it must not be understood that no other possible mode would be acceptable.

[L. S.] Given under my hand at the city of Washington, the 8th day of December, A. D. one thousand eight hundred and sixty-three, and of the independence of the United States of America the eighty-eighth.

By the President: Abraham Lincoln.

William H. Seward, *Secretary of State*

TO FREDERICK STEELE[2]
JANUARY 20, 1864

Lincoln directed General Frederick Steele to oversee reconstruction in Arkansas. Consistent with his efforts to permanently end slavery through legal means, Lincoln proposed that Arkansas's constitution be revised to abolish human servitude.

EXECUTIVE MANSION WASHINGTON, D.C.
MAJOR GENERAL STEELE
JAN. 20, 1864.

Sundry citizens of the State of Arkansas petition me that an election may be held in that State, at which to elect a Governor thereof; that it be assumed at said election, and thenceforward, that the constitution and laws of the State, as before the rebellion, are in full force, except that the constitution is so modified as to declare that "There shall be neither slavery nor involuntary servitude, except in the punishment of crime whereof the party shall have been duly convicted; but the General Assembly may make such provision for the freed-people as shall recognize and declare their permanent freedom, provide for their education, and which may yet be consistent, as a temporary arrangement, with their present condition as a laboring, landless, and homeless class"; and also except that all now existing laws in relation to slaves are inoperative and void; that said election be held on the twentyeighth day of March next, at all the usual voting places of the

2. *CWAL,* VII, 141-142.

State, or all such as voters may attend for that purpose; that the voters attending at each place, at eight o'clock in the morning of said day, may choose Judges and Clerks of election for that place; that all persons qualified by said constitution and laws, and taking the oath prescribed in the Presidents proclamation of December the 8th. 1863, either before or at the election, and none others, may be voters provided that persons having the qualifications aforesaid, and being in the Volunteer military service of the United States, may vote once wherever this may be at voting places; that each sett of Judges and Clerks may make return directly to you, on or before the eleventh day of April next; that in all other respects said election may be conducted according to said modified constitution, and laws; that, on receipt of said returns, you count said votes, and that, if the number shall reach, or exceed, five thousand four hundred and six, you canvass said votes and ascertain who shall thereby appear to have been elected Governor; and that on the eighteenth day of April next, the person so appearing to have been elected, and appearing before you at Little Rock, to have, by you, administered to him, an oath to support the constitution of the United States and said modified constitution of the State of Arkansas, and actually taking said oath, be by you declared qualified, and be enjoined to immediately enter upon the duties of the office of Governor of said State; and that you thereupon declare the constitution of the State of Arkansas to have been modified and amended as aforesaid, by the action of the people as aforesaid.

You will please order an election immediately, and perform the other parts assigned you, with necessary incidentals, all according to the foregoing. Yours truly   A. LINCOLN

LETTER TO GOVERNOR MICHAEL HAHN
MARCH 13, 1864

Governor Hahn was the recently elected free state governor of Louisiana who was endorsed by General Banks under Lincoln's Ten Percent Reconstruction Plan. As seen, because the Emancipation did not apply to sections of Louisiana, there were fears that a reconstructed government may try to reestablish the institution. After black representatives petitioned him to grant suffrage to African-Americans in Louisiana, Lincoln wrote the letter to Hahn two days later. Although he maintained that it was beyond the authority of the national government to confer suffrage upon blacks (before the Fifteenth Amendment, the authority to confer suffrage upon citizens was left to the individual states), Lincoln suggested, in an advisory capacity only, that the State of Louisiana should grant suffrage to at least some of its African-American citizens, especially those who fought for the Union.

The efforts of Louisiana to do this would keep, "the jewel of liberty within the family of freedom." Thus, in Lincoln's view, suffrage was a precious heirloom to be bequeathed to the entire human family, not just those of white, European ancestry.

PRIVATE

EXECUTIVE MANSION,

WASHINGTON, MARCH 13, 1864.

HON. MICHAEL HAHN

MY DEAR SIR:

I congratulate you on having fixed your name in history as the first-free-state Governor of Louisiana Now you are about to have a Convention which, among other things, will probably define the elective franchise. I barely suggest for your private consideration, whether some of the colored people may not be let in—as, for instance, the very intelligent, and especially those who have fought gallantly in our ranks. They would probably help, in some trying time to come, to keep the jewel of liberty within the family of freedom. But this is only a suggestion, not to the public, but to you alone.

Yours truly

A. Lincoln

ADDRESS AT A SANITARY FAIR IN BALTIMORE
APRIL 18, 1864

During the Civil War, Sanitary Fairs functioned very much like the Red Cross in caring for wounded soldiers. In this speech, Lincoln philosophically examined the elusive term "liberty." As he emphasized in his House Divided Speech in 1858, the resolution of political conflict presumed a tacit moral consensus over the substantive meaning of political principles like liberty. The fundamental breakdown over the meaning of such principles helped to precipitate the war. Indeed, the liberty of the slaveholder to exploit human chattel was diametrically opposed to the liberty of the slave and the God given right of each human being to enjoy the fruits of his or her own labor. Lincoln's political thought developed as a concrete response to clarify and define the philosophical basis of the nation's first principles. He noted the paradox between liberty's elusiveness on the one hand, and its centrality to popular government on the other. A tone of righteous indignation also pervades the speech. Lincoln warned that those responsible for the Fort Pillow Massacre in which black soldiers were ruthlessly butchered after they had surrendered would be held accountable for their actions. One of the leaders of the Fort Pillow Massacre was the notorious cavalryman Nathan Bedford Forest, the future founder of the Ku, Klux, Klan.

LADIES AND GENTLEMEN—

Calling to mind that we are in Baltimore, we can not fail to note that the world moves. Looking upon these many people, assembled here, to serve, as they best may, the soldiers of the Union, it occurs at once that three years ago the same soldiers could not so much as pass through Baltimore. The change from then till now, is both great, and gratifying. Blessings on the brave men who have wrought the change, and the fair women who strive to reward them for it.

But Baltimore suggests more than could happen within Baltimore. The change within Baltimore is part only of a far wider change. When the war began, three years ago, neither party, nor any man, expected it would last till now. Each looked for the end, in some way, long ere to-day. Neither did any anticipate that domestic slavery would be much affected by the war. But here we are; the war has not ended, and slavery has been much affected—how much needs not now to be recounted. So true is it that man proposes, and God disposes.

But we can see the past, though we may not claim to have directed it; and seeing it, in this case, we feel more hopeful and confident for the future.

The world has never had a good definition of the word liberty, and the American people, just now, are much in want of one. We all declare for liberty; but in using the same *word* we do not all mean the same *thing*. With some the word liberty may mean for each man to do as he pleases with himself, and the product of his labor; while with others the same word may mean for some men to do as they please with other men, and the product of other men's labor. Here are two, not only different, but incompatable [*sic*] things, called by the same name—liberty. And it follows that each of the things is, by the respective parties, called by two different and incompatable [*sic*] names—liberty and tyranny.

The shepherd drives the wolf from the sheep's throat, for which the sheep thanks the shepherd as a *liberator,* while the wolf denounces him for the same act as the destroyer of liberty, especially as the sheep was a black one. Plainly the sheep and the wolf are not agreed upon a definition of the word liberty; and precisely the same difference prevails to-day among us human creatures, even in the North, and all professing to love liberty. Hence we behold the processes by which thousands are daily passing from under the yoke of bondage, hailed by some as the advance of liberty, and bewailed by others as the destruction of all liberty. Recently, as it seems, the people of Maryland have been doing something to define liberty; and thanks to them that, in what they have done, the wolf's dictionary, has been repudiated.

It is not very becoming for one in my position to make speeches at great length; but there is another subject upon which I feel that I ought to say a word.

A painful rumor, true I fear, has reached us of the massacre, by the rebel forces, at Fort Pillow, in the West end of Tennessee, on the Mississippi river, of some three hundred colored soldiers and white officers, who had just been overpowered by their assailants. There seems to be some anxiety in the public mind whether the government is doing it's duty to the colored soldier, and to the service, at this point. At the beginning of the war, and for some time, the use of colored troops was not contemplated; and how the change of purpose was wrought, I will not now take time to explain. Upon a clear conviction of duty I resolved to turn that element of strength to account; and I am responsible for it to the American people, to the Christian world, to history, and on my final account, to God. Having determined to use the negro as a soldier, there is no way but to give him all the protection given to any other soldier. The difficulty is not in stating the principle, but in practically applying it. It is a mistake to suppose the government is indiffent [sic] to this matter, or is not doing the best it can in regard to it. We do not to-day *know* that a colored soldier, or white officer commanding colored soldiers, has been massacred by the rebels when made a prisoner. We fear it, believe it, I may say, but we do not know it. To take the life of one of their prisoners, on the assumption that they murder ours, when it is short of certainty that they do murder ours, might be too serious, too cruel a mistake. We are having the Fort-Pillow affair thoroughly investigated; and such investigation will probably show conclusively how the truth is. If, after all that has been said, it shall turn out that there has been no massacre at Fort-Pillow, it will be almost safe to say there has been none, and will be none elsewhere. If there has been the massacre of three hundred there, or even the tenth part of three hundred, it will be conclusively proved; and being so proved, the retribution shall as surely come. It will be matter of grave consideration in what exact course to apply the retribution; but in the supposed case, it must come.

LETTER TO CHARLES D. ROBINSON[3]
AUGUST 17, 1864

Charles Robinson, a War Democrat and editor of a Wisconsin newspaper, asked Lincoln to clarify his war aims as stated in his reply to Horace Greeley's Prayer of Twenty Million (see above). If Lincoln demanded the abolition of slavery as a condition of peace, then Robinson made it clear that he could not support Lincoln's candidacy for reelection in 1864. Lincoln wrote, but never sent this reply to Robinson. Lincoln viewed the service of black regiments in the Union army as a prudent step toward black freedom. The sacri-

3. *CWAL*, VII, 499-502.

fice of blacks on the battlefield would help dispose public opinion toward the goal of black freedom: how could the public deny blacks their freedom and even the right to vote if they were willing to make the supreme sacrifice in serving their country? The letter reveals something of Lincoln's pathos regarding black freedom and his scorn for those who would return the freedmen to slavery.

HON. CHARLES D. ROBINSON
EXECUTIVE MANSION,
MY DEAR SIR:
WASHINGTON, AUGUST 17, 1864.

Your letter of the 7th. was placed in my hand yesterday by Gov. Randall.

To me it seems plain that saying re-union and abandonment of slavery would be considered, if offered, is not saying that nothing *else* or *less* would be considered, if offered. But I will not stand upon the mere construction of language. It is true, as you remind me, that in the Greeley letter of 1862, I said: "If I could save the Union without freeing any slave I would do it; and if I could save it by freeing all the slaves I would do it; and if I could save it by freeing some, and leaving others alone I would also do that." I continued in the same letter as follows: "What I do about slavery and the colored race, I do because I believe it helps to save the Union; and what I forbear I forbear because I do not believe it would help to save the Union. I shall do less whenever I shall believe what I am doing hurts the cause; and I shall do more whenever I shall believe doing more will help the cause." All this I said in the utmost sincerety; and I am as true to the whole of it now, as when I first said it. When I afterwards proclaimed emancipation, and employed colored soldiers, I only followed the declaration just quoted from the Greeley letter that "I shall do *more* whenever I shall believe *doing* more will help the cause" The way these measures were to help the cause, was not to be by magic, or miracles, but by inducing the colored people to come bodily over from the rebel side to ours. On this point, nearly a year ago, in a letter to Mr. Conkling, made public at once, I wrote as follows: "But negroes, like other people, act upon motives. Why should they do anything for us if we will do nothing for them? If they stake their lives for us they must be prompted by the strongest motive—even the promise of freedom. And the promise, being made, must be kept." I am sure you will not, on due reflection, say that the promise being made, must be *broken* at the first opportunity. I am sure you would not desire me to say, or to leave an inference, that I am ready, whenever convenient, to join in re-enslaving those who shall have served us in consideration of our promise. As matter of morals, could such treachery by any possibility, escape the curses of Heaven, or of any good man? As matter of policy, to *announce* such a purpose, would ruin the Union cause itself. All recruiting of colored men would instantly cease, and all colored men now in our service, would instantly desert us. And rightfully too. Why should they give their lives for us, with full notice of our purpose to betray them? Drive back to the support of the rebellion the physical force which the colored people now give, and promise us, and neither the present, nor any coming administration, *can* save the Union. Take from us, and give to the enemy, the hundred and thirty, forty, or fifty thousand colored persons now serving us as soldiers, seamen, and laborers, and we can not longer maintain the contest. The party who could elect a President on a War & Slavery Restoration platform, would, of necessity, lose the colored force; and that force being lost, would be as powerless to save the Union as to do any other impossible thing. It is not a question of sentiment or taste, but one of physical force, which may be measured, and estimated as horsepower, and steam power, are measured and estimated. And by measurement, it is more than we can lose, and live. Nor can we, by discarding it, get a white force in place of it. There is a witness in every white mans bosom that he would rather go to the war having the negro to help him, than to help the enemy against him. It is not the giving of one class for another. It is simply giving a large force to the enemy, for *nothing* in return.

In addition to what I have said, allow me to remind you that no one, having control of the rebel armies, or, in fact, having any influence whatever in the rebellion, has offered, or intimated a willingness to, a restoration of the Union, in any event, or on any condition whatever. Let it be constantly borne in mind that no such offer has been made or intimated. Shall we be weak enough to allow the enemy to distract us with an abstract question which he himself refuses to present as a practical one? In the Conkling letter before mentioned, I said: "Whenever you shall have conquered all resistance to the Union, if I shall urge you to continue fighting, it will be an apt time *then* to declare that you will not fight to free negroes." I repeat this now. If Jefferson Davis wishes, for himself, or for the benefit of his friends at the North, to know what I would do if he were to offer peace and re-union, saying nothing about slavery, let him try me.

LETTER TO HENRY W. HOFFMAN
OCTOBER 10, 1864

Henry W. Hoffman was a chairman of the Maryland Unconditional Union Central Committee. He asked Lincoln to attend a meeting to support the ratification of a new free state Maryland Constitution that would abolish slavery. Lincoln did not attend the meeting, but wrote this letter to Hoffman, which was to be read out loud to the assembly.

EXECUTIVE MANSION,
WASHINGTON, OCTOBER 10, 1864.
HON. HENRY W HOFFMAN
MY DEAR SIR:

A convention of Maryland has framed a new constitution for the State; a public meeting is called for this evening, at Baltimore, to aid in securing its ratification by the people; and you ask a word from me, for the occasion. I presume the only feature of the instrument, about which there is serious controversy, is that which provides for the extinction of slavery. It needs not to be a secret, and I presume it is no secret, that I wish success to this provision. I desire it on every consideration. I wish all men to be free. I wish the material prosperity of the already free which I feel sure the extinction of slavery would bring. I wish to see, in process of disappearing, that only thing which ever could bring this nation to civil war. I attempt no argument. Argument upon the question is already exhausted by the abler, better posted, and more immediately interested sons of Maryland herself. I only add that I shall be gratified exceedingly if the good people of the State shall by their votes, ratify the new constitution.

Yours truly
A. Lincoln

RESPONSE TO A SERENADE
NOVEMBER 10, 1864

After the election of 1864, a group came to celebrate the president's victory by serenading him on the White House lawn one evening. In his reply to the serenaders, Lincoln describes the wider significance of the election, demonstrating to the world and the nation that the democratic process would continue, even in a time of crisis.

(NOV. 10, 1864)

It has long been a grave question whether any government, not *too* strong for the liberties of its people, can be strong *enough* to maintain its own existence in great emergencies.

On this point the present rebellion brought our republic to a severe test; and a presidential election occurring in regular course during the rebellion added not a little to the strain. If the loyal people, *united,* were put to the utmost of their strength by the rebellion, must they not fail when *divided,* and partially par- alized [*sic*], by a political war among themselves?

But the election was a necessity.

We can not have free government without elections; and if the rebellion could force us to forego, or postpone a national election, it might fairly claim to have already conquered and ruined us. The strife of the election is but human-nature practically applied to the facts of the case. What has occurred in this case, must ever recur in similar cases. Human-nature will not change. In any future great national trial, compared with the men of this, we shall have as weak, and as strong; as silly and as wise; as bad and good. Let us, therefore, study the incidents of this, as philosophy to learn wisdom from, and none of them as wrongs to be revenged.

But the election, along with its incidental, and undesirable strife, has done good too. It has demonstrated that a people's government can sustain a national election, in the midst of a great civil war. Until now it has not been known to the world that this was a possibility. It shows also how *sound,* and how *strong* we still are. It shows that, even among candidates of the same party, he who is most devoted to the Union, and most opposed to treason, can receive most of the people's votes. It shows also, to the extent yet known, that we have more men now, than we had when the war began. Gold is good in its place; but living, brave, patriotic men, are better than gold.

But the rebellion continues; and now that the election is over, may not all, having a common interest, re-unite in a common effort, to save our common country? For my own part I have striven, and shall strive to avoid placing any obstacle in the way. So long as I have been here I have not willingly planted a thorn in any man's bosom.

While I am deeply sensible to the high compliment of a re-election; and duly grateful, as I trust, to Almighty God for having directed my countrymen to a right conclusion, as I think, for their own good, it adds nothing to my satisfaction that any other man may be disappointed or pained by the result.

May I ask those who have not differed with me, to join with me, in this same spirit towards those who have?

And now, let me close by asking three hearty cheers for our brave soldiers and seamen and their gallant and skilful commanders.

LETTER TO MRS. BIXBY
NOVEMBER 21, 1864

EXECUTIVE MANSION,
WASHINGTON, NOV. 21, 1864.
DEAR MADAM,—

I have been shown in the files of the war Department a statement of the Adjutant General of Massachusetts, that you are the mother of five sons who have died gloriously on the field of battle.

I feel how weak and fruitless must be any word of mine which should attempt to beguile you from the grief of a loss so overwhelming. But I cannot refrain from tendering to you the consolation that may be found in the thanks of the Republic they died to save.

I pray that our Heavenly Father may assuage the anguish of your bereavement, and leave you only the cherished memory of the loved and lost, and the solemn pride that must be yours, to have laid so costly a sacrifice upon the altar of Freedom.

Yours, very sincerely and respectfully,
A. Lincoln
Mrs. Bixby.

ANNUAL MESSAGE TO CONGRESS
DECEMBER 6, 1864

Lincoln's Annual Message to Congress on the State of the Union reviewed diverse topics ranging from the war, peace negotiations, General Sherman's march through Georgia, organization of new territories, immigration, and the recent abolition of slavery in Maryland. Towards the end of the speech, he expressed his support of the Thirteenth Amendment that would forever abolish slavery throughout the entire union, including the Border States. Although the House of Representatives failed to pass the amendment by the necessary two-thirds in the past session of Congress, it approved it in late January 1865 by two votes.

FELLOW-CITIZENS OF THE SENATE AND HOUSE OF REPRESENTATIVES:

Again the blessings of health and abundant harvests claim our profoundest gratitude to Almighty God.

The condition of our foreign affairs is reasonably satisfactory.

Mexico continues to be a theatre of civil war. While our political relations with that country have undergone no change, we have, at the same time, strictly maintained neutrality between the belligerents.

At the request of the states of Costa Rica and Nicaragua, a competent engineer has been authorized to make a survey of the River San Juan and the port of San Juan. It is a source of much satisfaction that the difficulties which for a moment excited some political apprehensions, and caused a closing of the interoceanic transit route, have been amicably adjusted, and that there is a good prospect that the route will soon be reopened with an increase of capacity and adaptation. We could not exaggerate either the commercial or the political importance of that great improvement.

It would be doing injustice to an important South American state not to acknowledge the directness, frankness, and cordiality with which the United States of Colombia have entered into intimate relations with this government. A claims convention has been constituted to complete the unfinished work of the one which closed its session in 1861.

The new liberal constitution of Venezuela having gone into effect with the universal acquiescence of the people, the government under it has been recognized, and diplomatic intercourse with it has opened in a cordial and friendly spirit. The long-deferred Aves Island claim has been satisfactorily paid and discharged.

Mutual payments have been made of the claims awarded by the late joint commission for the settlement of claims between the United States and Peru. An earnest and cordial friendship continues to exist between the two countries, and such efforts as were in my power have been used to remove misunderstanding and avert a threatened war between Peru and Spain.

Our relations are of the most friendly nature with Chile, the Argentine Republic, Bolivia, Costa Rica, Paraguay, San Salvador, and Hayti.

During the past year no differences of any kind have arisen with any of those republics, and, on the other hand, their sympathies with the United States are constantly expressed with cordiality and earnestness.

The claim arising from the seizure of the cargo of the brig Macedonian in 1821 has been paid in full by the government of Chile.

Civil war continues in the Spanish part of San Domingo, apparently without prospect of an early close.

Official correspondence has been freely opened with Liberia, and it gives us a pleasing view of social and political progress in that Republic. It may be expected to derive new vigor from American influence, improved by the rapid disappearance of slavery in the United States.

I solicit your authority to furnish to the republic a gunboat at moderate cost, to be reimbursed to the United States by instalments. Such a vessel is needed for the safety of that state against the native African races; and in Liberian hands it would be more effective in arresting the African slave trade than a squadron in our own hands. The possession of the least organized naval force would stimulate a generous ambition in the republic, and the confidence which we should manifest by furnishing it would win forbearance and favor towards the colony from all civilized nations.

The proposed overland telegraph between America and Europe, by the way of Behring's Straits and Asiatic Russia, which was sanctioned by Congress at the last session, has been undertaken, under very favorable circumstances, by an association of American citizens, with the cordial good-will and support as well of this government as of those of Great Britain and Russia. Assurances have been received from most of the South American States of their high appreciation of the enterprise, and their readiness to co-operate in constructing lines tributary to that world-encircling communication. I learn, with much satisfaction, that the noble design of a telegraphic communication between the eastern coast of America and Great Britain has been renewed with full expectation of its early accomplishment.

Thus it is hoped that with the return of domestic peace the country will be able to resume with energy and advantage its former high career of commerce and civilization.

Our very popular and estimable representative in Egypt died in April last. An unpleasant altercation which arose between the temporary incumbent of the office and the government of the Pacha resulted in a suspension of intercourse. The evil was promptly corrected on the arrival of the successor in the consulate, and our relations with Egypt, as well as our relations with the Barbary powers, are entirely satisfactory.

The rebellion which has so long been flagrant in China, has at last been suppressed, with the co-operating good offices of this government, and of the other western commercial states. The judicial consular establishment there has become very difficult and onerous, and it will need legislative revision to adapt it to the extension of our commerce, and to the more intimate intercourse which has been instituted with the government and people of that vast empire. China seems to be accepting with hearty good-will the conventional laws which regulate commercial and social intercourse among the western nations.

Owing to the peculiar situation of Japan, and the anomalous form of its government, the action of that empire in performing treaty stipulations is inconstant and capricious. Nevertheless, good progress has been effected by the western powers, moving with enlightened concert. Our own pecuniary claims have been allowed, or put in course of settlement, and the inland sea has been reopened to commerce. There is reason also to believe that these proceedings have increased rather than diminished the friendship of Japan towards the United States.

The ports of Norfolk, Fernandina, and Pensacola have been opened by proclamation. It is hoped that foreign merchants will now consider whether it is not safer and more profitable to themselves, as well as just to the United States, to resort to these and other open ports, than it is to pursue, through many hazards, and at vast cost, a contraband trade with other ports which are closed, if not by actual military occupation, at least by a lawful and effective blockade.

For myself, I have no doubt of the power and duty of the Executive, under the law of nations, to exclude enemies of the human race from an asylum in the United States. If Congress should think that proceedings in such cases lack the authority of law, or ought to be further regulated by it, I recommend that provision be made for effectually preventing foreign slave traders from acquiring domicile and facilities for their criminal occupation in our country.

It is possible that, if it were a new and open question, the maritime powers, with the lights they now enjoy, would not concede the privileges of a naval belligerent to the insurgents of the United States, destitute, as they are, and always have been, equally of ships-of-war and of ports and harbors. Disloyal emissaries have been neither less assiduous nor more successful during the last year than they were before that time in their efforts, under favor of that privilege, to embroil our country in foreign wars. The desire and determination of the governments of the maritime states to defeat that design are believed to be as sincere as, and cannot be more earnest than our own. Nevertheless, unforeseen political difficulties have arisen, especially in Brazilian and British ports, and on the northern boundary of the United States, which have required, and are likely to continue to require, the practice of constant vigilance, and a just and conciliatory spirit on the part of the United States as well as of the nations concerned and their governments.

Commissioners have been appointed under the treaty with Great Britain on the adjustment of the claims of the Hudson's Bay and Puget's Sound Agricultural Companies, in Oregon, and are now proceeding to the execution of the trust assigned to them.

In view of the insecurity of life and property in the region adjacent to the Canadian border, by reason of recent assaults and depredations committed by inimical and desperate persons, who are harbored there, it has been thought proper to give notice that after the expiration of six months, the period conditionally stipulated in the existing arrangement with Great Britain, the United States must hold themselves at liberty to increase their naval armament upon the lakes, if they shall find that proceeding necessary. The condition of the border will necessarily come into consideration in connection with the question of continuing or modifying the rights of transit from Canada through the United States, as well as the regulation of imposts, which were temporarily established by the reciprocity treaty of the 5th of June, 1854.

I desire, however, to be understood, while making this statement, that the Colonial authorities of Canada are not deemed to be intentionally unjust or unfriendly towards the United States; but, on the contrary, there is every reason to expect that, with the approval of the imperial government, they will take the necessary measures to prevent new incursions across the border.

The act passed at the last session for the encouragement of emigration has, so far as was possible, been put into operation. It seems to need amendment which will enable the officers of the government to prevent the practice of frauds against the immigrants while on their way and on their arrival in the ports, so as to secure them here a free choice of avocations and places of settlement. A liberal disposition towards this great national policy is manifested by most of the European States, and ought to be reciprocated on our part by giving the immigrants effective national protection. I regard our emigrants as one of the principal replenishing streams which are appointed by Providence to repair the ravages of internal war, and its wastes of national strength and health. All that is necessary is to secure the flow of that stream in its present fullness, and to that end the government must, in every way, make it manifest that it neither needs nor designs to impose involuntary military service upon those who come from other lands to cast their lot in our country.

The financial affairs of the government have been successfully administered during the last year. The legislation of the last session of Congress has beneficially affected the revenues, although sufficient time has not yet elapsed to experience the full effect of several of the provisions of the acts of Congress imposing increased taxation.

The receipts during the year, from all sources, upon the basis of warrants signed by the Secretary of the Treasury, including loans and the balance in the treasury on the first day of July, 1863, were $1,394,796,007.62; and the aggregate disbursements, upon the same basis, were $1,298,056,101.89, leaving a balance in the treasury, as shown by warrants, of $96,739,905.73.

Deduct from these amounts the amount of the principal of the public debt redeemed, and the amount of issues in substitution therefor, and the actual cash operations of the treasury were: receipts, $884,076,646.57; disbursements, $865,234,087.86; which leaves a cash balance in the treasury of $18,842,558.71.

Of the receipts, there were derived from customs, $102,316,152.99; from lands, $588,333.29; from direct taxes, $475,648.96; from internal revenue, $109,741,134.10; from miscellaneous sources, $47,511,448.10; and from loans applied to actual expenditures, including former balances, $623,443,929.13.

There were disbursed, for the civil service, $27,505,599.46; for pensions and Indians, $7,517,930.97; for the War Department, $690,791,842.97; for the Navy Department, $85,733,292.77; for interest of the public debt, $53,685,421.69;— making an aggregate of $865,234,087.86, and leaving a balance in the treasury of $18,842,558.71, as before stated.

For the actual receipts and disbursements for the first quarter, and the estimated receipts and disbursements for the three remaining quarters of the current fiscal year, and the general operations of the treasury in detail, I refer you to the report of the Secretary of the Treasury. I concur with him in the opinion that the proportion of moneys required to meet the expenses consequent upon the war derived from taxation should be still further increased; and I earnestly invite your attention to this subject, to the end that there may be such additional legislation as shall be required to meet the just expectations of the Secretary.

The public debt on the first day of July last, as appears by the books of the treasury, amounted to $1,740,690,489.49. Probably, should the war continue for another year, that amount may be increased by not far from five hundred millions. Held as it is, for the most part, by our own people, it has become a substantial branch of national though private, property. For obvious reasons, the more nearly this property can be distributed among all the people the better. To favor such general distribution, greater inducements to become owners might, perhaps, with good effect, and without injury, be presented to persons of limited means. With this view, I suggest whether it might not be both competent and expedient for Congress to provide that a limited amount of some future issue of public securities might be held by any bona-fide purchaser exempt from taxation, and from seizure for debt, under such restrictions and limitations as might be necessary to guard against abuse of so important a privilege. This would enable every prudent person to set aside a small annuity against a possible day of want.

Privileges like these would render the possession of such securities, to the amount limited, most desirable to every person of small means who might be able to save enough for the purpose. The great advantage of citizens being creditors as well as debtors, with relation to the public debt, is obvious. Men readily perceive that they cannot be much oppressed by a debt which they owe to themselves.

The public debt on the first day of July last, although somewhat exceeding the estimate of the Secretary of the Treasury made to Congress at the commencement of the last session, falls short of the estimate of that officer made in the preceding December, as to its probable amount at the beginning of this year, by the sum of $3,995,097.31. This fact exhibits a satisfactory condition and conduct of the operations of the treasury.

The national banking system is proving to be acceptable to capitalists and to the people. On the twenty-fifth day of November five hundred and eighty-four national banks had been organized, a considerable number of which were conversions from State banks. Changes from State systems to the national system are rapidly taking place, and it is hoped that, very soon, there will be in the United States, no banks of issue not authorized by Congress, and no bank-note circulation not secured by the government. That the government and the people will derive great benefit from this change in the banking systems of the country can hardly be questioned. The national system will create a reliable and permanent influence in support of the national credit, and protect the people against losses in the use of paper money. Whether or not any further legislation is advisable for the suppression of State bank issues, it will be for Congress to determine. It seems quite clear that the treasury cannot be satisfactorily conducted unless the government can exercise a restraining power over the bank-note circulation of the country.

The report of the Secretary of War and the accompanying documents will detail the campaigns of the armies in the field since the date of the last annual message, and also the operations of the several administrative bureaus of the War Department during the last year. It will also specify the measures deemed essential for the national defence, and to keep up and supply the requisite military force.

The report of the Secretary of the Navy presents a comprehensive and satisfactory exhibit of the affairs of that Department and of the naval service. It is a subject of congratulation and laudable pride to our countrymen that a navy of such vast proportions has been organized in so brief a period, and conducted with so much efficiency and success.

The general exhibit of the navy, including vessels under construction on the 1st of December, 1864, shows a total of 671 vessels, carrying 4,610 guns, and

510,396 tons, being an actual increase during the year, over and above all losses by shipwreck or in battle, of 83 vessels, 167 guns, and 42,427 tons.

The total number of men at this time in the naval service, including officers, is about 51,000.

There have been captured by the navy during the year 324 vessels, and the whole number of naval captures since hostilities commenced is 1,379, of which 267 are steamers.

The gross proceeds arising from the sale of condemned prize property, thus far reported, amount to $14,396,250.51. A large amount of such proceeds is still under adjudication and yet to be reported.

The total expenditures of the Navy Department of every description, including the cost of the immense squadrons that have been called into existence from the 4th of March, 1861, to the 1st of November, 1864, are $238,647,262.35.

Your favorable consideration is invited to the various recommendations of the Secretary of the Navy, especially in regard to a navy yard and suitable establishment for the construction and repair of iron vessels, and the machinery and armature for our ships, to which reference was made in my last annual message.

Your attention is also invited to the views expressed in the report in relation to the legislation of Congress at its last session in respect to prize on our inland waters.

I cordially concur in the recommendation of the Secretary as to the propriety of creating the new rank of vice-admiral in our naval service.

Your attention is invited to the report of the Postmaster General for a detailed account of the operations and financial condition of the Post Office Department.

The postal revenues for the year ending June 30, 1864, amounted to $12,438,253.78 and the expenditures to $12,664,786.20; the excess of expenditures over receipts being $206,652.42.

The views presented by the Postmaster-General on the subject of special grants by the government in aid of the establishment of new lines of ocean mail steamships, and the policy he recommends for the development of increased commercial intercourse with adjacent and neighboring countries, should receive the careful consideration of Congress.

It is of noteworthy interest that the steady expansion of population, improvement and governmental institutions over the new and unoccupied portions of our country have scarcely been checked, much less impeded or destroyed, by our great civil war, which at first glance would seem to have absorbed almost the entire energies of the nation.

The organization and admission of the State of Nevada has been completed in conformity with law, and thus our excellent system is firmly established in the mountains, which once seemed a barren and uninhabitable waste between the Atlantic States and those which have grown up on the coast of the Pacific Ocean.

The territories of the Union are generally in a condition of prosperity and rapid growth. Idaho and Montana, by reason of their great distance and the interruption of communication with them by Indian hostilities, have been only partially organized; but it is understood that these difficulties are about to disappear, which will permit their governments, like those of the others, to go into speedy and full operation.

As intimately connected with, and promotive of, this material growth of the nation, I ask the attention of Congress to the valuable information and important recommendations relating to the public lands, Indian affairs, the Pacific railroad, and mineral discoveries contained in the report of the Secretary of the Interior, which is herewith transmitted, and which report also embraces the subjects of patents, pensions and other topics of public interest pertaining to his department.

The quantity of public land disposed of during the five quarters ending on the 30th of September last was 4,221,342 acres, of which 1,538,614 acres were entered under the homestead law. The remainder was located with military land warrants, agricultural scrip certified to States for railroads, and sold for cash. The cash received from sales and location fees was $1,019,446.

The income from sales during the fiscal year, ending June 30, 1864, was $678,007.21, against $136,077.95 received during the preceding year. The aggregate number of acres surveyed during the year has been equal to the quantity disposed of; and there is open to settlement about 133,000,000 acres of surveyed land.

The great enterprise of connecting the Atlantic with the Pacific States by railways and telegraph lines has been entered upon with a vigor that gives assurance of success, notwithstanding the embarrassments arising from the prevailing high prices of materials and labor. The route of the main line of the road has been definitely located for one hundred miles westward from the initial point at Omaha City, Nebraska, and a preliminary location of the Pacific railroad of California has been made from Sacramento eastward to the great bend of the Truckee River, in Nevada.

Numerous discoveries of gold, silver and cinnabar mines have been added to the many heretofore known and the country occupied by the Sierra Nevada and Rocky Mountains, and the subordinate ranges, now teems with enterprising labor, which is richly remunerative. It is believed that the product of the mines of precious metals in that region has, during the year, reached, if not exceeded, one hundred millions in value.

It was recommended in my last annual message that our Indian system be remodelled. Congress, at its last session, acting upon the recommendation, did provide for reorganizing the system in California, and it is believed that under the present organization the management of the Indians there will be attended with reasonable success. Much yet remains to be done to provide for the proper government of the Indians in other parts of the country to render it secure for the advancing settler, and to provide for the welfare of the Indian. The Secretary reiterates his recommendations, and to them the attention of Congress is invited.

The liberal provisions made by Congress for paying pensions to invalid soldiers and sailors of the republic, and to the widows, orphans, and dependent mothers of those who have fallen in battle, or died of disease contracted, or of wounds received in the service of their country, have been diligently administered. There have been added to the pension rolls, during the year ending the 30th day of June last, the names of 16,770 invalid soldiers, and of 271 disabled seamen; making the present number of army invalid pensioners 22,767, and of navy invalid pensioners 712.

Of widows, orphans, and mothers, 22,198 have been placed on the army pension rolls, and 248 on the navy rolls. The present number of army pensioners of this class is 25,433, and of navy pensioners, 793. At the beginning of the year the number of Revolutionary pensioners was 1,430; only twelve of them were soldiers, of whom seven have since died. The remainder are those who, under the law, receive pensions because of relationship to revolutionary soldiers. During the year ending the 30th of June, 1864, $4,504,616.92 have been paid to pensioners of all classes.

I cheerfully commend to your continued patronage the benevolent institutions of the District of Columbia, which have hitherto been established or fostered by Congress, and respectfully refer, for information concerning them, and in relation to the Washington aqueduct, the Capitol, and other matters of local interest, to the report of the Secretary.

The Agricultural Department, under the supervision of its present energetic and faithful head, is rapidly commending itself to the great and vital interest it was created to advance. It is peculiarly the people's department, in which they feel more directly concerned than in any other. I commend it to the continued attention and fostering care of Congress.

The war continues. Since the last annual message all the important lines and positions then occupied by our forces have been maintained, and our arms have steadily advanced, thus liberating the regions left in rear; so that Missouri, Kentucky, Tennessee, and parts of other States have again produced reasonably fair crops.

The most remarkable feature in the military operations of the year is General Sherman's attempted march of three hundred miles, directly through the insurgent region. It tends to show a great increase of our relative strength that our General-in-Chief should feel able to confront and hold in check every active force of the enemy, and yet to detach a well-appointed large army to move on such an expedition. The result not yet being known, conjecture in regard to it is not here indulged.

Important movements have also occurred during the year to the effect of moulding society for durability in the Union. Although short of complete success, it is much in the right direction, that twelve thousand citizens in each of the States of Arkansas and Louisiana have organized loyal State governments with free constitutions, and are earnestly struggling to maintain and administer them. The movements in the same direction, more extensive, though less definite in Missouri, Kentucky and Tennessee, should not be overlooked. But Maryland presents the example of complete success. Maryland is secure to Liberty and Union for all the future. The genius of rebellion will no more claim Maryland. Like another foul spirit, being driven out, it may seek to tear her, but it will woo her no more.

At the last session of Congress a proposed amendment of the Constitution abolishing slavery throughout the United States, passed the Senate, but failed for lack of the requisite two-thirds vote in the House of Representatives. Although the present is the same Congress, and nearly the same members, and without questioning the wisdom or patriotism of those who stood in opposition, I venture to recommend the reconsideration and passage of the measure at the present session. Of course the abstract question is not changed; but an intervening election shows, almost certainly, that the next Congress will pass the measure if this does not. Hence there is only a question of *time* as to when the proposed amendment will go to the States for their action. And as it is to so go, at all events, may we not agree that the sooner the better? It is not claimed that the election has imposed a duty on members to change their views or their votes, any further than, as an additional element to be considered, their judgment may be affected by it. It is the voice of the people now, for the first time, heard upon the question. In a great national crisis, like ours, unanimity of action among those seeking a common end is very desirable—almost indispensable. And yet no approach to such unanimity is attainable, unless some deference shall be paid to the will of the majority, simply because it is the will of the majority. In this case the common end is the maintenance of the Union; and, among the means to secure that end, such will, through the election, is most clearly declared in favor of such constitutional amendment.

The most reliable indication of public purpose in this country is derived through our popular elections. Judging by the recent canvass and its result, the purpose of the people, within the loyal States, to maintain the integrity of the Union, was never more firm, nor more nearly unanimous, than now. The extraordinary calmness and good order with which the millions of voters met and mingled at the polls, give strong assurance of this. Not only all those who supported the Union ticket, so called, but a great majority of the opposing party also, may be fairly claimed to entertain, and to be actuated by, the same purpose. It is an unanswerable argument to this effect, that no candidate for any office whatever, high or low, has ventured to seek votes on the avowal that he was for giving up the Union. There have been much impugning of motives, and much heated controversy as to the proper means and best mode of advancing the Union cause; but on the distinct issue of Union or no Union, the politicians have shown their instinctive knowledge that there is no diversity among the people. In affording the people the fair opportunity of showing, one to another and to the world, this firmness and unanimity of purpose, the election has been of vast value to the national cause.

The election has exhibited another fact not less valuable to be known—the fact that we do not approach exhaustion in the most important branch of national resources—that of living men. While it is melancholy to reflect that the war has filled so many graves, and carried mourning to so many hearts, it is some relief to know that, compared with the surviving, the fallen have been so few. While corps, and divisions, and brigades, and regiments have formed, and fought, and dwindled, and gone out of existence, a great majority of the men who composed them are still living. The same is true of the naval service. The election returns prove this. So many voters could not else be found. The States regularly holding elections, both now and four years ago, to wit, California, Connecticut, Delaware, Illinois, Indiana, Iowa, Kentucky, Maine, Maryland, Massachusetts, Michigan, Minnesota, Missouri, New Hampshire, New Jersey, New York, Ohio, Oregon, Pennsylvania, Rhode Island, Vermont, West Virginia, and Wisconsin cast 3,982,011 votes now, against 3,870,222 cast then; showing an aggregate now of 3,982,011. To this is to be added 33,762 cast now in the new States of Kansas and Nevada, which States did not vote in 1860, thus swelling the aggregate to 4,015,773, and the net increase during the three years and a half of war to 145,551. A table is appended showing particulars. To this again should be added the number of all soldiers in the field from Massachusetts, Rhode Island, New Jersey, Delaware, Indiana, Illinois, and California, who, by the laws of those States, could not vote away from their homes, and which number cannot be less than 90,000. Nor yet is this all. The number in organized Territories is triple now what it was four years ago, while thousands, white and black, join us as the national arms press back the insurgent lines. So much is shown, affirmatively and negatively, by the election. It is not material to inquire *how* the increase has been produced, or to show that it would have been *greater* but for the war, which is probably true. The important fact remains demonstrated, that we have *more* men *now* than we had when the war *began;* that we are not exhausted, nor in process of exhaustion; that we are *gaining* strength, and may, if need be, maintain the contest indefinitely. This as to men. Material resources are now more complete and abundant than ever.

The national resources, then, are unexhausted, and, as we believe, inexhaustible. The public purpose to re-establish and maintain the national authority is unchanged, and, as we believe, unchangeable. The manner of continuing the effort remains to choose. On careful consideration of all the evidence accessible it seems to me that no attempt at negotiation with the insurgent leader could result in any good. He would accept nothing short of severance of the Union—precisely what we will not and cannot give. His declarations to this effect are explicit and oft-repeated. He does not attempt to deceive us. He affords us no excuse to deceive ourselves. He cannot voluntarily reaccept the Union; we cannot voluntarily yield it. Between him and us the issue is distinct, simple, and inflexible. It is an issue which can only be tried by war, and decided by victory. If we yield, we are beaten; if the Southern people fail him, he is beaten. Either way, it would be the victory and defeat following war. What is true, however, of him who heads the insurgent cause, is not necessarily true of those who follow. Although he cannot reaccept the Union, they can. Some of them, we know, already desire peace and reunion. The number of such may increase. They can, at any moment, have peace simply by laying down their arms and submitting to the national authority under the Constitution. After so much, the government could not, if it would, maintain war against them. The loyal people would not sustain or allow it. If questions should remain, we would adjust them by the peaceful means of legislation, conference, courts, and votes, operating only in constitutional and lawful channels. Some certain, and other possible, questions are, and would be, beyond the Executive power to adjust; as, for instance, the admission of members into Congress, and whatever might require the appropriation of money. The Executive power itself would be greatly diminished by the cessation of actual war. Pardons and remissions of forfeitures, however, would still be within Executive control. In what spirit and temper this control would be exercised can be fairly judged of by the past.

A year ago general pardon and amnesty, upon specified terms, were offered to all, except certain designated classes; and, it was, at the same time, made known that the excepted classes were still within contemplation of special clemency. During the year many availed themselves of the general provision, and many more would, only that the signs of bad faith in some led to such precautionary measures as rendered the practical process less easy and certain. During the same time also special pardons have been granted to individuals of the excepted classes, and no voluntary application has been denied. Thus, practically, the door has been, for a full year, open to all, except such as were not in condition to make free choice—that is, such as were in custody or under constraint. It is still so open to all. But the time may come—probably will come—when public duty shall demand that it be closed; and that, in lieu, more rigorous measures than heretofore shall be adopted.

In presenting the abandonment of armed resistance to the national authority on the part of the insurgents, as the only indispensable condition to ending the war on the part of the government, I retract nothing heretofore said as to slavery. I repeat the declaration made a year ago, that "while I remain in my present position I shall not attempt to retract or modify the emancipation proclamation, nor shall I return to slavery any person who is free by the terms of that proclamation, or by any of the Acts of Congress." If the people should, by whatever mode or means, make it an Executive duty to re-enslave such persons, another, and not I, must be their instrument to perform it.

In stating a single condition of peace, I mean simply to say that the war will cease on the part of the government, whenever it shall have ceased on the part of those who began it.

Abraham Lincoln
December 6, 1864

SECOND INAUGURAL ADDRESS
MARCH 4, 1865

The Second Inaugural has been described correctly as "an expression of Lincoln's living faith." The speech was delivered in the context of the North's imminent victory and the public outcry for revenge against a defeated South. Theologically, the public expression of biblical faith in the Second Inaugural corresponds to Lincoln's private Meditation on the Divine Will in September 1862. A careful reading of the address reveals that Lincoln pointed to the culpability of both North and South before God. For this reason, the

Second Inaugural was a grave disappointment to some who demanded the triumphalist assertion of the North's righteousness now that the war was coming to an end. Instead, Lincoln stated that, "the prayers of both could not be answered; that of neither has been answered fully." Although slavery could not be reconciled with the conception of a just God and was clearly contrary to Genesis 3:19's injunction to earn "bread from the sweat of thy brow", Lincoln refrained from an ultimate judgment upon southern people's motives, citing Matthew 7:1 "judge not that we be not judged."

Furthermore, those who argue that Lincoln was speaking directly for God in the address are equally mistaken. It is noteworthy that he used the conditional when speculating about the Divine Will, concluding that ultimately it is inscrutable: "The Almighty has his own purposes." Nonetheless, whatever God has willed, however ultimately inscrutable, must be trusted; for the "judgments of the Lord, are true and righteous altogether." Here Lincoln's reference to Psalm 19 testified to the benevolence of a living God who would bring good out of suffering. The public view of biblical faith manifested in the Second Inaugural is further consistent with Lincoln's private interpretation of this faith in his letter to Joshua Speed in 1842 and his replies to Mrs. Gurney in 1863. Finally, Lincoln called for a generous and magnanimous peace: "With malice toward none; with charity for all; with firmness in the right, as God gives us to see the right."

At this second appearing to take the oath of the presidential office, there is less occasion for an extended address than there was at the first. Then a statement, somewhat in detail, of a course to be pursued, seemed fitting and proper. Now, at the expiration of four years, during which public declarations have been constantly called forth on every point and phase of the great contest which still absorbs the attention, and engrosses the energies of the nation, little that is new could be presented. The progress of our arms, upon which all else chiefly depends, is as well known to the public as to myself; and it is, I trust, reasonably satisfactory and encouraging to all. With high hope for the future, no prediction in regard to it is ventured.

On the occasion corresponding to this four years ago, all thoughts were anxiously directed to an impending civil war. All dreaded it—all sought to avert it. While the inaugeral [sic] address was being delivered from this place, devoted altogether to *saving* the Union without war, insurgent agents were in the city seeking to *destroy* it without war—seeking to dissole [sic] the Union, and divide effects, by negotiation. Both parties deprecated war; but one of them would *make* war rather than let the nation survive; and the other would *accept* war rather than let it perish. And the war came.

One eighth of the whole population were colored slaves, not distributed generally over the Union, but localized in the Southern part of it. These slaves constituted a peculiar and powerful interest. All knew that this interest was, somehow, the cause of the war. To strengthen, perpetuate, and extend this interest was the object for which the insurgents would rend the Union, even by war; while the government claimed no right to do more than to restrict the territorial enlargement of it. Neither party expected for the war, the magnitude, or the duration, which it has already attained. Neither anticipated that the *cause* of the conflict might cease with, or even before, the conflict itself should cease. Each looked for an easier triumph, and a result less fundamental and astounding. Both read the same Bible, and pray to the same God; and each invokes His aid against the other. It may seem strange that any men should dare to ask a just God's assistance in wringing their bread from the sweat of other men's faces; but let us judge not that we be not judged. The prayers of both could not be answered; that of neither has been answered fully. The Almighty has his own purposes. "Woe unto the world because of offences! for it must needs be that offences come; but woe to that man by whom the offence cometh!" If we shall suppose that American Slavery is one of those offences which, in the providence of God, must needs come, but which, having continued through His appointed time, He now wills to remove, and that He gives to both North and South, this terrible war, as the woe due to those by whom the offence came, shall we discern therein any departure from those divine attributes which the believers in a Living God always ascribe to Him? Fondly do we hope—fervently do we pray—that this mighty scourge of war may speedily pass away. Yet, if God wills that it continue, until all the wealth piled by the bond-man's two hundred and fifty years of unrequited toil shall be sunk, and until every drop of blood drawn with the lash, shall be paid by another drawn with the sword, as was said three thousand years ago, so still it must be said "the judgments of the Lord, are true and righteous altogether."

With malice toward none; with charity for all; with firmness in the right, as God gives us to see the right, let us strive on to finish the work we are in; to bind up the nation's wounds; to care for him who shall have borne the battle, and for his widow, and his orphan—to do all which may achieve and cherish a just and lasting peace, among ourselves, and with all nations.

LAST PUBLIC ADDRESS
APRIL 11, 1865

Lincoln's last public address was delivered two days after Lee's surrender to Grant and only three days before his assassination on April 14, 1865. Here he spoke to a crowd that had gathered outside of the White House in celebration of the Union's imminent victory. He alluded to dissatisfaction with his reconstruction plan. While Lincoln once again expressed his personal view that suffrages should be conferred upon black soldiers and more intelligent African-Americans, he nevertheless asked the nation to support Louisiana's new free state government, even if it had fallen short in this regard.

WE MEET THIS EVENING, not in sorrow, but in gladness of heart. The evacuation of Petersburg and Richmond, and the surrender of the principal insurgent army, give hope of a righteous and speedy peace whose joyous expression can not be restrained. In the midst of this, however, He from whom all blessings flow, must not be forgotten. A call for a national thanksgiving is being prepared, and will be duly promulgated. Nor must those whose harder part gives us the cause of rejoicing, be overlooked. Their honors must not be parcelled out with others. I myself was near the front, and had the high pleasure of transmitting much of the good news to you; but no part of the honor, for plan or execution, is mine. To Gen. Grant, his skilful officers, and brave men, all belongs. The gallant Navy stood ready, but was not in reach to take active part.

By these recent successes the re-inauguration of the national authority—reconstruction—which has had a large share of thought from the first, is pressed much more closely upon our attention. It is fraught with great difficulty. Unlike a case of a war between independent nations, there is no authorized organ for us to treat with. No one man has authority to give up the rebellion for any other man. We simply must begin with, and mould from, disorganized and discordant elements. Nor is it a small additional embarrassment that we, the loyal people, differ among ourselves as to the mode, manner, and means of reconstruction.

As a general rule, I abstain from reading the reports of attacks upon myself, wishing not to be provoked by that to which I can not properly offer an answer. In spite of this precaution, however, it comes to my knowledge that I am much censured for some supposed agency in setting up, and seeking to sustain, the new State government of Louisiana. In this I have done just so much as, and no more than, the public knows. In the Annual Message of Dec. 1863 and accompanying Proclamation, I presented *a* plan of re-construction (as the phrase goes) which, I promised, if adopted by any State, should be acceptable to, and sustained by, the Executive government of the nation. I distinctly stated that this was not the only plan which might possibly be acceptable; and I also distinctly protested that the Executive claimed no right to say when, or whether members should be admitted to seats in Congress from such States. This plan was, in advance, submitted to the then Cabinet, and distinctly approved by every member of it. One of them suggested that I should then, and in that connection, apply the Emancipation Proclamation to the theretofore excepted parts of Virginia and Louisiana; that I should drop the suggestion about apprenticeship for freed-people, and that I should omit the protest against my own power, in regard to the admission of members to Congress; but even he approved every part and parcel of the plan which has since been employed or touched by the action of Louisiana. The new constitution of Louisiana, declaring emancipation for the whole State, practically applies the Proclamation to the part previously excepted. It does not adopt apprenticeship for freed-people; and it is silent, as it could not well be otherwise, about the admission of members to Congress. So that, as it applies to Louisiana, every member of the Cabinet fully approved the plan. The message went to Congress, and I received many commendations of the plan, written and verbal; and not a single objection to it, from any professed emancipationist, came to my knowledge, until after the news reached Washington that the people of Louisiana had begun to move in accordance with it. From about July 1862, I had corresponded with different persons, supposed to be interested, seeking a reconstruction of a State government for Louisiana. When the message of 1863, with the plan before mentioned, reached New-Orleans, Gen. Banks wrote me that he was confident the people, with his military co-operation, would reconstruct, substantially on that plan. I wrote him, and some of them to try it; they tried it, and the result is known. Such only has been my agency in getting up the Louisiana government. As to sustaining it, my promise is out, as before stated. But, as bad promises are better broken than kept, I shall treat this as a bad promise, and break it, whenever I shall be convinced that keeping it is adverse to the public interest. But I have not yet been so convinced.

I have been shown a letter on this subject, supposed to be an able one, in which the writer expresses regret that my mind has not seemed to be definitely fixed on the question whether the seceded States, so called, are in the Union or out of it. It would perhaps, add astonishment to his regret, were he to learn that since I have found professed Union men endeavoring to make that question, I have *purposely* forborne any public expression upon it. As appears to me that question has not been, nor yet is, a practically material one, and that any discussion of it, while it thus remains practically immaterial, could have no effect other than the mischievous one of dividing our friends. As yet, whatever it may hereafter become, that question is bad, as the basis of a controversy, and good for nothing at all—a merely pernicious abstraction.

We all agree that the seceded States, so called, are out of their proper practical relation with the Union; and that the sole object of the government, civil

and military, in regard to those States is to again get them into that proper practical relation. I believe it is not only possible, but in fact, easier to do this, without deciding, or even considering, whether these States have ever been out of
the Union, than with it. Finding themselves safely at home, it would be utterly
immaterial whether they had ever been abroad. Let us all join in doing the acts
necessary to restoring the proper practical relations between these States and the
Union; and each forever after, innocently indulge his own opinion whether, in
doing the acts, he brought the States from without, into the Union, or only gave
them proper assistance, they never having been out of it.

The amount of constituency, so to speak, on which the new Louisiana government rests, would be more satisfactory to all, if it contained fifty, thirty, or
even twenty thousand, instead of only about twelve thousand, as it does. It is
also unsatisfactory to some that the elective franchise is not given to the colored
man. I would myself prefer that it were now conferred on the very intelligent,
and on those who serve our cause as soldiers. Still the question is not whether
the Louisiana government, as it stands, is quite all that is desirable. The question is, "Will it be wiser to take it as it is, and help to improve it; or to reject,
and disperse it?" "Can Louisiana be brought into proper practical relation with
the Union *sooner* by *sustaining,* or by *discarding* her new State government?"

Some twelve thousand voters in the heretofore slave-state of Louisiana have
sworn allegiance to the Union, assumed to be the rightful political power of the
State, held elections, organized a State government, adopted a free-state constitution, giving the benefit of public schools equally to black and white, and
empowering the Legislature to confer the elective franchise upon the colored
man. Their Legislature has already voted to ratify the constitutional amendment
recently passed by Congress, abolishing slavery throughout the nation. These
twelve thousand persons are thus fully committed to the Union, and to perpetual freedom in the state—committed to the very things, and nearly all the things
the nation wants—and they ask the nations recognition and its assistance to make
good their committal. Now, if we reject, and spurn them, we do our utmost to
disorganize and disperse them. We in effect say to the white men "You are
worthless, or worse—we will neither help you, nor be helped by you." To the
blacks we say "This cup of liberty which these, your old masters, hold to your
lips, we will dash from you, and leave you to the chances of gathering the spilled
and scattered contents in some vague and undefined when, where, and how." If
this course, discouraging and paralyzing both white and black, has any tendency
to bring Louisiana into proper practical relations with the Union, I have, so far,
been unable to perceive it. If, on the contrary, we recognize, and sustain the new

government of Louisiana the converse of all this is made true. We encourage the hearts, and nerve the arms of the twelve thousand to adhere to their work, and argue for it, and proselyte for it, and fight for it, and feed it, and grow it, and ripen it to a complete success. The colored man too, in seeing all united for him, is inspired with vigilance, and energy, and daring, to the same end. Grant that he desires the elective franchise, will he not attain it sooner by saving the already advanced steps toward it, than by running backward over them? Concede that the new government of Louisiana is only to what it should be as the egg is to the fowl, we shall sooner have the fowl by hatching the egg than by smashing it? Again, if we reject Louisiana, we also reject one vote in favor of the proposed amendment to the national Constitution. To meet this proposition, it has been argued that no more than three fourths of those States which have not attempted secession are necessary to validly ratify the amendment. I do not commit myself against this, further than to say that such a ratification would be questionable, and sure to be persistently questioned; while a ratification by three-fourths of all the States would be unquestioned and unquestionable.

I repeat the question. "Can Louisiana be brought into proper practical relation with the Union *sooner* by *sustaining* or by *discarding* her new State Government?"

What has been said of Louisiana will apply generally to other States. And yet so great peculiarities pertain to each state, and such important and sudden changes occur in the same state; and, withal, so new and unprecedented is the whole case, that no exclusive, and inflexible plan can safely be prescribed as to details and collaterals [sic]. Such exclusive, and inflexible plan, would surely become a new entanglement. Important principles may, and must, be inflexible.

In the present *"situation"* as the phrase goes, it may be my duty to make some new announcement to the people of the South. I am considering, and shall not fail to act, when satisfied that action will be proper.

VI.

Lincoln's "Political Faith"

A T GETTYSBURG LINCOLN RESOLVED that "this nation, under God," would not perish from the earth, and in his Second Inaugural Address he called for "firmness in the right, as God gives us to see the right." How are we to understand these and the many other invocations of Divine authority and religious belief in the speeches and writings of America's most admired president? Following a precedent established by George Washington, Lincoln proclaimed various national days of religious thanksgiving and fasting as Chief Executive during the Civil War. The nondenominational character of these executive proclamations affirmed the sacred sphere of religion in the American regime within the constitutional boundaries of the nonestablishment clause and the ban on religious tests. In the first of many such pronouncements dated August 12, 1861, Lincoln quoted verbatim from a proclamation made by the First Congress of the United States announcing a "day of public humiliation, prayer and fasting, to be observed by the people of the United States with religious solemnities, and the offering of fervent supplications to Almighty God for the safety and welfare of these States, His blessings on their arms, and a speedy restoration of peace...." And it should not be forgotten that Lincoln's Thanksgiving Day Proclamation of 1863 established the customary date of our national holiday: "I do, therefore, invite my fellow citizens in every part of the United States, and also those who are at sea and those who are sojourning in foreign lands, to set apart and observe the last Thursday of November next as a day of Thanksgiving and Praise to our beneficent Father who dwelleth in heaven."[1]

Among the many reasons Abraham Lincoln's political thought and leadership is of enduring significance was his profound recognition that political order derives its legitimacy from an ultimate, transcendent order. Indeed, Lincoln situated the politics of his day in a wider theological and philosophical context. He discerned that ostensible conflicts over social, economic, and political claims were themselves predicated upon some overarching vision of God, history, man, and society. In response to his proslavery rivals who invoked the Bible to legitimize their policies, Lincoln offered a compelling and comprehensive interpretation of

---

1. I have developed this cursory overview of Lincoln's religion and politics in much greater depth in my book, *Abraham Lincoln's Political Faith*. DeKalb: Northern Illinois University Press, 2003.

political order founded in American democratic and religious traditions. Because his interpretation of American public life combined the biblical tradition of Judeo-Christian faith and the Founder's republican tradition of self-government, it may be described as Biblical Republicanism. He often used the expressions "political faith," "political religion," "the early faith of the republic," " the national faith," "those sacred principles enunciated by our fathers," and the "ancient faith" to describe the American political creed enshrined in the Declaration. He thus likened the transformation of public opinion on slavery from that of a necessary evil to that of a positive good as tantamount to the nation "giving up" its Old Faith" in the Declaration for a "New Faith" based on racial supremacy and human inequality. Indeed, even a cursory reading of Lincoln's speeches and writings would recognize that they abound with allusions from the Bible. With his proslavery opponents claiming to fight for God's just cause, Biblical Republicanism provided Lincoln with a deeply felt moral justification for difficult political choices in a time of unprecedented crisis and upheaval.

The South's proslavery theology invoked the Bible to sanction human servitude, and it implied a corresponding critique of northern free society as decadent, corrupt, and heartless. In particular, George Fitzhugh, whom Lincoln had read, wrote two influential works defending slavery as a positive good and a social and political blessing: *Cannibals All* and *Sociology for the South*. Fitzhugh, Hammond, and others propounded what became known as the "Mud Sill Theory" critique of northern free labor, which claimed that every society rested on an underclass or bottom rung. In contrast to southern black slaves who were paternalistically cared for by benevolent masters, northern wage slaves, who occupied the bottom rung or mud sill in northern society, were callously abandoned to the vagaries of the free market. Fitzhugh's overarching critique motivated Lincoln to clarify the foundations of free society. To be sure, Lincoln's defense of the American Dream of equal opportunity and advancement in the race of life was in response to southern philosophical critiques of free society, which denied that free laborers (black or white) could ever improve their moral or material condition. While apologists like Fitzhugh and Presbyterian minister Frederick Ross preached that the South's "peculiar institution" was "ordained of God," abolitionist clergymen from the North like Gerritt Smith urged disunion over slavery in order to preserve the moral purity of the Republic. Even Stephen Douglas, who tried to avoid mixing religion and politics, invoked the Bible's precept in Matthew 7:1: "judge not lest ye be judged" to justify popular sovereignty's moral relativism toward slavery. Each of these alternatives attempted to provide an ultimate moral justification for public life during the

Civil War era. Each attempted to derive its legitimacy, either implicitly or explicitly, from the Bible. Each attempted to mould the climate of public opinion in accordance with its own peculiar interpretation of the public good. Indeed, each claimed to be the most authoritative representative of American republicanism.

The core religious experience and outlook that guided Lincoln's view of personal and political order is best described as "biblical faith." The adjective "biblical" is wholly appropriate to the non-sectarian character of his faith, which was based primarily on his own personal encounter with the Bible. While elements of Lincoln's biblical faith may correspond with various religious traditions, it is well known that he avoided formal church membership. Nonetheless, the core elements of his biblical faith are revealed in two early letters he wrote to his friend Joshua Speed in 1842. Moreover, these early private religious utterances are remarkably consistent with his subsequent public and private religious statements. Though Lincoln's personal faith deepened with maturity—especially after the death of his son, Willie, and during the turbulent years of war—his articulation and interpretation of this faith remained fairly consistent.

Lincoln manifested biblical faith in different ways throughout his life by humbly seeking to know God's will, by avoiding self-righteous vindictiveness towards his enemies, and by trusting in a higher power to guide him and the nation through its "fiery trial." His articulation of the experience of biblical faith in private letters and public speeches conveys a trust in the benevolence of a living God who will bring good out of suffering. St. Paul's exhortation in *Roman's 8:28* provides a parallel expression of the experience of biblical faith found in Lincoln's speeches and writings: "And we know that all things work together for good to them that love God, to them who are called according to his purpose." On several occasions, Lincoln referred to himself as "instrument of God" (See below: Letter to Speed, July 4, 1842; Remarks to a Delegation of Progressive Friends, June 20, 1862; Reply to Mrs. Gurney, Oct. 26, 1862). This self-interpretation did not mean that he saw himself as a secular messiah who had direct access to the will of God; rather it conveyed his struggle as a suffering servant to bear witness to God's design, whatever that may be, and however vaguely discerned. Thus, it is more accurate to say that Lincoln was an instrument of God insofar as he bore witness to God's goodness and providential design in the face of trials and tribulations. Avoiding the extremes of self-righteousness and despair, he affirmed and embodied the paradox of faith, humbly acknowledging the inscrutability of God's ultimate design, yet nevertheless trusting in God's ultimate benevolence. Some scholars have alleged a dichotomy between Lincoln's private and public religious views. They argue that Lincoln was privately a religious skeptic who publicly invoked religion for its social utility. Thus they view Lincoln's religious utterances as purely rhetorical and poetical expressions that stir the hearts of the common people to action, inducing them to sacrifice for a higher cause. On the contrary, the primary sources in this collection demonstrate a remarkable continuity between Lincoln's private and public religious belief.

Lincoln also embodied a biblical magnanimity that combined the seemingly incompatible elements of a Christian humility and a pagan grandeur. While he may well have recognized his own ambition and his superiority over other men, he also humbly confessed his own limitations and his dependence upon a higher power. Ambition was, and remains, an important spur to greatness. Ambition is not evil per se, but good or evil depending upon the end it serves. Thus, one may distinguish between a diabolical ambition that is unbounded by any external moral standard, as was the case with Napoleon, and a benign ambition that is circumscribed by moral boundaries, as was the case with Lincoln.

Some scholars have accused Lincoln of dangerously confounding religion and politics, of even being messianic in his combination of the two. They argue that Lincoln sought to arrogate divine authority to himself and that he sought to make the Union an object of holy veneration. This interpretation ignores Lincoln's prudence, his consistent affirmation of the mysterious character of the divine will, and his affirmation of sacred sphere beyond the reach of the state. For example, during the war, Lincoln pursued a policy of nonintervention with rebel churches suspected of disloyalty, and he countermanded his generals for such interference if the actions of the church presented no manifest danger to the public good. After suspending an order to remove a Missouri minister suspected of Confederate sympathies, Lincoln wrote the following to the Union general in charge on January 2, 1863:

> But I must add that the U.S. government must not . . . undertake to run the churches. When an individual, in a church or out of it, becomes dangerous to the public interest, he must be checked; but let the churches, as such take care of themselves. It will not do for the U.S. to appoint Trustees, Supervisors, or other agents for the churches.

Lincoln's policy of noninterference with rebel churches may be contrasted to the actions of actual secular messiahs like Adolf Hitler, Joseph Stalin, and Mao

Tse Tung, all of who sought to crush any institution, sacred or secular, whose authority challenged their claim to omnipotence. To argue that there is moral equivalence between the totalitarian tyrants of the Twentieth Century and Lincoln is to confound the wicked with the just. The failure to distinguish clearly between actual secular messiahs and a prudent statesman who acknowledged being bound to a higher power but whose moral and religious convictions were applied within the framework of the constitution, impairs our capacity to recognize either.

In sum, Lincoln's biblical opposition to slavery was based primarily on the following precepts: the affirmation of a common humanity created in the image of God in *Genesis 1:27*; The Golden Rule to "do unto others as you would have them do unto you" in *Matthew 7:12*; The Great Commandment "to love your neighbor as yourself" in *Matthew 22:37–40*; and the injunction to "earn bread by the sweat of thy brow" in *Genesis 3:19*. On the other hand, the South's proslavery theology was based upon a literal interpretation of the following biblical passages: *Genesis 9:18–27*; *Exodus 21:2–5, 7–11, 20–21*; *Leviticus 25:44–46*; *Colossians 3:22*—"servants, obey in all things your masters"; *Colossians 4:1*—"Masters, Give unto your servants that which is just and equal; knowing that ye also have a Master in heaven"; *1 Timothy 6:1–6*—"Let as many servants as are under the yoke count their own masters worthy of all honour"; *Titus 2:9*—"Exhort servants to be obedient unto their own masters"; *Ephesians 6:5–9*—"Servants, be obedient to them that are your masters according to the flesh, with fear and trembling, in singleness of your heart, as unto Christ; *Romans 13:1*: "Let every soul be subject unto the higher powers. For there is no power but of God: the powers that be are ordained of God"; and *1 Peter II: 18*: "Servants, be obedient to them that are your masters according to the flesh, with fear and trembling. . . . " Lincoln repudiated proslavery theology as a sophistry, claiming that it perverted the Bible and was utterly incompatible with a just God. In a letter to a Baptist group on May 30, 1864, he argued that the disingenuousness of proslavery theology was comparable to Satan's exploitation of the Bible to tempt Jesus Christ, as related in *Matthew 4: 1–11*.

It is important to emphasize, however, that Lincoln's opposition to slavery did not rely solely upon a literal interpretation of Scripture, but was complemented by the Three R's of his biblical republicanism: reason, republicanism, and revelation. That is to say, for Lincoln, the moral precepts of the Bible were confirmed through the insights of reason (common experience), and the Founders' tradition of republicanism. The reverse was true as well: the Founders' republicanism was confirmed by the teachings of the Bible and the self-evident apprehensions of reason and conscience. In his struggle against slavery, Lincoln translated the moral precepts of the Bible into the universal language of reason, thus making it publicly authoritative rather than privately sectarian.

A biblical view of human nature likewise informed Lincoln's political thought. His belief that all men were created equal; that human life was sacred; that rights came from the hand of God—all implied a Judeo-Christian interpretation of order derived from the Bible. Elements of this biblical view of human nature included a realistic view of man's capacity for both good and evil, the existence of a universal moral law, and the affirmation of a common humanity created in the image of God. After he had won a bitter election in 1864, Lincoln replied to a group of serenaders, "Human nature will not change. In any future great national trial, compared with the men of this, we shall have as weak, and as strong; as silly and as wise; as bad as good. Let us, therefore, study the incidents of this, as philosophy to learn wisdom from, and none of them as wrongs to be revenged." This realistic view of human nature recognized man's proclivity toward selfishness as a consequence of sin and his fallen nature. Lincoln thus maintained that slavery was "founded in the self-ishness of man's nature." However, while the selfishness of human nature pulled man in one direction, he was pulled in another direction by more noble forces. Lincoln's biblical view of human nature accounted for the higher dimensions of human experience as well as the lower. To be sure, it affirmed the existence of an immutable moral law impressed upon man's nature and known by him through the activity of conscience. Lincoln argued that slavery's moral repugnance could be apprehended intuitively despite all efforts of people to delude themselves that it was good. Thus, at Peoria, he asked southern people of good will why they considered the slave trader a contemptible figure among them. And why did they forbid their children to associate with him, "instinctively shrinking from his snaky contact." Moreover, if slavery was a social and political blessing, why did so many Southerners of good will seek to free their slaves, as George Washington did? At Peoria, Lincoln's appeal to a tacit moral sense attempted to reawaken the *conditio humana*— human condition—in his listeners. In addition to more discursive arguments against slavery, he compelled his listeners to discern their own internal contradictions by pricking their conscience and forcing them to consult honestly the inner recesses of their own heart.

In sum, Lincoln sincerely believed in a biblical faith that affirmed a living God who guided individuals and nations towards some ultimate good. And he turned to the Bible to bring himself and the American nation into closer communion with the Creator and his moral law. The evolution of Lincoln's political faith hinted at in his youthful Lyceum Address and more fully developed in his mature Peoria Address culminated with his Second Inaugural Address—the ultimate statement of his "political faith" and the preeminent expression of his living faith.

THE PERPETUATION OF OUR POLITICAL INSTITUTIONS: ADDRESS BEFORE THE YOUNG MEN'S LYCEUM OF SPRINGFIELD, ILLINOIS
JANUARY 27, 1838

The Lyceum Address has been viewed by many scholars as central to understanding Lincoln's teaching on religion and politics. Straussian scholars like Harry V. Jaffa, George Anastaplo, Glen Thurow, et. al. argue that a combined reading of Lincoln's Lyceum Address and Temperance Address of 1842 offer a systematic guide for understanding his "political religion." The distinction between Lincoln's exoteric (overt) teaching on religion and politics addressed to the general public and his esoteric (covert) teaching addressed to those with "superior minds and education" is crucial to the Straussian interpretation of his "political religion." In short, the Straussians maintain that publicly Lincoln invoked religious symbolism for its political utility; however, privately, he questioned it between the lines to the careful reader as metaphysically false. Southern conservative scholars M.E. Bradford and Willmoore Kendall insist that Lincoln's reference to "political religion" and his biblical allusion to St. John's gospel at the end of the speech imply a messianic fusion of religion and politics. They revile Lincoln as an American Cromwell who saw politics not as the art of compromise, but as an Armageddon struggle between "the children of light and children of darkness." Failing to recognize Lincoln's prudence and to distinguish between the Sixteenth President and the radical abolitionists whom he disagreed with in practice, they portray him as a secular messiah who waged a crusade against the South's "peculiar institution" with the millenarian expectation of transfiguring the imperfections of political life into an egalitarian utopia. However, as noted in the first section of this volume, Lincoln's reference to "political religion" should not be overemphasized since it was a rhetorical flourish delivered within a rhetorical context. While certain elements of the Lyceum Address anticipate the mature Lincoln's combination of the biblical and republican traditions—namely, the importance of adherence to the rule of law and the role of religion in buttressing the nation's republican institutions—I contend that the Peoria Address of 1854 constitutes a far more profound and mature expression of his political faith (see "I Am Young and Unknown" for the Peoria Address).

As A SUBJECT FOR THE REMARKS of the evening, *THE PERPETUATION OF OUR POLITICAL INSTITUTIONS,* is selected.

In the great journal of things happening under the sun, we, the American People, find our account running, under date of the nineteenth century of the Christian era.—We find ourselves in the peaceful possession, of the fairest portion of the earth, as regards extent of territory, fertility of soil, and salubrity of climate. We find ourselves under the government of a system of political institutions, conducing more essentially to the ends of civil and religious liberty, than any of which the history of former times tell us. We, when mounting the stage of existence, found ourselves the legal inheritors of these fundamental blessings. We toiled not in the acquirement or establishment of them—they are a legacy bequeathed us, by a *once* hardy, brave, and patriotic, but *now* lamented and departed race of ancestors. Their's was the task (and nobly they performed it) to possess themselves, and through themselves, us, of this goodly land; and to uprear upon its hills and its valleys, a political edifice of liberty and equal rights; 'tis ours only, to transmit these, the former, unprofaned by the foot of an invader; the latter, undecayed by the lapse of time and untorn by usurpation, to the latest generation that fate shall permit the world to know. This task gratitude to our fathers, justice to ourselves, duty to posterity, and love for our species in general, all imperatively require us faithfully to perform.

How then shall we perform it?—At what point shall we expect the approach of danger? By what means shall we fortify against it?—Shall we expect some transatlantic military giant, to step the Ocean, and crush us at a blow? Never!— All the armies of Europe, Asia and Africa combined, with all the treasure of the earth (our own excepted) in their military chest; with a Buonaparte for a commander, could not by force, take a drink from the Ohio, or make a track on the Blue Ridge, in a trial of a thousand years.

At what point then is the approach of danger to be expected? I answer, if it ever reach us, it must spring up amongst us. It cannot come from abroad. If destruction be our lot, we must ourselves be its author and finisher. As a nation of freemen, we must live through all time, or die by suicide.

I hope I am over wary; but if I am not, there is, even now, something of ill-omen, amongst us. I mean the increasing disregard for law which pervades the country; the growing disposition to substitute the wild and furious passions, in lieu of the sober judgment of Courts; and the worse than savage mobs, for the executive ministers of justice. This disposition is awfully fearful in any community; and that it now exists in ours, though grating to our feelings to admit, it would be a violation of truth, and an insult to our intelligence, to deny. Accounts of outrages committed by mobs, form the every-day news of the times. They have pervaded the country, from New England to Louisiana;— they are neither peculiar to the eternal snows of the former, nor the burning suns of the latter;—they are not the creature of climate—neither are they confined to the slave-holding, or the non-slave-holding States. Alike, they spring up among the pleasure hunting masters of Southern slaves, and the order loving citizens of the land of steady habits.—Whatever, then, their cause may be, it is common to the whole country.

It would be tedious, as well as useless, to recount the horrors of all of them. Those happening in the State of Mississippi, and at St. Louis, are, perhaps, the most dangerous in example and revolting to humanity. In the Mississippi case, they first commenced by hanging the regular gamblers; a set of men, certainly not following for a livelihood, a very useful, or very honest occupation; but one which, so far from being forbidden by the laws, was actually licensed by an act of the Legislature, passed but a single year before. Next, negroes, suspected of conspiring to raise an insurrection, were caught up and hanged in all parts of the State: then, white men, supposed to be leagued with the negroes; and finally, strangers, from neighboring States, going thither on business, were, in many instances subjected to the same fate. Thus went on this process of hanging, from gamblers to negroes, from negroes to white citizens, and from these to strangers; till, dead men were seen literally dangling from the boughs of trees upon every road side; and in numbers almost sufficient, to rival the native Spanish moss of the country, as a drapery of the forest.

Turn, then, to that horror-striking scene at St. Louis. A single victim was only sacrificed there. His story is very short; and is, perhaps, the most highly tragic, of anything of its length, that has ever been witnessed in real life. A mulatto man, by the name of McIntosh, was seized in the street, dragged to the suburbs of the city, chained to a tree, and actually burned to death; and all within a single hour from the time he had been a freeman, attending to his own business, and at peace with the world.

Such are the effects of mob law; and such are the scenes, becoming more and more frequent in this land so lately famed for love of law and order; and the stories of which, have even now grown too familiar, to attract any thing more, than an idle remark.

But you are, perhaps, ready to ask, "What has this to do with the perpetuation of our political institutions?" I answer, it has much to do with it. Its direct consequences are, comparatively speaking, but a small evil; and much of its danger consists, in the proneness of our minds, to regard its direct, as its only consequences. Abstractly considered, the hanging of the gamblers at Vicksburg, was of but little consequence. They constitute a portion of population, that is worse than useless in any community; and their death, if no pernicious example be set by it, is never matter of reasonable regret with any one. If they were annually swept, from the stage of existence, by the plague or small pox, honest men would, perhaps, be much profited, by the operation.—Similar too, is the correct reasoning, in regard to the burning of the negro at St. Louis. He had forfeited his life, by the perpetration of an outrageous murder, upon one of the most worthy and respectable citizens of the city; and had he not died as he did, he must have died by the sentence of the law, in a very short time afterwards. As to him alone, it was as well the way it was, as it could otherwise have been.—But the example in either case, was fearful.—When men take it in their heads to day, to hang gamblers, or burn murderers, they should recollect, that, in the confusion usually attending such transactions, they will be as likely to hang or burn some one who is neither a gambler nor a murderer as one who is; and that, acting upon the example they set, the mob of to-morrow, may, and probably will, hang or burn some of them by the very same mistake. And not only so; the innocent, those who have ever set their faces against violations of law in every shape, alike with the guilty, fall victims to the ravages of mob law; and thus it goes on, step by step, till all the walls erected for the defence of the persons and property of individuals, are trodden down, and disregarded. But all this even, is not the full extent of the evil.— By such examples, by instances of the perpetrators of such acts going unpunished, the lawless in spirit, are encouraged to become lawless in practice; and having been used to no restraint, but dread of punishment, they thus become, absolutely unrestrained.—Having ever regarded Government as their deadliest bane, they make a jubilee of the suspension of its operations; and pray for nothing so much, as its total annihilation. While, on the other hand, good men, men who love tranquility, who desire to abide by the laws, and enjoy their benefits, who would gladly spill their blood in the defence of their country; seeing their property destroyed; their families insulted, and their lives endangered; their persons injured; and seeing nothing in prospect that forebodes a change for the better; become tired of, and disgusted with, a Government that offers them no protection; and are not much averse to a change in which they imagine they have nothing to lose. Thus, then, by the operation of this mobocratic spirit, which all must admit, is now abroad in the land, the strongest bulwark of any Government, and particularly of those constituted like ours, may effectually be broken down and destroyed—I mean the *attach-ment* of the People. Whenever this effect shall be produced among us; when-ever the vicious portion of population shall be permitted to gather in bands of hundreds and thousands, and burn churches, ravage and rob provision-stores, throw printing presses into rivers, shoot editors, and hang and burn obnox-ious persons at pleasure, and with impunity; depend on it, this Government cannot last. By such things, the feelings of the best citizens will become more or less alienated from it; and thus it will be left without friends, or with too few, and those few too weak, to make their friendship effectual. At such a time and under such circumstances, men of sufficient talent and ambition will not be wanting to seize the opportunity, strike the blow, and overturn that fair fabric, which for the last half century, has been the fondest hope, of the lovers of freedom, throughout the world.

I know the American People are *much* attached to their Government;—I know they would suffer *much* for its sake;—I know they would endure evils long and patiently, before they would ever think of exchanging it for another. Yet, notwithstanding all this, if the laws be continually despised and disre-garded, if their rights to be secure in their persons and property, are held by no better tenure than the caprice of a mob, the alienation of their affections from the Government is the natural consequence; and to that, sooner or later, it must come.

Here then, is one point at which danger may be expected.

The question recurs, "how shall we fortify against it?" The answer is sim-ple. Let every American, every lover of liberty, every well wisher to his poster-ity, swear by the blood of the Revolution, never to violate in the least particular, the laws of the country; and never to tolerate their violation by others. As the patriots of seventy-six did to the support of the Declaration of Independence, so to the support of the Constitution and Laws, let every American pledge his life, his property, and his sacred honor;—let every man remember that to vio-late the law, is to trample on the blood of his father, and to tear the character of his own, and his children's liberty. Let reverence for the laws, be breathed by every American mother, to the lisping babe, that prattles on her laplet it be taught in schools, in seminaries, and in colleges; let it be written in Primers, spelling books, and in Almanacs;—let it be preached from the pulpit, pro-claimed in legislative halls, and enforced in courts of justice. And, in short, let it become the *political religion* of the nation; and let the old and the young, the rich and the poor, the grave and the gay, of all sexes and tongues, and colors and conditions, sacrifice unceasingly upon its altars.

While ever a state of feeling, such as this, shall universally, or even, very generally prevail throughout the nation, vain will be every effort, and fruitless every attempt, to subvert our national freedom.

When I so pressingly urge a strict observance of all the laws, let me not be understood as saying there are no bad laws, nor that grievances may not arise, for the redress of which, no legal provisions have been made.—I mean to say no such thing. But I do mean to say, that, although bad laws, if they exist, should be repealed as soon as possible, still while they continue in force, for the sake of example, they should be religiously observed. So also in unprovided cases. If such arise, let proper legal provisions be made for them with the least possible delay; but, till then, let them, if not too intolerable, be borne with.

There is no grievance that is a fit object of redress by mob law. In any case that arises, as for instance, the promulgation of abolitionism, one of two positions is necessarily true; that is, the thing is right within itself, and therefore deserves the protection of all law and all good citizens; or, it is wrong, and therefore proper to be prohibited by legal enactments; and in neither case, is the interposition of mob law, either necessary, justifiable, or excusable.

But, it may be asked, why suppose danger to our political institutions? Have we not preserved them for more than fifty years? And why may we not for fifty times as long?

We hope there is *no sufficient* reason. We hope all dangers may be overcome; but to conclude that no danger may ever arise, would itself be extremely dangerous. There are now, and will hereafter be, many causes, dangerous in their tendency, which have not existed heretofore; and which are not too insignificant to merit attention. That our government should have been maintained in its original form from its establishment until now, is not much to be wondered at. It had many props to support it through that period, which now are decayed, and crumbled away. Through that period, it was felt by all, to be an undecided experiment; now, it is understood to be a successful one.—Then, all that sought celebrity and fame, and distinction, expected to find them in the success of that experiment. Their *all* was staked upon it:—their destiny was *inseparably* linked with it. Their ambition aspired to display before an admiring world, a practical demonstration of the truth of a proposition, which had hitherto been considered, at best no better, than problematical; namely, *the capability of a people to govern themselves.* If they succeeded, they were to be immortalized; their names were to be transferred to counties and cities, and rivers and mountains; and to be revered and sung, and toasted through all time. If they failed, they were to be called knaves and fools, and fanatics for a fleeting hour; then to sink and be forgotten. They succeeded. The experiment is successful; and thousands have won their deathless names in making it so. But the game is caught; and I believe it is true, that with the catching, end the pleasures of the chase. This field of glory is harvested, and the crop is already appropriated. But new reapers will arise, and *they,* too, will seek a field. It is to deny, what the history of the world tells us is true, to suppose that men of ambition and talents will not continue to spring up amongst us. And, when they do, they will as naturally seek the gratification of their ruling passion, as others have so done before them. The question then, is, can that gratification be found in supporting and maintaining an edifice that has been erected by others? Most certainly it cannot. Many great and good men sufficiently qualified for any task they should undertake, may ever be found, whose ambition would aspire to nothing beyond a seat in Congress, a gubernatorial or a presidential chair; *but such belong not to the family of the lion, or the tribe of the eagle.* What! think you these places would satisfy an Alexander, a Caesar, or a Napoleon?—Never! Towering genius disdains a beaten path. It seeks regions hitherto unexplored.—It sees *no distinction* in adding story to story, upon the monuments of fame, erected to the memory of others. It *denies* that it is glory enough to serve under any chief. It *scorns* to tread in the footsteps of *any* predecessor, however illustrious. It thirsts and burns for distinction; and, if possible, it will have it, whether at the expense of emancipating slaves, or enslaving freemen. Is it unreasonable then to expect, that some man possessed of the loftiest genius, coupled with ambition sufficient to push it to its utmost stretch, will at some time, spring up among us? And when such a one does, it will require the people to be united with each other, attached to the government and laws, and generally intelligent, to successfully frustrate his designs.

Distinction will be his paramount object, and although he would as willingly, perhaps more so, acquire it by doing good as harm; yet, that opportunity being past, and nothing left to be done in the way of building up, he would set boldly to the task of pulling down.

Here then, is a probable case, highly dangerous, and such a one as could not have well existed heretofore.

Another reason which *once was;* but which, to the same extent, is *now no more,* has done much in maintaining our institutions thus far. I mean the powerful influence which the interesting scenes of the revolution had upon the *passions* of the people as distinguished from their judgment. By this influence, the jealousy, envy, and avarice, incident to our nature, and so common to a state of peace, prosperity, and conscious strength, were, for the time, in a great measure smothered and rendered inactive; while the deep-rooted principles of *hate,* and the powerful motive of *revenge,* instead of being turned against each other, were directed exclusively against the British nation. And thus, from the force of circumstances, the basest principles of our nature, were either made to lie dormant, or to become the active agents in the advancement of the noblest of cause—that of establishing and maintaining civil and religious liberty.

But this state of feeling *must fade, is fading, has faded,* with the circumstances that produced it.

I do not mean to say, that the scenes of the revolution *are now* or *ever will* be entirely forgotten; but that like every thing else, they must fade upon the memory of the world, and grow more and more dim by the lapse of time. In history, we hope, they will be read of, and recounted, so long as the bible shall be read;—but even granting that they will, their influence *cannot be* what it heretofore has been. Even then, they *cannot be* so universally known, nor so vividly felt, as they were by the generation just gone to rest. At the close of that struggle, nearly every adult male had been a participator in some of its scenes. The consequence was, that of those scenes, in the form of a husband, a father, a son or a brother, *a living history* was to be found in every family—a history bearing the indubitable testimonies of its own authenticity, in the limbs mangled, in the scars of wounds received, in the midst of the very scenes related—a history, too, that could be read and understood alike by all, the wise and the ignorant, the learned and the unlearned.—But *those* histories are gone. They *can* be read no more forever. They *were* a fortress of strength; but, what invading foeman could *never do,* the silent artillery of time *has done;* the leveling of its walls. They are gone.—They *were* a forest of giant oaks; but the all-resistless hurricane has swept over them, and left only, here and there, a lonely trunk, despoiled of its verdure, shorn of its foliage; unshading and unshaded, to murmur in a few more gentle breezes, and to combat with its mutilated limbs, a few more ruder storms, then to sink, and be no more.

They *were* the pillars of the temple of liberty; and now, that they have crumbled away, that temple must fall, unless we, their descendants, supply their places with other pillars, hewn from the solid quarry of sober reason. Passion has helped us; but can do so no more. It will in future be our enemy. Reason, cold, calculating, unimpassioned reason, must furnish all the materials for our future support and defence.—Let those materials be moulded into *general intelligence, sound morality,* and, in particular, *a reverence for the constitution and laws:* and, that we improved to the last; that we remained free to the last; that we revered his name to the last; that, during his long sleep, we permitted no hostile foot to pass over or desecrate his resting place; shall be that which to learn the last trump shall awaken our WASHINGTON.

Upon these let the proud fabric of freedom rest, as the rock of its basis; and as truly as has been said of the only greater institution, *"the gates of hell shall not prevail against it."*

TEMPERANCE ADDRESS DELIVERED BEFORE THE SPRINGFIELD WASHINGTON TEMPERANCE SOCIETY
FEBRUARY 22, 1842

The crusade for temperance was part of a broad social reform movement along with abolitionism, women's rights, and care for the mentally ill that swept the nation during the Antebellum Period. Lincoln's Temperance Speech reveals some of his insights on human nature as well as his political moderation. As with his opposition to slavery, Lincoln spoke against a moral evil while avoiding the self-righteousness. A close look at the speech shows that he sought "to prick the conscience" of his audience by eliciting compassion for the addicts. Although he was not a member of the Temperance Society, Straussian scholars have emphasized the philosophical implications of Lincoln's exaltation of the mind over the body at the end of the speech. They interpret the following passage not as a rhetorical flourish, but as evidence of Lincoln's secular rationalism and his deterministic ontology: "Happy day, when all appetites controlled, all passions subdued, all matters subjected, mind, all conquering mind, shall live and move the monarch of the world. Glorious consummation! Hail fall of Fury! Reign of Reason, all hail!" Indeed, in his masterful work, Crisis of the House Divided, *Harry V. Jaffa once noted that "Lincoln's temperance speech contains a theological critique which parallels his critique of the dogmas of the Revolution [in the Lyceum Address]."*

ALTHOUGH THE TEMPERANCE CAUSE has been in progress for near twenty years, it is apparent to all, that it is, *just now,* being crowned with a degree of success, hitherto unparalleled.

The list of its friends is daily swelled by the additions of fifties, of hundreds, and of thousands. The cause itself seems suddenly transformed from a cold abstract theory, to a living, breathing, active, and powerful chieftain, going forth "conquering and to conquer." The citadels of his great adversary are daily being stormed and dismantled; his temples and his altars, where the rites of his idolatrous worship have long been performed, and where human sacrifices have long been wont to be made, are daily desecrated and deserted. The trump of the conqueror's fame is sounding from hill to hill, from sea to sea, and from land to land, and calling millions to his standard at a blast.

For this new and splendid success, we heartily rejoice. That that success is so much greater *now* than *heretofore,* is doubtless owing to rational causes; and if we would have it to continue, we shall do well to enquire what those causes are. The warfare heretofore waged against the demon of Intemperance, has, some how or other, been erroneous. Either the champions engaged, or the tactics they adopted, have not been the most proper. These champions for the most part, have been Preachers, Lawyers, and hired agents.—Between these and the mass of mankind, there is a want of *approachability,* if the term be admissible, partially at least, fatal to their success. They are supposed to have no sympathy of feeling or interest, with those very persons whom it is their object to convince and persuade.

And again, it is so easy and so common to ascribe motives to men of these classes, other than those they profess to act upon. The *preacher,* it is said, advocates temperance because he is a fanatic, and desires a union of the Church and State; the *lawyer,* from his pride and vanity of hearing himself speak; and the *hired agent,* for his salary. But when one, who has long been known as a victim of intemperance, bursts the fetters that have bound him, and appears before his neighbors "clothed, and in his right mind," a redeemed specimen of long lost humanity, and stands up with tears of joy trembling in eyes, to tell of the miseries *once* endured, *now* to be endured no more forever; of his once naked and starving children, now clad and fed comfortably; of a wife, long weighed down with woe, weeping, and a broken heart, now restored to health, happiness and renewed affection; and how easily it all is done, once it is resolved to be done; however simple his language, there is a logic, and an eloquence in it, that few, with human feelings, can resist. They cannot say that *he* desires a union of church and state, for he is not a church member; they can not say *he* is vain of hearing himself speak, for his whole demeanor shows, he would gladly avoid speaking at all; they cannot say *he* speaks for pay for he receives none, and asks for none. Nor can his sincerity in any way be doubted; or his sympathy for those he would persuade to imitate his example, be denied.

In my judgment, it is to the battles of this new class of champions that our late success is greatly, perhaps chiefly, owing.—But, had the old school champions themselves, been of the most wise selecting, was their *system* of tactics, the most judicious? It seems to me, it was not. Too much denunciation against dram sellers and dram drinkers was indulged in. This, I think, was both impolitic and unjust. It was *impolitic,* because, it is not much in the nature of man to be driven to any thing; still less to be driven about that which is exclusively his own business; and least of all, where such driving is to be submitted to, at the expense of pecuniary interest, or burning appetite. When the dram-seller and drinker, were incessantly told, not in the accents of entreaty and persuasion, diffidently addressed by erring man to an erring brother, but in the thundering tones of anathema and denunciation, with which the lordly Judge often groups together all the crimes of the felon's life, and thrusts them in his face just ere he passes sentence of death upon him, that *they* were the authors of all the vice and misery and crime in the land; that *they* were the manufacturers and material of all the thieves and robbers and murderers that infested the earth; that *their* houses were the workshops of the devil; and that *their persons* should be shunned by all the good and virtuous, as moral pestilences—I say, when they were told all this, and in this way, it is not wonderful that they were slow, *very slow,* to acknowledge the truth of such denunciations, and to join the ranks of their denouncers, in a hue and cry against themselves.

To have expected them to do otherwise than as they did—to have expected them not to meet denunciation with denunciation, crimination with crimination, and anathema with anathema, was to expect a reversal of human nature, which is God's decree, and never can be reversed. When the conduct of men is designed to be influenced, *persuasion,* kind, unassuming persuasion, should ever be adopted. It is an old and a true maxim "that a drop of honey catches more flies than a gallon of gall."—So with men. If you would win a man to your cause, *first* convince him that you are his sincere friend. Therein is a drop of honey that catches his heart, which, say what he will, is the great high road to his reason, and which, when once gained, you will find but little trouble in convincing his judgment of the justice of your cause, if indeed that cause really be a just one. On the contrary, assume to dictate to his judgment, or to command his action, or to mark him as one to be shunned and despised, and he will retreat within himself, close all the avenues to his head and his heart; and though your cause be naked truth itself, transformed to the heaviest lance, harder than steel, and sharper than steel can be made, and tho' you throw it with more than Herculean force and precision, you shall be no more able to pierce him, than to penetrate the hard shell of a tortoise with a rye straw.

Such is man, and so *must* he be understood by those who would lead him, even to his own best interest.

On this point, the Washingtonians greatly excel the temperance advocates of former times. Those whom *they* desire to convince and persuade, are their old friends and companions. They know they are not demons, nor even the worst of men. *They* know that generally, they are kind, generous, and charitable, even beyond the example of their more staid and sober neighbors. *They* are practical philanthropists; and *they* glow with a generous and brotherly zeal, that mere theorizers are incapable of feeling.—Benevolence and charity possess *their* hearts entirely; and out of the abundance of their hearts, their tongues give utterance. "Love through all their actions runs, and all their words are mild." In this spirit they speak and act, and in the same, they are heard and regarded. And when such is the temper of the advocate, and such of the audience, no good cause can be unsuccessful.

But I have said that denunciations against dram-sellers and dram-drinkers are *unjust,* as well as impolitic. Let us see.

I have not enquired at what period of time the use of intoxicating drinks commenced; nor is it important to know. It is sufficient that to all of us who now inhabit the world, the practice of drinking them, is just as old as the world itself,—that is, we have seen the one, just as long as we have seen the other. When all such of us, as have now reached the years of maturity, first opened our eyes upon the stage of existence, we found intoxicating liquor, recognized by every body, used by every body, and repudiated by nobody. It commonly entered into the first draught of the infant, and the last draught of the dying man. From the sideboard of the parson, down to the ragged pocket of the houseless loafer, it was constantly found. Physicians prescribed it in this, that, and the other disease. Government provided it for its soldiers and sailors; And to have a rolling or raising, a husking or hoe-down, any where without it was *positively insufferable.*

So too, it was every where a respectable article of manufacture and of merchandize. The making of it was regarded as an honorable livelihood; and he who could make most, was the most enterprising and respectable. Large and small manufactories of it were every where erected, in which all the earthly goods of their owners were invested. Wagons drew it from town to town—boats bore it from clime to clime, and the winds wafted it from nation to nation; and merchants bought and sold it, by wholesale and by retail, with precisely the same feelings, on the part of the seller, buyer, and by-stander as are felt at the selling and buying of flour, beef, bacon, or any other of the real necessaries of life. Universal public opinion not only tolerated, but recognized and adopted its use.

It is true, that even *then,* it was known and acknowledged, that many were greatly injured by it; but none seemed to think the injury arose from the *use* of a *bad thing,* but from the *abuse* of a *very good thing.*—The victims to it were pitied, and compassionated, just as now are, the heirs of consumptions, and other hereditary diseases. Their failing was treated as a *misfortune,* and not as a *crime,* or even as a *disgrace.*

If, then, what I have been saying be true, is it wonderful that *some* should think and act *now,* as *all* thought and acted *twenty years ago?* And is it *just* to assail, contemn, or despise them, for doing so? The universal *sense* of mankind, on any subject, is an argument, or at least an *influence,* not easily overcome. The success of the argument in favor of the existence of an overruling Providence, mainly depends upon that sense; and men ought not, in justice, to be denounced for yielding to it in any case, or for giving it up slowly, *especially,* where they are backed by interest, fixed habits, or burning appetites.

Another error, as it seems to me, into which the old reformers fell, was, the position that all habitual drunkards were utterly incorrigible, and therefore, must be turned adrift, and damned without remedy, in order that the grace of temperance might abound to the temperate *then,* and to all mankind some hundred years *thereafter.*—There is in this something so repugnant to humanity, so uncharitable, so cold-blooded and feelingless, that it never did, nor ever can enlist the enthusiasm of a popular cause. We could not love the man who taught it—we could not hear him with patience. The heart could not throw open its portals to it. The generous man could not adopt it. It could not mix with his blood. It looked so fiendishly selfish, so like throwing fathers and brothers overboard, to lighten the boat for our security—that the noble minded shrank from the manifest meanness of the thing.

And besides this, the benefits of a reformation to be effected by such a system, were too remote in point of time, to warmly engage many in its behalf. Few can be induced to labor exclusively for posterity; and none will do it enthusiastically. Posterity has done nothing for us; and theorise on it as we may, practically we shall do very little for it, unless we are made to think, we are, at the same time, doing something for ourselves. What an ignorance of human nature does it exhibit, to ask or expect a whole community to rise up and labor for the *temporal* happiness of *others,* after *themselves* shall be consigned to the dust, a majority of which community take no pains whatever to secure their own eternal welfare, at no greater distant day? Great distance, in either time or space, has wonderful power to lull and render quiescent the human mind. Pleasures to be enjoyed, or pains to be endured, *after* we shall be dead and gone, are but little regarded, even in our *own* cases, and much less in the cases of others.

Still, in addition to this, there is something so ludicrous in *promises* of good, or *threats* of evil, a great way off, as to render the whole subject with which they are connected, easily turned into ridicule. "Better lay down that spade you're stealing, Paddy,—if you don't you'll pay for it at the day of judgment." "By the powers, if ye'll credit me so long, I'll take another, jist."

By the Washingtonians, this system of consigning the habitual drunkard to hopeless ruin, is repudiated. *They* adopt a more enlarged philanthropy. *They* go for present as well as future good. *They* labor for all *now* living, as well as all *hereafter* to live.—*They* teach *hope* to all—*despair* to none. As applying to *their* cause, *they* deny the doctrine of unpardonable sin. As in Christianity it is taught, so in this *they* teach, that

> "While the lamp holds out to burn,
> The vilest sinner may return."

And, what is a matter of the most profound gratulation, they, by experiment upon experiment, and example upon example, prove the maxim to be no less true in the one case than in the other. On every hand we behold those, who but yesterday, were the chief of sinners, now the chief apostles of the cause. Drunken devils are cast out by ones, by sevens, and by legions; and their unfortunate victims, like the poor possessed, who was redeemed from his long and lonely wanderings in the tombs, are publishing to the ends of the earth how great things have been done for them.

To these *new champions,* and this *new* system of tactics, our late success is mainly owing; and to *them* we must chiefly look for the final consummation. The ball is now rolling gloriously on, and none are so able as *they* to increase its speed and its bulk—to add to its momentum, and its magnitude.—Even though unlearned in letters, for this task, none others are so well educated. To fit them for this work, they have been taught in the true school. *They* have been in *that* gulf, from which they would teach others the means of escape. *They* have passed that prison wall, which others have long declared impassable; and who that has not, shall dare to weigh opinions with *them,* as to the mode of passing?

But if it be true, as I have insisted, that those who have suffered by intemperance *personally,* and have reformed, are the most powerful and efficient instruments to push the reformation to ultimate success, it does not follow, that those who have not suffered, have no part left them to perform. Whether or not the world would be vastly benefitted by a total and final banishment from it of all intoxicating drinks, seems to me not *now* to be an open question. Three-fourths of mankind confess the affirmative with their *tongues,* and, I believe, all the rest acknowledge it in their *hearts.*

Ought *any,* then, to refuse their aid in doing what the good of the *whole* demands?—Shall he, who cannot do *much,* be for that reason, excused if he do *nothing?* "But," says one, "what good can I do by signing the pledge? I never drink even without signing." This question has already been asked and answered more than millions of times. Let it be answered once more. For the man to suddenly, or in any other way, to break off from the use of drams, who has indulged in them for a long course of years, and until his appetite for them has become ten or a hundred fold stronger, and more craving, than any natural appetite can be, requires a most powerful moral effort. In such an undertaking, he needs every moral support and influence, that can possibly be brought to his aid, and thrown around him. And not only so; but every moral prop, should be taken *from* whatever argument might rise in his mind to lure him to his backsliding. When he casts his eyes around him, he should be able to see, all that he respects, all that he admires, and all that [he?] loves, kindly and anxiously pointing him onward; and none beckoning him back, to his former miserable "wallowing in the mire."

But it is said by some, that men will *think* and *act* for themselves; that none will disuse spirits or anything else, merely because his neighbors do; and that *moral influence* is not that powerful engine contended for. Let us examine this. Let me ask the man who would maintain this position most stiffly, what compensation he will accept to go to church some Sunday and sit during the sermon with his wife's bonnet upon his head? Not a trifle, I'll venture. And why not? There would be nothing irreligious in it: nothing immoral, nothing uncomfortable.— Then why not? Is it not because there would be something egregiously unfashionable in it? Then it is the influence of *fashion;* and what is the influence of fashion, but the influence that *other* people's actions have on our actions, the strong inclination each of us feels to do as we see all our neighbors do? Nor is the influence of fashion confined to any particular thing or class of things. It is just as strong on one subject as another. Let us make it as unfashionable to withhold our names from the temperance pledge as for husbands to wear their wives' bonnets to church, and instances will be just as rare in the one case as the other.

"But," say some, "we are no drunkards; and we shall not acknowledge ourselves such by joining a reformed drunkards' society, whatever our influence might be." Surely no Christian will adhere to this objection.—If they believe, as they profess, that Omnipotence condescended to take on himself the form of sinful man, and as such, to die an ignominious death for their sakes, surely they will not refuse submission to the infinitely lesser condescension, for the temporal, and perhaps eternal salvation, of a large, erring, and unfortunate class of their own fellow creatures. Nor is the condescension very great.

In my judgment, such of us as have never fallen victims, have been spared more from the absence of appetite, than from any mental or moral superiority over those who have. Indeed, I believe, if we take habitual drunkards as a class, their heads and their hearts will bear an advantageous comparison with those of any other class. There seems ever to have been a proneness in the brilliant, and the warm-blooded, to fall into this vice—the demon of intemperance ever seems to have delighted in sucking the blood of genius and of generosity. What one of us but can call to mind some dear relative, more promising in youth than all his fellows, who has fallen a sacrifice to his rapacity? He ever seems to have gone forth, like the Egyptian angel of death, commissioned to slay if not the first, the fairest born of every family. Shall he now be arrested in his desolating career? In that arrest, all can give aid that will; and who shall be excused that *can* and will not? Far around as human breath has ever blown, he keeps our fathers, our brothers, our sons, and our friends prostrate in the chains of moral death. To all the living every where, we cry, "come sound the moral resurrection trump, that these may rise and stand up, an exceeding great army"—"Come from the four winds, O breath! and breathe upon these slain, that they may live."

If the relative grandeur of revolutions shall be estimated by the great amount of human misery they alleviate, and the small amount they inflict, then indeed, will this be the grandest the world shall ever have seen.—Of our political revolution of '76 we all are justly proud. It has given us a degree of political freedom, far exceeding that of any other of the nations of the earth. In it the world has found a solution of the long mooted problem, as to the capability of man to govern himself. In it was the germ which has vegetated, and still is to grow and expand into the universal liberty of mankind.

But with all these glorious results, past, present, and to come, it had its evils too.—It breathed forth famine, swam in blood and rode on fire; and long, long after, the orphan's cry, and the widow's wail, continued to break the sad silence that ensued. These were the price, the inevitable price, paid for the blessings it bought.

Turn now, to the temperance revolution. In *it* we shall find a stronger bondage broken; a viler slavery manumitted; a greater tyrant deposed. In *it,* more of want supplied, more disease healed, more sorrow assuaged. By *it* no orphans starving, no widows weeping. By *it,* none wounded in feeling, none injured in interest. Even the dram maker and dram seller, will have glided into other occupations *so* gradually, as never to have felt the shock of change; and will stand ready to join all others in the universal song of gladness.

And what a noble ally this, to the cause of political freedom. With such an aid, its march cannot fail to be on and on, till every son of earth shall drink in rich fruition, the sorrow quenching draughts of perfect liberty. Happy day, when, all appetites controlled, all passions subdued, all matters subjected, *mind,* all conquering *mind,* shall live and move the monarch of the world. Glorious consummation! Hail, fall of Fury! Reign of Reason, all hail!

And when the victory shall be complete—when there shall be neither a slave nor a drunkard on the earth—how proud the title of that *Land,* which may truly claim to be the birthplace and the cradle of both those revolutions, that shall have ended in that victory. How nobly distinguished that People, who shall have planted, and nurtured to maturity, both the political and moral freedom of their species.

This is the one hundred and tenth anniversary of the birthday of Washington.—We are met to celebrate this day. Washington is the mightiest name of earth—*long since* mightiest in the cause of civil liberty; *still* mightiest in moral reformation. On that name an eulogy is expected. It cannot be. To add brightness to the sun, or glory to the name of Washington, is alike impossible. Let none attempt it. In solemn awe pronounce the name, and in its naked deathless splendor, leave it shining on.

LETTER TO JOSHUA F. SPEED
JULY 4, 1842

Lincoln's letters to Joshua Speed on February 3 ("I Am Young and Unknown," above) and this one on July 4, 1842, manifest the core elements of his biblical faith. Though his faith deepened with maturity—especially after the death of his son, Willie, and during the turbulent war years—Lincoln's articulation of this faith remained consistent throughout his life. In this private correspondence, Lincoln assured his friend that life is guided by a providential design. Things happen for a reason; life is not a series of unconnected random events. Using biblical language existentially, Lincoln conveyed his personal experience of the divine at work in his own life. He believed that God had made him "an instrument" in bringing Speed and his fiance, Fanny together. The letter manifests Lincoln's trust in the graciousness of divine being and his personal reliance upon God's power. As a faithful servant, he bore witness to God's providence quoting Exodus 14:13: "Stand still and see the salvation of the Lord," which communicated existentially his own experience of biblical faith. Despite the inscrutability of God's, Lincoln trusted that God would bring about some greater good out of his present suffering.

SPRINGFIELD, ILLS—JULY 4TH, 1842—

DEAR SPEED:

Yours of the 16th. June was received only a day or two since. It was not mailed at Louisville till the 25th. You speak of the great time that has elapsed since I wrote you. Let me explain that. Your letter reached here a day or two after I started on the circuit; I was gone five or six weeks, so that I got the letter only a few weeks before Butler started to your country. I thought it scarcely worth while to write you the news, which he could and would tell you more in detail. On his return, he told me you would write me soon; and so I waited for your letter. As to my having been displeased with your advice, surely you know better than that. I know you do; and therefore I will not labor to convince you. True, that subject is painful to me; but it is not your silence, or the silence of all the world that can make me forget it. I acknowledge the correctness of your advice too; but before I resolve to do the one thing or the other, I must regain my confidence in my own ability to keep my resolves when they are made. In that ability, you know, I once prided myself as the only, or at least the chief, gem of my character; that gem I lost—how, and where, you too well know. I have not yet regained it; and until I do, I can not trust myself in any matter of much importance. I believe now that had you understood my case at the time, as well as I understood yours afterwards, by the aid you would have given me, I should have sailed through clear; but that does not now afford me sufficient confidence, to begin that, or the like of that, again.

You make a kind acknowledgment of your obligations to me for your present happiness. I am pleased with that acknowledgment; but a thousand times more am I pleased to know, that you enjoy a degree of happiness, worthy of an acknowledgment. The truth is, I am not sure that there was any merit, with me, in the part I took in your difficulty; I was drawn to it as by fate; if I would, I could not have done less than I did. I always was superstitious; and as part of my superstition, I believe God made me one of the instruments of bringing your Fanny and you together, which union, I have no doubt He had fore-ordained. Whatever he designs, he will do for *me* yet. "Stand *still,* and see the salvation of the Lord" is my text just now. If, as you say, you have told Fanny *all,* I should have no objection to her seeing this letter, but for its reference to our friend here. Let her seeing it, depend upon whether she has ever known anything of my affair; and if she has not, do not let her.

I do not think I can come to Kentucky this season. I am so poor, and make so little headway in the world, that I drop back in a month of idleness, as much as I gain in a year's rowing. I should like to visit you again. I should like to see that "Sis" of yours, that was absent when I was there; tho I suppose she would run away again, if she were to hear I was coming.

About your collecting business. We have sued Branson; and will sue the others to the next court, unless they give deeds of trust as you require. Col Allen happened in the office since I commenced this letter, and promises to give a deed of trust. He says he had made the arrangement to pay you, and would have done it, but for the going down of the Shawnee money. We did not get the note in time to sue Hall at the last Tazewell court. Lockridge's property is levied on for you. John Irwin has done nothing with that Baker & Van Bergen matter. We will not fail to bring the suits for your use, where they are in the name of James Bell & Co. I have made you a suscriber to the Journal; and also sent the number containing the temperance speech. My respect and esteem to all your friends there; and, by your permission, my love to your Fanny.

Ever yours—
Lincoln

RELIGIOUS VIEWS: LETTER TO THE EDITOR OF THE *ILLINOIS GAZETTE*
AUGUST 11, 1846

In the 1846 congressional election, Lincoln ran as the Whig candidate against Peter Cartwright, a Methodist frontier preacher and revivalist who was the Democratic candidate. After falling behind in the race, Cartwright spread a rumor that Lincoln was an infidel. This accusation had harmed Lincoln in a previous election. In response to Cartwright's allegations, Lincoln wrote to the editor of the Illinois Gazette *asking him to publish his personal reply to the charges against him in a handbill addressed "To the Voters of the Seventh District" (see below). This handbill (an article addressed directly to the people expressing a candidate's views) constitutes the only explicit public declaration of Lincoln's personal religious beliefs. Consonant with his avoidance of sectarianism and his personal reliance upon Scripture, he acknowledged that he was not a member of any Christian church or denomination. Characteristically, he chose his words carefully to describe his beliefs. To not "deny the truth of Scriptures" does not mean that you affirm their literal truth. In his youth, Lincoln seemed to have reservations about the literalism and emotionalism of frontier religion. When Joshua Speed, an old friend from Springfield days, asked the president years later about their youthful questioning of religion, Lincoln replied, ". . . take all of this book [the Bible] upon reason that you can, and the balance on faith, and you will live and die a happier and better man."*

SPRINGFIELD, AUGUST 11TH, 1846.

MR. FORD:—

I see in your paper of the 8th inst. a communication in relation to myself, of which it is perhaps expected of me to take some notice.

Shortly before starting on my tour through yours, and the other Northern counties of the District, I was informed by letter from Jacksonville that Mr. Cartwright was whispering the charge of infidelity against me in that quarter.—I at once wrote a contradiction of it, and sent it to my friends there, with the request that they should publish it or not, as in their discretion they might think proper, having in view the extent of the circulation of the charge, as also the extent of credence it might be receiving. They did not publish it. After my return from your part of the District, I was informed that he had been putting the same charge in circulation against me in some of the neighborhoods in our own, and one or two of the adjoining counties.—I believe nine persons out of ten had not heard the charge at all; and, in a word, its extent of circulation was just such as to make a public notice of it appear uncalled for; while it was not entirely safe to leave it unnoticed. After some reflection, I published the little hand-bill, herewith enclosed, and sent it to the neighborhoods above referred to.

I have little doubt now, that to make the same charge—to slyly sow the seed in select spots—was the chief object of his mission through your part of the District, at a time when he knew I could not contradict him, either in person or by letter before the election. And, from the election returns in your county, being so different from what they are in parts where Mr. Cartwright and I are both well known, I incline to the belief that he has succeeded in deceiving some honest men there.

As to Mr. Woodward, "our worthy commissioner from Henry," spoken of by your correspondent, I must say it is a little singular that he should know so much about me, while, if I ever saw *him,* or heard of him, save in the communication in your paper, I have forgotten it. If Mr. Woodward has given such assurance of my character as your correspondent asserts, I can still suppose him to be a worthy man; he may have believed what he said; but there is, even in that charitable view of his case, one lesson in morals which he might, not without profit, learn of even me—and that is, never to add the weight of his character to a charge against his fellow man, without *knowing* it to be true.—I believe it is an established maxim in morals that he who makes an assertion without knowing whether it is true or false, is guilty of falsehood; and the accidental truth of the assertion, does not justify or excuse him. This maxim ought to be particularly held in view, when we contemplate an attack upon the reputation of our neighbor. I suspect it will turn out that Mr. Woodward got his information in relation to me, from Mr. Cartwright; and I here aver, that he, Cartwright, never heard me utter a word in any way indicating my opinions on religious matters, in his life.

It is my wish that you give this letter, together with the accompanying handbill, a place in your paper.

Yours truly,

A. Lincoln

TO THE VOTERS OF THE SEVENTH CONGRESSIONAL DISTRICT.

FELLOW CITIZENS:

A charge having got into circulation in some of the neighborhoods of this District, in substance that I am an open scoffer at *Christianity,* I have by the advice of some friends concluded to notice the subject in this form. That I am not a member of any Christian Church, is true; but I have never denied the truth of the Scriptures; and I have never spoken with intentional disrespect of religion in general, or of any denomination of Christians in particular. It is true that in early life I was inclined to believe in what I understand is called the "Doctrine of Necessity"—that is, that the human mind is impelled to action, or held in rest by some power, over which the mind itself has no control; and I have sometimes (with one, two or three, but never publicly) tried to maintain this opinion in argument—the habit of arguing thus however, I have, entirely left off for more than five years—And I add here, I have always understood this same opinion to be held by several of the Christian denominations. The foregoing, is the whole truth, briefly stated, in relation to myself, upon this subject.

I do not think I could myself, be brought to support a man for office, whom I knew to be an open enemy of, and scoffer at, religion.—Leaving the higher matter of eternal consequences, between him and his Maker, I still do not think any man has the right thus to insult the feelings, and injure the morals, of the community in which he may live.—If, then, I was guilty of such conduct, I should blame no man who should condemn me for it; but I do blame those, whoever they may be, who falsely put such a charge in circulation against me.

A Lincoln.

July 31, 1846.

FRAGMENT: ON SLAVERY
[OCTOBER 1, 1858?]

The following reflection demonstrates the extent to which Lincoln's political thought developed as a concrete response to rival interpretations of public life like proslavery theology. Around the mid-nineteenth century, influential Southerners no longer apologized for their "peculiar institution", but defended it as a social and political blessing "ordained of God." They took to the offensive, condemning what they perceived as the moral decadence of the North. The South's defense of slavery as a way of life implied a corresponding critique of northern free society as heartless and corrupt. The foremost members of the southern cultural elite like George Fitzhugh attempted to dispose public opinion toward the moral acceptance of slavery as a positive good. Here, Lincoln referred to Reverend Frederick A. Ross, a Presbyterian minister who lectured throughout the country on proslavery theology and published a series of proslavery articles in an influential book entitled, Slavery Ordained of God.

SUPPOSE IT IS TRUE, that the negro is inferior to the white, in the gifts of nature; is it not the exact reverse justice that the white should, for that reason, take from the negro, any part of the little which has been given him? *"Give* to him that is needy" is the Christian rule of charity; but "Take from him that is needy" is the rule of slavery.

PRO-SLAVERY THEOLOGY

The sum of pro-slavery theology seems to be this: "Slavery is not universally *right,* nor yet universally *wrong;* it is better for *some* people to be slaves; and, in such cases, it is the Will of God that they be such."

Certainly there is no contending against the Will of God; but still there is some difficulty in ascertaining, and applying it, to particular cases. For instance we will suppose the Rev. Dr. Ross has a slave named Sambo, and the question is "Is it the Will of God that Sambo shall remain a slave, or be set free?" The Almighty gives no audable [sic] answer to the question, and his revelation—the Bible—gives none—or, at most, *none* but such as admits of a squabble, as to it's meaning. No one thinks of asking Sambo's opinion on it. So, at last, it comes to this, that *Dr. Ross* is to decide the question. And while he consider [sic] it, he sits in the shade, with gloves on his hands, and subsists on the bread that Sambo is earning in the burning sun. If he decides that God wills Sambo to continue a slave, he thereby retains his own comfortable position; but if he decides that God wills Sambo to be free, he thereby has to walk out of the shade, throw off his gloves, and delve for his own bread. Will Dr. Ross be actuated by that perfect impartiality, which has ever been considered most favorable to correct decisions?

But, slavery is good for some people!!! As a *good* thing, slavery is strikingly perculiar [*sic*], in this, that it is the only good thing which no man ever seeks the good of, *for himself.*

Nonsense! Wolves devouring lambs, not because it is good for their own greedy maws, but because it is good for the lambs!!!

FRAGMENT: NOTES FOR SPEECHES[2]
[OCTOBER 1, 1858?]

The exact date of this fragment cannot be ascertained although it does resemble argu-ments made by Lincoln just prior to the Lincoln-Douglas Debates. The fragment shows that Lincoln situated the politics of the Civil War era in terms of a wider philosophical context as a struggle between rival public philosophies that sought to define American republicanism. In condemning the Declaration of Independence, the nation's moral covenant, as a self-evident lie, Southerners actually sought to dispose public opinion to accepting the "natural, moral, and religious right to slavery." Because Lincoln viewed public opinion and public policy reciprocal, he believed that a change in the former would lead to a change in the latter. If public opinion accepted the substitution of the old politi-cal standard of equality for the new political standard of servitude, a radical transforma-tion of the republic's ethos, policies and institutions was likely to follow.

BUT THERE IS A LARGER ISSUE than the mere question of whether the spread of negro slavery shall or shall not be prohibited by Congress. That larger issue is stated by the Richmond "Enquirer," a Buchanan paper in the South, in the language I now read. It is also stated by the New York "Day-book," a Buchanan paper in the North, in this language.—And in relation to indigent white chil-dren, the same Northern paper says.—In support of the Nebraska bill, on its first discussion in the Senate, Senator Pettit of Indiana declared the equality of men, as asserted in our Declaration of Independence, to be a "self-evident lie." In his numerous speeches now being made in Illinois, Senator Douglas regularly argues against the doctrine of the equality of all men; and while he does not draw the conclusion that the superiors ought to enslave the inferiors, he evi-dently wishes his hearers to draw that conclusion. He shirks the responsibility of pulling the house down, but he digs under it that it may fall of its own weight.

2. *CWAL,* III, 205.

Now, it is impossible to not see that these newspapers and senators are laboring at a common objective, and in doing so are truly representing the controlling sentiment in their party.

It is equally important to not see that that common object is to subvert, in the public mind, and in practical administration, our old and only standard of free government, that "all men are created equal," and to substitute for it some different standard. What that substitute is to be is not difficult to perceive. It is to deny the equality of men, and to assert the natural, moral, and religious right of one class to enslave another.

LETTER TO H. L. PIERCE AND OTHERS
APRIL 6, 1859

After he gained notoriety through the Lincoln-Douglas Debates, Lincoln was invited by Henry L. Pierce, the head of a committee of Boston Republicans to attend a festival in honor of Thomas Jefferson's birthday. Lincoln was unable to attend, but sent this letter, which was widely circulated by the Republican press. As noted, Lincoln believed that the principles of Jefferson were under attack by proponents of slavery who derided the Declaration's assertion of equality as "a self-evident lie." He characterized the principles of Jefferson in Euclidean terms as "the definitions and axioms of free society." In his view, political order required a consensus on first principles as a necessary condition of civic discourse. Lincoln's praise of Thomas Jefferson, a Democrat, buttressed the authority of the Republican Party as the authentic representatives of American republicanism. Toward the end of the speech, he explained that slavery was incompatible with man's rudimentary understanding of the divine justice. The general precepts of the Declaration circumscribed the boundaries of a just government thereby preventing the nation from succumbing to the political idolatry of tyranny.

SPRINGFIELD, ILLS, APRIL 6, 1859
MESSRS. HENRY L. PIERCE, & OTHERS.
GENTLEMEN

Your kind note inviting me to attend a Festival in Boston, on the 13th. Inst. in honor of the birth-day of Thomas Jefferson, was duly received. My engagements are such that I can not attend.

Bearing in mind that about seventy years ago, two great political parties were first formed in this country, that Thomas Jefferson was the head of one of them, and Boston the head-quarters of the other, it is both curious and interesting that those supposed to descend politically from the party opposed to Jefferson should now be celebrating his birthday in their own original seat of empire, while those claiming political descent from him have nearly ceased to breathe his name everywhere.

Remembering too, that the Jefferson party were formed upon its supposed superior devotion to the *personal* rights of men, holding the rights of *property* to be secondary only, and greatly inferior, and then assuming that the so-called democracy of to-day, are the Jefferson, and their opponents, the anti-Jefferson parties, it will be equally interesting to note how completely the two have changed hands as to the principle upon which they were originally supposed to be divided.

The democracy of to-day hold the *liberty* of one man to be absolutely nothing, when in conflict with another man's right of *property*. Republicans, on the contrary, are for both the *man* and the *dollar;* but in cases of conflict, the man *before* the dollar.

I remember once being much amused at seeing two partially intoxicated men engage in a fight with their great-coats on, which fight, after a long, and rather harmless contest, ended in each having fought himself *out* of his own coat, and *into* that of the other. If the two leading parties of this day are really identical with the two in the days of Jefferson and Adams, they have performed the same feat as the two drunken men.

But soberly, it is now no child's play to save the principles of Jefferson from total overthrow in this nation.

One would start with great confidence that he could convince any sane child that the simpler propositions of Euclid are true; but, nevertheless, he would fail, utterly, with one who should deny the definitions and axioms. The principles of Jefferson are the definitions and axioms of free society.

And yet they are denied and evaded, with no small show of success.

One dashingly calls them "glittering generalities"; another bluntly calls them "self evident lies"; and still others insidiously argue that they apply only to "superior races."

These expressions, differing in form, are identical in object and effect—the supplanting the principles of free government, and restoring those of classification, caste, and legitimacy. They would delight a convocation of crowned heads, plotting against the people. They are the van-guard—the miners, and sappers—of returning despotism.

We must repulse them, or they will subjugate us.

This is a world of compensations; and he who would *be* no slave, must consent to *have* no slave. Those who deny freedom to others, deserve it not for themselves; and, under a just God, can not long retain it.

All honor to Jefferson—to the man who, in the concrete pressure of a struggle for national independence by a single people, had the coolness, forecast, and capacity to introduce into a merely revolutionary document, an abstract truth, applicable to all men and all times, and so to embalm it there, that to-day, and in all coming days, it shall be a rebuke and a stumbling-block to the very harbingers of re-appearing tyranny and oppression.

Your obedient Servant

A. Lincoln—

SPEECH AT CINCINNATI, OHIO[3]
SEPTEMBER 17, 1859

This Speech at Cincinnati, Ohio, on September 17, 1859, was delivered about a year after the Lincoln-Douglas Debates and before the presidential campaign of 1860. Two sections of the speech are particularly relevant to Lincoln's political faith: (1) The "See Saw" section where Lincoln replied to Douglas's invocation of the "Almighty's Dividing Line;" and (2) the "Bible Theory" where he criticized Douglas's racial supremacist views. In a speech delivered at Memphis on November 30, 1858, Douglas reputedly stated that, "The Almighty had drawn a line on this Continent, on one side on which the soil must be cultivated by slave labor; on the other by white labor." In effect, Douglas offered an implicit religious justification for popular sovereignty. God had sanctioned a permanent national division over slavery as part of his providential plan for diversity. He ordained that the culture and climate of the South would be conducive to slavery, while that of the North would be averse to the institution. Thus, slavery was not evil per se, but good or bad depending upon culture and climate. As an indication of how seriously Lincoln considered ultimate justifications of public life, he responded to the Dividing Line argument on at least eight different occasions, even though the metaphor occupied a single sentence in Douglas's speech.

SEPTEMBER 17, 1859

My fellow-citizens of the State of Ohio: This is the first time in my life that I have appeared before an audience in so great a city as this. I therefore—though I am no longer a young man—make this appearance under some degree of embarrassment. But, I have found that when one is embarrassed, usually the

3. *CWAL*, III, 438-462.

shortest way to get through with it is to quit talking or thinking about it, and go at something else. (Applause.)

What did Douglas say?

I understand that you have had recently with you, my very distinguished friend, Judge Douglas, of Illinois, (laughter) and I understand, without having had an opportunity, (not greatly sought to be sure,) of seeing a report of the speech, that he made here, that he did me the honor to mention my humble name. I suppose that he did so for the purpose of making some objection to some sentiment at some time expressed by me. I should expect, it is true, that Judge Douglas had reminded you, or informed you, if you had never before heard it, that I had once in my life declared it as my opinion that this government cannot "endure permanently half slave and half free; that a house divided against itself cannot stand," and, as I had expressed it, I did not expect the house to fall; that I did not expect the Union to be dissolved; but, that I did expect that it would cease to be divided; that it would become all one thing or all the other, that either the opponents of Slavery would arrest the further spread of it, and place it where the public mind would rest in the belief that it was in the course of ultimate extinction; or the friends of Slavery will push it forward until it becomes alike lawful in all the States, old or new, Free as well as Slave. I did, fifteen months ago, express that opinion, and upon many occasions Judge Douglas has denounced it, and has greatly, intentionally or unintentionally, misrepresented my purpose in the expression of that opinion.

I presume, without having seen a report of his speech, that he did so here. I presume that he alluded also to that opinion in different language, having been expressed at a subsequent time by Governor Seward of New York, and that he took the two in a lump and denounced them; that he tried to point out that there was something couched in this opinion which led to the making of an entire uniformity of the local institutions of the various States of the Union, in utter disregard of the different States, which in their nature would seem to require a variety of institutions, and a variety of laws, conforming to the differences in the nature of the different States.

Not only so; I presume he insisted that this was a declaration of war between the Free and Slave States—that it was the sounding to the onset of continual war between the different States, the Slave and Free States.

This charge, in this form, was made by Judge Douglas on, I believe, the 9th of July, 1858, in Chicago, in my hearing. On the next evening, I made some reply to it. I informed him that many of the inferences he drew from that expression of mine were altogether foreign to any purpose entertained by me, and in so far as he should ascribe those inferences to me, as my purpose, he was entirely mistaken; and in so far as he might argue that whatever might be my purpose, actions, conforming to my views, would lead to these results, he might argue and establish if he could; but, so far as purposes were concerned, he was totally mistaken as to me.

When I made that reply to him—when I told him, on the question of declaring war between the different States of the Union, that I had not said I did not expect any peace upon this question until Slavery was exterminated; that I had only said I expected peace when that institution was put where the public mind should rest in the belief that it was in course of ultimate extinction; that I believed from the organization of our government, until a very recent period of time, the institution had been placed and continued upon such a basis; that we had had comparative peace upon that question through a portion of that period of time, only because the public mind rested in that belief in regard to it, and that when we returned to that position in relation to that matter, I supposed we should again have peace as we previously had. I assured him, as I now assure you, that I neither then had, nor have, or ever had, any purpose in any way of interfering with the institution of Slavery, where it exists. [Long continued applause.] I believe we have no power, under the Constitution of the United States; or rather under the form of government under which we live, to interfere with the institution of Slavery, or any other of the institutions of our sister States, be they Free or Slave States. [Cries of "Good," and applause.] I declared then and I now re-declare, that I have as little inclination to so interfere with the institution of Slavery where it now exists, through the instrumentality of the general Government, or any other instrumentality, as I believe we have no power to do so. [A voice—"You're right."] I accidentally used this expression: I had no purpose of entering into the Slave States to disturb the institution of Slavery! So, upon the first occasion that Judge Douglas got an opportunity to reply to me, he passed by the whole body of what I had said upon that subject, and seized upon the particular expression of mine, that I had no purpose of entering into the Slave States to disturb the institution of Slavery! "Oh, no," said he, "he (Lincoln) won't enter into the Slave States to disturb the institution of Slavery; he is too prudent a man to do such a thing as that; he only means that he will go on to the line between the Free and Slave States, and shoot over at them. [Laughter.] This is all he means to do. He means to do them all the harm he can, to disturb them all he can, in such a way as to keep his own hide in perfect safety." [Laughter.]

OPPORTUNITY TO SHOOT ACROSS THE LINE.

Well, now, I did not think, at that time, that that was either a very dignified or very logical argument; but so it was, I had to get along with it as well as I could.

It has occurred to me here to-night, that if I ever do shoot over the line at the people on the other side of the line into a Slave State, and purpose to do so, keeping my skin safe, that I have now about the best chance I shall ever have. [Laughter and applause.] I should not wonder that there are some Kentuckians about this audience; we are close to Kentucky; and whether that be so or not, we are on elevated ground, and by speaking distinctly, I should not wonder if some of the Kentuckians would hear me on the other side of the river. [Laughter.] For that reason I propose to address a portion of what I have to say to the Kentuckians.

INTRODUCING HIMSELF TO KENTUCKIANS.

I say, then, in the first place, to the Kentuckians, that I am what they call, as I understand it, a "Black Republican." (Applause and laughter.) I think Slavery is wrong, morally, and politically. I desire that it should be no further spread in these United States, and I should not object if it should gradually terminate in the whole Union. (Applause.) While I say this for myself, I say to you, Kentuckians, that I understand you differ radically with me upon this proposition; that you believe Slavery is a good thing; that Slavery is right; that it ought to be extended and perpetuated in this Union. Now, there being this broad difference between us, I do not pretend in addressing myself to you, Kentuckians, to attempt proselyting you; that would be a vain effort. I do not enter upon it. I only propose to try to show you that you ought to nominate for the next Presidency, at Charleston, my distinguished friend Judge Douglas. [Applause.] In all that there is a difference between you and him, I understand he is as sincerely for you, and more wisely for you, than you are for yourselves. [Applause.] I will try to demonstrate that proposition. Understand now, I say that I believe he is as sincerely for you, and more wisely for you, than you are for yourselves.

ADVOCATES THE "GIANT'S CLAIMS."

What do you want more than anything else to make successful your views of Slavery,—to advance the outspread of it, and to secure and perpetuate the nationality of it? What do you want more than anything else? What is needed absolutely? What is indispensable to you? Why! if I may be allowed to answer the question, it is to retain a hold upon the North—it is to retain support and strength from the Free States. If you can get this support and strength from the Free States, you can succeed. If you do not get this support and this strength from the Free States, you are in the minority, and you are beaten at once.

If that proposition be admitted,—and it is undeniable, then the next thing I say to you, is that Douglas of all the men in this nation is the only man that affords you any hold upon the Free States; that no other man can give you any strength in the Free States. This being so, if you doubt the other branch of the proposition, whether he is for you—whether he is really for you as I have expressed it, I propose asking your attention for awhile to a few facts.

The issue between you and me, understand, is that I think Slavery is wrong, and ought not to be outspread, and you think it is right and ought to be extended and perpetuated. (A voice, "oh, Lord.") That is my Kentuckian I am talking to now. (Applause.)

I now proceed to try to show you that Douglas is as sincerely for you and more wisely for you than you are for yourselves.

DOUGLAS AT THE WORK OF THE SOUTH.

In the first place we know that in a Government like this, in a Government of the people, where the voice of all the men of the country, substantially enter into the execution,—or administration rather—of the Government—in such a Government, what lies at the bottom of all of it, is public opinion. I lay down the proposition, that Douglas is not only the man that promises you in advance a hold upon the North, and support in the North, but that he constantly moulds public opinion to your ends; that in every possible way he can, he constantly moulds the public opinion of the North to your ends; and if there are a few things in which he seems to be against you—a few things which he says that appear to be against you, and a few that he forbears to say which you would like to have him say—you ought to remember that the saying of the one, or the forbearing to say the other, would loose his hold upon the North, and, by consequence, would lose his capacity to serve you. (A voice, "That is so.")

Upon this subject of moulding public opinion, I call your attention to the fact—for a well-established fact it is—that the Judge never says your institution of Slavery is wrong; he never says it is right, to be sure, but he never says it is wrong. [Laughter.] There is not a public man in the United States, I believe, with the exception of Senator Douglas, who has not, at some time in his life, declared his opinion whether the thing is right or wrong; but, Senator Douglas never declares it is wrong. He leaves himself at perfect liberty to do all in your favor which he would be hindered from doing if he were to declare the thing to be wrong. On the contrary, he takes all the chances that he has for inveigling the sentiment of the North, opposed to Slavery, into your support, by never saying it is right. [Laughter.] This you ought to set down to his credit. [Laughter.] You ought to give him full credit for this much, little though it be, in comparison to the whole which he does for you.

SEE–SAW.

Some other things I will ask your attention to. He said upon the floor of the United States Senate, and he has repeated it as I understand, a great many times, that he does not care whether Slavery is "voted up or voted down." This again shows you, or ought to show you, if you would reason upon it, that he does not believe it to be wrong, for a man may say, when he sees nothing wrong in a thing, that he does not care whether it be voted up or voted down, but no man can logically say that he cares not whether a thing goes up or goes down, which to him appears to be wrong. You therefore have a demonstration in this, that to Douglas' mind your favorite institution which you would have spread out, and made perpetual, is no wrong.

Another thing he tells you, in a speech made at Memphis in Tennessee, shortly after the canvass in Illinois, last year. He there distinctly told the people, that there was a "line drawn by the Almighty across this continent, on the one side of which the soil must always be cultivated by slaves," that he did not pretend to know exactly where that line was, [laughter and applause,] but that there was such a line. I want to ask your attention to that proposition again; that there is one portion of this continent where the Almighty has designed the soil shall always be cultivated by slaves; that its being cultivated by slaves at that place is right; that it has the direct sympathy and authority of the Almighty. Whenever you can get these Northern audiences to adopt the opinion that Slavery is right on the other side of the Ohio; whenever you can get them, in pursuance of Douglas' views, to adopt that sentiment, they will very readily make the other argument, which is perfectly logical, that that which is right on that side of the Ohio, cannot be wrong on this, [laughter;] and that if you have that property on that side of the Ohio, under the seal and stamp of the Almighty, when by any means it escapes over here, it is wrong to have constitutions and laws, "to devil" you about it. So Douglas is moulding the public opinion of the North, first to say that the thing is right in your State over the Ohio river, and hence to say that that which is right there is not wrong here, [at this moment the cannon was fired; to the great injury of sundry panes of glass in the vicinity,] and that all laws and constitutions here, recognizing it as being wrong, are themselves wrong, and ought to be repealed and abrogated. He will tell you, men of Ohio, that if you choose here to have laws against Slavery it is in conformity to the idea that your climate is not suited to it, that your climate is not suited to slave labor, and therefore you have constitutions and laws against it.

Let us attend to that argument for a little while and see if it be sound. You do not raise sugar cane—[except the new fashioned sugar cane, and you won't raise that long] but they do raise it in Louisiana. You don't raise it in Ohio because you can't raise it profitably, because the climate don't suit it. [Here again the cannon interrupted. Its report was followed by another fall of window glass.] They do raise it in Louisiana because there it is profitable. Now, Douglas will tell you that is precisely the Slavery question. That they do have slaves there because they are profitable, and you don't have them here because they are not profitable. If that is so, then it leads to dealing with the one precisely as with the other. Is there then anything in the Constitution or laws of Ohio against raising sugar cane? Have you found it necessary to put any such provision in your law? Surely not! No man desires to raise sugar cane in Ohio; but, if any man did desire to do so, you would say it was a tyrannical law that forbid his doing so, and whenever you shall agree with Douglas, whenever your minds are brought to adopt his argument, as surely you will have reached the conclusion, that although Slavery is not profitable in Ohio, if any man wants it, it is wrong to him not to let him have it.

In this matter Judge Douglas is preparing the public mind for you of Kentucky, to make perpetual that good thing in your estimation, about which you and I differ.

THE CHANGES IN FIVE YEARS.

In this connection let me ask your attention to another thing. I believe it is safe to assert that five years ago, no living man had expressed the opinion that the negro had no share in the Declaration of Independence. Let me state that again: five years ago no living man had expressed the opinion that the negro had no share in the Declaration of Independence. If there is in this large audience any man who ever knew of that opinion being put upon paper as much as five years ago, I will be obliged to him now or at a subsequent time to show it.

If that be true I wish you then to note the next fact; that within the space of five years Senator Douglas, in the argument of this question, has got his entire party, so far as I know, without exception, to join in saying that the negro has no share in the Declaration of Independence. If there be now in all these United States, one Douglas man that does not say this, I have been unable upon any occasion to scare him up. Now if none of you said this five years ago, and all of you say it now, that is a matter that you Kentuckians ought to note. That is a vast change in the Northern public sentiment upon that question.

Of what tendency is that change? The tendency of that change is to bring the public mind to the conclusion that when men are spoken of, the negro is not meant; that when negroes are spoken of, brutes alone are contemplated. That change in public sentiment has already degraded the black man in the estimation of Douglas and his followers from the condition of a man of some sort, and assigned him to the condition of a brute. Now, you Kentuckians ought to give Douglas credit for this. That is the largest possible stride that can be made in regard to the perpetuation of your thing of Slavery.

A Voice—"Speak to Ohio men, and not to Kentuckians!"

Mr. Lincoln—I beg permission to speak as I please. (Laughter.)

THE BIBLE THEORY.

In Kentucky, perhaps, in many of the Slave States certainly, you are trying to establish the rightfulness of Slavery by reference to the Bible. You are trying to show that slavery existed in the Bible times by Divine ordinance. Now Douglas is wiser than you, for your own benefit, upon that subject. Douglas knows that whenever you establish that Slavery was right by the Bible, it will occur that that Slavery was the Slavery of the *white* man—of men without reference to color—and he knows very well that you may entertain that idea in Kentucky as much as you please, but you will never win any Northern support upon it. He makes a wiser argument for you; he makes the argument that the slavery of the *black* man, the slavery of the man who has a skin of a different color from your own, is right. He thereby brings to your support Northern voters who could not for a moment be brought by your own argument of the Bible-right of slavery. Will you not give him credit for that? Will you not say that in this matter he is more wisely for you than you are for yourselves.

Now having established with his entire party this doctrine—having been entirely successful in that branch of his efforts in your behalf; he is ready for another.

A SUM IN THE RULE OF THREE.

At this same meeting at Memphis, he declared that while in all contests between the negro and the white man, he was for the white man, but that in all questions between the negro and the crocodile he was for the negro. (Laughter.) He did not make that declaration accidentally at Memphis. He made it a great many times in the canvass in Illinois last year, (though I don't know that it was reported in any of his speeches there,) but he frequently made it. I believe he repeated it at Columbus, and I should not wonder if he repeated it here. It is, then, a deliberate way of expressing himself upon that subject. It is a matter of mature deliberation with him thus to express himself upon that point of his case. It therefore requires some deliberate attention.

The first inference seems to be that if you do not enslave the negro you are wronging the white man in some way or other, and that whoever is opposed to the negro being enslaved is in some way or other against the white man. Is not that a falsehood? If there was a necessary conflict between the white man and the negro, I should be for the white man as much as Judge Douglas; but I say there is no such necessary conflict. I say that there is room enough for us all to be free, (loud manifestations of applause,) and that it not only does not wrong the white man that the negro should be free, but it positively wrongs the mass of the white men that the negro should be enslaved; that the mass of white men are really injured by the effect of slave labor in the vicinity of the fields of their own labor. (Applause.)

But I do not desire to dwell upon this branch of the question more than to say that this assumption of his is false, and I do hope that that fallacy will not long prevail in the minds of intelligent white men. At all events, you Kentuckians ought to thank Judge Douglas for it. It is for your benefit it is made.

The other branch of it is, that in a struggle between the negro and the crocodile, he is for the negro. Well, I don't know that there is any struggle between the negro and the crocodile, either. (Laughter.) I suppose that if a crocodile (or as we old Ohio river boatmen used to call them, alligators) should come across a white man, he would kill him if he could, and so he would a negro. But what, at last, is this proposition? I believe it is a sort of proposition in proportion, which may be stated thus: As the negro is to the white man, so is the crocodile to the negro, and as the negro may rightfully treat the crocodile as a beast or reptile, so the white man may rightfully treat the negro as a beast or a reptile. (Applause.) That is really the "knip" of all that argument of his.

Now, my brother Kentuckians, who believe in this, you ought to thank Judge Douglas for having put that in a much more taking way than any of yourselves have done. (Applause.)

THE "GREAT PRINCIPLE."

Again, Douglas' *great principle,* "Popular Sovereignty," as he calls it, gives you, by natural consequence, the revival of the Slave-trade whenever you want it. If you question this, listen a while, consider a while, what I shall advance in support of that proposition.

He says that it is the sacred right of the man who goes into the Territories, to have Slavery if he wants it. Grant that for argument's sake. Is it not the sacred right of the man that don't go there equally to buy slaves in Africa, if he wants them? Can you point out the difference? The man who goes into the Territories of Kansas and Nebraska, or any other new Territory, with the sacred right of taking a slave there which belongs to him, would certainly have no more right to take one there than I would who own no slave, but who would desire to buy one and take him there. You will not say—you, the friends of Douglas— but that the man who does not own a slave, has an equal right to buy one and take him to the Territory, as the other does?

A VOICE. "I want to ask a question. Don't foreign nations interfere with the Slave-trade?"

MR. LINCOLN. Well! I understand it to be a principle of Democracy to whip foreign nations whenever they interfere with us. (Laughter and applause.)

VOICE. "I only asked for information. I am a Republican myself."

MR. LINCOLN. You and I will be on the best terms in the world, but I do not wish to be diverted from the point I was trying to press.

I say that Douglas' Popular Sovereignty, establishing a sacred right in the people, if you please, if carried to its logical conclusion, gives equally the sacred right to the people of the States or the Territories themselves to buy slaves, wherever they can buy them cheapest; and if any man can show a distinction, I should like to hear him try it. If any man can show how the people of Kansas have a better right to slaves because they want them, than the people of Georgia have to buy them in Africa, I want him to do it. I think it cannot be done. If it is "Popular Sovereignty" for the people to have slaves because they want them, it is Popular Sovereignty for them to buy them in Africa, because they desire to do so.

A CHAPTER ON COMPROMISES.

I know that Douglas has recently made a little effort—not seeming to notice that he had a different theory—has made an effort to get rid of that. He has written a letter addressed to somebody, I believe, who resides in Iowa, declaring his opposition to the repeal of the laws that prohibit the African Slave Trade. He bases his opposition to such repeal upon the ground that these laws are themselves one of the compromises of the Constitution of the United States. Now it would be very interesting to see Judge Douglas or any of his friends turn to the Constitution of the United States and point out that compromise, to show where there is any compromise in the Constitution or provision in the Constitution, express or implied, by which the Administrators of that Constitution are under any obligation to repeal the African Slave-trade. I know, or at least I think I know, that the framers of that Constitution did expect that the African Slave-trade would be abolished at the end of twenty years, to which time their prohibition against its being abolished extended. I think there is abundant contemporaneous history to show that the framers of the Constitution expected it to be abolished. But while they so expected, they gave nothing for that expectation, and they put no provision in the Constitution requiring it should be so abolished. The migration or importation of such persons as the States shall see fit to admit shall not be prohibited, but a certain tax might be levied upon such importation. But what was to be done after that time? The Constitution is as silent about that, as it is silent personally about myself. There is absolutely nothing in it about that subject— there is only the expectation of the framers of the Constitution that the Slave-trade would be abolished at the end of that time and they expected it would be abolished, owing to public sentiment, before that time, and they put that provision in, in order that it should not be abolished before that time, for reasons which I suppose they thought to be sound ones, but which I will not now try to enumerate before you.

But while they expected the Slave-trade would be abolished at that time, they expected that the spread of Slavery into the new Territories should also be restricted. It is as easy to prove that the framers of the Constitution of the United States, expected that Slavery should be prohibited from extending into the new Territories, as it is to prove that it was expected that the Slave-trade should be abolished. Both these things were expected. One was no more expected than the other, and one was no more a compromise of the Constitution than the other. There was nothing said in the Constitution in regard to the spread of Slavery into the Territory. I grant that, but there was something very important said about it by the same generation of men in the adoption of the old Ordinance of '87, through the influence of which you here in Ohio, our neighbors in Indiana, we in Illinois, our neighbors in Michigan and Wisconsin are happy, prosperous, teeming millions of free men. (Continued applause.) That generation of men, though not to the full extent members of the Convention that framed the Constitution, were to some extent members of that Convention, holding seats, at the same time in one body and the other, so that if there was any compromise on either of these subjects, the strong evidence is that that compromise was in favor of the restriction of Slavery from the new territories.

But Douglas says that he is unalterably opposed to the repeal of those laws; because, in his view, it is a compromise of the Constitution. You Kentuckians, no doubt, are somewhat offended with that! You ought not to be! You ought to be patient! You ought to know that if he said less than that, he would lose the power of "lugging" the Northern States to your support. Really, what you would push him to do would take from him his entire power to serve you. And you ought to remember how long, by precedent, Judge Douglas holds himself obliged to stick by compromises. You ought to remember that by the time you yourselves think you are ready to inaugurate measures for the revival of the African Slave-trade that sufficient time will have arrived by precedent, for Judge Douglas to break through that compromise. He says now nothing more strong than he said in 1849 when he declared in favor of the Missouri Compromise—that precisely four years and a quarter after he declared that compromise to be a sacred thing, which "no ruthless hand would ever dare to touch," he, himself, brought forward the measure, ruthlessly to destroy it. (A voice—"hit him again!" Applause.) By a mere calculation of time it will only be four years more until he is ready to take back his profession about the sacredness of the Compromise abolishing the slave trade. Precisely as soon as you are ready to have his services in that direction, by fair calculation you may be sure of having them. (Applause and laughter.)

UNFRIENDLY LEGISLATION.

But you remember and set down to Judge Douglas' debit, or discredit, that he, last year, said the people of the Territories can, in spite of the Dred Scott decision, exclude your slaves from those territories; that he declared by "unfriendly legislation," the extension of your property into the new Territories may be cut off in the teeth of the decision of the Supreme Court of the United States.

He assumed that position at Freeport on the 27th of August, 1858. He said that the people of the Territories can exclude Slavery in so many words. You ought, however, to bear in mind that he has never said it since. (Laughter.) You may hunt in every speech that he has since made, and he has never used that expression once. He has never seemed to notice that he is stating his views differently from what he did then; but, by some sort of accident, he has always really stated it differently. He has always since then declared that "the Constitution does not carry Slavery into the Territories of the United States beyond the power of the people legally to control it, as other property." Now, there is a difference in the language used upon that former occasion and in this latter day. There may or may not be a difference in the meaning, but it is worth while considering whether there is not also a difference in meaning.

What is it to exclude? Why, it is to drive it out. It is in some way to put it out of the Territory. It is to force it across the line, or change its character, so that as property it is out of existence. But what is the controlling of it "as other property?" Is controlling it as other property the same thing [as] destroying it, or driving it away? I should think not. I should think the controlling of it as other property would be just about what you in Kentucky should want. I understand the controlling of property means the controlling of it for the benefit of the owner of it. While I have no doubt the Supreme Court of the United States would say "God speed" to any of the Territorial legislatures that should thus control slave property, they would sing quite a different tune if by the pretense of controlling it they were to undertake to pass laws which virtually excluded it, and that upon a very well known principle to all lawyers, that what a legislature cannot directly do, it cannot do by indirection; that as, the legislature has not the power to drive slaves out, they have no power by indirection, by tax or by imposing burdens in any way on that property, to effect the same end, and that any attempt to do so would be held by the Dred Scott Court unconstitutional.

Douglas is not willing to stand by his first proposition that they can exclude it, because we have seen that that proposition amounts to nothing more nor less than the naked absurdity, that you may lawfully drive out that which has a lawful right to remain. He admitted at first that the slave might be lawfully taken into the Territories under the Constitution of the United States, and yet asserted that he might be lawfully driven out. That being the proposition, it is the absurdity I have stated. He is not willing to stand in the face of that direct, naked and impudent absurdity; he has, therefore, modified his language into that of being *"controlled as other property."*

SWEARING BY THE COURTS.

The Kentuckians don't like this in Douglas! I will tell you where it will go. He now swears by the Court. He was once a leading man in Illinois to break down a Court, because it had made a decision he did not like. But he now not only swears by the Court, the courts having got to working for you, but he denounces all men that do not swear by the Courts, as unpatriotic, as bad citizens. When one of these acts of unfriendly legislation shall impose such heavy burdens as to, in effect, destroy property in slaves in a Territory and show plainly enough that there can be no mistake in the purpose of the Legislature to make them so burdensome, this same Supreme Court will decide that law to be unconstitutional, and he will be ready to say for your benefit, "I swear by the Court; I give it up;" and while that is going on he has been getting all his men to swear by the Courts, and to give it up with him. In this again he serves you faithfully, and as I say, more wisely than you serve yourselves.

A WORD ABOUT PATRIOTIC SPEECHES.

Again! I have alluded in the beginning of these remarks to the fact, that Judge Douglas has made great complaint of my having expressed the opinion that this Government "cannot endure permanently half slave and half free." He has complained of Seward for using different language, and declaring that there is an "irrepressible conflict" between the principles of free and slave labor.

(A voice—"He says it is not original with Seward. That is original with Lincoln.")

I will attend to that immediately, sir. Since that time, Hickman, of Pennsylvania expressed the same sentiment. He has never denounced Mr. Hickman: why? There is a little chance, notwithstanding, that opinion in the mouth of Hickman, that he may yet be a Douglas man. That is the difference! It is not unpatriotic to hold that opinion, if a man is a Douglas man.

But neither I nor Seward, nor Hickman, is entitled to the enviable or unenviable distinction of having first expressed that idea. That same idea was expressed by the Richmond *Enquirer* in Virginia, in 1856; quite two years before it was expressed by the first of us. And while Douglas was pluming himself, that in his conflict with my humble self, last year, he had "squelched out" that fatal heresy, as he delighted to call it, and had suggested that if he only had had a chance to be in New York and meet Seward he would have "squelched" it there also, it never occurred [to him?] to breathe a word against Pryor. I don't think that you can discover that Douglas ever talked of going to Virginia to "squelch" out that idea there. No. More than that. That same Roger A. Pryor was brought to Washington City and made the editor of the *par excellence* Douglas paper, after making use of that expression, which, in us, is so unpatriotic and heretical. From all this, my Kentucky friends may see that this opinion is heretical in his view only when it is expressed by men suspected of a desire that the country shall all become free and not when expressed by those fairly known to entertain the desire that the whole country shall become slave. When expressed by that class of men, it is in no wise offensive to him. In this again, my friends of Kentucky, you have Judge Douglas with you.

ON GIGANTIC CAPACITY.

There is another reason why you Southern people ought to nominate Douglas at your convention at Charleston. That reason is the wonderful capacity of the man; [laughter] the power he has of doing what would seem to be impossible. Let me call your attention to one of these apparently impossible things.

Douglas had three or four very distinguished men of the most extreme anti-slavery views of any men in the Republican party, expressing their desire for his re-election to the Senate last year. That would, of itself, have seemed to be a little wonderful, but that wonder is heightened when we see that Wise of Virginia, a man exactly opposed to them, a man who believes in the Divine right of slavery, was also expressing his desire that Douglas should be re-elected, that another man that may be said to be kindred to Wise, Mr. Breckinridge, the Vice President, and of your own State, was also agreeing with the anti-slavery men in the North; that Douglas ought to be re-elected. Still, to heighten the wonder, a Senator from Kentucky, whom I have always loved with an affection as tender and endearing as I have ever loved any man; who was opposed to the anti-slavery men for reasons which seemed sufficient to him, and equally opposed to Wise and Breckinridge, was writing letters into Illinois to secure the re-election of Douglas. Now that all these conflicting elements should be brought, while at dagger's points, with one another, to support him, is a feat that is worthy for you to note and consider. It is quite probable, that each of these classes of men thought by the re-election of Douglas, their peculiar views would gain something, it is probable that the antislavery men thought their views would gain something that Wise and Breckinridge thought so too, as regards their opinions, that Mr. Crittenden thought that his views would gain something, although he was opposed to both these other men. It is probable that each and all of them thought that they were using Douglas, and it is yet an unsolved problem whether he was not using them all. If he was, then it is for you to consider whether that power to perform wonders, is one for you lightly to throw away.

AN ALTERNATIVE PROPOSED.

There is one other thing that I will say to you in this relation. It is but my opinion, I give it to you without a fee. It is my opinion that it is for you to take him or be defeated; and that if you do take him you may be beaten. You will surely be beaten if you do not take him. We, the Republicans and others forming the Opposition of the country, intend to "stand by our guns," to be patient and firm, and in the long run to beat you whether you take him or not. [Applause.] We know that before we fairly beat you, we have to beat you both together. We know that you are "all of a feather," [loud applause,] and that we have to beat you altogether, and we expect to do it. [Applause] We don't intend to be very impatient about it. We mean to be as deliberate and calm about it as it is possible to be, but as firm and resolved, as it is possible for men to be. When we do as we say, beat you, you perhaps want to know what we will do with you. [Laughter]

I will tell you, so far as I am authorized to speak for the Opposition, what we mean to do with you. We mean to treat you as near as we possibly can, like Washington, Jefferson and Madison treated you. [Cheers] We mean to leave you alone, and in no way to interfere with your institution; to abide by all and every compromise of the constitution, and, in a word, coming back to the original proposition, to treat you, so far as degenerated men (if we have degenerated) may, according to the examples of those noble fathers—Washington, Jefferson and Madison. [Applause] We mean to remember that you are as good as we; that there is no difference between us other than the difference of circumstances. We mean to recognise and bear in mind always that you have as good hearts in your bosoms as other people, or as we claim to have, and treat you accordingly. We mean to marry your girls when we have a chance—the white ones I mean—[laughter] and I have the honor to inform you that I once did have a chance in that way. [A voice, "Good for you," and applause]

I have told you what we mean to do. I want to know, now, when that thing takes place, what you mean to do. I often hear it intimated that you mean to divide the Union whenever a Republican, or anything like it, is elected President of the United States.

[A voice, "That is so."] "That is so," one of them says. I wonder if he is a Kentuckian? [A voice, "He is a Douglas man."] Well, then, I want to know what you are going to do with your half of it? [Applause and laughter] Are you going to split the Ohio down through, and push your half off a piece? Or are you going to keep it right alongside of us outrageous fellows? Or are you going to build up a wall some way between your country and ours, by which that moveable property of yours can't come over here any more, to the danger of your losing it? Do you think you can better yourselves on that subject, by leaving us here under no obligation whatever to return those specimens of your moveable property that come hither? You have divided the Union because we would not do right with you as you think, upon that subject; when we cease to be under obligations to do anything for you, how much better off do you think you will be? Will you make war upon us and kill us all? Why, gentlemen, I think you are as gallant and as brave men as live; that you can fight as bravely in a good cause, man for man, as any other people living; that you have shown yourselves capable of this upon various occasions; but, man for man, you are not better than we are, and there are not so many of you as there are of us. [Loud cheering.] You will never make much of a hand at whipping us. If we were fewer in numbers than you, I think that you could whip us; if we were equal it would likely be a drawn battle; but being inferior in numbers, you will make nothing by attempting to master us.

THE ORDINANCE OF '87.

But perhaps I have addressed myself as long, or longer, to the Kentuckians than I ought to have done inasmuch as I have said that whatever course you take we intend in the end to beat you. I propose to address a few remarks to our friends by way of discussing with them the best means of keeping that promise, that I have in good faith made. [Long continued applause.]

It may appear a little episodical for me to mention the topic of which I shall speak now. It is a favorite proposition of Douglas' that the interference of the General Government, through the Ordinance of '87, or through any other act of the General Government, never has made or ever can make a Free State; that the Ordinance of '87 did not make Free States of Ohio, Indiana or Illinois. That these States are free upon his "great principle" of Popular Sovereignty, because the people of those several States have chosen to make them so. At Columbus, and probably here, he undertook to compliment the people that they themselves have made the State of Ohio free and that the Ordinance of '87 was not entitled in any degree to divide the honor with them. I have no doubt that the people of the State of Ohio did make her free according to their own will and judgment, but let the facts be remembered.

In 1802, I believe, it was you who made your first constitution, with the clause prohibiting slavery, and you did it I suppose very nearly unanimously, but you should bear in mind that you—speaking of you as one people—that you did so unembarrassed by the actual presence of the institution amongst you; that you made it a Free State, not with the embarrassment upon you of already having among you many slaves, which if they had been here, and you had sought to make a Free State, you would not know what to do with. If they had been among you, embarrassing difficulties, most probably, would have induced you to tolerate a slave constitution instead of a free one, as indeed these very difficulties have constrained every people on this continent who have adopted slavery.

Pray what was it that made you free? What kept you free? Did you not find your country free when you came to decide that Ohio should be a Free State? It is important to enquire by what reason you found it so? Let us take an illustration between the States of Ohio and Kentucky. Kentucky is separated by this river Ohio, not a mile wide. A portion of Kentucky, by reason of the course of the Ohio, is further north than this portion of Ohio in which we now stand.

Kentucky is entirely covered with slavery—Ohio is entirely free from it. What made that difference? Was it climate? No! A portion of Kentucky was further north than this portion of Ohio. Was it soil? No! There is nothing in the soil of the one more favorable to slave labor than the other. It was not climate or soil that caused one side of the line to be entirely covered with slavery and the other side free of it. What was it? Study over it. Tell us, if you can, in all the range of conjecture, if there be anything you can conceive of that made that difference, other than that there was no law of any sort keeping it out of Kentucky? while the Ordinance of '87 kept it out of Ohio. If there is any other reason than this, I confess that it is wholly beyond my power to conceive of it. This, then, I offer to combat the idea that that ordinance has never made any State free.

I don't stop at this illustration. I come to the State of Indiana; and what I have said as between Kentucky and Ohio I repeat as between Indiana and Kentucky; it is equally applicable. One additional argument is applicable also to Indiana. In her Territorial condition she more than once petitioned Congress to abrogate the ordinance entirely, or at least so far as to suspend its operation for a time, in order that they should exercise the "Popular Sovereignty" of having slaves if they wanted them. The men then controlling the General Government, imitating the men of the Revolution, refused Indiana that privilege. And so we have the evidence that Indiana supposed she could have slaves, if it were not for that ordinance that she besought Congress to put that barrier out of the way; that Congress refused to do so, and it all ended at last in Indiana being a Free State. Tell me not, then, that the Ordinance of '87 had nothing to do with making Indiana a free state, when we find some men chafing against and only restrained by that barrier.

Come down again to our State of Illinois. The great Northwest Territory including Ohio, Indiana, Illinois, Michigan and Wisconsin, was acquired, first I believe by the British Government, in part at least, from the French. Before the establishment of our independence, it became a part of Virginia, enabling Virginia afterwards to transfer it to the general government. There were French settlements in what is now Illinois, and at the same time there were French settlements in what is now Missouri—in the tract of country that was not purchased till about 1803. In these French settlements negro slavery had existed for many years—perhaps more than a hundred, if not as much as two hundred years—at Kaskaskia in Illinois, and at St. Genevieve, or Cape Girardeau, perhaps, in Missouri. The number of slaves was not very great, but there was about the same number in each place. They were there when we acquired the Territory. There was no effort made to break up the relation of master and slave and

even the Ordinance of 1787 was not so enforced as to destroy that slavery in
Illinois; nor did the Ordinance apply to Missouri at all.

What I want to ask your attention to, at this point, is that Illinois and Missouri came into the Union about the same time, Illinois in the latter part of 1818,
and Missouri, after a struggle, I believe some time in 1820. They had been filling up with American people about the same period of time; their progress
enabling them to come into the Union [at] about the same [time]. At the end
of that ten years, in which they had been so preparing, (for it was about that
period of time) the number of slaves in Illinois had actually decreased; while in
Missouri, beginning with very few, at the end of that ten years, there were about
ten thousand. This being so, and it being remembered that Missouri and Illinois
are, to a certain extent, in the same parallel of latitude—that the Northern half
of Missouri and the Southern half of Illinois are in the same parallel of latitude—
so that climate would have the same effect upon one as upon the other, and that
in the soil there is no material difference so far as bears upon the question of
slavery being settled upon one or the other—there being none of those natural
causes to produce a difference in filling them, and yet there being a broad difference in their filling up, we are led again to inquire what was the cause of that
difference.

It is most natural to say that in Missouri there was no law to keep that country from filling up with slaves, while in Illinois there was the Ordinance of '87.
The Ordinance being there, slavery decreased during that ten years—the Ordinance not being in the other, it increased from a few to ten thousand. Can anybody doubt the reason of the difference?

I think all these facts most abundantly prove that my friend Judge Douglas'
proposition, that the Ordinance of '87 or the national restriction of slavery,
never had a tendency to make a Free State, is a fallacy—a proposition without
the shadow or substance of truth about it.

POPULAR SOVEREIGNTY CAUSING FREEDOM.

Douglas sometimes says that all the States (and it is part of this same proposition I have been discussing) that have become free, have become so upon his
"great principle"—that the State of Illinois itself came into the Union as a slave
State, and that the people upon the "great principle" of Popular Sovereignty have
since made it a Free State. Allow me but a little while to state to you what facts
there are to justify him in saying that Illinois came into the Union as a Slave State.

I have mentioned to you that there were a few old French slaves there. They
numbered, I think, one or two hundred. Besides that there had been a Terri-

torial law for indenturing black persons. Under that law, in violation of the Ordinance of '87, but without any enforcement of the Ordinance to overthrow the system, there had been a small number of slaves introduced as indentured persons. Owing to this the clause for the prohibition of slavery, was slightly modified. Instead of running like yours, that neither slavery nor involuntary servitude, except for crime of which the party shall have been duly convicted, should exist in the State, they said that neither slavery nor involuntary servitude should thereafter be introduced, and that the children of indentured servants should be born free; and nothing was said about the few old French slaves. Out of this fact, that the clause for prohibiting slavery was modified because of the actual presence of it, Douglas asserts again and again that Illinois came into the Union as a Slave State. How far the facts sustain the conclusion that he draws, it is for intelligent and impartial men to decide. I leave it with you with these remarks, worthy of being remembered, that that little thing, those few indentured servants being there, was of itself sufficient to modify a Constitution made by a people ardently desiring to have a free Constitution; showing the power of the actual presence of the institution of slavery to prevent any people, however anxious to make a Free State, from making it perfectly so.

I have been detaining you longer perhaps than I ought to do [Long and repeated cries of "go on."]

COMPARISONS.

I am in some doubt whether to introduce another topic upon which I could talk awhile. [Cries of "Go on," and "Give us it."] It is this then. Douglas' Popular Sovereignty as a principle, is simply this: If one man chooses to make a slave of another man, neither that other man or anybody else has a right to object. [Cheers and laughter.] Apply it to government, as he seeks to apply it and it is this—if, in a new Territory, into which a few people are beginning to enter for the purpose of making their homes, they choose to either exclude slavery from their limits, or to establish it there, however one or the other may affect the persons to be enslaved, or the infinitely greater number of persons who are afterwards to inhabit that Territory, or the other members of the family of communities, of which they are but an incipient member, or the general head of the family of states as parent of all—however their action may affect one or the other of these, there is no power or right to interfere. That is Douglas' Popular sovereignty applied. Now I think that there is a real popular sovereignty in the world. I think a definition of popular sovereignty, in the abstract, would be about this—that each man shall do precisely as he pleases with himself, and with all those things which exclusively concern him. Applied in government, this principle would be, that a general government shall do all those things which pertain to it, and all the local governments shall do precisely as they please in respect to those matters which exclusively concern them.

Douglas looks upon slavery as so insignificant that the people must decide that question for themselves, and yet they are not fit to decide who shall be their Governor, Judge or secretary, or who shall be any of their officers. These are vast national matters in his estimation but the little matter in his estimation, is that of planting slavery there. That is purely of local interest, which nobody should be allowed to say a word about. [Applause.]

Labor is the great source from which nearly all, if not all, human comforts and necessities are drawn. There is a difference in opinion about the elements of labor in society. Some men assume that there is a necessary connection between capital and labor, and that connection draws within it the whole of the labor of the community. They assume that nobody works unless capital excites them to work. They begin next to consider what is the best way. They say that there are but two ways; one is to hire men and to allure them to labor by their consent; the other is to buy the men and drive them to it, and that is slavery. Having assumed that, they proceed to discuss the question of whether the laborers themselves are better off in the condition of slaves or of hired laborers, and they usually decide that they are better off in the condition of slaves.

In the first place, I say, that the whole thing is a mistake. That there is a certain relation between capital and labor, I admit. That it does exist, and rightfully exists, I think is true. That men who are industrious, and sober, and honest in the pursuit of their own interests should after a while accumulate capital, and after that should be allowed to enjoy it in peace, and also if they should choose when they have accumulated it to use it to save themselves from actual labor and hire other people to labor for them is right. In doing so they do not wrong the man they employ, for they find men who have not of their own land to work upon, or shops to work in, and who are benefited by working for others, hired laborers, receiving their capital for it. Thus a few men that own capital, hire a few others, and these establish the relation of capital and labor rightfully. A relation of which I make no complaint. But I insist that that relation after all does not embrace more than one-eighth of the labor of the country.

The speaker proceeded to argue that the hired laborer with his ability to become an employer, must have every precedence over him who labors under the inducement of force. He continued:

HOW TO WIN THE FIGHT.

I have taken upon myself in the name of some of you to say, that we expect upon these principles to ultimately beat them. In order to do so, I think we want and must have a national policy in regard to the institution of slavery, that acknowledges and deals with that institution as being wrong. (Loud cheering) Whoever desires the prevention of the spread of slavery and the nationalization of that institution, yields all, when he yields to any policy that either recognizes slavery as being right, or as being an indifferent thing. Nothing will make you successful but setting up a policy which shall treat the thing as being wrong. When I say this, I do not mean to say that this general government is charged with the duty of redressing or preventing all the wrongs in the world; but I do think that it is charged with the duty of preventing and redressing all wrongs which are wrongs to itself. This government is expressly charged with the duty of providing for the general welfare. We believe that the spreading out and perpetuity of the institution of slavery impairs the general welfare. We believe—nay, we know, that that is the only thing that has ever threatened the perpetuity of the Union itself. The only thing which has ever menaced the destruction of the government under which we live, is this very thing. To repress this thing, we think is providing for the general welfare. Our friends in Kentucky differ from us. We need not make our argument for them, but we who think it is wrong in all its relations, or in some of them at least, must decide as to our own actions, and our own course, upon our own judgment.

I say that we must not interfere with the institution of slavery in the states where it exists, because the constitution forbids it, and the general welfare does not require us to do so. We must not withhold an efficient fugitive slave law because the constitution requires us, as I understand it, not to withhold such a law. But we must prevent the outspreading of the institution, because neither the constitution nor general welfare requires us to extend it. We must prevent the revival of the African slave trade and the enacting by Congress of a territorial slave code. We must prevent each of these things being done by either Congresses or courts. The people of these United States are the rightful masters of both Congresses and courts (Applause) not to overthrow the constitution, but to overthrow the men who pervent that constitution. (Applause.)

To do these things we must employ instrumentalities. We must hold conventions; we must adopt platforms if we conform to ordinary custom; we must nominate candidates, and we must carry elections. In all these things, I think that we ought to keep in view our real purpose, and in none do anything that stands adverse to our purpose. If we shall adopt a platform that fails to recognize or express our purpose, or elect a man that declares himself inimical to our purpose, we not only take nothing by our success, but we tacitly admit that we act upon no [other] principle than a desire to have "the loaves and fishes," by which, in the end our apparent success is really an injury to us.

I know that it is very desirable with me, as with everybody else, that all the elements of the Opposition shall unite in the next Presidential election and in all future time. I am anxious that that should be, but there are things seriously to be considered in relation to that matter. If the terms can be arranged, I am in favor of the Union. But suppose we shall take up some man and put him upon one end or the other of the ticket, who declares himself against us in regard to the prevention of the spread of slavery—who turns up his nose and says he is tired of hearing anything about it, who is more against us than against the enemy, what will be the issue? Why he will get no slave states after all—he has tried that already until being beat is the rule for him. If we nominate him upon that ground, he will not carry a slave state; and not only so, but that portion of our men who are high strung upon the principle we really fight for, will not go for him, and he won't get a single electoral vote anywhere, except, perhaps, in the state of Maryland. There is no use in saying to us that we are stubborn and obstinate, because we won't do some such thing as this. We cannot do it. We cannot get our men to vote it. I speak by the card, that we cannot give the state of Illinois in such case by fifty thousand. We would be flatter down than the "Negro Democracy" themselves have the heart to wish to see us.

After saying this much, let me say a little on the other side. There are plenty of men in the slave states that are altogether good enough for me to be either President or Vice President, provided they will profess their sympathy with our purpose, and will place themselves on the ground that our men, upon principle, can vote for them. There are scores of them, good men in their character for intelligence and talent and integrity. If such a one will place himself upon the right ground I am for his occupying one place upon the next Republican or Opposition ticket. [Applause] I will heartily go for him. But, unless he does so place himself, I think it a matter of perfect nonsense to attempt to bring about a union upon any other basis; that if a union be made, the elements will scatter so that there can be no success for such a ticket, nor anything like success. The good old maxims of the Bible are applicable, and truly applicable to human affairs, and in this as in other things, we may say here that he who is not for us is against us; he who gathereth not with us scattereth. [Applause] I should be glad to have some of the many good, and able, and noble men of the south to place themselves where we can confer upon them the high honor of an election upon one or the other end of our ticket. It would do my soul good to do that thing. It would enable us to teach them that inasmuch as we select one of their own number to carry out our principles, we are free from the charge that we mean more than we say.

But, my friends I have detained you much longer than I expected to do. I believe I may do myself the compliment to say that you have stayed and heard me with great patience, for which I return you my most sincere thanks.

FRAGMENT ON FREE LABOR[4]

This fragment most likely constitutes a missing part of the Cincinnati speech on free labor. Lincoln rejected the mud-sill theory, which contended the condition of southern slaves was better than northern laborers. He cited his own life as a testimonial to the American dream of equality of opportunity, the promise of an equal chance for the progressive improvement of one's condition in life. The hope to improve one's condition provided a powerful incentive to succeed in the race of life. Lincoln's reference to labor as the "common burthen of the race" of which no race or person was exempted was based upon the biblical precept in Genesis 3:19. Because toil and labor were immutable aspects of the human condition ordained of God, it was unjust to shift the burden of one's own labor on to another. This would exempt one from doing his fair share of toil. It was nothing less than stealing the person of another.

[SEPTEMBER 17, 1859?]

change conditions with either Canada or South Carolina? *Equality,* in society, alike beats *inequality,* whether the lat[t]er be of the British aristocratic sort, or of the domestic slavery sort.

We know, Southern men declare that their slaves are better off than hired laborers amongst us. How little they *know,* whereof they *speak!* There is no permanent class of hired laborers amongst us. Twenty-five years ago, I was a hired laborer. The hired laborer of yesterday, labors on his own account to-day; and will hire others to labor for him to-morrow. Advancement—improvement in condition—is the order of things in a society of equals. As Labor is the common *burthen* of our race, so the effort of *some* to shift their share of the burthen on to the shoulders of *others,* is the great, durable, curse of the race. Originally a curse for transgression upon the whole race, when, as by slavery, it is concentrated on a part only, it becomes the double-refined curse of God upon his creatures.

4. *CWAL,* III, 462–463.

Free labor has the inspiration of hope; pure slavery has no hope. The power of hope upon human exertion, and happiness, is wonderful. The slave-master himself has a conception of it; and hence the system of *tasks* among slaves. The slave whom you can not drive with the lash to break seventy-five pounds of hemp in a day, if you will task him to break a hundred, and promise him pay for all he does over, he will break you a hundred and fifty. You have substituted *hope,* for the *rod.* And yet perhaps it does not occur to you, that to the extent of your gain in the case, you have given up the slave system, and adopted the free system of labor.

SPEECH AT NEW HAVEN, CONNECTICUT [5]
MARCH 6, 1860

Lincoln's speech at New Haven, Connecticut was part of a northeastern tour, which began with his celebrated speech at Cooper Union in February of the same year. This tour increased his chances as a Republican Party candidate in the forthcoming presidential election in the fall of 1860. While the dominant theme of the Cooper Union Address is legal, dealing with the Founders' intentions on slavery, the dominant theme of the New Haven speech is moral and philosophical. At New Haven, Lincoln emphasized that the question of slavery must be "settled upon some philosophical basis." This "philosophical basis" represented an ultimate view of public life also known as a civil theology or political faith.

MARCH 6, 1860

MR. PRESIDENT AND FELLOW-CITIZENS OF NEW HAVEN: If the Republican party of this nation shall ever have the national house entrusted to its keeping, it will be the duty of that party to attend to all the affairs of national house-keeping. Whatever matters of importance may come up, whatever difficulties may arise in the way of its administration of the government, that party will then have to attend to. It will then be compelled to attend to other questions, besides this question which now assumes an overwhelming importance—the question of Slavery. It is true that in the organization of the Republican party this question of Slavery was more important than any other; indeed, so much more important has it become that no other national question can even get a hearing just at present. The old question of tariff—a matter that will remain one of the chief affairs of national housekeeping to all time—the question of the management of financial affairs; the question of the disposition of the public domain—how shall

5. *CWAL,* IV, 13-30.

it be managed for the purpose of getting it well settled, and of making there the homes of a free and happy people—these will remain open and require attention for a great while yet, and these questions will have to be attended to by whatever party has the control of the government. Yet, just now, they cannot even obtain a hearing, and I do not purpose to detain you upon these topics, or what sort of hearing they should have when opportunity shall come.

For, whether we will or not, the question of Slavery is *the* question, the all absorbing topic of the day. It is true that all of us—and by that I mean, not the Republican party alone, but the whole American people, here and elsewhere—all of us wish this question settled—wish it out of the way. It stands in the way, and prevents the adjustment, and the giving of necessary attention to other questions of national house-keeping. The people of the whole nation agree that this question ought to be settled, and yet it is not settled. And the reason is that they are not yet agreed *how* it shall be settled. All wish it done, but some wish one way and some another, and some a third, or fourth, or fifth; different bodies are pulling in different directions, and none of them having a decided majority, are able to accomplish the common object.

In the beginning of the year 1854 a new policy was inaugurated with the avowed object and confident promise that it would entirely and forever put an end to the Slavery agitation. It was again and again declared that under this policy, when once successfully established, the country would be forever rid of this whole question. Yet under the operation of that policy this agitation has not only not ceased, but it has been constantly augmented. And this too, although, from the day of its introduction, its friends, who promised that it would wholly end all agitation, constantly insisted, down to the time that the Lecompton bill was introduced, that it was working admirably, and that its inevitable tendency was to remove the question forever from the politics of the country. Can you call to mind any Democratic speech, made after the repeal of the Missouri Compromise, down to the time of the Lecompton bill, in which it was not predicted that the Slavery agitation was just at an end; that "the abolition excitement was played out," "the Kansas question was dead," "they have made the most they can out of this question and it is now forever settled." But since the Lecompton bill no Democrat, within my experience, has ever pretended that he could see the end. That cry has been dropped. They themselves do not pretend, now, that the agitation of this subject has come to an end yet. [Applause.]

The truth is, that this question is one of national importance, and we cannot help dealing with it: we must do something about it, whether we will or not. We cannot avoid it; the subject is one we cannot avoid considering; we can no more avoid it than a man can live without eating. It is upon us; it attaches to the body politic as much and as closely as the natural wants attach to our natural bodies. Now I think it important that this matter should be taken up in earnest, and really settled. And one way to bring about a true settlement of the question is to understand its true magnitude.

There have been many efforts to settle it. Again and again it has been fondly hoped that it was settled, but every time it breaks out afresh, and more violently than ever. It was settled, our fathers hoped, by the Missouri Compromise, but it did not stay settled. Then the compromises of 1850 were declared to be a full and final settlement of the question. The two great parties, each in National Convention, adopted resolutions declaring that the settlement made by the Compromise of 1850 was a finality—that it would last forever. Yet how long before it was unsettled again! It broke out again in 1854, and blazed higher and raged more furiously than ever before, and the agitation has not rested since.

These repeated settlements must have some fault about them. There must be some inadequacy in their very nature to the purpose for which they were designed. We can only speculate as to where that fault—that inadequacy, is, but we may perhaps profit by past experience.

I think that one of the causes of these repeated failures is that our best and greatest men have greatly underestimated the size of this question. They have constantly brought forward small cures for great sores—plasters too small to cover the wound. That is one reason that all settlements have proved so temporary—so evanescent. [Applause.]

Look at the magnitude of this subject! One sixth of our population, in round numbers—not quite one sixth, and yet more than a seventh,—about one sixth of the whole population of the United States are slaves! The owners of these slaves consider them property. The effect upon the minds of the owners is that of property, and nothing else—it induces them to insist upon all that will favorably affect its value as property, to demand laws and institutions and a public policy that shall increase and secure its value, and make it durable, lasting and universal. The effect on the minds of the owners is to persuade them that there is no wrong in it. The slaveholder does not like to be considered a mean fellow, for holding that species of property, and hence he has to struggle within himself and sets about arguing himself into the belief that Slavery is right. The property influences his mind. The dissenting minister, who argued some theological point with one of the established church, was always met by the reply, "I can't see it so." He opened the Bible, and pointed him to a passage, but the orthodox minister replied, "I can't see it so." Then he showed him a single word—"Can you see that?" "Yes, I see it," was the reply. The dissenter laid a guinea over the word and asked, "Do you see it now?" [Great laughter.] So here. Whether the owners of this species of property do really see it as it is, it is not for me to say, but if they do, they see it as it is through 2,000,000,000 of dollars, and that is a pretty thick coating. [Laughter.] Certain it is, that they do not see it as we see it. Certain it is, that this two thousand million of dollars, invested in this species of property, all so concentrated that the mind can grasp it at once—this immense pecuniary interest, has its influence upon their minds.

But here in Connecticut and at the North Slavery does not exist, and we see it through no such medium. To us it appears natural to think that slaves are human beings; *men,* not property; that some of the things, at least, stated about men in the Declaration of Independence apply to them as well as to us. [Applause.] I say, we think, most of us, that this Charter of Freedom applies to the slave as well as to ourselves, that the class of arguments put forward to batter down that idea, are also calculated to break down the very idea of a free government, even for white men, and to undermine the very foundations of free society. [Continued applause.] We think Slavery a great moral wrong, and while we do not claim the right to touch it where it exists, we wish to treat it as a wrong in the Territories, where our votes will reach it. We think that a respect for ourselves, a regard for future generations and for the God that made us, require that we put down this wrong where our votes will properly reach it. We think that species of labor an injury to free white men—in short, we think Slavery a great moral, social and political evil, tolerable only because, and so far as its actual existence makes it necessary to tolerate it, and that beyond that, it ought to be treated as a wrong.

Now these two ideas, the property idea that Slavery is right, and the idea that it is wrong, come into collision, and do actually produce that irrepressible conflict which Mr. Seward has been so roundly abused for mentioning. The two ideas conflict, and must conflict.

Again, in its political aspect, does anything in any way endanger the perpetuity of this Union but that single thing, Slavery? Many of our adversaries are anxious to claim that they are specially devoted to the Union, and take pains to charge upon us hostility to the Union. Now we claim that we are the only true Union men, and we put to them this one proposition: What ever endangered this Union, save and except Slavery? Did any other thing ever cause a moment's fear? All men must agree that this thing alone has ever endangered the perpetuity of the Union. But if it was threatened by any other influence, would not all men say that the best thing that could be done, if we could not or ought not to destroy it, would be at least to keep it from growing any larger? Can any man believe that the way to save the Union is to extend and increase the only thing that threatens the Union, and to suffer it to grow bigger and bigger? [Great applause.]

Whenever this question shall be settled, it must be settled on some philosophical basis. No policy that does not rest upon some philosophical public opinion can be permanently maintained. And hence, there are but two policies in regard to Slavery that can be at all maintained. The first, based on the property view that Slavery is right, conforms to that idea throughout, and demands that we shall do everything for it that we ought to do if it were right. We must sweep away all opposition, for opposition to the right is wrong; we must agree that Slavery is right, and we must adopt the idea that property has persuaded the owner to believe—that Slavery is morally right and socially elevating. This gives a philosophical basis for a permanent policy of encouragement.

The other policy is one that squares with the idea that Slavery is wrong, and it consists in doing everything that we ought to do if it is wrong. Now, I don't wish to be misunderstood, nor to leave a gap down to be misrepresented, even. I don't mean that we ought to attack it where it exists. To me it seems that if we were to form a government anew, in view of the actual presence of Slavery we should find it necessary to frame just such a government as our fathers did; giving to the slaveholder the entire control where the system was established, while we possessed the power to restrain it from going outside those limits. [Applause.] From the necessities of the case we should be compelled to form just such a government as our blessed fathers gave us; and, surely, if they have so made it, that adds another reason why we should let Slavery alone where it exists.

If I saw a venomous snake crawling in the road, any man would say I might seize the nearest stick and kill it; but if I found that snake in bed with my children, that would be another question. [Laughter.] I might hurt the children more than the snake, and it might bite them. [Applause.] Much more, if I found it in bed with my neighbor's children, and I had bound myself by a solemn compact not to meddle with his children under any circumstances, it would become me to let that particular mode of getting rid of the gentleman alone. [Great laughter.] But if there was a bed newly made up, to which the children were to be taken, and it was proposed to take a batch of young snakes and put them there with them, I take it no man would say there was any question how I ought to decide! [Prolonged applause and cheers.]

That is just the case! The new Territories are the newly made bed to which our children are to go, and it lies with the nation to say whether they shall have snakes mixed up with them or not. It does not seem as if there could be much hesitation what our policy should be! [Applause.]

Now I have spoken of a policy based on the idea that Slavery is wrong, and a policy based upon the idea that it is right. But an effort has been made for a policy that shall treat it as neither right or wrong. It is based upon utter indifference. Its leading advocate has said "I don't care whether it be voted up or down." [Laughter.] "It is merely a matter of dollars and cents." "The Almighty has drawn a line across this continent, on one side of which all soil must forever be cultivated by slave labor, and on the other by free;" "when the struggle is between the white man and the negro, I am for the white man; when it is between the negro and the crocodile, I am for the negro." Its central idea is indifference. It holds that it makes no more difference to us whether the Territories become free or slave States, than whether my neighbor stocks his farm with horned cattle or puts it into tobacco. All recognize this policy, the plausible sugar-coated name of which is *popular sovereignty.*" [Laughter.]

This policy chiefly stands in the way of a permanent settlement of the question. I believe there is no danger of its becoming the permanent policy of the country, for it is based on a public indifference. There is nobody that "don't care." ALL THE PEOPLE DO CARE! one way or the other. [Great applause.] I do not charge that its author, when he says he "don't care," states his individual opinion; he only expresses his policy for the government. I understand that he has never said, as an individual, whether he thought Slavery right or wrong— and he is the only man in the nation that has not! Now such a policy may have a temporary run; it may spring up as necessary to the political prospects of some gentleman; but it is utterly baseless; the people are not indifferent; and it can therefore have no durability or permanence.

But suppose it could! Then it could be maintained only by a public opinion that shall say "we don't care." There must be a change in public opinion, the public mind must be so far debauched as to square with this policy of caring not at all. The people must come to consider this as "merely a question of dollars and cents," and to believe that in some places the Almighty has made Slavery necessarily eternal. This policy can be brought to prevail if the people can be brought round to say honestly "we don't care;" if not, it can never be maintained. It is for you to say whether that can be done. [Applause.]

You are ready to say it cannot, but be not too fast! Remember what a long stride has been taken since the repeal of the Missouri Compromise! Do you know of any Democrat, of either branch of the party—do you know one who declares that he believes that the Declaration of Independence has any application to the negro? Judge Taney declares that it has not, and Judge Douglas even vilifies me personally and scolds me roundly for saying that the Declaration applies to all men, and that negroes are men. [Cheers.] Is there a Democrat here who does not deny that the Declaration applies to a negro? Do any of you know of one? Well, I have tried before perhaps fifty audiences, some larger and some smaller than this, to find one such Democrat, and never yet have I found one who said I did not place him right in that. I must assume that Democrats hold that, and now, *not one of these Democrats can show that he said that five years ago!* [Applause.] I venture to defy the whole party to produce one man that ever uttered the belief that the Declaration did not apply to negroes, before the repeal of the Missouri Compromise! Four or five years ago we all thought negroes were men, and that when *"all men"* were named, negroes were included. But *the whole Democratic party has deliberately taken negroes from the class of men and put them in the class of brutes.* [Applause.] Turn it as you will, it is simply the truth! Don't be too hasty then in saying that the people cannot be brought to this new doctrine, but note that long stride. One more as long completes the journey, from where negroes are estimated as men to where they are estimated as mere brutes—as rightful property!

That saying, "in the struggle between the white man and the negro," &c., which I know came from the same source as this policy—that saying marks another step. There is a falsehood wrapped up in that statement. "In the struggle between the white man and the negro" assumes that there is a struggle, in which either the white man must enslave the negro or the negro must enslave the white. There is no such struggle! It is merely an ingenious falsehood, to degrade and brutalize the negro. Let each let the other alone, and there is no struggle about it. If it was like two wrecked seamen on a narrow plank, when each must push the other off or drown himself, I would push the negro off or a white man either, but it is not; the plank is large enough for both. [Applause.] This good earth is plenty broad enough for white man and negro both, and there is no need of either pushing the other off. [Continued applause.]

So that saying, "in the struggle between the negro and the crocodile," &c., is made up from the idea that down where the crocodile inhabits a white man can't labor; it must be nothing else but crocodile or negro; if the negro does not the crocodile must possess the earth; [laughter;] in that case he declares for the negro. The meaning of the whole is just this: As a white man is to a negro, so is a negro to a crocodile; and as the negro may rightfully treat the crocodile, so may the white man rightfully treat the negro. This very dear phrase coined by its author, and so dear that he deliberately repeats it in many speeches, has a tendency to still further brutalize the negro, and to bring public opinion to the point of utter indifference whether men so brutalized are enslaved or not. When that time shall come, if ever, I think that policy to which I refer may prevail. But I hope the good freemen of this country will never allow it to come, and until then the policy can never be maintained.

Now consider the effect of this policy. We in the States are not to care whether Freedom or Slavery gets the better, but the people in the Territories may care. They are to decide, and they may think what they please; it is a matter of dollars and cents! But are not the people of the Territories detailed from the States? If this feeling of indifference—this absence of moral sense about the question—prevails in the States, will it not be carried into the Territories? Will not every man say, "I don't care, it is nothing to me?" If any one comes that wants Slavery, must they not say, "I don't care whether Freedom or Slavery be voted up or voted down?" It results at last in naturalizing [nationalizing?] the institution of Slavery. Even if fairly carried out, that policy is just as certain to naturalize [nationalize] Slavery as the doctrine of Jeff Davis himself. These are only two roads to the same goal, and "popular sovereignty" is just as sure and almost as short as the other. [Applause.]

What we want, and all we want, is to have with us the men who think slavery wrong. But those who say they hate slavery, and are opposed to it, but yet act with the Democratic party—where are they? Let us apply a few tests. You say that you think slavery is wrong, but you denounce all attempts to restrain it. Is there anything else that you think wrong, that you are not willing to deal with as a wrong? Why are you so careful, so tender of this one wrong and no other? [Laughter.] You will not let us *do* a single thing as if it was wrong; there is no place where you will allow it to be even *called* wrong! We must not call it wrong in the Free States, because it is *not* there, and we must not call it wrong in the Slave States because it *is* there; we must not call it wrong in politics because that is bringing morality into politics, and we must not call it wrong in the pulpit because that is bringing politics into religion; we must not bring it into the Tract Society or the other societies, because those are such unsuitable places, and there is no single place, according to you, where this wrong thing can properly be called wrong! [Continued laughter and applause.]

Perhaps you will plead that if the people of Slave States should themselves set on foot an effort for emancipation, you would wish them success, and bid them God-speed. Let us test that! In 1858, the emancipation party of Missouri, with Frank Blair at their head, tried to get up a movement for that purpose, and having started a party contested the State. Blair was beaten, apparently if not truly, and when the news came to Connecticut, you, who knew that Frank Blair was taking hold of this thing by the right end, and doing the only thing that you say can properly be done to remove this wrong—did you bow your heads in sorrow because of that defeat? Do you, any of you, know one single Democrat that showed sorrow over that result? Not one! On the contrary every man threw up his hat, and hallooed at the top of his lungs, "hooray for Democracy!" [Great laughter and applause.]

Now, gentlemen, *the Republicans desire to place this great question of slavery on the very basis on which our fathers placed it, and no other.* [Applause.] It is easy to demonstrate that "our Fathers, who framed this government under which we live," looked on Slavery as wrong, and so framed it and everything about it as to square with the idea that it was wrong, so far as the necessities arising from its existence permitted. In forming the Constitution they found the slave trade existing; capital invested in it; fields depending upon it for labor, and the whole system resting upon the importation of slave-labor. They therefore did not prohibit the slave trade at once, but they gave the power to prohibit it after twenty years. Why was this? What other foreign trade did they treat in that way? Would they have done this if they had not thought slavery wrong?

Another thing was done by some of the same men who framed the Constitution, and afterwards adopted as their own act by the first Congress held under that Constitution, of which many of the framers were members; they prohibited the spread of Slavery into Territories. Thus the same men, the framers of the Constitution, cut off the supply and prohibited the spread of Slavery, and both acts show conclusively that they considered that the thing was wrong.

If additional proof is wanting it can be found in the phraseology of the Constitution. When men are framing a supreme law and chart of government, to secure blessings and prosperity to untold generations yet to come, they use language as short and direct and plain as can be found, to express their meaning. In all matters but this of Slavery the framers of the Constitution used the very clearest, shortest, and most direct language. But the Constitution alludes to Slavery three times without mentioning it once! The language used becomes ambiguous, roundabout, and mystical. They speak of the "immigration of persons," and mean the importation of slaves, but do not say so. In establishing a basis of representation they say "all other persons," when they mean to say slaves—why did they not use the shortest phrase? In providing for the return of fugitives they say "persons held to service or labor." If they had said slaves it would have been plainer, and less liable to misconstruction. Why didn't they do it. We cannot doubt that it was done on purpose. Only one reason is possible, and that is supplied us by one of the framers of the Constitution—and it is not possible for man to conceive of any other—they expected and desired that the system would come to an end, and meant that when it did, the Constitution should not show that there ever had been a slave in this good free country of ours! [Great applause.]

I will dwell on that no longer. I see the signs of the approaching triumph of the Republicans in the bearing of their political adversaries. A great deal of their war with us now-a-days is mere bush-whacking. [Laughter.] At the battle of Waterloo, when Napoleon's cavalry had charged again and again upon the unbroken squares of British infantry, at last they were giving up the attempt, and going off in disorder, when some of the officers in mere vexation and complete despair fired their pistols at those solid squares. The Democrats are in that sort of extreme desperation; it is nothing else. [Laughter.] I will take up a few of these *arguments*.

There is "THE IRREPRESSIBLE CONFLICT." [Applause.] How they rail at Seward for that saying! They repeat it constantly; and although the proof has been thrust under their noses again and again, that almost every good man since the formation of our government has uttered that same sentiment, from Gen. Washington, who "trusted that we should yet have a confederacy of Free States," with Jefferson, Jay, Monroe, down to the latest days, yet they refuse to notice that at all, and persist in railing at Seward for saying it. Even Roger A. Pryor, editor of the Richmond Enquirer, uttered the same sentiment in almost the same language, and yet so little offence did it give the Democrats that he was sent for to Washington to edit the States—the Douglas organ there, while Douglas goes into hydrophobia and spasms of rage because Seward dared to repeat it. [Great applause.] This is what I call bushwhacking, a sort of argument that they must know any child can see through.

Another is JOHN BROWN! [Great laughter.] You stir up insurrections, you invade the South! John Brown! Harper's Ferry! Why, John Brown was not a Republican! You have never implicated a single Republican in that Harper's Ferry enterprise. We tell you that if any member of the Republican party is guilty in that matter, you know it or you do not know it. If you do know it, you are inexcusable not to designate man and prove the fact. If you do not know it, you are inexcusable to assert it, and especially to persist in the assertion after you have tried and failed to make the proof. You need not be told that persisting in a charge which one does not know to be true is simply malicious slander. Some of you admit that no Republican designedly aided or encouraged the Harper's Ferry affair; but still insist that our doctrines and declarations necessarily lead to such results. We do not believe it. We know we hold to no doctrines, and make no declarations, which were not held to and made by our fathers who framed the Government under which we live, and we cannot see how declarations that were patriotic when they made them are villainous when we make them. You never dealt fairly by us in relation to that affair—and I will say frankly that I know of nothing in your character that should lead us to suppose that you would. You had just been soundly thrashed in elections in several States, and others were soon to come. You rejoiced at the occasion, and only were troubled that there were not three times as many killed in the affair. You were in evident glee—there was no sorrow for the killed nor for the peace of Virginia disturbed—you were rejoicing that by charging Republicans with this thing you might get an advantage of us in New York, and the other States. You pulled that string as tightly as you could, but your very generous and worthy expectations were not quite fulfilled. [Laughter.] Each Republican knew that the charge was a slander as to himself at least, and was not inclined by it to cast his vote in your favor. It was mere bushwhacking, because you had nothing else to do. You are still on that track, and I say, go on! If you think you can slander a woman into loving you or a man into voting for you, try it till you are satisfied! [Tremendous applause.]

Another specimen of this bushwhacking, that "shoe strike." [Laughter.] Now be it understood that I do not pretend to know all about the matter. I am merely going to speculate a little about some of its phases. And at the outset, *I am glad to see that a system of labor prevails in New England under which laborers* CAN *strike,* when they want to [Cheers.] where they are not obliged to work under all circumstances, and are not tied down and obliged to labor whether you pay them or not! [Cheers.] I *like* the system which lets a man quit when he wants to, and wish it might prevail everywhere. [Tremendous applause.] One of the reasons why I am opposed to Slavery is just here. What is the true condition of the laborer? I take it that it is best for all to leave each man free to acquire property as fast as he can. Some will get wealthy. I don't believe in a law to prevent a man from getting rich; it would do more harm than good. So while we do not propose any war upon capital, we do wish to allow the humblest man an equal chance to get rich with everybody else. [Applause.] When one starts poor, as most do in the race of life, free society is such that he knows he can better his condition; he knows that there is no fixed condition of labor, for his whole life. I am not ashamed to confess that twenty five years ago I was a hired laborer, mauling rails, at work on a flat-boat—just what might happen to any poor man's son! [Applause.] I want every man to have the chance—and I believe a black man is entitled to it—in which he *can* better his condition—when he may look forward and hope to be a hired laborer this year and the next, work for himself afterward, and finally to hire men to work for him! That is the true system. Up here in New England, you have a soil that scarcely sprouts black-eyed beans, and yet where will you find wealthy men so wealthy, and poverty so rarely in extremity? There is not another such place on earth! [Cheers.] I desire that if you get too thick here, and find it hard to better your condition on this soil, you may have a chance to strike and go somewhere else, where you may not be degraded, nor have your family corrupted by forced rivalry with negro slaves. I want you to have a clean bed, and no snakes in it! [Cheers.] Then you can better your condition, and so it may go on and on in one ceaseless round so long as man exists on the face of the earth! [Prolonged applause.]

Now, to come back to this shoe strike,—if, as the Senator from Illinois asserts, this is caused by withdrawal of Southern votes, consider briefly how you will meet the difficulty. You have done nothing, and have protested that you have done nothing, to injure the South. And yet, to get back the shoe trade, you must leave off doing something that you are now doing. What is it? You must stop thinking slavery wrong! Let your institutions be wholly changed; let your State Constitutions be subverted, glorify slavery, and so you will get back the shoe trade—for what? You have brought owned labor with it to compete with your own labor, to underwork you, and to degrade you! Are you ready to get back the trade on those terms?

But the statement is not correct. You have not lost that trade; orders were never better than now! Senator Mason, a Democrat, comes into the Senate in homespun, a proof that the dissolution of the Union has actually begun! but orders are the same. Your factories have not struck work, neither those where they make anything for coats, nor for pants, nor for shirts, nor for ladies' dresses. Mr. Mason has not reached the manufacturers who ought to have made him a coat and pants! To make his proof good for anything he should have come into the Senate barefoot! (Great laughter.)

Another bushwhacking contrivance; simply that, nothing else! I find a good many people who are very much concerned about the loss of Southern trade. Now either these people are sincere or they are not. (Laughter.) I will speculate a little about that. If they are sincere, and are moved by any real danger of the loss of Southern trade, they will simply get their names on the white list,

and then, instead of persuading Republicans to do likewise, they will be glad to
keep you away! Don't you see they thus shut off competition? They would not
be whispering around to Republicans to come in and share the profits with
them. But if they are not sincere, and are merely trying to fool Republicans out
of their votes, they will grow very anxious about *your* pecuniary prospects; they
are afraid you are going to get broken up and ruined; they did not care about
Democratic votes—*Oh no, no, no!* You must judge which class those belong to
whom you meet; I leave it to you to determine from the facts.

Let us notice some more of the stale charges against Republicans. You say
we are sectional. We deny it. That makes an issue; and the burden of proof is
upon you. You produce your proof; and what is it? Why, that our party has
no existence in your section—gets no votes in your section. The fact is substantially true; but does it prove the issue? If it does, then in case we should,
without change of principle, begin to get votes in your section, we should
thereby cease to be sectional. You cannot escape this conclusion; and yet, are
you willing to abide by it? If you are, you will probably soon find that we have
ceased to be sectional, for we shall get votes in your section this very year.
[Applause.] The fact that we get no votes in your section is a fact of your making, and not of ours. And if there be fault in that fact, that fault is primarily
yours, and remains so until you show that we repel you by some wrong principle or practice. If we do repel you by any wrong principle or practice, the
fault is ours; but this brings you to where you ought to have started—to a discussion of the right or wrong of our principle. If our principle, put in practice,
would wrong your section for the benefit of ours, or for any other object, then
our principle, and we with it, are sectional, and are justly opposed and
denounced as such. Meet us, then, on the question of whether our principle,
put in practice, would wrong your section; and so meet it as if it were possible that something may be said on our side. Do you accept the challenge? No?
Then you really believe that the principle which our fathers who framed the
Government under which we live thought so clearly right as to adopt it, and
indorse it again and again, upon their official oaths, is, in fact, so clearly wrong
as to demand your condemnation without a moment's consideration.

Some of you delight to flaunt in our faces the warning against sectional parties given by Washington in his Farewell address. Less than eight years before
Washington gave that warning, he had, as President of the United States,
approved and signed an act of Congress, enforcing the prohibition of Slavery in
the northwestern Territory, which act embodied the policy of Government
upon that subject, up to and at the very moment he penned that warning; and

VI. "POLITICAL FAITH"   787

about one year after he penned it he wrote LaFayette that he considered that prohibition a wise measure, expressing in the same connection his hope that we should some time have a confederacy of Free States.

Bearing this in mind, and seeing that sectionalism has since arisen upon this same subject, is that warning a weapon in your hands against us, or in our hands against you? Could Washington himself speak, would he cast the blame of that sectionalism upon us, who sustain his policy, or upon you who repudiate it? We respect that warning of Washington, and we commend it to you, together with his example pointing to the right application of it. [Applause.]

But you say you are conservative—eminently conservative—while we are revolutionary, destructive, or something of the sort. What is conservatism? Is it not adherence to the old and tried, against the new and untried? We stick to, contend for, the identical old policy on the point in controversy which was adopted by our fathers who framed the Government under which we live; while you with one accord reject, and scout, and spit upon that old policy, and insist upon substituting something new. True, you disagree among yourselves as to what that substitute shall be. You have considerable variety of new propositions and plans, but you are unanimous in rejecting and denouncing the old policy of the fathers. Some of you are for reviving the foreign slave-trade; some for a Congressional Slave-Code for the Territories; some for Congress forbidding the Territories to prohibit Slavery within their limits; some for maintaining Slavery in the Territories through the Judiciary; some for the "gur-reat pur-rin-ciple" that "if one man would enslave another, no third man should object," fantastically called "Popular Sovereignty;" [great laughter,] but never a man among you in favor of Federal prohibition of Slavery in Federal Territories, according to the practice of our fathers who framed the Government under which we live. Not one of all your various plans can show a precedent or an advocate in the century within which our Government originated. And yet you draw yourselves up and say "We are eminently conservative!" [Great laughter.]

It is exceedingly desirable that all parts of this great Confederacy shall be at peace, and in harmony, one with another. Let us Republicans do our part to have it so. Even though much provoked, let us do nothing through passion and ill temper. Even though the Southern people will not so much as listen to us, let us calmly consider their demands, and yield to them if, in our deliberate view of our duty, we possibly can. Judging by all they say and do, and by the subject and nature of their controversy with us, let us determine, if we can, what will satisfy them?

Will they be satisfied if the Territories be unconditionally surrendered to them? We know they will not. In all their present complaints against us, the Territories are scarcely mentioned. Invasions and insurrections are the rage now. Will it satisfy them if, in the future, we have nothing to do with invasions and insurrections? We know it will not. We so know because we know we never had anything to do with invasions and insurrections; and yet this total obtaining does not exempt us from the charge and the denunciation.

The question recurs, what will satisfy them? Simply this: we must not only let them alone, but we must, somehow, convince them that we do let them alone. [Applause.] This, we know by experience, is no easy task. We have been so trying to convince them, from the very beginning of our organization, but with no success. In all our platforms and speeches, we have constantly protested our purpose to let them alone; but this has had no tendency to convince them. Alike unavailing to convince them is the fact that they have never detected a man of us in any attempt to disturb them.

These natural and apparently adequate means all failing, what will convince them? This, and this only; cease to call slavery *wrong,* and join them in calling it *right.* And this must be done thoroughly—done in *acts* as well as in *words.* Silence will not be tolerated—we must place ourselves avowedly with them. Douglas's new sedition law must be enacted and enforced, suppressing all declarations that Slavery is wrong, whether made in politics, in presses, in pulpits, or in private. We must arrest and return their fugitive slaves with greedy pleasure. We must pull down our Free State Constitutions. The whole atmosphere must be disinfected of all taint of opposition to Slavery, before they will cease to believe that all their troubles proceed from us. So long as we call Slavery wrong, whenever a slave runs away they will overlook the obvious fact that he ran because he was oppressed, and declare he was stolen off. Whenever a master cuts his slaves with the lash, and they cry out under it, he will overlook the obvious fact that the negroes cry out because they are hurt, and insist that they were *put up to it by some rascally abolitionist.* [Great laughter.]

I am quite aware that they do not state their case precisely in this way. Most of them would probably say to us, "Let us alone, do nothing to us, and say what you please about Slavery." But we do let them alone—have never disturbed them—so that, after all, it is what we say, which dissatisfies them. They will continue to accuse us of doing, until we cease saying.

I am also aware they have not, as yet, in terms, demanded the overthrow of our Free State Constitutions. Yet those Constitutions declare the wrong of Slavery, with more solemn emphasis than do all other sayings against it; and when all these other sayings shall have been silenced, the overthrow of these Constitutions will be demanded, and nothing be left to resist the demand. It is nothing to the contrary, that they do not demand the whole of this just now. Demanding what they do, and for the reason they do, they can voluntarily stop nowhere short of this consummation. Holding as they do, that Slavery is morally right, and socially elevating, they cannot cease to demand a full national recognition of it, as a legal right, and a social blessing.

Nor can we justifiably withhold this, on any ground save our conviction that Slavery is wrong. If Slavery is right, all words, acts, laws, and Constitutions against it, are themselves wrong, and should be silenced, and swept away. If it is right, we cannot justly object to its nationality—its universality; if it is wrong, they cannot justly insist upon its extension—its enlargement. All they ask, we could readily grant, if we thought Slavery right; all we ask, they could as readily grant, if they thought it wrong. Their thinking it right, and our thinking it wrong, is the precise fact upon which depends the whole controversy. Thinking it right as they do, they are not to blame for desiring its full recognition, as being right; but, thinking it wrong, as we do, can we yield to them? Can we cast our votes with their view, and against our own? In view of our moral, social, and political responsibilities, can we do this?

Wrong as we think Slavery is, we can yet afford to let it alone where it is, because that much is due to the necessity arising from its actual presence in the nation; but can we, while our votes will prevent it, allow it to spread into the National Territories, and to overrun us here in these Free States?

If our sense of duty forbids this, then let us stand by our duty, fearlessly and effectively. Let us be diverted by none of those sophistical contrivances wherewith we are so industriously plied and belabored—contrivances such as groping for some middle ground between the right and the wrong, vain as the search for a man who should be neither a living man nor a dead man—such as a policy of "don't care" on a question about which all true men do care—such as Union appeals beseeching true Union men to yield to Disunionists, reversing the divine rule, and calling, not the sinners, but the righteous to repentance—such as invocations of Washington, imploring men to unsay what Washington did.

Neither let us be slandered from our duty by false accusations against us, nor frightened from it by menaces of destruction to the Government, nor of dungeons to ourselves. Let us have faith that right makes might; and in that faith, let us, to the end, dare to do our duty, as we understand it.

ADDRESS TO THE NEW JERSEY SENATE AT TRENTON, NEW JERSEY[6]
FEBRUARY 21, 1861

While making the twelve-day journey from Springfield to Washington, D.C., Lincoln delivered speeches at numerous points in-between. His address to the New Jersey Senate at Trenton was made en route to the White House. In this brief but important speech, Lincoln noted the historical significance of Trenton claiming that the glorious deeds of George Washington had inspired him as a child. Establishing continuity between himself and the Founders, he made it clear to the audience that he was dedicated to perpetuating the "original idea" for which the nation fought for during its Independence—that is, the idea of liberty and equality in the Declaration. Finally, invoking divine providence, Lincoln characterized himself as a "humble instrument in the hands of the Almighty" and ironically referred to the American people as God's "almost chosen people." This designation of Americans as God's "almost chosen people" introduced an ambiguity and qualification that recognized both the nation's blessings and its obligations.

FEBRUARY 21, 1861

MR. PRESIDENT AND GENTLEMEN of the Senate of the State of New-Jersey: I am very grateful to you for the honorable reception of which I have been the object. I cannot but remember the place that New-Jersey holds in our early history. In the early Revolutionary struggle, few of the States among the old Thirteen had more of the battle-fields of the country within their limits than old New-Jersey. May I be pardoned if, upon this occasion, I mention that away back in my childhood, the earliest days of my being able to read, I got hold of a small book, such a one as few of the younger members have ever seen, "Weem's Life of Washington." I remember all the accounts there given of the battle fields and struggles for the liberties of the country, and none fixed themselves upon my imagination so deeply as the struggle here at Trenton, New-Jersey. The crossing of the river; the contest with the Hessians; the great hardships endured at that time, all fixed themselves on my memory more than any single revolutionary event; and you all know, for you have all been boys, how these early impressions last longer than any others. I recollect thinking then, boy even though I was, that there must have been something more than common that those men struggled for. I am exceedingly anxious that that thing which they struggled for; that something even more than National Independence; that something that held out a great promise to all the people of the

6. *CWAl*, IV, 235-236.

world to all time to come; I am exceedingly anxious that this Union, the Constitution, and the liberties of the people shall be perpetuated in accordance with the original idea for which that struggle was made, and I shall be most happy indeed if I shall be an humble instrument in the hands of the Almighty, and of this, his almost chosen people, for perpetuating the object of that great struggle. You give me this reception, as I understand, without distinction of party. I learn that this body is composed of a majority of gentlemen who, in the exercise of their best judgment in the choice of a Chief Magistrate, did not think I was the man. I understand, nevertheless, that they came forward here to greet me as the constitutional President of the United States—as citizens of the United States, to meet the man who, for the time being, is the representative man of the nation, united by a purpose to perpetuate the Union and liberties of the people. As such, I accept this reception more gratefully than I could do did I believe it was tendered to me as an individual.

REMARKS TO A DELEGATION OF PROGRESSIVE FRIENDS[7]
JUNE 20, 1862

The New York Tribune *reported this Lincoln's response to a Quaker delegation who urged immediate emancipation of the slaves on religious grounds. As with his early correspondence with Joshua Speed (see above), Lincoln referred to himself as "an instrument of God."*

JUNE 20, 1862

The President said that, as he had not been furnished with a copy of the memorial in advance, he could not be expected to make any extended remarks. It was a relief to be assured that the deputation were not applicants for office, for his chief trouble was from that class of persons. The next most troublesome subject was Slavery. He agreed with the memorialists, that Slavery was wrong, but in regard to the ways and means of its removal, his views probably differed from theirs. The quotation in the memorial, from his Springfield speech, was incomplete. It should have embraced another sentence, in which he indicated his views as to the effect upon Slavery itself of the resistance to its extension.

The sentiments contained in that passage were deliberately uttered, and he held them now. If a decree of emancipation could abolish Slavery, John Brown would have done the work effectually. Such a decree surely could not be more binding upon the South than the Constitution, and that cannot be enforced in

7. *CWAL,* V, 278.

that part of the country now. Would a proclamation of freedom be any more effective?

Mr. Johnson replied as follows:

"True, Mr. President, the Constitution cannot now be enforced at the South, but you do not on that account intermit the effort to enforce it, and the memorialists are solemnly convinced that the abolition of Slavery is indispensable to your success."

The President further said that he felt the magnitude of the task before him, and hoped to be rightly directed in the very trying circumstances by which he was surrounded.

Wm. Barnard addressed the President in a few words, expressing sympathy for him in all his embarrassments, and an earnest desire that he might, under divine guidance, be led to free the slaves and thus save the nation from destruction. In that case, nations yet unborn would rise up to call him blessed and, better still, he would secure the blessing of God.

The President responded very impressively, saying that he was deeply sensible of his need of Divine assistance. He had sometime thought that perhaps he might be an instrument in God's hands of accomplishing a great work and he certainly was not unwilling to be. Perhaps, however, God's way of accomplishing the end which the memorialists have in view may be different from theirs. It would be his earnest endeavor, with a firm reliance upon the Divine arm, and seeking light from above, to do his duty in the place to which he had been called.

REPLY TO EMANCIPATION MEMORIAL PRESENTED BY CHICAGO CHRISTIANS OF ALL DENOMINATIONS[8]
SEPTEMBER 13, 1862

A delegation representing an interdenominational group of Christians presented Lincoln with a memorial urging emancipation about a week before the official decree on September 22, 1862. Lincoln's response to the memorial affirmed a harmony between biblical precept and human discernment: the two cooperated in the determination of prudent judgment. According to Lincoln, the general moral precepts of the Bible do not provide, nor do they intend to provide, specific legal determinations of public policy. While earnestly seeking to discern God's will, Lincoln also humbly accepted the limits of human nature. His humble acknowl-

edgment that "good men do not agree" on the application of moral principles to specific circumstances may be contrasted to the self-righteous dogmatism of the ideologue.

SEPTEMBER 13, 1862

"The subject presented in the memorial is one upon which I have thought much for weeks past, and I may even say for months. I am approached with the most opposite opinions and advice, and that by religious men, who are equally certain that they represent the Divine will. I am sure that either the one or the other class is mistaken in that belief, and perhaps in some respects both. I hope it will not be irreverent for me to say that if it is probable that God would reveal his will to others, on a point so connected with my duty, it might be supposed he would reveal it directly to me, for, unless I am more deceived in myself than I often am, it is my earnest desire to know the will of Providence in this matter. *And if I can learn what it is I will do it!* These are not, however, the days of miracles, and I suppose it will be granted that I am not to expect a direct revelation. I must study the plain physical facts of the case, ascertain what is possible and learn what appears to be wise and right. The subject is difficult, and good men do not agree. For instance, the other day four gentlemen of standing and intelligence (naming one or two of the number) from New York called, as a delegation, on business connected with the war; but, before leaving, two of them earnestly beset me to proclaim general emancipation, upon which the other two at once attacked them! You know, also, that the last session of Congress had a decided majority of anti-slavery men, yet they could not unite on this policy. And the same is true of the religious people. Why, the rebel soldiers are praying with a great deal more earnestness, I fear, than our own troops, and expecting God to favor their side; for one of our soldiers, who had been taken prisoner, told Senator Wilson, a few days since, that he met with nothing so discouraging as the evident sincerity of those he was among in their prayers. But we will talk over the merits of the case.

"What *good* would a proclamation of emancipation from me do, especially as we are now situated? I do not want to issue a document that the whole world will see must necessarily be inoperative, like the Pope's bull against the comet! Would *my word* free the slaves, when I cannot even enforce the Constitution in the rebel States? Is there a single court, or magistrate, or individual that would be influenced by it there? And what reason is there to think it would have any greater effect upon the slaves than the late law of Congress, which I approved, and which offers protection and freedom to the slaves of rebel masters who come within our lines? Yet I cannot learn that that law has caused a single slave to come over to us. And suppose they could be induced by a proclamation of freedom from me to throw themselves upon us, *what should we do with them?* How can we feed and care for such a multitude? Gen. Butler wrote me a few days since that he was issuing more rations to the slaves who have rushed to him than to all the white troops under his command. They *eat,* and that is all, though it is true Gen. Butler is feeding the whites also by the thousand; for it nearly amounts to a famine there. If, now, the pressure of the war should call off our forces from New Orleans to defend some other point, what is to prevent the masters from reducing the blacks to slavery again; for I am told that whenever the rebels take any black prisoners, free or slave, they immediately auction them off! They did so with those they took from a boat that was aground in the Tennessee river a few days ago. And then *I am very ungenerously attacked for it!* For instance, when, after the late battles at and near Bull Run, an expedition went out from Washington under a flag of truce to bury the dead and bring in the wounded, and the rebels seized the blacks who went along to help and sent them into slavery, Horace Greeley said in his paper that the Government would probably do nothing about it. What *could* I do? [Here your delegation suggested that this was a gross outrage on a flag of truce, which covers and protects all over which it waves, and that whatever he could do if *white* men had been similarly detained he *could* do in this case.]

"Now, then, tell me, if you please, what possible result of good would follow the issuing of such a proclamation as you desire? Understand, I raise no objections against it on legal or constitutional grounds; for, as commander-in-chief of the army and navy, in time of war, I suppose I have a right to take any measure which may best subdue the enemy. Nor do I urge objections of a moral nature, in view of possible consequences of insurrection and massacre at the South. I view the matter as a practical war measure, to be decided upon according to the advantages or disadvantages it may offer to the suppression of the rebellion."

Thus invited, your delegation very willingly made reply to the following effect; it being understood that a portion of the remarks were intermingled by the way of conversation with those of the President just given.

We observed (taking up the President's ideas in order) that good men indeed differed in their opinions on this subject; nevertheless *the truth was somewhere,* and it was a matter of solemn moment for him to ascertain it; that we had not been so wanting in respect, alike to ourselves and to him, as to come a thousand miles to bring merely *our opinion* to be set over against the *opinion* of other parties; that the memorial contained facts, principles, and arguments which appealed to the intelligence of the President and to his faith in Divine Providence; that he could not deny that the Bible denounced oppression as one of the highest of crimes, and threatened Divine judgments against nations that practice it; that our country had been exceedingly guilty in this respect, both at the North and South; that our just punishment has come by a slaveholder's rebellion; that the virus of secession is found wherever the virus of slavery extends, and no farther; so that there is the amplest reason for expecting to avert Divine judgments by putting away the sin, and for hoping to remedy the national troubles by striking at their cause.

We observed, further, that we freely admitted the probability, and even the certainty, that God would reveal the path of duty to the President as well as to others, provided he sought to learn it in the appointed way; but, as according to his own remark, Providence wrought by means and not miraculously, it might be, God would use the suggestions and arguments of other minds to secure that result. We felt the deepest personal interest in the matter as of national concern, and would fain aid the thoughts of our President by communicating the convictions of the Christian community from which we came, with the ground upon which they were based.

That it was true he could not now enforce the Constitution at the South; but we could see in that fact no reason whatever for not proclaiming emancipation, but rather the contrary. The two appealed to different classes; the latter would aid, and in truth was necessary to re-establish the former; and the two could be made operative together as fast as our armies fought their way southward; while we had yet to hear that he proposed to abandon the Constitution because of the present difficulty of enforcing it.

As to the inability of Congress to agree on this policy at the late session, it was quite possible, in view of subsequent events, there might be more unanimity at another meeting. The members have met their constituents and learned of marvellous conversions to the wisdom of emancipation, especially since late reverses have awakened thought as to the extreme peril of the nation, and made bad men as well as good men realize that we have to deal with God in this matter. Men of the most opposite previous views were now uniting in calling for this measure.

That to proclaim emancipation would secure the sympathy of Europe and the whole civilized world, which now saw no other reason for the strife than national pride and ambition, an unwillingness to abridge our domain and power. No other step would be so potent to prevent foreign intervention.

Furthermore, it would send a thrill through the entire North, firing every patriotic heart, giving the people a glorious principle for which to suffer and to fight, and assuring them that the work was to be so thoroughly done as to leave our country free forever from danger and disgrace in this quarter.

We added, that when the proclamation should become widely known (as the law of Congress has *not* been) it would withdraw the slaves from the rebels, leaving them without laborers, and giving us *both laborers and soldiers*. That the difficulty experienced by Gen. Butler and other Generals arose from the fact that *halfway measures could never avail*. It is the inherent vice of half-way measures that they create as many difficulties as they remove. It is folly merely to receive and feed the slaves. They should be welcomed and fed, and then, according to Paul's doctrine, that they who eat must work, be made to labor and to fight for their liberty and ours. With such a policy the blacks would be no incumbrance and their rations no waste. In this respect we should follow the ancient maxim, and learn of the enemy. What the rebels most fear is what we should be most prompt to do; and what they most fear is evident from the hot haste with which, on the first day of the present session of the Rebel Congress, bills were introduced threatening terrible vengeance if we used the blacks in the war.

The President rejoined from time to time in about these terms:

"I admit that slavery is the root of the rebellion, or at least its *sine qua non*. The ambition of politicians may have instigated them to act, but they would have been impotent without slavery as their instrument. I will also concede that emancipation would help us in Europe, and convince them that we are incited by something more than ambition. I grant further that it would help *somewhat* at the North, though not so much, I fear, as you and those you represent imagine. Still, some additional strength would be added in that way to the war. And then unquestionably it would weaken the rebels by drawing off their laborers, which is of great importance. But I am not so sure we could do much with the blacks. If we were to arm them, I fear that in a few weeks the arms would be in the hands of the rebels; and indeed thus far we have not had arms enough to equip our white troops. I will mention another thing, though it meet only your scorn and contempt: There are fifty thousand bayonets in the Union armies from the Border Slave States. It would be a serious matter if, in consequence of a proclamation such as you desire, they should go over to the rebels. I do not think they all would—not so many indeed as a year ago, or as six months ago—not so many to-day as yesterday. Every day increases their Union feeling. They are also getting their pride enlisted, and want to beat the rebels. Let me say one thing more: I think you should admit that we already have an important principle to rally and unite the people in the fact that constitutional government is at stake. This is a fundamental idea, going down about as deep as any thing."

We answered that, being fresh from the people, we were naturally more hopeful than himself as to the necessity and probable effect of such a proclamation. The value of constitutional government is indeed a grand idea for which to contend; but the people know that *nothing else has put constitutional government in danger but slavery;* that the toleration of that aristocratic and despotic element among our free institutions was the inconsistency that had nearly wrought our ruin and caused free government to appear a failure before the world, and therefore the people demand emancipation to preserve and perpetuate constitutional government. Our idea would thus be found to go deeper than this, and to be armed with corresponding power. ("Yes," interrupted Mr. Lincoln, "that is the true ground of our difficulties.") That a proclamation of general emancipation, "giving Liberty and Union" as the national watch-word, would rouse the people and rally them to his support beyond any thing yet witnessed—appealing alike to conscience, sentiment, and hope. He must remember, too, that present manifestations are no index of what would then take place. If the leader will but utter a trumpet call the nation will respond with patriotic ardor. No one can tell the power of the right word from the right man to develop the latent fire and enthusiasm of the masses. ("I know it," exclaimed Mr. Lincoln.) That good sense must of course be exercised in drilling, arming, and using black as well as white troops to make them efficient; and that in a scarcity of arms it was at least worthy of inquiry whether it were not wise to place a portion of them in the hands of those nearest to the seat of the rebellion and able to strike the deadliest blow.

That in case of a proclamation of emancipation we had no fear of serious injury from the desertion of Border State troops. The danger was greatly diminished, as the President had admitted. But let the desertions be what they might, the increased spirit of the North would replace them two to one. One State alone, if necessary, would compensate the loss, were the whole 50,000 to join the enemy. The struggle has gone too far, and cost too much treasure and blood, to allow of a partial settlement. Let the line be drawn at the same time between freedom and slavery, and between loyalty and treason. The sooner we know who are our enemies the better.

In bringing our interview to a close, after an hour of earnest and frank discussion, of which the foregoing is a specimen, Mr. Lincoln remarked: "Do not misunderstand me, because I have mentioned these objections. They indicate the difficulties that have thus far prevented my action in some such way as you desire. I have not decided against a proclamation of liberty to the slaves, but hold the matter under advisement. And I can assure you that the subject is on my mind, by day and night, more than any other. Whatever shall appear to be God's will I will do. I trust that, in the freedom with which I have canvassed your views, I have not in any respect injured your feelings."

MEDITATION ON THE DIVINE WILL
SEPTEMBER [30?], 1862

Lincoln wrote this private reflection while pondering the ultimate theological significance of the Civil War. The reflection was discovered in his personal notebook shortly after his assassination by his secretaries Nicolay and Hay who then entitled it "Meditation on the Divine Will." Significantly, Nicolay and Hay published the meditation as a testimony to the sincerity of Lincoln's faith in response to allegations made after his death by his law partner, William Herndon, that he was a skeptic. They claimed that the meditation was, "not written to be seen of men" and that it was "penned in the awful sincerity a perfectly honest soul trying to bring itself in closer communication with its maker." The articulation of biblical faith in this meditation bears comparison to the Second Inaugural Address.

THE WILL OF GOD prevails. In great contests each party claims to act in accordance with the will of God. Both may be, and one must be, wrong. God cannot be for and against the same thing at the same time. In the present civil war it is quite possible that God's purpose is something different from the purpose of either party; and yet the human instrumentalities, working just as they do, are of the best adaptation to effect his purpose. I am almost ready to say that this is probably true; that God wills this contest, and wills that it shall not end yet. By his mere great power on the minds of the now contestants, he could have either saved or destroyed the Union without a human contest. Yet the contest began. And, having begun, he could give the final victory to either side any day. Yet the contest proceeds.

REPLY TO MRS. ELIZA P. GURNEY[9]
OCTOBER 26, 1862

Mrs. Gurney was the widow of an English Quaker who came to the White House to provide "spiritual guidance" to the president. After she addressed the president, Lincoln, in an almost spontaneous profession of faith, replied to her on this occasion, and on another, in a private letter, written two years later. The fact that Lincoln remembered his encounter with Gurney and that he wrote her a private letter two years later conveys the extent to which this Quaker woman must have elicited the president's spiritual yearnings. The intimate tone of the Lincoln-Gurney correspondence suggests that the Quaker woman's piety sincerely touched Lincoln. Perhaps it was her humble effort to serve the president in a time of anguish and suffering? The response to Mrs. Gurney is also consistent with the biblical faith manifested in Lincoln's letter to Joshua Speed. In both cases, Lincoln referred to himself as "humble instrument" in the hands of God. Being called by God as a witness, however, required self-sacrifice and humility, not self-assertion and pride. Lincoln well recognized that worldly success was not a sign of divine favor. He trusted that God would ultimately bring good out of the conflict even though he could not comprehend the vast human suffering around him. Lincoln described the Civil War as a "fiery trial", a reference to 1 Peter 4:12, which described the experienced of martyrdom. Indeed, Lincoln viewed the Civil War as a trial in several senses: to preserve the republican form of government on earth; to test the viability of popular government; to vindicate the American experiment from the blight of slavery; and to remain faithful to the nation's moral covenant in the Declaration.

OCTOBER 26, 1862

I am glad of this interview, and glad to know that I have your sympathy and prayers. We are indeed going through a great trial—a fiery trial. In the very responsible position in which I happen to be placed, being a humble instrument in the hands of our Heavenly Father, as I am, and as we all are, to work out his great purposes, I have desired that all my works and acts may be according to his will, and that it might be so, I have sought his aid—but if after endeavoring to do my best in the light which he affords me, I find my efforts fail, I must believe that for some purpose unknown to me, He wills it otherwise; If I had had my way, this war would never have been commenced; If I had been allowed my way this war would have been ended before this, but we find it still continues; and we must believe that He permits it for some wise purpose of his own, mysterious and unknown to us; and though with our limited understandings we may not be able to comprehend it, yet we cannot but believe, that he who made the world still governs it.

ADDRESS DELIVERED AT THE DEDICATION OF THE CEMETERY AT GETTYSBURG
November 19, 1863

In November, Lincoln was invited to make "a few appropriate remarks" at the dedication of a national cemetery created on the site of the battle of Gettysburg, which was fought in July 1863. The feature speaker, however, was not Lincoln, whose presence was required to dignify the occasion, but the notable orator, Edward Everett. Everett's speech lasted about two hours while Lincoln's speech lasted about three minutes. Lincoln's 272 words at Gettysburg poetically distilled the essence of the American creed. The "Four score of seven years" of the speech—the term score was used by the King James Bible to designate a period of twenty years—placed the nation's birth at 1776, the year of the Declaration thereby emphasizing that equality was the "central idea" of the American experiment. A biblical cadence, ethos and style pervaded the speech. The religious metaphors of death, redemption, and re-birth symbolically conveyed the nation's sacrificial suffering for its political faith in the Declaration. The blood of the nation's soldiers symbolically redeemed the nation from the original sin of slavery leading to "a new birth of freedom," a Union freed from the stain of human servitude. Significantly, when speaking of the dead, Lincoln made no distinction between the South and the North, implicitly recognizing the courage and sacrifice of both sides. The memorable expression "of the people, by the people, and for the people" continues to resonate throughout the world as one of the tersest definitions of democracy. Lincoln inserted the term, "under God," spontaneously during the speech; it was not included in his original draft.

FOUR SCORE AND SEVEN years ago our fathers brought forth on this continent, a new nation, conceived in Liberty, and dedicated to the proposition that all men are created equal.

Now we are engaged in a great civil war, testing whether that nation, or any nation so conceived and so dedicated, can long endure. We are met on a great battle-field of that war. We have come to dedicate a portion of that field, as a final resting place for those who here gave their lives that that nation might live. It is altogether fitting and proper that we should do this.

But, in a larger sense, we can not dedicate—we can not consecrate—we can not hallow—this ground. The brave men, living and dead, who struggled here, have consecrated it, far above our poor power to add or detract. The world will little note, nor long remember what we say here, but it can never forget what they did here. It is for us the living, rather, to be dedicated here to the unfinished work which they who fought here have thus far so nobly advanced. It is rather for us to be here dedicated to the great task remaining before us—that from these honored dead we take increased devotion to that cause for which they gave the last full measure of devotion—that we here highly resolve that these dead shall not have died in vain—that this nation, under God, shall have a new birth of freedom—and that government of the people, by the people, for the people, shall not perish from the earth.

ABRAHAM LINCOLN
November 19, 1863

TO EDWIN M. STANTON[10]
FEBRUARY 5, 1864

This memo reveals the extent to which a biblical ethos imbued Lincoln's politics. The memo pertained to the oath rebels would have to swear to qualify for public office in reconstructed Tennessee. The Radicals demanded that former rebels should swear an oath of past purity and future loyalty in order to regain citizenship. Lincoln, on the contrary, thought this oath too punitive: it was enough that the offender swear to do no wrong in the future.

FEBRUARY 5, 1864

Submitted to the Sec. Of War. On principle I dislike an oath which requires a man to swear he *has* not done wrong. It rejects the Christian principle of forgiveness on terms of repentence. I think it is enough if the man does no wrong hereafter.

A. Lincoln

Feb. 5. 1864

10. *CWAL,* VII, 169.

TO ALBERT G. HODGES[11]
APRIL 4, 1864

Albert G. Hodges, editor of the Frankfort, Kentucky Commonwealth, *spoke with Lincoln about difficulties in the Border States, including those who opposed the use of slaves as soldiers. Shortly after their meeting on March 26, Hodges asked Lincoln for a written copy of remarks the president had made to him. Lincoln declined, claiming that he had not written anything down, but subsequently mailed Hodges the following letter. In anticipation of the Second Inaugural Address, Lincoln's letter to Hodges assigned culpability to both North and South for the war.*

A. G. HODGES, ESQ
EXECUTIVE MANSION,
FRANKFORT, KY.
WASHINGTON, APRIL 4, 1864.

My dear Sir: You ask me to put in writing the substance of what I verbally said the other day, in your presence, to Governor Bramlette and Senator Dixon. It was about as follows:

"I am naturally anti-slavery. If slavery is not wrong, nothing is wrong. I can not remember when I did not so think, and feel. And yet I have never understood that the Presidency conferred upon me an unrestricted right to act officially upon this judgment and feeling. It was in the oath I took that I would, to the best of my ability, preserve, protect, and defend the Constitution of the United States. I could not take the office without taking the oath. Nor was it my view that I might take an oath to get power, and break the oath in using the power. I understood, too, that in ordinary civil administration this oath even forbade me to practically indulge my primary abstract judgment on the moral question of slavery. I had publicly declared this many times, and in many ways. And I aver that, to this day, I have done no official act in mere deference to my abstract judgment and feeling on slavery. I did understand however, that my oath to preserve the constitution to the best of my ability, imposed upon me the duty of preserving, by every indispensable means, that government—that nation—of which that constitution was the organic law. Was it possible to lose the nation, and yet preserve the constitution? By general law life *and* limb must be protected; yet often a limb must be amputated to save a life; but a life is

11. *CWAL*, VII, 281–282.

never wisely given to save a limb. I felt that measures, otherwise unconstitutional, might become lawful, by becoming indispensable to the
preservation of the constitution, through the preservation of the nation.
Right or wrong, I assumed this ground, and now avow it. I could not
feel that, to the best of my ability, I had even tried to preserve the constitution, if, to save slavery, or any minor matter, I should permit the
wreck of government, country, and Constitution all together. When,
early in the war, Gen. Fremont attempted military emancipation, I forbade it, because I did not then think it an indispensable necessity. When
a little later, Gen. Cameron, then Secretary of War, suggested the arming of the blacks, I objected, because I did not yet think it an indispensable necessity. When, still later, Gen. Hunter attempted military
emancipation, I again forbade it, because I did not yet think the indispensable necessity had come. When, in March, and May, and July 1862
I made earnest, and successive appeals to the border states to favor compensated emancipation, I believed the indispensable necessity for military emancipation, and arming the blacks would come, unless averted by
that measure. They declined the proposition; and I was, in my best judgment, driven to the alternative of either surrendering the Union, and
with it, the Constitution, or of laying strong hand upon the colored element. I chose the latter. In choosing it, I hoped for greater gain than loss;
but of this, I was not entirely confident. More than a year of trial now
shows no loss by it in our foreign relations, none in our home popular
sentiment, none in our white military force,—no loss by it any how or
any where. On the contrary, it shows a gain of quite a hundred and thirty
thousand soldiers, seamen, and laborers. These are palpable facts, about
which, as facts, there can be no cavilling. We have the men; and we
could not have had them without the measure.

["]And now let any Union man who complains of the measure, test
himself by writing down in one line that he is for subduing the rebellion
by force of arms; and in the next, that he is for taking these hundred and
thirty thousand men from the Union side, and placing them where they
would be but for the measure he condemns. If he can not face his case
so stated, it is only because he can not face the truth.["]

I add a word which was not in the verbal conversation. In telling this tale I
attempt no compliment to my own sagacity. I claim not to have controlled
events, but confess plainly that events have controlled me. Now, at the end of
three years struggle the nation's condition is not what either party, or any man

devised, or expected. God alone can claim it. Whither it is tending seems plain. If God now wills the removal of a great wrong, and wills also that we of the North as well as you of the South, shall pay fairly for our complicity in that wrong, impartial history will find therein new cause to attest and revere the justice and goodness of God. Yours truly

    A. LINCOLN

TO GEORGE B. IDE, JAMES R. DOOLITTLE, AND A. HUBBELL[12] MAY 30, 1864

Lincoln's response to a group of Baptists manifests his righteous indignation over proslavery theology. While extremely patient and compassionate towards others, Lincoln particularly reserved his most bitter scorn for members of the cultural elite who exploited the Bible to justify slavery and rebellion. In this speech, he appealed to the biblical precepts of Genesis 3:19 and Matthew 7:12 (the Golden Rule) against the proslavery interpretation of the Bible.

REV. DR. IDE} EXECUTIVE MANSION,
HON. J. R. DOOLITTLE} COMMITTEE WASHINGTON,
& HON. A. HUBBELL} MAY 30, 1864.

In response to the preamble and resolutions of the American Baptist Home Mission Society, which you did me the honor to present, I can only thank you for thus adding to the effective and almost unanamous support which the Christian communities are so zealously giving to the country, and to liberty. Indeed it is difficult to conceive how it could be otherwise with any one professing christianity, or even having ordinary perceptions of right and wrong. To read in the Bible, as the word of God himself, that "In the sweat of *thy* face shalt thou eat bread,["] and to preach therefrom that, "In the sweat of *other mans* faces shalt thou eat bread," to my mind can scarcely be reconciled with honest sincerity. When brought to my final reckoning, may I have to answer for robbing no man of his goods; yet more tolerable even this, than for robbing one of himself, and all that was his. When, a year or two ago, those professedly holy men of the South, met in the semblance of prayer and devotion, and, in the name of Him who said "As ye would all men should do unto you, do ye even so unto them" appealed to the christian world to aid them in doing to a whole race of men, as they would have no man do unto themselves, to my thinking, they contemned and insulted God and His church, far more than did Satan when he tempted the Saviour with the Kingdoms of the earth. The dev-

12. *CWAL,* VII, 368.

ils attempt was no more false, and far less hypocritical. But let me forbear, remembering it is also written "Judge not, lest ye be judged."

LETTER TO MRS. ELIZA P. GURNEY
SEPTEMBER 4, 1864

Mrs. Gurney wrote to Lincoln on August 8, 1863 conveying her prayers for the president in his time of trial. She expressed her belief that God had made him "instrumental" in carrying out his providential design. Remembering their prior meeting, Lincoln responded to Mrs. Gurney by thanking her for strengthening his "reliance on God." (See above October 26, 1862).

EXECUTIVE MANSION,
WASHINGTON, SEPTEMBER 4, 1864.
ELIZA P. GURNEY.
MY ESTEEMED FRIEND.

I have not forgotten—probably never shall forget—the very impressive occasion when yourself and friends visited me on a Sabbath forenoon two years ago. Nor has your kind letter, written nearly a year later, ever been forgotten. In all, it has been your purpose to strengthen my reliance on God. I am much indebted to the good Christian people of the country for their constant prayers and consolations; and to no one of them, more than to yourself. The purposes of the Almighty are perfect, and must prevail, though we erring mortals may fail to accurately perceive them in advance. We hoped for a happy termination of this terrible war long before this; but God knows best, and has ruled otherwise. We shall yet acknowledge His wisdom and our own error therein. Meanwhile we must work earnestly in the best light He gives us, trusting that so working still conduces to the great ends He ordains. Surely He intends some great good to follow this mighty convulsion, which no mortal could make, and no mortal could stay.

Your people—the Friends—have had, and are having, a very great trial. On principle, and faith, opposed to both war and oppression, they can only practically oppose oppression by war. In this hard dilemma, some have chosen one horn, and some the other. For those appealing to me on conscientious grounds, I have done, and shall do, the best I could and can, in my own conscience, under my oath to the law. That you believe this I doubt not; and believing it, I shall still receive, for our country and myself, your earnest prayers to our Father in heaven.

Your sincere friend
A. Lincoln.

REPLY TO LOYAL COLORED PEOPLE OF BALTIMORE UPON PRESENTATION OF A BIBLE[13]
SEPTEMBER 7, 1864

In a gesture of appreciation for Lincoln's efforts towards black freedom, the "Loyal Colored People of Baltimore" presented him with a Bible. Its inscription read: "To Abraham Lincoln, President of the United States, the Friend of Universal Freedom, from the Loyal Colored People of Baltimore, as a token of respect and Gratitude. Baltimore July 4th, 1864."

SEPTEMBER 7, 1864

This occasion would seem fitting for a lengthy response to the address which you have just made. I would make one, if prepared; but I am not. I would promise to respond in writing, had not experience taught me that business will not allow me to do so. I can only now say, as I have often before said, it has always been a sentiment with me that all mankind should be free. So far as able, within my sphere, I have always acted as I believed to be right and just; and I have done all I could for the good of mankind generally. In letters and documents sent from this office I have expressed myself better than I now can. In regard to this Great Book, I have but to say, it is the best gift God has given to man.

All the good the Saviour gave to the world was communicated through this book. But for it we could not know right from wrong. All things most desirable for man's welfare, here and hereafter, are to be found portrayed in it. To you I return my most sincere thanks for the very elegant copy of the great Book of God which you present.

STORY WRITTEN FOR NOAH BROOKS[14]
DECEMBER 6, 1864

Reciting this story to his friend Noah Brooks, Lincoln remarked, "here is one speech of mine that has never been printed, and I think it worth printing." Brooks copied the speech verbatim and had it printed in the Washington Daily Chronicle *a day later on December 7, 1864. Lincoln signed his name and added the caption, "The President's Last, Shortest, and Best Speech."*

13. *CWAL*, VII, 542.
14. *CWAL*, VIII, 154–155.

[DECEMBER 6, 1864]

THE PRESIDENT'S LAST, SHORTEST, AND BEST SPEECH.

On thursday of last week two ladies from Tennessee came before the President asking the release of their husbands held as prisoners of war at Johnson's Island. They were put off till friday, when they came again; and were again put off to saturday. At each of the interviews one of the ladies urged that her husband was a religious man. On saturday the President ordered the release of the prisoners, and then said to this lady "You say your husband is a religious man; tell him when you meet him, that I say I am not much of a judge of religion, but that, in my opinion, the religion that sets men to rebel and fight against their government, because, as they think, that government does not sufficiently help *some* men to eat their bread on the sweat of *other* men's faces, is not the sort of religion upon which people can get to heaven!"

A. LINCOLN.

SECOND INAUGURAL ADDRESS
MARCH 4, 1865

The Second Inaugural has been described correctly as "an expression of Lincoln's living faith." The theology of the speech was likely influenced by the preaching of the celebrated Presbyterian minister Phineas Densmore Gurney, whose New York Avenue Church Lincoln attended during the war years. The speech was delivered in the context of the North's imminent victory and the public outcry for revenge against a defeated South. Theologically, the public expression of biblical faith in the Second Inaugural corresponds to Lincoln's private Meditation on the Divine Will and his letter to Albert Hodges. All of these ponder the ultimate theological significance of the war using similar language. The shallow interpretation of the speech as a self-righteous assertion that God had punished the South for slavery is inadequate. A more careful reading of the address reveals that Lincoln suggested that both North and South were culpable before God. For this reason, the Second Inaugural was a grave disappointment to radical abolitionists who demanded the triumphalist assertion of the North's righteousness now that the war was coming to an end. Lincoln stated that, "the prayers of both could not be answered; that of neither has been answered fully." Although slavery could not be reconciled with the conception of a just God and is clearly contrary to Genesis 3:19's injunction to earn "bread from the sweat of thy brow", Lincoln refrained from an ultimate judgment upon southern people's motives citing Matthew 7:1 "judge not that we be not judged."

Furthermore, those who argue that Lincoln was speaking directly for God in the address are equally mistaken. It is noteworthy that Lincoln used the conditional when speculating about the divine will. "The Almighty has his own purposes." Nonetheless, Lincoln suggested that whatever God had willed, however ultimately inscrutable, must be trusted; for the "judgments of the Lord, are true and righteous altogether." Here Lincoln's reference to Psalm 19 testified to God's justice and his ability to bring goodness out of suffering. Finally, the concluding paragraph's admonition of "With malice toward none; with charity for all; with firmness in the right, as God gives us to see the right" was stated in response to the North's demand for vengeance against the South. Lincoln invoked God's mercy to heal the nation's suffering. He also reminded his listeners that the expectation of divine mercy and compassion implies a corresponding responsibility of man to follow the Lord's example.

AT THIS SECOND APPEARING to take the oath of the presidential office, there is less occasion for an extended address than there was at the first. Then a statement, somewhat in detail, of a course to be pursued, seemed fitting and proper. Now, at the expiration of four years, during which public declarations have been constantly called forth on every point and phase of the great contest which still absorbs the attention, and engrosses the energies of the nation, little that is new could be presented. The progress of our arms, upon which all else chiefly depends, is as well known to the public as to myself; and it is, I trust, reasonably satisfactory and encouraging to all. With high hope for the future, no prediction in regard to it is ventured.

On the occasion corresponding to this four years ago, all thoughts were anxiously directed to an impending civil war. All dreaded it—all sought to avert it. While the inauyeral [sic] address was being delivered from this place, devoted altogether to *saving* the Union without war, insurgent agents were in the city seeking to *destroy* it without war—seeking to dissole [sic] the Union, and divide effects, by negotiation. Both parties deprecated war; but one of them would *make* war rather than let the nation survive; and the other would *accept* war rather than let it perish. And the war came.

One eighth of the whole population were colored slaves, not distributed generally over the Union, but localized in the Southern part of it. These slaves constituted a peculiar and powerful interest. All knew that this interest was, somehow, the cause of the war. To strengthen, perpetuate, and extend this interest was the object for which the insurgents would rend the Union, even by war; while the government claimed no right to do more than to restrict the territorial enlargement of it. Neither party expected for the war, the magnitude, or the duration, which it has already attained. Neither anticipated that the *cause* of the conflict might cease with, or even before, the conflict itself should cease. Each looked for an easier triumph, and a result less fundamental and astounding. Both read the same Bible, and pray to the same God; and each invokes His aid against the other. It may seem strange that any men should dare to ask a just God's assistance in wringing their bread from the sweat of other men's faces; but let us judge not that we be not judged. The prayers of both could not be answered; that of neither has been answered fully. The Almighty has his own purposes. "Woe unto the world because of offences! for it must needs be that offences come; but woe to that man by whom the offence cometh!" If we shall suppose that American Slavery is one of those offences which, in the providence of God, must needs come, but which, having continued through His appointed time, He now wills to remove, and that He gives to both North and South, this terrible war, as the woe due to those by whom the offence came, shall we discern therein any departure from those divine attributes which the believers in a Living God always ascribe to Him? Fondly do we hope—fervently do we pray—that this mighty scourge of war may speedily pass away. Yet, if God wills that it continue, until all the wealth piled by the bond-man's two hundred and fifty years of unrequited toil shall be sunk, and until every drop of blood drawn with the lash, shall be paid by another drawn with the sword, as was said three thousand years ago, so still it must be said "the judgments of the Lord, are true and righteous altogether."

With malice toward none; with charity for all; with firmness in the right, as God gives us to see the right, let us strive on to finish the work we are in; to bind up the nation's wounds; to care for him who shall have borne the battle, and for his widow, and his orphan—to do all which may achieve and cherish a just and lasting peace, among ourselves, and with all nations.

LETTER TO THURLOW WEED
MARCH 15, 1865

Lincoln wrote this letter to editor Thurlow Weed in response to perceived criticisms of his Second Inaugural Address. Because the Second Inaugural Address affirmed the inscrutability of God's will and assigned culpability to both sides of the conflict, it was not received well by radicals who demanded a triumphal assertion of the North's righteousness. Contrary to those who allege that Lincoln's religious political views were millenarian, the letters to Thurlow Weed and Albert Hodges provide a different view. In both, Lincoln acknowledged the mystery of God's providence, and distinguished between human pretenses and divine intention.

EXECUTIVE MANSION,
WASHINGTON, MARCH 15, 1865.
THURLOW WEED, ESQ
MY DEAR SIR.

Every one likes a compliment. Thank you for yours on my little notification speech, and on the recent Inaugeral [*sic*] Address. I expect the latter to wear as well as—perhaps better than—anything I have produced; but I believe it is not immediately popular. Men are not flattered by being shown that there has been a difference of purpose between the Almighty and them. To deny it, however, in this case, is to deny that there is a God governing the world. It is a truth which I thought needed to be told; and as whatever of humiliation there is in it, falls most directly on myself, I thought others might afford for me to tell it.

Yours truly

A. Lincoln

PROCLAMATIONS OF PRAYER AND THANKSGIVING

The following are a selection of Lincoln's proclamations of national days of prayer and thanksgiving. Through these proclamations, Lincoln accommodated the religious beliefs and practices of the American people and affirmed the transcendent claim of religion in American public life.

APRIL 10, 1862

BY THE PRESIDENT OF THE UNITED STATES OF AMERICA.

A PROCLAMATION.

It has pleased Almighty God to vouchsafe signal victories to the land and naval forces engaged in suppressing an internal rebellion, and at the same time to avert from our country the dangers of foreign intervention and invasion.

It is therefore recommended to the People of the United States that, at their next weekly assemblages in their accustomed places of public worship which shall occur after notice of this proclamation shall have been received, they especially acknowledge and render thanks to our Heavenly Father for these inestimable blessings; that they then and there implore spiritual consolations in behalf of all who have been brought into affliction by the casualties and calamities of sedition and civil war, and that they reverently invoke the Divine Guidance for our national counsels, to the end that they may speedily result in the restoration of peace, harmony, and unity throughout our borders, and hasten the establishment of fraternal relations among all the countries of the earth.

In witness whereof, I have hereunto set my hand and caused the seal of the United States to be affixed.

Done at the City of Washington, this tenth day of April, in the year of our Lord one thousand eight hundred and sixty-two, and of the Independence of the United States the eighty-sixth.

By the President: ABRAHAM LINCOLN

WILLIAM H. SEWARD, Secretary of State.

JULY 15, 1863

BY THE PRESIDENT OF THE UNITED STATES OF AMERICA.

A PROCLAMATION.

It has pleased Almighty God to hearken to the supplications and prayers of an afflicted people, and to vouchsafe to the army and the navy of the United States victories on land and on the sea so signal and so effective as to furnish reasonable grounds for augmented confidence that the Union of these States will be maintained, their constitution preserved, and their peace and prosperity permanently restored. But these victories have been accorded not without sacrifices of life, limb, health and liberty incurred by brave, loyal and patriotic citizens. Domestic affliction in every part of the country follows in the train of these fearful bereavements. It is meet and right to recognize and confess the presence of the Almighty Father and the power of His Hand equally in these triumphs and in these sorrows:

Now, therefore, be it known that I do set apart Thursday the 6th. day of August next, to be observed as a day for National Thanksgiving, Praise and Prayer, and I invite the People of the United States to assemble on that occasion in their customary places of worship, and in the forms approved by their own consciences, render the homage due to the Divine Majesty, for the wonderful things he has done in the Nation's behalf, and invoke the influence of His Holy Spirit to subdue the anger, which has produced, and so long sustained a needless and cruel rebellion, to change the hearts of the insurgents, to guide the counsels of the Government with wisdom adequate to so great a national emergency, and to visit with tender care and consolation throughout the length and breadth of our land all those who, through the vicissitudes of marches, voyages, battles and sieges, have been brought to suffer in mind, body or estate, and finally to lead the whole nation, through the paths of repentance and submission to the Divine Will, back to the perfect enjoyment of Union and fraternal peace.

In witness whereof, I have hereunto set my hand and caused the seal of the United States to be affixed.

Done at the city of Washington, this fifteenth day of July, in the year of our Lord one thousand eight hundred and sixty-three, and of the Independence of the United States of America the eighty-eighth.

By the President: ABRAHAM LINCOLN
WILLIAM H. SEWARD, Secretary of State.

OCTOBER 3, 1863
BY THE PRESIDENT OF THE UNITED STATES OF AMERICA.

A PROCLAMATION.

The year that is drawing towards its close, has been filled with the blessings of fruitful fields and healthful skies. To these bounties, which are so constantly enjoyed that we are prone to forget the source from which they come, others have been added, which are of so extraordinary a nature, that they cannot fail to penetrate and soften even the heart which is habitually insensible to the ever watchful providence of Almighty God. In the midst of a civil war of unequalled magnitude and severity, which has sometimes seemed to foreign States to invite and to provoke their aggression, peace has been preserved with all nations, order has been maintained, the laws have been respected and obeyed, and harmony has prevailed everywhere except in the theatre of military conflict; while that theatre has been greatly contracted by the advancing armies and navies of the Union. Needful diversions of wealth and of strength from the fields of peaceful industry to the national defence, have not arrested the plough, the shuttle or the ship; the axe has enlarged the borders of our settlements, and the mines, as well of iron and coal as of the precious metals, have yielded even more abundantly than heretofore. Population has steadily increased, notwithstanding the waste that has been made in the camp, the siege and the battle-field; and the country, rejoicing in the consciousness of augmented strength and vigor, is permitted to expect continuance of years with large increase of freedom. No human counsel hath devised nor hath any mortal hand worked out these great things. They are the gracious gifts of the Most High God, who, while dealing with us in anger for our sins, hath nevertheless remembered mercy. It has seemed to me fit and proper that they should be solemnly, reverently and gratefully acknowledged as with one heart and one voice by the whole American People. I do therefore invite my fellow citizens in every part of the United States, and also those who are at sea and those who are sojourning in foreign lands, to set apart and observe the last Thursday of November next, as a day of Thanksgiving and Praise to our beneficent Father who dwelleth in the Heavens. And I recommend to them that while offering up the ascriptions justly due to Him for such singular deliverances and blessings, they do also, with humble penitence for our national perverseness and disobedience, commend to His tender care all those who have become widows, orphans, mourners or sufferers in the lamentable civil strife in which we are unavoidably engaged, and fervently implore the interposition of the Almighty Hand to heal the wounds of the nation and to restore it as soon as may be consistent with the Divine purposes to the full enjoyment of peace, harmony, tranquillity and Union.

In testimony whereof, I have hereunto set my hand and caused the Seal of the United States to be affixed.

Done at the City of Washington, this Third day of October, in the year of our Lord one thousand eight hundred and sixty-three, and of the Independence of the United States the Eighty-eighth.

By the President: ABRAHAM LINCOLN
WILLIAM H. SEWARD, Secretary of State.

EXECUTIVE MANSION, WASHINGTON CITY SEPTEMBER 3D. 1864

The signal success that Divine Providence has recently vouchsafed to the operations of the United States fleet and army in the harbor of Mobile and the reduction of Fort-Powell, Fort-Gaines, and Fort-Morgan, and the glorious achievements of the Army under Major General Sherman in the State of Georgia, resulting in the capture of the City of Atlanta, call for devout acknowledgement to the Supreme Being in whose hands are the destinies of nations. It is therefore requested that on next Sunday, in all places of public worship in the United-States, thanksgiving be offered to Him for His mercy in preserving our national existence against the insurgent rebels who so long have been waging a cruel war against the Government of the United-States, for its overthrow; and also that prayer be made for the Divine protection to our brave soldiers and their leaders in the field, who have so ofen and so gallantly perilled their lives in battling with the enemy; and for blessing and comfort from the Father of Mercies to the sick, wounded, and prisoners, and to the orphans and widows of those who have fallen in the service of their country, and that he will continue to uphold the Government of the United-States against all the efforts of public enemies and secret foes. ABRAHAM LINCOLN

OCTOBER 20, 1864

BY THE PRESIDENT OF THE UNITED STATES OF AMERICA:

A PROCLAMATION.

It has pleased Almighty God to prolong our national life another year, defending us with his guardian care against unfriendly designs from abroad, and vouchsafing to us in His mercy many and signal victories over the enemy, who is of our own household. It has also pleased our Heavenly Father to favor as well our citizens in their homes as our soldiers in their camps and our sailors on the rivers and seas with unusual health. He has largely augmented our free population by emancipation and by immigration, while he has opened to us new sources of wealth, and has crowned the labor of our working men in every department of industry with abundant rewards. Moreover, He has been pleased to animate and inspire our minds and hearts with fortitude, courage and resolution sufficient for the great trial of civil war into which we have been brought by our adherence as a nation to the cause of Freedom and Humanity, and to afford to us reasonable hopes of an ultimate and happy deliverance from all our dangers and afflictions.

Now, therefore, I, Abraham Lincoln, President of the United States, do, hereby, appoint and set apart the last Thursday in November next as a day, which I desire to be observed by all my fellow-citizens wherever they may then be as a day of Thanksgiving and Praise to Almighty God the beneficent Creator and Ruler of the Universe. And I do farther recommend to my fellow-citizens aforesaid that on that occasion they do reverently humble themselves in the dust and from thence offer up penitent and fervent prayers and supplications to the Great Disposer of events for a return of the inestimable blessings of Peace, Union and Harmony throughout the land, which it has pleased him to assign as a dwelling place for ourselves and for our posterity throughout all generations.

In testimony whereof, I have hereunto set my hand and caused the seal of the United States to be affixed.

Done at the city of Washington this twentieth day of October, in the year of our Lord one thousand eight hundred and sixty four, and, of the Independence of the United States the eighty-ninth.

By the President: ABRAHAM LINCOLN

WILLIAM H SEWARD Secretary of State.

INDEX

NOTE ON THE EDITOR

Joseph R. Fornieri is Associate Professor of Political Science at the Rochester Institute of Technology where he teaches American politics, political philosophy, and constitutional rights and liberties. He is the author of *Abraham Lincoln's Political Faith,* 2003, which explores Lincoln's combination of religion and politics, co-editor of *Lincoln's America*, 2008, with Sara V. Gabbard. He received RIT's Eisenhart Provost's Award for Excellence in Teaching. He lives in upstate New York with his wife Pam and their two daughters, Isabella and Natalie. On the side, he plays in a blues band and strives to master the delta styles of Son House and Mississippi John Hurt.